The **Rough Guide** to

England DISCARDED

written and researched by

Robert Andrews, Jules Brown, Phil Lee and Rob Humphreys

with additional contributions from
Tara Dougal, Matthew Hancock, Dan Hodgkinson,
Claire Saunders, Jos Simon, Matthew Teller,
Amanda Tomlin and Lucy White

D0064487

www.roughguides.com

Contents

Coastal England colour
section following p.216

Pubs and pints colour
section following p.696

◀◀ Newcastle waterfront ◀ Palace Pier, Brighton

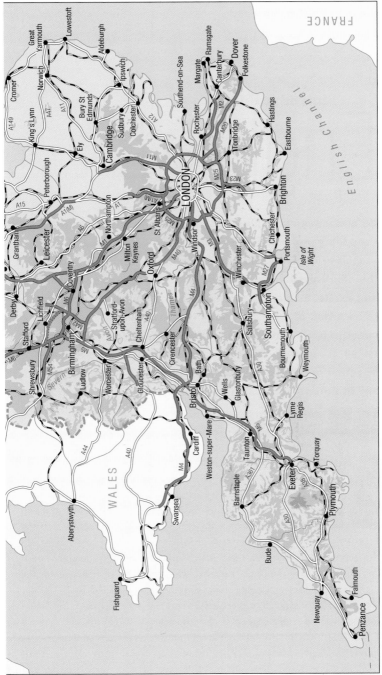

The Isles of Scilly

5

Introduction to

England

No one enjoys knocking England more than the English, but – modesty and self-deprecation aside – it's a great place to visit or explore, and whether you're a resident or tourist the country retains a boundless capacity to surprise, charm and excite. England has always had a history and heritage to be proud of, and a glorious regional diversity – from coast to hills, festivals to foodstuff – with few parallels. But for all the glories of the past, in recent times it's had an injection of life that makes it as thrilling a destination as any in Europe.

 As more and more people choose to holiday at home, it's worth recalling just how much England has changed in the last two decades for locals and visitors alike. Who could have predicted city breaks and shopping sprees in Leeds and Bristol, or the all-conquering march of music and arts festivals, or that camping would become cool? Accommodation and food in particular, the two essentials on any trip, were once a lottery, with many English hotels and restaurants seemingly intent on removing hospitality from the hospitality industry. Not any more. In boutique B&Bs, designer hotels and yurt-festooned campsites, there's an embarrassment of rich beds for the night, while an ever-expanding choice of real English food and drink – locally sourced and championed in cafés, restaurants and pubs, at food festivals and farmers' markets – challenges every lazy stereotype.

The English also do heritage amazingly well. There are first-class museums all over the country (many of them free), while what's left of England's green and pleasant land is protected with great passion and

skill. Indeed, ask an English person to define their country in terms of what's worth seeing and you're most likely to have your attention drawn to the golden rural past. The classic images are found in every brochure – the village green, the duckpond, the country lane and the farmyard. And it's true that it's impossible to overstate the bucolic attractions of the various English regions, from Cornwall to the Lake District, or the delights they provide – from walkers' trails and prehistoric stone circles to traditional pubs and obscure festivals. But despite celebrating their rural heritage, the modern-day English have an ambivalent attitude towards "the countryside". Farming today forms only a tiny proportion of the national income and there's a real dislocation between the population of the burgeoning towns and suburbs and the small, struggling rural communities.

Fact file

• As part of the United Kingdom of Great Britain and Northern Ireland ("the UK"), England is a parliamentary democracy, with Queen Elizabeth II as its head of state. Its traditional industries – fishing, farming, mining, engineering, shipbuilding – are all in decline and business today is dominated by banking and finance, the media and technology, steel production, oil and gas, and tourism.

• Bordered by Scotland to the north and Wales to the west, England is the largest country in Great Britain, occupying an area of 50,085 sq miles (129,720 sq km). The terrain is diverse, from plains to peaks, cliffs to beaches, though the superlatives are all modest on a world scale – the largest lake, Windermere, is 10 miles (16km) long, the highest mountain, Scafell, just 3205ft (978m) above sea level.

• The population of nearly 52 million is dense for a country of its size, but settlement is concentrated in the southeast around London, and in the large industrial cities of the Midlands and the North.

• This is one of the world's most multiethnic countries, made up largely of people of Anglo-Saxon, Scots, Welsh and Irish descent, but with sizeable communities from the Caribbean, Africa, the Indian subcontinent, China, Southeast Asia and Eastern Europe.

▼ Canterbury

So perhaps the heart of England is found in its towns and cities instead? Many, it's true, have a restless energy and a talent for reinvention. So for every person who wants to stand outside the gates of Buckingham Palace or visit the Houses of Parliament, there's another who makes a beeline for the latest show at Tate Modern, the cityscape of downtown Manchester or the revitalized Newcastle waterfront. Yet this flowering of urban civic pride is not a new phenomenon. In fact, it's been steady since the Industrial Revolution, and industry – and the Empire it inspired – has provided a framework for much of what you'll see as you travel around. Virtually every English town bears a mark of former wealth and power, whether it be a magnificent Gothic cathedral financed from a monarch's treasury, a parish church funded by the tycoons of the medieval wool trade, or a triumphalist civic building raised on the back of the slave and sugar trades. In the south of England you'll find old dockyards from which the navy patrolled the oceans, while in the north there are mills that employed entire town populations. England's museums and galleries – several of them ranking among the world's finest – are full of treasures trawled from its imperial conquests. And in their grandiose stuccoed terraces and wide esplanades, the old seaside resorts bear testimony to the heyday of English holiday towns, at one time as fashionable as any European spa.

Where to go

To begin to get to grips with England, **London** is the place to start. Nowhere else in the country can match the scope and innovation of the metropolis, a colossal, frenetic city that's going through a convulsion of improvements as it gears up to host the 2012 Olympics. It's here that you'll find England's best spread of nightlife, cultural events, museums, galleries, pubs and restaurants. However, each of the other large cities –

Only in England

However long you spend in England, you'll never figure out its inhabitants. The famous English reserve, sarcasm and sense of humour, the belief that a cup of tea is a universal panacea, the all-consuming obsession with weather – all form a nigh-on impenetrable barrier to the English soul. So we've come up with a list of unique places and experiences that might help lift the lid on the national character. At the end, you may be no closer to knowing what the English are really like – but you'll have seen another side to the country than just Big Ben and Beefeaters.

A day at the seaside Blackpool. The quintessential coastal trip is to England's loudest, brashest and best resort, where the sun never sets on the rollercoasters, karaoke bars and candy-floss kiosks. Fake breasts and party wig optional. See p.629.

A nice snack Melton Mowbray. France gives protected status to its champagne, Italy to its succulent ham from Parma, and England? Step forward the humble but heroic pork pie. See box, p.571.

The Olimpick Games Chipping Campden. Never mind London 2012, what you really need from a world-class sports meet is rustic wrestling, shin-kicking contests and dancing around in Tudor dress. See p.290.

Cerne Abbas Giant Dorchester. Flummoxed by the English love of *Carry On* films and tabloid double-entendres? A visit to see a large naked man carved into a Dorset hillside is in order. See p.248.

On the pier Southwold. Arcade games on the traditional seaside pier get a makeover in Southwold's brilliantly inventive Under the Pier Show of handmade slots and simulators. See p.448.

Time for tea Brighton. The tea ceremony, Brighton style, requires a tolerance for high-camp kitsch, knowledge of the national anthem and impeccable manners at the *Tea Cosy Tea Rooms*. See p.195.

Full steam ahead Haworth. Time was, every right-thinking English boy a) had a thing for Jenny Agutter in *The Railway Children* and b) wanted to work on a steam railway. Here's where they get to indulge both passions. See p.711.

Bed and breakfast Whitby. English B&Bs have come a long way since scary landladies and lace doilies, but quite what's going on at *La Rosa* (eclectic antiques, Victorian giggles and car-boot chic) no one rightly knows. See p.761.

Snowshill Manor The Cotswolds. Eyes glazing over at the fancy plates and Old Masters at stately home Number 32? Charles Paget Wade collected the stuff we really want to see, from beetles to boneshaker bikes. See p.291.

Birmingham, **Bristol**, **Newcastle**, **Leeds**, **Sheffield**, **Manchester** and **Liverpool** – makes its own claim for historic and cultural diversity, and you certainly won't have a representative view of England's cities if you venture no further than the capital. For the most part it's in these regional centres that the most exciting architectural and social developments are taking place, though for many visitors they rank a long way behind ancient cities like **Lincoln**, **Canterbury**, **York**, **Salisbury**, **Durham** and **Winchester** – to name a few of those with the most celebrated of England's cathedrals – or the university cities of **Cambridge** and **Oxford**, arguably the two most beautiful seats of learning in the world. Most beguiling of all, though, are the long-established **villages** of England, hundreds of which amount to nothing more than a pub, a shop, a gaggle of cottages and a farmhouse offering bed and breakfast. **Devon**, **Cornwall**, the **Cotswolds** and the **Yorkshire Dales** harbour some especially picturesque specimens, but every county can boast a decent showing of photogenic hamlets.

Evidence of England's pedigree is scattered between its settlements as well. Wherever you're based, you're never more than a few miles from a majestic **country house** or **ruined castle** or **monastery**, and in many parts of the country you'll come across the sites of civilizations that thrived here before England existed as a nation. In the southwest there are remnants of a **Celtic** culture that elsewhere was all but eradicated by the **Romans**, and from the south coast to the northern border you can find traces of **prehistoric** settlers, the most famous being the megalithic circles of Stonehenge and Avebury.

Then of course there's the English **countryside**, an extraordinarily diverse terrain from which Constable, Turner, Wordsworth, Emily Brontë and a host of other native luminaries took inspiration. Most dramatic and best known are the moors and uplands – **Exmoor**, **Dartmoor**, **Bodmin Moor**, the **North York Moors** and the **Lake District** – each of which has its over-visited spots, though a brisk walk will usually take you out of the throng. Quieter areas are tucked away in every corner of England, from the flat wetlands of the eastern Fens to the chalk downland of Sussex, the latter now protected as England's newest national park. It's a similar story on the coast, where the finest sands and most rugged cliffs have long been discovered, and sizeable resorts have grown to exploit many of the choicest locations. But again, if it's peace you're after, you can find it by heading for the exposed strands of **Northumberland**, the pebbly flat horizons of **East Anglia** or the crumbling headlands of **Dorset**.

When to go

Considering the temperateness of the English **climate**, it's amazing how much mileage the locals get out of the subject – a two-day cold snap is discussed as if it were the onset of a new Ice Age, and a week above 25°C (upper 70s °F) starts rumours of drought. However, on the whole, English summers rarely get very hot and the winters don't get very cold, and there's not a great deal of regional variation, as the chart shows, though in general, it's wetter in the west than the east, and the south gets more

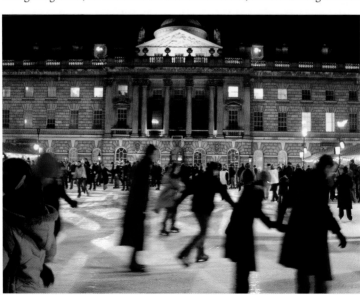

▶ Ice skating at Somerset House, London

hours of sunshine than the north. Differences between the regions are slightly more marked in winter, when the south tends to be appreciably milder and wetter than the north. Despite the general temperateness of the climate, extreme weather patterns are becoming more frequent and recent years have seen summer temperatures well into the 30s (over 90°F) and catastrophic winter and spring flooding in many parts of the country.

The bottom line is that it's impossible to say with any degree of certainty that the weather will be pleasant in any given month. May might be wet and grey one year and gloriously sunny the next, and the same goes for the autumnal months. November stands an equal chance of being crisp and clear or foggy and grim. Obviously, if you're planning to camp or go to the beach, you'll want to visit between June and September – a period when you shouldn't go anywhere without booking your accommodation well in advance. Elsewhere, if you're balancing the likely fairness of the weather against the density of the crowds, the best time would be between **April and early June** or in **September** or **October**.

Average temperatures and rainfall

	Jan	Feb	Mar	Apr	May	Jun	Jul	Aug	Sep	Oct	Nov	Dec
Birmingham												
(°F)	42	43	48	54	60	66	68	68	63	55	48	44
(°C)	5	6	9	12	16	19	20	20	17	13	9	7
(inches)	3	2.1	2	2.1	2.5	2	2.7	2.7	2.4	2.7	3.3	2.6
(mm)	74	54	50	53	64	50	69	69	61	69	84	67
London												
(°F)	43	44	50	56	62	69	71	71	65	58	50	45
(°C)	6	7	10	13	17	20	22	21	19	15	10	7
(inches)	2.1	1.6	1.5	1.5	1.8	1.8	2.2	2.3	1.9	2.2	2.5	1.9
(mm)	54	40	37	37	46	45	57	59	49	57	64	48
Plymouth												
(°F)	47	47	50	54	59	64	66	67	64	58	52	49
(°C)	8	8	10	12	15	18	19	19	18	15	11	10
(inches)	3.9	2.9	2.7	2.1	2.5	2.1	2.8	3	3.1	3.6	4.5	4.3
(mm)	99	74	69	53	63	53	70	77	78	91	113	110
York												
(°F)	43	44	49	55	61	67	70	69	64	57	49	45
(°C)	6	7	10	13	16	19	21	20	18	14	10	7
(inches)	2.3	1.8	1.5	1.6	2	2	2.4	2.7	2.2	2.2	2.6	2
(mm)	59	46	37	41	50	50	62	68	55	55	65	50

35

things not to miss

It's not possible to see everything England has to offer in one trip – and we don't suggest you try. What follows is a selective taste of the country's highlights: architecture, dramatic landscapes, great things to eat and drink, and fun activities. They're arranged in five colour-coded categories, which you can browse through to find the very best things to see, do and experience. All highlights have a page reference to take you straight into the Guide, where you can find out more.

01 Lake District National Park Page **650** • England's largest national park is also many peoples' favourite, boasting sixteen major lakes, including Wast Water (pictured here) and scores of mountains, not least the country's highest peak, Scafell Pike.

02 Dartmoor Page **376** • Southern England's greatest expanse of wilderness is perfect for hikers and riders.

04 The Cotswolds Page **282** • Take time out in England's largest Area of Outstanding Natural Beauty, poised between Oxford and Gloucester – rolling hills, honey-stone villages and great walking.

05 Northumbrian castles Page **812** • Symbols of a turbulent past, Northumberland's many fortresses are worth a visit, especially mighty Alnwick Castle (pictured), with its stunning medieval gardens.

03 Houses of Parliament Page **84** • One of London's most majestic buildings, where you can see the "Mother of all Parliaments" at work from the public gallery or take a summertime tour.

06 **Oxford** Page **265** • The Radcliffe Camera (pictured) stands at the centre of this old university town, famed for its sublime architecture and lively restaurants.

07 **Hay Festival** Page **508** • A rural outpost on the English–Welsh border, Hay-on-Wye may be remote, but it cuts a bibliographic dash with the size and variety of its second hand bookshops and prestigious literary festival.

08 Avebury stone circle Page **256** • Stonehenge might get all the publicity, but the stones at nearby Avebury have a raw appeal and are far more accessible.

09 Hadrian's Wall Path Page **802** • Walk or cycle the length of this atmospheric Roman monument, which snakes its way for 84 miles over rough, sheep-strewn countryside.

10 Music festivals
Page **45** • Mud, mud, glorious mud … Glastonbury (pictured) may be the biggest and best-known music and arts fest, but every summer weekend sees celebrations of anything from folk to trance on greenfield sites nationwide.

11 Surfing, Newquay Page **414** • The beaches strung along the northern coast of Devon and Cornwall offer some great breaks, with Newquay the place to see and be seen.

12 Bath Page **325** • Admire England's most elegant Georgian terrace, visit the Roman baths or do some serious shopping in one of the country's most beautiful cities.

13 Fish and chips Page **38** • There's nothing better than fish and chips, nor any better way to eat them than wrapped in paper and eaten on the beach.

14 Eden Project Page **393** • With its strong ecological thrust, the West Country's most spectacular attraction presents a refreshing alternative to the hard sell of most of the region's crowd-pullers.

16 Imperial War Museum North, Manchester

Page **608** • The striking modern building at Salford Quays addresses the themes of war and conflict in equally dramatic ways.

15 The Lizard peninsula, Cornwall Page **399** • This

headland has none of the razzmatazz of Land's End, which is all to its favour, yet still has the views; there are some great beaches within a short coastal hike, too.

17 New Forest Page **229** • Famed for its ponies, this ancient hunting ground is a magnet for cyclists and walkers.

18 Farmers' markets

Page **51** • Plug into England's sense of rural community at the growing network of markets where farmers and producers sell direct – not just fruit and veg but local cheeses, breads, pies, deli items, ales and more.

19 Durham Cathedral Page **775** • Arguably the greatest Norman building in England, Durham's imposing cathedral perches on a peninsula overlooking the city's quaint, cobbled old town.

20 Royal Armouries, Leeds Page **703** • Housing the wonderful national collection of arms and armour, the Royal Armouries also puts on a range of falconry displays, weapon demonstrations and colourful tournaments.

21 **St Ives, Cornwall** Page **408** • Bustling seaside resort with great beaches and the southwest's best arts collection.

22 **Punting on the Cam** Page **473** • A flat-bottomed boat that's easy to fall out of, with no paddles but a pole… Unnecessarily complicated it may be, but punting on the River Cam is the best way to see some of Cambridge's beautiful university buildings.

23 **The Peak District** Page **533** • A stirring landscape of moors and peaks, deep-green dales, tumbling rivers and jagged cliffs, the Peak District attracts outdoors enthusiasts by the thousand.

24 York Minster Page **735** • Soaring above York's medieval streets, Britain's biggest Gothic church has a thousand-year history and treasures to match.

25 Sutton Hoo Page **442** • Preserved in the burial mounds of Sutton Hoo were some of the most remarkable Anglo-Saxon archeological finds ever discovered – and the top-notch Exhibition Hall explains it all.

26 Stately homes Page **281** • Blenheim Palace (pictured) near Oxford is one of England's most majestic stately homes, but dozens more up and down the country offer cultured days out.

27 Canterbury Cathedral Page **164** • Mother Church of the Church of England, this cathedral is famous for its shrine to the murdered Archbishop, Thomas à Becket, and the tales that Chaucer weaved round a fictitious pilgrimage to the martyr's tomb.

28 Southwold Page **446** • George Orwell didn't like the place, but everyone else does: with its wide sandy beach and brightly painted beach huts, Southwold is the most beguiling of seaside towns.

29 Newcastle nightlife Page **795** • From chic wine bars to first-rate theatres, Newcastle's nightlife is growing in sophistication – though there are still plenty of places for a traditionally raucous night out on the Toon.

30 The Royal Pavilion, Brighton Page **190** • George IV's pleasure dome, designed by Nash, is the supreme example of Oriental-Gothic architecture.

31 **Tate Modern** Page **110** • Housed in a spectacular former power station, the world's largest modern art gallery is simply awesome.

32 **The Seven Sisters** Page **186** • The soaring Seven Sisters cliffs are just one of the highlights of the southeast's newly created national park, best explored on the long-distance South Downs Way footpath.

33 Blackpool Page **629** • The British seaside's best-known landmark provides the Blackpool skyline with a touch of grace.

34 Afternoon tea Page **133** • London's top hotels are the most wickedly indulgent places for a calorific afternoon tea of sandwiches, scones and cakes – though a Devonshire cream tea can give the capital a run for its money.

35 Durdle Door Page **240** • This distinctive limestone arch is the highlight of Dorset's Jurassic Coast and sits on one of the loveliest stretches of the South West Coast Path, close to some fine beaches.

Basics

Basics

Getting there

London is one of the world's busiest transport hubs. Stiff competition among airlines around the world on routings into the British capital ensures good deals on international travel.

Most **long-haul flights** come into London Heathrow or London Gatwick, although it's also worth exploring options into less crowded hubs outside London – notably Manchester, Birmingham or Newcastle. European **short-haul flights** also arrive at all these airports, and at a host of others including London Stansted, London Luton, London City, Bristol, Liverpool, East Midlands Airport near Nottingham, Leeds-Bradford, and many more around the country. Since routes and carriers can change at short notice, to get the latest up-to-date information the best advice is to check the website of your preferred arrival airport (see p.28) for details of who flies there, and from where.

Overland routes from neighbouring countries include high-speed **trains** into London through the Channel Tunnel – passenger-only services as well as special car-carrying trains for those on a self-drive tour – as well as a range of **ferry** routes.

Package tours of England, where all flights, accommodation and ground transport are arranged for you, can sometimes be cheaper than organizing things yourself. All-inclusive **city breaks** from North America can provide a good introduction to England, though many cover limited ground outside London. Many companies at home and in the UK offer **tours** of England's historic highlights by coach (bus), or help you explore some aspect of the country's heritage, such as art and architecture, or gardens and stately homes. Some companies offer budget versions of their holidays, staying in hostels or B&Bs. For **activity holidays**, see p.49.

Flights from the US and Canada

Many airlines fly nonstop to London and other English hubs. **Flight time** from the east coast is around seven hours, nearer ten hours from the west.

From the US take your pick of dozens of scheduled and charter flights out of New York, Washington DC, Boston, Chicago, Atlanta, Miami, Las Vegas, San Francisco and Los Angeles, among other cities. The route between New York JFK and London Heathrow, for example, is the busiest air corridor in the world, with somewhere between twenty and thirty flights a day in each direction. This level of competition pushes prices down: low-season return fares from New York start around US$400, from Los Angeles US$500–600.

From Canada, look for nonstop scheduled and charter routings to London and other English cities, mainly from Toronto, Montréal, Calgary and Vancouver, with return fares roughly covering the range Can$500–900.

As well as checking for deals on all the usual airlines, look out for low fares on unusual carriers. Air India, for instance, flies nonstop Toronto–London at bargain rates, as does Kuwait Airways out of JFK.

Flights from Australia and New Zealand

Routes **from Australia and New Zealand** to London are highly competitive, with return fares out of Sydney, Melbourne or Perth usually Aus$1500–2500, or NZ$2000–3000 out of Auckland. Check out the obvious carriers first, such as Qantas, British Airways and Air New Zealand – but then explore options on, for instance, Emirates, Etihad or Qatar Airways via the Gulf, Air Asia via Kuala Lumpur, or even taking a low-cost hop on a budget airline to, say, Bangkok or Singapore from where you can pick up super-cheap deals on scheduled carriers to London. Travel time is over twenty hours, even with the best connections; most airlines will let you stop over for no extra charge, and many of the cheaper flights involve a change of planes in any case.

Flights from South Africa

From South Africa direct flights – mostly from Johannesburg – cost roughly ZAR6000 –8000 return, though you might find lower rates on, for instance, Emirates via Dubai. Flight time is eleven hours nonstop. Cape Town has fewer direct flights; they take slightly longer and cost a bit more.

From Ireland

Stiff competition on flights between **Ireland** and England keeps fares low. It's easy to find a seat for €30–50 on routes out of Dublin, Cork, Kerry, Knock or Shannon to any of a dozen English airports, on airlines such as Ryanair, bmibaby, Flybe, Aer Lingus and others.

If you're driving, your best bet is a **ferry** from Dublin to Liverpool. Other routes, such as to Holyhead, Fishguard or Pembroke, leave you a long drive from the English border.

You can buy a **train** ticket from almost any station in Ireland to any station in England for €36–40 one way, including the ferry crossing. Dublin–London takes under seven hours. The **bus**/ferry options offered by Bus Éireann/ Eurolines cost about the same but take roughly twice as long.

From mainland Europe

Numerous **airlines** fly from cities across Europe to airports all over England. The best advice when researching routes and options is to check the website of your preferred arrival airport, to find out who flies there from your country.

Trains to London St Pancras run roughly hourly from Lille (1hr 20min), Paris (2hr 15min) and Brussels (2hr), with connections coming into those cities from all around Europe. Some trains include a stop before London at Ashford or Ebbsfleet – handy if you're planning to tour Kent. Fares vary widely depending on your starting point: Eurostar (www.eurostar.com) sells tickets online for journeys from certain stations in western Europe (see website for list) to any arrival point in the UK; otherwise consult a rail agent in your home country. A great resource for rail travel is www.seat61.com – it's designed to be used by UK travellers heading abroad, but has plenty to offer travellers seeking to avoid flights as a way to reach (and tour) England.

Drivers have a choice of **ferry** routes. The cheapest services are on the shortest cross-Channel hops from the French ports of Calais, Boulogne and Dunkerque to Dover. Other routes abound, from elsewhere in France, Belgium, the Netherlands, Spain, Denmark, Norway and Sweden into ports spread around the southern and eastern coasts of England. Consult www.directferries.com, www.ferrybooker.com or www.seaview.co.uk for up-to-date information on who sails where. Fares vary between operators according to the date, time and type of crossing.

Often quicker and more convenient are the drive-on/drive-off shuttle trains operated by **Eurotunnel** (www.eurotunnel.com) through the Channel Tunnel from Calais to Folkestone. Book well ahead for the lowest prices, which start from under €70 for a car with all passengers.

Eurolines (www.eurolines.com) coordinates international **bus** services from dozens of cities to London, though the small savings over equivalent airfares are outweighed by the marathon journey times.

Airports in England

Take your pick of England's twenty busiest airports, ranked by passenger traffic.
London Heathrow (LHR) www.heathrow airport.com.
London Gatwick (LGW) www.gatwickairport .com.
London Stansted (STN) www.stanstedairport .com.
Manchester (MAN) www.manchesterairport .co.uk.
London Luton (LTN) www.london-luton.co.uk.
Birmingham (BHX) www.bhx.co.uk.
Bristol (BRS) www.bristolairport.co.uk.
Liverpool (LPL) www.liverpoolairport.com.
East Midlands (EMA) www.eastmidlands airport.com.
Newcastle (NCL) www.newcastleairport.com.
London City (LCY) www.londoncityairport .com.
Leeds-Bradford (LBA) www.leedsbradford airport.co.uk.

Southampton (SOU) ⓦ www.southamptonairport
.com.
Bournemouth (BOH) ⓦ www.bournemouthairport
.com.
Doncaster Sheffield (DSA) ⓦ www
.robinhoodairport.com.

Exeter (EXT) ⓦ www.exeter-airport.co.uk.
Isle of Man (IOM) ⓦ www.iom-airport.com.
Norwich (NWI) ⓦ www.norwichairport.co.uk.
Newquay (NQY) ⓦ www.newquaycornwallairport
.com.
Humberside (HUY) ⓦ www.humbersideairport.com.

Getting around

Most places in England are accessible by train or bus. However, public transport costs are among the highest in Europe: travel can eat up a large part of your budget. It pays to investigate all the special deals and passes, some of which are only available outside England – and for some journeys it may be worth flying. It's often cheaper to drive yourself around the country, though fuel and car rental are expensive – and traffic congestion can be very bad.

By train

Despite some poor infrastructure and a tiresomely London-centric network, **trains** are still the best, most scenic and most pleasurable way to get around England. Overall reliability remains fairly good. Mainline routes into and out of London have fast and frequent services – the 200-mile journeys to York or Exeter, for instance, are covered in two hours – but travelling between other cities, or trying to go east–west across the country, can be a lengthy business, often involving numerous connections. The essential first call for information on routes, timetables, fares and special offers is **National Rail Enquiries** (☏ 0845/748 4950, ⓦ www.nationalrail.co.uk). The key to getting the best fares is to book early and bear in mind that your best bet may well be to go for a rail pass (see below). Point-to-point tickets, in general, offer the least flexibility and the highest prices.

Rail passes

Several rail passes are targeted specifically at visitors, led by the **BritRail pass** (ⓦ www .britrail.com). This comes in many different varieties, covering various areas and validity periods: for England alone, go for the

BritRail England pass, which is valid for 4, 8, 15, 22 or 30 consecutive days of travel or as a flexi-pass (3, 4, 8 or 15 days of travel in any two months). These currently cost US$285 for eight consecutive days, or US$369 for any eight days in two months. Numerous discounts are available, including for young people (under 26), seniors (over 60), parties (with discounts for more than two people travelling together), and so on. A free Family Pass add-on gives free travel to one child (under 15) for each adult in a family group. Note that you must buy your BritRail pass outside the UK before you arrive. Any good travel agent or tour operator can supply up-to-date information; see opposite for a list of rail contacts.

Eurail passes (ⓦ www.eurail.com) are not valid in the UK, though they do provide discounts on Eurostar trains to England and some ferry routes. If you've been resident in Europe for at least six months, you can buy an **InterRail** Great Britain Pass (ⓦ www .interrailnet.com), which provides unlimited train travel (plus discounts on Eurostar and some ferries) for 3, 4, 6 or 8 days within one month. Discounted passes are available for children (under 11) and youth (under 26).

Otherwise, numerous options exist for locals and visitors to cut the cost of rail travel

– all are detailed in full on the National Rail website. There are dozens of **"Ranger" and "Rover"** regional passes, covering travel on specified lines for varying periods – anything from two weeks on the entire national network down to, for example, the Cotswold Line Railcard, which gives one-third off the standard fare between six named stations near Oxford. For discounts off fares nation-wide, people aged between 16 and 25 (and full-time students of any age) qualify for the **16-25 Railcard**; people over 60 can get a **Senior Railcard**; groups of up to four adults and four children travelling together (they don't have to be related) can get a **Family & Friends Railcard**. Each of these passes costs £26 per year, and there are more available. Check restrictions and validity carefully on the National Rail website, where you can also buy online.

Rail fares

Individual point-to-point **fares** vary wildly. Each train operating company offers its own ticketing options, broadly grouped under three titles. Cheapest are **"advance"** fares: these cannot be bought on the day of travel and come with several restrictions (most notably that you must travel only on the train specified on the ticket: miss it, and you pay a surcharge). Advance fares sell out quickly: book as far ahead as possible. **"Off-peak"** fares can be bought in advance or on the day of travel, but are only valid for travel at quieter times, which vary depending on the location (generally after 9.30am Mon-Fri, all day at weekends). Most expensive are **"anytime"** tickets, which permit travel on any train. Expect extraordinary price variations: from London to Manchester, for instance, an advance fare is £11, an off-peak fare £65 and an anytime ticket £131.

A **seat reservation** is usually included with the ticket – these are essential, since most inter-city trains are crowded, especially on Fridays, weekends and public holidays. Many train companies let you upgrade your ticket by buying a **first-class supplement** for around £15, either in advance or on board – worth it if you're facing a long journey on a popular route.

For any journey, you can **buy** a ticket in person at any station, or by phone or online

from any train operator. These are listed on the National Rail Enquiries website, which also offers direct links from its journey planner for purchasing specific fares.

If the ticket office at your departure station is closed or there is no ticket machine, you can buy your ticket on the train. Otherwise, **boarding without a ticket** will render you liable to paying the full fare plus, possibly, a surcharge.

Megatrain (ⓦ www.megatrain.com) offers a limited number of budget fares on certain routes around the country. If you accept the restrictions (specified off-peak trains only, no changes, no amendments, and so on), you could travel from London to Birmingham, for instance, for only £3. Check the website for details.

Rail contacts

Britain on Track US & Canada ☎ 1-888/667-9734, ⓦ www.britainontrack.com.
BritRail US & Canada ☎ 1-866/BRITRAIL, ⓦ www.britrail.com.
National Rail UK ☎ 0845/748 4950, Worldwide ☎ +44 20 7278 5240; ⓦ www.nationalrail.co.uk. The official source for UK train information, with timetables, maps, links for purchasing and more.
Rail Europe US ☎ 1-800/622-8600, Canada ☎ 1-800/361-RAIL; ⓦ www.raileurope.com.
Rail Plus Australia ☎ 03/9642 8644, ⓦ www.railplus.com.au; New Zealand ☎ 09/377 5415, ⓦ www.railplus.co.nz.
Seat 61 ⓦ www.seat61.com. Top resource for rail travel worldwide, including a detailed section on travelling around Britain, with plenty of information, tips and links.

By bus and coach

Travel by **bus** (or, to use the more common term for long-distance bus services, **"coach"**) is generally much cheaper than by train. Though some coach services duplicate rail journeys, many others follow routes that would otherwise be tortuous or impossible by rail.

The biggest coach operator is **National Express** (☎ 0871/781 8181, ⓦ www.nationalexpress.com), with an extensive nationwide network. On busy routes, and on any route at weekends and during holidays, it's advisable to book ahead, rather than just turn up. Fares are very reasonable, with big discounts for

Airport transfers to UK towns, cities and airports

York

Liverpool

Birmingham

London

National Express is the UK's only nationwide scheduled coach operator, offering luxury transfers from all major airports.

On National Express coaches, you can sit back and relax in a leather reclining seat with air conditioning and WiFi on selected services.

Your luggage is stowed in a secure compartment and your seat is reserved when you buy your coach ticket.

- Leeds
- Liverpool
- Manchester
- Manchester Airport
- Nottingham
- Leicester
- Birmingham
- Birmingham International Airport
- Cambridge
- Luton Airport
- Stansted Airport
- Swansea
- Heathrow Airport
- Cardiff
- Bristol
- London
- Gatwick Airport
- Brighton
- Bournemouth

Travelling around England made easy

If you're travelling around England then there's no easier way to get to the heart of every city or see the beautiful countryside than with National Express coaches.

Whether its sightseeing, shopping or visiting friends and family sit back, relax and enjoy.

For our best fares book early at **nationalexpress.com**

national express

under-26s, over-60s and families, while advance-purchase fares and special deals are common – "FunFares" from £1, for example. Non-UK passport holders can buy a **Brit Xplorer** pass, which comes in 7-, 14- or 28-day versions. **Megabus** (ⓦwww .megabus.com) also operates low-budget coaches around England for very low prices, though restrictions apply and services can be infrequent. Rather more comfortable services are run by **Greyhound** (ⓦwww.greyhounduk .com), who operate luxury-style buses (with free wi-fi) on a regular timetable from London to various towns on the south coast – including an economical bus-and-ferry deal to the Isle of Wight.

Local **buses** within individual regions are run by a huge array of companies. In many cases, timetables and routes are well integrated, though some firms duplicate the busiest routes and leave the more remote spots neglected. As a rule, the further away from urban areas you get, the less frequent and more expensive bus services become.

The impartial official service **Traveline** (ⓣ0871/200 2233, ⓦwww.traveline.org.uk) has full details and timetable information for every bus route in the country.

By plane

If time is short and you want to cross the country quickly (Brighton/Gatwick to Newcastle, for instance, or Manchester to Newquay), you might consider **flying**. Leading airlines include Ryanair, easyJet, Flybe, bmibaby and British Airways, though routes and carriers can (and do) change: check the list of airport websites on p.28 to find out who serves your chosen destination, and from where. Often, though, if you calculate total journey time door to door, going by train can be just as quick and – if you book in advance – considerably cheaper.

By car or motorbike

Driving yourself around England brings the convenience of personal transport – but it can be both expensive and time-consuming.

In England you **drive on the left**. Motorways – "M" roads – and main "A" roads may have up to four lanes in each direction, but even these can get very congested, with long tailbacks a regular occurrence, especially at peak travel times and on public holidays. In the country, on "B" roads and minor roads, there might only be one lane (single track) for both directions. Keep your speed down, and be prepared for abrupt encounters with tractors, sheep, ponies and other hazards in remote spots.

Don't underestimate the **weather**: driving conditions can deteriorate quickly during rain, snow, ice, fog and high winds – on motorways as much as in rural areas. BBC Radio Five Live (693 or 909 AM nationwide) and local stations feature regularly updated traffic bulletins, as does the Highways Agency website.

Fuel is pricey: at more than £1.15 a litre, unleaded petrol (gasoline) and diesel are three times more expensive than in the US. The cheapest places to fill up are out-of-town supermarkets.

Rules of the road

Drive on the left. You must have your current full driving licence with you to show on demand: an international licence is not necessary. If you're bringing your own vehicle into the country you should also carry your vehicle registration, ownership and insurance documents. Left-hand-drive cars require minor adjustments to the headlights. Seat belts must be worn by everybody in the vehicle, in front and back. Motorcyclists and their passengers must wear a helmet.

Distances, weights and measures

England uses a confusing mixture of metric and imperial systems. Distances on road signs are marked in miles, and speed limits are given in miles per hour – but fuel is dispensed by the litre. You'll find milk and beer sold in pints, but meat and vegetables in kilograms. People are measured in imperial (height in feet and inches, weight in stones and pounds), but buildings and objects are metric (height in metres, weight in kilograms). None of it makes much sense.

Speed limits are clearly marked: 20 miles per hour in residential streets, 30 or 40mph in built-up areas, 60mph on out-of-town single carriageway roads (often signed by a white circle with a black diagonal stripe), 70mph on dual carriageways and motorways. The last two are reduced to 50 and 60mph if you're towing a caravan or trailer. Assume that in any area with street lighting the speed limit is 30mph unless otherwise stated.

The AA (⊛www.theaa.com), RAC (⊛www.rac.co.uk) and Green Flag (⊛www.greenflag.co.uk) all operate **24-hour emergency breakdown** services, and offer useful online route planners. You may be entitled to free assistance through a reciprocal arrangement with a motoring organization in your home country – check before setting out. You can make use of these emergency services if you are not a member of the organization, but you will need to become a member at the roadside and will also incur a hefty surcharge.

Parking

Parking in towns, cities and popular tourist spots can be limited and is often very expensive. A painted **yellow line** beside the kerb indicates time restrictions on parking; there will be a sign nearby (often attached to a lamp post) detailing exactly what they are. Two yellow stripes (a "**double yellow line**") means parking is prohibited at all times, though you can stop briefly to unload or pick up. A **red line** means no stopping at all. Do not park on the white zigzag lines painted near pedestrian crossings. **Fines** for parking transgressions are high – often more than £50 – and if you are wheel-clamped, expect to pay £200 or more to be released.

If you're in a tourist city for a day, look out for **park-and-ride** (**P&R**) options (⊛www.parkandride.net), whereby you park on the outskirts and take a cheap or free bus to the centre. Urban **car parks** (parking lots) often use a "pay and display" system: put your money into the machine, take the ticket and display it on your dashboard. A few are ticketless, requiring you to key in your registration (license plate) rather than take a ticket. All these will be cheaper than using on-street meters, which often restrict parking time to one or two hours maximum. Some towns operate free **disc-zone parking**, which allows limited parking in designated areas: if that's what roadside signs indicate, you need to pick up a cardboard disc from any local shop and display it on your dashboard.

Vehicle rental

Car rental is usually cheaper arranged in advance from home through one of the global chains or through your tour operator as part of a fly-drive package.

If you rent a car locally, expect to pay around £30 per day, £50 for a weekend or from £120 per week. You can sometimes find deals under £20 per day, though you'll need to book well in advance for the cheapest rates and be prepared for surcharges for extras like damage excess waiver (CDW) and an additional driver. Small **local agencies** often undercut the major chains. Few companies will rent to drivers with less than one year's experience and most will only rent to people between 21 and 75 years of age. Rental cars will be manual (stick shift) unless you specify otherwise.

Just Go (☎01582/842888, ⊛www.justgo.uk.com) can rent quality **motorhomes** sleeping four to six people, equipped with full bathrooms, kitchenette and bike racks, for £300–1000 per week, depending on the season.

Car rental agencies

Avis ⊛www.avis.com.
Budget ⊛www.budget.com.
easycar ⊛www.easycar.com.
Europcar ⊛www.europcar.com.
Hertz ⊛www.hertz.com.
National ⊛www.nationalcar.com.
SIXT ⊛www.sixt.com.
Thrifty ⊛www.thrifty.com.

Cycling

No one would choose to get around England by **cycling** on the main "A" roads – there's simply too much traffic. It's far better to stick to the quieter "B" roads and country lanes – or, best of all, follow one of the **traffic-free trails** of the extensive National Cycle Network (see p.48).

Cycle helmets are not compulsory – but if you're planning on tackling the congestion, pollution and aggression of city traffic, you're well advised to wear one. You do have to have a **rear reflector** and front and back **lights** when riding at night, and you're not allowed to carry children without a special **child seat**. It is also illegal to cycle on pavements and in most public parks. **Off-road** cyclists must stick to bridleways and byways designated for their use.

Bike rental is available at cycle shops in most large towns, and at villages within national parks and other scenic areas. Expect to pay around £10–15 per day, with discounts for longer periods; you may need to provide credit card details, or leave a passport as a deposit.

Accommodation

Accommodation in England ranges from motorway lodges to old-fashioned country retreats, and from budget guesthouses to chic boutique hotels. Characterful old buildings – former coaching inns in towns, converted mansions and manor houses in rural areas – offer heaps of historic atmosphere.

Nearly all tourist offices will **reserve rooms** for you. In some areas you pay a deposit that's deducted from your first night's bill (usually ten percent); in others the office will take a percentage or flat-rate commission – usually around £3. Also useful is the "Book-a-bed-ahead" scheme, which reserves accommodation in your next destination – again for a charge of about £3.

A nationwide **grading system** awards stars to hotels, guesthouses and B&Bs. There's no hard and fast correlation between rank and price, but the grading system does lay down minimum levels of standards and service.

Hotels

Hotels vary wildly in size, style, comfort and price. The starting price for a one-star establishment is around £60 per night for a double/twin room, breakfast usually included; two- and three-star hotels can easily cost £100 a night, while four- and five-star properties may charge £200 a night – considerably more in London or in resort or country-house hotels. Many city hotels offer cut-price **weekend rates** to fill the rooms vacated by the weekday business trade. It's worth noting, however, that many upper-end urban hotels quote a "room-only" rate only – breakfast can be another whopping £10 or £15 on top.

Budget hotel chains including easyHotel (@www.easyhotel.com), Tune Hotels (@www.tunehotels.com), Premier Inn (@www.premierinn.com), Travelodge (@www.travelodge.co.uk), Holiday Inn Express (@www.hiexpress.com), Jurys Inn (@www.jurysinn.com), Ibis (@www.ibishotel.com), Campanile (@www.campanile.com) and Comfort/Quality/Sleep Inn (all @www.choicehotelsuk.co.uk) have properties usefully located in city centres across the country. Their style is generic, with no frills – breakfast is charged extra – but with special offers bringing en-suite room rates down to £20–30 if booked in advance, they're a bargain.

B&Bs and guesthouses

At its most basic, a **B&B (bed-and-breakfast)** is an ordinary private house with a couple of bedrooms set aside for paying guests. Larger establishments with more rooms, particularly in resorts, style themselves **guesthouses**, but they are pretty much the same thing. Either way, these are a great option for travellers looking for character and a local experience: the best – with fresh, house-proud rooms, hearty home-cooked food and a wealth of local knowledge – can match or beat a hotel stay at any price.

Don't assume that a B&B is no good if it is ungraded in official listings: many places

Accommodation price codes

Throughout this guide, accommodation is graded on a scale of ❶ to ❽, the number indicating the lowest price you could expect to pay per night for a **double room in high season**. Breakfast is included unless otherwise stated. We've given the actual price for **dorm accommodation** in youth and backpackers' hostels, as well as price codes for those hostels that have private rooms.

❶ £50 and under	❹ £91–120	❼ £201–250
❷ £51–70	❺ £121–150	❽ £251 and above
❸ £71–90	❻ £151–200	

At the lower end of this scale (❶–❷) – often B&Bs rather than hotels – you'll normally experience small rooms, spartan facilities and shared bathrooms, though generally with a washbasin, TV and electric kettle for making tea in the room. You'll pay a few pounds more for en-suite shower and toilet facilities. Above category ❸ you can expect more space and comfort. Categories ❹–❺ usually guarantee a good location, decent en-suite rooms and some extras. Paying the top rates (❻–❽) – for instance in superior city-centre hotels, seaside palaces or rural mansions – you can expect to be properly pampered, with first-class amenities including spa and/or fitness facilities.

simply choose not to enter into a grading scheme. In countryside locations some of the best accommodation is to be found in **farmhouses** and other properties whose facilities may technically fall short of official standards.

Many village **pubs** also offer B&B, again often not graded. Standards vary wildly – some are great, others truly awful – but at best you'll be staying in a friendly spot with a sociable bar on hand, and you'll rarely pay more than £70 a room.

However, **single travellers** should be aware that many B&Bs and guesthouses don't have single rooms, and sole occupancy of a double/twin room may be charged at seventy or eighty percent of the standard rate.

B&B My Guest ☏0870/444 3840, ⊛www.beduk .co.uk. Online bookings at 300 traditional or historic B&B properties.

Distinctly Different ☏01225/866842, ⊛www .distinctlydifferent.co.uk. Unusual buildings converted into accommodation: stay the night in an old brothel, ex-chapel, windmill or lighthouse.

Farm Stay UK ☏024/7669 6909, ⊛www .farmstay.co.uk. The UK's largest network of farm-based accommodation.

Wolsey Lodges ☏01473/822058, ⊛www .wolseylodges.com. Superior B&B in inspected properties across England, from Elizabethan manor houses to Victorian rectories.

Hostels and student halls

The **Youth Hostel Association** (YHA; ☏01629/592700, ⊛www.yha.org.uk) has over 220 properties across England (and Wales), offering bunk-bed accommodation in single-sex dormitories and smaller rooms of two, four or six beds. Some hostels also offer tipi accommodation, some have pitches for camping, and most offer kitchens, laundry facilities, lounges, cycle stores and bike rental. In cities, resorts and national park areas the facilities can be as good as some budget hotels. Depending on the season, most hostels **charge** around £15–22 for a bed – less in quieter places, more in popular locations. Many also offer private twin/double and family rooms (roughly £30–65). **Meals** – breakfast, packed lunch or dinner – are good value (around £5).

The YHA is affiliated to the global network of **Hostelling International** (⊛www .hihostels.com). If you're already an HI member, you qualify for the YHA's standard rates. Otherwise, you must pay a membership supplement of £3 a night (£1.50 for under-18s) – or you can join HI in person at any hostel, or online, for £16 a year (£10 for under-26s). Family deals are available. Members qualify for perks and discounts on various UK travel providers, detailed on the website.

A comparable network of **independent hostels** (Ⓦwww.independenthostelsuk.co.uk) offers similar facilities in a more youthful, backpacker-oriented ambience, generally at lower prices and with fewer restrictions. Their *Independent Hostel Guide*, linked on the website, has full details.

In university towns over the summer (July–Sept), plus at Easter and Christmas, **student halls** can offer great value, generally in single rooms or self-catering apartments. Check Ⓦwww.budgetstayuk.com and www.universityrooms.co.uk for details.

Camping and camping barns

Camping in England has undergone something of a renaissance in recent years, and there are hundreds of **campsites**, ranging from rustic, family-run places to large sites with laundries, shops and sports facilities. Costs vary from around £5 per adult in the simplest sites up to around £20 per tent (including two adults) in the most sought-after places. Many campsites also offer accommodation in permanently fixed **caravans**, mostly large, fully equipped units. *The Rough Guide to Camping in Britain* has detailed reviews of the best campsites, and Ⓦwww.campingandcaravanningclub.co.uk, www.ukcampsite.co.uk and www.theaa.com are useful resources as well. You can also camp in the grounds (and use the facilities) of several YHA hostels: details at Ⓦwww.yha.org.uk. **Farmers** may offer pitches for as little as £5 per night, but setting up a tent without asking first will not be well received. **Camping rough** is illegal in national parks and nature reserves, with the exception of Dartmoor (see p.376).

The wilder parts of England offer accommodation in **camping barns** and **bunk-houses**, often administered by the YHA. Conditions are very basic, but they are weatherproof and cheap (from £5 a night). Check Ⓦwww.campingbarns.net for listings.

Self-catering accommodation

Holiday **self-catering** properties range from city penthouses to secluded **cottages**. The minimum rental period is usually a week:

THE ROALD DAHL MUSEUM AND STORY CENTRE

Discover the stories behind the stories...

HP16 0AL **T** 01494 892192
www.roalddahlmuseum.org

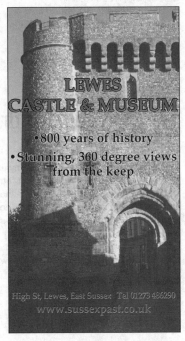

LEWES CASTLE & MUSEUM

• 800 years of history
• Stunning, 360 degree views from the keep

High St, Lewes, East Sussex Tel 01273 486290
www.sussexpast.co.uk

depending on the season, expect to pay around £300 a week for a small cottage in an out-of-the-way location, maybe three or four times that for a larger property in a popular spot. We've given some agencies below; otherwise, every tourist board has details of self-catering rentals in its area. **Serviced apartments**, available by the night in many English cities, offer an attractive alternative to hotel stays, with prices from around £100 (more in London).

Holiday cottages

Cornish Cottage Holidays ℡01326/573808, Ⓦwww.cornishcottageholidays.co.uk. Lots of thatched cottages and seaside places in Cornwall.
Cottages Direct ℡0845/268 0947, Ⓦwww.cottagesdirect.com. Massive choice of properties around the country, offering direct booking.
Cottages4You ℡0845/268 0760, Ⓦwww.cottages4you.co.uk. Wide range of graded properties all over the UK.
Heart of the Lakes ℡015394/32321, Ⓦwww.heartofthelakes.co.uk. Excellent choice of over 300 quality properties in the Lake District.
Helpful Holidays ℡01647/433593, Ⓦwww.helpfulholidays.com. Everything from cottages to a castle, exclusively in the West Country.
HomeAway ℡020/8827 1971, Ⓦwww.homeaway.co.uk. Lists thousands of holiday properties nationwide.

Landmark Trust ℡01628/825925, Ⓦwww.landmarktrust.org.uk. A preservation charity which lists over 180 historic properties converted into holiday accommodation, ranging from restored forts and Martello towers to a tiny radio shack used in World War II.
Marsdens ℡01271/813777, Ⓦwww.marsdens.co.uk. Great selection of graded properties in Devon and Cornwall.
National Trust ℡0844/800 2070, Ⓦwww.nationaltrustcottages.co.uk. The NT owns more than 350 cottages, houses and farmhouses, most set in their own gardens or grounds.
Rural Retreats ℡01386/701177, Ⓦwww.ruralretreats.co.uk. Upmarket accommodation, often in restored historic buildings. Especially strong on the Cotswolds and East Anglia, though with dozens of properties nationwide.

Serviced apartments

Apartment Service ℡020/8944 1444, Ⓦwww.apartmentservice.com. Properties in and around London.
City Base Apartments ℡0845/226 9831, Ⓦwww.citybaseapartments.com. Wide range of apartments across the country.
Holiday Serviced Apartments ℡01923/820077, Ⓦwww.holidayapartments.co.uk. Family business handling apartments in towns around England.

Food and drink

Changing tastes have transformed England's food and drink over the last decade. Much importance is being placed on "ethical" eating – notably sourcing products locally, but also using organic, humanely produced, quality ingredients. Good, moderately priced restaurants can now be found everywhere: increasingly, England's best meals are being served in otherwise modest, independently owned establishments, frequently lying off the beaten track. The old-fashioned English pub – seemingly impervious to fashion – remains an enduring social institution, often the best introduction to town or village life.

Traditional food

England's best-known traditional dish is **fish and chips** – a plate-sized fillet of cod or haddock, battered and deep-fried until crispy, served with freshly fried chips (thick-cut French fries) and doused in malt vinegar and salt. Restaurants will add a wedge of lemon and a blob of tartare sauce; at a takeaway counter you'll be asked whether you want it "open" – served in a paper cone for eating on the hoof – or "wrapped", for eating later. At its best, fish and chips is a light and succulent treat, but quality is very variable; too often it ends up as just more limp, greasy fast food. Local knowledge is the key: most towns, cities and resorts have at least one standout "chip shop". Some – like Whitby's *Magpie Café* or *Stein's Fish & Chips* in Padstow – are destinations in themselves. See ⓦwww.seafish.org for regional listings of quality-assured outlets.

Other **traditional English dishes** are just as ubiquitous – steak and kidney pie, lamb chops and others (for more, see box below) figure on menu after menu in cafés, pubs

and restaurants across the land, but **regional specialities** are increasingly important. As always, quality varies, but for every dismal meal being churned out, there's invariably a café or restaurant somewhere nearby serving up excellent, local food at reasonable prices. Even in fashionable fine-dining restaurants you'll find a revival of traditional English cuisine, with creative takes on the classics entering the realms of *haute cuisine*.

Breakfast remains sacrosanct: the gut-busting "Full English" (see box below) is still hugely popular. If you don't fancy a big fry-up first thing, you can generally ask for scrambled, boiled or poached eggs instead, while better establishments might offer

Some traditional English dishes

The Full English
The traditional **English breakfast**, or "Full English" – mainstay of almost every B&B and hotel – usually kicks off with a choice of cereals, followed by a plate of eggs, sausage, bacon, tomatoes, mushrooms – all of which (particularly if you're in the north) may well be fried – plus baked beans, toast (or sometimes fried bread) and tea or coffee. Travellers in northern England may also be offered black pudding, a sausage made from pork fat, onions, oatmeal and congealed blood.

The Sunday roast
Heartiest meal of the week used to be – and for many families still is – the **Sunday roast**; the tradition is continued every Sunday lunchtime in pubs and restaurants across England. Expect a choice of roast beef, lamb, pork or chicken, carved from the joint, and accompanied by boiled vegetables, Yorkshire pudding (though purists say this should only be served with roast beef), roast potatoes, gravy and a sauce on the side (horseradish for beef, mint for lamb, apple for pork or bread sauce for chicken). Wash it down with a pint or two of ale and say hello to a long, lazy Sunday afternoon.

Some other specialities
Bubble-and-squeak – fried potato and cabbage (and sometimes other veg).
Chip butty – a chip sandwich.
Crumble – an oven-baked dessert of stewed fruit with a crunchy topping made from butter, flour and sugar.
Faggots – offal meatballs.
Mushy peas – boiled marrowfat peas reduced almost to a paste, served alongside fish and chips.
Piccalilli – a mustard pickle.
Ploughman's lunch – a plate of crusty bread, cheese, pickle and salad.
Shepherd's pie – an oven-baked dish of minced lamb topped with mashed potato. A "cottage pie" is the same thing made with minced beef.
Spotted dick – a dessert of suet pudding with currants or sultanas.
Toad-in-the-hole – sausages baked in Yorkshire pudding.
Yorkshire pudding – baked batter, usually served to accompany a traditional Sunday roast.

dishes like muesli and yoghurt, fresh fruit salad, pancakes, kippers (smoked herring) and other delights. "Continental" breakfasts, of orange juice, croissants and coffee, are also widely available.

Cafés and tearooms

Every town, city and resort has dozens of **cafés**, characteristically unassuming places offering nonalcoholic drinks, all-day breakfasts, snacks and meals. Most are only open during the daytime (roughly 8am–5pm), and tend to be cash-only establishments with few airs and graces. **Teashops** or **tearooms** are more genteel, and serve a range of sandwiches, cakes and light meals as well as, of course, tea. Almost all the old-fashioned chrome-and-formica **coffee bars** have been replaced by US-style chain outlets, such as *Starbucks*, *Costa* and *Caffè Nero*.

Café-bars and gastropubs

Licensed (that is, alcohol-serving) **café-bars** on the European model are increasingly common. Although primarily places to drink, many serve reasonably priced food. Many pubs – if they serve food at all – still rely on their microwave and deep-fat fryer, but others have embraced the change in British tastes. The term "**gastropub**" – implying a pub that serves restaurant-quality food – is an urban affectation, but nonetheless reflects the fact you can often find great, affordable, high-quality "pub grub" in unlikely-looking rural hostelries and city drinking dens alike.

Restaurants

Chip shops aside, it's surprisingly hard to find a **restaurant** that serves traditional English food, though many showcase "**Modern British**" cuisine. At its best this inventive style marries local, seasonal produce with ingredients and techniques from the Mediterranean, Southeast Asia and further afield. It's an often idiosyncratic fusion that, these days, frequently relies upon "Slow Food" ideals (Ⓦ www.slowfood.org.uk).

More common are restaurants serving **Indian** (more properly Bangladeshi or Pakistani, in most cases) and **Chinese** (mostly Cantonese) cuisine: in many ways, the "curry house" now offers the quintessential English

dining experience. Most of these places are authentic and inexpensive – the best are to be found within their home communities in parts of London and the post-industrial cities of the Midlands (Birmingham, Leicester), the north (Leeds, Bradford) and the northwest (Manchester, Liverpool). Otherwise, other than **Thai** food – another Asian cuisine which has caught the British imagination and is widely represented – reliable budget stand-bys are ubiquitous **Italian** pizza/pasta joints and **French** chain bistros.

London has the best selection of **top-class restaurants**, and the widest choice of cuisines, but wherever you are you're rarely more than half an hour's drive from a really good meal – and some of the very best dining experiences are just as likely to be found in a suburban backstreet or quiet village as in a metropolitan hot-spot.

Costs and opening hours

The biggest deterrent to enjoying England's gastronomic delights is the expense. While a great curry in Birmingham's Balti Triangle or a Cantonese feast in Manchester's Chinatown can be had for well under £15 a head, the going rate for a full meal with drinks in most modest restaurants is more like £20–25 per person. Even in a pub, with main courses averaging £8–10, the price soon mounts up. If a restaurant has any sort of reputation, you can expect to be spending £30–40 each, while tasting menus at Michelin-starred restaurants cost upwards of £80 per person.

Restaurants usually open for **lunch** (generally noon to 2 or 3pm) and **dinner** (7 to 10 or 11pm); in our reviews we've stated any significant variations. Pub kitchens tend to close between 2.30 or 3pm and 6pm, often on Sunday and/or Monday evenings as well, and will stop serving around 9pm. **Reservations** are recommended everywhere, especially at weekends; the most celebrated places will require advance reservations weeks (or months) in advance.

Specialist **vegetarian** places are rare outside the cities, but most restaurants and pubs have at least one veggie option on their menus, while Italian, Indian and Chinese restaurants usually provide a decent choice of meat-free dishes. Veg Dining (Ⓦ www .vegdining.com) has good nationwide listings.

Pubs and bars

Originating as wayfarers' hostelries and coaching inns, **pubs** have outlived the church and marketplace as the focal points of many English towns and villages. They are as varied as the country's townscapes: in larger market towns you'll find huge oak-beamed inns with open fires and polished brass fittings; in remoter upland villages there are stone-built pubs no larger than a two-bedroomed cottage. At its best, the pub can be as welcoming as the full name – "public house" – suggests. Sometimes, particularly in the more inward-looking parts of post-industrial England, you might have to dig deeper for a welcome: in such places, the **public bar** is where working men bond over a pint while the plusher **saloon bar** is the preferred haunt of couples and women.

In many urban areas, especially with a younger population, traditional pubs face a challenge from contemporary **café-bars**. Most are chain properties – *All Bar One*, *Pitcher & Piano* and others – but we've highlighted some more characterful independent places in relevant city accounts.

Most pubs and bars keep **opening hours** of 11am to 11pm (usually 10.30pm on Sundays), though cities and popular resorts host many places open into the small hours.

Beer and wine

Although **lager** – pale, industrially produced, infused with bubbles and served chilled – is most popular by far (leading brands include Carling, Foster's, Kronenbourg and Stella Artois), the classic English **beer** is known as **bitter**. It should be physically pumped by hand from a barrel in the cellar and served at ambient temperature: if what's in your glass is ice-cold, fizzy or came out of an electric pump, it isn't the real McCoy.

The big brewing conglomerates still distribute some good bitters but the real glory of English beer is in the local detail. Dozens of regional breweries, many of them

No smoking

Smoking is illegal in all enclosed public spaces, including restaurants, cafés, pubs and offices, and on all public transport. Hotel rooms that are designated specifically as smoking rooms are exempt – but the vast majority of hotels and B&Bs impose smoking bans throughout their premises anyway.

with long histories, and contemporary micro-breweries produce nuanced, highly flavourful and distinctive styles of bitter, known as **"real ale"**, to traditional recipes. For more on these, and on the West Country's favourite tipples – **cider** and **perry** – see the *Pubs and pints* colour section.

Large breweries own most of England's fifty thousand pubs – and naturally favour their own beers for sale, though generally alongside one or two "guest ales". For the best choice, though, try to find a pub labelled as a **"free house"** – these are independently run, and therefore able to sell whichever brands of beer they like, often including idiosyncratic, locally brewed gems. Depending on the pub (and how busy it is), you could legitimately ask the bar staff for a bit of guidance – or even for a sample of one or two beers before buying – to find out what's to your taste. CAMRA (the Campaign for Real Ale; ⑩www.camra.org.uk) produces a *Good Beer Guide* which rates 4500 quality pubs nationwide.

The English also consume an ever-increasing quantity of **wine**, but although restaurants (and supermarkets) commonly stock an excellent range, wine sold in pubs can vary in quality. Although a few English wines (for more on which, see the box on p.177) make it onto menus and pub boards, they're a rarity in among the welter of French, Italian, German, Spanish, Bulgarian, Chilean, Australian and Californian wines which dominate.

The media

The English are avid consumers of mass media, from newspapers (national and local) and innumerable magazines to hundreds of TV and radio stations, both terrestrial and digital.

The press

The UK's national **daily newspapers** are commonly identified as either "quality" (that is, publishing serious, news-led journalism) or "tabloid" (devoted more to populist muck-raking and celebrity/royal gossip). On the quality side are the left-leaning *Guardian*, broadly centrist *Independent*, right-leaning *Times* and staunchly Conservative *Daily Telegraph*, along with the business-minded *Financial Times*. All are outsold by the tabloids, led by the right-wing *Sun* and left-ish *Daily Mirror*, along with the tub-thumping, frequently xenophobic *Daily Mail* and *Daily Express*.

All of these appear Monday to Saturday only. On Sundays, each gives way to a sister title from the same stable. Most are identifiable (ie *Sunday Times*, *Independent on Sunday* and so on), though the *Guardian* becomes the *Observer* – England's oldest Sunday newspaper – and the *Sun* mutates into the laughably mistitled gossip-rag *News of the World*.

You'll also see mostly weekly **local newspapers** along with racks of **magazines** from the parochial to familiar global titles. One to look out for is the satirical bi-weekly *Private Eye*, which prides itself on printing the stories the rest of the press won't touch, and on riding the consequent stream of libel suits. Australians, New Zealanders and South Africans in London should look out for the weekly free magazine *TNT*, which provides news from home as well as classified ads.

TV

The UK has five terrestrial **TV channels** available pretty much everywhere: BBC1 and BBC2 (Ⓦwww.bbc.co.uk), ITV1 (Ⓦwww.itv .com), Channel 4 (Ⓦwww.channel4.com) and Five (Ⓦwww.five.tv). Most hotels – and a fair sprinkling of other forms of tourist accommodation – will offer **cable** or, more frequently, **satellite** channels as well.

Radio

The BBC runs five analogue **radio** stations. All are available nationwide, though the exact frequency varies according to your location: Radio 1 (chart and urban music; 97–99FM), Radio 2 (light pop and specialist music; 88–91FM), Radio 3 (classical music; 90–93FM), Radio 4 (current affairs and serious speech; 92–95FM) and Five Live (rolling news and sport; 693 or 909 AM). Other national stations include Classic FM (light classical music; 100–102FM), Absolute (pop music; 1215 AM plus 105.8FM in London) and TalkSport (sports phone-ins; 1053 or 1089 AM). There's also a host of local stations in each area, both BBC (mostly speech-led) and commercial (almost entirely music-led).

All these can also be picked up **digitally** – either online, or through a digital TV, or with a special DAB digital radio – which also gives you access to countless more digital-only stations, from classic rock to Christian worship.

Festivals and events

Many of the showpiece events marketed to tourists – Trooping the Colour, the Lord Mayor's Show and the like – say little about contemporary England and nothing about the country's regional folk history. For a more instructive idea of what makes the English tick, you'd do better to sniff out some grassroots, local-led festivities – a wacky village celebration, for instance, or London's exuberant Notting Hill Carnival.

Most major towns and cities host public festivals, some dating back centuries, others more recent inventions, but everywhere there's a general willingness both to revive the traditional and to experiment with the new – from medieval jousting through to performing arts. The events calendar below picks out some of the best; for detailed local listings contact tourist offices.

January/February

London Parade (Jan 1; ⓦ www.londonparade .co.uk). Floats, marching bands, clowns, cheerleaders and classic cars wend their way through the centre of London.
Chinese New Year (on or near Feb 3, 2011; Jan 23, 2012; Feb 10, 2013; ⓦ www.londonchinatown.org). Processions, fireworks and festivities in the country's two main Chinatowns in London and Manchester.
Shrove Tuesday (aka Mardi Gras/"Fat Tuesday"; March 8, 2011; Feb 21, 2012; Feb 12, 2013). The last day before Lent, also known as "Pancake Day": it's traditional to eat pancakes and, famously in Olney, Buckinghamshire (ⓦ www.visitolney.com), to race with them. Ashbourne in Derbyshire (ⓦ www.ashbourne-town.com) hosts the world's oldest, largest, longest, maddest game of "Shrovetide Football".

Easter

British & World Marbles Championship (Good Friday; ⓦ www.britishmarbles.org.uk). Held at Tinsley Green in Sussex.
Bacup Nutters Dance (Easter Saturday; ⓦ www .coconutters.co.uk). Blacked-up clog dancers mark the town boundaries of Bacup in Lancashire.
Hare Pie Scramble and Bottle-Kicking (Easter Monday). Chaotic village bottle-kicking contest at Hallaton, Leicestershire.
World Coal-Carrying Championship (Easter Monday; ⓦ www.gawthorpe.ndo.co.uk). Competitors lug 50kg of coal through Gawthorpe village in West Yorkshire.

April

St George's Day (April 23; ⓦ www .stgeorgesholiday.com). Also, by happy chance, the birthday of William Shakespeare – and the Queen's birthday falls two days earlier, on April 21. Traditional St George's Day events include Morris dancing at Stoke Bruerne in Northamptonshire, Yate in Gloucestershire and elsewhere, as well as full-blown street festivals in Birmingham, Leicester, Manchester and London, where the Globe Theatre (ⓦ www.shakespeares-globe.org) hosts a day of Shakespeare events. Also reckon on parades, folk dancing and celebrations at Stratford-upon-Avon (ⓦ www.shakespearesbirthday.org.uk).

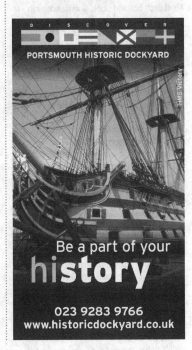

May

Padstow Obby Oss (May 1; @www.padstow .com). Processions, music and dancing in Padstow, Cornwall; the name is dialect for "hobby horse". See p.415.

Helston Furry Dance (May 8). A courtly procession and dance through the Cornish town by men in top hats and women in formal dresses. See p.401.

Glyndebourne Opera Festival (mid-May to end Aug; @www.glyndebourne.com). One of England's classiest arts events, in East Sussex. See p.188.

Cheese Rolling (last Mon in May; @www.cheese -rolling.co.uk). Mass pursuit of a cheese wheel down Cooper's Hill in Gloucestershire – one of the weirdest knees-ups in England. See p.293.

Chelsea Flower Show (late May; @www.rhs .org.uk). Essential event for England's green-fingered legions, at Chelsea in London.

Hay Festival (late May; @www.hayfestival.com). The nation's bookish types descend on Hay, on the Welsh border, for this literary shindig. See p.508.

Bath Music Festival (end May to early June; @www.bathmusicfest.org.uk). Arts jamboree, with a concurrent fringe festival. See p.333.

June

Aldeburgh Festival (June; @www.aldeburgh .co.uk). Suffolk jamboree of classical music, established by Benjamin Britten. See p.443.

Beating Retreat (early June; @www .guardsbeatingretreat.com) A colourful ceremony of pageantry and military music on Horse Guards Parade in London.

Strawberry Fair (1st Sat; @www.strawberry-fair .org.uk). Free festival of music, arts and crafts in Cambridge.

Appleby Horse Fair (2nd week; @www .applebyfair.org). Appleby in Cumbria hosts England's landmark annual gypsy gathering. See p.682.

Trooping the Colour (2nd Sat; @www.royal.gov .uk). Massed bands, equestrian pageantry, gun salutes and fly-pasts on Horse Guards Parade, London.

World Worm-Charming Championships (last Sat; @www.wormcharming.com). Worm-charming and other zany pastimes, at Willaston, Cheshire.

July

Pride London (early July; @www.pridelondon .org). Lesbian, gay, bisexual and transgender rally followed by a parade and music events. In 2012 London hosts WorldPride.

Rushbearing Festival (1st Sat; @www .amblesideonline.co.uk). Symbolic procession of crosses and garlands at Ambleside in the Lake District, dating back centuries.

Hobby Horse Festival (1st week; @www .hobbyhorsefestival.co.uk). Quirky shindig in Banbury, Oxfordshire, with costumed parades, folk dancing and lots of hobby horses.

York Early Music Festival (mid-July; @www .ncem.co.uk). The country's premier festival of medieval and Renaissance music. See p.741.

Great Yorkshire Show (2nd week; @www .greatyorkshireshow.com). England's largest region celebrates its heritage, culture and cuisine at Harrogate, North Yorkshire. See p.729.

The Proms (mid-July to mid-Sept; @www.bbc .co.uk/proms). Top-flight international classical music festival in London, with very cheap standing tickets. See p.146.

Swan Upping (3rd week; @www.royal.gov.uk). Ceremonial counting of the swan population on the upper stretches of the River Thames, dating back to the twelfth century. At Windsor, all the oarsmen stand to attention in their boats and salute the Queen.

Cambridge Folk Festival (last week; @www .cambridgefolkfestival.co.uk). Biggest event of its kind in England, with lots more than just folk music. See p.482.

Whitstable Oyster Festival (late July; @www .whitstableoysterfestival.com). A congenial mixing of oysters, Champagne, Guinness, parades and music. See p.156.

August

Brighton Pride (1st week; @www.brightonpride .org). A week of events celebrating lesbian, gay, bisexual and transgender culture, culminating in a huge carnival parade. See p.197.

Cowes Week (1st week; @www.cowesweek .co.uk). Sailing extravaganza in the Isle of Wight, with partying and star-studded entertainment. See p.223.

Sidmouth Folk Week (1st week; @www .sidmouthfolkweek.co.uk). Folk and roots performers in this Devon town, plus theatre and dance. See p.363.

Whitby Folk Week (last week; @www.whitbyfolk .co.uk). Traditional folk music, morris and sword dancing, storytelling and more. See p.765.

Grasmere Sports and Show (last Sun; @www .grasmeresportsandshow.co.uk). Wrestling, fell-running, ferret-racing and other curious Lake District pastimes. See p.660.

Notting Hill Carnival (last Sun & Mon; @www .thenottinghillcarnival.com). Vivacious Caribbean-style costumed celebration in the streets of west London, also including everything from Punjabi drummers to Brazilian salsa, plus music, food and floats. See p.119.

Music festivals

England has gone **music festival** crazy. Every weekend from June to September now sees some kind of musical happening – and in July and August literally dozens of outdoor events take place simultaneously in parks, town centres, farms, beaches and disused airfields up and down the country, often drawing tens of thousands of people to camp out for a weekend of partying under (hopefully) sunny skies. Here are ten to choose from; check ⓦ www.efestivals.co.uk for details of hundreds more.

Sunrise Celebration (early June; ⓦ www.sunrisecelebration.com). Hippyish "festival of organic arts and culture", held in Somerset as a prelude to summer.

Isle of Wight Festival (mid-June; ⓦ www.isleofwightfestival.com). Three days of established rock and pop acts for thirty/forty-something groovers.

Glastonbury (late June; ⓦ www.glastonburyfestivals.co.uk). Top-class musical line-up – nothing can dampen the trippy-hippy vibe. See p.339.

Latitude (mid-July; ⓦ www.latitudefestival.co.uk). Genteel, family-friendly fest, strong on the wider arts and comedy, in a gorgeous part of Suffolk.

Secret Garden (mid-July; ⓦ uk.secretgardenparty.com). A gorgeous lake and wacky art installations distinguish this genial Cambridgeshire hippie-fest.

WOMAD (late July; ⓦ www.womad.org). Renowned three-day world music event at Charlton Park, outside Malmesbury, Wiltshire.

Global Gathering (late July; ⓦ www.globalgathering.com). A weekend of top DJs and the odd crossover live act at Long Marston Airfield near Stratford-upon-Avon.

Cambridge Folk Festival (late July/early Aug; ⓦ www.cambridgefolkfestival.co.uk). Mellow and unpretentious folk festival that's still going strong almost five decades after it began.

Leeds Festival (late Aug; ⓦ www.leedsfestival.com). Raucous weekend of rock, punk and indie acts, both new and established.

Bestival (early Sept; ⓦ www.bestival.net). Quirky event on the Isle of Wight, featuring big names, wild electronica and fancy dress.

Leeds West Indian Carnival (last Mon; ⓦ www.leedscarnival.co.uk). England's oldest carnival, featuring processions, dancing and barbecues.

September

Blackpool Illuminations (early Sept to early Nov; ⓦ www.blackpool-illuminations.net). Five miles of extravagantly kitsch light displays on the Blackpool seafront. See p.629.

Abbots Bromley Horn Dance (early Sept; ⓦ www.abbotsbromley.com). Vaguely pagan mass dance in mock-medieval costume – one of the most famous of England's ancient customs, at Abbots Bromley, Staffordshire.

St Ives September Festival (mid-Sept; ⓦ www.stivesseptemberfestival.co.uk). Eclectic Cornish festival of art, poetry, literature, jazz, folk, rock and world music.

Heritage Open Days (mid-Sept; ⓦ www.heritageopendays.org.uk). A once-a-year opportunity to peek inside hundreds of buildings that don't normally open their doors to the public. For London-specific events see "Open House London" (ⓦ www.open-city.org.uk).

October

World Conker Championship (2nd Sun; ⓦ www.worldconkerchampionships.com). Thousands flock to Ashton, Northamptonshire, to watch modern-day gladiators fight for glory armed only with a conker and twelve inches of string.

State Opening of Parliament (late Oct; ⓦ www.royal.gov.uk). The Queen arrives at Westminster in a fancy coach with much pageantry to give a speech and officially open Parliament. Also takes place whenever a new government is sworn in after an election.

Halloween (Oct 31). All Hallows' Eve – and Samhain, last day of the Celtic calendar. Now swamped by commercialized US-style costumes and trick-or-treating, although druidic ceremonies survive at a few sites (the Rollright Stones, for example; ⓦ www.rollrightstones.co.uk).

November

London to Brighton Veteran Car Run (1st Sun; www.lbvcr.com). Ancient machines cough and splutter their way 57 miles down the A23.

Bonfire Night (Nov 5). Fireworks and bonfires held in communities all round the country to commemorate the foiling of the Gunpowder Plot in 1605 (see p.578) – most notably at York (www.yorkmaze.com), Ottery St Mary in Devon (www.otterytarbarrels.co.uk), and Lewes in East Sussex (www.bonco.org.uk; see p.188).

Lord Mayor's Show (2nd Sat; www.lordmayorsshow.org). Held annually in the City of London since 1215, and featuring a daytime cavalcade and night-time fireworks to mark the inauguration of the new Lord Mayor.

December

New Year's Eve (Dec 31). The biggest celebration takes place in London (www.london.gov.uk/newyearseve), with a fireworks display over the Thames and thousands of inebriates in Trafalgar Square, but there are huge parties in city centres nationwide. In Allendale village, Northumberland, locals turn up with trays of burning tar on their heads to parade round a large communal bonfire.

Sports and outdoor activities

As the birthplace of many global sports, including football, rugby, cricket and tennis, England can boast sporting events which attract a world audience. If you prefer participating to spectating, the country caters for just about every outdoor activity, too: we've concentrated below on walking, cycling and watersports, but there are also opportunities for anything from rock climbing to pony-trekking.

Spectator sports

Football (soccer) is the national game, with professional matches taking place every Saturday afternoon from early August to early May, plus plenty of Sunday and midweek fixtures too. It's very difficult to get tickets to Premier League matches involving the most famous teams (Chelsea, Arsenal, Manchester United, Liverpool): you'll have more success at Championship (second-tier) games.

Rugby is less popular than football, though no less entertaining to watch. It comes in two forms, which have completely different rules: Rugby Union is played largely in the south of England, while Rugby League dominates in the north. Securing tickets for a top game shouldn't be a problem, whether you go for a weekly match in Union's Premiership (Sept–May) or League's Super League (Feb–Sept) – or one of the many internationals.

Cricket (played April–Sept) has broken out of its idiosyncratically dotty roots to become big business, thanks largely to the invention of the "Twenty20" format, designed to encourage flamboyant, decisive play in short three-hour matches. Big crowds result. Watch English county sides competing for the Twenty20 Cup – or opt for a full-day game in the domestic knock-out competition or a four-day match in the County Championship. Every summer visiting countries play a cycle of international five-day "Test" matches against the English national side at grounds around the country.

Tennis fever bites for two weeks in late June/early July, during the famous Wimbledon championships, with wall-to-wall TV coverage and breathless recountings of how well (or badly) any British players do. The rest of the year, no one gives a hoot.

Cheltenham Gold Cup (mid-March; www.cheltenham.co.uk). Centrepiece of this hugely popular steeplechase (fence-jumping) horse race meeting.

Boat Race (Sat in late March; www.theboatrace.org). Two crews from Oxford and Cambridge universities race along the River Thames in London.

Grand National (1st Sat in April; www.aintree.co.uk). Thrills and spills in the world's greatest steeplechase, staged at Aintree in Liverpool.

London Marathon (April; ⓦwww.london
-marathon.co.uk). The country's biggest running
race, as vicars in gorilla suits trail in behind the
speedy pros.

FA Cup Final (mid-May; ⓦwww.thefa.com).
Climax of the biggest domestic football competition,
staged at London's Wembley stadium.

Premiership Final (late May; ⓦwww
.guinnesspremiership.com). The top two teams
in Rugby Union battle for honours at Twickenham
stadium in London.

The Derby (1st week June; ⓦwww.epsomderby
.co.uk). A parade of top-class nags compete in
the 200-year-old Derby horse race, at Epsom near
London.

Wimbledon (late June & early July; ⓦwww
.wimbledon.org). The world's top tennis players slug
it out at Wimbledon in southwest London.

Twenty20 Cup (mid-Aug; ⓦwww.ecb.co.uk).
A fast and furious riot of cricket: both semi-finals
and the final take place at the same ground on the
same day.

Challenge Cup Final (last Sat in Aug; ⓦwww
.superleague.co.uk). Culmination of the biggest
knockout competition for Rugby League clubs.

Great North Run (mid-Sept; ⓦwww.greatrun
.org). Europe's most popular half-marathon sees
50,000 competitors running across the Tyne Bridge in
Newcastle-Gateshead.

Walking

England's finest **walking areas** are the granite
moorlands and spectacular coastlines of
Devon and Cornwall in the southwest, and the
highlands further north – notably the Peak
District, the Yorkshire Dales, the North York
Moors, and the Lake District. We've
highlighted local walks, climbs, rambles and
trails, but it goes without saying that even for
short hikes you need to be **properly
equipped**, follow local advice and listen out
for local weather reports. England's climate
may be relatively benign, but the weather is
changeable in any given season and people
die on the moors and mountains every year.

Keen hikers might want to tackle one of
England's dozen or so **National Trails**
(ⓦwww.nationaltrail.co.uk), which amount to
some 2500 miles of waymarked path and
track. The toughest is the **Pennine Way**
(268 miles; usually takes 16 days), stretching
from the Derbyshire Peak District to the
Scottish Borders, while the challenging
South West Coast Path (630 miles; 56
days) through Somerset, Devon, Cornwall
and Dorset tends to be tackled in shorter
sections. Other trails are less gung-ho in

character, like the **South Downs Way** (101 miles; 8 days) or the fascinating **Hadrian's Wall Path** (84 miles; 7 days). You'll find more details on all these walks online and in relevant accounts throughout this book.

The large-scale topographic **maps** published by Ordnance Survey (@www.ordnancesurvey.co.uk) are renowned for their accuracy and clarity. Choose from the Landranger series (1:50,000) or Explorer series (1:25,000).

Cycling

The **National Cycle Network** (@www.sustrans.org.uk) is made up of 10,000 miles of signed cycle routes, a third on traffic-free paths (including disused railways and canal towpaths), the rest mainly on country roads. You're never very far from one of the numbered routes, all of which are detailed online and covered by an excellent series of waterproof maps (1:100,000) published by

Sustrans. Major routes include the northern coast-to-coast routes **C2C** (Sea-to-Sea), 140 miles from the Cumbrian to Northumberland coasts, and the new **Way of the Roses** (169 miles) from Morecambe to Bridlington, the **Cornish Way** (123 miles), from Bude to Land's End, and routes that cut through the heart of England, such as from Derby to York (154 miles) or Gloucester to Reading (128 miles). Most local tourist offices stock a range of **cycling guides**, with maps and detailed route descriptions.

Watersports

Sailing and **windsurfing** are especially popular along the south coast (particularly the Isle of Wight and Solent) and in the southwest (around Falmouth in Cornwall, and Salcombe and Dartmouth in Devon). Here, and in the Lake District, you'll be able to rent boards, dinghies and boats, either by the hour or for longer periods of instruction –

England's national parks

England has nine national parks (@www.nationalparks.gov.uk), plus the Norfolk and Suffolk Broads, which has equivalent legal status and is effectively a tenth. They account for around 8 percent of England's land area and attract over 110 million visitors a year.

The Broads See p.456; @www.broads-authority.gov.uk. Fine place for a boating holiday: the rivers, marshes, fens and canals of Norfolk and Suffolk make up one of Europe's most important wetlands, ideal for birdwatching. Forget a car: cyclists and walkers have the best of it. *Don't miss:* a wildlife-viewing trip on the *Electric Eel* (p.457).

Dartmoor See p.376; @www.dartmoor-npa.gov.uk. In deepest Devon, England's largest wilderness attracts back-to-nature hikers and trippy stone-chasers in equal measure – the moorland walks can be pretty hardcore, while the standing stones are famous. *Don't miss:* Grimspound Bronze Age village (p.379).

Exmoor See p.345; @www.exmoor-nationalpark.gov.uk. A slightly tamer version of Dartmoor, straddling the Somerset/Devon border with high, hogsback hills overlooking the sea. Crisscrossed by trails and also accessible from the South West Coast Path, it's ideal for walking and pony-trekking. *Don't miss:* Tarr Steps, a 17-span medieval bridge (p.346).

Lake District See p.649; @www.lake-district.gov.uk. The biggest national park, located in Cumbria amid a near-Alpine landscape of glacial lakes and rugged mountains. It's great for hiking, rock climbing and watersports, but also has strong literary connections and thriving cultural traditions. *Don't miss:* Honister's hard-hat mine tour (p.671).

New Forest See p.229; @www.newforestnpa.gov.uk. Amid the domesticated landscape of Hampshire, England's best surviving example of a medieval hunting forest can be surprisingly wild. The majestic woodland is interspersed by tracts of heath, and a good network of paths and bridleways offers plenty of scope for biking and pony rides. *Don't miss:* off-road cycling from Brockenhurst (p.231).

from around £25 for a couple of hours of windsurfing to around £140 for a two-day non-residential sailing course. The UK Sailing Academy (⊛www.uksa.org) on the Isle of Wight is England's finest instruction centre for windsurfing, dinghy sailing, kayaking and more.

Newquay in Cornwall is England's undisputed **surfing** centre, whose main break, Fistral, regularly hosts international contests. But there are quieter spots all along the north coast of Cornwall and Devon, as well as a growing scene on the northeast coast from Yorkshire to Northumberland. There are plenty of places where you can rent or buy equipment, which means that prices are kept down to reasonable levels, say around £10 per day each for board and wetsuit.

Activity holiday operators

Most operators offering **activity holidays** feature escorted (guide-led) trips and self-guided options, the latter usually cheaper. On all holidays you can expect luggage transfer each night, pre-booked accommodation, detailed route instructions, a packed lunch and support. Below is a small selection of favourites.

Above The Line ℗019467/26229, ⊛www .wasdale.com. Lake District company operating from the *Wasdale Head Inn*, birthplace of British mountaineering, offering hill walking, guided ascents, and more.

Big Friday ℗020/8960 2471, ⊛www.bigfriday .com. Surf weekend packages from London to Newquay, with accommodation, travel and tuition laid on.

Blakes Holiday Boating ℗0845/604 3985, ⊛www.blakes.co.uk. Cruisers, yachts and narrowboats on the Norfolk Broads, the River Thames and canals.

Capital Sport ℗01296/631671, ⊛www.capital -sport.co.uk. Gentle self-guided cycling tours in Kent, Oxford and the Cotswolds, in either B&B or "fine" accommodation.

Northumberland See p.807; ⊛www.northumberlandnationalpark.org.uk. Where England meets Scotland, Northumberland is adventure country. The long-distance Pennine Way runs the length of the park, while the Romans left their mark in the shape of Hadrian's Wall, along which you can hike or bike. *Don't miss:* the Chillingham cattle wildlife safari (p.811).

North York Moors See p.748; ⊛www.northyorkmoors.org.uk. A stunning mix of heather moorland, gentle valleys, ruined abbeys and wild coastline in North Yorkshire. Walking and mountain biking are the big activities, but you can also tour the picturesque stone villages or sample the sea at Whitby. *Don't miss:* a day out at Ryedale Folk Museum (p.754).

Peak District See p.533; ⊛www.peakdistrict.gov.uk. England's first national park (1951) is also the most visited, located between the big cities of the Midlands and the northwest. It's rugged country, with some dramatic underground caverns, tempered by stately homes and spa and market towns. *Don't miss:* a trip down Speedwell Cavern (p.542).

South Downs See p.179; ⊛www.southdowns.gov.uk. These rolling chalk downlands in Hampshire and Sussex extend to the sea cliffs at Beachy Head and include ancient beech and oak forests as well as open heath. More than 100,000 people live within the park boundaries: this is less a wilderness than a lovely place for long walks on London's doorstep. *Don't miss:* following prehistoric droving paths on the South Downs Way (p.179).

Yorkshire Dales See p.712; ⊛www.yorkshiredales.org.uk. Probably the best choice for walking, cycling and pony-trekking, Yorkshire's second national park spreads across twenty dales (valleys) at the heart of the Pennines. England's scenic Settle–Carlisle Railway is another draw, while caves, waterfalls and castles provide the backdrop. *Don't miss:* the train ride across Ribblehead Viaduct (p.718).

Set yourself free!

Situated in the middle of the Irish Sea the **Isle of Man** is one of the best kept secrets of the British Isles.

This unique self-governing kingdom can be quickly and easily reached by air or sea from a range of destinations across the UK. In the current climate the Isle of Man is a perfect cost effective destination as it uses sterling currency in the same way as the UK.

The Island itself encompasses beautiful scenery, rugged coastlines, unspoilt beaches and a variety of activities for all to enjoy. There is also a wealth of cultural heritage sites to explore including one of the most preserved castles in Europe, Castle Rushen, and the imposing ancient castle and island fortress of Peel Castle.

The Isle of Man is a haven for visitors who want to experience the outdoor lifestyle or those looking for a relaxing break amid the Island's tranquil shores. Team this with quality accommodation and award winning local produce and you'll soon see why the Isle of Man is a perfect holiday destination.

For more information on the Isle of Man and to start planning your break log on to www.visitisleofman.com or phone 01624 686766.

Contours ℡ 017684/80451, ⓦ www.contours
.co.uk. Short breaks or longer walking holidays and
self-guided hikes in every region.
Country Lanes ℡ 01590/622627, ⓦ www
.countrylanes.co.uk. Ranging from one-day bike
rides to week-long holidays in the New Forest and
Isle of Wight.
Doone Valley Trekking ℡ 01598/741234,
ⓦ www.doonevalleytrekking.co.uk. Horseriding
holidays on Exmoor, for all ages and levels, with
self-catering farmhouse accommmodation.
Footpath Holidays ℡ 01985/840049, ⓦ www
.footpath-holidays.com. Guided and self-guided
walking packages to various hill and coastal areas.
Global Boarders ℡ 01736/711404, ⓦ www
.globalboarders.com. Tailor-made surf packages in
Cornwall, with a variety of options and transport.

Ramblers Holidays ℡ 01707/331133, ⓦ www
.ramblersholidays.co.uk. Sociable guided walking
tours (scenic, themed or special interest).
Saddle Skedaddle ℡ 0191/265 1110, ⓦ www
.skedaddle.co.uk. Biking adventures and classic road
rides – includes guided and self-guided tours, from a
weekend to a week.
Sherpa Expeditions ℡ 020/8577 2717, ⓦ www
.sherpa-walking-holidays.co.uk. At-your-own-pace,
self-guided walks (and cycle tours) in Yorkshire, the
Lakes and the southwest.
Xplore Britain ℡ 01740/650900, ⓦ www
.xplorebritain.com. Escorted and independent walking
and cycling holidays nationwide.
YHA ℡ 01629/592700, ⓦ www.yha.org.uk. Range of
good-value hostel-based activity weekends and holidays,
from walking and biking to kayaking and caving.

Shopping

Although shopping is now one of the chief leisure activities of the English, it can be a rather soulless experience. High streets up and down the country feature the same bland chain-stores selling similar ranges of mass-produced items. Nonetheless it is still possible to track down neighbourhoods, stores and the occasional oddity that make for a more enjoyable retail experience.

Most places, for example, have a **market** at least once a week, which may vary from the sprawling, commercialized affairs of Camden, Portobello and Spitalfields in London (see p.148), to sedate, community-minded village jamborees. Street markets or covered markets are often the best places to pick up craft items, though you may have to wade through a proliferation of scented candles and twee bric-a-brac to find anything truly original. Markets are also the only places (apart from antique shops and some second-hand shops) where **haggling** is acceptable. Country Markets (ⓦ www.country-markets .co.uk) has nationwide listings that make it easy to find when a market takes place close to you. Many towns also have a weekly or monthly **farmers' market** (see ⓦ www .farmersmarkets.net), selling local foods and artisan products. You'll find similarly authentic local items in **farm shops**, usually signposted by the side of the road in rural areas.

Particular districts and towns specialize in certain items – Birmingham's Jewellery Quarter (see p.528) for silver and gold, for example, or Hay-on-Wye (see p.508) for books. Antiques feature strongly everywhere – and in Cotswold villages in particular.

Most goods, with the chief exceptions of books and food, are subject to 20 percent **VAT** (Value Added Tax, or sales tax). VAT is always included in the marked price of goods. Visitors from non-EU countries can benefit from the **Tax-Free Shopping scheme**. Participating stores allow you to fill out a form at the time of purchase, which you then show to customs officials when you leave the UK: as long as you are taking that item out of the country, they will refund the VAT you paid. See (among others) ⓦ www.gbtaxfree.com or www.globalrefund .com. You cannot reclaim VAT charged on hotel bills or other services.

Travel essentials

Costs

England is expensive. Even if you're camping or hostelling, using public transport, buying picnic lunches and eating in pubs and cafés your minimum expenditure will be around £35/US$55/€40 per person per day. Couples staying in B&Bs, eating at unpretentious restaurants and visiting some attractions should expect roughly £70/US$110/€80 per person, while if you're renting a car, staying in hotels and eating well, budget for £120/US$185/€135 each. Double that figure if you choose to stay in stylish city hotels or grand country houses. On any visit to London, work on the basis that you'll need an extra £30/US$45/€35 per day to get the best out of the city.

Many of England's **historic attractions** – from castles to stately homes – are owned and/or operated by either the **National Trust** (℡0844/800 1895, ⊛www.nationaltrust.org.uk) or **English Heritage** (℡0870/333 1181, ⊛www.english-heritage.org.uk), whose properties are denoted throughout this book with "NT" or "EH". Both usually charge entry fees (roughly £6–12), though some sites are free. If you plan to visit more than half a dozen places owned by either, it's worth considering an annual membership (around £40). You can join online or in person at any staffed attraction. US members of the Royal Oak Foundation (⊛www.royal-oak.org) get free admission to all National Trust properties.

Non-UK residents can buy a **Great British Heritage Pass** (4/7/15/30 days £38/54/72/96; ⊛www.britishheritagepass.com), which gives free entry to 600 cultural and historic properties, including National Trust and English Heritage. Family discounts are available. You can buy it online, at equivalent rates from travel agents in your home country, or at major tourist offices in the UK.

Many **stately homes** remain privately owned, charging £8–18 for admission. Other old buildings are owned by local authorities, which generally charge less or allow free access.

Municipal **art galleries and museums** often have free admission, as do the big state museums (British Museum, National Gallery, National Railway Museum, Royal Armouries and many others). Private museums and other collections rarely charge more than £6 admission. Most **cathedrals** and churches either charge modest admission or ask for donations.

Throughout this book, admission prices quoted are the full adult rate, unless otherwise stated. Concessionary rates – generally half-price – for **senior citizens** (over 60), under-26s and **children** (aged 5–17) apply almost everywhere, from tourist attractions to public transport; you'll need official ID as proof of age. Children under 5 are rarely charged.

Full-time **students** are often entitled to discounts too. They can benefit from an ISIC (International Student Identity Card), while people under 26 can get an IYTC (International Youth Travel Card) and full-time teachers qualify for the ITIC (International Teacher Identity Card). All these are valid for special air, rail and bus fares and discounts

Tipping

Although there are no fixed rules for **tipping**, a ten to fifteen percent tip is anticipated by restaurant waiters. Tipping taxi drivers is purely optional. Some restaurants levy a "discretionary" or "optional" **service charge** of 10 or 12.5 percent, which must be clearly stated on the menu and on the bill. You are not obliged to pay it, and certainly not if the food or service wasn't what you expected. You don't usually tip in a pub; if you want to, you could offer the bar person a drink – and then give them enough money to cover it. In upmarket hotels, porters and bell boys expect (and usually get) a pound or two.

England on a budget

Faced with another £3 pint, a £40 theatre ticket and a £20 taxi ride back to your £100-a-night hotel, England might seem like the most expensive country in Europe. However, there are ways to stick to a **budget** and still get the most out of your stay.

▶▶ Entry is free to many showpiece **museums and galleries**, including some of the world's finest art and historical collections in London, Leeds, York, Birmingham, Manchester, Liverpool and Bristol.

▶▶ Take every **discount card/ID** you're entitled to: students, young travellers, hostellers and seniors get free or discounted entry to many sights and attractions.

▶▶ Set meals can be a steal, even at the poshest of **restaurants**, where a two- or three-course lunch or a "pre-theatre" menu might cost less than half the usual price.

▶▶ Book **transport** tickets as far in advance as possible, and always ask about Day Rovers and other special deals.

▶▶ Don't ride or drive: **walk**. Often the easiest and most enjoyable way to get around is on your own two feet.

▶▶ Visit **markets** – from grungy urban stalls to rural farmers' markets, you can browse for free and pick up some bargains.

at attractions. Each costs around £10/€14/US$22) – see ⓦ www.isic.org for details.

Crime and personal safety

It's highly unlikely that you'll be at any risk as you travel around England. Despite what the media might have you believe, **terrorism** is exceptionally rare – and, as a holiday-maker, you won't be visiting the toughest urban estates where **crime** flourishes. You can walk more or less anywhere without fear of harassment, though all the big cities have their edgy districts and it's always better to err on the side of caution, especially late at night, when – for instance – you should avoid dark streets and give drunken groups a wide berth. Leave your passport and valuables in a hotel or hostel safe (carrying **ID** is not compulsory), and exercise the usual caution on public transport. If you're taking a cab make sure it's officially licensed: plan ahead by noting down local taxi numbers beforehand, or ask bar or restaurant staff for a recommendation. If you're robbed, report it straight away to the police: your insurance company will require a **crime report number**.

Most visitors rarely come into contact with the **police**, who are approachable and helpful – though they can get tetchy at

football matches, political demonstrations and in the late evenings when pubs close.

Being caught in possession of a small quantity of "soft" **drugs** – mainly marijuana and cannabis – will probably result in a police caution. If, on the other hand, the police suspect you are dealing, you can expect to be held in custody and ultimately prosecuted.

Customs

Travellers arriving directly from most other **EU countries** can carry 3200 cigarettes, 200 cigars or 3kg of loose tobacco, plus 10 litres of spirits, 90 litres of wine and 110 litres of beer. Any more than this and you'll have to provide proof that it's for personal use only. Limits are lower from some newer EU member states. If you're arriving from a **non-EU country**, you can buy a limited amount of **duty-free goods**: 200 cigarettes or 50 cigars or 250g of tobacco, plus 4 litres of wine, 1 litre of spirits, 16 litres of beer, and 60ml of perfume. For full details, see ⓦ www .hmrc.gov.uk.

In emergency

Call ☎999 or ☎112, then ask for police, fire, ambulance, mountain rescue or coastguard.

Electricity

The current is 240v AC. North American appliances will need a transformer and adaptor; those from Europe, South Africa, Australia and New Zealand only need an adaptor.

Entry requirements

EU citizens can travel to – and settle in – the UK with just a passport or identity card. US, Canadian, South African, Australian and New Zealand citizens can stay for up to six months without a visa, provided they have a valid passport. Many other nationalities require a **visa**, obtainable from the British consular office where you live. Check with the UK Border Agency (@www.ukvisas.gov.uk) for up-to-date information on visa applications, extensions and all other aspects of residency.

Gay and lesbian travellers

England offers one of Europe's most diverse and accessible **lesbian and gay** scenes. Nearly every sizeable town has some kind of organized gay life, from bars and clubs to community groups – with the widest choice in London, Manchester and Brighton. Many venues are listed in this book, and virtually every town has a free local listings sheet. Other listings and news can be found at @www.pinkpaper.com and in the glossy magazine *Gay Times* (@www.gaytimes.co .uk). For information and links, go to @www .gaybritain.co.uk and www.gaytravel.co.uk. The age of consent is 16.

Health

No vaccinations are required for entry into Britain. Citizens of all EU and EEA countries are entitled to free medical treatment within the UK's National Health Service (NHS), on production of their **European Health Insurance Card** (**EHIC**). The same applies to those Commonwealth countries which have reciprocal healthcare arrangements with the UK – for example Australia and New Zealand. Everyone else will be charged: you should definitely take out health insurance before you travel.

Pharmacists (usually known as **chemists** in England) can dispense a limited range of drugs without a doctor's prescription. Most are open standard shop hours; check on signs in the window (or in local newspapers) for which local chemists are due to be staying open late and/or at the weekend. For generic painkillers, cold remedies and the like, the local supermarket is usually the cheapest option.

For medical advice 24 hours a day, call **NHS Direct** (℡0845/4647, @www.nhsdirect .nhs.uk). The website is packed with useful information, and also has directories of doctors' surgeries and walk-in centres nationwide.

Otherwise, minor issues can be dealt with at the surgery of any local **doctor**, also known as a **GP** (General Practitioner); get directions from NHS Direct or your hotel. For serious injuries, go to the emergency room of the nearest hospital – generally known as "**casualty**" or "**A&E**" (accident and emergency) and open 24 hours. In a life-or-death situation, call for an ambulance on ℡999 or ℡112.

Insurance

Always take out an **insurance policy** before travelling to cover against theft, loss and illness or injury. A typical policy will provide cover for loss of baggage, tickets and – up to a certain limit – cash or travellers' cheques, as well as cancellation or curtailment of your journey. Most exclude so-called dangerous

---

British embassies and high commissions abroad

Australia ℡02/6270 6666, @ukinaustralia.fco.gov.uk.
Canada ℡613/237-1530, @ukincanada.fco.gov.uk.
Ireland ℡01/205 3700, @britishembassyinireland.fco.gov.uk.
New Zealand ℡04/924 2888, @ukinnewzealand.fco.gov.uk.
South Africa ℡012/421-7733, @ukinsouthafrica.fco.gov.uk.
USA ℡202/588-7800, @ukinusa.fco.gov.uk.

sports unless an extra premium is paid: in England this can mean watersports, rock climbing and mountaineering, though hiking and kayaking would probably be covered. **Medical cover** is strongly advised. Always ascertain beforehand whether benefits will be paid as treatment proceeds or only after you return home, and whether there is a 24-hour medical emergency number. When securing **baggage cover**, make sure that the per-article limit will cover your most valuable possession. Keep receipts for medicines and medical treatment, and in the event you have anything stolen you must obtain a crime report number from the police.

Mail

Royal Mail (☏0845/774 0740, ⓦwww .royalmail.com) runs the mail system, but post offices are operated by a separate company, **Post Office** (☏0845/722 3344, ⓦwww.postoffice.co.uk). Confused? Most Britons are too.

Virtually all **post offices** are open Monday to Friday 9am to 5.30pm, and on Saturdays 9am to 12.30pm. Small branches sometimes close on Wednesday afternoons, while main offices in larger towns and cities stay open all day Saturday. In villages general stores often host "sub-post office" counters; even if the shop is open for longer, post office services are only available during the hours above.

Rates depend on the size and weight of the item, as well as delivery speed. For UK desti-nations, postcards and ordinary letters (up to 100g, and smaller than 240x165x5mm) sent first class for next-day delivery cost 41p. Postcards and letters (up to 10g) cost 60p to Europe or 67p worldwide. Check online for

other options. You can buy **stamps** at post offices and at a wide variety of ordinary shops, supermarkets and filling stations.

Maps

For an overview of the whole of England on one (double-sided) map, Collins' 1:550,000 and Ordnance Survey's 1:625,000 maps are probably the best; both include some city plans. Ordnance Survey (OS; ⓦwww .ordnancesurvey.co.uk) and Michelin also produce useful regional maps at a scale of 1:250,000 and 1:400,000 respectively, while Philips, in conjunction with OS, produce detailed county maps at a scale of 1:18,000. Otherwise, for general route-finding the most useful resources are the road atlases produced by AA, RAC, Geographers' A–Z and Collins, among others, at a scale of around 1:250,000.

These and others are widely available from bookshops, and online from the likes of **Stanfords** (ⓦwww.stanfords.co.uk), England's premier map and travel specialist.

Money

UK currency is the **pound sterling** (£), divided into 100 pence (p). Coins come in denominations of 1p, 2p, 5p, 10p, 20p, 50p, £1 and £2. Notes are in denominations of £5, £10, £20 and £50. Very occasionally you may receive Scottish or Northern Irish banknotes: they're legal tender throughout the UK, but many businesses in England may be unwilling to accept them. If you're handed one, you'd be well advised to cheerfully hand it back and ask for a "normal" note (or coins) instead.

Every sizeable town and village has a branch of one or other of the retail ("high

---

Rough Guides travel insurance

Rough Guides has teamed up with WorldNomads.com to offer great **travel insurance** deals. Policies are available to residents of over 150 countries, with cover for a wide range of **adventure sports**, 24hr emergency assistance, high levels of medical and evacuation cover and a stream of **travel safety information**. Roughguides.com users can take advantage of their policies online 24/7, from anywhere in the world – even if you're already travelling. And since plans often change when you're on the road, you can extend your policy and even claim online. Roughguides.com users who buy travel insurance with WorldNomads.com can also leave a positive footprint and donate to a community development project. For more information go to ⓦ**www.roughguides.com/shop**.

street") **banks**, along with a sprinkling of smaller "building societies" (which operate in more or less the same way). The easiest way to get hold of cash is to use your **debit card** in a "cash machine" (ATM); check in advance with your home bank whether you will be subject to a daily withdrawal limit. **ATMs** are ubiquitous: inside and outside banks, at all major points of arrival and motorway service areas, at large supermarkets, petrol stations and even inside some pubs, rural post offices and village shops – though a charge of about £1.50 may be levied on cash withdrawals at small, stand-alone ATMs: the screen will notify you if so and give you an option to cancel.

Some people still rely on **travellers' cheques** in sterling. American Express is the most commonly accepted brand, followed by Visa. Amex will not charge commission if you exchange cheques at their own offices, nor will some banks – otherwise you will be charged 2–3 percent commission. Note that in the UK you cannot use travellers' cheques as cash: you'll always have to cash them first, making them an unreliable source of funds in more remote areas.

Outside banking hours, you can change cheques or cash at **post offices** and **bureaux de change** – the latter tend to be open longer hours and are found in most city centres, and at major airports and train stations. Avoid changing in hotels, where the rates are normally poor.

Paying by plastic involves inserting your card into a "**chip-and-pin**" terminal beside the till, then keying in your secret PIN number to authorize the transaction: the only person handling your card is you. Many restaurants use wireless chip-and-pin handsets: your waiter will bring it to your table when it's time to pay. At establishments with older swipe systems, never let your card leave your sight: take it yourself to the till and watch while staff are doing the swiping.

Credit cards are widely accepted in hotels, shops and restaurants – MasterCard and Visa are almost universal – **charge cards** such as American Express and Diners Club less so. Smaller establishments may accept cash only. At supermarkets and some other shops, you may be asked at the checkout if you want "**cash back**": that is, they let you pay (by card) for up to £50 more than the cost of your goods and receive the change in cash – very handy.

Opening hours and public holidays

Opening hours for most businesses, shops and offices are Monday to Saturday 9am to 5.30 or 6pm, with many shops also open on Sundays, generally 10.30 or 11am until 4.30 or 5pm. Big supermarkets have longer hours (except on Sundays), sometimes round the clock. Some towns have an **early closing day** (usually Wednesday) when most shops close at 1pm. **Banks** are usually open Monday to Friday 9am to 4pm, and Saturday 9am to 12.30pm or so. You can usually get fuel any time of the day or night in larger towns and cities. We've quoted full opening hours for specific museums, galleries and other attractions throughout this book; where these are seasonal (summer means Easter–Oct, winter Nov–Easter), they are shown in the format 9/10am–5/6pm. For the usual opening hours of cafés, restaurants and pubs, see p.39, p.40 & p.41.

Confusingly, several of England's public holidays are termed "**bank holidays**" – though it's not just the banks who have a day off: businesses and most shops also close, though large supermarkets, small corner shops and many tourist attractions stay open. On Christmas Day the whole country shuts down (including public transport),

England's public holidays

New Year's Day January 1
Good Friday Variable March/April
Easter Monday Variable March/April
Early May Bank Holiday First Monday in May
Spring Bank Holiday Last Monday in May
Summer Bank Holiday Last Monday in August
Christmas Day December 25
Boxing Day December 26
(If Jan 1, Dec 25 or Dec 26 fall on a Sat or Sun, the next weekday becomes a public holiday.)

Useful numbers

Domestic operator ☎100
International operator ☎155

Calling England from home
Dial your international access code, then **44** for the UK, then the area code (excluding the zero), then the number.

Calling home from England
Australia 0061 + area code (excluding the zero) + number.
New Zealand 0064 + area code (excluding the zero) + number.
US and Canada 001 + area code + number.
Republic of Ireland 00353 + area code (excluding the zero) + number.
South Africa 0027 + area code (excluding the zero) + number.

though you'll find occasional signs of life on Boxing Day and New Year's Day.

Phones

England's **phone numbers** are a mess. Most (though not all) have eleven digits, including a prefix beginning ☎01, 02 or 03 which generally denotes a fixed landline, or ☎07 which almost invariably denotes a mobile phone/cellphone. The ☎08 prefix is totally random: ☎0800 and 0808 are free to call if you're using a landline, but very expensive if you're calling off a mobile/cell; ☎0844 and 0845 are cheap if you're with one phone company but expensive otherwise; ☎0870 and 0871 are pricey whatever you do. Beware the "premium rate" ☎09 prefix, common for pre-recorded information services (used by some tourist authorities), which can be charged at anything up to £1.50 a minute.

Public **pay phones** (or "phone boxes") are plentiful and take coins (minimum charge 40p); most also accept credit cards. You can make international calls from any phone box, though it's usually cheaper to buy a **phonecard**, available from many newsagents in denominations of £5, £10 and upwards. You dial the company's local access number, key in the pin number on the card and then make your call.

Mobile phone access is universal in towns and cities. Rural areas are well covered too, but sometimes patchy, with occasional blind spots. To use your own mobile/cellphone, check with your provider before you leave home that roaming is activated – and that your phone will work in the UK (if you're coming from North America, you will need a multi-band model). If you're planning to stay for any length of time, it's often simpler to buy a handset plus local SIM card when you arrive: basic pre-pay ("pay as you go") phones start at around £50, usually including some credit.

Phoning UK **directory enquiries** is expensive; instead look online at ⓦwww .bt.com. Business and service numbers are searchable at ⓦwww.yell.com.

Time

From the last Sunday in March until the last Sunday in October, the UK is on GMT+1 – known as "British Summer Time" (**BST**). For the rest of the year, it follows **GMT**. Apart from a short period around the changeovers, England is consistently five hours ahead of the US east coast, one hour behind most of Europe and ten hours behind Sydney. Full details at ⓦwww.timeanddate.com.

Tourist information

The body promoting inbound tourism to the UK is **VisitBritain** (ⓦwww.visitbritain.com), with offices worldwide and a comprehensive website, packed with useful tips and ideas. Its partner agency VisitEngland operates under the branding "**Enjoy England**" (ⓦwww.enjoy england.com) – another excellent source of information. Within England, responsibility for promoting particular areas is in the hands of regional tourism boards (see p.58) and smaller local bodies.

Virtually every town has a **tourist office** (called a Tourist Information Centre, or "TIC"). They tend to follow standard shop hours (Mon–Sat 9am–5.30pm), sometimes also open on Sundays. Hours are curtailed in winter (Nov–Easter). Staff will nearly always be able to book accommodation, reserve space on guided tours, and sell guidebooks, maps and walks leaflets. They can also provide lists of local cafés, restaurants and pubs, and though they aren't supposed to recommend particular places you'll often be able to get a feel for the best local places to eat.

Areas designated as **national parks** (see box, pp.48–49) usually have their own dedicated information centres, which offer similar services to TICs but can also provide expert guidance on local walks and outdoor pursuits.

Regional tourism organizations

East of England ⓦ www.visiteastofengland.com. Bedfordshire, Cambridgeshire, Hertfordshire, Essex, Norfolk and Suffolk.
East Midlands ⓦ www.enjoyeastmidlands.com. Derbyshire, Lincolnshire, Nottinghamshire, Leicestershire, Rutland and Northamptonshire.
England's Northwest ⓦ www.visitenglands northwest.com. Cumbria and the Lake District, Cheshire, Lancashire, Manchester, Liverpool and Merseyside.
Heart of England ⓦ www.visittheheart.co.uk. Birmingham, Worcestershire, Herefordshire, Shropshire, Staffordshire and Warwickshire.
London ⓦ www.visitlondon.com.
North East England ⓦ www.visitnortheast england.com. County Durham, Northumberland, Tees Valley, and Tyne and Wear.
South East England ⓦ www.visitsoutheast england.com. Sussex, Kent, Surrey, Berkshire, Hampshire, Oxfordshire, Buckinghamshire and the Isle of Wight.
South West England ⓦ www.visitsouthwest .co.uk. Bath, Bristol, Devon, Cornwall, Dorset, Gloucestershire and the Cotswolds, Somerset and Wiltshire.
Yorkshire Tourist Board ⓦ www.yorkshire.com.

Travellers with disabilities

The UK has good facilities for **travellers with disabilities**. All new public buildings – including museums, galleries and cinemas – must provide wheelchair access, train stations and airports are fully accessible, many buses have easy-access boarding ramps, while kerbs and signalled crossings have been dropped in many towns and cities. The number of accessible hotels and restaurants is also growing, and reserved parking bays are available almost everywhere. If you have specific requirements, it's always best to talk first to your travel agent, chosen hotel or tour operator.

Access-Able ⓦ www.access-able.com. US-based resource for travellers with disabilities.
Door-to-Door ⓦ dptac.independent.gov.uk/door -to-door. Travel website offering information and advice.
RADAR ⓦ www.radar.org.uk. Campaigning organization with links and advice.
Tourism for All ⓣ 0845/124 9971, ⓦ www .tourismforall.org.uk. Excellent resource, with advice, listings and useful information.

Travelling with children

If you're **travelling with children**, facilities in England are no worse than in most other European countries. Breastfeeding is legal in all public places, including restaurants, cafés and public transport, and baby-changing rooms are available widely, including in malls and train stations. Under-5s aren't charged on public transport or at attractions; 5- to 16-year-olds usually get a fifty-percent discount. Children aren't allowed in certain licensed (that is, alcohol-serving) premises – though this doesn't apply to restaurants, and many pubs have family rooms or beer gardens where children are welcome. Some B&Bs and hotels won't accept children under a certain age (often 12) – our reviews state where this applies. Check ⓦ www .travellingwithchildren.co.uk and ⓦ www .babygoes2.com for tips and ideas.

Guide

Guide

London

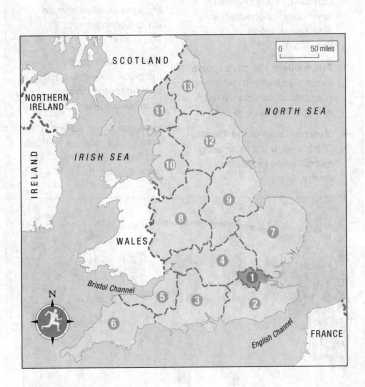

CHAPTER 1 Highlights

✳ **Houses of Parliament** The Mother of all Parliaments is a magnificently confident piece of Gothic Revival architecture. See p.84

✳ **British Museum** Quite simply one of the world's greatest museums. See p.94

✳ **London Eye** The universally loved observation wheel is now a key London landmark. See p.108

✳ **Tate Modern** The city's superb modern-art museum is housed in a spectacularly converted power station. See p.110

✳ **Shakespeare's Globe Theatre** Catch a show in this amazing reconstructed Elizabethan theatre. See p.111

✳ **Highgate Cemetery** The steeply sloping terraces of the West Cemetery's overgrown graves are the last word in Victorian Gothic gloom. See p.123

✳ **Greenwich** Picturesque riverside spot, boasting a weekend market, the National Maritime Museum and old Royal Observatory. See p.124

✳ **Kew Gardens** Stroll amid the exotic trees and shrubs, or head for the steamy glasshouses. See p.128

✳ **Hampton Court Palace** Tudor interiors, architecture by Wren and vast gardens make this a great day out. See p.129

▲ Great Court, British Museum

London

W hat strikes visitors more than anything else about **LONDON** is the sheer size of the place. Stretching for more than thirty miles east to west, on either side of the River Thames, and with an ethnically diverse population of just under eight million, it's the largest city in the EU. Londoners tend to cope with all this by compartmentalizing the city, identifying with the neighbourhoods in which they work or live, and just making occasional forays into the city centre or West End, London's shopping and entertainment heartland.

London dominates the national horizon, too: this is where the country's news and money are made, it's where central government resides and, as far as its inhabitants are concerned, provincial life begins beyond the circuit of the city's traffic-clogged orbital motorway. Londoners' sense of superiority causes enormous resentment in the regions, yet it's undeniable that the capital has a unique aura of excitement and success – in most walks of British life, if you want to get on, you've got to do it in London.

Monuments from the capital's glorious past are everywhere, from medieval banqueting halls and the great churches of Christopher Wren to the eclectic Victorian architecture of the triumphalist British Empire. The capital's traditional **sights** – Big Ben, Westminster Abbey, Buckingham Palace, St Paul's Cathedral, the Tower of London and so on – continue to draw in millions of tourists every year. Things change fast, though, and the regular emergence of new attractions ensures that there's plenty to do even for those who've visited before. In the last decade, all of London's world-class **museums**, **galleries** and institutions have been reinvented, from the Royal Opera House to the British Museum. And with Tate Modern and the London Eye, the city can now boast the world's largest modern art gallery and Europe's largest Ferris wheel as twenty-first century landmarks. And the tourist and transport infrastructure has had a major overhaul, too, ready for the 2012 Olympics. Away from the big sights, there's also much enjoyment to be had from the city's quiet Georgian squares, the narrow alleyways of the City of London, the riverside walks, and the assorted quirks of what is still identifiably a collection of villages. And London is offset by surprisingly large **expanses of greenery**, with several public parks right in the centre as well as wilder spaces such as Hampstead Heath and Richmond Park on the outskirts.

You could spend days just **shopping** in London too, mixing it with the upper classes in Harrods, or sampling the offbeat weekend markets of Portobello Road, Camden and Spitalfields. The **music**, **clubbing** and **gay/lesbian** scenes are second to none, and mainstream arts are no less exciting, with regular opportunities to catch brilliant **theatre** companies, dance troupes, exhibitions and opera. **Restaurants** these days are an attraction, too, with over fifty Michelin-starred

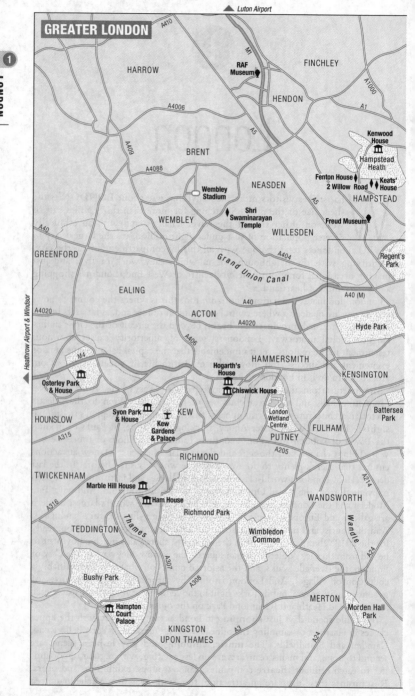

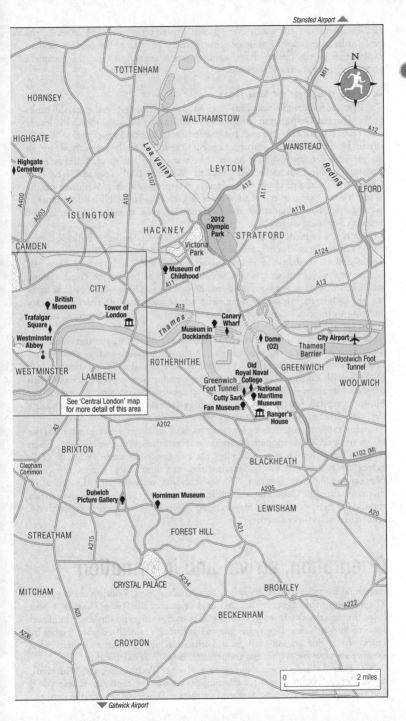

Stansted Airport ▲

N

TOTTENHAM

HORNSEY

WALTHAMSTOW

HIGHGATE

WANSTEAD

◆Highgate
  Cemetery

LEYTON

ILFORD

A12

A400

A503

A1

A107

A10

Lea Valley

Roding

A11

A118

ISLINGTON

HACKNEY

2012
Olympic
Park

STRATFORD

CAMDEN

Victoria
Park

A124

♟Museum of
  Childhood

A11

A13

CITY

British
♟Museum

A13

Thames

Canary
♟Wharf

Tower of
London

Museum in
Docklands

♦Dome
  (O2)

City Airport ✈

Trafalgar
◆Square

Westminster
◆Abbey

♟

Thames
Barrier

WESTMINSTER

LAMBETH

ROTHERHITHE

Old
Royal Naval
College

GREENWICH

Woolwich Foot
Tunnel

Greenwich
Foot Tunnel

WOOLWICH

See 'Central London' map
for more detail of this area

Cutty Sark♟

♟National
  Maritime
  Museum

Fan Museum♟

🏛Ranger's
  House

A202

BRIXTON

Clapham
Common

BLACKHEATH

A102 (M)

A3

Dulwich
Picture Gallery♟

♟Horniman Museum

A205

LEWISHAM

A20

STREATHAM

A215

FOREST HILL

A21

A20

MITCHAM

CRYSTAL PALACE

A234

BROMLEY

A222

A23

BECKENHAM

A236

CROYDON

0   2 miles

Gatwick Airport ▼

establishments and just about every global cuisine represented. Meanwhile, the city's **pubs** have heaps of atmosphere, especially away from the centre – and an exploration of the farther-flung communities is essential to get the complete picture of this dynamic metropolis.

A brief history of London

The Romans founded **Londinium** in 43 AD as a stores depot on the marshy banks of the Thames. Despite frequent attacks – not least by Boudica, the Celtic leader who razed it in 61 AD – the port became secure in its position as capital of Roman Britain by the end of the century. London's expansion really began, however, in the eleventh century, when it became the seat of the last successful invader of Britain, the Norman duke who became **William I of England** (aka "the Conqueror"). Crowned king of England in Westminster Abbey, William built the White Tower – centrepiece of the Tower of London – to establish his dominance over the merchant population, the class that was soon to make London one of Europe's mightiest cities.

Little is left of medieval or Tudor London. Many of the finest buildings were wiped out in the course of a few days in 1666 when the **Great Fire of London** annihilated more than thirteen thousand houses and nearly ninety churches, completing a cycle of destruction begun the year before by the Great Plague, which killed as many as a hundred thousand people. Chief beneficiary of the blaze was the architect Christopher Wren, who was commissioned to redesign the city and rose to the challenge with such masterpieces as St Paul's Cathedral and the Royal Naval Hospital in Greenwich.

Much of the public architecture of London was built during the eighteenth and nineteenth centuries – the Georgian and Victorian periods – when grand structures were raised to reflect the city's status as the financial and administrative hub of the **British Empire**. And though postwar development peppered the city with concrete brutalism – giving London a bland appearance compared to some other European capitals – more recent essays in high-tech modern architecture, a charge led by the likes of the Gherkin, have given the city a new gloss.

London's special atmosphere comes not from its buildings, though, but from the life on its streets. A cosmopolitan city since at least the seventeenth century, when it was a haven for Huguenot immigrants escaping persecution in Louis XIV's France, today it is truly multicultural, with over a third of its permanent population originating from overseas. The last hundred years has seen the arrival of thousands from the Caribbean, the Indian subcontinent, the Mediterranean, Africa and the Far East, all of whom play an integral part in defining a metropolis that is unmatched in its sheer diversity.

Orientation, arrival and information

Stretching for more than thirty miles at its broadest point, **London** is a big place. The majority of its sights are situated to the north of the **River Thames**, which loops through the city from west to east. However, there is no single predominant focus of interest, since the city has grown not through centralized planning but by a process of agglomeration – villages and urban developments that once surrounded the core are now lost within the amorphous mass of Greater London.

One of the few areas that is manageable on foot is **Westminster** and **Whitehall**, the city's royal, political and ecclesiastical power base for centuries, where you'll find some of London's most famous landmarks: Downing Street, Big Ben, the

Houses of Parliament, Westminster Abbey and, across St James's Park, Buckingham Palace. The grand streets and squares of **St James's**, **Mayfair** and **Marylebone**, to the north of Westminster, have been the playground of the rich since the Restoration, and now contain the city's busiest shopping zones.

East of Piccadilly Circus, **Soho** and **Covent Garden** are also easy to walk around and form the heart of the West End entertainment district, containing the largest concentration of theatres, cinemas, clubs, offbeat shops, cafés and restaurants. To the north lie the university quarter of **Bloomsbury**, home to the ever-popular British Museum, and the secluded quadrangles of **Holborn**'s Inns of Court, London's legal heartland.

The City – the City of London, to give it its full title – is both the most ancient and the most modern part of London. Settled since Roman times, it's now one of the world's great financial centres, yet retains its share of historic sights, notably the **Tower of London** and a fine cache of Wren churches that includes **St Paul's Cathedral**. Despite creeping gentrification, the **East End**, to the east of the City, is not conventional tourist territory, but to ignore it entirely is to miss out a crucial element of multiethnic London – and, of course, it is set to host the Olympics in 2012. **Docklands** is a mixture of abandoned warehouses now converted into swanky flats and modern apartment blocks of dubious architectural merit – at its centre is the **Canary Wharf** tower, the country's tallest building, epitomizing the aspirations of the Docklands dream.

A slice of central London south of the Thames is definitely worth exploring. First off, there's the **Southbank Centre**, London's little-loved concrete culture-bunker, which is enjoying a new lease of life thanks to inspired artistic direction and its proximity to the **London Eye**, Europe's biggest observation wheel. Further east along the river in Bankside is **Tate Modern**, one of the world's greatest modern art museums, linked to the City by the pedestrian-only Millennium Bridge.

In **Hyde Park** and **Kensington Gardens**, you'll find the largest park in central London, a segment of greenery which separates wealthy **Kensington** and **Chelsea** from the West End. The **museums** of South Kensington – the Victoria and Albert Museum, the Science Museum and the Natural History Museum – are a must; and if you have shopping on your agenda, you may well want to investigate the hive of plush stores in the vicinity of Harrods, superstore to the upper echelons.

The capital's most hectic weekend market takes place around **Camden Lock** in north London. Further out, in the literary suburbs of Hampstead and Highgate, there are unbeatable views across the city from half-wild **Hampstead Heath**, the favourite parkland of thousands of Londoners. The glory of southeast London is **Greenwich**, with its nautical associations, royal park and observatory. Finally, there are plenty of rewarding day-trips along the Thames from Chiswick to Windsor, most notably to **Hampton Court Palace** and **Windsor Castle**.

Arrival

Flying into London, you'll arrive at one of the capital's five **international airports**: Heathrow, Gatwick, Stansted, Luton or City Airport, all of which are less than an hour from the city centre.

At Heathrow

Heathrow (℗0870/000 0123, ⓦwww.heathrowairport.com), fifteen miles west of the centre, is the busiest airport, with five terminals and three train/tube stations: one for terminals 1, 2 and 3, and separate ones each for terminals 4 and 5. The fastest **trains** into London are the high-speed Heathrow Express to Paddington Station (every 15min; journey 15–23min); tickets cost £16.50 one-way or £32 return (more if you purchase your ticket on board the train). Less pricey are

Heathrow Connect trains, which stop at some intermediate stations (every 30min; journey 25min), but tickets cost just £7 single and £14 return. An even cheaper alternative is to take the Piccadilly **Underground** line (℡020/7222 1234, ⓦwww.tfl.gov.uk), which connects the airport to numerous tube stations across central London (every 5min; journey 50min); tickets cost £4 single, or, if you can, buy a One-Day Travelcard (Zones 1–6) for £7.50 (see box opposite).

At Gatwick

Gatwick (℡0870/000 2468, ⓦwww.gatwickairport.com) is around thirty miles south of London: nonstop **Gatwick Express** trains run between the airport's South Terminal and Victoria Station (every 15min; journey 30min) for £17 one-way, £29 return. Other train options include the Southern services to Victoria (every 15min; 35min) for £10 one-way, or First Capital Connect to St Pancras (every 15–30min; journey 30–40min), also for around £10 one-way.

At Stansted

Stansted (℡0870/000 0303, ⓦwww.stanstedairport.com) lies roughly 35 miles northeast of the capital, and is served by the **Stansted Express** to Liverpool Street (every 15–30min; journey 45min), which costs £20 one-way, £30 return. **Buses** to Baker Street tube (every 20min; journey 1hr 30min), run by easyBus (ⓦwww.easybus.co.uk), have online tickets for as little as £2 single (£10 if you buy on board).

At Luton

Luton Airport (℡01582/405100, ⓦwww.london-luton.com) is roughly thirty miles north of London, and mostly handles charter flights. A free shuttle bus takes five minutes to transport passengers to **Luton Airport Parkway** station, which is connected by train to King's Cross St Pancras (every 15–30min; journey 35–40min) and other stations in central London; single tickets cost around £11. All year round, 24 hours a day, **Green Line** and **easyBus** (ⓦwww.easybus.co.uk) run up to three buses an hour from Luton to Victoria Station (every 15–30min; journey 1hr 20min), stopping at several locations en route, including Baker Street; tickets cost as little as £2 if you book in advance online, or as much as £12 single (£15 return).

At City

City Airport (℡020/7646 0000, ⓦwww.londoncityairport.com), London's smallest, used primarily by business folk, is situated in Docklands, ten miles east of central London. The **Docklands Light Railway** (**DLR**) will take you straight to Bank in the City (every 8–15min; 20min), where you can change to the tube; tickets cost around £4.

By train and bus

Eurostar trains arrive at **St Pancras International**, north of the centre, next door to King's Cross. Arriving by train from elsewhere in Britain, you'll come into one of London's numerous main-line stations, all of which have adjacent Underground stations linking into the city-centre's tube network. Coming into London **by coach**, you're most likely to arrive at **Victoria Coach Station**, a couple of hundred yards south down Buckingham Palace Road from the train and Underground stations of the same name.

Information

The chief tourist office in London is the **Britain & London Visitor Centre**, 1 Regent St, SW1 (April–Sept Mon 9.30am–6.30pm, Tues–Fri 9am–6.30pm, Sat 9am–5pm, Sun 10am–4pm; times vary slightly in winter and June–Sept;

@ www.visitbritain.com; ⊖Piccadilly Circus); there's also the **London Information Centre**, a tiny window in the tkts kiosk on Leicester Square, WC2 (daily 10am–6pm; ☎020/7292 2333, @ www.londontown.com; ⊖Leicester Square). Individual boroughs also run tourist offices, the most central one being on the south side of St Paul's Cathedral (Mon–Sat 9.30am–5.30pm, Sun 10am–4pm; @ www .visitthecity.co.uk).

London: The Rough Guide Map is a comprehensive full-colour, waterproof and non-tearable **map** detailing restaurants, bars, shops and visitor attractions. If you want to find your way around every nook and cranny of the city you'll need to invest in either an *A–Z Street Atlas* or a *Nicholson Streetfinder*, both of which have a street index covering every street in the capital. You can get them at most bookshops and newsagents for less than £5.

The only comprehensive weekly **listings** magazine is *Time Out* (@ www .timeout.com/london), which comes out every Tuesday afternoon. It carries critical appraisals of much of the week's theatre, film, music, exhibitions, children's events and much more besides.

City transport

London's transport network is among the most complex and expensive in the world. **Transport for London** (**TfL**) provides excellent free maps and details of bus and tube services from its **Travel Information Centres**: the most central one is at Piccadilly Circus tube station (daily 7.15am–7pm), and there are other desks at Heathrow and various other tube and train stations. There's also a **24-hour helpline** for information on all bus and tube services (☎020/7222 1234) and a very useful website (@ www.tfl.gov.uk). One word of warning – avoid travelling during the **rush hour** (roughly Mon–Fri 8–9.30am & 5–7pm), when tubes become unbearably crowded (and the lack of air conditioning doesn't help) and some buses get so full they literally won't let you on.

Children under 11 travel for free; children aged 11–15 travel free on all buses and trams and at child-rate on the tube; those aged 16 or 17 can travel at child-rate on all forms of transport. However, all children over 10 must have an Oyster

---

Oyster cards and Travelcards

The cheapest, easiest way to get about London is to use an **Oyster card**, London's transport smartcard, available from all tube stations and Travel Information Centres (see above), and valid on the bus, tube, Docklands Light Railway (DLR), Tramlink, Overground and all suburban rail services. Oyster cards function in two different ways: the card can be used simply to store a weekly/monthly/yearly **Travelcard**, or you can use it as a **pay-as-you-go** card – cards can be topped up at all tube stations and at most newsagents. As you enter the tube or bus, simply touch in your card at the card reader – if you're using pay-as-you-go, the fare will be taken off your card. If you're using the tube or train, you need to touch out again or a £4 maximum cash fare will be deducted. A pay-as-you-go Oyster operates daily price-capping so that when you've paid (slightly less than) the equivalent of a daily Travelcard, it will stop taking money off your card, though you still need to touch in (and out). Oyster cards are free for those purchasing monthly or yearly tickets. Everyone else needs to hand over a £3 refundable deposit; visitors can buy a pay-as-you-go Oyster card for just £2.

If you don't have an Oyster card, you can still buy a paper **Travelcard**. Anytime Day Travelcards start from £7.20 (zones 1 & 2); Off-Peak Travelcards are valid after 9.30am on weekdays and all day at the weekend, and start from £5.60 (zones 1 & 2).

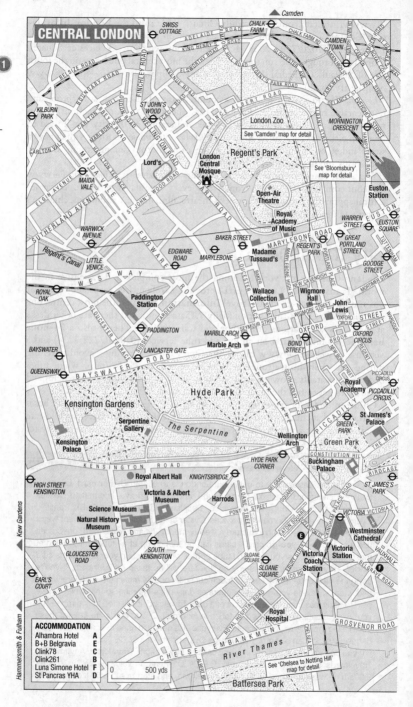

CENTRAL LONDON

ACCOMMODATION

Alhambra Hotel	A
B+B Belgravia	E
Clink78	C
Clink261	B
Luna Simone Hotel	F
St Pancras YHA	D

0   500 yds

Almeida Theatre

King's Cross Station

St Pancras Station

British Library

EUSTON

Foundling Museum

RUSSELL SQUARE

British Museum

HOLBORN

TOTTENHAM COURT ROAD

COVENT GARDEN

LEICESTER SQUARE

Covent Garden

National Gallery

CHARING CROSS

Charing Cross Station

EMBANKMENT

St James's Park

London Eye

WESTMINSTER

Houses of Parliament

Westminster Abbey

Lambeth Palace

See 'The West End and Westminster' map for detail

Tate Britain

PIMLICO

VAUXHALL

The Oval

OVAL

ANGEL

Sadler's Wells

KING'S CROSS-ST PANCRAS

See 'The City and around' map for detail

CITY ROAD

OLD STREET

Regent's Canal

HOXTON

Geffrye Museum

SHOREDITCH HIGH STREET

CLERKENWELL ROAD

BARBICAN

CHANCERY LANE

FARRINGDON

Smithfield

Lincoln's Inn

HOLBORN

Barbican Centre

MOORGATE

ST PAUL'S

St Paul's

Liverpool St Station

LIVERPOOL STREET

Bank of England

The Gherkin ALDGATE

FLEET STREET

BLACKFRIARS

Temple

TEMPLE

BLACKFRIARS BR.

Blackfriars Station

MILLENNIUM BRIDGE

Tate Modern

BANK

CHEAPSIDE

THREADNEEDLE

Lloyd's Building

MANSION HOUSE

CANNON STREET

MONUMENT

Cannon St Station

TOWER HILL

Tower of London

River Thames

Southwark Cathedral

LONDON BRIDGE

TOOLEY ST

London Bridge Station

Greenwich

South Bank Centre

SOUTHWARK

WATERLOO

Waterloo Station

LAMBETH NORTH

See 'Bankside and Southwark' map for detail

BOROUGH

LONG LANE

Bermondsey Market

See 'The South Bank' map for detail

Imperial War Museum

ELEPHANT & CASTLE

NEW KENT ROAD

OLD KENT ROAD

KENNINGTON

CAMBERWELL NEW ROAD

NIGHTLIFE

Ministry of Sound	4
Scala	3
Union Chapel	1

GAY BARS & CLUBS

Area	5
Central Station	2
Duckie	6
Fire	7
Popstarz	3

Lambeth

photocard to be eligible for free travel – these should be applied for in advance online. Without a photocard, you can buy an Off-Peak Day Travelcard (zones 1–9) for children aged 11–15 for just £1, providing they're travelling with an adult.

The tube

Except for very short journeys, the fastest way of moving around the city is by **Underground** or **tube**, as it's known to all Londoners. The twelve different tube lines cross much of the metropolis, although London south of the river is not very well covered. Each line has its own colour and name – all you need to know is which direction you're travelling in: northbound or southbound, eastbound or westbound. Services operate from around 5.30am until 12.30am Monday to Saturday, and from 7.30am until 11.30pm on Sundays; you rarely have to wait more than five minutes for a train from central stations. **Tickets** must be bought in advance; if you're caught without a valid ticket, you'll be charged an on-the-spot Penalty Fare of £20. Since the introduction of the **Oyster card** (see box, p.69), most Londoners don't bother with paper tickets any more.

Buses

London's famous red **double-decker buses** are fun to ride on, but tend to get stuck in traffic jams, which prevent them running to a regular timetable. In central London, and on all the extra-long "bendy buses", you must **have a valid ticket before boarding**. The standard walk-on fare is £2. Some buses run a 24-hour service, but most run between about 5am and midnight, with a network of **night buses** (prefixed with the letter "N") operating outside this period. Night bus routes radiate out from Trafalgar Square at approximately twenty- to thirty-minute intervals, more frequently on some routes and on Friday and Saturday nights. At night-time all stops are treated as request stops, so you must signal to get the bus to stop, and press the bell in order to get off.

Boats

Boat services on the Thames are much improved, but they still do not form part of a fully integrated public transport system. As a result fares are quite expensive, though you should ask about the regular discounts. Typical **fares** are £5 single, with an unlimited hop-on, hop-off River Roamer day-ticket costing £12, and a weekly ticket costing £36. A Rail Rover ticket (including unlimited travel on the DLR and hop-on, hop-off on City Cruises services) costs £13.50. **Timetables** and services are complex, and there are numerous companies and small charter operators – for a full list check with TfL.

Taxis and minicabs

Compared to many capital cities, London's metered **black cabs** are an expensive option unless there are three or more of you – a ride from Euston to Victoria, for example, costs around £12–15 (Mon–Fri 6am–8pm). After 8pm on weekdays and all day during the weekend a higher tariff applies, and after 10pm, a much higher one. A yellow light over the windscreen tells you if the cab is available – just stick your arm out to hail it. To order a black cab in advance, phone ☎0871/871 8710, and be prepared to pay an extra £2.

Minicabs look just like regular cars and are considerably cheaper than black cabs. The best way to pick a company is to take the advice of the place you're at; if you want to be certain of a woman driver, call Ladycabs (☎020/7272 3300), or if you want a gay/lesbian-friendly driver, call Freedom Cars (☎020/7739 9080).

Last, and definitely least, there's currently a plague of pedicabs or **bicycle taxis** in the West End. The oldest and biggest of the bunch are Bugbugs (☎020/7353 4028, ⓦwww.bugbugs.com), who have rickshaws operating Monday to Saturday from 7pm until the early hours of the morning. The rickshaws take up to three passengers and fares are negotiable, so you should always agree a price beforehand based on a fare of around £3–5 per person.

Accommodation

There's no getting away from the fact that **accommodation** in London is expensive. Compared with most European cities, you pay over the odds in every category. Aside from **campsites**, the cheapest option is to go to one of the independent **hostels**, where dorm beds start at around £12. Going up a notch, even the most basic **B&Bs** struggle to bring their tariffs below £60 for a double with shared facilities, which is why so many people head for the budget **chain hotels** (see box, p.74). For a really decent hotel room, you shouldn't expect much change out of £100 a night.

All London tourist offices (see p.68) operate a **room-booking service**, for which a small fee is levied (they also take the first night's fee in advance). The **British Hotel Reservation Centre** (☎020/7592 3055, ⓦwww.bhrc.co.uk) desks at Heathrow, Gatwick and Victoria train and coach stations don't charge a fee for booking rooms, however; most of their offices are open daily from 6am till midnight. You can also book for free **online** at ⓦwww.londontown.com; payment is made directly to the hotel on checking out and they can offer discounts of up to fifty percent. Booking online direct with a hotel or B&B can also be a good idea, as rates often vary according to availability.

Hotels and B&Bs

With **hotels** you get less for your money in London than elsewhere in the country – generally breakfasts are more meagre and rooms more spartan than in similarly priced places in the provinces. Whatever the time of year, you should phone as far in advance as you can if you want to stay within a couple of tube stops of the West End. When choosing your area, bear in mind that the West End – Soho, Covent

---

London postcodes

A brief word on London **postcodes**: the name of each street is followed by a letter giving the geographical location (E for "east", WC for "west central" and so on) and a number that specifies the postal area. However, this is not a reliable indication of the remoteness of the locale – W5, for example, lies beyond the more remote sounding NW10 – so it's always best to check a map before taking a room in what may sound like a fairly central area.

Budget chain hotels

Chain hotels have pretty much got the **budget hotel** market sewn up in London. B&Bs may offer a more personal touch, but the franchises are often in unbeatable central locations. Bumping along at the bottom are **easyHotel**, whose prices start at just £25 for an en-suite double – if you want a window, TV use or room cleaning, it's extra; there are branches in Victoria, South Kensington, Paddington and Earls Court. **Tune Hotel** offers equally tiny doubles for £35 – its first branch is close to Waterloo, with more due to open in the near future. Serious bargains can also be had at **Travelodge**, which has some handily situated hotels in Covent Garden, Farringdon, Marylebone and Southwark; rooms are utilitarian, but online en-suite doubles can cost less than £50. **Premier Inn** is the other real budget option. It's generally considered a cut above *Travelodge*, though it doesn't have quite the online bargains; there are centrally located branches near the London Eye, Tate Modern and the Tower of London. The rest of the chain gang aren't worth considering as you can get better value elsewhere.

Garden, St James's, Mayfair and Marylebone – and the western districts of Knightsbridge and Kensington are dominated by expensive, upmarket hotels and chains, whereas Bloomsbury is relatively inexpensive and very central. For cheaper rooms, the widest choice is close to the main train termini of Victoria and Paddington. Where possible, we've marked the following on the maps in this chapter.

Westminster, Whitehall and Victoria

B+B Belgravia 64–66 Ebury St, SW1 ☏ 020/7259 8570, ⓦ www.bb-belgravia .com ⊖ Victoria. See map, pp.70–71. A real rarity in this neck of the woods – a B&B with flair, very close to the train and coach station. The 17 rooms are of boutique-hotel quality, with original cornicing and large sash windows and have stylish modern touches – all have flat-screen TVs and funky bathrooms with mosaic tiling. Staff are welcoming and enthusiastic. Free in-room internet access. ❹

The Grand Trafalgar Square, WC2 ☏ 020/7839 8877, ⓦ www.thegrandattrafalgarsquare.com ⊖ Covent Garden. See map, pp.80–81. Grandiloquent building on Trafalgar Square itself, with fully equipped, modern rooms. It's part of an American business-orientated chain that uses minimal staff – there's no check-in and no breakfast. Rates vary according to availability – check weekend and holiday rates at their Club Quarters website (ⓦ www.clubquarters.com). ❻

Luna Simone Hotel 47–49 Belgrave Rd, SW1 ☏ 020/7834 5897, ⓦ www.lunasimonehotel .com ⊖ Victoria. See map, pp.70–71. Inexpensive B&B with a bright foyer, very friendly staff and plain well-maintained, en-suite rooms. Big breakfasts. ❸

Sanctuary House 33 Tothill St, SW1 ☏ 020/7799 4044, ⓦ www.fullershotels.co.uk ⊖ St James's Park. See map, pp.80–81. A Fuller's hotel above a Fuller's pub, and decked out like one too, in comfortable pseudo-Victoriana. Breakfast is extra, and is served in the pub, but the location by St James's Park is terrific. Rates vary – ask about the weekend deals. ❹

Mayfair and Marylebone

Edward Lear 28–30 Seymour St, W1 ☏ 020/7402 5401, ⓦ www.edlear.com ⊖ Marble Arch. See map, pp.114–115. Lear's former home enjoys a great location close to Oxford St and Hyde Park, with lovely flower boxes and a plush foyer. Rooms themselves need a bit of a makeover, but the low prices reflect both this and the fact that most only have shared facilities. ❸

Lincoln House Hotel 33 Gloucester Place, W1 ☏ 020/7486 7630, ⓦ www.lincoln-house-hotel .co.uk ⊖ Marble Arch or Baker Street. See map, pp.114–115. Dark wood panelling gives this Georgian B&B in Marylebone a ship's-cabin feel. All the rooms are en suite and well equipped; rates vary according to the size of the bed and length of stay. Breakfast not included. ❸

Wigmore Court 23 Gloucester Place, W1 ☏ 020/7935 0928, ⓦ www.wigmore-court-hotel .co.uk ⊖ Marble Arch or Baker Street. See map, pp.114–115. The ruched curtains and floral decor may not be to everyone's taste, but this Georgian townhouse in Marylebone is a better-than-average B&B, boasting a high tally of returning clients. Comfortable rooms with en-suite facilities, plus two cheaper doubles with shared facilities. No lift, but there's a laundry and basic kitchen for guests' use. ❹

Soho and Covent Garden

The Fielding Hotel 4 Broad Court, Bow St, WC2 ⊕ 020/7836 8305, ⊛ www .thefieldinghotel.co.uk ⊖ Covent Garden. See map, pp.80–81. Quietly situated on a traffic-free, gas-lit court, this excellent hotel is one of Covent Garden's hidden gems. Its en-suite rooms are a firm favourite with visiting performers, since it's just a few yards from the Royal Opera House. No lift and no breakfast. ❺

Hazlitt's 6 Frith St, W1 ⊕ 020/7434 1771, ⊛ www .hazlittshotel.com ⊖ Tottenham Court Road. See map, pp.80–81. Located off the south side of Soho Square, this early eighteenth-century building is a hotel of real character and charm, offering en-suite rooms decorated and furnished as close to period style as convenience and comfort allow. There's a small sitting room, but no dining room; continental breakfast (served in the rooms) is extra. ❼

Seven Dials Hotel 7 Monmouth St, WC2 ⊕ 020/7681 0791, ⊛ www.sevendialshotellondon .com ⊖ Covent Garden. See map, pp.80–81. Pleasant family-run B&B hotel on a lovely street in the heart of the West End. The staircase is narrow and winding (no lift) and the rooms are small, but all are en suite, with TV and tea/coffee-making facilities. ❸

Bloomsbury

Alhambra Hotel 17 Argyle St, WC1 ⊕ 020/7631 4115, ⊛ www.alhambrahotel.com ⊖ Goodge Street or Euston Square. See map, pp.70–71. Clean, modern, functional place just a stone's throw from St Pancras. Cheapest rooms have shared facilities and there's no lift, but free wi-fi is available. ❷

Arran House Hotel 77–79 Gower St, WC1 ⊕ 020/7535 2186, ⊛ www.arranhotel-london.com ⊖ Goodge Street. See map, p.95. Comfortable and clean B&B, with pink furnishings. All doubles are en suite, but there are a few bargain singles with shared facilities. ❸

Charlotte Street Hotel 15–17 Charlotte St, W1 ⊕ 020/7806 2000, ⊛ www.firmdale.com ⊖ Goodge Street or Tottenham Court Road. See map, p.95. Smart but comfortable townhouse hotel just north of Oxford St. Rooms are sumptuously decorated, but resolutely modern in style, with en-suite granite bathrooms complete with flat-screen TVs, and Tivoli radios at the bedsides. ❼

Ridgemount 65–67 Gower St, WC1 ⊕ 020/7636 1141, ⊛ www.ridgemounthotel.co.uk ⊖ Goodge Street. See map, p.95. Very friendly, old-fashioned, family-run place, with small rooms (half with shared facilities), a garden and free hot-drinks machine. A reliable, basic bargain. ❷

Hotel Russell 1–8 Russell Square, WC1 ⊕ 020/7837 6470, ⊛ www.londonrussellhotel.co.uk ⊖ Russell Square. See map, p.95. From its grand 1898 exterior to its opulent interiors of marble, wood and crystal, this late Victorian landmark fully retains its period atmosphere in all its public areas (though not in the rooms themselves). Service could often be better, and the rack rates are pretty high, but online you can get good deals. Breakfast not included. ❺

Clerkenwell and Hoxton

Fox & Anchor 115 Charterhouse St, EC1 ⊕ 0845/347 0100, ⊛ www.foxandanchor.com ⊖ Farringdon. See map, pp.100–101. This traditional Clerkenwell pub has six small but luxuriously furnished rooms, up a narrow flight of stairs, with all the mod cons you could desire. The only issue is noise from nearby clubs so ask for a room at the back. Check-in is at *Malmaison* (seepp.100–101). ❹

Hoxton Hotel 81 Great Eastern St, EC2 ⊕ 020/7550 1000, ⊛ www.hoxtonhotels.com ⊖ Old Street. See map, pp.100–101. Fittingly trendy hotel in über-hip Hoxton, with contemporary art on the walls and fashionably lugubrious decor in the rooms, plus flat-screen TVs and duck-down duvets. The tiny breakfast is delivered to your room. Free wi-fi and cheap phone calls. Price depends entirely on availability; rooms are occasionally even sold for £1. ❶–❻

Malmaison 18–21 Charterhouse Square, EC1 ⊕ 020/7012 3700, ⊛ www.malmaison-london. com ⊖ Farringdon. See map, pp.100–101. Set in a quiet, cobbled square in the heart of Clerkenwell, this is the London branch of a slowly expanding chain of British boutique hotels. The tone is dark, modern and quite clubby in deference to the nearby City. Service and facilities are difficult to fault. ❺

The Rookery 12 Peter's Lane, Cowcross St, EC1 ⊕ 020/7336 0931, ⊛ www.rookeryhotel .com ⊖ Farringdon. See map, pp.100–101. Rambling Georgian townhouse on the edge of the City that makes a fantastically discreet little hideaway. Each room has been individually designed in a deliciously camp, modern take on the Baroque period, and all have super bathrooms with lots of character. ❼

The Zetter 86–88 Clerkenwell Rd, EC1 ⊕ 020/7324 4444, ⊛ www.thezetter.com ⊖ Farringdon. See map, pp.100–101. A warehouse converted with real style and a dash of 1960s glamour. Rooms are simple and minimalist, with fun touches such as lights that change colour and decorative floral panels; ask for a room at the back, overlooking quiet, cobbled St John's Square. Water for guests is supplied from *The Zetter*'s own well, beneath the building. ❻

The City

Apex City of London Hotel 1 Seething Lane, EC3 ☎020/7977 9593, ⓦwww.apexhotels.co.uk ⊖Tower Hill. See map, pp.100–101. A swish hotel on a secluded City street, designed for corporate clientele – the rooms are very masculine, in black, grey and burgundy, with the pricier ones enjoying more light and better views. Rates vary enormously according to availability so book early. The gym, sauna and steam room are free for guests. ②–⑤

The King's Wardrobe 6 Wardrobe Place, Carter Lane, EC4 ☎020/7792 2222, ⓦwww .bridgestreet.com ⊖St Paul's. See map, pp.100–101. In a quiet courtyard just behind St Paul's Cathedral, this place is part of an international chain that caters largely for business customers. The apartments offer fully equipped kitchens and workstations, a concierge service and housekeeping. Though the building is fourteenth century, and once contained Edward III's royal regalia, the interior is modern. ⑤

South Bank and Southwark

London Marriott Hotel County Hall Belvedere Rd, SE1 ☎020/7928 5200, ⓦwww.marriott.com ⊖Waterloo or Westminster. See map, p.109. The *Marriott* has taken over some of the finest rooms in historic County Hall, former home to London's government, with over three-quarters offering river views, many with small balconies. It's all suitably pompous inside, and there's a full-sized indoor pool and well-equipped gym. ⑧

Mad Hatter 3–7 Stamford St, SE1 ☎020/7401 9222, ⓦwww.fullershotels.co.uk ⊖London Bridge. See map, p.109. Plush pseudo-Victorian Fuller's hotel above a modern pub on Blackfriars Rd. Breakfast is extra on weekdays, and is served in the pub, but this is a great location, a short walk from Tate Modern and the South Bank. Rates depend on availability – weekends are usually cheapest. ④

Southwark Rose 43–47 Southwark Bridge Rd, SE1 ☎020/7015 1490, ⓦwww .southwarkrosehotel.co.uk ⊖London Bridge. See map, pp.110–111. The *Southwark Rose* has nice contemporary design touches that raise the rooms several notches above the bland chain hotels in the area. Giant aluminium lamps hover over the lobby, which is lined with funky photographs, while the penthouse restaurant offers breakfast with a rooftop view and free wi-fi. Rates depend on availability. ⑤

Kensington and Chelsea

Aster House 3 Sumner Place, SW7 ☎020/7581 5888, ⓦwww.asterhouse.com ⊖South Kensington. See map, pp.114–115. Pleasant, award-winning B&B in a luxurious South Ken white-stuccoed street. There's a lovely garden at the back and a large conservatory where breakfast is served. ⑥

Caring Hotel 24 Craven Hill Gardens, W2 ☎020/7262 8708, ⓦwww.caringhotel.com ⊖Bayswater. See map, pp.114–115. The decor isn't to all tastes, but the rooms are clean; the cheaper ones have shared facilities. ②

The Halkin 5 Halkin St, SW1 ☎020/7333 1000, ⓦwww.halkin.como.bz ⊖Hyde Park Corner. See map, pp.114–115. A luxury hotel that spurns the chintzy country-house theme: elegant, East-meets-West minimalism prevails in each of the 41 rooms. The contemporary theme is continued in the Michelin-starred Thai restaurant, which overlooks a private garden. ⑧

Miller's Residence 111a Westbourne Grove, W2 ☎020/7243 1024, ⓦwww.millersuk.com ⊖Bayswater. See map, pp.114–115. Every inch of this grandiose and eccentric B&B is littered with nineteenth-century antiques, from the sumptuous baronial drawing room (much in demand for fashion shoots) to the bedrooms. Some rooms are a little small and dark for the price, but the welcome is warm and the ambience unique. Access from Hereford Rd. ⑥

The Pavilion 34–36 Sussex Gardens, W2 ☎020/7262 0905, ⓦwww.pavilionhoteluk.com ⊖Paddington. See map, pp.114–115. A decadent rock star's home from home, with outrageously over-the-top decor and every room individually themed, from "honky-tonk Afro" to "Highland Fling". Service can be erratic but it's perfect for those who like their hotels a bit quirky. ④

Portobello Gold 95–97 Portobello Rd, W11 ☎020/7460 4900, ⓦwww.portobellogold.com ⊖Notting Hill Gate or Holland Park. See map, pp.114–115. A fun and friendly option above a cheery modern pub/seafood restaurant. The seven rooms are plain and some are tiny, with miniature en-suite bathrooms, but the hotel also has a great apartment (sleeps 6 – at a bit of a pinch), with a dinky Caribbean-themed bathroom and fantastic roof terrace (and putting green). Breakfast not included. ③

St David's 14–20 Norfolk Square, W2 ☎020/7723 3856 or 4963, ⓦwww.stdavidshotels.com ⊖Paddington. See map, pp.114–115. Inexpensive, family-run B&B, famed for its English breakfast. Most rooms are en suite, and the large family rooms make it a good option for families on a budget. ②

Vicarage Hotel 10 Vicarage Gate, W8 ☎020/7229 4030, ⓦwww.londonvicaragehotel.com ⊖Notting Hill Gate or Kensington High Street. See map, pp.114–115. Ideally located B&B on a quiet street a step away from Kensington Gardens. Clean and smart floral rooms with shared facilities; full English breakfast included. ④

Hampstead

Hampstead Village Guesthouse 2 Kemplay Rd, NW3 ☎ 020/7435 8679, Ⓦ www.hampsteadguesthouse.com ⊖ Hampstead. Lovely B&B in a freestanding Victorian house on a quiet backstreet between Hampstead Village and the Heath. Rooms (most en suite) are tiny but characterful, crammed with books, pictures and handmade and antique furniture. ❸

Hostels and campsites

London's official **Youth Hostel Association (YHA) hostels** (Ⓦ www.yha.org.uk) are generally the cleanest, most efficiently run hostels in the capital. However, they charge around fifty percent or more above the rates of private hostels, and tend to get booked up several months in advance. **Independent hostels** are cheaper and more relaxed, but can be less reliable in terms of facilities. A good website for booking independent places online is Ⓦ www.hostellondon.com. London's **campsites** are all on the perimeter of the city, though they are without doubt the cheapest accommodation available.

Where possible we've marked the location of hostels on one of the maps in this chapter.

Hostels

Central YHA 104 Bolsover St, W1 ☎ 0845/371 9154, @elondoncentral@yha.org.uk ⊖ Great Portland Street. See map, p.95. The YHA's newest hostel is in a quiet location, and yet walking distance from the West End. Free wi-fi, kitchen and a 24hr café-bar. No groups. Dorms only (4–8 beds) from £20.

Clink78 78 King's Cross Rd, WC1 ☎ 020/7183 9400, Ⓦ www.clinkhostel.com ⊖ King's Cross. See map, pp.70–71. This 300-bed place has funky decor, bargain pod beds, and plenty of period features from the days when it was a Victorian courthouse, like the spacious internet courtroom – you can even stay in one of the old prison cells. Breakfast included; kitchen facilities from noon; 4–16-bed dorms available. Dorms from around £10; doubles £40. ❶

Clink261 261–265 Gray's Inn Rd, WC1 ☎ 020/7833 9400, Ⓦ www.ashleehouse.co.uk ⊖ King's Cross. See map, pp.70–71 A clean and friendly 170-bed hostel in a converted office block near King's Cross Station, with laundry and kitchen facilities. Breakfast included. Dorms (4–16 beds) available from £14; doubles £50. ❶

Generator Compton Place, off Tavistock Place, WC1 ☎ 020/7388 7666, Ⓦ www.generatorhostels.com ⊖ Russell Square or Euston. See map, p.95. A huge hostel, with over 800 beds, in a converted police barracks tucked away down a cobbled street. The neon and UV lighting and post-industrial decor may not be to everyone's taste, but this is without doubt the best bargain in Bloomsbury. There's a young, party atmosphere with themed nights in the late-night bar. Laundry, but no kitchen; breakfast included, plus cheap café;

4–12-bed dorms available. Dorms from £15; doubles £50. ❷

Holland House YHA Holland Walk, W8 ☎ 0845/371 9122, @hollandpark@yha.org.uk ⊖ Holland Park or High Street Kensington. See map, pp.114–115. Idyllically situated in Holland Park and fairly convenient for the centre. Kitchen available and café. Popular with groups. Dorms (4–10 beds) from £18.

Meininger Baden Powell House, 65–67 Queen's Gate, SW7 ⊖ Gloucester Road or South Kensington. ☎ 020/3051 8173, Ⓦ www.meininger-hostels.com. See map, pp.114–115. Bright and cheerful modern hostel, part of a German chain, run with Teutonic efficiency and located near the South Ken museums. Free wi-fi. Kitchen, but no laundry; breakfast not included. Dorms (4–6 beds) available. Dorms from £19; doubles £45. ❷

Oxford Street YHA 14 Noel St, W1 ☎ 0845/371 9133, @oxfordst@yha.org.uk ⊖ Oxford Circus or Tottenham Court Road. See map, pp.80–81. The Soho location and modest size mean this hostel tends to be full year-round. No groups, no café, but a large kitchen. Dorms (4–6 beds) from £18, plus doubles/twins £50. ❷

Piccadilly Backpackers 12 Sherwood St, W1 ☎ 020/7434 9009, Ⓦ www.piccadillybackpackers.com ⊖ Piccadilly Circus. See map, pp.80–81. Vast, 700-bed hostel with small rooms and an institutional feel. Not the quietest place to crash out, but it's incredibly cheap and central. You can pay more for pod bunks and en-suite facilities. Breakfast not included; laundry but no kitchen. Dorms £12; doubles £65. ❷

St Christopher's Village 161–165 Borough High St, SE1 ☎ 020/7407 1856, Ⓦ www.st-christophers.co.uk ⊖ Borough. See map, pp.110–111. St Christopher's run seven hostels across London, with no fewer than three near London Bridge, with branches in Camden, Greenwich, Shepherd's Bush and Hammersmith. The decor is upbeat and cheerful, the hostels are efficiently run and there's a party-animal ambience, fuelled by the hostel bars. The *Inn* has a pub attached, the *Oasis* is women only, while the *Village* has a nightclub and cinema, plus a rooftop hot tub and sauna. Free breakfast and laundry facilities but no kitchen. Dorms from £18; doubles/twins from £50. ❷

St Pancras YHA 79–81 Euston Rd, NW1 ☏0845/371 9344, ✉stpancras@yha.org.uk ⊖King's Cross or Euston. See map, pp.70–71. Hostel on the busy Euston Rd; rooms are very clean, bright, triple-glazed and air-conditioned. All doubles, and some dorms, are en suite and family rooms are available, all with TVs. Dorms from £22; doubles £50. ❷

St Paul's YHA 36 Carter Lane, EC4 ☏0845/371 9012, ✉stpauls@yha.org.uk ⊖St Paul's. See map, pp.100–101. Large 190-bed hostel in a superb location opposite St Paul's Cathedral. Breakfast included and a café for dinner, but no kitchen. Small groups only. Dorms (4–8 beds) £25 and twins £50. ❷

Smart Backpackers ☏020/7221 7773, ⓦwww.smartbackpackers.com. Hard-partying mini-chain of hostels, with basic, functional furnishings, and the city's cheapest dorm beds. Only the Russell Square hostel (see map, p.95) and the *Hyde Park Inn* (see map, pp.114–115) have kitchens; *Smart Hyde Park View* (see map, pp.114–115) also has en-suite doubles and a bar, and there are other branches in Camden and Bayswater. Dorm beds from around £12 (including breakfast); en-suite doubles from £80. ❸

Thameside YHA 20 Salter Rd, SE16 ☏0845/371 9756, ✉thameside@yha.org.uk ⊖Rotherhithe. London's largest purpose-built hostel, with 320 beds, is located in a quiet spot near the river, 15min from the nearest tube. Can feel a bit out on a limb, but has space when more central places are full. Kitchen available, plus café. Dorms (4–10 beds) from £16; doubles/twins £55. ❷

Campsites

Crystal Palace Crystal Palace Parade, SE19 ☏020/8778 7155, ⓦwww.caravanclub.co.uk. Crystal Palace train station from Victoria or London Bridge. A decent Camping & Caravanning Club site on south London's most famous woody hill, best suited for caravans and campervans. Station is five minutes' walk or bus #3 will take you all the way to Oxford St. Open all year.

Lea Valley Leisure Centre Caravan Park Meridian Way, Edmonton, N9 ☏020/8803 6900, ⓦwww.leevalleypark.org.uk; Ponders End train station from Liverpool St. Well-equipped site at Pickett's Lock on the River Lea, backing onto a vast reservoir. Multiplex cinema and 18-hole golf course on your doorstep. Open all year.

Westminster and Whitehall

Political, religious and regal power has emanated from **Whitehall** and **Westminster** for almost a millennium. It was King Edward the Confessor who first established this spot as London's royal and ecclesiastical power base in the eleventh century. He built his palace and abbey some three miles upstream from the City of London, and it was in the abbey that the embryonic English parliament met from the fourteenth century onwards.

Nowadays, **Whitehall** is synonymous with the faceless, pinstriped bureaucracy which runs the various governmental ministries located here, while **Westminster** remains home to the **Houses of Parliament**. Both are popular with visitors thanks to the **Changing of the Guard**, and familiar landmarks such as **Nelson's Column**, **Big Ben** and **Westminster Abbey**, London's most historic church.

Trafalgar Square

As one of the few large public squares in London, **Trafalgar Square** has been a focus for political demonstrations since it was laid out in the 1820s. Most days, however, it's scruffy urban pigeons that you're more likely to encounter, as they wheel around the square hoping some unsuspecting visitor will feed them (though, it is, in fact, illegal to do so). Along with its fountains, the square's central focal point is the deeply patriotic **Nelson's Column**, which stands 170ft high and is topped by a 17ft statue of the one-eyed, one-armed admiral who defeated the French at the 1805 Battle of Trafalgar. Nelson himself is actually quite hard to see – not so the giant bronze lions at the base of the column, which provide a popular photo opportunity.

Stranded on a traffic island to the south of the column, and predating the entire square, is an **equestrian statue of Charles I**, erected shortly after the Restoration on the very spot where eight of those who had signed the king's death warrant were disembowelled. Charles's statue also marks the original site of the thirteenth-century **Charing Cross**, from where all distances from the capital are measured – a Victorian imitation now stands outside Charing Cross train station. Don't miss the fourth plinth, in the northwest corner, originally earmarked for an equestrian statue of William IV. In fact, it remained empty until 1999, since when it has been used to display specially commissioned works of modern sculpture (Ⓦwww.london.gov.uk/fourthplinth).

The northeastern corner of the square is occupied by James Gibbs's church of **St Martin-in-the-Fields** (Mon–Wed 10am–7pm, Thurs–Sat 10am–10pm, Sun noon–7pm; free; Ⓦwww.stmartin-in-the-fields.org), fronted by a magnificent Corinthian portico. Completed in 1726, the interior is purposefully simple, though the Italian plasterwork on the barrel vaulting is exceptionally rich; it's best appreciated while listening to one of the church's free **lunchtime concerts** (Mon, Tues & Fri). There's a licensed café in the roomy **crypt**, not to mention a shop, gallery and brass-rubbing centre (Mon–Sat 10am–6pm, Sun noon–6pm).

London for free

London can be an expensive place for locals and tourists alike, with some of the city's top attractions – and in particular its royal palaces – charging a fortune for entry. However, there are lots of things to enjoy in the capital that are one hundred percent free.

Thanks to the last Labour government, the permanent collections of the city's **national museums** – from the British Museum to the South Kensington trio of the Science, Natural History and V&A museums – are all free. So too are the permanent **art collections** of the National Gallery, National Portrait Gallery, Tate Modern and Tate Britain, all of which also offer free guided tours, and lesser-known collections such as the Wallace Collection, Kenwood House, Saatchi Gallery and even the Courtauld (Mon 10am–2pm only). Then, there are the city's trendy commercial galleries, where you can see oodles of contemporary art for free. It's also worth checking out the **auction houses**, such as Sotheby's, where you can view hundreds of works of museum quality.

There's enough free music to keep you amused morning, noon and night. Free **lunchtime concerts** of classical chamber works or organ recitals take place Monday to Friday at various churches, mostly in the City, while at St Paul's Cathedral and Westminster Abbey you can hear the country's top choristers perform **choral evensong**. Two good venues to catch live foyer music are the Royal Festival Hall and the Barbican, and look out too for regular performances at other famous venues such as the National Gallery (Fri 6pm) and the V&A (Fri 6.30pm).

The Queen provides her own bit of free **royal pageantry** each day with the Changing of the Guard on Whitehall and elsewhere – she also gets out and about in her golden coach several times a year, as does the Lord Mayor of the City of London. Republicans will find more entertainment at **Speakers' Corner**, a traditional free-speech spot in Hyde Park. Finally, there are all the other wonderful green spaces the city boasts, from landscaped **royal parks** to peaceful inner-city churchyards.

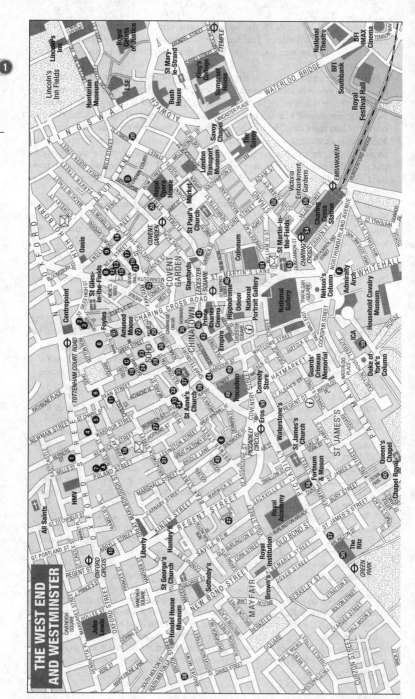

THE WEST END AND WESTMINSTER

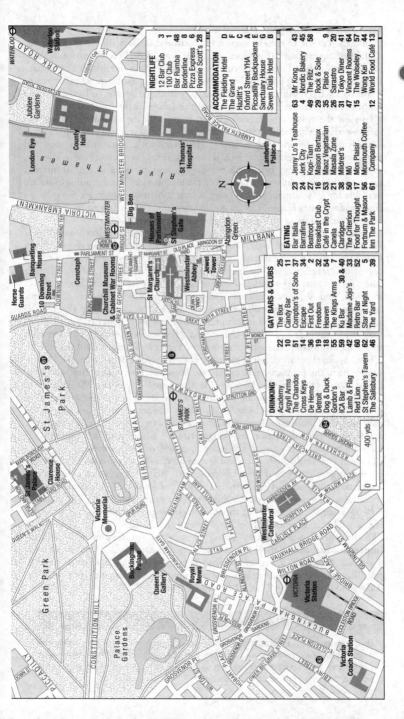

NIGHTLIFE

12 Bar Club	3
100 Club	1
Bar Rumba	48
Borderline	8
Pizza Express	6
Ronnie Scott's	28

ACCOMMODATION

The Fielding Hotel	D
The Grand	F
Hazlitt's	C
Oxford Street YHA	A
Piccadilly Backpackers	E
Sanctuary House	G
Seven Dials Hotel	B

EATING

Bar Italia	25	Jenny Lo's Teahouse	23
Barrafina	11	Jerk City	24
Beatroot	37	Kopi-Tiam	27
Breakfast Club	2	Maison Bertaux	16
Café in the Crypt	32	Maoz Vegetarian	53
Canela	54	Masala Zone	21
Claridges	7	Mildred's	26
The Criterion	30 & 40	Mô	50
Food for Thought	33	Mon Plaisir	17
Fortnum & Mason	5	Monmouth Coffee	56
Inn The Park	39	Company	61
Mr Kong	63		
Nordic Bakery	4		
The Ritz	49		
Rock & Sole	29		
Plaice	35		
Sarastro	20		
Tokyo Diner	31		
Vincent Rooms	47		
The Wolseley	15		
Wong Kei	44		
World Food Café	13		

GAY BARS & CLUBS

The Box	25
Candy Bar	11
Compton's of Soho	34
Escape	2
First Out	32
Freedom	54
Heaven	7
The Kings Arms	30 & 40
Ku Bar	33
Madame Jojo's	52
Retro Bar	5
Star at Night	56
The Yard	39

DRINKING

Academy	22
Argyll Arms	10
The Chandos	51
Cross Keys	34
De Hems	14
Detroit	19
Dog & Duck	18
Gordon's	55
ICA Bar	59
Lamb & Flag	42
Red Lion	60
St Stephen's Tavern	62
The Salisbury	46

Unlike the Louvre or the Hermitage, the **National Gallery**, on the north side of Trafalgar Square (daily 10am–6pm, Wed until 9pm; free; ⓦ www.nationalgallery .org.uk), is not based on a royal collection; in fact it was the British government that started procuring works as late as 1824. The gallery's subsequent canny acquisition policy has resulted in more than 2300 paintings, but the collection's virtue is not so much its size, but the range, depth and sheer quality of its contents.

To view the collection chronologically, begin with the **Sainsbury Wing**, the softly-softly, postmodern 1980s adjunct which is linked to – and playfully imitates – the original Neoclassical building. However, with more than a thousand paintings on permanent display, you'll need stamina to see everything in one day, so if time is tight your best bet is to home in on your areas of special interest, having picked up a gallery plan at one of the information desks. **Audioguides** are available for a "voluntary contribution" – much better, though, are the gallery's **free guided tours** (daily 11.30am & 2.30pm), which set off from the Sainsbury Wing foyer, and focus on a representative sample of works.

Among the National's **Italian** masterpieces are Leonardo's melancholic *Virgin of the Rocks*, Uccello's *Battle of San Romano*, Botticelli's *Venus and Mars* (inspired by a Dante sonnet) and Piero della Francesca's beautifully composed *Baptism of Christ*, one of his earliest works. The fine collection of Venetian works includes Titian's colourful early masterpiece *Bacchus and Ariadne*, his very late, much gloomier *Death of Acteon*, and Veronese's lustrous *Family of Darius before Alexander*. Elsewhere, Bronzino's erotic *Venus, Cupid, Folly and Time* and Raphael's trenchant *Pope Julius II* keep company with Michelangelo's unfinished *Entombment*. Later Italian works to look out for include a couple by Caravaggio, a few splendid examples of Tiepolo's airy draughtsmanship, and glittering vistas of Venice by Canaletto and Guardi.

From **Spain** there are dazzling pieces by El Greco, Goya, Murillo and Velázquez, among them the provocative *Rokeby Venus*. From the **Low Countries**, standouts include Van Eyck's *Arnolfini Marriage*, Memlinc's perfectly poised *Donne Triptych*, and a couple of typically serene Vermeers. There are numerous genre paintings, such as Frans Hals' *Family Group in a Landscape*, and some superlative landscapes, most notably Hobbema's *Avenue, Middleharnis*. An array of Rembrandt paintings that features some of his most searching portraits – two of them self-portraits – is followed by abundant examples of Rubens' expansive, fleshy canvases.

Holbein's masterful *Ambassadors* and several of Van Dyck's portraits were painted for the English court, and there's home-grown **British** art, too, represented by important works such as Hogarth's satirical *Marriage à la Mode*, Gainsborough's translucent *Morning Walk*, Constable's ever-popular *Hay Wain*, and Turner's *Fighting Temeraire*. Highlights of the **French** contingent include superb works by Poussin, Claude, Fragonard, Boucher, Watteau and David.

Finally, there's a particularly strong showing of **Impressionists** and **Post-Impressionists**, among them Manet's unfinished *Execution of Maximilian*, Renoir's *Umbrellas*, Monet's *Thames below Westminster*, Van Gogh's *Sunflowers*, Seurat's pointillist *Bathers at Asnières*, a Rousseau junglescape, Cézanne's proto-Cubist *Bathers* and Picasso's Blue Period *Child with a Dove*.

Blue plaques

Blue plaques on buildings across England – but especially in London, where there are around 800 – celebrate **historical figures** and the buildings they inhabited. Follow the links at ⓦ www.english-heritage.org.uk to track down the former homes of the famous, from Matthew Arnold to Emile Zola.

National Portrait Gallery

Founded in 1856 to house uplifting depictions of the good and the great, the **National Portrait Gallery** (daily 10am–6pm, Thurs & Fri till 9pm; free; @www .npg.org.uk) has some fine works in its collection. However, many of the studies are of less interest than their subjects, and the overall impression is of an overstuffed shrine to famous Brits rather than a museum offering any insight into the history of portraiture. Nevertheless, it is fascinating to trace who has been deemed worthy of admiration at any moment: aristocrats and artists in previous centuries, warmongers and imperialists in the early decades of the twentieth century, writers and poets in the 1930s and 1940s, and latterly, sportsmen and women, politicians and film and pop stars. The NPG's audioguide (£2) gives useful biographical background information and the gallery's **special exhibitions** (for which there's often an entrance charge) are well worth seeing – the photography shows, in particular, are usually excellent.

Whitehall

During the sixteenth and seventeenth centuries **Whitehall** served as the permanent residence of England's kings and queens. Originally the London seat of the Archbishop of York, Whitehall Palace was confiscated and embellished by Henry VIII after a fire at Westminster made him homeless; it was here that he celebrated his marriage to Anne Boleyn in 1533, and where he died fourteen years later. From the sixteenth century onwards, the key governmental ministries and offices migrated here, rehousing themselves on an ever-increasing scale. The royalty, meanwhile, moved out to St James's after a fire destroyed most of Whitehall Palace in 1698.

One of the few sections of Whitehall Palace to escape the 1698 fire, **Banqueting House** (Mon–Sat 10am–5pm; £4.50; @hrp.org.uk), was one of the first Palladian buildings to be built in England. The one room open to the public has no original furnishings, but is well worth seeing for the superlative **Rubens ceiling paintings** commissioned by Charles I in the 1630s, depicting the union of England and Scotland, the peaceful reign of his father, James I, and finally his apotheosis. Charles himself walked through the room for the last time in 1649, when he stepped onto the executioner's scaffold from one of its windows.

On the west side of Whitehall, two mounted sentries of the Queen's Household Cavalry and two horseless colleagues, all in ceremonial uniform, are posted daily from 10am to 4pm. Ostensibly they are protecting the **Horse Guards** building, (once the old palace guard house). The mounted guards are changed hourly, and those standing every two hours; try to coincide your visit with the Changing of the Guard (see box, p.84). Round the back of Horse Guards, you'll find the **Household Cavalry Museum** (daily: March–Sept 10am–6pm; Oct–Feb 10am–5pm; £6; @www.householdcavalrymuseum.co.uk), where you can try on a trooper's elaborate uniform, complete a horse quiz and learn about the regiments' history. With the stables immediately adjacent, it's a sweet-smelling place, and – horse-lovers will be pleased to know – you can see the beasts in their stalls through a glass screen. Don't miss the pocket Riot Act on display, which ends with the wise warning: "must read correctly: variance fatal".

Further down this west side of Whitehall is London's most famous address, **Number 10 Downing Street** (@www.number-10.gov.uk), the seventeenth-century terraced house that has been the residence of the prime minister since it was presented to Sir Robert Walpole, Britain's first PM, by George II in 1732. Facing Downing Street's locked gates, in the middle of the road, stands Edwin Lutyens' **Cenotaph**, eschewing any kind of Christian imagery, and inscribed

The Changing of the Guard

The **Changing of the Guard** takes place at two separate London locations: the Foot Guards hold their ceremony outside **Buckingham Palace** (April–July daily 11.30am; Sept–March alternate days; no ceremony if it rains), but the more impressive one is held on **Horse Guards Parade** in Whitehall, where a squad of mounted Household Cavalry in full livery arrives from Hyde Park to relieve the guards (Mon–Sat 11am, Sun 10am). Alternatively, if you miss the whole thing, turn up at Horse Guards at 4pm for the elaborate daily inspection by the Officer of the Guard, who checks the soldiers haven't knocked off early. A ceremony also takes place regularly at **Windsor Castle** (see p.130).

simply with the words "The Glorious Dead". The memorial remains the focus of the Remembrance Sunday ceremony in November.

In 1938, in anticipation of Nazi air raids, the basements of the civil service buildings on the south side of King Charles Street, south of Downing Street, were converted into the **Cabinet War Rooms** (daily 9.30am–6pm; £12; ⓦcwr.iwm .org.uk). It was here that Winston Churchill directed operations and held Cabinet meetings for the duration of World War II. The rooms have been left pretty much as they were when they were finally abandoned on VJ Day 1945, making for an atmospheric underground trot through wartime London. Also in the basement is the excellent **Churchill Museum**, where you can hear snippets of Churchill's most famous speeches and check out his trademark bowler, spotted bow-tie and half-chewed Havana, not to mention his wonderful burgundy zip-up "romper suit".

The Houses of Parliament

Clearly visible at the south end of Whitehall is one of London's best-known monuments, the Palace of Westminster, better known as the **Houses of Parliament** (ⓦwww.parliament.uk). The city's finest Gothic Revival building and symbol of a nation once confident of its place at the centre of the world, it's distinguished above all by the ornate, gilded clocktower popularly known as **Big Ben**, after the thirteen-tonne main bell that strikes the hour (and is broadcast across the world by the BBC).

The original medieval palace burned down in 1834, and everything you see now – save for **Westminster Hall**, the westernmost building – dates from Victorian times. You get a glimpse of the hall en route to the public galleries; its huge oak hammerbeam roof makes it one of the most magnificent secular medieval halls in Europe. The **Jewel Tower** (daily: April–Oct 10am–5pm; Nov–March 10am–4pm; £3; EH), across the road from parliament, is another remnant of the medieval palace, now housing an excellent exhibition on the history of Parliament – worth visiting before you queue up to get into Parliament itself.

To watch the proceedings in either the House of Commons or the Lords, simply join the queue for the **public galleries** (known as Strangers' Galleries) outside St Stephen's Gate. The public are let in slowly (from 4pm Mon, 1pm Tues–Thurs, 10am Fri); the security checks are very tight, and the whole procedure can take an hour or more. If you want to avoid the queues, turn up an hour or more later, when the crowds have usually thinned; phone ⓣ020/7219 4272 to check the place isn't closed for the holidays.

To see **Question Time** (Mon 2.30pm, Tues–Thurs 11.30am), when the House is at its most raucous and entertaining, UK citizens must book a ticket several weeks in advance from their local MP. If you're here in late summer, you can also see Parliament by way of a **guided tour** (Mon–Sat only; £7; booking line

℗0870/906 3773), in which visitors get to walk through the two chambers, see some of the state rooms reserved for the Queen, and admire Westminster Hall. It's a good idea to book in advance, or you can simply head for the ticket office on Abingdon Green, opposite Victoria Tower and its adjacent gardens.

Westminster Abbey

The Houses of Parliament dwarf their much older neighbour, **Westminster Abbey** (hours can vary, but normally Mon–Fri 9.30am–4.30pm, Wed until 6pm, Sat 9.30am–2.30pm; £12; ⓦ www.westminster-abbey.org), yet this single building embodies much of the history of England: it has been the venue for all coronations since the time of William the Conqueror, and was the site of more or less every royal burial for some five hundred years between the reigns of Henry III and George II. Scores of the nation's most famous citizens are honoured here, too (though many of the stones commemorate people buried elsewhere), and the interior is crammed with hundreds of monuments and statues.

Entry is via the north transept, cluttered with monuments to politicians and traditionally known as **Statesmen's Aisle**, shortly after which you come to the abbey's most dazzling architectural set-piece, the **Lady Chapel**, added by Henry VII in 1503 as his future resting place. With its intricately carved vaulting and fan-shaped gilded pendants, the chapel represents the final spectacular gasp of the English Perpendicular style. The public are no longer admitted to the **Shrine of Edward the Confessor**, the sacred heart of the building (except on a guided verger tour; £4) though you do get to inspect Edward I's **Coronation Chair**, a decrepit oak throne dating from around 1300 and still used for coronations.

Nowadays, the abbey's royal tombs are upstaged by **Poets' Corner**, in the south transept, though the first occupant, **Geoffrey Chaucer**, was in fact buried here not because he was a poet, but because he lived nearby. By the eighteenth century this zone had become an artistic pantheon, and since then, the transept has been filled with tributes to all shades of talent. From the south transept, you can view the central sanctuary, site of the coronations, and the wonderful **Cosmati floor mosaic**, constructed in the thirteenth century by Italian craftsmen, and often covered by a carpet for protection.

Doors in the south choir aisle (plus a separate entrance from Dean's Yard) lead to the **Great Cloisters** (daily 8am–6pm; free), rebuilt after a fire in 1298. At the eastern end of the cloisters lies the octagonal **Chapter House** (daily 10.30am–4pm; free), where the House of Commons met until 1395. The thirteenth-century decorative paving tiles and apocalyptic wall-paintings have survived intact. Close by is the **Abbey Museum** (daily 10.30am–4pm; free), filled with generations of bald royal death masks and wax effigies. From the cloisters you can make your way to the little-known **College Garden** (Tues–Thurs: April–Sept 10am–6pm; Oct–March 10am–4pm; free), a 900-year-old stretch of green which now provides a quiet retreat; brass band concerts take place in July and August between 12.30 and 2pm.

It's only after exploring the cloisters that you get to see the **nave** itself: narrow, light and, at over a hundred feet in height, by far the tallest in the country; you exit via the west door.

Westminster Cathedral

Begun in 1895, the stripy neo-Byzantine, Roman Catholic **Westminster Cathedral** (Mon–Fri 7am–7pm, Sat 8am–7pm, Sun 8am–8pm; free; ⓦ www .westminstercathedral.org.uk), halfway down Victoria Street, is one of London's most surprising churches, as well as one of the last – and the wildest – monuments to the Victorian era. Brick-built and decorated with hoops of Portland stone, it culminates in a magnificent 274ft tapered **campanile**, served by a lift (daily 9.30am–12.30pm & 1–5pm; £3). The interior is still only half-finished, so to get an idea of what the place should eventually look like, explore the series of **side chapels** whose rich, multicoloured decor makes use of over one hundred different types of marble from around the world. Be sure, too, to check out the low-relief **Stations of the Cross**, sculpted by Eric Gill during World War I.

Tate Britain

A purpose-built gallery founded in 1897 with money from Henry Tate, inventor of the sugar cube, **Tate Britain** (daily 10am–5.50pm; free; Ⓦ www.tate.org.uk), half a mile south of Parliament, is devoted exclusively to British art from 1500 to the present day. In addition, the gallery also showcases contemporary British artists and continues to sponsor the Turner Prize, the country's most prestigious modern-art award.

The pictures are rehung more or less annually, but always include a fair selection of works by British artists such as Hogarth, Constable, Gainsborough, Reynolds and Blake, plus foreign artists like Van Dyck who spent much of their career over here. The ever-popular **Pre-Raphaelites** are well represented, as are established twentieth-century greats including Stanley Spencer and Francis Bacon alongside living artists such as David Hockney and Lucian Freud. Lastly, don't miss the Tate's outstanding **Turner collection**, displayed in the Clore Gallery.

St James's

An exclusive little enclave sandwiched between St James's Park and Piccadilly, **St James's** was laid out in the 1670s close to the royal seat of St James's Palace. Regal and aristocratic residences overlook nearby Green Park and the stately avenue of **The Mall**, while gentlemen's clubs cluster along Pall Mall and St James's Street, and jacket-and-tie restaurants and expense-account gentlemen's outfitters line Jermyn Street. Hardly surprising, then, that most Londoners rarely stray into this area. Plenty of folk, however, frequent **St James's Park**, with large numbers heading for the Queen's chief residence, **Buckingham Palace**, and the adjacent Queen's Gallery and Royal Mews.

The Mall and St James's Park

The tree-lined sweep of **The Mall** – London's nearest equivalent of a Parisian boulevard – was laid out in the early twentieth century as a memorial to Queen Victoria. The bombastic **Admiralty Arch** was erected to mark the eastern entrance to The Mall, from Trafalgar Square, while at the other end, in front of Buckingham Palace, stands the ludicrously overblown **Victoria Memorial**, Edward VII's tribute to his mother. The Mall is best visited on a Sunday, when it's closed to traffic.

Flanking nearly the whole length of The Mall, **St James's Park** is the oldest of the royal parks, having been drained and enclosed for hunting purposes by Henry VIII. It was landscaped by Nash in the 1820s, and today its tree-lined lake is a favourite picnic spot for Whitehall's civil servants. Pelicans chill out at the eastern end, and there are exotic ducks, swans and geese aplenty. From the bridge across the lake there's also a fine view over to Westminster and the jumble of domes and pinnacles along Whitehall, with the London Eye peeking over it all.

Buckingham Palace and the Royal Mews

The graceless colossus of **Buckingham Palace** (Aug & Sept daily 9.45am–6pm; £16.50; ℗ www.royal.gov.uk), popularly known as "Buck House", has served as the monarch's permanent London residence only since the accession of Victoria. Bought by George III in 1762, the building was overhauled in the late 1820s by Nash and again in 1913, producing a palace that's as bland as it's possible to be.

For two months of the year, the hallowed portals are grudgingly nudged open to the public; timed tickets are sold from the marquee-like box office in Green Park at the western end of The Mall. The interior, however, is a bit of an anticlimax: of the palace's 775 rooms, you're permitted to see around 20, and there's little sign of life as the Queen decamps to Scotland every summer. If the decor is disappointing, at least the art on display is top-notch, with several Van Dycks, two Rembrandts, two Canalettos, a Poussin, a de Hooch and a wonderful Vermeer hanging in the Picture Gallery.

For the other ten months of the year, the palace is closed to visitors – not that this deters the crowds who mill around the railings and gather in some force to watch the **Changing of the Guard** (see box, p.84). If the Queen is at home, the Royal Standard flies from the roof of the palace and four guards patrol; if not, the Union flag flutters aloft and just two guards stand out front.

The public can also pay through the nose to view a small portion of the Royal Collection at the rebuilt **Queen's Gallery** (daily 10am–5.30pm; £8.50; ℗ www .royal.gov.uk), on the south side of the palace. Exhibitions change regularly, drawn from a collection which is three times larger than the National Gallery's, and includes masterpieces by Michelangelo, Reynolds, Gainsborough, Vermeer, Van Dyck, Rubens, Rembrandt and Canaletto, as well as the odd Fabergé egg and heaps of Sèvres china.

There's more pageantry on show at the Nash-built **Royal Mews** (Aug & Sept daily 10am–5pm; Oct–July daily except Fri 11am–4pm; £7.50; ℗ www.royal .gov.uk), further along Buckingham Palace Road. The royal carriages, lined up under a glass canopy in the courtyard, are the main attraction, in particular the Gold State Coach. Smothered in 22-carat gilding and weighing four tonnes, its axles supporting four life-size figures, it was made for George III in 1762. The Mews also houses the Royal Family's gleaming fleet of five Rolls-Royce Phantoms and three Daimlers.

Waterloo Place to St James's Palace

Away from Buckingham Palace, St James's does contain some interesting architectural set-pieces, such as **Waterloo Place**, at the centre of which stands the **Guards' Crimean Memorial**, fashioned from captured Russian cannon and featuring a statue of Florence Nightingale. Clearly visible, beyond, is the "Grand Old" **Duke of York's Column**, erected in 1833, ten years before Nelson's more famous one in Trafalgar Square.

Cutting across Waterloo Place, Pall Mall leads west to **St James's Palace**, whose main red-brick gate-tower is pretty much all that remains of the Tudor palace erected here by Henry VIII. When Whitehall Palace burned down in 1698, St James's became the principal royal residence and, in keeping with tradition, an ambassador to the UK is still accredited to the "Court of St James's", even though the court has since moved down the road to Buckingham Palace. The modest, rambling, crenellated complex is off limits to the public, with the exception of the **Chapel Royal** (Oct to Easter Sun 8.30am & 11.15am), situated within the palace, and the **Queen's Chapel** (Easter Sun to July Sun 8.30am & 11.15am), on the other side of Marlborough Road; both are open for services only.

Clarence House (Aug & Sept daily 10am–4pm; £8; ⓦ www.royal.gov.uk), built by John Nash for the future William IV and connected to the palace's southwest wing, is best known as the former home of the late Queen Mum. It now serves as chief London residence of **Prince Charles and Camilla**, and a handful of rooms can be visited over the summer; tickets must be booked in advance and visits are by guided tour only, Apart from a peek behind the scenes of a royal palace, the main draw is the selection of paintings by the likes of Walter Sickert and Augustus John.

Mayfair and Marylebone

A whiff of exclusivity still pervades the streets of **Mayfair**, particularly Bond Street and its tributaries, where designer clothes emporia jostle for space with jewellers, bespoke tailors and fine-art dealers. Most Londoners, however, stick to the more prosaic pleasures of Regent and Oxford streets, home to the flagship branches of the country's most popular chain stores. It's here that Londoners are referring to when they talk of the **West End**. **Marylebone**, to the north of Oxford Street, may not have quite the pedigree and snob value of Mayfair, but it's still a wealthy and aspirational area, and its mesh of smart Georgian streets and squares are a pleasure to wander, especially the chi-chi, village-like quarter around the High Street.

Piccadilly Circus

Anonymous and congested it may be, but for many Londoners, **Piccadilly Circus** is the nearest their city comes to having a centre. It's by no means a picturesque place, and is probably best seen at night when the spread of vast illuminated signs (a feature since the Edwardian era) provides a touch of Las Vegas dazzle, and the human traffic is at its most frenetic. Somewhat inexplicably, Piccadilly Circus attracts a steady flow of tourists, who come here to sit on the steps of the central fountain, topped by an aluminium statue popularly known as **Eros**. Despite the bow and arrow, it depicts not the god of love but the Angel of Christian Charity, and was erected to commemorate the Earl of Shaftesbury, a Bible-thumping social reformer who campaigned against child labour.

Originally an opulent restaurant from 1896 until its closure in 1965, **Trocadero** (Mon–Thurs & Sun 10am–midnight, Fri & Sat 10am–1am; ⓦ www .londontrocadero.com) has since become a tacky, glorified amusement arcade, casino and multiplex cinema that has had millions poured into it in an unsuccessful attempt to find a winning formula. Among the current incumbents is **Ripley's Believe It or Not!** (daily 10am–midnight; £17.95; ⓦ www.ripleys london.com), the world's largest odditorium – a sort of waxwork version of a Victorian freak show.

Regent Street

Drawn up by John Nash in 1812 as both a luxury shopping street and a new, wide triumphal approach to Regent's Park (to the north; see p.120), **Regent Street** was the city's first real attempt at dealing with traffic congestion. At the same time, it helped clear away a large swath of slums, and create a tangible borderline to shore up fashionable Mayfair against the chaotic maze of Soho. Even today, it's still possible to admire the stately intentions of Nash's plan, particularly evident in the Quadrant, the street's partially arcaded section which curves westwards

from Piccadilly Circus. During the course of the nineteenth century, however, the increased purchasing power of the city's middle classes brought the tone of the street "down", and heavyweight stores catering for the masses now predominate. Among the best known are **Hamley's**, reputedly the world's largest toyshop, and **Liberty**, the department store that popularized Arts and Crafts designs in the early 1900s.

Piccadilly and around

Piccadilly apparently got its name from the ruffs or "pickadills" worn by the dandies who used to promenade here in the late seventeenth century. Despite its fashionable pedigree, it's no place for promenading in its current state, with traffic careering down it nose to tail most of the day and night. Infinitely more pleasant places to window-shop are the various nineteenth-century **arcades** leading off the street, originally built to protect shoppers from the mud and horse-dung on the streets, but now equally useful for escaping exhaust fumes.

Piccadilly may not be the shopping heaven it once was, but it does still have **The Ritz**, a byword for decadence since it first wowed Edwardian society in 1906. The hotel's design, with its two-storey French-style mansard roof and long arcade, was based on the buildings of Paris's rue de Rivoli. For a prolonged look inside, you'll need to be in good appetite and dress appropriately, and book in advance for the famous afternoon tea (see box, p.133).

Royal Academy of Arts

The **Royal Academy of Arts** (daily 10am–6pm, Fri until 10pm; £6–12; Ⓦwww.royalacademy.org.uk) occupies one of the few surviving aristocratic mansions that once lined the north side of Piccadilly. The country's first-ever formal art school, the Academy was founded in 1768 by a group of English painters including Thomas Gainsborough and Joshua Reynolds, the first president, whose statue now stands in the main courtyard, palette in hand. The Academy usually has two or three art exhibitions on at any one time, but is best known for its **Summer Exhibition**, which opens in June and runs until mid-August. Anyone can enter paintings in any style, and the lucky winners' works get exhibited and sold. In addition, RA "Academicians" are allowed to display six of their own works – no matter how awful. The result is a bewildering display, which gets annually panned by the critics. As well as hosting exhibitions, the RA has a small selection of works from its own collection on **permanent display** in the newly restored white-and-gold John Madejski Fine Rooms (Tues–Fri 1–4.30pm, Sat & Sun 10am–6pm; free; free guided tours Tues, Thurs & Fri 1pm, Wed 1 & 3pm & Sat 11.30am). Highlights include a Rembrandtesque self-portrait by Reynolds, as well as works by the likes of John Constable, Stanley Spencer and David Hockney.

Royal Institution

Founded in 1799 "for teaching by courses of philosophical lectures and experiments the application of science to the common purposes of life", the **Royal Institution**, at 21 Albemarle St (Mon–Fri 9am–9pm; free; Ⓦwww.rigb.org), is a scientific body whose professors have included Humphry Davy (inventor of the miner's lamp), Michael Faraday and Lord Rutherford. The building's basement houses a **museum** devoted to Faraday, who was a pioneer in the fields of electricity and electromagnetism. Faraday was also the man responsible for inaugurating the Royal Institution's six Christmas Lectures in 1826, a continuing tradition designed to popularize science among schoolchildren.

Bond Street and around

While Oxford Street, Regent Street and Piccadilly have all gone downmarket, **Bond Street**, which runs parallel with Regent Street, has carefully maintained its exclusivity. It is, in fact, two streets rolled into one: the southern half, laid out in the 1680s, is known as Old Bond Street; its northern extension, which followed less than fifty years later, is New Bond Street. They are both pretty unassuming streets architecturally, yet the shops that line them are among the flashiest in London, dominated by perfumeries, **jewellers** and designer clothing stores. In addition to fashion, Bond Street is also renowned for its fine-art galleries and its auction houses, the oldest of which is **Sotheby's**, 34–35 New Bond St (Ⓦwww .sothebys.com), whose viewing galleries are open free of charge.

Handel House Museum

The German-born composer **George Frideric Handel** (1685–1759) spent the best part of his life in London, producing all his best-known works at what's now the **Handel House Museum**, 25 Brook St (Tues–Sat 10am–6pm, Thurs till 8pm, Sun noon–6pm; £5; Ⓦwww.handelhouse.org). The composer used the ground floor of the building as a sort of shop where subscribers could buy scores, while the first floor was employed as a rehearsal room. Although containing few original artefacts, the house has been painstakingly restored, and further atmosphere is provided by music students who come to practise on the house's harpsichords. For information on more formal **recitals** that regularly take place, see the website. Access to the house is via the chic cobbled yard at the back.

Oxford Street and around

The old Roman road to Oxford has been London's main **shopping** destination for the last century, and this aesthetically unremarkable two-mile hotchpotch of shops remains one of London's busiest streets. East of Oxford Circus, it forms the northern border of Soho; to the west, the one great landmark is **Selfridges**, a huge Edwardian pile fronted by giant Ionic columns, with the Queen of Time riding the ship of commerce and supporting an Art Deco clock above the main entrance. The store was opened in 1909 by Chicago millionaire Gordon Selfridge, who flaunted its 130 departments under the slogan, "Why not spend a day at Selfridges?"; he was later pensioned off after running into trouble with the Inland Revenue.

Wallace Collection

Immediately north of Oxford Street, on Manchester Square, stands Hertford House, a miniature eighteenth-century French-style chateau, housing the **Wallace Collection** (daily 10am–5pm; free; Ⓦwww.wallacecollection.org). This is an endearingly old-fashioned place, with exhibits piled high in glass cabinets, paintings covering every inch of wall space and a bloody great armoury. The collection is best known for its eighteenth-century **French paintings** (especially Watteau); look out, too, for Franz Hals' *Laughing Cavalier*, Titian's *Perseus and Andromeda*, Velázquez's *Lady with a Fan* and Rembrandt's affectionate portrait of his teenage son, Titus. Labelling can be pretty terse and paintings occasionally move about, so you might consider renting an audioguide.

Madame Tussauds

Madame Tussauds (Mon–Fri 9.30am–5.30pm, Sat & Sun 9am–6pm; from £22; Ⓣ0870/400 3000, Ⓦwww.madame-tussauds.co.uk), on Marylebone Road, has been pulling in the crowds ever since the good lady arrived in London from France in 1802 bearing the sculpted heads of guillotined aristocrats. The entrance fee is

extortionate, the likenesses occasionally dubious and the automated dummies inept, but you can still rely on finding London's biggest queues here – to avoid joining them, book your ticket online. There are photo opportunities galore throughout the first few sections, which are peppered with contemporary **celebrities** from the BBC to Bollywood. Keep your eyes out for the elderly and diminutive Madame Tussaud herself, and the oldest wax model, Madame du Barry, Louis XV's mistress, who gently respires as Sleeping Beauty – in reality she was beheaded in the French Revolution. The **Chamber of Horrors**, the most popular section of all, is irredeemably tasteless, and now features live, costumed actors who jump out at you in the dark (you can opt out of this). The Tussauds finale is a manic five-minute "ride" through the history of London in a miniaturized taxi cab, followed by a thirty-minute high-tech presentation, usually on a celebrity/Hollywood-inspired theme, projected onto the domed auditorium of the former Planetarium.

Sherlock Holmes Museum

Sherlock Holmes's fictional address was 221b Baker Street, hence the number on the door of the **Sherlock Holmes Museum** (daily 9.30am–6pm; £6; Ⓦwww .sherlock-holmes.co.uk), which is actually at no. 239. Unashamedly touristy, the place is stuffed full of Victoriana and life-size models of characters from the books. It's an atmospheric and very competent exercise in period reconstruction – you can even don a deerstalker to have your picture taken by the fireside, looking like the great detective himself.

Soho

Bounded by Regent Street to the west, Oxford Street to the north and Charing Cross Road to the east, **Soho** is very much the heart of the West End. It's been the city's premier red-light district for centuries, and retains an unorthodox and slightly raffish air that's unique for central London. Conventional sights are few and far between, yet it's a great area to wander through – whatever the hour, there's always something going on. Most folk head here to visit one of the big movie houses on **Leicester Square**, to drink in the latest designer bar or to grab a bite to eat at the innumerable cafés and restaurants, ranging from the inexpensive Chinese places that pepper the tiny enclave of **Chinatown**, to exclusive, Michelin-starred establishments in the backstreets of central Soho. The area is also now Europe's leading **gay hotspot**, especially in the bars and cafés concentrated around Old Compton Street.

Leicester Square and Chinatown

By night, when the big cinemas and nightclubs are doing brisk business and the buskers are entertaining passers-by, **Leicester Square** is one of the most crowded places in London; on a Friday or Saturday night, it can seem as if half the youth of the city's suburbs have congregated here to get drunk, supplemented by a vast number of tourists. It wasn't until the mid-nineteenth century that the square began to emerge as an entertainment zone, with accommodation houses (for prostitutes and their clients) and music halls such as the grandiose **Empire** and the **Hippodrome** (just off the square), both of which still stand today. Cinema moved in during the 1930s – a golden age evoked by the sleek black lines of the **Odeon** on the east side – and maintains its grip on the area. Now a cinema, the Empire is the favourite for big red-carpet premieres and, in a rather half-hearted imitation of the Hollywood tradition, there are even handprints-of-the-stars indented into the pavement of the square's southwestern corner.

Chinatown, hemmed in between Leicester Square and Shaftesbury Avenue, to the north, is a self-contained jumble of shops, cafés and restaurants that makes up one of London's most distinct and popular ethnic enclaves. **Gerrard Street**, Chinatown's main drag, has been endowed with ersatz touches – telephone kiosks rigged out as pagodas and fake oriental gates, or *paifang* – though few of London's 60,000 or so Chinese actually live in the enclave's three small blocks. Nonetheless, it remains a focus for the community, a place to do business or the weekly shopping, celebrate a wedding, or just meet up for meals, particularly on Sundays, when the restaurants overflow with Chinese families tucking into dim sum.

Old Compton Street

If Soho has a main drag, it has to be **Old Compton Street**, which runs parallel with Shaftesbury Avenue. The corner shops, peep shows, boutiques and trendy cafés here are typical of the area and a good barometer of the latest Soho fads. Soho has been a permanent fixture on the **gay scene** for the better part of a century, but the approach is much more upfront nowadays, with gay bars, clubs and cafés jostling for position on Old Compton Street and round the corner in Wardour Street.

The streets round here are lined with Soho institutions past and present. One of the best known is London's longest-running jazz club, *Ronnie Scott's* (see p.141), on Frith Street, founded in 1958 and still capable of pulling in the big names. Opposite is *Bar Italia* (see p.131), an Italian café with late-night hours popular with Soho's clubbers. It was in this building, appropriately enough for such a media-saturated area, that John Logie Baird made the world's first public television transmission in 1926.

Covent Garden and the Strand

Covent Garden is one of London's chief tourist attractions, thanks to its buskers, pedestrianized piazza and old Victorian market hall. More sanitized and brazenly commercial than neighbouring Soho, it's a far cry from the district's heyday when the piazza was the great playground (and red-light district) of eighteenth-century London. The buskers in front of St Paul's Church, the theatres round about, and the **Royal Opera House** on Bow Street are survivors of this tradition, and on a balmy summer evening, **Covent Garden Piazza** is still an undeniably lively place to be.

As its name suggests, the **Strand**, just to the south of Covent Garden, once lay along the riverbank: it achieved its present-day form when the Victorians shored up the banks of the Thames to create the Embankment. The Strand's most intriguing sight is **Somerset House**, sole survivor of the street's grandiose river palaces, now housing several museums and galleries as well as a lovely fountain courtyard.

Covent Garden Piazza

London's oldest planned square, laid out in the 1630s by Inigo Jones, **Covent Garden Piazza** was initially a great success, its novelty value alone attracting a rich and aristocratic clientele, but over the next century the tone of the place fell as the fruit and vegetable market expanded, and theatres and coffee houses began to take over the peripheral buildings. When the market closed in 1974, the piazza narrowly survived being turned into an office development. Instead, the elegant Victorian **market hall** and its environs were restored to house shops, restaurants and arts-and-crafts stalls. Of Jones's original piazza, the only remaining parts are the two rebuilt sections of north-side arcading, and **St Paul's Church**, facing the west side of the market building.

London Transport Museum

A former flower-market shed on the piazza's east side is now home to the **London Transport Museum** (daily 10am–6pm, Fri until 9pm; £8; Ⓦ www.ltmuseum .co.uk), a glorious celebration of the city's transport system over the last two centuries. The reconstructed 1829 Shillibeer's Horse Omnibus, which provided the city's first regular horse-bus service, is dwarfed by several wonderful double-decker electric trams, which, in the 1930s, formed part of the world's largest electric tram system. By 1952 the whole network had been dismantled, to be superseded by trolleybuses, of which the museum has several examples – these, in turn, bit the dust in the following decade. Look out, too, for the first "tube train", whose lack of windows earned it the nickname "the padded cell". The artistically inclined can buy reproductions of London Transport's stylish maps and posters, many commissioned from well-known artists, at the shop on the way out.

Royal Opera House

The arcading on the northeast side of the piazza was rebuilt as part of the redevelopment of the **Royal Opera House** (see also p.146), whose main Neoclassical facade dates from 1811 and opens onto Bow Street. Now, however, you can reach the opera house from a passageway in the corner of the arcading. The spectacular wrought-iron **Floral Hall** (daily 10am–3pm) serves as the opera house's main foyer, and is open to the public, as is the *Amphitheatre* bar/restaurant, which has a glorious terrace overlooking the piazza. **Backstage tours** (Mon–Fri 10.30am, 12.30 & 2.30pm, Sat 10.30am, 11.30am, 12.30 & 1.30pm; £9) of the opera house are also available.

Strand

Once famous for its riverside mansions, and later its music halls, the **Strand** – the main road connecting Westminster to the City – is a shadow of its former self. One of the few vestiges of glamour is **The Savoy**, London's grandest hotel, built in 1889 on the site of the medieval Savoy Palace on the south side of the street. César Ritz was the original manager, Guccio Gucci started out as a dishwasher here, and the list of illustrious guests is endless: Monet painted the Thames from one of the south-facing rooms, Sarah Bernhardt nearly died here, and Strauss the Younger arrived with his own orchestra.

Somerset House

Somerset House is the sole survivor of the grand edifices which once lined the riverfront, its four wings enclosing a large **courtyard** (daily 10am–11pm; free; Ⓦ www.somerset-house.org.uk) featuring a wonderful 55-jet fountain that spouts straight from the cobbles; in winter, an ice rink is set up in its place. The present building was begun in 1776 by William Chambers as a purpose-built governmental office development, but now also houses a series of museums and galleries.

In the house's north wing are the **Courtauld Institute galleries** (daily 10am–6pm; £5, free Mon 10am–2pm; Ⓦ www.courtauld.ac.uk), chiefly known for their dazzling collection of Impressionist and Post-Impressionist paintings. Among the most celebrated works is a small-scale version of Manet's *Déjeuner sur l'herbe*, Renoir's *La Loge*, and Degas' *Two Dancers*, plus a whole heap of Cézanne's canvases, including one of his series of *Card Players*. The Courtauld also boasts a fine selection of works by the likes of Rubens, Van Dyck, Tiepolo and Cranach the Elder. The collection has recently been augmented by the long-term loan of a hundred top-notch twentieth-century paintings and sculptures by, among others, Kandinksy, Matisse, Dufy, Derain, Rodin and Henry Moore.

The south wing has a lovely riverside terrace (daily 8am–6pm, Thurs until 9pm) with a café-restaurant and the Embankment Galleries (daily 10am–6pm, Thurs until 9pm; £8), which host innovative special exhibitions on contemporary art and design. Before you head off to one of the collections, however, make sure you go and admire the Royal Naval Commissioners' superb gilded eighteenth-century barge in the **King's Barge House**, below ground level in the south wing.

Bloomsbury

Bloomsbury was built over in grid-plan style from the 1660s onwards, and the formal bourgeois Georgian squares laid out then remain the area's main distinguishing feature. In the twentieth century, Bloomsbury acquired a reputation as the city's most learned quarter, dominated by the dual institutions of the **British Museum** and London University, and home to many of London's chief book publishers, but perhaps best known for its literary inhabitants, among them T.S. Eliot and Virginia Woolf. Today, the British Museum is clearly the star attraction, but there are other minor sights, such as the **Foundling Museum** and the **Charles Dickens Museum**. Only in its northern fringes does the character of the area change dramatically, becoming steadily seedier as you near the main-line train stations of Euston, St Pancras and King's Cross.

The British Museum

With seventy thousand exhibits ranged over two and a half miles of galleries, the **British Museum** (**BM**; daily 10am–5.30pm, Thurs & Fri until 8.30pm; free; Ⓦ www.britishmuseum.org) houses one of the largest and most comprehensive collections of antiquities, prints, drawings and books in the world. Begun in 1823, the building itself is the grandest of London's Greek Revival edifices, with its central **Great Court** (Mon–Wed & Sun 9am–6pm, Thurs–Sat 9am–11pm) featuring a remarkable curving glass-and-steel roof designed by Norman Foster. At the Court's centre stands the copper-domed former **Round Reading Room** of the British Library, where Karl Marx penned *Das Kapital*.

You'll never manage to see everything in one visit, so the best advice is to concentrate on one or two areas of interest, or else sign up with one of the museum's excellent **guided tours**. One place you could start is the BM's unparalleled collection of **Roman and Greek antiquities**, best known for the Parthenon sculptures, better known as the **Elgin Marbles** after the British aristocrat who walked off with the reliefs in 1801. Elsewhere, the **Egyptian collection** is easily the most significant outside Egypt, ranging from monumental sculptures to the ever-popular mummies and their ornate outer caskets. Also on display is the **Rosetta Stone**, which enabled French professor Champollion to finally unlock the secret of Egyptian hieroglyphs. Other highlights include a splendid series of **Assyrian reliefs** from Nineveh, and several extraordinary artefacts from **Mesopotamia** such as the enigmatic Ram in the Thicket (a goat statuette in lapis lazuli and shell) and the remarkable hoard of goldwork known as the Oxus Treasure.

The leathery half-corpse of the 2000-year-old **Lindow Man**, discovered in a Cheshire bog, and the Anglo-Saxon treasure from the **Sutton Hoo** ship burial, by far the richest single archeological find made in Britain, are among the highlights of the **Europe** collection, which ranges from the twelfth-century Lewis chessmen carved from walrus ivory, to twentieth-century exhibits such as the avant-garde Russian ceramics celebrating the 1917 revolution.

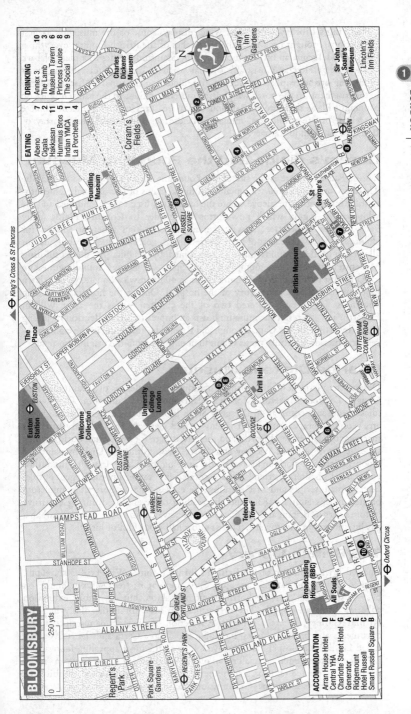

BLOOMSBURY

0 —— 250 yds

EATING
Abeno	7
Cigala	2
Hakkasan	11
Hummus Bros	5
Indian YMCA	1
La Porchetta	4

DRINKING
Annex 3	10
The Lamb	3
Museum Tavern	6
Princess Louise	8
The Social	9

ACCOMMODATION
Arran House Hotel	D
Central YHA	F
Charlotte Street Hotel	G
Generator	A
Ridgemount	E
Hotel Russell	C
Smart Russell Square	B

The **King's Library**, in the east wing, displays some of the museum's earliest acquisitions, brought back from the far reaches of the British Empire: everything from a model gamelan orchestra collected by Stamford Raffles to a piece of bark cloth made by Fletcher Christian's Tahitian partner. And don't miss the museum's expanding **ethnographic collection**, too, including the superb African galleries in the basement. In the north wing of the museum, closest to the back entrance on Montague Place, there are also fabulous **Asian** treasures including ancient Chinese porcelain, ornate snuffboxes, miniature landscapes and a bewildering array of Buddhist and Hindu statuary.

Coram's Fields and the Foundling Museum

East of Russell Square is the site of the Foundling Hospital, founded in 1756 by Thomas Coram, a retired sea captain. All that remains of the original eighteenth-century buildings is the alcove where the foundlings used to be abandoned and the whitewashed loggia which now forms the border to **Coram's Fields** (daily 9am–7pm or dusk; free; ⓦwww.coramsfields.org), an inner-city haven for children, with a whole host of hens, horses, sheep, goats and ducks. Adults are not allowed into the grounds unless accompanied by a child. At the **Foundling Museum** (Tues–Sat 10am–6pm, Sun 11am–5pm; £5; ⓦwww.foundlingmuseum.org.uk), just to the north of Coram's Fields, at 40 Brunswick Square, you can learn more about the fascinating story of the hospital. One of the hospital's founding governors – who even fostered two of the children – was the artist William Hogarth, and as a result the museum boasts an impressive **art collection** including works by artists such as Gainsborough and Reynolds, now hung in the eighteenth-century interiors carefully preserved in their entirety from the original hospital.

Charles Dickens Museum

Despite the plethora of blue plaques marking the residences of local luminaries, **Charles Dickens Museum** (Mon–Sat 10am–5pm, Sun 11am–5pm; £5; ⓦwww.dickensmuseum.com), at 48 Doughty St, in Bloomsbury's eastern fringes, is the area's only literary museum. Dickens moved here in 1837 shortly after his marriage to Catherine Hogarth, and they lived here for two years, during which time he wrote *Nicholas Nickleby* and *Oliver Twist*. Although Dickens painted a gloomy Victorian world in his books, the drawing room here, in which the author entertained his literary friends, was decorated in a rather upbeat Regency style. Letters, manuscripts and first editions, the earliest known portrait (a miniature painted by his aunt in 1830) and the reading copies he used during extensive lecture tours in Britain and the States are the rewards for those with more than a passing interest in the novelist. There's also a half-hour film of his life.

The British Library

The red-brick brutalism of the **British Library** (Mon & Wed–Fri 9.30am–6pm, Tues 9.30am–8pm, Sat 9.30am–5pm, Sun 11am–5pm; free; ⓦwww.bl.uk), on busy Euston Road, may be horribly out of fashion, but the public exhibition galleries inside are superb. The first gallery to head for is the dimly lit **John Ritblat Gallery**, where a superlative selection of ancient manuscripts, maps, documents and precious books, including the Magna Carta and the richly illustrated Lindisfarne Gospels, are displayed. One of the most appealing innovations is "**Turning the Pages**", a small room off the main gallery where you can "turn" the pages of selected texts on a computer terminal. The **temporary exhibitions**, for which there is sometimes an admission charge, are usually excellent.

Platform 9¾

Harry Potter and his wizarding chums leave for school on the *Hogwarts Express* each term from Platform 9¾ at **King's Cross Station**. The scenes from the films are, in fact, shot between platforms 4 and 5, though a station trolley is now half-embedded in the wall beside the side platforms of 9 and 10, providing a perfect photo opportunity for passing Potter fans.

Holborn

Holborn (pronounced "Ho-bun"), on the periphery of the financial district of the City, has long been associated with the law, and its **Inns of Court** make for an interesting stroll, their archaic, cobbled precincts exuding the rarefied atmosphere of an Oxbridge college, and sheltering one of the city's oldest churches, the twelfth-century **Temple Church**. Close by the Inns is the **Sir John Soane's Museum**, one of the most memorable and enjoyable of London's small museums, packed with architectural illusions and an eclectic array of curios.

Temple

Temple is the largest and most complex of the Inns of Court, where every barrister in England must study before being called to the Bar. A few very old buildings survive here and the maze of courtyards and passageways is fun to explore. Medieval students ate, attended lectures and slept in the **Middle Temple Hall** (Mon–Fri 10–11.30am & 3–4pm; free), across the courtyard, still the Inn's main dining room. The present building was constructed in the 1560s and provided the setting for many great Elizabethan masques and plays – probably including Shakespeare's *Twelfth Night*, which is believed to have been premiered here in 1602. The hall is worth a visit for its fine hammerbeam roof, wooden panelling and decorative Elizabethan screen.

The two Temple Inns share use of the complex's oldest building, **Temple Church** (Wed–Sun 11am–4pm; free), built in 1185 by the Knights Templar. An oblong chancel was added in the thirteenth century, and the whole building was damaged in the Blitz, but the original round church – modelled on the Church of the Holy Sepulchre in Jerusalem – still stands, with its striking Purbeck marble piers, recumbent marble effigies of knights, and tortured grotesques grimacing in the spandrels of the blind arcading.

Lincoln's Inn Fields, Hunterian Museum and Sir John Soane's Museum

To the north of Temple lies **Lincoln's Inn Fields**, London's largest square, laid out in the early 1640s with **Lincoln's Inn** (Mon–Fri 9am–6pm), the first – and in many ways the prettiest – of the Inns of Court, on its east side. The Inn's fifteenth-century **Old Hall** is open by appointment only (☎020/7405 1393), but you can view the early seventeenth-century **chapel** (Mon–Fri noon–2pm), with its unusual fan-vaulted open undercroft and, on the first floor, its late Gothic nave, hit by a zeppelin in World War I and much restored since.

The south side of Lincoln's Inn Fields is occupied by the gigantic Royal College of Surgeons, home to the **Hunterian Museum** (Tues–Sat 10am–5pm; free), a fascinating collection of pickled skeletons and body pieces. Also on view are the skeleton of the "Irish giant", Charles Byrne (1761–83), who was seven feet ten

Top 5: Offbeat museums in London

▶▶ **Hunterian Museum** A museum of grotesquely beautiful pickled bits and bobs in the Royal College of Surgeons. See p.97.

▶▶ **Sir John Soane's Museum** Part architectural set-piece, part art gallery, the Soane museum is small and perfectly formed. See p.98.

▶▶ **Dennis Severs' House** More of a theatrical experience than a museum proper, a visit here is unforgettable. See p.107.

▶▶ **Old Operating Theatre, Museum and Herb Garret** A stomach-churning pre-anaesthetic surgery hidden away at the top of a church tower. See p.112.

▶▶ **Horniman Museum** Gorgeous Art Nouveau building containing assorted curiosities collected by tea trader Frederick Horniman in the late nineteenth century. See p.126.

inches tall, and, in the adjacent McCrae Gallery, the Sicilian midget Caroline Crachami (d. 1824), who stood at only one foot ten and a half inches when she died at the age of nine.

A group of buildings on the north side of Lincoln's Inn Fields house **Sir John Soane's Museum** (Tues–Sat 10am–5pm; free; Ⓦ www.soane.org), one of London's best-kept secrets. Chief architect of the Bank of England, Soane (1753–1837) was an avid collector who designed this house not only as a home and office, but also as a place to stash his large collection of art and antiquities. Arranged much as it was in his lifetime, the ingeniously planned house has an informal, treasure-hunt atmosphere, with surprises in every alcove. The star exhibits are Hogarth's satirical *Election* series and his merciless morality tale *The Rake's Progress*, as well as the alabaster sarcophagus of Seti I. Note that the museum is extremely popular on Saturdays, when there's a fascinating hour-long **guided tour** (£5) at 11am, and on the **candlelit evenings** held on the first Tuesday of the month (6–9pm).

Hoxton

Hoxton (aka Shoreditch), on the northeastern edge of the City, has been colonized by artists, designers and architects and transformed into one of the city's most vibrant artistic enclaves, peppered with contemporary art galleries and a whole host of cool bars and clubs. Despite the area's lack of obvious aesthetic charm, it does have one or two formal sights.

A place of pilgrimage for Methodists all over the world, **Wesley's Chapel and House** (Mon–Sat 10am–4pm, Sun 12.30–2pm; free) was built in 1777, and heralded the coming of age of the faith founded by **John Wesley** (1703–91). The interior is uncharacteristically ornate, with powder-pink columns of French jasper and a superb, Adam-style gilded plasterwork ceiling. Predictably enough, the **Museum of Methodism** (Mon–Sat 10am–4pm, Sun 12.30–1.45pm; free) in the basement has only a passing reference to the insanely jealous 40-year-old widow Wesley married, and who eventually left him. Wesley himself spent his last two years in Wesley's House, a delightful Georgian place to the right of the main gates. On display inside are his deathbed and an early shock-therapy machine he was particularly keen on. Wesley's **grave** is round the back of the chapel, in the shadow of a modern office block.

The geographical focus of Hoxton's metamorphosis is **Hoxton Square**, a strange and not altogether happy assortment of light industrial units, many of them now converted into artists' studios arranged around a leafy, formal square. The chief landmark here is the **White Cube gallery** (Tues–Sat 10am–6pm; free), a sort of miniature Tate Modern: it's housed in an old piano factory, with a glass roof plonked on the top, and represents the likes of Damien Hirst, Tracey Emin and Sam Taylor-Wood.

Hoxton's one other conventional tourist sight is the **Geffrye Museum** (Tues–Sat 10am–5pm, Sun noon–5pm; free), a museum of furniture design, set back from Kingsland Road in a peaceful little enclave of eighteenth-century ironmongers' almshouses. A series of period living rooms, ranging from the oak-panelled seventeenth century through refined Georgian and cluttered Victorian, leads to the excellent twentieth-century section and a pleasant café/restaurant.

The City

The City is where London began, and its boundaries today are only slightly larger than those marked by the Roman walls and their medieval successors, hence its nickname, the "Square Mile". However, you'll find few visible leftovers of London's early days, since four-fifths of it burned down in the Great Fire of 1666. And though Wren's spires, and his masterpiece, **St Paul's Cathedral**, still punctuate the skyline, most of what you now see is the product of the Victorian construction boom, postwar reconstruction and modern redevelopment.

Aside from St Paul's, there are several rewarding sights in and around the City. At the eastern edge, the **Tower of London** still stands protected by some of the best-preserved medieval fortifications in Europe. Other relics, such as the area's few surviving medieval alleyways, Wren's **Monument** to the Great Fire, and London's oldest synagogue and church, are less conspicuous, and even locals have problems finding the more modern attractions of the **Museum of London** and the Barbican arts complex (see p.144).

Up until the eighteenth century, the majority of Londoners lived and worked in this area. Nowadays, over a million commuters spend the best part of Monday to Friday in the City, but only a few thousand actually live here, making the weekends very quiet indeed.

Fleet Street

Fleet Street offers one of the grandest approaches to the City, thanks to the view across to Ludgate Hill and beyond to St Paul's Cathedral. It's best known, however, for its associations with the printed press and particularly the newspaper industry. The press headquarters that once dominated the area have all now relocated, leaving just a handful of small publications and a few architectural landmarks to testify to five hundred years of printing history. The best source of information about the old Fleet Street is the church of **St Bride's** (Mon–Fri 9am–5pm, Sat 11am–3pm; free; ⓦ www.stbrides.com), which boasts Wren's tallest and most exquisite spire (said to be the inspiration for the tiered wedding cake), and whose crypt contains a little museum of Fleet Street history.

The western section of Fleet Street was spared the Great Fire, which stopped just short of **Prince Henry's Room** (Mon–Fri 11am–2pm; free; ⓦ www.cityoflondon.gov.uk/phr), a fine Jacobean house with timber-framed bay windows. The first-floor room now contains material relating to the diarist **Samuel Pepys**, who was born nearby in Salisbury Court in 1633 and baptized in St Bride's. Even if you've no interest in Pepys, the wooden-panelled room is worth a look – it contains one of the finest Jacobean plasterwork ceilings in London, and a lot of original stained glass.

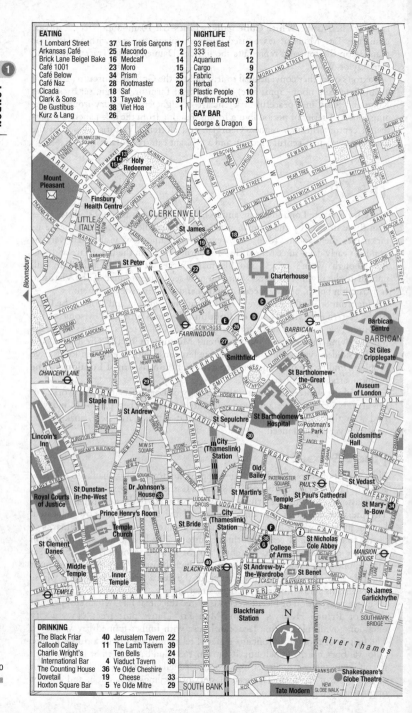

EATING

1 Lombard Street	37	Les Trois Garçons	17
Arkansas Café	25	Macondo	2
Brick Lane Beigel Bake	16	Medcalf	14
Café 1001	23	Moro	15
Café Below	34	Prism	35
Café Naz	28	Rootmaster	20
Cicada	18	Saf	8
Clark & Sons	13	Tayyab's	31
De Gustibus	38	Viet Hoa	1
Kurz & Lang	26		

NIGHTLIFE

93 Feet East	21		
333	7		
Aquarium	12		
Cargo	9		
Fabric	27		
Herbal	3		
Plastic People	10		
Rhythm Factory	32		

GAY BAR

George & Dragon	6

DRINKING

The Black Friar	40	Jerusalem Tavern	22
Callooh Callay	11	The Lamb Tavern	39
Charlie Wright's International Bar	4	Ten Bells	24
		Viaduct Tavern	30
The Counting House	36	Ye Olde Cheshire Cheese	33
Dovetail	19		
Hoxton Square Bar	5	Ye Olde Mitre	29

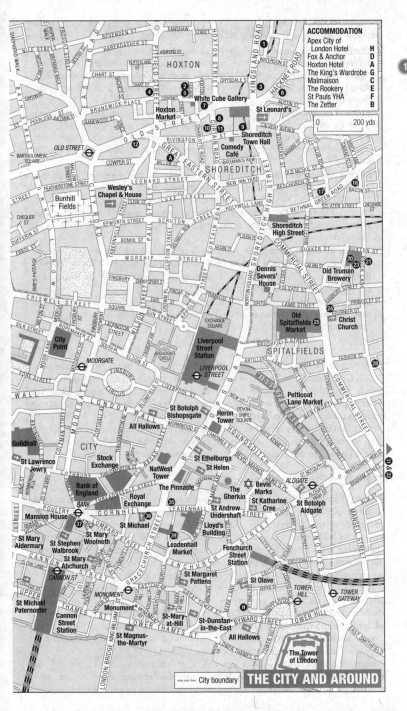

ACCOMMODATION

Apex City of London Hotel	H
Fox & Anchor	D
Hoxton Hotel	A
The King's Wardrobe	G
Malmaison	C
The Rookery	E
St Pauls YHA	F
The Zetter	B

0   200 yds

FANSHAW STREET
BEVENDEN ST
HABERDASHER ST
ASHFORD ST
HOXTON
BUTTESLAND ST
CHART ST
CHART ST
CORONET
White Cube Gallery
Hoxton Market
DRYSDALE ST
St Leonard's
AUSTIN ST
CALVERT AVENUE
Shoreditch Town Hall
RIVINGTON ST
Comedy Café
OLD STREET
COWPER ST
SHOREDITCH
WILLOW ST
NEW INN YARD
OLD NICHOL ST
REDCHURCH
BETHNAL GREEN ROAD
BACON ST
CHESHIRE ST
Wesley's Chapel & House
SCLATER STREET
BRICK LANE
Bunhill Fields
Shoreditch High Street
QUAKER ST
BUXTON ST
WORSHIP STREET
Old Truman Brewery
HANBURY STREET
PRINCELET ST
Dennis Severs' House
FOURNIER ST
Christ Church
EXCHANGE SQUARE
Old Spitalfields Market
BRUSHFIELD STREET
SPITALFIELDS
City Point
Liverpool Street Station
LIVERPOOL STREET
FASHION ST
MOORGATE
WHITE'S ROW
ARTILLERY LANE
FINSBURY CIRCUS
LONDON WALL
Petticoat Lane Market
Heron Tower
St Botolph Bishopsgate
DEVONSHIRE SQUARE
HOUNDSDITCH
WENTWORTH STREET
All Hallows
WORMWOOD ST
Guildhall
St Lawrence Jewry
CITY
Stock Exchange
St Ethelburga
St Helen
NatWest Tower
The Pinnacle
The Gherkin
Bevis Marks
ALDGATE
St Katharine Cree
St Botolph Aldgate
WHITECHAPEL HIGH STREET
Bank of England
Royal Exchange
CORNHILL
St Andrew Undershaft
Mansion House
St Michael
LEADENHALL STREET
Lloyd's Building
Fenchurch Street Station
St Mary Aldermary
St Stephen Walbrook
St Mary Woolnoth
St Mary Abchurch
Leadenhall Market
CANNON STREET
FENCHURCH STREET
St Margaret Pattens
St Olave
St Michael Paternoster
Cannon Street Station
Monument
St-Mary-at-Hill
St-Dunstan-in-the-East
All Hallows
St Magnus-the-Martyr
LONDON BRIDGE
LOWER THAMES ST
TOWER HILL
TOWER GATEWAY
The Tower of London
BYWARD STREET
EAST SMITHFIELD

City boundary   **THE CITY AND AROUND**

The City's churches

The City of London boasts over forty churches, the majority of them built or rebuilt by Wren after the Great Fire. As a general rule, weekday lunchtimes are the best time to visit these churches, as many put on **free lunchtime concerts** for the local wage slaves. Below is a list of six of the most varied and interesting churches within the Square Mile:

St Bartholomew-the-Great Cloth Fair. The oldest surviving church in the City and by far the most atmospheric. St Paul's aside, if you visit just one church in the City, it should be this one. Shame they charge, but it's worth it. Mon–Fri 8.30am–5pm (mid-Nov to mid-Feb till 4pm), Sat 10.30am–4pm, Sun 8.30am–8pm (except for services). £4.

St Mary Abchurch Abchurch Lane, Cannon St. Uniquely, the interior features a huge, painted, domed ceiling, plus the only authenticated Gibbons reredos. Mon 11am–3pm, Tues, Thurs & Fri 11am–4pm.

St Mary Aldermary Queen Victoria St. Wren's most successful stab at Gothic, with plasterwork fan vaulting in the aisles and a panelled ceiling in the nave. Mon–Fri 11am–3pm.

St Mary Woolnoth Lombard St. Hawksmoor church, with a Baroque clerestory that floods the church with light from its semicircular windows. Mon–Fri 9.30am–4.30pm.

St Olave Hart St. Built in the fifteenth century, and one of the few pre-Fire Gothic churches in the City. Mon–Fri 8am–5pm.

St Stephen Walbrook Walbrook. Wren's dress rehearsal for St Paul's, with a wonderful central dome and plenty of original woodcarving. Mon–Thurs 10am–4pm, Fri 10am–3pm.

Numerous narrow alleyways lead off the north side of Fleet Street, two of which – Bolt Court and Hind Court – eventually open out into Gough Square, on which stands **Dr Johnson's House** (Mon–Sat: May–Sept 11am–5.30pm; Oct–April 11am–5pm; £4.50; ⓦ www.drjohnsonshouse.org). The great savant, writer and lexicographer lived here from 1747 to 1759, while compiling the 41,000 entries for the first dictionary of the English language, two first editions of which can be seen in the grey-panelled rooms of the house. You can also view the open-plan attic, in which Johnson and his six helpers put together the dictionary.

St Paul's Cathedral

Designed by Christopher Wren and completed in 1711, **St Paul's Cathedral** (Mon–Sat 8.30am–4pm; £11; ⓦ www.stpauls.co.uk) remains a dominating presence in the City despite the encroaching tower blocks. Topped by an enormous lead-covered dome that's second in size only to St Peter's in Rome, its showpiece west facade is particularly magnificent. Compared to its great rival, Westminster Abbey, St Paul's may be soulless, but it's a perfectly calculated architectural set-piece – a burial place for captains rather than kings.

The best place to appreciate the building's glory is from beneath the **dome**, adorned (against Wren's wishes) by trompe l'oeil frescoes. The most richly decorated section of the cathedral is the **chancel**, where the late Victorian mosaics of birds, fish, animals and greenery are particularly spectacular. The intricately carved oak and lime-wood choir stalls, and the imposing organ case, are the work of Wren's master carver, Grinling Gibbons.

Beginning in the south aisle, a series of stairs lead to the dome's three galleries, the first of which is the internal **Whispering Gallery**, so called because of its acoustic properties – words whispered to the wall on one side are distinctly audible over one hundred feet away on the other, though you often can't hear much above the hubbub. Of the two exterior galleries, the best views are from the tiny **Golden Gallery**, below the golden ball and cross which top the cathedral.

Although the nave is crammed full of overblown monuments to military types, burials in St Paul's are confined to the crypt, reputedly the largest in Europe. The whitewashed walls and bright lighting make this one of London's least atmospheric mausoleums, but **Artists' Corner** here does boast as many painters and architects as Westminster Abbey has poets, including Christopher Wren himself. The star tombs, though, are those of Nelson and Wellington, both occupying centre stage and both with more fanciful monuments upstairs.

It's well worth attending one of the cathedral's **services**, if only to hear the ethereal choir, who perform during most evensongs (Mon–Sat 5pm), and on Sundays at 10.15am, 11.30am and 3.15pm.

Paternoster Square

The Blitz destroyed the area immediately to the north of St Paul's, incinerating all the booksellers' shops and around six million books. In their place, **Paternoster Square**, a modernist pedestrianized piazza was built, only to be torn down in the 1980s and replaced with post-classical office blocks in Portland stone and a Corinthian column topped by a gilded urn. One happy consequence of the square's redevelopment is that **Temple Bar**, the gateway which used to stand at the top of Fleet Street, has found its way back to London after over a hundred years of exile in a park in Hertfordshire. Designed by Wren himself, the triumphal arch, looking weathered but clean, now forms the entrance to Paternoster Square, with the Stuart monarchs, James I and Charles II, and their consorts occupying the niches.

Museum of London

Despite London's long pedigree, very few of its ancient structures are now standing. However, numerous Roman, Saxon and Elizabethan remains have been discovered during the City's various rebuildings, and many of these finds are now displayed at the **Museum of London** (daily 10am–5.50pm; free; ⓦ www.museumoflondon .org.uk), hidden above the western end of London Wall, in the southwestern corner of the Barbican complex. The museum's permanent exhibition is basically a superbly designed educational trot through London's past from prehistory to the present day via the Romans and the Great Fire; hence the large number of school groups who pass through. The museum also provides garage space for the Lord Mayor's heavily gilded coach and puts on excellent temporary exhibitions, lectures, walks and films throughout the year.

Guildhall

Situated at the geographical centre of the City, **Guildhall** (May–Sept daily 10am–5pm; Oct–April Mon–Sat 10am–5pm; free; ⓦ www.guildhall.city oflondon.gov.uk) has been the ancient seat of the City administration for over eight hundred years. It remains the headquarters of the Corporation of London, the City's version of local government, and is still used for many of the City's formal civic occasions. Architecturally, however, it is not quite the beauty it once was, having been badly damaged in both the Great Fire and the Blitz, and scarred by the addition of a 1970s concrete cloister and wing.

Nonetheless, the **Great Hall** still retains the walls of the fifteenth-century original, and is worth a brief look, as is the **Clockmakers' Museum** (Mon–Fri

9.30am–4.30pm; free; ⓦ www.clockmakers.org), a collection of over six hundred timepieces, including one of the clocks that won John Harrison the Longitude Prize (see p.125). Also worth a visit is the purpose-built **Guildhall Art Gallery** (Mon–Sat 10am–5pm, Sun noon–4pm; £2.50, free Fri and daily after 3.30pm), which contains one or two exceptional works, such as Rossetti's *La Ghirlandata*, and Holman Hunt's *The Eve of St Agnes*, plus a massive painting depicting the 1782 Siege of Gibraltar, commissioned by the Corporation, and a marble statue of Margaret Thatcher. In the basement, you can view the remains of a **Roman amphitheatre**, from around 120 AD, which was discovered during the gallery's construction.

Bank

Bank is the finest architectural arena in the City. Heart of the finance sector and the busy meeting point of eight streets, it's overlooked by a handsome collection of Neoclassical buildings – among them, the Bank of England, the Royal Exchange and Mansion House (the Lord Mayor's official residence) – each one faced in Portland stone.

Established in 1694 by William III to raise funds for the war against France, the **Bank of England** wasn't erected on its present site until 1734. All that remains of the building on which Sir John Soane spent the best part of his career from 1788 onwards is the windowless, outer curtain-wall, which wraps itself round the three-and-a-half-acre island site. However, you can view a reconstruction of Soane's Bank Stock Office, with its characteristic domed skylight, in the **museum** (Mon–Fri 10am–5pm; free; ⓦ www.bankofengland.co.uk/education), which has its entrance on Bartholomew Lane.

Mansion House, the Lord Mayor's sumptuous Neoclassical lodgings, offers weekly guided tours (Tues 2pm; £6). Designed in 1753 by George Dance, the building's grandest room is the columned "Egyptian" Hall, with its barrel-vaulted, coffered ceiling. Also impressive is the vast collection of gold and silver tableware, the mayor's 36lb gold mace and the pearl sword given by Elizabeth I and held out to the sovereign on visits to the City.

Bevis Marks Synagogue

Hidden away off Bevis Marks, north of the Gherkin (see box below), the **Bevis Marks Synagogue** (guided tours Wed & Fri noon, Sun 11.15am; £2; ⓦ www .bevismarks.org.uk) was built in 1701 by Sephardic Jews who had fled the Inquisition in Spain and Portugal. This is the country's oldest surviving synagogue, and

---

City skyscrapers

Until recently, most people's favourite modern building in the City was Richard Rogers' glitzy **Lloyd's Building** – a vertical version of Rogers' own Pompidou Centre – a startling array of glass and blue steel pipes. Lloyd's has subsequently been eclipsed by its near neighbour, Norman Foster's 590ft-high, glass-diamond-clad **Gherkin**, which has endeared itself to Londoners thanks to its cheeky shape. Meanwhile, the City skyline is about to sprout a new generation of skyscrapers, most significantly the **Heron Tower**, a 660ft skyscraper with a 144ft mast at 110 Bishopsgate, designed by Kohn Pedersen Fox, and **The Pinnacle** (945ft), a swirling helter-skelter of a tower (with a restaurant on the top floor) at 22–24 Bishopsgate, by the same architects. The City will then have outreached Canary Wharf, but it will still be ousted for the prize of the country's tallest building by Renzo Piano's 1017ft **Shard**, near London Bridge.

its roomy, rich interior gives an idea of just how wealthy the congregation was at the time. Nowadays, the Sephardic community has dispersed across London and the congregation has dwindled, though the magnificent array of chandeliers makes it popular for candle-lit Jewish weddings.

London Bridge and Monument

Until 1750, **London Bridge** was the only bridge across the Thames. The Romans were the first to build a permanent crossing here, but it was the medieval bridge that achieved world fame: built of stone and crowded with timber-framed houses, it became one of the great attractions of London – there's a model in the nearby church of **St Magnus-the-Martyr** (Tues–Fri 9.30am–4pm, Sun 10am–1pm). The houses were finally removed in the mid-eighteenth century, and a new stone bridge erected in 1831; that one now stands in the middle of the Arizona desert, having been bought in the late 1960s by a gentleman who, so the story goes, was under the impression he had purchased Tower Bridge. The present concrete structure – without doubt the ugliest yet – dates from 1972.

The only reason to go anywhere near London Bridge is to see the **Monument** (daily 9.30am–5.30pm; £2), designed by Wren to commemorate the Great Fire of 1666. Crowned with spiky gilded flames, this plain Doric column stands 202 feet high, making it the tallest isolated stone column in the world; if it were laid out flat it would touch the bakery where the Fire started, east of Monument. The bas-relief on the base, now in very bad shape, depicts Charles II and the Duke of York in Roman garb conducting the emergency relief operation. The 311 steps to the viewing gallery once guaranteed an incredible view; nowadays it is somewhat dwarfed by the buildings around it.

Tower of London

One of the most perfectly preserved medieval fortresses in the country, the **Tower of London** (March–Oct Mon & Sun 10am–6pm, Tues–Sat 9am–6pm; Nov–Feb closes 5pm; £17; ⒲hrp.org.uk) sits beside the Thames surrounded by a wide, dry moat. Begun by William the Conqueror, the Tower is chiefly famous as a place of imprisonment and death, though it has been used variously as a royal residence, armoury, mint, menagerie, observatory and – a function it still serves – a safe-deposit box for the Crown Jewels. Before you set off, join one of the free guided tours, given by the Tower's **Beefeaters** (officially known as Yeoman Warders). As well as giving a good introduction to the history, these ex-servicemen relish hamming up the gory stories.

Visitors today enter the Tower along Water Lane, but in times gone by most prisoners were delivered through **Traitors' Gate**, on the waterfront. The nearby **Bloody Tower** saw the murders of 12-year-old Edward V and his 10-year-old brother, and was used to imprison Walter Raleigh on three separate occasions. The central **White Tower** is the original "Tower", begun in 1076. Now home to the Royal Armouries, it's worth visiting if only for the beautiful Norman **Chapel of St John**, on the second floor. To the west of the White Tower is the execution spot on **Tower Green** where seven highly placed but unlucky individuals were beheaded, among them Henry VIII's second and fifth wives.

The **Crown Jewels** are the major reason so many people flock to the Tower. The oldest piece of regalia is the twelfth-century Anointing Spoon, but the vast majority of exhibits, including the Imperial State Crown, postdate the Commonwealth (1649–60). Among the jewels are the three largest cut diamonds in the world, including the legendary Koh-i-Noor, set into the Queen Mother's Crown in 1937.

Tower Bridge

Tower Bridge ranks with Big Ben as the most famous of all London landmarks. Completed in 1894, its neo-Gothic towers are clad in Cornish granite and Portland stone, but conceal a steel frame, which, at the time, represented a considerable engineering achievement, allowing a road crossing that could be raised to give tall ships access to the upper reaches of the Thames. The raising of the **bascules** (from the French for "see-saw") remains an impressive sight – phone ahead to find out when the bridge is opening (☏ 020/7940 3984). If you buy a ticket (daily: April–Sept 10am–6.30pm; Oct–March 9.30am–6pm; £6; Ⓦ www.towerbridge.org.uk), you get to walk across the elevated walkways linking the summits of the towers and visit the Tower's Engine Room, on the south side of the bridge, where you can see the now-defunct giant coal-fired boilers which drove the hydraulic system until 1976, and play some interactive engineering games.

The East End and Docklands

Few places in London have engendered so many myths as the **East End** (a catch-all title which covers just about everywhere east of the City, but has its heart closest to the latter). Its name is synonymous with slums, sweatshops and crime, as epitomized by antiheroes such as Jack the Ripper and the Kray Twins, and with rags-to-riches success stories of a whole generations of Jews who were born in these cholera-ridden quarters and then moved to wealthier pastures.

The area's first immigrants were **Huguenots**, French Protestants fleeing religious persecution in the late seventeenth century. Within three generations the Huguenots were entirely assimilated, and the Irish became the new immigrant population, but it was the influx of **Jews** escaping pogroms in Eastern Europe and Russia that defined the character of the East End in the late nineteenth century. Since the 1960s, the area has been at the heart of the **Bangladeshi** community. Racism has been a problem for each wave of immigrants, but nowadays it's bohemian gentrification, followed by City developers, that are probably the greatest threat.

As the area is not an obvious place for sightseeing, and certainly no beauty spot – Victorian slum clearances, Hitler's bombs and postwar tower blocks have all left their mark – most visitors to the East End come for its famous **Sunday markets**. Nearby, millions has been poured into the **Docklands** development, most of which can be gawped at from the overhead light railway, including vast **Canary Wharf**, which has to be seen to be believed. And there is of course one part of the East End that is set to be totally transformed: the lower Lea valley, a former industrial area between Bow and Stratford and venue for the 2012 **Olympic Park**.

Spitalfields

Spitalfields, within sight of the sleek tower blocks of the financial sector, lies at the old heart of the East End, where the French Huguenots settled in the seventeenth century, where the Jewish community was at its strongest in the late nineteenth century, and where today's Bengali community eats, sleeps, works and prays. If you visit just one area in the East End, it should be this zone, which preserves mementos from each wave of immigration and which is at its liveliest on Sundays, when there are market stalls all the way from Spitalfields to Brick Lane.

The easiest approach is from Liverpool Street Station, a short stroll west of **Old Spitalfields Market** (Mon–Fri 10am–4pm, Sun 9am–5pm), the red-brick and green-gabled market hall built in 1893, half of which was demolished in order to make way for more City offices. The dominant architectural presence in Spitalfields, however, is **Christ Church** (Tues 11am–4pm, Sun 1–4pm; free), built in 1714–29 to a characteristically bold design by Nicholas Hawksmoor, and now facing the market hall. Best viewed from Brushfield Street, the church's main features are its huge 225-foot-high spire and a giant Tuscan portico, raised on steps and shaped like a Venetian window (a central arched opening flanked by two smaller rectangles), a motif repeated in the tower and doors.

North of the market, at 18 Folgate St, is the highly atmospheric **Dennis Severs' House** (☎020/7247 4013, ⓦwww.dennissevershouse.co.uk). Severs, an American artist, created a theatrical experience which he described as "passing through a frame into a painting". The house is entirely candle-lit and log-fired, and decked out as it would have been two hundred years ago. Visitors are free to explore the ten rooms, and are left with the distinct impression that someone has literally just popped out. The house cat prowls, there's the smell of gravy bubbling on the hearth, and the sound of horses' hooves on the cobbled street outside. "The Experience" takes place on Sundays (noon–4pm; £8), and on Mondays following the first and third Sunday (noon–2pm; £5); for the Monday evening "Silent Night" you must book ahead (times vary; £12).

The East End's most popular museum is the **Museum of Childhood** (daily 10am–5.45pm; free; ⓦwww.vam.ac.uk/moc), opposite Bethnal Green tube station. The open-plan, wrought-iron hall, originally part of the V&A (see p.118), was transported here in the 1860s to bring art to the East End. On the ground floor there are clockwork toys, everything from classic robots to a fully functioning model railway, marionettes and puppets, teddies and Smurfs and even Inuit dolls. The most famous exhibits are the remarkable antique dolls' houses, dating back to 1673, which are now displayed upstairs, where you'll also find a play area for very small kids and the museum's space for temporary exhibitions.

Docklands

Built in the nineteenth century to cope with the huge volume of goods shipped along the Thames from all over the Empire, **Docklands** was once the largest enclosed cargo-dock system in the world. No one thought the area could be rejuvenated when the docks closed in the 1960s, but over the last thirty years warehouses have been converted into luxury flats, waterside penthouse apartments

2012 Olympics

The focus of the 2012 Olympic Games will be the **Olympic Park**, situated in an East End backwater between Hackney Wick and Stratford. The centrepiece is the 80,000-seat **Olympic Stadium**; close by is a 17,500-seat aquatic centre, designed by Zaha Hadid, a 6000-seat velodrome and an outdoor BMX track, a 15,000-seat hockey complex and several other multi-sports arenas. The **Olympic Village**, housing nearly 18,000 athletes, will also be here, and will be converted to public housing after the games.

The rest of the events will take place in and around London, mostly in existing venues: Wimbledon will host the tennis; Wembley the football; ExCel, by Royal Victoria Dock, will host everything from boxing to table tennis. Under the pseudonym, the "North Greenwich Arena", the Dome (aka the O2) will host the artistic gymnastics. Equestrian events are scheduled for Greenwich Park, while Hyde Park will host the triathlon and Regent's Park the road cycling. Archery will take place at Lord's, shooting at the Royal Artillery Barracks in Woolwich and – the one piece of planning that's really grabbed the headlines – beach volleyball will be staged on Horse Guards Parade. Only the sailing events will take place any great distance from the capital, at Weymouth in Dorset.

have been built and a huge high-rise office development has sprung up around Canary Wharf. Although Canary Wharf is on the Jubilee line, the best way to view Docklands is either from one of the boats that course up and down the Thames (see p.72), or from the driverless, overhead **Docklands Light Railway** or DLR, which sets off from Bank or Tower Gateway, close to Tower Hill tube.

The only really busy bit of Docklands, **Canary Wharf** is best known as the home of Britain's tallest building, Cesar Pelli's landmark tower, officially known as **One Canada Square**. The world's first skyscraper to be clad in stainless steel, it's an undeniably impressive sight, both from a distance (its flashing pinnacle is a feature of the horizon at numerous points in London) and close up. However, it no longer stands alone, having been joined by several other skyscrapers that stop just short of Pelli's stumpy pinnacle.

One of the few original warehouses left to the north of Canary Wharf has been converted into the **Museum in Docklands** (daily 10am–6pm; £5; Ⓦwww .museumindocklands.org.uk), an excellent stab at charting the history of the area from Roman times to the present day. Highlights include a great model of old London Bridge, an eight-foot-long watercolour and a soft play area for kids. Unless you're keen to visit the museum, though, there's little point in getting off the DLR at Canary Wharf. Instead, stay on the train as it cuts right through the middle of the office buildings under a parabolic steel-and-glass canopy and keep going until you reach Greenwich (see p.124).

The South Bank

The **South Bank** has a lot going for it. As well as the massive waterside **South Bank Centre**, it's home to a host of tourist attractions including the enormously popular **London Eye**. With most of London sitting on the north bank of the Thames, the views from here are the best on the river, and thanks to the wide, traffic-free riverside boulevard, the whole area can be happily explored on foot. And a short walk from the South Bank lies the absorbing **Imperial War Museum**, which contains the country's only permanent exhibition devoted to the Holocaust.

Southbank Centre

The **Southbank Centre** (see also p.146) is home to a whole variety of artistic institutions, the most attractive of which is the **Royal Festival Hall**, built in 1951 for the Festival of Britain and one of London's chief concert venues. Even the centre's most architecturally depressing parts are softened by their riverside location, the avenue of trees, fluttering banners, occasional buskers and skateboarders, and the weekend secondhand bookstalls outside the nearby **BFI Southbank**. The latter is the city's chief arts cinema, and runs **Mediathèque** (Tues–Sun 11am–8pm; free), where you can settle into one of the viewing stations and choose from a select archive of British films, TV programmes and documentaries.

London Eye and around

The **London Eye** (daily: May, June & Sept 10am–9pm; July & Aug 10am–9.30pm; Oct–April 10am–8pm; £17; Ⓦwww.ba-londoneye.com) is now one of the city's most famous landmarks. Standing an impressive 443ft high, it's the largest **Ferris wheel** in Europe, weighing over two thousand tonnes, yet as simple and delicate as a bicycle wheel. It's constantly in slow motion, which means a full-circle "flight" in one of its 32 pods should take around thirty minutes – that may seem a long

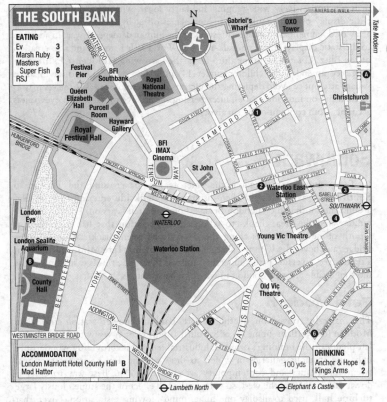

THE SOUTH BANK

N

Tate Modern

RIVERSIDE WALK

Gabriel's Wharf

OXO Tower

RENNIE STREET

PARIS GARDEN

COLOMBO ST

Christchurch

MEYMOTT ST

BRAD STREET

JOAN ST

ISABELLA STREET

SOUTHWARK ⊖

BLACKFRIARS RD

SHORT ST

WINDMILL WALK

CORNWALL ROAD

UPPER GROUND

BARGE HOUSE ST

DUCHY ST

HATFIELDS

BROADWALL

AQUINAS ST

COIN ST

DOON STREET

STAMFORD STREET

THEED STREET

WHITTLESEY ST

ROUPELL STREET

EXTON ST

ALASKA ST

WOOTTON ST

WEBBER STREET

MITRE ROAD

CHAPLIN CLOSE

VALENTINE PLACE

UPPER GROUND

WATERLOO ROAD

BAYLIS ROAD

YORK ROAD

TENISON WAY

LAKE STREET

ADDINGTON ST

LOWER MARSH

FRAZIER STREET

MEPHAM STREET

WATERLOO

EATING
Ev	**3**
Marsh Ruby	**5**
Masters Super Fish	**6**
RSJ	**1**

Festival Pier

BFI Southbank

Royal National Theatre

Queen Elizabeth Hall

Purcell Room

Hayward Gallery

Royal Festival Hall

BFI IMAX Cinema

St John

St John

Waterloo East Station

Young Vic Theatre

THE CUT

WATERLOO BRIDGE

HUNGERFORD BRIDGE

CONCERT HALL APPROACH

London Eye

London Sealife Aquarium

County Hall

BELVEDERE ROAD

WESTMINSTER BRIDGE ROAD

WATERLOO

Waterloo Station

Old Vic Theatre

CORAL STREET

WEBBER ROW

SIMONS BLACK

GRAY ST

BOUNDARY ROW

ACCOMMODATION
| London Marriott Hotel County Hall | **B** |
| Mad Hatter | **A** |

WESTMINSTER BRIDGE RD

0   100 yds

DRINKING
| Anchor & Hope | **4** |
| Kings Arms | **2** |

⊖ Lambeth North ▼   ⊖ Elephant & Castle ▼

time, though in fact it passes incredibly quickly. Book in advance (and online to save money), as on arrival you'll still have to queue to be loaded on.

Next to the London Eye is the only truly monumental building on the South Bank, **County Hall** (Ⓦwww.londoncountyhall.com), with its colonnaded crescent. Completed in 1933, it housed the LCC (London County Council), and later the GLC (Greater London Council), until 1986, and is now home to, among other things, several hotels, restaurants, an amusement arcade and a bizarre clutch of tourist attractions.

County Hall's most popular attraction is the **London Sealife Aquarium** (daily 10am–6pm; mid-July to Aug closes 7pm; £18; Ⓦwww.sealife.co.uk/london), laid out on two subterranean levels. With some super-large tanks, and everything from dog-face puffers and piranhas to robot fish (seriously), this is an attraction that's pretty much guaranteed to please kids. The Touch Pool, where children can stroke the (non-sting) rays, is particularly popular. Impressive in scale, the aquarium also has a walk-through underwater tunnel. Ask at the main desk for the times of the daily presentations.

Imperial War Museum

Housed in a domed building that was once the infamous "Bedlam" lunatic asylum, the **Imperial War Museum** (daily 10am–6pm; free; Ⓦwww.iwm.org.uk) holds by far the best collection of militaria in the capital. The treatment of the subject matter is impressively wide-ranging and fairly sober, with the main hall's militaristic display of guns, tanks and fighter planes offset by the lower-ground-floor array of documents and images attesting to the human damage of war. In addition to the static displays, there's a walk-through World War I trench and a re-creation of the Blitz. Entered from the third floor, the harrowing **Holocaust Exhibition** (not recommended for children under 14) pulls few punches, and has made a valiant attempt to avoid depicting the victims of the Holocaust as nameless masses by focusing on individual cases, interspersing the archive footage with eyewitness accounts from contemporary survivors.

Southwark

In Tudor and Stuart London, the chief reason for crossing the Thames to **Southwark** was to visit the then-disreputable **Bankside** entertainment district around the south end of London Bridge. Four hundred years on, Londoners have rediscovered the area, thanks to wholesale regeneration that has engendered a wealth of new attractions along the riverside between Blackfriars and Tower bridges and beyond – with the charge led by the mighty **Tate Modern**. And with a traffic-free, riverside path connecting most of the sights, this is easily one of the most enjoyable areas of London in which to hang out.

Tate Modern

The masterly conversion of the austere Bankside power station into **Tate Modern** (daily 10am–6pm, Fri & Sat until 10pm; free; ⓦ www.tate.org.uk) has left plenty of the building's original, industrial feel, while providing wonderfully light and spacious galleries in which to show off the Tate's vast international twentieth-century and contemporary art collection. The best way to enter is down the ramp from the west, so you get the full effect of the stupendously large **turbine hall**, used to display one huge, mind-blowing installation. Given that Tate Modern is the world's largest modern art gallery, you need to devote the best

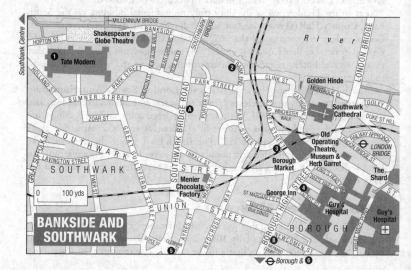

part of a day to do it justice – or be very selective. It's easy enough to find your way around: pick up a plan (and, for an extra £2, an audioguide), and take the escalator to level 3. This, and level 5, display the permanent collection; level 4 is used for fee-paying temporary exhibitions, and level 7 has a rooftop **café** with a great view over the Thames.

The curators have eschewed the usual chronological approach to display and gone instead for hanging (and re-hanging) works according to -isms. On the whole this works very well, though the early twentieth-century canvases, in their gilded frames, do struggle when made to compete with the attention-grabbing conceptual stuff. Although the displays change every six months or so, you're still pretty much guaranteed to see at least some works by **Monet** and Bonnard, Cubist pioneers **Picasso** and Braque, Surrealists such as **Dalí**, abstract artists like **Mondrian**, Bridget Riley and Pollock, and Pop supremos **Warhol** and Lichtenstein. There are seminal works such as a replica of **Duchamp**'s urinal, entitled *Fountain* and signed "R. Mutt", and Yves Klein's totally blue paintings. And such is the space here that several artists get whole rooms to themselves, among them **Joseph Beuys** and his shamanistic wax and furs, and **Mark Rothko**, whose abstract *Seagram Murals*, originally destined for a posh restaurant in New York, have their own shrine-like room in the heart of the collection.

Shakespeare's Globe

Seriously dwarfed by the Tate Modern but equally spectacular is **Shakespeare's Globe Theatre**, a reconstruction of the polygonal playhouse where most of the Bard's later works were first performed, and which was originally erected on nearby Park Street in 1598. To find out more about Shakespeare and the history of Bankside, the Globe's stylish **exhibition** (daily: mid-April to mid-Sept 9am–noon & 12.30–5pm; mid-Oct to mid-April 10am–5pm; £10.50; ⓦwww.shakespeares-globe.org) is well worth a visit. It begins by detailing the long campaign by American actor Sam Wanamaker to have the Globe rebuilt, but it's the imaginative hands-on exhibits that really hit the spot. You can have a virtual play on medieval instruments such as the crumhorn or sackbut, prepare your own edition of Shakespeare, and feel the thatch, hazelnut shell and daub used to build

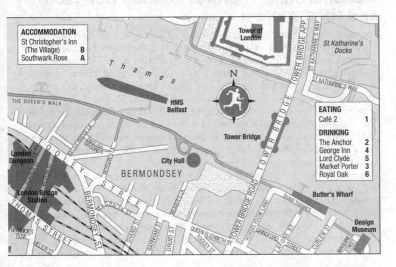

ACCOMMODATION
St Christopher's Inn
(The Village)   B
Southwark Rose   A

EATING
Café 2   1

DRINKING
The Anchor   2
George Inn   4
Lord Clyde   5
Market Porter   3
Royal Oak   6

the theatre. Visitors also get taken on an informative half-hour **guided tour** round the theatre itself, except in the afternoons during the summer, when you can only visit the exhibition (for a reduced fee).

Golden Hinde, Southwark Cathedral and Borough Market

An exact replica of the **Golden Hinde** (daily 10am–5.30pm; £6; Ⓦwww .goldenhinde.org), the galleon in which Francis Drake sailed around the world from 1577 to 1580, nestles in St Mary Overie Dock, at the eastern end of Clink Street. The ship is surprisingly small, and its original crew of eighty-plus must have been cramped to say the least. There's a lack of interpretive panels, so it's worth phoning ahead and booking a guided tour from one of the folk in period garb.

Close by the *Golden Hinde* stands **Southwark Cathedral** (Mon–Fri 7.30am–6pm, Sat & Sun 8.30am–6pm; free; Ⓦwww.southwark.anglican.org/cathedral), built as the medieval Augustinian priory church of St Mary Overie, and given cathedral status only in 1905. Of the original thirteenth-century church, only the choir and retrochoir now remain, separated by a tall and beautiful stone Tudor screen, making them probably the oldest Gothic structures left in London. The nave was entirely rebuilt in the nineteenth century, but the cathedral contains numerous interesting monuments, from a thirteenth-century oak effigy of a knight to an early twentieth-century memorial to Shakespeare (his brother is buried here). Above the memorial is a stained-glass window featuring a whole cast of characters from the plays.

Borough Market (Ⓦwww.boroughmarket.org.uk), squeezed underneath the railway arches by the cathedral, is one of the few wholesale fruit and vegetable markets still trading under its original Victorian wrought-iron shed. In recent years it's undergone a transformation from scruffy obscurity to a small foodie haven, with permanent outlets such as Neal's Yard Dairy and Konditor & Cook joined by **gourmet market stalls** on Thursdays (11am–5pm), Fridays (noon–6pm) and, particularly, Saturdays (9am–4pm).

Old Operating Theatre, London Dungeon and HMS Belfast

The most educative and strangest of Southwark's museums, the **Old Operating Theatre, Museum and Herb Garret** (daily 10.30am–5pm; £5.60; Ⓦwww .thegarret.org.uk) is located to the east of the cathedral on St Thomas Street, on the other side of Borough High Street. Built in 1821 up a spiral staircase at the top of a church tower, where the hospital apothecary's herbs were stored, this women's operating theatre dates from the pre-anaesthetic era. Despite being entirely gore-free, the museum is as stomach-churning as the London Dungeon (see below). The surgeons who used this room would have concentrated on speed and accuracy (most amputations took less than a minute), but there was still a thirty percent mortality rate, with many patients simply dying of shock, and many more from bacterial infection, about which very little was known.

There's usually an impressive queue beside the railway arches of London Bridge train station, on the south side of Tooley Street, home to the ever-popular **London Dungeon** (daily: Easter to mid-July, Sept & Oct 10am–5.30pm; mid-July to Aug 9.30am–7.30pm; Nov–Easter 10.30am–5pm; £17 online, £22 on the door; Ⓦwww.thedungeons.com). Young teenagers and the credulous probably get the most out of the life-sized waxwork tableaux of folk being hanged, drawn, quartered and tortured, the general hysteria being boosted by actors dressed as top-hatted Victorian vampires, executioners and monks pouncing out of the darkness. Visitors are led into the labyrinth, an old-fashioned mirror maze, before being herded through a series of live action scenarios, passing through the exploitative "Jack the Ripper Experience", and ending with a walk through a revolving tunnel of flames. Note that you can avoid the inevitable queues and save (some) money by pre-buying tickets online.

HMS Belfast (daily: March–Oct 10am–6pm; Nov–Feb 10am–5pm; £10.70; Ⓦhmsbelfast.iwm.org.uk), a World War II cruiser, is permanently moored between London Bridge and Tower Bridge. Armed with six torpedoes, and six-inch guns with a range of over fourteen miles, the *Belfast* spent over two years of the war in the Royal Naval shipyards after being hit by a mine in the Firth of Forth at the beginning of hostilities. It later saw action in the Barents Sea and during the Korean War, before being decommissioned. The maze of cabins is fun to explore but if you want to find out more about the *Belfast*, head for the exhibition rooms in zone 5; in the adjacent Life at Sea room, you can practise your Morse code and knots, and listen to accounts of naval life on board.

City Hall to Butler's Wharf

Bearing a striking resemblance to a giant car headlight, Norman Foster's startling glass-encased **City Hall** (Mon–Fri 8am–8pm, plus occasional weekends; Ⓣ020/7983 4000, Ⓦwww.london.gov.uk), downriver from the *Belfast*, is the headquarters for the **Greater London Authority** and the Mayor of London. Visitors are welcome to stroll up the helical walkway, visit the café and watch proceedings from the second floor. Contact in advance for access to "London's Living Room" on the ninth floor, which boasts the best views over the Thames.

In contrast to the brash offices on Tooley Street, **Butler's Wharf**, east of Tower Bridge, has retained its historical character. **Shad Thames**, the narrow street at the back of Butler's Wharf, has kept the wrought-iron overhead gangways by which the porters used to transport goods from the wharves to the warehouses further back from the river, and is one of the most atmospheric alleyways on the south bank of the Thames. The chief attraction in the vicinity is the superb riverside **Design Museum** (daily 10am–5.45pm; £7; Ⓦdesignmuseum.org), a stylish, Bauhaus-like conversion of a 1950s warehouse at the eastern end of Shad Thames. The museum has no permanent display, but instead hosts a series of temporary exhibitions (up to four at any one time) on important designers, movements or single products. The small coffee-bar in the foyer is a great place to relax, and there's a pricier restaurant on the top floor.

Kensington and Chelsea

London's wealthiest district, the Royal Borough of Kensington and Chelsea is particularly well-to-do in the area south of **Hyde Park**. Known popularly as the "Tiara Triangle", the moneyed feel here is evident in the flash shops and swanky bars as well as the plush houses and apartments. The most popular area for tourists, meanwhile, is **South Kensington**, where three of London's top museums stand side by side. Further south, **Chelsea** still has a slightly more bohemian pedigree, although these days, it's really just another wealthy west London suburb. To the north, **Notting Hill** is rammed solid with trendy – but wealthy – media folk, yet retains a strong Moroccan and Portuguese presence, as well as vestiges of the African-Caribbean community who initiated – and still run – Carnival, the city's (and Europe's) largest August Bank Holiday street party (see box, p.119).

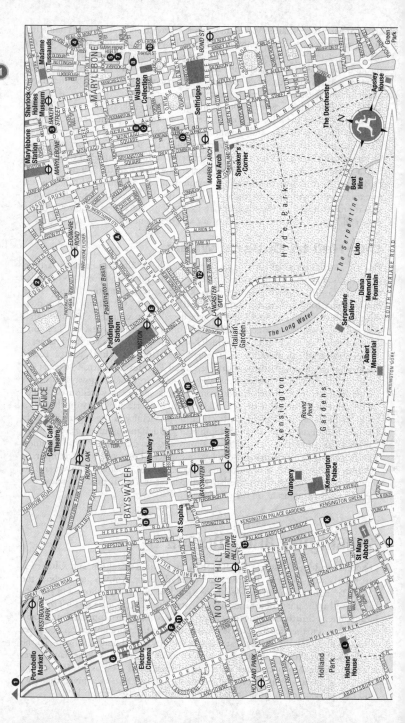

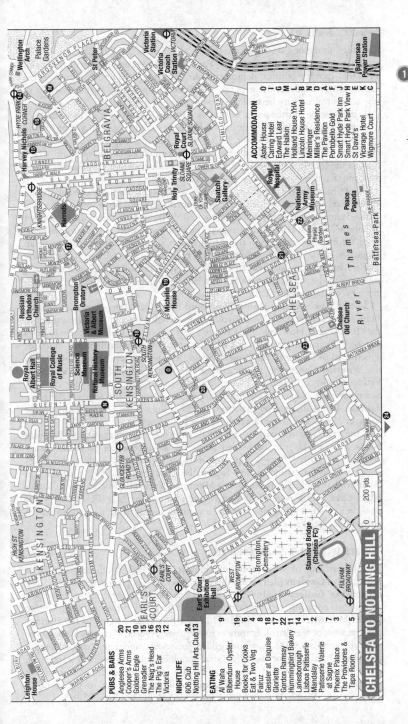

CHELSEA TO NOTTING HILL

ACCOMMODATION

Aster House	O
Caring Hotel	I
Edward Lear	G
The Halkin	M
Holland House YHA	L
Lincoln House Hotel	B
Meininger	N
Miller's Residence	D
The Pavilion	A
Portobello Gold	F
Smart Hyde Park Inn	J
Smart Hyde Park View	E
St David's	K
Vicarage Hotel	H
Wigmore Court	C

PUBS & BARS

Anglesea Arms	20
Cooper's Arms	21
Golden Eagle	10
Grenadier	15
The Nag's Head	16
The Pig's Ear	23
Victoria	12

NIGHTLIFE

606 Club	24
Notting Hill Arts Club	13

EATING

Al Waha	9
Bibendum Oyster House	19
Books for Cooks	6
Eat & Two Veg	4
Fairuz	8
Gessler at Daquise	18
Gloriette	17
Gordon Ramsay	22
Hummingbird Bakery	11
Lanesborough	14
Lisboa Patisserie	1
Mandalay	2
Patisserie Valerie at Sagne	7
Phoenix Palace	3
The Providores & Tapa Room	5

Hyde Park

Hangings, muggings, duels and the Great Exhibition of 1851 are just some of the events that have taken place in **Hyde Park** (daily 5am–midnight), which remains a popular spot for political demonstrations. For most of the time, however, the park is simply a lazy leisure ground – a wonderful open space that allows you to lose all sight of the city beyond a few persistent tower blocks.

At the treeless northeastern corner is **Marble Arch**, erected in 1828 as a triumphal entry to Buckingham Palace, but now stranded on a busy traffic island at the west end of Oxford Street. This is a historically charged piece of land, as it marks the site of Tyburn gallows, the city's main public execution spot until 1783. It's also the location of **Speakers' Corner**, a peculiarly English Sunday morning tradition, featuring an assembly of ranters and hecklers.

A more immediately appealing approach is to enter from the southeast around **Hyde Park Corner**, where the **Wellington Arch** (Wed–Sun: April–Oct 10am–5pm; Nov–March 10am–4pm; £3.50; EH) stands in the midst of another of London's busiest traffic interchanges. The arch was erected in 1828 to commemorate Wellington's victories in the Napoleonic wars; in 1846 it was topped by an equestrian statue of the Duke himself, later replaced by Peace driving a four-horse chariot. Inside, you can view an exhibition on London's outdoor sculpture and take a lift to the top of the monument where the exterior balconies offer a bird's-eye view of the swirling traffic.

Close by stands **Apsley House** (Wed–Sun: April–Oct 11am–5pm; Nov–March 11am–4pm; £5.10; EH), Wellington's London residence and now a museum to the "Iron Duke". However unless you're a keen fan of the Duke (or the building's architect, Benjamin Wyatt), the highlight here is the **art collection**, much of which used to belong to the King of Spain. Among the best pieces, displayed in the Waterloo Gallery on the first floor, are works by de Hooch, Van Dyck, Velázquez, Goya, Rubens and Murillo. The famous, more than twice life-size, nude statue of Napoleon by Antonio Canova stands at the foot of the main staircase. It was disliked by the sitter, not least for the figure of Victory in the emperor's hand, which appears to be trying to fly away.

At the centre of the park is the curvaceous lake, the **Serpentine**. **Rowing boats** and pedalos can be rented from the boathouse on the north bank (March–Oct daily 10am–6.30pm or dusk; £4 per hour), while the lake's popular **Lido** (mid-June to mid-Sept daily 10am–6pm; £3.50) is situated on the south bank. Nearby is the **Diana Memorial Fountain** (daily: March & Oct 10am–6pm; April–Aug 10am–8pm; Sept 10am–7pm; Nov–Feb 10am–4pm; free), less of a fountain, and more of a giant oval-shaped mini-moat, in which kids can dabble their feet.

Kensington Gardens

The western half of what most folk think is Hyde Park is officially known as **Kensington Gardens** (daily 6am–dusk). Its two most popular attractions are the **Serpentine Gallery** (daily 10am–6pm; free; ⓦ www.serpentinegallery.org), which hosts contemporary art exhibitions, and the richly decorated, High Gothic **Albert Memorial** erected in 1876. The latter is as much a hymn to the glorious achievements of the British Empire as to its subject, Queen Victoria's husband (he died of typhoid in 1861), whose gilded image sits under its central canopy, clutching a catalogue for the 1851 Great Exhibition. If you want to learn more about the 169 life-sized depictions of long-gone artists (all men) around the pediment, and the various other allegorical sculptures, join one of the monthly **guided tours** (March–Dec 1st Sun of month 2 & 3pm; 45min; £4.50).

The Exhibition's most famous feature, the gargantuan glasshouse of the Crystal Palace, no longer exists, but the profits were used to buy a large tract of land south of the park, now home to South Kensington's remarkable cluster of museums and colleges, plus the vast **Royal Albert Hall** (see also p.146), a splendid iron-and-glass-domed concert hall, with an exterior of red brick, terracotta and marble that became the hallmark of South Ken architecture. The hall is the venue for Europe's most democratic music festival, the Henry Wood Promenade Concerts, better known as **the Proms**. Daytime **guided tours** of the hall (daily except Wed 10.30am–3.30pm; £8) depart from the South Porch at Door 12 and last around an hour.

Kensington Palace

On the western edge of Kensington Gardens stands **Kensington Palace** (March–Oct daily 10am–6pm; Nov–Feb 10am–5pm; £12.50; Ⓦwww.hrp.org.uk), a modestly proportioned Jacobean brick mansion bought by William and Mary in 1689, and the chief royal residence for fifty years afterwards. KP, as it's fondly known in royal circles, is best known today as the place where **Princess Diana** lived until her death in 1997. Visitors don't get to see Diana's apartments, which were on the west side of the palace, where various minor royals still live. Instead, they get to view some of Diana's frocks – and also several worn by the Queen – and then the sparsely furnished, but lavishly decorated state apartments. The highlights are the trompe l'oeil ceiling paintings by William Kent, in particular the Cupola Room, and the oil paintings in the King's Gallery. En route, you also get to see the tastelessly decorated rooms in which the future Queen Victoria spent her unhappy childhood. To recover from the above, take tea in the exquisite **Orangery** (times as for palace).

Leighton House

A number of wealthy Victorian artists rather self-consciously founded an artists' colony in the streets that lay to the west of Kensington Gardens. It's possible to visit one of the most remarkable of these artist pads, **Leighton House**, at 12 Holland Park Rd (daily except Tues 10am–5.30pm; guided tour Wed 3pm; £5; Ⓦwww.rbkc.gov.uk/leightonhousemuseum). "It will be opulence, it will be sincerity," Lord Leighton opined before starting work on the house in the 1860s – he later became President of the Royal Academy and was ennobled on his deathbed. The big attraction is the domed Arab Hall, decorated with Saracen tiles, gilded mosaics and woodwork drawn from all over the Islamic world. The other rooms are less spectacular, but in compensation are hung with paintings by Lord Leighton and his Pre-Raphaelite chums.

Knightsbridge and Harrods

South of Hyde Park lies the irredeemably snobbish **Knightsbridge**, revelling in its reputation as the swankiest shopping area in London, a status epitomized by **Harrods** (Mon–Sat 10am–8pm, Sun noon–6pm) on Brompton Road. London's most famous department store started out as a family-run grocery store in 1849, with a staff of two. The current 1905 terracotta building is owned by the Qatari investors and employs in excess of three thousand staff. The store even has a few sections that are architectural sights in their own right, notably the Food Hall, with its exquisite Arts and Crafts tiling, and the Egyptian Hall, with its pseudo-hieroglyphs and sphinxes. Note that the store has a draconian **dress code**: no ripped jeans, no flip-flops or thong sandals, no shorts, no vest T-shirts, and no backpacks.

Victoria and Albert Museum (V&A)

In terms of sheer variety and scale, the **Victoria and Albert Museum**, on Cromwell Road (daily 10am–5.45pm, Fri until 10pm; free; Ⓦwww.vam.ac.uk) is the greatest museum of applied arts in the world. Beautifully but haphazardly displayed across a seven-mile, four-storey maze of halls and corridors, the V&A's treasures are impossible to survey in a single visit. Floor plans from the information desks can help you decide which areas to concentrate on.

The most celebrated of the V&A's exhibits are the **Raphael Cartoons**, seven vast biblical paintings that served as designs for a set of tapestries destined for the Sistine Chapel. Close by, you can view highlights from the UK's largest dress collection and theatre exhibition, and the world's biggest collection of Indian art outside India, plus extensive Chinese, Islamic and Japanese galleries. Elsewhere, there's a gallery of twentieth-century **objets d'art** to rival the Design Museum, and more Constable **paintings** than in Tate Britain. In addition, the V&A's temporary shows – for which you have to pay – are among the best in Britain.

Wading through the huge collection of European sculpture, you come to the surreal **plaster casts** gallery, filled with copies of European art's greatest hits, from Michelangelo's *David* to Trajan's Column from the forum in Rome (sawn in half to make it fit). Before you leave, make sure you check out the museum's trio of original refreshment rooms (now back to their original use) – the **Morris, Gamble and Poynter Rooms**, at the back of the main galleries.

Science Museum

The **Science Museum** (daily 10am–6pm; free; Ⓦwww.sciencemuseum.org .uk), on Exhibition Road, is undeniably impressive, filling seven floors with items drawn from every conceivable area of science, including space travel, digital technology, steam engines and carbon emissions. Keen to dispel the enduring image of museums devoted to its subject as boring and full of dusty glass cabinets, the Science Museum has updated its galleries with interactive displays, and puts on daily demonstrations to show that not all science teaching has to be deathly dry.

First off, ask at the information desk in the Power Hall for details of the day's (usually free) events and demonstrations. Most people will want to head for the four-floor **Wellcome Wing**, with its interactive computers and an IMAX cinema (tickets £8). To get there, you must pass through the **Making the Modern World**, a display of iconic inventions from Robert Stephenson's *Rocket* steam train of 1829 to the Ford Model T, the world's first mass-produced car.

If you've got kids, head for the **Launch Pad**, the museum's chief interactive gallery, where they can experiment with water, waves, light and sound and build a catenary arch (and knock it down again). "Explainers" are on hand to try and impart some educational input.

Natural History Museum

Alfred Waterhouse's purpose-built mock-Romanesque colossus ensures the **Natural History Museum** (daily 10am–5.50pm; free; Ⓦwww.nhm.ac.uk) its status as London's most handsome museum. The collections are as much an important resource for serious zoologists as they are a popular attraction.

The main entrance leads to the vast **Central Hall** dominated by an 85ft-long plaster cast of a Diplodocus skeleton. To one side, you'll find the **Dinosaur** gallery, where a raised walkway leads straight to the highlight for many kids, the grisly life-sized animatronic dinosaur tableau (currently a roaring Tyrannosaurus rex). Other child-friendly sections include the **Creepy-Crawlies** room, which features a live colony of leaf-cutter ants and the old-fashioned **Mammals** gallery with its life-size model of a blue whale.

For a visually exciting romp through evolution, head for the **Red Zone** (once the Geology Museum); popular sections include the slightly tasteless Kobe earthquake simulator, and the spectacular display of gems and crystals in the Earth's Treasury. Visitors can also view a selection of zoological bits and bobs in the giant, glass-encased, concrete Cocoon in the museum's **Darwin Centre** (Orange Zone), which houses 200 scientists, 28 million insects and 6 million plant specimens. Among the more bizarre items pickled in the glass jars are a 50-year-old piece of algae from Mauritius, a partially digested human head from a sperm whale's stomach and a brown rat found during the building's construction. To visit the Cocoon, you need to book ahead online or by phone.

Chelsea

From the Swinging Sixties and even up to the Punk era, **Chelsea** had a slightly bohemian pedigree; these days, it's just another wealthy west London suburb. On the south side of King's Road, a short stroll from Sloane Square, are the former **Duke of York's Barracks,** now housing shops and cafés. The main building, built in 1801 and fronted by a solid-looking Tuscan portico, houses the **Saatchi Gallery** (daily 10am–6pm; free; Ⓦ www.saatchi-gallery.co.uk), which puts on changing exhibitions of contemporary art in its fifteen white-washed rooms.

Among the most nattily attired of all those parading down the King's Road nowadays are the scarlet- or navy-blue-clad Chelsea Pensioners, army veterans from the nearby **Royal Hospital** (April–Sept daily 10am–noon & 2–4pm; Oct–March closed Sun; free; Ⓦ www.chelsea-pensioners.co.uk), founded by Charles II in 1681. The hospital's majestic red-brick wings and grassy courtyards became a blueprint for institutional and collegiate architecture all over the English-speaking world. The public are allowed to view the austere hospital chapel, and the equally grand wood-panelled dining hall opposite, which has a vast allegorical mural of Charles II.

The concrete bunker next door to the Royal Hospital, on Royal Hospital Road, houses the **National Army Museum** (daily 10am–5.30pm; free; Ⓦ www .national-army-museum.ac.uk). The museum harbours interesting historical artefacts, plus an impressive array of uniforms and medals, but for a more balanced view of war, you're better off visiting the Imperial War Museum (see p.109). Highlights include: a vast spot-lit model of the Battle of Waterloo (at 7pm before the Prussians arrived to save the day); the skeleton of Marengo, Napoleon's charger at the battle; the saw used to amputate the Earl of Uxbridge's leg; a paper lantern used by Florence Nightingale; and Richard Caton-Woodville's famous painting of *The Charge of the Light Brigade.*

Notting Hill Carnival

The two-day free festival **Notting Hill Carnival** is the longest-running and best-known street party in Europe. Originating in the 1960s, Carnival is a tumult of imaginatively decorated floats, eye-catching costumes, thumping sound systems, live bands, irresistible food and huge crowds. It takes place on the last weekend of August. For more, see Ⓦ www.rbkc.gov.uk.

North London

Almost all of **north London**'s suburbs are easily accessible by tube from the centre – indeed it was the expansion of the tube which encouraged the forward march of bricks and mortar into many of these areas – though just a handful of these satellite villages, now subsumed into the general mass of the city, are worth bothering with.

First off, is one of London's finest parks, **Regent's Park**, framed by Nash-designed architecture and home of London Zoo. Close by is **Camden Town**, where the weekend market is one of the city's big attractions – a warren of stalls selling street fashion, books, records and ethnic goods. The real highlights of north London, though, for visitors and residents alike, are the village-like suburbs of **Hampstead** and **Highgate**, which have the added advantage of proximity to one of London's wildest patches of greenery, **Hampstead Heath**.

Regent's Park

According to John Nash's masterplan, devised in 1811 for the Prince Regent (later George IV), **Regent's Park** (daily 5am–dusk) was to be girded by a continuous belt of terraces, and sprinkled with a total of 56 villas, including a magnificent pleasure palace for the Prince himself. The plan was never fully realized, due to lack of funds, but enough was built to create something of the idealized garden city that Nash and the Prince Regent envisaged. Prominent on the park's skyline is the minaret and shiny copper dome of **London Central Mosque** at 146 Park Rd, an entirely appropriate addition given the Prince Regent's taste for the Orient. Within the Inner Circle is the **Open Air Theatre**, which puts on summer performances of Shakespeare, opera and ballet, and **Queen Mary's Gardens**, by far the prettiest section of the park.

The northeastern corner of the park is occupied by **London Zoo** (daily: March–Oct 10am–5.30pm; Nov–Feb 10am–4pm; £18; ⓦ www.zsl.org/zsl-london-zoo). Founded in 1826 with the remnants of the royal menagerie, the enclosures here are as humane as any inner-city zoo could make them, and kids usually enjoy themselves. In particular they love **Animal Adventure**, the new children's zoo (and playground) where they can actually handle the animals, and the regular **"Animals in Action"** live shows. The invertebrate house, now known as **BUGS**, the **Gorilla Kingdom** and the walk-through rainforest and monkey forest are also guaranteed winners. The zoo boasts some striking architectural features, too, most notably the modernist, spiral-ramped 1930s concrete **penguin pool**.

Camden Town

For all its tourist popularity, **Camden Market** remains a genuinely offbeat place. More than 100,000 shoppers turn up here each weekend, and parts of the market

---

Regent's Canal by boat

Three companies run daily boat services on the Regent's Canal between Camden and Little Venice, passing through the Maida Hill tunnel. The narrowboat **Jenny Wren** (April–Oct only; ☏020/7485 4433) starts off at Camden, goes through a canal lock (the only company to do so) and heads for Little Venice, while **Jason's narrowboats** (☏020/7286 3428) start off at Little Venice; the **London Waterbus Company** (April–Sept daily; Oct Thurs–Sun only; Nov–March Sat & Sun only, weather permitting; ☏020/7482 2660) sets off from both places and calls in at London Zoo en route. Whichever you choose, you can board at either end; **tickets** cost around £9 return, and journey time is 45 minutes one way.

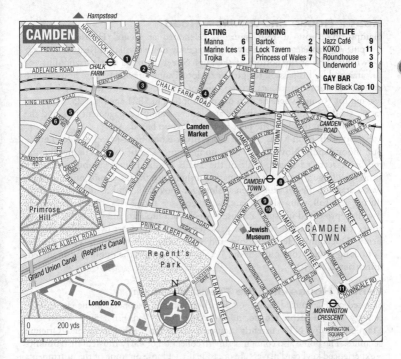

▲ Hampstead

CAMDEN

EATING		DRINKING		NIGHTLIFE	
Manna	6	Bartok	2	Jazz Café	9
Marine Ices	1	Lock Tavern	4	KOKO	11
Trojka	5	Princess of Wales	7	Roundhouse	3
				Underworld	8
				GAY BAR	
				The Black Cap	10

PROVOST ROAD · HAVERSTOCK HILL · CROSSLADE ROAD · FERDINAND ST · CLARENCE WAY · JEFFREY'S ST

ADELAIDE ROAD · CHALK FARM · REGENT'S PARK RD · CHALK FARM ROAD · HARTLAND RD · HAWLEY RD · CASTLE · PRINCE'S ST

CAMDEN ROAD · BAYNES ST

Camden Market

GLOUCESTER AVENUE · OVAL ROAD · HAWLEY CRES · KENTISH TOWN ROAD · CAMDEN ROAD · LYME STREET

CHALCOT ROAD · JAMESTOWN ROAD · CAMDEN HIGH ST · BLOK ST · GEORGIANA ST

PRIMROSE HILL RD · FITZROY RD · PRINCESS RD · GLOUCESTER CRESCENT · INVERNESS ST · GREENLAND ROAD · BARHAM STREET · MANDELA ST

CAMDEN TOWN

Primrose Hill · REGENT'S PARK ROAD · REGAL LA · PARKWAY · ARLINGTON ROAD · PRATT STREET · PLENDER STREET

CAMDEN TOWN

Jewish Museum

PRINCE ALBERT ROAD · DELANCEY STREET · ALBERT STREET · CAMDEN HIGH STREET · BAYHAM STREET

Grand Union Canal (Regent's Canal) · OUTER CIRCLE

Regent's Park

GLOUCESTER GATE · ALBANY STREET · MORNINGTON TERRACE · MORNINGTON ST · CARLOW · CROWNDALE RD

London Zoo

BROAD WALK · PARK VILLAGE EAST · MORNINGTON CRESCENT · HARRINGTON SQUARE

N

0   200 yds

Manna 6, Marine Ices 1, Trojka 5, Bartok 2, Lock Tavern 4, Princess of Wales 7, Jazz Café 9, KOKO 11, Roundhouse 3, Underworld 8, The Black Cap 10

now stay open week-long, alongside a similarly oriented crop of shops, cafés and bistros. The sheer variety of what's on offer, from bootleg tapes to furniture, along with a mass of street fashion and clubwear, and plenty of foodstalls, is what makes Camden so special. To avoid the crowds, which can be overpowering on a summer Sunday afternoon, you'll need to get here by 10am.

Despite having no significant Jewish associations, Camden is home to London's **Jewish Museum** (Mon–Wed & Sun 10am–5pm, Thurs 10am–9pm, Fri 10am–2pm; £7; Ⓦwww.jewishmuseum.org.uk), at 129 Albert St, just off Parkway. The displays aim both to tell the history of Jewish settlement in Britain, and also the rudiments of Judaism as a religion. One of the most remarkable exhibits is the medieval *mikveh* (ritual bath) excavated from the City, while the Holocaust gallery tells the story of the Shoah through the life of Leon Greenman, one of the few British Jews who experienced the horror of Auschwitz. The museum's temporary exhibitions are always thought-provoking and there's a café on site.

Hampstead and Highgate

The high points of north London, both geographically and aesthetically, the elegant, largely eighteenth-century developments of **Hampstead and Highgate** have managed to cling onto their village origins. Of the two, Highgate is slightly sleepier and more aloof, with fewer conventional sights, while Hampstead is busier and buzzier, with high-profile intelligentsia and discerning pop stars among its residents. Both benefit from direct access to **Hampstead Heath**, where you can enjoy stupendous views over London, kite flying and nude bathing, as well as outdoor concerts and high art in and around the Neoclassical country mansion of Kenwood House.

LONDON | North London

121

Keats' House and 2 Willow Road

Hampstead's most lustrous figure is celebrated at **Keats' House** (Tues–Sun 1–5pm; £5), an elegant, whitewashed Regency double villa on Keats Grove, off Downshire Hill at the bottom of the High Street. Inspired by the tranquillity of the area and by his passion for girl-next-door Fanny Brawne (whose house is also part of the museum), Keats wrote some of his most famous works here before leaving for Rome, where he died of consumption in 1821 aged just 25. The neat, rather staid interior contains books and letters, Fanny's engagement ring and the four-poster bed in which the poet first coughed up blood.

A short walk from Keats' House is **2 Willow Road** (mid-March to Oct Thurs–Sun noon–5pm; Nov Sat & Sun noon–5pm; £5.50; NT), an unassuming red-brick terraced house, built in the 1930s by the Hungarian-born architect Ernö Goldfinger, that gives a fascinating insight into the modernist mindset. This was a state-of-the-art pad when Goldfinger moved in, and as it changed little during the following sixty years, what you see today is a 1930s avant-garde dwelling preserved in aspic, a house at once both modern and old-fashioned. An added bonus is that the rooms are packed with **works of art** by the likes of Max Ernst, Duchamp, Henry Moore and Man Ray. Before 3pm, visits are by hour-long guided tour only (noon, 1 & 2pm); after 3pm the public has unguided, unrestricted access.

Fenton House and the Freud Museum

Situated on Hampstead Grove, off Heath Street, and decorated in the eighteenth-century taste, **Fenton House** (mid-March to Oct Wed–Fri 2–5pm, Sat & Sun 11am–5pm; £6; NT) currently houses a collection of European and Oriental ceramics. The house also contains a superb collection of **early musical instruments** – experienced keyboard players are occasionally let loose on some of the instruments during the day and you can sign up for one of the occasional demonstration tours (£10). Tickets for the house also allow you to take a stroll in the beautiful orchard, kitchen garden and formal **garden** (garden only; £1), which features some top-class topiary and herbaceous borders.

One of the most poignant of London's house museums is the **Freud Museum** (Wed–Sun noon–5pm; £5; Ⓦwww.freud.org.uk), hidden away in the leafy streets of south Hampstead at 20 Maresfield Gardens. Having lived in Vienna for his entire adult life, **Sigmund Freud** was forced to flee the Nazis, and arrived in London during the summer of 1938 as a semi-invalid (he died within a year). The ground-floor study and library look exactly as they did when Freud lived here – the collection of erotic antiquities and the famous couch, sumptuously draped in Persian carpets, were all brought here from Vienna. Upstairs, home movies of family life in Vienna are shown continually, and a small room is dedicated to his daughter, Anna, herself an influential child analyst, who lived in the house until her death in 1982.

Hampstead Heath and Kenwood

North London's "green lung", **Hampstead Heath** is the city's most enjoyable public park. It may not have much of its original heathland left, but it packs a wonderful variety of bucolic scenery into its 800 acres. At its southern end are the rolling green pastures of **Parliament Hill**, north London's premier spot for kite flying. On either side are numerous ponds, three of which – one for men, one for women and one mixed – you can swim in for free (see box, p.148). The thickest woodland is to be found in the **West Heath**, beyond Whitestone Pond, also the site of the most formal section, **Hill Garden**, a secretive and romantic little gem with eccentric balustraded terraces and a ruined pergola. Beyond lies **Golders Hill**

Park, where you can gaze at pygmy goats and fallow deer, and inspect the impeccably maintained aviaries, home to flamingoes, cranes and other exotic birds.

Finally, don't miss the landscaped grounds of Kenwood, in the north of the Heath, which are focused on the whitewashed Neoclassical mansion of **Kenwood House** (daily 11.30am–4pm; free; EH). The house is now home to a collection of seventeenth- and eighteenth-century art, including a handful of real masterpieces by the likes of Vermeer, Rembrandt, Boucher, Gainsborough and Reynolds. Of the house's period interiors, the most spectacular is Robert Adam's sky-blue and gold library, its book-filled apses separated from the central entertaining area by paired columns.

Highgate Cemetery

Receiving far more visitors than Highgate itself, **Highgate Cemetery** (Ⓦhighgate -cemetery.org), ranged on both sides of Swain's Lane, is London's best-known graveyard. The most illustrious incumbent of the **East Cemetery** (April–Oct Mon–Fri 10am–5pm, Sat & Sun 11am–5pm; Nov–March closes 4pm; £3) is **Karl Marx**. Erected by the Communist movement in 1954, his vulgar bronze bust surmounting a granite plinth is a far cry from the unfussy memorial he had requested; close by lies the much simpler grave of the author George Eliot. The East Cemetery's lack of atmosphere is in part compensated for by the fact that you can wander at will through its maze of circuitous paths.

On the other side of Swain's Lane, the overgrown **West Cemetery**, with its spooky Egyptian Avenue and terraced catacombs, is the ultimate Hammer Horror graveyard. Visitors can only enter by way of a **guided tour** (March–Nov Mon–Fri 2pm, Sat & Sun hourly 11am–4pm; Dec–Feb Sat & Sun hourly 11am–3pm; £5; no under 8s) – get there early on summer Sundays. Among the prominent graves usually visited are those of artist Dante Gabriel Rossetti, and of lesbian novelist Radclyffe Hall.

Hendon: The RAF Museum

A world-class assembly of historic military aircraft can be seen at the **RAF Museum** (daily 10am–6pm; free; Ⓦwww.rafmuseum.org.uk; ⊖Colindale), located in a godforsaken part of north London beside the M1 motorway. Enthusiasts won't be disappointed, but those looking for a balanced account of modern aerial warfare will – the overall tone is unashamedly militaristic, not to say jingoistic. Those with children should head for the hands-on Aeronauts gallery; those without might prefer to explore the often overlooked display galleries, ranged around the edge of the Historic Hangars section, which contain an art gallery and an exhibition on the history of flight, accompanied by replicas of some of the death-traps of early aviation.

Neasden: the Shri Swaminarayan Temple

Perhaps the most remarkable building in the whole of London lies just off the North Circular Road, in the glum suburb of **Neasden**. Here, rising majestically above the surrounding semi-detached houses like a mirage, is the **Shri Swaminarayan Mandir** (daily 9am–6pm; free; Ⓦwww.mandir.org; ⊖Neasden), a traditional Hindu temple topped with domes and shikharas, erected in 1995 in a style and scale unseen outside of India for more than a millennium. To reach the temple, you must enter through the adjacent Haveli, or cultural complex, with its carved wooden portico and balcony. After taking off your shoes, you can proceed to the Mandir (temple) itself, carved entirely out of Carrara marble, with every possible surface transformed into a honeycomb of arabesques, flowers and seated gods. Beneath the Mandir, an **exhibition** (daily 9am–6pm; £2) explains the basic tenets of Hinduism and details the life of Lord Swaminarayan, and includes a short film about the history of the building.

South London

Now largely built up into a patchwork of Victorian terraces, **south London** nevertheless boasts one outstanding area for sightseeing, and that is **Greenwich**, with its impressive ensemble of the Royal Naval College and the Queen's House, courtesy of Christopher Wren and Inigo Jones respectively. Most visitors, it has to be said, come to see the National Maritime Museum, the Royal Observatory, and the beautifully landscaped royal park, though Greenwich also pulls in an ever-increasing volume of Londoners in search of bargains at its Sunday **market**. The only other suburban sights that stand out are the **Dulwich Picture Gallery**, a public art gallery even older than the National Gallery, and the eclectic **Horniman Museum**, in neighbouring Forest Hill.

Greenwich

Greenwich is one of London's most beguiling spots, but Greenwich town centre, laid out in the 1820s with Nash-style terraces, is nowadays plagued with heavy traffic. In addition to the sights below, one of Greenwich's major draws has been the **Cutty Sark**, the world's last surviving tea-clipper. Launched from the Clydeside shipyards in 1869, the *Cutty Sark* was more famous in its day as a wool clipper, returning from Australia in just 72 days. Following a devastating fire in 2007, it has been undergoing a long restoration and is due to reopen in 2011. To reach Greenwich, you can take a **train** from London Bridge (every 30min), a **boat** from one of the piers in central London, or the **DLR** to Cutty Sark station.

Old Royal Naval College

To escape Greenwich's busy streets, head for the **Old Royal Naval College** (daily 10am–5pm; free; Ⓦwww.oldroyalnavalcollege.org), one of the few London buildings that really makes the most of its riverbank location. Initially intended as a royal palace, Wren's beautifully symmetrical Baroque ensemble was eventually converted into a hospital for disabled seamen in the eighteenth century. From 1873 until 1998 it was home to the Royal Naval College, but now houses the University of Greenwich and the Trinity College of Music. The two grandest rooms, situated underneath Wren's twin domes, are magnificently opulent and well worth visiting. The **Chapel**'s exquisite pastel-shaded plasterwork and spectacular decorative detailing on the ceiling were designed by James "Athenian" Stuart, after a fire in 1799 destroyed the original interior. The magnificent **Painted Hall** features trompe l'oeil fluted pilasters, and James Thornhill's gargantuan allegorical ceiling painting depicting William and Mary handing down Peace and Liberty to Europe, with a vanquished Louis XIV clutching a broken sword below them.

National Maritime Museum

Greenwich's excellent **National Maritime Museum** (daily 10am–5pm; July & Aug closes 6pm; free; Ⓦwww.nmm.ac.uk) houses a vast collection of boats and nauticalia, imaginatively displayed in modern, interactive galleries designed to appeal to visitors of all ages. The glass-roofed, central courtyard houses the museum's largest artefacts, among them the splendid 63ft-long gilded **Royal Barge**, designed in Rococo style for Prince Frederick, the much-unloved eldest son of George II.

The numerous themed galleries of the museum proper are superbly designed to appeal to visitors of all ages, but if you have kids in tow, head for Level 2 which boasts two hands-on galleries: "**The Bridge**", where you can navigate a catamaran, a paddle steamer and a rowing boat to shore; and "**All Hands**", where children can have a go at radio transmission, loading miniature cargo, firing a cannon and so forth.

The **Queen's House** is the focal point of Greenwich's riverside architectural ensemble and an integral part of the Maritime Museum. A bright white Palladian villa flanked by colonnades, it's modest for a royal residence, but as the first Neoclassical building in the country it has enormous significance. Inside, one or two features survive from Stuart times, most notably the cuboid Great Hall, and the beautiful Tulip Staircase, Britain's earliest cantilevered spiral staircase. The rooms now provide a permanent home for the museum's vast maritime **art collection**, including works by Reynolds, Hogarth, Gainsborough and Turner.

Royal Observatory

Greenwich's greatest claim to fame nowadays is, of course, as the home of **Greenwich Mean Time** (**GMT**) and the Prime Meridian. Since 1884, Greenwich has occupied zero longitude – hence the world sets its clocks by GMT. Perched on the crest of Greenwich Park's highest hill, the **Royal Observatory** (daily 10am–5pm; July & Aug closes 6pm; free; Ⓦ www.nmm.ac.uk) sits on the Prime Meridian, housed in a rather dinky Wren-built red-brick building, whose north-eastern turret sports a bright-red time-ball that climbs the mast at 12.58pm and drops at 1pm GMT precisely; it was added in 1833 to allow ships to set their clocks.

The observatory was built to house the first Astronomer Royal, John Flamsteed, whose chief task was to study the night sky in order to discover an astronomical method of finding the **longitude** of a ship at sea, the lack of which was causing enormous problems for the emerging British Empire. Astronomers continued to work here until the postwar smog forced them to decamp; the old observatory, meanwhile, is now a very popular **museum**.

Along the museum's **Meridian route**, you can see Flamsteed's restored apartments and the Octagon Room, designed for royalty to show off to their guests. The Time galleries beyond display four of the marine clocks designed by **John Harrison**, including "H4", which helped win the Longitude Prize in 1763. In the Meridian Building, you get to see several meridians, including the present-day Greenwich Meridian fixed by the cross hairs in Airy's "Transit Circle", the astronomical instrument that dominates the last room.

The museum's **Astronomy route** includes a visit to the new **Astronomy Centre**, housed in the fanciful, domed terracotta South Building. The high-tech galleries here give a brief rundown of the Big Bang theory of the universe, allow you to conduct some hands-on experiments to explain concepts such as gravity and spectroscopy, and then invite you to consider the big questions of astronomy today. You can also choose to watch one of the thirty-minute presentations in the

The Dome

Clearly visible from Greenwich Park, the Dome, or **O2** as it's now known, is a 23,000-seat events arena, designed by Richard Rogers for the millennium celebrations. Over half a mile in circumference, 160ft in height and held up by a dozen, 300ft-tall yellow steel masts, it's the largest of its kind in the world.

state-of-the-art **Planetarium** (daily 11am–4pm; £6), introduced by a Royal Observatory astronomer.

The Ranger's House and the Fan Museum

Southwest of the observatory, and backing onto Greenwich Park's rose garden, is the **Ranger's House** (April–Sept Mon–Wed & Sun 10am–5pm; £5.50; EH), an imposing red-brick Georgian villa that houses an art collection amassed by Julius Wernher, the German-born millionaire who made his money by exploiting the diamond deposits of South Africa. His taste was eclectic, ranging from medieval ivory miniatures to Iznik pottery, though he was definitely a man who placed technical virtuosity above artistic merit. Upstairs, the high points of the collection are Memlinc's *Virgin and Child*, a pair of sixteenth-century majolica dishes decorated with mythological scenes for Isabella d'Este; downstairs, take note of the Reynolds portraits and de Hooch interior.

Croom's Hill, running down the west side of the park, boasts some of Greenwich's finest Georgian buildings, one of which houses the **Fan Museum** at no. 12 (Tues–Sat 11am–5pm, Sun noon–5pm; £3.50; Ⓦ www.fan-museum.org). It's a fascinating little place (and an extremely beautiful house), revealing the importance of the fan as a social and political object. The permanent exhibition on the ground floor traces the history of the materials employed, from peacock feathers to straw, while temporary exhibitions on the first floor explore such subjects as techniques of production and changing fashion.

Dulwich Picture Gallery and the Horniman Museum

Dulwich Picture Gallery (Tues–Sun 10am–5pm; £5; Ⓦ www.dulwichpicture gallery.org.uk; West Dulwich train station from Victoria), on College Road, is the nation's oldest public art gallery, designed by John Soane and opened in 1817. Soane created a beautifully spacious building, awash with natural light and crammed with superb paintings – elegiac landscapes by Cuyp, one of the world's finest Poussin series, and splendid works by Hogarth, Gainsborough, Van Dyck, Canaletto and Rubens, plus **Rembrandt**'s tiny *Portrait of a Young Man*, a top-class portrait of poet, playwright and Royalist, the future Earl of Bristol. At the centre of the museum is a tiny mausoleum designed by Soane for the sarcophagi of the gallery's founders.

To the southeast of Dulwich Park, on the busy South Circular Road, is the wacky **Horniman Museum** (daily 10.30am–5.30pm; free; Ⓦ www.horniman.ac.uk; Forest Hill Overground), purpose-built in 1901 by Frederick Horniman, a tea trader with a passion for collecting. In addition to the museum's natural history collection of stuffed birds and animals, there's an amazingly eclectic **ethnographic collection**, and a **musical department** with more than 1500 instruments from Chinese gongs to electric guitars. Don't miss the museum's state-of-the-art aquarium in the basement, and look out for the special sessions at the **Hands on Base**, which allow you to handle and learn more about a whole range of the museum's artefacts.

Out west: Chiswick to Windsor

Most visitors experience **west London** en route to or from Heathrow Airport, either from the confines of the train or tube (which runs overground at this point), or the motorway. The city and its satellites seem to continue unabated, with only fleeting glimpses of the countryside. However, in the five-mile stretch from Chiswick to Osterley there are several former country retreats, now surrounded by

River transport

From April to October **Westminster Passenger Services** run a scheduled service from Westminster Pier to Kew, Richmond and Hampton Court. The full trip takes three hours one-way, and costs £13.50 one-way, £19.50 return. In addition, Turks runs a regular service from Richmond to Hampton Court (April to mid-Sept Tues–Sun) which costs £6.70 single or £8.20 return. For the latest on boat services on the Thames, see Ⓦwww.tfl.gov.uk.

suburbia, which are definitely worth digging out. The Palladian villa of **Chiswick House** is perhaps the best known of these attractions. However, it draws nothing like as many visitors as **Syon House**, most of whom come for the gardening centre rather than for the house itself, a showcase for the talents of Robert Adam, who also worked at **Osterley House**, another Elizabethan conversion.

The **River Thames**, once known as the "Great Highway of London", runs through these areas and is still the most pleasant way to travel in these parts during the summer (see box above). Boats plough up the Thames all the way from central London via the **Royal Botanic Gardens** at **Kew** and the picturesque riverside at **Richmond**, as far as **Hampton Court**, home of the country's largest royal residence and the famous maze. To reach the heavily touristed royal outpost of **Windsor Castle**, however, you need to take the train.

Chiswick

Chiswick House (April daily 10am–5pm; May–Oct Mon–Wed & Sun 10am–5pm; EH; £5; Chiswick train station from Waterloo) is a perfect little Neoclassical villa, designed in the 1720s by the Earl of Burlington, and set in one of the most beautifully landscaped gardens in London. Like its prototype, Palladio's Villa Rotonda near Vicenza, the house was purpose-built as a "temple to the arts" where, amid his fine-art collection, Burlington could entertain artistic friends such as Swift, Handel and Pope. Entertaining took place on the **upper floor**, a series of cleverly interconnecting rooms, each enjoying a wonderful view out onto the gardens – all, that is, except the **Tribunal**, the domed octagonal hall at the centre of the villa, where the earl's finest paintings and sculptures would have been displayed.

If you leave Chiswick House gardens by the northernmost exit, beyond the Italian garden, it's just a short walk along the thunderous A4 road to **Hogarth's House** (Tues–Fri 1–4pm, Sat & Sun 1–5pm; free), where the artist spent each summer with his wife, sister and mother-in-law from 1749 until his death in 1764. Nowadays it's difficult to believe Hogarth came here for "peace and quiet", but in the eighteenth century the house was almost entirely surrounded by countryside. In addition to scores of Hogarth's engravings, you can see copies of his satirical series *An Election*, *Marriage à la Mode* and *A Harlot's Progress*, and compare the modern view from the parlour with the more idyllic scene in *Mr Ranby's House*.

Syon House

From its rather plain, castellated exterior, you'd never guess that **Syon House** (house: Easter–Oct Wed, Thurs & Sun 11am–5pm; gardens: March–Oct daily 10.30am–5pm, Nov–Feb closes 4pm; gardens £4.50, house and gardens £9; Ⓦwww.syonpark.co.uk), across the water from Kew (see p.128), boasts London's most opulent eighteenth-century interior. The splendour of Robert Adam's refurbishment is immediately revealed in the pristine Great Hall, an apsed double cube

1

with a screen of Doric columns at one end and classical statuary dotted around the edges. There are several more Adam-designed rooms to admire, and a smattering of works by Van Dyck, Lely, Gainsborough and Reynolds adorn the walls. While Adam beautified Syon House, Capability Brown laid out its **gardens** around an artificial lake, surrounding the water with oaks, beeches, limes and cedars. The gardens' real highlight, however, is the crescent-shaped Great Conservatory.

To get here, take bus #237 or #267 to Brent Lea bus stop from Gunnersbury tube and train station or Kew Bridge train station, or else it's a fifteen-minute walk from Syon Lane train station.

Osterley Park and House

Robert Adam redesigned another colossal Elizabethan mansion three miles northwest of Syon at **Osterley Park** (daily 9am–7.30pm or dusk; free), which maintains the impression of being in the middle of the countryside, despite the presence of the M4 to the north of the house. The park itself is well worth exploring, and there's a great café in the Tudor stables, but anyone with a passing interest in Adam's work should pay a visit to **Osterley House** (March–Oct Wed–Sun noon–4.30pm; Dec Sat & Sun noon–3.30pm; NT; £8.80; ⊖Osterley). From the outside, Osterley bears some similarity to Syon, the big difference being Adam's grand entrance portico, with its tall, Ionic colonnade. From here, you enter a characteristically cool **Entrance Hall**, followed by the so-called State Rooms of the south wing. Highlights include the **Drawing Room**, with Reynolds portraits on the damask walls and a coffered ceiling centred on a giant marigold, and the **Etruscan Dressing Room**, in which every surface is covered in delicate painted trelliswork, sphinxes and urns, a style that Adam (and Wedgwood) dubbed "Etruscan", though it is in fact derived from Greek vases found at Pompeii.

Kew Gardens

Established in 1759, Kew's **Royal Botanic Gardens** (daily 9.30am–6.30pm or dusk; £13; Ⓦwww.kew.org; ⊖Kew Gardens) have grown from their original eight acres into a 300-acre site in which more than 33,000 species are grown in plantations and glasshouses. The beautiful landscaped parkland and steamy palmhouses attract over a million visitors every year. There's always something to see whatever the season, but to get the most out of the place come sometime between spring and autumn, bring a picnic and stay for the day.

The majority of people arrive at Kew Gardens tube and train station, a few minutes' walk east of the Victoria Gate. Immediately opposite the gate, the **Palm House** is by far the most celebrated of the glasshouses, a curvaceous mound of glass and wrought-iron designed by Decimus Burton in the 1840s. Its drippingly humid atmosphere nurtures most of the known palm species, while there's a small but excellent tropical aquarium in the basement. South of here is the largest of the glasshouses, the **Temperate House**, which contains plants from every continent, including the sixty-foot Chilean Wine Palm, one of the largest indoor palms in the world.

Elsewhere in the park, Kew's origins as an eighteenth-century royal pleasure garden are evident in the diminutive royal residence, **Kew Palace** (Easter–Sept Mon 11am–5pm, Tues–Sun 10am–5pm; £5), bought by George II as a nursery for his umpteen children. There are numerous follies dotted about the gardens, the most conspicuous of which is the ten-storey, 163-foot-high **Pagoda**, visible to the south of the Temperate House. A sure way to lose the crowds is to head for the thickly wooded southwestern section of the park around **Queen Charlotte's Cottage** (July & Aug Sat & Sun 10am–4pm; free), a tiny thatched summerhouse built in the 1770s as a royal picnic spot for George III's queen.

Richmond Park, Ham House and Marble Hill House

Richmond, upriver from Kew, basked for centuries in the glow of royal patronage, with Plantagenet kings and Tudor monarchs frequenting the riverside palace. Although most of the courtiers and aristocrats have gone, Richmond is still a wealthy district, with two theatres and highbrow pretensions. Richmond's greatest attraction, though, is enormous **Richmond Park** (daily: March–Sept 7am–dusk; Oct–Feb 7.30am–dusk; free), at the top of Richmond Hill – 2500 acres of undulating grassland and bracken, dotted with coppiced woodland and as wild as anywhere in London. Eight miles across at its widest point, this is Europe's largest city park, famed for its red and fallow deer, which roam freely, and for its ancient oaks. For the most part untamed, the park does have a couple of deliberately landscaped plantations that feature splendid springtime azaleas and rhododendrons, in particular the Isabella Plantation.

Back down the hill, if you continue along the towpath beyond Richmond Bridge, after a mile or so, you leave the rest of London far behind and arrive at **Ham House** (April–Oct Mon–Wed, Sat & Sun 1–5pm; £10.40; NT; ⊖Richmond), home to the earls of Dysart for nearly three hundred years. Expensively furnished in the seventeenth century, but little altered since then, the house boasts one of the finest Stuart interiors in the country, from the stupendously ornate Great Staircase to the Long Gallery, featuring six "Court Beauties" by Peter Lely. Elsewhere, there are several fine Verrio ceiling paintings, some exquisite parquet flooring and works by Van Dyck and Reynolds. Another bonus is the formal seventeenth-century **gardens** (Mon–Wed, Sat & Sun 11am–6pm; £3.50, free with ticket for house), especially the Cherry Garden, laid out with a pungent lavender parterre, surrounded by yew hedges and pleached hornbeam arbours. The Orangery, overlooking the original kitchen garden, currently serves as a tearoom.

On the opposite side of the river is **Marble Hill House** (April–Oct Sat 10am–2pm, Sun 10am–5pm. £5; EH), a stuccoed Palladian villa, set in rolling green parkland, built in 1729 for the Countess of Suffolk, mistress of George II for some twenty years and, conveniently, also a lady-in-waiting to his wife, Queen Caroline (apparently "they hated one another very civilly"). The few original furnishings are being slowly added to with reproductions and the place is beginning to have the feel of an eighteenth-century villa. **The Great Room**, on the *piano nobile*, is a perfect cube whose coved ceiling carries on up into the top-floor apartments. Copies of Van Dycks decorate the walls as they did in Lady Suffolk's day, but the highlight is **Lady Suffolk's Bedchamber**, with its Ionic columned recess – a classic Palladian device – where she died in 1767 at the age of 79. In the grounds, there are **open-air concerts** on occasional summer evenings.

Hampton Court

Hampton Court Palace (April–Oct daily 10am–6pm; Nov–March closes 4.30pm. £14; Ⓦhrp.org.uk; Hampton Court train station from Waterloo), a sprawling red-brick ensemble on the banks of the Thames, thirteen miles southwest of London, is the finest of England's royal abodes. Prickling with turrets, castellations, chimneypots and pinnacles, the Tudor **Great Gatehouse** is impressive and would have been five storeys high in its day. Despite the title, the only major survival from Tudor times in **Henry VIII's Apartments** is his Great Hall, which features a glorious double hammerbeam ceiling. The other highlight is the superbly ornate **Chapel Royal**, one of the most memorable sights in the whole palace, with its colourful plasterwork vaulting, heavy with pendants of gilded music-making cherubs.

Mary II's Apartments boast wonderful trompe l'oeil frescoes on the grandiose Queen's Staircase and in the Queen's Drawing Room, where Anne's husband is depicted riding naked and wigless on the back of a "dolphin". The gem of the **Georgian Private Apartments** is in fact the Wolsey Closet, a tiny Tudor room that gives a tantalizing glimpse of the splendour of the original palace. Next door is the **Communication Gallery**, linking the King's and Queen's apartments, now lined with Lely's "Windsor Beauties", flattering portraits of the best-looking women in the court of Charles II. **William III's Apartments**, built at the same time as Mary II's, are even more grand, particularly the militaristic trompe l'oeil paintings on the King's Staircase and the King's Great Bedchamber, which boasts a superb vertical Gibbons frieze and ceiling paintings by Verrio.

Several early Tudor rooms, with striking linenfold panelling and gilded strapwork ceilings, are now used to display **Young Henry VIII's Story**. This is a worthy attempt to portray Henry in his virile youth, during his happy, twenty-year marriage to his first wife, Catherine of Aragon. Last, but not least, are the earthy and evocative **Henry VIII's Kitchens**, which have been restored and embellished with historical reconstructions. To make the most of this route, you really do need to use the free **audioguide**, which helps to evoke the scene with contemporary accounts.

Windsor and Eton

Every weekend trains from Waterloo and Paddington are packed with people heading for **WINDSOR**, the royal enclave 21 miles west of London, where they join the human conveyor-belt round **Windsor Castle** (daily: March–Oct 9.45am–5.15pm; Nov–Feb 9.45am–4.15pm; £16; Ⓦ www.royalcollection.org .uk; Waterloo to Windsor & Eton Riverside train station). Towering above the town on a steep chalk bluff, the castle is an undeniably awesome sight, its chilly grey walls, punctuated by mighty medieval bastions, continuing as far as the eye can see. Inside, most visitors just gape in awe at the monotonous, gilded grandeur of the **State Apartments**, while the real highlights – the paintings from the Royal Collection that line the walls – are rarely given a second glance. More impressive is **St George's Chapel** (Mon–Sat 10am–4pm), a glorious Perpendicular structure ranking with Henry VII's chapel in Westminster Abbey (see p.85), and the second most important resting place for royal corpses after the Abbey. On a fine day, it pays to put aside some time for exploring **Windsor Great Park**, which stretches for several miles to the south of the castle.

Crossing the bridge at the end of Thames Avenue in Windsor town brings you to **ETON**, a one-street village lined with bookshops and antique dealers, but famous all over the world for **Eton College** (Easter, July & Aug daily 10.30am–4.30pm; April–June & Sept daily 1.30–4.30pm; guided tours £6.20; Ⓦ www .etoncollege.com), a ten-minute walk from the river. When the school was founded in 1440, its aim was to give free education to seventy poor scholars and choristers – how times have changed. The original fifteenth-century **schoolroom**, gnarled with centuries of graffiti, survives, but the real highlight is the **College Chapel**, completed in 1482, a wonderful example of English Perpendicular architecture. The self-congratulatory **Museum of Eton Life**, where you're deposited at the end of the tour, is well worth missing unless you have a fascination with flogging, fagging and bragging about the school's facilities and alumni – Percy Bysshe Shelley and George Orwell are among the few rebels in the school's roll call of Establishment figures that contains nineteen Prime Ministers, including David Cameron.

Eating

London is an exciting – though often expensive – place in which to eat out, and as it's home to people from all over the globe, you can sample pretty much any kind of cuisine here. The city boasts some of the best **Cantonese** restaurants in the whole of Europe, and is a noted centre for **Indian and Bangladeshi** food. As well as some excellent French, Greek, Italian, Japanese, Spanish and Thai restaurants, the capital also offers more unusual culinary options, from Polish and Peruvian to Sudanese and Brazilian. And of course, examples of **British** cuisine can be found all over town, from eel and pie caffs to Michelin-starred affairs.

Cafés and snacks

There are plenty of **cafés** and small, basic restaurants all over London that can fill you up for under £10, including tea or coffee. Several of the places listed are also open in the evening (for precise opening hours, phone ahead), but often the turnover is fast, so don't expect to linger – they're best seen as fuel stops. It's worth bearing in mind that most **pubs** (which are covered on pp.136–140) serve meals, and many take their food quite seriously.

Westminster and Whitehall

Café in the Crypt St Martin-in-the-Fields, Duncannon St, WC2 ☎020/7766 1129; see map, pp.80–81. The self-service buffet food is standard fare, but there are regular veggie dishes, and it has a handy (and atmospheric) location.

Jenny Lo's Teahouse 14 Ecclestone St, SW1 ☎020/7259 0399; see map, pp.80–81. Bright, bare and utilitarian yet somehow stylish and fashionable too, *Jenny Lo's* serves good Chinese food at low prices. Be sure to check out the therapeutic teas. Also open eve Mon–Sat; closed Sun.

St James's, Mayfair and Marylebone

Eat & Two Veg 50 Marylebone High St, W1 ☎020/7258 8595; see map, pp.114–115. A modern veggie diner, with an eclectic menu featuring Thai, Greek and Italian dishes; some vegan and soya protein choices.

Inn The Park St James's Park, SW1 ☎020/7451 9999; see map, pp.80–81. The panoramic windows of this curving wooden building look onto the park's lake. The restaurant serves delicious but pricey British food, while the classy takeaway section provides sandwiches, salads and cakes for a top-notch picnic.

Mô 25 Heddon St, W1 ☎020/7434 4040; see map, pp.80–81. Serving reasonably priced and delicious snacks, this is London's ultimate Arabic pastiche tearoom, with tables and hookahs spilling out onto the pavement of a quiet little Mayfair alleyway. Closed Sun.

Patisserie Valerie at Sagne 105 Marylebone High St, W1 ☎020/7935 6240; see map, pp.114–115. Founded as Swiss-run *Maison Sagne* in the 1920s, and preserving its wonderful decor from those days, the café is now run by Soho's fab patisserie makers, and is without doubt Marylebone's finest.

🏃 **The Wolseley** 160 Piccadilly, W1 ☎020/7499 6996; see map, pp.80–81. A lofty and stylish 1920s interior, attentive service and fairly pricey Viennese-inspired food. It's a great place for breakfast or a cream tea, but it's popular, so book ahead.

Soho

Bar Italia 22 Frith St, W1 ☎020/7437 4520; see map, pp.80–81. A tiny café that's a Soho institution, serving coffee, croissants and sandwiches more or less around the clock, as it has done since 1949.

Beatroot 92 Berwick St, W1 ☎020/7437 8591; see map, pp.80–81. Great little veggie café, doling out hot savoury bakes, stews and salads (plus delicious cakes) in boxes of varying sizes – all under £5. Closed Sun.

🏃 **Breakfast Club** 33 D'Arblay St, W1 ☎020/7434 2571; see map, pp.80–81. A laidback Aussie-style place with battered leather couches, offering substantial toasted sarnies, fresh juice, great coffee and free wi-fi.

Jerk City 189 Wardour St, W1 ☎020/7287 2878; see map, pp.80–81. Small Caribbean café that serves up big portions of jerk chicken and ackee and saltfish, as well as takeaway patties. Closed Sun.

Kopi-Tiam 9 Wardour St, W1 ☎020/7287 1113; see map, pp.80–81. Bright, cheap Malaysian café serving up curries, coconut rice, juices and "herbal soups", often to local Malays, all for around a fiver.

Maison Bertaux 28 Greek St, W1 ☎020/7437 6007; see map, pp.80–81. Long-standing, old-fashioned and terribly French patisserie, with tables on two floors (and one or two outside) and a loyal clientele that keeps things busy.

Maoz Vegetarian 43 Old Compton St, W1 ☎020/7851 1586; see map, pp.80–81. Kosher, vegan, late-night place that specializes in falafel in pitta, with a good salad bar and chips to boot.

Nordic Bakery 14a Golden Square, W1 ☎020/3230 1077; see map, pp.80–81. Fill up on crispbreads, cinnamon rolls, rye bread sandwiches and strong coffee at this super-sharp minimalist Scandinavian café.

Covent Garden

Canela 33 Earlham St, WC2 ☎020/7240 6926; see map, pp.80–81. A little Brazilian/Portuguese café-bar that serves up authentic snacks and cakes. The high-ceilinged, chandeliered interior makes it a nice place for a coffee, or you can sit outside and watch the action on Seven Dials.

Food for Thought 31 Neal St, WC2 ☎020/7836 9072; see map, pp.80–81. Long-established but minuscule bargain veggie restaurant and takeaway counter – the food is good, with the menu changing twice daily. Expect to queue and don't expect to linger at peak times.

Monmouth Coffee Company 27 Monmouth St, WC1 ☎020/7645 3516; see map, pp.80–81. The marvellous aroma hits you when you walk in. Pick and mix your coffee from a fine selection, then settle into one of the cramped wooden booths and flick through the daily newspapers on hand.

Rock & Sole Plaice 47 Endell St, WC2 ☎020/7836 3785; see map, pp.80–81. A no-nonsense Turkish-run fish-and-chip shop in central London. Eat in, or out at one of the pavement tables, or take away.

World Food Café 14 Neal's Yard, WC2 ☎020/7379 0298; see map,pp.80–81. First-floor veggie café where the windows are flung open in summer and you can gaze down upon trendy humanity as you tuck into filling dishes from all corners of the globe: Mexican tortillas, Indian thalis or Turkish meze. Closed Sun.

Bloomsbury

Abeno 47 Museum St, WC1 ☎020/7402 3211; see map, p.95. Small Japanese place that special-izes in *okonomiyaki* (£7–12): a cabbage, egg and dough pancake filled with pork, bacon, seafood or tofu, prepared before your very eyes.

Hummus Bros 37–63 Southampton Row, EC1 ☎020/7404 7079; see map, p.95. Hummus and a choice of topping with pitta bread on the side. You sit on benches at red lacquer tables; service is efficient and they often throw in mint tea on the house. Also takeaway. Closed Sat & Sun.

Indian YMCA 41 Fitzroy Square, W1 ☎020/7387 0411; see map, p.95. Ignore the signs saying the canteen is only for students – this place is open to all; just press the bell and pile in. The entire menu is portioned up into pretty little bowls; go and collect what you want and pay at the till. The food is great and the prices unbelievably low.

The City and around

Café Below St Mary-le-Bow, Cheapside, EC2 ☎020/7329 0789; see map, pp.100–101. City café serving imaginative dishes and delicious breakfast pastries in a wonderful Norman crypt. Closed Sat & Sun.

Clark & Sons 46 Exmouth Market, EC1 ☎020/7837 1974; see map, pp.100–101. With Exmouth Market having undergone something of a transformation, it's all the more surprising to find this genuine eel and pie shop still going strong. Closed Sun.

De Gustibus 53–55 Carter Lane, EC2 ☎020/7236 0056; see map, pp.100–101. Award-winning artisan bakery that creates a wide variety of sandwiches, bruschetta, *croques-monsieur* and quiches to eat in or take away. Closed Sat & Sun.

Kurz & Lang 1 St John St, EC1 ☎020/7253 6623; see map, pp.100–101. An *echt* German *Bratwurst* café in a prominent corner site off Smithfield. Choose from a variety of sausages, and help them down with bread, mustard and sauerkraut.

Hoxton

Macondo 8–9 Hoxton Square, N1 ☎020/7729 1119; see map, pp.100–101. Really relaxing Spanish café where you can hang out for hours, fuelling yourself with great tortillas and huge and delicious home-made cakes.

Viet Hoa 72 Kingsland Rd, E2 ☎020/7729 8293; see map, pp.100–101. Light and airy Vietnamese café not far from the Geffrye Museum, serving splendid "meals in a bowl" – soups and noodle dishes with everything from spring rolls to tofu.

The East End

Arkansas Café Unit 12, Old Spitalfields Market, E1 ☎020/7377 6999; see map, pp.100–101. American barbecue fuel stop, using only the very best free-range ingredients. Try chef Bubb's own smoked beef brisket and ribs, and be sure to taste his home-made barbie sauce. Closed Sat.

Brick Lane Beigel Bake 159 Brick Lane, E1 ☎020/7729 0616; see map, pp.100–101. Classic 24hr bagel takeaway shop in the heart of the East End – unbelievably cheap, even for your top-end filling, such as smoked salmon and cream cheese.
Café 1001 1 Dray's Lane, E1 ☎020/7247 9679, ⊛www.cafe1001.co.uk; see map, pp.100–101. Just off Brick Lane, this café has a beaten-up, studenty look, with lots of sofas to crash on and simple snacks and delicious cakes to sample. DJ sets every night; live jazz every Wed.
Rootmaster Ely's Yard, up Dray Walk, E1 ☎07912/389314; see map, pp.100–101. Tasty vegan food from all over the world, knocked up on the ground floor of an old red Routemaster bus; seating upstairs and outside.

The South Bank and Southwark

Café 2 Tate Modern, SE1 ☎020/7401 5014; see map, pp.110–111. Tate Modern's café on Level 2 has modest riverside views, and offers sophisticated British cuisine for around £10 a main course, though you can snack for less. Kids' menu's good, too.
Ev 97–99 Isabella St, SE1 ☎020/7620 6191; see map, p.109. Ev is a busy, buzzy Turkish enterprise with a lovely spacious garden terrace. You can choose between snacking in the deli or going for the full-on restaurant.
Marsh Ruby 30 Lower Marsh, SE1 ☎020/7620 0593; see map, p.109. Terrific filling lunchtime curries for under a fiver: the food is organic/free range and there's a basic but cheery communal dining area at the back.

Kensington and Chelsea

Books for Cooks 4 Blenheim Crescent, W11 ☎020/7221 1992; see map, pp.114–115. Tiny café/restaurant within London's top cookery bookshop. Conditions are cramped, but this is an experience not to be missed. Just wander in and have a coffee while browsing, or get there in time to grab a table for the set-menu lunch (noon–1.30pm). Closed Mon & Sun.
Gloriette 128 Brompton Rd, SW7 ☎020/7589 4750; see map, pp.114–115. Long-established Viennese café serving coffee and outrageous cakes as well as sandwiches, Wiener schnitzel, pasta dishes, goulash and fish and chips.
Hummingbird Bakery 133 Portobello Rd, W11 ☎020/7229 6446; see map, pp.114–115. A cute and kitsch place selling quality American home baking, from prettily garish cupcakes to sumptuous Brooklyn Blackout Cake. Tables outside make for great people-watching.
Lisboa Patisserie 57 Golborne Rd, W10 ☎0871/3327 7010; see map, pp.114–115. Authentic Portuguese *pastelaria*, with the best *pasteis de nata* (custard tarts) this side of Lisbon – also coffee, cakes and a friendly atmosphere.

Camden and Hampstead

Brew House Kenwood, Hampstead Lane, NW3 ☎020/8341 5384; bus #210 from ⊖Archway. Everything from full English breakfast to lunches, cakes and teas, all served in the old laundry at Kenwood, or enjoyed in the sunny garden courtyard.
Café Mozart 17 Swains Lane, N6 ☎020/8348 1384; Gospel Oak Overground. Conveniently located on the southeast side of Hampstead Heath, the best thing about this café is the Viennese cake selection and soothing classical music.
Louis Patisserie 32 Heath St, NW3 ☎020/7435 9908; ⊖Hampstead. Tiny, understated, old-fashioned Hungarian tearoom serving sticky cakes, tea and coffee to a mixed crowd.

Afternoon tea

The classic English **afternoon tea** – assorted sandwiches, scones and cream, cakes and tarts, and, of course, lashings of tea – is available all over London. The best venues are the capital's top hotels and most fashionable department stores; a selection of the best is given below. To avoid disappointment it's essential to book ahead. Expect to spend £15–30 a head, and leave your jeans and trainers at home – most hotels will expect "smart casual attire", though only The Ritz insists on jacket and tie.

Claridge's 49 Brook St ☎020/7409 6307; see map, pp.80–81. Daily 3–5.30pm.
Fortnum & Mason 181 Piccadilly ☎0845/602 5694; see map, pp.80–81. Mon–Sat 2–7pm, Sun 2–5pm.
Lanesborough Hyde Park Corner ☎020/7259 5599; see map, pp.114–115. Daily 3.30–6pm.
The Ritz 150 Piccadilly ☎020/7493 8181; see map, pp.80–81. Daily 11.30am, 1.30, 3.30, 5.30 & 7.30pm.

Marine Ices 8 Haverstock Hill, NW3 ⏲ 020/7482 9003; see map, p.121. Situated halfway between Camden and Hampstead, this is a splendid and justly famous old-fashioned Italian ice-cream parlour; pizza and pasta are served in a kiddie-friendly restaurant.

Greenwich

Biscuit 3–4 Nelson Rd, SE10 ⏲ 020/8858 8588; Cutty Sark DLR. This quirky modern café is great for those with kids: as well as serving soup, toast and cakes, you can paint your own design on their blank ceramics and they'll fire it for you within a week.

Tai Won Mein 39 Greenwich Church St, SE10 ⏲ 020/8858 1668; Cutty Sark DLR or Greenwich DLR/train station. Good-quality fast-food noodle bar that gets very busy at weekends. Decor is functional and minimalist; choose between rice, soup or various fried noodles, all for under a fiver.

Restaurants

Many of the restaurants we've listed will be busy on most nights of the week, particularly on Thursday, Friday and Saturday, and it's best to **reserve a table**. As for **prices**, you can pay an awful lot for a meal in London, and if you're used to North American portions, you're not going to be particularly impressed by the volume in most places. For cheaper eats, see the "Cafés and snacks" section above.

Westminster and Whitehall

Vincent Rooms 76 Vincent Square, SW1 ⏲ 020/7802 8391; see map, pp.80–81. Elegant lunchtime brasserie serving up dishes cooked by the student chefs of Westminster Kingsway College (where Jamie Oliver learnt his trade). Mains under £10 in the brasserie. Closed Sat & Sun, plus July, Aug & Christmas.

Mayfair and Marylebone

The Criterion 224 Piccadilly, W1 ⏲ 020/7930 0488; see map, pp.80–81. This is one of the city's most beautiful places to eat, with a sparkling gold mosaic ceiling and elegant food to match. Three courses for £20. Closed Sun.

Fairuz 3 Blandford St, W1 ⏲ 020/7486 8108; see map, pp.114–115. One of London's more accessible Middle Eastern restaurants, with an epic list of meze, a selection of charcoal grills and one or two oven-baked dishes. Mains £12–20.

Phoenix Palace 3–5 Glentworth St, W2 ⏲ 020/7486 3515; see map, pp.114–115. There's plenty to choose from here with dishes from all over China. Better still, the cooking is good and the portions large. Mains £8–11.

The Providores & Tapa Room 109 Marylebone High St, W1 ⏲ 020/7935 6175; see map, pp.114–115. Outstanding fusion restaurant run by an amiable New Zealander and split into two: snacky *Tapa Room* downstairs and an elegant restaurant upstairs. The food at both is original and wholly satisfying. Mains £18–26.

Soho

Barrafina 54 Frith St, W1 ⏲ 020/7440 1463; see map, pp.80–81. *Barrafina* means thin bar so you'll need to get here early to bag a seat (no bookings taken) in this very popular, stylish tapas bar, which serves superb (though very small) Spanish tapas. Tapas £4–7.

Hakkasan 8 Hanway Place, W1 ⏲ 020/7927 7000; see map, p.95. Impressively designed Chinese restaurant serving novel, well-presented, fresh, delicious and expensive food. Mains £10–40. Closed all Sat & Sun lunch.

Mildred's 45 Lexington St, W1 ⏲ 020/7494 1634; see map, pp.80–81. This has a fresher and more stylish feel than many veggie restaurants, and the stir-fries, pasta dishes and burgers are wholesome, delicious and inexpensive. Mains £8–10. Closed Sun.

Mr Kong 21 Lisle St, WC2 ⏲ 020/7437 7923; see map, pp.80–81. One of Chinatown's finest, with a huge choice of Cantonese dishes and friendly service. There's always something intriguing among the specials – anyone for jellyfish? Mains £8–25.

Tokyo Diner 2 Newport Place, WC2 ⏲ 020/7287 8777; see map, pp.80–81. Friendly place on the edge of Chinatown that shuns elaboration in favour of fast food, Tokyo-style. Minimalist decor lets the sushi do the talking. Mains £6–15.

Wong Kei 41–43 Wardour St, W1 ⏲ 020/7437 8408; see map, pp.80–81. Famous for dispensing large portions of cheap Chinese washed down with free tea. The place is enormous, with communal seating; have a look at the Art Nouveau exterior on the way in. Mains £6–12.

Covent Garden

Masala Zone 48 Floral St, W1 ⏲ 020/7379 0101; see map, pp.80–81. Smart restaurant, decorated with Rajastani puppets, serving modern Indian food, including lots of veggie options. Start with little dishes of "street food", then move on to the well-balanced, richly flavoured curries. Mains £5–15.

Mon Plaisir 21 Monmouth St, WC2 ☎ 020/7836 7243; see map, pp.80–81. An atmospheric and sometimes formidably French restaurant with an intimate vintage feel, serving classic and reliably excellent French meat and fish dishes. The pre- and post-theatre menu is a bargain at £12.50 for two courses, £14.50 for three. Mains £17–25. Closed Sat lunch & Sun.

Sarastro 126 Drury Lane, WC2 ☎ 020/7836 0101; see map, pp.80–81. Busy, over-the-top opera-themed restaurant, where you can hear young starlets perform live (Mon & Sun), while enjoying food from the eastern Med. Mains £9–15.

Bloomsbury

Cigala 54 Lamb's Conduit St, WC1; see map, p.95. Simple dishes, strong flavours, fresh ingredients and real passion are evident at this smart, Iberian restaurant. Mains cost £12–18 and there's a tapas menu (£2–8). Closed Sat & Sun.

La Porchetta 33 Boswell St, WC1; see map, p.95. Tiny, cramped, very loud, very Italian pizza and pasta place that dishes up huge portions (£6–10). Mains £6–10. Closed Sun.

Clerkenwell and Hoxton

Cicada 132 St John St, EC1 ☎ 020/7608 1550; see map, pp.100–101. Bar-restaurant set back from the street with alfresco seating and an unusual pan-Asian menu. Mains £10–17. Closed Sat lunch & Sun.

Medcalf 40 Exmouth Market, EC1 ☎ 020/7833 3533; see map, pp.100–101. A converted turn-of-the-century butcher's shop, fashionably unchic, which serves Modern British cuisine, with fresh ingredients and excellent puds. Mains £9–15.

Moro 34–36 Exmouth Market, EC1 ☎ 020/7833 8336; see map, pp.100–101. Modern, spartan restaurant that's a place of pilgrimage for disciples of the wood-fired oven and those who love food that is both Moorish and more-ish. Mains £16–19.

Saf 152–154 Curtain Rd, E2 ☎ 020/7613 0007; see map, pp.100–101. Modern, shiny new and totally unique vegan restaurant which specializes in exquisitely presented, mostly uncooked fruit and veg dishes. Mains £10–12.

The City

1 Lombard Street 1 Lombard St, EC3 ☎ 020/7929 6611; see map, pp.100–101. A former banking hall in the heart of the City with a spectacular glass dome above the buzzy circular French bar-brasserie, and a more intimate restaurant beyond. Mains (brasserie) £17–25; (restaurant) £25–35. Closed Sat & Sun.

Prism 147 Leadenhall St, EC3 ☎ 020/7256 3888; see map, pp.100–101. Another old banking hall, with the obligatory long bar, suave service and a menu comprising well-judged English favourites with modern influences. The bar menu has Plough-man's and sausage and mash for around a tenner; restaurant mains are in the range £20–30. Closed Sat & Sun.

The East End

Café Naz 46–48 Brick Lane, E1 ☎ 020/7247 0234; see map, pp.100–101. Self-proclaimed contemporary Bangladeshi restaurant that cuts an imposing modern figure on Brick Lane. The menu has all the standards plus a variety of baltis, the kitchen is open-plan, and the prices keen.

Les Trois Garçons 1 Club Row, E1 ☎ 020/7613 1924; see map, pp.100–101. The service can be iffy and the prices for the French cuisine are over-the-top, but then so is the whole experience: the decor's a surreal mixture of fantastic stuffed animals and art installations, and the punters aren't afraid to dress up. Set menus £42–50. Closed Sun.

Tayyab's 83–89 Fieldgate St, E1 ☎ 020/7247 9543; see map, pp.100–101. Smart place serving straightforward Pakistani fare for over thirty years: good, freshly cooked and served without pretension. Prices remain low, booking is essential and service is speedy and slick. Mains £6–10.

South Bank and Southwark

Masters Super Fish 191 Waterloo Rd, SE1 ☎ 020/7928 6924; see map, p.109. An old-fashioned, unpretentious fish-and-chip restaurant, which serves up huge portions with all the trimmings: gherkins, pickled onions, coleslaw and a few complimentary prawns. Mains £7–13.

RSJ 13a Coin St, SE1 ☎ 020/7928 4554; see map, p.109. Regularly high standards of Anglo-French cooking make this a good spot for a meal after or before an evening at a South Bank theatre or concert hall. Mains £11–19.

Kensington and Chelsea

Al Waha 75 Westbourne Grove, W2 ☎ 020/7229 0806; see map, pp.114–115. Arguably London's best Lebanese restaurant: delicious meze, but also mouthwatering main-course dishes. Mains £10–13.

Bibendum Oyster House Michelin House, 81 Fulham Rd, SW3 ☎ 020/7589 1480; see map, pp.114–115. A glorious tiled affair built in 1911, this former garage is a great place to eat shellfish. You can snack in the café for under a fiver, splash out on a *plateau de fruits de mer* for £30 a head at the oyster bar or enjoy a three-course lunch in the restaurant for around £30. Mains £15–27.

Gessler at Daquise 20 Thurloe St, SW7 ⓣ020/7589 6117; see map, pp.114–115. A South Ken institution since 1947, this small Polish café has recently been taken over by the people behind one of Warsaw's top restaurants, and now serves excellent Polish haute cuisine with prices to match.

Gordon Ramsay 68–69 Royal Hospital Rd, SW3 ⓣ020/7352 4441; see map, pp.114–115. The great man may be nowhere to be seen, but his small Chelsea restaurant is a class act through and through – book well in advance and dress up. Three-course lunch £45, dinner £90.

Mandalay 444 Edgware Rd, W2 ⓣ020/7258 3696; see map, pp.114–115. Pure and unexpurgated Burmese cuisine – a melange of Thai, Malaysian and a lot of Indian. The portions are huge, the service friendly and the prices low. Booking essential in the evening. Mains £4–8.

Camden and Hampstead

Jin Kichi 73 Heath St, NW3 ⓣ020/7794 6158; ⊖Hampstead. Eschewing the slick minimalism and sushi-led cuisine of most Japanese restaurants, *Jin Kichi* is cramped, homely and very busy

(so book ahead) and specializes in grilled skewers of meat. Closed Mon. Mains £6–12.

Manna 4 Erskine Rd, NW3 ⓣ020/7722 8028; see map, p.121. Smart vegetarian restaurant serving large portions of very good veggie and vegan food from around the world. Mains £10–13.

Trojka 101 Regent's Park Rd, NW1 ⓣ020/7483 3765; see map, p.121. The East European food here is inexpensive, filling and tasty, and features blinis and caviar, schnitzel and stroganoff, pierogi and pelmeni. Service can be a bit East European as well. Live Russian music (Fri & Sat eve). Mains £6–9.

Chiswick to Richmond

Chez Lindsay 11 Hill Rise, Richmond ⓣ020/8948 7473; ⊖Richmond. A wide choice of galettes, crêpes or more formal French main courses, including lots of fresh fish and shellfish. Mains £10–19.

The Gate 51 Queen Caroline St, W6 ⓣ020/8748 6932; ⊖Hammersmith. Located in a converted church with an outside courtyard that's lovely in summer, *The Gate* serves excellent and original vegetarian and vegan dishes with intense and satisfying tastes and textures. Mains £10–14. Closed Sun.

Drinking

London's great period of **pub** building took place under the Victorians, and genuine examples survive all over the capital, while the rest usually pay some kind of homage to the era. The emergence of **gastropubs**, where the food is as important as the drink, has had a knock-on effect on pubs; it's meant all pubs can now charge (and make) a lot more money out of food, but also that the overall standard of cooking has improved enormously. Alongside pubs, we've also listed a selection of the capital's **bars**, which go in and out of fashion with incredible speed.

Whitehall and Westminster

The Chandos 29 St Martin's Lane, WC2; see map, pp.80–81. If you can get one of the booths downstairs, or the leather sofas upstairs in the more relaxed Opera Room Bar, then you'll find it difficult to leave this cheap Sam Smith's pub.

St Stephen's Tavern 10 Bridge St, SW1; see map, pp.80–81. A beautifully restored, opulent Victorian pub, built in 1867, wall to wall with civil servants and MPs (there's a division bell), and serving good real ales.

St James's, Mayfair and Marylebone

Golden Eagle 59 Marylebone Lane, W1; see map, pp.114-115. Proper old one-room, neighbourhood

pub, with a good range of real ales, and sing-a-longs on the old "Joanna" (Tues, Thurs & Fri).

ICA Bar 94 The Mall, SW1; see map, pp.80–81. Cool late-opening drinking venue, with a noir dress-code observed by the arty crowd and staff. Sweaty DJ nights at the weekends.

Red Lion 23 Crown Passage, SW1; see map, pp.80-81. This is a genuinely warm and cosy local, with super-friendly bar staff, well-kept beer and excellent sandwiches. Closed Sun.

Soho

Academy 12 Old Compton St, W1; see map, pp.80–81. Two-floor retro cocktail bar that's considered one of the best in London; cocktail-school graduates serve up classics and new concoctions. DJs on Fri and every other Wed.

Top 5: Traditional London pubs

▶▶ **The Salisbury** One of the city's best-preserved Victorian pubs, with etched glass and all the trimmings. See below.

▶▶ **Ye Olde Cheshire Cheese** Just about London's most venerable pub, built just after the Great Fire of 1666. See p.138.

▶▶ **Jerusalem Tavern** Characterful converted Georgian coffee house in trendy Clerkenwell. See p.138.

▶▶ **The Black Friar** Fabulously ornate Art Nouveau pub with a monastic theme to the decor. See p.138.

▶▶ **The Holly Bush** Snug wood-panelled local in the picturesque backstreets of Hampstead. See p.138.

Annex 3 6 Little Portland St, W1; see map, p.95. *Annex Trois* (bien sur!) is a bizarre bar, decked with high-camp kitsch and fuelled by an imaginative range of cocktails. Closed Sun.

Argyll Arms 18 Argyll St, W1; see map, pp.80–81. Mobbed by shoppers and tourists alike, but this Victorian pub has preserved its beautifully crafted snugs, separated by mahogany and etched glass partitions, and offers a good range of real ales.

De Hems 11 Macclesfield St, W1; see map, pp.80–81. London's official Dutch pub since 1890. The frequently jam-packed downstairs bar is a simple wood-panelled affair, while the contemporary upstairs space is good for more relaxed drinking. Good selection of mainly Belgian and Dutch beers and food.

Dog & Duck 18 Bateman St, W1; see map, pp.80–81. Tiny Soho pub that retains much of its old character, beautiful Victorian tiling and mosaics, a good range of real ales and a loyal clientele. If it gets too busy downstairs, head upstairs to the George Orwell bar (he used to drink here).

The Social 5 Little Portland St, W1; see map, p.95. Industrial club-bar and diner with great DJs playing everything from rock to rap to a truly hedonistic-cum-alcoholic crowd.

Covent Garden

Cross Keys 31 Endell St, WC2; see map, pp.80–81. Welcoming pub that attracts an appealing blend of older Covent Garden residents, young workers and tourists – you'll do well to find a seat.

Detroit 35 Earlham St, WC2; see map, pp.80–81. Cavernous underground venue with an open-plan bar area, secluded Gaudíesque booths and a huge range of spirits. DJs take over at the weekends. Closed Sun.

Gordon's 47 Villiers St, WC2; see map, pp.80–81. Cavernous, shabby, atmospheric wine bar specializing in ports and sherries. The excellent and varied wine list, decent buffet food and genial atmosphere make this a favourite with local office workers, who spill outdoors in the summer.

Lamb & Flag 33 Rose St, WC2; see map, pp.80–81. Undeniably showing its age (more than 350 years old), this agreeably tatty yet much revered pub is tucked away down an alley between Garrick St and Floral St.

The Salisbury 90 St Martin's Lane, WC2; see map, pp.80–81. Easily one of the most beautifully preserved Victorian pubs in the capital – and certainly the most central – with cut, etched and engraved windows, bronze figures, red velvet seating and a fine lincrusta ceiling.

Bloomsbury

The Lamb 94 Lamb's Conduit St, WC1; see map, p.95. Pleasant Young's pub with a marvellously well-preserved Victorian interior of mirrors, old wood and "snob" screens.

Museum Tavern 49 Great Russell St, WC1; see map, p.95. Large and characterful old pub, right opposite the main entrance to the British Museum, and the erstwhile drinking hole of Karl Marx.

Princess Louise 208 High Holborn, WC1; see map, p.95. Architecturally, this is one of London's most impressive pubs, featuring gold-trimmed mirrors, gorgeous mosaics and a fine moulded ceiling. The Sam Smith's beer is very reasonably priced and there's always a lively crowd.

Clerkenwell and Hoxton

Callooh Callay 65 Rivington St, EC2; see map, pp.100–101. Hidden away off Shoreditch High St, this Jabberwocky-inspired camp-kitsch bar has a Narnia-style wardrobe separating its wacky rooms. Cocktails and wines are the drinks of choice.

Charlie Wright's International Bar 45 Pitfield St, N1 ⓦ www.charliewrights.com; see map, pp.100–101. Part of old-style – rather than trendy – Hoxton, this convivial bar-club, serving decent Thai food, has regular jazz nights and a useful late licence.

Dovetail 9 Jerusalem Passage, EC1; see map, pp.100–101. Marvellous, understated Belgian bar offering 101 varieties of beer (including a dozen or so on tap). The curious decor comprises pew-style seating, green-tiled tables and kitchen-style wall tiling. First-rate Belgian food, too. Closed Sun.

Hoxton Square Bar 2–4 Hoxton Square, N1 Ⓦwww.hoxtonsquarebar.com; see map, pp.100–101. Long-established modern bar and diner with regular gigs and DJ sets. It's generally heaving on the weekend, so get there early to bag a table overlooking the leafy square. Closed Sun

Jerusalem Tavern 55 Britton St, EC1; see map, pp.100–101. Converted Georgian coffee house – the frontage dates from 1810 – that has retained much of its original character. Better still, the excellent draught beers are from St Peter's Brewery in Suffolk. Something of a gem in these parts. Closed Sat & Sun.

Ye Olde Mitre 1 Ely Court, off Ely Place, EC1; see map, pp.100–101. Hidden down a tiny alleyway off Ely Place, this wonderfully atmospheric pub dates back to 1546, although it was actually rebuilt in the eighteenth century. Closed Sat & Sun.

The City

The Black Friar 174 Queen Victoria St, EC4; see map, pp.100–101. A gorgeous, utterly original pub, with Art Nouveau marble friezes of boozy monks and a wonderful highly decorated alcove, all dating from 1905.

The Counting House 50 Cornhill, EC2; see map, pp.100–101. Converted from a bank, with a magnificent interior featuring high ceilings, marble walls and mosaic flooring. The large, oval island bar – above which is an enormous glass dome – offers the full range of Fuller's ales. Closed Sat & Sun.

The Lamb Tavern 10–12 Leadenhall Market, EC3; see map, pp.100–101. Situated in the middle of a beautiful covered Victorian market, it's almost exclusively standing room only (both inside and out) at this super Young's pub. Excellent roast beef, pork and sausage sandwiches at lunchtime. Closed Sat & Sun.

Viaduct Tavern 126 Newgate St, EC1; see map, pp.100–101. Fuller's pub situated across from the Old Bailey, with a glorious Victorian interior from 1869. The red ceiling and walls are adorned with oils of faded ladies representing Commerce, Agriculture and the Arts. Closed Sat & Sun.

Ye Old Cheshire Cheese Wine Office Court, 145 Fleet St, EC4; see map, pp.100–101. A famous seventeenth-century watering hole – chiefly because of patrons such as Dickens and Dr Johnson – with several snug, dark-panelled bars and real fires. Popular with tourists, but by no means exclusively so. Closed Sun eve.

East End and Docklands

The Gun 27 Cold Harbour, E14; South Quay or Blackwall DLR, or ⊖Canary Wharf. Legendary dockers' pub, once the haunt of Lord Nelson, *The Gun* is now a classy gastropub, with a cosy back bar with a couple of snugs, and an outside deck offering an unrivalled view of the Dome.

Prospect of Whitby 57 Wapping Wall, E1; ⊖Wapping. Steeped in history, this is London's most famous riverside pub, with a pewter bar, flagstone floor, ancient timber beams and stacks of maritime memorabilia.

Ten Bells 84 Commercial St, E1; see map, pp.100–101. Stripped-down, pleasantly ramshackle pub, with some great Victorian tiling (and Jack the Ripper associations). Attracts a relentlessly hip and young crowd these days.

Town of Ramsgate 62 Wapping High St, E1; ⊖Wapping. Dark, narrow, medieval pub located by Wapping Old Stairs, which once led down to Execution Dock. Admiral Bligh and Fletcher Christian were regular drinking partners here in pre-mutiny days.

South Bank

Anchor & Hope 36 The Cut, SE1; see map, p.109. Gastropub that dishes up truly excellent, yet simple grub: soups, salads and mains such as slow-cooked pork with choucroute, as well as mouthwatering puds. You can't book a table so the bar is basically the waiting room. Closed Mon lunch & Sun eve.

Kings Arms 25 Roupell St, SE1; see map, p.109. Terrific local on a quiet Victorian terraced street: the front part is a traditional drinking area, while the rear is a tastefully cluttered, glass and wood conservatory-style space. Thai food.

Southwark

The Anchor 34 Park St, SE1; see map, pp.110–111. First built in 1770, this sprawling pub retains only a few vestiges of the past, but it does have one of the few riverside terraces in the centre of town – inevitably it's often mobbed by tourists.

George Inn 77 Borough High St, SE1; see map, pp.110–111. London's only surviving galleried coaching inn, dating from the seventeenth century; expect lots of wonky flooring, half-timbering, a good range of real ales and a fair smattering of tourists.

Lord Clyde 27 Clenham St, SE1; see map, pp.110–111. A genuinely hospitable, family-run boozer, with a good choice of ales, obliging staff and lots of good chatter. Before entering, take a look at the superb frontage, with its cream and green glazed earthenware dating from 1913. Closed Sun eve.

Market Porter 9 Stoney St, SE1; see map, pp.110–111. Handsome semicircular pub by Borough Market, with a vast and interesting range of real ales and decent food. Outrageously popular, as evidenced by the masses that spill out onto the surrounding pavements.

Royal Oak 44 Tabard St, SE1; see map, pp.110–111. Beautiful, lovingly restored Victorian pub that eschews jukeboxes and one-armed bandits, and opts simply for serving real ales from Lewes in Sussex and some good pub grub. Closed Sat lunch & Sun eve.

Kensington and Chelsea

Anglesea Arms 15 Selwood Terrace, SW7; see map, pp.114–115. Charming little local, with hanging flower baskets on the outside and dark wooden tables and green leather benches inside. In addition, there's an elegant dining area to the rear of the bar and a very pleasant courtyard area. There are half a dozen first-class ales on offer, including Brakspear and Hogs Back.

Cooper's Arms 87 Flood St, SW3; see map, pp.114–115. Very fine, popular, easy-going neighbourhood pub, with an attractively under-stated spacious interior, decorated with vintage travel posters and grandfather clocks, and offering first-rate beer and food.

Grenadier 18 Wilton Row, SW1; see map, pp.114–115. Located in a private mews, this quaint little pub was Wellington's local (his horse block survives outside) and his officers' mess; the original pewter bar survives, and there's plenty of military parapher-nalia to gawp at. Classy but pricey bar food.

The Nag's Head 53 Kinnerton St, SW1; see map, pp.114–115. A convivial, quirky and down-to-earth little pub in a posh cobbled mews, with dark wood-panelling, nineteenth-century china handpumps and old prints on a hunting, fishing and military theme. The unusual sunken backroom has a flagstone floor and fires in winter.

The Pig's Ear 35 Old Church St, SW1; see map, pp.114–115. Deep in Chelsea village, *The Pig's Ear* is a sympathetically converted and stylish panelled pub, where you can enjoy a leisurely board game, a pint of Pig's Ear or some classy pub grub.

Victoria 10a Strathearn Place, W2; see map, pp.114–115. Fabulously ornate corner pub, with two open fires, much Victorian brass and tilework, and gold-trimmed mirrors. The Fuller's beer is excellent, too.

Camden Town

Bartok 78–79 Chalk Farm Rd, NW1 ℡020/7916 0595; see map, p.121. Beauti-fully stylish bar where punters can sink into one of the deep red leather sofas and listen to a superb and quite unusual programme of live music, ranging from jazz and world to classical and opera. Acoustic evenings and DJ sets, too.

Lock Tavern 35 Chalk Farm Rd; see map, p.121. Rambling pub with large battered wooden tables, comfy sofas, a leafy upstairs terrace and beer garden down below, as well as posh pub grub and DJs playing anything from punk funk and electro to rock. Effortlessly cool.

Princess of Wales 22 Chalcot Rd, NW1 ℡020/7722 0354; see map, p.121. Smart, popular Victorian pub and restaurant with excellent though pricey food – get here early to eat in the pub, or book a table in the restaurant or lovely back garden.

Hampstead and Highgate

The Flask 14 Flask Walk, NW3; ⊖Hampstead. Convivial Young's pub that retains much of its original Victorian interior, tucked down one of Hampstead's more atmospheric lanes.

The Flask 77 Highgate West Hill, N6; ⊖Highgate. Ideally situated at the heart of Highgate village green, with a rambling, low-ceilinged interior and a summer terrace – as a result, it's very popular.

The Holly Bush 22 Holly Mount, NW3; ⊖Hampstead. A lovely old pub, with a real fire in winter, tucked away in the steep backstreets of Hampstead Village, which can get a bit too mobbed at weekends.

Dulwich and Greenwich

Crown & Greyhound 73 Dulwich Village, SE21; West Dulwich train station from Victoria. Grandiose Victorian pub, convenient for the Picture Gallery, with an ornate plasterwork ceiling and lots of polished wood and stained glass. The two-tiered beer garden is perfect for the summer barbecues that take place here. Young's, Harvey's and London Pride on tap.

Cutty Sark Ballast Quay, off Lassell St, SE10; Cutty Sark DLR or Maze Hill train station. This Georgian pub is the nicest place for a proper riverside pint in Greenwich, and slightly off the well-beaten tourist path.

Greenwich Union 56 Royal Hill, SE10 ℡020/8692 6258; Greenwich DLR & train station. A modern, laidback place with a youthful, unpretentious feel, fine gastro grub and a nice garden. Go for free samples of blonde ale, raspberry beer, chocolate stout or the house Union before committing yourself to a pint.

Chiswick to Richmond

Dove 19 Upper Mall, W6; ⊖Ravenscourt. Wonderful low-beamed old riverside pub with literary associations – Ernest Hemingway and

Graham Greene used to drink here – the smallest bar in the UK (4ft by 7ft), and very popular Sunday roast dinners. Take time to look at the fine selection of black-and-white photos.

White Cross Hotel Water Lane, Richmond; ⊖Richmond. With a longer pedigree and more character than its rivals, the *White Cross* has a very popular, large garden overlooking the river. In winter, you can decamp to the lovely upstairs lounge with its big bay windows and open fire.

Nightlife

On any night of the week London offers a bewildering range of things to do after dark, ranging from top-flight opera and theatre to clubs with a life span of a couple of nights. The **listings magazine** *Time Out*, which comes out every Tuesday afternoon, is essential if you want to get the most out of this city, giving full details of prices and access, plus previews and reviews.

Live music venues

Few cities in the world can match London for the sheer volume and diversity of its **live music**. Quite apart from its array of fine venues and impressive homegrown talent, the city's media spotlight makes it pretty much *the* place for young bands to break into the global mainstream.

General venues

100 Club 100 Oxford St, W1 ☏020/7636 0933, ⓦwww.the100club.co.uk; see map, pp.80–81. Fun jazz venue whose history stretches back to 1942 and takes in Louis Armstrong, Glen Miller and the Sex Pistols. Now mixes mostly trad bands with DJ-led nights.

Brixton Academy 211 Stockwell Rd, SW9 ☏020/7771 3000, ⓦwww.brixton-academy.co.uk; ⊖Brixton. The *Academy* has seen them all, from mods and rockers to Madonna. The 4000-capacity Victorian hall doesn't always deliver perfect sound quality, but remains a cracking place to see mid-level bands.

Cargo 83 Rivington St, EC2 ☏020/7739 3440, ⓦwww.cargo-london.com; see map, pp.100–101. *Cargo* plays host to a variety of excellent and often innovative club nights, from deep house to jazz, and often features live bands alongside the DJs.

Forum 9–17 Highgate Rd, NW5 ☏0207/428 4099, ⓦwww.meanfiddler.com; ⊖Kentish Town. One of the capital's best medium-sized venues, with a decent mix of new acts and groups inching their way onto the nostalgia circuit.

Hammersmith Apollo Queen Caroline St, W6 ☏020/8563 3800, ⓦwww.hammersmithapollo.net; ⊖Hammersmith. The former Hammersmith Odeon is a cavernous, theatre-style venue, host to everyone from Nick Cave to Kenny Rogers, plus stand-up and popular theatre.

Roundhouse Chalk Farm Rd, NW1 ☏0844/482 8008, ⓦwww.roundhouse.org.uk; see map, p.121.

Camden's barn-like former engine shed puts on theatrical spectacles and circus stuff interspersed with live gigs.

Shepherd's Bush Empire Shepherd's Bush Green, W12 ☏0844/477 2000, ⓦwww.shepherds-bush-empire.co.uk; ⊖Shepherd's Bush. Yet another grand old theatre, the *Empire* now plays host to a fine cross-section of mid-league UK and US bands. There's usually a superb atmosphere downstairs, while the upstairs balconies provide some of the best stage views around.

Union Chapel Compton Terrace, off Upper St, N1 ☏020/7226 1686, ⓦwww.unionchapel.org.uk; see map, pp.70–71. Wonderful, intimate venue that doubles as a church, hence the pew-style seating arrangements; the eclectic array of artists ranges from international contemporary stars to world music legends.

Rock, blues and indie

12 Bar Club Denmark St WC2 ☏020/7240 2622, ⓦwww.12barclub.com; see map, pp.80–81. Tiny, atmospheric bar, café and venue offering up-and-coming and often pleasantly eccentric indie acts as well as blues and folk.

Borderline Orange Yard, off Manette St, W1 ☏020/7734 5547, ⓦwww.meanfiddler.com; see map, pp.80–81. Small basement joint with a great sound and a diverse musical policy.

Half Moon Putney Lower Richmond Rd, SW15 ☏020/8780 9383, ⓦwww.halfmoon.co.uk; ⊖Putney Bridge. Long-running pub venue, good for blues, rock and soul. Acoustic on Mon, Jazz on Sun afternoon, folk on Sun night, plus regular cover bands and unsigned showcases.

Luminaire 311 High Rd, NW6 ℡ 020/7372 7123 ⓦ www.theluminaire.co.uk; ⊖ Kilburn. With a cracking music policy that incorporates electronica, world music and the groovier end of indie, plus a strict "no talking when the band's on" rule, this intimate space is one of London's best small venues.

Underworld 174 Camden High St, NW1 ℡ 020/7482 1932, ⓦ www.theunderworldcamden .co.uk; see map, p.121. Popular grungy venue under the *World's End* pub, that's a great place to check out metal, hard core, ska punk and heavy rock bands.

Jazz, world music and roots

606 Club 90 Lots Rd, SW10 ℡ 020/7352 5953, ⓦ www.606club.co.uk; see map, pp.114–115. Located just off the King's Rd, this rare all-jazz venue has a particular focus on home-bred talent. Licensing restrictions mean alcohol can only be served with food.

Jazz Café 5 Parkway, NW1 ℡ 0207/485 6834, ⓦ www.jazzcafelive.com; see map, p.121. Buzzing venue with an adventurous music policy exploring Latin, funk and hip-hop. If you fancy a sit-down book a seat at the restaurant tables. The clubbier late sessions start at 11pm on Fri and Sat.

Pizza Express 10 Dean St, W1 ℡ 0845/602 7017, ⓦ www.pizzaexpresslive.com; see map, pp.80–81. Also known as *Jazz Club Soho*, this chain pizza restaurant hosts consistent quality – with both established and new jazz artists.

Ronnie Scott's 47 Frith St, W1 ℡ 020/7439 0747, ⓦ www.ronniescotts.co.uk; see map, pp.80–81. The most famous jazz club in London, this small and atmospheric place has smartened up its decor and stretched its remit to more pop-oriented acts in recent years. Book for the big names; Wed's midweek jam sessions give the flavour of the place.

Clubs

London remains *the* place to come if you want to party after dark. The sheer diversity of dance music has enabled the city to maintain its status as the **world's dance capital** – and it's still a port of call for DJs from around the globe. Many of the city's **clubs** keep serving until 6am or even later; some are open six or seven nights a week, some keep irregular days, others just open at the weekend – and very often a venue will host a different club on each night of the week; for up-to-the-minute listings, pop into one of Soho's many record shops to pick up flyers or check *Time Out*.

Admission charges vary enormously, with small midweek nights starting at around £3–5 and large weekend events charging as much as £25; around £10–15 is the average, but bear in mind that profit margins at the bar are even more outrageous than at live music venues.

93 Feet East 150 Brick Lane, E2 ℡ 020/7247 5293, ⓦ www.93feeteast.co.uk; see map, pp.100–101. Cheerfully perched in Brick Lane's buzzing epicentre, this engaging small venue hosts indie, soul, electro and funk nights alongside its gigs, particularly on Fri, Sat and Sun nights – there's a daytime session on Sat too.

333 333 Old St, EC1 ℡ 020/7739 5949, ⓦ www .333mother.com; see map, pp.100–101. Rumours of closure haven't dented the popularity of this dressed-down, mashed-up Hoxton club. It's actually two clubs – *Mother* and the *333*, each spinning drum'n'bass, breakbeats and solid, scuzzy four/four.

Aquarium 256–264 Old St, EC1 ℡ 020/7253 3558, ⓦ www.clubaquarium.co.uk; see map, pp.100–101. Big, mainstream (disco, house and pop) venue with a splendid selling point – a good-sized pool and jacuzzi. The rather more hardcore after-hours Sat and Sun events (typically 4–11am) are dominated by electro and minimal techno.

Bar Rumba 36 Shaftesbury Ave, W1 ℡ 020/7287 6933, ⓦ www.barrumba.co.uk; see map, pp.80–81. Fun, smallish West End basement club – one of the few quality venues in the area – whose slant has edged towards guitars since 2008, when long-running indie night Blow Up took over the Sat residency. Tues is salsa and reggaeton, Thurs is R&B and Fri has live bands.

Fabric 77a Charterhouse St, EC1 ℡ 020/7336 8898, ⓦ www.fabriclondon.com; see map, pp.100–101. Despite big queues and a confusing layout that means you may take hours to find friends, jackets and some of its numerous rooms, this 1600-capacity club remains one of the world's finest. Drum'n'bass (most Fri) and techno (most Sat), but also live bands and lengthy DJ line-ups.

Herbal 12–14 Kingsland Rd, E2 ☎ 020/7613 4462, ⓦ www.herbaluk.com; see map, pp.100–101. This intimate venue, with a cool New York-style loft and sweaty ground-floor club, is a great place to check out drum'n'bass and breaks (Fri) and dirty house and electro (Sat).

KOKO 1a Camden High St, NW1 ⓦ www.koko.uk.com; see map, p.121. The old *Camden Palace* has slipped effortlessly back into London's indie club-and-gig scene, with Club NME combining the two in raucous style on Fri nights.

Ministry of Sound 103 Gaunt St, SE1 ☎ 020/7378 6528, ⓦ www.ministryofsound.com; see map, pp.70–710. The vast headquarters of this clubbing brand may sometimes seem peopled largely by corporate clubbers and gawping visitors, but the sound system is exceptional and it gets the pick of visiting DJs.

Notting Hill Arts Club 21 Notting Hill Gate, W11 ☎ 020/7460 4459, ⓦ www.nottinghillartsclub.com; see map, pp.114–115. Basement club that's popular for everything from Latin-inspired funk, jazz and disco through to soul, house and garage, and famed for its Sunday afternoon/evening deep-house session and "concept visuals".

Plastic People 147–149 Curtain Rd, EC2 ☎ 020/7739 6471, ⓦ www.plasticpeople.co.uk; see map, pp.100–101. Scuzzy, thumping basement club whose cheeringly broad booking policy stretches through punk, funk, rock'n'roll, Afro-jazz and dubstep.

Rhythm Factory 16–18 Whitechapel Rd, E1 ☎ 020/7375 3774, ⓦ www.rhythmfactory.co.uk; see map, pp.100–101. This textile factory turned cutting-edge club houses a bar area serving Thai food and two medium-sized rooms.

Scala 275 Pentonville Rd, N1 ☎ 020/7833 2022, ⓦ www.scala-london.co.uk; see map, pp.70–71. Once a cinema, the *Scala* stages some top-quality gigs, usually from established bands, while the weekend club nights take in hardcore rock, dubstep, tech-house and the nostalgia-fest that is School Disco.

Gay and lesbian London

London's **lesbian and gay scene** is so huge, diverse and well established that it's easy to forget just how much – and how fast – it has grown over the last couple of decades. **Soho** is the obvious place to start exploring, with a mix of traditional gay pubs, designer café-bars and a range of gay-run services. Details of most events appear in *Time Out*, while another excellent source of information is the London **Lesbian and Gay Switchboard** (☎ 020/7837 7324, ⓦ www.llgs.org.uk), which operates around the clock. The outdoor event of the year is **Pride London** (ⓦ www.pridelondon.org) in late June or early July, a colourful, whistleblowing march through the city streets followed at the end of the month by a huge, ticketed party in a central London park.

Many of London's gay **cafés**, **bars and pubs** have been around for years, but such is the fickle nature of the scene that some pop up and disappear within months. Our list is by no means exhaustive as every corner of the city has its own gay local. Many cafés and bars transform themselves into **drinking dens** at night and, as some open beyond licensing hours, they can be a cheap alternative to some **clubs**, which open up and shut down with surreal frequency – it's a good idea to check the gay press and listings mags before you set out. Bear in mind that although more and more lesbian bars admit gay men, mixed, as ever, tends to mean mostly men.

Mixed bars

The Black Cap 171 Camden High St, NW1 ⓦ www.theblackcap.com; see map, p.121. Venerable north London establishment offering cabaret and dancing almost every night. The upstairs bar is quieter, and opens onto the Fong Terrace in the summer.

The Box 32–34 Monmouth St, WC2 ☎ 020/7240 5828, ⓦ www.boxbar.com; see map, pp.80–81. Popular, bright café-bar serving hearty portions of simple food to a gay/straight crowd during the day, and attracting a muscly pre-clubbing crowd as the night goes on.

Central Station 37 Wharfdale Rd, N1 ☎ 020/7278 3294, ⓦ www.centralstation.co.uk; see map, pp.70–71. Award-winning, late-opening community pub offering cabaret, cruisey club nights and the UK's only gay sports bar. Mainly men, but Tuesdays see the ladies invade with *Bar Wotever*.

Escape 10a Brewer St, W1 ☎ 020/7734 2626, ⓦ www.escapesoho.com; see map, pp.80–81. Trendy DJ bar in the heart of Soho, attracting a young, mixed crowd and open until 3am Mon–Sat.

First Out 52 St Giles High St, WC2 ☎ 020/7240 8042; see map, pp.80–81. The West End's original gay café-bar, and still

permanently packed, serving good veggie food at reasonable prices. Girl Friday (Fri) is a busy pre-club session for grrrls; gay men are welcome as guests.
Freedom 60–66 Wardour St, W1 ☏ 020/7734 0071, ⓦ www.freedombarsoho.com; see map, pp.80–81. Hip metrosexual place, popular with a straight/gay Soho crowd. The basement becomes an intimate club at night, complete with pink banquettes and glitter balls.

🛦 **George & Dragon** 2–4 Hackney Rd, E2 ☏ 020/7012 1100; see map, pp.100–101. Dandies, fashionistas and locals meet in this lively, often rammed east London hangout. The interior setup is traditional, but then adorned with a fabulous collection of odd trinkets and curios.
Ku Bar 30 Lisle St, WC2 & 25 Frith St, W1 ☏ 020/7437 4303, ⓦ www.ku-bar.co.uk; see map, pp.80–81. The Lisle St original, with a downstairs club open late, is one of Soho's largest and best-loved gay bars, serving a scene-conscious yet low-on-attitude clientele. It's now joined by a stylish sibling bar on Frith St.

🛦 **Retro Bar** 2 George Court (off Strand), WC2 ☏ 020/7839 8760; see map, pp.80–81. Tucked down a quiet alleyway off the Strand, this friendly, indie/retro bar plays 1970s, 80s, rock, pop, goth and alternative sounds, and features regular DIY DJ nights.
The Yard 57 Rupert St, W1 ☏ 020/7437 2652; see map, pp.80–81. Attractive bar with courtyard, loft areas and a laidback, sociable atmosphere. *The Yard* attracts an over-25s crowd and in fine weather it's one of the best spots in the village for alfresco drinking.

Lesbian bars

Candy Bar 4 Carlisle St, WC2 ☏ 020/7494 4041, ⓦ www.candybarsoho.com; see map, pp.80–81. This Sapphic magnet has been in operation since 1996 and still has the same crucial, cruisey vibe that makes it the hottest girl bar in central London. Pole dancing is a regular feature.
Star at Night 22 Great Chapel St, W1 ☏ 020/7494 2488, ⓦ www.thestaratnight.com; see map, pp.80–81. Comfortable venue, popular with a slightly older crowd who want somewhere to sit, a decent glass of wine and good conversation. Open Tues–Sat from 6pm.

Gay men's bars

Compton's of Soho 53 Old Compton St, W1 ☏ 020/3238 0163; see map, pp.80–81. This large, traditional-style pub attracts a butch, cruising yet relaxed 25-plus crowd. Upstairs is more chilled and draws younger folks.
The Kings Arms 23 Poland St, W1 ☏ 020/7734 5907; see map, pp.80–81. London's best-known and perennially popular bear bar, with a traditional London pub atmosphere, DJ on Sat and karaoke night Sun.

Clubs

🛦 **Area** 67–68 Albert Embankment, SE1 ☏ 07500/667 874, ⓦ www.areaclublondon .com; see map, pp.70–71. With two dancefloors, chic decor and impressive laser and light displays, it hosts the after-hours club *Beyond*, as well as offering a London venue for big-name international DJs.

🛦 **Duckie** *Royal Vauxhall Tavern*, 372 Kennington Lane, SE11 ☏ 020/7737 4043, ⓦ www.duckie.co.uk; see map, pp.70–71. Modern, rock-based hurdy-gurdy provides a creative and cheerfully ridiculous antidote to the dreary forces of gay house domination.

🛦 **Fire** South Lambeth Rd, SW8 ⓦ www .fireclub.co.uk; see map, pp.70–71. *Fire* is London's superclub of choice for a mixed though mostly male crowd of disco bunnies. The party runs from Sat night to Sun morning, then on Sun afternoon, and from Sun night to Mon morning.
Heaven *Under the Arches*, Villiers St, WC2 ☏ 020/7930 2020, ⓦ www.heaven-london.com; see map, pp.80–81. Said to be the UK's most popular gay club, this 2000-capacity venue is now home to *G-A-Y* at the weekend, the queen of London's scene nights, with big-name DJs, PAs and shows. More Muscle Mary than Diesel Doris.
Madame Jojo's 8–10 Brewer St, W1 ☏ 020/7734 3040, ⓦ www.madamejojos.com; see map, pp.80–81. Lush, louche club offering cabaret and drag shows for office girls, gay boys and those in between, plus a variety of dance nights. Surrender your gender at Trannyshack on Wed.
Popstarz *Scala*, 275 Pentonville Rd, N1 ⓦ www .popstarz.org; see map, pp.70–71. The ground-breaking Fri-night indie club's still-winning formula of alternative tunes, 1970s and 80s trash, cheap beer and no attitude attracts a mixed, studenty crowd.

Theatre

The **West End** is the heart of London's "Theatreland", with Shaftesbury Avenue its most congested drag, but the term is more of a conceptual pigeon-hole than a geographical term. Despite the dominance of blockbuster musicals and revenue-spinning star vehicles, West End theatres still provide an occasional platform for innovation. The **Royal Shakespeare Company** (ⓦ www.rsc.org.uk) and the

National Theatre often put on extremely original productions of mainstream masterpieces, while some of the most exciting work is performed in what have become known as the **Off-West End** theatres. Further down the financial ladder still are the **Fringe** theatres, more often than not pub venues, where ticket prices are lower, and quality more variable. Below is a selection of some of the city's most interesting venues, large and small. To find out what's on, in addition to *Time Out*, check ⓦ www.londontheatre.co.uk.

Tickets for £10 are restricted to the Fringe; the box-office average is closer to £15–25, with £30–50 the usual top price. Tickets for the durable musicals and well-reviewed plays are like gold dust so book ahead. It's worth looking out for special deals: cheap Monday tickets or standby tickets. The cheapest way to buy your ticket is to go to the theatre box office in person; if you book over the phone or online, you may be charged a booking fee. Students, senior citizens and the unemployed can get **concessionary rates** on tickets for most shows, and many theatres offer reductions on standby tickets to these groups.

The Society of London Theatre (ⓦ www.officiallondontheatre.co.uk) runs **tkts** (Mon–Sat 10am–7pm, Sun noon–3pm), in Leicester Square, which sells on-the-day tickets for all the West End shows at discounts of up to fifty percent, though they tend to be in the top end of the price range, are limited to four per person, and carry a service charge of £3 per ticket.

Almeida Almeida St, N1 ☏ 020/7359 4404, ⓦ www.almeida.co.uk; ⊖ Angel or Highbury & Islington. Deservedly popular Off-West End venue in Islington that continues to premiere excellent new plays and excitingly reworked classics, and has attracted some big Hollywood names.

Barbican Centre Silk St, EC2 ☏ 020/7638 8891, ⓦ www.barbican.org.uk; ⊖ Barbican or Moorgate. The Barbican's two venues – the excellently designed Barbican Theatre and the much smaller Pit – put on a wide variety of theatrical spectacles from puppetry and musicals to new drama works, plus plays by the Royal Shakespeare Company who perform here (and elsewhere in London) on and off from autumn to spring each year.

Battersea Arts Centre 176 Lavender Hill, SW11 ☏ 020/7223 2223, ⓦ www.bac.org.uk; Clapham Junction train station from Victoria or Waterloo. The BAC is a triple-stage building, housed in an old town hall in south London, and has acquired a reputation for excellent productions, from straight theatre to comedy and cabaret.

Bush Shepherd's Bush Green, W12 ☏ 020/8743 5050, ⓦ www.bushtheatre.co.uk; ⊖ Goldhawk Road or Shepherd's Bush. This minuscule above-pub theatre is London's most reliable venue for new writing after the Royal Court, and it has turned out some great stuff.

Donmar Warehouse Thomas Neal's, Earlham St, WC2 ☏ 0870/060 6624, ⓦ www.donmarwarehouse.com; ⊖ Covent Garden. A small central performance space that's noted for new plays and top-quality reappraisals of the classics.

Drill Hall 16 Chenies St, WC1 ☏ 020/7307 5060, ⓦ www.drillhall.co.uk; ⊖ Goodge Street. This studio-style venue specializes in gay, lesbian, feminist and all-round politically correct new work.

ICA Nash House, The Mall, SW1 ☏ 020/7930 3647, ⓦ www.ica.org.uk; ⊖ Piccadilly Circus or Charing Cross. The Institute of Contemporary Arts attracts the most innovative practitioners in all areas of performance. It also attracts a fair quantity of modish junk, but the hits generally outweigh the misses.

Menier Chocolate Factory 51–53 Southwark St, SE1 ☏ 020/7907 7060, ⓦ www.menierchocolate factory.com; ⊖ London Bridge. Great name, great venue in an old Victorian factory; consistently good shows and has a decent bar and restaurant attached.

National Theatre South Bank Centre, South Bank, SE1 ☏ 020/7452 3000, ⓦ www.nationaltheatre .org.uk; ⊖ Waterloo. The Royal National Theatre, as it's now officially known, consists of three separate theatres. The country's top actors and directors perform here in a programme ranging from Greek tragedies to Broadway musicals. Twenty to thirty cheap tickets go on sale on the morning of each performance – get there by 8am for the popular shows.

Open Air Theatre Regent's Park, Inner Circle, NW1 ☏ 0844/826 4242, ⓦ www.openairtheatre.org; ⊖ Baker Street. If the weather's good, there's nothing quite like a dose of alfresco drama. This beautiful space in Regent's Park hosts a tourist-friendly summer programme of Shakespeare, musicals, plays and concerts.

Royal Court Sloane Square, SW1 ☎ 020/7565 5000, ⊛ www.royalcourttheatre.com; ⊖ Sloane Square. The Royal Court is one of the best places in London to catch radical new writing, either in the proscenium arch Theatre Downstairs, or the smaller-scale Theatre Upstairs studio space.

Shakespeare's Globe New Globe Walk, SE1 ☎ 020/7401 9919, ⊛ www.shakespeares-globe .com; ⊖ London Bridge, Blackfriars or Southwark. This thatch-roofed replica Elizabethan theatre uses only natural light and the minimum of scenery, and puts on fun Shakespearean shows from mid-May to mid-September, with "groundling" tickets (standing-room only) for around a fiver.

Tricycle Theatre 269 Kilburn High Rd, NW6 ☎ 020/7328 1000, ⊛ www.tricycle.co.uk; ⊖ Kilburn. One of London's most dynamic fringe venues, showcasing a mixed bag of new plays, often aimed at the theatre's multicultural neighbourhood, and often with a sharp political focus.

Wilton's Music Hall Grace's Alley, off Cable St, E1 ☎ 020/7702 2789, ⊛ www.wiltons.org.uk; ⊖ Tower Hill. A crumbling Victorian music hall, built in 1858, with barley-sugar wrought-iron columns holding up the gallery, intermittently provides a wonderful venue for theatre and music performances.

Comedy

The **comedy scene** continues to thrive in London, with the leading funny-persons catapulted to unlikely stardom on both stage and screen. Just about every London suburb now has a pub stage giving a platform to young hopefuls (full listings appear on ⊛ www.chortle.co.uk and in *Time Out*). Many venues only operate on Friday and Saturday nights, and August can be a lean month, as London's comedians head north for the Edinburgh Festival. Tickets at smaller venues can be had for £7–10, but in the more established places, you're looking at over £10.

Amused Moose Soho 17 Greek St, W1 ☎ 020/7287 3727, ⊛ www.amusedmoose.com; ⊖ Tottenham Court Rd. Top stand-up, and comedy courses too. Every Sat, plus other occasional nights. Branches in Covent Garden and Chalk Farm.

Canal Café Theatre Delamere Terrace, W2 ☎ 020/7289 6056, ⊛ www.canalcafetheatre.com; ⊖ Warwick Avenue. Perched on the water's edge in Little Venice, this venue is good for improvisation acts and is home to the NewsRevue team of topical gagsters; there's usually something going on from Thurs to Sun.

Comedy Café 66 Rivington St, EC2 ☎ 020/7739 5706, ⊛ www.comedycafe.co.uk; ⊖ Old Street.

Long-established, purpose-built club in Shoreditch/Hoxton, often with impressive line-ups, and free admission for the new-acts slot on Wed nights. Wed–Sat.

Comedy Store Haymarket House, 1a Oxendon St, SW1 ☎ 0844/847 1728, ⊛ www.thecomedystore .co.uk; ⊖ Piccadilly Circus. Widely regarded as the birthplace of alternative comedy, the *Comedy Store* has catapulted many a stand-up onto primetime TV. Improvisation by in-house comics on Wed and Sun, in addition to a stand-up bill; Fri and Sat are the busiest nights, with two shows, at 8pm and midnight – book ahead.

Cinema

There are an awful lot of **cinemas** in the West End, but very few places committed to independent films, and even fewer repertory cinemas programming serious films from the back catalogue. November's **London Film Festival** (⊛ www.lff.org.uk), which occupies half a dozen West End cinemas, is now a huge event, and so popular that many of the films sell out soon after publication of the festival's programme. Below is a selection of the cinemas that put on the most interesting programmes.

BFI IMAX South Bank, SE1 ☎ 0870/787 2525, ⊛ www.bfi.org.uk; ⊖ Waterloo. This glazed drum, in the middle of Waterloo roundabout, houses Europe's largest screen. It's stunning, state-of-the-art stuff alright, showing 2D and 3D films on a

massive screen, but, like all IMAX cinemas, it suffers from the paucity of good material that's been shot in the format.

BFI Southbank Belvedere Rd, South Bank, SE1 ☎ 020/7928 3232, ⊛ www.bfi.org.uk;

⊖Waterloo. Known for its attentive audiences and an exhaustive, eclectic programme that includes directors' seasons and thematic series. Around six films daily are shown in the vast NFT1 and the smaller NFT2 and NFT3.

Electric Cinema 191 Portobello Rd, W11 ☎020/7908 9696, Ⓦwww.the-electric.co.uk; ⊖Notting Hill Gate or Ladbroke Grove. One of the oldest cinemas in the country (opened 1910), the Electric has been filled out with luxury leather armchairs, footstools and two-seater sofas.

Everyman Hollybush Vale, NW3 ☎0870/066 4777, Ⓦwww.everymancinema.com; ⊖Hampstead. The city's oldest rep cinema, and still one of its best, with strong programmes of classics, cultish crowd-magnets and directors' seasons. Two screens and some very plush seating.

ICA Cinema Nash House, The Mall, SW1 ☎020/7930 3647, Ⓦwww.ica.org.uk; ⊖Piccadilly Circus or Charing Cross. Vintage and underground movies are shown on one of two tiny screens in the avant-garde HQ of the Institute of Contemporary Arts.

Prince Charles 2–7 Leicester Place, WC2 ☎020/7494 3654, Ⓦwww.princecharlescinema .com; ⊖Leicester Square or Piccadilly Circus. The Downstairs screen here is the bargain basement of London's cinemas (entry for most shows is just £4–5), with a programme of newish movies, classics and cult favourites, plus participatory "singalong" romps.

Classical music, opera and dance

London is spoilt for choice when it comes to **orchestras**. On most days you should be able to catch a concert by one of the five major orchestras – London Symphony Orchestra, Royal Philharmonic, Philharmonia Orchestra, BBC Symphony Orchestra and BBC Concert Orchestra – based in the capital or one of the more specialized ensembles. During the week, there are also **free lunchtime concerts** by students or professionals in numerous London churches, particularly in the City; performances in the **Royal College of Music**, behind the Royal Albert Hall (☎020/7589 3643 Ⓦwww.rcm.ac.uk; ⊖South Kensington), and **Royal Academy of Music** on Marylebone Road (☎020/7873/7373, Ⓦwww.ram.ac.uk; ⊖Regent's Park or Baker Street) are of an amazingly high standard, and the choice of work is often a lot riskier than at commercial venues.

The principal **large-scale venue** is the **Southbank Centre** (☎0871/663 2500, Ⓦwww.southbankcentre.co.uk), where the biggest names appear at the Royal Festival Hall, with more specialized programmes staged in the Queen Elizabeth Hall and Purcell Room. With the outstanding London Symphony Orchestra as its resident orchestra, and with top foreign orchestras and big-name soloists in regular attendance, the **Barbican** (see p.144) is one of the capital's best arenas for classical music. For chamber music, the intimate and elegant **Wigmore Hall**, 36 Wigmore St, W1 (☎020/7935 2141, Ⓦwww.wigmore-hall.org.uk; ⊖Bond Street), is many a Londoner's favourite.

From July to September each year, **the Proms** at the **Royal Albert Hall** (☎020/7589 8212, Ⓦww.royalalberthall.com; see also p.117) feature at least one concert daily, with hundreds of standing tickets sold for around £5 on the night. The acoustics aren't the world's best, but the calibre of the performers is unbeatable and the programme is a fascinating mix of standards and new or obscure works. The hall is so vast that if you turn up half an hour before the show starts there should be little risk of being turned away.

London is extremely well served for **opera**, with two opera houses, both of which have recently been refurbished. The **Royal Opera House** (☎020/7304 4000, Ⓦwww.royaloperahouse.org), in Covent Garden, is the pricier and more conservative of the two, with a fairly standard repertoire performed in the original language (with surtitles), while **English National Opera** at the Coliseum on St Martin's Lane (☎0871/911 0200, Ⓦwww.eno.org), just off Trafalgar Square, puts on lively, radical productions, sung in English.

From the time-honoured showpieces of the **Royal Ballet** to the diverse and exciting range of British and international dance that goes on at **Sadler's Wells**, on Rosebery Avenue (℡0844/412 4300, Ⓦwww.sadlerswell.com; ⊖Angel), and at the much smaller venue, **The Place**, 17 Duke's Rd (℡020/7121 1000, Ⓦwww.theplace.org.uk; ⊖Euston), there's always a **dance performance** of some kind afoot in London. The city also has a good reputation for international dance festivals showcasing the work of a spread of ensembles, the biggest of which is the annual **Dance Umbrella**, a six-week season (Sept–Nov; Ⓦwww .danceumbrella.co.uk) of new work from bright young choreographers and performance artists at venues across the city.

Shopping

From the *folie de grandeur* that is Harrods to the frenetic street markets of the East End, London is a shopper's playground. As befits a city of villages, London's **shopping districts** all have their own flavour, with some known for their specialities and others simply for their location.

In the centre of town, **Oxford Street** is the city's hectic chain-store hotspot, and, together with **Regent Street**, offers pretty much every mainstream clothing label you could wish for. Just off Oxford Street, expensive designer outlets clutter St Christopher's Place and South Molton Street, with even pricier designers and jewellers lining chic **Bond Street**.

Tottenham Court Road is best for electrical goods and, in its northern section, furniture and design shops. **Charing Cross Road** is the centre of London's book trade, both new and secondhand (see below). At its north end, and particularly on **Denmark Street**, you can find music shops selling everything from instruments to sound equipment and sheet music. **Soho** offers an offbeat mix of sex boutiques, specialist record shops and fabric stores, while the streets surrounding **Covent Garden** yield art and design shops, mainstream fashion chains, designer wear and camping gear; Neal Street is the place to go to indulge a shoe-shopping habit.

Just off Piccadilly, **St James's** is the natural habitat of the quintessential English gentleman, with Jermyn Street in particular harbouring shops dedicated to his grooming. **Knightsbridge**, further west, is home to Harrods, and the big-name fashion stores of Sloane Street and Brompton Road.

Books

The biggest bookstore in the capital is Waterstones' Piccadilly branch (⊖Piccadilly Circus), but the largest choice of bookshops is still on **Charing Cross Road**. Here you'll not only find most of the **chain stores** but also the long-established and idiosyncratic Foyles at no. 113–119, with its large feminist section, Ray's Jazz Shop and wi-fi café, as well as **secondhand stores**, including Any Amount of Books at no. 62. For travel books and maps, head to Stanfords, 12–14 Long Acre (Leicester Square tube).

Department stores

Fortnum & Mason, 181 Piccadilly (⊖Green Park or Piccadilly Circus), is fabulous for gorgeously presented and pricey food, plus upmarket clothes, furniture and stationery. **Harrods**, Knightsbridge (⊖Knightsbridge), is an enduring landmark of quirks and pretensions (for more on which, see p.117). Nearby, **Harvey Nichols**, 109–125 Knightsbridge, offers all the latest designer collections and famously frivolous luxury foods. Over at Oxford Circus, several major stores are close at hand, among them: **John Lewis**, 278–306 Oxford St (⊖Oxford Circus), which offers everything from buttons to stockings to furniture and household goods; **Liberty**, 210–220 Regent St (⊖Oxford Circus), founded as a retail outlet for the Victorian Arts and Crafts Movement, and still the main destination for regal fabrics and decorative household goods; and **Selfridges**, 400 Oxford St (⊖Bond Street), London's first great department store, which has a wide range of clothing, food and furnishings.

Markets

Camden Market, running from Camden High Street to Chalk Farm Road (⊖Camden Town), is top of the list for market shopping on most tourist itineraries. The atmosphere is a studenty mix of clubby and grungy and the stuff on sale is mainly cheap clothes and jewellery, though the stalls around Camden Lock are generally more interesting; it runs daily, but weekends are the best – and busiest – times to visit. For a real foody experience, head for **Borough Market** (see p.112). On Sundays, **Spitalfields**, Commercial Street (⊖Liverpool Street), offers good food, but is otherwise more of an arty-crafty market; it now spills over into nearby **Brick Lane**, whose market extends as far as Cheshire Street with everything from sofas and antiques to cheap junk. **Bermondsey (New Caledonian) Market**, Bermondsey Square (⊖Borough, London Bridge or Bermondsey), is a huge, unglamorous but highly regarded Friday antique market that kicks off at 5am. **Portobello** (Fri–Sun), Portobello Road (⊖Notting Hill or Ladbroke Grove), is mostly boho-chic clothes and (Sat only) portable antiques. South of the river, **Greenwich** (Sat & Sun), Market Square (Cutty Sark DLR or Greenwich train station), is another small arty-crafty market worth checking out.

Music

The **biggest store is** HMV, 150 Oxford St (⊖Oxford Circus). For **jazz**, try Ray's on the first floor of Foyles (see p.147). For **indie music**, there's Sister Ray, 94 Berwick St (⊖Oxford Circus or Piccadilly Circus). For **soul, funk**, R&B, rare groove, dance, world music and much more, head for Honest Jon's, 278 Portobello Rd (⊖Ladbroke Grove).

Swimming in London

Hampstead Ponds Hampstead Heath, NW3 ☏020/7485 5757; ⊖Hampstead. The Heath has three natural ponds: the Women's and Men's ponds are on the Highgate side, while the Mixed Bathing Pond is nearer Hampstead. Daily 7 or 8am–9pm or dusk.

Oasis 32 Endell St, WC2 ☏020/7831 1804; ⊖Tottenham Court Road. This place has an indoor and outdoor pool – the water is heated to a bath-like temperature and it's open all year. Mon–Fri 6.30am–10pm, Sat & Sun 9.30am–6pm.

Parliament Hill Lido Gordon House Rd, NW5 ☏020/7485 5757; ⊖Gospel Oak. Beautiful 200ft-by-90ft open-air pool with Art Deco touches and notoriously chilly water. Daily: May to mid-Sept 7am–8pm; mid-Sept to April 7am–noon.

Serpentine Lido Hyde Park, W2 ☏020/7706 3422, ⓦwww.serpentinelido.com; ⊖Knightsbridge. 110 yards of swimming in Hyde Park's lake, plus a paddling pool; deck chairs and sun loungers for hire. Mid-June to mid-Sept daily 10am–6pm.

Listings

Bike rental Barclays Cycle Hire is London's public bicycle sharing scheme, perfect for short journeys, with over 400 docking stations. It's £3 for a key, and £1 for access, after which the first 30min are free, the first hour's £1, increasing rapidly after that to £15 for three hours. Bikes can be rented from the London Bicycle Tour Company, 1a Gabriel Wharf, on the South Bank (☏020/7923 6838, ⓦwww.londonbicycle.com), costing around £20 a day or £50 a week.

Consulates and embassies Australian High Commission, Australia House, Strand, WC2 ⓦwww.australia.org.uk; ⊖Temple. Canadian High Commission, 1 Grosvenor Square ☏020/7528 6600, ⓦwww.dfait-maeci.gc.ca; ⊖Bond Street. Irish Embassy, 17 Grosvenor Place ☏020/7235 2171, ⓦwww.embassyofireland.co.uk; ⊖Hyde Park Corner. New Zealand High Commission, New Zealand House, 80 Haymarket ☏020/7930 8422, ⓦwww.nzembassy.com; ⊖Charing Cross. South African High Commission, South Africa House, Trafalgar Square ☏020/7451 7299, ⓦwww.southafricahouse.com; ⊖Charing Cross. US Embassy, 24 Grosvenor Square ☏020/7499 9000, ⓦwww.usembassy.org.uk; ⊖Bond Street.

Cricket Several Test matches are played in London each summer, normally two at Lord's (☏020/7432 1000, ⓦwww.lords.org; ⊖St John's Wood), the home of English cricket, and one at The Oval (☏0871/246 1100, ⓦwww.britoval.com; ⊖Oval). In tandem with the full-blown five-day Tests, there's also a series of One-Day and Twenty20 internationals, several of which are usually held in London.

Football Over the decades, London's most successful club by far has been Arsenal (☏020/7704 4040, ⓦwww.arsenal.com). However, since the arrival of Russian oil tycoon Roman Abramovich, fellow London club Chelsea (☏020/7386 9373, ⓦwww.chelseafc.com) have had a resurgence, winning the league for the first time in fifty years in 2005. Chelsea's closest rivals (geographically) are Fulham (☏0870/442 1234, ⓦwww.fulhamfc.com), while Arsenal's are Tottenham Hotspur (☏0870/420 5000, ⓦwww.tottenhamhotspur.com). East London's premier club is West Ham (☏0871/222 2700, ⓦwww.whufc.com). Tickets for most Premier League games start at £30–40 and are virtually impossible to get hold of on a casual basis, though you may be able to see one of the Cup fixtures. A better bet is to head to one of London's numerous, less illustrious clubs such as Charlton Athletic (☏0871/226 1905, ⓦwww.cafc.co.uk), Crystal Palace (ⓦwww.cpfc.co.uk), Millwall

(ⓦwww.millwallfc.co.uk) or Queens Park Rangers (ⓦwww.qpr.co.uk).

Hospitals If it's an emergency, you can turn up at the Accident and Emergency (A&E) department of University College London Hospital, Grafton Way, WC1 (⊖Euston Square), or phone for an ambulance (☏999). You can also go to a Minor Injuries Clinic such as the one at St Bartholomew's Hospital, West Smithfield (☏020/7601 7407; ⊖Farringdon), or get free medical advice from NHS Direct, the health service's 24hr helpline (☏0845/4647, ⓦwww.nhsdirect.nhs.uk).

Internet cafés Many hotels and hostels in London have internet access. After that, your best bet is a café with wi-fi like the café in Foyles bookshop (see p.147). Alternatively, log on to ⓦwww.easyinternetcafe.com to find an internet café (£2–5 per hour). In addition, some public libraries offer free access.

Left luggage Left luggage is available at all airports and major train terminals.

Police Central 24hr police stations include: Charing Cross, Agar St ⊖Charing Cross; Holborn, 10 Lambs Conduit St ⊖Holborn; Marylebone, 1–9 Seymour St ⊖Marble Arch; West End Central, 27 Savile Row ⊖Piccadilly Circus; ⓦwww.met.police.uk. The City of London Police are separate from the Metropolitan Police and have a police station at 182 Bishopsgate ⊖Liverpool Street; ☏020/7601 2222, ⓦwww.cityoflondon.police.uk. If there's an incident on public transport, call the British Transport Police on ☏0800/405040.

Post offices The only (vaguely) late-opening post office is the Trafalgar Square branch at 24–28 William IV St, WC2 ☏020/7930 9580 (Mon–Fri 8.30am–6.30pm, Tues opens 9.15am, Sat 9am–5.30pm); it's also the city's poste restante collection point. For general postal enquiries phone ☏0845/774 0740 (Mon–Fri 8am–6pm, Sat 8am–1pm), or visit the website ⓦwww.royalmail.com.

Tennis Tennis in England is synonymous with Wimbledon, the only Grand Slam tournament in the world to be played on grass. The championships last a fortnight over the last week of June and the first week of July. Getting hold of a ticket is a bit of a palaver. On weekdays, if you arrive early enough, you might get one of the 500 day-tickets for the show courts (prices around £40–100); otherwise, if you get there by 9am, you should get admission to the outside courts (where you'll catch some top players in the first week of the tournament), which costs £15–20. Avoid the middle Saturday, when thousands of people camp overnight.

Travel details

Buses

For information on all local and national bus services, contact Traveline ☏0871/200 2233, ⓦwww.traveline .org.uk.

London Victoria Coach Station to: Bath (every 1–1hr 30min; 3hr 30min); Birmingham (every 30min–hourly; 2hr 35min); Brighton (hourly; 2hr 10min); Bristol (hourly; 2hr 30min); Cambridge (hourly; 2hr); Canterbury (hourly; 2hr); Dover (hourly; 2hr 30min–3hr); Exeter (every 2hr; 4hr 15min); Gloucester (hourly; 3hr 20min); Liverpool (6 daily; 4hr 50min–5hr 30min); Manchester (9 daily; 4hr 50min–5hr 30min); Newcastle (5 daily; 6hr 25min–7hr 55min); Oxford (every 15min; 1hr 50min); Plymouth (6 daily; 5hr 20min); Stratford (4 daily; 3hr).

Trains

As a rough guide, Charing Cross handles services to Kent; Euston to the Midlands, northwest England and Glasgow; Fenchurch Street south Essex; King's Cross northeast England and Edinburgh; Liverpool Street East Anglia; Marylebone the Midlands; Paddington southwest England; St Pancras Eurostar, Kent, East Midlands and South Yorkshire; Victoria and Waterloo southeast England and the south coast. For information on all local and national rail services, contact National Rail Enquiries ☏08457/484950, ⓦwww .nationalrail.co.uk.

London Charing Cross to: Canterbury West (hourly; 1hr 40min); Dover Priory (Mon–Sat every 30min; 1hr 40min–1hr 50min); Hastings (2 hourly; 1hr 30min); Rochester (every 30min; 1hr 10min).

London Euston to: Birmingham New Street (every 20min; 1hr 25min); Carlisle (every 2hr; 3hr 15min); Lancaster (hourly; 2hr 30min); Liverpool Lime Street (hourly; 2hr 10min); Manchester Piccadilly (every 20min; 2hr 10min).

London King's Cross to: Brighton (Mon–Sat 4 hourly, Sun 2 hourly; 1hr); Cambridge (every 30min; 45min); Durham (hourly; 2hr 40min–3hr); Leeds (hourly; 2hr 25min); Newcastle (every 30min; 3hr); Peterborough (every 30min; 45min); York (every 30min; 2hr).

London Liverpool Street to: Cambridge (every 30min; 1hr 15min); Norwich (every 30min; 1hr 55min).

London Paddington to: Bath (every 30min–hourly; 1hr 30min); Bristol (every 30–45min; 1hr 40min); Cheltenham (every 2hr; 2hr 15min); Exeter (hourly; 2hr 15min); Gloucester (every 2hr; 2hr); Oxford (every 30min; 55min); Penzance (every 1–2hr; 5hr 30min); Plymouth (hourly; 3hr 15min–3hr 40min); Windsor (change at Slough; Mon–Fri every 20min, Sat & Sun every 30min; 30–40min); Worcester (hourly; 2hr 20min).

London St Pancras to: Brighton (every 20min; 1hr 20min); Canterbury (every 30min; 1hr); Dover Priory (hourly; 1hr 5min); Leicester (every 30min; 1hr 10min); Nottingham (every 30min; 1hr 40min–2hr); Rochester (every 30min; 40min); Sheffield (every 30min; 2hr 10min–2hr 30min).

London Victoria to: Arundel (Mon–Sat every 30min, Sun hourly; 1hr 30min); Brighton (every 30min; 50min); Canterbury East (every 30min–hourly; 1hr 25min); Chichester (Mon–Sat 2 hourly; 1hr 35min); Dover Priory (Mon–Sat every 30min; 1hr 40min–1hr 55min); Lewes (Mon–Sat every 30min, Sun hourly; 1hr 10min); Rochester (every 30min; 45min).

London Waterloo to: Portsmouth Harbour (every 30min; 1hr 35min); Southampton Central (every 30min; 1hr 15min); Winchester (every 30min; 1hr); Windsor (Mon–Sat every 30min, Sun hourly; 50min).

Kent, Sussex and Surrey

CHAPTER 2 # Highlights

✳ **Whitstable** Arty seaside retreat of picturesque clapboard houses and beach huts, famous for its oysters. See p.156

✳ **Canterbury Cathedral** An essential tourist stop stuffed with historical interest – for once transcending the hype. See p.164

✳ **The White Cliffs of Dover** Best seen from a boat, the famed chalky cliffs also offer walks and vistas over the Channel. See p.172

✳ **Walking the South Downs Way** Experience the best walking in the southeast – and some fantastic views – on this national trail, which spans England's newest national park. See p.179

✳ **Rye** Ancient hill-top town, offering some of the best places to stay and eat in Sussex. See p.182

✳ **Royal Pavilion, Brighton** The extraordinary palace of the decadent Prince Regent is the must-see sight in the south's favourite seaside town. See p.190

✳ **Petworth House** As well as being one of the country's most attractive stately homes, this place is home to a splendid art collection. See p.201

▲ Rye

Kent, Sussex and Surrey

The southeast corner of England was traditionally where London went on holiday. In the past, trainloads of Eastenders were shuttled to the hop fields and orchards of **Kent** for a working break from the city; boats ferried people down the Thames to the beach at Margate; and everyone from royalty to illicit couples enjoyed the seaside at Brighton, a blot of decadence in the otherwise sedate county of **Sussex**. **Surrey** is the least pastoral and historically significant of the three counties – the home of wealthy metropolitan professionals prepared to commute from what has become known as the "stockbroker belt".

Since their heyday, many of the old seaside resorts have struggled to keep their tourist custom in the face of ever more accessible foreign destinations combined with the vagaries of the English weather. There has, however, been something of a renaissance in recent years, with various celebrities and other big-city refugees choosing to settle in more congenial surroundings away from the metropolitan hubbub, while the whole region has maintained consistently high standards of both accommodation and gourmet dining. Narrow country lanes and verdant meadows preserve their picturesque charm – much of it now protected in the new **South Downs National Park** – and there are even pockets of comparative wilderness, not to mention the miles of bleak and cliffy coastline.

The proximity of Kent and Sussex to the Continent has dictated the history of this region, which has served as a gateway for an array of invaders, both rapacious and benign. **Roman** remains dot the coastal area – most spectacularly at **Bignor** in Sussex and **Lullingstone** in Kent – and many roads, including the main A2 London–Dover road, follow the arrow-straight tracks laid by the legionaries. When **Christianity** spread through Europe, it arrived in Britain on the **Isle of Thanet** – the northeast tip of Kent, since rejoined to the mainland by silting and subsiding sea levels. In 597 AD Augustine moved inland and established a monastery at **Canterbury**, still the home of the Church of England and the county's prime historic attraction.

The last successful invasion of England took place in 1066, when the **Normans** overran King Harold's army near **Hastings**, on a site now marked by **Battle Abbey**. The Normans left their mark all over this corner of the kingdom, and Kent remains unmatched in its profusion of medieval castles, among them **Dover's** sprawling cliff-top fortress guarding against continental invasion and **Rochester**'s huge, box-like citadel.

Away from the great historic sites, you can spend unhurried days in elegant old towns such as **Royal Tunbridge Wells**, **Rye** and **Lewes**, or enjoy the less-elevated charms of the traditional resorts, of which **Brighton** is far and away the best, combining the buzz of a university town with a blowsy good-time atmosphere and an excellent range of places to eat. The picturesque **South Downs Way** offers an expanse of rolling chalk uplands that, as much as anywhere in the crowded southeast, gets you away from it all. And of course Kent and Sussex harbour some of the country's finest **gardens**, ranging from Kew Gardens' country home at **Wakehurst Place** to the lush flowerbeds of **Sissinghurst** and the great landscaped estates of **Petworth** and **Sheffield Park**.

The commuter traffic in this corner of England is the heaviest in Europe, so almost everywhere of interest is close to a **train** station. National Express services from London and other parts of England to the region are pretty good, but local **bus** services are much less impressive.

Kent

Not so long ago Kent's tourist industry was focused chiefly on the resorts of its northern coast and the **Isle of Thanet**, the northeastern tip of the county. Nowadays these seaside towns have lost much of their gloss, but the county still boasts one of the most popular destinations in the entire country – the county town of **Canterbury**, site of one of the great English cathedrals. Kent can also boast its fair share of alluring castles and gardens, the best known of which are the estate of **Knole**, on the edge of Sevenoaks, **Leeds Castle**, to the east of Maidstone, and **Sissinghurst Gardens**, in the heart of the Weald. Exploration of the county's other scattered attractions – such as Winston Churchill's home at **Chartwell**, **Penshurst Place**, **Hever Castle** or the remnants of the Roman villa at **Lullingstone** – could fill a long and pleasurable weekend.

Transport links from London are good: the A2, M2 and M20 link the Channel ports of Ramsgate and Dover with London, and the country's first high-speed rail line connects the county's key towns to London's St Pancras station. Most of the major towns are well served by daily National Express bus services too, but local rail and bus links are slow.

The North Kent coast

Though most visitors only glimpse the northern part of Kent as they race to or from the Channel ports, the region merits a more prolonged exploration, with all its varied attractions easily accessible from London. There is a knot of historic sites at **Rochester** and **Chatham**, two of the five "Medway towns" – so-called because they are grouped around the River Medway – while the seaside resorts of **Whitstable**, **Margate** and **Broadstairs**, ranging from genteel to seedy, have a growing cachet among weekenders from the capital.

Rochester and around

ROCHESTER, the most pleasant of the Medway towns, boasts one of the best-preserved examples of Norman architecture in England: the **castle** (daily: April–Sept 10am–6pm; Oct–March 10am–4pm; £5), built in the eleventh century by Gundulf, architect of the White Tower at the Tower of London. The stark hundred-foot-high keep glowers over the town, while the interior is all the better for having lost its floors, allowing clear views up and down the dank interior. The foundations of the adjacent **cathedral** (daily 7.30am–6pm; free) were also Gundulf's work, but the building has been much modified over the past nine hundred years. Plenty of Norman touches have endured, however, particularly in the cathedral's west front, with its pencil-shaped towers, blind arcading and richly carved portal and tympanum above the doorway. Some fine paintings survived the Dissolution, most notably the thirteenth-century depiction of the Wheel of Fortune on the walls of the choir.

Rochester's long, semi-pedestrianized **High Street** is a handsome affair, lined with antique shops, cafés and pubs, many of which are housed within appealingly old half-timbered and weatherboarded buildings. The town's most famous son, **Charles Dickens**, spent his youth here, but would seem to have been less than impressed by the place – it appears as "Mudfog" in *The Mudfog Papers*, and "Dullborough" in *The Uncommercial Traveller*. Many of the buildings feature in his novels: the *Royal Victoria and Bull Hotel*, at the top of the High Street, became the *Bull* in *Pickwick Papers* and the *Blue Boar* in *Great Expectations*.

At the northwest end of the High Street, the excellent **Guildhall Museum** (Tues–Sun 10am–4.30pm, plus Mon in Aug; free) is home to a vivid model of the siege of Rochester Castle in 1215 by King John, and a chilling exhibition on the prison ships used to house convicts in the late eighteenth century before the establishment of Botany Bay.

Practicalities

Rochester **train station** is at the southeastern end of the High Street, where you'll also find the **tourist office** at no. 95, opposite the cathedral (Mon–Fri 9am–5pm, Sat 10am–5pm, Sun 10.30am–5pm; ℡01634/843666, ⓦwww.medway.gov.uk). From here you can join a free **guided tour** of the town (Easter–Sept Wed, Sat, Sun & public hols at 2.15pm; 1hr 30min).

As for **accommodation**, you can spend the night with some Dickensian ghosts at the ancient, and somewhat tired-looking, *Royal Victoria and Bull Hotel*, 16–18 High St (℡01634/846266, ⓦwww.rvandb.co.uk; ❸). Decent B&Bs include *Salisbury House*, 29 Watts Ave (℡01634/400182; ❷), a five-minute walk up the hill behind the castle, while the nearest **youth hostel** (℡0870/770 5964, ⓔmedway @yha.org.uk; dorm beds £14, rooms ❶) is at Capstone Farm, Gillingham, two miles southeast of Chatham.

The best **restaurant** in Rochester is *Topes*, just round the corner from the cathedral at 60 High St (℡01634/845270; closed Sun eve, Mon & Tues), which serves up inventive dishes such as sea bass with cardamom jam in a lovely dining room boasting sloping ceilings and wood-panelled walls. For a cup of tea, the cathedral's **tearooms** are an unbeatable spot in summer, with tables spilling out into the cathedral's beautiful gardens. As for **pubs**, the *Coopers Arms* on St Margaret's Street, between the castle and cathedral, serves good lunches in its small beer garden.

Chatham

CHATHAM, less than two miles east of Rochester, has none of the charms of its neighbour and is, in truth, rather a grim place. Its chief attraction is the **Historic Dockyard** (daily: mid-Feb to March & last two weeks of Oct 10am–4pm; April to

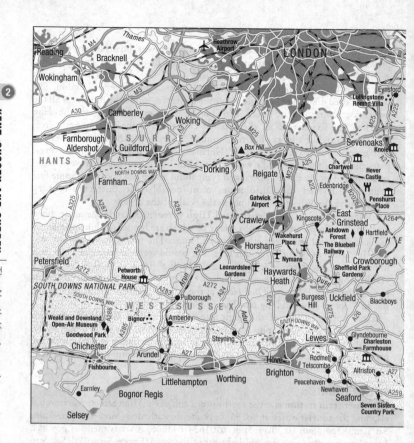

mid-Oct 10am–6pm; £15; ⓦ www.chdt.org.uk), originally founded by Henry VIII and once the major base of the Royal Navy, which commanded worldwide supremacy until the end of the Victorian age; the dockyards eventually closed in 1984. Inside the vast eighty-acre site, attractions include an array of historic ships and some architecturally fascinating buildings, including the former rope-making room – at a quarter of a mile long, it's the longest room in the country.

From the dockyard, **boat trips** run along the River Medway in Britain's last working coal-fired paddle steamer, the *Kingswear Castle*, built in 1924 (summer only; £10; ⓣ 01634/827648). The cruise takes you past **Upnor Castle** (April–Oct daily 10am–6pm; £5; EH), an atmospheric sixteenth-century gun fort built on the river to protect Elizabeth I's fleet.

The dockyard lies about one mile north of the town centre along the Dock Road; it's a fifteen-minute walk from Chatham town centre, or a short bus ride (either from bus stop B at Chatham Station, or take the Dockside Shuttle Bus from the bus station).

Whitstable

One of the few pleasant spots along the north Kent coast and a popular day-trip destination for Londoners, pretty, bohemian **WHITSTABLE** has been farming the oysters for which it is famed since classical times, when the Romans feasted on

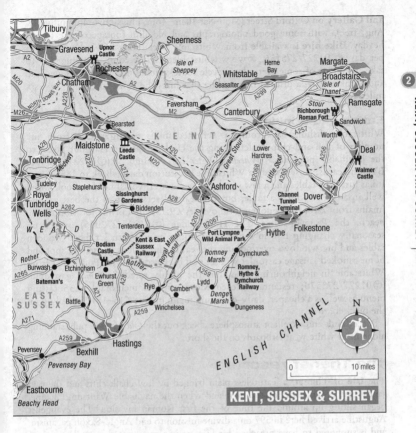

the region's marine delicacies. Oysters are still farmed in the area today – mostly the faster-growing Pacific oysters, which have displaced the original native oysters – but Whitstable is nowadays more dependent on its commercial port, fishing and seaside tourism. The town is at its most lively during the annual **Oyster Festival** (last two weeks of July), featuring lots of crustacean-crunching, jazz and parades.

Arrival and accommodation

Whitstable's **train station** is five minutes' walk along Cromwell Road, east of Oxford Street, the southern continuation of the High Street. For **B&B accommodation**, try the warm and friendly *Copeland House*, 4 Island Wall (℡01227/266207, ⓦwww.copelandhouse.co.uk; no credit cards; ❸), west of the High Street, with a garden that backs onto the beach, or *Victoria Villa*, 1 Victoria St (℡01227/779191, ⓦwww.victoria-villa.i12.com; ❹), a handsome Victorian house with stylish rooms and good breakfasts.

The Town and around

Walking along Whitstable's busy High Street, you'd never guess that you're just a stone's throw from the sea. Follow the signs at the top of the street to reach the seafront, a very pleasant, quiet shingle beach, backed by some pretty weatherboard cottages. For local maritime history, head for the **Whitstable Museum**

and Gallery on Oxford Street (Mon–Sat 10am–4pm, plus Sun 1–4pm in July & Aug; free), with some good photographs and old film footage of the town's heyday. **Bike hire** is available from Whitstable Cycle Hire, 56 Harbour St (£15 per day; ⊕01227/275156, ⓦwww.whitstablecyclehire.com), allowing you to take advantage of some pretty local cycle routes, including the picturesque Crab and Winkle Way, a disused railway line that links the town to Canterbury, six miles away.

Eating and drinking

Whitstable's fishing background is reflected in its **eating** places, from any number of fish-and-chip outlets along the High Street and Harbour Street to the justifiably popular 🍴 *Wheelers Oyster Bar*, 8 High St (⊕01227/273311; BYO, no cards; closed Wed), a Whitstable institution dating back to 1856; since it has just four tables and a few stools at the counter, you'll need to book ahead well in advance to get a table, but the seafood served up is the best around (mains from £18, half a dozen local oysters £9.75). In a prime location by the beach, the *Pearson's Arms*, The Horsebridge (⊕01227/272005), serves up seasonally changing fare in a first-floor dining room with scrubbed wooden tables and big windows overlooking the sea; mains such as goose, old spot and home-smoked sausage cassoulet will set you back around £16. Four miles from Whitstable in neighbouring Seasalter, the highly rated *Sportsman* gastropub (⊕01227/273370; restaurant closed Mon) offers a memorable £55 tasting menu as well as a cheaper, daily-changing menu (mains £15–18) chalked up on the blackboard.

For a **drink** and excellent atmosphere check out the *Old Neptune* pub, standing alone in its white weatherboards on the shore.

The Thanet resorts

The **Isle of Thanet**, a featureless plain fringed by low chalk cliffs and the odd sandy bay, became part of the mainland when the navigable Wantsum Channel began silting up around the time of the first Roman invasion. The evangelist Augustine arrived here in 597 on a divine mission to end Anglo-Saxon paganism, and is supposed to have preached his first sermon at a spot three miles west of Ramsgate – a cross marks the location at Ebbsfleet. Over the next thousand years or so, civilization advanced to the point at which, in 1751, one Mr Benjamin Beale (a resident of Margate) invented the bathing machine, which led to the growth of **seaside resorts**. By the mid-twentieth century the Isle's intermittent expanses of sand had become fully colonized as the "bucket and spade" resorts of the capital's leisure-seeking proletariat. That heyday has long passed, but these earliest of resorts still cling to their traditional attractions to varying degrees.

Getting to the Thanet resorts is straightforward: **trains** and **buses** make the ninety-minute journey from London to Margate, Ramsgate and Broadstairs several times a day, and there are local rail and bus services from Canterbury and Dover.

Margate

MARGATE – memorably summarized by Oscar Wilde as "the nom-de-plume of Ramsgate" – is a down-at-heel assortment of cafés, shops and amusement arcades wrapped around a broad bay. At the resort's peak thousands of Londoners were ferried down the Thames every summer's day, and on a fine summer weekend, the place is still heaving with day-trippers enjoying the traditional fish and chips, candyfloss and donkey rides. The town's depressed fortunes are set to change with the arrival of a spectacular new modern-art gallery, and in preparation hip little cafés and shops are starting to pop up around town.

Arrival, information and accommodation

Margate's **train station** is right by the seafront on Station Road, while all **buses** pull into Cecil Square, a few minutes away. The **tourist office** is nearby at 12–13 The Parade (Mon–Sat 9am–4/5pm; ℡0870/264 6111, Ⓦwww.visitthanet.co.uk). The town is packed with mainly mediocre **B&Bs** but it does have one gem: the uber-stylish ⚞ *Reading Rooms*, 31 Hawley Square (℡07932/611326, Ⓦwww .thereadingroomsmargate.co.uk; ❺), a handsome Georgian townhouse with artfully distressed walls, gorgeous furnishings and huge, luxurious bathrooms. Cheaper is the grand 1920s *Walpole Bay Hotel* on Fifth Avenue in Cliftonville, a few minutes' walk east of the centre (℡01843/221703, Ⓦwww.walpolebayhotel .co.uk; ❸), styled as a "living museum", whose motley exhibits – from urinals to fossils – you can browse around for free. There's a YHA **hostel** at 3–4 Royal Esplanade, by Westbrook Bay to the west of the train station (℡0870/770 5956, Ⓔmargate@yha.org.uk; dorm bed £15; rooms ❶).

The Town

Rearing up on the east side of the harbour, the sleek, modern lines of the **Turner Contemporary** gallery, scheduled to open in spring 2011 (check Ⓦwww.turner contemporary.org for details of hours; admission free), dominate the seafront; within the light-flooded gallery space will be changing exhibitions of contemporary art, and there will be at least one Turner on display at all times. Along the seafront, there's more regeneration at **Dreamland**, Margate's derelict theme park, which is set to reopen in 2011 as a living museum of seaside entertainment; the centrepiece of the traditional fairground rides will be the Scenic Railway, the UK's oldest surviving roller coaster.

Signs of Margate's regeneration can be found in the old town – or "cultural quarter" as it's now styled – where funky little cafés and retro **shops** have been springing up alongside the galleries and studio spaces: have a browse in Helter Skelter Boutique, 13 Market Place (for 1960s and 1970s furniture, homeware and collectables), and Betty B's, at the corner of Broad Street and King Street (for 1940s and 1950s vintage clothing); you can even get a retro hair and make-up makeover at the My Old Dutch salon on Fort Hill. The Ingoldsby Gallery, 2 Lombard St, is a good place to check out local art.

Elsewhere in town, Margate's main attraction is the intricately decorated **Shell Grotto** on Grotto Hill, off Northdown Road (Easter–Oct daily 10am–5pm; Nov–Easter Sat & Sun 11am–4pm; £3), which has been open to the public since its discovery by schoolchildren in 1835. There's also a small but agreeable sandy **beach**.

Eating and drinking

There's no shortage of lovely spots to eat in Margate, including one top-notch, award-winning **restaurant**. Most of Margate's **pubs** are a bit rough around the edges, and it's worth steering away from the seafront: try the tiny Victorian *Rose in June* on Trinity Square instead.

⚞ **The Ambrette** 44 King St ℡01843/231504. Margate's finest restaurant doesn't look like much from the outside, but promises superlative Indian food (mains £13–19). Closed Mon lunch.

BeBeached Harbour Arm ℡01843/226008. For brunch with a sea view you can't do better than an outside seat at this lovely café, in an unbeatable location on the harbour wall. Closed Mon & Tues.

Cupcake Café 3 Market Place. Cute little café in the old town decked out in polka dots and pastels

with tables on the street outside in summer. Closed Sun, plus Mon in winter.

Harbour Café Bar 10 The Parade ℡01843/290110. Hip, bohemian little hideout on the main seafront strip offering excellent coffee, tasty food and top-class jazz nights. Closed Mon; open late Thurs–Sat.

Mad Hatter Tea Garden 9 Lombard St. Eccentric tearoom in the old town, decorated with kitsch royal memorabilia and year-round Christmas decorations. Open Sat 11.30am–4.40pm only.

Broadstairs and around

From its cliff-top setting overlooking the pretty little Viking Bay, **BROAD-STAIRS** is the smallest, quietest and, undoubtedly, the most pleasant of Thanet's resort towns. The town comes to life every year for one of England's longest-standing folk music events, **Broadstairs Folk Week** (middle of Aug; Ⓦwww .broadstairsfolkweek.org.uk), which features singers, bands and dancing in locations around the town, both indoor and alfresco.

Arrival, information and accommodation

It's a ten-minute walk along the High Street from the **train station** to Broadstairs' seafront. The **tourist office** is at the Dickens House Museum (see below; April to mid-Sept daily 9am–5pm; mid-Sept to March Wed–Sat 2–5pm; Ⓣ0870/264 6111, Ⓦwww.visitthanet.co.uk). The nicest **place to stay** is the stylish, relaxed 🏃 *Belvidere Place*, Belvedere Road (Ⓣ01843/579850, Ⓦbelvidereplace.co.uk; ❹), which has beautiful rooms decorated with quirky individual artwork and furnishings. More modest is the *East Horndon Hotel* (Ⓣ01843/868306, Ⓦwww.east horndonhotel.com; ❷) on the Eastern Esplanade.

The Town and around

Broadstairs' main claim to fame is as Dickens' holiday retreat, and throughout his most productive years he stayed in various hostelries here. The **Dickens House Museum**, 2 Victoria Parade (daily: Easter–June, Sept & Oct 2–5pm; July–Sept 11am–5pm; £3), is in the house Dickens used as a model for Betsey Trotwood's house in *David Copperfield*, while the annual **Dickens Festival** (third week in June) features lectures, dramatizations of the author's works and a nightly Victorian music hall.

Viking Bay – the main bay in Broadstairs – is one of several **sandy coves** punctuating Thanet's eastern shore; between Broadstairs and Margate you'll find **Joss Bay**, the southeast's most popular **surfing** beach, with a beach café and excellent surf school (2hr beginner's lessons £35); **Botany Bay**, a quiet and undiscovered gem with rock pools and beautiful white cliffs; and **Kingsgate Bay**, which you can walk to from Botany Bay if the tide is out. A lovely way to reach the beaches is via the **Viking Coastal Trail cycle path** (Ⓦwww.vikingcoastaltrail.co.uk), which winds its way 27 miles around the Thanet peninsula; there's bike hire in Broadstairs at The Bike Shop, 98–100 Albion Rd; other bike-hire outlets are listed on the trail website.

Eating, drinking and entertainment

The diminutive *Oscar Café*, 15 Oscar Rd (July & Aug Tues–Sun; Sept–June Thurs–Sun only), decked out in pastels and bunting, serves up such old-fashioned delights as prawn cocktails, crab pots and Kentish pork pies alongside fabulous

---

Top 5: Outings for kids in the southeast

▸▸ **Broadstairs** Bucket-and-spade fun at Kent's nicest seaside resort. See p.160.

▸▸ **Port Lympne park** Spot elephants and rhinos on Kent's version of an African safari, with game drives and an overnight stay in a safari tent. See p.173.

▸▸ **Bodiam Castle** Travel by steam train to a picture-perfect castle. See p.184.

▸▸ **Drusillas Park** The southeast's best small zoo, by a mile, with plenty of animals and hands-on activities, a miniature railway and two fantastic adventure playgrounds. See p.186.

▸▸ **Ashdown Forest** Follow in the footsteps of Christopher Robin and Winnie-the-Pooh in the original Hundred Acre Wood. See p.199.

cakes. As for **restaurants**, the *Osteria Pizzeria Posillipo* on Albion Street (℡01843/601133) offers excellent pizza, pasta and other Italian standards, with a balcony overlooking the bay, while *Restaurant 54*, 54 Albion St (℡01843/867150; eve only, closed Mon & Tues), dishes up delicious Modern British cuisine in its elegant dining room and courtyard garden. Good **pubs** include *Neptune's Hall* and the *Tartar Frigate*, both on Harbour Street.

Also on Harbour Street, the diminutive Grade II-listed **Palace Cinema** ⓦ www.palacebroadstairs.co.uk) screens art-house films on Tuesday nights and mainstream releases the rest of the week.

Ramsgate

If Thanet had a capital, it would be **RAMSGATE**, a handsome Victorian red-brick resort, most of it set high on a cliff linked to the seafront and harbour by broad, sweeping ramps. Down by the Georgian harbour a collection of cosmopolitan cafés and bars overlooks the bobbing yachts, while the town's small, pleasant beach lies just a short stroll away.

Arrival, information and accommodation

Ramsgate is connected to Broadstairs by frequent **buses**, and its **train station** is about a mile northwest of the centre, at the end of Wilfred Road, at the top of the High Street. The **tourist office** is at 17 Albert Court, York Street (April to mid-Sept Tues–Sat 10am–6pm; mid-Sept to March Wed–Sat 10am–1pm; ℡0870/264 6111, ⓦ www.visitthanet.co.uk). For an overnight **stay**, book into the seafront *Royal Harbour Hotel*, 10–12 Nelson Crescent (℡01843/591514, ⓦ www.royalharbourhotel.co.uk; ❸), two interconnecting Georgian townhouses with a range of stylish rooms (from tiny "cabins" to four-posters with sea views) and a cosy lounge with real fires, newspapers and an honesty bar.

The Town

Housed in the nineteenth-century Clock House on the quayside, the **Ramsgate Maritime Museum** (Easter–Sept Tues–Sun 10am–5pm; Oct–Easter Thurs–Sun 11am–4.30pm; £1.50) chronicles municipal life from Roman times onwards. Its most interesting display is the section on the Goodwin Sands sandbanks, six miles southeast of Ramsgate – the occasional playing arena of the eccentric Goodwin Sands Cricket Club. If you're in Ramsgate midweek, don't miss the opportunity to visit **The Grange**, St Augustine's Road (Wed 2–4pm; by appointment only on ℡01843/596401), former family home of Augustus Pugin, the nineteenth-century architect best known as co-architect of the Houses of Parliament. Built in 1843–44, it was a revolution in house design, and is widely considered to be the first modern house. There's history of a different sort on display at the quirky **Pinball Parlour**, 2 Addington St (Sat & Sun 1–6pm; tokens 30p), where dozens of pinball machines from the 1930s onwards have been assembled under one roof by two pinball fanatics.

Eating and drinking

Among the town's **restaurants**, the *Surin Thai*, 30 Harbour St (℡01843/592001; closed Mon lunch & Sun), scores highly for its reasonably priced, quality Cambodian, Lao and Thai food, while *Eddie Gilbert's*, 32 King St (℡01843/852123; closed Sun eve & Mon), is the best for fish and seafood, serving up everything from fish and chips (from £7) to more imaginative creations such as crispy smoked-eel soldiers with soft-boiled duck egg. No foodie should leave Ramsgate without visiting the excellent ⚶ *Age & Sons*, Charlotte Court (℡01843/851515; closed Sun eve & Mon), which has something for everyone: a relaxed café on the ground floor, a restaurant on the first floor serving incredibly good-value cuisine with a Kentish twist (mains from £10.50), and a sleek and stylish bar in the basement. Finally, for harbour views, real ales and live music, head for the *Churchill Tavern* **pub** on The Paragon.

Canterbury

One of England's most venerable cities, **CANTERBURY** offers a rich slice through two thousand years of history, with Roman and early Christian ruins, a Norman castle and a famous cathedral that dominates a medieval warren of time-skewed Tudor dwellings. The city began as a Belgic settlement that was overrun by the Romans and renamed Durovernum. With the empire's collapse came the Saxons, who renamed the town Cantwarabyrig; it was a Saxon king, Ethelbert, who in 597 welcomed Augustine, despatched by the pope to convert the British Isles to Christianity. By the time of his death, Augustine had founded two Benedictine monasteries, one of which – Christ Church, raised on the site of the Roman basilica – was to become the first cathedral in England.

After the Norman invasion, Christianity increasingly became a tool of control, and a struggle for power developed between the archbishops, the abbots from the nearby Benedictine abbey and King Henry II, culminating in the assassination of Archbishop **Thomas à Becket** in 1170, a martyrdom that effectively established the autonomy of the archbishops and made this one of Christendom's greatest shrines. Geoffrey Chaucer's **Canterbury Tales**, written in the fourteenth century, portrays the unexpectedly festive nature of pilgrimages to Becket's tomb. Today the cathedral and compact town centre, enclosed on three sides by medieval walls, remain the focus for leisure-motivated pilgrims from across the globe.

Arrival, information and tours

Canterbury has two **train stations**, Canterbury East for services from London Victoria and Dover Priory, and Canterbury West for services from London St Pancras, London Charing Cross and the Isle of Thanet – each a ten-minute walk from the cathedral. National Express services and local **buses** use the bus station on St George's Lane. **Parking** can be problematic and drivers are best advised to use the signposted park-and-ride services available on Wincheap, Sturry Road and New Dover Road. The busy **tourist office** is in the Butter Market at 12–13 Sun St (Mon–Sat 9am–5.30pm, Sun 10am–5pm; ℡01227/378100, ⑩www .canterbury.co.uk), opposite the main entrance to the cathedral. For **internet** access, go to Dot Café, St Dunstans Street (daily 9am–9pm).

Canterbury is compact enough to find your own way around, but there are various **tours** available. The Guild of Guides runs informative walking tours of the city, leaving from the tourist office (daily: April–June & Oct 11am; July–Sept 11am & 2pm; 1hr 30min; £6), while the Canterbury Ghost Tour (Fri & Sat 8pm; 1hr 30min; £8) is a spicy mix of the supernatural and local folklore, leaving from *Alberry's Wine Bar* in St Margaret's Street. Alternatively, you can take a **boat trip** along the Stour – boats depart from the bridge next to Weaver's House (March–Oct daily 10am–5pm; 40min; ℡07790/534744; £7.50) – or hire a **chauffeured punt** at West Gate (Easter–Oct daily 10am–late; 35–65min; ℡07816/760869; from £8). **Bikes** can be rented from Downland Cycles on Malthouse Road, off St Stephens Road, a ten-minute walk from West Gate (℡01227/479643; £15 per day).

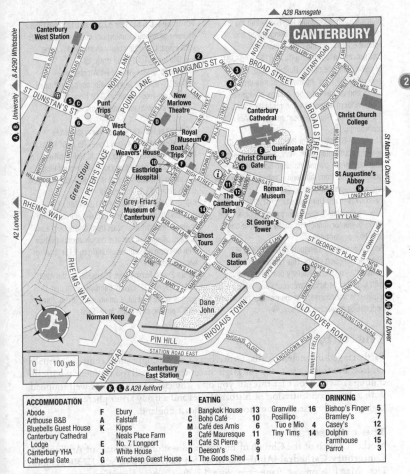

ACCOMMODATION		EATING				DRINKING	
Abode	F	Bangkok House	13	Granville	16	Bishop's Finger	5
Arthouse B&B	A	Boho Café	10	Posillipo		Bramley's	7
Bluebells Guest House	K	Café des Amis	6	Tuo e Mio	4	Casey's	12
Canterbury Cathedral Lodge	E	Café Mauresque	11	Tiny Tims	14	Dolphin	2
Canterbury YHA	J	Café St Pierre	8			Farmhouse	15
Cathedral Gate	G	Deeson's	9			Parrot	3
Ebury	C	The Goods Shed	1				
Falstaff							
Kipps							
Neals Place Farm	M						
No. 7 Longport	H						
White House	D						
Wincheap Guest House	L						

Accommodation

In the city centre, some old **hotels** offer all the creaking, authentic antiquity you could ask for, while there's a host of cheaper **B&Bs** to be found just outside the city walls.

Hotels and B&Bs

Abode 30 High St ☏ 01227/766266, ⓦ www
.abodehotels.co.uk/canterbury. The standard rooms
are very ordinary at this boutique hotel, but special
offers make a stay more reasonable. The priciest
rooms come with balconies overlooking the
cathedral, and there's also a top-notch restaurant
and champagne bar. ⑤

Arthouse B&B 24 London Rd ☏ 01227/
453032, ⓦ www.arthousebandb.com. Quirky,
artist-owned B&B situated in the old fire station, five
minutes' walk from West Gate. Two stylish double

rooms (each with private bathroom) share a lounge
and kitchen – or you can rent both rooms and have
the whole building to yourself. Excellent value. ②
Bluebells Guest House 248 Wincheap
☏ 01227/478842, ⓦ www.canterburybluebells
.com. Lovely Victorian B&B, fifteen minutes' walk
from the centre, with lots of original features,
stylishly decked-out rooms, and nice extra touches
like robes and fresh flowers in the rooms. ②
Canterbury Cathedral Lodge The Precincts
☏ 01227/865350, ⓦ www.canterburycathedral
lodge.org. Modern hotel with unfussy, contemporary

rooms and an unbeatable location within the grounds of the cathedral. Booking ahead and special offers bring the rates down. ❹
Cathedral Gate 36 Burgate ☎01227/464381, ⓦwww.cathgate.co.uk. Built in 1438, this venerable pilgrims' hostelry features crooked floors and exposed timber beams alongside more modern amenities and fantastic views of the cathedral. The cheapest rooms share bathrooms. ❸
Ebury 65–67 New Dover Rd ☎01227/768433, ⓦwww.eburyhotel.co.uk. Very comfortable and spacious family-owned Victorian hotel, fifteen minutes' walk from the centre, with an indoor pool and well-appointed rooms. ❹
Falstaff 8–10 St Dunstan's St ☎01227/462138, ⓦwww.thefalstaffincanterbury.com. Popular fifteenth-century coaching inn by the West Gate, with four-poster beds. ❹
No. 7 Longport 7 Longport ☎01227/455367, ⓦwww.7longport.co.uk. This fabulous little hideaway – a tiny, beautifully presented cottage with a double bedroom, wet room and lounge – is situated in the courtyard of the owners' home, just opposite St Augustine's Abbey. ❸

White House 6 St Peter's Lane ☎01227/761836, ⓦwww.whitehousecanterbury.co.uk. Popular B&B with elegant, contemporary rooms and a great location just off the main drag. ❸
Wincheap Guest House 94 Wincheap ☎01227/762309, ⓦwww.wincheapguesthouse .com. Good-value Victorian B&B close to Canterbury East Station, with en-suite rooms. ❷

Hostels and campsite
Canterbury YHA 54 New Dover Rd ☎0845/371 9010, ⓔcanterbury@yha.org.uk. Half a mile out of town, and 15min on foot from Canterbury East Station, this friendly hostel is set in a Victorian villa. Dorm beds £13.50, rooms ❶
Kipps 40 Nunnery Fields ☎01227/786121, ⓦwww.kipps-hostel.com. Popular self-catering hostel a few minutes' walk from Canterbury East Station, offering single and double rooms (❶) as well as dorm accommodation (from £16). Internet access available.
Neals Place Farm Neals Place Rd, off the A290 ☎01227/765632. Lovely campsite with just 18 pitches in the middle of an orchard, just a 20min walk from the city. Open April–Sept.

The City

Partly ringed by ancient **walls**, Canterbury's surprisingly small centre is virtually car free, but this doesn't stop the High Street seizing up all too frequently with the milling crowds. Don't let this put you off – the city's popularity is well founded, with a dense concentration of historical sites and a lively atmosphere, making it a highly rewarding stop on any tour of southeast England.

The cathedral

Mother Church of the Church of England and seat of the Primate of All England, **Canterbury Cathedral** (April–Oct Mon–Sat 9am–5.30pm, Sun 12.30–2.30pm; Nov–March Mon–Sat 9am–5pm, Sun 12.30–2.30pm; closed on some days in mid-July for university graduation ceremonies; £8; ⓦwww.canterbury -cathedral.org) fills the northeast quadrant of the old city with a befitting sense of authority. A cathedral has stood here since 602, but in 1070 the first Norman archbishop, Lanfranc, levelled the original Saxon structure to build a new cathedral. Over successive centuries the masterpiece was heavily modified, with the puritanical lines of the Perpendicular style gaining ascendancy in late medieval times. Though architecturally it's perhaps not among the country's most impressive, the cathedral derives its distinctiveness from the thrust of the 235-foot-high Bell Harry Tower, completed in 1505. The precincts (daily 7am–9pm) are entered through the superbly ornate early sixteenth-century **Christ Church Gate**, where Burgate and Mercery Lane meet. This junction, the city's medieval core, is known as the Buttermarket; here, religious relics were once sold to pilgrims hoping to prevent an eternity in damnation. Having paid your entrance fee, you pass through the gatehouse and get one of the finest views of the cathedral, foreshortened and crowned with soaring towers and pinnacles.

Once in the magnificent **interior**, look for the tomb of Henry IV and his wife, Joan of Navarre, and for the gilded effigy of Edward III's son, the Black Prince, all

Thomas à Becket and the Canterbury Tales

Appointed Archbishop of Canterbury in 1162 by his good friend and drinking partner Henry II, **Thomas à Becket** fell out with the king when the latter attempted to impose his jurisdiction over that of the Church. After a six-year spell in France, Becket was reconciled with Henry and returned home in 1170 – only to incur the king's wrath once more by refusing to absolve two bishops whom he had previously excommunicated, provoking Henry to utter the well-known words, "Will no one rid me of this turbulent priest?" Four knights took it upon themselves to seek out Becket and, finding him at prayer in the cathedral, murdered him on the spot. Almost immediately miracles were said to occur at his tomb, and Becket was canonized in 1173, by which time a steady stream of pilgrims had already begun to arrive at the shrine.

One such pilgrimage provided the setting for Geoffrey Chaucer's **Canterbury Tales**. Written between 1387 and 1400, the *Tales* are a collection of stories within a story, in which a group of thirty pilgrims exchange a series of fantastic yarns to while away the time as they journey. The group is a colourful cross-section of medieval society, including a knight, a monk, a miller, a squire and the oft-widowed Wife of Bath. Chaucer chose to write their earthy and often raunchy stories in English – at a time when French was very much the language of literature – and this, combined with their universal themes, has ensured their continuing popularity today.

of them to be found in the Trinity Chapel, behind the main altar. Also here, until demolished by Henry VIII's act of ecclesiastical vandalism in 1538, was the shrine of Thomas à Becket; the actual spot where he died, known as "The Martyrdom", is marked by the **Altar of the Sword's Point** in the northwest transept, where a jagged sculpture of the assassins' weapons is suspended on the wall. Steps from here descend to the low, Romanesque arches of the **crypt**, one of the few remaining relics of the Norman cathedral and considered the finest such structure in the country, with some amazingly well-preserved carvings on the capitals of the columns. Back upstairs, look out for the vivid medieval **stained glass**, much of which dates back to the twelfth and thirteenth centuries, notably in the Trinity Chapel, where the life and miraculous works of Thomas à Becket are depicted. Contemporary with the windows (1220) is the white marble **St Augustine's Chair** on which all archbishops of Canterbury are enthroned; it's located in the choir at the top of the steps beyond the high altar.

On the cathedral's north flank are the fan-vaulted colonnades of the **Great Cloister**, from where you enter the **Chapter House**, with its intricate web of fourteenth-century tracery supporting the roof and a wall of stained glass.

St Augustine's Abbey and St Martin's Church

Passing through the cathedral grounds and out through the city walls at the (exit-only) Queningate, you come to the vestigial remains of **St Augustine's Abbey** (April–June Wed–Sun 10am–5pm; July & Aug daily 10am–6pm; Sept & Oct Sat & Sun 11am–5pm; Nov–March Sat & Sun 11am–4pm; £4.50; EH), occupying the site of the church founded by Augustine in 598. It was built outside the city because of a Christian tradition that forbade burials within the walls, and became the final resting place of Augustine, Ethelbert and successive archbishops and kings of Kent, although no trace remains either of them or of the original Saxon church. Shortly after the Normans arrived, the church was demolished in the same building frenzy that saw the creation of the cathedral. It was replaced by a much larger abbey, most of which was destroyed in the Dissolution so that today only the ruins and foundations remain. To help bring the site to life, pick up an audioguide from the abbey's excellent interpretive centre.

Nearby, on the corner of North Holmes Road and St Martin's Lane is **St Martin's Church** (Tues, Thurs & Sat 10am–3pm, Sun 9.50–10.30am; free), one of England's oldest churches, built on the site of a Roman villa or temple and used by the earliest Christians. Although medieval additions obscure the original Saxon structure, this is perhaps the earliest Christian site in Canterbury – it was here that Queen Bertha welcomed St Augustine in 597, and her husband King Ethelbert was baptized.

Along the High Street and St Peter's Street

For the most part, the **High Street** is lined with picturesque and ancient buildings – the view up Mercery Lane towards Christ Church Gate is one of the most photographed scenes in the city: a narrow, medieval street of crooked, overhanging houses behind which loom the turreted gatehouse and the cathedral's towers.

Just before High Street becomes St Peter's Street, you come to the **Royal Museum and Art Gallery** (closed for refurbishment until summer 2011), housed on the first floor of a superbly preserved mock-Tudor building. Once reopened, the museum will house natural history displays, military memorabilia and an art collection that includes the odd Henry Moore and Gainsborough, as well as the city's library.

Where the street passes over a branch of the River Stour stands **Eastbridge Hospital** (Mon–Sat 10am–5pm; £1), founded in the twelfth century to provide poor pilgrims with shelter. Inside you can visit a refectory, a gallery showing the history of the hospital and sleeping quarters restored to their original medieval state. Over the road is the wonky, half-timbered **Weavers' House** – built around 1500 and now a restaurant – that was once inhabited by Huguenot textile workers who had been offered religious asylum in post-Reformation England.

St Peter's Street terminates at the two massive crenellated towers of the medieval **West Gate**, the only one of the town's seven city gates to have survived intact. Its prison cells and guard chambers house a small **museum** (Sat 11am–12.30pm & 1.30–3.30pm; £1.30), which displays contemporary armaments and weaponry used by the medieval city guard, as well as giving access to the battlements.

The Roman Museum, The Canterbury Tales and the Museum of Canterbury

Redevelopment of the Longmarket area (situated between Burgate and the High St) in the early 1990s exposed Roman foundations and mosaics that are now part of the **Roman Museum** (Mon–Sat 10am–4pm, plus June–Sept Sun 1.30–4pm; £3.10). The display of recovered artefacts is tasteful, but the remnants of the larger building are pretty dull, and better mosaics can be seen at Lullingstone (see p.178).

Turning in the other direction down St Margaret's Street leads to the former church that's now **The Canterbury Tales** (daily: March–June, Sept & Oct 10am–5pm; July & Aug 9.30am–5pm; Nov–Feb 10am–4.30pm; £7.75; Ⓦwww .canterburytales.org.uk), a quasi-educational show based on Geoffrey Chaucer's book. Equipped with an audioguide, visitors set off on a wander through mildly odour-enhanced galleries in which mannequins occupy idealized fourteenth-century tableaux and recount five of Chaucer's tales. Genuinely educational and better value is the **Museum of Canterbury**, round the corner in Stour Street (Mon–Sat 11am–4pm, plus June–Oct Sun 1.30–4pm; £3.60), an interactive

Museum passport

The **museum passport** (£6.40) gives entry to the Museum of Canterbury, the Roman Museum and the West Gate Museum and is available from the ticket offices of each.

exhibition spanning local history from the splendour of Durovernum through to the more recent literary figures of Joseph Conrad (buried in the cemetery on London Rd) and Oliver Postgate, originator of *Bagpuss* and *The Clangers*. The check-trousered philanthropist **Rupert Bear**, created by local-born Mary Tourtel, merits a museum of his own within the main museum.

Eating and drinking

The combination of a large student population and the tourist trade means Canterbury has a good selection of places to eat and drink, with many **restaurants** and **pubs** in genuinely old settings.

Restaurants and cafés

Bangkok House 13 Church St ☎01227/471141. Excellent, well-presented Thai food in this small, moderately priced restaurant near St Augustine's Abbey. Closed Mon lunch.

Boho Café 27 High St ☎01227/458931. This hip, relaxed little hangout, with its quirky decor, delicious home-cooked food and friendly vibe, is deservedly popular both in the daytime and in the evening. Closed Sun & Mon eve.

Café des Amis 93–95 St Dunstan's St ☎01227/464390. Very popular, authentic Mexican place close to Westgate; try the delicious paella (£26 for two) followed by a bubbling chocolate *fundido*.

Café Mauresque 8 Butchery Lane ☎01227/464300. Atmospheric North African restaurant tucked away in a cobbled sidestreet near the cathedral. Classic tagines and other mains will set you back £12–15.

Café St Pierre 41 St Peter's St. Excellent French patisserie and bakery with tables on the pavement and in the garden when the weather's fine.

Deeson's 25–26 Sun St ☎01227/767854. Delicious, Modern British cooking (mains £12–18) and a stylish interior are a winning combination at this popular little restaurant.

The Goods Shed Station Road West ☎01227/459153. Everything from a bowl of soup or sandwich to a first-class full meal, guaranteed super-fresh as it comes from the adjacent farmers' market. Closed Sun eve & all day Mon.

Granville Lower Hardres ☎01227/700402. Great gastropub a few miles from Canterbury, with wooden tables set around a huge wood-burning stove, and a daily changing seasonal menu featuring classics such as pork belly and roast leg of lamb (around £14). Closed Mon.

Posillipo Tuo e Mio 16 The Borough ☎01227/761471. Long-established restaurant serving classy Italian dishes, a range of pizzas and some delicious, home-made desserts. Closed Mon & Tues lunch.

Tiny Tims 34 St Margaret's St ☎01227/450793. Despite the name there's nothing twee about this elegant, contemporary tearoom, open for breakfast, lunch and afternoon tea. Closed Mon.

Pubs and bars

Bishop's Finger 13 St Dunstan's St. Popular wood-panelled bar just through the West Gate with a fine range of ales and a patio suntrap.

Bramley's 15 Orange St. Cool, eclectic bar decked out with mismatched furniture, squishy armchairs and assorted knick-knacks. Good bar food available. Closed Sun.

Casey's 5 Butchery Lane ☎01227/463252. Cosy, low-ceilinged Irish pub serving soda bread, pies and other pub grub, with occasional live folk music.

Dolphin 17 St Radigund's St. Nice old pub with a good selection of real ales, a log fire in winter and a popular beer garden in summer. Good food too.

Farmhouse 11 Dover St ☎01227/456118. Deservedly popular bar, live music venue and restaurant, just outside the city walls. Food served Tues–Sat (breakfast, lunch & dinner) & Sun (lunch only). Closed Mon.

Parrot Radigund's Hall, 1–9 Church Lane ☎01227/762355. Ancient hostelry – the oldest in Canterbury – with loads of character, good food and a decent selection of ales. Live music Thurs.

Nightlife and entertainment

Nightlife in Canterbury keeps a low profile – check out what there is going on in the free *What, Where and When* **listings magazine** available at the tourist office. The *Farmhouse* (see above) puts on **gigs**, as does the university on the other side of town.

The university also houses the **Gulbenkian Theatre** (☎01227/769075, ⓦwww .kent.ac.uk/gulbenkian), which hosts various cultural events. The **New Marlowe**

Theatre (☎01227/787787, ⓦwww.newmarlowetheatre.org.uk), named after the sixteenth-century Canterbury-born playwright, is currently being constructed on the site of the old Marlowe Theatre in The Friars and is due to open in September 2011. A good range of art **films** is shown at the university's Gulbenkian Cinema (same website as theatre). Finally, the **Canterbury Festival** (☎01227/452853, ⓦwww.canterburyfestival.co.uk), an international potpourri of music, theatre and arts, takes place annually during the last two weeks of October.

Sandwich to Dungeness

Dover, just 21 miles from mainland Europe, is Britain's principal cross-Channel port. As a town it is not immensely appealing, even though its key position has left it with a clutch of historic attractions. To the north lie pretty, medieval **Sandwich**, once the most important of the Cinque Ports but now no longer even on the coast, and the pleasant resort town of **Deal**. Southwest of Dover is a forty-square-mile area of shingle and marshland known as the **Romney and Denge marshes**, with the eerie headland of **Dungeness** at its southernmost tip.

There are frequent **train** – from St Pancras, Victoria and Charing Cross – and **bus** connections to Dover from London. A useful branch line offers connections from Dover up the coast to Deal and Sandwich and on to Ramsgate, and in the other direction there are regular buses west along the coast to Hythe. For late ferry arrivals, the last train service leaves Dover for London at 10.45pm.

Sandwich and around

SANDWICH, situated on the River Stour six miles north of Deal, is one of the best-preserved medieval towns in the country. It was chief among the Cinque Ports (see box below) until the Stour silted up; unlike at other former harbour inlets, however, the river hasn't silted up completely and still flows through town, its grassy willow-lined banks adding to the once great medieval port's charm today.

Arrival, information and accommodation

From the **train station**, it's a fifteen-minute walk north along New Street to the town centre, where you'll find the **tourist office**, housed in the Guildhall

---

The Cinque Ports

In 1278 **Dover**, **Hythe**, **Sandwich**, **New Romney** and **Hastings** – already part of a long-established but unofficial confederation of defensive coastal settlements – were formalized under Edward I's charter as the **Cinque Ports** (pronounced "sink", despite its French origin). In return for providing England with maritime support when necessary, the five ports were given trading privileges and other liberties, which enabled them to prosper while neighbouring ports struggled to survive. Some took advantage of this during peacetime, boosting their wealth by various nefarious activities such as piracy and the smuggling of tax-free contraband.

Later, **Rye** and **Winchelsea** were added to the confederation along with several other "limb" ports on the southeast coast. The confederation continued until 1685, when the ports' privileges were revoked. Their maritime services had become increasingly unnecessary after Henry VIII had founded a professional navy and, due to a shifting coastline, several of the ports' harbours had silted up anyway, leaving some of them several miles inland. Nowadays, only Dover is still a major working port.

(April–Oct Mon–Sat 10am–4pm; ☎01304/613565, ⓦwww.whitecliffscountry .org.uk). Pick of the **accommodation** is the *Bell Hotel* down on The Quay (☎01304/613388, ⓦwww.bellhotelsandwich.co.uk; ❹), a rambling nineteenth-century hostelry which has been converted in sleek, modern style. More affordable are the friendly *Le Trayas* bungalow, a ten-minute walk from The Quay at 10 Poulders Rd (☎01304/611056, ⓦwww.letrayas.co.uk; no credit cards; ❷), and the *St Crispin Inn* (☎01304/612081, ⓦwww.stcrispininn .com; ❷), an attractive fifteenth-century pub a couple of miles southeast of Sandwich in the village of Worth; the latter also has good bar food.

The Town
By the bridge over the Stour stands Sandwich's best-known feature, the sixteenth-century **Barbican**, a stone gateway decorated with chequerwork, where tolls were once collected. **Boat trips** (☎07958/376183; £6–20) run from here up to Richborough Roman Fort (see below) and down to the estuary to spot seals and birds. At the far corner of the quay you'll find the entrance to the 3.5-acre **Secret Gardens of Sandwich** (daily: mid-April to Sept 10am–6pm; Oct to mid-April 10am–4pm; closed for 2 weeks at Christmas; £5; ⓦwww.the-secretgardens.co .uk), designed by Sir Edward Lutyens and planted by his famous gardening partner Gertrude Jekyll, and recently restored after being lost to the wilderness for 25 years. Running parallel to the river is **Strand Street**, whose crooked half-timbered facades front antique shops and private homes while, back in the town centre, another fine sixteenth-century edifice, the **Guildhall**, houses both the tourist office (see opposite) and a small **museum** recounting the town's history (April–Sept Tues, Wed & Fri 10.30am–12.30pm & 2–4pm, Thurs & Sat 2–4pm; Oct–March Tues–Sat 2–4pm; £1). The genteel town is separated from the sandy beaches of Sandwich Bay by the **Royal St George Golf Course** (ⓦwww.royalstgeorges.com) – frequent venue of the British Open tournament (next due here in 2011) and open to all-comers on weekdays – and a mile of nature reserves. Three miles north of town, the **Gazen Salts Nature Reserve** is renowned for its diversity of sea birds.

Overlooking the doleful expanse of Pegwell Bay, two miles northwest of Sandwich, is **Richborough Roman Fort** (Easter–Sept daily 10am–6pm; £4.50; EH), one of the earliest coastal strongholds built by the Romans. Richborough's historical significance far outshines its present appearance, and all that remains within the well-preserved Roman walls are the relics of an early Saxon church.

Eating and drinking
Your best choice for excellent seafood and local game is the **restaurant** at the *Bell* (see above). Alternatively, the *George and Dragon*, 24 Fisher St, serves upmarket pub grub and has roaring real fires in winter and a courtyard garden for alfresco summer dining. For supplies for a riverside picnic look no further than the excellent No Name **deli** on No Name Street, just opposite the Guildhall, while the definitive cream tea can be found at the Secret Gardens **tearoom** (see above; no need to enter gardens for access), which has a fine outlook over Lutyens' handsome manor house and the gardens beyond.

Finally, you can't leave Sandwich without eating the famous snack it gave its name to when, in 1762, the Fourth Earl of Sandwich, passionately absorbed in a game of cards, ate his meat between two bits of bread; for the definitive Sandwich sandwich, head for the twee *Little Cottage Tearooms*, on The Quay.

Deal and around
One of the most unusual of Henry VIII's forts is the diminutive castle at **DEAL**, six miles south of Sandwich and site of Julius Caesar's first successful

landfall in Britain in 55 BC. Situated off the Strand at the south end of town, the **castle** (Easter–Sept Mon–Fri & Sun 10am–6pm, Sat 10am–5pm; £4.50; EH) is shaped like a Tudor rose when viewed from the air: the premise for its unusual form was that the rounded walls would be better at deflecting missiles. Inside the castle, you can see a comprehensive display on other similar forts built during Henry VIII's reign.

Out on the seafront, at the corner with Sondes Road, the **Timeball Tower** (Easter–Sept Wed–Sun noon–4pm; £2; ⓦ dealtimeball.tripod.com) was originally used as a semaphore tower for catching smugglers before a timeball was added in 1853; the ball dropped from the roof at exactly 1pm in summer, so providing an accurate time check for ships in the days before radio. It still drops regularly and the building also houses a small museum of horology and telegraphy.

Deal's **tourist office** is situated in the Landmark Centre on the High Street (Mon–Fri 10am–4pm, Sat 10am–2pm; ☎ 01304/369576, ⓦ www.whitecliffs country.org.uk). The nicest **place to stay** is the friendly and justifiably popular 🍴 *Number One B&B*, with stylish, contemporary rooms just a minute from the beach at 1 Ranelagh Rd (☎ 01304/364459, ⓦ www.numberonebandb.co.uk; ❸). A five-minute walk away along the seafront at 82 Beach St is the *Black Douglas Coffee House* (daily during the daytime, plus Fri & Sat eve for drinks & events), a cosy hideaway with scrubbed wooden tables, local art on the walls, newspapers and books for browsing, and a focus on quality, locally sourced, home-made **food**. Next door, there's good seasonal cooking at the brasserie *81 Beach Street* (☎ 01304/368136; closed Sun eve; mains around £15), while over the road at the end of Deal's concrete pier, *Jasin's Restaurant* serves up simple food (baked potatoes £4.50–5.50, fish and chips £7.50) in a striking, award-winning timber-and-glass building.

Walmer Castle

A mile south of Deal, **Walmer Castle** (March & Oct Wed–Sun 10am–4pm; April–Sept Mon–Fri & Sun 10am–6pm, Sat 10am–4pm; £7; EH) is another rotund Tudor-rose-shaped affair, commissioned in 1730. Now it more resembles a heavily fortified stately home than a military stronghold. The best-known resident was the Duke of Wellington, who died here in 1842, and not surprisingly, the house is devoted primarily to his life and times. The castle's terraced gardens, overlooking the Channel, are a good spot for a picnic, or you can have afternoon **tea** in *The Lord Warden's Tearooms* (April–Oct daily). To get to Walmer Castle from Deal, you can either catch one of the hourly buses or, if the weather's good, make the pleasant walk along the seafront (30min).

Dover

Badly bombed during World War II, **DOVER**'s town centre and seafront don't have what it takes to induce many travellers to linger. **Dover Castle** is by far the most interesting attraction, closely followed by a walk along Dover's legendary **White Cliffs**, which dominate the town and have long been a source of inspiration for travellers, lovers and soldiers sailing off to war.

Arrival, information and accommodation

There are frequent train services from both Charing Cross and Victoria stations in London to Dover Priory **train station**, situated off Folkestone Road, a ten-minute walk west of the centre; regular shuttle buses run to and from the Eastern and Western docks. Buses from London (hourly; 2hr 15min) run to the Eastern Docks and the town-centre **bus station** on Pencester Road. The **tourist office**, situated in the Old Town Gaol in Biggin Street (June–Aug daily

9am–5.30pm; Sept–May Mon–Fri 9am–5.30pm, Sat & Sun 10am–4pm; Oct–March closed Sun; ℡01304/205108, Ⓦwww.whitecliffscountry.org.uk), has a free *White Cliffs Trails* pamphlet that outlines many good walks near Dover, both coastal and inland.

Accommodation in Dover – mainly small hotels and B&Bs – is plentiful. The biggest concentration is to be found on the Folkestone Road, close to the train station, but those around the base of Castle Hill Road on the other side of town are generally nicer. The best nearby **campsite** is *The Warren*, a fifteen-minute drive away near Folkestone (℡01303/255093; closed Nov–Easter); the site boasts a lovely location, nestled underneath white cliffs by the beach.

B&Bs and guesthouses

Blakes of Dover 52 Castle St ℡01304/202194, Ⓦwww.blakesofdover.com. Small, comfortable en-suite rooms are available in this real-ale pub. ❷

Maison Dieu 89 Maison Dieu Rd ℡01304/204033, Ⓦwww.maisondieu.com. Warm and friendly B&B in a central location, with helpful on-site parking and wi-fi internet access. Some rooms have good views of Dover Castle. ❷

The Marquis at Alkham Alkham ℡01304/873410, Ⓦwww.themarquisatalkham .co.uk. The best upmarket option near Dover, this restaurant-with-rooms is housed in a 200-year-old inn in a picturesque village 10min from Dover. The five chic-boutique rooms have picture-perfect views across the Kent Downs, and the award-winning restaurant is well worth a splurge. ❹

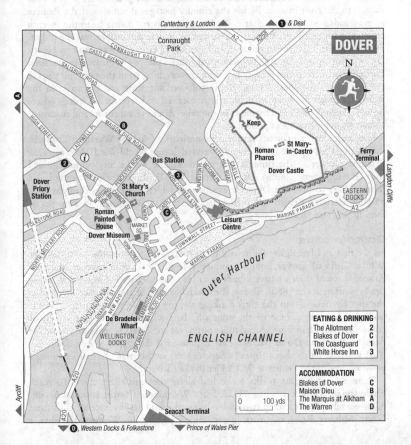

EATING & DRINKING

The Allotment	2
Blakes of Dover	C
The Coastguard	1
White Horse Inn	3

ACCOMMODATION

Blakes of Dover	C
Maison Dieu	B
The Marquis at Alkham	A
The Warren	D

The Town

Postwar rebuilding has made Dover town centre rather unprepossessing, but it does hold a couple of low-key attractions. The **Roman Painted House** on New Street (June–Aug Tues–Sat 10am–5pm; £3), once a hotel for official guests, boasts some reasonable Roman wall paintings, the remains of an underground Roman heating system and some mosaics. The nearby **Dover Museum** on the Market Square (Mon–Sat 10am–5.30pm, plus April–Aug Sun noon–5pm; £3) has three floors packed with informative displays on Dover's past, including a Bronze Age boat that was discovered in the town in 1992.

Dover Castle

It was in 1168, a century after the Conquest, that the Normans constructed the keep that now presides over the bulk of **Dover Castle** (Feb & March daily 10am–4pm; April–July & Sept daily 10am–6pm; Aug daily 9.30am–6pm; Oct daily 10am–5pm; Nov–Jan Mon & Thurs–Sun 10am–4pm; £13.90; EH), a superbly positioned defensive complex that was in continuous use as some sort of military installation right up to the 1980s. The castle's a stiff climb from the town centre, and there's a lot to see, so allow half a day for a thorough visit.

Dover was originally put on the map by the Romans, who chose the harbour as the base for their northern fleet, and erected a **lighthouse** (*pharos*) here to guide the ships into the river mouth. Beside the chunky hexagonal remains of the Roman *pharos* stands a Saxon-built church, **St Mary-in-Castro**, dating from the seventh century, with motifs graffitied by irreverent Crusaders still visible near the pulpit. Further up the hill is the impressive, well-preserved **Great Tower**, built by Henry II as a palace. Inside, Henry's opulent royal court – one of the greatest in medieval Europe – has been painstakingly re-created; everything from the pots and pans in the kitchen to the chess set and richly coloured furniture and tapestries in the King's Chamber has been meticulously researched and reproduced using, where possible, the materials and methods of the time. Audio visual effects and costumed characters complete the experience.

The castle's other main attraction is its network of **Secret Wartime Tunnels**, dug during the Napoleonic Wars and extended during World War II. You can tour "Hellfire Corner" – the tunnels' wartime nickname – on a fifty-minute guided tour (leaving every 20min). During World War II, the tunnels were used as a headquarters to plan the Dunkirk evacuation, which successfully brought back 330,000 stranded British and French troops from the Continent in a flotilla of local fishing and pleasure boats.

Dover's cliffs

As the first and last sight of England for travellers throughout the centuries, the **White Cliffs of Dover** hold a complex role in the English psyche. Matthew Arnold invoked their massive grandeur in his famous elegy for lost belief, *Dover Beach*, written in the 1860s. Today, the beach has little of the romance invested in the spot by Arnold, but the cliffs flanking the town retain their majesty, even if pollution has taken some of the edge off their whiteness. The best views, of course, are to be had from several miles out to sea and **boats** leave hourly from De Bradelei Wharf in Dover Marina (Easter–June Sat & Sun; July & Aug daily; call ☏01304/271388 to check times in Sept & Oct; £8), but an alternative vantage point on land is the Prince of Wales Pier in the harbour.

There are some great **walks** to be had along the cliffs themselves. To reach **Shakespeare Cliff**, catch bus #D2A from Worthington Street towards Aycliff. Alternatively, there's a steep two-and-a-half-mile climb to Shakespeare Cliff from North Military Road, off York Street, taking you by the **Western Heights**, a series of defensive battlements built into the cliff in the nineteenth century. From here there's a sweeping panorama of the Straits of Dover – the world's busiest shipping lanes – and a bird's-eye view of the harbour and the surrounding cliffs. It's even possible to catch a glimpse of France on a clear day.

At Langdon Cliffs, a couple of miles east of town, the **White Cliffs Visitor Centre** (daily: March–Oct 10am–5pm; Nov–Feb 11am–4pm; free; NT) has excellent displays explaining the ecology and history of the local coast and countryside. There's a coffee shop here, too, and regular countryside events and guided walks (T01304/202756).

Eating and drinking

Dover's **restaurant** scene is generally poor, with one shining exception: *The Allotment*, 9 High St (T01304/214467; closed Sun & Mon), a light-filled oasis on the shabby High Street serving up delicious breakfasts, lunches and dinners using ingredients sourced where possible from local allotments. For a **drink**, try the lovely wood-panelled cellar bar at *Blakes* (see p.171), or the eighteenth-century *White Horse Inn* on St James Street at the foot of the castle; the latter's a favourite hangout for English Channel swimmers, who get to add their names on the wall after a successful crossing. Four miles east of Dover in the pretty cove of St Margaret's Bay, *The Coastguard* pub is a perfect spot for lunch on a summer's day, with a terrace and beer garden that goes right down to the shingle.

Romney and Denge marshes

In Roman times, what is now the southernmost part of Kent was submerged beneath the English Channel, but the lowering of sea levels in the Middle Ages and later reclamation created a forty-square-mile area of shingle and marshland now known as the **Romney and Denge marshes**.

The forlorn, sheep-speckled expanse has an unearthly appearance today, which you can take in aboard the **Romney, Hythe & Dymchurch Railway** (RHDR; April–Oct daily; Nov–March Sat & Sun, plus school hols; £14 return; T01797/362353, Wwww.rhdr.org.uk), a fifteen-inch-gauge line which runs between the ancient town of **HYTHE**, on the eastern edge of the reclaimed marshes, and the headland of Dungeness. Built in the 1920s as a tourist attraction, its fleet of steam locomotives are mainly one-third scale models from the Twenties and Thirties – making the fourteen-mile ride a cramped one for most adults. The station is to the west of Hythe town centre, on the south bank of the canal by Station Bridge.

Five miles west of Hythe, the **Port Lympne Wild Animal Park** (daily: March–Oct 10am–6pm; Nov–Feb 10am–5pm; last admission 90min before closing; £16.95; Wwww.totallywild.net) is home to more than 650 beasts, including gorillas, African elephants, Barbary lions, Siberian and Indian tigers and the largest breeding herd of black rhinos outside Africa. The park offers fun **overnight safaris** (April to mid-Oct; from £110 per person), with game drives led by Zimbabwean rangers, and accommodation in a safari tent overlooking a watering hole; evening safaris are also available (Tues & Thurs May to mid-Sept; £40).

Dungeness

The spooky, shingle-swathed expanse of **DUNGENESS**, fourteen miles south of Hythe, was until the nineteenth century affected by malaria, and since the 1960s has been the appropriate setting for a nuclear power station. A more benign local landmark is the pair of lighthouses located close to the RHDR station. Decommissioned since the erection of its successor in 1961, the **Old Lighthouse** (10am–4.30pm: March, April & Oct Sat & Sun only; May, June &

Sept Thurs–Sun; July, Aug & school hols daily; £3), built in 1904, affords sweeping views and displays navigational equipment and information panels on its six floors.

The haunted landscape of Dungeness has become the abode of eccentric and reclusive characters living in basic fishermen's cabins or disused railway carriages, apparently relishing the area's bleak austerity. The late **Derek Jarman**, artist and filmmaker, made his home here at **Prospect Cottage**, and the shingle garden he created from beachcombed materials and plants has become something of a pilgrimage for garden lovers. The barren marshy environment also attracts huge colonies of gulls and terns, as well as smews and gadwalls, best appreciated at the **RSPB visitor centre** (daily: March–Oct 10am–5pm; Nov–Feb 10am–4pm; £3) off the Lydd road, three miles from Dungeness. The local floral ecology is also unique and all around you'll see tiny communities of wildflowers struggling against the unrelenting breeze.

Back towards Dungeness, you can refuel at the popular *Pilot Inn* **pub** on Battery Road, a stone's throw from the sea.

The Kent Weald

The Weald is usually taken to refer to the region around the spa town of **Royal Tunbridge Wells**. In fact it stretches across a much larger area between the North and South Downs and includes parts of both Kent and Sussex, though the majority of its attractions are just inside Kent. We've taken the wider definition to include the medieval manor at **Penshurst** and nearby **Hever Castle**, just northwest of Tunbridge Wells, as well as the town of **Sevenoaks**, on the edge of the North Downs.

The region is epitomized by gentle hills, sunken country lanes and somnolent villages as well as some of England's most beautiful gardens – **Sissinghurst** being the best known. Public transport to the area is good, but in order to explore the Wealden countryside in any depth, you'll need your own vehicle. If you are driving or on a bicycle, you may want to follow the signs indicating the **High Weald Country Tour**, a seventy-mile back-country loop stretching through the best of the Kentish Weald, from Penshurst in the west to Tenterden in the east. Ask for the leaflet and map at tourist offices in the area.

Royal Tunbridge Wells and around

ROYAL TUNBRIDGE WELLS – not to be confused with the more mundane Tonbridge, a few miles to the north – is the home of the mythical whingeing reactionary letter-writer known as "Disgusted of Tunbridge Wells". Most British people, therefore, view it with derision, but don't be misled – this prosperous spa town, which reached its height of popularity in the Regency period, is an elegant place surrounded by gorgeous countryside, and makes an excellent base for several local attractions.

Arrival, information and accommodation

The **train station**, on the London Charing Cross to Hastings line, is centrally located, close to the point where the High Street becomes Mount Pleasant Road. The **bus station** is north of the centre on St John's Road, but most buses stop on Mount Pleasant and at the train station. The **tourist office**, housed in the Old Fish Market in The Pantiles (Mon–Sat 9.30am–5pm; ℡01892/515675, ⓦwww .visittunbridgewells.com), can supply a town map.

Tunbridge Wells has a number of very plush **places to stay**, such as the chic *Brew House Hotel*, 1 Warwick Park (℡01892/520587, ⓦwww.thebrewhousehotel.net; ❹), a sleek boutique hotel in a great location near The Pantiles, with an excellent restaurant and bar attached. There's an attractive Regency-style **B&B** at *40 York Road* (℡01892/531342, ⓦwww.yorkroad.co.uk; ❸).

The spa and the town

The best place to start your wanderings is **The Pantiles**, an elegant colonnaded parade of shops ten minutes' walk south of the train station, where the fashionable once gathered to promenade and take the waters. Hub of The Pantiles is the original **Chalybeate Spring** (pronounced "Ka-*lee*-bee-at") in the Bath House (Easter–Sept Mon–Sat 10am–5pm, Sun 10am–4pm), where a "Dipper" has been employed since the late eighteenth century to serve the ferrous waters. In summer months a period-dressed incumbent will fetch you a glass from the cool spring for 40p. For a modern-day spa experience, the luxurious **Royal Day Spa** is just a five-minute walk away at 12 Vale Rd (℡01892/616191, ⓦwww.royal-dayspa.co.uk).

Ten minutes further north up the High Street, on Mount Pleasant Road, the **Museum and Art Gallery** (Mon–Sat 9.30am–5pm, Sun 10am–4pm; free; ⓦwww.tunbridgewellsmuseum.org) is worth a look for its exquisite collection of locally made wooden boxes, dating from the 1930s and known as "Tunbridge Ware". On the east side of the High Street, The Grove and, to the north, Calverley Grounds are havens of urban tranquillity, while **The Common**, spreading out on the west side of town, is laced with pathways carved by the original visitors to the spa.

Eating and drinking

The town has an excellent range of **restaurants**, the best being ♨ *Thackeray's House*, 85 London Rd (℡01892/511921; closed Sun eve & Mon), an ancient weatherboarded building that was briefly home to the writer; it's expensive (mains such as roast sloe-crusted venison cost £20–30, while the tasting menu is £65), but the three-course lunch is a bargain at £17.50. There's excellent Nepalese fare at *Mooli*, 57–59 Calverley Rd (℡01892/545499), while for top-notch seafood at moderate prices try the cosy basement brasserie at *Sankey's*, 39 Mount Ephraim (℡01892/511422; restaurant closed Sun); upstairs is a lovely **pub** decked out in enamel signs and brewery mirrors, with an open fire, secluded decked garden and great selection of specialist beers.

Penshurst Place and Hever Castle

Tudor timber-framed houses and shops line the high street of the attractive village of **PENSHURST**, five miles northwest of Tunbridge Wells (bus #231 or #233; not Sun). The main reason for coming here is to visit **Penshurst Place** (April–Oct daily noon–4pm, grounds 10.30am–6pm; March Sat & Sun only; £9.50, grounds only £7.50; ⓦwww.penshurstplace.com), home to the Sidney family since 1552 and birthplace of the Elizabethan soldier and poet, Sir Philip Sidney. The fourteenth-century Barons Hall is the chief glory of the interior, with its sixty-foot-high chestnut roof still in place, while the eleven acres of grounds include a formal Italian garden with clipped box hedges.

Three miles further west, the moated and much-altered **Hever Castle** (March, Nov & Dec Wed–Sun 10.30am–5pm; April–Oct daily 10.30am–6pm; last entry 1hr before closing; castle opens noon; £13, gardens only £10.50; ⓦwww.hever castle.co.uk) was the childhood home of Anne Boleyn, second wife of Henry VIII, and where Anne of Cleves, Henry's fourth wife, lived after their divorce. In 1903, having fallen into disrepair, the castle was bought by William Waldorf-Astor, American millionaire owner of *The Times*, who had the house assiduously restored, panelling the rooms with worthy reproductions of Tudor woodcarvings. In the Inner Hall hangs a fine portrait of Henry VIII by Holbein, who also painted the portrait of Elizabeth I on display on the middle floor. Upstairs, in Anne Boleyn's room, you can see the book of prayers she carried with her to the executioner's block. Outside in the **grounds** is Waldorf-Astor's beautiful Italian Garden, a traditional yew hedge maze, an adventure playground and a water maze. No bus routes serve Hever Castle, but there are **train stations** at Hever, a mile west of the castle, and Edenbridge, three miles northwest, from which taxis are usually available.

Sissinghurst

Sissinghurst, fourteen miles east of Tunbridge Wells (mid-March to Oct Mon, Tues & Fri–Sun 11am–6pm or dusk; £9.50; NT), was described by Vita Sackville-West as "a garden crying out for rescue" when she and her husband took it over in the 1920s. Over the following years they transformed the five-acre plot into one of England's greatest and most popular modern gardens. Spread over the site of a medieval moated manor (which was rebuilt into an Elizabethan mansion, of which only one wing remains today), the gardens were designed around the linear pattern of the former buildings' walls. The brick tower that Vita had restored and used as her study acts as a focal point and offers the best views of the walled gardens for which Sissinghurst is famous. Most impressive are the **White Garden**, composed solely of white flowers and silvery-grey foliage, and the **Cottage Garden**, featuring flora in shades of orange, yellow and red.

The gardens get extremely busy in summer when timed tickets for half-hourly visits are issued. Food options are limited and overpriced – your best bet is to bring a picnic. The nearest **train** station is Staplehurst (regular trains from Tunbridge Wells), from where there's a linking bus service to the gardens Tuesdays and Sundays; alternatively, **bus** #5, between Maidstone and Hastings, stops in Sissinghurst village en route. For a real treat, book in at the fabulous *Sissinghurst Castle Farmhouse* (℡01580/720992, Ⓦwww.sissinghurstcastlefarmhouse.com; ❻), a stunning Victorian farmhouse **B&B** less than 100m from the gardens, with luxurious rooms boasting fabulous views over the Sissinghurst estate.

Leeds Castle

Named after the local village, **Leeds Castle**, eighteen miles northeast of Tunbridge Wells and five miles east of Maidstone, off the A20 (daily 10am–6pm; last admission 4.30pm; castle & grounds £17.50 for an annual pass; Ⓦwww.leeds-castle.com), more closely resembles a fairytale palace than a defensively efficient fortress. Set half on an island in the middle of a lake and half on the mainland surrounded by landscaped parkland, the castle began life around 1120. Following centuries of regal and noble ownership (and, less glamorously, service as a prison) it is now run as a commercial concern, hosting conferences and sporting and cultural events. The castle's interior fails to match its stunning, much-photographed external appearance and, in places, twentieth-century renovations have quashed the historical charm; possibly the most unusual feature inside is the **Dog Collar Museum** in the gatehouse. In the grounds, there's a fine aviary, as well as manicured gardens and a maze.

Trains run to Bearsted Station from London Victoria via Maidstone East; there's a coach shuttle service from the station to the castle.

Sevenoaks and around

Set among the green sand ridges of west Kent, 25 miles from London, **SEVENOAKS** is a popular commuter town. The only real reason to make a trip here is to visit the immense baronial estate of **Knole**, or to use it as a base for seeing the mosaics at **Lullingstone Roman Villa** or memorabilia relating to Winston Churchill at his home of **Chartwell**.

Knole

Knole (house mid-March to Oct Wed–Sun noon–4pm; garden April–Sept Tues 11am–4pm; £9.50, garden £5; NT) is entered from the south end of Sevenoaks High Street, half an hour's walk from the train station or fifteen minutes from the bus station. Created in 1456 by Archbishop Thomas Bourchier, the palace was numerically designed to match the calendar, with 365 rooms, seven courtyards and 52 staircases. It was later appropriated by Henry VIII, who hunted in the thousand acres of **parkland** (free access throughout the year), still home to several hundred deer. Vita Sackville-West was brought up here, and her one-time lover Virginia Woolf derived inspiration for her novel *Orlando* from her frequent visits to the house. Only thirteen rooms are open to the public, featuring an array of fine, if well-worn, furnishings and tapestries, as well as paintings by Gainsborough, Van Dyck and Reynolds.

Practicalities

Sevenoaks' **tourist office** is within the Stag Theatre on the London Road (Mon–Sat: April–Oct 9.30am–5pm; Nov–March 9.30am–4.30pm; ℡01732/450305, Ⓦwww.visitheartofkent.com); the **train station** is fifteen minutes' walk north on the same road. The town's smartest **accommodation** is at the excellent *Royal Oak Hotel*, a seventeenth-century coaching inn at the south end of the High Street (℡01732/451109, Ⓦwww.brook-hotels.co.uk/royaloak; ❹), beyond the entrance to Knole. Alternatively, you could have a timber-clad cottage to yourself at *4 Old Timber Top Cottages*, Bethel Road (℡01732/460506, Ⓦwww.timbertopcottage.co.uk; ❷); breakfast is included in the nightly rate, though the cottage also has basic self-catering facilities.

For a **snack** (and really good coffee), pop into *Coffee Call* on Dorset Street. There are several excellent **restaurants** in Sevenoaks: try the stylish *House on the Hill*, 115 London Rd (℡01732/450120), for top-notch English classics (mains £14–20), or *The Vine*, 11 Pound Lane (℡01732/469510), with a lovely alfresco terrace overlooking the green and cricket ground (2 courses £15.50/18.50 lunch/dinner).

English wine: a sparkling success story

No longer is English wine regarded with derision. Today there are around four hundred English **vineyards** producing around two million bottles a year (more than eighty percent of it white), and the best of the harvest more than rivals the more famous names over the Channel. Sparkling wine is the biggest success story, with some English wines beating the best Champagnes in international blind-tasting competitions. With almost identical soil and geology to the Champagne region, and a helping hand from global warming, the southeast is home to many of the country's best vineyards, several of which now offer tours and tastings. In the Kent Weald, these include:

Biddenden Gribble Bridge Lane, Biddenden ℡01580/291726, Ⓦwww.biddendenvine yards.com. Kent's oldest commercial vineyard, producing wines from nine varieties of grape, as well as traditional Kentish ciders. Free vineyard tours and tastings Mon–Sat 10am–5pm, Sun 11am–5pm. Closed Sun in Jan & Feb.

Chapel Down Small Hythe, Tenterden ℡01580/763033, Ⓦwww.englishwinesgroup .com. Multi-award-winning winemaker, with a wine and English produce store on site, as well as a lovely terrace restaurant overlooking the vineyards. Guided tours and tastings (£7) daily June–Sept, weekends May & Oct.

See Ⓦwww.englishwineproducers.com for details of more vineyards around the country.

Lullingstone Roman Villa

Lullingstone Roman Villa, in a pleasant location alongside the trickle of the River Darent seven miles north of Sevenoaks (Feb, March, Oct & Nov daily 10am–4pm; April–Sept daily 10am–6pm; Dec & Jan Wed–Sun 10am–4pm; £5.90; EH), has some of the best-preserved Roman mosaics in southeast England. Believed to have been the first-century residence of a farmer, the site has yielded some fine marble busts (now on display in London's British Museum) and a superb floor depicting the killing of the Chimera, a mythical fire-breathing beast with a lion's head, goat's body and a serpent's tail. From Sevenoaks there are half-hourly trains to the village of Eynsford, from where it's a fifteen-minute walk west along the river.

Chartwell

The residence of Winston Churchill from 1924 until his death in 1965, **Chartwell**, six miles west of Sevenoaks (mid-March to Oct Wed–Sun 11am–5pm; July & Aug also Tues; £10.60; NT), is one of the most visited of the National Trust's properties. It's an unremarkable, heavily restored Tudor building whose main appeal is the wartime premier's memorabilia, including his paintings, which show an unexpectedly contemplative side to the famously gruff statesman. Entry to the house is by timed ticket at peak times – expect long queues. A direct bus service runs to Chartwell from Sevenoaks bus station four times daily on Sundays and public holidays.

Sussex

Although now separated into two counties, East and West, **Sussex** (deriving from "land of the south Saxons") retains a unified identity. Large areas of woodland contribute to its bucolic character, and nowhere is this rural atmosphere more evident than on the southeast's main long-distance footpath, the **South Downs Way** (see box opposite), which runs along the grassy ridge of the South Downs, giving dramatic views over some fine countryside as well as over the coast, where the Downs meet the sea at the chalk cliffs of **Beachy Head** and **Seven Sisters**.

However, Sussex also has its fair share of urban centres, many of which are populated by London commuters. The best known is the traditional seaside resort of **Brighton**, the counties' biggest and brashest city, while a few miles inland more sedate **Lewes**, the county town of East Sussex, is famed for its Bonfire Night celebrations. **Hastings**, further east, is best known for its historical connections, although the eponymous fight actually took place six miles away at **Battle**. Farther east still, on the edge of Romney Marsh, the former Cinque Port of **Rye** has cobbled streets and a well-preserved cluster of fifteenth-to-eighteenth-century buildings. In West Sussex, the main centres of interest are the attractive hill-top town of **Arundel**, surrounded by unspoilt countryside, and the county town of **Chichester**.

South Downs National Park and the South Downs Way

The tenth and newest member of the country's national park family, the **South Downs National Park** came into being in April 2010. Covering over six hundred square miles, it stretches for 70 miles from eastern Hampshire through the hills of West Sussex to the white chalk cliffs of East Sussex. The park is located in one of the most densely populated parts of the country, and in contrast to other "wilder" national parks, it contains a high proportion of farmland – around 85 percent of the park.

The **South Downs National Park Authority** becomes fully operational in April 2011. Until then, updated information can be found on the **websites** ⓦ www.south-downs.gov.uk and ⓦ www.southdownsonline.org. There are also **visitor centres** at the Queen Elizabeth Country Park in Hampshire, the Seven Sisters Country Park in East Sussex and at Beachy Head (see p.186).

The South Downs Way

One of the best ways to explore the park is to strike off into the countryside on the **South Downs Way**, which rises and dips over one hundred miles along the chalk uplands between the city of Winchester and the spectacular cliffs at Beachy Head, and offers the southeast's finest walks. If undertaken in its entirety, the bridle-path is best traversed from west to east, taking advantage of the prevailing wind, Eastbourne's better transport services and accommodation, and the psychological appeal of ending at the sea. **Steyning**, the halfway-point, marks a transition between predominantly wooded sections and more exposed chalk uplands – to the east of here you'll pass the modern **youth hostel** at Truleigh Hill (☎0845/371 9047, ℮truleigh@yha.org.uk; dorms £11.95; ●). Other hostels along the way are at Telscombe (see p.187) and at Alfriston (see p.186), where you can take a southern loop to Eastbourne along the cliffs of the Seven Sisters, and there's a bunkhouse at an old bothy (a small, stone-built outhouse) at *Gumber Farm* (☎01243/814730; closed Nov–Easter; £10), near Bignor Hill.

The OS Landranger **maps** #198 and #199 cover the eastern end of the route; you'll need #185 and #197 as well to cover the lot. Half a dozen guides are available, the best being by Kev Reynolds (written for following the route in either direction; published by Cicerone Press), or the more detailed guides by Paul Millmore (east–west; Aurum Press) and Jim Manthorpe (west–east; Trailblazer) – each is titled simply *South Downs Way*. You can also check the website ⓦ www.nationaltrail.co.uk/southdowns.

Hastings and around

Once an influential Cinque Port, and best known for the eponymous battle which took place nearby, **HASTINGS** is a curious mixture of unpretentious fishing port, run-down seaside resort and bohemian retreat popular with artists. In 1066, William, Duke of Normandy, landed at Pevensey Bay, a few miles west of town, and made Hastings his base, but his forces met Harold's army at **Battle**, six miles northwest of Hastings. Battle today boasts a magnificent abbey built by William in thanks for his victory, which makes a good afternoon's excursion from Hastings. Farther north, **Bateman's**, once the home of Rudyard Kipling, and the classic **Bodiam Castle** are both easily reached from Hastings in a day-trip, as is the atmospheric little town of **Rye**.

Arrival, information and accommodation

Hastings' **train station**, served by regular trains from London Victoria, is a ten-minute walk from the seafront along Havelock Road, while National Express **bus** services operate from the station at the junction of Havelock and Queen's roads. The **tourist office** is located within the town hall on Queen's Square (Mon–Fri 8.30am–6.15pm, Sat 9am–5pm, Sun 10.30am–4.30pm; ☎01424/451111, ⓦwww.visit1066country.com); there's another, smaller, office in the old town, within the Old Town Hall Museum on High Street (Easter–Oct Mon–Sat 10am–5pm, Sun 11am–5pm; Nov–Easter Mon–Fri 10am–4pm, Sat & Sun 11am–4pm; ☎01424/451120). You'll find **internet** access at Revolver Lounge, 26 George St (☎01424/439899), and **bikes** can be rented from Hastings Town Cycles (☎01424/444013) in St Andrews Market off Queens Road.

Hastings has a few luxurious **B&Bs**, and some decent cheaper options. The nearest **campsite**, *Shear Barn Holiday Park*, Barley Lane (☎01424/423583, ⓦwww.shearbarn.co.uk), is next to the seafront Hastings Country Park, a mile east of the town centre off All Saints Street.

Accommodation

Lavender and Lace 106 All Saints St
☎01424/716290, ⓦwww.lavenderlace1066.co.uk.
Popular, cosy, timber-framed guesthouse right in the middle of the old town. No credit cards. ❸
Senlac Guest House 46–47 Cambridge Gardens
☎01424/430080, ⓦwww.senlacguesthouse.co.uk.
Stylish yet affordable, this friendly B&B near the station is fantastic value for money. The cheapest rooms share bathrooms; self-contained apartments are also available. ❷

Swan House 1 Hill St ☎01424/430014,
ⓦwww.swanhousehastings.co.uk. Elegant, luxurious B&B in a half-timbered fifteenth-century building on one of the old town's most picturesque streets. ❹
Zanzibar 9 Everfield Place, St Leonards-on-Sea
☎01424/460109, ⓦwww.zanzibarhotel.co.uk.
Boutique B&B with rooms themed around the owner's travels, set in a beautifully styled Victorian townhouse overlooking St Leonard's seafront, a 20min walk from Hastings old town. ❹

The Town

Hastings **old town**, east of the pier, holds most of the resort's appeal. **All Saints Street** is by far the most evocative thoroughfare, punctuated with the odd, rickety, timber-framed dwelling from the fifteenth century. The thirteenth-century **St Clement's Church** stands in the High Street, which runs parallel to All Saints Street, on the other side of The Bourne. By a louvred window at the top of the church's tower rests a cannonball that was lodged there by a Dutch galleon in the 1600s – its poignancy rather dispelled by a companion fitted in the eighteenth century for the sake of symmetry.

Down by the seafront, the area known as **The Stade** is characterized by its tall, black weatherboard **net shops**, most dating from the mid-nineteenth century (and still in use), but which first appeared here in Tudor times. To raise Hastings' tone, the town council attempted to shift the fishermen and their malodorously drying nets from the beach by increasing rents per square foot, and these sinister-looking towers were their response. Somewhat remarkably, Hastings still boasts a working fishing fleet, and you can buy fresh fish from several of the net shops. Adjacent to the fishing quarter, the **Jerwood Gallery** (due to open in June 2011) will create a permanent home for the Jerwood Foundation's modern art collection, which includes works by Stanley Spencer, Walter Sickert and Augustus John; see ⓦwww.jerwoodgallery.org for more details.

There's a trio of nautical attractions on nearby Rock-a-Nore Road. The **Fishermen's Museum** (daily: April–Oct 10am–5pm; Nov–March 11am–4pm; free), a converted seaman's chapel, displays one of Hastings' last clinker-built luggers – exceptionally stout trawlers able to withstand being winched up and down the shingle beach. The neighbouring **Shipwreck Heritage Centre** (summer daily 10am–5pm; winter Sat & Sun 11am–4pm; free) details the dramas of unfortunate mariners, focusing on the wreck of the *Amsterdam*, beached in 1749 and now embedded in the sand three miles west of town.

Opposite is the small but well-presented **Underwater World** aquarium (daily: March–Sept 10am–4.30pm; Oct–Feb 11am–4pm; £7.95).

Castle Hill, separating the old town from the visually less interesting modern quarter, can be ascended by the **West Hill Cliff Railway** from George Street, off Marine Parade, one of two Victorian funicular railways in Hastings (daily: March–Oct 10am–5.30pm; rest of year call ☎01424/451111 for opening hours; £2.20), the other being the **East Cliff Railway**, on Rock-a-Nore Road (same times and price). Castle Hill is where William the Conqueror erected his first **castle** in 1066, one of several prefabricated wooden structures brought over from Normandy in sections. It was soon replaced by a more permanent stone structure, but in the thirteenth century storms caused the cliffs to subside, tipping most of the castle into the sea; the surviving ruins, however, offer an excellent prospect of the town. The castle is home to **The 1066 Story** (mid-Feb to Easter Sat & Sun 10am–4pm; Easter–Aug daily 10am–5pm; Sept & Oct daily 10am–4pm; £4.25), in which the events of the last successful invasion of the British mainland are described inside a mock-up of a siege tent.

Eating

Hastings has a good range of places to eat, most very central.

Boulevard Books 32 George St ☎01424/436521. The town's most unique eating experience, this tiny second-hand bookshop serves up Thai food in the evenings, with tables nestled among the bookshelves. BYO.

Dragon 71 George St ☎01424/423688. Great little hangout – part restaurant, part lounge bar – with delicious food (the locally sourced menu changes almost daily), changing art exhibitions and a good assortment of squishy sofas.

Maggies Above Hastings fish market, Rock-a-Nore ☎01424/430205. The best fish and chips (£5.90) in town are at this first-floor café, right on the

beach. Lunch only and very popular, so you'll need to book ahead. No cards.

St Clements 3 Mercatoria, St Leonards-on-Sea ☎01424/200355. Small, elegant restaurant tucked away in the backstreets of St Leonards but worth the journey for its seafood and other locally sourced fare. Mains £16.50–18.50; set menus also available. Closed Sun eve & Mon.

Webbes 1 Rock-A-Nore Rd ☎01424/721650. Contemporary seafood restaurant opposite the new Jerwood Gallery, with plenty of outside seating in summer. Mains such as steamed panache of fish cost around £14, or you can pick and choose from tasting dishes at £3.50 each.

Drinking and nightlife

There are more than thirty **pubs** to choose from in Hastings, and a thriving **live music** scene. In the old town, the ever-popular *First In Last Out*, 15 High St, has its own micro brewery; *Porter's Wine Bar*, on the same street at no. 56 (☎01424/427000, ⓦwww.porterswinebar.com), has jazz and acoustic music on Wednesday and Thursday nights and Sunday afternoons (including a regular spot by acclaimed jazz pianist and local resident Liane Carroll on Wed); and the friendly *Stag Inn*, 14 All Saints St (☎01424/425734), runs a folk session on Tuesdays and bluegrass on Wednesdays. The *Dragon* (see above) has DJs at weekends, while The Electric Palace, 39 High St (☎01424/720393, ⓦwww.electricpalacecinema.com), is a tiny independent **cinema** with a licensed bar. For comprehensive **listings** of what's on, get the free *Ultimate Alternative*, available in pubs, clubs and record shops and at ⓦwww.ua1066.co.uk.

Battle

The town of **BATTLE**, a ten-minute train ride inland from Hastings, occupies the site of the most famous land battle in British history. Here, on October 14, 1066, the invading Normans overcame the Anglo-Saxon army of King Harold, who is thought to have been killed not by an arrow through the eye – a myth resulting from a misinterpretation of the Bayeux Tapestry – but by a workaday clubbing about the head. Before the battle took place, William vowed that, should he win the engagement, he would build a religious foundation on the very spot of Harold's slaying to atone for the bloodshed, and, true to his word, **Battle Abbey** (daily: April–Sept 10am–6pm; Oct–March 10am–4pm; £7; EH) was built four years later and subsequently occupied by a fraternity of Benedictines. The magnificent structure, though partially destroyed in the Dissolution and much rebuilt and revised over the centuries, still dominates the town. You can wander through the ruins of the abbey to the spot where Harold was killed – the site of the high altar of William's abbey, now marked by a memorial stone – while a visitor centre holds an interactive exhibition and an auditorium where you can view a dramatic re-enactment of the battle using film and computer simulations.

You can eat well at the excellent *Nobles* **restaurant**, 17 High St (℡01424/774422; closed Sun), with mains such as saddle of Romney Marsh lamb setting you back around £16; good-value set-price meals are also available. The atmospheric *Pilgrims* (℡01424/772314), a fifteenth-century hall next to the abbey, is an ideal spot for afternoon **tea**, while the *Chequers Inn* at Lower Lake, on High Street, serves decent **pub** grub.

Rye and Winchelsea

Perched on a hill overlooking Romney Marsh, ten miles east of Hastings, sits the ancient town of **RYE**. Added as a "limb" to the original Cinque Ports (see box, p.168), the town then became marooned two miles inland with the retreat of the sea and the silting-up of the River Rother. It is now one of the most popular places in East Sussex – half-timbered, skew-roofed and quintessentially English, but also very commercialized.

From Strand Quay, head up The Deals to Rye's most picturesque lane, the sloping cobbled **Mermaid Street**, which brings you eventually to the peaceful oasis of Church Square. Henry James lived from 1898 until his death in 1916 in **Lamb House** at the east end of Mermaid Street (March–Oct Thurs & Sat 2–6pm; £4; NT). At the centre of Church Square stands **St Mary's Church**, home of England's oldest functioning pendulum clock; the ascent of the church tower – whose bells were looted by French raiders in 1377 and then retrieved with similar audacity – offers fine views over the clay-tiled roofs and grid of narrow lanes. In the far corner of the square stands the **Ypres Tower** (April–Oct Mon & Thurs–Sun 10.30am–1pm & 2–5pm; Nov–March Sat & Sun 10.30am–3.30pm; £2.95, joint ticket with Rye Castle Museum £5), formerly used to keep watch for cross-Channel invaders, and now a part of the **Rye Castle Museum** on nearby East Street (Mon, Thurs & Fri 2–5pm, Sat & Sun 10.30am–1pm & 2–5pm; £2.95, joint ticket with Ypres Tower £5; ⒲www.ryemuseum.co.uk), which houses a number of relics from Rye's past, including an eighteenth-century fire engine. Also worth seeking out is the **Rye Art Gallery**, 107 High St (daily except Tues 10.30am–1pm & 2–5pm; free; ⒲www.ryeartgallery.co.uk), which stages exhibitions by local contemporary artists; the gallery gives access to the associated Stormont Studio, which has a small permanent collection, including works by artists associated with Rye, such as Burra and Nash. Rye's acclaimed **literary festival** (⒲www.ryefestival.co.uk) takes place over two weeks in September and also features a wide range of musical and visual arts events.

WINCHELSEA, perched on a hill two miles southwest of Rye and easily reached by train, bus, foot or bike, was rebuilt by Edward I after the original settlement was washed away in the great storm of 1287. The village shares Rye's indignity of having become detached from the sea, but has a very different character. Rye gets all the visitors, whereas Winchelsea feels positively deserted, an impression augmented as you pass through the medieval Strand Gate and see the ghostly ruined **Church of St Thomas à Becket**. Head south for a mile and a half and you get to **Winchelsea beach**, a long expanse of pebbly sand. Three miles further east, **Camber Sands** is a two-mile stretch of sandy beach that has become a renowned centre of wind and water sports.

Practicalities

Hourly **trains** run to Rye and Winchelsea from Hastings; Rye's station is at the bottom of Station Approach, off Cinque Ports Street, while Winchelsea's is a mile north of the town. **Bus** #100 runs into the centre of both towns from Hastings. Rye's **tourist office** is at 4–5 Lion St (daily: April–Sept 10am–5pm; Oct–March 10am–4pm; ☎01797/229049, ⊛www.visitrye.co.uk), and there's more information on the town in the Heritage Centre on Strand Quay (daily 10am–5pm; ☎01797/226696, ⊛www.ryeheritage.co.uk), which also rents out audioguides (£4) and puts on a sound-and-light show (every 20min; £3.50) featuring a scaled-down model of the town. Rye Hire, 1 Cyprus Place (☎01797/223033), rents out **bikes**, useful if you fancy tackling the three-mile cycle path to Camber Sands.

The town's popularity with weekending Londoners gives it an excellent choice of **accommodation** and **places to eat**, much of it on the expensive side.

Hotels

Apothecary 1 East St ☎01797/229157, ⊛www.bedandbreakfastrye.com. Excellent-value, stylish B&B accommodation above Rye's nicest coffee house. **2**

The George 98 High St ☎01797/222144, ⊛www.thegeorgeinrye.com. Justifiably popular, this luxurious small hotel manages to get everything just right, from the tasteful, individually furnished rooms (complete with cashmere-covered hot-water bottles in winter) to the cosy, atmospheric bar and excellent restaurant. **5**

Haydens 108 High St ☎01797/224501, ⊛www.haydensinrye.co.uk. Eco-friendly boutique B&B with elegant, contemporary rooms set above a popular café-restaurant. **3**

The Place at the Beach New Lydd Rd, Camber ☎01797/225057, ⊛www.theplaceatthebeach.co.uk. Stylishly renovated motel set just back from the beach at Camber Sands, with a good restaurant attached. Special offers often available on their website. **5**

Strand House Tanyards Lane, Winchelsea ☎01797/226276, ⊛www.thestrandhouse.co.uk. At the foot of the cliff below Strand Gate, this Tudor hotel is Winchelsea's best accommodation option, with inglenook fireplaces and a grassy garden. Meals available, and special diets catered for. **2**

Cafés, restaurants and pubs

Apothecary See above. Leather armchairs, book-lined walls, scrubbed wooden tables and a wealth of original features make this lovely, atmospheric coffee shop, housed in the town's old apothecary, the best in town.

The George See above. Delicious, locally sourced food with a Mediterreanean influence is on offer at Rye's old coaching inn; there's formal dining in the restaurant, or you can settle down in front of an open fire in the snug bar.

Haydens See above. Local and organic produce is the thing at this small, environmentally friendly café-restaurant. The lunch menu covers favourites such as rarebit and soup, while in the evening (Fri & Sat only) you can choose between dishes such as local lamb cutlets (£14) and Rye Bay plaice (£12).

Mermaid Inn Mermaid St ☎01797/223065. This fifteenth-century, half-timbered hotel simply oozes character and charm, and a meal at its in-house restaurant is an excellent way to soak in the atmosphere without breaking the bank. Three courses will set you back £24 at lunch, £34 at dinner.

Tuscan Kitchen 8 Lion St ☎01797/223269. The delicious, authentic Tuscan cuisine on offer at this beamed, low-ceilinged restaurant has won it a lot of fans, and is excellent value too.

Winchelsea Farm Kitchen High St, Winchelsea ☎01797/226287. Small tearoom behind an excellent deli and butcher's on Winchelsea's main street. Courtyard seating in summer.

Ypres Castle Gun Gardens, down the steps behind the Ypres Tower. An unspoiled spot, with real ales, a beer garden with views over Romney Marsh, and live music on Friday nights.

Bodiam Castle

Ask a child to draw a castle and the outline of **Bodiam Castle**, nine miles north of Hastings (Jan to mid-Feb Sat & Sun 11am–4pm; mid-Feb to Oct daily 10am–6pm; Nov & Dec Wed–Sun 11am–4pm; £5.80; NT), would be the result: a classically stout square block with rounded corner turrets, battlements and a wide moat. When it was built in 1385 to guard what were the lower reaches of the River Rother, Bodiam was state-of-the-art military architecture, but during the Civil War a company of Roundheads breached the fortress and removed its roof to reduce its effectiveness as a possible stronghold for the king. Over the next 250 years Bodiam fell into neglect until restoration in the last century by Lord Curzon. The original portcullis is still in place, while the extremely steep spiral staircases, leading to the crenellated battlements, will test all but the strongest of thighs.

You can get here from Hastings by regular bus #349, or, from April to October, from Tenterden, ten miles northeast, on a full-scale steam train run by the **Kent & East Sussex Railway** (£12.80 all day; ☎01580/765155, ⓦwww.kesr.org.uk).

Burwash and Bateman's

Fifteen miles northwest of Hastings on the A265, halfway to Tunbridge Wells, **BURWASH**, with its red-brick and weather-boarded cottages and Norman church tower, exemplifies the pastoral idyll of inland Sussex. Half a mile south of the village lies the main attraction, **Bateman's** (house & garden: mid-March to Oct Mon–Wed, Sat & Sun 11am–5pm; house also open 2 weeks in Dec Sat & Sun 11.30am–3.30pm; garden only also open Nov & Dec Mon–Wed, Sat & Sun 11am–4pm; £7.45, garden free in Nov & Dec; NT), home of the Nobel Prize-winning writer and journalist **Rudyard Kipling** from 1902 until his death in 1936. Built in the seventeenth century and set amid attractive gardens, the house features a working watermill converted by Kipling to generate electricity, and which now grinds corn most Wednesdays and Saturdays at 2pm. Inside, the house is laid out as Kipling left it, with letters, early editions of his work and mementoes from his travels on display. Getting here without your own transport involves a three-mile walk from Etchingham station, which is served by regular trains from London and Hastings.

Bexhill and the De La Warr Pavilion

Seven miles west of Hastings, the seaside town of Bexhill-on-Sea would be unremarkable were it not for the iconic **De La Warr Pavilion** (Mon–Fri 10am–5pm, Sat & Sun 10am–6pm; free; ⓦwww.dlwp.com), a sleek modernist masterpiece overlooking the sea. Built in 1935 by architects Erich Mendelsohn and Serge Chermayeff, the Pavilion – the first modernist public building in the country, and the first to use a welded steel frame – was the brainchild of the progressive 9th Earl de la Warr, local landowner and socialist, who had a vision of a free-to-all seaside pavilion for the education, entertainment and health of the masses. In its brief heyday the Pavilion flourished, but slid gradually into disrepair after World War II. After decades hosting everything from bingo to wrestling while the building crumbled and corroded, today the Pavilion has been lovingly restored to its original glory – all crisp white lines and gleaming glass – and hosts changing **exhibitions** of contemporary art, and an eclectic mix of **live performances**, from big-name bands to comedy and film nights. Up on the first floor a **café** and restaurant offer glorious views from the floor-to-ceiling windows and balcony.

Eastbourne and around

Like so many of the southeast's seaside resorts, **EASTBOURNE** was kick-started into life in the 1840s, when the Brighton, Lewes & Hastings Rail Company built a branch line from Lewes to the sea. Past holiday-makers include George Orwell, the composer Claude Debussy, who finished writing *La Mer* here, as well as Marx and Engels. Nowadays Eastbourne has a solid reputation as a retirement town, and though the recently opened Towner Gallery has introduced a welcome splash of modernity, the town's charms remain for the most part sedate and old-fashioned. The greatest draw is the nearby South Downs, which the sea has ground into a series of dramatic chalk cliffs around **Beachy Head**, just southwest of town.

Arrival, information and accommodation

Eastbourne's **train station**, a splendid Italianate terminus, is ten minutes' walk from the seafront up Terminus Road, while the **bus station** is on Cavendish Place right by the pier. The **tourist office** is at 3 Cornfield Rd, just off Terminus Road (March–May & Oct Mon–Fri 9.30am–5.30pm, Sat 9.30am–4pm; June–Sept Mon–Fri 9.30am–5.30pm, Sat 9.30am–5pm; Nov–Feb Mon–Fri 9.30am–4.30pm, Sat 9.30am–1pm; ℡0871/663 0031, ⓦwww.visiteastbourne.com). The town's trackless **Dotto trains** ply up and down the seafront and into the centre (April–Oct daily 10.30am–5.30pm); a day-ticket (£5.50) allows visitors to hop on or off at a series of designated stops.

There are hundreds of places to **stay**, including the friendly *Sea Beach House Hotel*, 39–40 Marine Parade (℡01323/410458, ⓦwww.seabeachhouse.co .uk; ❷), and the budget boutique hotel *Big Sleep*, King Edward's Parade (℡01323/722676, ⓦwww.thebigsleephotel.com; ❷–❹), both on the seafront; the latter has a range of rooms, from basic, no-frills doubles to more luxurious suites, plus good-value family rooms. Eastbourne's modern **YHA** is a mile from the centre on East Dean Road (℡0845/3719316, ⒺEastbourne@yha.org.uk; dorms £13.95; closed mid-Oct to March). You can camp right by a sandy beach at the secluded *Bay View* **campsite** (℡01323/768688, ⓦwww.bay-view.co.uk), off the A259 east to Pevensey.

The Town

Conforming to tradition, the **pier** is the focal point of the elegant Grand Parade: opened in 1872, it was intended to match the best on the south coast, which it certainly does. To the west, on the promenade, the **Wish Tower** is the first of the prom's two prominent red-brick Martello towers. The **Redoubt Fortress**, half a mile east of the pier, now houses a military museum (April to early Nov Tues–Sun 10am–5pm; £4).

A few minutes' walk inland from the Wish Tower at Devonshire Park, the **Towner Art Gallery and Museum** (Tues–Sun 10am–6pm; free; ⓦwww .townereastbourne.org.uk) houses changing exhibitions of contemporary art within a sleek modern cube of glass and smooth concrete curves; up on the second floor there's a café-bar with a small terrace overlooking the rooftops of Eastbourne to the South Downs beyond. Just across the road in a distinctive corner house on Carlisle Road, the **Eastbourne Heritage Centre** (April–Oct daily 2–5pm; £2.50) tackles the history of the town, while the **"How We Lived Then" Museum of Shops** at 20 Cornfield Terrace (daily 10am–5pm; £4.50), just down from the tourist office, contains a staggering amount of artefacts from the last hundred years of consumerism crammed into mock-up shops.

Eating and drinking

Eastbourne has a clutch of decent **restaurants**, including *Pomodoro e Mozzarella*, a jolly and authentic Italian at 23 Cornfield Terrace (℡01323/733800), and the popular *Ashoka*, just up the road at 28 Cornfield Rd (℡01323/733344), for Indian food. For huge ice-cream sundaes, go to *Fusciardi's* on Marine Parade, an Eastbourne institution. The *Dolphin* **pub** at 14 South St is one of the town's nicest, a relaxed hangout with good food and locally brewed beers on tap. Up towards the station at 14 Station St, the stylish *Loft Lounge* has an extensive cocktail menu and live music on Sunday nights.

Beachy Head, Seven Sisters and the Cuckmere River Valley

A short walk west from Eastbourne takes you out along the most dramatic stretch of coastline in Sussex, where the chalk uplands of the Sussex Downs are cut by the sea into a sequence of splendid cliffs. The most spectacular of all, at 575ft high, is **Beachy Head**, a well-known suicide spot. An open-top bus runs at least hourly (April–Oct; £5 return; ⓦwww.city-sightseeing.co.uk) from Eastbourne Pier to the top of Beachy Head, where you'll find a visitor centre (daily: April–Oct 10am–4pm; Nov–March Sat & Sun 10am–3.30pm; ℡01323/737273).

West of the headland the scenery softens into a diminishing series of cliffs, a landmark known as the **Seven Sisters**. The eponymous country park provides some of the most impressive walks in the county, taking in the cliff-top path and the lower valley of the meandering **River Cuckmere**, into which the Seven Sisters subside. Head up to Seaford Head, on the western side of the estuary, for the iconic view of the cliffs you'll see on every postcard, with the picturesque coastguard's cottages in the foreground. There's **bike hire** (from £8) at the Seven Sisters Cycle Company, next door to the visitor centre (daily Easter–Oct 10.30am–4.30pm; ℡01323/870280) at the park entrance at Exceat, on the A259.

Three miles inland from the park in the picture-perfect village of **ALFRISTON**, the fourteenth-century timber-framed and thatched **Clergy House** (March–Oct Mon, Wed, Thurs, Sat & Sun 10.30am–5pm, plus Fri in Aug; Nov to mid-Dec Mon, Wed, Thurs, Sat & Sun 11am–4pm; £4.05; NT) was the first property to be acquired by the National Trust in 1896. Less edifying, but potentially more fun, is **Drusillas Park** (daily 10am–4/5pm; £11.30–14.30; ⓦwww.drusillas.co.uk), a mile or so up the valley. With penguins, meerkats, lemurs and more, a miniature railway, paddling pool and an excellent adventure playground, it's among the best small zoos in the country, though its popularity means it can get very crowded in the school holidays.

A couple of miles south of Alfriston, the Frog Firle **youth hostel** (℡0845/371 9101, ⓔalfriston@yha.org.uk; dorm bed £13.75) is beautifully situated in a traditional Sussex flint building in the Cuckmere Valley. The atmospheric fourteenth-century *George Inn* on Alfriston High Street (℡01323/870319) dishes up good bar **food** at lunchtime and more sophisticated fare in the evening, while *Moonrakers* (℡01323/871199), also on the High Street, serves imaginative food in its two elegant low-beamed dining rooms or outside on a lovely terrace overlooking the village green.

Lewes and around

East Sussex's county town, **LEWES** straddles the River Ouse as it carves a gap through the South Downs on its final stretch to the sea. Though new housing estates have spread from the town's fringes, the core of Lewes remains remarkably good-looking: Georgian and crooked older dwellings line the High Street, with narrow lanes – or "twittens" – leading off it and its continuations, with views onto the Downs. With some of England's most appealing chalkland right on its doorstep, numerous traces of a history that stretches back to the Saxons, and one of the houses most closely associated with the Bloomsbury group – **Charleston** – close by, Lewes is a worthwhile stopover on any tour – and an easy one, with good rail connections with London and along the coast.

Lewes made the headlines in 2008 when it introduced its own currency, the **Lewes pound**, created to encourage spending in the local economy. Available in £1, £5, £10 and £21 denominations, and with the same value as sterling, the currency is accepted by over a hundred businesses around town, and is issued at various locations including the town hall on the High Street and Mays General Store on Cliffe High Street.

Arrival, information and accommodation

The **train station** is south of High Street down Station Road, while the **bus station** is on Eastgate Street, near the foot of School Hill. At the junction of the High Street and Fisher Street, the **tourist office** (April–Sept Mon–Fri 9am–5pm, Sat 9.30am–5.30pm, Sun 10am–2pm; Oct–March Mon–Fri 9am–5pm, Sat 10am–2pm; ℡01273/483448, ⓦwww.lewes.gov.uk) provides free copies of the monthly **listings magazine**, *Viva Lewes* (ⓦwww.vivalewes.co.uk).

For **accommodation**, *Castle Banks Cottage*, 4 Castle Banks (℡01273/476291, ⓦwww.castlebankscottage.co.uk; no credit cards; ❷), is a beamed period house with great views and a small breakfast garden, tucked away off West Street, or try *Monty's*, just off the High Street at 4 Albion St (℡01273/474095, ⓦwww.montysaccommodation.co.uk; ❹), a lovely self-contained basement flat with its own entrance and a stylishly done-out bedroom, lounge and shower room; nice little touches such as a DVD library and plenty of books and magazines add to the charm. The nearest **youth hostel** is in the village of **Telscombe**, six miles south of Lewes (℡0845/371 9663; dorm bed £13.95; bus #123 from Lewes), with simple accommodation in two-hundred-year-old cottages. There's basic **camping** at *Spring Barn Farm Park* (℡01273/488450; April–Oct), a twenty-minute walk from town; the site's particularly good for families, with animals and an adventure playground on the doorstep, and there's a good café too.

The Town

The best way to begin a tour of the town from the train station is to walk up Station Road, then left down the High Street. Lewes's **castle** (Tues–Sat 10am–5.30pm, Mon & Sun 11am–5.30pm; closed Mon in Jan; winter closes at dusk; £6) is hidden from view behind the houses on your right. Inside the castle complex – unusual for being built on two mottes, or mounds – the shell of the eleventh-century keep remains, and both the towers can be climbed for excellent views over the town to the surrounding Downs. Tickets for the castle include admission to the **museum** (same hours as castle), by the castle entrance, holding a collection of archeological artefacts and a town model, among other items.

A few minutes' walk further west along the High Street, past **St Michael's Church** with its unusual twin towers, one wooden and the other flint, brings you to the steep, cobbled and much photographed **Keere Street**, down which the reckless Prince Regent is alleged to have driven his carriage. Keere Street leads to **Southover Grange**, with its lovely gardens (daily dawn–dusk; free). Built in 1572 from the remains of an earlier priory which was dismantled after the Dissolution, the Grange was also the childhood home of the diarist John Evelyn. Past

The bonfire societies

Each November 5, while the rest of Britain lights small domestic bonfires or attends municipal firework displays to commemorate the 1605 foiled Catholic plot to blow up the Houses of Parliament (see p.832), Lewes puts on a more dramatic show, whose origins lie in the deaths of the town's Protestant martyrs in 1556. By the end of the eighteenth century, Lewes' **Bonfire Boys** had become notorious for the boisterousness of their anti-Catholic demonstrations, in which they set off fireworks indiscriminately and dragged rolling tar barrels through the streets – a tradition still practised today, although with a little more caution. Lewes's first **bonfire societies** were established to try to get a bit more discipline into the proceedings, and in the early part of the last century they were persuaded to move their street fires to the town's perimeters.

Today's tightly knit bonfire societies, each with its quasi-militaristic motto ("Death or Glory", "True to Each Other", etc), spend much of the year organizing the Bonfire Night shenanigans, when their members dress up in traditional costumes and parade through the town carrying flaming torches, before marching off onto the Downs for their society's big fire. At each of the fires, effigies of Guy Fawkes and the pope are burned alongside contemporary, but equally reviled, figures – politicians are popular choices.

the gardens, a right turn down Southover High Street leads to the Tudor-built **Anne of Cleves House** (March–Oct Tues–Thurs 10am–5pm; £4.20, combined ticket with the castle £8.80), given to her in settlement after her divorce from Henry VIII – though she never actually lived here.

At the east end of the High Street, School Hill descends towards **Cliffe Bridge**, built in 1727 and the entrance to the commercial centre of the medieval settlement. For the energetic, a path leads up onto the Downs from the end of Cliffe High Street, passing close to an obelisk that commemorates the Lewes Martyrs, seventeen Protestants who were burned here in 1556 at the height of Mary Tudor's militant revival of Catholicism.

Eating, drinking and entertainment

No visit to Lewes would be complete without a trip to ⅍ *Bills*, 56 Cliffe High St (☎01273/476918), part **café**, part produce store, and a Lewes institution. Tucked away at the far end of Cliffe High Street, the *Buttercup Café*, within Pastorale Antiques at 15 Malling St (☎01273/477664), is another great spot, with plenty of outdoor seating in a sun-trap courtyard, and delicious salads, soups and bakes. For an evening meal try *Spice Merchant*, 18 West St (☎01273/470707), an always-buzzing Indian **restaurant**, or *Pelham House*, St Andrew's Lane (☎01273/488600), where mains such as lamb with carrot and vanilla puree (2 courses £17.50) can be enjoyed in the sixteenth-century interior or out on the lovely terrace.

Lewes is the home of the excellent Harvey's brewery and most of the **pubs** serve its beer – try the *Lewes Arms* tucked behind the Star Gallery, the *Brewers' Arms* on the High Street, or the *John Harvey Tavern* opposite the brewery. The lively *Snowdrop Inn* on the outskirts of town at 119 South St (☎01273/471018) serves excellent food and has **live music** several nights a week.

The annual **Glyndebourne** opera season runs from mid-May until the end of August, with performances held at the opera house at Glynde, three miles east of town. It's expensive and exclusive, though there are tickets available at reduced prices for dress rehearsals or for standing-room-only; call ☎01273/813813 for details or check the website at ⓦ www.glyndebourne.com.

Charleston Farmhouse

Six miles east of Lewes, off the A27, **Charleston Farmhouse** (April–Oct Wed–Sat 1–6pm, Sun & bank holiday Mondays 1–5.30pm; last entry 1hr before closing; £9, garden only £3.50; ⓦ www.charleston.org.uk) was home to Virginia Woolf's sister Vanessa Bell, Vanessa's husband, Clive Bell, and her lover, Duncan Grant. As conscientious objectors, the trio moved here during World War I so that the men could work on local farms (farm labourers were exempted from military service). The farmhouse became a gathering point for other members of the Bloomsbury Group, including the biographer Lytton Strachey, the economist John Maynard Keynes and the novelist E.M. Forster.

Unless it's a Sunday, you have to join a fifty-minute guided **tour** in order to view the interior of the farmhouse, where almost every surface is decorated and the walls are hung with paintings by Picasso, Renoir and Augustus John, alongside the work of the markedly less talented residents. Many of the fabrics, lampshades and other artefacts bear the unmistakeable mark of the Omega Workshop, the Bloomsbury equivalent of William Morris's artistic movement.

Brighton

Recorded as the tiny fishing village of Brithelmeston in the Domesday Book, **BRIGHTON** seems to have slipped unnoticed through history until the mid-eighteenth-century sea-bathing trend established it as a resort; it hasn't looked back since. The fad received royal approval in the 1780s when the decadent Prince of Wales (the future George IV) began patronizing the town in the company of his mistress, thus setting a precedent for the "dirty weekend", Brighton's major contribution to the English collective consciousness. Trying to shake off this blowsy reputation, Brighton now highlights its Georgian charm, its upmarket shops and classy restaurants, and a thriving conference industry. Yet, however much it tries to present itself as a comfortable middle-class town (granted city status in 2000), the essence of Brighton's appeal is its faintly bohemian vitality, a buzz that comes from a mix of English holiday-makers, thousands of young foreign students from the town's innumerable language schools, a thriving gay community and an energetic local student population from the art college and two universities.

Arrival and information

Brighton **train station** is at the head of Queen's Road, which descends to the Clock Tower, where it becomes West Street before continuing to the seafront – a distance of about half a mile. National Express and Stagecoach bus services arrive at Pool Valley **bus station**, tucked just in from the seafront on the south side of the Old Steine. Open-top **bus tours** (April to mid-Sept; every 30min; £8) operate on a circular route around the town and up and down the seafront, passing both the train station and tourist office; tickets are valid all day.

The **tourist office** is accessed through the Royal Pavilion's shop at 4–5 Pavilion Buildings (daily 10am–5pm; ⓣ 0300/300 0088, ⓦ www.visitbrighton.com).

Accommodation

Accommodation is pricey in Brighton, with prices rising through the roof (by as much as fifty percent) at weekends in the summer; accommodation codes given below refer to high-season weekend prices. Many places offer reductions for stays of two nights or more and at weekends there's often a two-night-stay minimum required. Brighton's official **campsite** is the *Sheepcote Valley* site (☎01273/626546), just north of Brighton Marina; take bus #1 or #1A to Wilsons Avenue; book early as it's popular.

Hotels, B&Bs and guesthouses

Blanch House 17 Atlingworth St ☎01273/603504, www.blanchhouse.co.uk. Luxury boutique hotel with twelve immaculate rooms, the most expensive of which come with roll-top baths. There's an excellent restaurant, but the main draw is the hotel's sleek, award-winning cocktail bar (see p.195). ❺

Brighton House Hotel 52 Regency Square ☎01273/323282, www.brighton-house.co.uk. Understated eco-friendly guesthouse with elegant, contemporary rooms and an all-organic breakfast buffet. Excellent value. ❹

Cavalaire House 34 Upper Rock Gardens ☎01273/696899, www.cavalaire.co.uk. Warm and welcoming B&B, with artwork from Brighton artists on the walls, fresh flowers in the cheery breakfast room, and a friendly resident dog. Rooms are clean and contemporary, though the cheapest standard rooms lack the charm of the others. ❹

Drakes Hotel 33–34 Marine Parade ☎01273/696934, www.drakesofbrighton.com. The unbeatable seafront location is the big draw at this chic, minimalist boutique hotel. All the luxuries you'd expect are there, and the most expensive rooms come with freestanding baths by floor-to-ceiling windows. The excellent in-house restaurant is one of Brighton's best. ❺

Hotel du Vin Ship St ☎01273/718588, www.hotelduvin.com. A Gothic Revival building in a contemporary style, luxuriously furnished in subtle seaside colours, with an excellent bar and bistro. ❻

Kemp Townhouse 21 Atlingworth St ☎01273/681400, www.kemptownhouse.com. Regency townhouse hotel with excellent service, chic, elegant rooms and excellent breakfasts. Sea-view rooms come with binoculars for gazing out to sea. ❹

Legends 31–34 Marine Parade ☎01273/624462, www.legendsbrighton.com. Large, buzzing, gay hotel on the seafront, with a late bar for residents and their guests, and regular cabaret nights. ❸

New Steine Hotel 10–11 New Steine ☎01273/681546, www.newsteinehotel.com. Rooms are stylish and modern at this excellent-value hotel, and there's a small in-house bistro too. Local artists exhibit regularly. ❸

Pelirocco 10 Regency Square ☎01273/327055, www.hotelpelirocco.co.uk. Self-styled rock'n'roll hangout with extravagantly themed rooms, a bohemian atmosphere and a late-opening bar. ❹

Snooze 25 St George's Terrace ☎01273/605797, www.snoozebrighton.com. Quirky 10-room B&B on a quiet road in the heart of Kemp Town Village. Rooms are individually styled with a hotchpotch of vintage furnishings. ❹

Hostels

Baggies Backpackers 33 Oriental Place ☎01273/733740, www.baggiesbackpackers.com. Spacious house a little west of the West Pier with private rooms and large bright dorms (starting at £13 a night), decent showers and plenty of room to spread out. No credit cards. ❶

Journeys 33 Richmond Place ☎01273/695866, www.visitjourneys.com. Friendly, modern hostel in a great central location close to North Laine. Free wi-fi and breakfasts, and a small bar. Dorm beds from £11. ❶

The City

Any visit to Brighton inevitably begins with a visit to its two most famous landmarks – the exuberant **Royal Pavilion** and the wonderfully tacky **Palace Pier**, a few minutes away – followed by a stroll along the seafront promenade or the pebbly beach. Just as interesting, though, is an exploration of Brighton's pedestrianized **Lanes**, where some of the town's diverse restaurants, bars and tiny bric-a-brac, jewellery and antique shops can be found, or an idle meander through the quaint, but more bohemian streets of **North Laine**.

The Royal Pavilion and the Brighton Museum

In any survey to find England's most loved building, there's always a bucketful of votes for Brighton's exotic extravaganza, the **Royal Pavilion** (daily: April–Sept 9.30am–5.45pm; Oct–March 10am–5.15pm; last entry 45min before closing;

A weekend in Brighton

Friday night

Start off the weekend in style with **champagne and oysters** at *Riddle and Finn* in the heart of the Lanes. Then head along to the hip Komedia theatre to catch some **comedy** or live music.

Saturday

Set aside a full morning to take in the splendours of the quirky **Pavilion**, George IV's pleasure palace by the sea. Then head down to the seafront for an **alfresco lunch**, whether it be divine mackerel sandwiches from *Jack and Linda's Smokehouse*, or a more substantial feast at the beachfront *Due South* restaurant. After an amble to the end of the garish **Palace Pier**, spend the afternoon exploring the winding passageways of the **Lanes**, and the **North Laine**'s quirky shops. Excellent cafés can be found on virtually every corner, but for something a bit different head towards Kemp Town to the quirky *Tea Cosy Tea Rooms* or *Bom-Bane's*, both on George Street; the latter is also a top tip for **dinner** if you happen to coincide your visit with one of their monthly musical dinners (check their website for details). Alternatively, check out the excellent *Terre-à-Terre*, for vegetarian cooking like no other. After dinner, head out on the town – Brighton has the best **nightlife** in the south outside of London, and is positively bursting at the seams with uber-cool bars and clubs, as well as a great collection of traditional boozers.

Sunday

There are plenty of great spots for a lazy **brunch**: try *The Dorset Street Bar* or *The Sanctuary*. Burn off the calories afterwards with a game of **beach volleyball** at Yellowave. If it's raining you can hunker down at Brighton's independent **cinema**, the Duke of York's, or take in the exhibits at the **Brighton and Hove Art Gallery**. If you fancy a complete change of scene, hop on a train to nearby **Lewes** (15min), where you can wander through the town's ancient twittens and visit an ancient castle before ending up at *Bills* for coffee and a fabulous flower-festooned cake.

£9.50; Ⓦ www.royalpavilion.org.uk), which flaunts itself in the middle of the Old Steine, the main thoroughfare along which most of the seafront-bound road traffic gets funnelled. Commissioned by the fun-loving Prince of Wales in 1815, the Pavilion was the design of John Nash, architect of London's Regent Street. What Nash came up with was an extraordinary confection of slender minarets, twirling domes, pagodas, balconies and miscellaneous motifs imported from India and China, all supported on an innovative cast-iron frame, creating an exterior profile that defines a genre of its own – Oriental-Gothic. George had the time of his life here, frolicking with his mistress, Mrs Fitzherbert, whom he installed in a house on the west side of the Old Steine.

Inside the Pavilion, one of the highlights – approached via the restrained Long Gallery – is the **Banqueting Room**, which erupts with ornate splendour and is dominated by a one-tonne chandelier hung from the jaws of a massive dragon cowering in a plantain tree. Next door, the huge, high-ceilinged kitchen, fitted with the most modern appliances of its time, has iron columns disguised as palm trees.

Nearby, the stunning **Music Room**, the first sight of which reduced George to tears of joy, has a huge dome lined with more than 26,000 individually gilded scales and hung with exquisite umbrella-like glass lamps. After climbing the famous cast-iron staircase with its bamboo-look banisters, you can go into Victoria's sober and seldom-used bedroom and the North Gallery where the king's portrait hangs, accompanied by a selection of satirical cartoons. More notable, though, is the **South Gallery**, decorated in sky blue with trompe-l'oeil bamboo trellises and a carpet that appears to be strewn with flowers.

Across the gardens from the Pavilion stands the **Dome**, once the royal stables and now the town's main concert hall. Adjoining it is the **Brighton Museum and Art Gallery** (Tues–Sun 10am–5pm; free; Ⓦ www.brighton-hove-rpml.org.uk), entered just around the corner on Church Street. It houses an eclectic mix of modern fashion and design, archeology, painting and local history, including a large collection of pottery. The collection of classic Art Deco and Art Nouveau furniture stands out, the highlight being Dalí's famous sofa based on Mae West's lips.

The seafront

Although its western end holds appealing Georgian terraces and squares, much of Brighton's seafront is an ugly mix of shops, entertainment complexes and hotels, ranging from the impressively pompous plasterwork of the *Grand Hotel* – scene of the IRA's attempted assassination of the Conservative Cabinet in October 1984 – to the green-glass monstrosity of the *Brighton Thistle Hotel*. To appreciate fully the tackier side of Brighton, take a stroll along the **Palace Pier**. Completed in 1899,

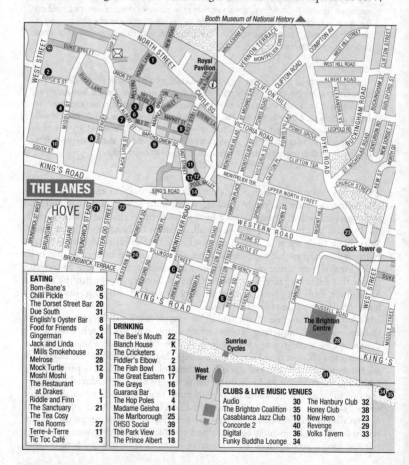

Booth Museum of National History ▲

EATING	
Bom-Bane's	26
Chilli Pickle	5
The Dorset Street Bar	20
Due South	31
English's Oyster Bar	8
Food for Friends	6
Gingerman	24
Jack and Linda Mills Smokehouse	37
Melrose	28
Mock Turtle	12
Moshi Moshi	9
The Restaurant at Drakes	L
Riddle and Finn	1
The Sanctuary	21
The Tea Cosy Tea Rooms	27
Terre-à-Terre	11
Tic Toc Café	3

DRINKING	
The Bee's Mouth	22
Blanch House	K
The Cricketers	7
Fiddler's Elbow	2
The Fish Bowl	13
The Great Eastern	17
The Greys	16
Guarana Bar	19
The Hop Poles	4
Madame Geisha	14
The Marlborough	25
OHSO Social	39
The Park View	15
The Prince Albert	18

CLUBS & LIVE MUSIC VENUES			
Audio	30	The Hanbury Club	32
The Brighton Coalition	35	Honey Club	38
Casablanca Jazz Club	10	New Hero	23
Concorde 2	40	Revenge	29
Digital	36	Volks Tavern	33
Funky Buddha Lounge	34		

its every inch is devoted to fun and money-making, from the cacophonous Palace of Fun and the Pleasure Dome to the state-of-the-art video games and the fairground rides and karaoke sessions at the end of the pier. Brighton's architecturally superior **West Pier**, built in 1866 half a mile west along the seafront, was damaged in World War II and then fell into disrepair, suffering partial collapse in 2002 and two separate fires in 2003, followed by further collapse. A 183-metre-tall viewing mast, the **i360**, is scheduled to open at the seafront here in 2012.

Underneath the arches between the Palace and West piers, there are two small museums: the **National Museum of Penny Slot Machines** (Easter–Oct Sat, Sun & school hols 11am–6pm; free) houses decrepit antique slot machines, and the **Brighton Fishing Museum** (daily 9am–5pm; free), which displays old photos and video footage of the golden days of the local fishing industry and houses a large Sussex clinker, a boat once common on Brighton beach.

Across the road from the Palace Pier, on Marine Parade, the **Sea Life Centre** (Mon–Fri 10am–5.30pm, Sat & Sun 10am–6.30pm, last entry 90min before closing; £12.50) is the world's oldest operating aquarium. Despite modern innovations, including a transparent tunnel passing through a huge aquarium tank, the

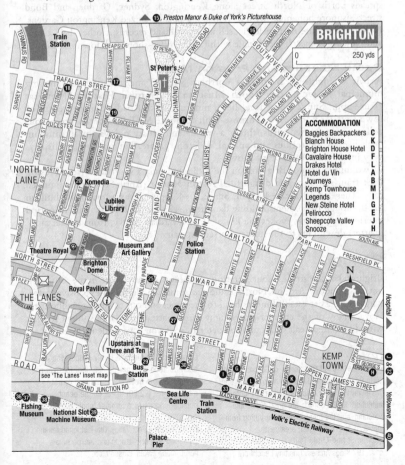

▲ ⑮ Preston Manor & Duke of York's Picturehouse

BRIGHTON

0   250 yds

ACCOMMODATION

Baggies Backpackers	C
Blanch House	K
Brighton House Hotel	D
Cavalaire House	F
Drakes Hotel	L
Hotel du Vin	A
Journeys	B
Kemp Townhouse	M
Legends	I
New Steine Hotel	G
Pelirocco	E
Sheepcote Valley	J
Snooze	H

whole thing is a bit tired-looking. Nearby, the antiquated locomotives of **Volk's Electric Railway** (Easter to mid-Sept Mon–Fri 10.15am–5pm, Sat & Sun 10.15am–6pm; £2.80 return; Ⓦwww.volkselectricrailway.co.uk) – the first electric train in the country – run eastward towards the Marina and the nudist beach, usually the preserve of just a few thick-skinned souls. Get off at the station at the halfway point – or walk fifteen minutes along Marine Parade – for the **Yellowave beach-sports centre** (March & April Mon & Fri 10am–5pm, Tues–Thurs 10am–9pm, Sat & Sun 10am–6pm; May–Sept Mon–Fri 10am–10pm, Sat & Sun 10am–8pm; Ⓣ01273/672222, Ⓦwww.yellowave.co.uk), which has six beach volleyball courts, a bouldering wall and excellent café.

The Lanes and North Laine

Tucked between the Pavilion and the seafront is a warren of narrow, pedestrianized thoroughfares known as **the Lanes** – the core of the old fishing village from which Brighton evolved. Long-established antiques shops, designer outlets and several bars, pubs and restaurants generate a lively and intimate atmosphere in this part of town. **North Laine** – "laine" was the local term for a strip of land – which spreads north of North Street along Kensington, Sydney, Gardner and Bond streets, is more bohemian with its hub along pedestrianized Kensington Gardens. Here the shops are more eclectic, selling secondhand records, clothes, bric-a-brac and New Age objects, and mingle with earthy coffee-shops and downbeat cafés.

Booth Museum and Preston Manor

A pair of sights in Brighton's northern suburbs merit a detour. The big municipal museum, the **Booth Museum of Natural History** (Mon–Sat 10am–5pm, Sun 2–5pm; free) lies a mile up Dyke Road from the centre of town (bus #27 or #27A). Purpose-built to house Mr E.T. Booth's prodigious collection of stuffed birds, this is a wonderfully fusty old Victorian museum with beetles, butterflies and animal skeletons galore, but which also displays very imaginative temporary shows.

Two miles north of Brighton on the A23 – but only a short walk from Preston Park train station – the delightful **Preston Manor** (April–Sept hourly guided tours Tues–Sat 10.15am–4.15pm, Sun 2.15–4.15pm; £5) was originally built in 1250, though the present building dates from 1738 and 1905. Its series of period interiors engagingly evokes the life of the Edwardian gentry, from the servants' quarters downstairs to the luxury nursery upstairs.

Eating

Brighton has the greatest concentration of **restaurants** anywhere in the southeast, outside London. Around North Laine are some wonderful, inexpensive **cafés**, while for classier establishments head to the Lanes and out towards neighbouring Hove. Many of the cheaper places fight hard to attract the large student market with discounted deals of around ten percent, so if you have student ID, use it.

Cafés

The Dorset Street Bar Corner of Gardner St and North Rd. Bar, café and restaurant rolled into one, this always bustling place is a bit of a Brighton institution. Tables outside are great for people-watching, and the menu covers everything from *moules* (£9) to full English breakfasts.

Jack and Linda Mills Smokehouse 197 Kings Arches. This tiny beachfront smokehouse is run by a lovely couple who've been traditionally smoking fish here for over a decade. Grab a fresh crab sandwich or hot mackerel roll (£2.80) to eat on the beach outside for a perfect summer lunch. Closed Jan & Feb.

Mock Turtle 4 Pool Valley. Old-fashioned teashop crammed with bric-a-brac and inexpensive home-made cakes. Closed Mon.

The Sanctuary 51–55 Brunswick St East, Hove ☎01273/770002. Arty vegetarian café with a cosy, relaxed ambience, and a cellar performance venue. Deservedly popular, despite its not-very-central location. Open till 10pm.

The Tea Cosy Tea Rooms 3 George St. Kitsch tearoom decked from head to foot with royal memorabilia. Cream teas are named after members of the royal family, and a strict code of etiquette forbids the dunking of biscuits in tea on pain of removal from the premises. Closed Mon & Tues.

Tic Toc Café 53 Meeting House Lane ☎01273/770115. Quirky little café in the heart of the Lanes, decked out with vintage wallpaper, yellow leather banquettes, formica tables and fairy lights. Excellent coffee, tasty food, and a few tables outside.

Restaurants

Bom-Bane's 24 George St ☎01273/606400, Ⓦwww.bom-banes.co.uk. Loveable, eccentric café-restaurant run by two professional musicians. The decor is homely and decidedly quirky – each of the extraordinary, individually designed tables holds a surprise in store – and the hearty Belgian-influenced food is delicious (*stoemp* and sausage £9.75). There are weekly live music (Tues) and film (Wed) nights, and a monthly musical night (£25), where dinner is interspersed with songs performed by the staff. Closed Tues & Wed lunch & all day Mon.

Chilli Pickle 42 Meeting House Lane ☎01273/328824. Stylish, buzzing little restaurant tucked away in the Lanes serving sophisticated, authentic Indian food: everything from *masala dosas* to oxtail Madras (£13). Closed Mon & Tues.

Due South 139 Kings Road Arches ☎01273/821218. Laid-back seafood restaurant right on the beach, with an emphasis on locally sourced, sustainable produce. Tables outside make the most of the sea views.

English's Oyster Bar 29–31 East St ☎01273/327980. Three fishermen's cottages knocked together to house a marble-and-brass oyster bar and a red-velvet dining room. Seafood's the speciality with a mouthwatering menu and better value than you might expect, especially the set menus (2 courses £15). Closed Sun eve.

Food for Friends 18 Prince Albert St ☎01273/202310. Brighton's ever-popular wholefood veggie eatery is imaginative enough to please die-hard meat-eaters too.

Gingerman 21a Norfolk Square ☎01273/326688. Small but perfectly formed one-room restaurant serving up some of the best food in Brighton. The set menus (2 courses for £15/26 at lunch/dinner) are excellent value. Closed Mon.

Melrose 132 King's Rd ☎01273/326520. Traditional seafront establishment that's been serving seafood, roasts and custard-covered puddings for over forty years. The next door *Regency Restaurant* is smaller and similar.

Moshi Moshi Bartholomew Square ☎01273/719195. Excellent, though pricey, conveyer-belt sushi restaurant housed in a sleek modernist cube, two sides of which slide open in summer months for alfresco dining. Extensive à la carte menu available too.

The Restaurant at Drakes 33–34 Marine Parade ☎01273/696934. Stylish, sumptuous restaurant in the basement of one of Brighton's finest boutique hotels; imaginative mains include rump of lamb served with sweetbreads and quinoa risotto (2/3-course dinner £28/37).

Riddle and Finn 12b Meeting House Lane ☎01273/328008. Friendly, bustling champagne and oyster bar where you can tuck into a huge range of shellfish and fish (mains £13–18) at communal marble-topped tables in a white-tiled, candlelit dining room. It's very popular, and they don't take bookings, so expect to wait for a table at busy times.

Terre-à-Terre 71 East St ☎01273/729051. Fabulous, inventive global veggie cuisine (mains around £13), served up in a modern arty restaurant. The Terre-à-Tapas taster plate for two (£20) is a good place to start if you're befuddled by the weird and wonderful creations on offer. Closed Mon in winter.

Drinking

Brighton's drinking scene ranges from hip beachfront **bars** to traditional boozers, and many **pubs** are open until at least midnight.

Pubs and bars

The Bee's Mouth 10 Western Rd, Hove ☎01273/770083. Quirky, sumptuously decorated bar on the Brighton/Hove border with exotic beers and live jazz.

Blanch House 17 Atlingworth St ☎01273/603504. This tiny, hip hotel bar serves the best cocktails in town, with a huge cocktail list that includes over 35 of their very own magnificent creations.

Brighton Festival

Every May the three-week-long **Brighton Festival** (☏01273/709709, ⓦwww .brightonfestival.org) takes over various venues around town. This arty celebration includes funfairs, exhibitions, street theatre and concerts from classical to jazz. Running at the same time is the **Brighton and Hove Fringe Festival** (☏01273/709709, ⓦwww.brightonfestivalfringe.org.uk), which also stages live music and drama, litera-ture readings and tonnes of club nights, and the **Artists' Open Houses Festival** (ⓦwww.aoh.org.uk), when over 250 private homes fling open their doors to show the work of local artists.

The Cricketers 15 Black Lion St ☏01273/ 329472. Brighton's oldest pub, immortalized by Graham Greene in *Brighton Rock*. Traditional feel with good daytime grub, real ales and a cosy courtyard bar.

Fiddler's Elbow 11 Boyce's St ☏01273/325850. Irish pub with regular live music and an annual St Patrick's Day street party.

The Fish Bowl 74 East St ☏01273/777505. A popular pre-club choice for its range of music; DJs four nights a week and free entry. Also a relaxing spot during the day, with a local, organic menu on offer.

The Great Eastern 103 Trafalgar St ☏01273/685681. Small and mellow pub with bare boards and bookshelves, lots of real ales and malt whiskies, and no fruit machines or TV.

The Greys 105 Southover St ☏01273/680734. Friendly pub with an open fire and a great menu. Frequent live music and Belgian beer nights, showcasing their wide range.

Guarana Bar 36 Sydney St ☏01273/600557. Brazilian-style daytime bar in the North Laine quarter serving herbal cocktails and shakes made with guarana (extract of Amazonian vine).

The Hop Poles 13 Middle St ☏01273/710444. Small and very popular pub, renowned for its real ales, excellent menu and generous portions.

Madame Geisha 75 East St ☏01273/770847. Lavishly decked-out bar, restaurant and lounge with private karaoke booths, exotic cocktails and Asian tapas.

The Marlborough 4 Prince's St ☏01273/570028. Friendly pub just off Old Steine, popular with Bright-on's gay and lesbian communities. The small theatre upstairs hosts readings and other performances.

OHSO Social 250a Kings Rd Arches ☏01273/ 746067. Get the full Brighton experience on the terrace of this late-night beachfront bar, with great cocktails and uninterrupted views of the Palace Pier.

The Park View 71 Preston Drove ☏01273/541663. Family-friendly pub adjacent to Preston Park with a great menu and a heated terrace. Regular weekly events include a quiz night, wine tasting and salsa dancing.

The Prince Albert 48 Trafalgar St ☏01273/730499. A listed building right by the train station, with real ale and big-screen football. Also one of the best venues for gigs and live music in Brighton.

Nightlife and entertainment

Nightlife is hectic and compulsively pursued throughout the year, making Brighton unique in the sedate southeast. As well as the mainstream **theatre** and **concert** venues, there are myriad **clubs**, lots of **live music** and plenty of **cinemas**. Midweek entry into the clubs can cost less than a fiver, and cinema seats are similarly priced before 6pm. Clubs are open until around 4am (often all night at weekends).

For up-to-date information, pick up the free monthly **listings** magazine *What's On* from the tourist office. Other similar magazines such as *Source* (ⓦwww.brighton source.co.uk), *Latest 7* (ⓦwww.thelatest.co.uk/7) and *Gscene* (see box opposite), can be found in various cafés and bars around the city. Also check out the **websites** ⓦwww.brighton.co.uk, ⓦwhatson.brighton.co.uk and ⓦmagazine.brighton.co.uk.

Clubs and live music venues

Audio 10 Marine Parade ☏01273/606906. Trendy hangout that boasts a terrace with sea views and a large bar on the first floor. The basement club is always packed, playing everything from indie rock to funky house and drum'n'bass.

The Brighton Coalition 171 King's Rd Arches
℡01273/772842, ⓦwww.brightoncoalition.co.uk.
Retro disco, Eighties pop, commercial house and
R&B.
Casablanca Jazz Club 2 Middle St
℡01273/321817, ⓦwww.casablancajazzclub.com.
Basement venue featuring live bands and all types
of funk, including Latin and jazz.
Concorde 2 Madeira Shelter, Madeira Drive
℡01273/673311, ⓦwww.concorde2.co.uk. A
Victorian tearoom in a former life, Brighton's
trendiest live music venue has featured everyone
from The White Stripes to Jarvis Cocker; it also hosts
weekend club nights and the popular Silent Disco.
Digital 187–193 King's Rd Arches ℡01273/227767,
ⓦwww.yourfutureisdigital.com. Stylish venue where
DJs spin a range of sounds from breaks to rock/indie,
and there are regular live bands. Expect laser shows
and a great sound system.
Funky Buddha Lounge 169 King's Rd Arches
℡01273/725541. Tiny venue renowned for
progressive house, breakbeats and soul.
The Hanbury Club 83 St George's Rd
℡01273/605789. Grade II-listed domed building,
offering an intimate venue for live music and
alternative club nights.
Honey Club 214 King's Rd Arches
℡01273/202807, ⓦwww.thehoneyclub.co.uk. One
of Brighton's most popular beachfront venues,
attracting a stylish crowd. Expect funky house,
R&B, hip-hop and big-name DJs.
New Hero 11 Dyke Rd ℡07944/762392, ⓦwww
.newhero.co.uk. Vibrant venue with an alternative
mix of Eighties, indie, electro and dance – as well
as regular live bands.

Revenge 32 Old Steine ℡01273/606064, ⓦwww
.revenge.co.uk. The south's largest gay club, with
cheesy pop, upfront dance and retro boogie on two
floors.
Volks Tavern 3 The Colonnade, Madeira Drive
℡01273/682828, ⓦwww.volksclub.co.uk.
Under the arches on Marine Parade you'll find
two rooms hosting live bands, reggae revival
nights, hip-hop and breakbeats, attracting an
eclectic crowd.

Arts centres, cinemas, theatres and comedy clubs

Brighton Dome 29 New Rd ℡01273/709709,
ⓦwww.brightondome.org. Three venues under one
roof – Pavilion Theatre, Dome Auditorium and Corn
Exchange – offering mainstream theatre, concerts,
ballet and even Viennese tea dances.
Duke of York's Picturehouse Preston Circus
℡0871/7042056, ⓦwww.picturehouses.co.uk.
Grade II-listed cinema with a licensed bar showing
art-house, independent and classic films.
Komedia Gardner St, North Laine ℡01273/
647100, ⓦwww.komedia.co.uk. Lively alternative
theatre-café notable for its regular roll call of
stand-up comedy and live music. Late bar.
Theatre Royal New Rd ℡01273/764400, ⓦwww
.ambassadortickets.com/theatreroyal. Mixture of
mainstream and progressive plays, opera, musicals
and one-man shows.
Upstairs at Three and Ten 10 Steine St
℡07800/983290, ⓦwww.otherplaceproductions
.co.uk. Tiny venue hosting live music, innovative
theatre, and regular comedy nights.

Listings

Bike rental Sunrise Cycles, West Pier, King's Rd
Arches ℡01273/748881.
Hospital Royal Sussex County, Eastern Rd
℡01273/696955.
Internet Eazinet, 47 West St (daily 9.30am–midnight),
or log on for free at Jubilee Library on North Rd (Mon
& Tues 10am–7pm; Wed, Fri & Sat 10am–5pm; Thurs
10am–8pm; Sun 11am–4pm).
Police John St ℡0845/607 0999.
Taxis ℡01273/205205, 204060 or 747474.

Gay and lesbian Brighton

Brighton has one of the longest established and most thriving **gay communities** in
Britain, with a variety of lively clubs and bars drawing people from all over the
southeast; for **listings** and events check out *Gscene* (ⓦwww.gscene.com). It also
hosts a number of gay events including the annual **Gay Pride Festival**, held over two
weeks at the beginning of July. It's a great excuse for a party with loads going on from
performing arts to exhibitions, not to mention the **Brighton Parade**, a day-and-night-
long jamboree. For details check out ⓦwww.gay.brighton.co.uk. Finally, for Brighton's
Lesbian and Gay Switchboard, contact ℡01273/204050 (daily 5–11pm; ⓦwww
.switchboard.org.uk).

Mid-Sussex

North of Brighton, the principal attraction of **mid-Sussex** is its wealth of fine gardens, ranging from the majestic **Sheffield Park** and the tree plantations of **Wakehurst Place** to the luscious flowerbeds of **Nymans** and the landscaped lakes of **Leonardslee**. Nearby **Ashdown Forest** is best known for its links with Winnie-the-Pooh. Exploring this region by public transport isn't really feasible unless you take your bike on the train; tourist information is thin on the ground too – it's best to get clued up at Brighton's tourist office beforehand, if you're interested in doing a thorough tour.

Sheffield Park and the Bluebell Railway

Around twenty miles northeast of Brighton lies the country estate of **Sheffield Park**, its centrepiece a Gothic mansion built for Lord Sheffield by James Wyatt. The house is closed to the public, but you can roam around the hundred-acre **gardens** (Jan to mid-Feb Sat & Sun 10.30am–4pm; mid-Feb to Oct daily 10.30am–5.30pm; Nov & Dec daily 10.30am–4pm; £7.40, combined ticket with Bluebell Railway £19; NT), which were laid out by Capability Brown.

A mile southwest of the gardens lies the southern terminus of the **Bluebell Railway** (April–Oct daily; Nov–March Sat, Sun & school hols; day-ticket with unlimited travel £12.50; 24hr information line ☏01825/722370, ⍟www .bluebellrailway.co.uk), whose vintage steam locomotives chuff nine miles north via Horsted Keynes to Kingscote. The service gets extremely crowded at weekends, especially in May, when the bluebells blossom in the woods through which the line passes. A vintage bus service connects the northern terminus of Kingscote (no car access) with East Grinstead train station (hourly trains from London Victoria).

A couple of miles away from Sheffield Park in the small village of **Fletchling**, the ⍟ *Griffin Inn* is a gorgeous old country **pub**, with a first-rate restaurant and a beer garden with far-reaching views over the Downs. The nearby *Wowo* campsite, at Waspsbourne Farm, Sheffield Park (☏01825/723414, ⍟www.wowo.co.uk), is a lovely back-to-nature **campsite**, with campfires encouraged and plenty of open spaces in which kids can run wild.

Wakehurst Place, Nymans and Leonardslee gardens

Wakehurst Place, a Jacobean mansion eighteen miles north of Brighton (daily: March–Oct 10am–6pm; Nov–Feb 10am–4.30pm; £10.75; NT), is the country home of Kew Royal Botanic Gardens. Guided tours take place at 11.30am and 2pm throughout the year. The 180-acre site is given over mainly to trees and shrubs in a variety of horticultural environments, and is also home to the Millennium Seed Bank, whose aim is to safeguard some 24,000 plant species by freezing the seeds in underground vaults. The nearest station is Haywards Heath, on the London–Brighton line, from where you can catch bus #82 (not Sun).

For one of the southeast's greatest gardens, head five miles southwest of Wakehurst Place to **Nymans** (Wed–Sun 10am–5pm; £7; NT), near the village of Handcross; bus #273 from Brighton to Crawley can drop you off on the A23 beside the village. The gardens are centred on the picturesque ruins of a mock-Tudor manor house and the highlight of the various enclosures is the large, romantic walled garden, housing a collection of rare Himalayan magnolia trees.

Arguably the most picturesque of all the mid-Sussex gardens is at **Leonardslee** (April–June daily 9.30am–6pm, last admission 4.30pm; £6.50, £8/£9 in May;

2

www.leonardsleegardens.com), four miles southwest of Nymans, near the village of Crabtree; bus #17 from Brighton to Horsham passes by the garden gates. Set in a wooded valley, the seventy-acre grounds are crisscrossed by steep paths linking six lakes, and wallabies, sika and fallow deer roam freely.

Ashdown Forest

Just a few miles north of Sheffield Park, the ten square miles of heathland and forest that make up **Ashdown Forest** are best known as the home of **Winnie-the-Pooh**, the much-loved creation of A.A. Milne. Milne wrote the classic children's books from his home in the small village of **Hartfield** on the forest's northeastern edge, Modelling Hundred Acre Wood closely on the area. Many of the spots featured in the stories can be visited today, with Pooh Sticks Bridge, a one-mile walk from the Pooh Car Park just off the B2026, the most popular spot. Alternatively, pick up the *Pooh Walks* leaflet, which details two walks from the car park at Gills Lap (the Galleon's Leap of the books) from the **Forest Centre** at Wych Cross (April–Sept Mon–Fri 2–5pm, Sat & Sun 11am–5pm; Oct–March Sat & Sun 11am–4pm; ℡01342/823583, www.ashdownforest.org). In the centre of Hartfield, a small shop, Pooh Corner, is devoted to all things Pooh.

Arundel and around

The hill-top town of **ARUNDEL**, eighteen miles west of Brighton, has for seven centuries been the seat of the dukes of Norfolk, whose fine castle looks over the valley of the River Arun. The medieval town's well-preserved appearance and picturesque setting draws in the crowds on summer weekends, but at any other time a visit reveals one of West Sussex's least spoilt old towns. North of here lie two contrasting sites: **Bignor Roman Villa**, containing some of the best Roman mosaics in the country, and the grand seventeenth-century **Petworth House**, replete with an impressive collection of paintings.

Arrival and information

Arundel's **train station** is half a mile south of the town centre over the river on the A27, with **buses** arriving either on High Street or River Road. The **tourist office** is at 1–3 Crown Yard Mews on River Rd (Easter–Sept Mon–Sat 10am–6pm, Sun 10am–4pm; Oct–Easter daily 10am–3pm; ℡01903/882268, www .sussexbythesea.com). **Boat rental** (motor boats £25/hour) and hourly riverboat **cruises** upstream to Arundel Castle (£7) are available from River Arun Cruises (℡01903/882609, www.riveraruncruises.com).

Arundel's **festival** takes place throughout the last week in August in a variety of locations around the town, and features everything from open-air theatre to pop and opera. For details see www.arundelfestival.co.uk.

Accommodation

The town has a range of accommodation to suit all pockets. You can pitch a tent at the youth hostel (see p.200), or there's more luxurious **camping** to be found at *Billycan Camping*, a fifteen-minute walk from town at Manor Farm (℡01903/882103, www.billycancamping.co.uk; 2-night minimum stay from £185 including hamper and Fri dinner), where pre-pitched canvas bell tents come decked out with bunting and fresh flowers, and campers are welcomed with a communal stew around the campfire on a Friday night.

Amberley Castle Amberley, four miles north of Arundel ☎01798/831992, ⓦwww.amberleycastle .co.uk. For a real splurge, head to this luxurious 600-year-old lodging, complete with gatehouse and portcullis. ❼

Arden Guest House 4 Queen's Lane ☎01903/882544, ⓦwww.ardenguesthouse.net. Comfortable family-run guesthouse, in a good central location. The cheapest rooms share bathrooms. ❷

Arundel House 11 High St ☎01903/882136, ⓦwww.arundelhouseonline.com. Stylish boutique hotel in a nineteenth-century merchant's house in a prime location opposite the castle, with a great restaurant downstairs (see below). Excellent value. ❸

Arundel YHA Warningcamp ☎0870/770 5676, ⓔarundel@yha.org.uk. This Georgian villa feels like a luxury B&B, a mile and a half northeast of town and connected by a riverside walk. Dorm beds from £16 (including breakfast), and you can camp here too.

Byass House 59 Maltravers St ☎01903/882129, ⓦwww.byasshouse.com. Elegant eighteenth-century building with a log fire in the drawing room, period furnishings and breakfast served in the conservatory or garden. No credit cards. ❸

The Town

Towering over the High Street, **Arundel Castle** (April–Oct Tues–Sun 10am–5pm; castle, keep, grounds & chapel £16, keep, grounds & chapel only £9; ⓦwww .arundelcastle.org) has an imposing medieval appearance, though most of what you see is little more than a century old. The structure dates from Norman times, but was ruined during the Civil War, then lavishly reconstructed from 1718 onwards by the eighth, eleventh and fifteenth dukes. From the top of the keep, you can see the current duke's spacious residence and the pristine castle grounds. Inside the castle, the renovated quarters include the impressive **Barons Hall** and the **library**, which boasts paintings by Gainsborough, Holbein and Van Dyck. On the edge of the castle grounds, the fourteenth-century **Fitzalan Chapel** houses tombs of past dukes of Norfolk including twin effigies of the seventh duke – one as he looked when he died and, underneath, one of his emaciated corpse. In the castle grounds, a new formal garden, the **Collector Earl's Garden**, is a playfully theatrical take on a Jacobean garden, with exotic planting, and pavilions, obelisks and urns made from green oak rather than stone.

Arundel's other major landmark is the towering Gothic bulk of **Arundel Cathedral** (daily 9am–6pm or dusk), constructed in the 1870s by the fifteenth duke of Norfolk. Inside are the enshrined remains of the fourth duke's canonized son, St Philip Howard, who was sentenced to death in 1585 when he was caught fleeing overseas after praying for Catholic Spanish victory against the Protestant English.

The rest of Arundel is pleasant to wander round, with the antique-shop-lined Maltravers and Arun streets being the most attractive thoroughfares.

Eating and drinking

Restaurants can be pricey, but a good range of snack bars and **pubs** ensures that sustenance is never hard to find. Pallant of Arundel, 17 High St, is a great **deli** selling everything you'll need for a picnic.

Arundel House See above. Sleek, contemporary restaurant with a locally sourced, seasonally changing menu; mains might include confit belly of Sussex pork, or roast loin of venison. Set-price menus cost £16 or £22 for lunch, £22/28 for dinner (£28/34 at weekends). No children. Closed Sun & Mon.

Bay Tree 21 Tarrant St ☎01903/883679. Cosy and relaxed little restaurant squeezed into three low-ceilinged beamed rooms, with a small terrace out the back. Mains such as pheasant breast wrapped in bacon cost £14–18 at dinner; lunch features simpler dishes. Closed Sun eve & Mon.

Black Rabbit Mill Rd, Offham. A pleasant half-hour's walk from town will bring you to this spot, overlooking the river, castle and surrounding wetlands. The pub grub is nothing special, but the idyllic setting still makes it well worth a visit, if only for a drink.

Fins 4–6 Queen St ☎ 01903/882844. You can feast on an array of fishy treats, from crab cakes (£9) to sushi (£8), at this relaxed, light-filled café with adjoining fish counter and deli. Tables outside in the summer. Daily 8.30am–5.30pm & Fri eve; closed Sun & Mon in winter.

King's Arms 36 Tarrant St. The best real-ale pub in town, though can be cramped. No food.

Bignor and Petworth

Six miles north of Arundel, the excavated second-century ruins of the **Bignor Roman Villa** (daily March–May, Sept & Oct 10am–5pm; June–Aug 10am–6pm; £5.50; ⓦ www.bignorromanvilla.co.uk) reveal some well-preserved mosaics, of which the Ganymede is the most outstanding. The site, first excavated between 1811 and 1819, is superbly situated at the base of the South Downs and features the longest extant section of mosaic in England, as well as the remains of a hypocaust, the underfloor heating system developed by the Romans. There are no public transport links to the site, so without your own transport you need to take a taxi from Arundel or Pulborough (about £15).

Adjoining the pretty little town of **PETWORTH**, replete with antiques shops, eleven miles north of Arundel, is **Petworth House** (mid-March to Oct Mon–Wed, Sat & Sun 11am–5pm; park daily 8am–dusk; house £9.90, Pleasure Ground £3.80, park free; NT), one of the southeast's most impressive stately homes. Built in the late seventeenth century, the house contains an outstanding art collection, with paintings by Van Dyck, Titian, Gainsborough, Bosch, Reynolds, Blake and Turner – the last a frequent guest here. Highlights of the interior decor are Louis Laguerre's murals around the **Grand Staircase** and the **Carved Room**, where work by Grinling Gibbons and Holbein's full-length portrait of Henry VIII can be seen. The seven-hundred-acre grounds – containing the 30-acre woodland garden known as the **Pleasure Ground** – were landscaped by Capability Brown and are considered one of his finest achievements. The extensive **Servants' Quarters**, connected by a tunnel to the main house, contain an impressive series of kitchens bearing the latest technological kitchenware of the 1870s. For an alternative and intriguing view of the life of one of the house's former employees, **Petworth Cottage Museum**, 346 High St (April–Oct Tues–Sun 2–4.30pm; £2.50), is well worth a visit. Seamstress Mary Cummings lived in this gas-lit abode, which has been restored using her own possessions to how it must have looked in 1910.

To get to Petworth from Arundel involves a **train** journey to Pulborough Station from where you can pick up the regular Stagecoach Coastline #1 **bus**. Petworth's **tourist office** is on Golden Square (Mon–Fri 9.30am–12.30pm & 1.30–4.30pm; ☎ 01798/343523, ⓦ www.visitchichester.org). For a memorable night's **stay**, book in at the converted *Old Railway Station* (☎ 01798/342346, ⓦ www.old-station.co.uk; ⑥), two miles south of Petworth on the A285 Chichester road.

Chichester and around

The county headquarters of West Sussex and its only city, **CHICHESTER** is an attractive, if stuffy, market town, which began life as a Roman settlement – the Roman cruciform street plan is still evident in the four-quadrant symmetry of the town centre, spread around the Market Cross. Chichester's chief attraction is its Gothic cathedral, while there are a handful of major draws in the surrounding area.

Arrival, information and accommodation

Chichester's **train station** is on Stockbridge Road, with the **bus station** across the road at South Street. From either station it's a ten-minute walk north to the Market Cross, passing the **tourist office** at 29a South St (April–Sept Mon 10.15am–5.15pm, Tues–Sat 9.15am–5.15pm, Sun 10.30am–3pm; Oct–March closed Sun; ℡01243/775888, ⊛www.visitchichester.org).

Seemingly every other house on the main roads out of Chichester offers **accommodation**, so there's no problem finding a place to stay other than during the festival (see opposite). You can **camp** at the *Red House Farm*, Brookers Lane, Earnley (℡01243/512959, ⊛www.rhfcamping.co.uk; closed Nov–Easter), six miles southwest of town, a mile or so from the beach.

Litten House 148 St Pancras, off East St ℡01243/774503, ⊛www.littenho.demon.co.uk. Good-value B&B in a great central location. Rooms share bathrooms. ❷

Richmond House 230 Oving Rd ℡01243/771464, ⊛www.richmondhouse chichester.co.uk. Lovely boutique B&B, just a 20min walk from the centre, with stylish rooms and fabulous breakfasts featuring home-baked bread and muffins. ❸

The Ship Hotel North St ℡01243/778000, ⊛www.theshiphotel.net. Stylish Georgian townhouse in the centre of town, with a good in-house bistro and bar. ❹

The City

The main streets lead off to the compass's cardinal points from the Gothic **Market Cross**, a bulky octagonal rotunda built in 1501 to provide shelter for the market traders. A short stroll down West Street brings you to the neat form of the **cathedral** (daily: June–Oct 7.15am–7pm; Nov–May 7.15am–6pm), whose slender spire – a nineteenth-century addition – is visible out at sea. Building began in the 1070s, but the church was extensively rebuilt following a fire a century later and has been only minimally modified since about 1300, except for the spire and the unique, freestanding fifteenth-century bell tower. The **interior** is renowned for its contemporary devotional art, which includes a stained-glass window by Marc Chagall and an enormous altar-screen tapestry by John Piper. However, the highlight is a pair of reliefs in the south aisle, close to the tapestry – created around 1140, they show the raising of Lazarus and Christ at the gate of Bethany. Originally highly coloured, the reliefs once featured semi-precious stones set in the figures' eyes and are among the finest Romanesque stone carvings in England.

There are several fine buildings up North Street, including a dinky little **Market House**, built by Nash in 1807 and fronted by a Doric colonnade, and a tiny flint **Saxon church** – now an ecclesiastical bookshop – with a diminutive wooden shingled spire. Finally, you come to the appealingly dumpy red-brick **Council House**, built in 1731, with Ionic columns and delightful intersecting tracery on its street facade, and crowned by a wonderful stone lion. East off South Street, in the well-preserved Georgian quadrant of the city known as the Pallants, you'll find **Pallant House Gallery**, 9 North Pallant (Tues, Wed, Fri & Sat 10am–5pm, Thurs 10am–8pm, Sun 12.30–5pm; £7.50; ⊛www.pallant.org.uk), a superlative collection of twentieth-century British art – the best in the country – housed in a Queen Anne townhouse and award-winning contemporary extension. Artists on display include Henry Moore, Lucian Freud, Walter Sickert and Peter Blake.

Eating, drinking and entertainment

For something to **eat**, *The Ship* has an excellent bistro (mains £10–15), while the *Field & Fork* café-restaurant at Pallant House Gallery (℡01243/770827; lunch daily, dinner Wed–Sat) has an imaginative, locally sourced menu and serves delicious afternoon teas. The candy-coloured *Swallow Bakery*, 81 North St, is popular for its fabulous cupcake creations, baked on site daily. Good **pubs** include the convivial *Park Tavern* at 11 Priory Rd, overlooking Priory Park, and the fourteenth-century *Fountain*, at the top of Southgate.

Chichester is one of southern England's major cultural centres, well known for its **Festival Theatre** in Oaklands Park (℡01243/781312, ⓦwww.cft.org.uk), with a season running roughly between Easter and October. In addition, **Chichester Festivities** (℡01243/528356, ⓦwww.chifest.org.uk), taking place over two weeks in late June and early July, features music from blues to classical, plus talks and other events.

Around Chichester

Chief among the attractions around Chichester are the restored Roman ruins at **Fishbourne**, one of the most visited ancient sites in the county, two miles west of town, while north of the city, one of England's most fashionable racing events takes place at **Goodwood Park**. A couple of miles further north, the **Weald and Downland Open-Air Museum** contains around fifty reconstructed historic buildings in a beautiful rural setting.

Fishbourne Roman Palace

Fishbourne (Jan Sat & Sun 10am–4pm; Feb daily 10am–4pm; March–Oct daily 10am–5pm; Nov & Dec daily 10am–4pm; £7.60; ⓦwww.fishbourneroman palace.com), is the largest and best-preserved Roman palace in the country. Roman relics have long been turning up in Fishbourne and in 1960 a workman unearthed their source – the site of a depot constructed by the invading Romans in 43 AD – which is thought later to have become the vast, hundred-room palace of the Romanized Celtic aristocrat, Cogidubnus. A pavilion has been built over the north, residential wing of the excavated remains, where floor mosaics depict Fishbourne's famous dolphin-riding cupid as well as the more usual geometric patterns. An audio-visual programme gives a fuller picture of the palace as it would have been in Roman times, and the extensive gardens attempt to re-create the palace grounds.

To get to Fishbourne take the train from Chichester to Fishbourne Station, turn right as you leave the station and the palace is a few minutes' walk away.

Goodwood

Three miles north of Chichester lies **Goodwood Sculpture Park** (April–Nov Tues–Sun 10.30am–4.30pm; £10; ⓦwww.sculpture.org.uk), an absolute must for anyone interested in contemporary art, with more than seventy large-scale works, some of which have been specially commissioned, sited in a unique woodland environment. The selection of pieces on display changes from year to year.

Goodwood Park (℡01243/774107, ⓦwww.goodwood.co.uk), four miles north of Chichester train station (and connected to it by bus on race days), hosts "Glorious Goodwood" in late July, one of the social events of the racing year. If you miss the main event, there are plenty of other meetings from May to October.

Weald and Downland Open-Air Museum

Five miles north of Chichester, the **Weald and Downland Open-Air Museum** (Jan & Feb Wed, Sat & Sun 10.30am–4pm; March, Nov & Dec daily 10.30am–4pm; April–Oct daily 10.30am–6pm; £9; ℡01243/811363, ⓦwww.wealddown .co.uk), just outside the village of Singleton, is one of the best rural museums in the southeast. More than forty old buildings – from a Tudor market hall to a medieval farmstead – have been saved from destruction and reconstructed at the fifty-acre museum site. There's a daily guided tour at 1.30pm of the latest building, the innovative timber Downland Gridshell, the museum's workshop and store, and there are also numerous special events and activities, particularly in July and August. The #60 bus from Chichester (every 30min) will drop you off in Singleton; passengers get a twenty percent discount on museum entrance.

Surrey

Effectively a rural suburb of southern London for those who can afford it, **Surrey** is bisected laterally by the chalk escarpment of the **North Downs** which rise west of Guildford, peak around **Box Hill** near **Dorking**, and continue east into Kent. The portion of Surrey within and around the M25 orbital motorway has little natural and virtually no historical appeal, being a collection of satellite towns and light industrial installations. But beyond the ring, the county takes on a more pastoral aspect, with the open heath-land of Surrey's western borders and **Farnham**, home to the county's only intact castle.

Farnham

The sleepy market town of **FARNHAM** lies tucked into Surrey's southwestern corner. Notwithstanding its thousand-year history, the majority of Farnham's architecture dates from the eighteenth century, when it enjoyed a boom period based on hop farming.

Farnham **castle** was built around 1138 by Henry de Blois, Bishop of Winchester, as a convenient residence halfway between his diocese and London. There are two parts to the castle: the motte and shell **keep** (April–Sept Fri, Sat & Sun 1–5pm; free; EH), from where there are good views over the rooftops to the downs beyond; and the privately owned **Bishop's Palace**, much altered over the years, which can be visited by guided tour (Wed 2–4pm year-round, Fri 2.30pm April–Aug only; £2).

Farnham's refined Georgian dwellings are at their best along the broad **Castle Street**, linking the town centre with the castle. To see inside one, however, head to 38 West St, where the **Museum of Farnham** (Tues–Sat 10am–5pm; free) is housed within the former home of a wealthy hop merchant. The museum contains a succinct rundown of the town's history.

Farnham **train station** is five minutes from the centre, over the river on the southern edge of town. The **tourist office** is in the council offices on South Street, midway between the station and the centre (Mon–Thurs 9am–5pm, Fri 9am–4.30pm; ℡01252/712667, ⓦwww.farnham.gov.uk). There's comfortable townhouse **accommodation** at *Meads Guest House*, 48 West St (℡01252/715298; no credit cards; ❷), or try the super-friendly *Farnham Bed and Breakfast*, a twenty-minute walk from the centre at 22 Abbot's Ride (℡01252/719580, ⓦwww.farnhambedandbreakfast.com; ❷). The *Caffe Piccolo*, 84 West St (℡01252/723277), serves inexpensive **meals**, while the more upmarket *Vienna* at 112 West St (℡01252/722978; closed Sun eve) is good for seafood. Among the local **pubs**, the oak-beamed *Nelson Arms* on Castle Street serves reasonable bar food. The community arts centre, **Farnham**

Maltings (Ⓦ www.farnhammaltings.com), hosts live music, theatre productions and art exhibitions throughout the year, and has a lovely riverside café.

Dorking and Box Hill

Set at the mouth of a gap carved by the River Mole through the North Downs, **DORKING**, 25 miles from London (frequent trains from London Victoria), has few sights of its own but makes a convenient base for exploring the surrounding countryside. If you want to **stay**, try *The White Horse Hotel* (Ⓣ 01306/881138; ❸) on the High Street, an oak-beamed former coaching inn dating from the seventeenth century. The town's best **food** option is *Two to Four*, 2–4 West St (Ⓣ 01306/889923; closed Sun & Mon), with both à la carte and great-value seasonal set menus available (two courses £12/15 lunch/dinner).

Box Hill, on the northern edge of town, is a popular draw for suburban weekenders. It's a three-hour climb to the top, but the snack bar (daily 9am–5pm), the view south over the town and the Weald's sandstone ridges reward the effort. Box Hill sits on the most interesting part of the 151-mile **North Downs Way**, a tame long-distance footpath that stretches from Farnham to Dover. Though walkable from Dorking (around 45min), the nearest **train station** to Box Hill is at Westhumble, on the Dorking–London line.

Travel details

Buses

For information on all local and national bus services, contact Traveline Ⓣ 0871/200 2233, Ⓦ www.traveline .org.uk.

Arundel to: Brighton (Mon–Sat every 30min, Sun 1; 50min–2hr 10min); Chichester (Mon–Sat hourly, Sun 1; 35min).

Battle to: Hastings (Mon–Sat hourly, Sun 1; 15–30min).

Brighton to: Arundel (Mon–Sat every 30min, Sun 1; 50min–2hr); Chichester (Mon–Sat every 30min, Sun hourly; 2hr 30min); Eastbourne (2–3 hourly; 1hr 15min); Lewes (Mon–Sat every 15min, Sun hourly; 25–30min); London Victoria (hourly; 2hr 20min); Portsmouth (Mon–Sat every 30min, Sun hourly; 3hr 30min); Tunbridge Wells (Mon–Sat every 30min, Sun hourly; 1hr 35min).

Broadstairs to: Canterbury (Mon–Sat every 20min, Sun every 30min; 1hr 30min); Margate (every 5–15min; 25min); Ramsgate (every 5–15min; 10min).

Canterbury to: Broadstairs (Mon–Sat every 20min, Sun every 30min; 1hr 30min); Deal (Mon–Fri 1–3 hourly, Sat hourly, Sun 5; 1hr 5min); Dover (Mon–Sat 1–2 hourly, Sun 6; 35min); London

Victoria (hourly; 1hr 50min); Margate (Mon–Sat every 20min, Sun every 30min; 50min); Ramsgate (Mon–Sat hourly; 45min); Sandwich (Mon–Sat 1–3 hourly, Sun 5; 40min); Whitstable (Mon–Sat every 5–15min, Sun every 30min; 30min).

Chatham to: Rochester (every 5min; 5min).

Chichester to: Arundel (Mon–Sat hourly, Sun 1; 35min), Brighton (Mon–Sat every 30min, Sun hourly; 2hr 30min); Portsmouth (hourly; 55min).

Deal to: Canterbury (Mon–Fri 1–3 hourly, Sat hourly, Sun 5; 1hr 5min); Dover (Mon–Sat hourly, Sun every 2hr; 40min); London Victoria (2 daily; 2hr 35min); Sandwich (Mon–Sat 1–2 hourly, Sun every 2hr; 30min).

Dover to: Canterbury (Mon–Sat hourly, Sun every 2hr; 35min); Deal (Mon–Sat hourly, Sun every 2hr; 40min); Hastings (Mon–Sat hourly, Sun every 2hr; 2hr 40min); Hythe (Mon–Sat every 30min, Sun hourly; 50min); London Victoria (every 30min; 2hr 30min–3hr); Sandwich (Mon–Sat hourly, Sun every 2hr; 55min).

Eastbourne to: Brighton (2–3 hourly; 1hr 15min); Hastings (Mon–Sat every 20min, Sun hourly; 1hr 10min); London Victoria (2 daily; 3–4hr).

Hastings to: Battle (Mon–Sat hourly, Sun 1; 15–30min); Dover (Mon–Sat hourly, Sun 6; 2hr 50min); Eastbourne (Mon–Sat every 20–30min, Sun hourly; 1hr 15min); London Victoria (2 daily;

205

2hr 35min–3hr 55min); Rye (Mon–Sat 2 hourly, Sun 6; 40min).

Hythe to: Dover (Mon–Sat every 30min, Sun hourly; 55min); London Victoria (2 daily; 3hr 20min); Rye (Mon–Sat 2 hourly, Sun 6; 1hr–1hr 15min).

Lewes to: Brighton (Mon–Sat every 15min, Sun hourly; 30min); Tunbridge Wells (Mon–Sat every 30min, Sun hourly; 1hr 10min).

Margate to: Broadstairs (every 5–15 min; 25min); Canterbury (Mon–Sat every 20min, Sun every 30min; 50min); London Victoria (4 daily; 2hr 30min); Ramsgate (every 5–15min; 30min).

Ramsgate to: Broadstairs (every 5–15 min; 10min); Canterbury (Mon–Sat hourly; 45min); London Victoria (4 daily; 2hr 50min); Margate (every 5–15 min; 30min); Sandwich (hourly; 30min).

Rochester to: Chatham (every 5min; 5min).

Rye to: Hastings (Mon–Sat 1–2 hourly, Sun 6; 40min); Hythe (Mon–Sat hourly, Sun 6; 1hr 10min).

Sandwich to: Canterbury (Mon–Sat every 30min, Sun 6; 45min); Deal (Mon–Sat 1–2 hourly, Sun 5; 25min); Dover (Mon–Sat hourly, Sun every 2hr; 55min); Ramsgate (hourly; 30min).

Sevenoaks to: Tunbridge Wells (Mon–Sat 2 hourly, Sun every 2hr; 40–55min).

Tunbridge Wells to: Brighton (Mon–Sat every 30min, Sun 9; 1hr 40min); Lewes (Mon–Sat every 30min, Sun 9; 1hr 10min); London (1 daily; 1hr 30min); Sevenoaks (Mon–Sat 2 hourly, Sun every 2hr; 40–50min).

Whitstable to: Canterbury (every 15–30min; 30min); London (4 daily; 1hr 50min).

Trains

For information on all local and national rail services, contact National Rail Enquiries: ☏ 08457/484950, Ⓦ www.nationalrail.co.uk.

Arundel to: Chichester (Mon–Sat 2 hourly, Sun hourly; 20min); London Victoria (Mon–Sat every 30min, Sun hourly; 1hr 30min); Portsmouth Harbour (2 hourly; 55min); Pulborough (Mon–Sat 2 hourly, Sun hourly; 10min).

Battle to: Hastings (2 hourly; 15min); London Charing Cross (2 hourly; 1hr 30min); Tunbridge Wells (2 hourly; 30min).

Brighton to: Chichester (Mon–Sat every 30min, Sun hourly; 50min); Eastbourne (2 hourly; 35min); Hastings (2 hourly; 1hr–1hr 20min); Lewes (every 10–20min; 15min); London Bridge (Mon–Sat 4 hourly, Sun 2 hourly; 1hr); London King's Cross (2–4 hourly; 1hr 15min); London Victoria (1–2 hourly; 55min–1hr 20min); Portsmouth Harbour (Mon–Sat 2 hourly, Sun hourly; 1hr 30min).

Broadstairs to: London St Pancras (Mon–Sat hourly; 1hr 20min); London Victoria (Mon–Sat every 30min, Sun hourly; 1hr 50min).

Canterbury East to: Dover Priory (Mon–Sat every 30min, Sun hourly; 30min); London Victoria (Mon–Sat every 30min; 1hr 35min).

Canterbury West to: London Charing Cross (Mon–Sat every 30min, Sun hourly; 1hr 45min); London St Pancras (Mon–Sat hourly; 55min); Margate (Mon–Sat hourly; 30min).

Chatham to: Dover Priory (Mon–Sat every 30min, Sun hourly; 1hr 10min); London Victoria (2 hourly; 45min–1hr).

Chichester to: Arundel (Mon–Sat 2 hourly, Sun hourly; 20min); London Victoria (Mon–Sat 2 hourly; 1hr 35min); Portsmouth Harbour (Mon–Sat every 30min, Sun hourly; 30–50min).

Dorking to: London Victoria (Mon–Sat every 30min; 50min); London Waterloo (Mon–Sat every 30min; 50min).

Dover Priory to: London Charing Cross (Mon–Sat 2 hourly; 1hr 55min); London St Pancras (hourly; 1hr 5min); London Victoria (Mon–Sat 2 hourly, Sun hourly; 1hr 50min).

Eastbourne to: Brighton (2 hourly; 35min); Hastings (every 20–30min; 30min); Lewes (every 20–30min; 20–30min); London Victoria (Mon–Sat every 30min, Sun hourly; 1hr 35min).

Farnham to: London Waterloo (hourly; 1hr).

Hastings to: London Charing Cross (2 hourly; 1hr 30min); London Victoria (hourly; 2hr–2hr 15min); Rye (hourly; 20min).

Lewes to: Brighton (every 10–20min; 15min); Eastbourne (every 20–30min; 20–30min); London Victoria (Mon–Sat every 30min, Sun hourly; 1hr 10min).

Margate to: Canterbury West (Mon–Sat hourly; 30min); London St Pancras (Mon–Sat hourly; 1hr 30min); London Victoria (Mon–Sat 2 hourly, Sun hourly; 1hr 45min).

Ramsgate to: London St Pancras (Mon–Sat hourly; 1hr 15min); London Victoria (Mon–Sat hourly; 1hr 45min).

Rochester to: Dover Priory (Mon–Sat every 30min, Sun hourly; 1hr–1hr 15min); London Charing Cross (every 30min; 1hr 10min); London St Pancras (every 30min; 40min); London Victoria (every 30min; 45min).

Rye to: Hastings (hourly; 20min).

Sandwich to: Dover Priory (hourly; 25min).

Sevenoaks to: London Blackfriars (Mon–Sat every 30min; 1hr); London Charing Cross (3–5 hourly; 35min); Tunbridge Wells (4 hourly; 20min).

Tunbridge Wells to: London Charing Cross (4 hourly; 55min).

Whitstable to: London Victoria (Mon–Sat every 30min, Sun hourly; 1hr 20min).

Hampshire, Dorset and Wiltshire

CHAPTER 3 # Highlights

* **Osborne House** Gain a real insight into Queen Victoria's family life at this fascinating Italianate villa, set in huge grounds with wonderful sea views. See p.223

* **Wykeham Arms, Winchester** Atmospheric, ancient tavern serving gourmet-standard food alongside the real ales. See p.226 & p.228

* **The New Forest** William the Conqueror's old hunting ground and home to wild ponies and deer, the New Forest is ideal for walking, biking and riding. See p.229

* **Corfe Castle** Picturesque ruins with a weathered, romantic charm. See p.238

* **Durdle Door** This crumbling natural arch stands at the end of a splendid beach – a great place for walkers and swimmers alike. See p.240

* **Avebury** Set in a peaceful village, this crude stone circle has a more powerful appeal than nearby Stonehenge, not least for its easy accessibility. See p.256

▲ Corfe Castle

Hampshire, Dorset and Wiltshire

The distant past is perhaps more tangible in **Hampshire** (often abbreviated to "Hants"), **Dorset** and **Wiltshire** than in any other part of England. Predominantly rural, these three counties overlap substantially with the ancient kingdom of **Wessex**, whose most famous ruler, Alfred, repulsed the Danes in the ninth century and came close to establishing the first unified state in England. Before Wessex came into being, earlier civilizations also left their stamp on the region. The chalky uplands of Wiltshire boast several of Europe's greatest Neolithic sites, including **Stonehenge** and **Avebury**, while in Dorset you'll find **Maiden Castle**, the most striking Iron Age hill fort in the country, and the **Cerne Abbas giant**, source of many a legend. The Romans left the most conspicuous signs of their occupation at the amphitheatre of **Dorchester** – though that town is more closely associated with the novels of Thomas Hardy and his vision of Wessex.

Much of the coastline is dramatic, incorporating the fossil-rich Jurassic Coast – particularly around **Lyme Regis** – while the inland countryside is consistently seductive, with the picturesque woodlands of the **New Forest** and the open curves of **Salisbury Plain**. The region's towns are generally modest, with the exceptions of the two great maritime cities of **Portsmouth** and **Southampton**, gateways to the genteel pleasures of the **Isle of Wight**. The area also boasts two of England's most venerable cities: **Salisbury** and **Winchester**, each of which possesses a stupendous cathedral amid an array of other historic sights. Of the area's great houses, **Wilton**, **Stourhead**, **Longleat** and **Kingston Lacy** are the ones that attract the crowds, but every cranny has its medieval church, manor house or unspoilt country inn – there are few parts of England in which an aimless meander can be so rewarding. If it's seaside fun you're after, **Bournemouth** leads the way, with **Weymouth** and Lyme Regis heading the ranks of the minor resorts, along with the yachtie havens on the Isle of Wight.

The counties' **roads** tend to get choked in summer, the bulk of the traffic heading either for the West Country, the Bournemouth beaches, or for the ferry ports. If you're heading for one particular spot, it's often easier to reach it by **rail**, on the direct services from London's Waterloo Station. For many inland areas, though, **buses** are more convenient; most regional services are run by Stagecoach (Ⓦ www.stagecoachbus.com/south), Wilts & Dorset (☎ 01983/827005, Ⓦ www.wdbus.co.uk) and First (Ⓦ www.firstgroup.com/ukbus), who also run the

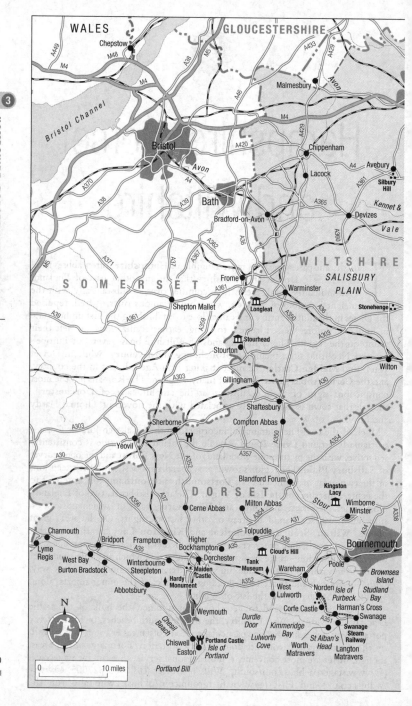

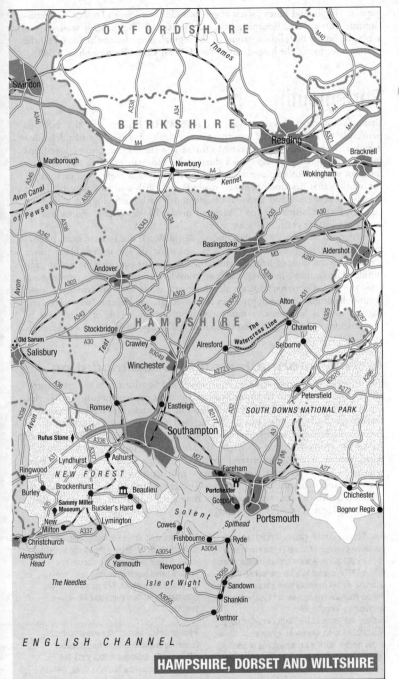

OXFORDSHIRE

Thames

M40

Swindon

M4

A346

BERKSHIRE

Reading

A321

A4

M4

Bracknell

Marlborough

Newbury

A4

Wokingham

A345

Avon Canal

A338

Kennet

of Pewsey

A342

A339

A33

A30

Avon

A336

A338

Basingstoke

M3

A287

Aldershot

Andover

A303

A303

A339

Alton

A31

A325

A267

A343

HAMPSHIRE

B3046

The Watercress Line

Chawton

A3

Stockbridge

A30

Crawley

B3049

Alresford

Selborne

B2070

A286

Old Sarum

Test

Winchester

A272

Salisbury

A36

A272

Petersfield

SOUTH DOWNS NATIONAL PARK

Romsey

Eastleigh

B2177

A32

A3

Avon

M27

Southampton

Rufus Stone

A336

M27

A338

Lyndhurst

Ashurst

Fareham

Chichester

Ringwood

NEW FOREST

Beaulieu

Portchester

A27

Burley

Brockenhurst

Gosport

Bognor Regis

Sammy Miller Museum

Buckler's Hard

Solent

Portsmouth

New Milton

Lymington

Cowes

Spithead

A337

Fishbourne

Ryde

Christchurch

A3054

A3054

Hengistbury Head

Yarmouth

Newport

A3055

Sandown

The Needles

Isle of Wight

Shanklin

A3055

Ventnor

ENGLISH CHANNEL

HAMPSHIRE, DORSET AND WILTSHIRE

popular Greyhound buses (Ⓦwww.greyhounduk.com) from London to South-ampton, Portsmouth, Bournemouth and the Isle of Wight. Keen **walkers** can avoid the hordes by following some of the region's many footpaths, including the southern section of the long-distance **South West Coast Path** (see box, p.348).

Portsmouth

Britain's foremost naval station, **PORTSMOUTH** occupies the bulbous peninsula of Portsea Island, on the eastern flank of a huge, easily defended harbour. The ancient Romans raised a fortress on the northernmost edge of this inlet, and a small port developed during the Norman era, but this strategic location wasn't fully exploited until Tudor times, when Henry VII established the world's first dry dock here and made Portsmouth a royal dockyard. It has flourished ever since and nowadays Portsmouth harbour is clogged with naval frigates, ferries bound for the Continent or the Isle of Wight, and swarms of tugs and pleasure craft.

Portsmouth was heavily bombed during World War II due to its military importance and, although the Victorian slums got what they deserved, bland tower blocks from the nadir of British architectural endeavour now give the city an ugly profile. The seafront, however, has been considerably smartened in recent years, with the new **Gunwharf Quays** development, while **Old Portsmouth**, based around the original harbour, preserves some Georgian and a little Tudor character. East of here is **Southsea**, a residential suburb with a rash of stoic military monuments overlooking its shingle beach, as well as a good selection of restaurants and places to stay.

Arrival, information and accommodation

Portsmouth's main **train station**, Portsmouth and Southsea, is in the city centre, but the line continues to **Harbour Station**, the most convenient stop for the main sights and old town, and where you'll also find the main **bus station**. Passenger **ferries** for Ryde, on the Isle of Wight, and Gosport, on the other side of Portsmouth Harbour, leave from the jetty at Harbour Station, while Wightlink car ferries for Fishbourne, Isle of Wight, depart from the ferry port off Gunwharf Road (see box, p.240). Hovertravel hovercraft to Ryde leave from Clarence Pier, Southsea. There are two **tourist offices** in Portsmouth (Ⓣ023/9282 6722, Ⓦwww.visitportsmouth.co.uk), one on The Hard (daily 9.30am–5.15pm), the other on Southsea's seafront, next to the Blue Reef Aquarium (March–Oct daily 9.30am–5.15pm; Nov–Feb daily except Thurs 9.30am–4.30pm).

Hotels and guesthouses

Fortitude Cottage 51 Broad St, Old Portsmouth Ⓣ023/9282 3748, Ⓦwww.fortitudecottage.co.uk. Stylish B&B in a great location overlooking the quayside. Its five rooms all have private bathrooms; the top-floor one has its own roof terrace and is worth paying extra for. ❷

Holiday Inn Express The Plaza, Gunwharf Quays Ⓣ023/9289 4240, Ⓦwww.hiexpress.co.uk. Rooms in this modern hotel are compact, and its position, right on Gunwharf Quays, can't be faulted. There's a large and airy breakfast room and bar too. ❹

The Retreat 35 Grove Rd South, Southsea Ⓣ023/9235 3701, Ⓦwww.theretreatguesthouse .co.uk. A clean, well-kept guesthouse in a Grade II listed building, an easy walk from the centre of Southsea. The rooms are bright with tasteful modern decor and flat-screen TVs. ❸

Hostels and campsites

Portsmouth and Southsea Backpackers 4 Florence Rd, Southsea Ⓣ023/9283 2495, Ⓦwww.portsmouthbackpackers.co.uk. Well-run hostel close to the seafront, with four- and six-bed dorms (£17 per person) along with doubles and twin rooms (①); there is also a communal kitchen, lounge, laundry, parking and use of the garden with a barbecue.

Southsea Leisure Park Melville Rd, Southsea ☏ 023/9273 5070, ⊛ www.southsealeisurepark .com. Useful and reasonably priced campsite right at the eastern end of Southsea Esplanade (bus #15 from Harbour Station).

The City

You are unlikely to spend any time in Portsmouth's modern **city centre**, a functional area of shops, offices and heavy traffic. Most items of interest, including the Historic Dockyard, lie west of here, in **Old Portsmouth** and the adjacent **waterfront district**. Across Portsmouth Harbour from here, and reachable by

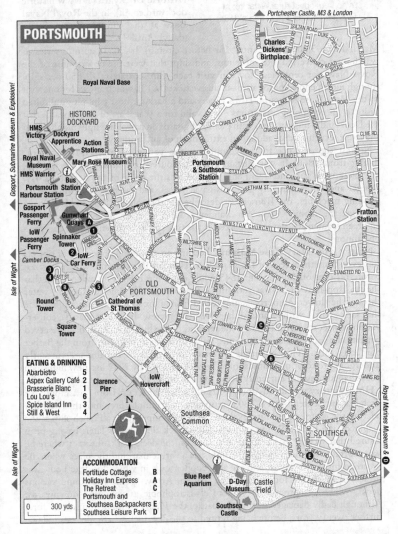

PORTSMOUTH

EATING & DRINKING
Abarbistro	5
Aspex Gallery Café	2
Brasserie Blanc	1
Lou Lou's	6
Spice Island Inn	3
Still & West	4

ACCOMMODATION
Fortitude Cottage	B
Holiday Inn Express	A
The Retreat	C
Portsmouth and Southsea Backpackers	E
Southsea Leisure Park	D

0   300 yds

Top 5: Outings for kids

▸▸ Visit **Beaulieu Motor Museum**, paradise for petrol-heads. See p.232.

▸▸ Take a boat to **Brownsea Island**. See box, p.236.

▸▸ Explore a 1940s schoolroom at **Tyneham** deserted village. See p.240.

▸▸ Go on a **fossil-hunting tour** at Charmouth. See p.245.

▸▸ Check out the lions, giraffes and rhino in deepest rural Wiltshire, at **Longleat Safari Park**. See p.258.

regular ferries, **Gosport** has a couple of naval museums, but little else worth lingering over. East of the old centre stretches **Southsea**, bounded to the south by Southsea Esplanade and the gravelly seafront, and holding a scattering of attractions as well as hotels and restaurants.

The Royal Naval Base

Portsmouth's biggest draw is the **Historic Dockyard** (Ⓦ www.historic dockyard.co.uk), in the **Royal Naval Base** at the end of Queen Street (daily: April–Oct 10am–6pm; Nov–March 10am–5.30pm; last entry 1hr before closing). It's made up of a series of warehouses converted into museums, and ships that were the powerhouse of the Royal Navy for centuries. You can visit each ship separately (£12.50 per ship) though most people opt for an all-inclusive ticket (£18), which allows for one visit to the Mary Rose Museum, HMS *Victory* and a harbour boat trip, plus unlimited visits to the remaining attractions – it is valid for a year. Part of the appeal is that the Dockland is unprettied, with plenty of guards on patrol and signs highlighting the latest security status adding an extra touch of authenticity.

Nearest the entrance to the complex is the youngest ship, **HMS Warrior**, dating from 1860. It was Britain's first armoured, or "iron-clad" battleship, complete with sails and steam engines, and was the pride of the fleet in its day. Longer and faster than any previous naval vessel, and the first to be fitted with washing machines, the *Warrior* was described by Napoleon III as a "black snake amongst the rabbits". You can wander around its main deck and see where eighteen seamen ate, slept and relaxed in the tiny spaces between each of the ship's 36 cannons.

Nearby is the **Mary Rose Museum**, housing an absorbing collection of objects retrieved from the wreck of the *Mary Rose*, Henry VIII's flagship, which capsized before his eyes off Spithead in 1545 while engaging French intruders. Whether she was top-heavy (she was certainly overloaded at the time) or took in water through her lower gunports having reeled from a broadside is uncertain, but the ship sank swiftly with almost all her 700-strong crew. In 1982 a massive conservation project successfully raised the remains of the hull, which silt had preserved beneath the sea bed, along with guns, gold coins and implements from the Barber Surgeon's cabin. The ship itself is not on display as its remains are currently undergoing restoration, but it should be back on view by 2012 in a new high-tech boat-shaped museum currently being built behind HMS *Victory*.

HMS Victory was already forty years old when she set sail from Portsmouth for Trafalgar on September 14, 1805, returning in triumph three months later, but bearing the corpse of Admiral Nelson. Shot by a sniper from a French ship at the height of the battle, Nelson expired below deck three hours later, having been assured that victory was in sight. A plaque on the deck marks the spot where he was mortally wounded, while the hold has a shrine marking the place where he breathed his last. You can also see the wooden cask in which his dead body was preserved in brandy for its return to Britain. Arrows point you round various decks, which get progressively more claustrophobic as you head downwards. Although badly damaged during the battle, the *Victory* continued in service for a further twenty years, before being retired to the dry dock where she rests today.

Opposite the *Victory*, various buildings house the exhaustive **Royal Naval Museum**, which traces British naval history from Alfred the Great's fleet to the present day, including the vivid and noisy **Trafalgar Experience**. Lastly, **Action Stations** has interactive games, videos and graphics to simulate life on board ship.

Gosport

The naval theme is continued at the **Submarine Museum** on Haslar Jetty in Gosport (daily: April–Oct 10am–5.30pm; Nov–March 10am–4.30pm; last tour 1hr before closing; £9; Ⓦwww.rnsubmus.co.uk), reached by taking the passenger ferry from Harbour train station jetty (every 10–15min: daily 5.30am–midnight; £2.30 return), just south of the entrance to the Royal Naval Base. Allow a couple of hours to explore these slightly creepy vessels – a guided tour inside HMS *Alliance* gives you an insight into life on board, and the museum elaborates evocatively on the long history of submersible craft. Nearby, housed in the old armaments depot at Priddy's Hard, **Explosion! The Museum of Naval Firepower** (Sat & Sun 10am–4pm; last entry at 3pm; £4; Ⓦwww.explosion.org.uk) tells the story of naval warfare from the days of gunpowder to the present, much helped by computer animations.

Gunwharf Quays, the Spinnaker Tower and Old Portsmouth

Back at the Harbour train station in Portsmouth, it's a short walk to the sleek **Gunwharf Quays**, with its waterfront cafés, restaurants, shops and nightspots, and which is also home to the soaring **Spinnaker Tower** (Sun–Thurs 10am–7.30pm, Fri & Sat 10am–6pm; £7.25; Ⓦwww.spinnakertower.co.uk), Portsmouth's most conspicuous attraction. Opened in 2005, the elegant, sail-like structure dominates the historic harbour, rising to 170m above the city and offering stunning vistas for up to twenty miles over land and sea. The three viewing decks can be reached by a high-speed lift, the highest one being open to the elements, though most people stick to View Deck 1, which has one of Europe's largest glass floors.

From the tower, it's a well-signposted fifteen-minute walk south to what remains of **Old Portsmouth**. Along the way, you pass the simple but elegant **Cathedral of St Thomas** on the High Street, whose original twelfth-century features have been obscured by rebuilding, first after the Civil War and again in the twentieth century. The High Street ends at a maze of cobbled Georgian streets huddling behind a fifteenth-century wall protecting the **Camber**, or old port, where Walter Raleigh landed the first potatoes and tobacco from the New World. Nearby, the Round and Square towers, which punctuate the Tudor fortifications, are popular vantage points for observing nautical activities.

Southsea

South of Old Portsmouth, **Southsea** is worth exploring above all for the **D-Day Museum** on Clarence Esplanade (daily: April–Sept 10am–5.30pm; Oct–March 10am–5pm; last entry 30min before closing; £6; Ⓦwww.ddaymuseum.co.uk), which relates how Portsmouth avenged its wartime bombing by being the main assembly point for the D-Day invasion, code-named "Operation Overlord". The museum's most striking exhibit is the 272-foot-long Overlord Embroidery, which tells the tale of the Normandy landings. Next door to the museum, the squat profile of **Southsea Castle** (April–Sept daily 10am–5.30pm; £3.50) may have been the spot from where Henry VIII watched the *Mary Rose* sink in 1545. A mile further along the shoreside South Parade, just past South Parade pier, the **Royal Marines Museum** (daily 10am–5pm; £6.95) describes the origins and greatest campaigns of the navy's elite fighting force.

Charles Dickens' Birthplace and Portchester Castle

The only other point of interest in Portsmouth itself is **Charles Dickens' Birthplace** at 393 Old Commercial Rd (May–Sept daily 10am–5.30pm; £3.50; Ⓦ www.charlesdickensbirthplace.co.uk), half a mile north of the town centre, where the writer was born in 1812. A couple of rooms have been fitted out as they were during his lifetime, though dedicated fans will find more of interest in Rochester (see p.155) and Broadstairs (see p.160) where Dickens wrote many of his greatest books.

More compelling is **Portchester Castle** (daily: April–Sept 10am–6pm; Oct–March 10am–4pm; £4.50; EH), six miles out of the centre, just past the marina development at Port Solent. Built by the Romans in the third century, this fortification boasts the finest surviving Roman walls in northern Europe – still over twenty feet high and incorporating some twenty bastions. The Normans felt no need to make any substantial alterations when they moved in, but a castle was later built within Portchester's precincts by Henry II, which Richard II extended and Henry V used as his garrison when assembling the army that was to fight the Battle of Agincourt. Today its grassy enclosure makes a sheltered spot for a kickabout with a football.

Eating and drinking

Gunwharf Quays has the usual selection of chain **restaurants and cafés**, while Southsea is home to a good variety of independent places, particularly for ethnic food. Old Portsmouth is your best bet for traditional waterfront **pubs**.

Restaurants and cafés

Abarbistro 58 White Hart Rd ☎023/9281 1585. Vibrant bar-restaurant with an outside terrace on the edge of Old Portsmouth. The menu ranges from salads and simple dishes such as burgers and baguettes (£4–8) to bistro classics including *moules* and fishcakes (£10), and generous mains such as salmon with dill sauce, pasta and steaks (from £13).

Aspex Gallery Café Vulcan Building, Gunwharf Quays. Enjoy great coffee, cakes and snacks inside the arty bare-brick interior of the Aspex art gallery, which hosts contemporary exhibitions. Closed eve.

Brasserie Blanc 1 Gunwharf Quays ☎023/9289 1320. Large modern brasserie from the Raymond Blanc empire, offering good-value early-evening deals (around £12 for two courses) along with tasty mains such as smoked haddock and leek fishcakes, scallops and fennel, and Spanish omelettes (£11–16).

Lou Lou's 37 Marmion Rd, Southsea ☎023/9282 5113. French-style brasserie with a lovely tiled interior, serving *croques monsieurs*, *tartiflette*, and goat's cheese salads as well as good breakfasts from around £5. Closed eve & all day Mon.

Pubs

Spice Island Inn 1 Bath Square, Old Portsmouth. Traditional pub in the old town with a lovely seafront terrace, wood-floored interior and good views from the upstairs rooms. It serves decent pub grub, such as steak and ale pie (£9), and has a takeaway fish-and-chips counter, so you can chomp away sitting on the harbour walls in true British fashion.

Still & West 2 Bath Square, Old Portsmouth. A waterfront terrace and cosy interior with views over the harbour make this pub worth a visit. The food ranges from traditional fish and chips (£9) to falafel and dips (£4.75) or smoked salmon risotto (£8.75).

Southampton

A glance at the map gives some idea of the strategic maritime importance of **SOUTHAMPTON**, which stands on a triangular peninsula formed at the place where the rivers Itchen and Test flow into Southampton Water, an eight-mile inlet from the Solent. Sure enough, Southampton has figured in numerous stirring events: it witnessed the exodus of Henry V's Agincourt-bound army, the Pilgrim

Coastal England

England, bound in with the triumphant sea
Whose rocky shore beats back the envious siege
Of watery Neptune.

Shakespeare, *Richard II*,
Act II, Scene 1

**With nowhere in England more than
75 miles from the coast, the sea –
bulwark against the Spanish Armada,
Napoleon and Hitler – occupies an
integral part of the English psyche.
Poets, painters and photographers have
been inspired through the centuries by
the bays and beaches, cliffs and creeks,
sand dunes and shingle of the country's
richly diverse coastline, which, at over
6000 miles in length (including islands),
ranges from stark wilderness to the
traditional seaside resort.**

Bamburgh Castle ▲

Par Beach, St Martin's, Isles of Scilly ▼

Minack Theatre, Porthcurno, Cornwall ▼

Beaches

Although rarely mentioned in the same breath as the sun-baked sands of the Mediterranean or Caribbean, England's beaches can compare with the best of them, both in terms of sheer natural beauty and for their cleanliness. For a combination of decent climate and good sand, the **southwest** of the country is hard to beat, especially the coasts of Cornwall and Devon. England's **southern coast** is perhaps less appealing for lounging, becoming more pebbly as you approach the southeastern corner of the country, but the low cliffs and gravel beaches of **East Anglia**'s shoreline give way to a string of wide sandy beaches between Cromer and Hunstanton. There are spectacular swathes of sand in the **northeast**, notably around Scarborough in Yorkshire and in Northumberland, though here the stiff North Sea breezes may require a degree of stoicism. Offshore **islands** too have some stunning coves and beaches, notably the Isles of Scilly and the Isle of Man.

Top five beaches

▶▶ **Par Beach**, St Martin's, Isles of Scilly. Perfect sands and crystal-clear water – and usually empty. See p.407

▶▶ **Bamburgh**, Northumberland. Sky, sea, dunes and acres of sand, with a dramatic castle backdrop. See p.817

▶▶ **Porthcurno**, Cornwall. Surrounded by cliffs, with the open-air Minack Theatre nearby. See p.404

▶▶ **Holkham Bay**, Norfolk. Beyond the pines and dunes lie three miles of pancake-flat sands. See p.465

▶▶ **Blackpool**, Lancashire. England's biggest resort has seven miles of clean beach. See p.629

Coastal paths

The cliffs and gently undulating slopes of England's coastline invite anything from a brief leisurely stroll to a vigorous long-distance hike. In the southeast, invigorating excursions can be made over the lovely **Seven Sisters** cliffs around Eastbourne, and over the iconic **white cliffs of Dover**, while in the northeast there are dramatic paths over the cliffs near **Whitby** and **Flamborough Head**. But almost every stretch of English coast is walkable, and mostly waymarked – check out the **Norfolk Coast Path**, or the **Cleveland Way** along the Yorkshire coast, or the 630-mile **South West Coast Path**, Britain's longest National Trail, which takes in some of the country's wildest and most picturesque scenery.

▲ South West Coast Path, Dorset

▼ Blackpool

Seaside resorts

The requisite ingredients of an English resort? A good beach, a pier or two, the piercing screech of gulls, fish and chips, saucy postcards, donkey rides, and lobster-red flesh at every turn. **Blackpool**, in the northwest, is the brilliant apotheosis of the genre – riotously full-on, glamorous and tawdry all at once. Other resorts mix the same basic family-friendly ingredients, blended with varying degrees of old-fashioned gentility, like **Scarborough** (Yorkshire) – said to be the country's oldest resort – and nearby **Bridlington**. The old seaside traditions also survive in places like **Skegness** (Lincolnshire), site of England's first Butlin's holiday camp, while elegance is the keynote in classy **Southwold** (Suffolk). On the south coast, **Bournemouth** (Dorset) and **Torquay** (Devon) are also both genteel and sedate by day, but with an energetic clubbing scene pulling in the punters at night. **Brighton** (Sussex), meanwhile, has a strong independent identity that combines

Georgian charm with a gay-friendly boho appeal, and has set a trend for regeneration that's inspired other traditional resorts from **Margate** (Kent) to **Morecambe** (Lancashire).

Beach huts, Southwold ▲

Calf of Man ▼

Top ten coastal beauty spots

▶▶ **Calf of Man**, Isle of Man. Take the boat across to this remote bird sanctuary for its high cliffs and grassy meadows. See p.645

▶▶ **Robin Hood's Bay**, Yorkshire. Honeycombed cliffs and rocky reefs set the scene at this erstwhile smugglers' haunt. See p.760

▶▶ **Lizard Point**, Cornwall. Raging seas surround the rocky promontory at England's southernmost point. See p.400

▶▶ **Holy Island**, Northumberland. A castle and priory ruins add to the brooding character of this ancient, legend-filled spot. See p.818

▶▶ **The Needles**, Isle of Wight. Spectacular pinnacles of rock thrust up from the sea. See p.223

▶▶ **Blakeney**, Norfolk. Picturesque retreat, with creeks, channels and sand banks to explore. See p.461

▶▶ **Hartland Point**, Devon. Fantastic, jagged slate cliffs give this remote headland an otherworldly feel. See p.387

▶▶ **Lulworth Cove**, Dorset. A gorgeous arc of beach beneath high chalk cliffs – though it can get crowded. See p.240

▶▶ **Heysham**, Lancashire. A pretty village with a ruined headland chapel that looks over the bay to the Lake District fells. See p.637

▶▶ **Cromer**, Norfolk. Pint-sized resort with a pier, sea cliffs, a wide sandy beach and a real gastronomic treat – the trusty Cromer crab. See p.458

Fathers' departure in the *Mayflower* in 1620 and the maiden voyages of such ships as the *Queen Mary* and the *Titanic*. Southampton suffered some disastrous postwar planning following a pummelling by the Luftwaffe, but despite this it's a lively place with two universities, a vibrant regenerated waterfront, some fine museums and a superb set of medieval walls. Its numerous retail areas have also turned it into a big draw for shoppers.

Arrival, information and accommodation

Services from London Waterloo arrive at the central **train station** in Blechynden Terrace, west of the Civic Centre; the **bus station** is immediately southeast of the Civic Centre. The **tourist office** is at 9 Civic Centre Rd (Mon–Sat 9.30am–5pm, Sun 10am–3.30pm; ☏023/8083 3333, ⓦwww.visit-southampton.co.uk).

A decent budget **accommodation** choice is *Eaton Court*, around half a mile west of the train station, at 32 Hill Lane (☏023/8022 3081, ⓦwww.eatoncourts outhampton.co.uk; ❷), for good-value, simple bed and breakfast with off-street parking. Alternatively, the stylish *White Star*, 28 Oxford St (☏023/8082 1990, ⓦwww.whitestartavern.co.uk; ❹), has contemporary rooms, with comfortable beds and modern decor, above a trendy bar-restaurant in a lively part of town. Southampton's most upmarket option is the plush steel-and-glass *De Vere Grand Harbour*, West Quay Road ☏023/8063 3033, ⓦwww.devere-hotels.com; ❺), with a pool, spa and restaurant, though the rooms feel slightly worn.

The Town

Core of the modern town is the **Civic Centre**. Its clocktower is the most distinctive feature of the skyline, and it houses an excellent **art gallery** (Mon–Fri 10am–5pm, Sat & Sun 11am–4pm; free; ⓦwww.southampton.gov.uk/art) with works by modern British artists such as Antony Gormley and Lucien Freud, through Impressionists such as Renoir and Monet, to Gainsborough. The **Western Esplanade**, curving southward from the station, runs alongside the best remaining bits of the old city **walls**. Rebuilt after a French attack in 1338, they feature towers with evocatively chilly names – Windwhistle, Catchcold and God's House – the last of these, at the southern end of the old town in Winkle Street, houses a **Museum of Archeology** (Thurs & Fri 10am–4pm, Sat & Sun 11am–4pm; £2.50). Best preserved of the city's seven gates is **Bargate**, at the opposite end of the old town at the head of the High Street; an elaborate structure, cluttered with lions, classical figures and defensive devices, it was formerly the guildhall and court house.

Other ancient buildings survive amid the piecemeal redevelopment of the High Street area. The oldest church is **St Michael's**, to the west of the High Street, with a twelfth-century font of black Tournai marble. The nearby **Tudor House Museum**, in Bugle Street (currently closed for refurbishment: contact tourist office for information), is an impressive fifteenth-century timber-framed building with a grand banqueting hall and reconstructed Tudor garden. Down at the southwest corner of the old town, by the seafront, the **Wool House** is a fine fourteenth-century stone warehouse, formerly used as a jail for Napoleonic prisoners and now home to a **Maritime Museum** (Mon–Fri 10am–4pm, Sat & Sun 11am–4pm; £2.50), focusing on the heyday of ocean liners, and including an exhibition on the *Titanic*.

Eating, drinking and nightlife

There's a cluster of lively **restaurants** on and around Oxford Street, including the *White Star* (see above) and the upmarket *Old Delhi Eatery*, 1 Oxford St (☏023/8023

3433), serving unusual Indian dishes such as water-buffalo bhuna; mains start around £8. For cheap and cheerful Italian cuisine, the small bustling *Piccolo Mondo*, 36 Windsor Terrace (☎023/8063 6890; closed Sun), dishes up filling, reasonably priced pizzas and home-made pasta. In a former Art Deco cruise liner terminal on the waterfront, ⚓ *Kuti's Royal Thai*, Gate House, Royal Pier (☎023/8033 9211), has an excellent all-you-can-eat Thai buffet (£10 for lunch, £20 for dinner) with fine views across the water.

The fifteenth-century *Duke of Wellington,* 36 Bugle St, is one of Southampton's oldest **pubs**, with an exterior that's barely changed since it first opened. Alternatively, for something less traditional, the *Orange Rooms*, 1–2 Vernon Walk, is a popular retro-themed lounge bar with regular DJs, and serves great cocktails and decent food. **Clubbers** should head to *Oceana*, West Quay Road (⊚www .oceanaclubs.com), one of the UK's biggest clubs, with various themed areas, such as a bar quarter, an alfresco courtyard and a New York-disco-style dancefloor.

The Isle of Wight

In recent years the **ISLE OF WIGHT** has begun to shake off its comfortable, unadventurous image, and has started to attract a younger, more lively crowd, with two major annual music festivals and a scattering of fashionable hotels. Measuring over twenty miles at its widest point with a chalk spine that runs from east to west across its centre, the island packs a surprising variety of landscapes and coastal scenery, with low-lying woodland and pasture contrasting with chalky downland fringed by high cliffs. Two **Heritage Coast** paths follow the best of the shoreline, one running from Totland to St Lawrence on the south coast, the other from east of Yarmouth to west of Cowes along the north coast. Blending into this background is a splendid array of well-preserved Victoriana – unsurprising perhaps, for the founding Victorian herself felt most at home here, with **Osborne House** becoming the monarch's permanent home after Albert died. Several other eminent Victorians also frequented the island, and you can't go far without coming across traces of Tennyson, Dickens, Swinburne and the photographer Julia Margaret Cameron, among others. Older remains include the castles at **Yarmouth** and **Carisbrooke**.

Ryde and around

A working town that came to prominence as a resort in the Victorian era, **RYDE** has some grand nineteenth-century architecture and decent beach amusements. Reaching out over the shallows of Ryde Sands, the half-mile-long **pier** is where the ferries dock and former London Underground rolling stock carries the seasonal throngs inland. Backed by sandy beaches, the **Esplanade** extends eastwards from the pier, with the small Gothic Revival folly of Appley Tower at its far end, celebrating the sailing of the First Fleet to Botany Bay from Mother Bank, off Ryde, in 1787.

Just outside the village of Binstead, two miles west of Ryde's centre, lies one of the island's earliest Christian relics. **Quarr Abbey** was founded in 1132 by Richard de Redvers as one of the first Cistercian monasteries in Britain. Its name derives from the nearby quarries, where stone was extracted for use in the construction of Winchester and Chichester cathedrals. Only stunted ruins survived the Dissolution and ensuing plunder of ready-cut stone, although an ivy-clad archway still hangs picturesquely over a farm track. In 1907 a new Benedictine abbey was founded just west of the ruins – a striking rose-brick building with Byzantine overtones, which can be visited on guided tours (check Ⓦwww.quarrabbey.co.uk for dates).

Due south of Ryde just off the busy Sandown road (A3055; bus #3), the **Brading Roman Villa** (daily 9.30am–5pm; £6.50; Ⓦwww.bradingromanvilla .org.uk) is the more impressive of two such villas on the island (the other is in Newport), both of which were probably sites of bacchanalian worship. Housed within an attractive modern museum, the villa is notable for its superbly preserved mosaics, including intact images of Medusa and depictions of Orpheus as well as a mysterious man with a cockerel's head. Brading is also a stop on the main Ryde–Shanklin train line, that connects at Smallbrook (one stop up from Brading) with the seasonal **Isle of Wight Steam Railway** (Ⓦwww.iwsteamrailway.co.uk). Its

Isle of Wight practicalities

Ferries

There are three **departure points** from the mainland to the Isle of Wight – Portsmouth, Southampton and Lymington. **Wightlink** (Ⓦwww.wightlink.co.uk) runs car ferries from **Lymington to Yarmouth** (30min) and from Gunwharf Terminal in **Portsmouth to Fishbourne** (40min), as well as a high-speed catamaran from Portsmouth Harbour to **Ryde Pier** (passengers only; 20min). **Hovertravel** (Ⓦwww.hovertravel.co.uk), meanwhile, runs hovercrafts from Clarence Esplanade in Southsea to Ryde (passengers only; 10min). From **Southampton**, **Red Funnel** (Ⓦwww.redfunnel.co.uk) operates a high-speed catamaran to **West Cowes** (passengers only; 25min) and a car ferry to **East Cowes** (55min). Fare structures and schedules on all routes are labyrinthine, so check the ferry companies' websites for details. A single foot-passenger ticket on the Southampton–West Cowes route can cost as little as £7 in low season, while a high-season return for a car and four passengers from Lymington to Yarmouth can cost up to £100.

Information and getting around

There are **tourist offices** in Ryde, Sandown, Shanklin, Yarmouth, Cowes and Newport (Ⓣ01983/813813, Ⓦwww.islandbreaks.co.uk); call for opening hours. Local **buses**, run by Southern Vectis (Ⓣ0871/200 2233, Ⓦwww.islandbuses.info), sell good-value tickets giving unlimited travel on the network (£10 for one day, £20 for a week). There are two **train** lines on the island: the seasonal **Isle of Wight Steam Railway** (see above) and the east-coast **Island line** from Ryde to Shanklin (Mon–Sat every 20–40min, Sun hourly; 25min; Ⓦwww.islandlinetrains.co.uk).

Cycling is a popular way of getting around the island, though in summer the narrow lanes can get very busy. For bike **rental**, contact Wight Cycle Hire (Ⓣ01983/761800, Ⓦwww.wightcyclehire.co.uk): its offices are in Yarmouth and Brading but it can deliver bikes anywhere on the island (£8 for half-day, or £14 per day).

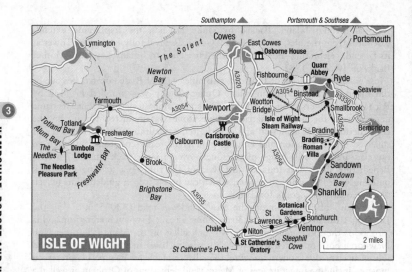

Southampton ▲   Portsmouth & Southsea ▲

Lymington

Cowes
East Cowes
Osborne House
Portsmouth

The Solent

Newton
Bay

Fishbourne
Quarr
Abbey
Ryde

Seaview

Yarmouth

A3054 Binstead

B3330

Newport
Wootton
Bridge
Smallbrook

Isle of Wight
Steam Railway

Wootton

A3054

Totland
Bay
Freshwater

Dimbola
Lodge

Alum Bay

Totland
Bay

The
Needles

The Needles
Pleasure Park

Freshwater Bay

Calbourne

Carisbrooke
Castle

A3054

Brading

Bembridge

Brading
Roman
Villa

A3055

A3056

Sandown
Sandown
Bay
Shanklin

N

Brook

Brighstone
Bay

A3055

Botanical
Gardens

Bonchurch

St
Lawrence
Ventnor

Chale
Niton

Steephill
Cove

0   2 miles

St Catherine's Point

St Catherine's
Oratory

ISLE OF WIGHT

impeccably restored carriages in traditional green livery make the delightful
ten-mile return trip to Wootton Bridge, between Ryde and Newport, through
lovely unspoilt countryside.

Practicalities

Ryde's **tourist office**, **bus station**, **hovercraft terminal** and **Esplanade train
station** (the northern terminus of the Island Line train line) are all located near the
base of the pier; there's also a **taxi** rank close by.

The comfortable *Yelf's Hotel* on Union Street (℡01983/564062, Ⓦwww
.yelfshotel.com; ❹) is one of Ryde's oldest **hotels**, while the nearby *Kasbah* at
76 Union St (℡01983/810088, Ⓦwww.kas-bah.co.uk; ❷) has stylish, Moroccan-
themed rooms above a funky café/bar. In a wonderful setting with lawns leading
down to a private beach, the elegant ⚑ *Priory Bay Hotel* in nearby Seaview, a couple
of miles east of Ryde (℡01983/613146, Ⓦwww.priorybay.com; ❻), has a
luxurious but unstuffy, child-friendly atmosphere and a great restaurant. Back in
Ryde, Union Street has a good selection of **places to eat**, including *Kasbah*'s
Moroccan café, while the friendly, seafront *Michelangelo*, 30 St Thomas St, serves
good-value pizzas and pasta.

Sandown and Shanklin

The two eastern resorts of **SANDOWN** and **SHANKLIN** merge into each other
across the sandy reach of **Sandown Bay**, and form the island's holiday-making
epicentre. Frequently recorded as among Britain's sunniest spots, Sandown is a
traditional bucket-and-spade resort while Shanklin nestles into its auburn cliffs,
with its Old Village and scenic chine. Sandown's **tourist office** is located at 8 High
St, and Shanklin's at 67 High St. There's no shortage of **accommodation** in the
two resorts, with *The Reef*, The Esplanade, Sandown (℡01983/403219, Ⓦwww
.thereefsandown.co.uk; ❷), having bargain-priced seaview rooms, while Shanklin's *Luccombe Hall* on Luccombe Road (℡01983/869000, Ⓦwww.luccombehall
.co.uk; ❺) sits in lovely grounds on the cliff top with sea views and a pool.

Aside from the long sandy beach, Sandown's main attractions are the **Isle of
Wight Zoo** at the northern end of the Esplanade (mid-Feb to March & Oct daily

10am–4pm; April–Sept daily 10am–6pm; Nov Sat & Sun 10am–4pm, weather permitting; £7.45; @www.isleofwightzoo.com) and **Dinosaur Isle**, next door (daily: April–Sept 10am–6pm; Oct 10am–5pm; Nov–March 10am–4pm; £5; @www.dinosaurisle.com), which showcases some of the prehistoric finds on the island, one of Europe's richest sites for dinosaur remains.

Separated from the shore by hundred-foot cliffs, Shanklin's touristy **Old Village** has a certain rose-clad, thatched charm. Leading from the village down to the beach, **Shanklin Chine** (daily: April–May & mid-Sept to Oct 10am–5pm; June to mid-Sept 10am–10pm; £3.80) is a picturesque, twisting pathway descending a mossy ravine and decorated on summer nights with fairy lights. In the village itself, the *Old Thatched Teashop*, 4 Church Rd, is the place for home-made cakes, cream teas and light lunches, while the thatched *Fisherman's Cottage* **pub** sits right on the beach at the bottom of the chine and serves decent pub meals in good-sized portions.

Ventnor and Bonchurch

The seaside resort of **VENTNOR** sits at the foot of St Boniface Down, the island's highest point at 787ft. The down periodically disintegrates into landslides, creating the **Undercliff**, a series of jumbled terraces with a sheltered, south-facing aspect, mild winter temperatures and thick undergrowth. Today, the former fishing village is a characterful place, with Gothic Revival buildings clinging dizzily to zigzagging bends, and some fine places to stay.

The floral terraces of the **Cascade** curve down to the slender Esplanade and narrow beach, where fresh fish is sold from former boat-builders' cottages and **boat trips** (@www.oceanblueseacharters.co.uk) are on offer. From here, it's a pleasant mile-long stroll to Ventnor's famous **Botanical Gardens**, where 22 landscaped acres of subtropical vegetation flourish. Displays are divided thematically, ranging from the South African and Australian banks to the Culinary Herb and the Medicinal gardens.

To the east of Ventnor, the ancient village of **BONCHURCH** exudes an alluring rustic charm with its duck pond and rows of quaint cottages set on the Undercliff's wooded slopes. Behind high stone walls loom grand Victorian country houses where writers such as Dickens, Thackeray and Swinburne once stayed. At Bonchurch's east end is the spartan, towerless edifice of the eleventh-century **Old Church of St Boniface** with its mature trees and wreath of skewed gravestones. There's a great, if steep, walk that starts on the beach below Bonchurch, heads up the **Devil's Chimney**, a dramatic series of steps winding up through woods, and then squeezes through a narrow crevice in the cliffs. You end up at the *Smuggler's Haven Tea Rooms* on St Boniface Downs, where you can reward your exertions with a cream tea.

Accommodation

Hambrough Hotel Hambrough Rd, Ventnor ☏01938/856333, @www.thehambrough.com. Small but stylish, modern hotel above a top-notch restaurant run by Britain's youngest Michelin-Star chef, Robert Thompson. The minimalist rooms come with all the luxuries; most have sea views, and some have balconies. ❻

Horseshoe Bay House Horseshoe Bay, Bonchurch ☏01983/856800, @www.horseshoebayhouse.co .uk. A lovely, comfortable B&B right on the beach, with sea views from all rooms. ❸

The Lake Shore Rd, Lower Bonchurch ☏01983/852613, @www.lakehotel.co.uk. Family-run hotel in a nineteenth-century country manor with lovely grounds, a short walk from Bonchurch village and the beach. It has an attractive sun-lounge and terrace and twenty large, comfortable rooms, all en suite. ❹

The Troubadour Hotel 25 High St, Ventnor ☏01983/856537, @www.troubadourhotel .co.uk. Simple but good-value en-suite rooms in a Victorian house, in the centre of Ventnor. ❷

Restaurants and pubs

El Toro Contento 2 Pier St ☎01983/857600. A cosy restaurant serving home-made tapas, such as chorizo in cider, and spicy squid, most for under a fiver. Also serves Spanish hams and cheeses and will cook paella for £10.50 a head (minimum 4 people) with 24hr notice. Closed Sun.

The Pond Café Bonchurch Village Rd, Bonchurch ☎01938/855666. Small and smart, this well-regarded restaurant overlooking the village pond is also run by Robert Thompson, but is cheaper and less formal than *The Hambrough* (see p.221). Its short menu features dishes such as fish and shellfish stew (£15) and roast pigeon (£17). Good value.

Spyglass Inn Ventnor Esplanade ☎01983/855338. Lively pub in a great location on the seafront with outdoor tables on the terrace. The meals are mostly pub staples in giant portions, such as fish pie for £9, while the home-made daily specials often include locally caught fish.

Wheelers Crab Shed Steephill Cove, 15min walk west of Ventnor along the Esplanade ☎01983/852177. Delicious home-made crab pasties, sandwiches and ciabattas served from a pretty shack on the seashore. April–Nov 11.30am–3.30pm.

The southwest coast

The western Undercliff begins to recede at the village of **NITON**, where a footpath continues to the most southerly tip of the island, **St Catherine's Point**, marked by a modern lighthouse. A prominent landmark on the downs behind is **St Catherine's Oratory**, known locally as the "Pepper Pot". In fact it's a medieval lighthouse, reputedly built in 1325 as an act of expiation by a local landowner, Walter de Goditon, who had attempted to pilfer a cargo of wine owned by a monastic community.

From St Catherine's Point, the road follows the cliff top westwards to Freshwater Bay, where **Dimbola Lodge** (Tues–Sun, plus Mon in school summer hols & bank hols: March–Oct 10am–5pm; Nov–Feb 10am–4pm; £4) was the home of pioneer photographer **Julia Margaret Cameron**, who moved here after visiting her friend and local resident Tennyson in 1860. The building now houses a gallery of her work, including an impressive range of portraits of some of the foremost society figures of her day, plus other visiting exhibitions of photography. There's a bookshop and good tearoom/restaurant on the premises too.

Just up the road, on Bedbury Lane, Tennyson's former home **Farringford** (☎01983/868344, ⓦ www.farringford.co.uk) provides several self-catering cottages (from £520 a week; shorter stays sometimes possible) in lovely grounds with an outdoor pool, putting green and tennis courts. On the way, you'll pass **FRESHWATER**'s unusual ninety-year-old thatched **Church of St Agnes**, containing memorials to Tennyson and Thackeray's daughter, Lady Ritchie; Tennyson's wife is buried in the churchyard. Between Freshwater Bay and the Needles, the breezy four-mile ridge of **Tennyson Down** is one of the island's most satisfying walks, with another monument to the poet at its 485-foot summit and vistas onto rolling downs and vales.

Alum Bay and The Needles

One of the two major focal points of the Isle's western tip is the multichrome cliffs of **Alum Bay**. To get here during the summer months, you can make use of an open-top bus that circulates every thirty minutes between Yarmouth, Freshwater Bay and **The Needles Pleasure Park** (daily from 10am; free; ⓦ www.theneedles .co.uk), comprising a collection of fairground amusements and a glass studio where you can watch the manufacture of glass objects. A chair lift (£4 return) runs down from the cliff top down to Alum Bay, whose ochre-hued sands, used as pigments for painting local landscapes in the Victorian era, contrast brightly with the chalk face of the Needles headland: from here, **boat trips** (every 15–30min

Easter–Oct daily 10.30am–4pm; 25min; £5; Ⓦwww.needlespleasurecruises
.co.uk) leave for cruises of The Needles and the Bay.

From the Pleasure Park, it's a twenty-minute walk to the lookout opposite the
three tall chalk stacks known as **The Needles**, where Tennyson Down slips into
the Channel. There are fine views from the end of the tunnel that burrows through
the cliffs at the **Old Battery**, a gun emplacement built 250ft above the sea in 1863
(mid-March to Oct daily 10.30am–5pm; £4.85; NT). The fort may be closed in
bad weather; call to check on Ⓣ01983/754772.

Yarmouth

Situated at the mouth of the River Yar, the relaxed town of **YARMOUTH**
stretches east along the seashore from its pocket-sized harbour. The island's first
purpose-built port, it was razed by the French in 1377 on their way to
Carisbrooke (see p.224), but regained prosperity in the sixteenth century after
Henry VIII ordered the construction of **Yarmouth Castle** (Easter–Sept
Mon–Thurs & Sun 11am–4pm; £3.80; EH). Amid a warren of chambers and
corridors, the castle has exhibitions on local history and the development of
Henry's fortress, while stairs lead up to a small green from where there are
splendid views across to the mainland.

Yarmouth's **tourist office** is just back from the harbour. The best place in town
to **stay** is *The George*, on Quay Street (Ⓣ01983/760331, Ⓦwww.thegeorge.co
.uk; Ⓖ), a seventeenth-century hotel right by the ferry dock, with elegantly
furnished rooms; Charles II stayed here when he visited the island. It also has a
superb if pricey seafood **restaurant** with tables in the garden overlooking the sea,
as well as a pleasant panelled bar. For cheaper meals, *Gossips Café* on the pier has
lovely views and serves good-value sandwiches, hot meals and cream teas.

Cowes and Osborne House

COWES, at the island's northern tip, is inextricably associated with sailing and
boat building: Henry VIII built a castle here to defend the Solent's expanding
naval dockyards from the French and Spanish, and in the 1950s the world's first
hovercraft made its test runs here. In 1820 the Prince Regent's patronage of the
yacht club gave the port its cachet with the Royal Yacht Squadron, now one of the
world's most exclusive sailing clubs. The first week of August sees the international yachting festival known as **Cowes Week** (Ⓦwww.cowesweek.co.uk),
which visiting royalty turns into a high-society gala, although the presence of
serious sailors helps to lift the event above the merely ceremonial. There are
dozens of organized events, including a spectacular fireworks display on the Friday
night, and a great party atmosphere.

The town is bisected by the River Medina, with **West Cowes** being the older
and more interesting half, its High Street meandering up from the waterfront
Parade. Along the High Street you'll find shops reflecting the town's gentrified
heritage, interspersed with boatyards and chandlers. The more industrial East
Cowes, where you'll find Osborne House, is connected to West Cowes by a
"floating bridge", or chain ferry (Mon–Sat 5am–12.30am, Sun 7am–12.30am;
pedestrians free, cars £1.50).

Queen Victoria's family home, **Osborne House** (Jan–March Wed–Sun
10am–4pm; April–Sept daily 10am–6pm; Oct daily 10am–4pm; Nov & Dec
Wed–Sun 10am–4pm pre-booked tours only; £8.40; EH) lies a mile southeast of
East Cowes; take bus #4 from Ryde or #5 from Newport, or either from East
Cowes. The house was built in the late 1840s by Prince Albert and Thomas Cubitt,
with extensions such as the Household Wing and the exotic, Indian-style Durbar

③

Room added over the next half-century. Albert designed the private family home as an Italianate villa, with balconies and large terraces overlooking the landscaped gardens towards the Solent. The state rooms, used for entertaining visiting dignitaries, exude formality, while the private apartments feel more homely, like an affluent family holiday residence. Following Albert's death, the desolate Victoria spent much of her time here, eventually dying here in 1901. Since then, the house has remained virtually unaltered, allowing an unexpectedly intimate glimpse into Victoria's family life. Included in the entry ticket is a minibus to the Swiss Cottage, built in the grounds for Victoria's children to play and study.

Practicalities

Cowes' **tourist office** is at the Arcade, Fountain Quay, West Cowes, with extended opening hours during Cowes Week. **Boat trips** upriver and around the harbour and the Solent leave from Thetis Wharf, near the chain ferry; for details contact Solent & Wight Line Cruises (℡01983/564602, ⓦwww.solentcruises .co.uk).

Accommodation options include the comfortable *Fountain Inn*, High Street, West Cowes (℡01983/292397; ❸), with views over the harbour, and *Crossways House Hotel* (℡01983/298282, ⓦwww.bedbreakfast-cowes.co.uk; ❸), opposite Osborne House on Crossways Road in East Cowes, with four-poster beds and a garden. All accommodation prices rise steeply during Cowes Week, when most places are booked up well in advance.

For all-day breakfasts, a good range of sandwiches and some more filling hot specials, the Beatles-themed *Octopus Garden*, 63 High St, is a fun spot for lunch (daytime only). Traditional **pub** meals are served at the *Union Inn* on Watch House Lane, while *Mojacs*, 10a Shooters Hill, is a more upmarket **restaurant**, offering a good-value set menu (three courses for £20); its puddings are particularly good.

Newport and Carisbrooke Castle

NEWPORT, the capital of the Isle of Wight, sits at the centre of the island at a point where the River Medina's commercial navigability ends. Apart from a few pleasant old quays dating from its days as an inland port, the town merits a visit principally for the hilltop fortress of **Carisbrooke Castle** (daily: April–Sept 10am–5pm; Oct–March 10am–4pm; £7; EH), on the southwest outskirts (buses #6, #7, #11 or #38 from Newport). The austere Norman keep was greatly extended over the years, initially in the thirteenth century by the imperious Countess Isabella who inherited much of the island and ruled it as a petty kingdom. Carisbrooke's most famous visitor was Charles I, detained here (and caught one night ignominiously jammed between his room's bars while attempting escape) prior to his execution in London. The **museum** in the centre of the castle features many relics from his incarceration, as well as those of the last royal resident, Princess Beatrice, Queen Victoria's youngest daughter – you can wander around her pretty private garden which has been redesigned with fountains, orchards and Edwardian-style planting. The castle's other notable curiosity is the sixteenth-century well-house, where donkeys still trudge inside a huge treadmill to raise a barrel 160ft up the well shaft. A stroll around the battlements provides several lofty perspectives of the castle's interior as well as sweeping views across the centre of the island.

Newport's **tourist office** is at the Guildhall on the High Street. Your best bet for a coffee or lunch is the *Quay Arts Café*, Sea Street, while the nearby *Bargeman's Rest* **pub** serves real ales, decent pub grub and has live music. For excellent Italian **food**, *Olivo*, 15 St Thomas Square (℡01983/530001), serves the usual pastas and pizzas plus some more adventurous Mediterranean dishes, such as wild boar stew (£14).

Winchester and around

Nowadays a tranquil, handsome market town, set amid docile hay-meadows and watercress beds, **WINCHESTER** was once one of the mightiest settlements in England. Under the Romans it was Venta Belgarum, the fifth largest town in Britain, but it was **Alfred the Great** who really put Winchester on the map when he made it the capital of his Wessex kingdom in the ninth century. For the next couple of centuries Winchester ranked alongside London, its status affirmed by William the Conqueror's coronation in both cities and by his commissioning of the local monks to prepare the **Domesday Book**. As the site of the shrine of St Swithun, King Alfred's tutor, Winchester attracted innumerable pilgrims, and throughout the medieval era the city continued to command enormous ecclesiastical and political influence – Bishop **William of Wykeham**, founder of Winchester College and Oxford's New College, was twice chancellor of England. It wasn't until after the Battle of Naseby in 1645, when Cromwell took the city, that Winchester began to decline into provinciality.

Hampshire's county town now has a scholarly and slightly anachronistic air, embodied by the ancient almshouses that still provide shelter for senior citizens of "noble poverty" – the pensioners can be seen wandering round the town in medieval black or mulberry-coloured gowns with silver badges. A trip to this secluded old city is a must – not only for the magnificent **cathedral**, chief relic of Winchester's medieval glory, but for the all-round, well-preserved ambience of England's one-time capital. The city also makes a good base from which to explore a trio of villages to the east: **Alresford**, **Chawton**, home of Jane Austen, and **Selbourne**.

Arrival, information and accommodation

Winchester **train station** is about a mile northwest of the cathedral on Stockbridge Road. If you arrive by **bus**, you'll find yourself on the Broadway, opposite the **tourist office** in the imposing Guildhall (May–Sept Mon–Sat 9.30am–5.30pm, Sun 11am–4pm; Oct–April Mon–Sat 10am–5pm; ☏01962/840500, ⓦwww.visitwinchester.co.uk), which has plenty of information about the city and its environs, and distributes excellent visitors' guides, walks leaflets and literature on the eighty-mile South Downs Way (see box, p.179). Ask here too about daily **guided walks** of the city (1hr 30min; £4.50).

Hotels and B&Bs

29 Christchurch Road 29 Christchurch Rd ☏01962/868661, ⓦwww.fetherstondilke.com. Reliable B&B accommodation in a charming Regency house located in a quiet residential part of town. ❸

Dawn Cottage 99 Romsey Rd ☏01962/869956, ⒺEdawncottage@hotmail.com. Classy B&B about a mile west of the centre and connected by frequent buses (#5). The three comfortable rooms have en-suite bathrooms and great views over the Itchen valley. ❷

Dolphin House 3 Compton Rd ☏01962/853284, ⓦwww.dolphinhousestudios.co.uk. Good-value rooms in a lovely townhouse in a quiet part of town. Double or twin rooms share their own kitchenette and have access to the gardens; off-street parking. ❷

Hotel du Vin Southgate St ☏01962/841414, ⓦwww.hotelduvin.com. The first of the classy *Hotel du Vin* chain: a lovely Georgian townhouse that's been given a stylish makeover. Rooms are plush – some cottage-style ones have their own private entrances and terraces – and there's a lovely patio garden, chic bar and great restaurant. First choice for accommodation in Winchester, especially if you can bag one of their good-value special offers. ❼

The Old Vine 8 Great Minster St ☏01962/854616, ⓦwww.oldvinewinchester.com. The spacious, comfortable and sumptuously furnished rooms above this old tavern include three at the front and a top-floor suite, which all have cathedral views (costing extra). Breakfast is served in your room. ❹

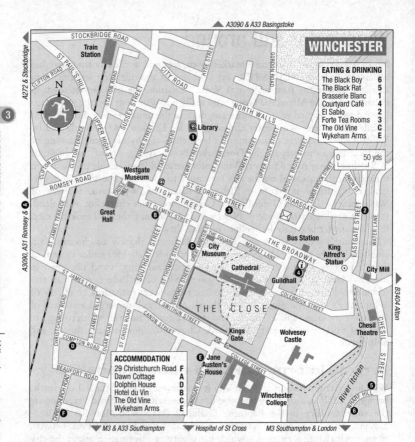

Wykeham Arms 75 Kingsgate St ☎ 01962/853834, ⓦ www.fullershotels.com. Fine old hostelry where the art of classy inn-keeping has not yet vanished. Fourteen beamed and quirkily shaped rooms are adorned with assorted antiques and curios. ⓖ

The City

Winchester is a compact city, easily toured on foot – indeed, a car is a liability here, and should be parked up at the first opportunity. Once away from the streams of traffic threading through the centre you can relax – the lanes are peppered with refreshment stops, and the Cathedral Close makes a pleasant spot for a quiet sit-down.

The cathedral

The first minster to be built in Winchester was raised by Cenwalh, the Saxon king of Wessex in the mid-seventh century and traces of this building have been unearthed near the present **cathedral** (Mon–Sat 8.30am–6pm, Sun 12.30pm–3pm; £6 donation requested; ⓦ www.winchester-cathedral.org.uk). Begun in 1079, the cathedral was completed some three hundred years later, producing a church whose elements range from early Norman to Perpendicular styles.

The exterior is not the cathedral's best feature – squat and massive, it crouches stumpily over the tidy lawns of the Cathedral Close. The interior is rich and complex, however, and its 556-foot **nave** makes this Europe's longest medieval church. Outstanding features include its carved Norman font of black Tournai marble, the fourteenth-century misericords (the choir stalls are the oldest complete set in the country) and some amazing monuments – **William of Wykeham's Chantry**, halfway down the nave on the right, is one of the best. **Jane Austen**, who died in Winchester, is commemorated close to the font by a memorial brass and slab beneath which she's interred, though she's recorded simply as the daughter of a local clergyman. Above the high altar lie the mortuary chests of pre-Conquest kings, including Knut, or **Canute** (though the bones were mixed up after Cromwell's Roundheads broke up the chests in 1645); William Rufus (see p.231), killed while hunting in the New Forest in 1100, lies in the presbytery. The statuary on the impressive **screen** at the end of the presbytery, showing Queen Victoria and Alfred the Great among many others, was added in the Victorian era to replace the original images destroyed during the Reformation. Beyond the screen, near Cardinal Beaufort's Chantry Chapel, look out too for the memorial shrine to **St Swithun**. Originally buried outside in the churchyard, his remains were later interred inside the cathedral where the "rain of heaven" could no longer fall on him, whereupon he took revenge and the heavens opened for forty days – hence the legend that if it rains on St Swithun's Day (July 15) it will continue for another forty. His exact burial place is unknown.

Accessible from the north transept, the Norman **crypt** is only rarely open, since it's flooded for much of the time – the cathedral's original foundations were dug in marshy ground. If you catch it open, though, have a look inside at the two fourteenth-century statues of William of Wykeham as well as Antony Gormley's standing figure, *Sound II*, one of the country's most adventurous ecclesiastical commissions in recent years.

The City Museum and the Great Hall
Outside the cathedral, the **City Museum** (April–Oct Mon–Sat 10am–5pm, Sun noon–5pm; Nov–March Tues–Sat 10am–4pm, Sun noon–4pm; free), a basic local history display, sits on The Square. Head up the nearby High Street to the **Westgate Museum** (Feb & March Tues–Sat 10am–4pm, Sun noon–4pm; April–Oct Mon–Sat 10am–5pm, Sun noon–5pm; free), a medieval gateway used for years as a debtors' prison; you can still see prisoners' graffiti and a Tudor ceiling, and there are fine views from the roof. Walk west, and then south, from here and you'll soon arrive at the **Great Hall** on Castle Avenue (daily 10am–5pm; July & Aug until 7pm on Fri; free), the vestigial remains of a thirteenth-century castle destroyed by Cromwell. Sir Walter Raleigh heard his death sentence here in 1603, though he wasn't finally dispatched until 1618, and Judge Jeffreys held one of his Bloody Assizes in the castle after the Monmouth Rebellion in 1685. The main interest now, however, is a large, brightly painted disc slung on one wall like some curious antique dartboard. This is alleged to be **King Arthur's Round Table**, though the woodwork is probably fourteenth-century, later repainted as a PR exercise for the Tudor dynasty – the portrait of Arthur at the top of the table bears an uncanny resemblance to Henry VIII. Below the table, the floor of the Great Hall is dominated by a gaudy sculpture of Queen Victoria, carved by Sir Alfred Gilbert (responsible for *Eros* in London's Piccadilly Circus) to mark her Golden Jubilee in 1887. Adjoining the Great Hall, an illuminating exhibition relates the history of the Norman castle and Great Hall, and you can also take a brief wander in Queen Eleanor's Medieval Garden – a re-creation of a noblewoman's shady retreat.

3

East and south of the cathedral

Head east along the High Street and you'll pass the striking, neo-Gothic Guildhall and the bronze statue of King Alfred on The Broadway, which marks the western-most boundary of the South Downs National Park, created in 2010 (see box, p.179). Just beyond sits the River Itchen and the restored **City Mill** (see Ⓦ www.nationaltrust.org.uk/winchestercitymill for opening hours; £3.50). Turn right before the bridge along the riverside path and you'll soon pass what remains of the Saxon walls, which bracket the ruins of the twelfth-century **Wolvesey Castle** (early April to Sept daily 10am–5pm; free; EH), former palace of the Bishops of Winchester and built by Christopher Wren. Immediately to the west up College Street stand the buildings of **Winchester College**, the oldest public school in England – established in 1382 by William of Wykeham for "poor scholars", it now educates the wealthy and privileged. The cloisters and chantry are open during term time and the chapel is open all year. Beyond the college at 8 College St, you'll pass the house where Jane Austen died, having moved here from Chawton in 1817 (see opposite) when already ill with Addison's Disease. At the top of College Street, the thirteenth-century **Kings Gate** is one of the city's original medieval gateways, housing the tiny St Swithun's Church.

About a mile south of College Walk, reached by a pleasant stroll across the water meadows of the Itchen, lies the **Hospital of St Cross** (April–Oct Mon–Sat 9.30am–5pm, Sun 1–5pm; Nov–March Mon–Sat 10.30am–3.30pm; £3). Founded in 1136 as a hostel for poor brethren, it boasts a fine church, begun in that year and completed a century or so later, where you can see a triptych by the Flemish painter Mabuse. Needy wayfarers may still apply for the "dole" at the porter's lodge – a tiny portion of bread and beer.

Eating and drinking

Winchester has a good selection of restaurants and pubs as well as one of the country's biggest **farmers' markets**, taking place on the second and last Sunday of each month (until around 2pm).

Cafés and restaurants

The Black Rat 88 Chesil St ☎ 01962/844465. Quality Modern British cuisine served in a cosy former pub. Ingredients are locally sourced with dishes such as wood pigeon, home-made black pudding, pork loin and English cheeses, though expect to pay at least £30 a head for three courses. Reservations advised. Eve only except Sat & Sun.

Brasserie Blanc 19–20 Jewry St ☎ 01962/810870. Smart but laid-back French bistro set in a former butcher's bedecked with chandeliers. Quality mains (from around £12) include tasty *moules* and fine pancakes.

Courtyard Café Guildhall, The Broadway. Excellent lunches and teas are served at this inexpensive, relaxed café by the tourist office. Closed eve.

El Sabio 60 Eastgate St ☎ 01962/820233. Vibrant Spanish bar-restaurant serving a fine range of inexpensive tapas, great fish platters and a tempting paella, as well as Spanish wines and beers. Closed Mon lunch.

Forte Tea Rooms 78 Parchment St. Animated upstairs dining room with warming soups, vegetable tagine and Thai red chicken curry on the menu, as well as a range of snacks, including renowned scones. Closed Mon–Wed eve & Sun all day. Inexpensive.

Pubs

The Black Boy Wharf Hill. Fantastic old pub with log fires in winter, walls lined with books and low ceilings hung with old coins and miniature bottles. Good cask ales and reasonable pub grub (from £8), as well as a small outdoor terrace.

The Old Vine 8 Great Minster St ☎ 01962/854616. Close to the cathedral, this inn has oak beams, a log fire in winter, patio in summer, and real ales on tap. Full meals such as Thai curry and fish pie from around £12.

Wykeham Arms 75 Kingsgate St ☎ 01962/853834. Winchester's most famous pub is somewhat unprepossessing from the outside, but inside it's a maze of characterful, intimate spaces where top-class food is served daily (not Sun eve) at school desks. Main courses are £12–19. Booking advised.

Alresford, Chawton and Selborne

The attractive Georgian town of **ALRESFORD** (pronounced Allsford) grew up on the cotton and tanning trades. The best way to explore the town is to walk the well-marked mile-long **Millennium Trail**, which takes you along the River Arle, a tributary of the Itchen, along which you'll see various watercress beds. Watercress has long grown wild in the local chalky streams, and Hampshire is still the main producer of watercress in England today. It was not until the advent of the railway that it became viable to grow it commercially, hence the so-called **Mid-Hants Watercress Line** (℡01962/733810, www.watercressline.co.uk; adults £12, £30 for family ticket), along which jolly, steam-powered locomotives chuff the ten miles to **Alton**; check the website for the varied timetable which includes special events such as gourmet dinners and real-ale evenings.

A mile southwest of Alton lies the pretty village of **CHAWTON**, where Jane Austen lived from 1809 to 1817, and where she wrote or revised most of her six books, including *Sense and Sensibility* and *Pride and Prejudice*. Fans flock to **Jane Austen's House** (Jan to mid-Feb Sat & Sun 10.30am–4.30pm; mid-Feb to May & Sept–Dec daily 10.30am–4.30pm; June–Aug daily 10.30am–5pm; £7; www.jane-austens-house-museum.org.uk) in the centre of the village, a plain red-brick building containing first editions of some of her greatest works, with a new multi-media visitor centre attached. A short walk away, you can take a guided tour of the house, gardens and library at **Chawton House** (tours March–Dec Tues & Thurs at 2.30pm; Jan & Feb Tues only; £6; www.chawton.org), which belonged to Jane's brother Edward and now houses an impressive collection of women's writing in English between 1600 and 1830; tours should be booked in advance on ℡01420/541010.

Four miles south of Chawton, the little village of **SELBORNE** is where the eighteenth-century naturalist Gilbert White wrote his ecological treatise, *The Natural History and Antiquities of Selborne*. In the High Street his house, now the **Gilbert White House and Oates Museum** (Jan–March Tues–Sun 11am–4pm; April, May & Sept Tues–Sun plus bank hols 10.30am–5.30pm; June–Aug daily 10.30am–5.30pm; £7.50; www.gilbertwhiteshouse.org.uk), is preserved as a memorial to his work, and contains the original manuscript as well as a small museum commemorating Captain Oates, a member of Scott's ill-fated Antarctic expedition in 1912. White constructed the Zig Zag Path with his brother and made many of his observations on Selborne Hill, just southwest of the village, the top of which is a pleasant hour's walk up from his house.

The New Forest

Covering about 220 square miles, the **New Forest** (www.thenewforest.co.uk) is one of southern England's main rural playgrounds, attracting some 13.5 million day-visits annually. The name itself is misleading, for much of this region's woodland was cleared for agriculture and settlement long before the Normans arrived, and its poor sandy soils support only a meagre covering of heather and gorse in many areas. The forest was requisitioned by William the Conqueror in 1079 as a game reserve, and the rights of its inhabitants soon became subservient to those of his precious deer. Fences to impede their progress were forbidden and terrible punishments were meted out to those who disturbed the animals. Later monarchs less passionate about hunting than the Normans gradually restored the forest-dwellers' rights, and today the New Forest enjoys a unique set of ancient laws and privileges, alongside the regulations applying to its National Park status.

The trees of the forest are now much more varied than they were in pre-Norman times, with birch, holly, yew, Scots pine and other conifers interspersed with the ancient oaks and beeches. One of the most venerable is the much-visited **Knightwood Oak**, just a few hundred yards north of the A35 three miles southwest of Lyndhurst, which measures about 22ft in circumference at shoulder height. The most conspicuous species of New Forest fauna are the New Forest **ponies**, reputedly descendants of the survivors of the small Spanish horses of the Armada and now thoroughly domesticated – you'll see them grazing nonchalantly by the roadsides and ambling through villages. The local **deer** are less likely to be seen, although several species still roam the woods, including the tiny sika deer, descendants of a pair that escaped from nearby Beaulieu in 1904.

The main wooded areas are around **Lyndhurst**, the "capital" of the New Forest, though **Brockenhurst** makes a more pleasant stopover. On the edge of the region lies the stately home and motor-vehicle museum of **Beaulieu**, while on the coast, **Lymington** is a charming yachting town, popular with weekending city types.

Practicalities

Trains from London Waterloo serve Brockenhurst twice hourly; the nearest station to Lyndhurst is Ashurst, a couple of miles northeast. There are **bus** routes from Lyndhurst and Brockenhurst to most parts of the forest, and between June and September the open-top New Forest tour bus (ⓦwww.thenewforesttour .info) circulates between Lyndhurst, Brockenhurst, Lymington and Beaulieu eight times a day; you can get on or off anywhere along the route and it also take bikes (all-day tickets £9).

To get the best from the region, however, you need to walk or **cycle** through it. There are 150 miles of car-free gravel roads in the forest, making cycling an appealing prospect – pick up a book of route maps from tourist offices or bike rental shops. The *Ordnance Survey OS Explorer Map 22* of the New Forest is worth getting if you want to explore in any detail, and tourist offices sell numerous walking itineraries, specialist walking books and natural history guides.

Both Lyndhurst and Brockenhurst have plenty of reasonably priced places to stay, though there are also several expensive country-house hotels and restaurants scattered in isolated settings. The forest has ten **campsites** run by the Forestry Commission (ⓣ0845/130 8226, ⓦwww.forestholidays.co.uk); most are open from late March to late September. There's an excellently situated **youth hostel** in Cottesmore House, Cott Lane, Burley, in the west of the Forest (ⓣ0870/770 5734, ⓔburley@yha.org.uk; closed Nov–Feb; from £18), which also has a few camping pitches in the garden. The hostel is a quarter-mile walk from Durmast Corner (buses #X34/35 from Bournemouth, Lyndhurst and Southampton), and half a mile from Burley (buses #105 & 126 from Christchurch). Drinks and meals are available next door at the *White Buck Inn*, which has a spacious garden.

Lyndhurst and around

LYNDHURST, its town centre skewered by an agonizing one-way system, isn't a particularly interesting place, but it has a concentration of useful services. At the **New Forest Visitor Centre**, in the central car park off the High Street (daily 10am–5pm; ⓣ023/8028 2269), you can buy maps and bus passes, and pick up a list of riding outlets; the adjoining **museum** (last entry at 4pm; £3) has child-friendly displays focusing on the forest, its history, wildlife and industries. Otherwise, Lyndhurst is mainly interesting for its brick **parish church**, which boasts William Morris glass, a fresco by Lord Leighton and the grave of one Mrs Reginald Hargreaves, better known as Alice Liddell, Lewis Carroll's model for Alice.

The forest's most visited site, the **Rufus Stone** stands a few hundred yards from the A31, three miles northwest of Lyndhurst. Erected in 1745, the monument marks the putative spot where the Conqueror's ghastly son and heir, **William II** – aka William Rufus after his ruddy complexion – was killed in 1100. The official version is that a crossbow bolt fired by a member of the royal hunting party glanced off a stag and struck the king in the heart, though it's quite likely that this was a political assassination. The stone is remarkably unimpressive for such a landmark: the Victorians encased it in a protective layer of metal to deter vandals, and now it can't be seen at all clearly.

Three miles southwest of Lyndhurst, the **Ornamental Drives** of Bolderwood and Rhinefield are Victorian plantations of exotic trees, suggestive of overgrown ancient woodland, which are popular for a stroll: stop at any of the marked car parks.

Practicalities

Near the visitor centre, in Gosport Lane, **bikes** can be rented from AA Bike Hire (☏023/8028 3349, ⓦ www.aabikehirenewforest.co.uk; £10 a day). For **accommodation**, try *Forest Cottage*, at the west end of the High Street (☏023/8028 3461, ⓦ www.forestcottage.co.uk; no credit cards; ❷), with a flowery garden and well-stocked library, or the *Forest Lodge Hotel*, Pikes Hill, Romsey Road ☏023/8028 3677, ⓦ www.newforesthotels.co.uk; ❹), in a quiet location a short walk from the High Street; rooms are comfortable and there's an indoor pool and sauna. For a spot of luxury, *Limewood Hotel* (☏023/8028 7177, ⓦ www .limewoodhotel.co.uk; ❼), a mile and a half outside Lyndhurst on the Beaulieu road, has smart, spacious designer-style rooms in a country-house atmosphere, and a highly rated restaurant.

The *Parisien* **café**, 64 High St, serves coffee, pastries and lunches such as inexpensive *croques monsieurs* and baguettes, that you can eat in its small garden in summer, while *Les Chocolats*, 23 High St, has wonderful croissants and hot chocolate and sells delicious slabs of handmade French chocolate. For a more substantial meal, the *Crown Brasserie* in the *Crown Hotel*, High Street (☏023/8028 2922), is a reasonably priced, informal brasserie serving main courses such as seafood tagliatelle (£10) and rabbit casserole (£12.50). The best **pub** by far is ☘ *The Oak Inn* on Pinkney Lane (☏023/8028 2350), a mile out of Lyndhurst in the village of Bank, with low wooden ceilings, an open fire, and a garden for summer. It serves fine ales and great, if pricey food, featuring local ingredients such as river fish and venison – book in advance.

Brockenhurst

BROCKENHURST, four miles south of Lyndhurst, is a useful centre for visitors without their own transport; it's also attractive, with a village green, wide ford and surrounding woods. There's a train station right in town and **bikes for rent** at Cycle Experience (☏01590/623407, ⓦ www.cyclex.co.uk) by the level-crossing for £13.50 a day. For **accommodation**, the *Thatched Cottage Hotel*, 16 Brookley Rd ☏01590/623090, ⓦ www.thatched-cottage.co.uk; ❷), has tiny, low-beamed rooms and a restaurant serving local produce such as New Forest mushrooms, wild fish and game. For more luxury, the *Whitley Ridge Hotel*, Beaulieu Road (☏01590/622354, ⓦ www.whitleyridge.com; ❹), a couple of miles out of Brockenhurst, is an attractive Georgian country house with a good brasserie-style restaurant serving more locally sourced food.

For snacks, **lunch** and picnic provisions, *French Confection*, 76 Brookley Rd, is a great little patisserie with a couple of outdoor tables, selling spinach pies, quiches, baguettes and strawberry tarts. For a full meal, the atmospheric *Il Palio* on Station Approach (℡01590/622730; closed Mon), in a former engine shed, serves vast portions of traditional Italian dishes – try the fried mixed fish or the seafood risotto. The *Rose and Crown*, Lyndhurst Road, is a traditional thirteenth-century forest **pub** with a pleasant garden and a skittle alley; it serves large portions of good-value pub grub, and a selection of real ales.

Beaulieu and Buckler's Hard

The village of **BEAULIEU** (whose name originates from the French meaning "Beautiful Place", but is pronounced "Bewley") was the site of one of England's most influential monasteries, a Cistercian house founded in 1204 by King John – in remorse, it is said, for ordering a group of supplicating Cistercian monks to be trampled to death. Built using stone ferried from Caen in northern France and Quarr on the Isle of Wight, the **abbey** managed a self-sufficient estate of ten thousand acres and became a famous sanctuary, offering shelter to Queen Margaret of Anjou among many others. It was dismantled soon after the Dissolution, and its refectory now forms the parish church, which, like everything else in Beaulieu, has been subsumed by the Montagu family, who have owned a large chunk of the New Forest since one of Charles II's illegitimate progeny was created duke of the estate.

The **Beaulieu** estate (daily: June–Sept 10am–6pm; Oct–May 10am–5pm; £15.75, children £8.50; Ⓦwww.beaulieu.co.uk) comprises the Montagu family's home, Palace House, the adjacent remains of Beaulieu Abbey and the celebrated National Motor Museum, with a mini-monorail and an old London bus running around the attractive grounds. **Palace House**, formerly the abbey's gatehouse, contains masses of Montagu-related memorabilia while the undercroft of the **abbey** houses an exhibition depicting medieval monastic life. The highlight, however, is the celebrated **Motor Museum**, whose collection of 250 cars and motorcycles includes a £650,000 McLaren F1, celebrity-owned cars, spindly antiques, recent classics, some svelte land-speed racers, and attractions such as the *Top Gear* exhibition featuring cars from the TV show.

There's a pleasant two-mile signed riverside walk from Beaulieu to **Buckler's Hard** (Ⓦwww.bucklershard.co.uk), also part of the Montagu estate, and with an even more wonderful setting. It doesn't look much like a shipyard now, but from Elizabethan times onwards dozens of men o' war were assembled here from giant New Forest oaks. Several of Nelson's ships, including HMS *Agamemnon*, were launched here, to be towed carefully by rowing boats past the sandbanks and across the Solent to Portsmouth. The **Maritime Museum** (daily 10am–4.30/5.30pm; £5.90) traces the history of the great ships and incorporates a labourer's cottage as it was in the 1790s, as well as the New Inn, shipwright's cottage and chapel – all preserved in their eighteenth-century form. The largest house in the hamlet of shipwrights' cottages belonged to Henry Adams, the master builder responsible for most of the Trafalgar fleet; it's now an attractive **hotel** and **restaurant**, the *Master Builder's House* (℡01590/616253, Ⓦwww.themasterbuilders.co.uk; ❹), with quirky, good-value rooms and a laid-back atmosphere.

Lymington and around

The most pleasant point of access for the Isle of Wight (for details of ferries, see box, p.219) is **LYMINGTON**, a sheltered haven that's linked by ferry to Yarmouth and has become one of the busiest leisure harbours on the south coast. Rising from the attractive quay, the old town is full of cobbled streets and Georgian houses with one unusual building – the thirteenth-century church of **St Thomas the Apostle**, whose cupola-topped tower was added in 1670. Eight miles

③

west of Lymington, just outside New Milton, the **Sammy Miller Museum** (daily 10am–4.30pm; Dec to mid-Feb Sat & Sun only; £5.90; Ⓦwww.sammymiller .co.uk) gives classic motorcycles the "Beaulieu" treatment. Many of the once-eminent British marques, from Ariel to Vincent, are displayed, as well as exotica from MV, NSU and several acclaimed trials bikes ridden by Sammy Miller himself, one of Britain's most successful trials riders.

Information is available in summer from the local **visitor centre** in Lymington's New Street, off the High Street (Mon–Sat: July–Sept 10am–5pm; Oct–June 10am–4pm; Ⓣ01590/689000). **Places to stay** in town include the friendly B&B *Britannia House*, Mill Lane (Ⓣ01590/672091, Ⓦwww.britannia-house.com; ❸), with smallish rooms and a fine sitting room commanding views over the yachts. More upmarket is the boutique-style *Stanwell House* (Ⓣ01590/677123, Ⓦwww .stanwellhouse.com; ❺), in a handsome Georgian house on the High Street; its individually designed rooms come with rolltop baths and flat-screen TVs, and it has a smart dining room (mains from around £17), as well as a less formal bistro. ⁂*Graze*, 9 Gosport St (Ⓣ01590/675595; closed Sun & Mon), is the liveliest **place to eat**, serving excellent-value fusion food such as courgette fritters and prawn tempura for around £15 a head; it also has a trendy bar, serving great cocktails, and a small garden area. For a more traditional pub atmosphere, the harbourfront *Ship Inn*, The Quay, has a waterside terrace, nautical-themed interior, and serves good-value pub food, with main courses from around £8.

Bournemouth and around

Renowned for its clean sandy beaches, the resort of **Bournemouth** has a single-minded holiday-making atmosphere. The town dates only from 1811, when a local squire, Louis Tregonwell, built a summerhouse on the wild, unpopulated heathland that once occupied this stretch of coast, and planted the first of the pine trees that now characterize the area. By the end of the century Bournemouth's mild climate, sheltered site and glorious sandy beach had attracted nearly sixty thousand inhabitants. Today the resort's traditional genteel, elderly image is tempered by burgeoning numbers of language schools and a university whose students fuel a lively nightclub scene. The construction of Europe's first artificial surf reef in Boscombe has also helped to bring in younger visitors, giving the town a more alternative vibe.

More interesting than Bournemouth historically are neighbouring towns of **Poole** and **Christchurch**. North of the town, pleasant **Wimborne Minster** has one of the area's most striking churches, while the stately home of **Kingston Lacy** contains an outstanding collection of old masters and other paintings.

Arrival, information and accommodation

Trains from London Waterloo stop just under a mile east of Bournemouth town centre; from the **bus station** opposite, frequent buses run into town. The **tourist office**, right in the centre of town on Westover Road (mid-July to mid-Sept daily 10am–5pm; mid-Sept to mid-July Mon–Sat 10.30am–4.30pm; Ⓣ0845/051 1701, Ⓦwww.bournemouth.co.uk), books bus tours and boat trips.

Hotels and B&Bs

Blue Palms 26 Tregonwell Rd, West Cliff Ⓣ01202/554986, Ⓦwww.bluepalmshotel.com. Small, friendly hotel in a quiet street a short walk from the centre. Rooms are a good size and there

is a comfortable communal living area and small garden. ❷

Miramar East Overcliff Drive Ⓣ01202/556581, Ⓦwww.miramar-bournemouth.com. Built as a diplomat's home with its own lovely gardens on the

cliff top, this pleasant hotel, where J.R.R. Tolkien was a regular, has a friendly atmosphere and good-sized rooms. It's worth paying £10 extra for a sea view or, even better, a sea-facing balcony. ⑤
Premier Inn Westover Rd ☎0870/423 6462, ⓦwww.premierinn.com. In a well-refurbished 1930s Art Deco building where the cover of a Beatles album, *With the Beatles*, was shot, this chain hotel is very central and offers good-value

rooms – all rooms, including family rooms, are the same price, so request one with sea views. ③
Urban Beach Hotel 23 Argyll Rd, Boscombe ☎01202/301509, ⓦwww.urbanbeachhotel.co.uk. Boutique-style hotel in an old Victorian townhouse a short (but steep) walk from Boscombe's surf beach. The rooms are stylish with designer furniture, comfy beds and DVDs, and there's a lively downstairs bar-restaurant. ④

The Town

Little remains today of Bournemouth's Victorian heyday, though the River Bourne still runs down from the mostly pedestrianized town centre through attractive **Pleasure Gardens** to **Bournemouth Pier**. Other than sunbathing along the pristine sandy beach – one of southern England's cleanest – the town's greatest attraction is its unusually high proportion of green space, with more than three million pine trees, and around two thousand acres of gardens. A couple of miles east, the lively suburb of **Boscombe** has a more earthy, alternative air and is home to an innovative man-made **surf reef**; constructed in 2009, the reef has been a controversial project and doubts remain as to its effectiveness.

Aside from the beach and reef, Bournemouth's main attraction is the excellent **Russell-Cotes Art Gallery and Museum** on East Cliff Promenade (Tues–Sun 10am–5pm; free; ⓦwww.russell-cotes.bournemouth.gov.uk) which houses an impressive collection of Victoriana gathered from around the world by the Russell-Cotes family. Inside the lavishly decorated former home, featuring unusual stained glass and ornate painted ceilings, are some fascinating Japanese artefacts as well as excellent examples of Pre-Raphaelite art, including Rosetti's *Venus Verticordia*.

In the centre of town, just east of The Square, the graveyard of **St Peter's Church** houses the body of Mary Shelley, author of the Gothic horror tale *Frankenstein*, and the heart of her husband, the poet Percy Bysshe Shelley, former residents of Boscombe. The tombs of Mary's parents – radical thinker William Godwin and early feminist Mary Wollstonecraft – are also here.

Eating, drinking and nightlife

With a constant stream of visitors, Bournemouth's restaurants don't have to try too hard, particularly those in prime seafront locations – and, with a few noteworthy exceptions, the result is a motley collection of fairly average eateries and chain restaurants.

Cafés and restaurants

Boscanova 650 Christchurch Rd, Boscombe Pedestrian Precinct ☎01202/395596. Laid-back café with a good-value Mediterranean-influenced menu. The food is all freshly cooked and the Middle Eastern meze are superb, as are the soups, unusual brunch combinations and fresh juices. Closed eve.
Chez Fred 10 Seamoor Rd, Westbourne ☎01202/761023. The region's best fish and chips are served at this sit-down restaurant and takeaway a couple of miles west from town, which regularly wins awards and is popular with locals and visiting celebs – hence the queues at peak times.

The Print Room Richmond Hill ☎01202/789669. Set in a lovely 1920s-style Art Deco building with wooden booths and chandeliers, this lively restaurant serves brasserie-style classics, such as steak, oysters, half a lobster (£25) and a charcuterie platter (£10), while breakfast includes eggs Florentine and pancakes.
Urban Reef Undercliff Drive, Boscombe ☎01202/443960. With great views of the new surf reef, this stylish restaurant/bar/café has quirky decor, tables on the promenade and is open from breakfast, for dishes such as pancakes with fruit (£5), through sandwiches (£6–7) and mussels (£7.50) for lunch, to steaks (£17) and line-caught sea bass (£14) for dinner.

West Beach Pier Approach ☎01202/587785. This award-winning seafood restaurant has a prime position on the beach, with tables out on the promenade. Local fish dishes such as Bournemouth Bay cod (£17.50) and Lulworth Cove scallops (£9) feature on the menu.

Bars, clubs and venues

Aruba Bar Pier Approach. A stylish Caribbean-themed bar above the entrance to Bournemouth pier; its outdoor terrace has comfy swing seats and overlooks the beach. Inside, soaring ceilings, palm trees and a resident parrot make it a great place to hang out, enjoy a reasonably priced cocktail and watch what's going on.

O2 Academy (formerly the Opera House) 570 Christchurch Rd, Boscombe ☎01202/399922, Ⓦwww.o2academybournemouth.co.uk. A great venue for gigs, this Grade II-listed Victorian building hosts regular club nights and a wide range of bands.

The Old Fire Station 36 Holdenhurst Rd ☎01202/963889, Ⓦwww.oldfirestation.co.uk. DJs, such as Rob da Bank, club nights, live bands and comedy in this popular venue in a converted fire station. Also hosts Bournemouth's student chart night, Lollipop, on a Friday.

Sixty Million Postcards 19 Exeter Rd ☎01202/292697. One of Bournemouth's best bars, attracting an unpretentious but trendy student crowd. There are DJs, craft nights and quiz nights, or you can simply chill out over board games and a cosy chat in the private alcoves. Serves a good range of beers, drinks and inexpensive snacks.

Christchurch

The attractive harbourside market town of **CHRISTCHURCH**, five miles east of Bournemouth, is best known for its colossal parish church, **Christchurch Priory** (Mon–Sat 9.30am–5pm, Sun 2.15–5.30pm; Ⓦwww.christchurchpriory.org), which is England's largest and bigger than most cathedrals. Built on the site of a Saxon minster dating from 650 AD, but exhibiting chiefly Norman and Perpendicular features, the church is 311ft long, and its fan-vaulted North Porch is the country's biggest. The choir contains what is probably the oldest misericord in England, dating from 1210, and complemented by a 1960s mural by Hans Feibush.

The area around the old town quay has a carefully preserved charm, with the **Red House Museum and Gardens** on Quay Road (Tues–Sat 10am–5pm, Sun 2–5pm; free) containing an affectionate collection of local memorabilia, and hosting various temporary exhibitions. **Boat trips** (Easter–Oct daily; ☎01202/429119) leave from the riverside quay east to Hengistbury Head (30min; £7 return) or upriver to the *Tuckton Tea Rooms* (15min; £3 return). Rowing boats (£15 per hour) and self-drive motor boats (£25 per hour) are also available.

Christchurch has become rather a foodie destination in recent years, with the annual **food festival** in mid-May attracting celebrity chefs, cooking demonstrations and market stalls galore (Ⓦwww.christchurchfoodfest.co.uk). The town has several upmarket **restaurants**, including two run by Gary Rhodes: the brasserie-style *Kings Rhodes*, 18 Castle St (☎01202/588933, Ⓦwww.thekings-christchurch .co.uk; ❹), specializes in grilled steaks (£13.50–20) and has stylish rooms, while the upmarket waterfront *Rhodes South* in the *Christchurch Harbour Hotel*, 95 Mudeford (☎01202/438434, Ⓦwww.christchurch-harbour-hotel.co.uk; ❻), offers fine dining, with main courses such as halibut with lentils (£21.50); the hotel has comfortable rooms, some with harbour views, and a smart pool and spa. For decent **pub** grub and fine local ales, *Ye Old George Inn*, 2a Castle St, is Christchurch's oldest pub, while *The Thomas Tripp*, 10 Wick Lane, also serves good pub meals and has live music.

Poole and around

Five miles west of Bournemouth's centre – though effectively joined to the town – **POOLE** is an ancient seaport on a huge, almost landlocked harbour. The port developed in the thirteenth century and was successively colonized by pirates, fishermen and timber traders, more recently replaced by companies prospecting for oil in the shallow waters – though the extraction process is carefully disguised. The **old quarter** by the lively quayside is worth exploring, with the old Custom House, Scaplen's Court and Guildhall the most striking of over a hundred historic buildings within a fifteen-acre site.

At the bottom of Old High Street, the well-presented **Poole Museum** (April–Oct Mon–Sat 10am–5pm, Sun noon–5pm; Nov–March Tues–Sat 10am–4pm, Sun noon–4pm; free) traces the town's development over the centuries and features local ceramics and tiles and a rare Iron Age log boat; the upstairs terrace has good views over the town. From Poole Quay, **boat trips** run to Brownsea Island (see box below), Swanage, and upriver to Wareham, depending on the tides (check ⓦ www.poolequay.com/cruises.html for details).

One of the area's most famous gardens lies on the outskirts of Poole, **Compton Acres** (daily 9/10am–4/6pm; £6.95; ⓦ www.comptonacres.co.uk), signposted off the A35 Poole Road towards Bournemouth. Here you'll find seven gardens, each with a different international theme, including an elegantly understated Japanese Garden, and a classical Italian Garden. Nearby is the opulent **Sandbanks peninsula** with its long sandy beach, millionaire's houses and clanking chain ferry over to Purbeck (see p.239).

Practicalities

Poole's **train station** is on Serpentine Lane, by the Dolphin Shopping Centre, a fifteen-minute walk from the waterfront down the High Street. The **bus station**, also close to the shopping centre, is on Kingland Road. The **tourist office** is on Poole Quay (May, June, Sept & Oct daily 10am–5pm; July & Aug daily 9.15am–6pm; Nov–April Mon–Fri 10am–5pm, Sat 10am–4pm; ⓣ01202/253253, ⓦ www.pooletourism.com). The best place **to stay** is at the stylish ⚸ *Hotel du Vin*, Thames Street (ⓣ01202/685666, ⓦ www.hotelduvin.com; ⓰), a fine old mansion house with plush rooms, a superb restaurant and a cosy bar. Alternatively, at the bottom of the High Street on the Quay, the café-restaurant *Corkers* (ⓣ01202/681393, ⓦ www.corkers.co.uk; ❷) offers B&B in its upstairs rooms, two with harbour-facing balconies.

There's a collection of good **restaurants** on the High Street, among them *Storm* at no. 16 (ⓣ01202/674970; closed Sun lunch), which specializes in pricey seafood. In a former warehouse, *Da Vinci's*, 7 The Quay (ⓣ01202/667528), is an old-fashioned Italian serving inexpensive pizza and pasta downstairs, and upmarket Italian cuisine upstairs. Of the **pubs**, the green tile-fronted *Poole Arms* on The Quay serves seafood and pub grub at reasonable prices, while the historic Georgian *Customs House*, The Quay, is a lively bar with a great outdoor terrace overlooking the harbour; it also serves reasonably priced brasserie-style meals.

Brownsea Island

In the middle of Poole harbour, the five-hundred-acre **Brownsea Island** (mid-March to Nov daily 10am–5pm; £5.50; NT) is famed for its red squirrels, wading birds and other wildlife, which you can spot along themed trails. The surprisingly diverse landscape – including heath, woodland and fine beaches – affords striking views. The most regular visitors here are scouts and guides: the Boy Scout movement was formed in the wake of a camping expedition to the island led by Lord Baden-Powell in 1907, and scouts are the only people allowed to camp here. The island is now managed by the National Trust, and linked by regular **ferries** to Poole Quay (ⓦ www .greensladepleasureboats.co.uk; £8.50 return) and the Sandbanks peninsula (ⓦ www .brownseaislandferries.com; £5 return).

Wimborne Minster and around

An ancient town on the banks of the Stour, just a few miles north of Bournemouth, **WIMBORNE MINSTER** is mainly of interest for its great church, the **Minster of St Cuthberga** (daily 9.30am–5.30pm, till 4pm Jan & Feb). Built on the site of an eighth-century monastery, its massive twin towers of mottled grey and tawny stone dwarf the rest of the town; at one time the church was even more imposing – its spire crashed down during morning service in 1602. What remains today is basically Norman, though the Perpendicular west tower, with its figure of a Napoleonic-era grenadier who strikes every quarter-hour with a hammer, was added later. Inside, look out for the orrery clock, with the sun marking the hours and the moon marking the days of the month, and for the organ with trumpets pointing towards the congregation instead of pipes. The **Chained Library** above the choir vestry (Easter–Oct Mon–Fri 10.30am–12.30pm & 2–4pm, Sat 10.30am–12.30pm; Nov–Easter Sat 10.30am–12.30pm), dating from 1686, is Wimborne's most prized possession and one of the oldest public libraries in the country.

Standing around the main square near the minster, Wimborne's older buildings and alleyways date mostly from the late eighteenth or early nineteenth century, while the **Priest's House Museum** on the High Street (April–Oct Mon–Sat 10am–4.30pm; £3.50) has each room furnished in the style of a different period; a working Victorian kitchen, a Georgian parlour and an ironmonger's shop are among its exhibits, and a walled garden at the rear provides teas. The best place for **lunch** is the ✳ *Long Crichel Bakery Tea Rooms*, 7 Cook Row, for good coffee and excellent home-made organic breads, pastries, quiches and soup (Mon–Sat 9am–4pm, Sun 9am–3pm).

Kingston Lacy

One of England's finest seventeenth-century country houses, **Kingston Lacy** (house: mid-March to Oct Wed–Sun 11am–4pm; gardens: Feb to mid-March Fri, Sat & Sun 10.30am–4pm; mid-March to Oct daily 10.30am–6pm; Nov & Dec Wed–Sun 10.30am–4pm; house & grounds £10, grounds only £5; NT), lies two miles northwest of Wimborne, in 250 acres of parkland. Designed for the Bankes family, who were exiled from Corfe Castle (see p.238) after the Roundheads reduced it to rubble, the brick building was clad in grey stone during the nineteenth century by Charles Barry, co-architect of the Houses of Parliament. William Bankes, then owner of the house, was a great traveller and collector, and the **Spanish Room** is a superb scrapbook of his Grand Tour souvenirs, lined with gilded leather and surmounted by a Venetian ceiling. Kingston Lacy also houses an outstanding collection of **pictures**, featuring Titian, Rubens, Velázquez and many other old masters, as well as England's largest private collection of Egyptian artefacts.

The Isle of Purbeck

Though not actually an island, the **Isle of Purbeck** – a promontory of low hills and heathland jutting out beyond Poole Harbour – does have an insular and distinctive feel. Reached from the east by the ferry from Sandbanks (see p.239), at the narrow mouth of Poole Harbour, or by a long and congested landward journey via the bottleneck of **Wareham**, Purbeck's villages are immensely pretty, none more so than **Corfe Castle**, with its majestic ruins. The low-key seaside resort of **Swanage** is flanked by a section of the World Heritage **Jurassic Coast**

(Ⓦwww.jurassiccoast.com), a 200-million-year-old stretch of coastline rich in fossils and accessible on the Dorset Coast Path: to one side the soft dunes of Studland Bay, to the other the cliffs of Durlston Head and Dancing Ledge, leading to the oily shales of **Kimmeridge Bay**, the spectacular cove at **Lulworth** and the much-photographed natural arch of **Durdle Door**. Like Portland, further west, the area is pockmarked with stone quarries – Purbeck marble is the finest grade of the local oolitic limestone. The villages and landscape hereabouts were the backdrop for Enid Blyton's Famous Five tales. Bus #50 runs from Bournemouth to Swanage along the Studland peninsula, via the Sandbanks ferry, hourly on weekdays and every half-hour at weekends: it's often open-top in summer.

Wareham and around

The grid pattern of its streets indicates the Saxon origins of **WAREHAM**, and the town is surrounded by even older earth ramparts known as the Walls. A riverside setting adds greatly to its charms, though there can be horrible traffic queues in summer, and the scenic stretch along The Quay gets fairly overrun: weather permitting, **boat trips** run from here up- and downriver (Easter–Sept; 45min; £5; Ⓣ01929/550688, Ⓦwww.warehamboathire.co.uk). Nearby lies an oasis of quaint houses around **Lady St Mary's Church**, which contains the marble coffin of Edward the Martyr, murdered at Corfe Castle in 978 by his stepmother to make way for her unready son Ethelred.

St Martin's Church, at the north end of town, dates from Saxon times and the chancel contains a faded twelfth-century mural of St Martin offering his cloak to a beggar, but the church's most striking feature is a romantic effigy of **T.E. Lawrence** in Arab dress, which was originally destined for Salisbury Cathedral, but was rejected by the dean there who disapproved of Lawrence's sexual proclivities. Lawrence was killed in 1935 in a motorbike accident on the road from Bovington (six miles west), after returning to Dorset from his Middle Eastern adventures. Some of his memorabilia is displayed in the small **museum** next to the town hall in East Street (Easter–Oct Mon–Sat 10am–4pm; free).

Lawrence's simply furnished cottage is at **Clouds Hill** (mid-March to Oct Thurs–Sun noon–5pm; £4.50; NT), seven miles northwest of Wareham, while further Lawrence effects are on show at the **Tank Museum** in Bovington Camp, five miles west of town (daily 10am–5pm; £11; Ⓦwww.tankmuseum.co.uk), along with a huge collection of tanks from many of the conflicts from World War I onwards. Exhibits include British Challenger I and Challenger II tanks, captured Iraqi tanks from both Gulf Wars, and a mock-up trench replicating conditions in the Somme.

Corfe Castle

The romantic ruins crowning the hill behind the village of **CORFE CASTLE** (daily: March & Oct 10am–5pm; April–Sept 10am–6pm; Nov–Feb 10am–4pm; £5.90; NT) are perhaps the most evocative in England. The family seat of Sir John Bankes, Attorney General to Charles I, this Royalist stronghold withstood a Cromwellian siege for six weeks, gallantly defended by Lady Bankes. One of her own men, Colonel Pitman, eventually betrayed the castle to the Roundheads, after which it was reduced to its present gap-toothed state by gunpowder. Apparently the victorious Roundheads were so impressed by Lady Bankes's courage that they allowed her to take the keys to the castle with her – they can still be seen in the library at the Bankes's subsequent home, Kingston Lacy (see p.237).

The village is well stocked with tearooms and gift shops and has a couple of fine **pubs** that serve good food too: *The Fox* on West Street, and *The Greyhound* on the

3

main square, both with gardens and views over the castle. The *National Trust Tearooms*, by the entrance to the castle, has a lovely garden and serves light lunches and afternoon teas, with delicious home-made cake. The smartest place **to stay** is the sixteenth-century *Mortons House* on East Street (℡01929/480988, Ⓦwww .mortonshouse.co.uk; ❺), with a beautiful walled garden and log fires in winter. Alternatively, a couple of miles southeast of Corfe Castle at Harman's Cross, ⚐ *Purbeck Vineyard* (℡01929/481525, Ⓦwww.vineyard.uk.com; ❹) has smart rooms with their own terraces overlooking a working vineyard.

Swanage and around

Purbeck's most northerly coastal stretch, **Shell Bay**, is a magnificent beach of icing-sugar sand backed by a remarkable heathland ecosystem that's home to all six British species of reptile – adders are quite common, so be careful. At the top end of the beach, a chain **ferry** (every 20min: 7am–11pm; pedestrians 90p, bikes 80p, cars £3) crosses the mouth of Poole Harbour connecting the Isle of Purbeck with the ostentatious **Sandbanks peninsula** in Poole. To the south the broad and sheltered sweep of **Studland Bay** holds one of the loveliest beaches on this coast – all white sands and dramatic white chalk-stacks at its southernmost end, with one section designated for naturists.

Beyond Studland Bay lies **SWANAGE**, a traditional seaside resort with a pleasant sandy beach and an ornate town hall, the facade of which once adorned the Mercers' Hall in the City of London and was brought back here as ballast on a cargo ship. The town's station is the southern terminus of the **Swanage Steam Railway** (April–Oct plus school hols daily; mid-Feb to March, Nov & Dec Sat & Sun; £9 all day; ℡01929/425800, Ⓦwww.swanagerailway.co.uk), which runs for six miles to Norden (on the A351). Swanage's **tourist office** is by the beach on Shore Road (Easter–Oct daily 10am–5pm; Nov–Easter closed Sun; ℡01929/422885, Ⓦwww.swanage.gov.uk), and there's a **youth hostel**, with good views across the bay, on Cluny Crescent (℡0870/770 6058, Ⓔswanage @yha.org.uk; open mainly during school hols, closed Dec & Jan), costing from £24.50 for a dorm bed including breakfast, with private rooms also available (❷). There are scores of **B&Bs** in Swanage, including a cluster just off the High Street along Park Road – try the spacious Victorian *Clare House*, at no. 1 (℡01929/422855, Ⓦwww.clare-house.com; ❹), 200m from the beach, or the good-value boutique-style ⚐ *Swanage Haven*, 3 Victoria Rd (℡01929/423088, Ⓦwww.swanagehaven .com; ❸), where the rooms are comfortable, there's a lovely decked garden with outdoor hot tub, and the organic breakfasts are delicious. There are several **campsites** around the town, but the nicest is a couple of miles out at Langton Matravers: the wonderfully sited and well-run ⚐ *Tom's Field Campsite* (℡01929/427110, Ⓦwww.tomsfieldcamping.co.uk), with direct access to the coast path. In town, good fish and chips can be had from the *Fisherman's Catch*, The Cabin, Shore Road (℡01929/426222), an unpretentious **café-restaurant** right on the seafront; or for something more upmarket, *Ocean Bay*, 1–7 Ulwell Rd (℡01929/422222), has a wonderful position facing the beach, with outdoor tables on a narrow terrace: mains (around £10–15), using mostly local produce, include Swanage Bay crab risotto and Purbeck venison sausages.

Highlights of the coast beyond Swanage are the cliffs of **Durlston Head**, topped by a lighthouse. Nearby stands a vast stone globe weighing forty tonnes, installed by George Burt, an eccentric Victorian building contractor from Swanage, who also erected the local castle folly. The cliffs continue to **St Alban's Head**, their ledges crowded with sea birds. Paths lead inland to the attractive village of **WORTH MATRAVERS**, with a fine Norman church and a great **pub**, the

⅃ *Square and Compass*, full of nooks and crannies, and with great views, delicious home-made pies, real ale and live music.

Kimmeridge Bay, Lulworth Cove and Durdle Door

Beyond St Alban's Head the coastal geology suddenly changes as the grey-white chalk and limestone give way to darker beds of shale. **Kimmeridge Bay** may not have a sandy beach but it does have a remarkable marine wildlife reserve much appreciated by divers. The amazing range of species is all the more surprising because the bay has been the site of small-scale industry for centuries. The Saxons crafted amulets from the shale and the extraction of alum (for glassmaking) and coal followed. Today a low-tech "nodding donkey" oil well fits unobtrusively into the landscape.

The Lulworth artillery ranges west of Kimmeridge are inaccessible during weekdays but generally open at weekends and in school holidays – watch out for the red warning flags and notices and always stick to the path. Roads in this area have similar restrictions, but generally open before 9am and after 5pm to allow commuters through. The coastal path passes close to the deserted village of **Tyneham** (ⓦtyneham.org.uk), whose residents were summarily evicted by the army in 1943; the abandoned stone cottages have an eerie fascination, and an exhibition in the church explains the history of the village. The army's presence has helped to preserve the local habitat, which hosts many species of flora and fauna long since vanished from farmed or otherwise developed areas.

The quaint thatch-and-stone village of West Lulworth forms a prelude to **Lulworth Cove**, a perfect shell-shaped bite formed when the sea broke through a weakness in the cliffs. Lulworth's scenic charms are well known, and as you descend the hill towards the cove in summer the sun glints off the metal of a thousand car roofs in the car park behind. Immediately west of the cove you come to **Stair Hole**, a roofless sea cave riddled with arches that will eventually collapse to form another Lulworth, and a couple of miles west is **Durdle Door**, a famous limestone arch that appeals to serious geologist and casual sightseer alike. A clear track leads steeply uphill from the car park along the dramatic cliffs, then steeply down to the arch itself: it's a twenty- to thirty-minute walk.

Practicalities

First choice **to stay** in Lulworth Cove is *The Beach House* (Ⓣ01929/400404, ⓦwww.lulworthbeachhouse.com; ❸–❺), with modern, bright, refurbished rooms – try and bag one with its own cove-view terrace. Alternatively, the *Lulworth Cove Inn*, just up the road (Ⓣ01929/400333, ⓦwww.lulworth-cove .com; ❸), has comfortable if less stylish rooms, some with sea-facing balconies. Up in West Lulworth, there's a very basic **youth hostel** at the end of School Lane (Ⓣ0870/770 5940, Ⓔlulworth@yha.org.uk; closed Dec–Feb, also Sun & Mon in low season; dorm beds from £16), a stone's throw from the Coast Path. **Campers** should head for the *Durdle Door Holiday Park*, high up on the cliff top with fantastic views, a mile west of West Lulworth (Ⓣ01929/400352, ⓦwww .lulworth.com; closed Nov–Feb).

For **food**, the *Castle Inn* in West Lulworth serves high-quality pub grub and a good range of local ales; while in Lulworth Cove, *Pebbles* at *The Beach House* has a lovely garden with views of the cove and specializes in fish dishes such as roasted sea bass (£12).

Weymouth to West Bay

Whether George III's passion for sea bathing was a symptom of his eventual madness is uncertain, but it was at the bay of **Weymouth** that in 1789 he became the first reigning monarch to follow the craze. Sycophantic gentry rushed into the waves behind him, and soon the town, formerly a workaday harbour, took on the elegant Georgian stamp it bears today. A likeness of the monarch on horseback is even carved into the chalk downs northwest of the town, like some guardian spirit. Weymouth nowadays is still a lively family-holiday destination, alternately seedy and sedate.

Just south of the town stretch the giant arms of Portland Harbour, and a long causeway links Weymouth to the strange five-mile-long excrescence of the **Isle of Portland**. West of the causeway, the bank of pebbles known as **Chesil Beach** runs eighteen miles northwest in the direction of **West Bay**.

Weymouth

WEYMOUTH had long been a port before the Georgians popularized it as a resort. It's possible that a ship unloading a cargo here in 1348 first brought the Black Death to English shores, and it was from Weymouth that John Endicott sailed in 1628 to found Salem in Massachusetts. A few buildings survive from these pre-Georgian times: the restored **Tudor House** on Trinity Street (Feb–April & mid-Oct to Dec first Sun of month 2–4pm; May to mid-Oct Tues–Fri 1–4pm; £3.50) and the ruins of **Sandsfoot Castle** (free access), built by Henry VIII, overlooking Portland Harbour. But Weymouth's most imposing architectural heritage stands along the Esplanade, a dignified range of bow-fronted and porticoed buildings gazing out across the graceful bay, an ensemble rather disrupted by the garish **clocktower** commemorating Victoria's jubilee. The more intimate quayside of the Old Harbour, linked to the Esplanade by the main pedestrianized thoroughfare, St Mary's Street, is lined with waterfront pubs and restaurants from where you can view the passing yachts and trawlers.

Weymouth boasts a number of all-weather attractions, the best of which is the **Sea Life Park** in Lodmoor Country Park, east of the Esplanade (daily 10am–5.30/6pm; winter sometimes closes earlier; £17, but cheaper online; Ⓦwww.sealifeeurope.com), home to sharks, turtles, penguins, otters, caymans and seals; and, over the river in the Brewers Quay complex on Hope Square, **Timewalk** (daily 10am–5.30pm; £4.75; Ⓦwww.brewers-quay.com), holding an entertaining and educational walk-through exhibition of Weymouth's maritime and brewing past.

From here, a fifteen-minute walk southwards leads to **Nothe Fort** (Easter, May–Sept & autumn half-term daily 10.30am–5.30pm; Oct–April Sun 11am–4.30pm; closed Jan; £6; Ⓦwww.nothefort.org.uk), built in 1860–72 to defend Portland Harbour. Inside, there are displays on military themes and a museum describing garrison life and the castle's role in coastal defence.

Practicalities

Weymouth's **train station** is on King Street, a short walk from where the buses pull in by the George III statue on the Esplanade; you'll also find the **tourist office** here (daily 9.30am–4/5pm; ☎01305/785747, Ⓦwww.visitweymouth .co.uk).

Accommodation

Bay View House 35 The Esplanade ⏱01305/782083, 🌐www.bayview -weymouth.co.uk. Excellent-value, clean, friendly and well-kept guesthouse, with comfortable rooms – ask for the one at the front of the house with a bay window overlooking the sea (just £60). Also has family rooms and free private garage parking. ❶

B+B Weymouth 68 The Esplanade ⏱01305/761190, 🌐www.bb-weymouth.com. Weymouth's first boutique B&B, with contemporary rooms and all mod cons. The rooms are clean and spacious, and there's a lovely lounge with a sea view and free tea and coffee. Breakfast is organic and local where possible, and they lend out bikes for free. ❸, or ❹ with a sea view.

The Chatsworth 14 The Esplanade ⏱01305/785012, 🌐www.thechatsworth.co.uk. Harbourside hotel with great views from the rooms (one has a balcony), and there's a nice terrace for eating out. ❸

Glenthorne Castle Cove, 15 Old Castle Rd ⏱01305/777281, 🌐glenthorne-holidays.co.uk. Former Victorian rectory, in a prime position overlooking the sea, with large gardens leading directly to Castle Cove beach. One of the three rooms has a sea view, and there's a heated outdoor pool, plus table tennis and trampoline. Also has self-catering accommodation in the grounds. ❹

Wilton Guest House 5 Gloucester St ⏱01305/782820, 🌐www.thewiltonguesthouse .co.uk. Just a few steps from the seafront and 400m from the train station, this agreeable B&B has bright, good-size rooms, all en suite, with crisp bed linen. There's also a small terrace. ❷

Restaurants, cafés and pubs

Crab House Café Portland Rd, Ferrybridge, a couple of miles from the town centre

⏱01305/788867. Right by the Fleet Lagoon with tables outside, this upmarket beach shack is renowned for its superb, locally caught fresh fish and seafood, including Fleet oysters and Portland crab. The menu changes daily according to the catch, but expect dishes such as skate wing with chorizo (£16). Closed Mon, Tues & Jan & Feb.

Daniels 159 Abbotsbury Rd. About a mile out of the centre, and a recent winner of the best fish-and-chip shop in the southwest of England, this immaculate takeaway serves the freshest fish and tastiest chips in the area (standard cod and chips £4.50). It also has good veggie options, such as pea fritters.

Enzos 110 The Esplanade ⏱01305/778666. Traditional Italian restaurant, but with clean, contemporary decor, tiled floors and modern furnishings; it's right on the seafront, but slightly away from the hubbub of the main drag. Serves authentic, freshly made pizzas (around £7), a range of pasta dishes (£7–8), as well as daily local specials such as sea bream.

Lazy Lizard 52–53 The Esplanade. Light and airy place overlooking the beach with wooden floors, quirky wooden furniture and a lively but laid-back atmosphere. Serves reasonably priced fish and chips, burgers and all-day breakfasts, and hosts live music and DJs in the evenings.

Perry's 4 Trinity Rd ⏱01305/785799. For seafood, you can't do better than this classy restaurant overlooking the quay. Main courses cost around £12–18, with daily changing fish specials, and there's a good-value two-course lunchtime menu for £15.

Red Lion Hope Square. Opposite Brewers Quay, this bustling pub is a good place for a drink, with outdoor tables on the square and a cosy interior. It serves a good choice of local real ales and reasonable pub grub.

Portland

Reached via a narrow pebbly causeway, the **Isle of Portland** is known for its hard white limestone, which has been quarried here for centuries – Wren used it for St Paul's Cathedral, and it clads the UN headquarters in New York – and the quarries remain prominent features of the island today. The stone was also used for the six-thousand-foot breakwater that protects Portland Harbour, itself surveyed by a 470-year-old Tudor fortress, **Portland Castle** (daily 10am–4/6pm; £4.20; EH), commissioned by Henry VIII. The island's small **Portland Museum** (11am–4.30pm: May, June, Sept & Oct Fri–Tues; July & Aug daily; £2.20) was founded by birth-control pioneer Marie Stopes, who lived in Portland's old lighthouse. The museum contains an exhibition on Stopes as well as displays on the history of the island.

Portland Bill, the southern tip of the island, is dominated by a lighthouse dating from 1906; you can climb its 153 steps for fantastic far-reaching views

(11am–5pm: April–June daily except Fri & Sat; July–Sept daily except Sat; £2.50). The lighthouse also houses Portland's **tourist office** (April–Sept daily 11am–5pm; Oct–March Sun only 11am–4pm; ☎01305/861233, ⓦwww .visitweymouth.co.uk), which can supply leaflets on the area's special features, including geology and wildlife. You're unlikely to want to stay on the island, but there are a few good **pubs** including the excellent ☘ *Cove House Inn* in Chiswell, which serves fresh local fish and seafood, such as mackerel (£6), fish pie (£8) and scallops (£10); it's cosy inside with a wood-burner and big windows with sea views, while the outside tables look over Chesil Beach. Nearby, the *Blue Fish Café* (☎01305/822911) is a friendly, laid-back **restaurant** serving excellent food, such as scallops with black pudding (£10), and *moules-frites* with a glass of wine or beer (£10); it has a nice garden outside beneath the shadow of the Chesil bank.

Chesil Beach to West Bay

Immortalized in Ian McEwan's moving eponymous 2007 novella, **Chesil Beach** is the strangest feature of the Dorset coast, a two-hundred-yard-wide, fifty-foot-high bank of pebbles that extends for eighteen miles, its component stones gradually decreasing in size from fist-like pebbles at Portland to "pea gravel" at Burton Bradstock in the west. This sorting is an effect of the powerful coastal currents, which make it one of the most dangerous beaches in Europe – churchyards in the local villages display plenty of evidence of wrecks and drownings. Though not a swimming beach, Chesil is popular with sea anglers, and its wild, uncommercialized atmosphere makes an appealing antidote to the south-coast resorts.

Chesil Beach encloses a brackish lagoon called **The Fleet** for much of its length – it was the setting for J. Meade Faulkner's classic smuggling tale, *Moonfleet*. At the point where the shingle beach attaches itself to the shore is the pretty village of **ABBOTSBURY**, all tawny ironstone and thatch. The three main attractions here draw people from far and wide (all open daily: mid-March to Oct 10am–5/6pm; last admission 1hr before closing; ⓦwww.abbotsbury-tourism.co.uk), and can be visited separately or on a passport ticket for £15. The most absorbing – and particularly impressive in May when the cygnets hatch – is the **Swannery** (£9.50), a wetland reserve for mute swans that dates back to medieval times, when it formed part of the abbot's larder. The eel-grass reeds through which the swans paddle were once harvested to thatch roofs throughout the region. One example can be seen on the fifteenth-century Tithe Barn, the last remnant of the village's Benedictine abbey; today it houses the **Children's Farm** (£8), whose highlights include goat-racing and pony rides. Lastly, in the **Subtropical Gardens** (£9.50), delicate species thrive in the microclimate created by Chesil's stones, which act as a giant radiator to keep out all but the worst frosts. Other local attractions are the hilltop, fifteenth-century **Chapel of St Catherine**, and, up on the downs a couple of miles inland from Abbotsbury, a monument to Thomas Hardy – not the usual one associated with Dorset, but the flag captain in whose arms Admiral Nelson expired. Near the tithe barn, ☘ *The Abbey House* (☎01305/871330, ⓦwww .theabbeyhouse.co.uk; ❸) has comfortable rooms with lovely views over the pretty gardens, which make the perfect spot for a cream tea or light lunch.

There are a couple of excellent seafront **restaurants** along this stretch of coast, both worth a visit in their own right. On the beach in **BURTON BRADSTOCK**, seven miles west of Abbotsbury, the laid-back ☘ *Hive Beach Café* (☎01308/897070) serves up top-quality seafood, such as West Bay plaice (£17) and Lyme Bay scallops (£17.50), as well as delicious home-made cakes. Three miles west in **WEST BAY**, the *Riverside Restaurant* is a renowned but informal fish place with good views over the river (☎01308/422011). There is a daily changing menu, but expect such delights as crab and scallop chowder and local lobster salad; the fixed-price lunches are good value at £16.50 and £21.

Lyme Regis

From the end of Chesil Beach an ever more dramatic sequence of cliffs runs westward, followed as closely as possible by the Dorset Coast Path, which has to deviate inland in a few places to avoid areas of landslip. This is a particularly fossil-rich section of the Jurassic Coast (see box opposite). **LYME REGIS**, Dorset's most westerly town, shelters snugly between steep hills, its intimate size and photogenic appeal making it a tourist honey-pot in high summer. For all that, the town lives up to the classy impression created by its regal name, which it owes to a royal charter granted by Edward I in 1284. It has some upmarket literary associations too – Jane Austen summered in a seafront cottage and set part of *Persuasion* here, while novelist **John Fowles** lived here until his death in 2005. It was the film adaptation of Fowles' book, *The French Lieutenant's Woman*, shot on location here, that did more than any tourist industry promotion to place the resort firmly on the map.

Though Lyme Regis now relies mostly on holiday-makers for its keep, it was for centuries a port for the wool traders of Somerset, and shipbuilding thrived here until Victorian times. Colourwashed cottages and elegant Regency and Victorian villas line its seafront and flanking streets, but Lyme's best-known feature is a briskly practical reminder of its commercial origins: **The Cobb**, the curving harbour wall, was first constructed in the thirteenth century but has undergone many alterations since, most notably in the nineteenth century, when its massive boulders were clad in neater blocks of Portland stone. As you walk along the seafront and out towards The Cobb, look for the outlines of ammonites in the walls and paving stones. Also on The Cobb is the small **Marine Aquarium** (March–Oct plus Feb half-term 10am–5pm; £5), where local fishermen bring their unusual catches, while up Church Street is the fifteenth-century **parish church** of St Michael the Archangel, which contains a seventeenth-century pulpit and a massive, chained Bible.

Practicalities

Lyme's nearest **train station** is in Axminster, five miles north, served by regular bus #31. The **tourist office** is on Church Street (April–Oct Mon–Sat 10am–5am, Sun 10am–4pm; Nov–March Mon–Sat 10am–3pm; ☎01297/442138, ⓦwww .lymeregistourism.co.uk).

Accommodation

Alexandra Hotel Pound St ☎01297/442010, ⓦwww.hotelalexandra.co.uk. Eighteenth-century manor house with lovely gardens overlooking the sea. The comfortable rooms are newly refurbished and many have sea views. ❺

Blue Sky 8 Pound St ☎01297/442339, ⓦwww .bluesky-lymeregis.co.uk. Friendly, newly refurbished B&B a steep walk uphill from the main street. The back rooms have good views over town, though the larger family rooms overlook the main road. Good breakfasts, though there's no parking. ❸

Royal Lion Broad St ☎01297/445622, ⓦwww .royallionhotel.com. Welcoming seventeenth-century coaching inn on the main street, complete with grandfather clock and a high-ceilinged dining room. Most rooms have balconies facing the sea, though the spacious family rooms downstairs have small outdoor patios. Off-street parking and a small indoor pool. ❹

Restaurants, cafés and pubs

Harbour Inn Marine Parade ☎01297/442299. Lively pub-cum-fish restaurant facing the seafront,

Fossil-hunting around Lyme

The cliffs around Lyme are made up of a complex layer of limestone, greensand and unstable clay, a perfect medium for preserving **fossils**, which are exposed by landslips of the waterlogged clays. In 1811, after a fierce storm caused parts of the cliffs to collapse, 12-year-old Mary Anning, a keen fossil-hunter, discovered an almost complete dinosaur skeleton, a thirty-foot ichthyosaurus now displayed in London's Natural History Museum.

Hammering fossils out of the cliffs is frowned on by today's conservationists, and in any case is rather hazardous. Hands-off inspection of the area's complex geology can be enjoyed on both sides of town: to the west lies the **Undercliff**, a fascinating jumble of overgrown landslips, now a nature reserve. East of Lyme, at **Charmouth** (Jane Austen's favourite resort), the **Heritage Centre** down on the beach runs excellent two-hour fossil-hunting tours (see ⓦwww.charmouth.org for times; £7, children £3). Beyond here is the headland of **Golden Cap**, whose brilliant outcrop of auburn sandstone is crowned with gorse.

Further fossil information can be gleaned from the **Lyme Regis Museum** on Bridge Street (Easter–Oct Mon–Sat 10am–5pm, Sun 11am–5pm; Nov–Easter Wed–Sun, daily in school hols 11am–4pm; £3; ⓣ01297/443370, ⓦwww.lymeregismuseum .co.uk) and from **Dinosaurland** on Coombe Street (daily 10am–5pm, though closed some weekdays in Nov–Feb so call to check; £5; ⓣ01297/443541, ⓦwww .dinosaurland.co.uk), which fills out the story on ammonites and other local finds.

with tables out the front. Fresh fish from around £14 along with fine meat dishes, though veggies are poorly catered for.

Hix Oyster and Fish House Cobb Rd
ⓣ01297/446910. In a lovely location overlooking The Cobb, this light and airy restaurant, owned by acclaimed chef Mark Hix, specializes in local fish and seafood: main courses such as squid ink squash, or Lyme Bay plaice, cost around £18, though there's a two-course set lunch for £17.
Royal Standard 25 Marine Parade
ⓣ01297/442637. Beachside inn dating back 400 years, with a log fire in winter and a sea-facing

terrace. It has some good real ales, serves decent bar food, plus reasonably priced but fine fresh fish.
Town Mill Bakery Mill Lane, off Coombe St. A wonderful rustic-chic bakery, café and restaurant with a superb array of freshly baked breads to take away. Also serves a range of local and largely organic produce, including sublime breakfasts – with local preserves and fresh mushrooms – lunches, such as focaccia and Dorset rarebit with cider and evening pizzas, which you can enjoy on low wooden benches. Daily 8.30am to 7 or 8pm, except Sun–Thurs in winter (closes 5pm).

Dorchester and around

The county town of Dorset, **DORCHESTER** still functions as the main agricultural centre for the region, and if you catch it on a Wednesday when the market is in full swing you'll find it at its liveliest. For the literature lover, however, this is essentially **Thomas Hardy**'s town: he was born at Higher Bockhampton, three miles east of here; his heart is buried in Stinsford, a couple of miles northeast (the rest of him is in Westminster Abbey); and he spent much of his life in Dorchester itself, where his statue now stands on High West Street. Even without the Hardy connection, Dorchester makes an attractive stop, with its pleasant central core of mostly seventeenth-century and Georgian buildings, and the prehistoric Maumbury Rings on the outskirts. To the southwest of town looms the massive hillfort of **Maiden Castle**, the most impressive of Dorset's many pre-Roman antiquities.

Arrival, information and accommodation

Dorchester has two **train stations**, both of them to the south of the centre: trains from Weymouth and London arrive at Dorchester South, while Bath and Bristol trains use the Dorchester West station. Most **buses** stop around the car park on Acland Road, to the east of South Street. The **tourist office** is in Antelope Walk (Mon–Sat: April–Oct 9am–5pm; Nov–March 9am–4pm; ☎01305/267992, Ⓦwww.westdorset.com). **Bikes** are available for rent at Dorchester Cycles, 31 Great Western Rd (☎01305/268787; £12 a day).

Dorchester has a reasonable selection of **accommodation**, though there's also a good choice of B&Bs in some of the lovely surrounding villages.

Hotels and B&Bs

Casterbridge Hotel 49 High East St ☎01305/264043, Ⓦwww.casterbridgehotel.co.uk. Friendly hotel on the main through-road with small but homely rooms. There's a relaxing communal lounge and small patio garden, with some rooms off it, including a family room (£150). ❹

Cornflowers 4 Durngate St ☎01305/751703, Ⓦwww.cornflowers.biz. Cosy B&B in a seventeenth-century townhouse a short walk from the centre. Just three double rooms, two en suite. ❸

Frampton House Frampton ☎01300/320308, Ⓦwww.frampton-house.co.uk. In a small village

five miles northwest of Dorchester, this grand Grade II-listed eighteenth-century manor house has played host to the likes of Thomas Hardy and Edwin Landseer. It has three very comfortable bedrooms, one with a four-poster bed, and a tennis court in the grounds, next to a park laid out by "Capability" Brown. ❹

The Old Rectory Winterbourne Steepleton, four miles west of Dorchester ☎01305/889468, Ⓦwww.theoldrectorybandb.co.uk. In a tiny, pretty village, this lovely former rectory from 1850 has four comfortable en-suite rooms, one with a four-poster, and attractive well-kept gardens. ❷

The Town

Dorchester was Durnovaria to the Romans, who founded the town in about 70 AD. The original Roman walls were replaced in the eighteenth century by tree-lined avenues called "Walks" (Bowling Alley Walk, West Walk and Colliton Walk), but some traces of the Roman period have survived. South of the centre of town, off Maumbury Road, **Maumbury Rings** is where the Romans held gladiatorial combats in an amphitheatre adapted from a Stone Age site; the gruesome traditions continued into the Middle Ages, when gladiators were replaced by bear-baiting and public executions or "hanging fairs".

Continuing the gory theme, after the ill-fated rebellion of the Duke of Monmouth (another of Charles II's illegitimate offspring) against James II, Judge Jeffreys was appointed to punish the rebels. His "Bloody Assizes" of 1685, held in the Oak Room of the **Antelope Hotel** on Cornhill, sentenced 292 men to death. In the event, 74 were hanged, drawn and quartered, and their heads stuck on pikes throughout Dorset and Somerset; the luckier suspects were merely flogged and transported to the West Indies.

In 1834 the **Shire Hall**, further down High West Street, witnessed another cause célèbre, when six men from the nearby village of Tolpuddle were sentenced to transportation for forming the Friendly Society of Agricultural Labourers in order to request a small wage increase on the grounds that their families were starving. After a public outcry the men were pardoned, and the **Tolpuddle Martyrs** passed into history as founders of the trade union movement. The **Old Crown Courts**, in which they were tried, is preserved as a memorial to the martyrs (Mon–Fri 10am–noon & 2–4pm; free), and you can find out more about them in Tolpuddle itself, eight miles east on the A35, where there's a fine little **museum** (April–Oct Tues–Sat 10am–5pm, Sun 11am–5pm; Nov–March Thurs–Sat 10am–4pm, Sun 11am–4pm; free; Ⓦwww.tolpuddlemartyrs.org.uk).

Hardy's Wessex

Thomas Hardy (1840–1928) resurrected the old name of **Wessex** to describe the region in which he set most of his fiction. In his books, the area stretched from Devon and Somerset ("Lower Wessex" and "Outer Wessex") to Berkshire and Oxfordshire ("North Wessex"), though its central core was Dorset ("South Wessex"), the county where Hardy spent most of his life. His books richly depict the life and appearance of the towns and countryside of the area, often thinly disguised under fictional names. Thus Salisbury makes an appearance as "Melchester", Weymouth (where he briefly lived) as "Budmouth Regis", and Bournemouth as "Sandbourne" in *Tess of the d'Urbervilles*. But it is **Dorchester**, the "Casterbridge" of his novels, that is portrayed in most detail, to the extent that many of the town's buildings and landmarks that still remain can be identified in the books (especially *The Mayor of Casterbridge* and *Far From the Madding Crowd*).

Hardy knew the town well; he was born and lived (1840–62 and 1867–70) in Higher Bockhampton, three miles northeast of town, in what is now **Hardy's Cottage** (April–Oct Sun–Thurs 11am–5pm; £4; NT), where a few bits of period furniture and some original manuscripts are displayed. Having worked as an architect in Cornwall and London, Hardy returned to Dorchester in 1885, spending the rest of his life in a house built to his own designs at **Max Gate**, on the A352 Wareham Road, a twenty-minute walk east from Dorchester's centre (April–Sept Mon, Wed & Sun 2–5pm; £3; NT). Here, the writer completed *Tess of the D'Urbervilles*, *Jude the Obscure* and much of his poetry, though only the garden and dining and drawing rooms are open to the public.

The best place to find out about Dorchester's history is the engrossing **Dorset County Museum** on High West Street (April–Oct Mon–Sat 10am–5pm; Nov–March Tues–Sat 10am–4pm; £6.50), where archeological and geological displays trace Celtic and Roman history, including a section on Maiden Castle. Pride of place goes to the re-creation of Thomas Hardy's study, where his pens are inscribed with the names of the books he wrote with them.

Dorchester has a weirdly eclectic range of other museums to visit, including a small **Dinosaur Museum** off High East Street on Icen Way (daily 9.30/10am–4.30/5.30pm; £6.95), chiefly aimed at children, and the formidably turreted **Keep Military Museum** (Mon–Sat 10am–4.30/5pm; Oct–March closed Mon; £6), at the top of High West Street, which traces the fortunes of the Dorset and Devonshire regiments over three hundred years and offers sweeping views over the town. Bizarrely, there's also **Tutankhamun: The Exhibition** on the High Street (April–Oct daily 9.30am–5.30pm; Nov–March Mon–Fri 9.30am–5pm, Sat & Sun 10am–5pm; £6.95), and the equally incongruous **Terracotta Warriors Museum** at the bottom of High East Street (daily 10am–4.30/5pm; £5.75).

Eating and drinking

As well as the usual high-street chains, Dorchester has a reasonable range of independent places to eat including Dorset's only Michelin-starred restaurant.

Café Jagos 8 High West St. With a minimalist interior and a courtyard garden, this easy-going café/restaurant near the tourist office offers panini and ciabattas, plus a range of mainly Mediterranean hot dishes (£7–11) and tasty desserts. Closed Sun.

The Old Ship 16 High West St. Dorchester's oldest pub dates from the 1600s, but has a contemporary feel inside, with wooden floors and comfy sofas. It has a good selection of real ales, with different guest beers each month, and serves the usual pub staples as well as, more unusually, some South American dishes.

Royal Oak 20–21 High West St. Inexpensive pub grub, such as scampi and chips and burgers, for around £6–7, at this old pub with a small patio behind.

Sienna 36 High West St ☏ 01305/250022. Dorset's only Michelin-starred restaurant, this tiny place is renowned for its Modern British cuisine such as poached West Country venison and Jurassic Coast

veal. Lunch menus start at around £22 for two courses up to £39 for three courses at dinner. Closed Sun & Mon.

Maiden Castle

One of southern England's finest prehistoric sites, **Maiden Castle** (free access) stands on a hill two miles or so southwest of Dorchester. Covering about 115 acres, it was first developed around 3000 BC by a Stone Age farming community and then used during the Bronze Age as a funeral mound. Iron Age dwellers expanded it into a populous settlement and fortified it with a daunting series of ramparts and ditches, just in time for the arrival of Vespasian's Second Legion. The ancient Britons' sling-stones were no match for the more sophisticated weapons of the Roman invaders, and Maiden Castle was stormed in a bloody massacre in 43 AD.

What you see today is a massive series of grassy concentric ridges about sixty feet high, creasing the surface of the hill. The site is best visited early or late in the day, when the low-angled sun casts the earthworks in shadow, showing them up more clearly. The main finds from the site are displayed in the Dorset County Museum (see p.247).

Inland Dorset

Heading north from Dorchester, the main pleasures of inland Dorset come from unscheduled meandering through its ancient landscapes and tiny rural settlements, many of which boast preposterously winsome names such as Ryme Intrinseca, Piddletrenthide, Up Sydling and Plush. Two of the most interesting of these villages are **Cerne Abbas** and **Milton Abbas**, the former distinguished by its rumbustious chalk-carved giant, the latter by its curious artificiality. The major tourist spots, however, are the towns of **Sherborne** and **Shaftesbury**.

Cerne Abbas and Milton Abbas

Eight miles north of Dorchester, just off the A352, the village of **CERNE ABBAS** has bags of charm in its own right, with gorgeous Tudor cottages and abbey ruins, not to mention a clutch of decent pubs. The main draw hereabouts, however, is the enormously priapic **giant** carved in the chalk hillside, standing 180ft high and flourishing a club over his disproportionately small head. The age of the monument is disputed, some authorities believing it to be pre-Roman, others thinking it might be a Romano-British figure of Hercules, but in view of his prominent feature it's probable that the giant originated as some primeval fertility symbol. Folklore has it that lying on the outsize member will induce conception, but the National Trust, which now owns the site, does its best to stop people wandering over it and eroding the two-foot trenches that form the outlines.

The village of **MILTON ABBAS**, ten miles east of Cerne Abbas and eleven miles northeast of Dorchester (from which it's reachable on bus #311), is an unusual English rural idyll. It owes its model-like neatness to the First Earl of Dorchester who, in the eighteenth century, found the medieval squalor of former "Middleton" a blot on the landscape of his estate. Although some see the earl as an enlightened advocate of modern town planning, the more likely truth is that he simply wanted to beautify his land, so he had the village razed and rebuilt in its present location as thirty semi-detached, whitewashed and thatched cottages on wide grassy verges. No trace remains of the old village, which once surrounded the fourteenth-century **abbey church** (now part of Milton Abbey school), a mile's walk away near the lake at the bottom of the village.

The best bet for a drink and a good **meal** in the village is the *Hambro Arms*, at the top of the hill, which serves good portions of pub food, such as steak and Dorset ale pie (£10). The pub also has comfortable, en-suite rooms (℡01258/880233, ⓌWwww.hambroarms.com; ❸).

Sherborne

Tucked away in the northwest corner of Dorset, the pretty town of **SHERBORNE** was once the capital of Wessex, its church having cathedral status until Old Sarum (see p.254) usurped the bishopric in 1075. This former glory is embodied by the magnificent **abbey church** (daily 8am–4/6pm), which was founded in 705, later becoming a Benedictine abbey. Most of its extant parts date from the fifteenth century, and it is one of the best examples of Perpendicular architecture in Britain, particularly noted for its outstanding **fan vaulting**. Among the church's many tombs are those of Alfred the Great's two brothers, Ethelred and Ethelbert, and the Elizabethan poet Thomas Wyatt. The **almshouse** on the opposite side of the Abbey Close dates from 1437 and is a rare example of a medieval hospital; another wing provides accommodation for Sherborne's well-known public school.

The town also has two "castles", both associated with Sir Walter Raleigh. Queen Elizabeth I first leased, then gave, Raleigh the twelfth-century **Old Castle** (daily: April–June & Sept 10am–5.30pm; July & Aug 10am–6pm; Oct 10am–4pm; £3.20; EH), but it seems that he despaired of feudal accommodation and built himself a more comfortable house, **Sherborne Castle**, in adjacent parkland (April–Oct Tues–Thurs, Sat & Sun 11am–4.30pm; Sat castle opens at 2pm; castle & gardens £9, gardens only £4.50; ⓌWwww.sherbornecastle.com). When Sir Walter fell from the queen's favour by seducing her maid of honour, the Digby family acquired the house and have lived here ever since; portraits, furniture and books are displayed in a whimsically Gothic interior, remodelled in the nineteenth century. The Old Castle fared less happily, and was pulverized by Cromwellian cannon fire for the obstinately Royalist leanings of its occupants.

On the London–Exeter train line, Sherborne is served by hourly trains from Waterloo. The **tourist office** is on Digby Road (Mon–Sat 9/10am–3/5pm; ℡01935/815341, ⓌWwww.westdorset.com), and the smartest place to stay in town is *The Eastbury*, Long Street (℡01935/813131, ⓌWwww.theeastburyhotel.co.uk; ❹), a fine Georgian house with comfortable rooms and a good restaurant. For lunch, the wonderful ✴ *Oliver's*, 19 Cheap St, is a friendly café-deli serving great cakes and snacks in a former butcher's adorned with the original tiles.

Shaftesbury

Fifteen miles north of Milton Abbas on the scenic A350, **SHAFTESBURY** perches on a spur of lumpy green-gold hills, with severe gradients on three sides. On a clear day, views from the town are terrific – one of the best vantage points is **Gold Hill**, quaint, cobbled and very steep, and familiar to many people from the 1970s Hovis ad, directed by Ridley Scott. The local history museum at the top of Gold Hill is currently closed for refurbishment, but is due to reopen in April 2011 as a **history centre**; check ⓌWwww.goldhillmuseum.org.uk for details. Its collection is likely to include include some locally made buttons, for which the area was once renowned, and a mummified cat.

Pilgrims used to flock to Shaftesbury to pay homage to the bones of Edward the Martyr, which were brought to the **abbey** in 978, though now only the footings of the abbey church survive, just off the main street (April–Oct daily 10am–5pm; £2.50). **St Peter's Church** on the marketplace is one of the few reminders of Shaftesbury's medieval grandeur, when it boasted a castle, twelve churches and four market crosses.

You can reach Shaftesbury on **buses** #26, #27 or #29 from Salisbury. The helpful **tourist office** on Bell Street (Mon–Sat 10am–3/5pm; ℡01747/853514, Ⓦwww.shaftesburydorset.com) can provide a full list of available **accommodation**: try *La Fleur de Lys*, Bleke Street ℡01747/853717, Ⓦwww.lafleurdelys .co.uk; ❺), which also has a highly rated, if pricey, restaurant. Alternatively, *The Retreat*, 47 Bell St (℡01747/850372, Ⓦthe-retreat.co.uk; ❸), offers good-value B&B in a Georgian former schoolhouse. For food, the ⚘ *Salt Cellar* **café** at the top of Gold Hill has wonderful views and serves inexpensive snacks and daily specials from around £7, including home-made pies; it closes at 5pm. *The Mitre* **pub** on the High Street also has lovely views from its outside terrace, and dishes up reasonably priced pub grub, such as venison and red wine casserole (£9).

Salisbury

"Salisbury Cathedral is the single most beautiful structure in England, and the Close around it the most beautiful space"

Bill Bryson, *Notes from a Small Island*

SALISBURY, huddled below Wiltshire's chalky plain in the converging valleys of the Avon and Nadder, looks from a distance very much as it did when Constable painted his celebrated view of it from across the water meadows, even though traffic may clog its centre. Prosperous and well kept, Wiltshire's only city is designed on a pleasantly human scale, with no sprawling suburbs or high-rise buildings to challenge the supremacy of the cathedral's immense spire – unusually, the local planners have imposed a height limit on new construction.

The town sprang into existence in the early thirteenth century, when the bishopric was moved from **Old Sarum**, an ancient Iron Age hillfort settled by the Romans and their successors, as the monks there were unhappy with activities at the garrison. The new town thrived due to its location on the London – Exeter road, with a stone bridge being built to allow travellers to cross the River Avon here. Salisbury became a busy market town, its success down to the wool trade, with cloth exported via nearby Southampton, and by the fifteenth century it was one of the largest towns in England with a population of around 8000. By the eighteenth century, cloth manufacturing had begun to decline and Salisbury was pretty much bypassed by the Industrial Revolution, leaving it the market town it remains today.

Arrival and information

Trains arrive half a mile west of the centre, on South Western Road, with the **bus station** a short way north of the Market Square on Endless Street. For a **taxi**, call ℡01722/743828. The **tourist office** is on Fish Row, just off Market Square (Mon–Sat 9.30am–5/6pm, plus May–Sept Sun 10am–4pm; ℡01722/334956, Ⓦwww.visitsalisbury.com), and is the starting point for informative **guided walks** of the city (1hr 30min: April–Oct daily at 11am; Nov–March Sat & Sun only; £4; ℡07873/212941, Ⓦwww.salisburycityguides.co.uk); in summer there are also themed walks, including a Friday-night Ghost Walk. **Bike rental** is available from Hayball's Cycle Shop, 30 Winchester St (℡01722/411378), for £10 a day (with £25 cash deposit). Bus **tours** to Stonehenge and Old Sarum (℡01722/336855, Ⓦwww.thestonehengetour.info; £11, or £17.50 including admission to both sites) leave from the train station on the hour in winter, and every thirty minutes in summer; they also pick up from the bus station.

Accommodation

With its year-round stream of visitors, Salisbury has plenty of accommodation within a short walk of the centre, though booking ahead is always advised. There's a well-appointed **campsite** a mile and a half north of Salisbury, close to Old Sarum: *Salisbury Camping and Caravanning Club Site*, Hudson's Field (☏01722/320713, ⓦwww.campingandcaravanningclub.co.uk).

HAMPSHIRE, DORSET AND WILTSHIRE | Salisbury

Byways House 31 Fowlers Rd ☏01722/328364, ⓦwww.bed-breakfast-stonehenge.co.uk. Plush Victorian house in a quiet location, offering spacious, comfortable rooms with or without bath. Two rooms have a view of the cathedral. ❸

Old Mill Town Path, Harnham ☏01722/327517, ⓦwww.signature -hospitality.com. The fully equipped rooms of this riverside pub have great views across the meadows to the cathedral. The location feels really rural but is just a short walk from the city centre. Real ales are on tap in the bar, and there's an adjoining 800-year-old restaurant serving moderately priced meals. ❹

Old Rectory 75 Belle Vue Rd ☏01722/502702, ⓦwww.theoldrectory-bb.co.uk. Three rooms with private or en-suite bathrooms in a light and modern conversion of a 1920s building. Breakfast is in the conservatory overlooking the garden. No credit cards. ❸

Rose & Crown Harnham Rd ☏0844/411 9046, ⓦwww.legacy-hotels.co.uk. Riverside hostelry dating from the thirteenth century, with traditional oak beams, grand four-poster beds and a huge pavilion restaurant; the rooms have been recently refurbished to mix traditional style with modern facilities. ❹

St Anns House 32–34 St Ann St ☏01722/335657, ⓦwww.stanneshouse.co.uk. A well-restored Georgian townhouse with stylish, comfortable rooms in a quiet street a short walk from the cathedral. ❸

Salisbury YHA Milford Hill ☏0870/770 6018, ⓔsalisbury@yha.org.uk. A 220-year-old building in its own spacious grounds, 10min walk east of the cathedral. Dorm bed and breakfast costs £22. Camping pitches available in summer. ❷

Sarum College 19 The Close ☏01722/424800, ⓦwww.sarum.ac.uk. By no means luxurious but in the best location in Salisbury, this friendly ecumenical college rents out simple en-suite doubles with views over The Close and cathedral, plus others without private facilities. There's also a decent common room, and breakfast is included. ❷

The City

Begun in 1220, **Salisbury Cathedral** (Mon–Sat 7.15am–6.15pm, June–Aug closes 7.15pm; Sun 12.30–2.30pm & 4–6.15pm; £5 suggested donation; ⓦwww .salisburycathedral.org.uk) was mostly completed within forty years and is thus unusually consistent in its style, with one extremely prominent exception – the **spire**, which was added a century later and at 404ft is the highest in England. Its survival is something of a miracle, for the foundations penetrate only about six feet into marshy ground, and when Christopher Wren surveyed it he found the spire to be leaning almost two and a half feet out of true. He added further tie-rods, which finally arrested the movement.

The cathedral's interior is over-austere after James Wyatt's brisk eighteenth-century tidying, but there's an amazing sense of space and light in its high nave, despite the sombre pillars of grey Purbeck marble, which are visibly bowing beneath the weight they bear. Monuments and carved tombs line the walls, where they were neatly placed by Wyatt, and in the north aisle is Europe's oldest working clock dating from 1386. Other features not to miss are the vaulted colonnades of the **cloisters**, and the octagonal **chapter house** (Mon–Sat 9.30/10am–4.30/6.45pm, Sun 12.45pm–4.30/5.30pm), which displays a rare original copy of the Magna Carta, and whose walls are decorated with a frieze

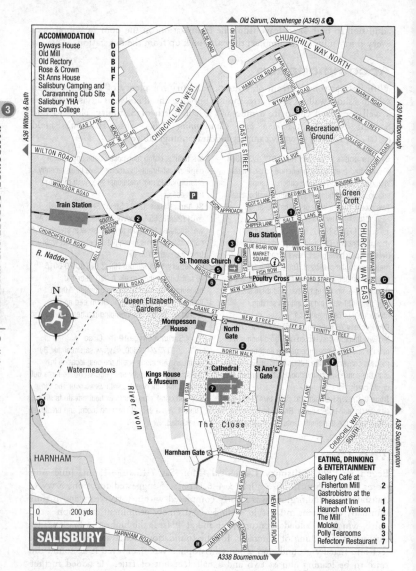

▲ Old Sarum, Stonehenge (A345) & Ⓐ

ACCOMMODATION
Byways House	D
Old Mill	G
Old Rectory	B
Rose & Crown	H
St Anns House	F
Salisbury Camping and Caravanning Club Site	A
Salisbury YHA	C
Sarum College	E

EATING, DRINKING & ENTERTAINMENT
Gallery Café at Fisherton Mill	2
Gastrobistro at the Pheasant Inn	1
Haunch of Venison	4
The Mill	5
Moloko	6
Polly Tearooms	3
Refectory Restaurant	7

0   200 yds

SALISBURY

A338 Bournemouth ▼

of scenes from the Old Testament. On most days, you can join a free 45-minute tour of the church leaving two or more times a day, and there are also 90-minute tours to the roof and tower, involving a climb of more than 300 steps (Mon–Sat 1–4 times daily, plus 2 daily on Sun May–Sept; call ☎01722/555156 for times and booking; £8).

Surrounding the cathedral is the peaceful precinct of lawns and mellow old buildings that makes up **The Close**, the largest and most impressive in the country. Most of the houses have seemly Georgian facades, though some, like the Bishop's Palace and the deanery, date from the thirteenth century. **Mompesson**

House (mid-March to Oct Mon–Wed, Sat & Sun 11am–5pm; £5.20, garden only £1; NT), built by a wealthy merchant in 1701, contains some beautifully furnished eighteenth-century rooms and a superbly carved staircase, as displayed to great effect in the film *Sense and Sensibility*. The other building to head for in The Close is the Kings House, home of the **Salisbury and South Wiltshire Museum** (Mon–Sat 10am–5pm plus Sun noon–5pm in July & Aug; £6; ⓦ www .salisburymuseum.org.uk) – an absorbing account of local history. It includes a good section on Stonehenge and also focuses on the life and times of General Pitt-Rivers, the father of modern archeology, who excavated many of Wiltshire's prehistoric sites, including Avebury (see p.256).

The Close's **North Gate** opens onto the centre's older streets, where narrow pedestrianized alleyways bear names like Fish Row and Salt Lane, indicative of their trading origin. Many half-timbered houses and inns have survived all over the centre, and the last of four market crosses, **Poultry Cross**, stands on stilts in Silver Street, near the Market Square. The **market**, held on Tuesdays and Saturdays, still serves a large agricultural area, as it did in earlier times when the city grew wealthy on wool. Nearby, the church of **St Thomas** – named after Thomas à Becket – is worth a look inside for its carved timber roof and "Doom painting" over the chancel arch, depicting Christ presiding over the Last Judgement. Dating from 1475, it's the largest of its kind in England.

Lastly, to best appreciate the city's inspiring silhouette – the view made famous by Constable – take a twenty-minute walk through the water meadows southwest of the centre to **Harnham**, pausing at the *Old Mill* (see p.251).

Eating, drinking and entertainment

Salisbury has a good selection of decent **pubs and cafés**, though nightlife is fairly limited.

Gallery Café at Fisherton Mill 108 Fisherton St ⓣ 01722/500200. Great café within a renovated mill serving delicious soups (£4), sandwiches on stone-baked bread (£5) and main courses such as sausage with lentils (£10). Upstairs, you can watch artists at work in their studios, weaving and making jewellery. Also open for dinner one Fri & Sat a month; phone to reserve. Closed Sun & Mon.

Gastrobistro at the Pheasant Inn 19 Salt St ⓣ 01722/414926. Friendly, good-value gastropub with low beams, bare walls, wooden floors and occasional live music. The cuisine has a French influence, with starters such as snails Bourgogne (£5.50) followed by Toulouse sausages (£13). Closed Sun & Mon eve.

Haunch of Venison Minster St. One of the city's most atmospheric pubs, with a wonderful warren of rooms. The quirky, sloping-floored upstairs restaurant serves good-value dishes such as shellfish and curly kale risotto (£10.50) and wild boar steaks (£13). Its best-known artefact, the mummified hand of a nineteenth-century card player still clutching his

cards, had just been stolen at the time of writing, but may well be returned, as it has a history of disappearing and re appearing.

The Mill Bridge St. Large, popular pub with riverside seating, right in the city centre. Standard pub meals and real ales are available, as well as tea and coffee until 9pm.

Moloko 5 Bridge St ⓣ 01722/507050, ⓦ www .themolokobar.co.uk. Lively vodka bar over three floors with dancing in the basement; hosts regular club nights and guest DJs.

Polly Tearooms 8 St Thomas's Square. Lovely old-fashioned tearooms and patisserie right outside St Thomas' church, with outdoor tables. Service is friendly, the coffee good, the lunches large and they serve their own home-made cakes, chocolates and children's biscuits. Open daily 8.30am–5pm.

Refectory Restaurant Salisbury Cathedral. Child-friendly café with great views of the cathedral spire through its glass roof. Serves delicious cakes, pastries and good coffee: lunch dishes include home-made soup and bread (£4) or main courses such as salmon and spinach pie (£8). Closes at 5.30pm.

Around Salisbury

North of Salisbury stretches a hundred thousand acres of chalky upland, known as **Salisbury Plain**; it's managed by the Ministry of Defence whose presence has protected it from development and intensive farming, thereby preserving species that are all but extinct elsewhere in England. Its empty expanses are home to the country's only colony of great bustards, the world's heaviest flying bird, which became extinct in the UK in the 1840s. Chicks were reintroduced from Russia in 2004 to a secret location on the Plain, and the first great bustard to be born in the UK in nearly two hundred years appeared in 2009.

Though now largely deserted, in previous times Salisbury Plain positively throbbed with communities. Stone Age, Bronze Age and Iron Age settlements left hundreds of burial mounds scattered over the chalklands, as well as major complexes at Danebury, Badbury, Figsbury, **Old Sarum**, and, of course, the great circle of **Stonehenge**, England's most famous historial monument. To the west, Salisbury's hinterland also includes one of Wiltshire's great country mansions: **Wilton House**.

Wilton

WILTON, five miles west of Salisbury, is renowned for its carpet industry and the splendid **Wilton House** (first week in April, May–Aug Mon–Thurs, Sun & occasional Sat 11am–5pm; grounds also Sat & Sun in Sept; last entry 3.45pm; £12.50, grounds only £5.50; Ⓦwww.wiltonhouse.com), of which Daniel Defoe wrote: "One cannot be said to have seen any thing that a man of curiosity would think worth seeing in this county, and not have been at Wilton House." The Tudor house, built for the First Earl of Pembroke on the site of a dissolved Benedictine abbey, was ruined by fire in 1647 and rebuilt by Inigo Jones, whose classic hallmarks can be seen in the sumptuous Single Cube and Double Cube rooms, so called because of their precise dimensions. Sir Philip Sidney, illustrious Elizabethan courtier and poet, wrote part of his magnum opus *Arcadia* here – the dado round the Single Cube Room illustrates scenes from the book – and the Double Cube room was the setting for the ballroom scene in Ang Lee's film, *Sense and Sensibility*. The easel **paintings** are what makes Wilton really special, however – the collection includes works by Van Dyck, Rembrandt, two of the Brueghel family, Poussin, Andrea del Sarto and Tintoretto. In the grounds, the famous **Palladian Bridge** has been joined by attractions including an adventure playground, garden centre and an audio-visual show on the colourful earls of Pembroke. Frequent city buses #60, #60A and #61 connect Wilton with Salisbury's centre.

Old Sarum

The ruins of **Old Sarum** (daily: Feb, March & Oct 10am–4pm; April–June & Sept 10am–5pm; July & Aug 9am–6pm; Nov–Jan 11am–3pm; £3.50; EH) occupy a bleak hilltop site two miles north of the city centre – it's an easy walk, or take buses #5, #6 or #69. Possibly occupied up to five thousand years ago, then developed as an Iron Age fort – whose double protective ditches remain – it was settled by Romans and Saxons before the Norman bishopric of Sherborne was moved here in the 1070s. Within a couple of decades a new cathedral had been consecrated at Old Sarum, and a large religious community was living alongside the soldiers in the central castle. Old Sarum was an uncomfortable place, parched and windswept, and in 1220 the dissatisfied clergy – additionally at loggerheads with the castle's occupants – appealed to the pope for permission to decamp to Salisbury (still known officially as New Sarum). When permission was granted, the stone from the cathedral was commandeered for Salisbury's gateways, and once the church had gone the population waned. By the nineteenth century Old Sarum was deserted, but it continued to exist as a political constituency – William Pitt was one of its representatives. The most notorious of the "rotten boroughs", it returned two MPs at a time to Westminster until the 1832 Reform Act put a stop to it. Huge earthworks, banks and ditches are the dominant features of the site today, with a broad trench encircling the promontory, on which lie the rudimentary remains of the Norman palace, castle and cathedral.

Stonehenge

No ancient structure in England arouses more controversy than **Stonehenge** (daily: mid-March to May & Sept to mid-Oct 9.30am–6pm; June–Aug 9am–7pm; mid-Oct to mid-March 9.30am–4pm; £6.90; NT & EH), a mysterious ring of monoliths nine miles north of Salisbury. There are no public buses, but the Stonehenge Tour bus runs regular trips here; see p.250 for details. While archeologists argue over whether it was a place of ritual sacrifice and sun worship, an astronomical calculator or a royal palace, conservation of the UNESCO-designated World Heritage Site remains an urgent priority. Visitors are no longer permitted to walk among the stones, though special access to the inner ring (outside normal hours) can be arranged on ☎01722/343830; check dates and times at ⓦwww .english-heritage.org.uk/stonehenge. There is also open access to the stones during the summer solstice celebrations when crowds of 35,000 or more gather to watch the sunrise. There have long been plans to build a new visitor centre and car park away from the stones themselves, with a transit system connecting the two; however, various different schemes have been afoot for years, with a lack of general consensus and the daunting cost leading to interminable delays.

The site

While some people may find Stonehenge distinctly underwhelming, understanding a little of its history and ancient significance gives an insight into its mystical appeal. What exists today is only a small part of the original prehistoric complex, as many of the outlying stones were probably plundered for building materials. The construction of Stonehenge is thought to have taken place in several stages. In about 3000 BC the outer circular bank and ditch were created, just inside which was dug a ring of 56 pits, which at a later date were filled with a mixture of earth and human ash. Around 2500 BC the first stones were raised within the earthworks, comprising approximately forty great blocks of dolerite (bluestone), whose original source was Preseli in South Wales. Some archeologists have suggested that these monoliths were found lying on Salisbury Plain, having been borne down from the Welsh mountains by a glacier in the last Ice Age, but the lack of any other glacial debris on the plain would seem to disprove this theory. It really does seem to be the case that the stones were cut from quarries in Preseli and dragged or floated here on rafts, a prodigious task which has defeated recent attempts to emulate it.

The crucial phase in the creation of the site came during the next six hundred years, when the incomplete bluestone circle was transformed by the construction of a circle of twenty-five **trilithons** (two uprights crossed by a lintel) and an inner horseshoe formation of five trilithons. Hewn from Marlborough Downs sandstone, these colossal stones (called sarsens), ranging from 13ft to 21ft in height and weighing up to thirty tonnes, were carefully dressed and worked – for example, to compensate for perspective distortion the uprights have a slight swelling in the middle, the same trick as the builders of the Parthenon were to employ hundreds of years later. More bluestones were arranged in various patterns within the outer circle over this period.

The purpose of all this work remains baffling, however. The symmetry and location of the site (a slight rise in a flat valley with even views of the horizon in all directions), as well as its alignment towards the points of sunrise and sunset on the summer and winter solstices, tend to support the supposition that it was some sort of observatory or time-measuring device. The site ceased to be used at around 1600 BC, and by the Middle Ages it had already become a "landmark". Recent excavations have revealed the existence of a much larger settlement here than had previously been thought – in fact the most substantial Neolithic village of this period to be found on the British mainland – covering a wide area. Nothing is to be seen of the new finds as yet, though there are plans to re-create a part of the ancient complex.

Woodhenge

There's a lot less charisma about the reputedly significant Bronze Age site of **Woodhenge** (dawn–dusk; free), two miles northeast of Stonehenge. The site consists of a circular bank about 220ft in diameter enclosing a ditch and six concentric rings of post holes, which would originally have held timber uprights, possibly supporting a roofed building of some kind. The holes are now marked less romantically (if more durably) by concrete pillars. A child's grave was found at the centre of the rings, suggesting that it may have been a place of ritual sacrifice.

North and west Wiltshire

North of Salisbury Plain is another cluster of ancient sites, including the huge stone circle of **Avebury**, the mysterious grassy mound of **Silbury Hill** and the chamber graves of **West Kennet**. On the western edges of Wiltshire, the villages of **Lacock** and **Bradford-on-Avon** and the landscaped garden at **Stourhead** offer picturesque glimpses into a past era of provincial life, with the brasher stately home at **Longleat** an unlikely hybrid of safari park and historic monument.

Avebury, Silbury Hill and West Kennet

The village of **AVEBURY** stands in the midst of a **stone circle** (free access; NT & EH) that rivals Stonehenge – the individual stones are generally smaller, but the circle itself is much wider and more complex. A massive earthwork 20ft high and 1400ft across encloses the main circle, which is approached by four causeways across the inner ditch, two of them leading into wide avenues that stretch over a mile beyond the circle. The best guess is that it was built soon after 2500 BC, and presumably had a similar ritual or religious function to Stonehenge. The structure of Avebury's diffuse circle is quite difficult to grasp, but there are plans on the site, and you can get an excellent overview at the **Alexander Keiller Museum**, at the western entrance to the site (daily: April–Oct 10am–6pm; Nov–March 10am–4.30pm; £4.20, including Barn Gallery; NT & EH), which displays excavated material, while the nearby **Barn Gallery** holds a permanent exhibition on Avebury and the surrounding country.

In the village, the sixteenth-century **Avebury Manor** (April–Oct Mon, Tues & Fri–Sun: house noon–5pm; garden 11am–5pm; £4.20, garden only £3.15; NT) has four or five panelled and plastered rooms, for which you are issued with over-shoes to protect the wooden floors from the chalk dust, and a **garden** with topiary and medieval walls.

Just outside Avebury, the neat green mound of **Silbury Hill** is probably overlooked by the majority of drivers whizzing by on the A4. At 130ft it's no great height, but when you realize it's the largest prehistoric artificial mound in Europe, and was made by a people using nothing more than primitive spades, it commands more respect. It was probably constructed around 2600 BC, and no one knows quite what it was for, though the likelihood is that it was a burial mound. You can't walk on the hill anyway, so cross the road to the footpath that leads half a mile to the **West Kennet Long Barrow** (free access; NT & EH). Dating from about 3250 BC, this was definitely a chamber tomb – nearly fifty burials have been discovered here.

Practicalities

Good **bus** routes connect Avebury with Salisbury. There's a **tourist office** (Easter–Oct daily 9.30am–5pm; Nov–Easter Thurs–Sun 9.30am–4.30pm; ☏ 01380/734669, ⓦ www.visitwiltshire.co.uk) in the Avebury Chapel Centre on Green Street, which sells local walking guides. You can wake up to views of the stones at *Manor Farm*, a B&B on the High Street (☏ 01672/539294, ⓦ www.manorfarmavebury.com; ④), which has a private guests' sitting room. *The Circle* restaurant, next to the Barn Gallery, offers good vegetarian **meals** and snacks, while the *Red Lion* pub also serves reasonable meals (☏ 01672/539266).

Lacock

Photogenic **LACOCK**, eleven miles west of Avebury, is the perfect English feudal village, albeit one gentrified by the National Trust to within a hair's breadth of natural life, and besieged by tourists all summer. Appropriately for such a regular TV and film location – starring in the recent *Harry Potter* films and *Cranford* among others – the village has a fascinating museum dedicated to the founding father of photography, Henry Fox Talbot, a member of the dynasty that has lived in the local abbey since it passed to Sir William Sharington on the Dissolution of the Monasteries in 1539. Ten years later Sharington was arrested for colluding with Thomas Seymour, Treasurer of the Mint, in a plot to subvert the coinage: he narrowly escaped with his life by shopping his partner in crime – who was beheaded – and after a period of disgrace managed to buy back his estates. His descendant, William Henry Fox Talbot, was the first to produce a photographic negative, and the **Fox Talbot Museum**, in a sixteenth-century barn by the abbey gates (Jan to mid-Feb & Nov to mid-Dec Sat & Sun 11am–4pm; mid-Feb to Oct daily 11am–5.30pm; £11, including abbey garden and cloisters, £8 without access to grounds; NT), captures something of the excitement he must have experienced as the dim outline of an oriel window in the abbey steadily imprinted itself on a piece of silver nitrate paper. The **abbey** itself preserves a few monastic fragments amid the eighteenth-century Gothic, while the **church of St Cyriac** in its grounds contains the opulent tomb of the nefarious Sir William Sharington, buried beneath a splendid barrel-vaulted roof.

The village's delightfully Chaucerian-sounding hostelry, *At the Sign of the Angel*, is a good **hotel** and **restaurant** (☏ 01249/730230, ⓦ www.lacock.co.uk; ⑤), with four-poster beds and a lovely garden, while *Lacock Pottery* (☏ 01249/730266, ⓦ www.lacockbedandbreakfast.com; ③) has three B&B rooms in a lovely old building overlooking the church. For a drink or decent **pub** food, the *George Inn* on West Street is a rambling spot with roaring fires.

Bradford-on-Avon

With its buildings of mellow auburn stone and lovely river- and canalside walks, **BRADFORD-ON-AVON** is the most appealing town in Wiltshire's northwest corner. Sheltering against a steep wooded slope, it takes its name from its "broad ford" across the Avon, though the original fording place was replaced by a **bridge** dating mainly from the seventeenth century. The domed structure at one end is a quaint old jail converted from a chapel.

The local industry, based on textiles, was revolutionized with the arrival of Flemish weavers in 1659, and many of the town's handsome buildings reflect the prosperity of this period. Yet Bradford's most significant building is the tiny **St Lawrence** on Church Street, an outstanding example of Saxon church architecture dating from about 700 AD. Its distinctive feature is its carved angels over the chancel arch.

Trains call regularly at Bradford from Salisbury, Dorchester, Bath and Bristol; the **train station** is on St Margaret's Street close to the town centre. The well-equipped **tourist office** is at 50 St Margaret's St (Mon–Sat 10am–4/5pm, Sun 10/11am–3/4pm; ☎01225/865797, ⊛www.bradfordonavon.co.uk). For easy biking along the Kennet & Avon Canal west to Bath you can **rent bikes** from *The Lock Inn Café* (see below); they also rent out **canoes**.

Bradford has a good range of **accommodation**, none more characterful than *Bradford Old Windmill*, a B&B up the hill at 4 Mason's Lane (☎01225/866842, ⊛www.bradfordoldwindmill.co.uk; two-night minimum stay; closed Nov–Jan; ❹). *Priory Steps*, closer to the centre on Newtown (☎01225/862230, ⊛www.priory steps.co.uk; ❹), is a family home converted from seventeenth-century weavers' cottages, with well-prepared dinners (by prior arrangement; £25) and excellent views over the rooftops. The quirky *Lock Inn Café* (closed eve Sun & Mon) by the canal is the best place for an inexpensive **meal** at any time of the day, with pub-grub meals (from £5) which you can eat in a series of Wendy houses or inside a moored canalboat. The best **pub** is the atmospheric *Bunch of Grapes* on Silver Street, which has good wines and beers and serves great food, particularly their home-made pies.

Longleat

In 1946 the sixth marquess of Bath raised eyebrows when he became the first stately home owner to open his house to the paying public on a regular basis to make ends meet. In 1966 he caused even more amazement when **Longleat's** Capability Brown landscapes were turned into England's first drive-through **safari park** with lions, tigers, giraffes, rhinos, elephants, zebras and hippos on show (house: April–Oct plus Feb half-term daily 10am–5/5.30pm; Nov–March guided tours 2–4 times daily; safari park: March Sat & Sun 10am–3pm; April–Oct plus Feb half-term daily – check website for times; house £12, safari park £12; all attractions £24; ⊛www .longleat.co.uk). More traditionally, there's an exquisitely furnished Elizabethan **house**, built for Sir John Thynne, Elizabeth I's High Treasurer, with the largest private library in Britain and a fine collection of pictures, including Titian's *Holy Family*. Today, the African savanna contrasts bizarrely with the classical stately home, and both have been joined by other attractions including the world's largest hedge maze, safari boat trips, a mini-railway and the seventh marquess's steamy murals encapsulating his interpretation of life and the universe.

Stourhead

Landscape gardening – the creation of an artificially improved version of nature – was a favoured mode of display among the grandest eighteenth-century landowners, and **Stourhead** (house: mid-March to Oct Mon, Tues & Fri–Sun 11.30am–5pm; garden: daily 9am–6pm; house & garden £12.30, house or garden £7.40; NT), six miles south of Longleat, is one of the most accomplished survivors of the genre. The Stourton estate was bought in 1717 by Henry Hoare, who commissioned Colen Campbell to build a new villa in the Palladian style. Hoare's heir, another Henry, returned from his Grand Tour in 1741 with his head full of the paintings of Claude and Poussin, and determined to translate their images of well-ordered, wistful classicism into real life. He dammed the Stour to create a lake, then planted the terrain with trees, domed temples, stone bridges, grottoes and statues, all mirrored vividly in the water. In 1772, the folly of **King Alfred's Tower** (11am–5pm: April–Aug Mon, Tues & Fri–Sun; Sept & Oct Sat & Sun only; £2.80) was added and today affords fine views across the estate and into neighbouring counties. The rhododendrons and azaleas that now make such a splash in early summer are a later addition to this dream landscape. The **house**, in contrast, is fairly run-of-the-mill, though it has some good Chippendale furniture.

Travel details

Buses

Details of minor and seasonal local bus services are frequently given in the text. For information on all other local and national bus services, contact Traveline ⊕0871/200 2233, ⓦwww.traveline.org.uk.

Bournemouth to: London (hourly; 2hr 40min); Lymington (Mon–Sat hourly, Sun every 2hr; 1hr 30min); Salisbury (Mon–Sat every 30min, Sun 7; 1hr 10min); Southampton (11 daily; 45min–1hr 50min); Weymouth (4 daily; 1hr 20min); Wimborne Minster (Mon–Sat every 30min, Sun every 2hr; 1hr); Winchester (4 daily; 1hr 45min).

Dorchester to: London (1 daily; 4hr); Lyme Regis (hourly; 1hr 15min); Sherborne (4 daily; 40–50min); Weymouth (3–6 hourly; 25min).

Portsmouth to: London (15 daily; 2hr); Salisbury (1 daily; 1hr 35min); Southampton (Mon–Sat 13 daily, Sun 6; 40–50min).

Salisbury to: Bournemouth (Mon–Sat every 30min, Sun 7; 1hr 10min); London (3 daily; 2hr 50min–4hr); Portsmouth (1 daily; 1hr 35min); Shaftesbury (10 daily; 50min–1hr 15min); Southampton (Mon–Sat 1–2 hourly, Sun 6; 45min–1hr); Winchester (Mon–Sat 5–7 daily; 1hr 20min).

Southampton to: Bournemouth (11 daily; 45min–1hr 50min); Brockenhurst (every 30min; 45min); London (hourly; 2hr 25min–3hr); Lymington (every 30min; 1hr 10min); Lyndhurst (every 30min; 30min); Portsmouth (Mon–Sat 13 daily, Sun 6; 40–50min); Salisbury (Mon–Sat 1–2 hourly, Sun 6; 45min–1hr); Weymouth (2 daily; 2hr 40min); Winchester (every 15–30min; 35–45min).

Weymouth: to Bournemouth (4 daily; 1hr 20min); Dorchester (3–6 hourly; 25min); Southampton (2 daily; 2hr 40min).

Winchester to: Alresford (every 30min; 15–30min); Alton (Mon–Sat hourly, Sun every 2hr; 40min); Bournemouth (4 daily; 1hr 45min); London (8 daily; 2hr); Salisbury (Mon–Sat 5–7 daily; 1hr 20min); Southampton (every 15–30min; 35–45min).

Trains

For information on all local and national rail services, contact National Rail Enquiries ⊕0845/748 4950, ⓦwww.nationalrail.co.uk.

Bournemouth to: Brockenhurst (3–4 hourly; 15–25min); Dorchester (hourly; 45min); London Waterloo (2 hourly; 2hr); Poole (2–3 hourly; 10–15min); Southampton (3 hourly; 30–50min); Wareham (every 30min; 25min); Weymouth (hourly; 55min); Winchester (2–3 hourly; 45min–1hr).

Dorchester to: Bath (Mon–Sat 8 daily, Sun 3; 2hr); Bournemouth (hourly; 45min); Bradford-on-Avon (Mon–Sat 8 daily, Sun 3; 1hr 45min); Brockenhurst (hourly; 1hr); London Waterloo (hourly; 2hr 40min); Southampton (every 2hr; 1hr 30min); Weymouth (2–3 hourly; 10–15min).

Poole to: Bournemouth (2–3 hourly; 10–15min); London Waterloo (1–2 hourly; 2hr 5min–2hr 50min); Weymouth (hourly; 45min).

Portsmouth to: London Waterloo (3–4 hourly; 1hr 35min–2hr 15min); Salisbury (hourly; 1hr 20min);

Southampton (2 hourly; 45min–1hr); Winchester (hourly; 1hr).

Salisbury to: Bath (hourly; 1hr); Bradford-on-Avon (hourly; 45min); London Waterloo (2 hourly; 1hr 30min); Portsmouth (hourly; 1hr 20min); Sherborne (hourly; 45min); Southampton (1–2 hourly; 30min).

Southampton to: Bournemouth (3 hourly; 30–50min); Brockenhurst (2–3 hourly; 15–30min); Dorchester (every 2 hr; 1hr 30min); London Waterloo (2–3 hourly; 1hr 20min); Portsmouth (2 hourly; 45min–1hr); Salisbury (1–2 hourly; 30min);

Weymouth (2 hourly; 1hr 30min–1hr 45min); Winchester (3–4 hourly; 15–30min).

Weymouth to: Bournemouth (hourly; 55min); Dorchester (2–3 hourly; 10–15min); Southampton (2 hourly; 1hr 30min–1hr 45min); London Waterloo (hourly; 2hr 50min–3hr 35min); Poole (hourly; 45min).

Winchester to: Bournemouth (2–3 hourly; 45min–1hr); London Waterloo (3–4 hourly; 1hr–1hr 15min); Portsmouth (hourly; 1hr); Southampton (3–4 hourly; 15–30min).

Oxfordshire, the Cotswolds and around

CHAPTER 4 # Highlights

* **Christ Church College, Oxford** Oxford boasts many beautiful old buildings, with Christ Church holding several of the most fascinating. See p.271

* **Northleach** A charming Cotswold village without the crowds, easily reached from Oxford and Cirencester. See p.287

* **Kingham Plough, Kingham** One of the Cotswolds' best eating experiences – fine dining in an updated but still pleasantly rustic village pub. See p.289

* **Chipping Campden** Perhaps the most handsome of the Cotswolds towns, with honey-coloured stone houses flanking the superb church of St James. See p.290

* **Winchcombe** The "walking capital of the Cotswolds" offers leg-stretching excursions in the hills. See p.291

* **Gloucester Cathedral** One of England's finest churches – a magnificently atmospheric array of Gothic cloisters and stained glass. See p.296

* **White Horse Hill** The huge, prehistoric horse cut into the bright-white chalk of the Berkshire Downs is a stunning sight. See p.301

▲ Chipping Campden

Oxfordshire, the Cotswolds and around

With its superb architecture, world-class museums and lively student population, the university city of **Oxford** is one of England's star turns. Close to London – and also to Heathrow Airport, making it viable as a first-night arrival point – it offers easygoing charm set against a classically English backdrop of historic buildings, with open countryside on the doorstep.

On Oxford's edge, **Woodstock**, a handsome little town, abuts one of England's most imposing country homes, **Blenheim Palace**, while beyond lie the gently rolling **Cotswold** hills, occupying west **Oxfordshire**, most of **Gloucestershire** and bits of neighbouring Warwickshire and Worcestershire. Dotted with picturesque villages made from the local honey-coloured stone, the Cotswolds became rich from the medieval wool trade, evidence of which remains all around in a multitude of beautiful old churches and handsome mansions. The region attracts visitors by the coachload, though this should not deter you from visiting: it's easy to dodge the crowds. Top draws include the engaging market town of **Chipping Campden**, the delightful village of **Northleach** and bustling **Cirencester**. Ultimately, however, the Cotswolds' charms only reveal themselves when you take to the hills and valleys along its dense network of footpaths and trails, in particular the **Cotswold Way**, a hundred-mile national trail that runs along the edge of the Cotswold escarpment from Chipping Campden in the northeast to Bath in the southwest. Heading west, the land drops sharply from the Cotswold escarpment down to **Cheltenham**, an appealing Regency spa town famous for its horse racing – and for hosting some of the region's best restaurants and bars. Nearby, a superb cathedral dominates the old county town of **Gloucester**.

Approaching Oxford from the southwest, the 85-mile-long **Ridgeway**, a prehistoric track – and now a national trail – offers fine walks on the downs straddling the Berkshire–Oxfordshire border, where you can visit the gigantic prehistoric depiction of a horse in chalk that gives the **Vale of White Horse** its name. The Ridgeway continues to traverse the **Chiltern Hills**, a picturesque band of chalk uplands

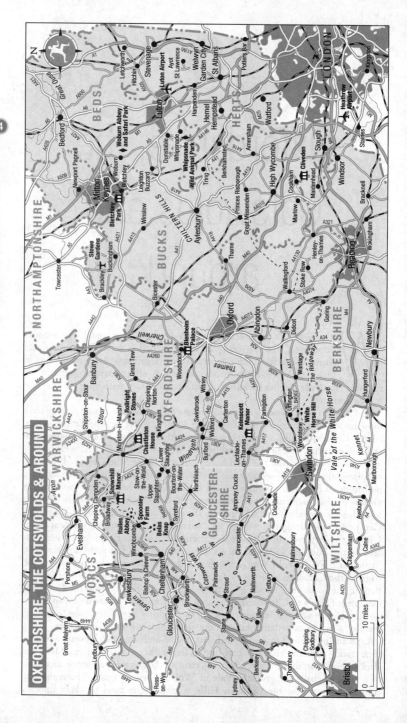

OXFORDSHIRE, THE COTSWOLDS & AROUND

The Cotswolds lie in the triangle formed by three **motorways**, the M5, M4 and M40, which give swift access from all directions – as do the M1 and A1(M) further east. Long-distance **buses** provide an efficient service to larger towns, but local services between villages are patchy. **Mainline trains** from London Paddington serve Oxford and several Cotswold villages including Kingham and Moreton-in-Marsh, as well as Gloucester and Cheltenham. Oxford is also on the cross-country main line between Birmingham New Street and Winchester, Southampton and Bournemouth, bypassing London. Other trains serve Henley from Paddington, and St Albans and Bedford from London St Pancras.

extending from Reading northeast to Luton: for the casual visitor one target in the area is **Henley-on-Thames**, an attractive old town famous for its rowing regatta.

Moving north and east, modest **Buckingham** is within easy reach of **Stowe Gardens**, which holds a remarkable collection of outdoor sculptures, monuments and follies. Further east, another whopping stately home, **Woburn Abbey** – and **Woburn Safari Park** – prelude the town of **Bedford**, while adjacent Hertfordshire boasts the ancient and dignified town of **St Albans**, now sadly marooned amid a knot of motorways on the fringes of the capital.

Oxford and around

When visitors think of **OXFORD**, they almost always imagine its **university**, revered as one of the world's great academic institutions, inhabiting honey-coloured stone buildings set around ivy-clad quadrangles. The image is accurate enough, but although the university dominates central Oxford both physically and mentally, the wider city has an entirely different character, its economy built on the factories of Cowley to the south. It was here that Britain's first mass-produced cars were manufactured in the 1920s and, although there have been more downs than ups in recent years, the plants are still vitally important to the area.

Oxford started late, in Anglo-Saxon times, and blossomed even later, under the **Normans**, when the cathedral was constructed and Oxford was chosen as a royal residence. The origins of the university are obscure, but it seems that the reputation of **Henry I**, the so-called "Scholar King", helped attract students in the early twelfth century, their numbers increasing with the expulsion of English students from Paris in 1167. The first **colleges** were founded mostly by rich bishops, and most still share common architectural features: the private rooms of the students, and most of the communal rooms – the chapels, dining halls and libraries – arranged around **quadrangles** (quads).

Though they share a similar history, each of the university's 39 colleges has its own character and often a particular label, whether it's the richest (St John's), most left-wing (Wadham and Balliol) or most public-school-dominated (Christ Church), and collegiate rivalries are long established, usually revolving around sports. Tension between the city and the university – "**Town**" and "**Gown**" – has existed as long as the university itself: relations became especially fractious during the Civil War, when the colleges sided with Charles I (who turned Oxford into a Royalist stronghold) while the city backed the Parliamentarians. The privileges enjoyed by the colleges – until 1950 the university had two MPs of its own – have also stoked resentment, which occasionally flares into confrontation, but a non-communicative coexistence is more typical. Given that thousands of tourists and foreign-language students also invade Oxford throughout the year, it is no surprise that the city's 140,000 permanent inhabitants often choose to keep themselves to themselves.

Despite – indeed, partly because of – its idiosyncrasies, Oxford should be high on anyone's itinerary, and can keep you occupied for several days. The university buildings include some of England's finest architecture, and the city can also boast some excellent museums and a good range of bars and restaurants. Getting there is easy, too: from London Paddington the journey takes just an hour by train, a little longer by bus.

Arrival

From Oxford **train station**, it's a ten-minute walk east to the centre. Long-distance and many county-wide buses terminate at Gloucester Green **bus station**, in the city centre adjoining George Street. The Oxford Bus Company works in tandem with Stagecoach to operate most local and city buses, many of which terminate on George Street, Magdalen Street and/or St Aldates. The former also runs the **park-and-ride** scheme, with buses (Mon–Sat 6am–11pm, Sun 9am–7pm) travelling into the centre (every 15min at peak times, less in the evenings) from five large and clearly signed free car parks on the main approach roads into the city. Parking in the city centre is deliberately expensive and hard to find.

Wherever you arrive, an efficient – and very green – option for getting you and/or your bags to your hotel is to call **Oxon Carts** (℡07747/024600, ⓦwww.oxoncarts .com), a cycle-rickshaw firm charging roughly £6–8 for a trip across the city centre.

Information and guided tours

The **tourist office** is plumb in the centre of town at 15 Broad St (Mon–Sat 9.30am–5pm, Sun 10am–4pm; ℡01865/252200, ⓦwww.visitoxford.org). They have a wealth of information about the city and its sights, little of which is issued free, though the monthly **listings booklet** *In Oxford* is an exception. The tourist

---

A weekend in Oxford

Friday night
Toast your weekend with a **champagne cocktail** in the Randolph's *Morse Bar* and a slap-up **dinner** at *Al Shami*, *Gee's* or *Jamie's Italian*.

Saturday
Start the day with a visit to the **Covered Market**, to watch the butchers and fishmongers lay out the new day's wares and grab coffee while getting a flavour of town life. Extend the theme by dropping into the **Museum of Oxford**, or join one of the introductory **walking tours** offered by the tourist office. Grab lunch on the hoof and then devote the afternoon to "gown" life: choose two or three of the **colleges** (Christ Church, Merton and New would make a fine hat-trick) and pick up the atmosphere of the old city-centre streets (Broad, Merton, Turl) – or the water meadows behind Christ Church – as you go. End the day with a **punt**, before setting off down the **Cowley Road** to sample Oxford's lounge bars and ethnic restaurants, and perhaps stumble across a gig or a club.

Sunday
Begin with a lazy brunch in one of **Jericho**'s taverns and cafés before tackling the wonder that is the **Ashmolean Museum**. Sample more history at **Oxford Castle Unlocked**, or opt for a country walk in the deer park of **Magdalen College** before sloping off to the *Half Moon* for their regular Sunday folk session.

office also offers excellent **guided walking tours**, including a two-hour gambol round the city centre and its colleges (several tours daily; £7) and specialist themed walks which vary week by week; the schedule is posted online. Further along Broad Street, the main Blackwell's bookshop (℡01865/792792) also runs specialist walking tours. Their main offering is a literary tour of Oxford (2 weekly; £7), but there are others running less frequently, such as their Inklings Tour – Inklings being the group of writers, Tolkien and C.S. Lewis included, who met regularly in Oxford in the 1930s. In all cases, advance booking is recommended. Other guided walks depart several times a day from Trinity College gates on Broad Street: placards onsite give details and booking isn't required.

Accommodation

With supply struggling to keep pace with demand, Oxford's central **hotels** can be expensive, though there are one or two inexpensive options. Generally, however, at the budget end of the market you're better off choosing a **guesthouse** or **B&B**, which are plentiful if usually some distance out. In the summer months (July–Sept) many colleges open their **student halls** to the public as B&Bs or self-catering apartments. The *Isis Guest House* (Ⓦwww.isisguesthouse.com) is a great example; check Ⓦwww .budgetstayuk.com and Ⓦwww.universityrooms.co.uk for others. Wherever you stay, **book ahead** – either direct or (for a £5 fee) through the tourist office.

Hotels

Bath Place 4 Bath Place ℡01865/791812, Ⓦwww .bathplace.co.uk. This unusual hotel comprises a handful of higgledy-piggledy medieval cottages around a tiny cobbled courtyard off Holywell Street. There are sixteen rooms, each individually decorated in attractive, antique style – canopied beds, exposed beams and so forth. The central location is excellent. Secure parking nearby (£10 per night). **④**

Eastgate 73 High St ℡01865/248332, Ⓦwww .mercure.com. Modern four-star Mercure chain hotel insinuated into a seventeenth-century ex-coaching inn. There's not much character left in the rooms, but this is still a reliable choice in a central location. **④**

Malmaison Oxford Castle, New Rd ℡01865/268400, Ⓦwww.malmaison.com. Classy and hugely atmospheric designer hotel occupying what was a Victorian prison. Rooms – which take up two or three cells, knocked through – are nothing short of glamorous, featuring contemporary bathrooms and high-tech gadgets, with bigger mezzanine suites in C wing. Book ahead for bargain rates. Parking £20 per night. **④**

Old Bank 91 High St ℡01865/799599, Ⓦwww .oldbank-hotel.co.uk. Great location for a slick and sleek hotel, a glistening conversion of an old bank. All forty-plus bedrooms are decorated in crisp, modern style – pastel shades and whites – and some have great views over All Souls College. **⑥**

Old Parsonage 1 Banbury Rd ℡01865/310210, Ⓦwww.oldparsonage-hotel.co.uk. Lovely hotel occupying a charming, wisteria-clad stone building by the church at the top of St Giles. The thirty-odd rooms are tastefully furnished in a bright modern manner, the only problem being some minor traffic noise. **⑥**

Randolph 1 Beaumont St ℡0844/879 9132, Ⓦwww.randolph-hotel.com. Oxford's most famous hotel, long the favoured choice of the well-heeled visitor, occupies a well-proportioned brick building with a distinctive neo-Gothic interior – the carpeted staircase is especially handsome. Now part of the Macdonald chain, but with impeccable service and well-appointed bedrooms. Top-floor rooms are quietest. **⑦**

Guesthouses and B&Bs

Acorn 260 Iffley Rd ℡01865/247998, Ⓦwww .oxford-acorn.co.uk. Huge Edwardian house a couple of miles southeast of the centre offering a friendly, efficient welcome and a well-kept interior. The fourteen guest rooms are fresh and pretty, all en suite (bar a single and small twin), with quiet ones overlooking the rear garden. Great value. **②–③**

Becket House 5 Becket St ℡01865/724675, Ⓦwww.beckethouse.co.uk. Modest but proficient bay-windowed guesthouse in a plain terrace close to the train station. Most rooms en suite. **②**

Browns Guest House 281 Iffley Rd ℡01865/246822, Ⓦwww.brownsguesthouse.co.uk. Well-maintained guesthouse in a pleasing Victorian property with fourteen rooms, mostly en suite. Just under two miles southeast of the centre. **③**

Buttery 11 Broad St ℡01865/811950, Ⓦwww .thebutteryhotel.co.uk. Slap-bang central

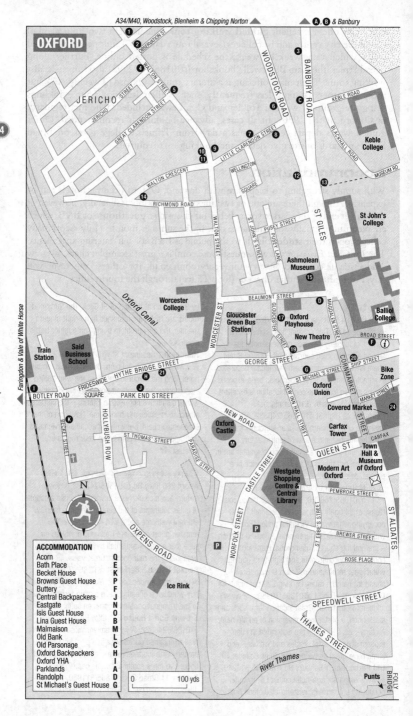

OXFORD

◀ Faringdon & Vale of White Horse

ACCOMMODATION

Acorn	Q
Bath Place	E
Becket House	K
Browns Guest House	P
Buttery	F
Central Backpackers	J
Eastgate	N
Isis Guest House	O
Lina Guest House	B
Malmaison	M
Old Bank	L
Old Parsonage	C
Oxford Backpackers	H
Oxford YHA	I
Parklands	A
Randolph	D
St Michael's Guest House	G

0   100 yds

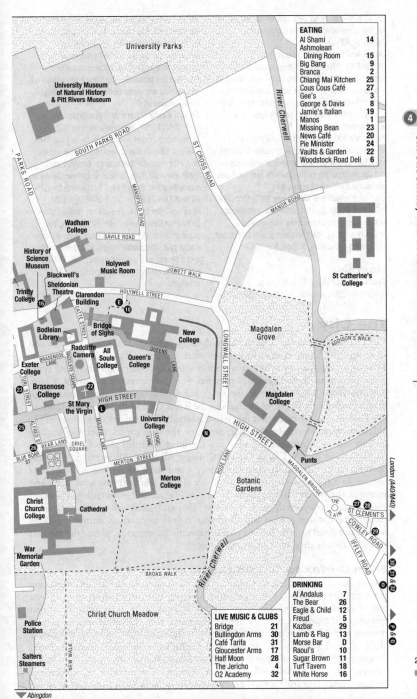

EATING

Al Shami	14
Ashmolean Dining Room	15
Big Bang	9
Branca	2
Chiang Mai Kitchen	25
Cous Cous Café	27
Gee's	3
George & Davis	8
Jamie's Italian	19
Manos	1
Missing Bean	23
News Café	20
Pie Minister	24
Vaults & Garden	22
Woodstock Road Deli	6

LIVE MUSIC & CLUBS

Bridge	21
Bullingdon Arms	30
Café Tarifa	31
Gloucester Arms	17
Half Moon	28
The Jericho	4
O2 Academy	32

DRINKING

Al Andalus	7
The Bear	26
Eagle & Child	12
Freud	5
Kazbar	29
Lamb & Flag	13
Morse Bar	D
Raoul's	10
Sugar Brown	11
Turf Tavern	18
White Horse	16

guesthouse-cum-hotel, with sixteen modest rooms (including one single), plainly but decently decorated. ③–④

Lina Guest House 308 Banbury Rd ☏01865/511070, ⓦwww.linaguesthouse.com. Spotless, well-maintained establishment occupying a Victorian house in Summertown, a short bus ride north of the centre. Completely renovated in 2009: all rooms are en suite and stylishly appointed. Great service. Free parking. ③

Parklands 100 Banbury Rd ☏01865/554374, ⓦwww.parklandsoxford.co.uk. Pleasant fourteen-room B&B in a large Victorian house with a garden and bar. North of the centre towards Summertown, but served by frequent buses. ④

🏃 **St Michael's Guest House** 26 St Michael's St ☏01865/242101. Often full, this friendly, well-kept B&B, in a cosy three-storey terrace house, has unsurprising furnishings and fittings but a charming city-centre location. A snip. ②

Hostels

Central Backpackers 13 Park End St ☏01865/242288, ⓦwww.centralbackpackers.co.uk.

Award-winning hostel, independently owned and operated, with fifty beds in 4-, 6-, 8- and 12-bed dorms (including female-only), 24hr access, a good range of facilities and a friendly can-do attitude. Located on a lively street midway between the train and bus stations: expect late-night noise from nearby bars and clubs. Beds £18–21 including breakfast and wi-fi.

Oxford Backpackers 9a Hythe Bridge St ☏01865/721761, ⓦwww.hostels.co.uk. Independent hostel with 120 beds in 4-, 8-, 10-, 14- and 18-bed dorms (including female-only) and 24hr access – but a touch scruffier and more make-do than its near-neighbour. Similarly handy location. Beds £14–17 including breakfast.

Oxford YHA 2a Botley Rd ☏0845/371 9131, ⓔoxford@yha.org.uk. In a clumpy modern block behind the train station, with 24hr access, this popular YHA hostel has 187 beds in 4- and 6-bed dorms plus nine double rooms, with good facilities and a decent café and restaurant. Beds £16–20 including breakfast (YHA non-members pay £3 supplement).

The City

The compact **centre** of Oxford is wedged in between the rivers Thames and Cherwell, just to the north of the point where they join. Most maps rename the Thames within the city as the "Isis", but few locals – other than university types – use the term. Central Oxford's principal point of reference is **Carfax**, a busy junction from where three of the city's main thoroughfares begin: the **High Street** runs east to Magdalen Bridge and the River Cherwell; **St Aldates** south to the Thames; and **Cornmarket** north to the broad avenue of St Giles. Many of the oldest **colleges** face onto the High Street or the side streets adjoining it, their mellow stonework combining to create the most beautiful part of Oxford; the most attractive of all is **Christ Church College**. All colleges have restricted public opening hours – generally afternoons only – and some of the more visited ones impose an admission charge. However it's always worth trying your luck and asking at the porter's lodge, invariably located beside the main college entrance: you may just be waved through regardless. That said, some colleges do not permit public access at any time – and all impose tighter restrictions during the exam season (late April to early June). For more specific information, phone the relevant college – details are given in the text below.

From Carfax to Oxford Castle

Always busy, the distinctive **Carfax** crossroads is overlooked by an interesting remnant of the medieval town, a chunky fourteenth-century **tower**, adorned by a pair of clocktower jacks dressed in vaguely Roman attire. The tower is all that remains of St Martin's Church, where legend asserts that William Shakespeare stood sponsor at the baptism of one of his friends' children. You can climb the **tower** (daily 10am–5.30pm, winter closes 3pm; £2.20) for wide views over the centre, though other vantage points – principally St Mary's (see p.276) – have the edge.

Spreading down St Aldates from Carfax, Oxford's **Town Hall** is an ostentatious Victorian confection that reflects a municipal determination not to be overwhelmed by the university. A staircase on its south side gives access to the fine **Museum of Oxford** (Mon–Wed 10am–5pm, Thurs–Sat 10am–10pm, Sun noon–5pm; free; ⓦ www.museumofoxford.org.uk) – often ignored, though it does a great job of telling the history of the city.

From the town hall, cross St Aldates and it's a few paces to Pembroke Street, where you'll find the outstanding **Modern Art Oxford** gallery (Tues–Sat 10am–5pm, Sun noon–5pm; free; ⓦ www.modernartoxford.org.uk), hosting an excellent programme of temporary exhibitions.

A five-minute stroll around (or through) the massive Westgate shopping centre and onto New Road leads to the remains of **Oxford Castle**, a classic medieval motte-and-bailey castle – the motte (mound) survives – which served as a prison right through to 1996. Now well restored, and taking in the *Malmaison* luxury hotel as well as restaurants and cafés, the complex includes **Oxford Castle Unlocked** (every 20min daily 10am–5pm; 40min; £7.75; ⓦ www.oxfordcastleunlocked.co.uk), offering memorable guided tours, during which costumed warders lead you up St George's Tower, dating from the Saxon era, down into the Romanesque crypt and through the old prison, telling tales of wars, executions and hauntings along the way.

Christ Church College and Cathedral

Fronting St Aldates south of Carfax is the main facade of **Christ Church College** (Mon–Sat 9am–5pm, Sun 2–5pm; £6; ⓣ 01865/276150, ⓦ www.chch .ox.ac.uk), whose distinctive Tom Tower was added by Christopher Wren in 1681 to house the weighty "Great Tom" bell. The tower lords it over the main entrance of what is Oxford's largest and most prestigious college, but visitors have to enter from the south, a signed five-minute walk away – through the tiny War Memorial Garden and alongside **Christ Church Meadow**. Popular with strollers, the Meadow fills in the tapering gap between the rivers Cherwell and Thames; if you decide to delay visiting Christ Church College, either head east along Broad Walk for the Cherwell or keep straight down tree-lined (and more appealing) New Walk for the Thames.

The college

Albert Einstein and no fewer than thirteen British prime ministers, including William Gladstone, were educated at Christ Church. The college also claims the distinction of having been founded three times, firstly by Cardinal Wolsey in 1525, then by Henry VIII after the cardinal's fall from favour and finally, after the Reformation – when the second college was suppressed – in 1545, when it assumed its present name.

Entering the college from the south, it's a short step to the striking **Tom Quad**, the largest quad in Oxford, so large in fact that the Royalists penned up their mobile larder of cattle here during the Civil War. Guarded by the Tom Tower, the Quad's soft, honey-coloured stone makes a harmonious whole, but it was actually built in two main phases: the southern side dates back to Wolsey, the north was finally finished in the 1660s. A wide stone staircase in the southeast corner of the Quad leads up to the **Dining Hall**, the grandest refectory in Oxford – famously featuring as Hogwarts' Great Hall in the *Harry Potter* films – with a fanciful hammer-beam roof and a set of stern portraits of past scholars by a roll-call of well-known artists, including Reynolds, Gainsborough and Millais. Charles I held court here when the Parliamentarians were in control of London, and Lewis Carroll, author of *Alice's Adventures in Wonderland* (who, under his real name Charles Dodgson, was a mathematics tutor at Christ Church), is commemorated with a portrait by the door – and with images of characters from his books set into the fifth stained-glass window on the left.

The cathedral

Just to the rear of the Tom Quad stands **Oxford Cathedral**, which is also – in a most unusual arrangement – Christ Church's college chapel. The Anglo-Saxons built a church on this site in the seventh century as part of St Frideswide Priory. The priory was suppressed in 1524, but the church survived, becoming a cathedral forty years later, though in between Wolsey knocked down the west end to make space for the Tom Quad. It's an unusually discordant church, with all sorts of bits and bobs from different periods, but it's fascinating all the same. The dominant feature is the sturdy circular columns and rounded arches of the Normans, but there are also early Gothic pointed arches, and the chancel ceiling is a particularly fine example of fifteenth-century stone vaulting. The battered **shrine of St Frideswide**, in the Latin Chapel – to the far left (northeast) of the entrance – was destroyed during the Dissolution, but the pieces were found down an old well and gamely assembled by the Victorians. Today, it exhibits some of the earliest natural foliage in English sculpture, a splendid filigree of leaves dating from around 1290. The shrine is overlooked by an equally rare two-storey stone-and-timber **watching loft**, from where custodians would keep a close eye on the tomb of the saint, and by a cluttered but deeply coloured stained-glass window by **Edward Burne-Jones**. The window, crammed with biblical bodies, was completed in 1858, long before Jones got into his Pre-Raphaelite stride, but there are three examples from his later period along the rest of the back of the chancel, with the **St Catherine Window**, in the right-hand corner of the church, being the finest.

To the Canterbury Quad

A passage at the northeast corner of the Tom Quad leads through to the **Peckwater Quad**, whose pleasantries are overwhelmed by the whopping Neoclassical library. A few paces more and you're in the pocket-sized **Canterbury Quad**, where the **Picture Gallery** (May–Sept Mon–Sat 10.30am–5pm, Sun 2–5pm; Oct–April Mon–Sat 10.30am–1pm & 2–4.30pm; £1.50 extra, or £3 for gallery only) is home to works by many of Italy's finest artists from the fifteenth to eighteenth centuries, including Leonardo da Vinci and Michelangelo. There's also a good showing by the Flemish and Dutch – Van Dyck, Frans Hals and so forth. The Canterbury Quad abuts **Oriel Square** with Merton College beckoning just beyond, or you can return to the college's south entrance for Christ Church Meadow (see p.271).

Merton College

Just a few yards from Christ Church, on Merton Street, stands **Merton College** (Mon–Fri 2–5pm, Sat & Sun 10am–4pm; £2; ☏01865/276310, ⓦwww.merton .ox.ac.uk), historically the city's most important college. Balliol and University colleges may have been founded earlier, but it was Merton – opened in 1264 – which set the model for colleges in both Oxford and Cambridge, being the first to gather its students and tutors together in one place. Furthermore, unlike the other two, Merton retains some of its original medieval buildings, with the best of the thirteenth-century architecture clustered around **Mob Quad**, a charming courtyard with mullioned windows and Gothic doorways to the right of the Front Quad. The quad's **Library** is of interest too, built in the 1370s and the first library in England to store books upright on shelves, rather than in piles. Much of the woodwork, including the panelling, screens and bookcases, dates from the Tudor period, but some fittings are original. From the Mob Quad, an archway leads through to the **Chapel**, which dates from 1290. The chapel has never had a nave, leaving the choir as the main body of the church and the transepts as ante-chapels. In the latter is the curious funerary plaque of **Thomas Bodley** – founder of Oxford's most important library (see p.275) – his bust surrounded by ungainly, boyish-looking women in classical garb. The windows of the choir were donated by the egocentric Henry de Mamesfeld, who appears as a kneeling figure no less than 24 times. Famous Merton alumni include T.S. Eliot, Angus Wilson, Louis MacNeice and Kris Kristofferson.

University and Queen's colleges

From Merton, narrow Magpie Lane cuts through to the west end of **University College** (no set opening times; ☏01865/276602, ⊛www.univ.ox.ac.uk), whose long sweeping facade and twin gateway towers spread along the High Street. Known as "Univ", the college claims Alfred the Great as its founder, but things really got going with a formal endowment in 1249, making it Oxford's oldest college – though nothing of that period survives. A year the college may prefer to forget is 1811, when it expelled **Percy Bysshe Shelley** for distributing a paper called *The Necessity of Atheism*. Guilt later induced the college to accept a memorial to the poet, who drowned in Italy in 1822: the white marble monument, showing the limp body of the poet borne by winged lions and mourned by the Muse of Poetry, occupies a shrine-like domed chamber in the northeast corner of the Front Quad. The college's most famous recent alumnus was Rhodes Scholar Bill Clinton; the former Australian premier Bob Hawke also studied here, as did Stephen Hawking, Clement Attlee and poet Andrew Motion.

Across the High Street from Univ stands **Queen's College** (no set opening times; ☏01865/279120, ⊛www.queens.ox.ac.uk), whose handsome Baroque buildings cut an impressive dash. Built between 1682 and 1765, Queen's benefited from the skills of several talented architects, most notably Nicholas Hawksmoor and Christopher Wren. Wren designed (or at least influenced the design of) the

On the river

Punting is a favourite summer pastime among both students and visitors, but handling a **punt** – a flat-bottomed boat ideal for the shallow waters of the Thames and Cherwell rivers – requires some practice. The punt is propelled and steered with a long pole, which beginners inevitably get stuck in riverbed mud: if this happens, let go of it and paddle back, otherwise you're likely to be pulled overboard. The Cherwell, though much narrower than the Thames and therefore trickier to navigate, provides more opportunities for pulling to the bank for a picnic, an essential part of the punting experience.

There are two central **boat rental** places: Magdalen Bridge boathouse (☏01865/202643, ⊛www.oxfordpunting.co.uk), beside the Cherwell at the east end of the High Street; and the Thames boat station at Folly Bridge (☏01865/243421), a ten-minute stroll south of the centre along St Aldates. Opening times vary: call for details, or try and arrive early (around 10am) to avoid the queues which build up on sunny summer afternoons. At both boathouses, expect to pay about £14 per hour plus a £30 deposit; ID is required. Punts can take a maximum of five people: four sitting and one punting. Both boathouses also rent out **chauffeured punts** (about £20 for 30min) and cheaper **pedaloes**. Alternatively, Salter's Steamers (☏01865/243421, ⊛www .salterssteamers.co.uk) runs **passenger boats** along the Thames from Oxford's Folly Bridge to Abingdon, about eight miles south, between late May and late September. There are two boats daily in each direction; the return trip takes four hours (£16.40).

The other boats most commonly seen on the Thames belong to the university's **rowing clubs**, which started up in the early nineteenth century. The first Oxford–Cambridge boat race – now staged in London – took place in 1829. Rowers mostly practise along the wide stretch of river south of Folly Bridge, which is also used for college races – the **Torpids**, held in February, and the more prestigious **Eights**, in May.

college's most diverting building, the **Chapel**, whose ceiling is filled with cherubs amid dense foliage.

Magdalen College and the University Botanic Gardens

Heading east along the High Street from Queen's, it's a short hop to **Magdalen College** (pronounced "Maud-lin"; daily: July–Sept noon–7pm; rest of year 1–6pm or dusk; £4.50; ℡01865/276000, ⓦwww.magd.ox.ac.uk), whose gaggle of stone buildings is overshadowed by its chunky medieval bell tower. Steer right from the entrance and you soon reach the **Chapel**, which has a handsome reredos, though you have to admire it through the windows of an ungainly stone screen. The adjacent **cloisters**, arguably the finest in Oxford, are adorned by standing figures, some biblical and others folkloric, most notably a tribe of grotesques. Magdalen also boasts better **grounds** than most other colleges, with a bridge – at the back of the cloisters – spanning the River Cherwell to join **Addison's Walk**, which you can follow along the river and around a water meadow; rare wild fritillaries flower here in spring, while deer roam here and in the adjacent meadow, depending on the season. Magdalen's alumni include Oscar Wilde, C.S. Lewis, John Betjeman, Julian Barnes and Ian Hislop.

Across the High Street from Magdalen lie the **University of Oxford Botanic Gardens** (daily 9am–6pm; March, April, Sept & Oct closes 5pm; Nov–Feb closes 4.30pm; £3.50, free on weekdays in winter; ⓦwww.botanic-garden.ox.ac.uk), whose greenery is bounded by a graceful curve of the Cherwell. First planted in 1621, the gardens comprise several different zones, from a lily pond, a bog garden and a rock garden through to borders of bearded irises and variegated plants. There are also six large **glasshouses** featuring tropical and desert species.

The gardens are next to **Magdalen Bridge**, where you can rent punts (see box, p.273).

New College and the Bridge of Sighs

Doubling back along the High Street, cut north up Queen's Lane and you'll dog-leg your way to **New College** (daily: Easter to early Oct 11am–5pm; rest of year 2–4pm; £2; ℡01865/279555, ⓦwww.new.ox.ac.uk). Founded in 1379, the college kicks off with an attractive **Front Quad**, though the splendid Perpendicular Gothic architecture of the original was spoiled by the addition of an extra storey in 1674. The adjoining **Chapel** can lay claim to being the finest in Oxford, not so much for its design as its contents. The ante-chapel contains some superb fourteenth-century stained glass and the west window – of 1778 – holds an intriguing (if somewhat unsuccessful) Nativity scene based on a design by Sir Joshua Reynolds. Beneath it stands the wonderful *Lazarus* by Jacob Epstein; Khrushchev, after a visit to the college, claimed that the memory of this haunting sculpture kept him awake at night. The entire east wall of the main chapel is occupied by a magnificent nineteenth-century stone reredos, consisting of about fifty canopied figures, mostly saints and apostles, with Christ Crucified as the centrepiece. An archway on the east side of the Front Quad leads through to the modest **Garden Quad**, with the thick flowerbeds of the **College Garden** beckoning beyond. The north side of the garden is flanked by the largest and best-preserved section of Oxford's medieval **city wall**, but the conspicuous earthen **mound** in the middle is a later decorative addition. Notable New College alumni include Tony Benn, John Fowles and Kate Beckinsale.

From the entrance to New College, it's the briefest of walks along the narrow lane to the **Bridge of Sighs**, an archway completed in 1914 to link two buildings of Hertford College which bears little resemblance to its Venetian namesake but nonetheless has an Italianate elegance. Walking beneath the bridge, and right on Catte Street, brings you to a crossroads at the eastern end of Broad Street.

The Sheldonian Theatre and the Clarendon Building

The east end of Broad Street abuts much of Oxford's most monumental architecture, beginning with the **Sheldonian Theatre** (Mon–Sat 10am–12.30pm & 2–4.30pm; Nov–Feb closes 3.30pm; £2.50; ⓦwww.sheldon.ox.ac.uk), ringed by a series of glum-looking, pop-eyed classical heads. The Sheldonian was Christopher Wren's first major work, a reworking of the Theatre of Marcellus in Rome, semicircular at the back and rectangular at the front. It was conceived in 1663, when the 31-year-old Wren's main job was as professor of astronomy. Designed as a stage for university ceremonies, nowadays it also functions as a concert hall, but the interior lacks any sense of drama.

Wren's colleague Nicholas Hawksmoor designed the **Clarendon Building**, a domineering, solidly symmetrical edifice topped by allegorical figures that is set at right angles to – and lies immediately east of – the Sheldonian. The Clarendon was erected to house the University Press, but is now part of the **Bodleian Library** – the UK's largest after the British Library in London – with an estimated eighty miles of shelves distributed among its several buildings. The heart of the Bodleian is located straight across from the Clarendon in the Old Schools Quadrangle.

The Bodleian Library

Occupied by the **Bodleian Library**, the beautifully proportioned **Old Schools Quadrangle** was built in the early seventeenth century in the ornate Jacobean-Gothic style that distinguishes many of the city's finest buildings. On the quad's east side is the handsome **Tower of the Five Orders**, which gives a lesson in architectural design, with tiers of columns built according to the five Classical styles – Tuscan, Doric, Ionic, Corinthian and Composite. On the west side is the library's main entrance and, although most of the complex is out of bounds to the general public, you should pop into the stunning **Divinity School** (Mon–Fri 9am–5pm, Sat 9am–4.30pm, Sun 11am–5pm; £1), one large room where, until the nineteenth century, degree candidates were questioned in detail about their subject by two interlocutors, with a professor acting as umpire. Begun in 1424, and sixty years in the making, the Divinity School is an exquisite example of late Gothic architecture, boasting an extravagant vaulted ceiling, a riot of pendants and decorative bosses. However, this elaborate design was never carried right through – funding was a constant problem – and parts of the school were finished off in a much plainer style with the change being especially pronounced on the south wall.

You can also sign up for a forty-minute **guided tour** (Mon–Fri 10.30am, 11.30am, 2pm & 3pm, Sat 11.30am, 2pm & 3pm; £6.50) of the Bodleian, which includes visits to **Convocation House**, adjacent to the Divinity School, and **Duke Humfrey's Library**, immediately above. The former is a sombre wood-panelled chamber graced by a fancy fan-vaulted ceiling, completed in 1759 but designed to look much older. The latter is distinguished by its painted beams and carved corbels, dating from the fifteenth century, but restored and remodelled by Thomas Bodley over a century later.

The Radcliffe Camera

Behind the Bodleian rises Oxford's most imposing – or vainglorious – building, the **Radcliffe Camera**, accessible to the public only on the Bodleian's bookable "extended tours" (Sun 11.15am plus some Sat; £13; 90min). This mighty rotunda, built between 1737 and 1748 by James Gibbs, architect of London's St Martin-in-the-Fields church, displays no false modesty. Dr John Radcliffe was,

4

according to a contemporary diarist, "very ambitious of glory" and when he died in 1714 he bequeathed a mountain of money for the construction of a library – the "Radcliffe Mausoleum" as one wag termed it. Gibbs was one of the few British architects of the period to have been trained in Rome and his library was thoroughly Italian in style, its limestone columns ascending to a delicate balustrade, decorated with pin-prick urns and encircling a lead-sheathed dome. For a less overpowering perspective, climb the tower of the church of St Mary the Virgin (see below) to the rear of the rotunda – from where there's also a charming view of All Souls College (see below).

St Mary the Virgin and All Souls College

Flanking the High Street just behind the Radcliffe Camera, **St Mary the Virgin** (daily 9am–5pm; free) is a hotchpotch of architectural styles, but mostly dates from the fifteenth century. The church's saving graces are its elaborate, thirteenth-century pinnacled spire and its distinctive Baroque **porch**, flanked by chunky corkscrewed pillars. The interior is disappointingly mundane, though the carved poppy-heads on the choir stalls are of some historical interest: the tips were brusquely flattened off when a platform was installed here in 1554 to stage the heresy trial of Cranmer, Latimer and Ridley, leading Protestants who had run foul of Queen Mary. In a desperate bid to avoid being burned at the stake, **Cranmer** (1489–1556) had previously confessed to heresy and at his public trial he was expected to repeat his recantation. Instead, he rounded on his accusers and confirmed his Protestant faith, an action which stunned Mary and gave new heart to her religious opponents. The church's other diversion is the **tower** (same times; £3), with wonderful views across to the Radcliffe Camera (see p.275) and east over **All Souls College** (Mon–Fri 2–4pm; free; ℡01865/279379, ⓦwww.all-souls .ox.ac.uk), with its twin mock-Gothic towers (the work of Hawksmoor) and conspicuous, brightly decorated sundial designed by Wren.

History of Science Museum, Trinity and Balliol

Back on Broad Street, the classical heads that shield the Sheldonian (see p.275) continue along the front of the **History of Science Museum** (Tues–Fri noon–5pm, Sat 10am–5pm, Sun 2–5pm; free; ⓦwww.mhs.ox.ac.uk), whose two floors display an amazing clutter of antique microscopes and astrolabes, sundials, quadrants and sextants. More obscure items include a thirteenth-century geared calendar and an "equatorium" for finding the position of the planets. The highlights are Elizabeth I's own astrolabe and Einstein's blackboard.

Across the street, **Trinity College** (no set opening times; free; ℡01865/279900, ⓦwww.trinity.ox.ac.uk) is fronted by three dinky lodge-cottages. Behind them the manicured lawn of the Front Quad stretches back to the richly decorated **Chapel**, awash with Baroque stuccowork. Its high altar is flanked by an exquisite example of

Oxford Covered Market

For refreshment on the hoof – as well as a fascinating glimpse into the everyday life of Oxford away from all the pomp and history of the colleges – drop into the **Covered Market** (Mon–Sat 9am–5.30pm, Sun 10am–4pm), wedged between Market Street, Turl Street and the High Street. Opened in 1774, it remains full of atmosphere, home to butchers, bakers, fishmongers, greengrocers and cheese sellers as well as a welter of excellent cafés, patisseries and even some clothes boutiques and shoeshops. Whatever you do, don't miss the *Ben's Cookies* stall, where sensational cookies are baked continuously throughout the day and sold by weight.

the work of Grinling Gibbons – a distinctive performance, with cherubs' heads peering out from delicate foliage. Behind the chapel stands **Durham Quad**, an attractive ensemble of old stone buildings begun at the end of the seventeenth century. Trinity alumni include explorer Richard Burton and playwright Terence Rattigan.

Next door, **Balliol College** (no set opening times; free; ☎01865/277777, ⓦwww.balliol.ox.ac.uk), founded in 1260, is Trinity's arch-rival, the collegiate antipathy ritualized in the tradition of Gordouli, when Balliol students chant abuse at their adversaries across the wall, usually at unsociable hours of the night. Despite its antiquity, Balliol has little to offer architecturally: remodelled and rebuilt in the nineteenth century, it now presents an unexceptional assembly of buildings, haphazardly gathered around two quads. Among many notable alumni are Adam Smith, Hilaire Belloc, Graham Greene and Aldous Huxley, plus a raft of politicians, including Harold Macmillan, Edward Heath, Denis Healey and Boris Johnson.

Exeter College to the Oxford Union

From the south side of Broad Street, take Turl Street and you'll soon reach – on the left – the entrance to **Exeter College** (daily 2–5pm; free; ☎01865/279600, ⓦwww.exeter.ox.ac.uk), another medieval foundation whose original buildings were chopped about in the nineteenth century. On this occasion, however, the Victorians did create something of interest in the elaborate neo-Gothic **Chapel**, whose intricate, almost fussy detail was conceived by Gilbert Scott in the 1850s. The chapel contains a fine set of stained-glass windows illustrating scores of biblical stories – St Paul on the road to Damascus and Samson bringing down the pillars of the Philistine temple for example – but their deep colours put the nave in permanent shade. The chapel also holds a superb **Pre-Raphaelite** tapestry, the *Adoration of the Magi*, a fine collaboration between William Morris and Edward Burne-Jones. Morris and Burne-Jones were both students here, as were J.R.R. Tolkien and Alan Bennett.

Broad Street leads into the **Cornmarket**, a busy, pedestrianized shopping strip lined by major stores. There's precious little here to fire the imagination, but St Michael's Street – the first turning on the right – is a pleasant residential street and the location of the **Oxford Union** (no public access), the university debating society, where scores of budding British politicians have flexed their oratorical muscles.

The Ashmolean

Occupying a mammoth Neoclassical building on the corner of Beaumont Street and St Giles, the **Ashmolean** (Tues–Sun 10am–6pm; free; ⓦwww.ashmolean .org) is the university's principal museum. It grew from the collections of the magpie-like **John Tradescant**, gardener to Charles I, who bequeathed a huge assortment of artefacts and natural specimens to his friend and sponsor, the lawyer Elias Ashmole, who in turn gave it to the university. Today the Ashmolean possesses a vast and far-reaching collection, showcased to superb effect in bright, uncluttered contemporary galleries.

The **Egyptian** rooms are not to be missed, featuring unusual frescoes, rare textiles from the Roman and Byzantine periods and several fine examples of relief carving, such as those on the Taharqa shrine. Look out, too, for superb Islamic ceramics, before moving onto the **Chinese art** section, which boasts some remarkable early Chinese pottery. The archeologist Arthur Evans gifted the museum a stunning collection of **Minoan** finds from his years working at Knossos in Crete (1900–06): pride of place goes to the storage jars, sumptuously decorated with sea creatures and marine plants. A further highlight is the **Alfred Jewel**, a tiny gold, enamel and rock crystal piece of uncertain purpose. The inscription translates as "Alfred ordered me to be made" – almost certainly a reference to King Alfred the Great.

The museum is also strong on **European art**. Among the **Italian** works, watch out for Piero di Cosimo's *Forest Fire* and Paolo Uccello's *Hunt in the Forest*. **French paintings** make a strong showing too, with works by Pissarro, Monet, Manet and Renoir hanging alongside Cézanne and Bonnard, and there's also a selection of eighteenth- and nineteenth-century **British artists**, including lashings of Pre-Raphaelite stuff by Rossetti, Holman Hunt and others.

Finally, don't miss the basement displays – **Powhatan's mantle**, a handsome deerskin wall-hanging which belonged to the father of Pocahontas, alongside Guy Fawkes' lantern, Oliver Cromwell's death mask and Elizabeth I's gloves.

The Natural History and Pitt-Rivers museums

From the Ashmolean, it's a brief walk north up St Giles to the *Lamb & Flag* pub, beside which an alley cuts through to the **University Museum of Natural History** (daily 10am–5pm; free; Ⓦwww.oum.ox.ac.uk) on Parks Road. The building, constructed under the guidance of John Ruskin, looks like a cross between a railway station and a church – and the same applies inside, where a High Victorian-Gothic fusion of cast iron and glass features soaring columns and capitals decorated with animal and plant motifs. Exhibits include some impressive dinosaur skeletons, though the museum's natural history displays are outdone by the **Pitt-Rivers Museum** (Mon noon–4.30pm, Tues–Sun 10am–4.30pm; free; Ⓦwww.prm.ox.ac.uk), reached through a door at the far end. Founded in 1884 from the bequest of grenadier guard turned archeologist Augustus Henry Lane-Fox Pitt-Rivers, this is one of the world's finest ethnographic museums and an extraordinary relic of the Victorian Age, arranged like an exotic junk shop with each bulging cabinet labelled meticulously by hand. The exhibits, brought to England by several explorers, Captain Cook among them, range from totem poles and mummified crocodiles to African fetishes and gruesome shrunken heads.

Eating and drinking

With so many students and tourists to cater for, Oxford has a wide choice of places to eat and drink. You'll have no difficulty finding somewhere congenial and affordable for a midday bite – we've listed some of the better **cafés** and delis below, but there are lots more. Oxford's **restaurant** scene has skyrocketed recently: for the best choice, avoid the city centre and instead stroll either northwest to the characterful district of **Jericho**, where Walton Street and Little Clarendon Street offer a string of pleasant places to eat, or southeast to the **Cowley Road**, which buzzes with after-work lounge bars and ethnic restaurants of all kinds. Below we also pick out a selection of **pubs** and **bars**, notable for their beer and/or their atmosphere.

Cafés

George & Davis 55 Little Clarendon St. Great little café offering everything from (delicious) ice cream to bagels and full breakfasts. The cow mural is good fun too. Also try "brother" establishments *George & Danver* (94 St Aldates, near Carfax) and *George & Delila* (104 Cowley Rd). Daily till midnight.

Missing Bean 14 Turl St. Conversation swirls and great coffee goes down at this fine, friendly spot with plate-glass windows looking out onto pleasant old Turl Street.

News Café 1 Ship St. Breakfasts, bagels and daily specials, plus beer and wine, are served in this brisk and efficient café. Plenty of local and international newspapers are on hand too. Daily till 10pm.

Vaults & Garden Radcliffe Square. In an atmospheric stone-vaulted room attached to the church of St Mary the Virgin, this café serves up good-quality organic, locally sourced wholefood, as well as coffee and cake. A small outside area gazes up at the Radcliffe Camera. Cash only.

Woodstock Road Deli 15 Woodstock Rd. A stroll along St Giles lies this fabulous little locals' deli and café, with a range of veggie and vegan salads and mains – all organic, prepared daily.

Restaurants

Al Shami 25 Walton Crescent ℡ 01865/310066. Splendid Lebanese restaurant on a Jericho backstreet – coincidentally, opposite Oxford's synagogue – serving authentic meze, grills and kebabs to a knowledgeable local clientele. Plenty for veggies. Meze £2–3, mains £6–8.

Ashmolean Dining Room Ashmolean Museum, Beaumont St ℡ 01865/553823. Contemporary, open-plan restaurant occupying a stunning space on the museum's rooftop level, with an outside terrace. Cuisine is international, from chorizo, crêpes and squid to lamb and sea bream, alongside a range of cheeses and charcuterie. Mains £11–17. Has its own opening hours, independent of the museum: Tues–Sat 10am–10pm, Sun 10am–6pm.

Big Bang 124 Walton St ℡ 01865/511441. Friendly little independent Jericho restaurant serving bangers and mash to die for, gourmet Cumberland sausages, wild venison sausages and more (including veggie options). The style is eclectic: menus are pasted into antiquarian cloth-bound novels, the shabby-chic furniture is mix-and-match, and there's live jazz in the cellar. Book for a table in their lovely upstairs room.

Branca 111 Walton St ℡ 01865/556111. Large and informal brasserie-restaurant in proto-industrial premises offering a wide-ranging menu, though Italian dishes predominate. Excellent daily specials – and a weekday lunch from £7 including wine.

Chiang Mai Kitchen 130a High St ℡ 01865/202233. Oxford's best Thai restaurant, a smart little place in a seventeenth-century timber-framed house off the High Street. Serves all the classics – and then some – and it's particularly strong on vegetarian dishes. Mains around £8.

Cous Cous Café 19 St Clement's ℡ 01865/722350. Cheery little Moroccan deli and casual restaurant serving delicious, authentic, low-priced nosh – lentil soup, hummus, salads, lamb tagine, baklava, mint tea – in a relaxed Moorish-style setting. Mains roughly £3–7. Closes Mon–Sat 8pm, Sun 6pm.

Gee's 61 Banbury Rd ℡ 01865/553540. Well-established restaurant set in a chic conservatory, where the inventive menu includes such items as chargrilled vegetables with polenta, roasted beetroot, a variety of steaks and a wide choice of breads. Strong on fish, too, with seafood main courses for around £16. Book ahead. Live jazz on Sun eve.

Jamie's Italian 24 George St ℡ 01865/838383. Flagship Italian restaurant under the Jamie Oliver banner – always busy, featuring a laid-back interior of exposed bricks, graffitied walls and hams hanging above the salad station. Food is exquisite, with a

trademark informality: mixed antipasti arrive on a plank of wood, the pasta menu takes in "beautiful bucatini" and old-school spaghetti bolognese, while mains include "flash steak" and "lamb chop lollipops". Mains £10–15. Book well ahead.

Manos 105 Walton St ℡ 01865/311782. Family-run Greek deli and restaurant on a sunny Jericho corner, offering budget meals of salads and wraps alongside delicious Mediterranean mains and, of course, coffee and pastries. Mon–Wed 9.30am–9pm, Thurs–Sat 9.30am–10pm, Sun 11.30am–8pm. Also hosts beer and whisky tastings from one of Oxford's artisan brewers – see ⓦ www.compassbrewery.com for dates.

Pie Minister Covered Market ℡ 01865/241613. Your nose will lead you to this fantastic pie shop and sit-down restaurant inside the Covered Market. The wide choice includes porky pie (outdoor-reared pork and apple), moo pie (beef and ale), Heidi pie (goat's cheese, sweet potato and spinach), and so on, all accompanied by creamy mashed potato, gravy and minty peas for around £5–6. Unmissable. Open daily, daytimes only.

Pubs

The Bear 6 Alfred St. Tucked away down a narrow side-street in the centre of town, this popular pub (the oldest in Oxford, founded more than 800 years ago) has not been themed up – and a good job too. Offers a wide range of beers amid and among its traditional decor.

Eagle & Child 49 St Giles. Dubbed the "Bird & Baby", this was once the haunt of J.R.R. Tolkien and C.S. Lewis. The beer is still good and the old wood-panelled rooms at the front are great, but the pub is no longer independently owned – and feels it. The food (and atmosphere) are corporate, and the modern rear extension is a travesty. Pop over the road to the *Lamb & Flag* to compare.

Lamb & Flag 12 St Giles. Generations of university types have relished this quiet old tavern, which comes complete with low-beamed ceilings and a series of cramped but cosy rooms in which to enjoy hand-drawn ale and genuine pork scratchings. Cash only.

Turf Tavern Bath Place, off Holywell St. Small, atmospheric medieval pub, reached via narrow passageways off Holywell St or New College Lane, with a fine range of beers, and mulled wine in winter. Abundant seating outside. Typical pub grub on offer includes Sunday roast from £8.

White Horse 52 Broad St. A tiny, old pub beside Blackwell's bookshop in the town centre with snug rooms, pictures of old university sports teams on the walls, real ales and good food.

Bars

Al Andalus 10 Little Clarendon St. Congenial tapas bar with a good selection of Spanish wines, great tapas (around £5), cosy decor and live flamenco. Daily noon till late.

Freud 119 Walton St. Occupying a nineteenth-century former church in Classical style, this fashionable café-bar is an upmarket spot for cocktails and chitchat, along with good Italian/Mediterranean food (mains from £6). Live music some nights too.

Kazbar 27 Cowley Rd. Atmospheric lounge bar-cum-restaurant in a hippyish/Moorish style – adobe, incense, lanterns, bar stools in cracked tan leather and bartenders in embroidered jackets. Food and cocktails are great, and there's always a buzz. Mon–Fri 4pm till late, Sat & Sun noon till late. Near here, bar-hop your way to the similarly alluring *Café Tarifa* (see below).

Morse Bar *Randolph Hotel*, Beaumont St. Traditional hotel bar – roaring fire, club armchairs, wood panelling – which featured so often in *Inspector Morse* that the hotel renamed it to match. Specializes in whisky and champagne cocktails.

Raoul's 32 Walton St. Award-winning Jericho cocktail bar, with a retro 70s theme, great tunes and a devoted clientele who know (and love) their drinks. Daily 4pm till late.

Sugar Brown 30 Walton St. Funky neighbour to *Raoul's* which manages to hold its own, with cocktails (including an original 1931 mojito), comfy sofas and decent bar food. Mon–Thurs 4pm till late, Fri–Sun 11am till late.

Entertainment and nightlife

Oxford's buzzing **live music** scene spawned – among others – Radiohead and Supergrass, and continues to unearth new discoveries at a clutch of venues around town. Devotees of **classical music** are also well catered for, with halls and some college chapels – primarily Christ Church and Merton – offering concerts and recitals. Live **theatre** is another option, with high-quality productions supplemented by more casual open-air Shakespeare in summer. For **listings**, consult *In Oxford*, available free from the tourist office, or check ⓦ www.dailyinfo.co.uk.

Live music & clubs

Bridge 6 Hythe Bridge St ⓦ www.bridgeoxford.co .uk. Popular bar and club with smooth DJing on three floors. Open 10pm till late (student nights Mon–Thurs). Closed Sun.

Bullingdon Arms 162 Cowley Rd. Lively pub and venue that is famous for its long-running Monday night blues sessions, as well as regular gigs and comedy nights.

Café Tarifa 56 Cowley Rd. Atmospheric lounge bar in Moorish/Arabian style, with cocktails and cushions, which also hosts a variety of generally chilled live music and DJ nights.

Gloucester Arms Friars Entry. Grungy back-alley pub off Gloucester Green showcasing rock and punk acts in a suitably downbeat setting.

Half Moon 18 St Clements ⓦ www.halfmoonoxford .com. Legendary pub that hosts live folk every Sunday, in among a regular timetable of jazz, blues and DJing.

The Jericho 56 Walton St ⓦ www.thejericho.co .uk. Much-loved Jericho tavern which doubles up as a leading indie venue.

O2 Academy 190 Cowley Rd ⓦ www.o2academy oxford.co.uk. Oxford's biggest indie, mainstream and dance venue, with a good programme of live bands and guest DJs.

Classical music & theatre

Creation Theatre ⓦ www.creationtheatre.co.uk. Unattached troupe, best known for its summer season of Shakespeare at unusual venues around town – Headington Hill Park, the roof of the Said Business School, on the factory floor of BMW's Mini production plant, and so on.

Holywell Music Room 32 Holywell St ⓦ www .musicatoxford.com. This small, plain, Georgian building was opened in 1748 as the first public music hall in England. It offers a varied programme, from straight classical to experimental, with occasional bouts of jazz. Sunday morning "coffee concerts" (ⓦ www.coffeeconcerts.com) run year-round.

New Theatre George St ⓣ 01865/320760, ⓦ www.newtheatreoxford.org.uk. Popular – and populist – programme of theatre, dance, pop music, musicals and opera.

Oxford Playhouse 11 Beaumont St ⓣ 01865/305305, ⓦ www.oxfordplayhouse.com. Touring companies perform a mixture of plays, opera and concerts at the city's leading theatre.

Sheldonian Theatre Broad St ⓣ 01865/277299, ⓦ www.sheldon.ox.ac.uk. This seventeenth-century edifice is Oxford's top concert hall, despite rather dodgy acoustics, with the Oxford Philomusica (ⓦ www.oxfordphil.com) in residence.

Listings

Bike rental Bike Zone, 6 Lincoln House, Market St, off Cornmarket (℡01865/728877, Ⓦwww .bikezoneoxford.co.uk).

Bookshops The leading university bookshop is Blackwell's (Ⓦwww.blackwell.co.uk), with several outlets including the main shop at 48–51 Broad St (℡01865/792792).

Buses Most local buses, including park-and-ride, are operated by the Oxford Bus Company (℡01865/785400, Ⓦwww.oxfordbus.co.uk), which also offers fast and frequent services to central

London, as well as Heathrow and Gatwick airports. Most other services – including competing buses to London – are in the hands of Stagecoach (℡01865/772250, Ⓦwww.stagecoachbus.com).

Hospital John Radcliffe Hospital, Headley Way ℡01865/741166.

Police St Aldates, near Carfax ℡01865/841148.

Post office 102 St Aldates, near Carfax.

Taxis There are taxi ranks throughout the city centre, as well as at the train station. Radio Taxis is on ℡01865/242424.

Around Oxford

As a base for exploring some of the more delightful parts of central England, Oxford is hard to beat. It's a short trip west into the Cotswolds (see p.282), south to the Vale of White Horse (p.300), east to Buckingham (p.305) or north to Stratford-upon-Avon (p.489). Nearer still – a brief bus ride away – is the charming little town of **Woodstock** and its imperious neighbour, **Blenheim Palace**, birthplace of Winston Churchill.

Woodstock

WOODSTOCK, eight miles northwest of Oxford, has royal associations going back to Saxon times, with a string of kings attracted by its excellent hunting. Henry I built a royal lodge here and his successor, Henry II, enlarged it to create a grand manor house-cum-palace, where the Black Prince was born in 1330. The Royalists used Woodstock as a base during the Civil War, but, after their defeat, Cromwell never got round to destroying either the town or the palace: the latter was ultimately given to (and flattened by) the Duke of Marlborough in 1704 when work started on Blenheim Palace of today. Long dependent on royal and then ducal patronage, Woodstock is now both a well-heeled commuter town for Oxford and a provider of food, drink and beds for visitors to Blenheim. It is also an extremely pretty little place, its handsome stone buildings gathered around the main square, at the junction of Market and High streets. This is also where you'll find the town's one specific sight, the **Oxfordshire Museum** (Tues–Sat 10am–5pm, Sun 2–5pm; free), a well-composed review of the county's archeology, social history and industry.

The museum shares its premises with the town's **tourist office** (Mon–Sat 10am–5pm; ℡01993/813276, Ⓦwww.oxfordshirecotswolds.org), which has a useful range of information on the Cotswolds. Part of the Macdonald **hotel** chain, the *Bear* (℡0870/400 8202, Ⓦwww.bearhotelwoodstock.co.uk; ❹) – an old coaching inn across from the museum – has fifty or so luxurious rooms kitted out in an attractive, country-house style. Its bar, with low-beamed ceilings and an open fire, is the most atmospheric of Woodstock's several good **pubs**. Just as enticing is the nearby *King's Arms*, 19 Market St (℡01993/813636, Ⓦwww.kings -hotel-woodstock.co.uk; ❺), with fifteen chic, pastel-painted rooms, and a great **restaurant**, with main courses starting at about £11.

Stagecoach **bus** #20 leaves Oxford bus station for Woodstock every thirty minutes or so; some continue to Chipping Norton in the Cotswolds (see p.288).

Blenheim Palace

Nowadays, successful British commanders get medals and titles, but in 1704, as a thank-you for his victory over the French at the Battle of Blenheim (in Bavaria),

Queen Anne gave **John Churchill**, Duke of Marlborough (1650–1722), the royal estate of Woodstock, along with the promise of enough cash to build himself a palace. Marlborough was a brilliant general, but the gift had more to do with Anne's fear of Louis XIV – and the relief she felt after the battle – than a recognition of his genius, as events were to prove.

Work started promptly on **Blenheim Palace** (mid-Feb to Oct daily 10.30am–5.30pm, last admission 4.45pm; Nov to mid-Dec Wed–Sun same times; £18 including parking; ⓦ www.blenheimpalace.com) with the principal architect being Sir John Vanbrugh, who was also responsible for Castle Howard in Yorkshire (see p.742). However, Marlborough's formidable wife, Sarah Jennings, who had wanted Christopher Wren as architect, was soon at loggerheads with Vanbrugh, while Queen Anne had second thoughts, stifling the flow of money. Construction work was halted and the house was finished only after the duke's death at the instigation of his widow, who ended up paying most of the bills and designing much of the interior herself. The end result is England's grandest example of Baroque civic architecture, an Italianate palace of finely worked yellow stone.

The **interior** of the main house is stuffed with paintings and tapestries, plus all manner of objets d'art, including furniture from Versailles. Marlborough's martial skills are celebrated with assorted murals in the Great Hall, though you may find more of interest in the **Churchill Exhibition** – Winston was born at Blenheim in 1874 and the displays provide a brief introduction, accompanied by recordings of some of his speeches. Churchill died in 1965 and was buried alongside his wife in the graveyard of Bladon church just outside the estate.

Blenheim's formal **gardens** (same hours & ticket; park and gardens only £10.30 including parking) have several distinct areas, including a rose garden and an arboretum, though the open **park** (daily 9am–5.30pm or dusk, last admission 45min before closing) is more enticing, leading from the front of the house down to an artificial lake, **Queen Pool**. Vanbrugh's splendid Grand Bridge crosses the lake to the hill-top **Column of Victory**, topped by a heroic statue of Marlborough. It's said that Capability Brown, who landscaped the park, laid out the trees and avenues to represent the Blenheim battlefield.

There are two **entrances** to Blenheim, one just south of Woodstock on the Oxford road and another through the Triumphal Arch at the end of Park Street in Woodstock village. Stagecoach **bus #S3** runs to Blenheim Palace from Oxford's bus station every thirty minutes.

The Cotswolds

The limestone hills that make up the **Cotswolds** are preposterously photogenic, dotted with a string of picture-book villages built by wealthy cloth merchants. **Wool** had been important here for centuries, but the greatest fortunes were made between the fourteenth and sixteenth centuries, off the back (literally) of the local breed of sheep, nicknamed the Cotswold Lion, which grazed on the Cotswolds' fields of rich limestone grasses. By the thirteenth century it had become England's biggest breed, producing heavy fleeces that were exported to the Flemish weaving towns. The income from this lucrative trade, initially controlled by the clergy but later by a handful of wealthy merchants, financed the construction of many of the region's fine manors and churches. Largely bypassed by the Industrial Revolution, which heralded the area's commercial decline, the Cotswolds has held on to much of its medieval architecture. Numerous **churches** are decorated with beautiful carving, for which the local limestone was ideal: soft and easy to carve when first

Angel, Burford Splendid Cotswold gastropub with a creative, innovative approach that blends a wide range of styles and flavours. See p.284.

Kingham Plough, Kingham Outstanding rural gastropub, using locally sourced ingredients and state-of-the-art methods to encapsulate the best of the region's flavours. See p.289.

Falkland Arms, Great Tew The food is not in the same class as others in this list, but the atmosphere of this wonderful old pub more than makes up. See p.290.

Eight Bells, Chipping Campden Fine traditional inn on the edge of one of the Cotswolds' most beautiful villages, serving posh pub grub to remember. See p.291.

White Hart, Winchcombe Classy, upmarket inn serving classic British fare (with an emphasis on sausages) alongside fine wines. See p.292.

quarried, but hardening after long exposure to the sunlight. The use of this **local stone** is a strong unifying characteristic across the region, though its colour modulates as subtly as the shape of the hills, ranging from a deep golden tone in the north to a silvery grey further south.

The consequence is that the Cotswolds have become one of the country's main tourist attractions, with many towns afflicted by plagues of coaches, tearooms and souvenir shops. To see the Cotswolds at their best, avoid the most popular towns and aim instead for the smaller villages and the countryside: while tourist honeypots like **Stow-on-the-Wold** and **Bourton-on-the-Water** can be packed with visitors, even in high season the charms of towns like **Chipping Campden**, **Winchcombe** and **Northleach** remain evident. This might be a tamed landscape, but there's good scope for **walking**, either in the gentler valleys that are most typical of the Cotswolds or along the escarpment that marks the boundary with the Severn Valley. A national trail, the **Cotswold Way**, runs along the top of the ridge, stretching about one hundred miles from Chipping Campden past Cheltenham, Gloucester and Stroud as far as Bath. A number of prehistoric sites provide added interest along the route, with some – such as **Belas Knap** near Winchcombe – being well worth a diversion.

Main-line **trains** from London Paddington and Oxford to Worcester/Hereford stop at half a dozen of the region's villages – notably **Kingham**, from where buses shuttle to Chipping Norton, and **Moreton-in-Marsh**, with buses to Stow-on-the-Wold or Chipping Campden. Otherwise, the **bus** network does a reasonable job connecting the larger towns and villages, though service is poor on Sundays.

Burford

Twenty miles west of Oxford you get your first real taste of the Cotswolds at **BURFORD**, where the long and wide **High Street**, which slopes down to a bridge over the River Windrush, is magnificent – despite the traffic. The street is flanked by a remarkably homogeneous line of old buildings that exhibit almost every type of peccadillo known to the Cotswolds, from wonky mullioned windows and half-timbered facades with bendy beams through to spiky brick chimneys, fancy bow-fronted stone houses, and grand horse-and-carriage gateways.

What's more, Burford also possesses the fascinating **church of St John the Baptist**, by the river and down a lane off the High Street. Of all the Cotswold churches, this has the most historical resonance, with architectural bits and pieces surviving from every phase of its construction, beginning with the Normans and ending in the wool boom of the seventeenth century. Most unusually, its clutter of mausoleums, chapels and chantries survived the Reformation. The most impressive **mausoleum** is that of Lawrence Tanfield, James I's Chancellor of the Exchequer, who lies on his canopied table-tomb with his wife, both decked out in their Jacobean finery. Even more striking, however, is the funerary plaque of Edmund Harman, Henry VIII's barber and surgeon, stuck to the wall of the nave and sporting four Amazonian figures, the first representation of Native Americans in Britain. It is unlikely that Harman met any, but rather he seems to have been linked to a Spanish company trading with South America. The **churchyard** is strewn with so-called "bale tombs", whose rounded tops symbolize wool. A modern plaque just to the left of the entrance pays tribute to three **Levellers**, loyal members of Cromwell's New Model Army who believed all men possessed equal rights under the law – yet who were shot in the churchyard on Cromwell's orders in May 1649. The drama is commemorated annually with a day of festivities (ⓦwww.levellers.org.uk).

A beautiful **footpath** heads east along the River Windrush through **Widford**, a hamlet with an idyllic medieval chapel built in the middle of a field on the site of a Roman villa, and on to **Swinbrook**, just under three miles from Burford. Here, the church of St Mary holds a monument showing six members of the Fettiplace family reclining comically on their elbows: the Tudor effigies rigid and stony-faced, their Stuart counterparts stylish and rather camp.

Practicalities

Buses to Burford pull in along the High Street. One of the most useful services is the three times daily – once on Sundays – Swanbrook bus (ⓣ01452/712386, ⓦwww.swanbrook.co.uk) from Oxford to Gloucester via Burford, Northleach and Cheltenham. The **tourist office** is located just off the High Street on Sheep Street (March–Oct Mon–Sat 9.30am–5.30pm; Nov–Feb Mon–Sat 9.30am–4pm; ⓣ01993/823558, ⓦwww.oxfordshirecotswolds.org).

Burford has two first-class **hotels**. The *Bay Tree*, on Sheep Street (ⓣ01993/822791, ⓦwww.cotswold-inns-hotels.co.uk; ⓞ), occupies a wisteria-clad stone house dating from the seventeenth century. It has twenty-odd rooms – both in the main house and in a couple of annexes – though the period styling can get a bit overwhelming at times. The *Lamb Inn*, just along Sheep Street (ⓣ01993/823155, ⓦwww.cotswold-inns-hotels.co.uk; ⓞ), is another great choice, a tad more traditional than its neighbour from the bar's flagstoned floor up. Alternatively head for 🍴 *The Angel*, 14 Witney St (ⓣ01993/822714, ⓦwww.theangelatburford.co.uk; ⓞ), which has three pleasant, traditional guest rooms in another very old stone house. *The Angel* is also where you should **eat**: they offer a lively, creative menu with mains from £14 – roast chicken in Madeira, crab linguine with chilli, and so forth.

Kelmscott Manor

Kelmscott Manor (April to late Sept Wed 11am–5pm, plus 1st & 3rd Sat of the month 11am–5pm; £8.50; ⓣ01367/252486, ⓦwww.kelmscottmanor.org.uk), about eight miles south of Burford, is a place of pilgrimage for devotees of **William Morris** (see box opposite), who used this Tudor manor as a summer home from 1871 to his death in 1896. The simple beauty of the house is enhanced by the furniture, fabrics, wallpapers and tapestries created by Morris and his Pre-Raphaelite friends, including Burne-Jones and Rossetti. Entry is by timed ticket and it's wise to call ahead to confirm the opening hours. There are no buses and the easiest way to get there by **car** from Burford is to drive south on the A361 to Lechlade, from where you take the A417 east – watch for the sign after a couple of miles. The car park is a ten-minute walk from the house.

William Morris and the Pre-Raphaelites

Socialist, artist, writer and craftsman **William Morris** (1834–1896) had a profound influence on his contemporaries and on subsequent generations. In some respects he was an ally of Karl Marx, railing against the iniquities of private property and the squalor of industrialized society, but – in contrast to Marx – he believed machines enslave the individual, and that people would be liberated only through a sort of communistic, crafts-based economy. His prose/poem story *News from Nowhere* vaguely described his Utopian society, but his main legacy turned out to be the **Arts and Crafts Movement**.

Morris's career as an artist began at Oxford, where he met **Edward Burne-Jones**, who shared his admiration for the arts of the Middle Ages. After graduating they both ended up in London, painting under the direction of Dante Gabriel Rossetti, the leading light of the **Pre-Raphaelites** – a loose grouping of artists intent on regaining the spiritual purity characteristic of art before Raphael and the Renaissance "tainted" the world with humanism. In 1861 Morris founded **Morris & Co** ("The Firm"), whose designs came to embody the ideas of the Arts and Crafts Movement, one of whose basic tenets was formulated by its founder: "Have nothing in your houses that you do not know to be useful or believe to be beautiful." Rossetti and Burne-Jones were among the designers, though Morris's own designs for fabrics, wallpapers and numerous other products were to prove a massive influence in Britain. The Laura Ashley aesthetic is a lineal descendant of Morris's rustic nostalgia.

Not content with his artistic endeavours, in 1890 Morris set up the **Kelmscott Press**, named after (but not located at) his summer home, whose masterpiece was the so-called *Kelmscott Chaucer*, the collected poems of one of the Pre-Raphaelites' greatest heroes, with woodcuts by Burne-Jones. Morris also pioneered interest in the architecture of the Cotswolds and, in response to the Victorian penchant for modernizing churches and cottages, he instigated the **Society for the Protection of Ancient Buildings** (Ⓦwww.spab.org.uk), still an active force in preserving the country's architectural heritage.

Cirencester and around

CIRENCESTER, some twenty miles southwest of Burford, is a somewhat old-fashioned town on the southern fringes of the Cotswolds. It made an early start, when, as Corinium, it became a provincial capital and a centre of trade under the **Romans**. The town flourished for three centuries, and even had one of the largest forums north of the Alps, but the Saxons destroyed almost all of the Roman city and it only revived with the wool boom of the Middle Ages. Nowadays, with its handsome stone buildings, Cirencester is an affluent little place that lays claim to be the "Capital of the Cotswolds". It's also within easy striking distance of **Malmesbury**, where the big deal is the Norman abbey.

Arrival, information and accommodation

Buses to Cirencester stop in the Market Place, where resides the **tourist office** (Mon–Sat 10am–5pm, Sun 2–5pm; Nov–March closes 4pm; ℡01285/654180, Ⓦwww.cotswolds.com), in the Corn Hall. The choicest **B&B** is *107 Gloucester Street* (℡01285/657861, Ⓦwww.107gloucesterstreet.co.uk; no cards; ❸), in an old and attractively furnished Georgian house down a narrow alley just north of the Market Place. Alternatively, a string of B&Bs line up along Victoria Road, a short walk east of the Market Place, including *The Ivy House*, in high-gabled Victorian premises at no. 2 (℡01285/656626, Ⓦwww.ivyhousecotswolds.com; ❷), which has four en-suite guest rooms, modestly but pleasantly done up. More upmarket is the *Crown of Crucis* **hotel** (℡01285/851806, Ⓦwww.thecrownofcrucis.co.uk; ❹), a modified ex-coaching inn with riverside gardens just over two miles east of town in Ampney Crucis.

The Town

Cirencester's heart is the delightful, swirling **Market Place**, packed with traders' stalls on Mondays and Fridays. An irregular line of eighteenth-century facades along the north side contrasts with the heavier Victorian structures opposite, but the parish church of **St John the Baptist** (Mon–Sat 9.30am–5pm, Sun 2.15–5pm; £3 suggested donation), built in stages during the fifteenth century, dominates. The flying buttresses that support the tower had to be added when it transpired that the church had been constructed over a filled-in ditch. Its grand three-tiered south **porch**, the largest in England and big enough to function at one time as the town hall, leads to the nave, where slender piers and soaring arches create a superb sense of space, enhanced by clerestory windows that admit a warm light. The church contains much of interest, including a colourful wineglass **pulpit**, carved in stone around 1450 and one of the few pre-Reformation pulpits to have survived in Britain. North of the chancel, superb fan vaulting hangs overhead in the **chapel of St Catherine**, who appears in a vivid fragment of a fifteenth-century wall painting. Outside, one of the best views of the church is from the **Abbey Grounds**; site of the Saxon abbey, it's now a small park skirted by the modest River Churn and a fragment of the Roman city wall.

Few other medieval buildings have survived in Cirencester. The houses along the town's most handsome streets – Park, Thomas and Coxwell – date mostly from the seventeenth and eighteenth centuries. One of those on Park Street, just west of the Market Place, houses the sleek **Corinium Museum** (Mon–Sat 10am–5pm, Sun 2–5pm; £4.50), which mostly devotes itself to Roman and Saxon artefacts, including several **mosaic pavements**. There's a reconstruction of a Romano-British garden, as well as finds from a cemetery excavated at Lechlade-on-Thames in 1985. A yew hedge the height of telegraph poles runs along Park Street, concealing **Cirencester House**, the home of the Earl of Bathurst. At no point can you actually see the building (it's rather plain anyway), but the attached three-thousand-acre **park** is open to the public: you enter it from Cecily Hill, a lovely street except for the eccentric Victorian barracks. The park's **polo** pitches attract some of the country's top players, with games held almost daily between May and September.

Just south of the Market Place off Cricklade Street, the **New Brewery Arts Centre** (Mon–Sat 9am–5pm, Sun 10am–4pm; free; ⓦ www.breweryarts.org.uk) has more than a dozen resident artists, whose studios you can visit and whose work you can buy.

Eating and drinking

For **snacks**, you can't do much better than *Keith's Coffee Shop* on Black Jack Street, and the inexpensive café in the New Brewery Arts Centre, which serves interesting vegetarian food. The best choice for a relaxing **evening meal** is *Harry Hare's*, 3 Gosditch St (☎01285/652375), just behind the church, which specializes in classy renditions of down-to-earth English dishes at moderate prices.

Cirencester has plenty of **pubs**, aided by the presence nearby of the Royal Agricultural College. Try the *Kings Head* on the Market Place or, for **bar meals**, the *Waggon & Horses* on London Road.

Malmesbury

The small hill-town of **MALMESBURY** lies on the periphery of the Cotswolds twelve miles south of Cirencester, just over the county boundary from Gloucestershire in Wiltshire. The town may have lost most of its good looks with a rash of modern development, but there's no gainsaying the beauty of its partly ruinous Norman abbey, a majestic structure boasting some of the finest Romanesque sculpture in the country.

Malmesbury's **High Street** begins at the bottom of the hill by the old silk mills and heads north across the river and past a jagged row of cottages to the octagonal **Market Cross**, built around 1490. Nearby, the eighteenth-century **Tolsey Gate** leads through to the **abbey** (daily 10am–5pm; Nov–Easter closes 4pm; £2 suggested donation), once a rich and powerful Benedictine monastery. The first abbey burnt down in about 1050, the second was roughed up during the Dissolution, but the beautiful Norman **nave** of the abbey church has survived, its south porch sporting a multitude of exquisite if badly worn figures. Three bands of figures surround the doorway, depicting scenes from the Creation, the Old Testament and the life of Christ, while inside the porch the apostles and Christ are carved in deep relief – stately figures in flowing folds surmounted by a flying angel. The tympanum shows Christ on a rainbow, supported by gymnastic angels. Within the main body of the church, the pale stone brings a dramatic freshness, particularly to the carving of the nave arches (look out for the Norman beak-heads) and of the clerestory. To the left of the high altar, the pulpit virtually hides the **tomb of King Athelstan**, grandson of Alfred the Great and the first Saxon to be recognized as king of England; the tomb, however, is empty and the location of the king's body is unknown. The abbey's greatest surviving treasures are housed in the **parvis** (room above the porch), reached via a narrow spiral staircase right of the main doorway, where pride of place is given to four Flemish **medieval Bibles**, written on parchment and sumptuously illuminated with gilt ink and exquisite miniature paintings.

Buses pull into the Market Place, a short walk from the **tourist office**, on the corner of Cross Hayes and Market Lane (Mon–Thurs 9am–4.50pm, Fri 9am–4.20pm, Easter–Sept also Sat 10am–4pm; ☏01666/823748, ⊛www.malmesbury.gov.uk). The *Old Bell* in Abbey Row (☏01666/822344, ⊛www.oldbellhotel.co.uk; ⑥) provides a strong incentive to **stay**: originally built as a guesthouse for the abbey, it has loads of atmosphere, pleasantly appointed rooms, and a good **restaurant**.

Northleach

Secluded in a shallow depression ten miles north of Cirencester, **NORTHLEACH** is one of the Cotswolds' most appealing villages. This, together with its location within easy reach of Oxford and the picturesque Windrush Valley, makes it a perfect base: **walking trails** radiate in all directions across the grassy hills or along the river.

Around the **Market Place** cluster rows of immaculate late-medieval cottages, with more framing the adjoining **Green**, but the outstanding feature is the handsome Perpendicular **church of St Peter and St Paul**, erected in the fifteenth century at the height of the wool boom. Its porch – suitably ostentatious – is overseen by a set of finely carved corbel heads, while wide clerestory windows light the beautifully proportioned nave. The floor is inlaid with an exceptional collection of **memorial brasses**, marking the tombs of the merchants whose endowments paid for the church. On several, you can make out the woolsacks laid out beneath the owner's feet – a symbol of wealth and power that survives in the House of Lords, where a woolsack is placed on the Lord Chancellor's seat.

Two minutes' walk along the High Street from Market Place is **Keith Harding's World of Mechanical Music** (daily 10am–5pm; £8; ⊛www.mechanicalmusic .co.uk), a bewildering one-room collection of antique musical boxes, barrel organs and automata. The entrance fee includes an hour-long demonstration tour, of which the highlight is hearing the likes of Rachmaninov, Gershwin or Paderewski playing their own masterpieces on piano rolls.

Northleach has **buses** from Cirencester (Mon–Sat approx every 90min) and from Oxford, Burford, Cheltenham and Gloucester (Mon–Sat 3 daily, 1 on Sun). There is no tourist office. At the excellent *Wheatsheaf Hotel* (T01451/860244, Wwww .cotswoldswheatsheaf.com; ❸), a former coaching inn just along from the Market Place on West End, the old stone exterior has been left intact, but the public areas and guest rooms have been remodelled in a bright modern style softened by period furniture. Its **restaurant** is first-rate, offering delicious traditional English cuisine – roast duck, loin of pork and so forth – with mains around £15.

Bourton-on-the-Water and the Slaughters

At the epicentre of Cotswold tourism, **BOURTON-ON-THE-WATER** lies six miles northeast of Northleach. The reason for all the attention is the five (admittedly very picturesque) mini-bridges that straddle the River Windrush in the centre of the village. Add to this a few purpose-built attractions – a Model Village here, a Dragonfly Maze there – and you have enough to draw in an army of tourist coaches.

Much more enticing, though still on the day-trippers' circuit, is the hamlet of **LOWER SLAUGHTER** (as in *slohtre*, Old English for "marshy place"), a mile or so northwest of Bourton on the other side of the A429. Here, the River Eye snakes its way through the village, overlooked by a string of immaculate and very old stone cottages. The village **church** blends in well, but in fact it's largely Victorian. There is a small **museum** (and souvenir shop) in a former mill, but you're better off walking up the river valley to **UPPER SLAUGHTER**, another pretty little place buried deep in a wooded dell about an hour from its twin. There are several **places to stay**, the most alluring being *Lords of the Manor*, a luxurious hotel in Upper Slaughter's old rectory (T01451/820243, Wwww.lordsofthemanor.com; ❻–❼).

Stow-on-the-Wold

Ambling over a steep hill some ten miles northeast of Northleach, **STOW-ON-THE-WOLD** sucks in a disproportionate number of visitors for its size and attractions, which essentially comprise an old **marketplace** surrounded by cafés, pubs, antiques and souvenir shops. The narrow walled alleyways, or "tchures", running into the square were designed for funnelling sheep into the market, which is itself dominated by an imposing Victorian hall.

Stow is, however, easy to reach by **bus** from the likes of Cheltenham and Cirencester (as well as the train station at nearby Moreton-in-Marsh), with services pulling in on the High Street, just off the main square. There's a tiny **tourist office** at 12 Talbot Court (Mon–Sat 10am–5pm, Sun 11am–4.30pm; T01451/870150, Wwww.go-stow.co.uk). **Accommodation** is in reasonable supply, including the *Tall Trees B&B* (T01451/831296; no credit cards; ❷), on the edge of town off the Oddington road, with sweeping views and a cosy, modern ambience. Stow has the Cotswolds' only ⚜ **youth hostel**, in a good-looking Georgian townhouse on the main square (T0845/371 9540, Estow@yha.org.uk), with fifty beds (around £16) in four- to eight-person rooms.

For **food**, the *Royalist Hotel*, just off the main square on the corner of Park and Digbeth streets, offers light meals in its *Eagle & Child* bar and also has the very good *947AD* restaurant (T01451/830670), where a two-course meal costs around £30. Stow's best **teashop** is the *Cotswold Garden Tearoom* on Digbeth Street.

Chipping Norton and around

The bustling market town of **CHIPPING NORTON**, eight miles east of Stow – "Chipping" comes from *ceapen*, Old English for market – is not the prettiest place in the Cotswolds, but it is flanked to the north and east by one of the least explored and most scenic corners of the region, where the limestone uplands are patterned by long dry-stone walls and sprinkled with tiny stone villages. King John granted a **wool fair** charter to the town in the twelfth century, but it reached its peak three hundred years later, when it acquired many of the stalwart stone buildings that now line up along the sloping **Market Square**.

Also paid for by wealthy wool merchants, **St Mary's Parish Church**, just below the square – and beyond a handsome row of almshouses – looks every inch the country church, the modesty of its tower offset by the slender windows of its Perpendicular Gothic nave. The vaulted porch is equally striking, not least for the ugly grinning devils and green men that peer down from the roof. By comparison, the interior is rather routine, though the nave is well-lit and airy and the east window of the south aisle is a splendid affair, spiralling out from a central tulip; look out also for two superbly carved alabaster table-tombs commemorating sixteenth-century merchants and their wives.

Down in the valley west of the centre, the old **Bliss Tweed Mill** (no public access) – its whopping chimneystack unmistakeable beside the A44 – recalls the textile mini-boom Chipping Norton enjoyed in the nineteenth century.

Practicalities

Buses to Chipping Norton – including useful shuttles from Kingham train station – pull in on West Street, a few yards from the town hall. **Accommodation** is thin on the ground, but there are well-appointed rooms behind the Georgian facade of the *Crown and Cushion* (℡01608/642533, ⓦwww.crown-cushion.co.uk; ❸–❹) on the main square, or you could try one of the three cosy, stylish rooms at the *Wild Thyme* **restaurant**, 10 New St (℡01608/645060, ⓦwww.wildthymerestaurant .co.uk; ❷–❸) – whose Modern British cuisine is also the best in town. For lighter bites try the lovely **café** in the splendid *Jaffé & Neale* bookshop on the square, or sample the atmospheric *Chequers* **pub** nearby – but if you have your own transport, book ahead for a meal to remember at the superb ⚏*Kingham Plough* in **Kingham** village, five miles southwest (℡01608/658327, ⓦwww.thekinghamplough.co.uk). The epitome of a Cotswolds gastropub, this is one of the region's best restaurants, atmospherically housed in an old stone building by the village green; come here for local, seasonal produce of all kinds, expertly prepared though not cheap (mains £15–25). They also have seven country-style rooms (❹).

The Rollright Stones

Driving west from Chipping Norton along the A44, it only takes a few minutes to reach the signed country lane that leads off to the right to the **Rollright Stones** (ⓦwww.rollrightstones.co.uk), a scattering of megalithic monuments in the fields either side of the lane. The eerie array consists of large natural stones moved here – no one is sure why – plus several burial chambers and barrows. The largest group is the **King's Men**, comprising over seventy irregularly spaced stones forming a circle thirty metres in diameter, one of the most important such monuments in the country. Signed just off the lane, it's also the easiest to find. The circle gets its name from a legend about a witch who turned a king and his army (of unknown identity) into these gnarled rocks to stop them invading England. Across the lane stands the **King's Stone** monolith, offering pensive views across the Warwickshire countryside, while the **Whispering Knights** lie a short walk southeast on the field margin.

Great Tew

GREAT TEW, about five miles east of Chipping Norton via the A361 and B4022, is one of the most beautiful of all Cotswold villages, its thatched cottages and honey-coloured stone houses weaving around grassy hillocks with woodland on all sides. Here also is the idyllic, locally renowned ⚲ *Falkland Arms* (☏01608/683653, ⓦwww.falklandarms.co.uk), which rotates guest beers in addition to its Wadworth cask ales, and sells a fine selection of single malts, herbal wines, snuff and clay pipes you can fill with tobacco for a smoke in the flower-filled garden. Little has changed in the flagstone-floored **bar** since the sixteenth century, although the snug is now a small **dining room** serving home-made food (mains from £9). It's also a popular place to **stay**: there are five rooms (❸), sympathetically renovated and attractively furnished.

Chastleton House

About four miles west of Chipping Norton along the A44 – also easily reached from Stow-on-the-Wold – stands **Chastleton House** (Wed–Sat: April–Sept 1–5pm; Oct 1–4pm; £8.65; timed tickets, pre-bookable on ☏01494/755560; NT). Built between 1605 and 1612 by Walter Jones, a wealthy Welsh wool merchant, this ranks among England's most splendid Jacobean properties, set amid ornamental gardens that include the country's first-ever croquet lawn (croquet's rules were codified here in 1865). Inside, the house looks stuck in time, with unwashed upholstery, unpolished wood panelling and miscellaneous clutter clogging some of the corners. This dishevelled air partly derives from the previous owners, the Jones family, who lost their fortune in the aftermath of the Civil War – they were Royalists – and never had enough cash to modernize thereafter. It's also a credit to the National Trust, who took on the property in 1991, but wisely decided to stick to the "lived-in look". Among the highlights are the barrel-vaulted long gallery and, in the beer cellar, the longest ladder (dated 1805) you're ever likely to see. There's also a wonderful topiary garden.

Chipping Campden

CHIPPING CAMPDEN, some fifteen miles northwest of Chipping Norton, gives a better idea than anywhere else in the Cotswolds as to what a prosperous wool town might have looked like in the Middle Ages. The short **High Street** is hemmed in by ancient houses, whose undulating, weather-beaten roofs jag against each other, while down below are twisted beams and mullioned windows. The seventeenth-century **Market Hall** has survived too, a barn-like affair in the middle of the High Street, where farmers once gathered to sell their harvests. From the High Street, it's a brief walk east past a splendid sequence of old stone houses to the **church of St James** (March–Oct Mon–Sat 10am–5pm, Sun 2–6pm; rest of year Mon–Sat 11am–3pm, Sun 2–3pm; free), built in the fifteenth century, the zenith of the town's wool-trading days. Inside, the airy nave is bathed in light from the clerestory windows and there's a delicate and carefully considered balance between height and length. Here also is the ostentatious **funerary chapel** of the Hicks family, with the fancily carved marble effigies of Sir Baptist and Lady Elizabeth lying on their table-tomb.

A fine panoramic view rewards those who make the short but severe hike up the Cotswold Way north from the High Street (along West End Terrace/Hoo Lane) to **Dover's Hill**. Since 1612 this natural amphitheatre has been the stage for an Olympics of rural sports, though the event was suspended in the mid-nineteenth century when games such as shin-kicking began to attract too many undesirables. A more civilized version, the **Cotswold Olimpick Games** (ⓦwww.olimpickgames.co.uk), has been staged here each June since 1963 with a tug-of-war, falconry and hammer-throwing plus a bit of shin-kicking for old times' sake.

Practicalities

Chipping Campden heaves with day-trippers in the summer: try to stay overnight so you can explore in the evening or early morning, when the streets are empty and the golden hues of the stone at their richest. Getting here by **bus** is easiest from Cheltenham, Moreton-in-Marsh (for Chipping Norton and Oxford) and Stratford-upon-Avon. The **tourist office** is very central, on the High Street (daily 9.30am–5pm; ☏01386/841206, ⓦwww.chipping-campden .net). They will book accommodation on your behalf.

The town's best **B&B** is *Badgers Hall* (☏01386/840839, ⓦwww.badgershall .com; ④), in an old stone house on the High Street, above their own tearoom. Guest rooms are en suite and come with period detail – but a two-night minimum stay may apply. There's also the smart, contemporary styled *Cotswold House Hotel*, which occupies an immaculately maintained Regency townhouse and its older neighbours on the main square (☏01386/840330, ⓦwww.cotswoldhouse.com; ⑥), but choicest accommodation is in the *Lygon Arms* (☏01386/840318, ⓦwww .lygonarms.co.uk; ③–④), a family-run hotel in a sixteenth-century coaching inn on the High Street: go for one of the pricier rooms on the internal courtyard.

Pick of the **pubs** is the 🍴 *Eight Bells Inn* (☏01386/840371), a cosy spot in a charming old stone building on the way up to the church. The restaurant here is first-rate, with a menu encompassing dishes such as ham and cloves or pheasant and mushrooms (mains from £13). Otherwise aim for the *Lygon Arms* or the half-timbered *Red Lion*, a High Street pub with mains about £12.

Broadway and Snowshill

BROADWAY, five miles west of Chipping Campden, is a handsome little village at the foot of the steep escarpment that rolls along the western edge of the Cotswolds. It seems likely that the Romans were the first to settle here, but Broadway's zenith was as a stop for stagecoaches plying between London and Worcester. This has defined much of the village's present appearance – its long, wide main street framed by stone cottages and shaded by chestnut trees. Broadway can attract more visitors than is comfortable, but things quieten down in the evening: the *Olive Branch*, 78 High St (☏01386/853440, ⓦwww.theolivebranch-broadway .com; ④), is a very pleasant **B&B** in an old stone house with half a dozen cosy guest rooms. **Buses** (not Sun) arrive from Chipping Campden and Winchcombe.

Down a country lane two miles south, **Snowshill Manor** (March–Oct Wed–Sun noon–5pm; £9; NT) is a good-looking Cotswold manor house holding a trove of exotic curiosities. The architect, craftsman and poet Charles Wade (1883–1956) – inspired as a boy by his grandmother's Chinese cabinet, now on display in the house – spent decades hunting down objects that were not rare or valuable but "of interest as records of various vanished handicrafts". The results of his forays include model carts, boneshaker bicycles, children's prams, wooden toys, beds, beetles, all kinds of musical instruments and other curios; they were crammed into the house, while he himself lived in a cottage in the garden. Most dramatic is the arrangement of 26 Samurai warriors dating from the seventeenth to the nineteenth centuries in the Green Room. Note that it's a ten-minute walk to reach the house from the car park.

Winchcombe and around

About eight miles southwest of Broadway – and nine miles northeast of Cheltenham – **WINCHCOMBE** has a long main street flanked by a fetching medley of stone and half-timbered buildings. Placid today, Winchcombe was an important Saxon town and one-time capital of the kingdom of Mercia. It flourished during the medieval cloth boom too, one of the results being **St Peter's**, the town's main church, a mainly fifteenth-century structure distinguished by forty alarming gargoyles that ring the exterior. With access to the Cotswold Way as well as a host of lesser walks round and about, Winchcombe sets itself up as the **walking** capital of the Cotswolds, with plenty of information and route maps at the **tourist office** on the High Street (April–Oct Mon–Sat 10am–5pm, Sun 10am–4pm; rest of year Sat & Sun 10am–4pm; ℗01242/602925, ⓦwww.cotswolds.com) and at the dedicated website ⓦwww.winchcombewelcomeswalkers.com.

Three or four **buses** a day (not Sun) serve Winchcombe from Cheltenham and Broadway. Of the town's many **B&Bs**, *Gower House*, 16 North St (℗01242/602616; no credit cards; ❷), offers three comfortable rooms – two en suite – in an attractively modernized, seventeenth-century house in the town centre. The ⚔ *White Hart Inn* (℗01242/602359, ⓦwww.whitehartwinchcombe.co.uk; ❸), in a good-looking old building on the High Street, has eight rooms decorated in traditional-meets-folksy manner – and this is also the best place to **eat**. Its speciality is simple British cooking – chiefly sausages in gourmet varieties like venison and red wine or lamb, mint and apricot. Dine in the restaurant (mains from about £10) or at the bar (from £5).

Spoonley Wood

The three-and-a-half-hour hiking loop from Winchcombe through **Spoonley Wood** to Spoonley Farm, two miles southeast of town, takes in a ruined Roman villa with a beautifully preserved **mosaic** *in situ*. It starts in the same place as the Cotswold Way, opposite the church at the south end of the main street, but shortly after peels left towards **Sudeley Castle**, a restored Tudor mansion with magnificent gardens. After crossing the castle grounds, it follows the contour of the hill to Spoonley Wood, site of the Roman villa. From there, strike uphill to a farm track, which you can follow southwest, turning right at Cole's Hill towards Waterhatch Farm. The path then drops gently down to river level and wends its way back to Winchcombe.

Hailes Abbey

Hailes Abbey (daily: April–June & Sept 10am–5pm; July & Aug 10am–6pm; Oct 10am–4pm; £3.40; NT & EH), a two-mile stroll or drive northeast of Winchcombe, was once one of England's great Cistercian monasteries. Pilgrims came here from all over the country to pray before the abbey's phial of Christ's blood – that is, until the Reformation, during which the relic was discredited and most of the thirteenth-century monastery demolished. The principal remains are an assortment of foundations, but some cloister arches survive, worn by wind and rain. The ruins may lack drama, but Hailes is still worth visiting for its **museum**, where you can examine thirteenth-century bosses at close quarters, and for the nearby **church**, which is older than the abbey and contains beautiful wall paintings dating from around 1300.

Belas Knap

Up on the ridge of Cleeve Hill, south of Winchcombe, the Neolithic long barrow of **Belas Knap** occupies one of the wildest – and highest – spots in the Cotswolds. Dating from around 3000 BC, this is the best-preserved burial chamber in England, stretching out like a strange sleeping beast cloaked in green velvet. The views from the top are exceptional. The best way to get there is to **walk** – it's a two-mile climb up the Cotswold Way from Winchcombe. The path strikes off to the right near the entrance to Sudeley Castle and afterwards, when you reach the country lane at the top, turn right and then left for the ten-minute hike to the barrow. It's also possible to **drive** to Belas Knap along this same country lane: follow the signs to the roadside pull-in where you can park before the short walk to the site. Continue on the country lane for an exhilarating drive south, scuttling over the hills and through dense woods to join the A40 Cheltenham–Oxford road near Syreford.

Cheltenham

Until the eighteenth century **CHELTENHAM** was like any other Cotswold town, but the discovery of a spring in 1716 transformed it into Britain's most popular **spa**. During Cheltenham's heyday, a century or so later, royalty and nobility descended in droves to take the waters, which were said to cure anything from constipation to worms. The super-rich have since moved on to sunnier climes, but the town has maintained a lively, bustling atmosphere, holds lots of good restaurants and boasts some of England's best-preserved Regency architecture.

Cheltenham is also a thriving arts centre, famous for its **festivals** of folk (Feb), jazz (April/May), science (June), classical music (July) and literature (April & Oct) – for information on these check Ⓦ www.cheltenhamfestivals.com – and, of course, the **races** (see box below). In addition, the steep **Coopers' Hill**, six miles southwest near Brockworth, hosts the annual **Cheese Rolling Festival** (Ⓦ www.cheese-rolling .co.uk) on the last Monday in May, when a round of Double Gloucester cheese is pursued down the slope by dozens of (mostly drunken) folk. The resultant string of hospitalizations has resulted in the race often being banned; the 2010 version was officially cancelled and the future of the event remains uncertain.

Arrival, information and accommodation

Long-distance buses arrive at the **bus station** in Royal Well Road, just west off the main drag, the Promenade. Cheltenham Spa **train station** is on Queen's Road, southwest of the centre; local buses run into town every fifteen minutes, otherwise it's a twenty-minute walk. The **tourist office** is at 77 Promenade (Mon, Tues & Thurs–Sat 9.30am–5.15pm, Wed 10am–5.15pm; Ⓣ 01242/522878, Ⓦ www .visitcheltenham.co.uk). **Hotels** and **guesthouses** abound, many of them in fine Regency houses, and rooms are easy to come by – except during the races and festivals, when you should book weeks in advance.

Abbey Hotel 14–16 Bath Parade Ⓣ 01242/516053, Ⓦ www.abbeyhotel-cheltenham .com. Rooms here are attractively and individually furnished and wholesome breakfasts are taken overlooking the garden. Friendly service. ❸
Big Sleep Wellington St Ⓣ 01242/696999, Ⓦ www.thebigsleephotel.com. Excellent contemporary hotel in the centre, with a retro designer feel and high-tech gadgetry but no frills – and, more important, low prices. ❷

Brennan 21 St Luke's Rd Ⓣ 01242/525904, Ⓦ www.brennanguesthouse.co.uk. A good-value B&B in a small Regency building on a quiet square. No credit cards. ❷
Crossways 57 Bath Rd Ⓣ 01242/527683, Ⓦ www .crosswaysguesthouse.com. Very central, this comfortable Regency house has period trimmings and well-equipped rooms. ❸
Hotel du Vin Parabola Rd Ⓣ 01242/588450, Ⓦ www.hotelduvin.com. Swanky boutique hotel in

---

Cheltenham races

Cheltenham racecourse (Ⓣ 0844/579 3003, Ⓦ www.cheltenham.co.uk), on the north side of town, a ten-minute walk from Pittville Park at the foot of Cleeve Hill, is Britain's main steeplechasing venue. The principal event of the season (Oct–April) is the four-day **National Hunt Festival** in March, which attracts forty thousand people each day. For the cheapest but arguably the best view, pay £10 (£25 during the Festival) for entry to the pen opposite the main stand, known as Best Mate Enclosure.

the sought-after Montpellier district, with 49 stylish rooms and suites. ⑤–⑥

Lypiatt House Lypiatt Rd ☏01242/224994, ⓦwww.lypiatt.co.uk. Victorian villa set in its own grounds, with open fires and a conservatory with a small bar. ③

Willoughby House 1 Suffolk Square ☏01242/522798, ⓦwww.willoughbyhousehotel .co.uk. South of the centre, in a handsome Regency building, this hotel has ornate, opulent rooms and a restaurant. ⑤

The Town

The broad **Promenade**, focus of the town, sweeps majestically south from the High Street, lined with some of Cheltenham's grandest houses and smartest shops. It leads into **Imperial Square**, whose greenery is surrounded by proud Regency

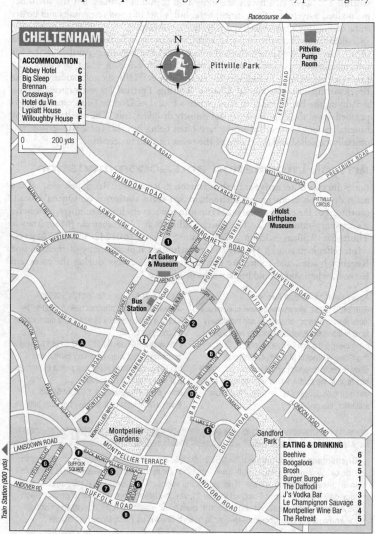

Map legend — CHELTENHAM:

ACCOMMODATION
Abbey Hotel — C
Big Sleep — B
Brennan — E
Crossways — D
Hotel du Vin — A
Lypiatt House — G
Willoughby House — F

EATING & DRINKING
Beehive — 6
Boogaloos — 2
Brosh — 5
Burger Burger — 1
The Daffodil — 7
J's Vodka Bar — 3
Le Champignon Sauvage — 8
Montpellier Wine Bar — 4
The Retreat — 5

Train Station (900 yds)

terraces that herald the handsome and harmonious terraces and squares of the **Montpellier** district, which stretches south in a narrow block to Suffolk Road, making a delightful detour.

Back in the centre, just north of the Promenade on Clarence Street, is the enjoyable **Cheltenham Art Gallery and Museum** (Mon–Sat 10am–5pm, Nov–March closes 4pm; free; ⓦwww.cheltenhammuseum.org.uk). This is very good on social history, with different eras represented by table displays of personal belongings and a typical dinner of the time. There's also a fine room dedicated to the Arts and Crafts Movement and a section devoted to Edward Wilson, a local man who died on Scott's ill-fated expedition to the Antarctic. A brief stroll north lies the **Holst Birthplace Museum**, 4 Clarence Rd (Feb to mid-Dec Tues–Sat 10am–4pm; £4.50; ⓦwww.holstmuseum.org.uk). Once the home of the composer of *The Planets*, the intimate rooms hold plenty of Holst memorabilia and give a good insight into Victorian family life.

It's about ten minutes' walk north to the **Pittville** district, where a certain Joseph Pitt began work on his own grand spa in the 1820s – soon afterwards running out of cash. Most of the area is now parkland, though Pitt did manage to complete the domed **Pump Room** (daily except Tues 10am–4pm) before he hit the skids. A lovely Classical structure with an imposing colonnaded facade, it is now used as a concert hall, but you can still sample the **spa waters** from the marble fountain in the main auditorium for free. Very pungent they are too.

Eating and drinking

Cheltenham caters for all tastes and pockets: its **restaurants**, **bars** and **pubs** manage to draw in punters from nearby Gloucester as well as from around the Cotswolds.

Cafés and restaurants

Beehive 1–3 Montpellier Villas ☎01242/702270. Friendly ambience and great French food in a lofty, blue-draped restaurant above the pub (see below). Mains from £13. Reservations advised; closed Sun eve.

Boogaloos 16 Regent St. The salads and sandwiches are good at this coffee house, where you can either chill out in the relaxed sofa basement or join the crowd in the buzzing, brightly coloured upstairs rooms. Closed Sun.

Brosh 8 Suffolk Parade ☎01242/227277. Unusually good Middle Eastern restaurant, mixing modern Israeli cooking with familiar meze-style presentation, and using local Cotswolds ingredients – Gloucestershire lamb chargrilled with a sweet Moroccan-style salsa, *kreplach* (small wonton-style dumplings) made from local forest mushrooms, and so on. Mains £16–20, but lighter bar meals available (Wed–Fri). Eve only. Closed Sun–Tues.

Burger Burger The Brewery, Henrietta St ☎01242/248886. Upmarket take on fast food, with gourmet, hand-prepared nosh – beef sourced from local herds, chicken all free-range, bread baked fresh daily by an artisan bakery in nearby Nailsworth – served in a chic, minimalist setting. Mains £6–8.

The Daffodil 18–20 Suffolk Parade ☎01242/700055. Eat in the circle bar or auditorium of this former cinema, where the screen has been replaced with a hubbub of chefs. Great atmosphere and first-class British cuisine (mains around £15).

Le Champignon Sauvage 24 Suffolk Rd ☎01242/573449. Chic and intimate restaurant serving Michelin-starred French cuisine, including scrumptious desserts. Two-course set menu £45, three courses £55. Book well ahead. Closed Sun & Mon.

Pubs and bars

Beehive 1–3 Montpellier Villas. Easy-going Cheltenham institution with games shed, courtyard garden and cosy snug.

J's Vodka Bar 6 Regent St. Killer drinks from a range of 24 vodkas, served to the accompaniment of DJs playing house and funk. Closed Sun–Tues.

Montpellier Wine Bar Bayshill Lodge, Montpellier St. Stylish wine bar and restaurant, with lovely bow-fronted windows. Good breakfasts are also served, and Friday is fish night.

The Retreat 10–11 Suffolk Parade. Lively venue which caters to the business fraternity at lunchtimes and a Cheltenham Ladies' College set in the evening. Good lunches too. Closed Sun.

Gloucester

For centuries life was good for **GLOUCESTER**, which lies ten miles west of Cheltenham. The Romans chose this spot for a garrison to guard the River Severn and spy on Wales, and later for a *colonia* or home for retired soldiers – the highest status a provincial Roman town could dream of. Commercial success came with traffic up the Severn, which developed into one of the busiest trade routes in Europe, and the city's political importance hit its peak under the Normans, with William the Conqueror a regular visitor. Gloucester became a religious centre too, as exemplified by the construction of what is now the cathedral, but by the fifteenth century it was on the skids: navigating the Severn this far upstream was so difficult that most trade shifted south to Bristol. In an attempt to reverse the decline, a canal was opened in 1827 to link Gloucester to Sharpness, on a broader stretch of the Severn further south. Trade picked up for a time, but it was only a temporary stay of economic execution.

Today, the **canal** is busy once again, though this time with pleasure boats, and the Victorian **docks** have undergone a facelift, their assorted warehouses turned into offices, apartments, a large antiques centre and a museum. The main reason for a visit, though, is Gloucester's magnificent **cathedral**, the city's one and only outstanding attraction. There's no strong reason to stay overnight: a day-trip (from Cheltenham) is sufficient.

Arrival, information and accommodation

Gloucester's **bus and train stations** are opposite one another on Bruton Way, a five-minute walk east of the centre, with the **tourist office** very central at 28 Southgate St (Mon 10am–5pm, Tues–Sat 9.30am–5pm; July & Aug also Sun 11am–3pm; ℡01452/396572, ⓦwww.thecityofgloucester.co.uk). Central **accommodation** includes the *New Inn*, 16 Northgate St (℡01452/522177, ⓦwww.newinn-hotel .co.uk; ❷), with 33 pleasant, well-maintained rooms, and the *Albert Hotel*, 56 Worcester St (℡01452/502081, ⓦwww.alberthotel.com; ❸), a nineteenth-century townhouse with good, modern facilities.

The City

Gloucester lies on the east bank of the Severn, its centre spread around a curve in the river. **The Cross**, once the entrance to the Roman forum, marks the heart of the city and the meeting-point of Northgate, Southgate, Eastgate and Westgate streets, all Roman roads. **St Michael's Tower**, the remains of an old church, overlooks it. The main shopping area lies east of the Northgate–Southgate axis, while the **cathedral** and **docks** are the focus of interest to the west.

Gloucester Cathedral

The superb condition of **Gloucester Cathedral** (daily 7.30am–6pm; suggested donation £5; ⓦwww.gloucestercathedral.org.uk) is striking in a city that has lost so much of its history. The Saxons founded an abbey here, and four centuries later, Benedictine monks arrived intent on building their own church; work began in 1089. As a place of worship it shot to importance after the murder of King Edward II at Berkeley Castle (see p.299) in 1327: Gloucester took his body and the king's shrine became a major place of pilgrimage. The money generated helped finance the conversion of the church into the country's first and greatest example of the **Perpendicular style**, crowned by the magnificent 225-foot tower. Henry VIII recognized the church's prestige by conferring the status of cathedral.

Beneath the fourteenth- and fifteenth-century reconstructions, some Norman aspects remain, best seen in the **nave**, which is flanked by sturdy pillars and arches adorned with immaculate zigzag carvings. Only when you reach the choir and transepts can you see how skilfully the new church was built inside the old, the Norman masonry hidden beneath the finer lines of the Perpendicular panelling and tracery. The **choir** has extraordinary fourteenth-century misericords, and also provides the best vantage point for admiring the **east window**, completed in around 1350 and – at almost 80 feet tall – the largest medieval window in Britain. Beneath it, to the left (as you're facing the east window) is the **tomb of Edward II** in alabaster and marble. In the nearby **Lady Chapel**, delicate carved tracery holds a breathtaking patchwork of stained-glass windows. In the **south ambulatory**, the tomb of Robert, Duke of Normandy – and eldest son of William the Conqueror – forms a painted wooden effigy dating from around 1290 (though Robert died in 1134). Dressed as a Crusader, he lies in a curious pose, his arms and legs crossed.

The innovative nature of the cathedral's design can also be appreciated in the beautiful **cloisters**, completed in 1367 and featuring the first fan vaulting in the country; the intricate quality of the work is outdone only by Henry VII's Chapel in Westminster Abbey, which it inspired. The setting was used to represent the corridors of Hogwarts in the *Harry Potter* films.

Back inside, the north transept holds the entrance to the **treasury** (April–Oct Mon–Fri 10.30am–4pm, Sat 10.30am–3.30pm; free), of minor interest, and also

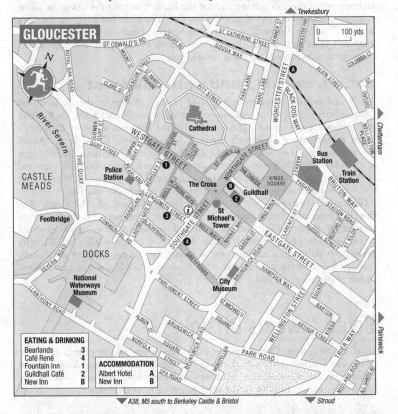

serves as the entrance to the **upstairs galleries** (same hours; £2) where an exhibition explains the east window and allows you to view it at close quarters, while the **Whispering Gallery** enables you to pick up the tiniest sounds from across the vaulting. You can also climb the **tower** for outstanding views (Wed–Fri 2.30pm, Sat 1.30pm & 2.30pm; also Mon & Tues in school hols 2.30pm; £3).

City Museum and docks

From the cathedral, it's a brief stroll over to **Westgate Street**, quieter and more pleasant than its three Roman counterparts, and another short step to **Southgate Street**, from where Greyfriars runs east to the **City Museum**, housed in a Victorian building on Brunswick Road (Tues–Sat 10am–5pm; free). The museum has a diverting archeological collection which includes a decorative bronze mirror dating to about 50 AD and an exquisite set of twelfth-century bone and antler playing pieces – the Gloucester Tables Set – bearing designs representing everything from the signs of the Zodiac to biblical stories.

Roughly 500m west of the centre, **Gloucester Docks** hold fourteen **warehouses** built for storing grain following the opening of the Sharpness canal to the River Severn in 1827. Most have been turned into offices and shops, but the southernmost Llanthony Warehouse is now occupied by the **National Waterways Museum** (April–June, Sept & Oct Mon–Fri 11am–4.30pm, Sat & Sun 10.30am–4.30pm; July & Aug daily 10.30am–5pm; Nov–March daily 11am–4pm; £4.25; Ⓦ www.nwm.org.uk), which delves into every watery nook and cranny, from the engineering of the locks to the lives of the horses that trod the towpaths, along with plenty of interactive displays. Out from the main building you can also practise "walking the wall" in the time-honoured manner of boatmen, who propelled their narrowboats through the tunnels by their feet, and explore the boats themselves moored up along the quayside.

Eating, drinking and entertainment

You'll find reliable if undemanding food at the **café-bar** in the Guildhall on Eastgate Street; it's open for lunch and dinner and always lively (closed Sun & Mon). Alternatively, there are well-prepared British and European dishes at *Bearlands*, a smart **restaurant** on Longsmith Street (Ⓣ01452/419966; closed Sun & Mon), where a two-course set meal is £25. Or head for *Café René*, Greyfriars, 31 Southgate St (Ⓣ01452/309340, Ⓦ www.caferene.co.uk), whose walls and ceilings are covered with bottles; good burgers and other more substantial dishes are on the menu, while the Sunday barbecues in summer are worth going out of your way for.

Gloucester's best **pubs** are all within spitting distance of The Cross. The rambling fifteenth-century *New Inn* in Northgate Street (see p.296) has plenty of atmosphere, a splendid galleried courtyard and inexpensive meals, or for tasty food at rock-bottom prices try the *Fountain Inn*, down a narrow alley off Westgate Street; this pub pulls a sublime pint of Abbot ale and has tables in an adjacent courtyard – ideal for a sunny day. *Café René* hosts live blues, jazz and acoustic **music** in its cellar bar (Wed & Fri).

South towards Bristol

Heading south from Cheltenham or Gloucester, most visitors thump down the M5 bound for Bristol (see p.313) and/or Bath (see p.325). En route, however, you could divert to the elaborate shrubbery of **Painswick**'s **Rococo Garden**, the picturesque hamlet of **Uley** or the magnificent castle at **Berkeley**.

Painswick

Heading south from Cheltenham on the A46, it's ten miles to the congenial old wool town of **PAINSWICK**, where ancient buildings jostle for space on narrow streets running downhill off the busy main street. The fame of Painswick's **church** stems chiefly from the surrounding graveyard, where 99 yew trees, cut into bizarre bulbous shapes, surround a fine collection of eighteenth-century table-tombs. However, the main attraction is the **Rococo Garden** (mid-Jan to Oct daily 11am–5pm; £6; Ⓦ www.rococogarden.co.uk), about half a mile north up the Gloucester road. Created in the early eighteenth century, it's England's only example of Rococo garden design, a short-lived fashion typified by a mix of formal geometrical shapes and more naturalistic, curving lines. The garden was later abandoned but has been restored to its original form with the aid of a painting dated 1748. In February and March people flock to see the snowdrops that smother the slopes. For the best vistas, walk around anticlockwise.

Bus #46 (approx hourly) links Cheltenham with Painswick, where the **tourist office** is housed in the library on the main street (April–Oct Tues–Sat 10am–5pm, Sun 10am–1pm; Ⓣ01452/813552, Ⓦ www.cotswolds.com). A fine **hotel** is *Cardynham House* on St Mary's Street (Ⓣ01452/814006, Ⓦ www.cardynham .co.uk; ❻), which has themed rooms, most with four-posters. You can eat well at the atmospheric *Royal Oak* **pub** on the same street.

Stroud and Uley

South of Painswick, the A46 slips into the humdrum market town of **Stroud**, once the centre of the local cloth industry, now famed for its Saturday-morning farmers' market. From here, the B4066 cuts a glorious route southwest along the valley ridge, passing through **ULEY**, six miles out. Boasting a superb setting, the village **church** lords it over the small green and the *Old Crown* pub. **Uley Bury**, among the largest hillforts in Britain, extends along the ridge above the village. The path from the church takes you up the shortest and steepest route – or you could drive up to the summit car park. Fences prevent you from clambering on top of the bury, but you can walk around the edge – about two miles in total – and take in some staggering views.

Berkeley Castle

Though secluded within a swathe of meadows and gardens, **Berkeley Castle** (April, May, Sept & Oct Sun & Thurs 11am–5.30pm; June–Aug Sun–Thurs same hours; £7.50; Ⓦ www.berkeley-castle.com) dominates the little village of **BERKELEY**, about nine miles west of Uley. The stronghold has a turreted medieval look, its twelfth-century austerity softened by its gradual transforma-tion into a family home. The interior is packed with mementoes of its long history, including its grisliest moment when, in 1327, **Edward II** was murdered here – purportedly by a red-hot poker thrust into his backside. You can view the cell where the event took place, along with dungeons, dining room, kitchen, picture gallery and the Great Hall. Outside, the grounds include an Elizabethan terraced garden.

For a lunchtime stop nearby, follow the narrow High Street out of the village for about a mile to reach the *Salutation Inn* (Ⓣ01453/810284), an unpretentious country **pub** with a beer garden.

Vale of White Horse

East of Malmesbury and Cirencester, the humdrum working town of Swindon anchors the southern fringes of the Cotswolds. From here extends the **Vale of White Horse** (Ⓦwww.visitvale.com), a shallow valley whose fertile farmland is studded with tiny villages. It runs east–west between Faringdon and Wantage, roughly twenty miles southwest of Oxford, and takes its name from the prehistoric figure cut into the chalk downs above two of its smaller hamlets – **Uffington** and **Woolstone**. Carved in the first century BC, the horse is the most conspicuous of a string of prehistoric remains that punctuate these open downs and include burial mounds and Iron Age forts. The **Ridgeway National Trail** (see box below), running along or near the top of the downs, links several of these sites, offering wonderful, breezy views and skirting the White Horse itself. Day-trips are easiest, but you might opt to stay locally in the attractive hostel on the ridge above **Wantage**, or in one of the Vale's quaint villages. **Buses** are sporadic: you'll need to plan ahead.

Wantage

Workaday **WANTAGE** is an unassuming market town, its crowded Market Place overseen by a rather uninspiring Victorian statue of its most famous son, Alfred the Great (849–99), the most distinguished of England's Saxon kings. From the south side of the Market Place a couple of alleys lead through to Church Street, where you'll find the **tourist office** (Mon–Sat 10am–4.30pm; Ⓣ01235/760176, Ⓦwww.wantage.com), which sells local hiking maps, and a small museum.

Nearby begins the finest stretch of the **Ridgeway**, running seven miles west along the downs to White Horse Hill (see opposite). In prime position a stone's throw from the trail – two miles south of Wantage – the 🜨 *Court Hill Centre* **hostel** (Ⓣ01235/760253, Ⓦwww.courthill.org.uk; dorm beds £17) consists of several converted timber barns set around a courtyard, with 59 beds in dorms, plus one double, as well as budget meals and space for pitching a tent. Book at least 24 hours ahead.

The Ridgeway National Trail

The Iron Age inhabitants of Britain developed the **Ridgeway** as a major thoroughfare, a fast route that beetled across the chalky downs of modern-day Berkshire and Oxfordshire, negotiated the Thames and then traversed the Chiltern Hills. It was probably once part of a longer route extending from the Dorset coast to the Wash in Norfolk. Today, the Ridgeway is one of the country's National Trails, running from **Overton Hill**, near Avebury in Wiltshire, to **Ivinghoe Beacon**, 87 miles to the northeast near Tring. Crossing five counties, it avoids densely populated areas, keeping to the hills, except where the Thames slices through the trail at **Goring Gap**, marking the transition from the open Berkshire–Oxfordshire downs to the wooded valleys of the Chilterns.

By and large, the Ridgeway is fairly easy hiking and over half is accessible to cyclists. The prevailing winds mean that it is best walked in a northeasterly direction. The trail is strewn with prehistoric monuments, though the finest archeological remains are on the downs edging the **Vale of White Horse** and around **Avebury** (see p.256). There are several **hostels** within reach of the trail – most notably the *Court Hill Centre* near Wantage (see above) – and numerous B&Bs. Maps and detailed guides are available from the National Trails Office (Ⓣ0300/060 0507, Ⓦwww.nationaltrail.co.uk).

White Horse Hill

White Horse Hill, overlooking the B4507 six miles west of Wantage, follows close behind Stonehenge (see p.255) and Avebury (see p.256) in the hierarchy of Britain's ancient sites, though it attracts nothing like the same number of visitors. Carved into the north-facing slope of the downs above the villages of Uffington and Woolstone, the 374-foot-long **horse** looks like something created with a few swift strokes of an immense brush, and there's been no lack of theories as to its origins. Some have suggested it was a glorified signpost, created to show travellers where to join the Ridgeway; others that it represented the horse (or even the dragon) of St George. In Victorian times, the best-loved legend – popularized in a ballad by G.K. Chesterton – claimed that it was cut by King Alfred to celebrate his victory over the Danes at the Battle of Ashdown, fought around here in 871 AD. In fact, burial sites excavated in the surrounding area point to the horse having some kind of sacred function. The first written record of the horse's existence dates from the time of Henry II, but it was cut much earlier, probably in the first century BC. A detailed study in 1994 showed that its creators dug out the soil to a depth of a metre and then filled the hollow with clear white chalk taken from a nearby hill top.

Just below the horse is **Dragon Hill**, a small flat-topped hillock that has its own legend. Locals long asserted that this was where St George killed and buried the dragon, a theory proved, so they argued, by the bare patch at the top and the channel down the side, where blood trickled from the creature's wounds. Here also, at the top of the hill, is the Iron Age earthwork of **Uffington Castle**, which provides wonderful views over the Vale.

The Ridgeway runs alongside the horse and continues west to reach, after one and a half miles, **Wayland's Smithy**, a 5000-year-old burial mound encircled by trees. It is one of the best Neolithic remains along the Ridgeway, though heavy restoration has rather detracted from its mystery. In ignorance of its original function, the invading Saxons named it after Weland (hence Wayland), an invisible smith who, according to their legends, made invincible armour and shod horses without ever being seen.

The B4507 passes the narrow lane that leads – after 500 yards – to the car park just below the White Horse. There are no regular buses.

Woolstone and Uffington

About three-quarters of a mile below the White Horse car park, on the north side of the B4057, is the hamlet of **WOOLSTONE**, where the attractive *White Horse Inn* (☎01367/820726, ⓦwww.whitehorsewoolstone.co.uk; ❸) occupies a half-timbered old building and offers both good-quality pub food and straightforward **accommodation**, mostly in a modern annexe. A mile or so north, the larger village of **UFFINGTON** has the outstanding *Craven* **B&B** on Fernham Road (☎01367/820449, ⓦwww.thecraven.co.uk; ❷), with five cosy guest rooms in a delightful thatched cottage. Breakfast is served in the old farmhouse kitchen.

Reading and the Chiltern Hills

The **Chiltern Hills** extend from Thames-side towns south of Oxford, bumping northeast across Buckinghamshire all the way to Luton in Bedfordshire. At their best, the hills offer handsome countryside, comprising a band of forested chalk hills with steep ridges and deep valleys interrupted by rolling farmland. The Chilterns are also one of England's wealthier areas, liberally sprinkled with exclusive commuter hideaways-cum-country homes. An obvious target is **Henley-on-Thames**, a pleasant riverside town within easy striking distance of the area's key attractions, which offers a reasonable range of accommodation. Nearby highlights include the sumptuous country house and estate of **Cliveden** and the village of **Cookham**, home to the fascinating Stanley Spencer Gallery. Leave time also for the inventive Roald Dahl Museum in docile **Great Missenden**, and **Reading**, a busy town straddling the River Thames just beyond the Chilterns. Crossing the Chilterns to the north and west of Henley, the Ridgeway National Trail (see box, p.300) offers splendid hiking.

Henley, Reading and Great Missenden are well served from London by **train** and there's a branch line up to Cookham from Maidenhead, but to get to Cliveden you'll need your own transport.

Reading

READING, thirty miles southeast of Oxford (and forty miles west of London), is a modern, prosperous town on the south bank of the River Thames. Guarding the western approaches to the capital, it has always been important, long a stopping-off point for kings and queens. Since the 1980s the town has reinvented itself, attracting a raft of IT companies that have made it the epicentre of England's own "Silicon Valley" along the M4 corridor.

Reading also boasts a couple of Victorian curiosities: the **prison** (no public access), a severe-looking structure on Forbury Road, where Oscar Wilde was incarcerated in the 1890s and wrote his poignant *Ballad of Reading Gaol*; and a replica of the **Bayeux Tapestry** recording William the Conqueror's invasion of England in 1066. The original is in France, but in the 1880s thirty-five embroiderers worked on this 70-metre-long copy, now displayed in a purpose-built gallery at the **Museum of Reading**, in the town hall, on the northeast side of the main shopping precinct (Tues–Sat 10am–4pm, Sun 11am–4pm; free; ⓦwww .readingmuseum.org.uk).

Reading boasts a flourishing **arts scene**, with both the Reading Film Theatre (ⓦwww.readingfilmtheatre.co.uk) and Hexagon Theatre (ⓦwww.readingarts .com) offering a programme of concerts and shows. The **Reading Festival** (ⓦwww.readingfestival.com) is a raucous three-day rock and dance music festival held in late August.

The **train station**, with frequent services from London Paddington, is on the north side of town, a five- to ten-minute walk from the centre.

Henley-on-Thames

Oxfordshire, Berkshire and Buckinghamshire meet at **HENLEY–ON–THAMES**, long a favourite stopping-place for travellers between London and Oxford. It's a good-looking, affluent commuter town that's best renowned for its five-day **Royal Regatta** (ⓦwww.hrr.co.uk) in late June or early July, the world's most important amateur rowing tournament, established in 1839. Though it features Olympic rowers past, present and future, the regatta has effectively become a parade ground

---

Thames passenger boats

Salter's Steamers (ⓣ01865/243421, ⓦwww.salterssteamers.co.uk) run **passenger boats** along scenic stretches of the River Thames (mid-May to late Sept). There are services between Oxford and Abingdon, Reading and Henley, Henley and Marlow, and between Marlow, Cookham and Windsor – one or two boats daily on the more popular routes, three weekly on others. Prices are reasonable: Reading to Henley, for example, costs £15.50 return.

for the rich, aristocratic and aspiring, whose champagne-swilling antics are inexplicably found thrilling by large numbers of ordinary folk.

Arrival, information and accommodation

It takes about an hour to get to Henley by **train** from London's Paddington Station, but you almost always have to change twice (at Reading/Slough and Twyford). From Henley **train station**, it's a five-minute walk north to Hart Street, along Station Road and its continuation Thames Side. Regular **buses** from Reading, Oxford, London and nearby villages (including Cookham) stop on or just off Hart Street. The **tourist office** (daily 10am–5pm; Nov–March closes 4pm; ℡01491/578034, ⓦwww.visitsouthoxfordshire.co.uk) is across from the town hall.

Henley has several first-rate **B&Bs**, including *Lenwade*, 3 Western Rd (℡01491/573468, ⓦwww.lenwade.com; ❸), an attractive Edwardian house with six en-suite guest rooms, comfortable furnishings and an unusual stained-glass window in the hallway. Of the **hotels**, top choice is the distinctively slick, contemporary styled *Hotel du Vin* (℡01491/848400, ⓦwww.hotelduvin.com; ❺), in the creatively revamped old Brakspear's Brewery, very central on New Street.

The Town

Henley is at its prettiest among the old brick and stone buildings that flank the short main drag, **Hart Street**, at one end of which is the Market Place and its fetching **town hall**, while at the other rise the easy Georgian curves of **Henley Bridge**. Overlooking the bridge is the **parish church of St Mary**, whose sturdy square tower sports a set of little turrets worked in chequerboard flint and stone, a popular decorative motif hereabouts in the fifteenth and sixteenth centuries. Several operators run **boat trips** on the Thames from the jetties just south of the bridge, including Hobbs & Sons (℡01491/572035, ⓦwww.hobbs-of-henley .com), who offer hour-long jaunts (March–Sept; £7.75); see also box opposite. The imaginative **River and Rowing Museum** (daily 10am–5.30pm; Sept–April closes 5pm; £7.50; ⓦwww.rrm.co.uk), a ten-minute walk south along the riverbank from the foot of Hart Street via Thames Side, focuses on the history of Henley, the development of rowing and the life of the Thames. One of the galleries is devoted to Kenneth Grahame's children's book *Wind in the Willows*, set near Henley where Grahame (1859–1932) lived as a boy.

Eating and drinking

The *Hotel du Vin* has the best **restaurant** in town, emphasizing British cuisine (mains £14–18) – think Yorkshire roast grouse, fillet of Cornish sea bass, Lincolnshire pork cutlet, and so on. *Bloc 2*, across from the town hall at the top of Hart Street, is a great coffee shop, and, among a platoon of downtown **pubs**, *The Angel*, by the bridge, has the advantage of an outside deck overlooking the river. Five miles west of Henley in **Stoke Row** is the seventeenth-century *Crooked Billet* (℡01491/681048), one-time hideout of highwayman Dick Turpin, with an open fireplace and low-beamed ceilings. Their food is excellent, drawing in all sorts of English, French and Italian flourishes (mains around £17; book ahead).

Cookham: Stanley Spencer Gallery

Heading east out of Henley on the A4155, it's eight leafy miles to the riverside town of Marlow, then three more to tiny **COOKHAM**, former home of **Stanley Spencer** (1891–1959), one of Britain's greatest – and most eccentric – artists. The son of a Cookham music teacher, Spencer took inspiration from the Bible: many of his paintings depict biblical tales transposed to his Cookham surroundings – remarkable, visionary works in which the village is turned into a sort of earthly paradise. Spencer made his name in the 1920s, first as an official war artist and then for his *Resurrection: Cookham*, which attracted rave reviews when it was exhibited in London in 1927.

Much of Spencer's best work is in London's Tate Britain (see p.86), but there's a fine sample here at the **Stanley Spencer Gallery** (April–Oct daily 10.30am–5.30pm; Nov–April Thurs–Sun 11am–4.30pm; £3; Ⓦwww.stanleyspencer.org .uk), in the old Methodist Chapel on the High Street, including *View from Cookham Bridge*, the unsettling *Sarah Tubb and the Heavenly Visitors*, and the wonderful (but unfinished) *Christ Preaching at Cookham Regatta*. The gallery has a leaflet detailing a Spencer-themed walk round Cookham (1hr).

From Cookham **train station** (change at Maidenhead if you're coming from Reading or London Paddington), the gallery is a fifteen-minute walk east along the High Street. It stands opposite the antique, half-timbered *Bel & The Dragon* **pub** – a good spot for a pint.

Cliveden

Perched on a ridge overlooking the Thames about four circuitous miles east of Cookham, **Cliveden** (pronounced "clivd'n") is a grand Victorian mansion, designed with sweeping Neoclassical lines by Sir Charles Barry, architect of the Houses of Parliament. Its most famous occupant was **Nancy Astor**, the first woman MP and leading light of the **"Cliveden set"**, a group of influential right-wing politicians who gathered here in the 1930s, though the house remains best known for the party antics of William Waldorf Astor, the third Viscount, in the 1960s – and notably the **Profumo Affair**.

This complicated tale of sex and spies centred on **Stephen Ward**, a society go-between. At one of Cliveden's many parties, he introduced **John Profumo**, then Secretary of State for War, to showgirl **Christine Keeler**. They had an affair, but unluckily for Profumo, Keeler was also sleeping at the time with Yevgeny Ivanov, a naval attaché at the Soviet embassy. It's uncertain whether Keeler passed information from pillow to pillow – and whether Profumo betrayed any secrets – but many historians believe Ward was a Soviet agent, manipulating Keeler. Whatever the truth, when the story broke in 1962, it created an intense scandal. Profumo lied about it to Parliament and was forced to resign; Ward was prosecuted for living off immoral earnings, but committed suicide on the last day of the trial, before the jury reached their verdict. A couple of months later, Prime Minister Harold Macmillan resigned.

The National Trust now owns Cliveden and leases the house as a luxury **hotel** (☎01628/668561, Ⓦwww.clivedenhouse.co.uk; ❻). The extraordinarily lavish interiors feature acres of wood panelling, portraits of past owners and fancy chimneypieces, culminating in the French Dining Room, containing the complete fittings and furnishings of Madame de Pompadour's eighteenth-century dining room, bought as a job lot in Paris by one of the Astors. Most of the hotel is only open to guests, but visitors are permitted limited access on timed, same-day tickets (April–Oct Thurs & Sun 3–5.30pm; £9 including grounds; NT). More satisfying are the **grounds** (daily: mid-March to Oct 11am–6pm; Nov to late Dec 11am–4pm; £8), where a large slice of broadleaf woodland is intercepted by several themed gardens – the water garden is perhaps the most striking. There are also superb views of the Thames, none better than from the Yew Walk just beyond the house.

Great Missenden: Roald Dahl Museum

Enmeshed in suburbia eighteen miles north of Henley, **GREAT MISSENDEN** was home for many years to **Roald Dahl** (1916–1990), one of the world's greatest children's storywriters. Born in Wales, the son of Norwegian parents, Dahl had a tragic life, suffering a harrowing air crash in the Libyan desert during World War II, the death of one of his children from measles and serious injury to another in a car crash. In 1965 his wife, Patricia Neal, suffered three strokes during pregnancy, sinking into a coma. She eventually re-learned to walk and talk with Dahl's help. During and after all this, Dahl was writing a series of extraordinary books, tales infused with menace and comedy, malice and eccentricity, most memorably *James and the Giant Peach* (1961), *Charlie and the Chocolate Factory* (1964), *Fantastic Mr Fox* (1970) and *The BFG* (1982). His house remains in private hands, but nearby is the **Roald Dahl Museum and Story Centre**, 81 High St (Tues–Fri 10am–5pm, Sat & Sun 11am–5pm; £6; Ⓦwww.roalddahlmuseum.org), an unmissable treat for Dahl fans. As well as chronicling the author's life, it explores the nature of creative writing, supported by hints from contemporary writers and interactive games.

Trains serve Great Missenden from London Marylebone (half-hourly; 40min). The museum is a five-minute walk from the station – veer right down the hill and then turn right along High Street.

North Buckinghamshire and Bedford

The untidy landscapes of north **Buckinghamshire** and **Bedfordshire** mark the transition between London's satellite towns and the Midlands. Since 1945, the character of the region has been transformed by the attempt to solve London's overcrowding, and suburbs now encircle many of what were once small country towns: in 1967, Milton Keynes swallowed more than a dozen villages to become the country's largest "New Town". Nonetheless, north Buckinghamshire boasts a couple of fine attractions: **Stowe Gardens**, dotted with a remarkable assortment of outdoor sculptures and follies, and the World War II code-breaking centre of **Bletchley Park**. Meanwhile, Bedfordshire's most distinctive attraction – aside from the wriggling **River Ouse**, whose banks were once lined with watermills and brickworks – is the whopping country mansion of **Woburn Abbey** and nearby safari park. **Bedford** itself is mainly of interest for its links with John Bunyan.

Local **buses** link all the larger towns and there is a fast and frequent **train** service from London to Bedford and Milton Keynes.

Buckingham

Unassuming **BUCKINGHAM** is tucked into a sharp bend in the River Ouse about 25 miles northeast of Oxford. It became the county town of Buckingham-shire in the tenth century and flourished during medieval times, but was bypassed by the Industrial Revolution and remained a backwater until a wave of incomers created the modern suburbs that now surround it. The town centre is at its prettiest along the wide, sloping Market Hill, in the middle of which is the **Old Gaol**, a chunky, stone structure that houses the tourist office (see p.306) and a small local history museum. Otherwise, you might take a peek inside the sombre **Church of St Peter and St Paul**, which perches on the hill where the castle once stood – follow Castle Street from the west end of Market Hill.

Buckingham has no train service, but **buses** from neighbouring towns – principally Milton Keynes – stop on the High Street a few yards from the tourist office in the Old Gaol (Mon–Sat 10am–4pm; July & Aug also Sun noon–4pm; ☎01280/823020, ⓦwww.visitbuckinghamshire.org), which can book **B&Bs**. The *Villiers* is a fine **hotel** in an imaginatively modernized old inn at 3 Castle St (☎01280/822444, ⓦwww.villiers-hotel.co.uk; ❹); most rooms flank the rear courtyard. The best spot for **food** is *Dipalee*, 18 Castle St (☎01280/813151), an Indian restaurant with a good range of main courses from about £8.

Stowe Gardens

Three miles northwest of Buckingham off the A422, the extensive **Stowe Landscape Gardens** (March–Oct Wed–Sun 10am–5.30pm; Nov–Feb Sat & Sun 10.30am–4pm; £7.50; NT) contain an extraordinary collection of outdoor sculptures, monuments and decorative buildings by some of the eighteenth century's greatest designers and architects. They worked at the behest of the prodigiously wealthy Temple and Grenville families, and later the dukes of Buckingham and Chandos. The thirty-odd structures are spread over a sequence of separate, carefully planned landscapes, from the lake views of the Western and Eastern gardens to the wooded delights of the Elysian Fields and the gentle folds of the Grecian Valley, **Capability Brown**'s first large-scale design. The gardens were planned in detail, but the romantic rural idyll they represented was a break with the strictly formal garden tradition that had dominated Europe for decades. There was a political agenda too: the owners were Whigs, proudly committed to the constitutional monarchy and liberal (albeit class-based) notions of political liberty, their *bêtes-noires* being the absolutist Stuarts, whom they had helped depose in the Glorious Revolution of 1688. Several of the monuments hammer home the Whig agenda, especially the **Temple of British Worthies**, whose fourteen busts represent a selection of leading figures of whom the family approved. Many buildings are of interest, most memorably the Neo-Romanesque **Hermitage**, the eccentric **Gothic Temple**, the magnificent **Grecian Temple** (Temple of Concord and Victory) and the beautifully composed **Palladian Bridge**, one of only three such bridges in the country.

At the heart of the gardens, the main **Stowe House**, with its whopping Neoclassical facade, is separate from the estate: it is used by Stowe School, which offers regular guided tours (schedule at ⓦwww.stowe.co.uk; joint ticket with gardens £10.70).

Bletchley Park

Marooned on the edge of Milton Keynes, thirteen miles east of Buckingham, **Bletchley Park** (April–Oct Mon–Fri 9.30am–5pm, Sat & Sun 10.30am–5pm; Nov–March daily 10.30am–4pm; £10 including audioguide; ⓦwww .bletchleypark.org.uk) was the headquarters of Britain's leading code-breakers during World War II, known as "Station X". This was where the British built the first programmable digital computer, Colossus, in 1943, and it was here that they famously broke the German "**Enigma**" code which was encrypting communications within Hitler's armed forces. Much of Station X has survived, its Nissen huts spread over a leafy parcel of land that surrounds the original Victorian mansion. Inside are displays exploring the workings of Station X as well as the stolen Enigma machine that was crucial in deciphering the German code. You can choose to explore independently or book ahead for one of the excellent **guided tours** (see website for details). Bletchley **train** station – with good service from London Euston, Milton Keynes, Birmingham New Street, Northampton and Bedford – is 300 yards from the park.

Woburn

Roughly four miles east of Bletchley Park, the little village of **WOBURN** makes a healthy living from its location beside Woburn Abbey and Safari Park. Little more than one main street lined with Georgian buildings, its most interesting feature is **St Mary's Church**, whose cumbersome stonework is guarded by a couple of peculiar gargoyles, one of which looks like a prototype Tolkien hobgoblin. The interior was refitted in fancy Gothic style by the Duke of Bedford in the 1860s and supplemented with an elaborate reredos a few years later.

Woburn has several good **restaurants**, where you can get set for – or unwind after – an excursion into the Abbey and the Safari Park. Among them, *Nicholls Brasserie*, 13 Bedford St (℡01525/290896), is a chic establishment with an imaginative menu that ranges from guinea fowl to fishcakes, with main courses averaging £15.

Woburn Abbey and Safari Park

The grandiloquent Georgian facade of **Woburn Abbey** (March–Oct daily 11am–5.30pm, last entry 4pm; £12.50; Ⓦwww.woburn.co.uk/abbey) overlooks a chunk of landscaped parkland on the eastern edge of Woburn village. Called an abbey because it was built on the site of a Cistercian foundation, the house is the ancestral pile of the dukes of Bedford, whom Queen Victoria once dismissed as a dull lot. Judging by the family's penchant for canine portraits, she may have had a point, but the lavish state rooms also contain some fine paintings, including an exquisite set of **Tudor portraits**, most notably the famous *Armada Portrait* of Elizabeth I by George Gower. Elsewhere are works by Van Dyck, Velázquez, Gainsborough, Rembrandt and Reynolds, as well as a fine selection of Canalettos.

Another part of the duke's enormous estate is home to **Woburn Safari Park** (March–Oct daily 10am–6pm, last entry 5pm, £18.50; Nov–Feb Sat & Sun 11am–4pm, last entry 3pm, £11; Ⓦwww.woburn.co.uk/safari), Britain's largest drive-through wildlife reserve. The animals – which appear to be in excellent health – include endangered species such as the African white rhino and bongo antelope. Rangers watch out for drivers in distress, but the main danger is an overheated engine rather than a wildlife attack: the park is extraordinarily popular and in high season the traffic can achieve rush-hour congestion. Arrive early for a quieter experience. The park may close in bad weather.

Bedford

BEDFORD, twelve miles northeast of Woburn (and 45 miles north of London), has struggled to retain character in the face of redevelopment, but is pleasant enough, its neat centre hugging the north bank of the River Great Ouse. The town makes the most of its connections with **John Bunyan** (1628–88), a blaspheming tinker turned Nonconformist preacher, who lived most of his life in and around Bedford. Bunyan fought for Parliament in the Civil War and became a well-known public speaker during Cromwell's Protectorate, but in 1660 he was arrested for breaking Charles II's new religious legislation and spent most of the next seventeen years in Bedford prison. During his incarceration he wrote *The Pilgrim's Progress*, whose simple language and powerful allegories were to have a profound influence on generations of Nonconformists and their progressive causes, most notably the campaign for the abolition of slavery.

Built in 1850 on the spot where Bunyan founded his first Independent Congregation, the **Bunyan Meeting Free Church** (Tues–Sat 10.15am–3.45pm), just east of the High Street on Mill Street, is still a Nonconformist church. It bears several memorials to Bunyan, beginning with the splendid bronze doors, decorated with ten finely worked panels inspired by *Pilgrim's Progress*. Inside, the stained-glass windows develop the theme; one shows Bunyan scribbling away in prison. Next door, the modest **Bunyan Museum** (March–Oct Tues–Sat 11am–4pm; free) explores the author's life and times.

Practicalities

Bedford **train station** – on the line from London St Pancras to Corby, Leicester and Sheffield – is a ten-minute walk west of the centre. From the **bus station** on All Hallows, it's a couple of minutes' walk east to the short High Street, which runs north–south and crosses the river. The **tourist office** (Mon–Sat 9am–4.30pm; ℡01234/221712, ⓦwww.visitbedford.co.uk) is in the old town hall, just off the High Street on St Paul's Square. The riverside *Swan* **hotel** is at the foot of the High Street on The Embankment (℡01234/346565, ⓦwww.bedfordswanhotel .co.uk; ④), its Georgian stonework concealing a tastefully modernized interior.

Bedford's unusually large Italian community – a third of the town claims Italian descent – adds a bit of zip to the local **restaurant** scene. Pick of the bunch, serving some of the tastiest pizzas and pastas in town (from £5), is *Pizzeria Santaniello*, 9 Newnham St (℡01234/353742), immediately east of Mill Street's Bunyan Meeting Free Church. Further down Newnham Street, at no. 36, the *Cappuccino Bar* serves up fabulous coffee, ice cream and pizzas.

St Albans

About 25 miles south of Bedford towards London, **ST ALBANS** in Hertfordshire is one of the most appealing towns on the northern peripheries of the capital, its blend of medieval and modern features grafted onto the site of **Verulamium**, the town founded by the Romans soon after their successful invasion of 43 AD. Boudicca burned this settlement to the ground eighteen years later, but reconstruction was swift and the town grew into a major administrative base. It was here, in 209 AD, that a Roman soldier by the name of Alban became the country's first Christian martyr, when he was beheaded for giving shelter to a priest. Pilgrims later flocked to the town that had come to bear his name, with the place of execution marked by a hill-top cathedral that was once one of the largest churches in the Christian world.

Not just a religious centre, St Albans also flourished as a trading town and a staging post on the route to London from the north, its economy buttressed by two local industries, brewing and straw-hat-making. In the nineteenth century, the coaching trade faded away with the coming of the railways, but when St Albans was connected to London by train in 1868, it rapidly reinvented itself as a prosperous and pleasant commuter town, a description that fits well today.

Arrival, information and accommodation

First Capital Connect **trains** from London St Pancras to Bedford stop at St Albans station, from where it's a ten-minute walk west up the hill along Victoria Street to the **main street**, comprising Chequer Street, which begins at the clocktower, and its northern continuation St Peter's Street. Running parallel, immediately to the west, is the Market Place; here, in the town hall, is the **tourist office** (Easter–Oct Mon–Sat 10am–4.30pm; ℡01727/864511, ⓦwww.stalbans.gov.uk).

Of **places to stay**, try the very competent B&B *Wren Lodge*, 24 Beaconsfield Rd (℡01727/855540, ⓦwww.wrenlodge.co.uk; ②), a well-maintained Edwardian house near the station with four attractively furnished bedrooms. A pricier option is *St Michael's Manor Hotel,* in a handsome Georgian house amid terraced grounds on Fishpool Street (☎01727/864444, ⓦwww.stmichaelsmanor.com; ◉), with thirty rooms tastefully decorated in a modern rendition of country-house style.

The City

One good way to start a tour is by climbing to the top of the fifteenth-century **clocktower** (Easter–Sept Sat & Sun 10.30am–5pm; 80p), plumb in the centre of town where the High Street and Market Place meet – worth it for the view over the **cathedral** (daily 8.30am–5.45pm; donation requested; ⓦwww.stalbanscathedral .org), a vast brick-and-flint edifice immediately to the south, reached down a narrow passageway across from the foot of the tower. An abbey was constructed here in 1077 on the site of a Saxon monastery founded by King Offa of Mercia, and despite subsequent alterations – including the ugly nineteenth-century west front – the legacy of the Normans remains the most impressive aspect. The sheer scale of their design is breathtaking: the **nave**, almost 300 feet long, is the longest medieval nave in Britain, even if it isn't the most harmonious – the massive Norman pillars on the north side stand out from those in the later Early English style opposite. Some of the Norman pillars retain thirteenth- and fourteenth-century paintings, their detail clear despite much-faded ochre colouring. Two- and three-tone geometric designs decorate the Norman **arches** in the nave and at the central crossing, where the impact of the original design reaches its peak with the mighty Norman tower.

Behind the high altar an elaborate stone **reredos** (a clumsy construction compared with the splendid Gothic rood screen) hides the fourteenth-century **shrine of St Alban**. The tomb was smashed up during the Reformation, but the Victorians discovered the pieces and gamely put them all together again. Some of the carving on the Purbeck marble is now remarkably clear – look out for the scene on the west end depicting the saint's martyrdom.

Verulamium

From the abbey gateway, a few yards west of the cathedral's main entrance, Abbey Mill Lane leads down past the *Fighting Cocks* (one of England's oldest pubs) and across the trickle of the River Ver to **Verulamium Park**, whose sloping lawns and duck ponds occupy the site of the Roman city. The park holds a scattering of Roman remains, including fragments of the old city wall and the **Hypocaust** (April–Sept Mon–Sat 10am–4.30pm, Sun 2–4.30pm; Oct–March Mon–Sat 10am–3.45pm, Sun 2–3.45pm; free), comprising the foundations of a townhouse complete with an *in situ* mosaic and the original underfloor heating system of the bath suite.

However, this is small beer in comparison with the **Verulamium Museum** (Mon–Sat 10am–5.30pm, Sun 2–5.30pm; £3.50), which occupies an attractive circular building on the northern edge of the park. Inside, a series of well-conceived displays illustrate and explain life in Roman Britain, but these are eclipsed by the **mosaics**, a set of wonderful floor mosaics exhibited in one gallery and unearthed hereabouts in the 1930s and 1950s. Dating from about 200 AD, the Sea God Mosaic has created its share of academic debate, with some arguing it depicts a god of nature with stag antler horns rather than a sea god with lobster claws – but there's no disputing the subject of the Lion Mosaic, in which a lion carries the bloodied head of a stag in its jaws. The most beautiful of the five is the Shell Mosaic, a gorgeous work of art whose semicircular design depicts a beautifully crafted scallop shell within a border made up of rolling waves.

Just to the west, across busy Bluehouse Hill, the **Roman Theatre of Verulamium** (daily 10am–5pm; Nov–Feb closes 4pm; £2.50) was built around 140 AD, but was reduced to the status of a municipal rubbish dump by the fifth century. Little more than a small hollow now, the site nonetheless gives a real sense of how these theatres would once have looked.

From the theatre, you can walk back to the centre along **St Michael's Street**, over one of the prettier stretches of the Ver and past an antique watermill. At the end of St Michael's Street, steer right up the gently curving **Fishpool Street**, a quiet road lined with medieval inns and handsome Georgian houses that leads back to the clocktower.

Eating and drinking

St Albans holds the headquarters of CAMRA, the Campaign for Real Ale: excellent, hand-pumped beers are available in many a local **pub**. Good choices include the *Farmer's Boy*, a short stroll east of the clocktower at 134 London Rd, where they brew their own beers on site, and the antique *Ye Old Fighting Cocks*, on Abbey Mill Lane, which gets crowded on sunny summer days, but still has lots of enjoyable nooks and crannies in which to nurse a pint. Just east of the cathedral, the *Goat Inn*, 37 Sopwell Lane (☎01727/833934), serves great **pub food** (mains £6–9).

Travel details

Buses

For information on all local and national bus services, contact Traveline ☎0871/200 2233, ⓦwww.traveline .info.

Buckingham to: Bedford (hourly; 1hr 30min); Oxford (every 30min; 1hr 15min).

Cheltenham to: Gloucester (Mon–Sat every 15min, Sun 2 hourly; 15–40min); London (11–13 daily; 2hr 35min–3hr 20min); Painswick (Mon–Sat hourly, Sun 6 daily; 30min).

Cirencester to: Cheltenham (Mon–Sat hourly; 45min); Gloucester (Mon–Sat 5 daily; 40min–1hr); Moreton-in-Marsh (Mon–Sat every 2–3hr; 1hr); Northleach (Mon–Sat every 2–3hr; 30min).

Gloucester to: Cheltenham (Mon–Sat hourly; 15–40min); Cirencester (6 daily; 1hr 40min); London (12 daily; 3hr 20min–3hr 50min).

Henley to: London (every 30min; 1hr 20min); Oxford (hourly; 1hr); Reading (hourly; 40min); Wantage (hourly; 1hr 40min).

Oxford to: Buckingham (hourly; 1hr 15min); Henley (hourly; 1hr); London (up to 3 hourly; 1hr 15min);

Reading (every 2hr; 1hr 30min); Wantage (hourly; 45min).

Reading to: Henley (hourly; 20min); Oxford (every 2hr; 1hr 30min).

Trains

For information on all local and national rail services, contact National Rail Enquiries ☎0845/748 4950, ⓦwww.nationalrail.co.uk.

Bedford to: London (2–3 hourly; 30min–1hr); St Albans (4–6 hourly; 40min).

Cheltenham to: Bristol (3 hourly; 45min–1hr); Gloucester (3–4 hourly; 10–15min); London (every 2hr; 2hr 10min).

Gloucester to: Bristol (hourly; 50min); Cheltenham (3–4 hourly; 10–15min); London (every 2hr; 1hr 50min).

Henley to: London (every 30min with 1 or 2 changes; 1hr).

Oxford to: Birmingham (hourly; 1hr 30min); London (1–2 hourly; 1hr).

St Albans to: Bedford (1–2 hourly; 40min); London (14 daily; 20–40min).

Bristol, Bath and Somerset

CHAPTER 5 # Highlights

✳ **Clifton Suspension Bridge**
Brunel's iconic construction
soars above the impressive
Avon Gorge. See p.322

✳ **Thermae Bath Spa** Indulge
yourself with spa treatments
and a rooftop bathe at Bath's
chic, modern spa complex.
See p.329

✳ **Wells Cathedral** A gem of
medieval masonry, not least
for its richly ornamented west
front. See p.335

✳ **Cheddar Gorge** Despite
the coach parties, a truly
impressive rockscape, with

opportunities for scenic walks
in the Mendips. See p.338

✳ **Glastonbury Abbey**
Evocative and picturesque
ruins are a fitting setting for
a complexity of Christian
legends and Arthurian myths.
See p.340

✳ **Exmoor** Explore the wilds
of this national park, along
the dramatic coast or on
moorland tracks. See p.345

✳ **South West Coast Path** The
ever-changing vistas ensure
constant variety on Britain's
longest national trail, which
begins in Somerset. See p.348

▲ Clifton Suspension Bridge

5

Bristol, Bath and Somerset

T he rural allure of England's West Country is encapsulated by the undulating green swards of **Somerset**, where tidy cricket greens and well-kept country pubs contrast with wilder, more dramatic landscapes. A world away from this bucolic charm, the dynamic and cosmopolitan city of **Bristol** has a busy go-ahead vibe, while preserving traces of its long maritime and engineering history. Just a few miles away, the graceful, honey-toned terraces of Georgian **Bath** combine with the city's beautifully preserved Roman baths and a vivacious cultural scene to make an unmissable stop on any itinerary. Within easy reach to the south is the exquisite cathedral city of **Wells**, and the ancient town of **Glastonbury**, steeped in Christian lore and Arthurian legend, and popular with New Age mystics. The nearby **Mendip Hills** are pocked by cave systems, such as **Wookey Hole** and **Cheddar Gorge**, while to the west, **Bridgwater** makes a useful base for exploring the **Quantock Hills** – best experienced on foot or on saddle. West of the Quantocks, and straddling the border between Somerset and Devon, are the heathery slopes of **Exmoor**, whose cliffy seaboard offers strenuous but scenic hikes.

Trains from London's Paddington Station provide easy access to Bristol, Bath and Bridgwater. From these centres, a network of **bus routes** connects with all the places covered in this chapter, with the exception of the heights of the Mendip and Quantock hills. For First, the major bus operator in these parts, see Ⓦwww.firstgroup.com, or check Ⓦwww.travelinesw.com for all services. The M4 and M5 **motorways**, which meet outside Bristol, are the main through-routes for the region.

Bristol

On the borders of Gloucestershire and Somerset, **BRISTOL** has harmoniously blended its mercantile roots with an innovative, modern culture, fuelled in recent years by technology-based industries, a lively arts and media community and a large student population. Its vibrant youth scene ensures the region's best nightlife, while daytime sights range from medieval churches to cutting-edge attractions highlighting the city's scientific achievements.

Weaving through its centre, the River Avon forms part of a system of waterways that made Bristol a great inland port, in later years booming on the transatlantic trafficking of such goods as rum, tobacco and slaves (see box, p.321). In the nineteenth century the illustrious **Isambard Kingdom Brunel** laid the foundations of a tradition of engineering, creating two of Bristol's greatest monuments – the SS *Great Britain* and the lofty Clifton Suspension Bridge. More recently, spin-offs from the aerospace industry have placed the city at the forefront of the fields of communications, computing, design and finance.

Arrival, information and accommodation

Trains from London Paddington arrive at Bristol Temple Meads, a twenty-minute walk from The Centre and served by frequent buses (#8 and #9), which pass through the city centre on their way to Clifton. The circular #500 "Harbour Link" goes through The Centre en route to the Floating Harbour and the river, or you could take advantage of the river ferry, which leaves for The Centre every 20 to 40 minutes. **Cyclists** can take advantage of marked cycle routes (few of them off-road, though), including one between Temple Meads

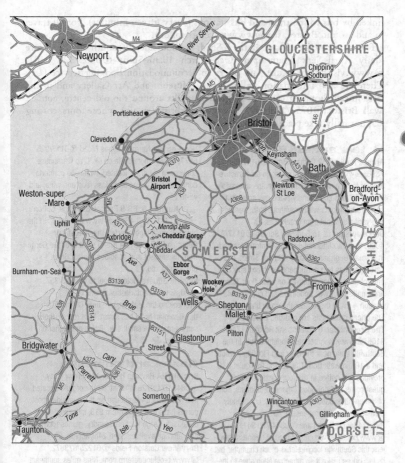

station and the SS *Great Britain*. Pick up *Cycling Bristol*, a free booklet detailing the best bike-friendly routes, from the tourist office, and see Ⓦwww .betterbybike.info for maps and resources. The **bus station** in Marlborough Street has regular National Express services from London; Megabus services from London stop opposite Colston Hall, off The Centre – the name given to the busy traffic intersection at the heart of the modern city, where most local buses stop. **Bristol International Airport** is at Lulsgate, eight miles southwest of town on the A38 (Ⓣ0871/334 4444, Ⓦwww.bristolairport.co.uk), and

Bristol's ferries

A daily **ferry service** operated by Bristol Ferry Boat Co. (Ⓣ0117/927 3416, Ⓦwww .bristolferry.com) connects the various parts of the Floating Harbour including Temple Meads station, The Centre, SS *Great Britain* and various waterside pubs. Leaving twice hourly between 10.30am and 5.50pm, it makes a fun and nifty way to explore Bristol's waterways. Buy tickets on board (£1.60–3.30 one-way; £2.70–4.90 return; £7 all-day ticket).

linked by bus to the train and bus stations (every fifteen minutes). For all travel in and around Bristol, see Ⓦwww.travelbristol.org.

The main **tourist office** is in the E Shed, Harbourside, just south of The Centre (daily April–Sept 10am–6pm; Oct–March 10am–5pm; ☎0333/321 0101, Ⓦwww.visitbristol.co.uk), and offers an accommodation booking service (£3). There are also information desks in City Museum and Art Gallery and in the Broadmead shopping centre. For **guided walks** around the old centre, contact Walk Bristol (☎0753/105 6592, Ⓦwww.walkbristol.co.uk), whose tours, costing £5, normally take place at weekends.

Hotels and B&Bs

Arches House 132 Cotham Brow ☎0117/924 7398, Ⓦwww.arches-hotel.co.uk. In an attractive area of town a mile north of the centre, accessible on bus #9, this eco-friendly place has small but comfortable rooms with or without bath, free wi-fi and vegan or vegetarian breakfasts. ❷

Berkeley Square 15 Berkeley Square ☎0117/925 4000, Ⓦwww.cliftonhotels.com. Centrally located in a smart Georgian building off Park Street, this "art hotel" has two permanent exhibition spaces and rotating works displayed on each floor. Rooms are smallish but well appointed and comfortable enough – avoid those near the noisy basement bar. The pricey breakfasts are charged extra. ❺

The Greenhouse 61 Greenbank Rd ☎0117/902 9166, Ⓦwww.thegreenhousebristol.co.uk. In the Southville area, near the river and Floating Harbour and a 10min walk from The Centre, this quiet B&B provides real coffee in the four pastel-shaded guestrooms and delicious organic breakfasts. Some of the en-suite bathrooms are small, but friendly owners and wi-fi compensate. ❹

Hotel24Seven Dean Lane ☎0844/770 9411, Ⓦwww.hotel24seven.com. Aimed at business travellers, this Southville lodging lacks much character, but its low prices make it an attractive alternative to the usual B&B/hotel. The varied rooms are clean and functional, and there's a shared kitchen for self-caterers and free wi-fi. Needs booking. ❶

Hotel du Vin Narrow Lewins Mead ☎0117/925 5577, Ⓦwww.hotelduvin.co.uk. Chic warehouse conversion, centrally located, with solid comforts, contemporary decor, first-class food and wine, and wi-fi. ❻

Number 9. PB 9 Princes Buildings, Clifton ☎0117/973 4615, Ⓦwww.9pb.co.uk. In the chic Clifton Village quarter, this five-storey Georgian B&B enjoys a grand vista over the Gorge from its elegant and spacious rooms. Great breakfasts, too. ❸

Victoria Square Victoria Square ☎0843/357 1490, Ⓦwww.victoriasquarehotel.co.uk. Overlooking the leafy square near Clifton Village, this Georgian hotel has smart, light rooms, though some are on the small side. Rates are higher on weekdays. ❸–❺

Hostel and campsite

Bristol YHA Hayman House, 14 Narrow Quay ☎0845/371 9726, Ⓔbristol@yha.org.uk. Located in a refurbished warehouse on the quayside; most dorms have four beds (from £18, including breakfast). Large kitchen, laundry, games room and bike storage available, and 24hr access. ❶

Bury View Corston Fields ☎01225/873672, Ⓦwww.brooklodgefarm.com. Nine miles southeast of Bristol, off the A39 near Keynsham, this rural site is flat, spacious and clean. The *Wheatsheaf* pub is just 5min away. Check winter opening.

The City

Once a quay-lined dock but now the traffic-ridden nucleus of the city, **The Centre** makes a good place to kick off an exploration of Bristol, just a few steps from the cathedral and the oldest quarter of town. At its southern end is a branch of the **Floating Harbour**, the waterway network that links up with the **River Avon**. You could cover Bristol's other central attractions on foot without too much sweat, but buses are useful for the **Clifton** district, at the highest part of town on the edge of the Avon Gorge.

College Green: the cathedral and Lord Mayor's Chapel

A short walk west of The Centre, the grassy expanse of **College Green** is dominated by the crescent-shaped Council House, from the 1950s, and the contrasting medieval lines of **Bristol Cathedral** (Mon–Fri 8am–6.30pm, Sat &

A weekend in Bristol

Friday night

Spend the evening by the water at the **Floating Harbour**, where either the Watershed or Arnolfini arts centres would make a congenial spot for a drink. Have a meal at the waterside *Severnshed* or *riverstation* restaurants, then stroll over to King Street to catch some live **jazz** at the *Old Duke* pub.

Saturday

Head for **St Nicholas Markets**, browse the stalls here and pick up a coffee or a juice. From Corn Street, cross The Centre to the bottom of Park Street and College Green, where two faithfully preserved **churches** – Bristol Cathedral and the Lord Mayor's Chapel – merit a leisurely look. Make your way up Park Street, turning off at Great George Street to see the **Georgian House**, a fascinating insight into the lives of the merchants who created the city's wealth. Have a bite to eat at the *Boston Tea Party* or one of the other eateries on Park Street, then continue up the hill to immerse yourself in **art and antiquity** at the City Museum and Art Gallery. In the evening, you might try one of the restaurants in **Easton**, for example *Café Maitreya* or the *Thali Café*, before unwinding in a pub or lounge bar. If you're up for it, sample Bristol's up-to-the-minute **clubbing** scene to round off the night.

Sunday

In the morning, take a tour round **SS Great Britain**, Brunel's beautifully restored iron ship. Then head up to **Clifton**, window-shop among the boutiques and antiques shops of Clifton Village, and soak up the views of Clifton Suspension Bridge from the terrace bar of the *Avon Gorge Hotel*. Have a drink or lunch here, then stretch your legs on the grassy expanse of Clifton Downs. Alternatively, spend the afternoon in **Clifton Zoo**, bordering the Downs.

Sun 8am–5pm; Ⓦwww.bristol-cathedral.co.uk). Founded around 1140 as an abbey on the supposed spot of St Augustine's convocation with Celtic Christians in 603, this became a cathedral church with the Dissolution of the Monasteries. Among the many later additions are the two towers on the west front, erected in the nineteenth century. The cathedral's interior offers a unique example among Britain's cathedrals of a German-style "hall church", in which the aisles, nave and choir rise to the same height. The choir offers one of the country's most exquisite illustrations of the early Decorated style of Gothic, while the adjoining thirteenth-century Elder Lady Chapel contains some fine tombs and eccentric carvings of animals, including a monkey playing the bagpipes accompanied by a ram on the violin. From the south transept, a door leads through to the Chapter House, a richly carved piece of late Norman architecture.

Across College Green, take a glance at the **Lord Mayor's Chapel** (Wed–Sun 10am–noon & 1–4pm), conspicuous by its large Perpendicular window. The interior has some lovely French and Flemish stained glass, and striking effigies of the thirteenth-century founders of the hospital of which the church once formed a part.

Park Street and around

Elegant Georgian streets lead off the shop-lined **Park Street**, which climbs steeply up from College Green. On Great George Street, the **Georgian House** (Mon–Wed, Sat & Sun 10am–5pm; free) is the former home of a local sugar merchant, its spacious and faithfully restored rooms filled with sumptuous examples of period furniture. Upstairs, illustrated panels tell the engrossing story of the family's dealings in the West Indies, including their involvement in slavery.

BRISTOL

B, C, 3 & Clifton

Queen's Road

M5 & Clifton Suspension Bridge

ST PAUL'S ROAD

WHITELADIES ROAD

ELMDALE ROAD

PRIORY ROAD

WOODLAND ROAD

ST MICHAEL'S PARK

TYNDALL AVENUE

ST MICHAEL'S HILL

HORFIELD ROAD

UPPER MAUDLIN STREET

LOWER

Bristol Royal Infirmary

LEWINS

RUPERT

ELTON ROAD

COTHAM

UNIVERSITY WALK

UNIVERSITY ROAD

WOODLAND ROAD

BERKELEY PLACE

City Museum & Art Gallery

7

N

BERKELEY SQUARE

E

PARK ROW

Red Lodge

COLSTON STREET

CHRISTMAS STEPS

COLSTON AVENUE

Megabus Bus Stop

D

SMALL ST

CORN

9

JACOB'S WELLS ROAD

Cabot Tower

Brandon Hill Park

CHARLOTTE STREET

GREAT GEORGE STREET

PARK STREET

11

13

Georgian House

FROGMORE STREET

DENMARK STREET

12

Specialized Concept Store

TRENCHARD STREET

10

PARADE

ST AUGUSTINE'S

St Stephen's

The Centre

14

BROAD QUAY

BALDWIN

HIGH STREET

ST

The Council House

College Green

Lord Mayor's Chapel

Quayhead

MARSH STREET

Theatre Royal

KING ST

QUEEN SQUARE

ST GEORGE'S ROAD

DEANERY RD

Cathedral

Ferry Stop

i

Central Library

Blue Reef Aquarium

17

@

Watershed Media Centre

HOTWELL ROAD

ANCHOR ROAD

At-Bristol

18

CANONS ROAD

MILLENNIUM SQUARE

20

Pero's Bridge

F

PRINCE STREET

THE GROVE

QUEEN SQUARE

P

HARBOURSIDE

SS Great Britain

Ferry Stop

P

Floating Harbour

Ferry Stop

Arnolfini Arts Centre

WAPPING ROAD

GASFERRY ROAD

M Shed

CUMBERLAND ROAD

CORONATION ROAD

SOUTHVILLE

G

BALLEY ROAD

River Avon

DEAN LANE

CORONATION ROAD

BEDMINSTER

H

CLUBS & LIVE MUSIC	
Bierkeller	8
Colston Hall	10
Fiddlers	24
Flamingos	6
Lakota	2
Motion	19
O2 Academy	12
St George's	13
Thekla	22
Timbuk 2	9

From Great George Street, or from Berkeley Square further up the hill, you can access the steep **Brandon Hill Park**, where you can climb the 105-foot **Cabot Tower** (open daily until dusk; free) – built in 1897 to commemorate the four-hundredth anniversary of John Cabot's voyage to America – for the city's best panorama.

At the top of Park Street, on Queen's Road, the **City Museum and Art Gallery** (daily 10am–5pm; free) has the usual sections on local archeology, geology and

MARLBOROUGH ST

BOND STREET

NEWFOUNDLAND STREET

Bus Station

THE HAYMARKET

HORSEFAIR

WELLINGTON ROAD

MAUDLIN ST

MEAD

MEAD STREET

New Room

PENN ST

UNION STREET

Broadmead Shopping Centre

Cabot Circus Shopping Centre

❻

WEST STREET

Police Station

NELSON STREET

BROAD WEIR

TOWER CASTLE

OLD MARKET STREET

❹ ❺ & A420 Chippenham

❽

FAIRFAX

BROAD STREET

WINE STREET

Castle Green

CASTLE STREET

CASTLE STREET

QUEEN STREET

TOWER HILL

St Nicholas Markets

NICHOLAS ST

Ferry Stop

Ferry Stop

AVON STREET

STREET

VICTORIA STREET

TEMPLE BACK

ST THOMAS STREET

TEMPLE WAY

TEMPLE BACK

BRISTOL-BATH CYCLEWAY

❶⑤

❶⑥

QUEEN CHARLOTTE STREET

WELSH BACK

REDCLIFFE STREET

Ferry Stop

Temple Meads Train Station

❶⑨

❷② ❷③ ❷①

REDCLIFFE WAY

Ferry Stop

REDCLIFFE WAY

REDCLIFFE PARADE

REDCLIFFE HILL

St Mary Redcliffe

REDCLIFFE MEAD LANE

SOMERSET STREET

TEMPLE GATE

GUINEA STREET

REDCLIFFE

BATH ROAD

COMMERCIAL ROAD

CLARENCE ROAD

River Avon

YORK ROAD

BEDMINSTER PARADE

0 ___ 200 yds

▼ ❷④ , A38 & Bristol Airport A37 & A39 Wells ▼ ▼ ❶ & A4 Bath

ACCOMMODATION

Arches House	A
Berkeley Square	E
Bristol YHA	F
Bury View	I
The Greenhouse	G
Hotel24Seven	H
Hotel du Vin	D
Number 9. PB	B
Victoria Square	C

EATING

Bordeaux Quay	20
Browns	7
Café Maitreya	5
riverstation	23
Severnshed	21
Thali Café	4

DRINKING

Avon Gorge Hotel	3
Boston Tea Party	11
Canteen	1
Grain Barge	18
Llandoger Trow	16
Old Duke	15
Start the Bus	14
Watershed	17

natural history that you'd expect in a provincial museum, but its scope is occasionally surprising – it has an important collection of Chinese porcelain, glassware, stoneware and ivory, and some magnificent Assyrian reliefs carved in the eighth century BC. The second-floor gallery of paintings and sculptures includes work by English Pre-Raphaelites and French Impressionists, as well as a few choice older pieces, among them a portrait of Martin Luther by Cranach and Giovanni Bellini's unusual *Descent into Limbo*.

The Banksy phenomenon

An integral part of Bristol's cultural profile, the street artist known as **Banksy** has managed to maintain his anonymity despite his global celebrity, with exhibitions pulling crowds from London to Los Angeles. It was in Bristol, though, a city known since the 1980s for its **graffiti art**, that he first made his mark, leaving his stencilled daubs and freehand murals on walls throughout the inner city. The sly wit that undercuts his social satire has led to his works becoming accepted and even protected by the city supremos, culminating in a wildly successful exhibition in the City Museum in 2009. Websites such as Ⓦ www.bristol-street-art.co.uk will allow you to track down his surviving murals, though it's easy enough to locate his more iconic works such as *The Mild Mild West* on Stokes Croft and *The Naked Man* off Park Street.

Turning right at the top of Park Street onto Park Row, the **Red Lodge** (Mon–Wed, Sat & Sun 10am–5pm; free) was originally a merchant's home when built in the sixteenth century, and later became England's first girls' reform school. Highlight is the Great Oak Room, featuring a splendid carved stone fireplace and lavish oak panelling.

From The Centre to Broadmead

One of Bristol's oldest churches, **St Stephen's**, stands at the northern end of The Centre. Established in the thirteenth century, rebuilt in the fifteenth and thoroughly restored with plenty of neo-Gothic trimmings in 1875, the parish church has some flamboyant tombs inside, mainly of various members of the merchant class who were the church's main patrons.

On nearby **Corn Street**, in the city's financial quarter, you'll find the Georgian Corn Exchange, designed by John Wood of Bath, and now holding the covered **St Nicholas Markets**, which include a great range of delis, cafés and juice bars. Outside the entrance stand four engraved bronze pillars, dating from the sixteenth and seventeenth centuries and transferred from a nearby arcade where they served as trading tables.

The area north of here holds the modern, partly pedestrianized shopping centre of **Broadmead**, within which survives one older building, the **New Room** (Mon–Sat 10am–4pm; free), accessible from both the central strip of Broadmead and from the Horsefair. Established by John Wesley in 1739, this was the country's first Methodist chapel, and today looks very much as Wesley left it, with a double-deck pulpit beneath a hidden upstairs window, from which the evangelist could observe the progress of his trainee preachers.

King Street and Queen Square

King Street, a short walk southeast from The Centre, was laid out in 1633 and still holds some fine seventeenth- and eighteenth-century buildings, among them the **Theatre Royal**, the oldest working theatre in the country. Opened in 1766 and preserving many of its original Georgian features, the theatre hosted most of the famous names of its time, including Sarah Siddons, whose ghost is said to stalk the building. Further down, the timber-framed **Llandoger Trow** pub derives its name from the flat-bottomed boats that were used to trade between Bristol and the Welsh coast, and is reputed to have been the meeting place of Daniel Defoe and Alexander Selkirk, the model for Robinson Crusoe.

South of King Street, **Queen Square** is an elegant grassy area with a statue of William III by Flemish sculptor John Michael Rysbrack at its centre, reckoned to be the best equestrian statue in the country. The square was the site of some of the worst civil disturbances ever seen in England when the Bristolians rioted in support of the Reform Bill of 1832.

St Mary Redcliffe

The southeast corner of Queen Square leads to Redcliffe Bridge, across which the spire of **St Mary Redcliffe** (Mon–Sat 9am–5pm, Sun 8am–7.30pm) provides one of the distinctive features of the city's skyline. Described by Elizabeth I as "the goodliest, fairest, and most famous parish church in England", the church was largely paid for and used by merchants and mariners. The present building was begun at the end of the thirteenth century, though it was added to in subsequent centuries and the spire dates from 1872. Inside, memorials and tombs recall some of the figures associated with the building, including the arms and armour of Sir William Penn, admiral and father of the founder of Pennsylvania, on the north wall of the nave, and the Handel Window in the North Choir aisle, installed in 1859 on the centenary of the death of Handel, who composed on the organ here. The whale bone above the entrance to the Chapel of St John the Baptist is said to have been brought back from Newfoundland by John Cabot. The poets Samuel Taylor Coleridge and Robert Southey were both married in St Mary, within six weeks of each other in 1795.

Around the harbourside

At the southern end of The Centre, **St Augustine's Reach**, part of the Floating Harbour, is flanked by pubs, clubs, and the **Arnolfini** and **Watershed** arts centres, both housed in refurbished Victorian warehouses and the venues for

> ## The slave trade in Bristol
>
> The statue of Edward Colston that stands in Bristol's Centre has more than once been the subject of graffiti attacks and calls for its removal. Although the eighteenth-century sugar magnate is revered as a great philanthropist – his name given to numerous buildings, streets and schools in Bristol – he is reviled by many as a leading light in the London-based Royal African Company, which held the monopoly on the **slave trade** until the market was opened in 1698. From that date until the abolition of the British slave trade in 1807, merchants throughout the country were able to participate in the "triangular trade" whereby vast numbers of slaves were shipped from West Africa to plantations in the Americas, the vessels returning to Europe with cargoes of sugar, cotton, tobacco and other slave-produced commodities. By the 1730s, Bristol had become – along with London and Liverpool – one of the main beneficiaries of the trade, sending out a total of more than two thousand ships in search of slaves on the African coast; in 1750 alone, Bristol ships transported some eight thousand of the twenty thousand slaves sent that year to British colonies in the Caribbean and North America. The direct profits, together with the numerous spin-offs, helped to finance some of the city's finest Georgian architecture.
>
> Bristol's primacy in the trade had already been long supplanted by Liverpool by the time opposition to the trade began to gather force: first the Quakers and Methodists, then more powerful forces, voiced their discontent. By the 1780s the Anglican Dean Josiah Tucker and the Evangelical writer Hannah More had become active abolitionists, and Samuel Taylor Coleridge made a famous anti-slavery speech in Bristol in 1795.
>
> Today, Bristol's Caribbean link is maintained by an active West Indian population largely concentrated in the St Paul's district – scene of a flamboyant carnival in early July. To learn more about the city's involvement in the slave trade, visit the small but informative exhibition at the Georgian House (see p.317).

5

BRISTOL, BATH AND SOMERSET | Bristol

exhibitions and art-house films. Opposite the Arnolfini is the site for **M Shed**, a new museum dedicated to Bristol, due to open in 2011: see Ⓦmshed.org for opening details.

Behind the Watershed, off Anchor Road, the pricey **Blue Reef Aquarium** (Mon–Fri 10am–5pm; Sat, Sun & school hols 10am–6pm; £13.50; Ⓦwww .bluereefaquarium.co.uk) allows you to get close up to a fabulous array of mainly tropical fish, from conger eels and rays to sharks, and there are talks and Imax cinema screenings. Next to the aquarium, the interactive science centre **At-Bristol** (same times as Aquarium; £10.80; Ⓦwww.at-bristol.org.uk) is chiefly aimed at families and schoolkids, though there's a good half-day's worth of entertainment for everyone here, with opportunities to view the blood in your veins, freeze your shadow and create animations (including input from Aardman Animations). The spherical, stainless-steel **planetarium** attached to the complex has five to ten half-hour daily shows illustrating the night sky; book a slot when you buy your entry tickets.

SS Great Britain and the Matthew

A quick ride on the ferry west, or a ten-minute walk, brings you to the **SS Great Britain** (daily: April–Oct 10am–5.30pm; Nov–March 10am–4.30pm; last entry 1hr before closing; £11.95; Ⓦwww.ssgreatbritain.org), the first propeller-driven, ocean-going iron ship, built by Brunel in 1843. After circumnavigating the globe 32 times, her sea-faring days ended in 1886 when she was caught in a storm off Cape Horn and abandoned in the Falkland Islands. Salvaged and returned to Bristol in 1970, she is now berthed in the same dry dock in which she was built. Visitors can peer into the immense engine room, see the restored cabins – the bunks occupied by eerily breathing mannequins – and take in the various displays illustrating the background and history of the vessel. Alongside the ship may be moored a much smaller affair, a replica of the **Matthew** (same ticket; Ⓦwww .matthew.co.uk), the vessel in which John Cabot sailed to America in 1497 – though the ship is frequently absent on sailing excursions.

Clifton

The long Whiteladies Road leads northwest of the centre to **Clifton**, once an aloof spa resort and now Bristol's most elegant quarter. **Clifton Village**, its select enclave, is centred on the Mall, close to **Royal York Crescent**, the longest Georgian crescent in the country, offering splendid views over the steep drop to the River Avon below.

A few minutes' walk behind the Crescent is Bristol's most famous symbol, **Clifton Suspension Bridge**, 702-foot long and poised 245ft above high water. Money was first put forward for a bridge to span the Avon Gorge by a Bristol wine merchant in 1753, though it was not until 1829 that a competition was held for a design, won by Isambard Brunel on a second round, and not until 1864 that the bridge was completed, five years after Brunel's death. Hampered by financial difficulties, the bridge never quite matched the engineer's original ambitious design, which included Egyptian-style towers topped by sphinxes on each end. You can see copies of Brunel's drawings in the **Interpretation Centre**, located at the far side of the bridge (daily 10am–5pm; free; Ⓦwww .cliftonbridge.org.uk), alongside other designs proposed by Brunel's rivals, some of them frankly bizarre.

Stretching north of the bridge at the top of the gorge is the broad expanse of **Clifton Downs**, adjoining which **Bristol Zoo** (daily: April–Oct 9am–5.30pm; Nov–March 9am–5pm; £11.81; Ⓦwww.bristolzoo.org.uk) is renowned for its animal conservation work, and also features a collection of rare trees and shrubs.

Eating and drinking

Bristol's numerous **pubs** and **restaurants** are nearly always buzzing – especially those around King Street and Corn Street.

Restaurants

Bordeaux Quay V-Shed, Harbourside ☎0117/943 1200. Housed in a former warehouse, this has an elegantly minimalist restaurant upstairs (closed Sat lunch, Sun eve & all Mon) with harbour views and mains costing £13–22, and a downstairs brasserie (open all week), which is less formal and cheaper (main dishes around £10). The food in both is mainly Mediterranean, using local and organic ingredients. There's also a bar and an excellent deli.

Browns 38 Queen's Rd ☎0117/930 4777. Spacious and relaxed place for breakfast, a superior burger (£10), seafood platter (£13.50) or a late cocktail; it's housed in the former Art Museum, modelled on the Doge's Palace, Venice.

Café Maitreya 89 St Mark's Rd ☎0117/951 0100. Tucked away in the multicultural Easton neighbourhood (bus #48/49 from The Centre), this casual-smart eatery is rated one of the country's best vegetarian restaurants, with a constantly changing menu of innovative dishes. Fixed-price menus are £10–13 at lunchtime, £20–23 for dinner. Open Wed–Sat only.

riverstation The Grove ☎0117/914 4434. A former river-police station artfully transformed, with the downstairs *Bar Kitchen* serving deli-type snacks and drinks (some tables on an outdoor deck), and a more formal upstairs restaurant offering Modern European dishes. Set-price lunches here cost around £10, while main courses in the evening are £14–20. Try to bag a table by the window for the dockside views. Closed Sun eve, restaurant also Mon eve.

Severnshed The Grove ☎0117/925 1212. Right next to *riverstation* with a waterside terrace, this serves light, tasty food, ranging from fish and chips "with Yorkshire caviar" (mushy peas) to lobster and asparagus risotto – respectively £9.75 and £12. Two-course meals are offered for £10 (Mon–Sat

noon–3pm & 6–7pm), and tapas and good cocktails are also available.

Thali Café 64–66 St Mark's Rd ☎0117/951 4979. *Dhaba*-style South Asian food in vibrant surroundings in the heart of Easton (bus #48/49): a combination of spicy dishes is served on a steel plate (around £7.50). Live acoustic music on Sun eve. There are also branches in Clifton and Montpelier. Closed Mon daytime.

Pubs, bars and cafés

Avon Gorge Hotel Sion Hill. On the edge of the Gorge in Clifton Village, the mediocre bar is compensated for by a broad terrace with magnificent views. Meals available.

Boston Tea Party 75 Park St. Cosy spot in the centre of town for teas and coffees as well as soups and pies, with seating upstairs and a heated terrace garden. Closed eve.

Canteen 80 Stokes Croft ☎0117/924 9599, ⓦthecanteenbristol.wordpress.com. Overlooked by one of Banksy's most famous murals, a drab 1960s office block now accommodates Coexist (ⓦwww .coexistuk.org), dedicated to community enterprises in the neighbourhood, and including workshops, studios and meeting spaces. There's also a chilled-out bar for coffee, beer, cider, good cheap food and live music most nights. It's a 10min walk up Stokes Croft from Broadmead.

Grain Barge Hotwell Rd ☎0117/929 9347, ⓦwww.grainbarge.com. A floating pub, café and restaurant with a tranquil ambience, real ales and regular live music on Fri eve.

Llandoger Trow King St. Seventeenth-century tavern full of historical resonance (see p.320), with cosy nooks and armchairs.

Old Duke King St. Jolly, trad-jazz pub with live bands nightly and lunchtime on Sun, and tables outside.

Start the Bus 7 Baldwin St ☎0117/930 4370, ⊚www.startthebus.tv. Indie hangout, though with an eclectic choice of music and food (including Hippy Burgers). Art students have been let loose on the decor, and there are board games, comfy sofas and live music or DJs in the evening.

Watershed 1 Canon's Rd, Harbourside. This arts complex (see below) overlooking the boats has a great bar and café, with food available until 10pm (7pm on Sun) and free internet access.

Nightlife and entertainment

Nightlife is equally lively; for a full list of **clubs** and events, pick up a copy of the weekly **listings** magazine *Venue*, or consult ⊚bristolnightlife.com. Bristol's handful of multimedia **arts centres** – two of them are listed below – are always worth checking out, while the Theatre Royal is the most famous of the local **theatres**; for other venues and to see what's on, see ⊚theatrebristol.net.

Clubs and live venues

Bierkeller All Saints St, off Broadmead ☎0117/926 8514, ⊚www.bristolbierkeller.co.uk. Live music of the metal and punk ilk in this sweaty cellar venue. Live oompah band on Sat.

Colston Hall Colston St ☎0117/922 3686, ⊚www.colstonhall.org. Major names appear in this stalwart of mainstream venues. Lunchtime classical recitals cost £5.

Fiddlers Willway St, Bedminster ☎0117/987 3403, ⊚www.fiddlers.co.uk. Mainly folk, ska and world bands at this relaxed live music venue on the south side of the river, off Bedminster Parade. It's a 10min walk from St Mary Redcliffe, or take buses #52, #75–77, #89 or #90 from The Centre (#N5 or #N6 at night).

Flamingos 23–25 West St, Old Market ⊚www.flamingosbristol.com. In the heart of Bristol's "gay village", this lively club boasts of being the biggest LGBT club in the southwest, with two main rooms and four bars. If you don't like the vibe, there are several alternatives steps away.

Lakota 6 Upper York St ⊚www.lakota.co.uk. The *grande dame* of Bristol's club scene, it's neither state-of-the-art nor particularly salubrious, but it can still serve up the goods, churning out hardcore and drum'n'bass, with Tribe of Frog taking over on the last Sat of the month.

Motion 74 Avon St ☎0117/972 3111, ⊚www.motionbristol.com. It's worth the effort to reach this out-of-the-way place near Temple Meads station for all-night raves and big-name acts pumping out dubstep, drum'n'bass and electro. There's a huge main room, an outdoor area, and by day it's a skate park.

02 Academy Frogmore St ☎0844/477 2000, ⊚www.o2academybristol.co.uk. Near The Centre, this spacious, multi-level place stages almost nightly live gigs.

St George's Great George St ☎0845/402 4001, ⊚www.stgeorgesbristol.co.uk. This elegant Georgian church with near-perfect acoustics has regular lunchtime and evening concerts of classical, world and jazz music.

Thekla The Grove ☎0117/929 3301, ⊚www.theklabristol.co.uk. Riverboat venue popular with students, staging regular live bands plus dub, house and indie club nights. Can get rammed. Look out for the Banksy artwork on the hull.

Timbuk 2 22 Small St ☎0117/945 8459, ⊚www.tb2.co.uk. Central, intimate (and slightly grungy) basement club for dubstep, drum'n'bass and house music. Open Thurs–Sat eve and 24hr as a café Mon–Sat.

Arts and culture

Arnolfini 16 Narrow Quay, Harbourside ☎0117/917 2300, ⊚www.arnolfini.org.uk. Arts complex including a cinema, gallery, bookshop and café-bar, with tables on the quay.

Theatre Royal King St ☎0117/987 7877, ⊚www.bristololdvic.org.uk. Home to the Old Vic company, Bristol's main theatre venue has a continuous programme of quality productions.

Watershed 1 Canon's Rd, Harbourside ☎0117/927 5100, ⊚www.watershed.co.uk. Exhibitions and talks are held here, while art-house films are shown at the three screens – it's also the venue for regular film festivals.

Listings

Bike rental Blackboy Hill Cycles, 180 Whiteladies Rd, Clifton ☎0117/973 1420; Specialized Concept Store, 12–14 Park St ☎0117/929 7368.

Buses Local services ☎0845/602 0156, ⊚www.firstgroup.com. In addition to National Express and Megabus, Bakers Dolphin (☎01934/415000,

The monumental new shopping precinct at the eastern end of Broadmead, **Cabot Circus** is the place for the big stores, including an outpost of the exclusive Harvey Nichols. **Clifton Village** (see p.322) offers antiques and chic boutiques aplenty. For humbler ware, delve into **St Nicholas Markets** (see p.320), a rich warren of stalls selling everything from posters and secondhand books to trendy clothes and jewellery. For comestibles, check out the **Slow Food Market**, held on the first Sunday of the month on adjacent Corn Street, also the venue for a good **Farmers' Market** (Wed 9.30am–2pm).

Ⓦwww.bakersdolphin.com) operates a limited service to London.
Hospital Bristol Royal Infirmary, Marlborough St ℡0117/923 0000.
Internet Free access at the Central Library, College Green (Mon, Tues & Thurs 9.30am–7.15pm, Wed 10am–4.45pm, Fri & Sat 9.30am–4.45pm, Sun

1–4.45pm; book at ℡0117/903 7234), and the Watershed, St Augustine's Reach (daily roughly 9.30am–11pm).
Police Rupert St ℡0845/456 7000.
Taxis Ranks at train and bus stations, and in The Centre. Call ℡0117/925 1111 or 0117/955 9999.

Bath

Though only twelve miles from Bristol, **BATH** has a very different feel from its neighbour – more harmonious, compact, leisurely and complacent. Jane Austen set *Persuasion* and *Northanger Abbey* here, it is where Gainsborough established himself as a portraitist and landscape painter, and the city's elegant crescents and Georgian buildings are studded with plaques naming Bath's eminent inhabitants from its heyday as a spa resort. Nowadays Bath ranks as one of Britain's top tourist cities, yet the place has never lost the exclusive air those names evoke.

Bath owes its name and fame to its **hot springs** – the only ones in the country – which made it a place of reverence for the local Celtic population, though it had to wait for Roman technology to create a fully-fledged bathing establishment. The baths fell into decline with the departure of the Romans, but the town later regained its importance under the Saxons, its abbey seeing the coronation of the first king of all England, Edgar, in 973. A new bathing complex was built in the sixteenth century, popularized by the visit of Elizabeth I in 1574, and the city reached its fashionable zenith in the eighteenth century, when **Beau Nash** ruled the town's social scene. It was at this time that Bath acquired its ranks of Palladian mansions and townhouses, all of them built in the local **Bath stone**, which is still the city's leitmotif today. The acres of parkland between the Georgian developments lend modern Bath a spacious feel, with theatrical vistas at every turn.

Arrival, information and accommodation

Bath Spa **train station** and the city's **bus station** are both a short walk south of the centre. Drivers are advised to use one of the **park-and-ride** car parks around the periphery. If you're coming from Bristol, note that you can **cycle** all the way along the route of a disused railway line, following the course of the River Avon for much of the way.

The **tourist office**, right next to the abbey on Abbey Churchyard (June–Sept Mon–Sat 9.30am–6pm, Sun 10am–4pm; Oct–May Mon–Sat 9.30am–5pm, Sun

Tours in and around Bath

A tour with a knowledgeable commentary can be the best way to take in a lot of Bath in a short time. Free **walking tours** of Bath leave daily from Abbey Churchyard at 10.30am and 2pm (℡01225/477411, ⓦwww.bathguides.org.uk; no 2pm tour on Sat; May–Sept also Tues & Fri 7pm; 2hr), while Bizarre Bath offers **"comedy walks"** around the city every evening from April to October (℡01225/335124, ⓦwww .bizarrebath.co.uk; 1hr 30min; £8); meet at 8pm outside the *Huntsman Inn* on North Parade Passage). Two-hour **ghost walks** leave from outside the *Garrick's Head* pub next to the Theatre Royal at 8pm (℡01225/350512, ⓦwww.ghostwalksofbath.co.uk; Thurs–Sat; £7). The **Jane Austen Centre** arranges ninety-minute walks in the author's footsteps, leaving from Abbey Churchyard (℡01225/443000, ⓦwww .janeausten.co.uk; Sat & Sun all year at 11am, also July & Aug Fri & Sat at 4pm; £6).

There is a plethora of open-top **bus tours** available all year, leaving from Grand Parade or the bus station (all-day tickets about £11). Between Easter and October, various **river trips** can be made from Pulteney Bridge and weir (one-hour trips £7), and there are cruises on the Kennet & Avon Canal from Sydney Wharf, near Bathwick Bridge.

Outside Bath, Mad Max Tours offers half- or full-day minibus **excursions** to the pretty villages of Lacock and Castle Combe, Stonehenge, Avebury and the Cotswolds (℡07990/505970, ⓦwww.madmax.abel.co.uk; £15–32), while Scarper Tours conducts daily tours to Stonehenge (℡07739/644155, ⓦwww.scarpertours.com; £14).

10am–4pm; ℡0906/711 2000, ⓦvisitbath.co.uk), offers an accommodation booking service (£3); note that this phone number is premium rate.

Although Bath has an abundant choice of **places to stay**, most establishments are small and fill up quickly at weekends, when many places demand a two-night minimum stay.

Hotels and B&Bs

Bath Paradise House 88 Holloway ℡01225/317723, ⓦwww.paradise-house .co.uk. The wonderful view justifies the 10min uphill trudge from the centre to this lovely Georgian villa, while croquet or boules in the lush garden and open fires in the winter provide alternative attractions. Some rooms have four-posters, and three open straight onto the garden. ⑤

Belmont 7 Belmont, Lansdown Rd ℡01225/423082, ⓦwww.belmontbath.co.uk. Mostly huge rooms – though the single's a bit poky – and most en suite, in a house designed by John Wood, very near to the Assembly Rooms, Circus and Royal Crescent. No credit cards. ②

Cranleigh 159 Newbridge Hill ℡01225/310197, ⓦwww.cranleighguesthouse.com. A mile or so west of the centre, this period Victorian house has fine views from the back rooms, three four-posters and seven breakfast options. The garden has a hot tub. Buses #14, #17, #319 and #332 (#632 Sun). ③

Harington's Queen St ℡01225/461728, ⓦwww .haringtonshotel.co.uk. Very central hotel in a converted townhouse with small but quiet, modern and well-equipped rooms, and friendly service. ⑤

The Henry 6 Henry St ℡01225/424052, ⓦwww.thehenry.com. Excellent guesthouse close to the abbey, with eight large rooms with private and en-suite bathrooms, and friendly owners. ③

Holly Villa 14 Pulteney Gardens ℡01225/310331, ⓦwww.hollyvilla.com. Neat and friendly B&B, close to the Kennet & Avon Canal, with six en-suite rooms (including a triple) and a small, flower-filled front garden. No credit cards. ③

The Queensberry Russel St ℡01225/447928, ⓦwww.thequeensberry .co.uk. Occupying four Georgian townhouses built for the eponymous marquis, Bath's most luxurious boutique hotel lays on the chic charm, with taste-fully minimalist white-walled rooms, a fantastic basement restaurant (see p.333) and a walled garden. ⑤–⑥

Three Abbey Green 3 Abbey Green ℡01225/428558, ⓦwww.threeabbeygreen .com. Top-class B&B in a beautifully renovated Georgian house just steps from the abbey. The airy rooms are wi-fi-enabled; the more spacious ones overlooking a peaceful square are in a higher price category. ④

Hostels and campsite

Bath Backpackers 13 Pierrepont St
℡ 01225/446787, ⓦ www.hostels.co.uk. Clean and
friendly place right in the centre of things. There's
no curfew, no lockout, a kitchen, internet access
and a "party dungeon". Beds in 4–10-bed dorms
cost £11–22, breakfast included.

Bath YHA Bathwick Hill ℡ 0845/371 9303,
ⓔ bath@yha.org.uk. An Italianate mansion a mile
from the centre, with gardens and panoramic
views. Dorm beds (from £16) and double rooms
available, also evening meals and 24hr access.
Buses #18, #U18, #418 or #94 from the bus
station. ❶

Newton Mill Touring Centre ℡ 01225/333909,
ⓦ www.newtonmillpark.co.uk. The nearest
campsite, three miles west of the centre at Newton

St Loe (bus #5 to Newton Mill), with the Bristol–
Bath cycleway nearby. The site has a laundry, bar/
restaurant and shop, but it's pricey.

🏃 **White Hart** Widcombe Hill, a ten-minute
walk from the train station ℡ 01225/313985,
ⓦ www.whitehartbath.co.uk. The comfiest of
Bath's hostels has a kitchen, a first-class restaurant and a sunny courtyard. Dorm beds are £15,
and a range of neat doubles and twins are
available. Midnight curfew. ❶

YMCA International House, Broad Street Place
℡ 01225/325900, ⓦ www.bathymca.co.uk. Clean
and central, with lots of room, this place charges
£17–19 for dorm beds, £28–32 for singles and
£46–52 for twins, with reductions for weekly stays;
all prices include breakfast, but there's no kitchen.
Free wi-fi, laundry and gym (costing extra). ❶

The City

Although Bath could easily be seen on a day-trip from Bristol, it really deserves a
stay of a couple of days. The city is chock-full of museums, but some of the
greatest enjoyment comes simply from wandering the streets, with their pale gold
architecture and sweeping vistas. With limited time you might consider viewing
these on a walking or open-top bus tour (see box opposite).

The Roman Baths

Bath's focal point is the pedestrianized Abbey Churchyard, two interlocking
squares usually milling with buskers, tourists and traders, and site of both the
Baths and the abbey. Although ticket prices are high for the **Roman Baths** (daily:
March–June, Sept & Oct 9am–6pm; July & Aug 9am–10pm; Nov–Feb 9.30am–
5.30pm; last entry 1hr before closing; £11.50, £12.25 in July & Aug, £15
combined ticket with Fashion Museum; ⓦ www.romanbaths.co.uk), there's two
or three hours' worth of well-balanced, informative entertainment here, with
hourly guided tours and audioguides available (both free). Highlights are: the
Sacred Spring, part of the temple of the local deity Sulis Minerva, where water
still bubbles up at a constant 46.5°C; the open-air (but originally covered) Great
Bath, its vaporous waters surrounded by nineteenth-century pillars, terraces and
statues of famous Romans; the Circular Bath, where bathers cooled off; and the
Norman King's Bath. Among a quantity of coins, jewellery and sculpture
exhibited are the gilt bronze head of Sulis Minerva and a grand, Celtic-inspired
gorgon's head from the temple's pediment. Models of the complex at its greatest
extent give some idea of the awe which it must have inspired, while the graffiti
salvaged from the Roman era – mainly curses and boasts – give a nice personal
slant on this antique leisure centre. You can get a free glimpse into the baths from
the next-door **Pump Room**, the social hub of the Georgian spa community and
still redolent of that era, housing a formal tearoom and restaurant (see p.333).

Bath Abbey

Although there has been a church on the site since the seventh century, **Bath
Abbey** (Mon–Sat 9am–4.30/6pm, Sun 1–2.30pm & 4.30–5.30pm; requested
donation £2.50) did not take its present form until the end of the fifteenth
century, when work began on the ruins of the previous Norman building, some
of which were incorporated into the new church. Much of the building underwent

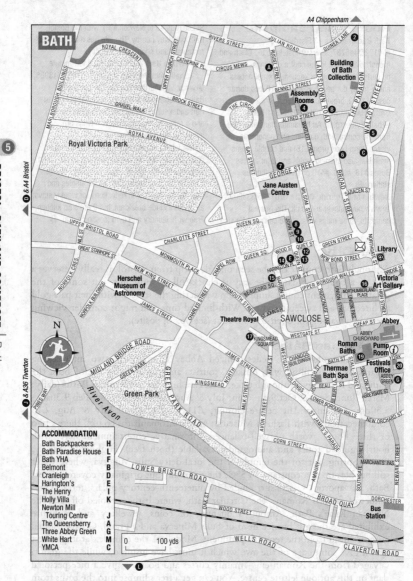

BATH

A4 Chippenham

Building of Bath Collection

RIVERS STREET

JULIAN ROAD

GUINEA LANE

ROYAL CRESCENT

UPPER CHURCH STREET

CATHERINE PL

CIRCUS MEWS

RUSSEL STREET

LANSDOWN ROAD

THE PARAGON

WALCOT STREET

BENNETT STREET

Assembly Rooms

BARTLETT STREET

BROCK STREET

THE CIRCUS

GRAVEL WALK

MARLBOROUGH BUILDINGS

ALFRED STREET

SARACEN ST

BROAD STREET

ROYAL AVENUE

Royal Victoria Park

GAY STREET

GEORGE STREET

MILSOM STREET

GREEN STREET

NORTHUMB ST

Jane Austen Centre

UPPER BRISTOL ROAD

GREAT STANHOPE ST

CHARLOTTE STREET

QUEEN SQUARE

JOHN ST

WOOD ST

QUIET ST

NEW BOND STREET

Library

NORFOLK K.CRES

NEW KING STREET

MONMOUTH PLACE

CHAPEL ROW

QUEEN SQ

HARINGTON PL

BRIDGE ST

HIGH STREET

Herschel Museum of Astronomy

NORFOLK BUILDINGS

CHARLES STREET

JAMES STREET

MONMOUTH STREET

BEAUFORD SQ

BARTON ST

TRIM ST

UPPER BOROUGH WALLS

PASSAGE LANE

UNION ST

NORTHUMBERLAND PLACE

CHEAP ST

Victoria Art Gallery

Theatre Royal

ST JOHN'S PL

SAWCLOSE

Abbey

ABBEY CHURCHYARD

KINGSMEAD SQUARE

WESTGATE ST

WESTGATE BUILDINGS

Roman Baths

Pump Room

Festivals Office

MIDLAND BRIDGE ROAD

GREEN PARK

JAMES STREET

CHANDOS BUILDINGS

BATH ST

STALL ST

YORK STREET

ABBEY GREEN

GREEN PARK ROAD

KINGSMEAD NORTH

AVON ST

Thermae Bath Spa

BEAU ST

LOWER BOROUGH WALLS

ABBEYGATE ST

Green Park

River Avon

KINGSMEAD

MILK ST

ST JAMES'S PARADE

NEW ORCHARD ST

PINES WAY

CORN STREET

SOUTHGATE STREET

MARCHANTS PAS.

DORCHESTER ST

LOWER BRISTOL ROAD

OAK ST

WOOD STREET

AVON ST

BROAD QUAY

Bus Station

N

ACCOMMODATION	
Bath Backpackers	H
Bath Paradise House	L
Bath YHA	F
Belmont	B
Cranleigh	D
Harington's	E
The Henry	I
Holly Villa	K
Newton Mill Touring Centre	J
The Queensberry	A
Three Abbey Green	G
White Hart	M
YMCA	C

0   100 yds

WELLS ROAD

CLAVERTON ROAD

restoration following the destruction that took place under Henry VIII; his daughter, Queen Elizabeth I, played a large part in the repairs. The interior is in a restrained Perpendicular style, and boasts splendid fan vaulting on the ceiling, which was not properly completed until the nineteenth century. The floor and walls are crammed with elaborate monuments and memorials, and traces of the grander Norman building are visible in the Norman Chapel.

Below the abbey, reached from a door to the right of the Choir, the **Heritage Vaults** (Mon–Sat 10am–4pm; free) give some background to the construction of the building, and display examples of statuary and precious silver.

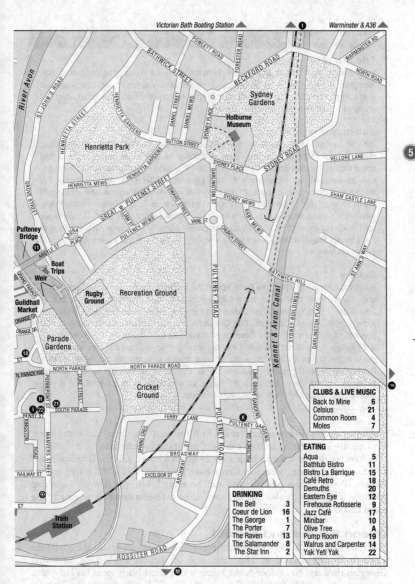

River Avon

POWLETT ROAD

FORESTER ROAD

BECKFORD ROAD

WARMINSTER RD

NORTH ROAD

BATHWICK STREET

ST JOHN'S ROAD

HENRIETTA STREET

HENRIETTA GARDENS

DANIEL STREET

DANIEL MEWS

SUTTON STREET

SYDNEY PLACE

Sydney Gardens

Holburne Museum

SYDNEY ROAD

VELLORE LANE

Henrietta Park

HENRIETTA MEWS

HENRIETTA GARDENS

GREAT PULTENEY STREET

EDWARD STREET

WILLIAM ST

GROVE STREET

SYDNEY PLACE

SYDNEY MEWS

DARLINGTON ST

SHAM CASTLE LANE

VANE ST

RABY MEWS

ST ANN'S WAY

Pulteney Bridge ⑪

LAURA PLACE

ARGYLE ST

PULTENEY MEWS

CHURCH STREET

BATHWICK HILL

Boat Trips

Weir

GRAND PARADE

Guildhall Market

ORANGE GR.

ORANGE GR.

Rugby Ground

Recreation Ground

PULTENEY ROAD

Kennet & Avon Canal

SYDNEY BUILDINGS

DARLINGTON PLACE

Parade Gardens

ST ⑱

NORTH PARADE

NORTH PARADE ROAD

N. PARADE PAS.

H

PIERREPONT ST

DUKE STREET

Cricket Ground

LIME GROVE GARDENS

⑤

① ㉒

HENRY ST

SOUTH PARADE

FERRY LANE

PULTENEY GARDENS

K

CLUBS & LIVE MUSIC
Back to Mine	6
Celsius	21
Common Room	4
Moles	7

LINGSTON

ROAD

MANVERS STREET

SPRING CRES.

ARCHWAY ST

BROADWAY

PULTENEY ROAD

PULTENEY GARDENS

EATING
Aqua	5
Bathtub Bistro	11
Bistro La Barrique	15
Café Retro	18
Demuths	20
Eastern Eye	12
Firehouse Rotisserie	9
Jazz Café	17
Minibar	10
Olive Tree	A
Pump Room	19
Walrus and Carpenter	14
Yak Yeti Yak	22

EXCELSIOR ST

RAILWAY ST

@

ST

Train Station

DRINKING
The Bell	3
Coeur de Lion	16
The George	1
The Porter	7
The Raven	13
The Salamander	8
The Star Inn	2

ROSSITER ROAD

▼ Ⓜ

Thermae Bath Spa

Thermae Bath Spa, at the bottom of the elegantly colonnaded Bath Street (daily 9am–10pm; ☎0844/888 0844, ⓦwww.thermaebathspa.com), allows you to take the local waters in much the same way that visitors to Bath have done throughout the ages, but with state-of-the-art spa facilities. The complex is heated by the city's thermal waters and offers every treatment from massages to dry flotation. Its centrepiece is the **New Royal Bath**, a sleekly futuristic "glass cube" designed by Nicholas Grimshaw, incorporating a curving indoor pool with massage jets, fragrant steam-rooms and a rooftop pool with glorious views. In a separate

A weekend in Bath

Friday night

Bath is a city for strolling, and there's no better place for an introductory amble than alongside the river and over graceful Pulteney Bridge. You could combine a wander with information and entertainment by joining one of the **themed walks** that point out some of the city's more recondite corners.

Saturday

No visit to Bath should omit the **Roman Baths**, worth two or three hours at least. Have a snack lunch at the *Pump Room* adjoining the Baths – or at any of the dining spots on nearby York Street and North Parade Passage – then cross Abbey Churchyard to **Bath Abbey**, also worth a prolonged look. After sightseeing, wander the warren of lanes north of here, crammed with independent **shops** and minuscule **pubs**. Dine at any of Bath's rich choice of **restaurants** (book ahead – essential at weekends); standouts include *Demuths* for superior veggie fare, *Bistro La Barrique* for French tapas and *Yak Yeti Yak* for a Nepalese curry. Check out what's showing at the **Theatre Royal** or, for a less sedate evening, who's playing at **Moles**, Bath's most venerable venue.

Sunday

Book in a session at **Thermae Bath Spa** in the morning, for a memorable spa, sauna and dip in the rooftop pool. Have lunch here or in one of the options on nearby Sawclose or Barton Street. From here, head up Gay Street to admire John Wood the Elder's architectural ensemble, **The Circus**. A few steps away, you can take in 400 years of clothes design at the **Fashion Museum**, while in the other direction, there's the younger John Wood's majestic masterpiece, the Royal Crescent, an exquisite arc of Georgian construction – for an inside view, take a whirl around the restored **No 1 Royal Crescent**. The grassy meadow below – launching site for hot-air balloons on a Sunday afternoon – merges into Royal Victoria Park, a great spot for a late afternoon promenade or game of pitch and putt.

building, a small **visitor centre** (April–Oct Mon–Sat 10am–5pm, Sun 10am–4pm; free) has displays relating to Bath's thermal waters and a brief film.

Tickets for the New Royal Bath are £24 for two hours, £34 for four hours and £54 for a full day; for the smaller **Cross Bath** pool, they cost £14 for a 90-minute session. Towels, robes and slippers can be rented, but you'll need a bathing costume. The complex also houses an excellent **café-restaurant** with nourishing soups and salads.

Queen Square and around

North of Hot Bath Street, Westgate Street and Sawclose are presided over by the **Theatre Royal**, opened in 1805 and one of the country's finest surviving Georgian theatres. Next door is the house where Beau Nash spent his last years, now a restaurant. Up from the Theatre Royal, off Barton Street, the graceful **Queen Square** was the first Bath venture of the architect **John Wood**, who with his son (see box opposite) was chiefly responsible for the Roman-inspired developments outside the confines of the medieval city. Wood himself lived at no. 24, giving him a vista of the northern terrace's palatial facade.

Just north of the square, at 40 Gay St, the **Jane Austen Centre** (mid-March to early Nov daily 9.45am–5.30pm, July & Aug Thurs–Sat open till 7pm; early Nov to mid-March daily except Sat 11am–4.30pm, Sat 9.45am–5.30pm; £6.95; Ⓦwww.janeausten.co.uk) helps you to tie the various Austen threads together with an overview of the author's connections with the city, illustrated by extracts from her writings, contemporary costumes, furnishings and household items. Austen herself, who wasn't entirely enamoured of the city, lived just down the road at 25 Gay St – one of a number of places the author inhabited while in Bath.

West of Queen Square, at 19 New King St, another typical Bath townhouse contains the small **Herschel Museum of Astronomy** (Feb to mid-Dec Mon, Tues, Thurs & Fri 1–5pm, Sat & Sun 11am–5pm; £4.50; Ⓦ www.bath-preservation-trust .org.uk), where the musician and astronomer Sir William Herschel, in collaboration with his sister Caroline, discovered the planet Uranus in 1781. The museum displays contemporary furnishings, musical instruments, a replica of the telescope with which Uranus was identified and various knick-knacks from the Herschels' lives.

The Circus and the Royal Crescent

Up from Queen Square, at the end of Gay Street, the elder John Wood's masterpiece, **The Circus**, consists of three crescents arranged in a tight circle of three-storey houses, with a carved frieze running round the entire circle. Wood died soon after laying the foundation stone for this enterprise, and the job was finished by his son. The painter Thomas Gainsborough lived at no. 17 from 1760 to 1774.

The Circus is connected by Brock Street to the **Royal Crescent**, grandest of Bath's crescents, begun by the younger John Wood in 1767. The stately arc of thirty houses is set off by a spacious sloping lawn from which a magnificent vista extends to green hills and distant ribbons of honey-coloured stone. The interior of **No. 1 Royal Crescent**, on the corner with Brock Street, has been restored to reflect as nearly as possible its original Georgian appearance at the end of the eighteenth century (Tues–Sun: mid-Feb to late Oct 10.30am–5pm; late Oct to mid-Dec 10.30am–4pm; £6; Ⓦ www.bath-preservation-trust.org.uk). The furnishings,

---

Bath's Golden Age

Covering the first four decades of the eighteenth century, Bath's golden age was dominated by a handful of individuals who laid down the rules in architecture and social style. Among the arbiters of etiquette, none enjoyed greater prestige than **Richard "Beau" Nash**, an ex-army officer, ex-lawyer, dandy and gambler, who became Bath's Master of Ceremonies in 1704, conducting public balls of an unprecedented splendour. Wielding dictatorial powers over dress and behaviour, Nash orchestrated the social manners of the city and even extended his influence to cover road improvements and the design of buildings.

Bath's distinctive Georgian style of architecture, however, was largely attributable to a father and son team, both called **John Wood** ("the elder", c.1704–54, and "the younger", 1727–81), and both champions of the Neoclassical Palladianism that originated in Renaissance Italy. Their "speculative developments", designed to cater to the seasonal floods of fashionable visitors, were constructed in the soft oolitic limestone from local quarries belonging to **Ralph Allen** (c.1694–1764), a deputy postmaster who made a fortune by improving England's postal routes and later from Bath's building boom. Allen was nicknamed "the man of Bath", and was known for his association with Pope, Fielding and other luminaries who were frequent visitors.

Lastly, the name of **William Oliver** should not be forgotten in the story of Georgian Bath. A physician and philanthropist, Oliver did more than anyone to boost the city's profile as a therapeutic centre, thanks to publications such as his *Practical Essay on the Use and Abuse of Warm Bathing in Gouty Cases* (1751), and by founding the Bath General Hospital to enable the poor to make use of the waters. On a less elevated note, he is also remembered for his invention, the Bath Oliver biscuit.

drapes and Laura Ashley-style wallpaper are all authentic or else faithful re-creations, as explained by the attendants providing commentaries in each room.

At the bottom of the Crescent, Royal Avenue leads onto **Royal Victoria Park**, the city's largest open space, containing an aviary and botanical gardens.

The Assembly Rooms and the Building of Bath Museum

The younger John Wood's **Assembly Rooms**, east of The Circus on Bennett Street, were, with the Pump Room, the centre of Bath's social scene. The building houses the entertaining **Fashion Museum** (daily: March–Oct 10.30am–6pm; Nov–Feb 10.30am–5pm; £7, or £15 with the Baths; ⓦ www.museumofcostume.co.uk), with clothing from the Stuart era to the latest Milanese designs.

From the Assembly Rooms, Alfred Street leads to the area known as **The Paragon**. Here, accessed from the raised pavement, the Georgian-Gothic Countess of Huntingdon's Chapel houses the **Building of Bath Collection** (mid-Feb to Nov Mon, Sat & Sun 10.30am–5pm; £4; ⓦ www.bath-preservation-trust.org .uk), a fascinating exploration of the construction and architecture of Bath.

Pulteney Bridge to Holburne Museum

East of the abbey, Grand Parade looks down onto the formal Parade Gardens and the River Avon. At the top of Grand Parade, the **Victoria Art Gallery** (Tues–Sat 10am–5pm, Sun 1.30–5pm; free; ⓦ www.victoriagal.org.uk) has an impressive exhibition space upstairs where you can see works by artists who worked locally, including Gainsborough, while subjects of the numerous portraits include Beau Nash; the ground-floor rooms are used for temporary exhibitions. Across the road, the flow of the river is interrupted by a graceful V-shaped weir just below the shop-lined **Pulteney Bridge**, an Italianate structure designed by the eighteenth-century Scottish architect Robert Adam. The bridge leads on to **Great Pulteney Street**, a handsome avenue originally planned as the nucleus of a large residential quarter; the work ran into financial difficulties, however, which is why the roads running off it stop short after a few yards. There is, however, a lengthy vista to the imposing classical facade of the **Holburne Museum** at the end of the street (due to reopen in 2011 after refurbishment; check ⓦ www.bath.ac.uk/holburne). The three-storey building contains an impressive range of decorative and fine art, mostly furniture, silverware, porcelain and paintings, including work by Stubbs and the famous *Byam Family* by Gainsborough, his biggest portrait.

Behind Holburne House, **Sydney Gardens** make a delightful place to take a breather. When Holburne House was a bustling hotel, the pleasure gardens were the venue for concerts and fireworks, as witnessed by Jane Austen, a frequent visitor here – the family had lodgings across the street at 4 Sydney Place in the autumn of 1801. Today, the gardens' slopes are cut through by the railway and the Kennet & Avon Canal, along which it's a pleasant one-and-a-half mile saunter to *The George* pub (see p.334).

If you want to explore the river itself, rent a skiff, punt or canoe from the **Victorian Bath Boating Station** at the end of Forester Road, behind the Holburne Museum (Easter–Sept daily 10am–6pm; £7 per person for 1hr, then £3 per hour; ⓦ www.bathboating.co.uk).

Eating and drinking

Bath has a huge range of **eating** outlets, from expensive gourmet cuisine to decent, inexpensive cafés. Most places offer set-price meals at certain times. Booking in the evening is usually advised. Numerous congenial **pubs** also offer good-value food in atmospheric surroundings.

Restaurants and cafés

Aqua 88 Walcot St ☎01225/471371. In a converted Arts and Crafts church house, this Italian place has loads of atmosphere, with chandeliers suspended from the high-beamed roof, and a gallery. The menu ranges from pastas and pizzas (£7.50–13) to grilled swordfish with Sicilian dressing (£14.25), and the desserts are exquisite. Fixed-price menus are £12–16.50.

Bathtub Bistro 2 Grove St ☎01225/460593. Just off Pulteney Bridge, this restaurant looks tiny from the outside but reveals several eating areas on three levels. The eclectic dishes – including spicy chorizo chicken stew and grilled aubergine – mostly cost £12–15. Closed Sun eve.

Bistro La Barrique 31 Barton St ☎01225/463861. This place has cornered the market in "French tapas", or *petits plats*, ideal for grazing on such dishes as mushroom flan, chicken and mushroom *croustade* and *boeuf bourguignon*, each costing £5–6. The room is nothing special, but there's a nice walled garden where you can eat alfresco. Closed Sun.

Café Retro 18 York St. A cosy place near the abbey for a cappuccino and a bite, accompanied by a mellow soundtrack. Hot meals such as ratatouille and organic burgers cost around £6, and the *Retro-to-Go* takeaway next door sells rolls and salads. Closed eve.

Demuths 2 North Parade Passage ☎01225/446059. Bath's favourite veggie and vegan restaurant offers "quick bites" (2 for £10.50) or hot stews and curries (around £10) at lunchtime, and original and delicious dishes from around the world in the evening (around £14). Organic beers and wines are available, and the ambience is smooth and civilized.

Eastern Eye 8 Quiet St ☎01225/422323. This traditional curry house occupies a Georgian bank, with a spectacular domed ceiling. The food's good too (mains £9–15), and briskly served.

Firehouse Rotisserie 2 John St ☎01225/482070. Delicious, outsized Californian pizzas (about £11) and grills (£15) are the main items in this busy place with a pleasant woody interior on two floors. Closed Sun.

Jazz Café 1 Kingsmead Square. Big breakfasts, snack fodder and dishes such as Moroccan pork skewers (£8.50) are served at this boho hangout. Beers and wines are served, newspapers are on hand, and there's some outside seating. Open until 6pm (4pm on Sun).

Minibar 1 John St. Small, chic tapas bar, all mirrors and stainless steel, where the ham croquettes, cold meats and *calamares fritos* are expertly prepared (all £5–7), and there's a great view over Bath. Closed Sun & Mon.

Olive Tree Russel St ☎01225/447928. In the basement of *The Queensberry* hotel (see p.326), this is one of Bath's top restaurants, offering French-inspired dishes, a romantic ambience and discreetly attentive service. The menu changes regularly, but look out for crab risotto, Portland scallops or cauliflower soup for starters, and fantastic desserts such as caramel mousse; there's also an extensive wine list. Expect to pay around £40–60 per person in the evening; set-price lunches are £16–20.

Pump Room Abbey Churchyard ☎01225/444477. Splash out on an eggs Benedict brunch, try the excellent lunchtime menu, or succumb to a Bath bun or a range of cream teas, all accompanied by a pianist or a classical trio. It's a bit hammy, and you may have to queue, but you get a good view of the Baths. Open daytime only, plus evenings during the Bath Festival, Aug and Christmas, when three-course menus are around £25.

Walrus and Carpenter 28 Barton St ☎01225/314864. You'll find an extensive vegetarian menu in this warren of small rooms

Bath's festivals

Bath has a great range of festivals throughout the year, offering talks, gigs and other events in often sumptuous surroundings. If you're visiting during one of these occasions, you'll find the city's mellow pace livened up a notch or two, though you should be aware that accommodation gets very scarce. Best of the bunch are: the **Bath International Music Festival** (⊛www.bathmusicfest.org.uk), held between late May and early June and featuring big names in classical music, jazz, folk and world, plus fireworks, literary and art events and lots of busking; the **Bath Fringe Festival** (⊛www.bathfringe.co.uk), running from late May to mid-June, with the accent on art and performance; and **Bath Literature Festival** (⊛www.bathlitfest.org.uk), taking place over nine days in February/March. There's also a Jane Austen festival in September and a film festival in October/November. For further information on each, call ☎01225/463362, click on ⊛www.bathfestivals.org.uk, visit the festivals office at 2 Church St, Abbey Green, or check out the individual websites above.

near the Theatre Royal – though organic and free-range steaks, burgers and poultry dishes are also available (£10–18). The atmosphere is friendly and funky.

Yak Yeti Yak 12 Pierrepont St ☏01225/442299. This authentic Nepalese restaurant has a series of cellar rooms with hanging puppets and a choice of chairs or floor cushions. There's a rich vegetarian selection and meat dishes are stir-fried or spicily marinated, all £5–7.50.

Pubs

The Bell 103 Walcot St ⓦwww.walcotstreet .com. Excellent, easy-going pub with a great atmosphere. There's a beer garden, bar billiards, free internet access and live music three times a week (Mon & Wed eve, plus Sun lunchtime).

Coeur de Lion Northumberland Place. Centrally located tavern on a flagstoned shopping alley, with a few tables outside (and more upstairs). It's Bath's smallest boozer and a regular tourist stop, but persevere for the good lunchtime food.

The George Mill Lane, Bathampton. Popular canal-side pub 20min walk from the centre and with better-than-average bar food.

The Porter Miles Buildings, George St ⓦwww .theporter.co.uk. Very relaxed café/pub serving good beer, coffees and all-veggie food until 9pm, with free wi-fi. There are tables outside and pool in the *Cellar Bar*, where, in the evenings, there's free live music (Mon–Thurs) and DJs (Fri & Sat). Comedy nights (Sun) cost £7.

The Raven 7 Queen St. Civilized watering hole with first-rate local ales (try the Raven Gold), served both downstairs and in the less crowded upstairs room. Food available, including great pies.

The Salamander 2 John St. Local brewer Bath Ales pub with a traditional, dark-wood interior, a relaxed atmosphere and tasty dishes available at the bar or in the upstairs restaurant.

The Star Inn 23 The Vineyards, The Paragon. First licensed in 1760, this Abbey Ales pub has a classic Victorian interior, and beers that include the award-winning Bellringer and draught Bass served from a jug.

Nightlife and entertainment

First and foremost of the town-centre **clubs** is 𝕏 *Moles* (☏01225/404445, ⓦwww.moles.co.uk) on George Street, a Bath institution which features a mix of live music and DJs playing club sounds. *Celsius*, 1 South Parade (☏07854/638260, ⓦwww.celsiusclub.co.uk), is another option, for party tunes, funk and cheese (Mon is students' night), and it contains a frosty Ice Bar with frozen sculptures. For a slightly older clientele, there's *Back to Mine*, The Paragon (☏01225/444162, ⓦwww.backtomineclub.co.uk; closed Sun), for everything from retro to reggae (and even poker), and the *Common Room*, 2 Saville Row (☏01225/424952), for late-night chat and chilled sounds. For **live music**, head for *Moles* or the *Cellar Bar* in the next-door *Porter* (see above).

Theatre and ballet fans should check out what's showing at the Theatre Royal on Sawclose (☏01225/448844, ⓦwww.theatreroyal.org.uk), which stages fairly traditional productions in the main house and more experimental material in its Ustinov Studio. Big names in all genres of music play during the International Music Festival (see box, p.333), while for **concerts**, gigs and other events during the rest of the year, check *Venue*, the weekly **listings** magazine (ⓦwww.venue .co.uk). Another useful site for event listings is ⓦwww.thepigguide.com.

Shopping in Bath

Bath is a centre for antiques, rare books and galleries, with small stores scattered throughout the city, but particularly in the lanes around **Bartlett Street** and **Brock Street**, while architectural bric-a-brac can be found along **Walcot Street**. The indoor **Guildhall Market**, between High Street and Grand Parade, is worth a rummage for its delicatessens, craft shops and general bric-a-brac. Bath's **Christmas Market**, which sets up in Abbey Churchyard for around seventeen days in November and December, gets very congested, but might provide inspiration for prezzie-buying.

Listings

Wells, the Mendips and Glastonbury

Wells, twenty miles south of Bristol and the same distance southwest of Bath, is a miniature cathedral city that has not significantly altered in eight hundred years. You could spend a good half-day kicking around here, and you might decide to make it an accommodation stop for visiting nearby attractions in the **Mendip Hills**, such as the **Wookey Hole** caves and **Cheddar Gorge**. On the southern edge of the range, and just a jump away from Wells, the town of **Glastonbury** has for centuries been one of the main Arthurian sites of the West Country, and is now the country's most enthusiastic centre of New Age cults.

Wells

Technically England's smallest city, **WELLS** is compact and pedestrian-friendly, easily negotiated from its High Street axis, at the top of which lie all the main sights.

Arrival, information and accommodation

Wells **bus station**, off Market Street, has regular connections with Bristol and Bath. Drivers should head straight for the large **car parks** off the A39 west of the centre. The **tourist office**, where discounted tickets for Cheddar Gorge and Wookey Hole are sold, is on Market Place (April–Oct Mon–Sat 10am–5pm, Sun 10am–4pm; Nov–March Mon–Sat 11am–4pm; ℡01749/672552, ⓦwww .wellstourism.com).

Accommodation

Ancient Gatehouse Hotel Sadler St
℡01749/672029, ⓦwww.ancientgatehouse.co.uk.
The fourteenth-century origins of this hostelry are evident in the sagging floors and winding staircase, but – apart from poor sound insulation – the wi-fi-enabled rooms are comfortable; some have four-posters and carved wooden ceilings, and four of them overlook the cathedral. ❹

Canon Grange Cathedral Green
℡01749/671800, ⓦwww.canongrange.co
.uk. Beautifully located B&B, with three rooms facing the west front of the cathedral. Breakfast,

which can cover various dietary requirements, is taken overlooking the green. ❷
The Crown Market Place ℡01749/673457,
ⓦwww.crownatwells.co.uk. Fifteenth-century coaching inn with an authentically antique flavour, where William Penn was arrested in 1695 for illegal preaching. Can be noisy from the bar and bistro below or the Saturday market. ❸
Swan Hotel Sadler St ℡01749/836300, ⓦwww
.swanhotelwells.co.uk. This rambling inn is old-fashioned in places, but it has character and a great restaurant. Go for one of the rooms with cathedral views. ❺

The cathedral

Wells owes its city status to the existence of its **cathedral** (daily: April–Sept 7am–7pm; Oct–March 7am–6pm; suggested donation £5.50; ⓦwww.wells cathedral.org.uk), well hidden from sight until you pass into its spacious close from the central Market Place. Fronted by the broad lawn of the former graveyard, the building presents a majestic spectacle, its west front teeming with some three hundred thirteenth-century figures of saints and kings – once brightly painted and gilded, though their present honey tint has a subtle splendour of its own. The facade was constructed about fifty years after work on the main building was begun in 1180. The **interior** is a supreme example of early English Gothic, the long nave punctuated by a dramatic "scissor arch", one of three that were constructed in 1338 to take the extra weight of the newly built tower. Though some wax enthusiastic about the ingenuity of these so-called "strainer" arches, others argue that they're "grotesque intrusions" from an artistic point of view.

Other features worth scrutinizing are the narrative carvings on the **capitals and corbels** in the transepts – including men with toothache and an old man caught raiding an orchard. In the north transept, don't miss the 24-hour astronomical clock, dating from 1390, whose jousting knights charge each other every quarter-hour. Opposite the clock, a doorway leads to a graceful, much-worn flight of steps rising to the **Chapter House**, an octagonal room elaborately ribbed in the Decorated style. There are some gnarled old tombs to be seen in the aisles of the **Quire**, at the end of which is the richly coloured stained glass of the fourteenth-century **Lady Chapel**. The best way to see it all is on one of the **free guided tours**, which take place up to five times daily (twice daily in winter; none on Sun). If you want to take pictures, you have to buy a photographic permit (£3); the use of flash is banned in the Quire. Evensong takes place at 5.15pm (3pm on Sun).

The museum and Vicar's Close

The row of clerical houses on the north side of the cathedral green are mainly seventeenth- and eighteenth-century, though one, the **Old Deanery**, shows traces of its fifteenth-century origins. The chancellor's house is now a **museum** (Easter–Oct Mon–Sat 10am–5.30pm, Sun 11am–4pm; Nov–Easter daily 11am–4pm; £3), displaying, among other items, some of the cathedral's original statuary, as well as a good geological section with fossils from the surrounding area, including Wookey Hole.

Beyond the arch, a little further along the street, the cobbled medieval **Vicars' Close** holds more clerical dwellings, linked to the cathedral by the Chain Gate and fronted by small gardens. The cottages were built in the mid-fourteenth century – though only no. 22 has not undergone outward alterations – and have been continuously occupied by members of the cathedral clergy ever since.

The Bishop's Palace

On the other side of the cathedral – and accessible through the cathedral shop – are the cloisters, from which you can enter the tranquil grounds of the **Bishop's Palace** (daily: mid-Feb to March 10.30am–4.30pm; April–Oct 10.30am–6pm; last entry 1hr before closing; £5), also reachable from Market Place through the Bishop's Eye archway. The residence of the Bishop of Bath and Wells, the palace was walled and moated as a result of a rift with the borough in the fourteenth century, and the imposing gatehouse still displays the grooves of the portcullis and a chute for pouring oil and molten lead on would-be assailants.

Within, the tranquil gardens contain the springs from which the city takes its name and the scanty but impressive remains of the **Great Hall**, built at the end of the thirteenth century and despoiled during the Reformation. Across the lawn, which is used for regular croquet matches in summer, stands the square **Bishop's Chapel** and the **Undercroft**, holding state rooms, displays relating to the history of the site and a café. Outside, a stroll along the rampart walk reveals glimpses of Glastonbury Tor to the south.

Eating and drinking

Wells has a good concentration of **places to eat** to suit all pockets. Market Place is the scene of a small but busy **market** on Wednesday and Saturday, good for trinkets and locally sourced snacks.

City Arms Cuthbert St. Formerly the city jail, this is a good place for a drink or a full meal in its moderately priced restaurant. There's also seating in the plant-filled courtyard.

Good Earth Priory Rd. Excellent organic produce is on hand at this inexpensive vegetarian café near the bus station, with pizzas and flans to eat in and delicious takeaway goodies. Expect queues at lunchtime. Closed eve & all Sun.

Goodfellows 5 Sadler St ☎ 01749/673866. You can pick up superb sandwiches and pastries at the patisserie here, or a set-price lunch or dinner with wine for £10 and £20 respectively. The separate restaurant is famed for its innovative seafood dishes (£16.50 or £19.50 for lunch, £35 for a three-course dinner). Patisserie closed eve Mon &

Tues and all Sun, restaurant closed Tues eve and all Sun & Mon.

Old Spot 12 Sadler St ☎ 01749/689099. Spacious, easy-going place with first-rate food on set-price menus (lunch £12.50 and £15, dinner £23.50 and £27.50 for two and three courses respectively). The eclectic Modern British menu includes wood pigeon salad with quince, and mushroom polenta with cheddar.

Rugantino's 20 Sadler St ☎ 01749/672029. Italian-run restaurant (attached to the *Ancient Gatehouse Hotel*) serving quality Mediterranean cuisine in gorgeous medieval surroundings. You can have lunch for £8.50, or dine more formally in the evening, when main courses are around £15 and the set-price menu is £21.50.

The Mendips

The **Mendip Hills**, rising to the north of Wells, are chiefly famous for **Wookey Hole** – the most impressive of many caves in this narrow limestone chain – and for **Cheddar Gorge**, where a walk through the narrow cleft might make a starting point for more adventurous trips across the Mendips.

Wookey Hole and around

Hollowed out by the River Axe a couple of miles north of Wells, **Wookey Hole** is an impressive cave complex of deep pools and intricate rock formations, but it's folklore rather than geology that takes precedence on the hour-long guided tours (daily: April–Oct 10am–5pm; Nov–March 10am–4pm; £16; ⓦ www.wookey .co.uk). Highlight of the tour is the alleged petrified remains of the Witch of Wookey, a "blear-eyed hag" who was said to turn her evil eye on crops, young lovers and local farmers until the Abbot of Glastonbury intervened; he dispatched a monk who drove the witch into the inner cave, sprinkled her with holy water and turned her into stone.

At the end of the tour, you can use your ticket to visit a functioning Victorian paper mill by the river, and rooms containing speleological exhibits. On a less earnest note, the range of amusements includes a collection of gaudy, sometimes ghoulish, Edwardian fairground pieces.

For food, drinks – including a great selection of Belgian beers – or a **place for the night**, head for the ⚐ *Wookey Hole Inn* (☎ 01749/676677, ⓦ www.wookeyholeinn .com; ❹), just along the street from the caves. In contrast with the traditional exterior, the five guest-rooms are furnished in contemporary style with widescreen TVs and CD players, and continental breakfast is delivered in a basket. At lunchtime you can just have a soup or a sandwich, while in the evening the **restaurant** (for which advance booking is essential; closed Sun eve) cooks up exquisite dishes (£14–23 for mains); there's also a sculpture garden and regular live music.

A walkable couple of miles uphill west of Wookey Hole, **Ebbor Gorge** offers a wilder alternative to the more famous Cheddar Gorge, with tranquillity guaranteed on the wooded trails that follow the ravine up to the Mendip plateau.

Cheddar Gorge

Six miles west of Wookey on the A371, **Cheddar** has given its name to Britain's best-known cheese – most of it now mass-produced far from here – but the biggest selling point of this rather plain village is **Cheddar Gorge**, lying beyond the neighbourhood of Tweentown about a mile to the north.

Cutting a jagged gash across the Mendip Hills, the limestone gorge is an impressive geological phenomenon, though its natural beauty is undermined by the road running through it and by the Lower Gorge's mile of shops and parking areas. Beyond these, the first few curves of the gorge hold its most dramatic scenery, though each turn of the two-mile length presents new, sometimes startling vistas, which can be seen from the open-top bus that plies up and down between February and October (free to Cheddar Caves ticket-holders; see below). At its narrowest the road squeezes between cliffs towering almost five hundred feet above. Those in a state of honed fitness can climb the 274 steps of **Jacob's Ladder** to a **lookout tower** that offers views towards Glastonbury Tor and occasional glimpses of the sea and even Exmoor – if you don't want to tackle the muscle-wrenching climb you can reach the same spot with a great deal more ease via the narrow lane winding up behind the cliffs.

There's a circular three-mile clifftop Gorge Walk, with marked paths branching off to such secluded spots as **Black Rock**, two miles west of Cheddar, and **Black Down**, at 1067ft the Mendips' highest peak. The tourist office can also provide details of the **West Mendip Way**, a forty-mile route extending from Uphill, near Weston-super-Mare, to Wells and Shepton Mallet.

Beneath the gorge, the **Cheddar Caves** (daily: Easter, July & Aug 10am–5.30pm; Sept–June excluding Easter 10.30am–5pm; £17; Ⓦwww.cheddarcaves.co.uk) were scooped out by underground rivers in the wake of the Ice Age, and subsequently occupied by primitive communities. The bigger of the two main groups, **Gough's Caves**, is a sequence of chambers with names such as Solomon's Temple, Aladdin's Cave and the Swiss Village, all arrayed with tortuous rock formations that resemble organ pipes, waterfalls and giant birds. **Cox's Caves** (same ticket), entered lower down the main drag, are floodlit to pick out the subtle pinks, greys, greens and whites in the rock, as well as a set of lime blocks known as "the Bells", which produce a range of tones when struck.

Practicalities

Cheddar's **tourist office** stands at the bottom of the gorge (Easter to mid-Sept daily 10am–5pm; mid-Sept to Oct daily 10.30am–4.30pm; Nov–Easter Sun 11am–4pm; Ⓣ01934/744071, Ⓦwww.visitsomerset.co.uk). Among the village's handful of **B&Bs**, *Chedwell Cottage*, on Redcliffe Street (Ⓣ01934/743268; no credit cards; ❷), has three en-suite rooms and a garden, while another option is the **youth hostel**, in a modernized Victorian house opposite the fire station, off the Hayes (Ⓣ0845/371 9730, Ⓔcheddar@yha.org.uk; dorm bed from £12; call to check opening). There are two **campsites** nearby, most centrally *Cheddar Bridge*, a camping and caravan complex opposite the church on Draycott Road (Ⓣ01934/743048, Ⓦwww .cheddarbridge.co.uk; no under-18s; closed Nov–Feb), with the River Yeo running through and spotless facilities, while the fully equipped, family-orientated *Broadway House* lies on the northwestern outskirts of the village, off the A371 to Axbridge (Ⓣ01934/742610, Ⓦwww.broadwayhousepark.co.uk; closed Nov–Feb).

Glastonbury

Six miles south of Wells, and reachable from there in twenty minutes on frequent buses, **GLASTONBURY** lies at the centre of the so-called **Isle of Avalon**, a region rich with mystical associations. At the heart of it all is the early Christian legend that the young Christ once visited this site, a story that is not as far-fetched as it sounds. The Romans had a heavy presence in the area, mining lead in the Mendips, and one of these mines was owned by **Joseph of Arimathea**, a well-to-do merchant said to have been related to Mary. It's not completely impossible that the merchant took his kinsman on one of his many visits to his property, during a period of Christ's life of which nothing is recorded. It was this possibility to which William Blake referred in his *Glastonbury Hymn*, better known as *Jerusalem*: "And did those feet in ancient times/Walk upon England's mountains green?"

Another legend relates how Joseph was imprisoned for twelve years after the Crucifixion, miraculously kept alive by the **Holy Grail**, the chalice of the Last Supper in which the blood was gathered from the wound in Christ's side. The Grail, along with the spear that had caused the wound, were later taken by Joseph to Glastonbury, where he founded the abbey and commenced the conversion of Britain.

Arrival, information and accommodation

Buses #375, #376 and #377 run up to four times hourly from Wells, dropping you outside the abbey on Magdalene Street. Round the corner on the High Street, housed in the Tribunal, Glastonbury's **tourist office** (Mon–Thurs 10am–4pm, Fri & Sat 10am–4.30pm; ℡01458/832954, ⓦwww.glastonburytic.co.uk) sells discounted tickets to such local attractions as Cheddar Caves and Wookey Hole. You can log on to the **internet** here, or else across the road at the Assembly Rooms.

Glastonbury's **accommodation** takes in everything from medieval hostelry to backpacker hostel, with most places a brief walk from the town centre. There's also a clean, friendly **campsite** within sight of the Tor, the *Isle of Avalon* (℡01458/833618), ten minutes' walk up Northload Street on Godney Road.

Hotels and B&Bs

1 Park Terrace Street Rd ℡01458/835845, ⓦwww.no1parkterrace.co.uk. Large Victorian house, 5min walk from the centre, with traditionally furnished rooms en suite or with shared facilities, internet and wi-fi access, and Spanish-influenced evening meals. ❷

George & Pilgrim 1 High St ℡01458/831146, ⓦwww.relaxinnz.co.uk. This fifteenth-century oak-panelled inn brims with medieval atmosphere. ❷

Meadow Barn Middlewick Farm, Wick Lane ℡01458/832351, ⓦwww.middlewickholiday cottages.co.uk. A mile and a half north of town, this Canadian-run place offers peace and quiet in rural surroundings, with an indoor pool, a steam room and wi-fi. ❸

White House 21 Manor House Rd ℡01458/830886, ⓦwww.theglastonburywhitehouse.com. Lovely B&B with two en-suite rooms. Everything is eco-friendly and organic, including the optional breakfast (£5–7) – which can be served in your room and is well worth taking. Aromatherapy and reflexology treatments are available, and there's free internet access. No credit cards. ❷

Hostels

Glastonbury Backpackers Market Place ℡01458/833353, ⓦwww.glastonburyback packers.com. Centrally located former coaching inn

Glastonbury Festival

Glastonbury Festival takes place most years over four days in late June outside the nearby village of Pilton. Having started in the 1970s, the festival has become the biggest and best organized in the country, without shedding too much of its alternative feel. Bands cover all musical spectrums, from up-and-coming indie groups to huge acts – recent headliners have included Lady Gaga and Stevie Wonder. Ticket prices are steep (around £200), but they're invariably snapped up within hours of going on sale around October of the previous year: for ticket sales and general information, see ⓦwww.glastonburyfestivals.co.uk.

with lively café/bar, kitchen, pool table, internet access and no curfew. Advance booking recommended. Dorm beds £15, twins ❶ **YHA Street** Ivythorn Hill, Street ☎ 0845/371 9143, ⓔ street@yha.org.uk. The nearest YHA lies a

couple of miles south of Glastonbury, but is easily accessed by bus (#29 or #377; alight at Marshall's Elm crossroads and follow signs). Camping pitches available, and dorm beds from £14.

Glastonbury Abbey

Aside from its mythological origins, **Glastonbury Abbey**, with its entrance near the town centre on Magdalene Street (daily: Feb 10am–5pm; March 9.30am–5.30pm; April, May & Sept 9.30am–6pm; June–Aug 9am–6pm; Oct 9.30am–5pm; Nov 9.30am–4.30pm; Dec & Jan 10am–4.30pm; £5.50; ⓦ www .glastonburyabbey.com), can safely claim to be the oldest Christian foundation in England, dating back to the seventh century and possibly earlier. Three kings (Edmund, Edgar and Edmund Ironside) were buried here, and in the tenth century, funded by a constant procession of pilgrims, the Saxon church was enlarged by St Dunstan (later archbishop of Canterbury), under whom it became the richest Benedictine abbey in the country, with a widely renowned library. Further expansion took place under the Normans, though most of the additions were destroyed by fire in 1184. Rebuilt, the abbey was later a casualty of the Dissolution in the 1530s, and the ruins, now hidden behind walls and nestled among grassy parkland, can only hint at its former extent. The most prominent and photogenic remains are the transept piers and the shell of the Lady Chapel, with its carved figures of the Annunciation, the Magi and Herod.

The abbey's **choir** introduces another strand to the Glastonbury story, for it holds what is alleged to be the tomb of **Arthur and Guinevere**. As told by William of Malmesbury and Thomas Malory, the story relates how, after being mortally wounded in battle, King Arthur sailed to Avalon where he was buried alongside his queen. The discovery of two bodies in an ancient cemetery outside the abbey in 1191 – from which they were transferred here in 1278 – was taken to confirm the popular identification of Glastonbury with Avalon. In the grounds, the fourteenth-century abbot's kitchen is the only monastic building to survive intact, with four huge corner fireplaces and a great central lantern above.

Behind the main entrance to the grounds, look out for the thorn-tree that is supposedly from the original **Glastonbury Thorn** said to have sprouted from the staff of Joseph of Arimathea when he landed here to convert the country. The plant grew for centuries on a nearby hill known as Wyrral, or Weary-All, and despite being hacked down by Puritans, lived long enough to provide numerous cuttings, descendants of which still bloom twice a year (Easter & Dec). Only at Glastonbury do they flourish, it is claimed – everywhere else they die after a couple of years.

The Town

At the bottom of Glastonbury's High Street, abbots once presided over legal cases in the fourteenth-century **Tribunal**; it later became a hotel for pilgrims, and now holds the tourist office and the small **Glastonbury Lake Village Museum**, which displays finds from the Iron Age villages that fringed the former marshland below the Tor (same hours as tourist office; £2.50; EH).

Further up the High Street, take a glance at the fifteenth-century **church of St John the Baptist**: the tower is reckoned to be one of Somerset's finest, and the interior has a fine oak roof and stained glass illustrating the legend of St Joseph of Arimathea, both from the period of the church's construction. The Glastonbury thorn in the churchyard is the biggest in town.

At the top of the High Street, walk down Lambrook and Chilkwell streets to find, at the southeastern edge of the abbey grounds, the medieval **Abbey Barn**, centrepiece of the engaging **Somerset Rural Life Museum** (Tues–Sat 10am–5pm; free), which illustrates a range of local rural occupations, from cheese- and cider-making to peat-digging, thatching and farming. A collection of heavy-duty farm machinery is on show in the fourteenth-century tithe barn, which originally held the produce of the abbey's 24 acres of arable estates. Today, the adjacent Barn Orchard holds twenty different types of cider-apple tree.

Further down Chilkwell Street, the **Chalice Well** (daily: April–Oct 10am–5.30pm; Nov–March 10am–4pm; £3.50) stands in the middle of a lush garden intended for quiet contemplation. The iron-red waters of the well – which is fondly supposed to be the hiding-place of the Holy Grail – were considered to have curative properties, making the town a spa for a brief period in the eighteenth century, and they are still prized (there's a tap in Wellhouse Lane).

Glastonbury Tor

From Chilkwell Street, turn left into Wellhouse Lane and immediately right for the footpath that leads up to **Glastonbury Tor**, at 521ft a landmark for miles around. The conical hill – topped by the dilapidated **St Michael's Tower**, sole remnant of a fourteenth-century church – commands stupendous views encompassing Wells, the Quantocks, the Mendips, the Somerset Levels, and, on very clear days, the Welsh mountains. Pilgrims once embarked on the stiff climb here with hard peas in their shoes as penance – nowadays people come to feel the vibrations of crossing ley-lines.

You can save some legwork by taking advantage of the **Glastonbury Tor Bus** (April–Sept daily 9.30am–7pm; £2.50 valid all day), which ferries people from the abbey car park to the base of the Tor every thirty minutes, with stops at the Rural Life Museum and the Chalice Well.

Eating, drinking and entertainment

Wedged between the esoteric shops of Glastonbury's High Street are numerous **cafés** and informal **restaurants** serving inexpensive meals, usually with an accent on organic and vegetarian food. The Assembly Rooms (Ⓦwww .assemblyrooms.org.uk) are the venue for talks and musical and theatrical **performances**, usually on Thursday to Saturday evenings, while big-name concerts, miracle plays and exhibitions are held in the abbey grounds – call Ⓣ01458/832267 or see Ⓦwww.glastonburyabbey.com for details. Various talks and workshops are also held throughout the year at the Chalice Well (Ⓣ01458/831154, Ⓦwww.chalicewell.org.uk).

Blue Note Café 4 High St. A relaxed place to hang out over inexpensive coffees and cakes with some seating in the courtyard. Sometimes open eve in summer.

Glastonbury Backpackers Market Place. A convivial spot for drinks and snacks at all hours, with TVs showing live sport, DJs, bands on Fri & Sat eve, and jazz on Sun.

Hawthorns 8 Northload St Ⓣ01458/831255. Bar and restaurant with an eclectic menu, including a curry buffet at lunchtime, regional curries on Thurs eve (£12) and some great vegetarian choices; most main courses cost £10–15. Closed Sun eve in winter & Mon lunch.

Hundred Monkeys 52 High St Ⓣ01458/833386. Mellow café-restaurant with a courtyard. Wholesome snacks include a renowned seafood soup. Stays open until 8pm (Mon & Tues) or 9pm (Fri & Sat) for meals (mains around £12). Closed Wed, Thurs & Sun eve.

Mocha Berry Market Place. Small café with a buzzy feel, serving up traditional grub such as sausage and mash and bubble and squeak for around £7.

Who'd a Thought It 17 Northload St. Quirkily decorated pub with garden, serving pies (£11.50), Cornish mussels (£15) and vegetarian dishes (£10.50).

Bridgwater and the Quantocks

Travelling west through the reclaimed marshland of the Somerset Levels, your route could take you through **Bridgwater**, a handy starting-point for excursions into the gently undulating **Quantock Hills**, where snug villages nestle among scenic wooded valleys or "combes". Public transport is fairly minimal around here, but you can see quite a lot on the **West Somerset Railway** between Bishops Lydeard and the coastal resort of Minehead, which stops at some of the thatched, typically English villages along the west flank of the Quantocks, and there are **horse riding** facilities at many local farms.

Bridgwater

Sedate **BRIDGWATER** has seen little excitement since it was embroiled in the Civil War and its aftermath, in particular the events surrounding the **Monmouth Rebellion** of 1685. Having landed from his base in Holland, the Protestant Duke of Monmouth, an illegitimate son of Charles II, was enthusiastically proclaimed king at Bridgwater, but his disorganized rebel army was mown down by the forces of the Catholic James II on nearby **Sedgemoor**. Monmouth himself was captured and later beheaded, and a period of repression was unleashed under the infamous Judge Jeffreys, whose Bloody Assizes resulted in gibbets and gutted carcasses displayed around Somerset.

Bridgwater's most striking monument today is the thirteenth- to fourteenth-century **St Mary's Church**, immediately identifiable by its polygonal, angled steeple that soars over the town centre. Within, you can admire the oak pulpit and a seventeenth-century Italian altarpiece – the impressive hammer-beam roof, however, was added in the 1850s. Elsewhere in town – just round the corner from the red-brick Christ Church, where Coleridge preached in 1797 and 1798 – the **Blake Museum**, by the River Parrett on Blake Street (Tues–Sat 10am–4pm; free), shows relics, models and a short film relating to the Battle of Sedgemoor. The sixteenth-century building is reputedly the birthplace of local hero Robert Blake, admiral under Oliver Cromwell, whose swashbuckling career against Royalists, the Dutch and the Spanish is chronicled and illustrated here.

Practicalities

Bridgwater's **tourist office**, in King Square (Mon–Fri 8.45am–5pm; ℡01278/436438, Ⓦwww.visitsomerset.co.uk), provides details of **accommodation** hereabouts. Central choices include the *Old Vicarage* right opposite St Mary's Church (℡01278/458891, Ⓦwww.theoldvicaragebridgwater.com; ❸), one of the town's oldest buildings, and the more up-to-date *Tudor Hotel*, 27 St Mary St (℡01278/422093, Ⓦwww.tudorhotel.co.uk; ❷), which has wi-fi. Both hotels

---

Carnival at Bridgwater

A good time to be in Bridgwater is for the **carnival** celebrations, said to be the largest illuminated procession in Europe, attracting up to 150,000 people. The festivities usually take place on the nearest Thursday or Friday to Bonfire Night (one of the Catholic conspirators of the Gunpowder Plot hailed from nearby Nether Stowey; see opposite). Grandly festooned floats belonging to Somerset's seventy-odd carnival clubs roll through town, before heading off to do the same in various other local towns and villages, including Glastonbury and Wells. See Ⓦwww.somersetcarnivals .co.uk for dates.

serve teas, light lunches and full **meals**. The Bridgwater Arts Centre on Castle Street (℡01278/422700, ⓦwww.bridgwaterartscentre.co.uk) is worth seeking out for its concerts, films, plays and comedy.

The Quantock Hills

West of Bridgwater, crossed by clear streams and grazed by red deer, the **Quantock Hills** measure just twelve miles in length and are mostly 800- to 900-foot high. The secluded hamlets within the range are linked by a tangle of narrow lanes, connected by rather sporadic local **bus** services from Bridgwater and Taunton, Somerset's county town, and by a restored **steam railway** along the western edge of the range. There are unstaffed **information** points in various Quantock villages, or see ⓦwww.thequantockhills.co.uk or www.quantock online.co.uk, where you can also download walking itineraries.

Nether Stowey and around

On the northern edge of the hills, eight miles west of Bridgwater on the A39, the pretty village of **NETHER STOWEY** is best known for its association with **Samuel Taylor Coleridge**, who walked here from Bristol at the end of 1796 to join his wife and child at their new home (see box below). In **Coleridge Cottage** (April–Sept Thurs–Sun 2–5pm; £4; NT), you can see the poet's parlour and reading room, and, upstairs, his bedroom and an exhibition room containing various letters and first editions. You can pick up leaflets here (or consult the website ⓦwww.coleridgeway.co.uk) on the **Coleridge Way**, a walking route that supposedly follows the poet's footsteps between Nether Stowey and Porlock on the Exmoor coast (see p.348). Waymarked with quill signs, the 36-mile hike takes you through some of the most scenic parts of the Quantocks and Exmoor.

From Nether Stowey, a minor road winds south off the A39 to the highest point on the Quantocks at **Wills Neck** (1260ft); park at Triscombe Stone, on the edge of Quantock Forest, from where a footpath leads to the summit about a mile distant. Stretching between Wills Neck and the village of Aisholt, the bracken- and heather-grown moorland plateau of **Aisholt Common** is the heart of the Quantocks – the best place to begin exploring this central tract is near **West Bagborough**, where a five-mile path starts at Birches Corner. Lower down the slopes, outside Aisholt, the banks of **Hawkridge Reservoir** make a lovely picnic stop.

Coleridge and Wordsworth in the Quantocks

Shortly after moving into their new home – or this "miserable cottage", as Sara Coleridge called it – in **Nether Stowey**, the **Coleridges** were visited by **William Wordsworth** and his sister Dorothy, who soon afterwards moved into the somewhat grander Alfoxden House, near Holford, a couple of miles down the road. The year that Coleridge and Wordsworth spent as neighbours was extraordinarily productive – Coleridge composed some of his best poetry at this time, including **The Rime of the Ancient Mariner** and **Kubla Khan**, and the two poets in collaboration produced the **Lyrical Ballads**, the poetic manifesto of early English Romanticism. Many of the greatest figures of the age made the trek down to visit the pair, among them Charles Lamb, Thomas De Quincey, Robert Southey, Humphry Davy and William Hazlitt, and it was the coming and going of these intellectuals that stirred the suspicions of the local authorities in a period when England was at war with France. Spies were sent to track them and Wordsworth was finally given notice to leave in June 1798, shortly before Lyrical Ballads rolled off the press.

The Quantocks are notorious for confrontations between hunting parties and anti-hunt activists, but if you want to indulge in less contentious **pony-trekking**, contact *Mill Farm* at Fiddington, near Nether Stowey (see below).

Practicalities

There are a couple of good **accommodation** choices on Castle Street in Nether Stowey: *Stowey Brooke House*, at no. 18 (℡01278/733356; no credit cards; ❷), handsomely renovated with all rooms en suite (one has its own sitting area), and the *Old Cider House* at no. 25 (℡01278/732228, ⓦwww.theoldciderhouse.co.uk; ❷), which has fully equipped rooms, great evening meals and a microbrewery on site; themed walking breaks taking in good pubs and accommodation in the area are also run from here. Alternatively, the *Rose & Crown* on St Mary Street offers decent en-suite rooms (℡01278/732265, ⓦwww.roseandcrown-netherstowey. co.uk; ❷), as well as real ales, bar **meals** and a walled garden. **Campers** should head for *Mill Farm* (℡01278/732286, ⓦwww.millfarm.biz), a couple of miles east of Nether Stowey outside the village of Fiddington; there's also a stables here, and indoor and outdoor pools.

Five miles further west along the A39, the village of **Holford**, a stop on the #14 bus from Bridgwater, has the *Plough Inn*, where Virginia and Leonard Woolf spent their honeymoon, today serving simple **snacks**.

Bishops Lydeard to Crowcombe

The other main road route fringing the Quantocks – the A358 heading northwest from Taunton – is accompanied for most of the way by the **West Somerset Railway** (℡01643/704996, ⓦwww.west-somerset-railway.co.uk), a restored branch line running some twenty miles between Bishops Lydeard, five miles out of Taunton (reachable on bus #28), to Minehead on the Somerset coast. Between late March and October (plus some winter dates), up to eight steam and diesel trains depart daily from Bishops Lydeard, stopping at renovated stations on the way; the full ticket to Minehead costs £10.40 one-way, £14.80 return. Buses #23 and #28 link the terminus with Taunton's train station.

BISHOPS LYDEARD itself is worth a wander, not least for the **church of St Mary**, with a splendid tower in the Perpendicular style and carved bench-ends inside, one of them illustrating the allegory of a pelican feeding its young with blood from its own breast – a symbol of the redemptive power of Christ's blood. The church is constructed of the pink-red sandstone characteristic of Quantock villages; **COMBE FLOREY**, a couple of miles north, is almost exclusively built in this material. For over fifteen years (1829–45), the rector here was the unconventional cleric Sydney Smith, called "the greatest master of ridicule since Swift" by the essayist Macaulay; more recently it's been home to Evelyn Waugh. A little over three miles further along the A358, and the first stop on the West Somerset Railway (though the station lies around four miles west of the village), **CROWCOMBE** is another typical cob-and-thatch Quantock village, with a well-preserved Church House from 1515. Opposite, the parish church has some pagan-looking carved bench-ends from around the same time that are worth a look.

There's **camping** at *Quantock Orchard* (℡01984/618618, ⓦwww.quantock orchard.co.uk), south of Crowcombe towards Triscombe, which has a heated pool and also rents out **mountain bikes**. The cycle, hike or drive across the Quantocks from Crowcombe to Nether Stowey takes in some of the range's loveliest wooded scenery.

Exmoor

A high, bare plateau sliced by wooded combes and splashing rivers, **Exmoor** (@www.exmoor-nationalpark.gov.uk) can be one of the most forbidding landscapes in England, especially when its sea mists fall. When it's clear, though, the moorland of this national park reveals rich displays of colour and an amazing diversity of wildlife, from buzzards to the unique **Exmoor ponies**, a species closely related to prehistoric horses. In the treeless heartland of the moor around **Simonsbath**, in particular, it's not difficult to spot these short and stocky animals, though fewer than twelve hundred are registered, and of these only about two hundred are free-living on the moor. Much more elusive are the **red deer**, England's largest native wild animal, of which Exmoor supports the country's only wild population. Hunting through the centuries accounted for a drastic depletion in numbers, though they have a strong recovery rate, and a healthy population of about two and a half thousand is thought to inhabit the moor today; their annual culling is a regular point of issue among conservationists and nature-lovers.

Endless permutations of **walking routes** are possible along a network of some six hundred miles of footpaths and bridleways. In addition, the National Park Authority and other local organizations have put together a programme of guided walks, graded according to distance, speed and duration, and costing £3–5 per person. Contact any of the local visitor centres or the park headquarters at Dulverton for details. **Horseback** is another option for getting the most out of Exmoor's desolate beauty, and stables are dotted throughout – the most convenient are mentioned below; expect to pay around £20 an hour. Whether walking or riding, bear in mind that over seventy percent of the national park is privately owned and that access is theoretically restricted to public rights of way; special permission should certainly be sought before camping, canoeing, fishing or similar. Check the website @www.activeexmoor.com for **organized activity** operators on Exmoor, as well as details of the 60-mile on-road **Exmoor Cycle Route**.

There are four obvious inland bases, all on the Somerset side of the county border: **Dulverton** in the southeast, site of the main information facilities; **Simonsbath** in the centre; **Exford**, near Exmoor's highest point of Dunkery

Getting around Exmoor

Minehead is the northern terminus of the **West Somerset Railway** (see opposite), but otherwise you have to rely on infrequent local **buses** for public transport. On the coast, the most useful route is the daily #300, connecting Minehead with Porlock, Lynton and Ilfracombe, while the #39 runs frequently between Minehead and Porlock and #398 links Minehead, Dunster, Dulverton and Tiverton, where there's a main-line train station; both the latter services operate all year, but not on Sunday. In summer, the #400 Exmoor Explorer vintage bus service, which is open-top in fine weather, links Minehead, Dunster, Exford and Porlock (May–Sept Sat & Sun; late July to late Aug also Tues & Thurs), while winter sees a few once- or twice-weekly community buses connecting Dulverton, Minehead and Lynton. If you're planning to make good use of First buses (@www.firstgroup.com), the major bus operator in these parts, buy a "FirstDay South West" ticket from the bus driver (£6.90–7.70 valid all day). In summer, you can also make use of the Moor Rover, a bookable **minibus** service that can transport people, bikes and luggage for a flat fee (June–Oct; ☏01398/323841, @www.atwest.org.uk; passengers £5, bikes £1, bags £5); reservations must be made on the previous day of travel or earlier, and routes cover all areas of the national park lying within Somerset.

Beacon, and **Winsford**, close to the A396 on the eastern side of the moor. Exmoor's coastline offers an alluring alternative to the open moorland, all of it accessible via the **South West Coast Path** (see box, p.348), which embarks on its long coastal journey at **Minehead**, though there is more charm to be found farther west at the sister villages of **Lynmouth** and **Lynton**, just over the Devon border.

Dulverton

The village of **DULVERTON**, on the southern edge of the national park, is the Park Authority's headquarters and so makes a good introduction to Exmoor. Information on the whole moor is available at the **visitor centre**, 7 Fore St (daily: April–Oct 10am–1.15pm & 1.45–5pm; Nov–March 10.30am–3pm; ☏01398/ 323841). Moorland **horseriding** and tuition is offered at West Anstey Farm (☏01398/341354), a couple of miles west of Dulverton.

Dulverton's smartest **accommodation** is ⚲ *Town Mills* (☏01398/323124, Ⓦwww.townmillsdulverton.co.uk; no under-12s; ❸), an old mill house in the centre of the village, while the nearby *Lion Hotel* in Bank Square (☏01398/324437, Ⓦwww.lionhoteldulverton.com; ❸) has a traditional feel, with beams and four-posters. Alternatively, there's the modern *Tongdam*, a Thai restaurant at 26 High St (☏01398/323397, Ⓦwww.tongdamthai.com), offering two doubles with shared bathroom (❷) and a suite with a sitting room and private bathroom (❸). A mile north of Dulverton, *Northcombe Farm* (☏01398/323602) has two YHA-affiliated camping barns (£8) as well as basic **camping** facilities.

Both the *Lion* and *Tongdam* offer moderately priced **meals**, while *Woods*, 4 Bank Square (☏01398/324007), serves more expensive but high-quality food, including local slow-roast pork, seafood and home-made ice cream – worth booking for.

Winsford, Exford and Dunkery Beacon

Just west of the A396, five miles north of Dulverton, **WINSFORD** lays good claim to being the moor's prettiest village. A scattering of thatched cottages ranged around a sleepy green, it is watered by a confluence of streams and rivers – one of them the Exe – giving it no fewer than seven bridges. On Halse Lane, *Karslake House* (☏01643/851242, Ⓦwww.karslakehouse.co.uk; no under-12s; ❹) offers excellent **B&B** in pretty rooms, while there's a well-equipped **campsite** a mile southwest of the village at *Halse Farm* (☏01643/851259, Ⓦwww.halsefarm .co.uk; closed Nov to mid-March). The rambling old thatched *Royal Oak* serves drinks, snacks and full restaurant **meals**, and also offers plush accommodation (☏01643/851455, Ⓦwww.royaloak-somerset.co.uk; ❺).

The hamlet of **EXFORD**, an ancient crossing-point on the River Exe four miles northwest of Winsford, is popular with hunting folk as well as with walkers

---

Walks from Dulverton and Tarr Steps

The most popular short walk from Dulverton goes along the east bank of the Barle to the seventeen-span medieval bridge at **Tarr Steps**, five miles to the northwest. You could combine this walk with a hike up **Winsford Hill** (a circular route of less than four hours from Tarr Steps), from where there are views as far as Dartmoor. From Winsford Hill you can make easy excursions to the **Punchbowl**, a bracken-grown depression resembling an amphitheatre, and the **Caractacus Stone**, an inscribed stone thought to date from around the year 500. Back at Tarr Steps, the *Tarr Farm* restaurant provides food, refreshment and pricey accommodation (☏01643/851507, Ⓦwww.tarrfarm.co.uk; ❺). Pick up route maps from Dulverton's tourist office.

here for the four-mile hike to **Dunkery Beacon**, Exmoor's highest point at 1700ft. There's a good range of **accommodation**, including *Exmoor Lodge*, a friendly B&B on Chapel Street (℡01643/831694, ⓦwww.exmoor-lodge.co .uk; ❷), and the village also holds Exmoor's main YHA **hostel**, a rambling Victorian house in the centre (℡0845/371 9634, Ⓔexford@yha.org.uk; from £10). Two and a half miles northwest of Exford off the Porlock Road, *Westermill Farm* (℡01643/831238, ⓦwww.exmoorcamping.co.uk) provides a tranquil **campsite** on the banks of the Exe.

Exmoor Forest and Simonsbath

At the heart of the national park stands **Exmoor Forest**, the barest part of the moor, scarcely populated except by roaming sheep and a few red deer – the word "forest" denotes simply that it was a hunting reserve. In the middle of it stands the village of **SIMONSBATH** (pronounced "Simmonsbath"), at a crossroads between Lynton, Barnstaple and Minehead on the River Barle. The village was home to the Knight family, who bought the forest in 1818 and, by introducing tenant farmers, building roads and importing sheep, brought systematic agriculture to an area that had never before produced any income.

Simonsbath would make a useful base for hikes on the moor, but there are only two **accommodation** possibilities: the *Exmoor Forest Inn* (℡01643/831341, ⓦwww.exmoorforestinn.co.uk; ❹), with comfortable rooms as well as space for camping, and the *Simonsbath House Hotel* (℡01643/831259, ⓦwww.simonsbath house.co.uk; no under-12s; ❹), former home of the Knights and now a cosy bolt-hole offering elegant rooms and a good but fairly expensive **restaurant**. In a converted barn next to the hotel, *Boevey's* offers coffees, lunches and internet access (closed Dec & Jan), while a couple of miles southwest of the village on the Brayford Road is the *Poltimore Arms* at **Yarde Down**, a classic country **pub** serving excellent food.

Minehead and Dunster

A chief port on the Somerset coast, **MINEHEAD** quickly became a favourite Victorian watering-hole with the arrival of the railway, and it has preserved an old-fashioned holiday-town atmosphere ever since. Steep lanes link the two quarters of **Higher Town**, on North Hill, containing some of the oldest houses, and **Quay Town**, the harbour area. It's in Quay Town that the **Hobby Horse** performs its dance in the town's three-day May Day celebrations, snaring maidens under its prancing skirt and tail in a fertility ritual resembling the more famous festivities at the Cornish port of Padstow (see p.415).

The **tourist office** lies on the seafront and close to the West Somerset Railway station on Warren Road (March–Oct Mon–Sat 10am–5pm, plus Sun 10am–2pm in July & Aug; Nov–Feb Mon–Sat 10am–3pm; ℡01643/702624). For **accommodation** in Minehead, try ⚥ *Baytree* at 29 Blenheim Rd (℡01643/703374, Ⓔderekcole@onetel.com; no credit cards; closed Nov–March; ❷), a friendly B&B with spacious rooms, or, right by the harbour on Quay Road, the *Old Ship Aground* pub (℡01643/702087, ⓦwww.theoldshipaground.co.uk; ❷), convenient for the coast path. There's a YHA **hostel** a couple of miles southeast, outside the village of Alcombe (℡0845/371 9033, Ⓔminehead@yha.org.uk; from £10), in a secluded combe on the edge of Exmoor.

Minehead is crammed with **places to eat**, mostly very mediocre. However, you could do a lot worse than an evening at the *Queen's Head*, on Holloway Street, off the Parade and near the tourist office, offering a range of ales and bar meals, as well as darts and pool.

5

The South West Coast Path

Britain's longest National Trail, the **South West Coast Path** (ⓦwww.southwest coastpath.com), starts at Minehead and tracks the coastline along Somerset and Devon's northern seaboard, round Cornwall, back into Devon, and on to Dorset, where it finishes close to the entrance to Poole Harbour. The path was conceived in the 1940s, but it was thirty years ago that – barring a few significant gaps – the full **630-mile route** opened, much of it on land owned by the National Trust, and all of it well signposted with the acorn symbol of the Countryside Agency.

Some degree of **planning** is essential for any long walk along the South West Coast Path, in particular on the south Devon stretch, where there are six ferries to negotiate and one ford to cross between Plymouth and Exmouth. **Accommodation** needs to be considered too: don't expect to arrive late in the day at a holiday town in season and immediately find a bed. Even campsites can fill to capacity, though campers have the flexibility of asking farmers for permission to pitch in a corner of a field.

Aurum Press publishes four **National Trail Guides** describing different parts of the path and using Ordnance Survey maps, while the **South West Coast Path Associa-tion** (ⓣ01752/896237, ⓦwww.swcp.org.uk) publishes an annual guide (£10.50, including postage) to the whole path, including accommodation lists, ferry timetables and transport details.

Dunster

As well as being the start of the South West Coast Path (see box above), Minehead is a terminus for the **West Somerset Railway**, which curves eastwards into the Quantocks as far as Bishops Lydeard. The area's major attraction, the old village of **DUNSTER**, is about a mile from the line's first stop, three miles inland. Dunster's main street is dominated by the towers and turrets of its **castle** (castle: mid-March to Oct daily except Thurs 11am–5pm; grounds: mid-March to Oct daily 11am–5pm; Nov to mid-March daily 11am–4pm; £8.10, grounds only £4.50; NT). Most of its fortifications were demolished after the Civil War, after which time the castle became something of an architectural showpiece, and Victorian restoration has made it more like a Rhineland *schloss* than a Norman stronghold. A tour of the castle will take you past various portraits of the Luttrells, owners of the house for six hundred years, as well as a bedroom once occupied by Charles I, a fine seventeenth-century carved staircase and a richly decorated banqueting hall. The grounds include terraced gardens and riverside walks, all overlooked by a hill-top folly, **Conygar Tower**, dating from 1776.

In the High Street below the castle stands the octagonal **Yarn Market**, dating from 1609, while the three-hundred-year-old **water mill** at the end of Mill Lane is still used commercially for milling the various grains which go to make the flour and muesli sold in the shop (April–Oct daily 11am–4.30pm; £3.25; NT) – the café, overlooking its riverside garden, is a good spot for lunch. For somewhere to **stay**, try the atmospheric *Luttrell Arms* on the High Street (ⓣ01643/821555, ⓦwww.luttrellarms.co.uk; ❹–❺), a fifteenth-century inn with open fires and beamed rooms, some with four-posters. There's a **National Park Centre** at the top of Dunster Steep by the main car park (Easter–Oct daily 10am–5pm; some weekends in winter 10.30am–3pm; ⓣ01643/821835).

Porlock and around

PORLOCK, six miles west of Minehead, lies in a deep hollow cupped on three sides by the hogbacked hills of Exmoor. The thatch-and-cob houses and dripping charm of the village's long main street have led to invasions of tourists, some of whom are also drawn by the place's literary links. According to Coleridge's own less than reliable testimony, it was a "man from Porlock" who broke the opium trance in which he was composing *Kubla Khan*, while the High Street's beamed *Ship Inn* prides itself on featuring prominently in the Exmoor romance *Lorna Doone* and, in real life, having sheltered the poet Robert Southey, who staggered in rain-soaked after an Exmoor ramble. There's little specific to do in Porlock, but the **Dovery Manor Museum** (May–Sept Mon–Fri 10am–1pm & 2–5pm, Sat 10.30am–12.30pm & 2–4pm; free; ⓦwww.doverymanormuseum.org.uk), in a fifteenth-century house at the eastern end of the High Street, holds a couple of cramped rooms showing traditional domestic and agricultural tools of Exmoor – including a man-trap – together with some material on the local wildlife. The most impressive items here though are the beautiful window and huge fireplace on the ground floor.

Practicalities

Porlock's **tourist office** is at West End, High Street (April–Oct Mon–Sat 10am–1pm & 2–5pm, Sun 10am–1pm; Nov–Easter Tues–Fri 10am–1pm, Sat 10am–2pm; ⓣ01643/863150, ⓦwww.porlock.co.uk). You can **stay** comfortably at ⅄ *Glen Lodge*, Hawkcombe (ⓣ01643/863371, ⓦwww.glenlodge.net; no credit cards; ❸), a ten-minute walk up Parsons Street off the High Street, a secluded and beautifully furnished B&B with distant sea views from the rooms and direct access to the moor. Back on the High Street, the Victorian *Lorna Doone Hotel* (ⓣ01643/862404, ⓦwww.lornadoonehotel.co.uk; ❶) has an endearing old-fashioned style, with rooms in three sizes, all comfy and with bathrooms. You can also pick up snacks, meals and teas here, or alternatively the *Whortleberry Tearoom* (closed Mon & Tues, also Wed & Sun in winter), further up the High Street, offers whortleberry jam on muffins among other home-made goodies. Porlock has a good, central **campsite**, *Sparkhayes Farm* (ⓣ01643/862470; closed Nov–Feb), signposted off the main road near the *Lorna Doone Hotel*.

Around Porlock

Two miles west over the reclaimed marshland, the tiny harbour of **PORLOCK WEIR** gives little inkling of its former role as a hard-working port trafficking with Wales. It's a peaceful spot, giving onto a bay that enjoys the mildest climate on Exmoor, and there's a top-notch **restaurant**, *Andrew's on the Weir* (ⓣ01643/863300, ⓦwww.andrewsontheweir.co.uk; closed Mon & Tues), which cooks up local lamb and seafood to perfection and also offers luxury **accommodation** (❻). An easy two-mile stroll west from Porlock Weir along the South West Coast Path brings you to **Culbone**, where a tiny church – claimed to be the country's smallest – lies buried within woods once inhabited by charcoal-burners.

East of Porlock, it's only a couple of miles to the National Trust-owned village of **Selworthy**, a parade of whitewashed thatched cottages, and a church with a notable barrel-vaulted ceiling.

Lynton and Lynmouth

West from Porlock, the road climbs 1350ft in less than three miles, though cyclists and drivers might prefer the gentler and more scenic toll-road alternative to the direct uphill trawl (cars £2.50). Nine miles along the coast, on the Devon side of the county line, the Victorian resort of **Lynton** perches above a lofty gorge with splendid views over the sea and its sister resort of **Lynmouth** down at sea level.

Lynton

Almost completely cut off from the rest of the country for most of its history, **LYNTON** struck lucky during the Napoleonic wars, when frustrated Grand

Tourists – unable to visit their usual continental haunts – discovered here a domestic slice of Swiss landscape. Coleridge and Hazlitt trudged over to Lynton from the Quantocks, but the greatest spur to the village's popularity came with the publication in 1869 of R.D. Blackmore's Exmoor melodrama *Lorna Doone*, a book based on the outlaw clans who inhabited these parts in the seventeenth century. Since then the area has become indelibly associated with the swashbuckling romance.

Opposite the school on Market Street, one of the oldest houses in the village is home to the **Lyn and Exmoor Museum** (Easter–Oct Mon–Fri 10am–4pm, Sun 2–5pm; £1), holding a motley selection of relics from the locality and a reconstructed Exmoor kitchen c.1800. Lynton's imposing **town hall** on Lee Road epitomizes the Victorian–Edwardian accent of the village. It was the gift of publisher George Newnes, who also donated the nearby **cliff railway** connecting Lynton with Lynmouth (daily: mid-Feb to March & early Oct to early Nov 10am–5pm; April to mid-June & mid-Sept to early Oct 10am–6pm; mid-June to late July & early Sept 10am–7pm; late July & Aug 10am–9pm; £3 return; ⓦwww.cliffrailwaylynton.co.uk). The device is an ingenious hydraulic system, its two carriages counterbalanced by water tanks, which fill up at the top, descend, and empty their load at the bottom.

Practicalities

The local **tourist office** is in Lynton's town hall (April–Oct Mon–Sat 9.30am–5pm, Sun 10am–4pm; Nov–March Mon–Sat 10am–4pm, Sun 10am–2pm; ☎0845/660 3232, ⓦlynton-lynmouth-tourism.co.uk). The town has a better choice of budget **B&Bs** than Lynmouth, among them the friendly ⚘ *North Walk House*, North Walk (☎01598/753372, ⓦwww.northwalkhouse.co.uk; ❸), in a panoramic position overlooking the sea, with rugs, wooden floors and free wi-fi in the rooms, and great organic food. More central is the *St Vincent Hotel* (☎01598/752244, ⓦwww .st-vincent-hotel.co.uk; ❸; closed Nov–March), a whitewashed Georgian house on Castle Hill with spacious, beautifully furnished bedrooms, and an excellent **restaurant** open to all, which specializes in French and Belgian recipes using local ingredients (eve only; closed Mon & Tues); two- and three-course menus cost £24 and £27, and Belgian beers are on hand. Elsewhere, you'll eat more cheaply at *Kensington Tea Room*, a traditional teashop and restaurant at 1 Castle Hill (☎01598/753972), offering

---

Walks from Lynton and Lynmouth

As well as the draws of the coastal path, there are several popular walks inland in this region. The one-and-a-half-mile tramp to **Watersmeet**, for example, follows the East Lyn River to where it's joined by Hoar Oak Water, a tranquil spot transformed into a roaring torrent after a bout of rain. From the fishing lodge here – now owned by the National Trust and open as a café and shop in summer – you can branch off on a range of less-trodden paths, such as the three-quarters-of-a-mile route south to **Hillsford Bridge**, the confluence of Hoar Oak and Farley Water.

North of Watersmeet, a path climbs up **Countisbury Hill** and the higher **Butter Hill** (nearly 1000ft) giving riveting views of Lynton, Lynmouth and the north Devon coast, and there's also a track leading to the lighthouse at **Foreland Point**, close to the coastal path. East from Lynmouth you can reach the point via a fine sheltered shingle beach at the foot of Countisbury Hill – one of a number of tiny coves that are easily accessible on either side of the estuary.

From Lynton, an undemanding expedition takes you west along the North Walk, a mile-long path leading to the **Valley of Rocks**, a steeply curved heathland dominated by rugged rock formations. At the far end of the valley, herds of wild goats range free, as they have done here for centuries.

daytime sandwiches, steak pies and hearty Sundays roasts, and evening meals between May and September (Thurs–Sat only).

Lynmouth

Five hundred feet below Lynton, **Lynmouth** lies at the junction and estuary of the East and West Lyn rivers, in a spot described by Gainsborough as "the most delightful place for a landscape painter this country can boast". Shelley spent nine weeks here with his 16-year-old bride Harriet Westbrook in the summer of 1812, during which time he wrote his polemical *Queen Mab* – two different houses claim to have been the Shelleys' love-nest. R.D. Blackmore stayed in **Mars Hill**, the oldest part of the town, its creeper-covered cottages framing the cliffs behind the Esplanade. At the back of the village you can explore the **Glen Lyn Gorge**, a wooded valley with walks, waterfalls and displays of waterpower, including hydro-electric turbines and a water-cannon (Easter–Oct daily 10am–1hr before dusk; £4). The gorge was the conduit of ferocious floodwaters streaming off Exmoor in 1952, a disaster that almost washed away the village and is recalled here.

You can also ask at the gorge (or call) about **boat trips** from Lynmouth harbour with Exmoor Coast Boat Cruises (Easter–Sept; ☎01598/753207); the hour-long excursion to Woody Bay and back (£10) allows you to view the abundant birdlife on the cliffs between May and July. Other trips, including fishing expeditions, are available at the harbour.

Practicalities

Lynmouth has a **National Park Visitor Centre** opposite *Shelley's Hotel* in the Lyndale car park (April to early Nov daily 10am–5pm; late Nov & March Sat & Sun 10am–3.30pm; ☎01598/752509). Central **accommodation** choices include *Shelley's*, right next to the Glen Lyn Gorge (☎01598/753219, ⓦwww.shelley shotel.co.uk; ❸; closed Nov–Easter), where you can sleep in the room occupied by the poet – he apparently left without paying his bill. Among other options, try *Sea View Villa*, at the top of a steep ascent at 6 Summer House Path (☎01598/753460, ⓦwww.seaviewvilla.co.uk; ❹), with elegant rooms and splendid views; evening meals and gourmet picnics are also available. For **food**, you'll find loads of atmosphere and fairly expensive prices at the traditional *Rising Sun* inn, Harbourside, or for cheaper eats, try the nearby *Rock House Hotel*, which has a tea garden, snacks at the bar and meals in its restaurant.

Travel details

Buses

For information on all local and national bus services, contact Traveline ☎0871/200 2233, ⓦwww.traveline .org.uk.

Bath to: Bradford-on-Avon (every 30min; 40min); Bristol (Mon–Sat every 10–15min, Sun every 30min; 45min); London (10 daily; 3hr–3hr 50min); Wells (Mon–Sat hourly, Sun 9 daily; 1hr 20min).

Bridgwater to: Glastonbury (Mon–Sat hourly, Sun 4; 1hr–1hr 15min); Holford (4–6 daily; 30–50min); Nether Stowey (7–10 daily; 25–40min); Taunton (2–4 hourly, Sun every 1–2hr; 30–45min); Wells (Mon–Sat hourly, Sun 4; 1hr 15min–1hr 30min).

Bristol to: Bath (Mon–Sat every 10–15min, Sun every 30min; 50min); Glastonbury (hourly; 1hr 20min); London (1–2 hourly; 2hr 30min); Wells (1–2 hourly; 1hr).

Glastonbury to: Bridgwater (Mon–Sat hourly, Sun 4; 55min–1hr 15min); Bristol (hourly; 1hr 20min); Wells (2–4 hourly; 20min).

Wells to: Bath (Mon–Sat hourly, Sun 8 daily; 1hr 20min); Bridgwater (Mon–Sat hourly, Sun 4; 1hr 10min–1hr 30min); Bristol (1–2 hourly; 1hr); Glastonbury (2–4 hourly; 20min); Wookey Hole (Mon–Sat every 1hr–1hr 30min, Sun 8 daily; 10–30min).

Trains

For information on all local and national rail services, contact National Rail Enquiries ☏ 0845/748 4950, ⓦ www.nationalrail.co.uk.

Bath to: Bristol (2–3 hourly; 15min); London (1–2 hourly; 1hr 30min); Salisbury (1–2 hourly; 1hr).

Bristol to: Bath (2–3 hourly; 15min); Birmingham (every 30min; 1hr 30min); Bridgwater (hourly; 45min); Cheltenham (2 hourly; 40min); Exeter (1–3 hourly; 1hr–1hr 40min); Gloucester (Mon–Sat hourly, Sun every 2hr; 50min); London (every 30min; 1hr 45min).

6

Devon and Cornwall

CHAPTER 6

Highlights

* **Sidmouth Folk Week** Great folk and roots music from around the country, with workshops, ceilidhs and busking galore. See p.363

* **Hiking on Dartmoor** Experience this bleakly beautiful landscape along a good network of paths. See p.369

* **Eden Project** A disused clay pit is home to a fantastic array of exotic plants and crops. See p.393

* **Lizard Point** This unspoiled headland is the starting point for some inspiring walks. See p.399

* **Isles of Scilly** England's most stunning offshore islands with majestic beaches and crystal-clear waters. See p.406

* **Tate St Ives** Iconic beachside showcase for local and contemporary art. See p.409

* **Surfing in Newquay** Ranks of Atlantic rollers draw enthusiasts from far and wide to the beaches here. See p.414

* **Seafood in Padstow** The local catch goes straight to the excellent restaurants of this gastronomic hotspot. See p.417

▲ Padstow harbour

Devon and Cornwall

At the western extremity of England, the counties of **Devon and Cornwall** encompass everything from genteel, cosy villages to wild expanses of granite moorland and vast Atlantic-facing strands of golden sand. The combination of rural peace and first-class beaches has made the peninsula perennially popular with tourists, so much so that tourism has replaced the traditional occupations of fishing and farming as the main source of employment and income. Enough remains of these beleaguered communities to preserve the region's authentic character, however – even if this can be occasionally obscured during the peak summer season.

Of the major cities of Devon and Cornwall, **Exeter** is the most interesting, dominated by the twin towers of its medieval cathedral and offering a rich selection of restaurants and nightlife. Much of the old city was destroyed by bombing during World War II, though **Plymouth** suffered far worse, due to its historic role as a great naval port. Here, bland postwar development inflicted almost as much damage as the Luftwaffe, although enough of Plymouth's Elizabethan core has survived to merit a visit.

While the human history of the area has left a strong stamp in the form of churches, castles and stately piles, it's the natural landscape of Devon and Cornwall that is the biggest draw, not least the long, deeply indented coastline. Warmed by the Gulf Stream, and enjoying more hours of sunshine than virtually anywhere else in England, part of the peninsula can appear almost Mediterranean, and indeed Devon's principal resort, **Torquay**, styles itself the capital of the "English Riviera". St Tropez it ain't, but there's no denying a certain glamour, far removed from the old-fashioned charm of the seaside towns of **east Devon**, or the cliff-backed resorts of the county's northern seaboard.

Britain's longest National Trail, the South West Coast Path (see box, p.348), which starts in Minehead, provides the best way of exploring the coast. Inland, hikers and others can escape the crowds on **Dartmoor**, the greatest of the West Country's granite massifs, whose national park status has preserved its remoter tracts of wilderness.

Like Devon, Cornwall owes much of its allure to the powerful presence of the ocean, which is never more than half an hour's drive away. The restless waves lend the county's old fishing ports an almost embattled character, especially on the north coast, where the bleak ruins of **Tintagel** – the most famous of the many places hereabouts to boast a connection with King Arthur and his knights – and the rock-walled harbour of **Boscastle** encapsulate the county's craggy appeal. The full elemental power of the Atlantic can best be appreciated on the headlands of **Lizard Point** and **Land's End**, where the splintered cliffs resound to the constant thunder of the waves. The sea also attracts legions of tourists to such resorts as

Falmouth and Newquay, the first of these a sailing centre, the second a magnet for surfers. St Ives, too, has long attracted the crowds, though the town has a separate identity as a magnet for the arts.

In counterpoint to all the seaside frivolity, Cornwall's granite coasts are dotted with the remnants of its now-defunct mining industries. Outside St Austell, a disused clay pit has been transformed into a brilliantly successful ecological gallery, the Eden Project, which highlights the diversity of the planet's plant systems with the help of science-fiction "biomes" that re-create tropical and Mediterranean climates and conditions.

Getting around by public transport in the West Country can be a convoluted and lengthy process, especially if you're relying on the often deficient bus network. By train, you can reach Exeter, Plymouth and Penzance, with a handful of branch lines wandering off to the major coastal resorts.

Devon

With its rolling meadows, narrow lanes and remote thatched cottages, Devon has long been idealized as a vision of a pre-industrial, "authentic" England, and a quick tour of the county might suggest that this is largely a region of cosy, gentrified villages inhabited mainly by retired folk and urban refugees. But the county's appeal goes deeper than the merely picturesque – the serene beauty of the landscape, from moorland villages to quiet coves on the majestic coastline, seeps into everyday life here, and it's the genuine article.

Intensely agricultural, Devon has also played a leading part in England's maritime history, and you can't go far without meeting some reminder of the great names of Tudor and Stuart seafaring, particularly in the two cities of Exeter and Plymouth. These days the nautical tradition is continued on a domesticated scale by yachties taking advantage of Devon's numerous creeks and bays, especially on its southern coast, where ports such as Dartmouth and Salcombe are awash with amateur sailors. Land-bound tourists flock to the sandy beaches and seaside resorts, of which Torquay, on the south coast, and Ilfracombe, on the north, are the busiest – though the most attractive are those which have retained something of their nineteenth-century elegance, such as Sidmouth, in east Devon. Occasionally, the nostalgia is overplayed, as in the case of Clovelly, frozen in a stilted olde-worlde image of itself, though even here the spectacular cliffside location will melt the most cynical heart. Inland, Devon is characterized by swards of lush pasture and a scattering of sheltered villages, the county's low population density dropping to almost zero on Dartmoor, the wildest and bleakest of the region's moors.

Exeter and Plymouth are on the main rail lines from London and the Midlands, with branch lines from Exeter linking the north coast at Barnstaple and the south-coast towns of Exmouth and Torquay. Buses fan out along the coasts and into the interior, though the service can be rudimentary for the smaller villages.

DEVON & CORNWALL

0 _____ 10 miles

ATLANTIC OCEAN

ENGLISH CHANNEL

Lundy Island

Isles of Scilly
Tresco · St Martin's
Bryher · St Mary's
St Agnes

Land's End
Penwith Peninsula
St Just
St Ives
Penzance
St Agnes
Perranporth
Redruth
Camborne
Helston
Newquay
Newquay Airport
Coverack
Lizard
Lizard Point
Lizard Peninsula
Falmouth
Truro
St Mawes
Veryan
Gorran Haven
Mevagissey
Lost Gardens of Heligan
St Austell
Eden Project
Par
Fowey
Polperro
Looe
Lanhydrock
St Neot
Liskeard
Bolventor
Bodmin Moor
Bodmin
Wadebridge
Rock
Padstow
Polzeath
Port Isaac
Tintagel
Boscastle
Camelford
Bude
Morwenstow
Hartland
Hartland Point
Clovelly
Appledore
Woolacombe
Ilfracombe
Great Torrington
Bideford
Barnstaple
Meeth
Eggesford
Dulverton
Minehead
EXMOOR NATIONAL PARK
Weston-super-Mare
Bridgwater
Taunton
SOMERSET
Honiton
Lyme Regis
Seaton
Beer
Sidmouth
Budleigh Salterton
A La Ronde
Topsham
Exmouth
Teignmouth
Torquay
Paignton
Paignton & Dartmouth Steam Railway
Brixham
Dartmouth
Kingsbridge
Salcombe
South Hams
Totnes
R. Dart
Newton Abbot
Buckfastleigh
Princetown
DARTMOOR NATIONAL PARK
Saltram House
Plymouth
Mount Edgcumbe
Calstock
Tavistock
Buckland Abbey
Lydford
Okehampton
Launceston
R. Tamar
R. Torridge
R. Taw
R. Exe
Crediton
Tiverton
Exeter
DEVON
CORNWALL
SOUTH WEST COAST PATH

SOUTH WEST COAST PATH

N

Exeter

EXETER's sights are richer than those of any other town in Devon or Cornwall, the legacy of an eventful history since its Celtic foundation and the establishment of the most westerly Roman outpost. After the Roman withdrawal, Exeter was refounded by Alfred the Great and by the time of the Norman Conquest had become one of the largest towns in England, profiting from its position on the banks of the River Exe. The expansion of the wool trade in the Tudor period sustained the city until the eighteenth century, and Exeter has maintained its status as commercial centre and county town, despite having much of its ancient centre gutted by World War II bombing. The city's sturdy cathedral and other remnants of its compact old quarter survived, which, along with its vibrant cultural life – infused by a lively student population and a series of festivals throughout the year – merits an extended visit.

Arrival, information and accommodation

Exeter has two **train stations**, Exeter Central and St David's, the latter a little further out from the centre of town, though connected by frequent city buses. South West trains on the London Waterloo–Salisbury line stop at both, as do trains on the Tarka Line to Barnstaple (see p.383) and those to Exmouth, though Exeter Central is not served by most other long-distance trains. **Buses** stop on Paris Street, which is opposite the **tourist office** at Dix's Field, off Princesshay (Mon–Sat 9am–5pm, plus Sun 10am–4pm in July & Aug; ℡01392/665700, ⓦ www.exeterandessentialdevon.com). There's a second visitor centre in the Quay House on Exeter's Quay (April–Oct daily 10am–5pm; Nov–Easter Sat & Sun 11am–4pm; ℡01392/271611). **Internet** access is available at the *New Horizon* café at 47 Longbrook St (daily 9am–9pm), where you can also nibble on Moroccan snacks.

Most of Exeter's B&B **accommodation** lies north of the centre, near the two stations.

Hotels and B&Bs

Abode Exeter Cathedral Yard ℡01392/319955, ⓦ www.abodehotels.co.uk. Built in 1769 and reputedly the first inn in England to be described as a "hotel", the former Royal Clarence is now part of an upmarket chain. It boasts a superb location, with contemporary bedrooms and a celebrated restaurant on the ground floor (see p.361). ❺

The Garden House 4 Hoopern Ave ℡01392/256255, ⓦ www.exeterbedandbreakfast .co.uk. In a quiet cul de sac just 10min north of the High Street, this B&B has charming owners and immaculate rooms with DVD and CD players and wi-fi. The immense, multi-choice breakfasts can be taken in the lovely garden. ❸

Raffles 11 Blackall Rd ℡01392/270200, ⓦwww .raffles-exeter.co.uk. An elegant Victorian house whose rooms are furnished with Pre-Raphaelite etchings and other items from the owner's antique business. Breakfasts make use of the organic garden produce. ❸

Silversprings 12 Richmond Rd ℡01392/494040, ⓦwww.silversprings.co.uk. Friendly service, free wi-fi and great breakfasts make this an excellent choice. Rooms have comfortable beds and DVDs, and there's a patio garden. Advance booking advised. ❸

Townhouse 54 St David's Hill ℡01392/494994, ⓦwww.townhouseexeter.co.uk. Contemporary rooms in an appealing Edwardian guesthouse, midway between the train stations, with wi-fi access. Some bathrooms and shower rooms are small. ❸

White Hart 66 South St ℡01392/279897, ⓦwww.whitehartpubexeter.co.uk. Old coaching inn with period trappings and a lovely old bar, though rooms have a bland business ambience. Prices drop at weekends. ❷

Hostels

Exeter YHA 47 Countess Wear Rd ℡0845/371 9516, ⓔ exeter@yha.org.uk. A country house three miles southeast of the centre, with dorm beds from £14 and bike rental. Take minibus #K or #T from High Street or South Street (#57 and others from the bus station) to the Countess Wear post office on Topsham Rd, a fifteen-minute ride, then a 10min walk. Also reachable on the footpath alongside the River Exe from The Quay.

Globe Backpackers 71 Holloway St ☏ 01392/215521, ⓦ www.exeterbackpackers.co.uk. Clean

and central (though a bit of a hike from the stations), this hostel has good showers and an upbeat atmosphere. Facilities include kitchen and free wi-fi. Bunk beds in dorms of six to ten cost from £16.50 for one night, or £75 for a week.

The City

Most of Exeter's sights are concentrated in the area between the High Street and the river. The city is easily negotiated on foot, but if you envisage using the buses on an intensive one-day visit, pick up a bus map from the tourist office and buy a "Day Rider" bus ticket from the bus station or on board (£4).

St Peter's Cathedral

The most distinctive feature of Exeter's skyline, **St Peter's Cathedral** (Mon–Sat 9am–4.45pm; £5), is a stately monument made conspicuous by the two great Norman towers flanking the nave. Close up, it's the facade's ornate Gothic screen

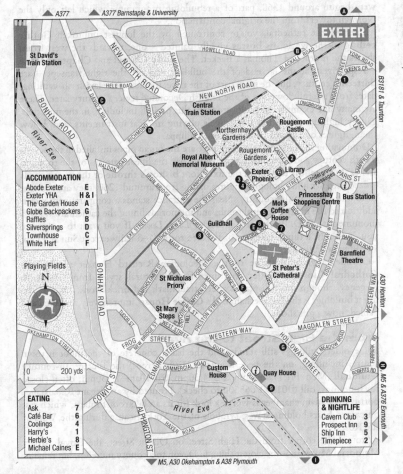

EXETER

▲ A377
▲ A377 Barnstaple & University

HOWELL ROAD

St David's Train Station

NEW NORTH ROAD

HELE ROAD

NEW NORTH ROAD

BONHAY ROAD

River Exe

ST DAVID'S HILL

RICHMOND RD

QUEEN ST

Central Train Station

Northernhay Gardens

Rougemont Castle

Rougemont Gardens

Royal Albert Memorial Museum

HALDON ROAD

IRON BRIDGE

NORTHERNHAY ST

Exeter Phoenix

Library

HIGH STREET

PARIS ST

Underground Passages

ⓘ

Princesshay Shopping Centre

Bus Station

HOWELL ROAD

BLACKALL ROAD

YORK ROAD

QUEEN'S CR.

B3181 & Taunton

LONGBROOK ST

LONGBROOK ST

CHURCH

BADGROVE ST

ACCOMMODATION
Abode Exeter	E
Exeter YHA	H & I
The Garden House	A
Globe Backpackers	G
Raffles	B
Silversprings	D
Townhouse	C
White Hart	F

PAUL STREET

EXE STREET

BARTHOLOMEW ST W

NORTH STREET

Guildhall

Mol's Coffee House

MARY ARCHES ST

CATHEDRAL YARD

HIGH STREET

BEDFORD ST

SOUTHERNHAY WEST

SOUTHERNHAY EAST

BARNFIELD RD

BARNFIELD ROAD

Barnfield Theatre

A30 Honiton ▶

WESTERN WAY

Playing Fields

N

BONHAY ROAD

BARTHOLOMEW ST

St Nicholas Priory

St Mary Steps

TUDOR ST

SMYTHEN ST

KING ST

PRESTON STREET

ST GEORGE'S

MARKET STREET

FORE STREET

St Peter's Cathedral

PALACE

CATHEDRAL CLOSE

SOUTHERNHAY

MAGDALEN STREET

BULL MEADOW RD

A30 Honiton ▶

A30 & A376 Exmouth ▶

0   200 yds

OKEHAMPTON STREET

FROG STREET

NEW BRIDGE ST

EDMUND STREET

COMMERCIAL ROAD

COWICK ST

WEST STREET

QUAY HILL

THE QUAY

Custom House

ⓘ Quay House

HOLLOWAY STREET

ROBERTS RD

M5 & A376 Exmouth ▶

River Exe

ALPHINGTON ST

HAVEN ROAD

EATING
Ask	7
Café Bar	6
Coolings	4
Harry's	1
Herbie's	8
Michael Caines	E

DRINKING & NIGHTLIFE
Cavern Club	3
Prospect Inn	9
Ship Inn	5
Timepiece	2

▼ M5, A30 Okehampton & A38 Plymouth

Top 5 Devon and Cornwall festivals

▶▶ **Exeter Festival** Twice-yearly celebration of music, from classical to jazz, with theatre, cabaret and comedy also on the menu. See p.362.

▶▶ **Sidmouth Folk Week** Rollicking jamboree of all kinds of folk and roots music in an otherwise genteel resort, with good vibes and smiles all round. See box, p.363.

▶▶ **St Ives Festival** The town's September knees-up is an essential cultural highlight in Cornwall, with the accent on music from around the world, plus films and theatre. See p.408.

▶▶ **Boardmasters Festival, Newquay** Increasingly popular beach festival combining big-name rock acts with surf and skate competitions – book early. See box, p.415.

▶▶ **Obby Oss, Padstow** Boisterous and deeply traditional May Day caper, permeated with raunchy symbolism. See p.415.

that commands attention: its three tiers of sculpted (and very weathered) figures – including Alfred, Athelstan, Canute, William the Conqueror and Richard II – were begun around 1360, part of a rebuilding programme which left only the Norman towers from the original construction.

Entering the cathedral, you're confronted by the longest unbroken **Gothic ceiling** in the world, its **bosses** vividly painted – one, towards the west front, shows the murder of Thomas à Becket. The **Lady Chapel** and **Chapter House** – respectively at the far end of the building and off the right transept – are thirteenth century, but the main part of the nave, including the lavish rib-vaulting, dates from the full flowering of the English Decorated style, a century later. There are many fine examples of sculpture from this period, including, in the minstrels' gallery high up on the left side, angels playing musical instruments, and, below them, figures of Edward III and Queen Philippa.

Dominating the cathedral's central space are the organ pipes installed in the seventeenth century and harmonizing perfectly with the linear patterns of the roof and arches. In the **choir** don't miss the sixty-foot **bishop's throne** or the **misericords** – decorated with mythological figures dating from around 1260, they are thought to be the oldest in the country. Near the entrance stands a comparatively recent addition to the many medieval tombs and memorials lining the cathedral's walls: a monument to R.D. Blackmore, author of *Lorna Doone*. If you want to make sure you don't miss a thing, take one of the free **tours** (1–3 daily except Sun at 11am, 12.30pm & 2.30pm).

Outside, a graceful statue of the theologian Richard Hooker surveys the **Cathedral Close**, a motley mixture of architectural styles from Tudor to Regency, though most display Exeter's trademark red-brick work. One of the finest buildings is the Elizabethan **Mol's Coffee House**, impressively timbered and gabled, now a gift shop.

From the High Street to the river

Some older buildings still stand amid the banal concrete of the modern town centre, including, on the pedestrianized **High Street**, the fourteenth-century **Guildhall** (Mon–Fri 11am–1pm & 2–4.30pm, Sat 10am–12.30pm; often closed for functions, call ☎01392/665500 to check). Fronted by an elegant Renaissance portico, the main chamber is worth a look for its arched roof timbers, which rest on carved bears holding staves, symbols of the Yorkist cause during the Wars of the Roses.

Around the corner from the High Street on Queen Street, the **Royal Albert Memorial Museum** is the closest thing in Devon to a county museum, but remains closed for a major refit until 2012. Behind the museum, Rougemont and North-ernhay Gardens hold what remains of **Rougemont Castle**, once a Norman fortress, now little more than a perimeter of red-stone walls. Off the top end of the High Street, Paris Street holds the entrance to a network of **underground passages** (June–Sept & school hols Mon–Sat 9.30am–5.30pm, Sun 10.30am–4pm; Oct–May Tues–Fri 11.30am–5.30pm, Sat 9.30am–5.30pm, Sun 11.30am–4pm; £5), first excavated in the thirteenth century to bring water to the cathedral precincts, and now visitable on a guided **tour**; it's not recommended for claustrophobes.

Exeter's centre is bounded to the southwest by the River Exe, where the port area is now mostly devoted to leisure activities, particularly around **The Quay**. Pubs, shops and cafés share the space with handsomely restored nineteenth-century warehouses and the smart **Custom House**, built in 1681, its opulence reflecting the former importance of the cloth trade. Next door, the Quay House from the same period has an information desk, and shows footage of Exeter's history upstairs. The area comes into its own at night, but is worth a wander at any time, and you can **rent bikes** and **canoes** at Saddles & Paddles on The Quay (T 01392/424241, W www.sadpad.com) to explore the **Exeter Canal**, which runs five miles to Topsham and beyond.

Eating and drinking

Exeter is well supplied with **places to eat** to suit every pocket. Good **pubs** are harder to find, though The Quay makes a lively spot to while away an evening over a pint or two.

Restaurants and cafés

Ask 5 Cathedral Close T 01392/427127. This lovely old building facing the cathedral makes a superb setting for the standard chain pizzas and pastas (£8–10). Outdoor seating in the courtyard.
Café Bar Cathedral Yard T 01392/223626. Opposite the cathedral, this is a modish spot for a coffee, lunch (toasties, salads, burgers and pasta) or a full evening meal (set menus for £10 & £14). There's live jazz on alternate Fridays, for which booking is advised.
Coolings Gandy St T 01392/434184. Buzzy wine bar and bistro serving tasty meals (around £8) until 9pm daily – it's open until 11pm (midnight at weekends) and has a cellar bar open for cocktails Wed–Sat eve.
Harry's 86 Longbrook St T 01392/202234. Set in a converted church, this place offers good-value Mexican, Italian and American staples (around £9) and usually attracts a cheery crowd.

Herbie's 15 North St T 01392/258473. Friendly spot for delicious wholefood dishes (mostly £9) and organic beers, wines and ice cream. Closed all Sun & Mon eve.
Michael Caines *Abode Exeter* hotel, Cathedral Yard T 01392/223638. Exeter's classiest restaurant offers sophisticated Modern European cuisine in sleek surroundings. Prices are fairly high (mains around £24), but there are reasonable fixed-price menus (£14.50 & £19.50) at lunchtime. Closed Sun.

Pubs

Prospect Inn The Quay. You can eat and drink outside at this seventeenth-century waterside pub, setting for 1970s TV drama *The Onedin Line*.
Ship Inn St Martin's Lane. Claiming to have once been Francis Drake's local, this place serves bar meals (baguettes, jacket potatoes and curries) in the low-ceilinged bar, adorned with sailors' knots and clay pipes, or upstairs at lunchtime.

Nightlife and entertainment

A veteran of Exeter's **clubbing** scene, the subterranean *Cavern Club* (T 01392/495370, W www.cavernclub.co.uk), with entrances on Queen and Gandy streets, alternates DJ sets with **live bands**, mainly post-punk, dub, electro and indie. *Timepiece*, occupying a former prison on Little Castle Street (T 01392/493096, W www.timepiecenightclub.co.uk), has pop and cheese (Mon), Latin (Tues), students' night (Wed), r'n'b (Thurs), dance mixes (Fri & Sat) and world (Sun). Off Gandy Street, live music is among the cultural pursuits at **Exeter**

Phoenix (☎01392/667080, ⓦwww.exeterphoenix.org.uk), an arts centre which also hosts art-house films, exhibitions and readings.

Of the town's **theatres**, the Northcott, on the university campus on Stocker Road (☎01392/493493, ⓦwww.exeternorthcott.co.uk), and the Barnfield, on Barnfield Road (☎01392/270891, ⓦwww.barnfieldtheatre.org.uk), have the best productions – both also stage music performances in a range of genres. The **Exeter Festival** (☎01392/265200, ⓦwww.exeter.gov.uk/festival) takes over various venues around town over two weeks in June/July and again in October/November, featuring a range of cultural events, and in March, **Vibraphonic** (ⓦwww.2020vibraphonic.co.uk), based at the Phoenix, focuses on modern and world music.

The east Devon coast

The coast south and east of Exeter holds an architectural oddity, **A La Ronde**, as well as a string of old-fashioned seaside resorts, stretching towards the Dorset border. None of them is over-commercialized, but all are still best seen outside the summer peak, with **Sidmouth** and the neighbouring village of **Beer** being good choices for an overnight stop.

Frequent **trains** connect Exeter with Exmouth on the Avocet Line, while A La Ronde and Exmouth are both served by **bus** #57 from Exeter's bus station. For Budleigh Salterton and Sidmouth take bus #157 or #357 from Exmouth; #52A and #52B connect Sidmouth directly with Exeter. The #899 service links Sidmouth with Beer (Mon–Sat), while the #X53 from Exeter stops in Beer en route to the Jurassic Coast (see p.237).

A La Ronde

The Gothic folly of **A La Ronde** (mid-March to Oct Mon–Wed, Sat & Sun 11am–5pm, also Fri July & Aug; £6.70; NT), a couple of miles north of Exmouth off the A376, was the creation of two cousins, Jane and Mary Parminter, who in the 1790s were inspired by their European Grand Tour to construct a sixteen-sided house, possibly based on the Byzantine basilica of San Vitale in Ravenna. The end product is filled with mementoes of the Parminters' travels as well as a number of their more offbeat creations, such as a frieze made of feathers culled from game birds and chickens. In the upper rooms are a gallery and staircase completely covered in shells, too fragile to be visited, though part can be glimpsed from the completely enclosed octagonal room on the first floor – a closed-circuit TV system enables visitors to home in on details. Superb views extend over the Exe Estuary.

Exmouth and Budleigh Salterton

EXMOUTH started as a Roman port and went on to become the first of the county's resorts to be popularized by holiday-makers in the late eighteenth century. Overlooking lawns, rock pools and a respectable two miles of beach, Exmouth's Georgian terraces once accommodated such folk as the wives of Nelson and Byron – installed at nos. 6 and 19 The Beacon respectively (on a rise overlooking the seafront, above the public gardens). From Easter to October, Exmouth is linked by an hourly **ferry** to Starcross, on the other side of the Exe estuary (£4.50 one-way), where you can pick up a bus to Torquay (see p.364). There's a **tourist office** on Alexandra Terrace (Mon–Sat: Easter–Oct 10am–5pm; Nov–Easter 10am–2pm; ☎01395/222299, ⓦwww.exmouthguide.co.uk).

Four miles east of Exmouth, bounded on each side by red sandstone cliffs, **BUDLEIGH SALTERTON** has a more genteel air – its thatched and white-washed cottages attracted such figures as Noël Coward and P.G. Wodehouse, and John Millais painted his famous *Boyhood of Raleigh* on the shingle beach here (Sir Walter Raleigh was born in pretty East Budleigh, a couple of miles inland). Three miles east, **Ladram Bay** is a popular pebbly beach sheltered by woods and beautiful eroded cliffs. If you want to stay in the area, contact Budleigh's **tourist office** on Fore Street (Easter–Oct Mon–Sat 10am–1pm & 2–4.30pm; Nov–Easter Mon–Sat 10am–1pm; ☎01395/445275, ⊛www.visitbudleigh.com).

Sidmouth

Set amid a shelf of crumbling red sandstone, cream-and-white **SIDMOUTH** is the chief resort on this stretch of coast and boasts nearly five hundred buildings listed as having special historic or architectural interest, among them the stately Georgian homes of **York Terrace** behind the Esplanade. Moreover, the **beaches** are better tended than many along this stretch, not only the mile-long main town beach but also Jacob's Ladder, a cliff-backed shingle-and-sand strip beyond Connaught Gardens to the west of town. To the east, the coast path climbs steep Salcombe Hill to follow cliffs that give sanctuary to a range of birdlife including yellowhammers and green woodpeckers, as well as the rarer grasshopper warbler. Further on, the path descends to meet one of the most isolated and attractive beaches in the area, **Weston Mouth**.

Practicalities

Sidmouth's **tourist office** is on Ham Lane, off the eastern end of the Esplanade (March & April Mon–Thurs 10am–4pm, Fri & Sat 10am–5pm, Sun 10am–1pm; May–July, Sept & Oct Mon–Sat 10am–5pm, Sun 10am–4pm; Aug Mon–Sat 10am–6pm, Sun 10am–5pm; Nov–Feb Mon–Sat 10am–1.30pm; ☎01395/516441, ⊛www.visitsidmouth.co.uk).

Among the town's vast range of **accommodation**, ♣ *The Hollies* is a winning blend of traditional elegance and contemporary fittings, a ten-minute walk from the seafront on Salcombe Road (☎01395/514580, ⊛www.holliesguesthouse.co .uk; no credit cards; ❷). To stay nearer the sea, try *Dukes*, The Esplanade (☎01395/513320, ⊛www.hotels-sidmouth.co.uk; ❹), a busy bar and hotel in the heart of things, with functional, modern rooms. For old-fashioned style seek out the Georgian Gothic *Woodlands Hotel*, a few minutes' walk up Station Road from the Esplanade (☎01395/513120, ⊛www.woodlands-hotel.com; ❺), with antiques in the bedrooms and a conservatory in the grounds. The nearest **campsite** lies a mile and a half east of town at Salcombe Regis: *Salcombe Regis Camping and Caravan Park* (☎01395/514303, ⊛www.salcombe-regis.co.uk; closed Nov to mid-March).

For **meals** in town, *Mocha Restaurant* on The Esplanade (☎01395/512882; daytime only, eve in July & Aug) serves jacket potatoes, paninis and hot lunches,

---

Sidmouth Folk Week

Sidmouth hosts what many consider to be the country's best **folk festival** over eight days in early August. It's an upbeat affair: folk and roots artists from around the country perform in marquees, pubs and hotels around town, and there are numerous ceilidhs and pavement buskers. Accommodation during this period is at a premium but campsites are laid on outside town with shuttle buses to the centre. Tickets can be bought for specific days, for the weekend or the entire week. For detailed information, call ☎01395/578627 or see ⊛www.sidmouthfolkweek.co.uk. Book early for the main acts.

including crab and a seafood platter for under £13, while *Brown's Bistro and Wine Bar* at 33 Fore St (℡01395/516724; closed Mon & Tues in winter) offers tasty meals with a good-value early-evening menu (£14). Among the **pubs**, head for the agreeable *Swan Inn*, near the tourist office at 37 York St, which has real ales, bar meals and a garden – a fun place to linger at festival time.

Beer

Eight miles east along the coast, the fishing village of **BEER** lies huddled within a small sheltered cove between gleaming white headlands. A stream rushes along a deep channel dug into Beer's main street, and if you can ignore the crowds in high summer much of the village looks unchanged since the time when it was a smugglers' eyrie. The area is best known for its quarries, which were worked from Roman times until the nineteenth century: **Beer stone** has been used in many of Devon's churches and houses, not to mention some of London's greatest monuments. A mile or so west of the village, you can take a guided tour around **Beer Quarry Caves** (Easter–Sept 10am–6pm; Oct daily 10am–5pm; last tour 1hr before closing; £6), which includes a small exhibition of pieces carved by medieval masons. Take something warm to wear.

Bay View (℡01297/20489, ⓦwww.bayviewbeer.com; no credit cards; closed Nov–Easter; ❷), overlooking the sea on Fore Street, is the best of the **B&Bs**, and east Devon's only **youth hostel** is half a mile northwest, at Bovey Combe, Townsend (℡0845/371 9502, ⓔbeer@yha.org.uk; from £14; call to check opening). For **food**, head for the *Barrel o' Beer* pub (℡01297/20099), on Fore Street, where the moderately priced restaurant menu includes oysters and home-smoked fish, or, at the bottom of the street, the *Anchor Inn*, where you can enjoy your beer and snacks with sea views from the cliff-top garden, or choose from the range of seafood on offer in the separate restaurant.

The "English Riviera" region

The wedge of land between Dartmoor and the sea contains some of Devon's most fertile pastures, backing onto some of the West Country's most popular coastal resorts. Chief of these is **Torbay**, an amalgam of **Torquay**, **Paignton** and **Brixham**, together forming the nucleus of an area optimistically known as "**The English Riviera**". South of the Torbay conurbation, the yachting port of **Dartmouth** offers a calmer alternative, and is linked by riverboat to historic and almost unspoiled **Totnes**. West of the River Dart, the rich agricultural district of **South Hams** extends as far as Plymouth, cleft by a web of rivers flowing off Dartmoor. The main town here is **Kingsbridge**, at the head of an estuary down which you can ferry to the sailing resort of **Salcombe**.

Trains from Exeter to Plymouth run down the coast as far as Teignmouth before striking inland for Totnes – to get to Torbay, change at Newton Abbot. The frequent #X46 **bus** takes an hour to connect Exeter and Torquay. For the hinterland and points south and west along the coast, you can rely on a network of buses from Torquay, and travellers to Totnes and Dartmouth could make use of the **South Devon Railway** and **boats** along the River Dart.

Torquay

TORQUAY, the largest component of the super-resort of **Torbay**, comes closest to living up to the self-penned "English Riviera" sobriquet, sporting a mini-corniche and promenades landscaped with flowerbeds. The much-vaunted palm trees and the coloured lights that festoon the harbour by night contribute to the town's unique flavour, a slightly frayed combination of the exotic and the classically English. Two of the most famous figures associated with Torquay – genteel crimewriter Agatha Christie and fictional angst-ridden hotelier Basil Fawlty – perfectly encapsulate the resort's muddled identity.

Arrival, information and accommodation

The **train station** is off Rathmore Road, next to the Torre Abbey gardens; most **buses** leave from outside the Pavilion, including the frequent #12 and #12A service linking Torquay with Paignton and Brixham. Torquay's well-organized **tourist office** is on Vaughan Parade, by the harbour (June–Sept Mon–Sat 9.30am–5.30pm, Sun 10am–4pm; Oct–May Mon–Sat 9.30am–5pm; ☎01803/211211, ⒲www.englishriviera.co.uk). Tourist offices in Paignton and Brixham share the same times and telephone number.

Torquay has plenty of **accommodation**, but you'll need to book in advance during peak season. Most of the budget choices lie along and around Belgrave Road and, slightly further out, Avenue Road. The nearest **campsite** is the peaceful *Widdicombe Farm*, an adults-only site near Compton accessed from the A380 ring road (☎01803/558325, ⒲www.widdicombefarm.co.uk; closed mid-October to late March).

Allerdale 21 Croft Rd ☎01803/292667, ⒲www .allerdalehotel.co.uk. The place to come for views and stately surroundings, with a long, sloping, lawned garden and a snooker room. Free wi-fi. ❸

The Exton 12 Bridge Rd ☎01803/293561, ⒲www.extonhotel.co.uk. Small, clean and quiet hotel, close to Belgrave Rd and a 10min walk from the train station. Evening meals available. ❷

Lanscombe House Cockington ☎01803/606938, ⒲www.lanscombehouse.co.uk. A couple of miles west of the centre outside the touristy village of Cockington, this elegant B&B offers rural seclusion, with airy rooms and a walled garden. ❸

Torquay Backpackers 119 Abbey Rd ☎01803/299924, ⒲www.torquaybackpackers .co.uk. Central, cheap and friendly hostel, a ten-minute walk from the station. Dorm beds cost £16 a night (£12 in winter), and there's a double with shared bathroom. ❶

The Town

Torquay's seafront is centred on the small **harbour** and marina off The Strand, where the mingling crowds can make the place seem almost Mediterranean, especially at night. To one side stands the copper-domed **Pavilion**, an Edwardian building that originally housed a ballroom and assembly hall and is now refurbished with shops. Behind the Pavilion, limestone cliffs sprouting white high-rise hotels and apartment blocks separate the harbour area from Torquay's main beach, **Abbey Sands**. Good for chucking a frisbee about but too busy in summer for serious relaxation, it takes its name from **Torre Abbey**, sited in ornamental gardens behind the beachside road (March–Oct daily 10am–6pm; Nov, Dec & Feb Tues–Sun 10am–5pm; £5.75; ⒲www.torre-abbey.org.uk). The Norman church that once stood here was razed by Henry VIII, though a gatehouse, tithe barn, chapterhouse and tower escaped demolition, and recent excavations have uncovered medieval walls. The present **Abbey Mansion** is a seventeenth- and eighteenth-century construction, now containing a suite of period rooms and a good museum, with collections of silver and glass, window designs by Edward Burne-Jones, illustrations by William Blake, and nineteenth-century and contemporary works of art.

A more down-to-earth collection can be viewed at **Torquay Museum**, a short walk up from the harbour at 529 Babbacombe Rd (Mon–Sat 10am–5pm, also Sun in summer school hols 1.30–5pm; £4.65), which includes a section devoted to

Agatha Christie, who was born and raised in Torquay, though most of the space here is given over to local and natural history displays.

At the northern end of the harbour, **Living Coasts** (daily: Easter–Sept 10am–5pm; £8.35, or £17.55 with Paignton Zoo, see below; Ⓦwww.living coasts.org.uk) is home to a variety of fauna and flora found on British shores, including puffins, penguins and seals. You can see the animals in their carefully re-created habitats, and feed them at various intervals throughout the day. The rooftop café and restaurant have splendid panoramic views. Beyond here, the coast path leads round a promontory to reach some good sandy beaches: **Meadfoot Beach** is one of the busiest, reached by crossing Daddyhole Plain, an open green space named after a large chasm in the adjacent cliff caused by a landslide, but locally attributed to the devil ("Daddy"). North of the Hope's Nose promontory, the coast path leads to a string of less crowded beaches, including **Babbacombe Beach** and, beyond, **Watcombe** and **Maidencombe**.

Eating and drinking

Torquay offers a surprisingly high standard of **restaurants**, with fairly high prices, though cheaper places are thick on the ground too.

Hole in the Wall Park Lane Ⓣ01803/200755. Among the central pubs, this place is strong on atmosphere – it was the Irish playwright Sean O'Casey's boozer when he lived in Torquay – and has a good range of beers. There's a separate restaurant, and weekly live music.

Number 7 Fish Bistro Beacon Terrace Ⓣ01803/295055. Just above the harbour, this place is a must for seafood fans, with a menu covering everything from seafood broth to grilled turbot – or whatever else the boats have brought in. Most mains cost about £17. Closed lunch

Sun–Tues, also Sun eve Oct–June, Mon eve Nov–May.

Orange Tree 14 Parkhill Rd Ⓣ01803/213936. Just up from the harbour, this demure little restaurant serves up classy Modern British dishes, such as duck breast with pok choi and cashew nuts, at around £17. Eve only, closed Sun.

Sea Spray 8 Victoria Parade Ⓣ01803/293734. Good-value informal restaurant by the harbour, specializing in fresh seafood – try the grilled lemon sole with a cider and mushroom sauce. Meat dishes also available; all main courses are £8–15.

Nightlife

Torquay has the hottest and rowdiest **nightlife** in Devon; the main clubs are all near the harbour, including, on Torwood Street, *Venue* (Ⓣ01803/213903, Ⓦwww.venueclubbing.co.uk) and *Bohemia* (Ⓣ01803/292079), and *Valbonne* on Higher Union Street (Ⓣ01803/290458, Ⓦwww.thevalbonne.co.uk). On The Strand, *Café Mambo* (Ⓣ01803/291112, Ⓦwww.cafemambo.co.uk) has three floors including a terrace, with Thai food on hand and nightly DJs playing chart tunes, hip-hop and r'n'b. *Candyfloss* (Ⓣ01803/292279), near the Pavilion on Rock Road (off Abbey Rd), is a good-time, long-established gay club with party sounds.

Paignton

Not so much a rival to Torquay as its complement, **PAIGNTON** lacks the gloss of its neighbour, but also its pretensions. Activity is concentrated at the southern end of the wide town beach, around the small harbour that nestles in the lee of the appropriately named Redcliffe headland. Otherwise, diversion-seekers could wander over to **Paignton Zoo** (daily 10am–6pm in summer, 10am–4pm or dusk in winter, last entry 1hr before closing; £11.35, or £17.75 with Living Coasts, see above), a mile out on Totnes Road, or board the **Paignton & Dartmouth Steam Railway** at Paignton's Queen's Park train station near the harbour (Ⓣ01803/555872, Ⓦwww.paignton-steamrailway.co.uk). Running almost daily from Easter to October, plus a few dates in December, the line connects with Paignton's other main beach – **Goodrington Sands** – before trundling alongside the Dart estuary to Kingswear, seven miles away. If you can stomach the heavy-handed Victorian trappings, it's a pleasant way to view the scenic countryside, and you could make a day of it by using the ferry connection from Kingswear to Dartmouth (see p.369), then taking a river boat up the Dart to Totnes, from where you can catch any bus back to Paignton – a "Round Robin" ticket (£19.50) lets you do this.

Paignton's bus and train stations are next to each other off Sands Road. Five minutes away, there's a **tourist office** on the seafront (see p.365 for details).

Brixham

From Paignton, it's a fifteen-minute bus ride down to **BRIXHAM**, the prettiest of the Torbay towns. Fishing was for centuries Brixham's lifeblood, its harbour extending some way farther inland than it does now to afford a safe anchorage – a function performed today by an extensive breakwater. Indeed, at the beginning of the nineteenth century, this was the major fish market in the West Country, and it still supplies fish to restaurants as far away as London. The harbour is overlooked by an unflattering statue of William III, a reminder of his landing in Brixham to claim the Crown of England in 1688. Among the trawlers moored here is a full-size reconstruction of the **Golden Hind** (March–Oct daily 10am–4pm, with longer opening in summer; £3.50), in which Francis Drake circumnavigated the world – though it has no real connection with the port. The boat is surprisingly small, and below decks you can see the extremely cramped surgeon's and carpenter's cabins, and the only slightly grander captain's quarters.

From the quayside, steep lanes and stairways climb up to the older centre around Fore Street, where the bus from Torquay pulls in. East of the harbour, you can reach the promontory of **Berry Head** along a path winding up from the *Berry Head House Hotel*. Fortifications built during the Napoleonic Wars are still standing on this southern limit of Torbay, which is now a conservation area, attracting colonies of nesting sea birds and affording fabulous views.

Practicalities

On the quayside, the town's **tourist office** (see p.365 for details) can help with finding **accommodation**. The best places are on King Street, overlooking the harbour, for example *Harbour View* at no. 65 (☎01803/853052, ⓦwww .harbourviewbrixhambandb.co.uk; ❷), a B&B with spotless en-suite rooms. Away from the seafront, there's *Brookside* at 160 New Rd (☎01803/858858, ⓦwww.brooksidebrixham.co.uk; no under-16s; ❸), a bungalow with a more contemporary style and organic breakfasts. There's a YHA **hostel** four miles away outside the village of Galmpton, on the banks of the Dart (☎0845/371 9531, ⓔriverdart@yha.org.uk; sporadic opening; from £14), a two-mile walk from Churston Pottery, accessible on frequent bus #12 and on the Paignton & Dartmouth Steam Railway (see opposite).

When it comes to **eating** options, Brixham offers fish and more fish – from the stalls selling cockles, whelks and mussels on the harbourside to the *Poopdeck* at 14 The Quay (☎01803/858681) with some tables overlooking the harbour, and the fairly expensive restaurant at the *Quayside Hotel* on King Street (☎01803/855751). Otherwise the local **pubs** serve decent food; try the *Blue Anchor* at the bottom of Fore Street, with its coal fires and low beams.

Totnes

Trains from Exeter, and most of the Plymouth buses from Paignton and Torquay, stop at **TOTNES** on the west bank of the River Dart. The town has an ancient pedigree, its period of greatest prosperity occurring in the sixteenth century when this inland port exported cloth to France and brought back wine. Some handsome structures from that era remain, and there is still a working port down on the river, but these days Totnes has mellowed into a residential market town, enjoying an esoteric fame as a centre of the New Age arts-and-crafts crowd. With its arcaded High Street and secretive flowery lanes, Totnes has its syrupy side, partly the result of its proximity to the Torbay tourist hive, but so far its allure has survived more or less intact.

Arrival, information and accommodation

Totnes **train station** lies a few minutes north of the centre, while **buses** pull into The Plains at the bottom of the main street. Signposted off The Plains, the **tourist office** is in the Town Mill, near the Morrisons car park (April–Oct Mon–Fri 9.30am–5pm, Sat 10am–4pm; Nov–March Mon–Fri 10am–4pm, Sat 10am–1pm; ℡01803/863168, ⓦwww.totnesinformation.co.uk). **Bike rental** is available from B.R. Trott, Warland Garage, Warland, off The Plains (℡01803/862493, ⓦwww .brtrott.co.uk).

You'll find a range of **accommodation** in and around town, though it can fill up quickly. The nearest **campsite** is peaceful *Beara Farm*, five miles northwest of Totnes and close to the River Dart, on Colston Road, Buckfastleigh (℡01364/642234).

3 Plymouth Rd 3 Plymouth Rd ℡01803/866917, ⓦwww.mlfen.freeserve.co.uk. Friendly, good-value B&B off the High Street, with simple rooms, with and without en-suite facilities, and a small roof terrace. No credit cards. Closed Nov–Feb. ❶

Dart Villas 3 Dart Villas, Totnes Down Hill ℡01803/865895, ⓦwww.dartvillasbb.co.uk. Tastefully furnished Georgian B&B with hill-top views, a 10min walk from The Plains. Breakfasts are organic and vegetarian. Treatments, therapies and internet available. ❷

The Great Grubb Fallowfields, Plymouth Rd ℡01803/849071, ⓦwww.thegreatgrubb .co.uk. Friendly owners, restful colours, healthy breakfasts and a patio are the main attractions at this stylish B&B. ❷

Royal Seven Stars The Plains ℡01803/862125, ⓦwww.royalsevenstars.co.uk. Central, atmospheric coaching inn, whose modernized rooms have a smart boutiquey feel. ❺

The Town

Totnes centres on the long main street that starts off as Fore Street, site of the town's **Elizabethan House Museum** (mid-March to Oct Mon–Fri 10.30am–5pm; £2.50), which occupies a four-storey Elizabethan house at no. 70. Showing how wealthy clothiers lived at the peak of Totnes's fortunes, it's packed with domestic objects and furniture, and also has a room devoted to local mathematician Charles Babbage, whose "analytical engine" was the forerunner of the computer. There are a number of other houses along Fore and High streets in an equally good state of preservation: the late eighteenth-century, mustard-yellow **Gothic House**, a hundred yards up Fore Street on the left; 28 High St, overhung by some curious grotesque masks; and 16 High St, a house built by pilchard merchant Nicholas Ball, whose initials are carved outside. His wealth, inherited by his widow, was eventually bequeathed by her second husband, Thomas Bodley, to found Oxford's Bodleian Library.

Fore Street becomes the High Street at the **East Gate**, a much retouched medieval arch. Beneath it, Rampart Walk trails off along the old city walls, curling round the fifteenth-century **church of St Mary**, inside which you can admire the exquisitely carved rood-screen that stretches across the full width of the red sandstone building. Behind the church, the eleventh-century **Guildhall** (April–Oct Mon–Fri 10.30am–4pm; £1.25) was originally the refectory and kitchen of a Benedictine priory. Granted to the city corporation in 1553, the building still houses the town's Council Chamber, which you can see together with the former jail cells, used until the end of the nineteenth century, and the courtroom, which only ceased to function in 1974. **Totnes Castle** (daily: late March to June & Sept 10am–5pm; July & Aug 10am–6pm; Oct 10am–4pm; £3.20; EH) on Castle Street – leading off the High Street – is a classic Norman structure of the motte and bailey design, its simple crenellated keep set atop a grassy mound offering wide views of the town and Dart valley.

Along the river

Totnes is the highest navigable point on the **River Dart** for seagoing vessels, and the quayside at the bottom of Fore Street is the departure point for cruises to Dartmouth – the best way to see the river's deep creeks. Services depart between Easter and October from Steamer Quay, on the far side of the Dart (1hr 15min; £12 return; ☏01803/834488, ⓦwww.riverlink.co.uk). Riverside walks in either direction pass some congenial pubs, and near the railway bridge you can board a steam train of the **South Devon Railway** (late March to Oct; ☏0845/345 1420, ⓦwww.southdevonrailway.co.uk) on its run along the course of the Dart to Buckfastleigh, on the edge of Dartmoor (£10 return).

A walkable couple of miles north of Totnes, both rail and river pass near the estate of **Dartington Hall**, the arts and education centre set up in 1925 by US millionairess Dorothy Elmhirst and her husband. You can walk through the sculpture-strewn gardens and – when it's not in use – visit the fourteenth-century Great Hall, rescued from dereliction by the Elmhirsts. There's a constant programme of films, plays, concerts, dance and workshops; for details, call ☏01803/847070 or see ⓦwww.dartington.org/arts.

Eating and drinking

You don't need to stray off the Fore Street/High Street axis to find good **places to eat** in Totnes, most of which are fairly laid back. There are several decent **pubs** in town apart from *The Steampacket* listed below: both the *Castle Inn* on Fore Street and the *Bull Inn* at the top of the High Street have a lively atmosphere, bar meals and local ales.

Barrel House 58–59 High St ☏01803/863000. At street level there's a café, and upstairs there's a lounge in a former ballroom with chandeliers and cinema seats, where you can eat salads, burgers and full meals (£7–10). Stays open late for gigs, poetry readings and DJ nights, usually Thurs–Sun.

Rumour 30 High St ☏01803/864682. Lively place, good for coffees, snacks or good-value full meals – English or Mediterranean, including burgers and pizzas. Most mains are around £15. Closed Sun lunch.

The Steampacket St Peter's Quay ☏01803/863880. Riverside inn with a conservatory and patio, reached by walking west along The Plains. Well-prepared traditional meals (around £10) and real ales are served, and there's live folk every Tues.

Willow 87 High St ☏01803/862605. Vegetarian and vegan food and organic wines are offered here, with an Indian menu on Wed night and live music on Fri night. Evening dishes cost around £9. The courtyard's good for lunches and teas. Closed Sun, also Mon, Tues & Thurs eve. No credit cards.

Dartmouth and around

South of Torbay, and eight miles downstream from Totnes, **DARTMOUTH** has thrived since the Normans recognized the potential of this deepwater port for trading with their home country. Today its activities embrace fishing, freight and a booming leisure industry, as well as the education of the senior service's officer class at the Royal Naval College, built at the start of the last century on a hill overlooking the port.

Arrival, information and accommodation

Coming from Torbay, visitors to Dartmouth can save time and a long detour through Totnes by using the frequent **ferries** crossing the Dart estuary, either the Higher Ferry from the A379 (£1 one-way, £3.50 for cars with passengers), or the Lower Ferry from Kingswear and the B3205 (£1 one-way, £3.20 for cars with passengers); the last ones leave at around 10.45pm. Dartmouth's **tourist office** is opposite the car park on Mayor's Avenue (Easter–Sept Mon–Sat 9.30am–5pm, Sun 10am–2pm; Oct–Easter Mon, Tues & Thurs–Sat 9.30am–5pm, Wed 9.30am–1pm; ☎01803/834224, ⓦwww.discoverdartmouth.com) and has **internet** access.

The town's less expensive **accommodation** is scattered along Victoria Road, a continuation of Duke Street, though it's worth paying a little more for the views that the hill-top choices can boast, such as the spacious and elegant *Avondale* at 5 Vicarage Hill (☎07968/026449, ⓦwww.avondaledartmouth.co.uk; no credit cards; ❸). More centrally, for character and funky charm you can't beat the rooms above the 🎋 *Café Alf Resco* on Lower Street (☎01803/835880, ⓦwww.cafealfresco .co.uk; no credit cards; ❸), while for something a little different there's the *Resnova Inn*, a barge moored mid-river (☎07770/628967, ⓦwww.resnova.co.uk; closed Sun & Mon and all Jan & Feb; ❸), which has seven compact but comfy cabins with shared bathroom – guests are ferried to and from town by arrangement.

The Town

Behind the enclosed boat basin at the heart of town stands Dartmouth's most photographed building, the four-storey **Butterwalk**, built in the seventeenth century for a local merchant. Richly decorated with wood carvings, the timber-framed construction overhangs the street on eleven granite columns, and is home to Dartmouth's small **museum** (Mon–Sat: April–Oct 10am–4pm; Nov–March 11am–3pm; £1.50), mainly devoted to maritime curios, including old maps, prints and models of ships. Nearby **St Saviour's**, rebuilt in the 1630s from a fourteenth-century church, has long been a landmark for boats sailing upriver. The building stands at the head of Higher Street, the old town's central thorough-fare and the site of another tottering medieval structure, the *Cherub Inn*. More impressive is **Agincourt House** on the parallel Lower Street, built by a merchant after the battle for which it is named, then restored in the seventeenth century and again in the twentieth.

Lower Street leads down to **Bayard's Cove**, a short cobbled quay lined with well-restored eighteenth-century houses, where the Pilgrim Fathers stopped en route to the New World. A twenty-minute walk from here along the river takes you to **Dartmouth Castle** (April–June & Sept daily 10am–5pm; July & Aug daily 10am–6pm; Oct daily 10am–4pm; Nov–March Sat & Sun 10am–4pm; £4.50; EH), one of two fortifications on opposite sides of the estuary dating from the fifteenth century. The site includes coastal defence works from the nineteenth century and from World War II. If you don't wish to return on foot, you can take advantage of a **ferry** back to town (Easter–Oct; £2).

Blackpool Sands and along the Dart

Continuing south along the coastal path brings you through the pretty hill-top village of **Stoke Fleming** to **Blackpool Sands** (45min from the castle), the best and most popular beach in the area. The unspoilt cove, flanked by steep, wooded cliffs, was the site of a battle in 1404 in which Devon archers repulsed a Breton invasion force sent to punish the privateers of Dartmouth for their raiding across the Channel.

From Dartmouth's quay there are regular ferries across the river to **Kingswear**, terminus of the **Paignton & Dartmouth Steam Railway** (see p.366), as well as various **cruises** around the harbour and up the River Dart to Totnes (see p.367), affording good views of the **Royal Naval College**. The river is also the best way to get to **Greenway** (March to mid-July, Sept & Oct Wed–Sun 10.30am–5pm; mid-July to Aug also Tues same hours; £8, or £7.40 if not arriving by car; NT), birthplace of Walter Raleigh's three seafaring half-brothers, the Gilberts, and later rebuilt for **Agatha Christie**. The house contains a low-key collection of memorabilia belonging to the Christie family, including archeological scraps, silverware, ceramics and books, while the very steep wooded grounds – the climb to the house is challenging – afford lovely views over the river.

You can also arrive by road on a circuitous ten-mile route via Dittisham, but it gets very congested, and parking at Greenway must be booked at ☎01803/842382.

Eating and drinking

The *Café Alf Resco* (open until 2pm) is good for breakfasts, **snack** lunches and steaming coffees, and has an outdoor area where live music evenings take place monthly in summer; internet access is also available. The *Resnova Inn* (closed all Mon & Tues lunchtime, and mid-Jan to mid-Feb; call for winter opening) is open for breakfast, lunch and dinner, with the menu covering everything from bangers and mash to lobster at reasonable prices. Dartmouth's top **restaurant** is the *New Angel*, 2 South Embankment (☎01803/839425; closed Sun & Mon), run by celebrity chef John Burton-Race; it provides high-class Modern British dishes in an informal atmosphere, with great riverside views. The ancient *Cherub Inn*, 13 Higher St, is one of the most atmospheric **pubs** in town, and serves meals in its small restaurant upstairs.

The South Hams

The area between the Dart and Plym estuaries, the **South Hams**, holds some of Devon's comeliest villages and most striking stretches of coastline. Frequent buses from Dartmouth and Totnes run to **Kingsbridge**, at the top of the Kingsbridge estuary, the "capital" of the region and the hub of local services to the South Hams villages. However, you'll spend more time in the yacht resort of **Salcombe**, near the mouth of the estuary and connected to Kingsbridge by a ferry in summer, and on the less crowded coast hereabouts.

Kingsbridge

Fine Tudor and Georgian buildings distinguish the busy market town of **KINGS-BRIDGE**, especially along the steep Fore Street, where the colonnaded Shambles is largely Elizabethan on the ground floor, its granite pillars supporting an upper floor added at the end of the eighteenth century. There are various **markets** throughout the year at the town hall and on The Quay; the latter is right by the **tourist office**, which has information on the whole region (Easter–Oct Mon–Sat 9am–5.30pm, Sun 10am–4pm; Nov–Easter Mon–Sat 9am–5pm; ☎01548/853195, ⓦwww.kingsbridgeinfo.co.uk).

Salcombe and around

Once a nondescript fishing village, **SALCOMBE** is now a full-blown sailing and holiday resort, its calm waters strewn with yachts and dinghies. There's still some fishing activity here, and a few working boatyards, and you can bone up on boating and local history at **Salcombe Maritime Museum** on Market Street, off the north end of the central Fore Street (Easter–Oct 10.30am–12.30pm & 2.30–4.30pm; £1.50).

From the quay off Fore Street, a **ferry** provides transport to the beach at South Sands (April–Oct every 30min until 5.15pm; £3), while the ferry across to **East Portlemouth** (Easter–Oct continuous service 8am–7pm; Nov–Easter every 30min 8am–5.30pm; £1.30) enables you to follow the coastal path east to the craggily photogenic **Gammon Point** and, half a mile further, Devon's most southerly tip at **Prawle Point**. Around four miles east, at the far end of Lannacombe Bay, the headland of **Start Point** has a raw elemental grandeur – an inspiring spot for a picnic.

Salcombe's **tourist office** is on Market Street (Easter to late July and early Sept to Oct daily 10am–5pm; late July to early Sept Mon–Sat 9am–6pm, Sun 10am–4pm; Nov–Easter Mon–Sat 10am–3pm; ℡01548/843927, ⓦwww .salcombeinformation.co.uk). Out of the small range of **accommodation**, try *Rocarno* on Grenville Road above Fore Street, for excellent estuary views (℡01548/842732, ⓦwww.rocarno.co.uk; no credit cards; ❷), or, on the edge of town a fifteen-minute walk from the centre, *Beadon Farmhouse* (℡01548/843020, ⓦwww.beadonfarmhouse.homecall.co.uk; no credit cards; no under-12s; ❸), a Victorian B&B on Beadon Road with neat, chintz-free en-suite rooms and great rural views. **Campers** have lots of choice in the area, for example *Higher Rew* at Rew Cross (℡01548/842681, ⓦwww.higherrew.co.uk; closed Nov–March), a clean, panoramic site one mile southwest of Salcombe and about the same distance from South Sands beach.

For **food** and refreshment, the *Winking Prawn*, right on the beach on North Sands (℡01548/842326), makes an alluring stop for a cappuccino, baguette or ice cream by day, or a steak or chargrilled chicken in the evening (closed Sun–Wed eve late Oct to Easter). In town, the *Island Street Bar and Grill* on Island Street (℡01548/844007) has a range of food available all day, late cocktails and live music.

Sharpitor

At **SHARPITOR**, a couple of miles south of Salcombe, the National Trust runs **Overbeck's Museum** (mid-March to Oct daily except Fri 11am–5pm; school hols daily same hours; garden as above plus Feb to mid-March, Nov & Dec Mon–Thurs 11am–4pm; £6.70 including garden, garden free in winter; NT), which is mainly given over to natural history and shares its building with a spacious **youth hostel** (℡0845/371 9341, ⓔsalcombe@yha.org.uk; call to check opening; from £16). You can reach the site from Salcombe on the South Sands ferry (see above), from where it's a ten-minute climb.

South of Sharpitor, the six-mile hike from Bolt Head to **Bolt Tail** takes you along a ragged coast where shags and cormorants swoop over the rocks, and wild thyme and sea thrift grow underfoot.

Plymouth and around

PLYMOUTH's predominantly bland and modern face belies its historic importance as a great naval base, dating back to the sixteenth century when it was the home port of such national heroes as John Hawkins – known as chief architect of the Elizabethan navy (and also the first English slave-trader) – and his kinsman, Francis Drake, who sailed from here to defeat the Spanish Armada in 1588. Thirty-two years later the port was the last embarkation point for the Pilgrim Fathers, whose New Plymouth colony became the nucleus for the English settlement of North America.

The city's dockyards were a target for the Luftwaffe in World War II, when most of the old centre was reduced to rubble, apart from the compact area around the **Barbican**. Postwar reconstruction has done nothing to enhance what is now Devon's largest city, though nothing can spoil the glorious vista over **Plymouth Sound**, the basin of calm water at the mouth of the combined Plym, Tavy and Tamar estuaries, which has remained largely unchanged since Drake played his famous game of bowls on the Hoe before joining battle with the Armada. You could also spend a couple of hours wandering around the Elizabethan warehouses and inns of the Barbican, where a gamut of restaurants specialize in freshly caught seafood.

Although this area is easy to stroll around, you could also make use of the regular and frequent circular **bus** service (#25) for getting around the town, with stops at Sutton Harbour, the Hoe and near the train station. Plymouth makes a good starting point for forays onto Dartmoor and a base for visiting a trio of elegant **country houses** with both aesthetic appeal and historical resonance, though transport connections are not always easy.

Arrival, information and accommodation

Plymouth's **train station** is a mile north of the Hoe off Saltash Road; the **bus station** is near the harbour at Bretonside and has left-luggage lockers. The **tourist office**, at 3–5 The Barbican (April–Oct Mon–Sat 9am–5pm, Sun 10am–4pm; Nov–March Mon–Fri 9am–5pm, Sat 10am–4pm; ℡01752/306330, Ⓦwww .visitplymouth.co.uk), can provide details of tours of the city and surrounding areas. **Internet** access is available at the central library off Drake Circus (Mon–Fri 9am–7pm, Sat 9am–5pm).

Plymouth has plenty of choice when it comes to **accommodation**: try first the row of B&Bs edging the Hoe on Citadel Road if you want to be near the sights.

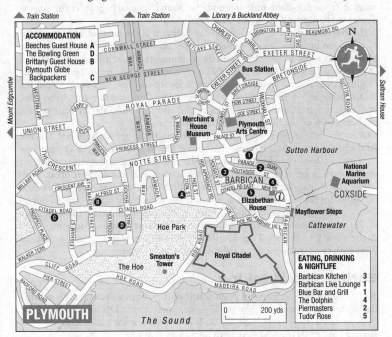

Beeches Guest House 177 Citadel Rd
☎01752/266475. A good choice on this row close
to the Barbican, with views over the Hoe and all
rooms en suite except for a couple of singles. ❷
The Bowling Green 9–10 Osborne Place, Lockyer
St ☎01752/209090, ⓦwww.bowlingreen
plymouth.com. Smart establishment with bright
rooms overlooking Francis Drake's fabled haunt on
the Hoe. Wi-fi access. ❸

Brittany Guest House 28 Athenaeum St
☎01752/262247, ⓦwww.brittanyguesthouse.co.uk.
Easy-going place with en-suite rooms, a choice of
breakfasts and a car park (a bonus around here). ❶
Plymouth Globe Backpackers 172 Citadel Rd
☎01752/225158, ⓦwww.plymouthbackpackers
.co.uk. Relaxed hostel west of the Hoe, with kitchen,
free tea and coffee, free wi-fi and a courtyard garden.
Book ahead. Dorm beds from £13, doubles ❶

The City

A good place to start a tour of the city is **Plymouth Hoe**, an immense esplanade
studded with reminders of the great events in the city's history, including a rather
portly statue of Sir Francis Drake gazing grandly out to sea – appropriately, there's
a bowling green back from the brow. Resplendent in fair weather, with glorious
views over the sea, the Hoe can also attract some pretty ferocious winds, making
it well-nigh impossible to explore in wintry conditions.

In front of the memorials stands the red-and-white-striped **Smeaton's Tower**
(Tues–Sat 10am–noon & 1–3/4.30pm; £2), originally erected in 1759 by the
renowned engineer John Smeaton on the treacherous Eddystone Rocks, fourteen
miles out to sea. When replaced by a larger lighthouse in 1882, it was reassembled
here, where it gives the loftiest view over Plymouth Sound. Following the
seafront round to the east, past the formidable seventeenth-century Royal Citadel,
you'll reach the old town's quay at **Sutton Harbour**, where the **Mayflower Steps**
commemorate the sailing of the 102 Pilgrim Fathers and a nearby plaque lists their
names and professions. Nowadays, the harbour is the starting point for **boat trips**,
ranging from one-hour tours around the Sound to a four-hour cruise up the
Tamar to the Cornish village of Calstock.

The **Barbican** district, which edges the harbour, is the heart of old Plymouth.
Most of the buildings are now shops and restaurants, but off the quayside New
Street holds some of the oldest buildings, among them the **Elizabethan House**
(April–Sept Tues–Sat 10am–5pm; £2), a captain's dwelling retaining most of the
original architectural features, including a lovely old pole staircase. Above the
tourist office at 3–5 The Barbican, the **Mayflower Centre** (Mon–Sat 10am–4pm,
Sun in summer 10am–3pm; £2) traces the story of the Pilgrim Fathers, and
explains much of the history of the Barbican area.

Cross the bridge over Sutton Harbour to reach the grand **National Marine
Aquarium** (daily 10am–5/6pm; last entry 1hr before closing; £11; ⓦwww
.national-aquarium.co.uk). On four levels, the complex represents a range of
marine environments from moorland stream to coral reef and deep-sea ocean, with
wildlife including sharks and an extensive collection of seahorse species. Talks and
presentations take place throughout the day, and the feeding times – carried out by
divers – are among the highlights. Back in the centre of town, the handsome
timber-framed, mainly seventeenth-century **Merchant's House Museum**, 33 St
Andrew's St (April–Sept Tues–Sat 10am–5pm; £2), explores various aspects of
Plymouth's history by means of themed rooms and reconstructions.

Eating and drinking

You'll find an eclectic range of **restaurants and pubs** in and around Plymouth's
Barbican area. If you feel like staying out, you'll catch DJs and live music at
Barbican Live Lounge (☎01752/672127, ⓦwww.barbicanlivelounge.com) or *Blues
Bar and Grill* (☎01752/257345), both on Sutton Harbour.

Barbican Kitchen 60 Southside St ☎01752/604448. Set in an attic of the ancient Black Friars Distillery, this relaxed bistro serves everything from baguettes to salads, beer-battered fish and chips (£9.50), burgers (£9.50) and steaks (£15–17.50). Closed Sun lunch.

The Dolphin 14 The Barbican. A venerable fisherman's pub with authentic character and Bass beer straight from the barrel.

Piermasters 3 Southside St ☎01752/229345. One of Plymouth's finest fish restaurants, whose ingredients are supplied straight from the nearby harbour; it's plain but elegant, with lunchtime and early evening set menus at £10–16 and evening mains around £18. Closed Sun.

Tudor Rose 36 New St. Cosy tearoom and restaurant, where you can tuck into such snacks as cottage pie and Welsh rarebit (£4–6), with a garden open in summer. Closed eve.

Around Plymouth

One of the best local excursions from Plymouth is to **Mount Edgcumbe**, where woods and meadows provide a welcome antidote to the urban bustle and a fabulous beach is within easy reach. East of Plymouth, the aristocratic opulence of **Saltram House** includes some fine art and furniture, while to the north of town you can visit Drake's old residence at **Buckland Abbey**.

Mount Edgcumbe

Lying on the Cornish side of Plymouth Sound and visible from the Hoe, **Mount Edgcumbe** features a Tudor house, landscaped gardens and acres of rolling parkland and coastal paths. The **house** (Easter–Sept Mon–Thurs & Sun 11am–4.30pm; £6; ⓦwww.mountedgcumbe.gov.uk) is a reconstruction of the bomb-damaged Tudor original, though inside the predominant note is eighteenth century, the rooms elegantly restored with authentic Regency furniture. Far more enticing than the house however, are the **grounds**, which include impeccable gardens divided into French, Italian and English sections – the first two a blaze of flowerbeds adorned with classical statuary, the last an acre of sweeping lawn shaded by exotic trees. The **park**, which is free and open all year, covers the whole of the peninsula facing the estuary and the sea, including a part of the Cornish Coastal Path, and gives access to **Whitsand Bay**, a long bathing beach that's subject to dangerous shifting sands and fierce currents. From the peninsula's two headlands, Rame Head and Penlee Point, extensive views show Plymouth in its best light.

You can reach the house by the passenger **ferry** to Cremyll (£1.50), leaving twice hourly from Admiral's Hard, a small mooring in the Stonehouse district of town (bus #34 from Royal Parade), or on the thrice-daily ferry from the pontoon below Mayflower Steps (April–Oct; £9.50 return, including entry to Mount Edgcumbe).

Saltram House

Showing little of its Tudor origins, **Saltram House** (mid-March to Oct daily except Fri noon–4.30pm: £8.70, including garden; NT), two miles east of Plymouth off the A38, is Devon's largest country house. The mansion features work by the great architect Robert Adam and fourteen portraits by **Joshua Reynolds** (1723–92), who was born nearby in Plympton. The showpiece, however, is the **Saloon**, a fussy but exquisitely furnished room dripping with gilt and plaster, and set off by a huge Axminster carpet specially commissioned in 1770. Saltram's landscaped **garden** (daily except Fri 11am–4/5pm; £4.50) provides a breather from this riot of interior design, though it's marred by the proximity of the road. You can get here on the hourly #22 bus (not Sun) from Royal Parade to Merafield Road, from where it's a fifteen-minute signposted walk.

Six miles north of Plymouth, close to the River Tavy and on the edge of Dartmoor, stands **Buckland Abbey** (late Feb to early March & early Nov to mid-Dec Fri–Sun 11am–4.30pm; mid-March to Oct daily 10.30am–5.30pm; £7.80, or free with grounds ticket in winter; grounds only £4; NT). After its dissolution Buckland was converted to a family home by the privateer Richard Grenville (cousin of Walter Raleigh), from whom the estate was acquired by Sir Francis Drake in 1582, the year after he became mayor of Plymouth. It remained his home until his death, but the house reveals few traces of Drake's residence, as he spent most of his retirement years plundering on the Spanish main. There are, however, numerous maps, portraits and mementoes of his buccaneering exploits on show, most famous of which is Drake's Drum, which was said to beat a supernatural warning of impending danger to the country. More eye-catching are the architectural embellishments in the oak-panelled **Great Hall**, dated 1576 but previously the nave of the abbey, while the majestic grounds contain a fine fourteenth-century **monastic barn**, buttressed and gabled and larger than the abbey itself. To get here from Plymouth, take any bus to Tavistock, changing at Yelverton for the hourly #55, or, on Sunday, take the #48 direct from Royal Parade.

Dartmoor

Occupying the main part of the county between Exeter and Plymouth, **Dartmoor** is southern England's greatest expanse of wilderness, some 365 square miles of raw granite, barren bogland, sparse grass and heather-grown moor. It was not always so desolate, as testified by the remnants of scattered Stone Age settlements and the ruined relics of the area's nineteenth-century tin-mining industry. Today desultory flocks of sheep and groups of ponies are virtually the only living creatures to be seen wandering over the central fastnesses of the national park, with solitary birds – buzzards, kestrels, pipits, stonechats and wagtails – wheeling and hovering high above.

The core of Dartmoor, characterized by tumbling streams and high tors chiselled by the elements, is **Dartmoor Forest**, which has belonged to the Duchy of Cornwall since 1307, though there is almost unlimited public access as long as certain guidelines are followed. Camping is permitted out of sight of houses and roads, but fires are strictly forbidden. The *Dartmoor Guide* free newspaper, available from national park visitor centres and other information points, has info on accommodation, events, activities, disabled facilities and firing-range schedules (see box, p.382).

Princetown, at the heart of the moor, has the Dartmoor National Park's main information centre and a selection of stores, pubs and places to stay. A few other villages, such as **Chagford** and **Widecombe**, have B&Bs and shops, though for the widest choice of both you have to go to the towns and villages edging the moor – chief among them **Tavistock**, **Okehampton** and **Moretonhampstead**. It would not be impossible to base yourself in Exeter or Plymouth, neither more than an hour's ride from the central **Two Bridges**, at the intersection of the B3212 and B3357, which gives access to some of Dartmoor's wildest tracts. Always plan ahead and book places to stay – availability can be extremely restricted at weekends in high season.

Getting around

The Transmoor **bus** (#82) runs twice daily on Sundays between Exeter and Plymouth, stopping at Moretonhampstead, Postbridge, Two Bridges and

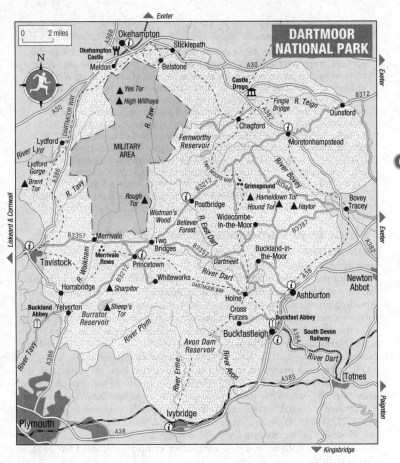

Princetown. From Exeter, the #173 goes to Castle Drogo, Chagford and Moretonhampstead, #359 (not Sun) goes to Moretonhampstead, and #X9 (not Sun), #510 and #599 go to Okehampton. The infrequent #179 links Okehampton, Chagford and Moretonhampstead (not Sun). Buses #83, #84 and #86 connect Plymouth with Tavistock, while #98 connects Tavistock with Princetown (not Sun) and #118 runs from Tavistock to Okehampton via Lydford (not Sun). Apart from these, there's little except the occasional Sunday service in summer and once-weekly runs to remote villages.

There are also a couple of **train** services: the **Tamar Valley Line**, running 5 to 9 times daily all year between Plymouth and Gunnislake, five miles southwest of Tavistock, and the **Dartmoor Railway** (Ⓦ www.dartmoor-railway.co.uk), which currently runs at weekends and bank holidays from June to mid-September linking Sampford Courtenay, three miles northeast of Okehampton, Okehampton and Meldon, a couple of miles southwest. It is likely, however, that the Dartmoor Railway will be extended in 2010 to connect Okehampton with Exeter daily in less than an hour (to check call ℡01837/55164). The **Sunday Rover ticket** (£6.50, valid all day), covers all transport on the moor on Sundays, including the two rail lines.

Princetown and Wistman's Wood

PRINCETOWN owes its growth to the presence of Dartmoor Prison, a high-security jail originally constructed for POWs captured in the Napoleonic Wars. The grim presence seeps into the village, some of whose functional grey stone houses – as well as the parish church of St Michael – were built by French and American prisoners. What Princetown lacks in beauty is amply compensated for by the surrounding countryside, the best of which lies immediately to the north.

On the village's central green, information on all of Dartmoor is supplied by the main **National Park information centre** (daily: Easter–Oct 10am–5pm; Nov–Easter 10am–4pm; ℡01822/890414, Ⓦ www.dartmoor-npa.gov.uk).

One of the best **places to stay** is *Duchy House*, two hundred yards from the centre on Tavistock Road (℡01822/890552, Ⓦ www.duchyhouse.co.uk; closed early Nov; ❷), which has rooms with and without private bath. Two pubs on Princetown's central square also offer accommodation: the *Railway Inn* (℡01822/890240; ❸), with all rooms en suite, and, under the same management, the *Plume of Feathers*, supposedly the oldest building in town, which has two bunkhouses (£17.50) as well as a convenient **campsite**; standard bar food is always available.

Northeast of Princetown, two miles north of the crossroads at Two Bridges, the dwarfed and misshapen oaks of **Wistman's Wood** are an evocative relic of the original Dartmoor Forest, cluttered with lichen-covered boulders and a dense undergrowth of ferns. The gnarled old trees are alleged to have been the site of druidic gatherings, a story unsupported by any evidence but quite plausible in this solitary spot.

Postbridge and Bellever Forest

Three miles northeast of Two Bridges, the largest and best preserved of Dartmoor's **clapper bridges** crosses the East Dart river at **POSTBRIDGE**. Used by tin-miners and farmers since medieval times, these simple structures consist of huge slabs of granite supported by piers of the same material; another more basic example is at Two Bridges. Postbridge has a useful tourist office in the car park near the bridge (Easter–Oct daily 10am–5pm; Nov & Dec Sat & Sun 10am–4pm; ℡01822/880272), which provides advice about local walks. One popular trail leads south through **Bellever Forest** to the open moor where **Bellever Tor** (1453ft) affords outstanding views.

On the edge of the forest, a couple of miles south of Postbridge on the banks of the East Dart river, lies a **YHA hostel** (☎0845/371 9622, ✉bellever@yha.org.uk; from £12) – it's on a minor road from Postbridge, accessible on the rare #98 from Tavistock (not Sun); alternatively, walk the mile from Postbridge. Close to Bellever Forest, *Runnage Farm* (☎01822/880222, ⌨www.runnagecampingbarns .co.uk) offers **camping barns** (£8.50) and outdoor camping facilities.

Two miles northeast of Postbridge, the solitary *Warren House Inn* (☎01822/880208) offers warm, fire-lit comfort and **meals** in an unutterably bleak tract of moorland.

Grimspound and Hound Tor

To the east of the B3212, reachable on a right turn towards Widecombe-in-the-Moor, the Bronze Age village of **Grimspound** lies below Hameldown Tor, about a mile off the road. Inhabited some three thousand years ago, when Dartmoor was fully forested and enjoyed a considerably warmer climate than it does today, this is the most complete example of Dartmoor's prehistoric settlements, consisting of 24 circular huts scattered within a four-acre enclosure. A stone wall nine-feet thick surrounds the huts, several of which have raised sleeping areas, and you can see how the villagers ensured a constant water supply by enclosing part of a stream with a wall. Grimspound itself is thought to have been the model for the Stone Age settlement in which Sherlock Holmes camped in *The Hound of the Baskervilles*, while **Hound Tor**, an outcrop three miles to the southeast, was the inspiration for Conan Doyle's tale – according to local legend, phantom hounds were sighted racing across the moor to hurl themselves on the tomb of a hated squire following his death in 1677. There's a basic **camping barn** here, *Great Houndtor*, with two upstairs sleeping areas, a cooking area and showers (☎01629/592700, ⌨www .yha.org.uk; £6.50).

Buckland-in-the-Moor and the southeastern moor

Four miles east of the crossroads at Two Bridges, **Dartmeet** marks the place where the East and West Dart rivers merge after tortuous journeys from their remote sources. Crowds home in on this beauty spot, but the valley is memorably lush and you don't need to walk far to leave the car park and ice-cream vans behind. From here the Dart pursues a more leisurely course, joined by the River Webburn near the pretty moorland village of **BUCKLAND-IN-THE-MOOR**, one of a cluster of moorstone-and-thatch hamlets on this southeastern side of the moor.

Four miles north is another candidate for most popular Dartmoor village, **WIDECOMBE-IN-THE-MOOR**, set in a hollow amid high granite-strewn ridges. Its **church of St Pancras** provides a famous local landmark, its pinnacled tower dwarfing the fourteenth-century main building, whose interior boasts a beautiful painted rood-screen. Look out too for the carved one-eared rabbits above the communion rail. The nearby **Church House** was built in the fifteenth century for weary churchgoers from outlying districts, and was later converted into almshouses. Widecombe's other claim to fame is the traditional song, *Widdicombe Fair*: the **fair** is still held annually on the second Tuesday of September.

You could **stay** in Widecombe at the elegant *Old Rectory* (☎01364/621231, ✉rachel.belgrave@care4free.net; no credit cards; closed Nov–Easter; ❷), opposite the post office and set in a lovely garden, or, signposted next to it, *Manor Cottage* (☎01364/621218, ✉di.richard@btinternet.com; no credit cards; ❷), which has an inglenook fireplace in the dining room, a nice garden and accommodation in a converted barn. There's basic **camping** at *Cockingford Farm*, one and a half miles south of Widecombe (☎01364/621258; closed mid-Nov to mid-March). Just south of the village, Shilstone Rocks **pony-trekking** centre (☎01364/621281, Ⓦwww.dartmoorstables.com) offers tuition and excursions.

South of Buckland, the village of **HOLNE** is another rustic idyll surrounded on three sides by wooded valleys. The vicarage here was the birthplace of Charles Kingsley, author of *The Water Babies* and such Devon-based tales as *Westward Ho!* – a window commemorates him in the village church. The next-door *Church House Inn* offers excellent **meals** and **rooms** (☎01364/631208, Ⓦwww.church houseinn-holne.co.uk; ❸). On the edge of Holne, on the route of the Two Moors Way, there's a **camping barn** at *The Stone Barn*, with good facilities (☎01364/631544; £5), backing onto a small camping field.

The northeastern moor

The peaceful village of **MORETONHAMPSTEAD**, lying on the northeastern edge, makes an attractive entry point to the moor from Exeter. Local **information** is handled by a visitor information point at 10 The Square (April–Oct daily 10am–4pm; Nov–March Thurs–Sat 10am–4pm, Sun 11am–3pm; ☎01647/440043). There's classy **accommodation** in the centre of the village, where the *White Hart*, The Square (☎01647/441340, Ⓦwww.whitehartdart moor.co.uk; ❸), makes a stylish spot for a getaway break, with elegant and fully equipped bedrooms and a smart brasserie, while, at 18 Court St, *The Old Post House* (☎01647/440900, Ⓦwww.theoldposthouse.com; no credit cards; ❷) offers friendly B&B with clean and spacious en-suite rooms. The village also has a first-rate, centrally located vegetarian **hostel**, *Sparrowhawk Backpackers*, at 45 Ford St (☎01647/440318, Ⓦwww.sparrowhawkbackpackers.co.uk), with dorm beds (£16) and a private room sleeping up to four (❶).

Moretonhampstead has a historic rivalry with neighbouring **CHAGFORD**, a Stannary town (a chartered centre of the tin trade) that also enjoyed prosperity as a centre of the wool industry. Standing on a hillside above the River Teign, and with a fine fifteenth-century church, it makes a great base for the area, with a selection of pubs and **accommodation**, such as the ancient *Three Crowns Hotel*, facing the church (☎01647/433444, Ⓦwww.threecrowns-chagford.co.uk; ❸), some of whose comfortable rooms are subject to noise from the church clock. A quieter alternative is the sixteenth-century *Cyprian's Cot*, 47 New St (☎01647/432256, Ⓦwww.cyprianscot.co.uk; no credit cards; ❷), where you can warm your bones by an inglenook fireplace. There's also a renowned **restaurant** in the village, *22 Mill Street* (☎01647/432244, Ⓦwww.22millstreetrestaurant.co.uk; closed Sun eve and all Mon), which offers top-quality Modern European cuisine; two-course set menus cost £15 for lunch and £36 for dinner; there are also two luxury rooms available for B&B (❹).

Numerous pleasant **walks** are available in the immediate vicinity, for instance to Fernworthy Reservoir, four miles to the southwest along signposted narrow lanes, or downstream along the Teign to the twentieth-century extravaganza of **Castle Drogo** (mid-Feb to late Feb & April to early Sept daily 11am–5pm; early March Sat & Sun 11am–5pm; mid-March to late March and early Sept to Oct daily except Tues 11am–5pm; late Nov to mid-Dec Sat & Sun 11am–4.30pm; £7.80, or £5 in winter, grounds only £5, or £2.30 in winter; NT), which occupies a stupendous site overlooking the Teign Gorge. Having retired at the age of 33, grocery magnate Julius Drewe unearthed a link that suggested his descent from a Norman baron, and set about creating a castle befitting his pedigree. Begun in 1910 to a design by **Sir Edwin Lutyens**, it was not completed until 1930, but the result was an unsurpassed synthesis of medieval and modern elements. The croquet lawn is available for use (June–Sept), with all equipment available for rent.

Paths lead from Drogo east to **Fingle Bridge**, one of Dartmoor's most noted beauty spots, where shaded green pools hold trout and the occasional salmon. The *Fingle Bridge Inn* here has an adjoining **restaurant** (℡01647/281287; closed Sun–Thurs eve in winter, Sun eve in summer).

Okehampton and around

The main centre on the northern fringes of Dartmoor, **OKEHAMPTON** grew prosperous as a market town for the medieval wool trade, and some fine old buildings survive between the two branches of the River Okement that meet here, among them the prominent fifteenth-century tower of the **Chapel of St James**. Across the road from the seventeenth-century town hall, a granite archway leads into the **Museum of Dartmoor Life** (April–Oct Mon–Fri 10.15am–4.30pm, Sat 11am–3pm; Nov to mid-Dec Mon–Sat 11am–3pm; £3.50), an excellent overview of habitation on the moor since earliest times. Loftily perched above the West Okement on the other side of town, **Okehampton Castle** (daily: April–June & Sept 10am–5pm; July & Aug 10am–6pm; £3.50; EH) is the shattered hulk of a stronghold laid waste by Henry VIII; its ruins include a gatehouse, Norman keep and the remains of the Great Hall, buttery and kitchens. Four miles east of Okehampton at Sticklepath (buses #X9, #179, #510 or #599), **Finch Foundry** (late March to Oct Mon & Wed–Sun 11am–5pm; £4.40; NT) is a Victorian forge with working machinery and demonstrations.

Practicalities

Okehampton's station, which provides a useful Sunday **rail** connection from Exeter (between late May and late Sept), lies a fifteen-minute walk up Station Road from Fore Street in the town centre, where the **tourist office** (Easter–Oct Mon–Sat 10am–5pm; Nov–Easter Mon, Fri & Sat 10am–4.30pm; ℡01837/53020, Ⓦwww.okehamptondevon.co.uk) can be found next to the museum.

Local **accommodation** options include the *Fountain Hotel*, east along Fore Street (℡01837/53900; ❷), a beamed old coaching inn with smallish rooms, and the Victorian *Meadowlea*, 65 Station Rd (℡01837/53200, Ⓦwww.meadowleaguest house.co.uk; ❷), a no-frills B&B near the station. For more rural surroundings, try *Upcott House* on Upcott Hill, half a mile north of the centre (℡01837/53743, Ⓦwww.upcotthouse.com; no credit cards; ❷), an Edwardian schoolhouse with comfy rooms. Okehampton's **youth hostel** (℡0845/371 9651, Ⓔokehampton @yha.org.uk; from £14) provides bunkrooms in a converted goods shed at the station, **rents bikes** and offers a range of outdoor activities including canoeing and rock climbing. The nearest **campsite** is at the small *Betty Cottles Inn* (℡01837/55339, Ⓦwww.bettycottles.co.uk), two miles southwest of town on the B3260; it also offers **bunks** (£15).

Okehampton offers no great choice when it comes to **eating**, though the *White Hart Hotel* on Fore Street has bar food, pizzas and more formal restaurant meals, while *Panache*, across Fore Street in Red Lion Yard is good for coffees and inexpensive lunches, with some outdoor tables (closed Sun). Best of all is the mellow ⚑ *Pickled Walnut*, a cellar restaurant with an international menu, hidden behind the church on Fore Street (℡01837/54242; closed eve Tues–Thurs and all Sun & Mon). For **riding** on the moor, contact Skaigh Riding Stables (℡01837/840917, Ⓦwww.skaighstables.co.uk; closed Nov–March).

The western moor

Southwest from Princetown, walkers can trace the grassy path of the defunct rail line to **Burrator Reservoir**, four miles away; flooded in the 1890s to provide water for

Dartmoor's firing ranges

A significant portion of northern Dartmoor, containing some of its highest tors and most famous beauty spots, has been appropriated by the **Ministry of Defence**. The firing ranges are marked by red and white posts; when firing is in progress, red flags or red lights signify that entry is prohibited. As a general rule, if no warning flags are flying by 9am between April and September, or by 10am from October to March, there is to be no firing on that day; alternatively, check at ☎0800/458 4868 or ⓦwww .dartmoor-ranges.co.uk.

Plymouth, this is the biggest stretch of water on Dartmoor. The wooded lakeside teems with wildlife, and the boulder-strewn slopes are overlooked by the craggy peaks of **Sharpitor** (1312ft) and **Sheep's Tor** (1150ft). From here, the best walk is to strike northwest to meet the valley of the **River Walkham**, which rises in a peat bog at Walkham Head, five miles north of Princetown, then scurries through moorland and woods to join the River Tavy at Double Waters, two miles south of Tavistock. The fast-flowing water attracts herons, kingfishers and other colourful birdlife, to be seen darting in and out of dense woods of alder, ash and sycamore.

The river crosses the B3357 Tavistock road four miles west of Princetown at **MERRIVALE**, a tiny settlement amounting to little more than a **pub**, the *Dartmoor Arms*. Merrivale makes another good starting point for moorland walks – it's only half a mile west of one of Dartmoor's most important prehistoric sites, the **Merrivale Rows**. Just a few yards from the B3357, the upright stones form a stately procession, stretching 850ft across the bare landscape. Dating from between 2500 BC and 750 BC, and probably connected with burial rites, the rows are known locally as "Potato Market" or "Plague Market" in memory of the time when provisions for plague-stricken Tavistock were deposited here. A mile to the southwest, on the western slopes of the Walkham valley, the sphinx-like pinnacle of **Vixen Tor** looms over the barren moor.

Tavistock and around

Five miles west of Merrivale, the main town of the western moor, **TAVISTOCK**, owes its distinctive Victorian appearance to the building boom that followed the discovery of copper deposits here in 1844. Originally, however, this market and Stannary town on the River Tavy grew around what was once the West Country's most important Benedictine abbey, established in the eleventh century and, at the time of its dissolution, owning land as distant as the Isles of Scilly. Some scant remnants survive in the churchyard of **St Eustace**, a mainly fifteenth-century building with stained glass from William Morris's studio in the south aisle.

Tavistock's **tourist office**, on Bedford Square (Easter–Oct Mon–Sat 9.30am–5pm; Nov–Easter Mon, Tues, Fri & Sat 10am–4.30pm; ☎01822/612938), can supply you with information on the western moor. Among the town's good range of **accommodation**, try *Westward*, 15 Plymouth Rd (☎01822/612094, ⓦwww .westward-tavistock.co.uk; ❷), a Victorian B&B five minutes' walk south of Bedford Square, or, about half a mile east of town off the B3357 Princetown Road, *Mount Tavy Cottage* (☎01822/614253, ⓦwww.mounttavy.co.uk; ❸), set in a lush garden and offering organic breakfasts, evening meals and a self-catering option. For a splurge, there's *Browns* on West Street, off Bedford Square (☎01822/618686, ⓦwww.brownsdevon.co.uk; ❺), a plush boutique hotel. For **camping**, head two miles north of Tavistock to the riverside *Harford Bridge Holiday Park*, Peter Tavy (☎01822/810349, ⓦwww.harfordbridge.co.uk), just off the A386. **Bikes** can be rented from Tavistock Cycles, Paddons Row, Brook Street (☎01822/617630).

North of Tavistock, a four-mile lane wanders up to **Brent Tor**, 1130ft high and dominating Dartmoor's western fringes. Access to its conical summit is easiest along a path gently ascending through gorse on its southwestern side, leading to the small church of St Michael at the top. Bleak, treeless moorland extends in every direction, wrapped in silence that's occasionally pierced by the shrill cries of stonechats and wheatears. A couple of miles eastwards, **Gibbet Hill** looms over Black Down and the ruined stack of the abandoned Wheal Betsy silver and lead mine.

Lydford

Six miles north of Tavistock, the village of **LYDFORD** boasts the sturdy but small-scale Lydford Castle, a Saxon outpost, then a Norman keep and later used as a prison. The chief attraction here, though, is **Lydford Gorge** (daily: mid-March to Sept 10am–5pm; Oct 10am–4pm; Nov to mid-March 11am–3.30pm; £5.50, £3 in winter; NT), whose main entrance is a five-minute walk downhill. Two routes – one above, one along the banks – follow the ravine burrowed through by the River Lyd as far as the hundred-foot White Lady Waterfall, returning on the opposite bank. The full course takes roughly two hours at a leisurely pace, though there is a separate entrance at the south end of the gorge if you only want to visit the waterfall. In winter, when the river can flood, only the waterfall is open to the public.

Back in the village, the picturesque *Castle Inn* sits right next to the castle, and provides a fire-lit sixteenth-century bar where you can drink and snack amid curios and memorabilia; it also has an extensive beer garden. The inn offers en-suite **accommodation** in low-ceilinged oak-beamed rooms (℡01822/820241, Ⓦwww.castleinnlydford.co.uk; ❷), and there's a separate **restaurant** too. Cheaper rooms are available at *Heathergate* (℡01822/820486, Ⓦwww.heathergate-lydford .co.uk; no credit cards; ❷), a working farm less than a mile west of Lydford on the Coryton road. The renowned 🍴 *Dartmoor Inn* (℡01822/820221, Ⓦwww .dartmoorinn.com; closed Sun eve & Mon lunchtime), on the A386 opposite the Lydford turning, serves superior bar meals and pricier British and European dishes – evening meals usually need to be booked – and offers three spacious rooms furnished with antiques (❸).

North Devon

From Exeter the A377 runs alongside the scenic Tarka Line railway to **North Devon**'s major town, **Barnstaple**. Within easy reach of here, the resorts of **Ilfracombe** and **Woolacombe** draw the crowds, though the fine sandy beaches surrounding the latter give ample opportunity to find your own space. West of the river port of **Bideford**, the precipitous village of **Clovelly** is one of Devon's most famous beauty spots, while stormy **Hartland Point** offers dramatic scenery and inspiring coastal walks. For a complete break and further scope for stretching the legs and clearing the lungs, head over to the tiny island of **Lundy**, twelve miles out to sea, reachable from Ilfracombe or Bideford.

Barnstaple

BARNSTAPLE, at the head of the Taw estuary, makes an excellent north Devon base, being well connected to the resorts of Bideford Bay, Ilfracombe and Woolacombe, as well as to the western fringes of Exmoor. The town's centuries-old role as a marketplace is perpetuated in the daily bustle around the huge timber-framed **Pannier Market** off the High Street, alongside which runs **Butchers Row**, its

33 archways now converted to a variety of uses. Also off the High Street, in the pedestrianized area, lies Barnstaple's **parish church** and the fourteenth-century **St Anne's Chapel**, converted into a grammar school in 1549 and later numbering among its pupils John Gay, author of *The Beggar's Opera*; it's now closed to the public (though can be visited as part of a guided tour – ask at the tourist office for details). At the end of Boutport Street on The Square, make time to visit the **Museum of North Devon** (Mon–Sat 9.30am–5pm; free), a lively miscellany including wildlife displays and a collection of eighteenth-century pottery for which the region was famous. The museum lies alongside the Taw, where footpaths make for a pleasant riverside stroll, with the colonnaded eighteenth-century **Queen Anne's Walk** – built as a merchants' exchange – providing some architectural interest and housing the **Barnstaple Heritage Centre** (April–Oct Tues–Sat 10am–5pm; Nov–March Tues–Fri 10am–4.30pm, Sat 10am–3.30pm; £3.50), which traces the town's social history by means of reconstructions and touch-screen computers.

Practicalities

Barnstaple's well-informed **tourist office** is inside the Museum of North Devon (Mon–Sat 9.30am–5pm; ☎01271/375000, ⓦwww.staynorthdevon.co.uk). You can **rent bikes** from Tarka Trail Cycle Hire at the train station (April–Oct; ☎01271/324202, ⓦwww.tarkatrail.co.uk).

Places to stay in town include *The Old Post Office*, 22 Pilton St (☎01271/859439, ⓦwww.theoldpostoffice-pilton.co.uk; no credit cards; ❸), half a mile north of the centre, with tasteful, period furnishings and a garden, and, a couple of miles southeast of the centre on Landkey Road, *Mount Sandford* (☎01271/342354; no credit cards; ❷), an elegant, porticoed Regency building. Outside town, you could have a more interesting stay at ⚓ *Broomhill Art Hotel*, Muddiford, signposted two miles north of Barnstaple off the A39 – a striking combination of gallery, restaurant and hotel (☎01271/850262, ⓦwww.broomhillart.co.uk; no credit cards; ❸), where the en-suite rooms look onto a sculpture garden. Half-board only is available at weekends.

By day, you can pick up coffees and **snacks** at the *Old School Coffee House* (closed Sun), a building dating from 1659 on Church Lane, near St Anne's Chapel, and from the *Owl Vegan Café*, 1 Maiden St, where all dishes cost less than £6, and board games and wi-fi are available (closed eve and all Sat & Sun, unless by booking ☎01271/371222). Out of town, the *Terra Madre* **restaurant** at the *Broomhill Art Hotel* lays on delicious bar meals, Mediterranean-style fixed-price lunches for £14 and dinners for £24 (closed Mon & Tues and eve Sun–Thurs).

Ilfracombe and around

The most popular resort on Devon's northern coast, **ILFRACOMBE** is essentially little changed since its evolution into a Victorian and Edwardian tourist centre, with any large-scale development restricted by the surrounding cliffs. In summer the place is heaving, but you can always escape on a coastal tour, cruise to Lundy Island (see box, p.388) or fishing trip from the harbour. For walkers, the coast path follows the attractive stretch east of town beyond the grassy cliffs of Hillsborough to a succession of unspoiled coves and inlets characterized by jagged slanting rocks and heather-covered slopes.

From Barnstaple, **buses** #3 and #301 run several times an hour to Ilfracombe (only #3 on Sun), while from Minehead and Lynton "Exmoor Coastlink" #300 runs to the town two or three times daily (weekends only in winter). The Ilfracombe **tourist office** is at the Landmark Theatre on the seafront (Easter–Oct daily 10am–5pm; Nov–Easter Mon–Fri 10am–5pm, Sat 10am–4pm; ☎01271/863001, ⓦwww.visitilfracombe.co.uk).

Henry Williamson's book *Tarka the Otter* (1927) relates the travels and travails of a young otter, and is frequently recalled in north Devon. The Exeter–Barnstaple rail route, which for half of its length follows the Taw valley – where parts of the book are set – has been dubbed the **Tarka Line**, while Barnstaple itself forms the centre of the figure-of-eight traced by the **Tarka Trail**, which tracks the otter's wanderings for a distance of over 180 miles. To the north, the trail penetrates Exmoor then follows the coast back, passing through Williamson's home village of Georgeham on its return to Barnstaple. South, the path takes in Bideford (see p.386), following a disused rail line to Meeth, and continuing as far as Okehampton (see p.381), before swooping up via Eggesford, the point at which the Tarka Line enters the Taw valley.

Twenty-one miles of the trail follow a former rail line that's ideally suited to **bicycles**; up to six bikes can be carried free on Tarka Line trains (booking advisable on ℡08457/000125); there are bike rental shops at Barnstaple (see p.384) and Bideford (see p.386). A good ride from Barnstaple is to **Great Torrington** (fifteen miles south), where you can eat at the *Puffing Billy* pub, formerly the train station. Pick up a leaflet on the Tarka Trail with a route map from tourist offices.

Smartest choice among Ilfracombe's extensive **accommodation** is *Westwood*, Torrs Park (℡01271/867443, ⓦwww.west-wood.co.uk; ❹), in a quiet area west of the centre: a B&B that's more like a small boutique hotel, it has three sleek, contemporary rooms and serves organic breakfasts. More central (though a steep climb from the harbour), off Hillsborough Road, is *Montpelier*, 20 Montpelier Terrace (℡01271/879646, ⓦwww.montpelierbandb.com; ❷), with comfortable en-suite rooms – two with sea views – and wi-fi. There's also an excellent **hostel**, ⚑ *Ocean Backpackers*, near the bus station and harbour at 29 St James Place (℡01271/867835, ⓦwww.oceanbackpackers.co.uk), offering dorm beds at £12–14 and double rooms (❶).

For a slap-up feed, head to *The Quay*, 11 The Quay (℡01271/868090; closed Sun eve, Mon & Tues), a harbourside **restaurant** co-owned by artist Damien Hirst (some of whose works are on display), with a Mediterranean menu using local ingredients; you can also order drinks and snacks in the relaxed ground-floor area.

Woolacombe, Croyde and around

Five miles west of Ilfracombe, a cluster of hotels, B&Bs and villas makes up the summer resort of **WOOLACOMBE**, at the northern end of one of the West Country's top beaches, **Woolacombe Sands**, a broad, west-facing expanse much favoured by surfers and families alike. The beach can get crowded around here, but you'll always find space at the quieter southern end, **Putsborough Sands**, a choice swimming spot bracketed by **Baggy Point**, where from September to November the air is a swirl of gannets, shags, cormorants and shearwaters. Woolacombe Bay is bounded to the north by **Morte Point**, a rocky promontory named after the menacing sunken reef of Morte Stone. A break in the rocks makes space for the pocket-sized **Barricane Beach**, famous for the tropical shells washed here from the Caribbean by the Atlantic currents, and a popular swimming spot.

South of Baggy Point, **Croyde Bay** is another surfers' delight, more compact than Woolacombe, with the beach lying half a mile west of the village of **CROYDE**. Shops in the village and stalls on the sand rent surfboards and wetsuits. South of Croyde Bay, **Saunton Sands** is a magnificent long stretch of coast pummelled by ranks of classic breakers and beloved of longboarders.

Woolacombe is linked to Barnstaple by bus #303 (not Sun in winter), and to Ilfracombe by #31 (Mon–Sat) and #302 (Sun in summer). Bus #308 (not Sun in winter) connects Barnstaple to Croyde, via Saunton. There's no service between Woolacombe and Croyde. Woolacombe's **tourist office** is on the Esplanade (Easter–Oct Mon–Sat 10am–5pm, Sun 10am–3pm; Nov–Easter Mon–Sat 10am–1pm; ☎01271/870553, ⓦwww.woolacombetourism.co.uk).

In Woolacombe, top **accommodation** choice is *The Rocks Hotel* (☎01271/870361, ⓦwww.therockshotel.co.uk; ➌), a surfer-friendly place close to the beach, with high-spec bedrooms and bathrooms, and a breakfast room in the style of a 1950s American diner. In Croyde, try the friendly 🍴 *Baggy's Surf Lodge*, right above the beach on Moor Lane (☎01271/890078, ⓦwww.baggys.co.uk), offering bunks (£25 including breakfast), double rooms (➋) and surf equipment rental. Most local **campsites** are around Morte Point, including *North Morte Farm*, Mortehoe (☎01271/870381, ⓦwww.northmortefarm.co.uk; closed Nov–March), with caravans for rent, panoramic sea views and access to Rockham Beach.

For **refreshments** in Woolacombe, surfers and day-trippers gather at the *Red Barn*, a bar/restaurant just behind the beach, while breakfasts, full meals and a buzzy atmosphere can be found further up at the stylish 🍴 *Electric*, West Road (☎01271/871411; Sept–Easter closed Sun eve & Mon–Wed), a restaurant and bar with a terrace and regular DJs.

Croyde's hangouts of choice are *The Thatch* **pub** and *The Blue Groove*, a contemporary café/restaurant (closed mid-Oct to Easter) – both on Hobbs Hill.

Bideford Bay

Bideford Bay (sometimes called Barnstaple Bay) ranges in tone from the twee village of **Clovelly** to the savage windlashed rocks of **Hartland Point**. Low-key **Bideford** is a useful transit centre, with some decent accommodation, bus connections to all the towns on the bay and regular boats for Lundy.

Bideford

Like Barnstaple, nine miles to the east, the estuary town of **BIDEFORD** formed an important link in the north Devon trade network, mainly due to its **bridge**, which still straddles the River Torridge. First built in 1300, the bridge was reconstructed in stone in the following century, and subsequently reinforced and widened, hence the irregularity of its 24 arches, no two of which have the same span.

From the Norman era until the eighteenth century, the port was the property of the Grenville family, whose most celebrated scion was **Richard Grenville**, commander of the ships that carried the first settlers to Virginia, and a major player in the defeat of the Spanish Armada.

The main sight here is the **Burton Art Gallery and Museum** on Kingsley Road (Mon–Sat 10am–4/5pm, Sun 11am–4pm; free; ⓦwww.burtonartgallery.co.uk), which exhibits paintings and craftwork, with regular exhibitions. The gallery also holds Bideford's **tourist office** (Easter–Sept Mon–Sat 10am–5pm, Sun 10am–4pm; Oct–Easter Mon–Sat 10am–4pm, Sun 11am–4pm; ☎01237/477676, ⓦwww .torridge.gov.uk). You can pick up information and tickets here (also sold on the quayside) for coastal cruises and the boat to Lundy (see box, p.388). Bideford Bicycle Hire, Torrington Street (☎01237/424123, ⓦwww.bidefordbicyclehire .co.uk), two hundred yards south of the old bridge on the far riverbank, **rents bikes** for exploring the Tarka Trail.

The town's best **accommodation** choice is the Georgian *Mount* on Northdown Road (☎01237/473748, ⓦwww.themountbideford.co.uk; ➌), set in its own peaceful garden and linked to the centre by a footpath, while the friendly *Corner*

House, 14 The Strand (℡01237/473722, ⓦwww.cornerhouseguesthouse.co.uk; no credit cards; ➋), has rooms with shared bathrooms, superb breakfasts and free wi-fi.

For a daytime **snack** or full Mediterranean-style evening **meal**, head for *Cafecino Plus*, 26 Mill St (closed Mon eve & Sun), a lively café/bistro with courtyard seating. You'll find a pair of first-class **pubs** a couple of miles downstream in the port of Appledore, where the *Royal George* and *Beaver Inn* on Irsha Street serve great seafood and enjoy wonderful estuary views.

Clovelly

Snuggled in a cleft in the cliff wall ten miles west of Bideford, **CLOVELLY** must have featured on more chocolate boxes than anywhere else in the West Country. The perfectly preserved antique charm of the village attracts a regular stream of visitors, though its rather unreal, manufactured flavour can also cloy. Privately owned, Clovelly's museum-like character is underlined by the presence of a **visitor centre** (daily: April–Oct 9am–6pm; Nov–March 9.30am–4pm; £5.95 including car park; ⓦwww.clovelly.co.uk), through which you'll have to pass to gain access.

Below the visitor centre, the cobbled, traffic-free main street plunges steeply down past neat, flower-smothered cottages where sledges are tethered for transporting goods – the only way to carry supplies since the use of donkeys ceased. A couple of buildings hold an exhibition devoted to the author Charles Kingsley, whose father was rector here for six years, and a restored nineteenth-century fisherman's home. At the bottom, a stony beach and tiny harbour lie next to the *Red Lion Inn*.

If you don't fancy the return climb, use the Land Rover service leaving every fifteen minutes from behind the *Red Lion Inn* back to the top of the village (Easter–Oct 9am–5.30pm; £2). Here, immediately below the visitor centre, it's worth strolling along the three-mile, thickly wooded **Hobby Drive** for some grand views over the village and sea.

Practicalities

You can reach Clovelly by **bus** #319 (not Sun in winter) from Barnstaple and Bideford. Of the two pricey **hotels** here, the luxurious *Red Lion Inn* enjoys the best position, right on the harbour (℡01237/431237, ⓔredlion@clovelly.co.uk; ➎). Halfway down the main street, *Donkey Shoe Cottage* (℡01237/431601, ⓦwww .donkeyshoecottage.co.uk; no credit cards; ➋) offers much more modest but still comfortable **B&B** accommodation, and needs booking well ahead in summer. You'll find greater availability a twenty-minute walk up from the visitor centre in Higher Clovelly: right at the top, near the A39 junction, try the two-hundred-year-old *East Dyke Farmhouse* (℡01237/431216, ⓦwww.bedbreakfastclovelly.co.uk; no credit cards; ➋), with its lovely beamed and flagstoned dining room, and guest rooms with fridges and private bathrooms. Clovelly's best **eating** option is the *Red Lion*, which offers snacks in the Harbour Bar, and full meals in the upstairs restaurant.

Hartland Point and around

You could drive along minor roads to **Hartland Point**, ten miles west of Clovelly, but the best approach is on foot along the coastal path. Shortly before arriving, the path touches the only sandy beach along this stretch of coast, **Shipload Bay**. The headland presents one of Devon's most dramatic sights, its jagged black rocks battered by the sea and overlooked by a solitary lighthouse 350ft up. South of Hartland Point, the saw-toothed rocks and near-vertical escarpments defiantly confront the waves, with spectacular waterfalls tumbling over the cliffs.

This sheer stretch of coast has seen dozens of shipwrecks over the centuries, though many must have been prevented by the sight of the tower of fourteenth-century **St Nectan's** – a couple of miles south of the point in the village of

STOKE – which acted as a landmark to sailors before the construction of the lighthouse. At 128ft, it is the tallest church tower in north Devon, and the wagon-roofed interior boasts a finely carved rood-screen and a Norman font. Opposite, tea and home-made scones are served at *Stoke Barton Farm* (Easter–Sept Sat & Sun).

Half a mile east of the church, gardens and lush woodland surround **Hartland Abbey** (April to late May Wed, Thurs & Sun 2–5pm; late May to early Oct also Mon & Tues; grounds April to early Oct daily except Sat noon–5pm; £9.50, grounds only £5), an eighteenth-century country house incorporating the ruins of an abbey dissolved in 1539, and displaying fine furniture, old photographs and recently uncovered frescoes. There's a nice walk through the grounds to the beach here.

HARTLAND itself, further inland, holds little appeal beyond its three pubs and café, but on the coast, **Hartland Quay** deserves a linger: once a busy port, financed in part by the mariners Raleigh, Drake and Hawkins, it was mostly destroyed by storms in the nineteenth century, and now holds a solitary pub and hotel, surrounded by beautiful slate cliffs. About one mile south of here, **Speke's Mill Mouth** is a select surfers' beach.

Lundy Island

There are fewer than twenty full-time residents on **Lundy**, a tiny windswept island twelve miles north of Hartland Point. Now a refuge for thousands of marine birds, Lundy has no cars, just one pub and one shop – indeed little has changed since the Marisco family established itself here in the twelfth century, making use of the shingle beaches and coves to terrorize shipping along the Bristol Channel. The family's fortunes only fell in 1242 when one of their number, William de Marisco, was found to be plotting against the king, whereupon he was hanged, drawn and quartered at Tower Hill in London. The castle erected by Henry III on Lundy's southern end dates from this time.

Today the island is managed by the Landmark Trust. Unless you're on a specially arranged diving or climbing expedition, **walking** along the interweaving tracks and footpaths is really the only thing to do here. The grass, heather and bog is crossed by dry-stone walls and grazed by ponies, goats, deer and the rare soay sheep. The shores – mainly cliffy on the west, softer and undulating on the east – shelter a rich variety of **birdlife**, including kittiwakes, fulmars, shags and Manx shearwaters, which often nest in rabbit burrows. The most famous birds, though, are the **puffins** after which Lundy is named – from the Norse *lunde* (puffin) and *ey* (island). They can only be sighted in April and May, when they come ashore to mate. Offshore, **grey seals** can be seen all year round.

Between April and October, the MS *Oldenburg* sails to Lundy up to four times a week from Ilfracombe, less frequently from Bideford, taking around two hours from both places. Day-return tickets cost £32.50, open returns £56; to reserve a place, call ☏01271/863636 (day-returns can also be booked from local tourist offices). **Accommodation** in a range of idiosyncratic properties on the island can be booked up months in advance, and B&B is only available in houses that have not already been taken for weekly rentals. Since B&B bookings can only be made within two weeks of the proposed visit, this limits the options, though it's still possible to find a double room for £60 per night (£75 in peak season), with a minimum two-night stay. **Bookings** for weekly rentals must be made through the Landmark Trust's office (☏01628/825925, ⓦwww.landmarktrust.org.uk), or call ☏01271/863636 for shorter B&B stays. There's also a **campsite** on the island open from April to October. More information can be found on the island's website, ⓦwww.lundyisland.co.uk.

Practicalities

Accommodation options in the area are scattered, and you'll need your own transport unless you stay in Hartland itself (bus #319 from Barnstaple), where you'll find a small, friendly B&B at ⚵ *Two Harton Manor*, The Square, off Fore Street (☏01237/441670, ⓦwww.twohartonmanor.co.uk; no credit cards; ❷), with two congenial rooms above an artist's studio. For proximity to the sea, you can't do better than the *Hartland Quay Hotel*, Hartland Quay (☏01237/441218, ⓦwww.hartlandquayhotel.com; ❸), but if you want to be nearer Shipload Bay and Hartland Point (and the coast path), try *West Titchberry Farm* (☏01237/441287; no credit cards; ❷), for which drivers should follow signs for Hartland Lighthouse. In nearby Stoke, *Stoke Barton Farm* provides basic **camping** facilities (☏01237/441238, ⓦwww.westcountry-camping.co.uk; closed Oct–Easter).

Cornwall

Virtually unaffected by the Roman conquest, **Cornwall** was for centuries the last haven for a **Celtic culture** elsewhere eradicated by the Saxons – a land where princes communed with Breton troubadours, chroniclers and scribes composed the epic tales of Arthurian heroism, and itinerant monks from Welsh and Irish monasteries disseminated an elemental and visionary Christianity. Primitive granite crosses and a crop of Celtic saints remain as traces of this formative period, and though the Cornish language had ebbed away by the eighteenth century, it is recalled in Celtic place names that have often grown more exotic as they have mutated over time.

The relics of once-thriving **industries** are far more conspicuous in Cornwall than in neighbouring Devon. Its more westerly stretches in particular are littered with the derelict stacks and castle-like ruins of the engine-houses that once powered the region's **copper** and **tin mines**, while deposits of **china clay** continue to be mined in the area around St Austell, as witnessed by the conical spoil heaps thereabouts. Also prominent throughout the county are the grey Nonconformist chapels that reflect the impact of Methodism on Cornwall's mining communities.

Nowadays, of course, Cornwall's biggest industry is tourism, though its impact has been uneven across the county: **Land's End**, for example, is cluttered with a tacky leisure complex while Cornwall's other great headland, **Lizard Point**, remains undeveloped. The resorts of **Falmouth**, site of the impressive National Maritime Museum, and **Newquay**, the chief surfing centre, throng with visitors, while the innate charm of smaller places such as **Mevagissey**, **Polperro**, **Mousehole** and **Padstow** can be hard to make out in peak season. Other villages, however, such as **Charlestown**, **Port Isaac** and **Boscastle**, are hardly touched, and even **Tintagel**, site of what is fondly known as King Arthur's castle, has preserved its sense of desolation. Near **St Austell**, the spectacular **Eden Project** has pioneered eco-friendly crowd-pulling, while other places – such as **St Ives**, **Fowey** and **Bude** – have absorbed the seasonal influx without losing their character. For true remoteness, head for **Bodmin Moor**, a tract of wilderness in the heart of Cornwall, or leave the mainland altogether for the exquisite **Isles of Scilly**. Throughout the county, the best advice is to avoid the peak holiday periods, though even in the height of summer it only requires a shift of a few miles to escape the crowds, and there are enough good beaches around for everyone to find a space.

The best way to explore the coast is along the **South West Coast Path** (see box, p.348), but a car is almost indispensable for anyone wanting to see a lot in a short time, as the **public transport** system is limited.

From Looe to Veryan Bay

The southeast strip of the Cornish coast from Looe to Veryan Bay holds a string of medieval harbour towns tarnished by various degrees of commercialization, but there are also a few spots where you can experience the best of Cornwall, including some wonderful coastline. The main rail stop is **St Austell**, the capital of Cornwall's china clay industry, though there is a branch line connecting nearby Par with the north coast at Newquay. To the east of St Austell Bay, the touristy **Polperro** and **Looe** are easily accessible by bus from Plymouth, and there's a rail link to Looe from Liskeard. The estuary town of **Fowey**, in a niche of Cornwall closely associated with the author Daphne du Maurier, is most easily reached by bus from St Austell and Par, as is **Mevagissey**, to the west.

Looe

LOOE was drawing crowds as early as 1800, when the first "bathing-machines" were wheeled out, but the arrival of the railway in 1879 was what really packed out its beaches. Though the village now touts itself as something of a shark-fishing centre, most people come here for the sand, the handiest stretch being the beach in front of East Looe, the busier half of the river-divided town. Away from the river mouth, you'll find a cleaner spot to swim a mile eastwards at **Millendreath**. Most of Looe's attractions are in boating and bathing, and in summer, you'll find various **boating and fishing trips** advertised on the long quayside, spread along the river parallel to the main Fore Street. The main diversion in the village is the **Old Guildhall Museum** (Easter & late May to Sept Mon–Fri & Sun 11am–4pm; £1.80), a diverse collection of maritime models and exhibits, though none so interesting as the building itself, a fifteenth-century construction preserving its prisoners' cells and raised magistrates' benches.

East Looe's **tourist office** is at the Guildhall on Fore Street (Easter to late Oct daily 10am–5pm; ℡01503/262072, Ⓦwww.visit-southeastcornwall.co.uk). The best **accommodation** lies outside the centre: on Shutta Road, try *Shutta House* (℡01503/264233, Ⓦwww.shuttahouse.co.uk; ❷), a neo-Gothic ex-vicarage with clean, airy en-suite rooms and free wi-fi. In West Looe, there's *Schooner Point*, 1 Trelawney Terrace (℡01503/262670, Ⓦwww.schoonerpoint.co.uk; no credit cards; ❷), with lofty river views from most of its good-value rooms.

For fresh, local seafood, the town has a couple of quality **restaurants** right next to each other on the quayside: the oak-beamed *Old Sail Loft* (℡01503/262131; closed lunchtime Tues & Sun) and the more formal *Trawlers* (℡01503/263593; eve only; closed Mon & Tues), though prices are steep. For simpler fare, try the inexpensive *Tom Sawyer's* on Marine Drive, West Looe (℡01503/263913; closed Sun eve & all Mon), good for a baguette, steak, or just a pint, with sea views.

Polperro

Looe is linked by hourly #573 buses (5 on Sun) with neighbouring **POLPERRO**, a smaller, quainter place, but equally inundated by tourists in summer. From the bus stop and car park at the top of the village, it's a five- or ten-minute walk alongside the River Pol to the pretty harbour. The surrounding cliffs and the tightly packed houses rising on each side of the stream have an undeniable charm, and the tangle of lanes is little changed since the village's heyday of smuggling and pilchard fishing, though its straggling main street – The Coombes – is now an unbroken row of tourist shops and food outlets.

Polperro's best **places to stay** include: *Penryn House* on The Coombes (℡01503/272157, ⊛www.penrynhouse.co.uk; ❷), a small hotel with a country feel and friendly management, and *The House on the Props*, Talland Street (℡01503/272310, ⊛www.houseontheprops.co.uk; ❷), a quirky B&B right next to the harbour with awesome views from its rooms.

The Old Mill House Inn on Mill Hill has a separate **restaurant** with decent dinners, though you'll find more sophisticated fare at *Couches Great House* (℡01503/272554; closed daytime), offering modern, beautifully executed dishes on fixed-price menus for £25–38. The snug *Blue Peter* **pub** on The Quay has chunky crab sandwiches and live music at weekends.

Fowey and around

A fetching cascade of neat, pale terraces at the mouth of one of the peninsula's greatest rivers, **FOWEY** (pronounced "Foy") was once a major port on the county's south coast, becoming so ambitious that Edward IV was provoked to strip the town of its military capability. Fowey continued to thrive commercially, however, and was the leading port for china clay shipments in the nineteenth century. The harbour today is crowded with yachts and other craft, giving the town a brisk, purposeful character.

Arrival, information and accommodation

Separated from eastern routes by its river, Fowey is most accessible by hourly #25 **buses** from St Austell and Par train stations. Travellers to or from the west might make use of the **ferry** linking Fowey with Mevagissey (see p.394), which operates three to six times daily between late April and September (35min; £7; ⊛www .mevagissey-ferries.co.uk). The **tourist office** is at 5 South St (Mon–Sat 9.30am–5pm, Sun 10am–4.30pm; ℡01726/833616, ⊛www.fowey.co.uk).

Most of the town's pubs offer **B&B**, including the two listed below. Three miles north, outside Golant, there's a YHA **hostel** at *Penquite House*, a Georgian mansion with views over the valley (℡0845/371 9019, ✉golant@yha.org.uk; from £14).

Coombe Farm ℡01726/833123, ⊛www .coombefarmbb.co.uk. This B&B provides perfect rural isolation just 20min walk from town, at the end of a lane off the B3269 – and there's a bathing area just 300m away. No credit cards. ❷
Old Quay House 28 Fore St ℡01726/833302, ⊛www.theoldquayhouse.com. At the top of the scale, this stylish boutique hotel has creamily opulent rooms – those with estuary views and patios cost extra. ❻

Safe Harbour Lostwithiel St ℡01726/833379, ⊛www.cornwall-safeharbour.co.uk. Above the centre, but right at the town's bus stop, this pub is not so strong on character but has comfortable rooms, good views and parking. ❷
Ship Inn Trafalgar Square ℡01726/832230, ⊛www.staustellbrewery.co.uk. Very central, sixteenth-century pub with small rooms, shared bathrooms and no breakfast – hence the low rates. ❷

The Town

Fowey's steep layout centres on the church of **St Fimbarrus**, a distinctive fifteenth-century construction that marks the end of the ancient **Saints' Way footpath** from Padstow, linking the north and south Cornish coasts. Beside St Fimbarrus on South Street, the **Literary Centre**, at the back of the tourist office (and sharing the same times; free), is worth a glance; it's mainly devoted to Daphne du Maurier, who spent her most creative years in and around Fowey. Fans can join a guided walk around scenes described in her books – contact the tourist office for details – while the nine-day **Daphne du Maurier Festival** each May delves more deeply into her life and work (℡0845/094 0428, ⓦwww.dumaurierfestival.co.uk).

Below St Fimbarrus, Fore Street, Lostwithiel Street and the **Esplanade** fan out from Trafalgar Square, the last leading to a footpath that gives access to some splendid walks around the coast. Past the remains of a blockhouse that once supported a defensive chain hung across the river's mouth, you'll soon reach the small beach of **Readymoney Cove** – so-called either because it was where smugglers buried their ill-gotten gains, or because it was where the flotsam of shipwrecks came ashore. Close by stand the ruins of **St Catherine's Castle**, built on the orders of Henry VIII, and offering fine views across the estuary.

Other scenic hikes include the **Hall Walk**, a circular four-mile ramble north of Fowey, passing a memorial to "Q", alias Sir Arthur Quiller-Couch, who lived on Fowey's Esplanade between 1892 and 1944, and whose writings helped popularize the place he called "Troy Town". Details of this and other local excursions are available from the tourist office. Further afield, you can reach the riverside hamlet of **Golant**, three miles north and just over a mile east of the Iron Age fort of **Castle Dore**, which features in Arthurian romance as the residence of King Mark of Cornwall, husband of Iseult.

Coastwalkers can trace the rocky shore westwards to **Gribbin Head** (less than four miles), near which stands Menabilly House, where Daphne du Maurier lived for 24 years – it was the model for the Manderley of *Rebecca*. The house is not open to the public, but the coast path takes you down to the twin coves of Polridmouth, where Rebecca met her watery end.

Heading east along the coast from Polruan, the ten-mile stretch west to Polperro (see p.390) is one of the most scenic parts of the coastal path in south Cornwall, giving access to some beautiful secluded sand beaches.

Eating and drinking

As well as a cluster of first-rate seafood eateries, Fowey is well stocked with fine **pubs** – the *Ship Inn* (see p.391) and the *King of Prussia* on the quayside are both worth a lingering drink or meal.

Old Quay House Hotel 28 Fore St ℡01726/833302. Perhaps the finest of Fowey's restaurants, this elegant but relaxed place has tables by the waterside and specializes in Modern British cuisine on set-price menus (£27.50 and £35). There's a more moderately priced menu at lunchtime. Closed Mon–Fri lunchtime in winter.

The Other Place 41 Fore St ℡01726/833636. If you don't fancy the contemporary restaurant upstairs, where paella, rump steak and locally caught seafood are on offer (£14–18), pick up a takeaway from the counter on the ground floor – burgers, fish and chips, and fabulous ice cream. Restaurant closed daytime, open Thurs–Sat only in winter.

Sam's 20 Fore St ℡01726/832273. With a menu ranging from burgers (£8–12) to seafood dishes (£12–15), this place has 1960s rock'n'roll decor and friendly service. It doesn't take bookings, so arrive early or be prepared to wait. There's a late-closing lounge bar upstairs.

St Austell Bay

It was the discovery of china clay, or kaolin, in the downs to the north of **St Austell Bay** that spurred the area's growth in the eighteenth century. An essential ingredient in the production of porcelain, kaolin had until then only been produced in northern China, where a high ridge, or *kao-ling*, was the sole known source of the raw material. Still a vital part of Cornwall's economy, the clay is now mostly exported for use in the manufacture of paper, as well as paint and medicines. The conical spoil heaps are a feature of the local landscape, the great green and white mounds making an eerie sight.

The town of **ST AUSTELL** itself is fairly unexciting, but makes a useful stop for trips in the surrounding area. The town's nearest link to the sea is at **CHARLESTOWN**, two miles south and an easy downhill walk from the centre of town. This unassuming and unspoilt port is named after the entrepreneur Charles Rashleigh, who in 1791 began work on the harbour in what was then a small fishing community, widening its streets to accommodate the clay wagons passing through daily. The wharves are still used, loading clay onto vessels that appear oversized beside the tiny jetties, and also providing a backdrop for the location filming that frequently takes place here – you'll often see period sailing vessels moored here too. Behind the harbour – the **Shipwreck and Heritage Centre** (March–Oct daily 10am–5pm; £5.95) is accessed through tunnels once used to convey the clay to the docks, and shows a good collection of photos and relics as well as tableaux of historical scenes.

On each side of the dock the coarse sand and stone **beaches** have small rock pools, above which cliff walks lead around St Austell Bay. Eastwards, you soon arrive at overdeveloped **Carlyon Bay**, whose main resort is **Par**. The beaches here get clogged with clay – the best swimming is to be found by pressing on to the sheltered crescent of **Polkerris**.

Practicalities

Trains on the main London–Penzance line serve St Austell, with most services stopping at Par, also connected to Newquay on the north coast. Frequent #25 and

---

The Eden Project

A disused clay pit four miles northeast of St Austell is home to Cornwall's most flamboyant attraction – the **Eden Project** (daily: April–Oct 10am–6pm; Nov–March 10am–4.30pm; last entry 90min before closing; £16; ⓦwww.edenproject.com). Occupying a 160ft-deep crater, the project showcases the diversity of the planet's plant life in an imaginative, sometimes wacky style. The whole site is stunningly landscaped with, at centre stage, vast geodesic "biomes", or conservatories made up of eco-friendly, Teflon-coated, hexagonal panels. One cluster holds groves of olive and citrus trees, cacti and other plants more usually found in the warm, temperate zones of the Mediterranean, southern Africa and southwestern USA, while the larger group contains plants from the tropics, including teak and mahogany trees. There's a waterfall and river gushing through, and things can get pretty steamy – you can take cool refuge in an air-conditioned bunker halfway along the course. Equally impressive are the external grounds (described as "Picasso meeting the Aztecs"), where plantations of bamboo, tea, hops, hemp and tobacco are interspersed with brilliant flower displays. The whole "living theatre" presents a constantly changing spectacle, and should ideally be visited in different seasons. Look out for news about the latest planned addition to the site: a third covered biome, using cutting-edge technology, dedicated to the warm desert regions and the impact of climate change.

Allow at least half a day for a full exploration, but arrive early to avoid congestion. There are timed "story-telling" sessions, and abundant good food is on hand. In summer, the grassy arena sees performances of a range of music – from Kasabian to Mika – and in winter a skating rink is set up; consult the website for all details.

The most useful **bus routes** to Eden are #101 and #527 from St Austell station all year. Bus #527 also connects the site with Newquay. Drivers will find the site signposted on most roads in the area, and there's a useful network of routes for walkers and cyclists, who can claim a £4 reduction off the adult entry fee.

#524 **buses** link St Austell with Par and Fowey, and #525 (not Sun) goes to Charlestown.

Charlestown is the most attractive **place to stay** hereabouts: try *T'Gallants* (℡01726/70203, ⓦwww.tgallants.co.uk; ❸), a smart Georgian B&B at the back of the harbour where cream teas are served in the garden. At *Broad Meadow House*, behind the Shipwreck Centre on Quay Road (℡01726/76636, ⓦwww.broad meadowhouse.com; no credit cards), you can have "tent and breakfast" (May–Sept; £20–25 per person) in family-size tents provided in a meadow by the sea, to which breakfast is brought in the morning; limited camping in small tents is also available. St Austell Bay has a range of official **campsites**, mostly closed October to Easter, including *Carlyon Bay* (℡01726/812735, ⓦwww.carlyonbay .net), near the beach at Bethesda and just a mile and a half from the Eden Project.

Behind *T'Gallants* in Charlestown, the *Rashleigh Arms* offers real **ales** and a lunchtime carvery, and the *Harbourside Inn* also serves a range of **food**.

Mevagissey to Veryan Bay

MEVAGISSEY was once known for the construction of fast vessels, used for carrying contraband as well as pilchards. Today the tiny port might display a few stacks of lobster pots, but the real business is tourism, and in summer the maze of backstreets is saturated with day-trippers, converging on the inner harbour and overflowing onto the large sand beach at **Pentewan** a mile to the north.

A couple of miles north of Mevagissey lie the **Lost Gardens of Heligan** (daily 10am–5/6pm; last entry 90min before closing; £10), a fascinating resurrection of a Victorian garden which had fallen into neglect and was rescued from a ten-foot covering of brambles by Tim Smit, the visionary instigator of the Eden Project (see box, p.393). The abundant palm trees, giant Himalayan rhododendrons, immaculate vinery and glasshouses scattered about all look as if they've been transplanted from warmer climes; a boardwalk takes you past interconnecting ponds, through a jungle and under a canopy of bamboo and ferns down to the Lost Valley, where there are lakes, wildflower meadows and leafy glades of oak, beech and chestnut.

Past the headland to the south of Mevagissey, the small sandy cove of **Portmellon** retains little of its boat-building activities but is freer of tourists. Further still, the village of **GORRAN HAVEN**, which was formerly known for its crab-fishing, has a neat rock-and-sand beach and a footpath that winds round to the even more attractive **Vault Beach**, half a mile south. South of here juts the most striking headland on Cornwall's southern coast, **Dodman Point**, cause of many a wreck and topped by a stark granite cross built by a local parson as a seamark in 1896. The promontory holds the substantial remains of an Iron Age fort, with an earthwork bulwark cutting right across the point.

Curving away to the west, the elegant parabola of **Veryan Bay** is barely touched by commercialism. Just west of Dodman Point lies one of Cornwall's most beautiful coves, **Hemmick Beach**, an excellent swimming spot with rocky outcrops affording a measure of privacy. Visually even more impressive is **Porthluney Cove**, a crescent of sand backed by green pastures and the battlemented **Caerhays Castle** (mid-March to May Mon–Fri noon–4pm; gardens mid-Feb to May daily 10am–5pm; last entry 1hr before closing; house £5.50, garden £5.50, combined ticket £9.50), built in 1808 by John Nash and surrounded by beautiful gardens.

Practicalities

From St Austell's bus and train station, **buses** #26 and #526 leave for Mevagissey and Heligan, with some #526 buses continuing to Gorran Haven. Veryan is reachable on #550 and #551 from Truro (not Sun). **Bike rental** is available from Pentewan Valley Cycle Hire (℡01726/844242), off the B3273 at Pentewan.

Right in the heart of Mevagissey, the best **accommodation** options are the fifteenth-century *Fountain Inn* (℡01726/842320; ❷) on Cliff Street, off East Quay, and *The Old Parsonage*, 58 Church St (℡01726/843709, ⓦwww.old parsonage.net; ❷), a B&B offering simply furnished rooms with private facilities. Outside the village, try the weathered old *Rising Sun Inn* (℡01726/843235, ⓦwww.risingsunmevagissey.com; closed late Dec to Feb; ❸), overlooking the sea at Portmellon. There's a YHA **hostel** (℡0845/371 9107, Ⓔboswinger @yha.org.uk; from £14) in a former farmhouse at Boswinger, a remote spot half a mile from Hemmick Beach and about a mile from the bus stop at Gorran Churchtown, served infrequently by #526 buses.

There's no shortage of **restaurants** in Mevagissey, most specializing in fish – for something a bit different, try the Portuguese ℀ *Alvorada*, 17 Church St (℡01726/842055; closed daytime Mon & Sat and all Sun except Sun eve in Aug; winter Fri & Sat eve only), offering generous portions and great flavours. The *Fountain Inn* and the *Ship Inn* on Fore Street both offer **pub** grub, and Portmellon's *Rising Sun* serves Cornish sausages as well as fresh fish.

Truro, Falmouth and St Mawes

Lush tranquillity collides with frantic tourist activity around the estuary basin of **Carrick Roads**. Connected by river to the estuary, **Truro** is a stop on the main rail line to Penzance and the region's main transport centre. At the end of a branch line from Truro and at the mouth of the Carrick Roads, **Falmouth** is the major resort around here, and the site of one of Cornwall's mightiest castles, **Pendennis**. Its sister fort lies across the Carrick Roads in **St Mawes**, the main settlement on the **Roseland peninsula**, a luxuriant backwater of woods and sheltered creeks between the River Fal and the sea.

Truro

Cornwall's county town, **TRURO**, presents a mixture of different styles, from the graceful Georgian architecture that came with the tin-mining boom of the 1800s to its modern shopping centre. Further blurring the town's overall identity, and its dominant feature, is Truro's faux-medieval **cathedral** (Mon–Sat 7.30am–6pm, Sun 9am–7pm), at the bottom of Pydar Street. Completed in 1910, it was the first Anglican cathedral to be built in England since St Paul's in London, though it incorporates part of the fabric of a much older parish church. The airy interior's best feature is its neo-Gothic baptistry, complete with emphatically pointed arches and elaborate roof-vaulting. To the right of the choir, St Mary's aisle is a relic of the original Perpendicular building, other fragments of which adorn the walls, including – in the north transept – a colourful Jacobean memorial to local Parliamentarian John Robartes and his wife. To get the full picture, join a **guided tour** of the cathedral (April–Oct Mon–Thurs & Sat 11am, Fri 11.30am, plus weekdays at 2pm during school hols).

Truro's other unmissable attraction is the **Royal Cornwall Museum** (Mon–Sat 10am–4.45pm; free), housed in an elegant Georgian building on River Street. The wide-ranging exhibits include minerals, Celtic inscriptions and paintings by Cornish artists. From Town Quay, Enterprise Boats runs scenic **river cruises** to Falmouth and St Mawes up to five times daily between May and October (£15 return; ℡01326/374241, ⓦwww.enterprise-boats.co.uk).

Practicalities

Buses stop nearby at Lemon Quay, or near the train station on Richmond Hill, and Truro's **tourist office** is on Boscawen Street (Mon–Fri 9am–5pm; Easter–Oct also Sat 9am–5pm; ℡01872/274555, ⓦtourism.truro.gov.uk). Best hotel **accommodation** in the centre of town is *Mannings* at the bottom of Lemon Street (℡01872/270345, ⓦwww.manningshotels.co.uk; ❸–❹), with a bright, modern feel and a good, informal brasserie. Among the **B&Bs**, try *Bay Tree*, a restored Georgian house at 28 Ferris Town (℡01872/240274, ⓦwww.baytree-guesthouse .co.uk; no credit cards; ❷), where rooms have shared bathrooms. There's also a comfortable **hostel** with real character, ⚡ *Truro Backpackers Lodge*, at 10 The Parade (℡01872/260857 or 07813/755210, ⓦwww.trurobackpackers.co.uk), offering dorm beds (£18) and single and double rooms (❶). Three miles southwest of Truro on the A39 Falmouth road, the five-star *Carnon Downs* **campsite** has fantastic washing facilities (℡01872/862283, ⓦwww.carnon-downs-caravanpark.co.uk).

Truro's best **restaurants** are fairly centrally located. For coffees, vegetarian lunches and a choice of organic wines and Belgian beers, head for *Lettuce & Lovage*, 15 Kenwyn St (℡01872/272546; closed eve & all Sun), while *Saffron*, 5 Quay St (℡01872/263771; closed Sun, also Mon eve Jan–May), also serves inexpensive lunches as well as a good-value early-evening menu and seafood specials. The *One Eyed Cat*, a cool, contemporary restaurant and "drinkery" in a converted church at 116 Kenwyn St (℡01872/222122; closed Sun eve in winter) has pastas, pizzas and seafood dishes on the menu and occasionally live music or DJs at weekends. Among the **pubs**, you'll find good ale, coffees and decent bar meals at the *Wig and Pen*, on the corner of Frances and Castle streets, and at the *Globe*, next door.

Falmouth

The construction of Pendennis Castle on the southern point of Carrick Roads in the sixteenth century prepared the ground for the growth of **FALMOUTH**, then no more than a fishing village. Falmouth's prosperity was assured when in 1689 it became chief base of the fast Falmouth Packets, which sped mail to the Americas, and the port has maintained its allure for sailors ever since. Recent years have seen the growth of a local arts scene, and the castle alone is reason enough to brave the waves of tourist traffic that engulf the town every summer, drawn to the lush beaches stretching south of town.

Arrival, information and accommodation

The branch **rail** line from Truro has stops at Falmouth Town, best for the centre, and Falmouth Docks, nearest to Pendennis Castle. Most **buses** stop on The Moor, close to the Prince of Wales Pier, site of Falmouth's **tourist office** (Mon–Fri 9.30am–5.15pm, plus Easter–Sept Sat 9.30am–5.15pm; ℡01326/312300, ⓦwww.discoverfalmouth.co.uk). You can access the **internet** at the library on The Moor (Mon, Tues, Thurs & Fri 9.30am–6pm, Sat 9.30am–4pm).

Falmouth has a vast range of **accommodation**, including some good central budget choices. Among the overdeveloped caravan parks on the coast south of Falmouth, the **campsite** at *Tregedna Farm* is more tent-friendly, two and a half miles from town and half a mile from Maenporth Beach and the coast path (℡01326/250529, ⓦwww .tregednafarmholidays.co.uk; closed Oct–Easter); bunkrooms are also available.

Arwenack Hotel 27 Arwenack St
℡01326/311185, ⓦwww.falmouthtownhotels
.co.uk. Basic, good-value rooms are available in this very central lodging, including two with good views. No credit cards. ❷

Falmouth Lodge 9 Gyllyngvase Terrace
℡01326/319996, ⓦwww.falmouthbackpackers
.co.uk. Clean and friendly backpackers' hostel near the beach, with a kitchen and internet access. Dorm beds £19, doubles ❶ (breakfast included)

The Town

From the **Prince of Wales Pier**, embarkation point for ferries to St Mawes and Truro as well as a plethora of other boat trips in summer, Falmouth's long **High Street** and its continuations Market and Church streets make up a busy parade of humdrum shops and cafés. At its southern end, Arwenack Street holds the Tudor remains of **Arwenack House** (closed to the public), residence of the Killigrews, an important local dynasty. The peculiar granite pyramid in front, dating from 1737, was probably intended to commemorate the family, though its exact significance has never been clear. On the seafront opposite stands Falmouth's chief attraction, the **National Maritime Museum Cornwall** (daily 10am–5pm; £9.50; ⓦwww
.nmmc.co.uk), an impressive collection of vessels from all over the world. Many of these are suspended in mid-air in the Flotilla Gallery, the cavernous centrepiece of the museum, which can be viewed from three different levels. Panels on the walkways explain the finer points of boat design, while smaller lateral galleries focus on boat building and repairing, Falmouth's packet ships and Cornwall's various other links with the sea, including fishing. A lighthouse-like lookout tower offers excellent views over the harbour and estuary.

Pendennis Castle and Falmouth's beaches

A few minutes' walk west of the museum, **Pendennis Castle** stands sentinel at the tip of the promontory that separates Carrick Roads from Falmouth Bay (April–June & Sept Mon–Fri & Sun 10am–5pm, Sat 10am–4pm; July & Aug Mon–Fri & Sun 10am–6pm, Sat 10am–4pm; Oct–March daily 10am–4pm; £6; EH). The extensive fortification shows little evidence of its five-month siege by the Parliamentarians during the Civil War, which ended only when half its defenders had died and the rest had been starved into submission. Though this is a less-refined contemporary of the castle at St Mawes (see p.398), its site wins hands down, facing right out to sea on its own pointed peninsula, the stout ramparts offering the best all-round views of Carrick Roads and Falmouth Bay. Jousting displays, concerts and drama productions are occasionally staged in the grounds in summer.

If you want to swim in the area, head for the long sandy bay round Pendennis Point, south of the centre, where a succession of sheltered **beaches** are backed by expensive hotels. From the popular **Gyllyngvase Beach**, you can reach the more attractive **Swanpool Beach** by cliff path, or walk a couple of miles further on to **Maenporth**, from where there are some fine cliff-top walks.

Eating and drinking

Arwenack Street holds the majority of **restaurants**, but for a quieter spot seek out *Café Cinnamon*, Old Brewery Yard (℡01326/211457; closed Sun & eve Mon–Wed), a wholefood, vegetarian and vegan café that offers lunchtime snacks and a selection of inexpensive "evening bites" and organic wines. You can tuck into grills and pizzas right on Gyllyngvase Beach at the lively ⚑ *Gylly Beach Café* (℡01326/312884; closed eves Mon–Wed), which has barbecues in summer and live music in the evenings, or go further afield to *Indaba*, Swanpool Beach (℡01326/311886; closed Sun eve), for another Mediterranean-style beachside experience, with fish at the top of the menu.

Drivers or boaters might venture upriver to the *Pandora Inn* at Restronguet, overlooking a creek four miles north of Falmouth; superior bar food is available at lunchtime, or you can eat fresh seafood in the upstairs restaurant (℡01326/372678).

St Mawes and the Roseland peninsula

Stuck at the tip of a prong of land at the bottom of Carrick Roads, the secluded, unhurried village of **ST MAWES** has an attractive walled seafront lying below a hillside of villas and abundant gardens. Just out of sight at the end of the seafront stands the small and pristine **St Mawes Castle** (April–June & Sept daily except Sat 10am–5pm; July & Aug daily except Sat 10am–6pm; Oct daily 10am–4pm; Nov–March Mon & Fri–Sun 10am–4pm; £4.20; EH), built during the reign of Henry VIII. The castle owes its excellent condition to its early surrender to Parliamentary forces during the Civil War, a move that hastened the bloody subjugation of Pendennis Castle over in Falmouth. Both castles adhere to the same cloverleaf design, with a round central keep surrounded by robust gun emplacements, but this is the more attractive of the pair. The dungeons and gun installations contain various artillery exhibits as well as some background on local social history.

Moving away from St Mawes, you could spend a pleasant afternoon poking around the **Roseland peninsula**. Between Easter and October, a twice-hourly passenger **ferry** (daily 10am–5pm; £5.50 return) crosses from the village to the southern arm of the peninsula, which holds the twelfth- to thirteenth-century church of **St Anthony-in-Roseland** and the **lighthouse** on St Anthony's Head, marking the entry into Carrick Roads. Two and a half miles north of St Mawes, the scattered hamlet of **ST JUST-IN-ROSELAND** holds the strikingly picturesque church of St Just, right next to the creek and surrounded by palms and subtropical shrubbery, its gravestones tumbling down to the water's edge.

The easiest way to visit St Mawes and the Roseland peninsula is on one of the frequent ferries from Falmouth's Prince of Wales Pier (£7.50 return). By road, the fastest route from Truro, Falmouth and west Cornwall involves crossing the River Fal on the chain-driven **King Harry Ferry** (every 20min: April–Sept daily 7.30am–9.30pm; Oct–March Mon–Sat 7.20am–7.20pm, Sun 9am–7.20pm; £4.50 per car, 50p per bike, 20p per foot passenger; ℡01872/862312). See Ⓦwww.kingharryscornwall.co.uk/frl for all ferry services.

The King Harry Ferry docks close to **Trelissick Garden** (daily: mid-Feb to Oct 10.30am–5.30pm; Nov to mid-Feb 11am–4pm; £7.40; NT), which is celebrated for its hydrangeas and other Mediterranean species, and has a splendid woodland walk along the Fal (free access all year). In summer, ferries from Falmouth, St Mawes and Truro also stop here, as does the year-round bus #93 (not Sun) from Truro.

Practicalities

Though lacking Falmouth's range of accommodation, St Mawes (Ⓦwww .stmawes.info) makes an attractive – if pricey – **place to stay**. The best budget choices are a ten-minute walk up from the seafront on Newton Road and run by the same family: *Little Newton* (℡01326/270664; ❷) and *Lowen Meadows* (℡01326/270036; ❸); both have spacious, en-suite rooms and friendly hosts (and neither takes credit cards). For location – and very steep rates – book in at the *Tresanton Hotel* (℡01326/270055, Ⓦwww.tresanton.com; ❽), an exclusive Mediterranean-style retreat with a fabulous **restaurant**. You can also eat and drink at the *Victory Inn*, a fine old oak-beamed **pub** just off the seafront.

The Lizard peninsula

The **Lizard peninsula** – from the Celtic *lys ardh*, or "high point" – preserves a thankfully undeveloped if sometimes bleak appearance. If this flat and treeless expanse can be said to have a centre, it is **Helston**, a junction for buses running from Falmouth and Truro to the spartan villages of the peninsula's interior and the tiny fishing ports on its coast. By public transport, you can reach Helston on **buses** #2 and #2A from Penzance, #82 and #82A from Truro and #2 and #35 from Falmouth. From Helston, #32 goes to the east-coast settlements of **St Keverne** and **Coverack**, and #33 goes via **Mullion** to the village of **The Lizard**.

Along the River Helford

To the north of the peninsula, the snug hamlets sprinkled in the valley of the **River Helford** provide a complete contrast to the rugged character of most of the Lizard. At the river's mouth stands **MAWNAN**, whose granite church of **St Mawnan-in-Meneage** is dedicated to the sixth-century Welsh missionary St Maunanus – Meneage (rhyming with "vague") means "land of monks".

Upstream, outside the village of Gweek, the **National Seal Sanctuary** (daily 10am–4/5pm; last entry 1hr before closing; £13.50) is a rehabilitation and release centre for the increasing number of injured seals being rescued from around Cornwall and beyond. Most entertaining are the seal pups, which can be seen during the winter months.

On the south side of the estuary, **Frenchman's Creek**, one of a splay of creeks and arcane inlets running off the river, was the inspiration for Daphne du Maurier's novel of the same name. Her evocation of it holds true: "still and soundless, surrounded by the trees, hidden from the eyes of men".

You can get over to the south bank on the seasonal ferry (Easter–June, Sept & Oct 9.30am–5.30pm; July & Aug 9.30am–9.30pm; £4) from Helford Passage to **HELFORD**, an agreeable old smugglers' haunt worth a snack stop – the *Shipwright's Arms* has pub lunches and a garden overlooking the river.

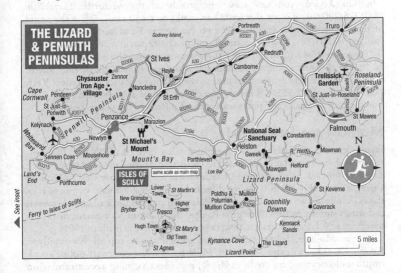

St Keverne and Coverack

South of Helford, the broad, windswept plateau of **Goonhilly Downs** is interrupted by ranks of wind turbines and the futuristic saucers of Goonhilly Satellite Station. The minor B3293 ends at the inland village of **ST KEVERNE**, whose tidy square is flanked by two inns and a church. Forking right onto the B3294, you'll come to **COVERACK**, a fishing port in a lovely sheltered bay, with a range of **accommodation**. Among the B&Bs, try *Fernleigh* (℡01326/280626, ⊛www.fernleighcoverack.co.uk; no credit cards; ❷), on Chymbloth Way, a turn-off from Harbour Road, whose amiable proprietors can cook up a homely three-course meal for around £15. Alternatively, you can stay right above the harbour at the *Paris Hotel* (℡01326/280258 ⊛www.pariscoverack.com; ❷), which offers sea views from all rooms. There's a YHA **hostel** just west of Coverack's centre overlooking the bay (℡0845/371 9014, ⓔcoverack@yha.org.uk; closed Nov–March; from £14), and a **campsite** outside the village, *Little Trevothan* (℡01326/280260, ⊛www.littletrevothan.com; closed Jan & Feb).

The *Paris Hotel* provides good **meals**; otherwise nip across to *The Old Lifeboat House* (℡01326/281212; closed Tues & Wed in winter & Nov to mid-March), which serves superb fresh fish; it's pricey and often fully booked, but you can always pick up first-rate fish and chips from the attached takeaway. Ask about **windsurfing** courses at the Coverack Windsurfing Centre, below the post office at Cliff Cottage (April–Oct; ℡01326/280939, ⊛www.coverack.co.uk).

Around Lizard Point

Mainland Britain's southernmost village, called simply **THE LIZARD**, is a nondescript but much visited place, with a handful of shops and B&Bs. A road and footpath lead a mile south to the tip of the promontory, **Lizard Point**, marked by a plain lighthouse. You can follow the coast path a mile or so northwest to the peninsula's best-known beach, **Kynance Cove**, with sheer hundred-foot cliffs, stacks and arches of serpentine rock, and offshore islands. The beach has a wild grandeur, and the water quality is excellent – but keep an eye on the tide, which can cut you off at its flood.

In The Lizard, you can **stay** comfortably at the Victorian *Caerthillian* (℡01326/290019, ⊛www.thecaerthillian.co.uk; no credit cards; ❷), at the centre of the village, or, with seaward views on Penmenner Road, at *Parc Brawse House* (℡01326/290466, ⊛www.cornwall-online.co.uk/parcbrawsehouse; ❷) or ⚐ *Penmenner House* (℡01326/290370, ⊛www.penmennerhouse.com; no credit cards; ❷) – the latter a sumptuous abode where the poet Rupert Brooke once stayed. A Victorian villa right on the coast next to the lighthouse houses an excellent YHA **hostel** (℡0845/371 9550, ⓔlizard@yha.org.uk; closed Nov–March; from £14). You can pick up snacks and **pub meals** at the *Top House* in the village centre.

Mullion and around

Four miles north of Kynance Cove, the inland village of **MULLION** has a fifteenth-to sixteenth-century church dedicated to the Breton **St Mellane** (or Malo), with a dog-door for canine churchgoers. A lane leads a mile and a quarter west to **Mullion Cove**, where a tiny beach is sheltered behind a delightful harbour and more rock stacks. A mile or two north, the sands at **Polurrian** and **Poldhu** are better, however, and attract surfers. At the cliff edge at Poldhu, the **Marconi Monument** marks the spot from which the first transatlantic radio transmission was made in 1901.

Back in Mullion, behind an enclosed garden at the top of Nansmellyon Road, *The Old Vicarage* (℡01326/240898, ⊛www.cornwall-online.co.uk/mullionoldvicarage; no credit cards; ❸) provides charming **accommodation** with period furnishings, while *Campden House*, north of the centre on The Commons, has plainer rooms and lies just a few minutes from Poldhu beach (☏01326/240365; no credit cards; closed Nov–Easter; ❷). In the village centre, you'll find **refreshment** at the sixteenth-century *Old Inn*, Churchtown, which serves bar food and real ales, and has outdoor tables.

Helston and around

The main transport hub and centre for the Lizard peninsula, the unassuming town of **HELSTON** is best known for its **Furry Dance** (or Flora Dance), which dates from the seventeenth century. Held on May 8 (unless this falls on a Sun or Mon, when the procession takes place on the nearest Sat), it's a stately procession of top-hatted men and summer-frocked women performing a solemn dance through the town's streets and gardens. You can learn something about it and absorb plenty of other local history and lore in the eclectic **Helston Folk Museum** (Mon–Sat 10am–1pm, closes 4pm school hols; free), housed in former market buildings behind the Guildhall on Church Street.

For a drink or a snack, head straight for the ✈ *Blue Anchor*, 50 Coinagehall St, a fifteenth-century monastery rest-house, now a snug **pub** with flagstone floors and mellow Spingo beer brewed on the premises in three strengths. Next door, under the same management, *No. 52* provides **meals** (closed daytime & Sun) as well as good-sized **rooms** (☏01326/569334 or 01326/562821, ⓦwww.spingoales.com; ❷).

Three miles southwest of Helston, **PORTHLEVEN** is a sizeable port that once served to export tin ore from the inland mines. There are plenty of good **beaches** within easy reach: the best for swimming are around **Rinsey Head**, three miles north along the coast, including the sheltered **Praa Sands**. One and a quarter miles south of Porthleven, strong currents make it unsafe to swim at the beautiful **Loe Bar**, a strip of shingle which separates the freshwater **Loe Pool** from the sea. The elongated pool is one of two places claiming to be where the sword Excalibur was restored to its watery source (the other is on Bodmin Moor), and there's a path running along its western shore as far as Helston, five miles north, making an excellent **walk**.

The Penwith peninsula

Though more densely populated than the Lizard, the **Penwith peninsula** is a more rugged landscape, with a raw appeal that is still encapsulated by the headland of **Land's End**, despite the commercial paraphernalia superimposed there. The seascapes, the quality of the light and the slow tempo of the local fishing communities made this area a hotbed of artistic activity towards the end of the nineteenth century, when the painters of **Newlyn**, near **Penzance**, established a distinctive school of painting. More innovative figures – among them Ben Nicholson, Barbara Hepworth and Naum Gabo – were soon afterwards to make **St Ives** one of England's liveliest cultural communities, and their enduring influence is illustrated in Tate St Ives, showcasing the modern artists associated with the locality.

Penwith is far more easily toured than the Lizard, with a road circling its coastline and a better network of public transport from the two main towns, St Ives and Penzance, which have most of the accommodation. From Penzance – the terminus for **rail** services from London and Birmingham – **buses** #1, #1A and #501 go to Land's End via Newlyn and Porthcurno, while the #6 and #504 also take in Mousehole. North of Land's End, St Just is served by buses #17, #17A, #17B, #504 and #509. The open-top #300 performs a useful and scenic summer service, following the coast on a long circuit between St Ives and Penzance, stopping at all villages en route. St Ives can be reached by branch rail line or numerous buses from Penzance and Truro.

Hikers might consider walking the eight miles separating Penzance from St Ives along the old St Michael's Way, a waymarked pilgrim's route for which the tourist office in both towns can provide a free route map.

Penzance and around

Occupying a sheltered position at the northwest corner of Mount's Bay, **PENZANCE** has always been a major port, but most traces of the medieval town were obliterated by a Spanish raiding party at the end of the sixteenth century. Today, much of the town has a graceful Georgian character, and it makes an attractive base, though it does get very busy in summer.

Arrival, information and accommodation

Penzance's **train** and **bus stations** are next to each other on the seafront. The **tourist office** (Mon–Fri 9am–5pm, plus Easter to mid-July & Sept Sat 10am–1pm, mid-July to Aug Sat 10am–4pm, Sun 10am–2pm; ⓣ01736/362207, ⓦwww .visit-westcornwall.com) is next to the bus station. For **bike rental** head for the Cycle Centre, 1 New St (ⓣ01736/351671). The library, at 62 Morrab Rd (Mon–Fri 9.30am–6pm, Sat 9.30am–4pm), provides **internet** access.

Morrab Road and the parallel Alexandra Road hold a concentration of Penzance's **accommodation** – places on or around the central Chapel Street are pricier.

Abbey Hotel Abbey St, off Chapel St ⓣ01736/366906, ⓦwww.theabbeyonline.com. Pamper yourself at this seventeenth-century homely hotel owned by former model Jean Shrimpton and her husband. Lashings of old-fashioned comfort, and superb views. ❻

Cornerways 5 Leskinnick St ⓣ01736/364645, ⓦwww.penzance.co.uk/cornerways. Small, friendly B&B very close to the bus and train stations, with simply furnished en-suite rooms. Evening meals and packed lunches are available. ❷

🏃 **Penzance Arts Club** Chapel House, Chapel St ⓣ01736/363761, ⓦwww.penzanceartsclub .co.uk. Formerly the Portuguese consulate, this has a cheerful Bohemian ambience and rooms combining modern art, antique furnishings and great views. There's wi-fi, a good café/restaurant in the basement, plus cabaret, music and poetry nights. ❹

Penzance Backpackers Alexandra Rd ⓣ01736/363836, ⓦwww.pzbackpack.com. Tidy and friendly hostel with dorm beds as well as doubles, plus self-catering, laundry and internet facilities. Dorm beds £15, doubles ❶

Penzance YHA Castle Horneck, Alverton ⓣ0870/770 5992, ⓔpenzance@yha.org.uk. Clean and comfortable hostel housed in a Georgian mansion, a two-mile hike from the station up Market Jew St into Alverton Rd, then right at the *Pirate Inn* (or take bus #5 or #6 from Penzance station as far as the *Pirate Inn*). Dorm beds from £14, camping available.

Union Hotel Chapel St ⓣ01736/362319, ⓦwww .unionhotel.co.uk. This centrally located Georgian hotel is a bit old-fashioned and tired-looking, but it has loads of atmosphere and there are terrific views from some rooms. ❷

The Town

Climbing up from the harbour and the train and bus stations, **Market Jew Street** (from *Marghas Jew*, meaning "Thursday Market") is Penzance's main traffic artery. At the top, in front of the silver-domed Victorian **Market House**, stands a statue of **Humphry Davy** (1778–1829), the local woodcarver's son who pioneered the science of electrochemistry and invented the life-saving miners' safety lamp. Turn left here into **Chapel Street**, which has some of the town's finest buildings, including the flamboyant **Egyptian House**, built in 1835 to house a geological museum but subsequently abandoned until its restoration thirty years ago. Across the street, the **Union Hotel** dates from the seventeenth century, and originally held the town's assembly rooms; the news of Admiral Nelson's victory at Trafalgar and the death of Nelson himself were first announced from the minstrels' gallery here in 1805.

Off Chapel and Market Jew streets in Princes Street, an old telephone exchange houses a modern art gallery and education centre, **The Exchange** (Mon–Sat 10am–5pm, closed Mon in winter; free), worth a visit for its sleek design and regular exhibitions. You'll find a more traditional collection of art at **Penlee House Gallery and Museum** (Mon–Sat 10/10.30am–4.30/5pm; £3, free on Sat; Ⓦwww.penleehouse.org.uk), off Morrab Road (walk up from the Promenade or down from Alverton St, a continuation of Market Jew St). The gallery holds the biggest collection of the works of the Newlyn School – impressionistic harbour scenes, sometimes sentimentalized but often bathed in an evocatively luminous light. There are frequent exhibitions, and also displays on local history.

On the seafront, bulging out of the Promenade into Mount's Bay, the Art Deco **Jubilee Pool** (late May to early Sept daily 10.30am–6pm; £4) is a tidal, salt water (though chlorinated) open-air swimming pool, built to mark the Silver Jubilee of George V in 1935. Non-swimmers can stroll around (£1.30) to get a closer view of the pool and bay.

From the Promenade, it's an easy walk to **NEWLYN**, Cornwall's biggest fishing port, lying immediately south of Penzance. The **art gallery**, near the harbour at 24 New Rd (Mon–Sat 10am–5pm, closed Mon in winter; free), merits a visit for its exhibitions of contemporary work.

Eating and drinking

Penzance has a decent range of **restaurants** scattered about town, as well as modern bars and traditional **pubs**.

Admiral Benbow 46 Chapel St. Crammed with gaudy ships' figureheads and other nautical items, this pub offers standard bar meals and heaps of atmosphere.

Archie Brown's Bread St. You can get tasty vegetarian and wholefood dishes – for example quiche and homity pie (£6–7) – at this café above a health shop off Causeway Head. Occasionally open for special theme nights, otherwise daytime only and closed Sun.

The Boatshed Wharf Rd ☏01736/368845. A relaxed snack stop during the day, this café-bar with granite walls and ship's timbers offers tasty vegetarian dishes, meat and seafood (all around £10–15) as well as pizzas in the evening. Some tables outside. Closed lunchtime Mon–Wed.

Harris's 46 New St ☏01736/364408. Traditional fine dining is offered at this formal restaurant, with the accent on seafood. Main courses are around £19. Leave room to sample one of the memorable desserts. Closed Sun, plus Mon in winter.

Renaissance Café Wharfside Centre, entered from Market Jew St or the Promenade. Casual and inexpensive café/restaurant with a small outdoor terrace that offers tapas (among other meals), great views over Mount's Bay and wi-fi access. Closed Sun eve.

Turk's Head 49 Chapel St. The town's oldest inn, reputedly dating back to the thirteenth century, has a maze of low-ceilinged rooms and a garden. Good beer and food served.

St Michael's Mount

The medieval chimneys and towers of **St Michael's Mount** (late March to June, Sept & Oct Mon–Fri & Sun 10.30am–5pm; July & Aug 10.30am–5.30pm; Nov to late March guided tours Tues & Fri at 11am & 2pm, book at ☏01736/710507; £7; NT) are a prominent feature of Mount's Bay. The fortress-isle lies a couple of hundred yards offshore of the village Marazion, five miles east of Penzance and reachable on frequent buses. A vision of the archangel Michael led to the building of a church on this granite pile around the fifth century, and within three centuries a Celtic monastery had been founded here. The present building originated as a chapel, constructed in the eleventh century by Edward the Confessor. It was then handed over to the Benedictine monks of Brittany's Mont St Michel, whose island abbey – also founded after a vision of St Michael – was the model for this one. The complex was appropriated by Henry V during the Hundred Years' War, and it became a fortress after its dissolution a century later. After the Civil War, when it was used to store arms for the Royalist forces, it became the residence of the St Aubyn family, who still live in the castle.

A good number of the fortress's buildings date from the twelfth century, but the later additions are more interesting, such as the battlemented **chapel** and the seventeenth-century decorations of the **Chevy Chase Room**, so called after the medieval hunting ballad, which is illustrated by a simple plaster frieze on the walls. Other rooms are crowded with paintings and general memorabilia.

At low tide the promontory can be approached on foot via a cobbled causeway; at high tide there are boats from Marazion (£1.50).

Mousehole to Land's End

Accounts vary as to the derivation of the name of **MOUSEHOLE** (pronounced "Mowzle"), though it may come from a smugglers' cave just south of town. In any case, the name evokes perfectly this minuscule harbour, cradled in the arms of a granite breakwater three miles south of Penzance. The village attracts more visitors than it can handle, so hang around until the crowds have departed before exploring its tight tangle of lanes. Among them, you'll come across Mousehole's oldest house, the fourteenth-century **Keigwin House**, a survivor of the sacking of the village by Spaniards in 1595. Finish off with a drink at the harbourside *Ship Inn*, which also has **meals** and en-suite **rooms** (℡01736/731234, Ⓦwww.shipmousehole.co.uk; ❸).

Eight miles west round the coast, **PORTHCURNO** is one of Penwith's best bathing spots. The name means "Port Cornwall", but its beach of tiny white shells suggests privacy and isolation rather than the movement of ships. Steep steps lead up from here to the cliff-hewn **Minack Theatre**, created in the 1930s and since enlarged to hold 750 seats (though the basic Greek-inspired design has remained intact). The spectacular backdrop of Porthcurno Bay makes this one of the country's most inspiring theatres. The summer season lasts seventeen weeks from May to September, presenting a gamut of plays, opera and musicals, with tickets costing just £8–9.50 (℡01736/810181, Ⓦwww.minack.com). Bring a cushion and a rug. The **Exhibition Centre** (daily: April–Oct 9.30am–5.30pm; Nov–March 10am–4pm; closed during performances; £3) allows you to view the theatre and illustrates the story of its creation.

The peculiar white pyramid on the shore to the east of Porthcurno marks the spot where the first transatlantic cables were laid in 1880. On the headland beyond lies an Iron Age fort, **Treryn Dinas**, close to the famous rocking stone called **Logan's Rock**, a seventy-tonne monster that was knocked off its perch by a nephew of playwright Oliver Goldsmith and a gang of sailors in 1824. Somehow they replaced the stone, but it never rocked again.

Land's End

The best way to reach **Land's End** is unarguably on foot along the coastal path. Although nothing can completely destroy the impact of this approach to the extreme western tip of England, the theme park behind this majestic headland comes close to irreparably violating the spirit of the place. The trivializing **Land's End Experience** (daily from 10/10.30am–3.30/5pm, closes later in Aug: call ℡0871/720 2244 to check) substitutes a tawdry panoply of lasers and unconvincing sound effects for the real open-air experience (£3–4 for individual attractions, £10 for all). The location, however, is a public right of way (though you'll have to pay to use the car park). Once past the theme park, nature takes over: turf-covered cliffs sixty feet high provide a platform to view the Irish Lady, the Armed Knight, Dr Syntax Head and the rest of the Land's End outcrops, beyond which you can spot the Longships lighthouse, a mile and a half out to sea, sometimes the Wolf Rock lighthouse, nine miles southwest, and even the Isles of Scilly, 28 miles away.

Whitesand Bay to Pendeen

To the north of Land's End the rounded granite cliffs fall away at **Whitesand Bay** to reveal a glistening mile-long shelf of beach that offers the best swimming on the Penwith peninsula. The rollers make for good surfing and boards can be rented at **Sennen Cove**, the more popular southern end of the beach. There are a few **B&Bs** here, including *Pengelly House* (℡01736/871866, ⊛www.pengellyhouse.com; no credit cards; ❷), offering three rooms with a shared bathroom but no breakfast. If you don't mind staying a short distance inland, there's *Whitesands Hotel* (℡01736/871776, ⊛www.whitesandshotel.co.uk), with themed en-suite guestrooms (❹) as well as bunkrooms (£21 per person) and tipis and yurts (from £16 per person). The **restaurant** and grill is open to all and has snacks, grills and seafood dishes (£10–17), and daily barbecues in summer.

Cape Cornwall, three miles northward, shelters another good beach, overlooked by an old mining chimney. Half a mile inland, the grimly grey village of **ST JUST-IN-PENWITH** was a centre of the tin and copper industry, and the rows of trim cottages radiating out from Bank Square are redolent of the close-knit community that once existed here. Just off the square, miracle plays were once staged on **Plen-an-Gwary**, a grassy open-air theatre that was later used by Methodist preachers as well as Cornish wrestlers.

Among St Just's small choice of **accommodation**, try *The Old Fire Station*, Nancherrow Terrace (℡01736/786463, ⊛www.oldfirestationstjust.co.uk; ❷), which has clean, modern en-suite rooms. There's a YHA **hostel** on the southern outskirts of the village (℡0845/371 9643, ✉landsend@yha.org.uk; from £14) – take the left fork past the post office. There's also an excellent secluded **campsite**, just outside the hamlet of Kelynack a couple of miles south of St Just: *Kelynack Caravan and Camping Park* (℡01736/787633, ⊛www.kelynackcaravans.co.uk; closed Nov–Easter), one of the few sheltered sites on Penwith, which also has B&B (❷) available all year. *Kegen Teg*, at 12 Market Square, serves mainly organic, vegetarian and locally sourced snacks and **meals** (℡01736/788562; closed eve, Sun Oct–Easter & all Jan). Just off Bank Square, the traditional *Star Inn* is the best of the **pubs**.

A couple of miles north of St Just, outside **PENDEEN**, you can get a close-up view of the Cornish mining industry at **Geevor Tin Mine** (daily except Sat 9am–4/5pm; last entry 1hr before closing; £9.50), where you can tour the surface machinery, explore an underground mine and visit the museum.

Zennor and around

East of Pendeen, the landscape is all rolling moorland and an abundance of granite, the chief building material of **ZENNOR**. D.H. Lawrence and Frieda came to live here in 1916 and were soon joined by John Middleton Murry and Katherine Mansfield, the intention being to form a writers' community. The new arrivals soon left for a more sheltered haven near Falmouth, but Lawrence stayed on to write *Women in Love*, spending in all a year and a half in Zennor before being given notice to quit by the local constabulary, who suspected Lawrence and his German wife of unpatriotic sympathies. His Cornish experiences were later described in *Kangaroo*.

At the bottom of the village, the **Wayside Museum** is dedicated to Cornish life from prehistoric times (Easter–May & Oct Mon–Fri & Sun 11am–5pm; June–Sept

The **Isles of Scilly** are a compact archipelago of about a hundred islands 28 miles southwest of Land's End, none of them bigger than three miles across, and only five of them inhabited – **St Mary's**, **Tresco**, **Bryher**, **St Martin's** and **St Agnes**. Free of traffic, theme parks and crowds, they offer a welcome respite from the mainland tourist trail.

In the annals of folklore, the Scillies are the peaks of the submerged land of Lyonnesse, a fertile plain that extended west from Penwith before the ocean broke in, drowning the land and leaving only one survivor to tell the tale. Geologically, the islands form part of the same granite mass as Land's End, Bodmin Moor and Dartmoor, and, though they rarely rise above a hundred feet and are largely treeless, they possess a remarkable variety of landscape. Each one has a distinctive character, at every turn revealing new perspectives over the extraordinary rocky seascape. The energizing briny air is filled with the cries of sea birds, while the **beaches** are well-nigh irresistible, ranging from minute coves to vast untrammelled strands – though swimmers must steel themselves for the chilly water. The waters hereabouts, free of plankton or silt, are said to be among the clearest in Britain, offering some of the country's best **diving** sites; non-divers too can go snorkelling among the seals.

For all information, including diving operator details, contact the **tourist office** on Hugh Street, Hugh Town, St Mary's (Easter–Oct Mon–Sat 8.30am–6pm, May–Sept also Sun 9am–2pm; Nov–Easter Mon–Fri 9am–4.30/5pm; ☎01720/424031, ⓦwww .simplyscilly.co.uk). Between May and September, on Wednesday and Friday evenings, islanders gather to watch the **gig races**, performed by six vessels over thirty feet long, and some over a hundred years old. The usual route starts at Nut Rock, to the east of Samson, and finishes at St Mary's Quay. You can follow the action from launches that leave about twenty minutes before the start of each race – see boards on St Mary's Quay or contact the tourist office.

Getting there

The islands are accessible by sea or air. **Boats** to St Mary's, operated by Isles of Scilly Travel (☎0845/710 5555, ⓦwww.islesofscilly-travel.co.uk), depart from Penzance's South Pier between Easter and October, the crossing taking about two and three-quarter hours. Saver returns, subject to certain restrictions, cost £80. The main departure points for **flights** (also operated by Isles of Scilly Travel) are Land's End (near St Just), Newquay, Exeter, Bristol and Southampton; in winter, there are departures only from Land's End and Newquay. From Land's End, a Saver return fare costs £125. British International (☎01736/363871, ⓦwww.islesofscillyhelicopter .com) runs year-round helicopter flights (20min) to St Mary's and Tresco from the heliport a mile east of Penzance; saver returns are £146. Note that there are no crossings by sea or air on Sunday.

Accommodation, eating and drinking

Although you can get a taste of the islands' highlights on a day-trip from Penzance, the Scillies deserve a much longer visit. Apart from the high cost of reaching them, the chief drawback is the shortage of **accommodation**, making advance booking essential in summer and school holidays. The vast majority of places to stay are on St Mary's, while Bryher, St Martin's and St Agnes each have three or four B&Bs only, and Tresco has just two very swanky choices. Prices are generally steep, especially at the trio of elite **hotels**: Tresco's *Island Hotel* (☎01720/422883, ⓦwww.tresco.co .uk), Bryher's *Hell Bay Hotel* (☎01720/422947, ⓦwww.tresco.co.uk) and St Martin's *St Martin's on the Isle* (☎01720/422090, ⓦwww.stmartinshotel.co.uk), all ⑧ and closed in winter.

As for **B&Bs**, most are in the ③–④ category in summer, less in the low season. Note that many offer – and often insist on – a dinner, bed and breakfast package, which is (apart from on St Mary's) the most convenient option in any case, considering the tiny choice of places to eat on the off islands. Many close in winter, but there's usually enough to cater for the trickle of visitors who come in these months. The alternatives are a **self-catering** deal, almost always available only by the week (you'll need to book some time in advance), and **camping**. There are very basic sites on St Mary's, Bryher, St Martin's and St Agnes, mostly unsheltered and all closed in winter; camping elsewhere is not allowed.

Groceries are available on all five inhabited islands (though cost more than on the mainland), and there are places to eat on each, though only St Mary's has any great choice. The best **restaurants** are attached to the above-mentioned hotels, though there are a few other places worth seeking out. In addition, each island also has at least one **pub** serving food, among which special mention should be made of the *New Inn* on Tresco, which also provides high-quality restaurant meals, and the *Turk's Head* on St Agnes, famous for its pasties.

Exploring the islands

Apart from beach and sea, the main attractions of the Isles of Scilly include Cornwall's greatest concentration of **prehistoric remains**, some fabulous **rock formations**, and masses of **flowers**, nurtured by the equable climate and long hours of sunshine (the archipelago's name means "Sun Isles"). Along with tourism, the main source of income here is flower-growing, and the heaths and pathways of the islands are also dense with a profusion of wildflowers, from marigolds and gorse to sea thrift, trefoil and poppies, not to mention a host of more exotic species introduced by visiting foreign vessels.

The majority of the resident population of just over two thousand is concentrated on the biggest island, **St Mary's**, which has the lion's share of facilities in its capital, **Hugh Town**, and the richest trove of prehistoric sites. The island has a limited bus service, but cycling is the ideal way to get around – you can **rent bikes** from St Mary's Bike Hire on The Strand, Hugh Town (☏01720/422289, or 07796/638506 in winter).

The "off islands", as the other inhabited members of the group are known, are always accessible on inter-island launches. The largest, **Tresco**, presents an appealing contrast between the orderly landscape around the remains of its ancient abbey and the bleak, untended northern half. The exuberant **Tresco Abbey Gardens** (daily 10am–4pm; £10), hosting an impressive collection of subtropical plants, are the archipelago's most popular visitor attraction. West of Tresco, **Bryher** has the smallest population, the slow routines of island life quickening only in the tourist season. The bracing, back-to-nature feel here is nowhere more evident than on the exposed western shore, where **Hell Bay** sees some formidable Atlantic storms. East of Tresco, **St Martin's** has a reputation as the least striking of the Scillies with the most introverted population, but its white-sand beaches are as majestically wild as any – Par Beach deserves a special mention – there are stunning views from its cliffy northeastern end, and the surrounding waters are much favoured by scuba enthusiasts. On the southwest rim of the main group, the tidy lanes and picturesque cottages of **St Agnes** are nicely complemented by the weathered boulders and craggy headlands of its indented shoreline.

A visit to the isles would be incomplete without a sortie to the **uninhabited islands**, sanctuaries for seals, puffins and a host of other marine birdlife. On the largest of them, **Samson**, you can poke around prehistoric and more recent remains that testify to former settlement. Some of the smaller islets are worth visiting for their delightfully deserted beaches, though the majority amount to no more than bare rocks. This chaotic profusion of rocks of all shapes and sizes, each bearing a name, is densest at the archipelago's extremities – the **Western Rocks**, lashed by ferocious seas and the cause of innumerable wrecks over the years, and the milder **Eastern Isles**.

Mon–Fri & Sun 10.30am–5.30pm but open daily during summer school hols; £4.75). At the top of the lane, the **church of St Sennen** displays a sixteenth-century bench carving of a mermaid who, according to local legend, was so entranced by the singing of a chorister that she lured him down to the sea, from where he never returned.

Next to the church, a fairly level path leads less than a mile northwest to the sea at **Zennor Head**, where there is some awe-inspiring cliff scenery above the sandy **Pendour Cove** (the fabled home of Zennor's mermaid). A couple of miles southeast of Zennor, located on a windy hillside off the minor road to Penzance, the Iron Age village of **Chysauster** (daily: April–June & Sept 10am–5pm; July & Aug 10am–6pm; Oct 10am–4pm; £3.20; EH) is the best-preserved ancient settlement in the southwest. Dating from about the first century BC, it contains two rows of four buildings, each consisting of a courtyard with small chambers leading off it, and a garden that was presumably used for growing vegetables.

Back in the village, if you don't mind sleeping up to six to a room, the ⚓ *Old Chapel Backpackers Hostel* makes a fun **place to stay**, right next to the Wayside Museum (☎01736/798307, ⓌWwww.backpackers.co.uk/zennor); bunkbeds cost £17.50, and there's a family room too (❷). Sea views from the rooms and a congenial atmosphere are added attractions, and a café provides meals for guests and visitors. The *Tinners Arms* is a cosy **place to eat** and drink, and west along the coast at Treen, the *Gurnard's Head* (☎01736/796928, ⓌWwww.gurnardshead .co.uk; ❹) is a relaxed gastropub with smallish rooms and simple but expertly prepared food, for which booking is recommended.

St Ives

East of Zennor, the road runs four hilly miles to the steeply built town of **ST IVES**, a place that has smoothly undergone the transition from major fishing port to holiday haunt. Virginia Woolf, who spent every summer here up to the age of 12, described St Ives as "a windy, noisy, fishy, vociferous, narrow-streeted town; the colour of a mussel or a limpet; like a bunch of rough shell fish clustered on a grey wall together". By the time the pilchard reserves dried up around the early years of the last century, the town was beginning to attract a vibrant **artists' colony**, precursors of the wave later headed by Ben Nicholson, his wife Barbara Hepworth, Naum Gabo and the potter Bernard Leach, who in the 1960s were followed by a third wave including Terry Frost, Peter Lanyon and Patrick Heron.

Arrival and information

To reach St Ives by **train**, change at St Erth on the main line to Penzance or take a direct service from Penzance (though most trains from Penzance still involve a change at St Erth). Regular and frequent **buses** connect Penzance with St Ives, which you can reach from Truro on #14 and National Express buses. The train station is off Porthminster Beach, just south of the bus station on Station Hill. The **tourist office** is in the Guildhall, in the nearby Street-an-Pol (June–Sept Mon–Fri 9am–5pm, Sat 10am–4pm, Sun 10am–2pm; Oct–May Mon–Fri 9am–5pm, Sat 10am–1pm; ☎01736/796297, ⓌWwww.visit-westcornwall.com). You can rent **surfing equipment** at Porthmeor Beach and from surf specialists on Fore Street and by the harbour. The **St Ives Festival**, mainly featuring folk, jazz and world music but also taking in films and theatre, takes place over two weeks in September (ⓌWwww.stivesseptemberfestival.co.uk).

Accommodation

Even with West Cornwall's greatest concentration of hotels and guesthouses, St Ives can still run short of available **accommodation** in peak season, and advance booking is essential. Most of the places listed below are central, and the majority offer one or two parking spaces.

Hotels and B&Bs

Cornerways The Square ☎01736/796706, ⓦwww.cornerwaysstives.com. Daphne du Maurier once stayed in this tastefully modern cottage conversion, which has friendly management and airy rooms with black slate bathrooms. No credit cards. ❸

The Nook Ayr, off Ayr Terrace ☎01736/795913, ⓦwww.nookstives.co.uk. In a quiet lane at the top of a steep hill a 15min walk from the centre, this modern B&B has spotless, well-equipped rooms, free wi-fi, a decked patio and parking spaces. ❸

Organic Panda 1 Pednolver Terrace ☎01736/793890, ⓦwww.organicpanda.co.uk. As the name suggests, everything is organic and sustainable in this stylish B&B close to the stations, including the plush cotton bedding and bamboo towels. There's free wi-fi and delicious breakfasts. No under-3s. ❹

Primrose Valley Porthminster Beach ☎01736/794939, ⓦwww.primroseonline .co.uk. Modernized Edwardian villa just above Porthminster Beach with friendly staff and fresh, light rooms. Three- or four-day minimum stays in July and Aug. ❺

Hostel and campsites

Ayr Higher Ayr ☎01736/795855, ⓦwww .ayrholidaypark.co.uk. Large complex with caravans and holiday homes, half a mile west of the centre above Porthmeor Beach, with good sea views. It's near the coast path, and buses #339 and #516 stop close by.

Higher Chellew Nancledra ☎01736/364532, ⓦwww.higherchellewcamping.co.uk. Out-of-town site, cheaper than the *Ayr*, with basic but clean facilities including washing machines. It's on the B3311, equidistant between St Ives and Penzance (bus #516). Closed Nov–Easter.

St Ives Backpackers The Stennack ☎01736/799444, ⓦwww.backpackers.co.uk /st-ives. Usefully located in the centre of St Ives, this hostel in a restored Wesleyan chapel school from 1845 has a games area, barbecues, a kitchen and wi-fi internet. Dorms have 4–8 beds for around £18 per head in peak season, and there are also double and twin rooms (❶).

The Town

Dozens of galleries are sandwiched between the town's restaurants and bars, but the only unmissable one is **Tate St Ives**, overlooking Porthmeor Beach on the north side of town (March–Oct daily 10am–5.20pm; Nov–Feb Tues–Sun 10am–4.20pm; closes two or three times a year for about ten days – call to check; £5.75, or £8.75 with Hepworth Museum; ☎01736/796226, ⓦwww.tate.org.uk/stives). The airy, gleaming white building is the perfect setting for the various paintings, sculptures and ceramics on display, most of which date from the period 1925 to 1975, though there are also specially commissioned contemporary works on view. The museum's rooftop **café** is one of the best places in town for tea and cake.

A short distance away on Barnoon Hill, the **Barbara Hepworth Museum** (same times as Tate; £4.75, or £8.75 with the Tate) gives another insight into the local arts scene. One of the foremost non-figurative sculptors of her time, Hepworth lived in the building from 1949 until her death in a studio fire in 1975. Apart from the sculptures, which are arranged in positions chosen by Hepworth in the house and garden, the museum has masses of background on her art, from photos and letters to catalogues and reviews.

Devotees of Bernard Leach's Japanese-inspired ceramics can visit his former studio, the **Leach Pottery**, in the Higher Stennack neighbourhood, three-quarters of a mile outside St Ives on the Zennor road (Mon–Sat 10am–4.30/5pm; Sun 11am–4pm; £4.50). Some examples of Leach's work are on display here, alongside pieces by his wife Janet Leach, Shoji Hamada and Michael Cardew, as well as more contemporary artworks.

The wide expanse of **Porthmeor Beach** dominates the northern side of St Ives, the stone houses tumbling almost onto the yellow sands. Unusually for a town beach, the water quality is excellent, and the rollers make it popular with surfers;

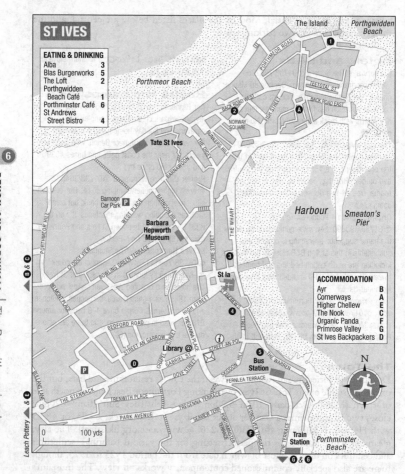

ST IVES

EATING & DRINKING
Alba	3
Blas Burgerworks	5
The Loft	2
Porthgwidden Beach Café	1
Porthminster Café	6
St Andrews Street Bistro	4

The Island

Porthgwidden Beach

Porthmeor Beach

Tate St Ives

Barnoon Car Park

Barbara Hepworth Museum

Harbour

Smeaton's Pier

ACCOMMODATION
Ayr	B
Cornerways	A
Higher Chellew	E
The Nook	C
Organic Panda	F
Primrose Valley	G
St Ives Backpackers	D

Library @

Bus Station

N

Train Station

Porthminster Beach

Leach Pottery ◀ & E

0   100 yds

there's also a good open-air café here. South of the station, the broader, usually less crowded **Porthminster Beach** is another favourite spot for sunbathing and swimming, while, heading east out of town, you'll find a string of magnificent golden beaches lining **St Ives Bay** – the strand is especially fine on the far side of the port of Hayle, at the mouth of the eponymous river.

Eating and drinking

The year-round tourist industry has given St Ives a dazzling range of **restaurants**, mostly concentrating on seafood. **Bar** life is fairly low-level, however, and there's little in the way of café culture.

Alba The Wharf ☎ 01736/797222. Sleek modern harbourside restaurant in a converted lifeboat house. Fixed-price menus (£13.50 and £16.50), available at lunchtime and in the evening before 7pm, include seafood and free-range roast chicken. Otherwise, mains are around £14.

Blas Burgerworks The Warren ☎ 01736/797272. Alternative burger-bar doling out fantastic burgers using local ingredients (£7.50–10). There's just one small room with four communal tables made from found or reclaimed wood. No reservations. Closed Sun & Mon in winter.

The Loft Norway Lane ⊤01736/794204. Bright and stylish eatery set in a long, conservatory-like space with an outdoor terrace. The Seafood Marinière (£17) is one of the most popular dishes; non-seafood items include duck, beef fillet and roast pepper with couscous. Lunch and early-evening menus cost £13 and £16. Closed Oct–Easter Sun & Mon.

Porthgwidden Beach Café Porthgwidden Beach ⊤01736/796791. A simpler and cheaper offshoot of the *Porthminster Café*, this beachside place with a stone terrace offers burgers, mussels, pastas and steaks, mostly £8–12. Breakfasts include scrambled egg and smoked salmon (£5). Nov–Easter closed Sun eve, all Mon & Tues–Thurs eve.

Porthminster Café Porthminster Beach ⊤01736/795352. With its sun deck and beach location, this makes a superb spot for coffees, cream teas and full meals. Seafood predominates, ranging from first-class fish and chips to monkfish curry. Prices are steep (£15–19 for mains). Nov–Easter closed Sun eve, all Mon & Tues–Thurs eve.

St Andrews Street Bistro 16 St Andrews St ⊤01736/797074. Rugs on the wooden floor, tall white walls filled with objets d'art and cool music help to create a low-lit, boho ambience. The food is good, with dishes such as Lebanese carrot pâté and chicken-and-apricot tagine. The two-course menu costs £15, and you can bring your own wine. Closed daytime, also Sun–Wed Oct–Easter.

Cornwall's north coast

Though generally harsher than the county's southern seaboard, the north Cornish coast is punctuated by some of the finest beaches in England, the most popular of which are set around **Newquay**, the surfers' capital. Other major holiday centres are to be found down the coast at the ex-mining town of **St Agnes** and north around the Camel estuary, where the port of **Padstow** makes a good base for some remarkable beaches as well as a fine inland walk. North of the Camel, the coast is an almost unbroken line of cliffs as far as the Devon border, the gaunt, exposed terrain making a melodramatic setting for **Tintagel**, though the wide strand at **Bude** attracts legions of surfers and holidaying families.

Newquay is the terminus for the cross-peninsula **train** route from Par, while the main line to Penzance stops at Redruth and Camborne. Redruth is more useful for St Agnes, connected by **bus** #315 (not Sun). Service #403 (not Sun) plies between Truro, St Agnes, Perranporth and Newquay. Frequent services link Newquay with Truro, while bus #510 connects Newquay with Okehampton and Exeter. Service #555 runs between Padstow and Bodmin, and #556 tracks the coast between Newquay and Padstow.

North of Padstow, bus #584 serves Polzeath and Port Isaac, #594 links Boscastle and Tintagel, and #595 connects Boscastle and Bude. Finally, buses #X9 and #599 run between Bude, Okehampton and Exeter, while National Express coaches run daily between Penzance, St Ives, Camborne, Redruth, Newquay, Bodmin and Plymouth, and Megabus run services between Newquay, Plymouth, Exeter and London.

St Agnes and around

East of St Ives Bay, surfers and other beach cognoscenti congregate at **Portreath** and, three miles further up the coast, **Porthtowan**, which together enjoy some of the cleanest water on this stretch. A couple of miles east of Porthtowan, **ST AGNES** makes a useful base. Though surrounded by ruined engine houses, the village gives little hint of the conditions in which its population once lived, the uniform grey ex-miners' cottages now fronted by immaculate flower-filled gardens, and its steep, straggling streets busy in summer with troops of holiday-makers.

At the end of a steep valley below St Agnes, **Trevaunance Cove** is the site of several failed attempts to create a harbour for the town, and now has a fine sandy beach. West of the village lies one of Cornwall's most famous vantage points, **St Agnes Beacon**, 630ft high, from which views extend inland to Bodmin Moor and even across the peninsula to St Michael's Mount. To the northwest, the headland of **St Agnes Head** has the area's largest colony of breeding kittiwakes, and the nearby cliffs also shelter fulmars and guillemots, while grey seals are a common sight offshore.

Three miles north of St Agnes, **PERRANPORTH** lies at the southern end of Perran Beach, a three-mile expanse of sand enhanced by caves and natural rock arches. It's very popular with surfers – boards and equipment are available to rent in summer.

Practicalities

The St Agnes **tourist office** is at 18 Churchtown (Mon–Sat 9.30am–5pm, also Sun in summer 10am–4pm; reduced hours in winter; ℡01872/554150, ⍟www .st-agnes.com).

The town's good choice of **accommodation** includes the relaxed ⚓ *Malthouse* in Peterville (the lower part of the village), an eighteenth-century brewing-house where you'll find rooms with shared or en-suite bathrooms, big breakfasts and use of the kitchen (℡01872/553318, ⍟www.themalthousestagnes.co.uk; no credit cards; ❷). On Penwinnick Road, *Penkerris* (℡01872/552262, ⍟www.penkerris .co.uk; ❷) is a spacious, creeper-clad house, with log fires in winter, a garden and home-cooked dinners. At Trevaunance Cove, the whitewashed seventeenth-century *Driftwood Spars* (℡01872/552428, ⍟www.driftwoodspars.com; ❸) has a range of smart, modern rooms – sea-facing ones cost more. On the cliff top at the southern end of Perranporth beach, a former coastguard station houses a YHA **hostel** (℡0845/371 9755, ✉perranporth@yha.org.uk; from £14), enjoying superb views.

You can have bar food or full **meals** in the dining room and three bars at the *Driftwood Spars*, which has live music at weekends. In St Agnes's centre, the *Tap House* **pub** on Peterville Square attracts a young and lively crowd with its eclectic menu and regular live music.

Newquay

It is difficult to imagine a lineage for **NEWQUAY** that extends more than a few decades, but the "new quay" was built in the fifteenth century in what was already a long-established fishing port more colourfully known as Towan Blistra. The town was given a boost in the nineteenth century when its harbour was expanded for coal import and a railway was constructed across the peninsula for china clay shipments. With the trains came a swelling stream of seasonal visitors, drawn to the town's superb position on a knuckle of cliffs overlooking fine golden sands and Atlantic rollers, natural advantages which have made Newquay the premier resort of north Cornwall.

Arrival, information and accommodation

Newquay's **airport** is five miles northeast of town at St Mawgan (℡01637/860600, ⍟www.newquaycornwallairport.com; bus #556). The town's **train station** is off Cliff Road, just east of the centre, and the **bus station** is on Manor Road. Five minutes from the bus station, Newquay's **tourist office** is on Marcus Hill (April–Sept Mon–Fri 9am–5.30pm, Sat & Sun 10am–4pm; Oct–March Mon–Fri 9am–4pm, Sat & Sun 10am–3pm; ℡01637/854020, ⍟www.visitnewquay.org) has **internet** access. The town has a plethora of **accommodation** in every category, though vacancies can still be scarce in July and August.

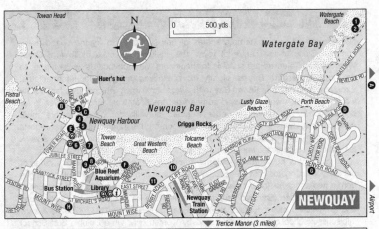

ACCOMMODATION				EATING		DRINKING & NIGHTLIFE			
Goofys	B	Pengilley Guest House	F	The Beach Hut	1	Barracuda	10	Koola	8
Harbour Hotel	C	Porth Beach	D	Café Irie	6	The Beach	9	Red Lion	3
Matt's Surf Lodge	H	Rockpool Cottage	E	Fifteen Cornwall	2	Berties	11	Sailors	4
The Metro	G	Trevelgue	A	New Harbour Restaurant	5	Fort Inn	7		

Hotels and B&Bs

Harbour Hotel North Quay Hill ☏01637/873040, ⓦwww.harbourhotel.co.uk. Small, luxurious hotel with fantastic views from its stylish rooms, all of which have balconies. There's a good restaurant, too. ⑤

The Metro 142 Henver Rd ☏01637/871638, ⓦwww.metronewquay.co.uk. Smart, contemporary B&B a mile or so east of the centre, with leather sofas, widescreen TVs and internet access. Buffet-style continental breakfasts are available until 11am, and you can use the breakfast room during the day. Closed Dec–Easter. ③

Pengilley Guest House 12 Trebarwith Crescent ☏01637/872039, ⓦwww.pengilley-guesthouse.co .uk. Very close to the main town beach, this amiable B&B has tasteful en-suite rooms. No credit cards. ②

Rockpool Cottage 92 Fore St ☏01637/870848, ⓦwww.rockpoolcottage.co.uk. Run by a former surfing champion, this B&B is convenient for the town centre and Fistral Beach. Breakfast is served in your room, where there are mini-fridges and en-suite bathrooms with good showers. Closed Jan–Easter. ②

Hostels and campsites

Goofys 5 Headland Rd ☏01637/872684, ⓦwww.goofys.co.uk. Family-run hostel, more minimalist and stylish than most, with single, double and bunk beds in clean, en-suite rooms costing £32.50–40 per person in peak season, when there's a three- or four-night minimum stay. It's very close to Fistral Beach and the harbour, with sea views. Included in the price are self-service breakfasts, a modern kitchen and a child-friendly lounge.

Matt's Surf Lodge 110 Mount Wise ☏01637/874651, ⓦwww.matts-surf-lodge.co.uk. Set slightly further out than other hostels, this place has free tea and coffee available all day and a licensed bar. In summer, dorm beds are £20–25 and en-suite double rooms ①, but prices in winter and for longer stays are much lower.

Porth Beach Porth ☏01637/876531, ⓦwww .porthbeach.co.uk. Located behind Porth Beach to the east of town, this campsite is clean with good washing facilities and free hot showers. Singles, couples or families only. Closed Nov–Feb.

Trevelgue Trevelgue Rd ☏0845/130 1515, ⓦwww.trevelgue.co.uk. Beyond Porth Beach, this place separates its caravan and family sites from groups. There's a restaurant, a large indoor pool and nightly entertainment in summer, though facilities are minimal in winter. Closed Nov & Dec.

The town and beaches

Aside from the allure of the sea, there are few specific sights in Newquay. The centre of town is a somewhat tacky parade of shops and fast-food outlets, partly

Surfing in Newquay

Newquay's surfing buzz tempts scores of non-surfheads to try their hand every summer. Close to the centre of town, the sheltered beaches of **Towan**, **Great Western** and **Tolcarne** are suitable for beginners with bodyboards, while further to the north **Watergate Bay** is slightly more exposed, so good for intermediates. Experts should head for **Fistral Bay** to the west of the town, which enjoys fast hollow waves, especially when the wind comes from the southwest, and is the venue for competitions. The beach is under lifeguard surveillance; conditions are most dangerous at low tide, especially mid-afternoon on the spring tide. For surf reports and webcam images, see any one of a number of websites – for example ⓦwww .a1surf.com or magicseaweed.com.

You can rent or buy **surfing equipment** from Newquay's beach stalls or a range of outlets in town; boards cost £5–15 a day, wetsuits around the same. **Surf tuition** ranges from a two-and-a-half-hour session (around £25) to a week (around £130). The British Surfing Association (ⓦwww.britsurf.co.uk) provides a list of approved schools, clubs and events, and offers courses at Fistral Beach. Hibiscus (ⓣ01637/879374, ⓦwww .hibiscussurfschool.co.uk) is run for and by women only, while Dolphin Surf School (ⓣ01637/873707, ⓦwww.surfschool.co.uk) and Reef Surf School (ⓣ01637/879058, ⓦwww.reefsurfschool.com) also offer accommodation (£60–160 per person, according to season, for a three-night surf-and-stay package). For **kite-surfing**, **land yachting**, **surf canoeing**, **paragliding** and other activities, head for The Extreme Academy on Watergate Bay (ⓣ01637/860543, ⓦwww.watergatebay.co.uk).

If you can, try to arrange your visit to Newquay to coincide with one of the surfing competitions and events that run all through the year – contact the tourist office (see p.412) for details.

pedestrianized, from which lanes lead to ornamental gardens and sloping lawns on the cliff tops. At the bottom of Beach Road, adjacent to the small harbour, the **Blue Reef Aquarium** (daily: March–Oct 10am–5pm; Nov–Feb 10am–4pm; £9.20) allows you to view tropical fish from an underwater tunnel; there are also tours, talks and feeding sessions. Below the aquarium, in the crook of the massive Towan Head, **Towan Beach** is the most central of the seven miles of firm sandy beaches that follow in an almost unbroken succession. You can reach all of them on foot, though for some of the further ones, such as **Porth Beach**, with its grassy headland, or the extensive **Watergate Bay**, two and a half miles north of the centre, you could use bus #556. The beaches can be unbearably crowded in full season, and all are popular with surfers, particularly Watergate and – west of Towan Head – **Fistral Bay**, the largest of the town beaches. On the other side of East Pentire Head from Fistral, **Crantock Beach** – reachable over the Gannel River by ferry or upstream footbridge, or by buses #585 or #587 – is usually less crowded, and has a lovely backdrop of dunes and undulating grassland.

Eating

Although most of Newquay's numerous **places to eat** are pretty bland, recent years have seen an influx of more stylish places, some of them out of town.

The Beach Hut Watergate Bay ⓣ01637/860877. Chilled hangout for surfers and a good venue for a sundowner, with terrific views. Breakfasts and snacks are available all day, alongside burgers, fish pie and vegetable tagine (£9.50–12.50). Nov–Easter closed eve Mon–Thurs & Sun.

Café Irie 38 Fore St ⓣ01637/859200. Funky, lattice-windowed cottage serving all-day breakfasts, soups, veggie food, cream teas and – during summer school hols – inexpensive evening meals, usually to mellow musical accompaniment. No credit cards. Closed Mon–Thurs Nov–Easter.

Fifteen Cornwall Watergate Bay ⓣ01637/861000. Overlooking the beach, this contemporary-looking place set up by TV chef Jamie Oliver showcases the culinary talents of trainee chefs. The mainly Italian but locally sourced dishes are inventive and delicious; set menus are £26 at lunchtime, £55 (£97 including select wines) in the evening, and breakfasts are also worth sampling.

New Harbour Restaurant Newquay Harbour ⓣ01637/874062. Great seafood and a harbourside location are the main draws of this eatery with a decked terrace, where you can choose from the lobsters scurrying around in the adjacent pools. There are hot and cold snacks at lunchtime (under £10), and a separate Crab Shack in summer. Main dishes cost £13–18. Closed Jan–March.

Drinking and nightlife

Newquay is easily Cornwall's biggest centre for **nightlife**, drawing in crowds from around the county at weekends. Among the good **pubs** are the *Red Lion*, North Quay Hill, with live music at weekends and meals available, and the more family-friendly *Fort Inn*, 63 Fore St, with sea views from its ranks of outdoor tables and barbecues in summer.

As for **clubbing**, the town's current top spots are: *Berties* on East Street (ⓣ01637/870369, ⓦwww.bertiesclub.com), which has its own lodge if you want to stay over; *Sailors* on Fore Street (ⓣ01637/872838, ⓦwww.sailorsnightclub.com); *The Beach* (ⓣ01637/872194, ⓦwww.beachclubnewquay.co.uk) and *Koola* (ⓣ01637/873415, ⓦwww.thekoola.com) on Beach Road; and *Barracuda*, 27–29 Cliff Rd (ⓣ01637/875800, ⓦwww.barracudanewquay.com), which also has occasional live acts. These mainstream places tend to be fairly glitzy and get overwhelmed in summer.

Padstow and around

The small fishing port of **PADSTOW** is nearly as popular as Newquay, but has a very different feel. Enclosed within the estuary of the Camel – the only river of any size that empties on Cornwall's north coast – the town long retained its position as the principal fishing port on this coast, and still has something of the atmosphere of a medieval town. Its chief annual festival is also a hangover from times past, the **Obby Oss**, a May Day romp when one of the locals garbs themselves as a horse and prances through the town preceded by a masked and club-wielding "teaser" – a spirited if rather institutionalized re-enactment of old fertility rites.

Arrival, information and accommodation

Bus #556 from Newquay pulls in near the harbour, site of Padstow's **tourist office** (Easter–Oct Mon–Sat 9am–5pm, Sun 10am–4pm; Nov–Easter Mon–Fri 10am–4pm, Sat 11am–2pm; ⓣ01841/533449, ⓦwww.padstowlive.com), which offers **internet** access.

If you're overnighting here, the **B&Bs** and **hostel** listed below should see you right; some of Rick Stein's restaurants also offer fairly pricey accommodation (④–⑦) – call ⓣ01841/532700 or go to ⓦwww.rickstein.com for reservations. **Campers** should head for *Dennis Cove Camping* (ⓣ01841/532349; closed Oct–Easter), about a ten-minute walk south of town; generally quiet and well tended, it sits right above the Camel Trail and the estuary.

The Town

On a hill overlooking Padstow, the **church of St Petroc** is dedicated to the Welsh or Irish monk supposed to have landed here in the sixth century, giving his name to the town – "Petrock's Stow". The building has a fine fifteenth-century font, an Elizabethan pulpit and some amusing carved bench-ends. The walls are lined with monuments to the local Prideaux family, who still occupy nearby **Prideaux Place**, an Elizabethan manor house with grand staircases, richly furnished rooms full of portraits, fantastically ornate ceilings and formal gardens (Easter & early May to early Oct Mon–Thurs & Sun 1.30–5pm, last tour at 4pm; grounds open from 12.30pm; £7.50, grounds only £3), all of which have been used in a plethora of films, such as *Twelfth Night* and *Oscar and Lucinda*. The grounds contain an ancient deer park, and afford wonderful views over the Camel estuary.

At the bottom of the town, Padstow's small **harbour** is jammed with launches and boats offering cruises in Padstow Bay, while a regular **ferry** (summer daily 7.50am–7.50pm; winter Mon–Sat 7.50am–4.30pm; £3 return) carries people and bikes across the river to Rock (see p.416). The ferry leaves from the harbour's North Pier except at low water when it goes from near the war memorial downstream.

Around Padstow

From Padstow's harbour, you can take the ferry to **ROCK** for the good beaches around Polzeath (see opposite) and, within a short walk, the low-slung **church of St Enodoc** (John Betjeman's burial place).

The coast on the **south side** of the estuary also offers some great **beaches**, reachable on bus #556, though walking would be preferable for exploring the terrific coastline. Round **Stepper Point** you can reach the sandy and secluded **Harlyn Bay** and, turning the corner southwards, **Constantine Bay**, the area's best surfing beach. The dunes backing the beach and the rock pools skirting it make this one of the most appealing bays on this coast; it boasts good water quality too, though the tides can be treacherous and bathing hazardous near the rocks.

Surfers are attracted to other beaches in the neighbourhood, but the surrounding caravan sites can make these claustrophobic in summer – the sands around **Porthcothan**, south of Constantine, might offer more seclusion.

Three or four miles further south lies one of Cornwall's most dramatic beaches, **Bedruthan Steps**. Said to be the stepping-stones of a giant called Bedruthan, these slate outcrops can be readily viewed from the cliff-top path, at a point which drivers can reach on the B3276. Steps lead down to the broad beach below (closed in winter), which has dangerous tides and thunderous waves and is not recommended for swimming.

The old railway line between Padstow and Wadebridge has been converted into an excellent **cycle track** that forms part of the **Camel Trail**, a fifteen-mile traffic-free path that follows the river up as far as Wenfordbridge, on the edge of Bodmin Moor, with a turn-off for Bodmin. The five-mile Padstow–Wadebridge stretch offers glimpses of a variety of birdlife, especially around the small **Pinkson Creek**, habitat of terns, herons, curlews and egrets.

You can **rent bikes** from Trail Bike Hire (℡01841/532594, ⓦwww.trailbikehire.co .uk) and Padstow Cycle Hire (℡01841/533533, ⓦwww.padstowcyclehire.com), both on South Quay, by the start of the Camel Trail. Further up the Trail at Wadebridge, Bridge Bike Hire (℡01208/813050, ⓦwww.bridgebikehire.co.uk) has a greater stock, though it's still advisable to reserve.

Padstow also marks one end of the thirty-mile cross-peninsula **Saints' Way**, linking up with Fowey on Cornwall's south coast (see p.391). Leaflets and books detailing the walk are available from the tourist offices at Padstow, Bodmin and Fowey.

Eating and drinking

Foodies know Padstow best for its high-class **restaurants**, particularly those associated with star chef Rick Stein; the waiting list for a table at one of his establishments can be months long, though a weekday reservation out of season can mean booking only a day or two ahead, and there's always the chance of a cancellation if you turn up on spec. If you want to savour the master's creations without breaking the budget, you can always opt for *Stein's Fish and Chips* on South Quay or his **deli** next door, which offers delicious takeaway items. Alternatively, you can eat and drink well in Padstow's **pubs**, such as the *Shipwright's* on the harbour's north side, or the eighteenth-century *Old Ship* on Mill Square, both with outdoor seating.

Paul Ainsworth at Number 6 6 Middle St ℡01841/532093. In a Georgian townhouse with stylish modern decor, this restaurant is Padstow's best alternative to the Stein empire. Main dishes cost around £15 and three-course lunches are £13.50. Closed Mon, also Sun Oct–May.

Rick Stein's Café 10 Middle St ℡01841/532700. The most relaxed of Stein's restaurants – and the best for atmosphere – serves snacks at lunch and moderately priced evening meals.

St Petroc's Bistro 4 New St ℡01841/532700. This fairly formal offshoot of the Stein family has a lighter, meatier and more restricted version of the *Seafood Restaurant*'s menu, with mains around £17.

Seafood Restaurant Riverside ℡01841/532700. Stein's flagship is one of England's top fish restaurants – and expensive, with most main courses around £29 (though cod, chips and mushy peas cost a more reasonable £17.50).

Polzeath to Port Isaac

Facing west into Padstow Bay, the beaches around **POLZEATH** are the finest in the vicinity, pelted by rollers which make **Hayle Bay**, in particular, one of the most popular **surfing** venues in the West Country. A mile south of Polzeath, **Daymer Bay** is more favoured by the windsurfing crowd. All the gear can be rented from shops on the beach, where you can get information on tuition, and there are campsites and bars in the vicinity.

Accommodation hereabouts is scarce, but there's a useful **campsite**, *Valley Caravan Park* (℡01208/862391, ⓦwww.valleycaravanpark.co.uk; closed Oct–Easter), just 200m from the beach, signposted up the lane behind the shop; it has a stream running through it attracting ducks and geese. *The Waterfront* (℡01208/869655; closed Mon–Wed & Sun in winter), a relaxed **café/restaurant** just back from the beach, has a first-floor terrace and an eclectic menu.

Heading east, the coastal path brings you through cliff-top growths of feathery tamarisk, which flower spectacularly in July and August. From the headland of **Pentire Point**, views unfold for miles over the offshore islets of **The Mouls** and **Newland**, which foster populations of grey seals and puffins. Half a mile east, the scanty remains of an Iron Age fort stand on **Rump's Point**, from where the path descends a mile or so to **Lundy Bay**, a pleasant sandy cove surrounded by green fields. Climbing again, you pass the shafts of an old antimony mine on the way to **Doyden Point**, which is picturesquely ornamented with a nineteenth-century castle folly once used for gambling parties.

Beyond the inlet of **Port Quin**, the next settlement of any size is **PORT ISAAC**, wedged in a gap in the precipitous cliff wall and dedicated to the crab and lobster trade. Only seasonal trippers ruffle the surface of life in this cramped village, whose narrow lanes lead down to a pebble beach where rock pools are exposed at low tide. The village makes a good place to **stay**: you can enjoy great views from both *The Gallery*, 44 Fore St (℡01208/881032, Ⓦwww.bed-and -breakfast-port-isaac.co.uk; ❷), which has stylish, contemporary rooms, a garden and wi-fi, and *The Old School Hotel* on the same street (℡01208/880721, Ⓦwww .theoldschoolhotel.co.uk; ❹), with its exposed beams and slate walls in school-room-themed rooms.

Food-wise, Port Isaac is most famous for crab, which you can sample from stalls at the harbour or from the **restaurants** at *The Old School* and the *Slipway Hotel* on the quayside. The *Slipway* bar is a congenial place for a pint, as is the neighbouring *Golden Lion*, which has a cellar bistro. In serene **Port Gaverne**, the next cove to the east, the snug *Port Gaverne Inn* offers bar food as well as fine dining in a separate restaurant.

Tintagel

East of Port Isaac, the coast is wild and unspoiled, making for some steep and strenuous walking, and interspersed with some stupendous strands of sandy beaches such as that at **Trebarwith** – a surfers' favourite. Two miles further north, the rocky littoral provides an appropriate backdrop for the black, forsaken ruins of **Tintagel Castle** (daily: Easter–Sept 10am–6pm; Oct 10am–5pm; Nov–Easter 10am–4pm; £5.20; EH). It was the medieval chronicler Geoffrey of Monmouth who first popularized the notion that this was the **birthplace of**

King Arthur, son of Uther Pendragon and Ygrayne, but by that time local folklore was already saturated with tales of King Mark of Cornwall, Tristan and Iseult, Arthur and the knights of Camelot. Tintagel is certainly a plausibly resonant candidate for the abode of the Once and Future King, but the **castle** ruins in fact belong to a Norman stronghold occupied by the earls of Cornwall, who after sporadic spurts of rebuilding allowed it to decay, most of it having been washed into the sea by the sixteenth century. However, remains of a Celtic monastery that occupied this site in the sixth century can still be seen. A visitor centre fills you in on the story.

The best approach to the site is the South West Coast Path from **Glebe Cliff** to the west, where the parish **church of St Materiana** sits in isolation; drivers, however, should park in the village of **TINTAGEL**, from which there's easy access on foot. For the most part a dreary collection of cafés and B&Bs, Tintagel has one other item of genuine interest: the **Old Post Office** on Fore Street (daily: mid-March to early April & Oct 11am–4pm; early April to late May 10.30am–5pm; late May to Sept 10.30am–5.30pm; £3.20; NT), a slate-built, rickety-roofed construction dating from the fourteenth century, now restored to its appearance in the Victorian era.

King Arthur in Cornwall

Did **King Arthur** really exist? If he did, it's likely that he was an amalgam of two figures: a sixth-century Celtic warlord who united local tribes in a series of successful battles against the invading Anglo-Saxons, and a local Cornish saint. Whatever his origins, his role was recounted and inflated by poets and troubadours in later centuries, and elaborated by the unreliable twelfth-century chronicler Geoffrey of Monmouth, who made Arthur the conqueror of Western Europe. The Arthurian legends were crystallized in Thomas Malory's epic, *Morte d'Arthur* (1485), further romanticized in Tennyson's *Idylls of the King* (1859–85) and resurrected in T.H. White's saga *The Once and Future King* (1937–58).

Many places throughout Britain and Europe claim some association with Arthur, but it's England's West Country, and **Cornwall** in particular, that has the greatest concentration. Here, influenced by tales from Celtic Brittany and Wales, the legends have established deep roots, so that, for example, the spirit of Arthur is said to be embodied in the Cornish chough – a bird now almost extinct. Cornwall's most famous Arthurian site is **Tintagel**, the king's supposed birthplace and where Merlin reputedly lived in a cave (a rock near Mousehole, south of Penzance, also claims this honour). Nearby **Bodmin Moor** is dotted with such places as "King Arthur's Bed" and "King Arthur's Downs", while Camlan, the battlefield where Arthur was mortally wounded fighting against his nephew Mordred, is associated with **Slaughterbridge**, near Camelford. Also on the moor, **Dozmary Pool** was apparently where the knight Bedivere was dispatched by the dying king to return the sword Excalibur to the mysterious hand emerging from the water (though some sources claim this happened at **Loe Pool** in Mount's Bay). According to legend, Arthur's body was carried after the battle to **Boscastle**, northeast of Tintagel, from where a funeral barge transported it to Avalon.

Cornwall is also the presumed home of **King Mark**, at the centre of a separate cycle of myths which later became interwoven with the Arthurian one. It was Mark who sent the knight Tristan to Ireland to fetch his betrothed, Iseult; his headquarters is supposed to have been at **Castle Dore**, north of Fowey. Out beyond Land's End, the fabled, vanished country of **Lyonnesse** was the birthplace of Tristan (according to Malory and Spenser's *Faerie Queene*) – and some sources name this as Arthur's native land.

Buses stop on the main Fore Street close to the **tourist office** on Bossiney Road (daily 10/10.30am–4/5pm; ℡01840/779084, Ⓦwww.visitboscastleandtintagel .com). The village has a couple of gems among its mostly banal **accommodation** choices. Near the centre on Atlantic Road, *The Avalon* (℡01840/770116, Ⓦwww .tintagelbedbreakfast.co.uk; closed late Nov to mid-Feb; ❸) has Gothic-style beds and Victorian fireplaces but contemporary comforts and amazing views. A few minutes' walk along the same road, the eco-friendly *Bosayne* (℡01840/770514, Ⓦwww.bosayne.co.uk; ❷) has sea views from some rooms, organic breakfasts and free wi-fi. Three-quarters of a mile outside the village at Dunderhole Point, past St Materiana, the offices of a former slate quarry now house a YHA **hostel**, which has great views of the coastline (℡0845/371 9145, Ⓔtintagel@yha.org.uk; from £12; call for winter opening). At the end of Atlantic Road, the *Headland* site offers scenic **camping** (℡01840/770239, Ⓦwww.headlandcaravanpark.co.uk; closed Nov–Easter). Among Tintagel's numerous **cafés and tearooms**, try *Wyldes*, opposite the tourist office on Bossiney Road (℡01840/770007; closed Sun and eve; no credit cards), whose options range from breakfasts to panini, pies and fried halloumi. The *Old Malt House* on Fore Street serves local ales and **meals**.

Boscastle

Three miles east of Tintagel, **BOSCASTLE** lies compressed within a narrow ravine drilled by the rivers Jordan and Valency and ending in a twisty harbour. The tidy riverfront bordered by thatched and lime-washed cottages was the scene of a devastating flash flood in 2004, but most of the damage has now been repaired. One of the gnarled old buildings here houses the **Museum of Witchcraft** (Easter–Oct Mon–Sat 10.30am–6pm, Sun 11.30am–6pm; £3), an intelligent, non-gimmicky account of witchcraft through the ages, displayed in themed galleries.

There's little else of specific interest to see in the village, though you can pick up a leaflet from the tourist office for local walks in the Valency valley, one of them leading a couple of miles east to the church of **St Juliot's**, restored by Thomas Hardy when he was plying his trade as a young architect. It was while working here that he met Emma Gifford, whom he married in 1874, a year after the publication of *A Pair of Blue Eyes*, the book that kicked off Hardy's literary career. It opens with an architect arriving in a Cornish village to restore its church, and is full of descriptions of the country around Boscastle.

Boscastle's **tourist office** is in the main car park in the lower village (daily 10/10.30am–4/5pm; ℡01840/250010, Ⓦwww.visitboscastleandtintagel.com). One of the most appealing **places to stay** is the whitewashed *Pencarmol*, in a fabulous position overlooking the harbour, offering three cottagey en-suite rooms with free wi-fi (℡01840/250435, Ⓦwww.pencarmol.co.uk; no credit cards; ❷). Hardy fans should book ahead for the *Old Rectory*, on the road to St Juliot (℡01840/250225, Ⓦwww.stjuliot.com; no under-12s; closed mid-Nov to mid-Feb; ❹), for the opportunity to stay in Hardy's or Emma's bedroom, or in a converted stable, and roam the extensive grounds. There's a YHA **hostel** right on the harbourfront (℡0845/371 9006, Ⓔboscastle@yha.org.uk; closed Dec–March; from £14) housed in a former stables. You can eat at one of the village's excellent **pubs**: in upper Boscastle, the *Napoleon* has a good seafood bistro and a spacious lawned garden, while the *Cobweb*, down near the harbour, scores highly on atmosphere and has bar food; both host live music evenings.

Bude and around

There is little distinctively Cornish in Cornwall's northernmost town of **BUDE**, four miles west of the Devon border. Built around an estuary surrounded by a fine expanse of sands, the town has sprouted a crop of holiday homes and hotels, though these have not unduly spoilt the place nor the magnificent cliffy coast surrounding it.

Of the excellent beaches hereabouts, the central and clean **Summerleaze** grows to immense proportions at low tide, though bathers can save themselves a lengthy trudge by taking advantage of a sea-water swimming pool near the cliffs. The mile-long **Widemouth Bay**, two and a half miles south of Bude, also draws the holiday hordes – though bathing can be dangerous near the rocks at low tide. Surfers congregate five miles down the coast at **Crackington Haven**, wonderfully situated between 430ft crags at the mouth of a lush valley. The cliffs hereabouts are characterized by remarkable zigzagging strata of shale, limestone and sandstone, a mixture which erodes into vividly contorted detached formations.

To the north of Bude, acres-wide **Crooklets** is the scene of **surfing** and life-saving demonstrations and competitions, while the pristine expanse of **Sandy Mouth**, a couple of miles further, has rock pools beneath encircling cliffs. It's a short walk from here to another surfers' delight, **Duckpool**, a tiny sandy cove flanked by jagged reefs at low tide and dominated by the three-hundred-foot **Steeple Point**.

Between Duckpool and the Devon border stretch five miles of strenuous but exhilarating coast. The only village along here is **MORWENSTOW**, just south of **Henna Cliff**, at 450ft the highest sheer drop of any sea cliff in England after Beachy Head, affording magnificent views along the coast and beyond Lundy to the Welsh coast.

Practicalities

Bude's **tourist office**, in the car park off the Crescent (daily 10am–4pm, may stay open later in summer; ℡01288/354240, ⓦwww.visitbude.info), offers **internet** access. You can rent **surfing equipment** from a number of outlets, including Zuma Jay on Belle Vue Lane.

A cluster of **B&Bs** overlooks the golf course near Crooklets Beach, among them *Dylan's* at 12 Downs View (℡01288/354705, ⓦwww.dylansguesthouseinbude.co .uk; no credit cards; ❷), with contemporary decor and airy, well-equipped rooms. Outside town, near Widemouth Bay, try *Elements* (℡01288/352386, ⓦwww .elements-life.co.uk; ❹), a boutiquey "surf hotel" on the coast road near Upton, with a gym and sauna, and *Bangors Organic*, a stylish B&B a mile inland at Poundstock (℡01288/361297, ⓦwww.bangorsorganic.co.uk; ❺), with spacious, beautifully designed modern rooms. There's a friendly backpackers' **hostel** not far from the beaches, *North Shore*, 57 Killerton Rd (℡01288/354256, ⓦwww.northshorebude .com; from £17), with a large garden, internet access and some double rooms (❶); there's a two-night minimum stay at weekends. Among the numerous **campsites** around Bude, *Upper Lynstone Caravan and Camping Park* (℡01288/352017, ⓦwww .upperlynstone.co.uk; closed Nov–Easter) lies just three-quarters of a mile south of the centre on the coast road to Widemouth Bay.

Both *Elements* and *Bangors Organic* have top-notch **restaurants** open to non-residents, but in Bude itself you can't beat ⚶ *Life's a Beach* on Summerleaze Beach for style, cuisine and location: a café by day, it becomes a romantic seafood bistro in the evening (℡01288/355222; closed Sun eve, also all Mon–Wed & Thurs daytime in winter; book ahead). For lower prices, there's the *Atlantic Diner*, 5–7 Belle Vue (closed Mon eve in summer, Sun–Thurs eve in winter; no credit cards), popular with shoppers and surfers alike for its burgers, steaks, curries and ice creams.

The **Bude Jazz Festival** attracts a range of stonking sounds for a week in August/September (ⓦwww.budejazzfestival.co.uk).

Bodmin and Bodmin Moor

Bodmin Moor, the smallest and mildest of the West Country's great moors, has some beautiful tors, torrents and rock formations, but much of its fascination lies in the strong human imprint, particularly the wealth of relics left behind by its **Bronze Age** population, including such important sites as **Trethevy Quoit** and the stone circles of the **Hurlers**. Separated from these by some three millennia, the churches in the villages of **St Neot**, **Blisland** and **Altarnun** are among the region's finest examples of fifteenth-century art and architecture.

The biggest centre in the area, **Bodmin**, stands outside the moor but can provide a useful base, with a good choice of accommodation and easy access – main-line trains stop just outside town and there are regular bus connections to Padstow and St Austell. The north moor village of **Camelford** also has good accommodation, and is connected by bus #584 to Polzeath and Port Isaac and by #594 to Tintagel and Boscastle. The only regular services on the moor, however, are #225 between Launceston and Altarnun (not Sat or Sun), and #575 between Liskeard and St Neot (not Sun). Otherwise, there's the Corlink community bus scheme, which must be booked (call ℡0845/850 5556 at least 1hr before) for journeys between Bodmin, Blisland and Camelford (not Sun).

Bodmin

The town of **BODMIN** lies on the western edge of Bodmin Moor, equidistant from the north and south Cornish coasts and the Fowey and Camel rivers, a position that encouraged its growth as a trading town. It was also an important ecclesiastical centre after the establishment of a priory by St Petroc, who moved here from Padstow in the sixth century. The priory disappeared but Bodmin retained its prestige through its church, **St Petroc's**, on Priory Road (open for services and April–Sept Mon–Sat 11am–3pm; at other times call ℡01208/73867). Dating from the fifteenth century, and still Cornwall's largest parish church, it contains an extravagantly carved twelfth-century font and an ivory casket that once held the bones of the saint, while the southwest corner of the churchyard contains a sacred well.

West of here on Berrycoombe Road, the notorious **Bodmin Jail** (daily 10am–dusk; £5.50) recalls the public executions that were guaranteed crowd-pullers until 1862, from which time the hangings continued behind closed doors until 1909. The jail finally closed in 1927. You can visit part of the original eighteenth-century structure, including the condemned cell and some grisly exhibits chronicling the lives of the inmates.

Further up Berrycoombe Road, there's access to a cycleway and footpath that after a mile links up to the main route of the Camel **Trail** (see p.417) at Boscarne Junction. From the station here, steam locomotives of the **Bodmin & Wenford Railway** run to the main-line station at Bodmin Parkway between March and October (℡0845/125 9678, ⓦwww.bodminandwenfordrailway.co.uk; £9.50 return or £11.50 all day). The trains make a stop at the restored old station on St Nicholas Street, and at Colesloggett, a good starting point for rambles in **Cardinham Woods**.

From Parkway it's less than two miles' walk to one of Cornwall's most celebrated country houses, **Lanhydrock** (house mid-March to Sept Tues–Sun 11am–5.30pm; Oct Tues–Sun 11am–5pm; gardens open daily 10am–6pm or dusk; £9.90, grounds only £5.80; NT), originally seventeenth century but rebuilt in 1881. Inside the granite exterior, the fifty-odd rooms include a long picture gallery with a plaster ceiling depicting scenes from the Old Testament, and servants' quarters that reveal the daily workings of a Victorian manor house. The grounds hold magnificent beds of magnolias, azaleas and rhododendrons, and a huge area of wooded parkland bordering onto the River Fowey.

Practicalities

Three miles outside town, Bodmin Parkway **train station** has a regular bus connection to the centre; all **buses** pull in on Mount Folly, site of the **tourist office** (Mon–Fri 10am–5pm, Easter to late Oct also Sat 10am–5pm; ☏01208/76616, ⓦwww.bodminlive.com). You can **rent bikes** from Bodmin Bikes at 3 Hamley Court, off Dennison Road (☏01208/73192).

There's eco-friendly **B&B** accommodation at *Bedknobs*, Polgwyn, Castle Street (☏01208/77553, ⓦwww.bedknobs.co.uk; ❸), a Victorian villa in an acre of wooded garden, close to the centre, or try *Roscrea*, 18 St Nicholas St (☏01208/74400, ⓦwww.roscrea.co.uk; no credit cards; ❸), a schoolmaster's house from 1805, offering breakfasts with home-laid eggs and superb dinners.

Bodmin Jail has an excellent café and **restaurant** open till late (☏01208/76292). Wholesome snacks are served at the tiny *Bara Café*, across from St Petroc's at 14 Honey St (closed Sun), while, on Fore Street, a Methodist chapel from 1840 is now a Wetherspoons **pub**, with tables outside and cheap food and beer all day.

Bodmin Moor

Just ten miles in diameter, **Bodmin Moor** is a wilderness on a small scale, its highest tor rising to just 1375ft from a platform of 1000ft. Yet the moor conveys a sense of loneliness quite out of proportion to its size, with scattered ancient remains providing in places the only distraction from an empty horizon. Aside from its tors, the main attractions of the landscape are the small Dozmary Pool, a site steeped in myth, and a quartet of rivers – the Fowey, Lynher, Camel and De Lank – that rise from remote moorland springs and effectively bound the moor to the north, east and south.

Blisland and the western moor

BLISLAND stands in the Camel valley on the western slopes of Bodmin Moor, three miles northeast of Bodmin. Georgian and Victorian houses cluster around a village green and a church whose well-restored interior has an Italianate altar and a startlingly painted screen. On **Pendrift Common** above the village, the gigantic

Jubilee Rock is inscribed with various patriotic insignia commemorating the jubilee of George III's coronation in 1809. From this 700ft vantage point you look eastward over the De Lank Gorge and the boulder-crowned knoll of **Hawk's Tor**, three miles away. On the shoulder of the tor stand the Neolithic **Stripple Stones**, a circular platform once holding 28 standing stones, of which just four are still upright.

On Blisland's village green, you can sample good **ales and food** at the *Blisland Inn*, which has outdoor seating.

Jamaica Inn, Dozmary Pool and Altarnun

On the A30 midway between Bodmin and Launceston, outside the uninspiring village of **Bolventor** in the heart of the moor, **Jamaica Inn** is one of the chief points of interest locally for walkers and sightseers alike. A staging-post even before the main road was first laid here in 1769, the inn was described by Daphne du Maurier as being "alone in glory, four square to the winds", though it has lost any trace of romance since its development into a bland hotel and restaurant complex (℡01566/86250, ⓌWwww.jamaicainn.co.uk; ➌). One corner exhibits the room where the author stayed in 1930, soaking up inspiration for her smugglers' yarn. Adjacent to the hotel, the **Smuggler's Museum** (daily 9/10am–4/5pm; £2.50) shows the diverse ruses used for concealing contraband.

The inn's car park makes a useful place to leave your vehicle and venture forth on foot. Just a mile south, **Dozmary Pool** is famous in Arthurian mythology (see box, p.419). The diamond-shaped lake has been known to run dry in summer, dealing a bit of a blow to the legend that it is bottomless.

Four miles northeast of Bolventor, the granite-grey village of **ALTARNUN** lies snugly sheltered beneath the eastern heights of the moor. Its prominent **church**, St Nonna's, contains a fine Norman font and 79 bench-ends carved at the beginning of the sixteenth century, depicting saints, musicians and clowns.

South of the village off the A30, the *King's Head* has old beams, saggy ceilings and plain **rooms** with shared bathrooms (℡01566/86241; ➊), as well as a range of **food and drink**.

Camelford and the northern tors

The northern half of Bodmin Moor is dominated by its two highest tors, both of them easily accessible from **CAMELFORD**, a town once associated with King Arthur's Camelot. The town has resisted trading on the Arthurian myths, but does have the diverting **North Cornwall Museum** on Clease Road (April–Sept Mon–Sat 10am–5pm; £3), containing domestic items and exhibits showing the development of the local slate industry. The same building houses a **tourist office** (same hours; ℡01840/212954).

Although it lacks excitement, Camelford makes a useful touring base. The best **accommodation** hereabouts is offered at ⚘ *Warmington House* on Fore Street (℡01840/214961, ⓌWwww.warmingtonhouse.co.uk; no credit cards; ➌), an elegant Queen Anne building with period furnishings and modern comforts. Alternatively, try the next-door thirteenth-century *Darlington Inn* (℡01840/213314; ➋). There's **camping** at *Lakefield Caravan Park*, Lower Pendavey Farm (℡01840/213279, ⓌWwww.lakefieldcaravanpark.co.uk; closed Nov–March), which also offers **horseriding**. Try the *Mason's Arms* on Fore Street for good pub **meals** and a beer garden (no credit cards).

Rough Tor, the second highest peak on Bodmin Moor at 1311ft, is four miles southeast of Camelford. The hill presents a different aspect from every angle: from the south an ungainly mass, from the west a nobly proportioned mountain. A short distance to the east are Little Rough Tor, home to the remains of an Iron Age camp, and Showery Tor, capped by a prominent formation of piled rocks.

Easily visible to the southeast, **Brown Willy** is, at 1375ft, the highest peak in Cornwall, as its original name signified – Bronewhella, or "highest hill". Like Rough Tor, Brown Willy shows various faces, its sugarloaf appearance from the north sharpening into a long multi-peaked crest as you approach. The tor is accessible by continuing from the summit of Rough Tor across the valley of the De Lank, or, from the south, by footpath from Bolventor. The easiest ascent is by the worn path which climbs steeply up from the northern end of the hill.

St Neot and the southeastern moor

Seven miles east of Bodmin, on the southern edge of the moor, **ST NEOT** is one of the region's prettiest villages. Its fifteenth-century **church** contains some of the most impressive stained-glass windows of any parish church in the country, the oldest glass being the fifteenth-century **Creation Window**, at the east end of the south aisle. Next along, **Noah's Window** continues the sequence, but the narration soon dissolves into windows portraying patrons and local bigwigs, while others present cameos of the ordinary men and women of the village.

This side of the moor is greener and more thickly wooded than the northern reaches, due to the confluence of a web of rivers into the Fowey. One of the best-known local beauty spots is a couple of miles east, below Draynes Bridge, where the Fowey tumbles through the **Golitha Falls**, less a waterfall than a series of rapids. Dippers and wagtails flit through the trees, and there's a pleasant woodland walk you can take to the dam at the Siblyback Lake reservoir just over a mile away.

North of Siblyback Lake, **Twelve Men's Moor** holds some of Bodmin Moor's grandest landscapes. The quite modest elevations of **Hawk's Tor** (1079ft) and the lower **Trewartha Tor** appear enormous from the north, though they are overtopped by **Kilmar**, highest of the hills on the moor's eastern flank at 1280ft. A quarter-mile northwest of **Minions**, Cornwall's highest village, you can see **The Hurlers**, a wide complex of three circles dating from about 1500 BC. The purpose of these stark upright stones is not known, though they owe their name to the legend that they were men turned to stone for playing the Celtic game of hurling on the Sabbath. A further half-mile or so north, **Stowe's Hill** is the site of the moor's most famous stone pile, **The Cheesewring**, a precarious pillar of balancing flat granite slabs that have been marvellously eroded by the wind. The disused Cheesewring Quarry, gouged out of the hillside nearby, is a centre for rock climbing.

Three miles south of Minions stands another Stone Age survivor, **Trethevy Quoit**, a chamber tomb nearly nine feet high, surmounted by a massive capstone. Originally enclosed in earth, the stones have been stripped by centuries of weathering to create Cornwall's most impressive megalithic monument.

Travel details

For information on all local and national bus services, contact Traveline ⓣ0871/ 200 2233, ⓦwww.travelines.com.
Bodmin to: Newquay (4 daily; 30–45min); Padstow (Mon–Sat hourly, Sun 5 daily; 40min); Plymouth (4 daily; 1hr); St Austell (Mon–Sat hourly, Sun 5 daily; 40min).

Exeter to: Bristol (4–5 daily; 1hr 45min–2hr); Newquay (3–5 daily; 2hr 30min–3hr 40min); Penzance (1–2 daily; 4hr–4hr 40min); Plymouth (every 1–2hr; 1hr–1hr 30min); Sidmouth (1–2 hourly; 50min); Torquay (every 1–2hr; 50min–1hr 15min); Truro (2 daily; 3hr 20min).
Falmouth to: Helston (Mon–Sat every 1–2hr, Sun 5 daily; 25min–1hr 10min); Penzance (Mon–Sat 9 daily, Sun 2 daily; 1hr–1hr 45min); St Austell

(2 daily; 1hr); Truro (Mon–Sat every 15min, Sun hourly; 25–45min).

Newquay to: Bodmin (4 daily; 30–50min); Exeter (3–5 daily; 2hr 40min–3hr 20min); Padstow (Mon–Sat hourly, Sun 5 daily; 1hr 20min); Plymouth (5 daily; 1hr 45min); St Austell (Mon–Sat hourly, Sun 5 daily; 40–55min); Truro (2–4 hourly; 50min–1hr 20min).

Penzance to: Falmouth (Mon–Sat 8 daily, Sun 2 daily; 1hr–1hr 40min); Helston (Mon–Sat hourly, Sun 6 daily; 35–50min); Plymouth (6 daily; 2hr 45min–4hr); St Austell (3 daily; 1hr 35min–2hr); St Ives (Mon–Sat 3–4 hourly, Sun hourly; 25–40min); Truro (Mon–Sat 1–2 hourly, Sun 4 daily; 1hr–1hr 30min).

Plymouth to: Bodmin (4 daily; 50min–1hr); Exeter (Mon–Sat hourly, Sun every 1–2hr; 1–2hr); Falmouth (2 daily; 2hr 15min); Newquay (5 daily; 1hr 35min); Penzance (6 daily; 2hr 40min–3hr 20min); St Austell (4 daily; 1hr 15min); St Ives (3 daily; 2hr 45min–3hr 10min); Torquay (Mon–Sat hourly, Sun 7 daily; 1hr 40min–2hr); Truro (5 daily; 1hr 50min).

St Austell to: Bodmin (Mon–Sat hourly, Sun 5 daily; 40min); Exeter (2 daily; 3hr); Falmouth (2 daily; 1hr); Newquay (Mon–Sat hourly, Sun 5 daily; 40min); Penzance (3 daily; 1hr 45min–2hr); Plymouth (4 daily; 1hr 20min); Truro (Mon–Sat every 30min, Sun every 2hr; 40min–1hr).

St Ives to: Penzance (Mon–Sat 3 hourly, Sun hourly; 30–40min); Plymouth (3 daily; 3hr 20min); Truro (Mon–Sat hourly, Sun 5 daily; 1hr 30min).

Torquay to: Exeter (Mon–Sat 1–2 hourly, Sun 12 daily; 1hr); Plymouth (4–7 daily; 1hr 40min–2hr).

Truro to: Exeter (2 daily; 3hr 30min); Falmouth (Mon–Sat every 15min, Sun hourly; 45min); Newquay (2–3 hourly; 40min–1hr 20min); Penzance (Mon–Sat 1–2 hourly, Sun 4 daily; 1hr 10min–1hr 40min); Plymouth (5 daily; 1hr 40min–2hr 20min); St Austell (Mon–Sat every 30min, Sun every 2hr; 30min–1hr); St Ives (Mon–Sat hourly, Sun 5 daily; 1hr–1hr 35min); St Mawes (Mon–Sat 8 daily, Sun 3 daily; 50min–1hr 15min).

Trains

For information on all local and national rail services, contact National Rail Enquiries ☎0845/748 4950, ⓦ www.nationalrail.co.uk.

Barnstaple to: Exeter (Mon–Sat hourly, Sun 5 daily; 1hr 20min).

Bodmin to: Exeter (every 1–2hr; 1hr 45min); Penzance (1–2 hourly; 1hr 25min); Plymouth (hourly; 40min).

Exeter to: Barnstaple (Mon–Sat hourly, Sun 6 daily; 1hr 30min); Bodmin (every 1–2hr; 1hr 45min); Bristol (1–2 hourly; 1hr–1hr 45min); Exmouth (1–2 hourly; 30min); Liskeard (every 1–2hr; 1hr 30min); London (hourly; 2–3hr); Par (every 1–2hr; 2hr); Penzance (every 1–2hr; 3hr 15min); Plymouth (2 hourly; 1hr); Torquay (1–2 hourly; 40min–1hr); Totnes (1–2 hourly; 35min); Truro (every 1–2hr; 2hr 20min).

Falmouth to: Truro (Mon–Sat every 30min, Sun 10 daily; 25–30min).

Liskeard to: Exeter (every 1–2hr; 1hr 30min); Looe (Mon–Sat hourly, Sun mid-May to mid-Sept 8 daily; 30min); Penzance (1–2 hourly; 1hr 35min); Plymouth (1–2 hourly; 30min); Truro (1–2 hourly; 50min).

Newquay to: Par (Mon–Sat 7 daily, Sun mid-May to mid-Sept 5 daily; 50min).

Par to: Exeter (every 1–2hr; 2hr); Newquay (Mon–Sat 7 daily, Sun mid-May to mid-Sept 5 daily; 50min); Penzance (hourly; 1hr 15min); Plymouth (hourly; 50min).

Penzance to: Bodmin (1–2 hourly; 1hr 15min); Exeter (every 1–2hr; 3hr); Plymouth (1–2 hourly; 2hr); St Ives (most via St Erth; hourly; 25–45min); Truro (1–2 hourly; 40min).

Plymouth to: Bodmin (hourly; 40min); Exeter (2 hourly; 1hr); Liskeard (1–2 hourly; 30min); Par (hourly; 50min); Penzance (1–2 hourly; 2hr); Truro (hourly; 1hr 15min).

St Ives to: Penzance (via St Erth; hourly; 30–50min).

Torquay to: Exeter (1–2 hourly; 45min–1hr).

Truro to: Exeter (every 1–2hr; 2hr 20min); Falmouth (Mon–Sat every 30min, Sun 10 daily; 25min); Liskeard (1–2 hourly; 50min); Penzance (1–2 hourly; 45min); Plymouth (hourly; 1hr 20min).

East Anglia

CHAPTER 7

Highlights

* **Sutton Hoo** The burial mounds of Sutton Hoo only revealed their Anglo-Saxon treasures in 1939, but what treasures they were. See p.442

* **Orford** Solitary hamlet with a splendid coastal setting that makes for a wonderful weekend away. See p.442

* **Southwold** Extraordinarily pretty and distinctly genteel seaside town that's perfect for walking and bathing – with the added incentive of the sage and inventive "Under the Pier Show". See p.446

* **Norwich Market** This open-air market is the region's biggest and best for everything from whelks to wellies. See p.453

* **Holkham Bay and beach** Wide bay holding Norfolk's finest beach – acres of golden sand set against hilly, pine-dusted dunes. See p.465

* **Ely** Isolated Cambridgeshire town, with a true fenland flavour and a magnificent cathedral. See p.469

* **Cambridge** With some of the finest late-medieval architecture in Europe, Cambridge is a must-see, its compact centre graced by dignified old colleges and their crisply manicured quadrangles. See p.472

▲ Holkham Bay

East Anglia

S trictly speaking, **East Anglia** is made up of just three counties – Suffolk, Norfolk and Cambridgeshire – which were settled by Angles from present-day Germany in the fifth century, though in more recent times it's come to be loosely applied to parts of Essex too. As a region it's renowned for its wide skies and flat landscapes, and of course such generalizations always contain more than a grain of truth – if you're looking for mountains, you've come to the wrong place. Nevertheless, East Anglia often fails to conform to its stereotype: parts of Suffolk are positively hilly, and its coastline can induce vertigo; the north Norfolk coast holds steep cliffs as well as wide sandy beaches; and even the pancake-flat fenlands are broken by wide, muddy rivers and hilly mounds, on one of which perches Ely's magnificent cathedral. Indeed, the whole region is sprinkled with fine medieval **churches**, the legacy of the days when this was England's most progressive and prosperous region.

Heading into East Anglia from the south almost inevitably takes you through **Essex**, whose proximity to London has turned much of the county into an unappetizing commuter strip. Amid the suburban gloom, there are, however, several worthwhile destinations, most notably **Colchester**, once a major Roman town and now a likeable sort of place with an imposing castle, and the handsome hamlets of the bucolic **Stour River Valley** on the Essex–Suffolk border. Essex's **Dedham** is one of the prettiest of these villages, but the prime attraction hereabouts is Suffolk's **Flatford Mill**, famous for its associations with the painter John Constable.

Pushing on deeper into the region, **Suffolk** boasts a string of extremely pretty, well-preserved little towns – **Lavenham** is the prime example – which enjoyed immense prosperity from the thirteenth to the sixteenth century, the heyday of the wool trade. Elsewhere, **Bury St Edmunds** can boast not just the ruins of its once-prestigious abbey, but also some fine Georgian architecture, while even the much maligned county town of **Ipswich** has its moments, especially down on its creatively revamped old docks. Nevertheless, for many visitors it's the north Suffolk coast that steals the local show. In **Southwold**, with its comely Georgian high street, Suffolk possesses a delightful seaside resort, elegant and relaxing in equal measure, while neighbouring **Aldeburgh** hosts one of the best music festivals in the country.

Norfolk, as everyone knows thanks to Noël Coward, is very flat. It's also one of the most sparsely populated counties in England, a remarkable turnaround from the days when it was an economic and political powerhouse – until, that is, the Industrial Revolution simply passed it by. Its capital, **Norwich**, is still East Anglia's largest city, renowned for its Norman cathedral and castle, and for its high-tech Sainsbury Centre, exhibiting a challenging collection of twentieth-century art.

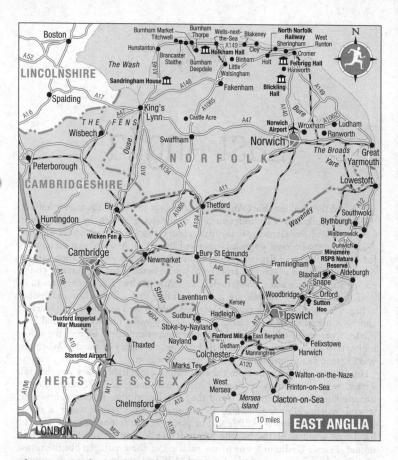

The most visited part of Norfolk is, however, the **Broads**, a unique landscape of reed-ridden waterways, which has been intensively exploited by boat-rental companies for the last thirty years. Almost as popular, the **north Norfolk coast** holds a string of busy, very English seaside resorts – **Cromer**, **Sheringham** and

Regional transport

East Anglia's principal international **airport** is Stansted – sometimes "London Stansted" – some thirty miles south of Cambridge, though Norwich airport is growing in size and importance too. The region's **train** network is at its best to and from London, with quick and frequent services from the capital to all of the region's major towns. One main line links Colchester, Ipswich and Norwich, another Cambridge, Ely and King's Lynn. These services are supplemented by a number of cross-country branch lines, most usefully between Peterborough, Ely and Norwich and Ipswich, Bury St Edmunds and Cambridge. Once you get away from the major towns, however, you'll have to rely on local **buses**. Services, operated by a multitude of companies, are very patchy, though at least the north Norfolk coast is well served by the **Coasthopper** (see p.458; ⓦwww.coasthopper.co.uk).

Long-distance footpaths

Given the prevailing flatness of the terrain, hiking in East Anglia is less strenuous than in most other English regions, and there are several **long-distance footpaths**. The main one is the **Peddars Way**, which runs north from Knettishall Heath, near Thetford, to the coast at Holme, near Hunstanton, where it continues east as the **Norfolk Coast Path** to Cromer – 93 miles in total (see ⊛ www.nationaltrail.co.uk for both). At Cromer, you can pick up the 57-mile **Weavers' Way**, which wends its way through the Broads to the coast at Great Yarmouth.

Hunstanton to name but three – but for the most part it's charmingly unspoilt, with marshes, creeks and tidal flats studded with tiny flint-stone villages, most enjoyably **Blakeney** and **Cley**. Meanwhile, sheltering inland, are two outstanding stately homes – **Blickling Hall** and **Holkham** – with a third, **Sandringham**, long a royal favourite, within easy striking distance of **King's Lynn**, a strange, almost disconcerting mixture of fenland town and ancient seaport.

Cambridge is the one place in East Anglia everyone visits, principally because of its world-renowned university, whose ancient colleges boast some of the finest medieval and early modern architecture in the country. The rest of Cambridgeshire is pancake-flat fenland, for centuries an inhospitable marshland but now comprising rich alluvial farming land. The one star turn here is the cathedral town of **Ely**, settled on one of the few areas of raised ground in the Fens and an easy day-trip from Cambridge.

Colchester

Perhaps more than anything else, **COLCHESTER**, a busy, bustling sort of place fifty miles or so northeast of London, prides itself on being England's oldest town – and there is indeed documentary evidence of a settlement here as early as the fifth century BC – though the oldest remains today date from the Roman period. By the first century AD, it was the region's capital under **King Cunobelin** – better known as Shakespeare's Cymbeline – and when the **Romans** invaded Britain in 43 AD they chose Colchester as their new capital, though it was soon eclipsed by London, becoming a retirement colony for legionaries instead. The first Roman temple in the country was erected here, and in 60 AD the colony was the target of Boudica's abortive revolt (see box, p.432). A millennium later, the conquering Normans built one of their mightiest strongholds in Colchester, but the conflict that most marked the town was the **Civil War**. In 1648, Colchester was subjected to a gruelling siege by the Parliamentarian army led by Lord Fairfax; after three months, during which the population ate every living creature within the walls, the town finally surrendered and the Royalist leaders were promptly executed for their pains.

Colchester is probably best visited on a **day-trip**, but it is a potential base for further exploration of the surrounding countryside – particularly the Stour Valley towns of Constable Country (see p.434), within easy reach a few miles to the north.

Arrival, information and accommodation

Colchester has two **train stations**, but most services stop at Colchester North, from where it's a fifteen-minute walk south into town; just southeast of town is Colchester Town train station, from which services leave for the Tendring coast (see

Betrayed and abused: Boudica of the Iceni

Boudica – aka Boadicea – was the wife of Prasutagus, chief of the Iceni tribe of Norfolk, who allied himself to the Romans during their conquest of Britain in 43 AD. Five years later, when the Iceni were no longer useful, the Romans attempted to disarm them and, although the Iceni rebelled, they were soon brought to heel. On Prasutagus's death, the Romans confiscated his property and when Boudica protested, they flogged her and raped her daughters. Enraged, Boudica determined to take her revenge, quickly rallying the Iceni and their allies before setting off on a rampage across southern Britain in 60 AD.

As the ultimate symbol of Roman oppression, the **Temple of Claudius** in Colchester was the initial focus of hatred, but, once Colchester had been razed, Boudica soon turned her sights elsewhere. She laid waste to London and St Albans, massacring over seventy thousand citizens and inflicting crushing defeats on the Roman units stationed there. She was far from squeamish, ripping traitors' arms out of their sockets and torturing every Roman and Roman collaborator in sight. The Roman governor Suetonius Paulinus eventually defeated her in a pitched battle, which cost the Romans just four hundred lives and the Britons untold thousands. Boudica knew what to expect from the Romans, so she opted for **suicide**, thereby ensuring her later reputation as a patriotic Englishwoman, who died fighting for liberty and freedom – claims which Boudica would have found incomprehensible.

box opposite). The **bus station** is off Queen Street, a couple of minutes' walk from the High Street and yards from both the castle and the **tourist office**, at 1 Queen St (Mon–Sat 10am–5pm; ℡01206/282920, ⓦwww.visitcolchester.com). Among the town's several **hotels and B&Bs**, easily the pick is *Charlie Brown's*, just to the east of the centre at 60 East St (℡01206/517541, ⓦwww.charliebrownsbedand breakfast.co.uk; ❷), where the three en-suite guest rooms are canny and strikingly good-looking amalgamations of the old – exposed wooden beams et al – and the new. Close by, also on East Street, is the dependable, half-timbered *Best Western Rose & Crown* (℡01206/866677, ⓦwww.bw-roseandcrownhotel.co.uk; ❸), which dates back to the fourteenth century; guests choose between the oak-beamed rooms in the original building or the attractively furnished rooms in the modern annexe.

The Town

At the heart of Colchester is its **castle**, or rather what remains of the medieval stronghold, a ruggedly imposing, honey-coloured keep, set in attractive parkland that stretches down to the River Colne. Begun less than ten years after the Battle of Hastings, the keep was the largest in Europe at the time, and was built on the site of the Temple of Claudius – the one that Boudica had attacked many centuries before (see box above). Inside the keep, a **museum** (Mon–Sat 10am–5pm, Sun 11am–5pm; £5.70) holds an excellent collection of Romano-British archeological finds, including a miscellany of coins, tombstones, statues and mosaics. Highlights are the so-called Colchester vase, decorated with gladiators and a hunting scene, and a fine if armless bronze of Mercury, the messenger of the gods. The museum also covers the history of the town and runs regular **guided tours** (45min; £2), giving access to parts of the castle that are otherwise out of bounds. Outside, down towards the river in Castle Park, is a section of the old **Roman walls**, whose battered remains are still visible around much of the town centre. They were erected after Boudica had sacked the city and, as such, are a case of too little too late.

The castle stands at the eastern end of the wide and largely pedestrianized **High Street**, which follows pretty much the same route as it did in Roman times. The

Jutting out into the North Sea to the east of Colchester is the wide and chunky **Tendring peninsula**, aka Essex's **"Sunshine Coast"**, though the name has as much to do with tourist flannel as the Essex climate. Nonetheless, seaside resorts do line up along the Tendring's south coast. Biggest and brassiest is **Clacton-on-Sea**, though rather more demure are **Frinton-on-Sea** and **Walton-on-the-Naze**, both smart little places with sandy beaches. Both towns are served hourly by train from Colchester Town Station (see p.431); it takes around thirty minutes to reach either town.

most arresting building here is the flamboyant **town hall**, built in 1902 and topped by a statue of St Helena, mother of Constantine the Great and daughter of Old King Cole of nursery-rhyme fame – after whom, some say, the town was named.

Looming above the western end of the High Street is **"Jumbo"**, a disused nineteenth-century water tower that has long served as a popular landmark. The tower rises high above the neighbouring **Balkerne Gate**, which marked the western entrance to Roman Colchester. Built in 50 AD, this is the largest surviving Roman gateway in the country, though with the remains at only a touch over six feet in height, it's far from spectacular. The gate is joined to another section of the town's Roman walls, though here the effect is spoiled by the neighbouring ring road.

Eating and drinking

Colchester has a good choice of first-rate **restaurants**, one of the best being *The Lemon Tree*, 48 St John's St (℡01206/767337; closed Sun), which offers a contemporary European menu in smart premises with main courses hovering around £13; St John's Street runs south of – and parallel to – the High Street. An excellent alternative is the *Warehouse Brasserie*, housed in an old Methodist chapel – complete with the original pews – some way to the south of the High Street at 12 Chapel St North (℡01206/765656; eve only, closed Sun & Mon). The emphasis here is on local, seasonal ingredients with a main course – for example stuffed slow-roast Suffolk pork belly, apple and cider gravy with mashed potatoes – costing £14.

Colchester's **oysters** have been highly prized since Roman times and down on the coast in West Mersea, on Mersea Island, about nine miles south of town, *The Company Shed*, 129 Coast Rd (℡01206/382700; daytime only, closed Mon), continues the tradition. Here, they serve locally cultivated oysters without any frills, at rickety tables. The oyster season runs from September to May.

The Stour Valley and the old wool towns of south Suffolk

Five miles or so north of Colchester, the **Stour River Valley** forms the border between Essex and Suffolk, and signals the beginning of East Anglia proper. Compared with much of the region it is positively hilly, a handsome landscape of farms and woodland latticed by dense, well-kept hedges and the thick grassy banks that once kept the Stour in check. The valley is dotted with lovely little villages too, where rickety, half-timbered Tudor houses and elegant Georgian dwellings cluster around medieval churches, proud buildings with square, self-confident towers. The Stour's prettiest villages are concentrated along its lower reaches – to the east of the A12 – in Dedham Vale, with **Stoke-by-Nayland** and **Dedham** arguably the most appealing of them all. The vale is also known as "**Constable Country**" as it was the home of John Constable (1776–1837), one of England's greatest artists, and the subject of his most famous works. Inevitably, there's a Constable shrine – the much-visited complex of old buildings down by the river at **Flatford Mill**.

The villages along the River Stour and its tributaries were once busy little places at the heart of East Anglia's weaving trade, which boomed from the thirteenth to the fifteenth century. By the 1490s, the region produced more cloth than any other part of the country, but in Tudor times production shifted to Colchester, Ipswich and Norwich and, although most of the smaller settlements continued spinning cloth for the next three hundred years or so, their importance slowly dwindled. Bypassed by the Industrial Revolution, south Suffolk had, by the late nineteenth century, become a remote rural backwater, an impoverished area whose decline had one unforeseen consequence: with few exceptions, the towns and villages were never prosperous enough to modernize, so the architectural legacy of medieval and Tudor times survived. The two best-preserved villages are **Lavenham** and **Kersey**, both of which heave with sightseers on summer weekends. Nearby **Sudbury** is also attractive and boasts an excellent museum devoted to the work of Thomas Gainsborough, another talented English artist who spent much of his time painting the local landscape.

Seeing the region by **public transport** is problematic – distances are small, but **buses** between the villages are infrequent and you'll find it difficult to get away from the towns. For bus timetable information, go to ⓦ www.suffolkonboard .com or ⓦ www.traveline.org.uk. By **train**, you need to make for Sudbury, which is on a branch line off the London Liverpool Street–Colchester mainline; change at Marks Tey. For walkers, **footpaths** crisscross the area, with some of the most enjoyable being in the vicinity of Dedham village. All the local tourist offices sell easy-to-use walking leaflets.

Flatford Mill

"I associate my careless boyhood to all that lies on the banks of the Stour," wrote **John Constable**, who was born the son of a miller in **East Bergholt**, nine miles northeast of Colchester in 1776. The house in which he was born has long since disappeared, so it has been left to **Flatford Mill**, a mile or so to the south, to take up the painter's cause. The mill was owned by his father and was where Constable painted his most famous canvas, *The Hay Wain* (now in London's National Gallery), which created a sensation when it was exhibited in 1824. To the chagrin of many of his contemporaries, Constable turned away from the landscape-painting conventions of the day, rendering his scenery with a realistic directness that harked back to the Dutch landscape painters of the seventeenth century. Typically, he justified this approach in unpretentious terms, observing that, after all "no two days are alike, nor even two hours; neither were there ever two leaves of a tree alike since the creation of the world."

The **mill** itself – not the one he painted, but a Victorian replacement – is not open to the public and neither is neighbouring **Willy Lott's Cottage**, which does actually feature in *The Hay Wain*, but the National Trust have colonized several local buildings, principally **Bridge Cottage** (Jan & Feb Sat & Sun 11am–3.30pm; March Wed–Sun 11am–4pm; April daily 11am–5pm; May–Sept daily 10.30am–5.30pm; Oct daily 11am–4.30pm; Nov & Dec Wed–Sun 11am–3.30pm; free, except for parking; NT), which was familiar to Constable and is now packed with Constabilia. None of the artist's paintings is displayed here, but there's a pleasant riverside tearoom to take in the view.

Practicalities

In summer, the National Trust organizes **guided walks** around the sites of Constable's paintings (call ☎01206/298260 for details), but there are many other pleasant walks to be had along this deeply rural bend in the Stour. One footpath connects the mill to the **train station** at Manningtree, two miles to the southeast, and another runs over to the village of Dedham (see below), a mile and a half to the west. Alternatively, you can rent a **rowing boat** from beside the bridge and potter peacefully along the river. There's a **B&B** here too, *The Granary* (☎01206/298111, ⓦwww.granaryflatford.co.uk; ❷), in the annexe to the old granary that was once owned by Constable's father. The en-suite rooms are cottage-style affairs with beamed ceilings and folksy furniture.

Dedham

Constable went to school in **DEDHAM**, just upriver from Flatford Mill and one of the region's most attractive villages, its wide main street graced by a handsome medley of old timber-framed houses and Georgian villas. The only sights as such are **St Mary's Church**, an early sixteenth-century structure that Constable painted on several occasions, and the **Sir Alfred Munnings Art Museum**, in Castle House (April–Oct Wed & Sun 2–5pm, plus Thurs & Sat in May, July & Sept 2–5pm; £5; ⓦwww.siralfredmunnings.co.uk), just south of the village on the road to Ardleigh. A locally born academician, Munnings (1875–1959) is barely remembered today, but in his time he was well known for his portraits of horses. In the 1940s, he became a controversial figure when, as president of the Royal Academy, he savaged almost every form of modern art there was. Few would say his paintings were inspiring, but seeing them is a pleasant way to fill a rainy afternoon.

Practicalities

It's a circuitous drive of around 5km from Flatford Mill to Dedham via the A12. Constable Coaches (ⓦwww.constablecoachesltd.co.uk) operates a **bus** service from Colchester to Dedham with buses stopping outside the *Marlborough Head* pub (Mon–Sat 3–4 daily; 40min). Among Dedham's several **pubs**, the pick is *The Sun Inn*, on the High Street (☎01206/323351, ⓦwww.thesuninndedham.com; ❹, weekends ❺), an ancient place that has been sympathetically modernized. The menu is strong on local ingredients and offers a tasty range of both Italian and British dishes, all washed down with real ales; main courses average around £12. *The Sun* also has five immaculate en-suite **rooms** decorated in a creative blend of country inn and boutique hotel, from four-poster beds through to billowy, caramel-cream curtains. A second option is *Dedham Hall* (☎01206/323027, ⓦwww.dedhamhall.co.uk; ❺), in an old manor house set in its own grounds on the east side of the village off Brook Street, a continuation of the High Street; be sure to ask for a room in the house itself.

Stoke-by-Nayland and Nayland

Heading northwest from Dedham, the B1029 dips beneath the A12 on its way to Higham, where you pick up the road to **STOKE-BY-NAYLAND**, four miles further west. This is the most picturesque of villages, where a knot of half-timbered and pastel-painted cottages cuddle up to one of Constable's favourite subjects, **St Mary's Church** (daily 9am–5pm; free), with its pretty brick-and-stone-trimmed tower. The doors of the south porch are covered by the beautifully carved if badly weathered figures of a medieval **Jesse Tree** and, although the interior is sombre and severe, it does boast a beautifully carved medieval font.

The village also has a pair of appealing **pub-restaurants**, beginning with the rustic beams and bare-brick walls of *The Angel Inn* (℡01206/263245, Ⓦwww .theangelinn.net; ❸), where they serve a straightforward range of English dishes – sausage and mash for example. There are half a dozen, en-suite guest **rooms** here too. Rather better, though, is the food at *The Crown* (℡01206/262001, Ⓦwww .crowninn.net; ❺), the menu being an adventurous amalgamation of British and European dishes with the ingredients sourced locally wherever possible – try the pork belly with leek mash; main courses cost in the region of £12–16. *The Crown* also has eleven guest rooms kitted out in an attractive country-house style with browns and greens to the fore.

Travelling southwest from Stoke-by-Nayland, it's two miles back to the River Stour at **NAYLAND**, a workaday little place where the most distinctive feature is the **church of St James**, whose square tower and copper-green spire poke high into the sky. Inside, Constable's *Christ Blessing the Bread and Wine* is one of only two attempts he made at a religious theme – and, dating from 1809, it was completed long before he found his artistic rhythm.

Sudbury

With a population of around 12,000, **SUDBURY** has doubled in size in the last forty years, to become by far the most important town in this part of the Stour Valley. A handful of timber-framed houses harks back to its days of wool-trade prosperity, but its salad days were underwritten by another local industry, **silk weaving**, which survives on a small scale to this day.

Sudbury's most famous export, however, is **Thomas Gainsborough** (1727–1788), the leading English portraitist of the eighteenth century, whose statue, with brush and palette, stands on Market Hill, the town's predominantly Victorian marketplace. A superb collection of the artist's work is on display a few yards away in the house where he was born – **Gainsborough's House**, at 46 Gainsborough St (Mon–Sat 10am–5pm; £4.50; Ⓦwww.gainsborough.org). Gainsborough left Sudbury when he was just 13, moving to London where he was apprenticed to an engraver, but it seems he was soon moonlighting and the earliest of his surviving portrait paintings – his *Boy and Girl*, a remarkably self-assured work dated to 1744 – is displayed here in two pieces as someone, somewhere, chopped up the original. In 1752, Gainsborough moved on to Ipswich, where he quickly established himself as a portrait painter to the Suffolk gentry with one of his specialities being wonderful "conversation pieces", so called because the sitters engage in polite chitchat – or genteel activity – with a landscape as the backdrop. Stints in Ipswich, Bath and London followed, and it was during these years that Gainsborough developed a fluid, flatteringly easy style that was ideal for his aristocratic subjects, who posed in becoming postures painted in soft, evanescent colours. Examples of Gainsborough's later work on display include the *Portrait of Harriet, Viscountess Tracy* (1763) and the particularly striking *Portrait of Abel Moysey, MP* (1771). In his last years, the artist also dabbled with romantic paintings of country scenes – as in *A Wooded Landscape with Cattle by a Pool* – a playful variation of the serious landscaping painting he loved to do best; the rest, he often said, just earned him a living. Gainsborough never bothered with assistants, with one exception, his nephew **Gainsborough Dupont**, whose work has a room devoted to it on the top floor.

Practicalities

Sudbury is just seven miles northwest of Nayland along the A134. It's accessible by **train** from Colchester, fifteen miles away, and is the hub of **bus** services to and from neighbouring towns and villages. The **tourist office** is on Gaol Lane, bang

Top 5: Places to stay in Suffolk and Norfolk

▶▶ **Great House** Lavenham. Antique luxury in a picture-postcard setting. See p.437.

▶▶ **Crown & Castle Hotel** Orford. Fantastically relaxing rural getaway in the prettiest of villages. See p.443.

▶▶ **Ocean House** Aldeburgh. Immaculate B&B right by the sea. See p.444.

▶▶ **Cley Windmill** Cley. Three cheers for whoever decided to turn this old windmill into a B&B. See p.460

▶▶ **White Horse** Brancaster Staithe. Walkers and twitchers alike can hardly do better than this comfortable hotel overlooking the marshes of the Norfolk coast. See p.466.

in the centre of town off Market Hill (Mon–Fri 9am–5pm, plus Sat April–Sept 10am–4.45pm, Oct–March 10am–2.45pm; ℡01787/881320, Ⓦwww.visit -suffolk.org.uk). With other, prettier places nearby, there's no strong reason to overnight here, but Sudbury does have one inexpensive, well-situated **hotel**, *Hotel Elizabeth The Mill*, by the river on the west side of town on Walnut Tree Lane (℡01787/375544, Ⓦwww.hotelelizabeththemill.co.uk; ❷). This occupies a large, appealing old mill, but many of the fifty-odd rooms are more than a little frugal. For **food**, head for *The Secret Garden*, 21 Friars St (Mon–Fri 9am–5pm, plus Fri & Sat 7–9.30pm; ℡01787/372030), a tearoom with bells, where the menu has lots of French flourishes and they do their best to source locally.

Lavenham

LAVENHAM, some eight miles northeast of Sudbury, was once a centre of the region's wool trade and is now one of the most visited villages in Suffolk, thanks to its unrivalled ensemble of perfectly preserved half-timbered houses. In outward appearance at least, the whole place has changed little since the demise of the wool industry, owing in part to a zealous local preservation society, which has carefully maintained the village's antique appearance by banning from view such modern frivolities as advertising hoardings.

Arrival, information and accommodation

Chambers **bus #753** (Mon–Sat hourly) connects Sudbury and Bury St Edmunds with Lavenham; buses pull in at the junction of Water Street and the High Street, a couple of minutes' walk from the Market Place. Lavenham **tourist office** is just south off the Market Place on Lady Street (Jan to mid-March Sat & Sun 11am–3pm; mid-March to Oct daily 10am–4.45pm; Nov & Dec daily 11am–3pm; ℡01787/248207, Ⓦwww.southandheartofsuffolk.org.uk). They sell a detailed, street-by-street walking guide and can help with **accommodation** – there's plenty of choice but rooms still get mighty tight in the high season.

Angel Gallery 17 Market Place ℡01787/248417, Ⓦwww.angelgallerylavenham.co.uk. Great location, on the main square above the eponymous gallery, this homely B&B has three modest rooms, two en suite, and is very reasonably priced – for Lavenham. ❸

🏃 **Great House** Market Place ℡01787/247431, Ⓦwww.greathouse.co.uk. Delightful family-run hotel bang in the centre of the village. There are five guest rooms here, each decorated in a thoughtful and extremely tasteful manner,

amalgamating the original features of the old – very old – house with the new. Deeply comfortable beds and a great breakfast to round it all off. Unbeatable. ❹, ❺ on the weekend

Guinea House 16 Bolton St ℡01787/249046, Ⓦwww.guineahouse.co.uk. In a dinky little house a short walk from the Market Place, this well-established B&B has two low-beamed, folksy-meets-cosy guest rooms. No credit cards. ❸

Lavenham Priory Water St ℡01787/247404, Ⓦwww.lavenhampriory.co.uk. The most luxurious

B&B in Lavenham, this deluxe place occupies a handsome, half-timbered complex of buildings that began life as a priory. There are half a dozen en-suite guest rooms, each kitted out in a fancy version of period style – four-poster beds are (almost) de rigueur. ⑤
The Swan Hotel High St ☎01787/247477, ⓦwww.theswanatlavenham.co.uk. One of a small chain of hotels, this splendid if somewhat dandified old inn incorporates a warren of lounges and courtyard gardens not to mention an authentic Elizabethan Wool Hall. Most of the guest rooms have original features – low wooden beams etc – and are decorated in warm pastel shades. ⑥

The village

The village is at its most beguiling in the triangular **Market Place**, an airy spot flanked by pastel-painted, medieval dwellings whose beams have been bent into all sorts of wonky angles by the passing of the years. It's here you'll find Lavenham's most celebrated building, the lime-washed, timber-framed **Guildhall of Corpus Christi** (March Wed–Sun 11am–4pm; April–Oct daily 11am–5pm; Nov Sat & Sun 11am–4pm; £3.90; NT), erected in the sixteenth century as the headquarters of one of Lavenham's four guilds. In the much-altered interior (used successively as a prison and workhouse), there are modest exhibitions on timber-framed buildings, medieval guilds, village life and the wool industry, though most visitors soon end up in the walled garden or the teashop next door. Back outside on the Market Place, the view down Prentice Street from beside the *Angel Hotel* is one of Lavenham's most exquisite – a line of creaky timber-framed dwellings dipping into the deep green countryside beyond.

Spare time also for the Perpendicular **church of St Peter and St Paul** (daily: April–Sept 8.30am–5.30pm; Oct–March 8.30am–3.30pm; free), which is sited a short walk southwest of the centre at the top of Church Street, and features gargoyle water-spouts and carved pigs above the entrance. Local merchants endowed the church with a nave of majestic proportions and a mighty flint tower, at 141ft the highest for miles around, partly to celebrate the Tudor victory at the Battle of Bosworth in 1485 (see p.571), but mainly to show just how wealthy they had become.

Eating and drinking

The *Angel Hotel*, on the Market Place, offers a good range of brews as well as tip-top **bar food** – tasty, unpretentious English cuisine with dishes such as steak and ale pie, a snip at just £11. Alternatively, the chic and smart ⌘ **restaurant** of the *Great House*, also on the Market Place (☎01787/247431; closed Sun eve, Mon & Tues lunchtime), specializes in classic French cuisine, with a three-course set meal costing £20 at lunch, £32 at night. With such delights as belly of Suffolk pork confit and duck in cider, they have garnered rave reviews all over the place, so book ahead.

Kersey

Minuscule **KERSEY**, eight miles southeast of Lavenham off the A1141, is one of the most photographed villages in Suffolk. Another old wool town, it seems to have dodged just about every historical bullet since the seventeenth century and now comprises little more than one exquisite street of timber-framed houses, which dips in the middle to negotiate a ford inhabited by a family of fearless ducks. Prime real-estate today, Kersey's more populous past is recalled by the large and austere parish **church of St Mary**, visible for miles around, perched on high ground above the village. There's nowhere to stay, but there is one good **pub**, the ancient, half-timbered *Bell Inn*, and you can drop by **Kersey Pottery** (Tues–Sat 10am–5.30pm, Sun 11am–5pm) to have a look at their distinctive stoneware.

Bury St Edmunds

An amiable, eminently likeable place, **BURY ST EDMUNDS**, ten miles north of Lavenham, is one of the prettiest towns in Suffolk. It started out as a Benedictine monastery, founded to accommodate the remains of Edmund, the last Saxon king of East Anglia, who was tortured and beheaded by the marauding Danes in 869. Almost two centuries later, England was briefly ruled by the kings of Denmark and the shrewdest of them, **King Canute**, made a gesture of reconciliation to his Saxon subjects by granting the monastery a generous endowment and building the monks a brand-new church. It was a popular move and the abbey prospered, so much so that by the time of its dissolution in 1539, it had become the richest religious house in the country. Most of the abbey disappeared long ago, and nowadays Bury is better known for its graceful Georgian streets, its flower gardens and its sugar-beet plant than for its ancient monuments.

Arrival, information and accommodation

From Bury St Edmunds' **train station**, it's ten minutes' walk south to central Angel Hill via Northgate Street. The **bus station** is on St Andrew Street North, just north of Cornhill, itself just five minutes' walk west of Angel Hill. The town's **tourist office**, at 6 Angel Hill (Easter–Oct Mon–Sat 9.30am–5.30pm, plus May–Sept Sun 10am–3pm; Nov–Easter Mon–Fri 10am–4pm, Sat 10am–1pm; ⓣ01284/764667, ⓦwww.visit-burystedmunds.co.uk), provides free town maps and has a useful range of leaflets. For a small town, Bury St Edmunds has a healthy supply of **hotels** and **B&Bs**.

Angel 3 Angel Hill ⓣ01284/714000, ⓦwww.theangel.co.uk. Long-established former coaching inn whose public areas have been remodelled in fairly uninspiring contemporary manner. Beyond are 75 comfortable bedrooms, some with a country-house feel, others with a more modern inflection. ④

Chantry Hotel 8 Sparhawk St ⓣ01284/767427, ⓦwww.chantryhotel.com. There are fifteen smart, modern guest rooms in this privately owned hotel which occupies two converted Georgian townhouses just to the south of the abbey ruins off Honey Hill. ④

Old Cannon 86 Cannon St ⓣ01284/768769, ⓦwww.oldcannonbrewery.co.uk. Arguably Bury's most distinctive B&B, with five spick-and-span guest rooms, all en suite, in an intelligently recycled brewhouse, which is itself attached to a microbrewery and bar. The brews are strong – so you might be glad your bed is near at hand, though the brewery is in a dull part of town, on the north side of the centre: to get there, take Northgate St from Angel Hill, then turn hard left at the roundabout. ③

The Town

The town centre has preserved much of its Norman street plan, a gridiron in which Churchgate was originally aligned with – and sloped up from – the abbey's high altar. It was the first planned town of Norman Britain and, for that matter, the first example of urban planning in England since the departure of the Romans.

Angel Hill and the abbey ruins

At the heart of the town is **Angel Hill**, a broad, spacious square partly framed by Georgian buildings, the most distinguished being the ivy-covered **Angel Hotel** (see above), which features in Dickens' *The Pickwick Papers*. Dickens also gave readings of his work in the **Athenaeum**, the Georgian assembly rooms at the far end of the square. A twelfth-century wall runs along the east side of Angel Hill, with the bulky fourteenth-century **Abbey Gate** forming the entrance to the abbey gardens and ruins beyond.

The **abbey ruins** themselves (Mon–Sat 7.30am–dusk, Sun 9am–dusk; free) are like nothing so much as petrified porridge, with little to remind you of the grandiose Norman complex that once dominated the town. Thousands of medieval pilgrims once sought solace at St Edmund's altar and the cult was of such significance that the barons of England gathered here to swear that they would make King John sign their petition – the Magna Carta of 1215. Today, the most significant remains are those of the old **abbey church** on the far (right) side of the abbey gardens and the neighbouring **Norman tower**, which was once the main gateway into the abbey and is now a solitary monument with dragon gargoyles and fancily decorated arcading.

The cathedral and the Greene King brewery

The Norman tower stands next to the Anglican **St Edmundsbury Cathedral** (daily 8.30am–6pm; £3 donation), a hangar-like affair with a beautiful painted roof whose chancel and transepts were added as recently as the 1960s. It was a toss-up between this church and **St Mary's** (Mon–Sat 10am–4pm, 3pm in winter; free), further down the street, as to which would be given cathedral status in 1914. The presence of the tomb of the resolutely Catholic Mary Tudor in the latter was the clinching factor. From St Mary's, it's a couple of minutes' walk south along Crown Street to the **Greene King brewery**, where the visitor centre sells tickets for guided brewery tours (1–3 daily; £8; Ⓦwww.greeneking.co.uk), during which you can wet your whistle on a range of their products – Old Speckled Hen is perhaps their most celebrated brew.

The rest of the centre

Bury's main commercial area is just to the west of Angel Hill up along Abbeygate. There's been some intrusive modern planning here, but sterling Victorian buildings flank both the L-shaped **Cornhill** and the **Buttermarket**, the two short main streets, as well as the narrower streets in between. Also between the two is **Bury St Edmunds Art Gallery** (Tues–Sat 10.30am–5pm; free; Ⓦwww.burystedmundsartgallery.org), which features a lively programme of temporary exhibitions focusing on contemporary fine and applied art. The streets to the south of the Cornhill are lined by an attractive medley of architectural styles, from elegant Georgian townhouses to Victorian brick terraces. You'll see the best by strolling along Guildhall Street and turning left down Churchgate, which brings you back to Angel Hill.

Eating, drinking and entertainment

The best **teashop** in town is *Bailey's*, a cosy, modern place just off Abbeygate at 5 Whiting St (closed Sun), where they serve a good line in toasties and an even better one in home-made cakes. The town has several good **restaurants**, but the pick is ⚜ *Maison Bleue*, 31 Churchgate St (Ⓣ01284/760623; closed Sun & Mon), which is noted for its outstanding (French-style) seafood, from crab through to sardines and skate; main courses kick off at around £15. *The Old Cannon*, (see p.439), is a good second choice, offering a delicious range of dishes and using locally sourced ingredients wherever possible in both its bar and brasserie; main courses, such as Lowestoft smoked haddock kedgeree with horseradish crumble, cost around £10.

Of the **pubs**, it's the *Old Cannon* again – they brew their own ales – or you might try the *Nutshell*, on The Traverse at the top of Abbeygate, which, at sixteen feet by seven and a half, claims to be Britain's smallest pub and serves a first-rate range of real ales. Finally, the **Theatre Royal**, at the junction of Crown and Westgate streets (Ⓣ01284/769505, Ⓦwww.theatreroyal.org), offers a year-round programme of cultural events, from Shakespeare to pantomime.

Ipswich

IPSWICH, situated at the head of the Orwell estuary, was a rich trading port in the Middle Ages, but its appearance today is mainly the result of a revival of fortunes in the Victorian era – give or take some clumsy postwar development. No one could say the town was actually pretty, but it does have the odd highlight, most notably **Christchurch Mansion**, with its collection of Gainsboroughs and Constables, and the recently renovated **waterfront** – altogether quite enough to keep you busy for half a day.

The Town

Cornhill, the ancient Saxon marketplace, is still the town's focal point, a likeable urban space flanked by a bevy of imposing Victorian edifices – the Italianate town hall, the old Neoclassical post office and the grandiose pseudo-Jacobean Lloyds building. From here, it's just a couple of minutes' walk southeast to Ipswich's most famous building, the **Ancient House**, on Buttermarket, near St Stephen's Lane. The building's exterior was decorated around 1670 in extravagant style, a riot of fancy plasterwork, which makes it one of the finest examples of Restoration artistry in the country. There are plasterwork reliefs of pelicans and nymphs as well as representations of the four continents known at the time: Europe is symbolized by a Gothic church, America a tobacco pipe, Asia an Oriental dome and Africa, eccentrically enough, by an African astride a crocodile. Since the house is now a shop, you're free to take a peek inside to view yet more of the decor, including the hammer-beam roof.

From the Ancient House, it's a short hop north to **Christchurch Mansion** (daily 10am–5pm; free), a handsome, if much-restored Tudor building sporting seventeenth-century Dutch-style gables and set in 65 acres of parkland – an area larger than the town centre itself. The mansion's labyrinthine interior is worth exploring, with period furnishings and a good assortment of paintings by Gainsborough and Constable, including the latter's wonderfully verdant *Vegetable Garden*.

On the other side of the town centre, about half a mile south of Cornhill, is the **Wet Dock**, which was the largest dock in Europe when it opened in 1845. After years in the doldrums, a sustained effort has been made to re-invigorate the area and now, although there are still blotches of decay, the quayside is flanked by a pleasant mix of apartments and offices, hotels and restaurants, some occupying the old marine warehouses. The architectural high-point here is the proud Neoclassical **Customs House**, which comes complete with a grand portico and a wide double stairway.

Practicalities

Ipswich **train station** is on the south bank of the river, about ten minutes' walk from Cornhill along Princes Street. The **bus station** is more central, on Turret Lane, a southerly extension of St Stephen's Lane, which is where you'll find the **tourist office**, in the converted St Stephen's Church (Mon–Sat 9am–5pm; ℡01473/258070, ⓦwww.visit-ipswich.com).

Ipswich has one really good **hotel**, the *Salthouse Harbour*, in an imaginatively converted old warehouse, down on the quayside of the Wet Dock (℡01473/226789, ⓦwww.salthouseharbour.co.uk; ⑤). It has great views over the harbourfront from its upper floors and the rooms are decorated in modern, minimalist style. The hotel **brasserie** is good too, with a surprisingly varied menu – from liver and parsnips to daily seafood specials; main courses average £14.

The Suffolk coast

The **Suffolk coast** feels detached from the rest of the county: the road and rail lines from Ipswich to the seaport of Lowestoft funnel traffic a few miles inland for most of the way, and patches of marsh and woodland make the separation still more complete. The coast has long been plagued by erosion and this has contributed to the virtual extinction of the local fishing industry, and, in the case of **Dunwich**, almost destroyed the whole town. What is left, however, is undoubtedly one of the most unspoilt shorelines in the country – if, that is, you set aside the Sizewell nuclear power station. Highlights include **Sutton Hoo**, where a National Trust exhibition hall provides an outstanding introduction to the Anglo-Saxon burial mounds that bump across the surrounding fields; the sleepy isolation of tiny **Orford**; and several genteel resorts, most notably **Southwold**, which has evaded the lurid fate of so many English seaside towns. There are scores of delightful **walks** hereabouts too, easy routes along the coast that are best followed with either the appropriate OS Explorer Map or the simplified Footpath Maps available at most tourist offices. The Suffolk coast is also host to East Anglia's most compelling cultural gathering, the **Aldeburgh Festival**, which takes place every June.

Getting along and around the Suffolk coast by **public transport** requires patience and planning and your best bet is to work out your route ahead of time on ⓦ www.traveline.org.uk. Some journeys are perfectly straightforward – there is, for example, a regular bus service from Ipswich to Aldeburgh – but some are more complicated: to get from Southwold to Aldeburgh, for instance, you catch the bus to Halesworth, the train from Halesworth to Saxmundham and then another bus to Aldeburgh, a somewhat epic journey that takes at least a couple of hours.

Sutton Hoo

In 1939, a local farmer-cum-archeologist by the name of Basil Brown investigated one of a group of burial mounds on a sandy ridge at **Sutton Hoo**, on a remote part of the Suffolk coast in between Ipswich and Orford. Much to everyone's amazement, including his own, he unearthed the forty-oar burial ship of an Anglo-Saxon warrior king, packed with his most valuable possessions, from a splendid iron and tinted-bronze helmet through to his intricately worked gold and jewelled ornaments. There's been much academic debate about the burial ship ever since, not least as to the identity of the body, though Raedwald, king of East Anglia, who died around 625 AD, remains the favourite. A series of supplementary digs has since explored the other burial mounds, but these were robbed centuries ago and have revealed little. Much of the Sutton Hoo treasure is now in London's British Museum (see p.94), but a scattering of artefacts – ship's rivets, belt buckles, a horse harness and so forth – can be seen in the **Sutton Hoo exhibition hall** (Jan to early March, Nov & Dec Sat & Sun 11am–4pm; mid- to late March Wed–Sun 10.30am–5pm; April–Oct daily 10.30am–5pm; £6.20; NT), which explains the history and significance of the finds. Afterwards, you can wander out onto the burial site itself, about 500 yards away.

Located some ten miles east of Ipswich, on the far side of the River Deben, Sutton Hoo is clearly signed from the A12 at Woodbridge. The site is beside the B1083; there's no public transport.

Orford and around

Some twenty miles from Ipswich, in one of the most secluded parts of Suffolk, two medieval buildings dominate the tiny, eminently appealing village of

ORFORD. The more impressive is the twelfth-century **castle** (April–June & Sept daily 10am–5pm; July & Aug daily 10am–6pm; Oct–March Mon & Thurs–Sun 10am–4pm; £5.30; EH), built on high ground by Henry II, and under siege within months of its completion from Henry's rebellious sons. Most of the castle disappeared centuries ago, but the lofty keep remains, its impressive stature hinting at the scale of the original fortifications. Today, the castle offers wide views over Orford Ness National Nature Reserve (see below) from its battlements and also holds a pocket-sized museum, which puts some flesh on local bones. Orford's other medieval edifice is **St Bartholomew's church**, where Benjamin Britten premiered his most successful children's work, *Noye's Fludde*, as part of the 1958 Aldeburgh Festival (see box, p.445).

The most popular excursion from Orford is out onto Orford Ness, but there are plenty of **walks** to be had around Orford itself. One of the best is the five-mile hike north along the river wall that guards the west bank of the River Alde, returning via Ferry Road, a narrow country lane.

Orford Ness

Lying tight against the coast, **Orford Ness National Nature Reserve** is a six-mile-long shingle spit that has all but blocked Orford from the sea since Tudor times. The spit's assorted mud flats and marshes nourish sea lavender beds, which act as prime feeding and roosting areas for wildfowl and waders, and the whole caboodle is now owned by the National Trust. The Trust offers **boat trips** (early April to June & Oct Sat only; July–Sept Tues–Sat; outward boats between 10am & 2pm, last ferry back 5pm; £7.20, NT members £4; ☎01394/450900) across to the Ness from Orford Quay, five hundred yards down the road from St Bartholomew's church, and a five-mile hiking trail threads its way along the spit. En route, the trail passes a string of abandoned military buildings. Some of the pioneer research on radar was carried out here, but the **radar station** was closed at the beginning of World War II for fear of German bombing – though the military stayed on until the 1980s.

Practicalities

Orford's gentle and unhurried air is best experienced by **staying** at the excellent ⚔ *Crown & Castle Hotel* (☎01394/450205, ⓦ www.crownandcastlehotel.co .uk; ❺), whose modest-looking exterior doesn't quite do justice to the eighteen stylish guest rooms within. Very much to its credit, the hotel manages to dodge the clichés of both the boutique and the country-house hotel, maintaining a fresh and welcoming appeal. The hotel also has an outstanding **restaurant**, where the emphasis is on local ingredients – rump of Suffolk lamb with broad-bean cream sauce for example – with main courses in the range of £17–20. Just along the street from the hotel is *Butley Orford Oysterage* (☎01394/450277; lunchtimes daily all year, plus eve April–May & mid-Sept to Oct Wed–Sat, June to mid-Sept daily, Nov–March Sat & Sun), a straightforward café-restaurant where they sell the seafood they have caught and smoked themselves. They run a shop too – Pinney's, down at the harbour.

Aldeburgh

Well-heeled **ALDEBURGH**, just along the coast from Orford, is best known for its annual arts festival, the brainchild of composer **Benjamin Britten** (1913–76), who is buried in the village churchyard alongside the tenor Peter Pears, his lover and musical collaborator. The festival, which takes place in June, is the highlight of Aldeburgh's busy summer season, though the town seldom feels too crowded – for the most part, it's a relaxed and low-key coastal resort, with a few fishing boats selling the daily catch from wooden shacks along the pebbled shore. Don't be deceived, however: Aldeburgh's slightly old-fashioned, time-warped appearance is no accident but a tribute to its citizens, many of whom have fought hard to keep the commercial Philistines at the door. At worst, however, this can morph into a distrust of anything modern, as borne out by the almighty rumpus – Barbours at dawn – when Maggi Hambling's thirteen-foot-high, steel **Scallop** sculpture appeared on the beach in 2003. Hambling described the sculpture as a conversation with the sea and a suitable memorial to Britten; many locals compared it to a mantelpiece ornament gone wrong.

Arrival, information and accommodation

Buses to Aldeburgh pull in along the High Street, which is where you'll find the **tourist office**, at no. 152 (Mon–Sat 9am–5pm, plus June–Sept Sun 10am–4pm; ☎01728/453637, ⓦwww.suffolkcoastal.gov.uk/tourism); they share their premises with the festival box office (see box opposite). The tourist office holds local bus timetables and can book **accommodation**, though during the summer you'd be well advised to reserve in advance. Aldeburgh is second-home territory, so the number of hotels and B&Bs is constrained.

Blaxhall YHA Heath Walk, Blaxhall ☎0845/371 9305, ⓔblaxhall@yha.org.uk. Standard-issue hostel accommodation in the old village school of Blaxhall, a tiny hamlet a couple of miles southwest of the concert facilities at Snape Maltings. The hostel has forty beds in two- to six-bed rooms, a self-catering kitchen, a café and a laundry. Dorm beds £16, doubles ❶

Martello Tower Slaughden Rd ☎01628/825925, ⓦwww.landmarktrust.org.uk. Let by the Landmark Trust (see p.38), the heavily fortified Martello Tower right on the edge of the ocean about half a mile south of Aldeburgh provides the town's most distinctive accommodation. The tower has two bedrooms, self-catering facilities and a shower (but not a bath). In summer, a four-night rental costs £985.

Ocean House B&B 25 Crag Path ☎01728/ 452094, ⓦwww.oceanhousealdeburgh.co.uk.

Housed in an immaculately maintained Victorian dwelling in a prime location right on the seafront in the centre of town, *Ocean House* has just three guest rooms – so advance booking is well-nigh essential – including a top-floor suite. All the guest rooms are en suite and are decorated in traditional style complete with period furnishings. The full English breakfasts, with home-made bread, are delicious too. ❹

Wentworth Hotel Wentworth Rd ☎01728/ 452312, ⓦwww.wentworth-aldeburgh.com. Popular with an older and distinctly genteel clientele, this traditional hotel, with its long series of Edwardian half-timber gables, is on the seafront just along from the Moot Hall. The interior is all thick carpets and polished wood and the bedrooms are relaxed and relaxing. ❻

The Town

Aldeburgh's wide **High Street** and its narrow side-streets run close to the beach, but this was not always the case – hence their quixotic appearance. The sea swallowed much of what was once an extensive medieval town long ago and today Aldeburgh's oldest remaining building, the sixteenth-century, red-brick, flint and timber **Moot Hall**, which began its days in the centre of town, now finds itself on the seashore. From here, it's a few paces to **Crag House**, a large and somewhat dishevelled pinkish house at 4 Crabbe St, named after the poet George Crabbe, who provided Benjamin Britten with his greatest inspiration (see box opposite). Britten and Pears supposedly grew tired of fans peering through the windows, prompting them to move to the **Red House**, a much grander home about a mile and a half away out in the country on the road to Leiston.

Several **footpaths** radiate out from Aldeburgh, with the most obvious trail leading north along the coast to Thorpeness, and others going southwest to the winding estuary of the **River Alde**.

Born in Lowestoft in 1913, **Benjamin Britten** was closely associated with Suffolk for most of his life. The main break was during World War II when, as a conscientious objector, Britten exiled himself to the US. Ironically enough, it was here that Britten first read the work of the nineteenth-century Suffolk poet, George Crabbe, whose *The Borough*, a grisly portrait of the life of the fishermen of Aldeburgh, was the basis of the libretto of Britten's best-known opera, *Peter Grimes*. The latter was premiered in London in 1945 to great acclaim.

In 1947 Britten founded the English Opera Group and the following year launched the **Aldeburgh Festival** as a showpiece for his own works and those of his contemporaries. He lived in the village for the next ten years and it was during this period that he completed much of his best work as a conductor and pianist. For the rest of his life he composed many works specifically for the festival, including his masterpiece for children, *Noye's Fludde*, and the last of his fifteen operas, *Death in Venice*.

By the mid-1960s, the festival had outgrown the parish churches in which it began, and moved into a collection of disused malthouses, the **Snape Maltings** (Ⓦwww .snapemaltings.co.uk), five miles west of Aldeburgh on the River Alde, just south of the small village of Snape. The main malthouse was converted into one of the finest concert venues in the country, and the complex now encompasses recording studios, various craft shops and galleries, a tearoom, and a pub, the *Plough & Sail*. Consequently, even if there's nothing specific on, it's worth calling in to nose around.

The Aldeburgh Festival takes place every June for two and a half weeks. Core performances are still held at the Maltings, but a string of other local venues is pressed into service as well. In addition, the Maltings hosts a wide-ranging programme of musical and theatrical events throughout the rest of the year, including the three-day Britten Festival in October. For more information, contact **Aldeburgh Music** (Ⓣ01728/687110, Ⓦwww.aldeburgh.co.uk), which operates two box offices, one at Snape Maltings, the other on Aldeburgh High Street in premises it shares with the tourist office. Tickets for the Aldeburgh Festival itself usually go on sale to the public towards the end of March, and sell out fast for the big-name recitals.

Eating and drinking

Aldeburgh's best **restaurant** is ⚼ *The Lighthouse*, a relaxed and informal place in cosy premises at 77 High St (Ⓣ01728/453377). Prominence is given to locally sourced ingredients, but the menu features both Modern British and Mediterranean-style dishes, from cod with a cheese sauce to venison tagine with couscous; main courses average around £12 at lunchtimes, a tad more in the evening. Aldeburgh also has two outstanding **fish-and-chip shops** – the original takeaway ⚼ *Fish & Chip Shop* at 226 High St, and its sister, *The Golden Galleon*, where you can sit in just along the street at no. 137. The best place for a **drink** is the unpretentious *White Hart Inn*, footsteps from the *Fish & Chip Shop* at 222 High St, where they serve a good pint of Adnams. Otherwise, the **Aldeburgh Food and Drink Festival** (Ⓦwww .aldeburghfoodanddrink.co.uk), in late September/early October, with its focus at Snape Maltings (see above), is generally reckoned to be one of the best of its sort in the region, a real celebration of Suffolk produce and culinary skill.

Dunwich and around

Tiny **DUNWICH**, about twelve miles up the coast from Aldeburgh, is probably the strangest and eeriest place on the Suffolk coast. The one-time seat of the kings of East Anglia, a bishopric and formerly a large port, Dunwich peaked in the twelfth century since when it's all been downhill: over the last millennium something like a mile of land has been lost to the sea, a process that continues at the rate of about a yard a year. As a result, the whole of the medieval city now lies under water, including all twelve churches, the last of which toppled over the cliffs in 1919. All that survives today are fragments of the **Greyfriars monastery**, which originally lay to the west of the city and now dangles near the sea's edge. For a potted history of the lost city, head for the **museum** (daily: April–Sept 11.30am–4.30pm; Oct noon–4pm; £1 donation) in what's left of Dunwich – little more than one small street of terraced houses built by the local landowner in the nineteenth century. The museum has an interesting section on those many locals who decided to ship out to Canada, including the grandmother of Lucy Maud Montgomery, the author of one of the most popular children's books of all time, *Anne of Green Gables*.

A sprawling, seashore **car park** gives ready access to both the village and this stretch of the coast. On the beach also is the extremely popular *Flora Tea Rooms*, a large hut-like affair where they serve steaming cups of tea and piping-hot fish and chips to an assortment of birdwatchers, hikers and anglers. In the village itself, there's one remaining **pub**, the *Ship Inn* (☎01728/648219, ⓦwww.shipinndunwich.co .uk), which, with its low wooden beams and open fire, is a good place for a drink. The inn also serves inexpensive bar food and has a few, recently revamped guest rooms (❹) – and it's at night that the spookiness of the place really strikes you.

Dunwich Heath and Minsmere Nature Reserve

From Dunwich car park, it's possible to walk south along the seashore and then cut inland up and over the dunes to **Dunwich Heath**, where heather and gorse spread over a slab of upland that is now owned by the National Trust. You can also drive here – the turning is clearly signed on the more southerly of the two byroads to Dunwich. At the end of this turning, on the heath immediately behind and above the coast – the views are fantastic – the old **coastguard cottages** accommodate a National Trust shop and tearoom (March to mid-July & mid-Sept to Dec Wed–Sun 10am–4pm; mid-July to mid-Sept daily 10am–5pm; free, but £4.40 for parking). The cottages are also available for rent with a minimum two-night stay costing £140 in low season, three nights £369 in peak; contact the National Trust for further details and reservations (☎0870/4584422, ⓦwww .nationaltrustcottages.co.uk).

From the coastguard cottages, it's a twenty-minute walk south along the dunes and then inland to the **Minsmere RSPB Nature Reserve Visitor Centre** (reserve: daily 9am–9pm or dusk; visitor centre: daily 9am–5pm, 4pm in the depths of winter; £5), though there's a road here too – just watch for the sign on the southerly byroad into Dunwich. The reserve covers a varied terrain of marsh, scrub and beach, and it's home to a small (and hard to spot) population of bitterns, one of England's rarest birds. In the spring, it attracts large flocks of avocets, for which it's famous, and in the autumn becomes a gathering place for hundreds of migrant wading birds and waterfowl. You can rent binoculars from the visitor centre and strike out on the trails to the birdwatching hides.

Southwold

Perched on robust cliffs just to the north of the River Blyth, **SOUTHWOLD** gained what Dunwich lost, and by the sixteenth century it had overtaken all its local rivals to become Suffolk's busiest fishing port. In turn, Southwold lost most of its fishery to Lowestoft, just up along the coast, and today, although a small fleet still brings in herring, sprats and cod, the town is primarily a seaside resort, a genteel and eminently appealing little place with none of the crassness of many of its coastal competitors. There are fine old buildings, a long **sandy beach**, open heathland, a dinky harbour and even a little industry – in the shape of the Adnams brewery – but no burger bars and certainly no tacky amusement arcades. This gentility was not to the liking of **George Orwell**, who lived for a time at his parents' house at 36 High St (a plaque marks the spot). Orwell heartily disliked the town's airs and graces, and has left no trace of his time here – apart from disguised slights in a couple of early novels. On the other hand, Orwell might well have approved of Southwold's major music festival, **Latitude** (ⓦwww.latitudefestival .co.uk), which began in 2006 and now spreads over four days in the middle of July with happy campers grubbing down in Henham Park beside the A12 about five miles west of town.

Arrival, information and accommodation

Buses to Southwold pull in on the High Street, yards from the **tourist office**, at 69 High St (April–Oct Mon–Fri 10am–5pm, Sat 10am–5.30pm, Sun 11am–4pm; Nov–March Mon–Fri 10.30am–3pm, Sat 10am–4.30pm; ℡01502/724729, ⓦwww.visit-sunrisecoast.co.uk). They have a reasonably long list of local **accommodation**, including two well-known hotels, but vacant rooms can get mighty thin on the ground in high season.

The Crown High St ℡01502/722186, ⓦadnams .co.uk/stay-with-us. Adnams the brewers owns two hotels in Southwold and this is the less expensive, offering fourteen rooms above a bar-restaurant. Some of the rooms are large and decorated in a pleasant contemporary style, others are poky and basic – a long-term revamp is under way. ⑤

Home@21 21 North Parade ℡01502/722573, ⓦwww.homeat21northparade.co.uk. Near the pier, this seafront guesthouse occupies a well-maintained Victorian terrace house, whose rooms have been sympathetically updated and opened out. There are three rooms: two en suite and two sea-facing. Incidentally, General Booth, the founder of the Salvation Army, was a regular visitor to 28 North Parade, the house with the mini-tower just along the street. ④

Northcliffe Guesthouse 20 North Parade ℡01502/724074, ⓦwww.northcliffe-southwold .co.uk. Of the several guesthouses that line up along the seafront promenade, near the pier on North Parade, this is one of the more pleasant with three en-suite guest rooms decorated in comfort-able if undramatic style. ④

The Swan Market Place ℡01502/722186, ⓦadnams.co.uk/stay-with-us. Delightful hotel which occupies a splendid Georgian building right at the heart of Southwold. The main building is a real period piece, its nooks and crannies holding all manner of Georgian details. Some of the guest rooms are here, others (the Lighthouse Rooms) are in the more modern garden annexe at the back. ⑤

The Town

Southwold's breezy **High Street** is framed by attractive, mostly Georgian buildings, which zero in on the pocket-sized **Market Place**. From here, it's a brief stroll along East Street to a cliff-top vantage point that offers a grand view over the **beach**, where row upon row of candy-coloured huts face out towards the ocean. Also on the cliff top is the curious **Sailors' Reading Room** (daily: April–Sept 9am–5pm; Oct–March 9am–3.30pm; free), where pensioners gather to shoot the breeze in the mornings amid a room full of model ships, seafaring texts and photos of local tars, all beards and sea boots.

To the harbour

Queen Street begins at the Market Place too, scuttling along to **South Green**, the prettiest of several greens dotted across town. In 1659, a calamitous fire razed much of Southwold and when the town was rebuilt the greens were left to act as firebreaks. Beyond South Green, both Ferry Road and the ferry footpath lead down to the **harbour**, at the mouth of the River Blyth, an idyllic spot, where fishing smacks rest against old wooden jetties and nets are spread out along the banks to dry. From the mouth of the river, a footpath leads west to a tiny passenger **ferry** (early April & June–Sept daily 10am–12.30pm & 2–5pm; late April, May & Oct Sat & Sun 10am–5pm; 80p), which shuffles across the river to Walberswick (see below). If you're heading back towards Southwold, however, keep going along the river until you pass the *Harbour Inn* and then take the path that leads back into town across **Southwold Common**. The whole circular walk takes about thirty minutes.

East Green and St Edmund's

Back on the Market Place, it's a couple of hundred yards north along Church Street to East Green, with the **Adnams Brewery** on one side and a stumpy **lighthouse** on another. Close by is Southwold's architectural pride and joy, the **church of St Edmund** (daily: June–Aug 9am–6pm; Sept–May 9am–4pm; free), a handsome fifteenth-century structure whose solid symmetries are balanced by a long sequence of elegantly carved windows. Inside, the slender, beautifully proportioned nave is distinguished by its panelled roof, embellished with praying angels, and its intricate rood-screen. The latter carries paintings of the apostles and the prophets, though Protestants defaced them during the Reformation. Beyond the screen, the choir stalls carry finely carved human and animal heads as well as grotesques – look out for the man in the throes of toothache. Look out also for "Southwold Jack", a brightly painted, medieval effigy of a man in armour nailed to the wall beside the font. No one knows when or why this very military carving was moved into the church – it certainly doesn't fit in – but the betting is that he was once part of a clock, nodding belligerently as he struck the hours.

The pier

Southwold **pier** is the latest incarnation of a structure that dates back to 1899. Built as a landing stage for passenger ferries, the pier has had a troubled history: it has been repeatedly damaged by storms, was hit by a sea-mine and then partly chopped up by the army as a protection against German invasion in World War II. Recently revamped and renovated, the pier houses the usual – if rather more polite than usual – cafés and souvenir shops, but its star turn is the **Under the Pier Show** (daily 9am–7pm), where a series of knowingly playful machines, handmade by the multi-talented Tim Hunkin, provide all sorts of arcade-style sensory surprises, from the "Autofrisk" to the "Rent-a-Dog" and, hurrah for Hunkin, the very satisfying "Whack-a-Banker".

Eating and drinking

Among Southwold's several **teashops**, the pick is *Tilly's*, 51 High St, where the service is electric fast and they do a great line in sandwiches and home-made cakes both inside and outside in the walled garden. The best **place to eat** in town is in the front bar of ✷ *The Crown*, 90 High St, where they serve delicious meals, effectively deluxe bar food, featuring local, seasonal ingredients, all washed down with Adnams fine ales. Mains here average around £16 and tables are allocated on a first-come, first-served basis. The main gastronomic competitor is *Sutherland House*, a smart hotel and restaurant in antique premises at 56 High St (☏01502/724544); the menu here once again has a strong local emphasis and there's a helpful food-miles chart attached (main courses £11–18). For a **drink**, sample Adnams' brews in *The Crown*'s wood-panelled back-bar or stroll along to the *Lord Nelson*, a lively neighbourhood pub of low, beamed ceilings on East Street.

Around Southwold: Walberswick

Just across the River Blyth from Southwold lies the pretty little village of **WALBERSWICK** (🖰 www.explorewalberswick.co.uk), another once-prosperous port now fallen (or risen) into well-heeled tranquillity. For many years it was the home of the English Impressionist painter Philip Wilson Steer (1860–1942) and, warming to the same theme, it's now a seaside escape with an arty, sometime celebrity undertow. There's not much to see as such, though you can stroll south along the coast to Dunwich (see p.445) and drop by the *Bell Inn* for a pint. Close to the river, this old village pub is a rabbit warren of a place, with all sorts of ancient nooks and crannies, and they serve filling bar food and Adnams beer. Close by, further along in the village, is Walberswick's second pub, *The Anchor* (℗01502/722112), a smart and urbane sort of place where they serve delicious food, anything from seared scallops in a fennel jus to fish and chips; mains average about £13.

There are two ways for **walkers** to get to Walberswick from Southwold – either via the ferry (see opposite) or over the bridge about a mile further inland. The footpath to the bridge begins on Station Road, a westerly continuation of Southwold's High Street.

Norwich

One of England's most appealing smaller cities, **NORWICH** has more in common with Cambridge than Ipswich, not least its prominent student population and lack of full-scale industry. Norwich was one of the five largest cities in Norman England and in medieval times it served a vast hinterland of East Anglian **cloth producers**, whose work was brought here by river and then exported to the Continent. The city's isolated position beyond the Fens meant that it enjoyed closer links with the Low Countries than with the rest of England – it was, after all, quicker to cross the North Sea than to go cross-country to London. The local textile industry, based on worsted cloth (named after the nearby village of Worstead), was further enhanced by an influx of Flemish and Huguenot weavers, who made up more than a third of the population in Tudor times. By 1700, Norwich was the second richest city in the country after London.

With the onset of the Industrial Revolution, however, Norwich lost ground to the northern manufacturing towns – the city's famous mustard company, Colman's, is one of its few industrial success stories – and this, together with its geographical isolation, has helped preserve much of the ancient street plan and many of the city's older buildings. Pride of place goes to the beautiful **cathedral** and the imposing **castle**, but the city's hallmark is its medieval **churches**, thirty or so squat flintstone structures with sturdy towers and sinuous stone tracery round the windows. Many are no longer in regular use and are now in the care of the **Norwich Historic Churches Trust** (ⓦwww.norwich-churches.org), whose excellent website describes each church in detail and gives opening times.

Norwich's relative isolation has also meant that the population has never swelled to any great extent and today, with just 130,000 inhabitants, it remains an easy and enjoyable city to negotiate. Yet Norwich is no provincial backwater. In the 1960s, the foundation of the **University of East Anglia** (UEA) made it more cosmopolitan and bolstered its arts scene, while in the 1980s it attracted new high-tech companies, who created something of a mini-boom, making it one of England's wealthier cities. It is also home to Britain's most revered television chef and cookbook writer **Delia Smith**: when Delia is about to recommend an unusual ingredient, the supermarkets supposedly ask for advance notice so that they can source extra supplies.

Finally, as East Anglia's unofficial capital Norwich also lies at the hub of the region's **transport network**, serving as a useful base for visiting the Broads and as a springboard for the north Norfolk coast. The largest local bus company hereabouts is First (Ⓦ www.firstgroup.com).

Arrival, information and getting around

Norwich's grandiose **train station** is on the east bank of the River Wensum, ten minutes' walk from the city centre along Prince of Wales Road. Long-distance **buses** mostly terminate at the Surrey Street station, from where it's about ten minutes' walk north to the town centre, though some services also stop in the centre on Castle Meadow. Norwich **tourist office** is in the glassy Forum building overlooking the Market Place (April–Oct Mon–Sat 9.30am–6pm, Sun 10.30am–4.30pm; Nov–March Mon–Sat 9.30am–5.30pm; Ⓣ01603/213990, Ⓦ www.visitnorwich.co.uk).

The best way to explore the city is on foot with the added diversion of a **boat trip**. From April to September, **City Boats** (Ⓣ01603/701701, Ⓦ www.cityboats.co.uk) operate cruises through Norwich along the River Wensum, starting at Station Quay near the railway station and proceeding to Elm Hill Quay near the cathedral (1 daily; 20min; £5, £8 return). The same company also offers longer cruises out from Norwich and into the Broads (see box, pp.456–457).

Accommodation

As you might expect, Norwich has **accommodation** to suit all budgets, though there's not very much in the city centre, which is really where you want to stay.

3 Princes St 3 Princes St Ⓣ01603/662693, Ⓦ www.3princes-norwich.co.uk. In a great location, up a narrow lane yards from the cathedral, this B&B looks pretty dour from the outside – it occupies a plain red-brick Georgian terraced house that was once a rectory – but the four en-suite guest rooms inside are attractively furnished in pastel shades, and three of them have views over Blackfriars Hall. ❸

38 St Giles 38 St Giles St Ⓣ01603/662944, Ⓦ www.38stgiles.co.uk. Slick and sleek B&B with just five guest rooms, each turned out in a tasteful contemporary manner. Delicious breakfasts and a handy central location too. ❹

175 Newmarket Road 175 Newmarket Rd Ⓣ01603/506160, Ⓦ www.bedandbreakfastinnorwich.co.uk. On the southwest edge of the city, this large Edwardian house, set in its own wooded grounds, has been turned into a country-house-style B&B with three en-suite guest rooms. Indoor pool and large conservatory too. ❸

Beeches Hotel 2–6 Earlham Rd Ⓣ01603/621167, Ⓦ www.beecheshotelnorwich.co.uk. The city's most improved hotel – formerly underwhelming, under new owners *The Beeches* has caught up fast. There's a good selection of rooms, ranging from the traditional to the slick and more modern, distributed among three attractive nineteenth-century buildings. ❸

Maid's Head Hotel Tombland Ⓣ01603/209955, Ⓦ www.maidsheadhotel.co.uk. Not everyone's cup of tea perhaps, but this chain hotel is delightfully idiosyncratic – a rabbit warren of a place with all sorts of architectural bits and pieces, from the mock-Tudor facade to the ancient, wood-panelled bar – though there is also a clumpy modern extension. The rooms are mostly large and very comfortable in a standard-issue sort of way and the location, bang in the centre opposite the cathedral, can't be beat. ❹

Number 17 17 Colegate Ⓣ01603/764486, Ⓦ www.number17norwich.co.uk. Family-run guesthouse with eight tidy guest rooms decorated in a brisk, modern style. Good location, in one of the nicest parts of the centre. ❸

St Giles House 41 St Giles St Ⓣ01603/275180, Ⓦ www.stgileshousehotel.com. This deluxe hotel, Norwich's fanciest, occupies a handsome Edwardian building that was designed to look something like a French imperial palace by George Skipper, for many years the city's leading architect and the man responsible for the Royal Arcade. The exterior, with its columns and balustrade, is impressive – perhaps overly so – and each of the 24 guest rooms beyond is different, though most combine new, sometimes adventurous pastel shades with retro flourishes. ❺

The City

Tucked into a wide bend of the River Wensum, **Norwich** has an irregular street plan, a Saxon legacy, which can make orientation difficult. There are, however, three obvious landmarks to help you find your way – the **cathedral** with its giant spire, the Norman **castle** on its commanding mound and the distinctive **clocktower** of City Hall. The cathedral and the castle are the town's premier attractions and the latter also holds one of the region's most satisfying collections of fine art.

The cathedral

Of all the medieval buildings in Norwich, it's the **cathedral** that fires the imagination, a mighty, sand-coloured structure finessed by its prickly octagonal spire, which rises to a height of 315ft, second only to Salisbury (daily 7.30am–6pm; free; Ⓦwww.cathedral.org.uk). From the front, the cathedral just looks imposing, but from the south – from the Lower Close (see p.452) – the full intricacy of the design becomes apparent, the thick curves of the flying buttresses and the rounded excrescences of the ambulatory chapels – unusual in an English cathedral – set against the straight symmetries of the main trunk.

Entered via a brand-new visitor centre, the **Hostry**, just to the right of the main doors, the **interior** is pleasantly light thanks to a creamy tint in the stone and the clear-glass windows of much of the **nave**, where the thick pillars are a powerful legacy of the Norman builders who began the cathedral in 1096. Look up to spy the nave's fan vaulting, delicate and geometrically precise carving adorned by

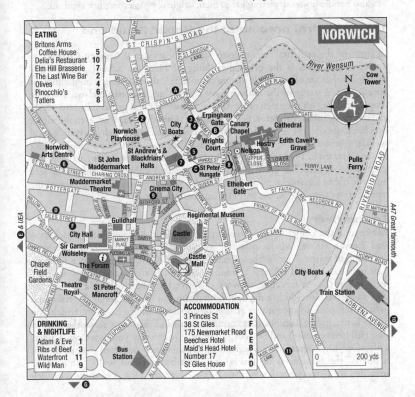

several hundred roof **bosses** recounting – from east to west – the story of the Old and New Testaments from the Creation to the Last Judgement.

St Luke's Chapel and the bishop's throne

Pushing on down the south (right) side of the ambulatory, you soon reach **St Luke's Chapel** where the cathedral's finest work of art, the *Despenser Reredos*, is a superb painted panel commissioned to celebrate the crushing of the Peasants' Revolt of 1381. Across the aisle, encased by the choir, is the **bishop's throne**, a sturdy stone structure dating back to the eighth century and possibly moved here from the long-gone cathedral at Dunwich (see p.445). Norman bishops were barons as much as religious leaders, and to emphasize their direct relationship with the Almighty they usually put their thrones behind the high altar. Most were relocated during the Reformation, but this one occupies its original position. Here in Norwich, the bishop also had a spiritual prop: a flue runs down from the back of the throne to a **reliquary recess** in the ambulatory, the idea being that divine essences would be transported up to him to help him do his job.

The cathedral cloisters

Accessible from the south aisle of the nave are the cathedral's unique **cloisters**. Built between 1297 and 1450, and the only two-storey cloisters left standing in England, they contain a remarkable set of sculpted **bosses**, similar to the ones in the main nave, but here they are close enough to be scrutinized without binoculars. The carving is fabulously intricate and the dominant theme is the **Apocalypse**, but look out also for the bosses depicting green men, originally pagan fertility symbols.

The cathedral precincts: the Upper Close and Tombland

In front of the cathedral's main doors stands the medieval **Canary Chapel** (no public access). This is the original building of Norwich School, whose blue-blazered pupils are often visible during term-time – the rambling school buildings are adjacent. A statue of the school's most famous boy, **Horatio Nelson**, faces the chapel, standing on the green of the **Upper Close**, which is guarded by two ornate and imposing **medieval gates**, Erpingham and, a hundred yards or so to the south, Ethelbert. Beside the Erpingham gate is a memorial to **Edith Cavell**, a local woman who was a nurse in occupied Brussels during World War I. She was shot by the Germans in 1915 for helping Allied prisoners to escape, a fate that made her an instant folk hero; her grave is outside the cathedral ambulatory. Both gates lead onto the old Saxon marketplace, **Tombland**, a wide and busy thoroughfare whose name derives from the Saxon word for an open space.

To the river

Just beyond the Upper Close, extending east towards the river, is the pedestrianized **Lower Close**, where attractive Georgian and Victorian houses flank a scattering of wispy silver birches. Keeping straight on from the Close, a footpath continues east to **Pull's Ferry**, a landing stage at the city's medieval water-gate, named after the last ferryman to work this stretch of the river. It's a picturesque spot and from here (during daylight hours) you can wander along the riverbank path either south to the railway station or north to Bishopgate, from which you can either return to Tombland or continue north and then west along the river to Elm Hill (see opposite) and St George's Street. On the way you pass **Cow Tower**, a fifty-foot-high watchtower where the bishop's retainers collected river tolls. This is one of the few surviving pieces of Norwich's **fortified walls**, which once stretched for over two miles, surrounding the city and incorporating thirty such circular towers and ten defensive gates. Up until the 1790s, the gates were closed at dusk and all day on Sundays.

Elm Hill

At the north end of Tombland, fork left into Wensum Street and cobbled **Elm Hill**, more a gentle slope than a hill, soon appears on the left. J.B. Priestley, in his *English Journey* of 1933, thought this part of Norwich to be overbearingly Dickensian, proclaiming it "difficult to believe that behind those bowed and twisted fronts there did not live an assortment of misers, mad spinsters, saintly clergymen, eccentric comic clerks, and lunatic sextons." Since then, the tourist crowds have sucked the atmosphere, but the quirky half-timbered houses still appeal and while you're here take a look at **Wright's Court**, down a passageway at no. 43, one of the few remaining enclosed courtyards which were once a feature of the city. Elm Hill quickly opens out into a triangular square centred on a plane tree, planted on the spot where the eponymous elm tree once stood. It then veers left up to **St Peter Hungate** (Thurs–Sat 10am–4pm; £3), a good-looking, fifteenth-century flint church equipped with a solid square tower and a batch of exquisite stained-glass windows.

The Halls and St John Maddermarket

Turn right at St Peter Hungate and it's just a few yards to **St Andrew's Hall** and **Blackfriars Hall**, two adjoining buildings that were originally the nave and chancel, respectively, of a Dominican monastery church. Imaginatively recycled, as **The Halls** these two buildings are now used for a variety of public events, including concerts, weddings and antique fairs; the crypt of the former now serves as a café (closed Sun).

It's another short haul from Blackfriars to **St John Maddermarket** (April–Oct Tues–Thurs 11am–3pm; free), one of the thirty medieval churches standing within the boundaries of the old city walls. Most are redundant and are rarely open to the public, but this is one of the more accessible, courtesy of dedicated volunteers. Apart from the stone trimmings, the church – which is named after madder, the yellow flower the weavers used to make red vegetable dye – is almost entirely composed of flint rubble, the traditional building material of east Norfolk, an area chronically short of decent stone. The exterior is a good example of the Perpendicular style, characterized by straight vertical lines – as you might expect from the name – and large windows framed by flowing, but plain, tracery. By comparison, the interior is something of a disappointment, its furnishings and fittings thoroughly remodelled at the start of the twentieth century, though there's compensation in a trio of finely carved Jacobean tombstones.

Back outside, the arch under the church tower leads through to the **Maddermarket Theatre**, built in 1921 in the style of an Elizabethan playhouse.

The Market Place

Norwich **Market Place** has long been the site of one of the country's largest open-air markets (closed Sun), with stalls selling everything from bargain-basement clothes to local mussels and whelks. Four very different but equally distinctive buildings oversee the market's stripy awnings, the oldest of them being the fifteenth-century **Guildhall**, a capacious flint-and-stone structure begun in 1407. Opposite, commanding the heights of the Market Place, are the austere **City Hall**, a lumbering brick pile with a landmark clocktower built in the 1930s in a Scandinavian style – it bears a striking resemblance to Oslo's city hall – and **The Forum**, a large, flashy, glassy structure completed in 2001. The latter is home to the city's main library and the tourist office.

On the south side of Market Place is the finest of the four buildings, **St Peter Mancroft** (Mon–Fri 10am–4pm; free), whose long and graceful nave leads to a mighty stone tower, an intricately carved affair surmounted by a spiky little spire. The church once delighted John Wesley, who declared "I scarcely ever remember to have seen a more beautiful parish church," a fair description of what remains an exquisite example of the Perpendicular style with the slender columns of the nave reaching up towards the delicate groining of the roof. Completed in 1455, the nave's open design was meant to express the mystery of the Christian faith with light filtering in through the stained-glass windows in a kaleidoscope of colours. Some of the original glass has survived, most notably in the east window.

Gentlemen's Walk and the Royal Arcade

Just below the church stands the **Sir Garnet Wolseley** pub, sole survivor of the 44 alehouses that once crowded the Market Place – and stirred the local bourgeoisie into endless discussions about the drunken fecklessness of the working class. Opposite the pub, on the far side of **Gentlemen's Walk**, the city's main promenade, which runs along the bottom of the Market Place, is the **Royal Arcade**, an Art Nouveau extravagance from 1899. The arcade has been beautifully restored to reveal the swirl of the tiling, ironwork and stained glass, though it's actually the eastern entrance, further from Gentlemen's Walk, which is the fanciest section.

The castle

Glued to the top of a grassy mound right in the centre of town – with a modern shopping mall drilled into its side – the stern walls of **Norwich Castle** date from the twelfth century. To begin with they were a reminder of Norman power and then, when the castle was turned into a prison, they served as a grim warning to potential law-breakers. Now lavishly refurbished, the castle holds the **Castle Museum and Art Gallery** (Mon–Sat 10am–4.30pm, Sun 1–5pm; £6.20), which is divided into three zones. The **Art and Exhibitions zone** is the pick, scoring well with its temporary displays and boasting an outstanding selection of work by the **Norwich School**. Founded in 1803, and in existence for just thirty years, this school of landscape painters produced – for the most part – richly coloured, formally composed land- and seascapes in oil and watercolour, paintings whose realism harked back to the Dutch landscape painters of the seventeenth century. The leading figures were **John Crome** (1768–1821) – aka "Old Crome" – and **John Sell Cotman** (1782–1842), who is generally acknowledged as one of England's finest watercolourists. Both have a gallery to themselves and, helpfully, there's also a gallery given over to those Dutch painters who influenced them.

The **Castle and History zone** includes the castle keep, though this is no more than a shell, its gloomy walls rising high above a scattering of local archeological finds. More unusual is a bloated model **dragon**, known as Snap, which was paraded round town on the annual guilds' day procession – a folkloric hand-me-down from the dragon St George had so much trouble finishing off. To see more of the castle, join one of the regular **guided tours** (£2.20 extra) that explore the battlements and the dungeons. Finally, a long, dark (and one-way) stairway leads down from the Castle Museum to the **Royal Norfolk Regimental Museum** (Tues–Fri 10am–4.30pm, Sat 10am–5pm; £3.50), which traces the history of the regiment with the aid of some excellent old photos and especially apt descriptions. The exit leaves you below the castle on Market Avenue.

The university

The **University of East Anglia** (UEA) occupies a sprawling campus on the western outskirts of the city beside the B1108. Its buildings are resolutely modern, an assortment of concrete-and-glass blocks of varying designs, some quite ordinary, others like the prize-winning "ziggurat" halls of residence, designed by Denys Lasdun, eminently memorable. The main reason to visit is the high-tech **Sainsbury Centre for Visual Arts** (Tues–Sun 10am–5pm, Wed till 8pm; free; Ⓦwww.scva.org.uk), built by Norman Foster in the 1970s. The interior houses one of the most varied collections of sculpture and painting in the country, donated by the family which founded the Sainsbury's supermarket chain, in which the likes of Degas, Seurat, Picasso, Giacometti, Bacon and Henry Moore rub shoulders with Mayan and Egyptian antiquities. The centre also runs a first-rate programme of temporary exhibitions (for which admission may be charged).

Buses #22, #25 and #35 run frequently to UEA from Castle Meadow.

Eating, drinking and nightlife

There are plenty of **cafés and restaurants** in the city centre, and many of them are very good value. Decent **pubs**, though, are harder to find, partly because previously serviceable places have been turned into ersatz "traditional" drinking dens for students.

Cafés and restaurants

Britons Arms Coffee House 9 Elm Hill. Home-made quiches, tarts, cakes and scones plus pies and salads in quaint Elm Hill premises. Closed Sun.

Delia's Restaurant Carrow Rd ℡01603/218704. Decorated in whites and creams, Delia Smith's smart hometown restaurant has set the local pulse racing. Reflecting her keen interest in Norwich Football Club – The Canaries – the restaurant is down at the football ground just beyond the train station. Most football fans are condemned to eat fast-food crap, but not here, though there are restrictions: the restaurant is only open on Fri and Sat eve (from 7pm) and it's a three-course set-meal only (for £35).

Elm Hill Brasserie 2 Elm Hill ℡01603/624847. This intimate, one-room bistro-brasserie, housed in an old shop, offers a creative menu with a French twist. Daily specials, written on a blackboard, are well considered and reasonably priced at around £13 per main course. Closed Mon; Sun open noon–6pm only.

The Last Wine Bar 76 St George's St ℡01603/626626. Imaginatively converted old shoe factory, a couple of minutes' walk north of the river, holding a relaxed and very amenable wine bar in one section and an excellent restaurant in the other. The food is firmly Modern British, with the likes of braised lamb shank with carrots and parsnips in a rosemary jus (around £14). Closed Sun.

Olives 40 Elm Hill. In antique, half-timbered premises, this agreeable little daytime café serves up a good line in salads and light meals – and it's not part of a chain (hurrah).

Pinocchio's 11 St Benedict's St ℡01603/613318. Relaxed Italian restaurant in a bright and lively conversion of what was once a general store. The menu covers all the classics and then some, and prices are very reasonable, with pizzas from £7. Closed Sun.

Tatlers 21 Tombland ℡01603/766670. Slick, contemporary restaurant – all plain-wood floors and deep-red walls – where the emphasis is on local, seasonal ingredients like wood pigeon and

Norwich Arts Centre

Housed in a redundant church, the inventive and creative **Norwich Arts Centre**, 51 St Benedict's St (Mon–Sat 9am–10pm; ℡01603/660352, Ⓦwww.norwichartscentre .co.uk), covers many bases, including a wide range of performing and media arts plus an enterprising programme of participatory workshops and activities with an arts bias. Some of the kids' workshops are really first rate, like "Revamp Pirates" in which household objects are turned into piratical paraphernalia.

Three rivers – the **Yare**, **Waveney** and **Bure** – meander across the flatlands to the east of Norwich, converging on **Breydon Water** before flowing into the sea at the old port and seaside resort of Great Yarmouth. In places these rivers swell into wide expanses of water known as "**broads**", which for years were thought to be natural lakes. In fact they're the result of extensive peat cutting, several centuries of accumulated diggings made in a region where wood was scarce and peat a valuable source of energy. The pits flooded when sea levels rose in the thirteenth and fourteenth centuries to create the **Broads**, now one of the most important wetlands in Europe – a haven for many birds such as kingfishers, grebes and warblers – and one of the county's prime tourist attractions.

The Broads' delicate **ecological balance** suffered badly during the 1970s and 1980s. The careless use of fertilizers poisoned the water with phosphates and nitrates encouraging the spread of algae; the decline in reed cutting – previously in great demand for thatching – made the Broads partly unnavigable; and the enormous increase in pleasure-boat traffic began to erode the banks. Protection equivalent to national park status was, however, accorded to the area in 1988, and efforts are now well under way to clear the waters and protect the ecosystem. Coordinating the clean up is the **Broads Authority** (Ⓦ www.broads-authority.gov.uk), which maintains a series of information centres throughout the region. At any of these, you can pick up a free copy of the *Broadcaster*, a useful newspaper guide to the Broads as a whole.

Exploring the Broads

The region is crisscrossed by roads and rail lines, but the best – really the only – way to see the Broads is **by boat**, and you could happily spend a week or so exploring the 125 miles of lock-free navigable waterways, visiting the various churches, pubs and windmills en route. Of the many **boat rental** companies, Norfolk Broads Direct (Ⓣ 01603/782207, Ⓦ www.broads.co.uk) is well established and has a rental outlet at

pork belly. The portions are a tad nouvelle, but there's a good wine cellar to compensate.

Pubs, bars and clubs

Adam & Eve Bishopgate. There's been a pub on this site for seven hundred years and it's still a top spot for the discerning drinker with a changing range of real ales and an eclectic wine list supplied by Adnams.

Ribs of Beef 24 Wensum St. Boisterous riverside drinking haunt popular with students and townies alike.

Waterfront 139–141 King St Ⓣ 01603/632717, Ⓦ www.waterfrontnorwich.com. Norwich's principal club and alternative music venue, with gigs and DJs most nights.

Wild Man 29 Bedford St. Long-established city-centre watering hole – a popular student hangout.

Entertainment

Norwich has an excellent art-house cinema, **Cinema City**, on St Andrew's Street (Ⓣ 0871/7042053, Ⓦ www.picturehouses.co.uk). The city also has several noteworthy theatres, starting with the **Theatre Royal**, on Theatre Street (Ⓣ 01603/630000, Ⓦ www.theatreroyalnorwich.co.uk), which has a wide-ranging programme of mainstream and more adventurous plays and dance. There's also the amateur **Maddermarket**, St John's Alley, off Pottergate (Ⓣ 01603/620917, Ⓦ www.maddermarket.co.uk), where they offer an interesting range of modern theatre, and **Norwich Playhouse**, on St George's Street (Ⓣ 01603/598598, Ⓦ www.norwichplayhouse.co.uk), which chips in with just about everything from blues concerts to panto.

Wroxham, seven miles to the northeast of Norwich and easy to reach by train, bus and car. Prices for cruisers start at around £900 a week for four people in peak season, but less expensive, short-term rentals are widely available, too. **Houseboats** are much cheaper than cruisers, but they are, of course, static.

Trying to explore the Broads by car is pretty much a waste of time, but **cyclists and walkers** can take advantage of the region's network of footpaths and cycle trails. There are Broads Authority **bike rental** points dotted around the region and walkers might consider the 56-mile **Weavers' Way**, a long-distance footpath that winds through the best parts of the Broads on its way from Cromer to Great Yarmouth, though there are many shorter options too.

Places to see

Boating round the Broads as the mood takes you is the way to go, but there are a couple of prime targets for landlubbers and boaters alike. First up is **Toad Hole Cottage** (April, May & Oct Mon–Fri 10.30am–1pm & 1.30–5pm, Sat & Sun 10.30am–5pm; June–Sept daily 9.30am–6pm; free), an old eel-catcher's cottage holding a small exhibit on the history of the trade, which was common hereabouts until the 1940s. The cottage is at How Hill, close to the hamlet of **Ludham**, six miles east of Wroxham on the A1062. Behind the cottage is the River Ant, where there are hour-long, wildlife-viewing **boat trips** in the *Electric Eel* (April, May & Oct Sat & Sun 11am–3pm; June–Sept daily 10am–5pm, hourly; £7; reservations on ☏01692/756096). Another enjoyable boat trip is on the *Helen of Ranworth*, a small, open boat that makes one-hour excursions (Easter to Oct 2 daily; £6; reservations on ☏01603/756095) out into the Broads from **Ranworth**, a tiny hamlet about twelve miles east of Norwich via the A1151 and B1140. The *Helen* also makes slightly longer (2hr; £9.50) but less frequent trips to the isolated ruins of **St Benet's Abbey** (open access; free), which date back to the twelfth century, though they are dwarfed by the remains of the windmill a local farmer built behind the abbey gatehouse six centuries later.

The north Norfolk coast

About forty miles from one end to the other, the **north Norfolk coast** begins at **Cromer**, a low-key seaside town whose blustery cliffs have drawn tourists for over a century. A few miles to the west is another well-established resort, **Sheringham**, but thereafter the shoreline becomes a ragged patchwork of salt marshes, dunes and shingle spits which form an almost unbroken series of nature reserves supporting a fascinating range of flora and fauna. It's a lovely stretch of coast and the villages bordering it, primarily **Cley**, **Blakeney** and possibly **Wells-next-the-Sea**, are prime targets for an overnight stay. The other major attractions here are a short distance inland, principally **Little Walsingham**, an ancient hamlet that was the country's most important place of pilgrimage throughout the medieval period, and a pair of stately homes, **Blickling Hall** and **Felbrigg Hall**. Wells-next-the-Sea has a good sandy beach, but the beach at neighbouring **Holkham Bay**, near **Holkham Hall**, a third stately home, is much better – indeed it's one of England's finest. To the west of Holkham lies the studied gentility of the Burnhams – especially **Burnham Market** and **Burnham Thorpe**, the childhood home of Nelson – and then there are more salt marshes and muddy creeks en route to **Hunstanton**, the westernmost resort on the north Norfolk coast.

There's an hourly **train** service on the Bittern Line (Ⓦwww.bitternline.com) from Norwich to two major stops on the north Norfolk coast – Cromer and Sheringham. A battery of local **buses** fills in (most of) the gaps, but easily the most useful is the Norfolk **Coasthopper** (℡01553/776980, 🌐www.coasthopper .co.uk), which runs from Cromer to King's Lynn via a whole gaggle of coastal towns and villages, including Blakeney, Sheringham, Wells and the Burnhams. Frequencies vary on different stretches of the route and there are more services in the summer than in the winter, but on the more popular stretches buses appear every thirty minutes or hourly, less frequently on Sundays. The Coasthopper Rover ticket (£6) gives a day's unlimited travel on the whole of the route. For walkers, the **Norfolk Coast Path** runs from Hunstanton to Cromer (where it joins the Weavers' Way, which presses on to the sea at Great Yarmouth), an exhilarating route through the dunes and salt marshes. A National Trail guide covers the route in detail; otherwise you'll need the appropriate OS Explorer map.

⑦ Cromer and around

Dramatically poised on a high bluff, **CROMER** should be the most memorable of the Norfolk coastal resorts, but its fine aspect is undermined by a certain shabbiness in its narrow streets and alleys – an "atrophied charm" as Paul Theroux called it. Things are on the mend, however, with the tentative beginnings of a clean-up and a spruce-up. It's no more than the place deserves: Cromer has a long history, first as a prosperous medieval port – witness the tower of **St Peter and St Paul**, at 160ft the tallest in Norfolk – and then as a fashionable watering-hole after the advent of the railway in the 1880s. The Victorians and then the Edwardians built a bevy of grand hotels along the seafront, but the gloss soon wore off and only the dishevelled **Hotel de Paris** has survived as a reminder of all the bustles and top hats. There are three things you must do here: take a walk on the beach, stroll out onto the **pier**, and, of course, grab a **crab**: Cromer crabs are famous right across England and J.W.H. Jonas, in the centre at 7 Chapel St (℡01263/514121), has some fine specimens.

Practicalities

Somewhat miraculously Cromer has managed to retain its rail link with Norwich and from the **train station** it's a five-minute walk east into the centre. **Buses** terminate outside *Julio's Café*, on Cadogan Road, two minutes from the **tourist office** (Jan to mid-May & Sept–Dec daily 10am–4pm; mid-May to Aug Mon–Sat 10am–5pm, Sun 10am–4pm; ℡0871/200 3071, 🌐www.visitnorthnorfolk.com).

There's no shortage of inexpensive **accommodation** – the tourist office has all the details – and one of the more appealing places is the *Beachcomber Guesthouse*, a cosy B&B with five en-suite rooms located on a suburban side-street just to the west of the centre at 17 Macdonald Rd (℡01263/513398, 🌐www.beachcomber -guesthouse.co.uk; no credit cards; ❷). Much grander is the *Cliftonville Hotel*, also just west of the centre along the coast road at 29 Runton Rd (℡01263/512543, 🌐www.cliftonvillehotel.co.uk; ❺). It occupies a large Edwardian mansion, complete with many of its original features, and most of its thirty bedrooms have smashing sea views. Just inland from Cromer on the A140, *Deer's Glade Caravan & Camping Park*, White Post Road, Hanworth (℡01263/768633, 🌐www.deers glade.co.uk; open all year), is a very rural but well-equipped **campsite** occupying a large field amid oak and pine woodland – hence the deer. There's bike and fishing-rod rental, useful as the site has its own pond stocked with carp and bream.

For **food**, the best place in town is the *Rocket House Café* (daily 10am–5pm, but kitchen closes 3pm, plus Sat 6–9pm) in the spankingly new RNLI building on the seafront at the foot of The Gangway, where local fishermen still haul their boats. The menu here is lively and portions are large to enormous – try the oak-smoked sprats and beets with seasonal salad (£7).

Felbrigg Hall

Felbrigg Hall (mid-March to Oct Mon–Wed, Sat & Sun 11am–5pm; £7.80, including park & garden; NT), situated just a couple of miles southwest of Cromer off the A148, is a charming Jacobean mansion. The main facade is particularly appealing, the soft hues of the ageing limestone and brick intercepted by three bay windows, which together sport a large, cleverly carved inscription – "Gloria Deo in Excelsis" – in celebration of the reviving fortunes of the family who then owned the place, the Windhams. The interior is splendid too, with the studied informality of both the dining and drawing rooms enlivened by their magnificent seventeenth-century plasterwork ceilings plus sundry objets d'art. Many of the **paintings** were purchased by William Windham II, who undertook his Grand Tour in the 1740s – hence the two paintings of the Battle of the Texel by Willem van de Velde the Elder, and the six oils and twenty-odd gouaches of Rome and southern Italy by Giovanni Battista Busiri.

The surrounding **parkland** (daily dawn to dusk; free) divides into two, with woods to the north and open pasture to the south. Footpaths crisscross the park and a popular spot to head for is the medieval **church of St Margaret's** in the south-eastern corner, which contains a fine set of brasses and a fancy memorial to William Windham I and his wife by Grinling Gibbons. Nearer the house, the extensive **walled garden** (March–Oct daily 11am–5pm; Nov & Dec Fri–Sun 11am–4pm; garden only £3.65; NT) features flowering borders and an octagonal dove-house, while the stables have been converted into particularly pleasant **tearooms**.

Blickling Hall

Blickling Hall (March to mid-July, Sept & Oct Wed–Sun 11am–5pm; mid-July to Aug daily except Tues 11am–5pm; house & gardens £9.30, gardens only £6.30; NT), set in a sheltered, wooded valley ten miles south of Cromer via the A140, is a second grand Jacobean pile. Built for Sir Henry Hobart, a Lord Chief Justice, the hall dates from the 1620s and although it was extensively remodelled over a century later, the modifications respected the integrity of the earlier design. As a result, the long facade, with its slender chimneys, high gables and towers, remained – and remains – the apotheosis of Jacobean design. Inside, highlights include a superb plasterwork ceiling in the Long Gallery and an extraordinarily grand main staircase. There's also a gargantuan tapestry depicting Peter the Great defeating the Swedes, given to one of the family by no less than Catherine the Great. The earthly remains of the last of the male Hobarts are stashed away in a weird pyramidal mausoleum that is located in the **parkland** (daily dawn to dusk) that encircles the house.

Sheringham and around

SHERINGHAM, a popular seaside town with a shingle beach just four miles west of Cromer, has an amiable, easy-going air and makes a reasonable overnight stop – though frankly you're still only marking time until you hit the more appealing places further to the west. One of the distinctive features of the town is the smooth beach pebbles that face and decorate the houses, a **flinting technique** used frequently in this part of Norfolk – the best examples here are on and around the High Street. The downside is that the power of the waves, which makes the pebbles smooth, has also forced the local council to spend thousands rebuilding the sea defences. The resultant mass of reinforced concrete makes for a less than pleasing seafront despite the best efforts of **The Mo** (Feb–Oct Tues–Sat 10am–4.30pm, Sun noon–4pm; £3.50; Ⓦwww.sheringhammuseum.co.uk), Sheringham's brand-new museum, whose various displays focus on the town's history alongside several lifeboats and fishing boats.

Sheringham Park and the North Norfolk Railway

One highlight of this section of the coast is **Sheringham Park** (daily dawn to dusk; free, but parking extra; NT), a sizeable chunk of woodland lying a couple of miles southwest of the town and laid out by Humphry Repton in the early 1800s. The park boasts wonderful battalions of rhododendrons and azaleas, at their best in late May and early June, and a series of lookout posts from which you can admire the view down to the coast. The other out-of-town jaunt is on the **North Norfolk Railway**, whose steam and diesel trains operate along the five miles of track southwest from Sheringham to the modest market town of **Holt** (April & Oct most days; May–Sept daily; Nov–March limited service; all-day ticket £10.50, dogs £1; ℡01263/820808, Ⓦwww.nnrailway.co.uk).

Practicalities

Sheringham's two **train stations** are opposite each other on either side of Station Road. The main station, the terminus of the Bittern Line from Norwich, is just to the east, the North Norfolk Railway station is to the west. The **tourist office** (March–Oct Mon–Sat 10am–5pm, Sun 10am–4pm; ℡0871/200 3071, Ⓦwww .visitnorthnorfolk.com) is next to the North Norfolk Railway station – and from here it's a five-minute walk north to the seafront down Station Road and its continuation, High Street. There is plenty of accommodation, mostly B&Bs, plus one good **hotel**, the *Two Lifeboats*, 2 High St (℡01263/822401, Ⓦwww.twolife boats.co.uk; ❸), a small, traditional place just yards from the seafront; most of the ten en-suite bedrooms have sea views. **Campers** should make for the sociable, well-set-up *Beeston Regis Caravan & Camping Park*, in a smashing location beside the sea cliffs on Cromer Road in West Runton, just to the east of Sheringham (℡01263/823614, Ⓦwww.beestonregis.co.uk; March–Oct). There's a steep path down to the beach and the Norfolk Coast Path (see p.431) passes close by.

The tastiest **fish and chips** for miles around are served up at *Dave's*, 50 High St. *Ellie's*, close by at 14 High St, sells Norfolk's own Ronaldo's ice cream in a mouth-watering battery of flavours, from chocolate and ginger to cinnamon and lavender.

Cley and around

Travelling west from Sheringham, the A149 meanders through a pretty rural landscape offering occasional glimpses of the sea and a shoreline protected by both a slab of marshland and a giant shingle barrier erected after the catastrophic flood of 1953. After seven miles you reach **CLEY-NEXT-THE-SEA**, once a busy wool port but now little more than a row of flint cottages and Georgian mansions set beside a narrow, marshy inlet that (just) gives access to the sea. The original village was destroyed in a fire in 1612, which explains why Cley's fine medieval **church of St Margaret** is located half a mile inland at the very southern edge of the current village, overlooking the green. The Black Death brought church construction to a sudden halt here, hence the contrast between the stunted, unfinished chancel and the splendid nave. Cley's main draws are, however, gastronomic: the excellent **Cley Smoke House** (℡01263/740282), housed in an old forge on the main street, sells local smoked fish among other delicacies, and neighbouring **Picnic Fayre** has long been one of the finest delis in East Anglia.

As for a **place to stay**, Cley holds the outstanding ⚘ *Cley Windmill* (℡01263/740209, Ⓦwww.cleywindmill.co.uk; ❺), which comes complete with sails and a balcony offering wonderful views over the surrounding salt marshes and seashore. The guest rooms, both in the windmill and the adjoining outhouses, are decorated in an attractive, suitably rustic manner and the best, like the Stone Room, have splendid beamed ceilings; self-catering arrangements are possible as well. At peak periods, there's a minimum two-night stay.

Blakeney Point

It's about 400 yards east from Cley to the mile-long byroad that leads to the shingle mounds of **Cley beach**. This is the starting point for the four-mile hike west out along the spit to **Blakeney Point**, a nature reserve famed for its colonies of terns and seals. The seal colony is made up of several hundred common and grey seals, and the old lifeboat house, at the end of the spit, is now a **National Trust information centre** (early April to Sept dawn to dusk). The shifting shingle can make walking difficult, so keep to the low-water mark – which also means that you won't accidentally trample any nests. The easier alternative is to take one of the boat trips to the point from Blakeney or Morston (see below). The Norfolk Coast Path passes close to Cley beach, too, and then continues along the edge of the **Cley Marshes**, which attract a wide variety of waders. One section of the marshes is protected as the **Cley Marshes Nature Reserve**, owned by the Norfolk Wildlife Trust. They run a **visitor centre** here (April to early Dec daily 10am–5pm), just east of Cley on the A149, and charge an entry fee of £4 for their part of the marshes and its assorted birdwatching hides.

Blakeney and around

Perhaps the prettiest of all the villages on the north Norfolk coast, **BLAKENEY**, a mile or so to the west of Cley, is simply delightful. Once a bustling port exporting fish, corn and salt, it's now a lovely little place with pebble-covered cottages sloping up from a muddy creek of a harbour. Crab sandwiches are sold from stalls at the quayside, family-run shops flank the dinky high street, and footpaths stretch out along the sea wall to east and west, offering fine views over the salt marshes. The only sights as such are the battered ruins of the medieval **Guildhall** (open access; free; EH), just back from the harbour, and the **church of St Nicholas**, beside the A149 at the south end of the village, where the sturdy tower and nave are made of flint rubble with stone trimmings, the traditional building materials of north Norfolk. Curiously, the church has a second, much smaller tower at the back. In the nineteenth century this was used as a lighthouse to guide ships into harbour, but its original function is unknown. Inside the church, the oak and chestnut hammer-beam roof and the delicate rood-screen are the most enjoyable features of the nave, which is attached to a late thirteenth-century chancel, the only survivor from the original Carmelite friary church.

Blakeney harbour and boat trips

Blakeney **harbour** is linked to the sea by a narrow channel, which wriggles its way through the salt marshes. The channel is, however, only navigable for a few hours at high tide, and at low tide the harbour is no more than a muddy creek (ideal for a bit of quayside crabbing and mud sliding). Depending on the tides, there are **boat trips** from either Blakeney or **Morston quay**, a mile or two to the west, to Blakeney Point (see above) – where passengers have a couple of hours at the point before being ferried back – and/or the seal colony just off the point. The main operators advertise departure times on blackboards by Blakeney quayside or you can reserve in advance with Beans Boats (℡01263/740505, Ⓦwww.beansboat trips.co.uk) or Bishop's Boats (℡01263/740753, Ⓦwww.norfolksealtrips.co.uk). Boat trips cost £8 per adult.

Practicalities

Buses to Blakeney pull in at the Westgate bus shelter, a couple of minutes' walk from the harbour; there's no tourist office. The village has several top-ranking hotels, but for longer stays contact *Quayside Cottages* (℡01462/768627, @www.blakeneycottages.co.uk), who rent out some quaint Blakeney cottages from £450 per week in high season, half that in winter.

Accommodation and eating

Blakeney Hotel The Quay ℡01263/740797, @www.blakeney-hotel.co.uk. One of the most charming seaside hotels in Norfolk, this family-owned establishment occupies a rambling building with high-pitched gables and pebble-covered walls. The hotel has a heated indoor swimming pool, secluded garden, and cosy lounges with exquisite sea views, and also serves outstanding lunches, afternoon teas and dinners. The cheaper rooms can be poky and somewhat airless, so it's worth paying a little more for one with splendid views across the harbour and the marshes. ❻

Blakeney White Horse 4 High St ℡01263/740574, @www.blakeneywhitehorse .co.uk. An old pub in the centre of the village, the *White Horse* offers nine guest rooms kitted out in a bright and cheerful manner. The food here is excellent, featuring such delights as beer-battered haddock and chips (for £13), and you can eat either informally in the bar or in the restaurant. ❹

Galley Hill Farm Camping Langham Rd ℡01263/741201, @www.glavenvalley.co.uk /galleyhillcamping. Pocket-sized campsite whose main draw is its location – just a mile's walk from Blakeney. Twenty pitches, no hook-ups. Reached from Blakeney along the B1156 Langham road. Open late May to Sept.

Kings Arms Westgate St ℡01263/740341, @www .blakeneykingsarms.co.uk. This traditional pub, with its low, beamed ceilings and seven modest, modern en-suite bedrooms, is situated just back from the quay. Very popular, not least for its first-rate bar food with local seafood the principal speciality. ❸

Manor Hotel The Quay ℡01263/740376, @www .blakeneymanor.co.uk. Flanking a courtyard, the flint-faced barns of the *Manor* were once adjuncts to the manor house, but they now hold 37 modern bedrooms. Smashing location, a few yards to the east of the harbour. ❹

Around Blakeney: Binham Priory

The substantial remains of **Binham Priory** (dawn to dusk; free; EH) boast a handsome rural setting about four miles southwest of Blakeney, on the edge of the hamlet of **Binham**. The Benedictines established a priory here in the late eleventh century, but long before its suppression in 1540, the priory had gained a bad reputation, its priors renowned for their fecklessness. One of the worst was William de Somerton, who funded his dabblings in alchemy by selling the church silverware and then the vestments in the fourteenth century. Neither were the monks a picture of contentment – one became insane through excessive meditation, so the prior had him flogged and then kept in solitary confinement until his death. Today, the ruins focus on the **priory church**, whose nave was turned into the parish church during the Reformation. Inside, the nave arcades are a handsome illustration of the transition between the Norman and Early English styles, a triple bank of windows that sheds light on the spartan interior. Among the fittings, look out for the delicately carved font and the remains of the former rood-screen kept at the back of the church. The Protestants whitewashed the screen and then covered it with biblical texts, but the paint is wearing thin and the saints they were keen to conceal have started to pop out again.

Wells-next-the-Sea

Despite its name, **WELLS-NEXT-THE-SEA**, some eight miles west of Blakeney, is situated a good mile or so from open water. In Tudor times, before the harbour silted up, this was one of the great ports of eastern England, a major player in the trade with the Netherlands. Those heady days are long gone and although today it's the only commercially viable port on the north Norfolk coast, this is hardly a major boast. More importantly, Wells is also one of the county's more attractive towns, and even though there are no specific sights among its narrow lanes, it does make a good base for exploring the surrounding coastline.

The town divides into three distinct areas, starting with **The Buttlands**, a broad rectangular green on the south side of town, lined with oak and beech trees and framed by an attractive medley of old houses and cottages; it takes its unusual name from the time it was used for archery practice (a butt being the earthen mound behind the target). North from here, across Station Road, lie the narrow lanes of the town centre with **Staithe Street**, the minuscule main drag, flanked by quaint old-fashioned shops. Staithe Street leads down to the **quay**, a somewhat forlorn affair inhabited by a couple of amusement arcades and fish-and-chip shops, and the mile-long byroad that scuttles north to the **beach**, a handsome sandy tract backed by pine-clad dunes. The beach road is shadowed by a high flood defence and a tiny narrow-gauge **railway**, which scoots down to the beach every twenty minutes or so (Easter–Oct from 10.30am; £1.20 each way).

Practicalities

Most **buses** to Wells stop on both The Buttlands and the quayside, from where it's the briefest of walks to the **tourist office**, at the foot of Staithe Street (late March to mid-July & Oct Mon–Sat 10am–5pm, Sun 10am–1pm; mid-July to Sept Mon–Sat 9.30am–7pm, Sun 9.30am–6pm; ℡0871/200 3071, ⊛www.visitnorthnorfolk.com). There are two recommendable **hotels** on The Buttlands. The more enticing is *The Crown* (℡01328/710209, ⊛www.thecrownhotelwells.co.uk; ⑤), in a good-looking, three-storey former coaching inn that has been tastefully modernized in slick contemporary style. There are twelve guest rooms here with pastel shades of cream and brown to the fore. The second hotel, owned by the Holkham estate, is *The Globe Inn* (℡01328/710206, ⊛www.holkham.co.uk; ⑤), whose seven rooms are decorated in a similar style as those at *The Crown*, though the building itself is really rather squat and dumpy. Wells also possesses the sprawling and extremely popular *Pinewoods Holiday Park*, right by the beach and complete with its own beach huts, **camping** pitches and caravan sites (℡01328/710439, ⊛www.pinewoods.co.uk; mid-March to Dec).

The best **place to eat** is *The Crown*, either in the restaurant or the bar, where the emphasis is on local ingredients with the likes of roast venison, parsnip mash, braised red cabbage and blackberry jam costing a very reasonable £14.25. A good second choice is *The Corner House*, Staithe Street (℡01328/710701), a bar-restaurant where the big deal is the local seafood.

Little Walsingham

For centuries, **LITTLE WALSINGHAM**, six miles south of Wells (and not to be confused with adjoining Great Walsingham), rivalled Bury St Edmunds and Canterbury as the foremost **pilgrimage site** in England. It all began in 1061 when the Lady of the Manor, a certain Richeldis de Faverches, was prompted to build a replica of the Santa Casa (Mary's home in Nazareth) in this remote part of Norfolk – inspired, it is said, by visions of the Virgin Mary. Whatever the reason, it brought instant fame and fortune to Little Walsingham and every medieval king from Henry III onwards made at least one trip, walking the last mile barefoot. Both the Augustinians and the Franciscans established themselves here and all seemed set fair when Henry VIII followed in his predecessors' footsteps in 1511. Yet, pilgrim or not, it didn't stop Henry from destroying the shrine in the Dissolution of the 1530s, and at a stroke the village's principal trade came to a halt. Pilgrimages resumed in earnest after 1922, when the local vicar, one Alfred

Hope Patten, organized an Anglo-Catholic pilgrimage, the prelude to the building of an Anglican shrine in the 1930s – much to the initial chagrin of the diocesan authorities. Nowadays, the village does good business out of its holy connections as well as the narrow-gauge **steam railway**, which links it with Wells (April–Oct 3–5 daily; 30min; £8 return; ☏01328/711630, ⓦwww .wellswalsinghamrailway.co.uk).

The village

Little Walsingham has a number of **shrines** catering to a variety of denominations – there's even a Russian Orthodox church – but the main one is the **Anglican shrine**, located beside Holt Road, a few yards to the east of the village's main square, Common Place. Flanked by a **Welcome Centre**, where there's a small exhibition on the history of the cult, and attractive gardens, the shrine itself is a strange-looking building, rather like a cross between an English village hall and an Orthodox church. Inside lies a series of small chapels and a Holy Well with healing waters as well as the idiosyncratic Holy House – **Santa Casa** – which contains the statue of Our Lady of Walsingham.

Shrines apart, Little Walsingham has an attractive and singularly old-fashioned centre, beginning with **Common Place**, whose half-timbered buildings surround a quaint octagonal structure built to protect the village pump in the sixteenth century. The **High Street** extends south from here, overlooked by antique brick and half-timbered houses. It's also overseen by the impressive, if badly weathered, fifteenth-century **abbey gatehouse** of the old Augustinian priory – look up and you'll spy Christ peering out from a window – though the **ruins** beyond, whose landscaped grounds stretch down to the River Stiffkey, can only be reached from Common Place through the **Shirehall Museum** (Feb & April–Oct daily 10am–4pm; March, Nov & Dec Sat & Sun only 10am–4pm; £3.50 for grounds & museum) for most of the year; if the museum is closed, try the Estate Office, footsteps away at 10 Common Place (Mon–Fri 9am–1pm & 2–5pm). Adjoining the south end of the High Street is the town's second square, **Friday Market Place**, a tiny crossroads edged by a pretty medley of very old houses.

Practicalities

Sanders Coaches (☏01263 712800, ⓦwww.sanderscoaches.com) operates a limited **bus** service to Little Walsingham's Anglican shrine from Wells and several nearby villages. The **train station** (for the steam train from Wells, see above) is a five-minute walk from Common Place – just follow the signs. The **tourist office** is part of the Shirehall Museum (same times as museum – see above; ☏01328/820510). They have details of local **accommodation**, though there's not much on offer and during major pilgrimages vacant rooms are impossible to find. The best local choice is the *Old Bakehouse Guest House*, in an old red-brick right in the centre at 33 High St (☏01328/820454, ⓦwww.glavenvalley.co.uk/oldbakehouse; ❸); they have just three comfortable, albeit very traditional, en-suite guest rooms. The **place to eat** is the *Norfolk Riddle*, 2 Wells Rd (☏01328/821903), a combined fish-and-chip shop and restaurant supplied – and owned – by local farmers; it's located a brief walk north of the Anglican shrine.

Holkham Hall and Holkham Bay

Holkham Hall (April–Oct Mon, Thurs & Sun noon–4pm; £9, plus £2.50 parking; ⓦwww.holkham.co.uk), three miles to the west of Wells, is a grand and self-assured (or vainglorious) stately home designed by the eighteenth-century architect William Kent for the first earl of Leicester, whose descendants still own the place. The severe sandy-coloured Palladian exterior belies the warmth and richness of the interior, which retains much of its original decoration, notably the much-admired marble hall, with its fluted columns and intricate reliefs. The rich colours of the state rooms are an appropriate backdrop for a wide selection of **paintings**, including canvases by Van Dyck, Rubens and Gainsborough. While you're here you could also pop into the **Bygones Museum**, but it does cost £2 extra.

The **grounds** (Jan–March Mon, Wed & Fri 7am–7pm, Tues & Thurs 9.30am–7pm; April–Oct Mon–Sat 7am–7pm, Sun 9am–7pm; free) are laid out on sandy, saline land, much of it originally salt marsh. The focal point is an eighty-foot-high obelisk, atop a grassy knoll, from where you can view both the hall to the north and the triumphal arch to the south. In common with the rest of the north Norfolk coast, there's plenty of **birdlife** – Holkham's lake attracts Brent geese, herons and grebes, and several hundred deer graze the open pastures.

Back on the A149, beside the main entrance to the Holkham estate, the conspicuous *Victoria Hotel* stands opposite Lady Anne's Drive, a half-mile byroad-cum-parking-lot that is as near as you can get by car and bike to **Holkham Bay**. The bay boasts one of the finest beaches on this stretch of coast, with golden sand and pine-studded sand dunes. Warblers, flycatchers and redstarts inhabit the drier coastal reaches, while waders paddle about the mud and salt flats.

Burnham Market and Burnham Thorpe

Heading west from Wells on the A149, it's about five miles to the postcard-pretty village of **BURNHAM MARKET**, where an attractive medley of Georgian and Victorian houses surrounds a dinky little green with an oh-so-cutesy stream flowing across the road whenever it rains. The village attracts a well-heeled, north London crowd, in no small measure because of the *Hoste Arms* (℡01328/738777, ⓦwww .hostearms.co.uk; ❺, ❼ on the weekend), a creatively modernized old coaching inn – with assorted outbuildings – that offers some of the best food on the coast. Some of the decor verges on the pretentious/preposterous, but the food cannot be criticized, either in the bar or in the restaurant. The menu is a well-balanced mixture of land and sea, anything from wood pigeon with strawberries to cod in beer batter with peas and chips; main courses range from £14 to £20. The guest rooms are round the back also and range from the small (verging on the cramped) to the much more expansive (and expensive). The same people also own the *Railway Inn* (same details), in the old train station on Creake Road, a ten-minute walk away.

BURNHAM THORPE, a mile or so to the southeast of Burnham Market, was the birthplace of **Horatio Nelson** (see box below), who was born in the village

Horatio Nelson

Born in Burnham Thorpe in 1758, **Horatio Nelson** joined the navy at the tender age of 12, and was sent to the West Indies, where he met and married Frances Nisbet, retiring to Burnham Thorpe in 1787. Back in action by 1793, his bravery cost him first the sight of his right eye, and shortly afterwards his right arm. His personal life was equally eventful – famously, his infatuation with **Emma Hamilton**, wife of the ambassador to Naples, caused the eventual break-up of his marriage. His finest hour was during the **Battle of Trafalgar** in 1805, when he led the British navy to victory against the combined French and Spanish fleets, a crucial engagement that set the scene for Britain's century-long domination of the high seas. The victory didn't do Nelson much good – he was shot in the chest during the battle and even the kisses of Hardy failed to revive him. Thereafter, Nelson was placed in a barrel of brandy and the pickled body shipped back to England, where he was laid in state at Greenwich and then buried at St Paul's Cathedral in London.

parsonage on September 29, 1758. The parsonage was demolished years ago, but the admiral is still celebrated in the village's **All Saints Parish Church**, where the lectern is made out of timbers taken from his last ship, the *Victory*, the chancel sports a Nelson bust, and the south aisle has a small exhibition on his life and times. It was actually Nelson's express wish that he should be buried here, but to no avail. The other place to head for is the village **pub** (no prizes for guessing the name; closed Mon eve), where Nelson held a farewell party for the locals in 1793. They have kept modernity at bay here – from the old wooden benches through to the serving hatch and tiled floor – and the bar food is very good: try the venison sausages and mash.

Burnham Deepdale, Brancaster Staithe and Titchwell

From Burnham Market, it's a couple of miles west to tiny **BURNHAM DEEPDALE**, where *Deepdale* (℡01485/210256, Ⓦwww.deepdalefarm.co.uk), situated beside the A149, is a lively and very amiable set up, operating a combined **campsite**, info centre, **café** and eco-friendly backpackers' **hostel** (dorm beds £9.50–13.50, doubles ❶) in creatively renovated former stables. Not only that but they have also diversified into **tipis and yurts**, which range in price and size from £85 per night (for 1–2 people) up to around £120 (for 3–6).

From the *Deepdale* complex, it's just a few hundred yards west to **BRANCASTER STAITHE**, where a strip of housing falls either side of the A149. First impressions of the village are not especially favourable, but it does possess the excellent ⚒ *White Horse* (℡01485/210262, Ⓦwww.whitehorsebrancaster.co.uk; ❹), a combined restaurant, pub and **hotel** that backs straight onto the marshes, lagoons and creeks of the coast – and, even better, the North Norfolk Coast Path runs along the bottom of the hotel garden. Brancaster is famous for its **oysters** and this is as good a place as any to try them, though the restaurant has all sorts of other temptations from local duck to local beef (mains average around £16). The hotel divides into two sections: there are seven en-suite rooms in the main building, one of which is split-level with a telescope thrown in for free, and eight more at the back with grass roofs. Decor is light and airy with a few nautical bits and pieces thrown in for good measure and many of the rooms – and all of those at the back – look out over the tidal marshes.

From Brancaster Staithe, it's two miles more to tiny **TITCHWELL**, where the thirty slick and ultra modern rooms at the roadside *Titchwell Manor Hotel* (℡01485/210221, Ⓦwww.titchwellmanor.com; ❺) occupy a rambling Victorian brick house and adjacent garden-cottage complex. The hotel is also a five-minute drive from the **Titchwell Marsh RSPB Nature Reserve** (daily dawn to dusk; free, but £4 parking) – head west on the A149 and watch for the signed turning – whose mix of marsh, reed bed, mudflat, lagoon and beach attracts a wide range of birds, including marsh harriers, bearded tits, avocets, gulls and terns.

From Titchwell, it's just six miles more to Hunstanton.

Hunstanton

The north Norfolk coast ends (or begins) at **HUNSTANTON**, a popular seaside resort whose centre has been mashed up by some pretty awful modern development. That said, Hunstanton does have a splendid beach, a sandy tract backed by stripy gateau-like cliffs that stretch north to **Old Hunstanton**, where a large and grassy park-cum-car-park offers superb sea views. There's no strong reason to stay the night here, but the **tourist office** has a long list of B&Bs (daily: April, May,

Sept & Oct 10.30am–4.30pm; June–Aug 10am–5pm; Nov–March 10.30am–3pm; ℡01485/532610, 🌐www.visitnorthnorfolk.com); it's in the town hall on the wide sloping green that serves as the resort's focal point.

Sandringham House

Built in 1870 on land purchased by Queen Victoria for her son, the future Edward VII, **Sandringham House** (April–Oct daily 11am–5.30pm; last entry 4.45pm; closed for 1–2 weeks late July or early Aug; £10, £7 museum & gardens only; 🌐www.sandringhamestate.co.uk) is located off the A149 about eight miles south of Hunstanton. The house is billed as a private home, but few families have a drawing room crammed with Russian silver and Chinese jade. The **museum** (same times), housed in the old coach and stable block, contains an exhibition of royal memorabilia from dolls to cars, but much more arresting are the beautifully maintained **gardens** (same dates daily from 10.30am; last entry 5pm), a mass of rhododendrons and azaleas in spring and early summer. The estate's sandy soil is also ideal for game birds, which was the attraction of the place for the terminally bored Edward, whose tradition of posh shooting parties is still followed by the royals of today.

Local **bus** #41 makes the journey to Sandringham Visitor Centre from King's Lynn every hour or so during opening hours.

King's Lynn and around

An ancient port, **KING'S LYNN** straddles the canalized mouth of the River Great Ouse a mile or so before it slides into The Wash. Before the river was tamed, the town occupied an improbably marshy location, but it was strategically placed for easy access to seven English counties. Consequently, the town's merchants grew rich importing fish from Scandinavia, timber from the Baltic and wine from France, while exporting wool, salt and corn to the Hanseatic ports. The good times came to an end when the focus of maritime trade moved to the Atlantic seaboard, but its port struggled on until it was reinvigorated in the 1970s by the burgeoning trade between the UK and its EU partners. Much of the old centre was demolished during the 1950s and 1960s to make way for commercial development and, as a result, most of Lynn is not especially enticing, but it does have a cluster of handsome old riverside buildings, which taken together are well worth a couple of hours. As an added incentive, King's Lynn's lively, open-air **markets** attract large fenland crowds – there's one on the Saturday Market Place every Saturday and two others on the Tuesday Market Place, on Tuesdays and Fridays.

Arrival, information and accommodation

From the **train station**, it's a short walk west along Waterloo Street to Railway Road, the principal north–south thoroughfare, which borders the eastern edge of the town centre on the east bank of the river. The **bus station** is right in the centre, amid the main shopping area about 150 yards to the west of Railway Road. The **tourist office** is by the river, in the Custom House on Purfleet Quay (April–Sept Mon–Sat 10am–4pm, Sun noon–5pm; Oct–March Mon–Sat 10.30am–4pm, Sun noon–4pm; ℡01553/763044, 🌐www.visitwestnorfolk.com). They have a wide range of information and will help arrange **accommodation**.

Bank House Hotel King's Staithe Square
☎01553/660492, ⓦwww.thebankhouse.co.uk.
In an intelligently converted Georgian townhouse
down by the river at the heart of the old town,
this classy hotel has eleven guest rooms. Most
have river views and the decor is a pleasant mix
of the old (timber beams) and the new (the
bathrooms). ④

The Old Rectory 33 Goodwins Rd
☎01553/768544, ⓦwww.theoldrectory-kingslynn
.com. Small and agreeable B&B whose bedrooms
are decorated in a reassuringly modern/cosy style,
though the house itself dates back to the 1840s.
Goodwins Road is on the southern side of town,
east off London Road, a southerly extension of
Railway Road. ②

The Town

King's Lynn's historic core is situated in the two blocks between the High Street
and the quayside. A good place to begin is the **Saturday Market Place**, the older
and smaller of the town's two marketplaces, presided over by the hybrid **church
of St Margaret**, whose chancel contains two of the most fanciful medieval brasses
in East Anglia. These are the Walsoken brass, adorned with country scenes, and the
Braunche brass, named after a certain Robert Braunche and depicting the lavish
feast he laid on for Edward III. Across the square is Lynn's prettiest building, the
Trinity Guildhall, its wonderful chequered flint and stone facade dating to 1421
and repeated in the Elizabethan addition and the Victorian town hall immediately
to the left. Close by, just across from – and to the south of – the church is the
former **Hanseatic Warehouse**, the most evocative of the medieval warehouses
that survive along the quayside. Built around 1475, its half-timbered upper floor
juts unevenly over the cobbles of St Margaret's Lane.

Heading north from the **Saturday Market Place** along the Georgian curve of
Queen Street, it only takes a couple of minutes to reach the splendid **Custom
House**, erected in 1683 in a style clearly influenced by the Dutch. There are
classical pilasters, petite dormer windows and a roof-top balustrade, but it's the
dinky little cupola that catches the eye. The Custom House holds the tourist office
and overlooks **Purfleet Quay**, a short harbour once packed with merchant ships.

Beyond the Custom House, King Street, with its much wider berth, continues
where Queen Street leaves off. On the left, just after Ferry Lane, stands Lynn's
most precious building, **St George's Guildhall**, dating from 1410 and one of the
oldest surviving guildhalls in England. It was a theatre in Elizabethan times and is
now part of the King's Lynn Arts Centre (see below). Beyond the Guildhall is the
Tuesday Market Place, where the pastel-pink *Duke's Head Hotel*, dating from
1689, and the Neoclassical Corn Exchange (see below) stand out.

From Tuesday Market Place, you can regain the **riverfront** for a stroll down the
old quayside – a pleasant way to finish off a visit.

Eating, drinking and entertainment

The best **café** in town is *Crofters Coffee Shop* (closed Sun), located in the undercroft
of St George's Guildhall at the King's Lynn Arts Centre, 29 King St. They serve
tasty salads and light meals plus sandwiches and soups. One of the better **restaurants** in town, though it does get mixed reviews, is the *Riverside*, 27 King St
(☎01553/773134; closed Sun), in a handsomely converted, fifteenth-century
warehouse overlooking the river from the back of the arts centre; main courses
here start at around £15.

Entertainment in Lynn revolves around the **King's Lynn Arts Centre**
(☎01553/764864, ⓦwww.kingslynnarts.co.uk), which stages a wide range of
performances and exhibitions both here and in several other downtown venues,
including the old **Corn Exchange**, on Tuesday Market Place (☎01553/764864,
ⓦwww.kingslynncornexchange.co.uk).

Ely and around

Perched on a mound of clay above the River Great Ouse about thirty miles south of King's Lynn, the attractive little town of **ELY** – literally "eel island" – was to all intents and purposes a true island until the draining of the Fens (see p.471) in the seventeenth century. Up until then, the town was encircled by treacherous marshland, which could only be crossed with the help of the local **"fen-slodgers"** who knew the firm tussock paths. In 1070, **Hereward the Wake** turned this inaccessibility to military advantage, holding out against the Normans and forcing William the Conqueror to undertake a prolonged siege – and finally to build an improvised road floated on bundles of sticks. Centuries later, the Victorian writer Charles Kingsley resurrected this obscure conflict in his novel *Hereward the Wake*. He presented the protagonist as the Last of the English who "never really bent their necks to the Norman yoke and ... kept alive those free institutions which were the germs of our British liberty" – a heady mixture of nationalism and historical poppycock that went down a storm.

Since then, Ely has always been associated with Hereward, which is really rather ridiculous as Ely is, above all else, an ecclesiastical town and a Norman one to boot. The Normans built the **cathedral**, a towering structure visible for miles across the flat fenland landscape and Ely's main sight. It's easy to see the town on a day-trip from Cambridge and Ely is also relatively close to Cambridgeshire's most important ecclesiastical sight – namely the cathedral at Peterborough (see box, p.471) – not to mention a rare chunk of undrained and unmolested fenland, the National Trust's **Wicken Fen**.

Arrival, information and accommodation

From Ely **train station**, it's a ten-minute walk to the cathedral, straight up Station Road and then Back Hill before veering right along The Gallery. **Buses** stop on Market Street immediately north of the cathedral, and the **tourist office** is a couple of minutes' walk northwest of the cathedral in Oliver Cromwell's House at 29 St Mary's St (April–Oct daily 10am–5pm; Nov–March Mon–Fri & Sun 11am–4pm, Sat 10am–5pm; ☏ 01353/662062, ⓦ visitely.eastcambs.gov.uk).

Among Ely's several **B&Bs**, one good choice is the *Cathedral House*, in an attractive Georgian townhouse a brief stroll from the cathedral at 17 St Mary's St (☏ 01353/662124, ⓦ www.cathedralhouse.co.uk; no credit cards; ❸). All the guest rooms here are en suite and each comes complete with period details, though they all tend to be a tad spartan. A second option is *Sycamore House*, which occupies a well-maintained detached house on the southwest edge of town at 91 Cambridge Rd (☏ 01353/662139, ⓦ sycamoreguesthouse.co.uk; ❸); they have three en-suite guest rooms and all are decorated in a cheerful, vaguely retro style.

The cathedral

Ely Cathedral (June–Sept daily 7am–7pm; Oct–May Mon–Sat 7.30am–6pm, Sun 7.30am–5pm; Mon–Sat £6, Sun free; ⓦ www.cathedral.ely.anglican.org) is one of the most impressive churches in England, but the **west facade**, where visitors enter, has been lopsided ever since one of its transepts collapsed in a storm in 1701. Nonetheless, the remaining transept, which was completed in the 1180s and is seen to best advantage from The Gallery running to the south, is an imposing structure, its dog-tooth windows, castellated towers and blind arcading possessing all the rough, almost brutal charm of the Normans.

The first things to strike you as you enter the **nave** are the sheer length of the building and the lively nineteenth-century painted ceiling, largely the work of amateur volunteers. The nave's procession of plain, late Norman arches, built around the same time as those at Peterborough (see box opposite), leads to the architectural feature that makes Ely so special, the **octagon** – the only one of its kind in England – built in 1322 to replace the collapsed central tower. Its construction, employing the largest oaks available in England to support some four hundred tonnes of glass and lead, remains one of the wonders of the medieval world, and the effect, as you look up into this Gothic dome, is simply breathtaking. From April to October, **Octagon Tower tours** (£4 extra, £6 on Sun; reservations & schedule ℡01353/660344) depart two to four times daily from the desk at the entrance, venturing up into the octagon itself.

When the central tower collapsed, it fell eastwards onto the **choir**, the first three bays of which were rebuilt at the same time as the octagon in the Decorated style – in contrast to the slightly plainer Early English of the choir bays beyond. In the floor of the choir, a commemorative plaque marks the site of the shrine of **St Ethelreda**, founder of the abbey in 673, who, despite being twice married, is honoured liturgically as a virgin. The shrine once attracted pilgrims from far and wide, but it was destroyed during the Reformation. At the east end of the cathedral is the thirteenth-century **presbytery**, where there are two medieval **chantry chapels**, the more charming of which (on the left) is an elaborate Renaissance affair dated to 1488. The other marvel is the **Lady Chapel**, a separate building accessible via the north transept. It lost its sculpture and its stained glass during the Reformation, but its fan vaulting remains, an exquisite example of English Gothic. Back near the main entrance, the south triforium holds the **Stained Glass Museum** (Mon–Sat 10.30am–5pm, Sun noon–6pm, closes 4.30pm in winter; £3.50), an Anglican money-spinner exhibiting examples of this applied art from 1200 to the 1970s, including some especially fine work by William Morris and his circle.

The rest of the town

The rest of Ely is pleasant and pretty enough, but hardly compelling after the wonders of the cathedral. To the immediate north of the church is the **High Street**, a slender thoroughfare lined by old-fashioned shops and cafés that makes for an enjoyable browse. At the east end of the High Street is the town's dinky little **Market Place**, from where Forehill and its continuation Waterside continue on down to the **riverside**, a relaxing spot with a large antique centre, a marina, a riverside footpath, a tearoom or two, a small art gallery and an entertainment and cinema complex housed in the splendidly restored **Old Maltings**. Alternatively, head northwest from the cathedral to get to **Oliver Cromwell's House** at 29 St Mary's St (April–Oct daily 10am–5pm; Nov–March Mon–Fri & Sun 11am–4pm, Sat 10am–5pm; £4.50), a timber-framed former vicarage, which holds a small exhibition on the Protector's ten-year sojourn in Ely when he was employed as a tithe collector; the tourist office is here as well.

Eating and drinking

For location, the most appealing **café** in town is *The Almonry*, on the High Street, where they serve a competent line in sandwiches and snacks with the added bonus of lovely views of the cathedral from a pleasant outside area. The food at *Peacocks Tearoom*, down by the river at 65 Waterside (closed Mon & Tues) is, however, a good bit better – and the salads are something of a local rave. The best **restaurant** in Ely is *The Boathouse*, a modern, bistro-style place also down by the river at 5 Annesdale (℡01353/664388). The menu, which features local, seasonal ingredients, is firmly British with the likes of pheasant and skate, mutton and – the house speciality – sausages and mash; mains average £13, but the sausages cost just £10.50. For a **pint**, try the *Prince Albert*, a cosy local at 62 Silver St; to get there, walk along The Gallery, which runs south from the cathedral's main entrance, and turn right.

Around Ely: the Fens

One of the strangest of all English landscapes, **the Fens** cover a vast area of eastern England from just north of Cambridge right up to Boston in Lincolnshire. For centuries, they were an inhospitable wilderness of quaking bogs and marshland, punctuated by clay islands on which small communities eked out a livelihood cutting peat for fuel, using reeds for thatching and living on a diet of fish and wildfowl. Piecemeal land reclamation took place throughout the Middle Ages, but it wasn't until the seventeenth century that the systematic draining of the Fens was undertaken – amid fierce local opposition – by the Dutch engineer **Cornelius Vermuyden**. This wholesale draining had unforeseen consequences: as it dried out, the peaty soil shrank to below the level of the rivers, causing frequent flooding, and the region's **windmills**, which had previously been vital in keeping the waters at bay, now compounded the problem by causing further shrinkage. The engineers had to do some rapid backtracking and the task of draining the Fens was only completed in the 1820s following the introduction of **steam-driven pumps**, leviathans which could control water levels with much greater precision than their windmill predecessors. Drained, the Fens now comprise some of the most fertile agricultural land in the Europe.

Wicken Fen

At **Wicken Fen National Nature Reserve** (daily 10am–5pm or dusk if earlier; ☎01353/720274; £5.75; NT), nine miles south of Ely via the A10 and A1123, you can visit one of the few remaining areas of undrained fenland. Its survival is thanks to a group of Victorian entomologists who donated the land to the National Trust in 1899, making it the oldest nature reserve in the UK. The seven

---

Peterborough Cathedral

For the casual visitor, the burgeoning city of **Peterborough**, about thirty-odd miles northwest of Ely, has just one distinct – but unmissable – attraction: its superb Norman **cathedral** (Mon–Fri 9am–5.15pm, Sat 9am–3pm, Sun noon–3.15pm; donation requested; ⑩www.peterborough-cathedral.org.uk). A site of Christian worship since the seventh century, the first two churches here were destroyed – the original Saxon monastery by the Danes in 870, its replacement by fire in 1116. Work on the present structure began a year after the fire and was largely completed within the century. The one significant later addition is the thirteenth-century west facade, one of the most magnificent in England, made up of three grandiloquent, deeply recessed arches, though the purity of the design is marred slightly by an incongruous central porch added in 1370.

The interior is a wonderful example of Norman architecture. Round-arched rib vaults and shallow blind arcades line the nave, while up above the painted wooden ceiling, dating from 1220, is an exquisite example of medieval art, one of the most important in Europe. There are several notable tombs in the cathedral, too, beginning with that of Henry VIII's first wife, **Catherine of Aragon**, who is buried in the north aisle of the presbytery under a slab of black Irish marble.

Peterborough **train station** is a short, signposted walk across the pedestrianized town centre from the cathedral.

hundred acres are undrained but not uncultivated – sedge and reed cutting are still carried out to preserve the landscape as it is. The reserve is readily explored by means of several easy and clearly marked **footpaths**, one of which – the easiest – is a three-quarter-of-a-mile stroll along a boardwalk and takes in one of the last surviving fenland wind-pumps. The reserve also holds about ten birdwatching hides, while at the main entrance, there's a **visitor centre** and an antique fenland thatched **cottage** (April–Oct Sat & Sun 2–5pm). The visitor centre organizes a variety of events and guided walks – call ahead for details.

Cambridge and around

On the whole, **CAMBRIDGE** is a much quieter and more secluded place than Oxford, its great scholarly rival, though for the visitor what really sets it apart is "**The Backs**" – the green sward of land that straddles the languid River Cam, providing exquisite views over the backs of the old **colleges**. At the front, the handsome facades of these same colleges dominate the layout of the city centre, lining up along the main streets. Most of the older colleges date back to the late thirteenth and early fourteenth centuries and are designed to a similar plan with the main gate leading through to a series of "courts", typically a carefully manicured slab of lawn surrounded on all four sides by college residences and offices. Many of the buildings are extraordinarily beautiful, but the most famous is **King's College**, whose magnificent **King's College Chapel** is one of the great statements of late Gothic architecture. There are 31 university colleges in total, each an independent, self-governing body, proud of its achievements and attracting – for the most part at least – a close loyalty from its students, among whom privately educated boys remain hopelessly over-represented. This intrinsic elitism is amplified by all sorts of eccentric (some say charming) rules and regulations and by an arcane vocabulary unfamiliar to ordinary mortals. "Heads of house" are heads of college – whether they be "Masters", "Provosts", "Principals", "Presidents" or "Wardens" – and most of them are elected by the "Fellows", graduates or senior members with teaching responsibilities. "The Other Place" is Oxford; "bedders" are college domestics; and "porters" man the gates and keep good order. There are three terms – Michaelmas (Oct–Dec), Lent (Jan–March) and Easter (April–June) – and the students' biggest annual knees-up, the "May balls", are held in June.

Cambridge is an extremely compact place, and you can walk round the centre, visiting the most interesting colleges, in an afternoon. A more thorough exploration, covering more of the colleges, a visit to the fine art of the **Fitzwilliam Museum** and a leisurely afternoon on a **punt**, will, however, take at least a couple of days. If possible, avoid coming in high summer, when the students are replaced by hordes of sightseers and posses of foreign-language students, though you can still miss the crowds by getting up early – the tourists only start to appear in numbers from around 10am.

Some history

Tradition has it that **Cambridge** was founded in the late 1220s by scholastic refugees from Oxford, who fled that town after one of their number was lynched by hostile townsfolk – though the first proper college wasn't founded until 1271. Rivalry has existed between the two institutions ever since – epitomized by the annual Boat Race on the River Thames – while internal tensions between "**Town and Gown**" have inevitably plagued a place where, from the late fourteenth century onwards, the university has tended to control local life. The first (but by no means the last) rebellion against the scholars occurred during the Peasants' Revolt of 1381, and had to be put down with armed troops by the Bishop of Norwich.

In the sixteenth century, Cambridge became a centre of **church reformism**, educating some of the most famous Protestant preachers in the country, including Cranmer, Latimer and Ridley, all of whom were martyred in Oxford by Mary Tudor. Later, during the Civil War, Cambridge once again found itself at the centre of events: **Oliver Cromwell** was both a graduate of Sidney Sussex and the local MP, though the university itself was largely Royalist. After the Restoration, the university regained most of its privileges, but by the eighteenth century it was in the doldrums, better known, as Byron put it, for its "din and drunkenness" than for its academic record.

The university finally lost its ancient **privileges** over the town in Victorian times, when the latter expanded rapidly thanks to the arrival of the railway. The town's population quadrupled between 1800 and 1900 and meanwhile the university expanded too, with the number of students increasing by leaps and bounds following the broadening of the curriculum to include new subjects such as natural science and history. Change was slower in coming in the battle for equality of the sexes. The first two **women's colleges** were founded in the 1870s, but it was only in 1947 that women were actually awarded degrees, and one or two colleges held out against accepting female students until the 1980s. In the meantime, the city and university acquired a reputation as a high-tech centre of excellence, known locally as "**Silicon Fen**". Cambridge has always been in the vanguard of scientific research – its alumni have garnered almost one hundred Nobel prizes – and it has now become a major international player in the lucrative electronic communications industry.

Arrival

Cambridge **train station** is a mile or so to the southeast of the city centre, off Hills Road. It's an easy but tedious twenty-minute walk into the centre, or take local bus #1, #3 or #7 to the **bus stops** on Emmanuel Street, which is itself yards from the Drummer Street long-distance **bus station**. Cambridge is just thirty miles north of **London Stansted airport**, from where there are hourly trains to the city; the journey time is 45 minutes. Arriving by **car**, you'll find much of the city centre closed to traffic and on-street parking well-nigh impossible to find; for a day-trip, at least, the best option is a **park-and-ride** car park; they are signposted on all major approaches.

Messing about on the water

Punting (see also p.273), the quintessential Cambridge activity, is a good deal harder than it looks. First-timers find themselves zigzagging across the water and "punt jams" are very common on the stretch of the River Cam beside The Backs in summer. **Punt rental** is available at several points, including the boatyard at Mill Lane (beside the Silver Street bridge), at Magdalene Bridge, and at the Garret Hostel Lane bridge at the back of Trinity College. It costs around £18 an hour (most places charge a deposit), and punts can hold up to six people. Alternatively, you can hire a **chauffeured punt** from any of the rental places for about £12 per person per hour. If you become proficient, one possible target is the village of **Grantchester** to the south of Cambridge, where you can collapse in a deckchair and take tea and scones at the idyllic *Orchard Tea Garden* (daily: March–May & Sept–Nov 9.30am–5.30pm; June–Aug 9.30am–7pm; Dec–Feb 9.30am–4.30pm), a short walk up from the banks of the Cam.

Information and getting around

Cambridge **tourist office** is bang in the centre of town on Peas Hill, just off King's Parade (Mon–Sat 10am–5pm, plus May–Sept Sun 11am–3pm; ☏0871/226 8006, ⓦwww.visitcambridge.org). They sell city maps (50p), coordinate a wide range of guided walking tours (from £11; reservations required), and can book accommodation.

The city centre is small enough to walk round comfortably, but **cycling** speeds things up and is extremely popular with locals and students alike. There are **bike rental** outlets dotted all over town (see p.483), but when and wherever you leave your bike, padlock it to something immovable as bike theft is far from rare.

Accommodation

Cambridge is light on central accommodation and those few **hotels and guest-houses** that do occupy prime locations are expensive. That said, there is a cluster of less pricey places, including a YHA **hostel**, around the train station and another on Chesterton Lane and its continuation, Chesterton Road, the busy street running east from the top of Magdalene Street. In high season, when vacant rooms are often thin on the ground, the tourist office's **accommodation booking service** can be very useful (for contact details, see above).

Arundel House Hotel 53 Chesterton Rd ☏01223/367701, ⓦwww.arundelhousehotels .co.uk. One of the better mid-range hotel choices, in a converted row of late Victorian houses overlooking the river and Jesus Green. Neat and tidy rooms, but mundane modern furnishings. ❹

Cambridge YHA 97 Tenison Rd ☏0845/371 9728, ⓔcambridge@yha.org.uk. This long-established hostel occupies a rambling Victorian house near the train station – Tenison Rd is a right turn a couple of hundred yards down Station Rd. Its facilities include laundry and self-catering, a cycle store, games room and a small courtyard garden. There are 100 beds in two- to eight-bed rooms and advance reservations are advised. Dorm beds £14, doubles ❶

City Roomz Station Rd ☏01223/304050, ⓦwww .cityroomz.com. This popular, bargain-basement hostel-style hotel is in a converted granary warehouse right outside the train station. Most of the rooms are kitted out with bunks, though there are a few doubles and twins too. All the rooms are en suite, but space is in short supply. ❷

Doubletree by Hilton Cambridge Granta Place, Mill Lane ☏01223/259988, ⓦdoubletree.hilton.co.uk. Though one of a chain, this is the city's most appealing hotel by a long chalk, occupying a strikingly modern 1960s building a couple of minutes' walk from the centre. The foyer is wide and expansive, the rooms well-appointed and well-equipped and the breakfasts are first-rate. The best rooms have balconies overlooking the river (though the views are hardly riveting). ❺

Hotel du Vin Trumpington St ☏01223/227330, ⓦwww.hotelduvin.com. Bijou luxury hotel in an immaculately refurbished old mansion just south of the town centre. Every facility, plus oodles of finessed details – from Egyptian-cotton bed linen onwards. One of a growing chain. ❻

Warkworth House Warkworth Terrace ☏01223/363682, ⓦwww.warkworthhouse.co.uk. Welcoming B&B with a handful of straightforward, unfussy en-suite rooms, in a Victorian house southeast of the bus station. ❸

Worth House 152 Chesterton Rd ☏01223/316074, ⓦwww.worth-house.co.uk. Very recommendable B&B in a pleasantly upgraded Victorian house, about 20min walk from the centre. All the bedrooms are en suite, the bathrooms are large and the facilities immaculate. Great breakfasts too. ❷

The City

Cambridge's **main shopping street** is Bridge Street, which becomes Sidney Street, St Andrew's Street and finally Regent Street; the other main thoroughfare is the procession of St John's Street, Trinity Street, King's Parade and Trumpington Street. The university developed on the land west of this latter route along the banks of the River Cam, and now forms a continuous half-mile parade of **colleges** from Peterhouse to Magdalene, with sundry others scattered about the

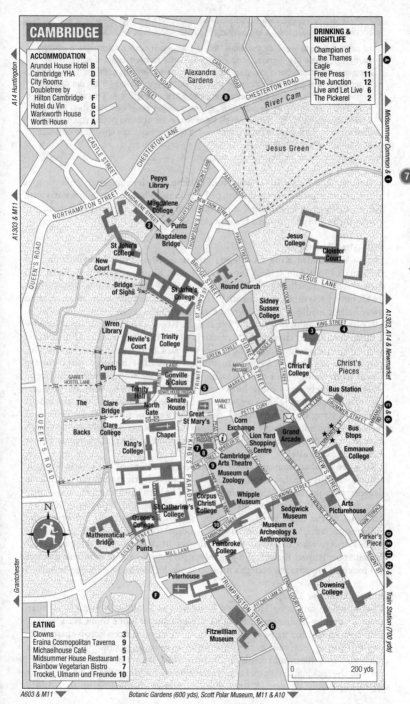

CAMBRIDGE

ACCOMMODATION
Arundel House Hotel	B
Cambridge YHA	E
City Roomz	D
Doubletree by	
Hilton Cambridge	F
Hotel du Vin	G
Warkworth House	C
Worth House	A

DRINKING & NIGHTLIFE
Champion of	
the Thames	4
Eagle	8
Free Press	11
The Junction	12
Live and Let Live	6
The Pickerel	2

EATING
Clowns	3
Eraina Cosmopolitan Taverna	9
Michaelhouse Café	5
Midsummer House Restaurant	1
Rainbow Vegetarian Bistro	7
Trockel, Ulmann und Freunde	10

A14 Huntingdon

A1303 & M11

Midsummer Common & ①

A1303, A14 & Newmarket

C & G

D, E, 11, 12 &

Train Station (700 yds)

Grantchester

A603 & M11

Botanic Gardens (600 yds), Scott Polar Museum, M11 & A10

475

periphery. The **Fitzwilliam Museum**, holding the city's finest art collection, is along Trumpington Street just south of Peterhouse. The account below starts with **King's College**, whose **chapel** is the university's most celebrated attraction, and covers the rest of the city in a broadly clockwise direction.

King's College

Henry VI founded **King's College** (term time: Mon–Fri 9.30am–3.30pm, Sat 9.30am–3.15pm, Sun 1.15–2.15pm; rest of year: Mon–Sat 9.30am–4.30pm, Sun 10am–5pm; £5 including chapel; ℡01223/331100, ⍟www.kings.cam.ac.uk) in 1441, but he was disappointed with his initial efforts, so four years later he cleared away half of medieval Cambridge to make room for a much grander foundation. His plans were ambitious, but the Wars of the Roses – and bouts of royal insanity – intervened and by the time of his death in 1471 very little had been finished and work on what was intended to be Henry's Great Court hadn't even started. This part of the site remained empty for no less than three hundred years and the **Great Court** complex of today – facing King's Parade from behind a long stone screen – is largely neo-Gothic, built in the 1820s to a design by **William Wilkins**. Henry's workmen did, however, start on the college's finest building, the much-celebrated **King's College Chapel,** on the north side of today's Great Court and reached – depending on the season – from either the main gatehouse on King's Parade or the North Gate beyond the Senate House at the end of Senate House Passage (see opposite).

King's enjoyed an exclusive supply of students from one of the country's public schools – in this case, Eton – and until 1851 claimed the right to award its students degrees without taking any examinations. The first non-Etonians were only accepted in 1873. Times have changed since those days, and, if anything, King's is now one of the more progressive colleges, having been one of the first men's colleges to admit women in 1972. Among its most famous alumni are E.M. Forster, who described his experiences in *Maurice*, film director Derek Jarman, poet Rupert Brooke, and John Maynard Keynes, whose economic theories did much to improve the college's finances when he became the college bursar.

King's College Chapel

Committed to canvas by Turner and Canaletto, and eulogized in no fewer than three sonnets by Wordsworth, **King's College Chapel** (same times as college), is now best known for its **boys' choir**, whose members process across the college grounds during term time in their antiquated garb to sing evensong (Mon–Sat at 5.30pm, Sun 6.30pm) and carols on Christmas Eve. Begun in 1446 and over sixty years in the making, the chapel is an extraordinary building. From the outside, it seems impossibly slender, its streamlined buttresses channelling up to a dainty balustrade and four spiky turrets, but the exterior was, in a sense at least, a happy accident – its design predicated by the carefully composed interior. Here, in the final flowering of the Gothic style, the high and handsome **nave** boasts an exquisite ceiling, whose fan-tail tracery is a complex geometry of extraordinary complexity and delicacy. The nave is flooded with kaleidoscopic patterns of light that filter in through copious stained-glass windows. Paid for by Henry VIII, the **stained glass** was largely the work of Flemish glaziers, with the lower windows portraying scenes from the New Testament and the Apocrypha, and the upper windows the Old Testament. Henry VIII also paid for the dark and clumpy wooden **choir organ screen**, one of the earliest examples of Italian Renaissance woodcarving in England, but the heavy-duty choir stalls beyond date from the 1670s. Above the altar hangs Rubens' *Adoration of the Magi*, a perfect setting for this most tender of paintings, and finally an exhibition in the side **chantries** puts more historical flesh on Henry's grand plans.

Great St Mary's and the Senate House

King's College dominates **King's Parade**, the town's medieval High Street, but the higgledy-piggledy shops and cafés opposite are an attractive foil to William Wilkins's architectural screen. At the northern end of King's Parade is **Great St Mary's** (May–Aug Mon–Sat 9am–5pm, Sun 12.30–5pm; Sept–April Mon–Sat 9am–4pm, Sun 12.30–4pm), the university's pet church. It's a sturdy Gothic structure dating from the fifteenth century, whose **tower** (Mon–Sat 10am–4pm, Sun 12.30–4pm; £2.50) offers a good overall view of the surrounding colleges. Opposite the church stands **Senate House**, an exercise in Palladian classicism by James Gibbs, and the scene of graduation ceremonies on the last Saturday in June, when champagne corks fly among the rabbit-fur collars and black gowns. It's not usually open to the public, though you can wander around its precincts if the gate is open.

Gonville and Caius College

The northern continuation of King's Parade is Trinity Street, which is where you'll find the cramped main entrance to **Gonville and Caius College** (no set opening hours; free; ℡01223/332400, ⓦwww.cai.cam.ac.uk), known simply as Caius (pronounced "keys") after the sixteenth-century co-founder John Keys, who latinized his name as was then the custom with men of learning. The design of the college owes much to Keys, who placed three **gates** on two adjoining courts, each representing a different stage on the path to academic enlightenment: the Gate of Humility is at the main entrance; the Gate of Virtue, sporting the female figures of Fame and Wealth, fronts Caius Court; and the exquisite Gate of Honour, capped with sundials and decorated with classical motifs, leads onto Senate House Passage.

Clare College

Senate House Passage proceeds past Caius College's Gate of Honour on its way to both **Trinity Hall College** – not to be confused with Trinity College (see p.478) – and **Clare College** (daily 10.45am–4.30pm; free, but £2 in summer; ℡01223/333200, ⓦwww.clare.cam.ac.uk), whose alumni include David Attenborough and Siegfried Sassoon. Clare's plain period-piece courtyards, completed in the early eighteenth century, lead to one of the most picturesque of all the bridges over the Cam, **Clare Bridge**. Beyond lies the **Fellows' Garden**, one of the loveliest college gardens open to the public (times as college). Back at the entrance to Clare, it's a few steps more to the North Gate of King's College, beside King's College Chapel.

Trinity College

Trinity College, on Trinity Street (daily 9am–4pm; £1; ☎01223/338400, ⓦwww.trin.cam.ac.uk), is the largest of the Cambridge colleges and also has the largest courtyard. It comes as little surprise then that its list of famous alumni is probably longer than any of its rivals: literary greats, including Dryden, Byron, Tennyson, Thackeray and Vladimir Nabokov; the Cambridge spies Blunt, Burgess and Philby; prime ministers, including Balfour and Baldwin; Isaac Newton, Vaughan Williams, Jawaharlal Nehru, Bertrand Russell and Ludwig Wittgenstein, plus a trio of (much less talented) royals, Edward VII, George VI and Prince Charles.

A statue of Henry VIII, who founded the college in 1546, sits in majesty over Trinity's **Great Gate**, his sceptre replaced long ago with a chair leg by a student wit. Beyond lies the vast asymmetrical expanse of **Great Court**, which displays a fine range of Tudor buildings, the oldest of which is the fifteenth-century clocktower – the annual race against its midnight chimes is now common currency thanks to the film *Chariots of Fire*. The centrepiece of the court is a delicate fountain, in which, legend has it, Lord Byron used to bathe naked with his pet bear – the college forbade students from keeping dogs.

On the far side of the Great Court, walk through "the screens" – the narrow passage separating the dining hall from the kitchens – to reach **Nevile's Court**, where Newton first calculated the speed of sound. The west end of Nevile's Court is enclosed by one of the university's most famous buildings, the **Wren Library**, which was completed in 1695 (Mon–Fri noon–2pm, plus Sat during term time 10.30am–12.30pm; free). Viewed from the outside, it's impossible to appreciate the scale of the interior thanks to Wren's clever device of concealing the internal floor level by means of two rows of stone columns. Natural light pours into the white stuccoed interior, which contrasts wonderfully with the dark lime-wood bookcases, also Wren-designed and housing numerous valuable manuscripts including Milton's *Lycidas* and A.A. Milne's *Winnie the Pooh*.

St John's College and the Round Church

Next door to Trinity, **St John's College**, on St John's Street (daily: March–Oct 10am–5.30pm; Nov–Feb 10am–3.30pm; £3.20; ☎01223/338600, ⓦwww.joh .cam.ac.uk), sports a grandiloquent Tudor gatehouse, which is distinguished by the coat of arms of the founder, Lady Margaret Beaufort, the mother of Henry VII, held aloft by two spotted mythical beasts. Beyond, three successive courts lead to the river, but there's an excess of dull reddish brickwork here – enough for Wordsworth, a student here, to describe the place as "gloomy". The stone arcade on the far side of Third Court leads through to the **Bridge of Sighs**, a chunky, covered bridge built in 1831 but in most respects very unlike its Venetian namesake. The bridge is best viewed from the much older – and much more stylish – Wren-designed bridge a few yards to the south. The Bridge of Sighs links the old college with the fanciful nineteenth-century **New Court**, a crenellated neo-Gothic extravaganza topped by a feast of dinky stone chimneys and pinnacles.

Back on St John's Street, it's a few seconds' walk to the **Round Church** (Tues–Sat 10am–5pm, Sun 1–5pm; £2), built in the twelfth century on the model of the Holy Sepulchre in Jerusalem. It's a curious-looking structure, squat with an ill-considered late medieval extension to the rear, but the Norman pillars of the original church remain, overseen by sturdy arcading and a ring of finely carved faces.

Magdalene College

Not far from the Round Church is **Magdalene Bridge** and then **Magdalene College** (daily 10am–6pm; free; ☎01223/332100, ⓦwww.magd.cam.ac.uk) –

pronounced "maudlin" – which was founded as a hostel by the Benedictines, became a university college in 1542 and was the last of the colleges to admit women, finally succumbing in 1988. The main focus of attention here is the **Pepys Library** (mid-Jan to mid-March, Oct & Nov Mon–Sat 2.30–3.30pm; late April to Aug Mon–Sat 11.30am–12.30pm & 2.30–3.30pm; free), in the second of the college's ancient courtyards and looking like a country house. Samuel Pepys, a Magdalene student, bequeathed his entire library to the college, where it has been displayed ever since in its original red-oak bookshelves – though his famous **diary**, which also now resides in the library, was only discovered in the nineteenth century.

Jesus College

Back at the Round Church, take neighbouring Jesus Lane to get to **Jesus College** (daily 10am–5pm; free; ☏01223/339339, Ⓦwww.jesus.cam.ac.uk), whose intimate cloisters are reminiscent of a monastery – appropriately, as the Bishop of Ely founded the college on the grounds of a suppressed Benedictine nunnery in 1496. The main red-brick gateway is approached via a distinctive walled walkway strewn with bicycles and known as **"the Chimney"**. Beyond, much of the ground plan of the nunnery has been preserved, especially around **Cloister Court**, the first court on the right after the entrance and the prettiest part of the college. Entered from the Cloister Court, the college **chapel** occupies the former priory chancel and looks like a medieval parish church, though it was imaginatively restored in the nineteenth century, using ceiling designs by William Morris. The poet Samuel Taylor Coleridge was the college's most famously bad student, absconding in his first year to join the Light Dragoons, and returning only to be kicked out for a combination of bad debts and unconventional opinions.

To Sidney Sussex College

Near Jesus, Malcolm Street cuts off Jesus Lane to reach King Street and its continuation **Hobson Street**, named after the owner of a Cambridge livery stable, who would only allow customers to take the horse nearest the door – hence "Hobson's choice". Leading off Hobson Street is a pleasant shopping **arcade**, which occupies the Victorian red-bricks of tiny Sussex Street. The arcade leads through to **Sidney Sussex College** (no set opening times; free; ☏01223/338800, Ⓦwww.sid.cam .ac.uk), whose sombre, mostly mock-Gothic facade glowers over Sidney Street. The interior is fairly unexciting too, though the long, slender **chapel** to the right of the entrance is noteworthy for its fancy marble floor, hooped roof and Baroque wood panelling, as well as for being the last resting place of the skull of its most famous alumnus, **Oliver Cromwell**. Originally buried with much pomp and circumstance in Westminster Abbey, Cromwell's body was exhumed after the Restoration on the orders of Charles II, and then dragged through the streets of the capital, before being hung on a gibbet and decapitated. The head was then stuck on a post, where it remained for a couple of decades, before it was blown down in a storm. It then disappeared from historical view until, finally, a Suffolk family donated it to Sidney Sussex in 1960. The skull was subsequently buried somewhere in the chapel – in a secret location so as to avoid the attentions of latter-day admirers and detractors alike.

Christ's College

Strolling south from Sidney Sussex College, along Sidney Street, you soon reach the hustle and bustle of the town's central shopping area and the turreted gateway of **Christ's College** (daily 9.30am–4.30pm; free; ☏01223/334900, Ⓦwww .christs.cam.ac.uk), which features the coat of arms of the founder, Lady Margaret

Beaufort, who also founded St John's. Passing through First Court you come to the Fellows' Building, attributed to Inigo Jones, whose central arch gives access to the **Fellows' Garden**. The poet John Milton is said to have either painted or composed beneath the garden's elderly mulberry tree, though there's no definite proof that he did either. Another of Christ's famous undergraduates was Charles Darwin, who showed little academic promise and spent most of his time hunting.

The university museums

Near Christ's, Downing Street and its continuation Pembroke Street cut west to King's Parade and Trumpington Street. To either side is a rambling assortment of large, mostly Victorian buildings, some of which contain scientific and specialist museums. Each museum is connected to one of the university faculties and forms an important resource for students, but is also open to the public. First up, on the left, is the **Sedgwick Museum of Earth Sciences** (Mon–Fri 10am–1pm & 2–5pm, Sat 10am–4pm; free; Ⓦwww.sedgwickmuseum.org), which displays fossils and skeletons of dinosaurs, reptiles and mammals, plus one of the oldest geological collections in the world. In the same complex is the **Museum of Archaeology and Anthropology** (Tues–Sat 10.30am–4.30pm; free; Ⓦwww.maa.cam.ac.uk), where a wide-ranging assortment of archeological finds is supplemented by an ethnographical gallery, whose prime exhibits are derived from the "cabinets of curiosities" collected by eighteenth-century explorers.

A little further down Downing Street are the **Museum of Zoology** (Mon–Fri 10am–4.45pm, Sat 11am–4pm; free; Ⓦwww.museum.zoo.cam.ac.uk), some of whose exhibits were donated by Darwin, and, round the corner on Free School Lane, the **Whipple Museum of the History of Science** (Mon–Fri 12.30–4.30pm; free; Ⓦwww.hps.cam.ac.uk/whipple), crammed with hundreds of antique scientific instruments.

Queens' College

At the west end of Pembroke Street, turn right up King's Parade and then first left along Silver Street to get to **Queens' College** (mid-March to mid-May & late June to Sept daily 10am–4.30pm; Oct to mid-March daily 2–4pm; £2.50 in summer, otherwise free; Ⓣ01223/335511, Ⓦwww.queens.cam.ac.uk), which is accessed through the visitors' gate on Queens' Lane. This is one of the most popular colleges with university applicants, and it's not difficult to see why. In the **Old Court** and the **Cloister Court**, Queens' possesses two fairy-tale Tudor courtyards, with the first of the two the perfect illustration of the original collegiate ideal with kitchens, library, chapel, hall and rooms all set around a tiny green. Flanking Cloister Court is the Long Gallery of the **President's Lodge**, the last remaining half-timbered building in the university, and the tower where Erasmus is thought to have beavered away during his four years here, probably from 1510 to 1514. Be sure also to pay a visit to the ornately decorated college **Old Hall**, off the screens passage between the two courts, which holds mantel tiles by William Morris and a portrait of Erasmus. Equally eye-catching is the wooden **Mathematical Bridge** over the River Cam (viewable for free from the Silver Street Bridge), a copy of the mid-eighteenth-century original, which – so it was claimed – would stay in place even if the nuts and bolts were removed.

Pembroke College

Doubling back to Trumpington Street, **Pembroke College** (no set opening times; free; Ⓣ01223/338100, Ⓦwww.pem.cam.ac.uk) holds Wren's first ever commission, the **college chapel**, paid for by his Royalist uncle, the erstwhile

Bishop of Ely, in thanks for his deliverance from the Tower of London after seventeen years' imprisonment. It holds a particularly fine, though modern, stained-glass east window and a delicate fifteenth-century marble relief of St Michael and the Virgin, the product of an unusually skilled English workshop. Close by, outside the Victorian library, is a statue of a toga-clad William Pitt the Younger, who entered Pembroke at fifteen and was prime minister ten years later. Pitt is just one of a long list of notable college alumni, which includes poets Edmund Spenser, Thomas Gray and Ted Hughes.

The Fitzwilliam Museum

The **Fitzwilliam Museum**, on Trumpington Street (Tues–Sat 10am–5pm, Sun noon–5pm; free; Ⓦ www.fitzmuseum.cam.ac.uk), displays the city's premier fine and applied art collection in a grandiloquent Neoclassical edifice that was built to house the vast hoard bequeathed by Viscount Fitzwilliam in 1816. Since then, the museum has been gifted a string of private collections, most of which follow a particular specialism. The **Lower Galleries,** on the ground floor, contain a wealth of antiquities including Egyptian sarcophagi and mummies, fifth-century BC black- and red-figure Greek vases, plus a bewildering display of early European and Asian ceramics and separate sections dedicated to armour, glass and pewterware.

The **Upper Galleries** boast an eclectic assortment of mostly eighteenth-, nineteenth- and early twentieth-century European paintings and sculptures. There are two rooms of French paintings, with works by Picasso, Matisse, Monet, Renoir, Delacroix, Cézanne and Degas, and two rooms of Italian works by the likes of Fra Filippo Lippi and Simone Martini, Titian and Veronese. Two further rooms feature British paintings, with canvases by William Blake, Constable and Turner, Hogarth, Reynolds, Gainsborough and Stubbs, and one is devoted to Dutch art, displaying paintings by Frans Hals, Steen and Ruisdael. Among the more modern works, there are pieces by Lucian Freud, David Hockney, Henry Moore, Ben Nicholson, Jacob Epstein and Barbara Hepworth.

Scott Polar Research Museum and Botanic Gardens

Past the Fitzwilliam, turn left along busy Lensfield Road to get to the recently revamped **Scott Polar Research Museum** (Tues–Fri 11am–1pm & 2–4pm, Sat noon–4pm; free; Ⓦ www.spri.cam.ac.uk), founded in 1920 in memory of the explorer, Captain Robert Falcon Scott (1868–1912). The displays here illustrate the expeditions of various polar adventurers along with native cultures of the Arctic.

Also of interest on this side of town is the **University Botanic Gardens** (daily: Feb, March & Oct 10am–5pm; April–Sept 10am–6pm; Nov–Jan 10am–4pm; £4; Ⓦ www.botanic.cam.ac.uk), whose main entrance is at the junction of Trumpington Road and Bateman Street – about 500 yards to the south of Lensfield Road. Founded in the 1840s and covering forty acres, the gardens incorporate glasshouses as well as bountiful outdoor displays such as the Fen Garden, the Woodland Garden and two Rock Gardens – one sandstone, one limestone.

Eating and drinking

With most Cambridge students eating at their college dining hall, good-quality **restaurants** are a little thin on the ground; in contrast, the **takeaway** and **café** scene is on a roll. Quality does, however, vary enormously, so it is well worth choosing carefully, particularly in the more touristy areas. Cambridge abounds in excellent **pubs**, and our list rounds up some of the best.

Cafés and restaurants

Clowns 54 King St. Italian-style cappuccino and cakes, sandwiches and snacks, plus newspapers to browse. Off the tourist route and not part of a chain – bonuses in anyone's books. Daily 8am–late.

Eraina Cosmopolitan Taverna 2 Free School Lane ☎ 01223/368786. Packed taverna, which satisfies the hungry hordes with huge platefuls of stews and grills, as well as pizzas, curries and a whole host of other menu madness. Try to avoid getting stuck in the basement, though at weekends (when you'll probably have to queue) you'll be lucky to get a seat anywhere. Mains from £7.

Michaelhouse Café Trinity St. Good-quality café food – snacks, salads and so forth – in an attractively renovated medieval church. Great, central location too. Closed Sun.

Midsummer House Restaurant Midsummer Common ☎ 01223/369299. Lovely riverside restaurant with a conservatory, specializing in top-flight French-influenced cuisine – pig's head with spices and spinach for example. A two-course set meal will rush you no less than £55. Located on the south side of the river, beside the footbridge that lies just to the east of Victoria Avenue. Reservations essential. Closed Sun & Mon, plus Tues lunchtime.

Rainbow Vegetarian Bistro 9a King's Parade ☎ 01223/321551. Cramped but very agreeable vegetarian restaurant with main courses – ranging from couscous to lasagne and tagine – for around £9, and organic wines served with meals. Handy location, opposite King's College, and New-Age-meets-hippy decor. Closed Sun eve, plus all day Mon.

Trockel, Ulmann und Freunde 13 Pembroke St. Café food at its best in bright, creatively decorated premises. The baguettes have imaginative fillings – hummus and avocado, for example; the soups are hot and tasty; and the cakes are simply delicious. Tends to get jam-packed during term time. Closed Sun.

Pubs and bars

Champion of the Thames 68 King St. Gratifyingly old-fashioned central pub with decent beer and a student/academic clientele.

Eagle 8 Bene't St. An ancient inn with a cobbled courtyard where Crick and Watson sought inspiration in the 1950s, at the time of their discovery of DNA. It's been tarted up since and gets horribly crowded, but is still worth a pint of anyone's time.

Free Press 7 Prospect Row. Classic, superbly maintained backstreet local with real-ale brews and delicious bar food. To get there, proceed south down St Andrew's St, turn left along Park Terrace, which runs beside the grassy expanse of Parker's Piece; then, turn right onto Parkside, cross over the road and take Melbourne Place, a narrow, pedestrian alley that intersects with Prospect Row.

Live and Let Live 40 Mawson Rd. The focus is very much on the beer (and cider) at this cosy and welcoming pub, not far from the train station. Simply and traditionally furnished with old wood floors and well-bottomed chairs.

The Pickerel 30 Magdalene St. Once a brothel and one of several pubs competing for the title of the oldest pub in town, *The Pickerel* has a lively atmosphere and offers a good range of beers beneath its low beams.

Entertainment and nightlife

The performing arts scene is at its busiest and best during the university's term time, with numerous student **drama** productions, **classical concerts** and **gigs**, culminating in the traditional whizzerama of excess following the exam season. The most celebrated concerts are those given by **King's College choir** (see p.476), though the choral scholars who perform at the chapels of St John's College and Trinity are also exceptionally good.

June and July are the busiest times in Cambridge's calendar of **events**. The fortnight of post-exam celebrations, which take place in the first two weeks of June – and is known confusingly as **May Week** – herald the ball and garden-party season, and include boat races, known as the "May Bumps", on the River Cam by Midsummer Common. There are also free jazz and brass-band performances in the city's parks and, at the end of July, the four-day **Cambridge Folk Festival** (Ⓦ www.cambridgefolkfestival.co.uk), one of the longest-running folk festivals in the world, is held in neighbouring Cherry Hinton. **Nightclubs** are not the city's forte, but there is one very good place that's popular with Town if not Gown. For upcoming events, the tourist office (see p.474) issues various free **listings** leaflets and brochures.

Arts Picturehouse 38–39 St Andrew's St
☎ 0871/704 2050, ⓦ www.picturehouses.co.uk.
Art-house cinema with an excellent, wide-ranging
programme.
Cambridge Arts Theatre 6 St Edward's Passage,
off King's Parade ☎ 01223/503333, ⓦ www
.cambridgeartstheatre.com. The city's main
repertory theatre, founded by John Maynard
Keynes, and launch pad of a thousand-and-one
famous careers; offers a top-notch range of
cutting-edge and classic productions.

Cambridge Corn Exchange Wheeler St
☎ 01223/357851, ⓦ www.cornex.co.uk. Revamped
nineteenth-century trading hall, now the main city-
centre venue for opera, ballet, musicals and
comedy as well as regular rock and folk gigs.
The Junction Clifton Way ☎ 01223/511511,
ⓦ www.junction.co.uk. Rock, indie, jazz, reggae or
soul gigs, plus theatre, comedy and dance at this
popular arts and entertainments venue-cum-club.
To get there, take Hills Rd from the centre, and turn
left along Cherry Hinton Rd; Clifton Rd is the
second on the left.

Listings

Bike rental Mikes Bikes, 28 Mill Rd
(☎ 01223/312591), and H. Drake, near the train
station at 56–60 Hills Rd (☎ 01223/363468).
Bookshops Cambridge University Press has a shop
at 1 Trinity St. For secondhand books try the shops
down St Edward's Passage off King's Parade: G.
David, at no.16, is an antiquarian's and hardback

hunter's paradise; the Haunted Bookshop, at no. 9,
is better for children's and illustrated books.
Post office The main office is at 9–11
St Andrew's St.
Taxis There are ranks at the train and bus
stations. Alternatively, call Diamond Taxis
☎ 01223/523523.

Around Cambridge: Duxford Imperial War Museum

Just eight miles south of Cambridge, and clearly visible from the M11 (Junction #10), the giant hangars of the **Duxford Imperial War Museum** dominate the eponymous airfield (daily: mid-March to late Oct 10am–6pm; late Oct to mid-March 10am–4pm; £16.50; ☎ 01223/835000, ⓦ duxford.iwm.org.uk). Throughout World War II, East Anglia was a centre of operations for the RAF and the USAF, with the region's flat, unobstructed landscape dotted by dozens of airfields, among which Duxford was one of the more important. In total, the museum holds over 150 historic aircraft, a wide-ranging collection of civil and military planes from the Sunderland flying boat and the Vulcan B2 bombers, which were used for the first and last time in the 1982 Falklands conflict, to Concorde; the Spitfires, however, remain the most enduringly popular. Most of the planes are kept in full working order and are taken out for a spin at **Duxford Air Shows**, which attract thousands of visitors. There are usually half a dozen air shows a year and advance bookings are strongly recommended – call ahead or consult the museum website.

During museum opening hours, **Stagecoach bus #C7** leaves for Duxford from the bus stop on Emmanuel Street in Cambridge every half-hour, hourly on Sundays.

Travel details

Buses

For information on all local and national bus services, contact Traveline ☎ 0871/200 2233, ⓦ www.traveline .org.uk. For details of the Norfolk

Coasthopper bus, which runs between Cromer and King's Lynn, see p.458.
Cambridge to: Bury St Edmunds (hourly; 1hr); Colchester (7 daily; 3hr 30min); Ely (every 30min; 50min); London (hourly; 2hr); Peterborough (hourly; 2hr 20min); Stansted Airport (hourly; 50min).

Colchester to: Bury St Edmunds (hourly; 2hr); Cambridge (7 daily; 3hr 30min); Ipswich (hourly; 1–2hr); Sudbury (hourly; 50min).

Ely to: Cambridge (every 30min; 50min); King's Lynn (7 daily; 2hr); Peterborough (every 2hr; 2hr).

Ipswich to: Aldeburgh (hourly; 1hr 30min); Bury St Edmunds (every 2hr; 2hr); Colchester (hourly; 1–2hr); Orford (every 2hr; 1hr 20min).

King's Lynn to: Bury St Edmunds (3 daily; 2hr 15min); Ely (7 daily; 2hr); Norwich (hourly; 1hr 45min); Peterborough (hourly; 1hr 20min).

Norwich to: Bury St Edmunds (hourly; 2–3hr); King's Lynn (hourly; 1hr 45min).

Peterborough to: Cambridge (hourly; 2hr 20min); Ely (every 2hr; 2hr); King's Lynn (hourly; 1hr 20min).

Trains

For information on all local and national rail services, contact National Rail Enquiries ☎ 08457/484950, ⓦ www.nationalrail.co.uk.

Cambridge to: Bury St Edmunds (8 daily; 40min); Ely (hourly; 15min); Ipswich (6 daily; 1hr 20min); King's Lynn (hourly; 45min); London (every 30min; 1hr); Norwich (hourly; 1hr); Peterborough (hourly; 50min); Stansted Airport (10 daily; 40min).

Colchester to: Ipswich (2 hourly; 25min); London (2 hourly; 50min); Norwich (hourly; 1hr); Sudbury (hourly; 1hr).

Ely to: King's Lynn (hourly; 30min); London (hourly; 1hr); Peterborough (hourly; 30min).

Ipswich to: Bury St Edmunds (10 daily; 30min); Ely (7 daily; 1hr); London (every 30min; 1hr 10min); Norwich (hourly; 45min); Peterborough (7 daily; 1hr 50min).

Norwich to: Cromer (every 1–2hr; 50min); Ely (hourly; 50min); London (hourly; 2hr); Peterborough (hourly; 1hr 30min); Sheringham (every 1–2hr; 1hr).

Peterborough to: Bury St Edmunds (6 daily; 1hr); Cambridge (hourly; 50min); London (2 hourly; 1hr); Norwich (hourly; 1hr 30min).

8

The West Midlands
and the Peak District

CHAPTER 8

Highlights

* **The theatres, Stratford-upon-Avon** The best place in the world to see Shakespeare's plays, performed by the pre-eminent Royal Shakespeare Company. **See p.494**

* **Mappa Mundi, Hereford Cathedral** This antique map, dating to around 1000, provides a riveting insight into the medieval mind. **See p.504**

* **Hay-on-Wye** Deep in the countryside, this dinky little town has more secondhand bookshops than anywhere else on earth. **See p.508**

* **Ironbridge Gorge** The first iron bridge ever constructed arches high above the River Severn – poetry in iron. **See p.511**

* **Ludlow** A postcard-pretty country town with a herd of half-timbered houses and a sprawling castle, once a frontier fortress. **See p.519**

* **Gilbert & Sullivan Festival, Buxton** Limber up for a night of Victorian whimsy at Buxton's prime-time festival in the heart of the Peak District. **See p.538**

▲ *Julius Caesar* at Stratford-upon-Avon

8

The West Midlands and the Peak District

With justification, the small country towns and untrammelled scenery of the **West Midlands** are the apple of the tourist eye, but there's no disputing the urban epicentre of the region – **Birmingham**, Britain's second city, once the world's greatest industrial metropolis with a slew of factories that powered the Industrial Revolution. Long saddled with a reputation as a culture-hating, car-loving backwater, Birmingham has redefined its image in recent years, initiating some ambitious architectural and environmental schemes, jazzing up its museums and industrial heritage sites and giving itself a higher profile on the nation's cultural map than it's ever had before. To some extent change was forced on Birmingham by the decline in its manufacturing base – it lost over a third of its manufacturing jobs between 1974 and 1983 – but things were even worse in the **Black Country**, that knot of industrial towns clinging to the western side of the city, where de-industrialization proved particularly painful.

The counties to the south and west of Birmingham and beyond the Black Country – **Warwickshire**, **Worcestershire**, **Herefordshire** and **Shropshire** – comprise a rural stronghold that maintains an emotional and political distance from the conurbation. For the most part, the four counties constitute a quiet, unassuming stretch of pastoral England whose beauty is rarely dramatic, but whose charms become more evident the longer you stay. Of the four, **Warwickshire** is the least obviously scenic, but draws by far the largest number of visitors, for – as the road signs declare at every entry point – this is "Shakespeare Country". The prime target is, of course, **Stratford-upon-Avon**, with its handful of Shakespeare-related sites and world-class theatre, but spare time also for the diverting town of **Warwick**, which has a superb church and a whopping castle.

Neighbouring **Worcestershire**, which stretches southwest from the urban fringes of the West Midlands, holds two principal places of interest: **Worcester**, which is graced by a mighty cathedral; and **Great Malvern**, a mannered inland resort spread along the rolling contours of the **Malvern Hills** – prime walking territory. From here, it's west again for **Herefordshire**, a large and sparsely populated county that's home to the amenable market town of **Ledbury** and to **Hay-on-Wye**, which boasts the largest concentration of secondhand bookshops in the world. There's also **Hereford**, where the remarkable medieval Mappa

Regional transport

Birmingham, the region's public transport hub, has a major **airport** and is easily accessible by **train** from London Euston, Liverpool, Manchester, Leeds, York and a score of other towns. It is also well served by the National Express **bus** network, with dozens of buses leaving every hour for destinations all over Britain. **Local bus** services are excellent around the West Midlands conurbation and very good in the Peak District, but fade away badly in among the villages of Worcestershire, Herefordshire and Shropshire.

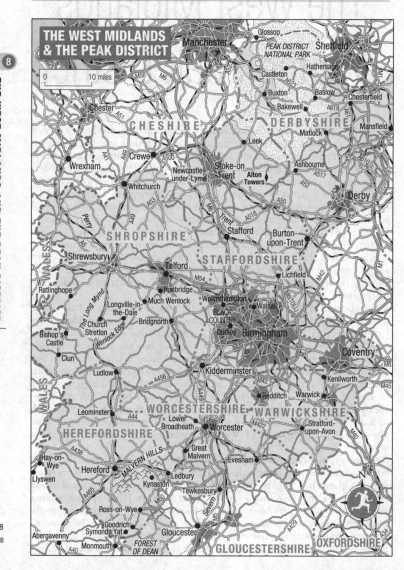

THE WEST MIDLANDS & THE PEAK DISTRICT

0   10 miles

Mundi map is displayed in the cathedral, and pocket-sized **Ross-on-Wye**, which is within easy striking distance of an especially scenic stretch of the **Wye River Valley**.

Next door, to the north, rural **Shropshire** weighs in with **Ludlow**, one of the region's prettiest towns, awash with antique half-timbered buildings, and the amiable county town of **Shrewsbury**, which is also close to the hiking trails of the **Long Mynd**. Shropshire has a fascinating industrial history, too, for it was here in the **Ironbridge Gorge** that British industrialists built the world's first iron bridge and pioneered the use of coal as a smelting fuel. These were two key events in the Industrial Revolution and, appropriately, the gorge's industrial heyday is recalled by a phalanx of museums.

To the east of Shropshire, sprawling north of the Birmingham conurbation, is **Staffordshire**, where **Lichfield** makes a good hand of its links with Samuel Johnson. Beyond lies **Derbyshire**, whose northern reaches incorporate the region's finest scenery in the rough landscapes of the **Peak District National Park**. The park's multitude of hiking trails attracts visitors by the thousand, its best base being the appealing former spa town of **Buxton**. The Peaks are also home to the limestone caverns of **Castleton**, the so-called "Plague Village" of **Eyam** and the grandiose stately pile of **Chatsworth House**, a real favourite hereabouts.

Stratford-upon-Avon

Despite its worldwide fame, **STRATFORD-UPON-AVON** is at heart an unassuming market town with an unexceptional pedigree. A charter for Stratford's weekly market was granted in the twelfth century and the town later became an important stopping-off point for stagecoaches between London, Oxford and the north. Like all such places, Stratford had its clearly defined class system. Within this typical milieu John and Mary **Shakespeare** occupied the middle rank, and would have been forgotten long ago had their first son, William, not turned out to be the greatest writer ever to use the English language. A consequence of their good fortune is that this ordinary little town is nowadays all but smothered by package-tourist hype and, in the summer at least, its central streets groan under the weight of thousands of tourists. Don't let that deter you: the **Royal Shakespeare Company** offers superb theatre, and dodging the multitudes is possible by avoiding the busiest attractions – principally the Birthplace Museum. Moreover, Stratford still has the ability to surprise and delight, whether in the excellence of some of its restaurants or by the gentle river views beside Holy Trinity Church.

Arrival and information

Stratford **train station** is on the northwest edge of town, a ten-minute walk from the centre. London Midland operates hourly services here from Birmingham (Moor Street and Snow Hill stations), and Chiltern Railways runs a direct train (every 2–3hr) from London Marylebone; Stratford is at the end of the line for both services. Local **buses** arrive and depart from the east end of Bridge Street; National Express services and most other long-distance buses pull into the **Riverside bus station** on the east side of the town centre, off Bridgeway.

Stratford's official **tourist office** is at 62 Henley St (℡01789/264293, ⓦwww.discover-stratford.com); at the time of writing opening hours (currently daily 10am–4pm) were due to be extended – phone for details.

Tickets for Stratford's key attractions

The **Shakespeare Birthplace Trust** (☎01789/204016, ⊛www.shakespeare.org.uk) owns five properties – three in the town centre (the Birthplace Museum, Nash's House and Hall's Croft) and two on the outskirts (Anne Hathaway's Cottage and Mary Arden's House). **Tickets** are not available for individual properties – instead you have to buy a ticket for all five (£19) or for the three in the centre (£12.50). Tickets are on sale at all five.

Accommodation

In peak months and during the Shakespeare birthday celebrations around April 23, it's pretty much essential to book accommodation well ahead. The town has a dozen or so **hotels**, the pick of which occupy old half-timbered buildings right in the centre, but most visitors choose to stay in a **B&B**, of which there's a particular concentration to the west of the centre around Grove Road, and Evesham Place.

Hotels

Best Western Grosvenor Warwick Rd ☎01789/269213, ⊛www.bwgh.co.uk. Close to the canal, just a couple of minutes' walk from the town centre, the *Grosvenor* occupies a row of pleasant, two-storey Georgian houses. The interior is crisp and modern and there's ample parking at the back. ❸

Falcon Chapel St ☎0844/411 9005, ⊛www .legacy-hotels.co.uk. Handily situated in the middle of town, this hotel has a half-timbered facade dating from the sixteenth century, though most of the rest is an unremarkable modern rebuild. Substantial discounts are commonplace. ❺

The Shakespeare Chapel St ☎01789/294997, ⊛www.mercure.com. Now part of a chain, this old hotel, with its mullioned windows and half-timbered facade, is one of Stratford's best known. The interior has low beams and open fires and represents a fairly successful amalgamation of the old and new. Right in the centre of town. ❹

Guesthouses and B&Bs

Adelphi Guest House 39 Grove Rd ☎01789/204469, ⊛www.adelphi-guest house.com. Extremely cosy B&B in a good-looking Victorian townhouse a short walk from the centre.

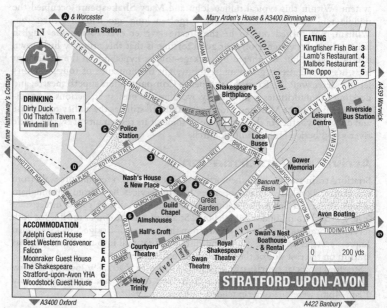

The owners have accumulated all sorts of interesting curios – from vintage theatrical posters and furniture to ornate chandeliers and lamps – and the five double guest rooms are all en suite. The best room, which comes complete with a four-poster, is in the attic and offers pleasant views. Top-ranking, home-cooked breakfasts too. ❷

Moonraker Guest House 40 Alcester Rd ☏01789/268774, ⓦwww.moonrakerhouse.com. This well-maintained place, in a large suburban house, has seven en-suite guest rooms, each decorated in smart modern-meets-period style (canopied beds, mini-chandeliers and so forth). Great breakfasts, too – either full English or vegetarian. Just beyond the train station, about 900 yards from the centre. ❸

Woodstock Guest House 30 Grove Rd ☏01789/299881, ⓦwww.woodstock-house.co.uk.

A smart and neatly kept B&B 5min walk from the centre, by the start of the path to Anne Hathaway's Cottage (see p.494). It has five extremely comfortable bedrooms, all en suite, decorated in frilly modern style. ❷

Hostel

Stratford-upon-Avon YHA Hemmingford House, Alveston, two miles east of the town centre on the B4086 ☏0845/371 9661, Ⓔstratford@yha.org.uk. This hostel occupies a rambling Georgian mansion on the edge of the pretty village of Alveston. There are dormitories, double and family rooms, some of which are en suite, plus laundry, cycle hire, internet access, car parking and self-catering facilities. Breakfasts and evening meals are on offer too. Served by local buses #18, #18A and #15 from Bridge St. Open all year. Dorm beds £16, doubles ❶

The Town

All of Stratford's leading attractions are dotted around the centre, a flat and compact slice of land spreading back from the River Avon. Top of the list are the extraordinarily popular **Shakespeare's Birthplace**, as well as **Nash's House** and **Hall's Croft**, all three of which are owned and operated by the Shakespeare Birthplace Trust (see box opposite). The other star turns are **Holy Trinity Church**, where Shakespeare lies buried, and the three theatres of the **Royal Shakespeare Company** (**RSC**). In addition, there are two outlying Shakespearean properties, **Anne Hathaway's Cottage** in Shottery and **Mary Arden's House** in Wilmcote – though you have to be a really serious sightseer to want to see them all.

Shakespeare's Birthplace

Top of everyone's bardic itinerary is **Shakespeare's Birthplace** on Henley Street (April–June, Sept & Oct daily 9am–5pm; July & Aug daily 9am–6pm; Nov–March Mon–Sat 10am–4pm, Sun 10.30am–4pm; £12.50 – see box opposite), which comprises an unappetizing modern visitor centre and the heavily restored half-timbered building where the great man was born. The **visitor centre** pokes into every corner of Shakespeare's life and times, making the most of what little hard evidence there is. His will is interesting in so far as he passed all sorts of goodies to his daughters and chums, but precious little to his wife – the museum commentary tries to gainsay this apparent meanness, but fails to convince.

Next door, the half-timbered **birthplace** dwelling is actually two buildings knocked into one. The northern, much smaller and later part was the house of Joan, Shakespeare's sister, and it adjoins the main family home, bought by John Shakespeare in 1556 and now returned to something like its original appearance. It includes a glover's workshop, where Shakespeare's father beavered away, though some argue that he was a wool merchant or a butcher. Neither is it certain that Shakespeare was born in this building nor that he was born on April 23, 1564 – it's just known that he was baptized on April 26, and it's an irresistible temptation to place the birth of the national poet three days earlier, on St George's Day. Despite these uncertainties, the house has been attracting visitors for centuries and upstairs one of the old mullioned windows, now displayed in a glass cabinet, bears the scratch-mark signatures of some of them, including those of Thomas Carlyle and Walter Scott.

Shakespeare: What's in a name?

Over the past hundred years or so, the deification of **William Shakespeare** (1564–1616) has been dogged by a loony backlash among a fringe of revisionist scholars and literary figures known as "**Anti-Stratfordians**". According to these heretics, the famous plays and sonnets were not written by a glover's son from Stratford at all, but by someone else, and William Shakespeare was merely a nom de plume. A variety of candidates has been proposed for the authorship of Shakespeare's works, ranging from the faintly plausible (Christopher Marlowe, Ben Jonson, and the earls of Rutland, Southampton and Oxford) to the manifestly whacko (Queen Elizabeth I, King James I and Daniel Defoe, author of *Robinson Crusoe*, who was born six years after publication of the First Folio). The wildest theories, however, have been reserved for **Francis Bacon**. In his book *The Great Cryptogram*, one-time American congressman Ignatius Donnelly postulated that the word "honorificabilitudinitatibus", which crops up in *Love's Labours Lost*, was actually an anagram for the Latin "Hi ludi F Baconis nati tuiti orbi" ("These plays, F. Bacon's offspring, are preserved for the world"). Others, like Sigmund Freud, have rallied around the Earl of Oxford's banner; Orson Welles agreed, saying that otherwise there were "… some awfully funny coincidences to explain away".

Lying at the root of the authorship debate are several **unresolved questions** that have puzzled scholars for years. How could a man of modest background from the provinces have such an intimate knowledge of royal protocol? How could he know so much about Italy without ever having travelled there? Why did he not leave a library in his will, when the author of the plays clearly possessed an intimate knowledge of classical literature? And why, given that Shakespeare was supposedly a well-known dramatist, did no death notice or obituary appear in publications of the day?

The speculation surrounding Shakespeare's work stems from the lack of definite information about his life. The few details that have been preserved come mostly from official archives – birth, marriage and death certificates and court records. From these we know that on April 22 or 23, 1564, a certain John Shakespeare, variously described as a glove-maker, butcher, wool merchant and corn trader,

Nash's House and New Place

Follow **High Street** south from the junction of Bridge and Henley streets, and you'll soon come to **Nash's House** on Chapel Street (April–June, Sept & Oct daily 10am–5pm; July & Aug daily 10am–6pm; Nov–March daily 11am–4pm; £12.50). Once the property of Thomas Nash, first husband of Shakespeare's granddaughter, Elizabeth Hall, the house's ground floor is kitted out with a pleasant assortment of period furnishings. Upstairs, one display provides a potted history of Stratford, including a scattering of archeological bits and pieces, and another focuses on the house itself with a cabinet of woodcarvings made from the **mulberry tree** that once stood outside. Reputedly planted by Shakespeare, the tree was chopped down in the 1750s by the owner, a certain Reverend Francis Gastrell, because he was fed up with all the pilgrims. An enterprising woodcarver bought the wood and carved Shakespearean mementoes from it – hence the carvings in the cabinet.

The adjacent gardens contain the foundations of **New Place** (same hours), Shakespeare's last residence, which was demolished by the same Reverend Gastrell, but for different reasons – Gastrell was in bitter dispute with the town council over taxation. The foundations have prompted all sorts of speculation, queries and questions that may be resolved by the **archeological dig** that is currently burrowing into the site.

and his wife, Mary, had their first son, William. We also know that the boy attended a local grammar school until financial problems forced him into his father's business, and that, at the age of 18, he married a local woman, **Anne Hathaway**, seven years his senior, who five months later bore a daughter, Susanna, the first of three children. Several years later, probably around 1587, the young Shakespeare was forced to flee Stratford after being caught poaching on the estate of Sir Thomas Lucy at nearby Charlecote. Five companies of players passed through the town on tour that year, and it is believed he absconded with one of them to London, where a theatre boom was in full swing. *Henry VI*, Shakespeare's first play, appeared soon after, followed by the hugely successful *Richard III*. Over the next decade, the playwright's output was prodigious. Thirty-eight plays appeared, most of them performed by his own theatre troupes based in the **Globe Theatre** on the south bank of the River Thames (see p.111), in which he had a one-tenth share.

Success secured Shakespeare the patronage of London's fashionable set, among them the dashing young courtier, Henry Wriothesley, 3rd Earl of Southampton, with whom the playwright may well have had a passionate affair (Southampton is thought to have been the "golden youth" of the Sonnets). The ageing Queen Elizabeth I regularly attended the Globe, as did her successor, James I, whose Scottish ancestry and fascination with the occult partly explain the subject matter of *Macbeth* – Shakespeare knew the commercial value of appealing to the rich and powerful. This, as much as his extraordinary talent, ensured his plays were the most acclaimed of the day, earning him enough money to retire comfortably to Stratford, where he largely abandoned literature in the last years of his life to concentrate on business and family affairs.

Ultimately, the sketchy details of Shakespeare's life are of far less importance than the plays, sonnets and songs he left behind. Whoever wrote them – and despite all the conjecture, William Shakespeare almost certainly did – the body of work attributed to this shadowy historical figure comprises some of the most inspired and exquisite English ever written.

The Great Garden and the Guild Chapel

Next door to Nash's House, along Chapel Lane, is the **Great Garden** (daily 9am–4pm; free), whose immaculate lawns and flowerbeds are flanked by some particularly fine topiary. On the other side of Chapel Lane stands the **Guild Chapel**, whose chunky tower and sturdy stonework shelter a plain interior enlivened by some rather crude stained-glass windows and a faded mural above the triumphal arch. The adjoining **King Edward VI Grammar School**, where it's assumed Shakespeare was educated, incorporates a creaky line of fifteenth-century **almshouses** running along Church Street.

Hall's Croft

From the almshouses, it's a brief stroll to Stratford's most impressive medieval house, **Hall's Croft** (daily: April–Oct 10am–5pm; Nov–March 11am–4pm; £12.50). The former home of Shakespeare's elder daughter, Susanna, and her doctor husband, John Hall, the immaculately maintained Croft, with its beamed ceilings and rickety rooms, holds a good-looking medley of period furniture and – mostly upstairs – a fascinating display on **Elizabethan medicine**. Hall established something of a reputation for his medical know-how and after his death some of his case notes were published in a volume entitled *Select Observations on English Bodies*. You can peruse extracts from Hall's book – noting that Joan Chidkin of Southam "gave two vomits and two stools" after being "troubled with trembling of the arms and thighs" – and then suffer vicariously at the displays of eye-watering forceps and other implements. The best view of the building itself is at the back, in the neat walled garden.

Holy Trinity Church
Near Hall's Croft, flanked by the yews and weeping willows of its graveyard, is **Holy Trinity Church** (March & Oct Mon–Sat 9am–5pm, Sun 12.30–5pm; April–Sept Mon–Sat 8.30am–6pm, Sun 12.30–5pm; Nov–Feb Mon–Sat 9am–4pm, Sun 12.30–5pm; free), whose mellow, honey-coloured stonework dates from the thirteenth century – though the recent application of a coat of preservative has made it very blotchy (locals are assured the effect will wear off soon-ish). Inside, the **nave** is flanked by a fine set of stained-glass windows, some of which are medieval, and bathed in light from the clerestory windows up above. Quite unusually, you'll see that the nave is built on a slight skew from the line of the chancel – supposedly to represent Christ's inclined head on the cross. In the north aisle, beside the transept, is the **Clopton Chapel**, where the large wall-tomb of George Carew is a Renaissance extravagance decorated with military insignia appropriate to George's job as master of ordnance to James I. But poor old George is long forgotten, unlike William Shakespeare, who lies buried in the **chancel** (£1.50), his remains overseen by a sedate and studious memorial plaque and effigy added just seven years after his death.

To the theatres
Doubling back from the church, turn right into the **park** just before you reach Southern Lane and you can stroll along – or at least near – the river bank, past the RSC's **Courtyard Theatre** and the dinky little **chain ferry** (50p) across the Avon, to reach the Royal Shakespeare Company's two main **theatres**, the Swan and the Royal Shakespeare. There was no theatre in Stratford in Shakespeare's day and indeed the first home-town festival in his honour was only held in 1769 at the behest of London-based David Garrick. Thereafter, the idea of building a permanent home in which to perform Shakespeare's works slowly gained momentum, and finally, in 1879, the first Memorial Theatre was opened on land donated by local beer baron Charles Flower. A fire in 1926 necessitated the construction of a new theatre, and the ensuing architectural competition produced the **Royal Shakespeare Theatre**, a cinema-like, red-brick edifice that has recently been remodelled and extended in fine style. Attached to it is the revamped **Swan Theatre**, a replica "in-the-round" Elizabethan stage.

The Gower Memorial and Bancroft Basin
In front of the Royal Shakespeare Theatre, the manicured lawns of a small riverside park stretch north as far as **Bancroft Basin**, where the Stratford Canal meets the river. The basin is usually packed with narrowboats and in the small park on the far side, over either of two pedestrian bridges, is the finely sculpted **Gower Memorial** of 1888 in which a seated Shakespeare is surrounded by characters from his plays. To round things off, stroll over the Clopton Bridge to **Avon Boating** (April–Oct 9am–dusk; ☎01789/267073, ⓦwww.avon-boating.co.uk), where you can rent out rowing boats, punts and canoes for £4 an hour; they also offer thirty-minute river trips (£4.50).

Anne Hathaway's Cottage
Anne Hathaway's Cottage (daily: April–Oct 9am–5pm; Nov–March 10am–4pm; £7.50) is located just over a mile west of the centre in the well-heeled

suburb of **Shottery**. The cottage – actually an old farmhouse – is an immaculately maintained, half-timbered affair with a thatched roof and dinky little chimneys. This was the home of Anne Hathaway before she married Shakespeare in 1582, and the interior holds a comely combination of period furniture, including a superb, finely carved four-poster bed. The garden is splendid too, crowded with bursting blooms in the summertime. The adjacent orchard and **Shakespeare Tree Garden** features a scattering of modern sculptures and over forty types of tree, shrub and rose mentioned in the plays, with each bearing the appropriate quotation inscribed on a plaque. The most agreeable way to get to the cottage from the town centre is on the signposted **footpath** from Evesham Place, at the south end of Rother Street.

Mary Arden's House

The Birthplace Trust also owns **Mary Arden's House** (March–Oct daily 10am–5pm; £8.50), three miles northwest of the town centre in the village of **Wilmcote**. Mary was Shakespeare's mother and the only unmarried daughter of her father, Robert, at the time of his death in 1556. Unusually for the period, Mary inherited the house and land, thus becoming one of the neighbourhood's most eligible women – John Shakespeare, eager for self-improvement, married her within a year. The house is a well-furnished example of an Elizabethan farmhouse and, though the labelling is rather scant, a platoon of guides fills in the details of family life and traditions.

Eating and drinking

Stratford is accustomed to feeding and watering thousands of visitors, so finding refreshment is never difficult. Standards may vary enormously, but there is a scattering of very good **restaurants**, several of which have been catering to theatre-goers for many years, and a handful of **pubs** and **cafés** offering good food, too.

Restaurants and cafés

Kingfisher Fish Bar 13 Ely St. The best fish-and-chip shop in town. Takeaway and sit-down. A 5min walk from the theatres. Closed Sun.

Lamb's Restaurant 12 Sheep St ☎01789/292554. Smart and immensely appealing restaurant serving a mouthwatering range of stylish English and Continental dishes in antique premises – beamed ceilings and so forth. Daily specials at around £9, other main courses £14–16. Closed Mon lunchtime.

Malbec Restaurant 6 Union St ☎01789/269106. Intimate bistro-style restaurant serving top-quality seafood and meat dishes, often with a Mediterranean slant. The emphasis is on local, seasonal ingredients. Mains around £15. Closed Sun & Mon.

The Oppo 13 Sheep St ℡01789/269980. International cuisine in pleasant old premises with a busy but amiable atmosphere. The dishes of the day, chalked up on a board inside, are good value at around £8; otherwise mains average £13.

Pubs

Dirty Duck 53 Waterside. The archetypal actors' pub, stuffed to the gunwales every night with a vocal entourage of RSC employees and hangers-on. Traditional beers in somewhat spartan premises plus a terrace for hot-weather drinking.
Old Thatch Tavern Market Place. Ancient pub with a convivial atmosphere and a good range of beers that attracts a mixed crew of tourists and locals.
Windmill Inn Church St. Popular pub with rabbit-warren rooms and low-beamed ceilings. Flowers beer, too.

Warwick

Pocket-sized **WARWICK**, just eight miles northeast of Stratford and easily reached by bus and train, is famous for its massive **castle**, but it also possesses several charming streetscapes erected in the aftermath of a great fire in 1694, not to mention an especially fine church chancel. An hour or two is quite enough time to nose around the town centre, though you'll need the whole day if, braving the crowds and the medieval musicians, you're also set on exploring the castle and its extensive grounds: either way, Warwick is the perfect day-trip from Stratford.

Arrival, information and accommodation

From Warwick **train station**, on the northern edge of town, it's about ten minutes' walk to the centre. More conveniently, **buses** stop on Market Street, close to the Market Place, from where it's a five-minute walk east to the **tourist office**, in the old Court House at the corner of Castle and Jury streets (Mon–Fri 9.30am–4.30pm, Sat 10am–4.30pm, Sun 10am–3.30pm; ℡01926/492212, ⓦwww.warwick-uk.co.uk). They have a list of local **hotels and B&Bs**, but with Stratford so near and easy to reach, there's no special reason to stay. That said, *The Rose and Crown*, 30 Market Place (℡01926/411117, ⓦwww.roseandcrown warwick.co.uk ; ❸), has five attractive guest rooms, all en suite and each decorated in a bright and breezy contemporary style.

The castle

Towering above the River Avon at the foot of the town centre, **Warwick Castle** (daily: April–Sept 10am–6pm; Oct–March 10am–5pm; £20; parking £4; ⓦwww.warwick-castle.co.uk) is often proclaimed the "greatest medieval castle in Britain". This claim is valid enough if bulk equals greatness, but actually much of the existing structure is the result of extensive nineteenth-century tinkering. It's likely that the Saxons raised the first fortress on this site, though things really took off with the Normans, who built a large motte and bailey here towards the end of the eleventh century. Almost three hundred years later, the eleventh Earl of Warwick turned the stronghold into a formidable stone castle, complete with elaborate gatehouses, multiple turrets and a keep.

The **entrance** to the castle is through the old stable block at the foot of Castle Street. Beyond, a footpath leads round to the imposing moated and mounded **East Gate**. Over the footbridge – and beyond the protective towers – is the main **courtyard**. You can stroll along the ramparts and climb the towers, but most visitors head straight for one or other of the special, very touristy displays installed inside the castle's many chambers and towers. The **grounds** are perhaps much more enjoyable, acres of woodland and lawn inhabited by peacocks and including

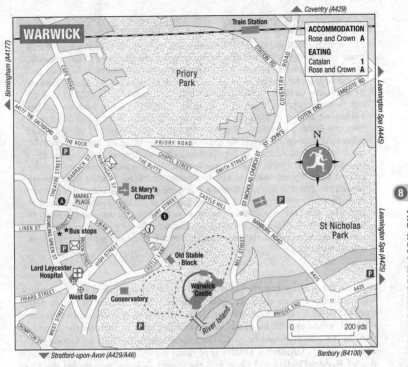

a large glass **conservatory**. A footbridge leads over the River Avon to **River Island**, the site of jousting tournaments and other such medieval hoopla.

The town centre

Re-emerging from the castle by the stables, **Castle Street** leads up the slope for a few yards to its junction with the High Street. Turn left and it's a brief stroll to another remarkable building, the **Lord Leycester Hospital** (daily except Mon: April–Oct 10am–5pm; Nov–March 10am–4.30pm; £4.90), a tangle of half-timbered buildings that lean at fairy-tale angles against the old West Gate. The complex represents one of Britain's best-preserved examples of domestic Elizabethan architecture. It was established as a hostel for old soldiers by Robert Dudley, Earl of Leicester – a favourite of Queen Elizabeth I – and incorporates several beamed buildings, principally the Great Hall and the Guildhall, as well as a wonderful galleried courtyard and an intimate chantry chapel. There's a **tearoom** too, plus a modest regimental museum – appropriately enough, as retired servicemen (and their wives) still live here.

St Mary's Church

Also near Castle Street is **St Mary's Church** (daily: April–Oct 10am–6pm; Nov–March 10am–4.30pm; £2 donation suggested), which was rebuilt in a weird Gothic-Renaissance amalgam after the fire of 1694. Most of the chancel, however, remained untouched, and it's simply glorious illustration of the Perpendicular style with a splendid vaulted ceiling of flying and fronded ribs. On the right-hand side of the chancel is the **Beauchamp Chantry Chapel**, which

Coventry Cathedral

At the outbreak of World War II, **Coventry**, eleven miles north of Warwick, was a major engineering centre and its factories attracted the attentions of the Luftwaffe, who well-nigh levelled the town in a huge bombing raid on November 14, 1940. Out of the ashes arose what is now Coventry's one sight of note, Basil Spence's **St Michael's Cathedral** (Mon–Sat 9am–5pm, Sun noon–3.45pm; £4.50, free on Sun; ⓦwww.coventrycathedral.org.uk), raised alongside the burnt-out shell of the old cathedral right in the centre of town and dedicated with a performance of Benjamin Britten's specially written *War Requiem* in 1962. One of the country's most successful postwar buildings, the cathedral's pink sandstone is light and graceful, the main entrance adorned by a stunningly forceful *St Michael Defeating the Devil* by Jacob Epstein. Inside, Spence's high and slender nave is bathed in light from the soaring stained-glass windows, a perfect setting for the magnificent and immense **tapestry** of *Christ in Glory* by **Graham Sutherland**. The choice of artist could not have been more appropriate. A painter, graphic artist and designer, Sutherland (1903–80) had been one of Britain's official war artists, his particular job being to record the effects of German bombing. A canopied walkway links the new cathedral with the old, whose shattered nave flanks the church tower and spire that somehow eluded the bombs.

contains the equally beautiful tomb of Richard Beauchamp, Earl of Warwick, who is depicted in an elaborate, gilded-bronze suit of armour of Italian design from the tip of his swan helmet down to his mailed feet. A griffin and a bear guard Richard, who lies with his hands half joined in prayer so that, on the Resurrection, his first sight would be of Christ triumphant at the Second Coming. The adjacent tomb of Ambrose Dudley is of finely carved and painted alabaster, as is that of Robert Dudley and his wife – the same Dudley who founded the **Lord Leycester Hospital**.

Eating and drinking

For a bite to eat, try the busy informality of the *Rose and Crown* (see p.496), where they serve good-quality bar food throughout the day, washed down by a prime selection of guest beers; mains cost anywhere between £10 and £16. Alternatively, the *Catalan*, 6 Jury St (☎01926/498930; closed Sun), is a slick, modern café-restaurant, which offers tasty tapas and light lunches during the day, and Mediterranean-inspired food at night, with mains from £13.

Worcester and around

In geographical terms, **Worcestershire** can be compared to a huge saucer, with the low-lying plains of the Severn Valley and the Vale of Evesham, Britain's foremost fruit-growing area, rising to a lip of hills, principally the Malverns in the west and the Cotswolds to the south. In character, the county divides into two broad belts. To the north lie the industrial and overspill towns – Droitwich and Redditch for instance – that have much in common with the Birmingham conurbation, while the south is predominantly rural as famously portrayed in *The Archers*, the BBC's long-running radio soap, which attracts a massive and extraordinarily dedicated audience.

Bang at the geographical heart of the county is **WORCESTER**, an amenable county town where a liberal helping of half-timbered Tudor and handsome

Georgian buildings stands cheek by jowl with some fairly charmless modern developments. Postwar clumsiness apart, the biggest single influence on the city has always been the **River Severn**, which flows along Worcester's west flank. It was the river that made the city an important settlement as early as Saxon times, though the river's propensity to breach its banks, inundating parts of the city in murky water, has prompted the construction of a battery of defences which tumble down the slope from the mighty bulk of the **cathedral**, easily Worcester's star turn.

Arrival, information and accommodation

Worcester has two **train stations**. The handiest for the city centre is **Foregate Street**, from where it's about half a mile south to the cathedral along Foregate Street and its continuation The Cross and then High Street. The other train station, **Shrub Hill**, is located further out, about a mile to the northeast of the cathedral. The **bus station** is at the back of the sprawling Crowngate shopping mall on The Butts, about six hundred yards northwest of the cathedral. The **tourist office** (Mon–Sat 9.30am–5pm; ℡01905/726311, ⓌÑwww.visitworcester .com) is in the Guildhall towards the cathedral end of the High Street.

There's no overriding reason to overnight in Worcester, but there are a couple of appealing **places to stay**, beginning with the *Diglis House Hotel*, a family-owned place in an attractive Georgian villa beside the river, about five minutes' walk south of the cathedral at the end of Severn Street (℡01905/353518, ⓌÑwww.diglishouse hotel.co.uk; ❸). Most of the 28 guest rooms here have recently been revamped in a pleasant version of country-house style, but the hotel's prime feature is the large conservatory overlooking the river. The pick of the town's **B&Bs** is *Barrington House*, in an immaculately restored Georgian property right by the river at 204 Henwick Rd (℡01905/422965, ⓌÑwww.barringtonhouse.eu; ❸), about a mile north of the centre along the A443 – and across the river from Worcester Racecourse. It comes complete with a large garden, has three en-suite guest rooms decorated in a broadly period style and the owners dish up tasty breakfasts.

The City

Worcester's centre is small and compact, and all the key sights plus the best restaurants are clustered within the immediate vicinity of the main landmark, the cathedral.

The cathedral

Towering above the River Severn, the soaring sandstone of **Worcester Cathedral** (daily 8am–6pm; free; ⓌÑwww.worcestercathedral.co.uk) comprises a rich stew of architectural styles dating from 1084. The bulk of the church is firmly medieval, from the Norman transepts through to the late Gothic cloister, though the Victorians did have a good old hack at the exterior. Inside, the pillars of the cavernous **nave** are decorated with bunches of fruit, initially carved by stonemasons from Lincoln, most of whom succumbed to the Black Death, leaving inferior successors to finish the job. Moving on, the **choir**, built between 1220 and 1260, is a beautiful illustration of the Early English style, with a forest of slender pillars rising above the intricately worked choir stalls. Here also, in front of the high altar, is the **table-tomb** of England's most reviled monarch, **King John** (1167–1216), who certainly would not have appreciated the lion that lies at his feet biting the end of his sword – a reference to the curbing of his power by the barons when they obliged him to sign the Magna Carta. Just beyond the tomb – on the right – is **Prince Arthur's Chantry**, a delicate lacy confection of carved stonework built in 1504 to commemorate Arthur, King Henry VII's son, who died at the age of 15 in Ludlow. He was on his honeymoon with Catherine of Aragon, who was soon passed on – with such momentous consequences – to his younger brother, Henry.

A stairway beside the chantry leads down to the **crypt**, the oldest part of the cathedral and the largest Norman crypt in the country. In addition, a doorway on the south side of the nave leads to the **cloisters**, with their delightful roof bosses, and the circular, largely Norman **chapter house**, which has the distinction of being the first such building constructed with the use of a central supporting pillar.

The Worcester Porcelain Museum

There was a time when Severn Street, tucked away just to the south of the cathedral, hummed with the activity of one of England's largest porcelain factories, **Royal Worcester**, but the company hit the skids and was finally rolled up in 2008 after over one hundred and fifty years in production. The old factory complex is currently being turned into apartments, but the **Worcester Porcelain Museum** (Easter–Oct Mon–Sat 10am–5pm; Nov–Easter Tues–Sat 10.30am–4pm; £6; Ⓦwww.worcesterporcelainmuseum.org) has survived, exhibiting a comprehensive collection of the ornate, indeed fancifully ornate, porcelain for which Royal Worcester was famous.

The Commandery

From the Porcelain Museum, double back along Severn Street and turn right along King Street to get to **The Commandery** (Mon–Sat 10am–5pm, Sun 1.30–5pm, Nov to Easter closed Fri; £5.40), just a few minutes' walk away on the far side of the busy Sidbury dual carriageway. This is the town's main history museum, its varied displays occupying Worcester's oldest building, a rambling, half-timbered structure dating from the early sixteenth century. Its moment of fame came when **King Charles II** used the building as his headquarters during the battle-cum-siege of Worcester in 1651, the end game of his unsuccessful attempt to regain the throne from Cromwell and the Parliamentarians, who had executed his father – King Charles I – in 1649. Much to Cromwell's chagrin, however, Charles managed to escape Parliament's clutches and reach safety in France by fleeing in disguise – no mean feat considering the would-be king was six feet and two inches tall, about ten inches above the average. Recently refurbished, the highlight of The Commandery is the **painted chamber**, whose walls are covered with intriguing cameos recalling the building's original use as a monastery hospital. Each of the cameos relates to a saint with healing powers – for example St Thomas à Becket is shown being stabbed in the head by a group of knights, enough to make him the saint for headaches.

Friar Street and Greyfriars

From the Commandery, it's a short step northwest along Sidbury to narrow **Friar Street**, whose hotchpotch of half-timbered houses and small, independent shops make it Worcester's prettiest thoroughfare. Here also is **Greyfriars** (March to mid–Dec Wed–Sun 1–5pm; £4.15; NT), a largely fifteenth-century townhouse, whose wonky timbers and dark-stained panelling shelter a charming collection of antiques. There's an attractive walled garden here too.

From Greyfriars, it's a couple of minutes walk west to the High Street, a couple more to the cathedral.

Eating and drinking

The best **restaurant** in town is *Brown's*, a smart, modern place in a handsomely converted old grain mill down by the river just west of the High Street at 24 Quay St (Ⓣ01905/26263; closed Sun eve). The menu here is Modern British, featuring the likes of lamb with pea and mint risotto, and main courses cost around £20 at night, much less at lunch times, when they also do sandwiches. A second good bet is *The Glasshouse*, a more informal brasserie-style affair housed in a glass-and-steel block in between the cathedral and The Commandery at 55 Sidbury (℡01905/611120; closed Sun). They probably try to cover too many gastronomic bases here, but the deluxe fish and chips, for one, are very, very good. As for **drinking**, *Brown's* has a slick cocktail bar and *The Glasshouse* doubles up as a lounge bar.

West of Worcester: Lower Broadheath

One of Worcestershire's most famous sons was **Sir Edward Elgar** (1857–1934), the first internationally acclaimed English composer for almost two hundred years. Elgar built his reputation on a series of lyrical works celebrating his abiding love of the Worcestershire countryside, quintessentially English pieces among which the most famous is the *Enigma Variations*. Elgar was born in **LOWER BROAD-HEATH**, a workaday hamlet just three miles west of Worcester on the B4204, and it's here you'll find the **Elgar Birthplace Museum** (daily 11am–5pm, last admission 4.15pm; £7; ℗www.elgarfoundation.org). This comprises a modern **visitor centre**, exploring Elgar's life and times with the assistance of some fascinating old photographs, and – just behind at the end of the path – the substantial brick **cottage** where he was born. Inside the cottage, the cramped rooms contain several of Elgar's musical scores, personal correspondence in his spidery handwriting, more photographs, and miscellaneous mementoes. The museum also organizes an imaginative programme of special events from illustrated talks to Elgar concerts and recitals. Lower Broadheath is not, however, of any scenic interest and if you want to see the green, quilted landscapes beloved of Elgar you'll have to push on to The Malverns.

The Malvern Hills and Great Malvern

One of the more prosperous parts of the West Midlands, **The Malverns** is the generic name for a string of towns and villages stretched along the eastern lower slopes of the **Malvern Hills**, which rise spectacularly out of the flatlands a few miles to the southwest of Worcester. About nine miles from north to south – between the A44 and the M50 – and never more than five miles wide, the hills straddle the Worcestershire–Herefordshire boundary. Of ancient granite rock, they are punctuated by over twenty summits, mostly around 1000 feet high, and in between lie innumerable dips and hollows. It's easy if energetic walking country, with great views, and there's an excellent network of **hiking trails**, most of which can be completed in a day or half-day with **Great Malvern** the obvious base, though Ledbury (see p.506), over in Herefordshire, is a possible base too.

Great Malvern

Among towns in the Malverns, it's **GREAT MALVERN** that grabs the attention, its pocket-sized centre clambering up the hillside with the crags of North Hill beckoning beyond. The town's grand but often rather faded old houses, which congregate on and around the top of the main drag, **Church Street**, mostly date from Great Malvern's nineteenth-century heyday as a spa town when the local **spring waters** drew the Victorians here by the trainload. As a first instalment, visitors were wrapped up in cold wet sheets for hours before being plunged and

8

Hiking the Malverns

Great Malvern tourist office (see below) sells hiking maps and issues half a dozen free **Trail Guide leaflets**, which describe circular routes up to and along the hills that rise behind the town. The shortest trail is just one and a half miles, the longest four. One of the most appealing is the 2.5-mile hoof up to the top – and back – of **North Hill** (1307ft), from where there are panoramic views over the surrounding countryside; this hike takes in *St Ann's Well Café* (see box below). Alternatively, the one-way hike along the top of the Malvern ridge is a sterner test that takes all day and is ten miles long. On the way, you'll pass through the vague remains of a brace of Iron Age hillforts. It's best to start at the southern end – at **Chase End Hill** – and work your way north.

dipped, all with varying degrees of success: Alfred Lord Tennyson, for one, took the full treatment, recording that he was "Half cured, half destroyed by it" – a common sentiment. You can still sample the waters today (see box below), but the town's principal sight is its splendid **priory**.

Arrival, information and accommodation

From Great Malvern's infinitely rustic **train station**, with its dainty ironwork and quaint chimneys, it's about half a mile to the town centre – take Avenue Road, which leads to **Church Street**, the steeply sloping main drag. The well-equipped **tourist office** is right in the centre at the top of Church Street (daily 10am–5pm; ℡01684/892289, ⊛www.visitthemalverns.org).

The most conspicuous **hotel** is *The Abbey* (℡01684/892332, ⊛www.sarova .com; ❸), the main part of which occupies a rambling, creeper-clad Victorian building executed in a sort of neo-baronial style and sitting pretty a few yards from the tourist office. It's part of a small chain and the guest rooms lack character, especially in the hotel's lumpy modern wing, though they are comfortable enough and some have attractive views back down over town. One recommendable **B&B** is *The Copper Beech House*, in a large Victorian family home near the train station at 32 Avenue Rd (℡01684/565013, ⊛www.copperbeechhouse.co.uk; ❷), with seven en-suite guest rooms, ranging from the large and plush to the small and really rather plain. Further afield, the cream of the hotel crop is *Colwall Park* (℡01684/540000, ⊛www.colwall.co.uk; ❺), an independently operated, country-house hotel with Edwardian half-timbered gables a few miles southwest of Great Malvern along the B4218. There are 22 extremely comfortable, modern bedrooms with thick carpets and heavy drapes.

The Town

The Benedictines built one of their abbeys at Great Malvern and, although Henry VIII closed the place down in 1538, the **Priory Church**, close to the top

Taking the waters

The gushing **Malvhina spring** in the mini-park at the top of Church Street is the obvious and certainly the most convenient way to taste Great Malvern's waters. There's also a spring at *St Ann's Well Café*, a sweet little café in an attractive Georgian building a steep 25-minute walk up the wooded hillside from town (normally Easter–Sept Tues–Sun 10am–4pm, plus Mon in July & Aug; call ℡01684/560285 or check ⊛www.stannswell.co.uk for winter opening hours); the signposted path begins beside the *Mount Pleasant Hotel*, on Belle Vue Terrace, just to the left (south) of the top of Church Street.

of Church Street (daily: 9am–5pm; free), has survived, the elaborate decoration of its exterior witnessing the priory's former wealth. Inside, the sternly Norman nave sweeps down to the chancel, which came later, a fine example of Perpendicular Gothic, its sinuous tracery serving to frame a simply fabulous set of **stained-glass windows** dating from the end of the fifteenth century. Among them, pride of place goes to the great east window, a giant flash of colour with several easily decipherable Biblical scenes, such as Palm Sunday and the Crucifixion. The north transept window is also of special interest as it holds a rare **Coronation of Mary** set against a blue-sky background, one of the few coronation windows to survive the attentions of the Protestants during the Reformation.

Behind the church is the delicately proportioned **Priory Gatehouse**, which now holds the tiny **Malvern Museum** of local history (Easter–Oct daily except Wed 10.30am–5pm; £2). The most interesting room looks at Great Malvern's days as a spa town with a small selection of old promotional cartoons showing patients packed into soaked sheets before, their ailments cured, they hop gaily away from their crutches.

Eating and drinking

With most visitors apparently eating where they sleep, the café and restaurant scene in Great Malvern is not as varied as you might expect. One good daytime choice is *Great Malvern Deli* (closed Sun), a combined shop and **café** a few paces from the top of Church Street, where they serve delicious home-made cakes. Otherwise, try *Pepper & Oz* (T01684/562676), a lively, informal place just along the street, which does a tasty line in Italian dishes with mains averaging about £11. The best **pub** in town is *The Morgan*, near the train station at 52 Clarence Rd, where you can sample the brews of Herefordshire's own Wye Valley Brewery.

Herefordshire

Over the Malvern Hills from Worcestershire, the rolling agricultural landscapes of **Herefordshire** have an easy-going charm, but the finest scenery hereabouts is along the banks of the **River Wye**, which wriggles and worms its way across the county linking most of the places of interest. Plonked in the middle of the county on the Wye is **Hereford**, a sleepy, rather old-fashioned sort of place whose proudest possession is a remarkable medieval map, the cathedral's **Mappa Mundi**. Hereford is also close to the pleasant little town of **Ledbury**, sitting near the edge of the Malvern Hills and distinguished by its Tudor and Stuart half-timbered buildings. Moving on, the southeast corner of the county has one attractive town, **Ross-on-Wye**, a genial little place with a picturesque river setting. Ross also serves as a convenient gateway to one of the wilder portions of the **Wye River Valley**, around **Symonds Yat**, where canoeists gather in their droves. To the west of Hereford, hard by the Welsh border, the key attraction is **Hay-on-Wye**, which – thanks to the purposeful industry of Richard Booth (see box, p.509) – has become both the world's largest repository of secondhand books and the host of a premium literary festival.

Herefordshire possesses one **rail line**, linking Ledbury and Hereford with points north to Shrewsbury and east to Great Malvern and Worcester. Otherwise, you'll be restricted to the tender mercies of the county's **buses**, which provide a reasonable service between the villages and towns, except on Sundays when there's very little. All the local tourist offices have bus timetables and there's local **bus information** on T0870/608 2608 and Wwww.herefordshire-buses.tbctimes.co.uk.

Hereford

A low-key country town with a spacious feel, **HEREFORD** was long a border garrison town held against the Welsh, its military importance guaranteed by its strategic position near the River Wye. It also became a religious centre after the Welsh murdered the Saxon king **Ethelbert** near here in 794. These were bloody times, so in itself the murder was pretty routine, but legend asserts that Ethelbert's ghost kept on turning up to insist his remains be interred here in Hereford – and eventually it got its way. Ethelbert's posthumous antics made him a military martyr and a Saxon cult soon grew up around his name, prompting the construction of the town's first cathedral. Today, with the fortifications that once girdled the city all but vanished, it's the second **cathedral**, dating from the eleventh century, which forms the main focus of architectural interest. It lies just to the north of the River Wye at the heart of the city centre, whose compact tangle of narrow streets and squares is boxed in by the ring road. Taken as a whole, Hereford makes for a pleasant overnight stay especially as it possesses a particularly fine hotel.

Arrival, information and accommodation

From Hereford **train station**, it's about half a mile southwest to the main square, High Town, via Station Approach, Commercial Road and its continuation Commercial Street. The long-distance **bus station** is just off Commercial Road. The **tourist office** is directly opposite the cathedral, at 1 King St (April–Sept daily 9.30am–4.30pm; Oct–March Mon–Sat 10am–4.30pm; bank holiday Mon 10am–4pm; ℡01432/268430, ⊛www.visitherefordshire.co.uk).

Easily the best **hotel** in town is the ⚡ *Castle House*, in an immaculately refurbished Georgian mansion just a couple of minutes' walk from the cathedral on Castle Street (℡01432/356321, ⊛www.castlehse.co.uk; ❻). It's hard to find fault with this hotel: the staff are welcoming and very obliging; the rooms are simply delightful with all sorts of period details including deep ruffle curtains; and the breakfast room has a lovely outside terrace beside what was originally the town moat. Hereford also has a substantial number of **B&Bs**, arguably the pick of which is *Charades*, 34 Southbank Rd (℡01432/269444, ⊛www.charadeshereford.co.uk; ❷), with fourteen comfortable, en-suite guest rooms in a large Victorian house a ten- to fifteen-minute walk northeast from the centre. To get there, take Commercial Street and then Commercial Road and cross the railway bridge; Southbank Road is the second on the right.

The cathedral

Hereford Cathedral (daily 9.15am–5.30pm; £4 donation suggested; ⊛www.herefordcathedral.org) is a curious building, an uncomfortable amalgamation of styles, with bits and pieces added to the eleventh-century original by a string of bishops and culminating in an extensive – and not especially sympathetic – Victorian refit. From the outside, the sandstone **tower** is the dominant feature, constructed in the early fourteenth century to eclipse the Norman western tower, which subsequently collapsed under its own weight in 1786. The crashing masonry mauled the **nave** and its replacement lacks the grandeur of most other English cathedrals, though the forceful symmetries of the long rank of surviving Norman arches and piers more than hint at what went before. The **north transept** is, however, a flawless exercise in thirteenth-century taste, its soaring windows a classic example of Early English architecture.

The Mappa Mundi and the New Library

In the 1980s, the cathedral's finances were so parlous that a plan was drawn up to sell its most treasured possession, the **Mappa Mundi**. There was an awful lot of cultural huffing and puffing about this controversial proposal, but the government and John Paul Getty Jr rode to the rescue, with the oil tycoon stumping up a million pounds to keep the map here and install it in a brand-new building, now the **New Library**, which blends in seamlessly with the older buildings it adjoins at the west end of the cloisters. Inside, the **Mappa Mundi and Chained Library Exhibition** (Mon–Sat: Easter–Oct 10am–5pm; Nov–Easter 10am–4pm, but some closures for maintenance in Jan; £4.50) begins with a series of interpretative panels that explain the historical background to – and the composition of – the Mappa. Included is a copy of the Mappa in English, which is a particularly helpful touch as the original, which is displayed in a dimly lit room just beyond the interpretative panels, is in Latin. Measuring 64 by 52 inches (1.58 x 1.33m) and dating to about 1300, the Mappa provides an extraordinary insight into the medieval mind. It is indeed a map (as we know it) in so far as it suggests the general geography of the world – with Asia at the top and Europe and Africa below, to left and right respectively – but it also squeezes in history, mythology and theology. In total, the three continents are adorned by over five hundred drawings, some signifying towns and cities, including Hereford, others Biblical events, plants, birds and animals as well as a menagerie of mythological creatures – from the manticoras (man-headed lions) and the essedones (cannibals), through to the blemyae, who have heads in their chests.

As if this wasn't enough, the New Library also holds the **Chained Library**, a remarkably extensive collection of books and manuscripts dating from the eighth to the eighteenth centuries. A selection is always open on display.

The rest of the city

After the Mappa, Hereford's other attractions can't help but seem rather pedestrian. Nonetheless, the **Hereford Museum and Art Gallery**, in a flamboyant Victorian building opposite the cathedral on Broad Street (Tues–Sat 10am–5pm; free), does hold a mildly diverting collection of geological remains and local memorabilia spruced up by temporary art exhibitions. From the gallery, Broad Street continues up and round into the main square, **High Town**, which is fringed by several good-looking Victorian buildings.

Eating and drinking

Hereford rustles up a couple of really good **cafés**, beginning with *Cafe@allsaints* (closed Sun), near the cathedral in the old church at the top of Broad Street, which serves a range of well-conceived and tasty veggie dishes – ricotta pie with salad leaves for instance – at around £8. An appealing alternative is *Nutters* (closed Sun), a vegan-friendly joint just north of the cathedral on Capuchin Yard, which is itself just off pedestrianized Church Street. The smartest **restaurant** in town is at the *Castle House* hotel (see opposite), where the emphasis is on local ingredients – Hereford beef and Gloucestershire pork for instance – with main courses starting at £15. The restaurant is fairly formal, but you can also eat in a more relaxed fashion in the hotel bar.

Don't leave town without sampling the favourite local tipple, **cider**. Every **pub** in town serves the stuff, but the place to head for is *The Barrels*, a popular local just five minutes' walk southeast of High Town, at 69 St Owen's St. *The Barrels* is also the home pub of the local Wye Valley Brewery, whose trademark **bitters** are much acclaimed.

Ledbury

Heading east from Hereford, it's an easy fifteen miles along the A438 to **LEDBURY**, an amenable little town glued to the western edge of the Malvern Hills. The focus of the town is the short and wide **High Street**, whose tiny **Market Place** is home to the dinky **Market House**, a Tudor beamed building raised on oak columns and with herringbone-pattern beams. From beside it, narrow **Church Lane** – not to be confused with adjacent Church Street – runs up the slope framed by an especially fine ensemble of half-timbered Tudor and Stuart buildings, sometimes called "Black and Whites". Among them, at the foot of the lane in the town council offices, is the so-called **Painted Room** (Easter–Sept Mon–Fri 11am–1pm & 2–4pm; free), featuring a set of bold symmetrical floral frescoes painted on wattle-and-daub walls sometime in the sixteenth century. Just beyond is the tiny **Butcher Row House Museum** (daily: Easter–Sept 11am–5pm; Oct 11am–3pm; free), which displays a number of antique musical instruments, and then, at the end of the lane, **St Michael's parish church**, whose strong and angular detached spire pokes high into the sky. The nucleus of the adjacent church is Norman, but there are early Gothic flourishes too, most importantly the nave's long and slender windows.

Practicalities

Ledbury **train station** is on the northern edge of town, about three-quarters of a mile from the High Street – straight along The Homend. **Buses** stop on the High Street, near the **tourist office**, which is down a little alley (April–Sept daily 10am–5pm; Oct–March Mon–Sat 10am–4.30pm; ☎01531/636147, ⓦwww.visitherefordshire.co.uk).

Accommodation is thin on the ground, but the *Feathers Hotel* (☎01531/635266, ⓦwww.feathers-ledbury.co.uk; ❺) occupies a smashing "Black and White" on the High Street. It possesses around twenty comfortable guest rooms, each appealingly kitted out in a warm, modern style. Further afield, just six miles west of Ledbury in tiny **Kynaston**, *Hall End House* (☎01531/670225, ⓦwww.hallendhouse.co.uk; ❹) is a large and immaculately restored Georgian farmhouse offering excellent B&B; it comes complete with a heated outside swimming pool.

For its size, Ledbury does well for **restaurants**. The pick are the exemplary *Malthouse Restaurant*, Church Lane (eve only Tues–Sat, plus Sat lunchtime; ☎01531/634443), which offers a creative menu featuring local ingredients with main courses averaging around £16, and the comparable restaurant at the *Feathers* (see above), where they also do first-rate bar and brasserie food.

Ross-on-Wye

The small market town of **ROSS-ON-WYE**, nestling above a loop in the river sixteen miles southeast of Hereford, is a relaxed and easy-going place with an artsy/New Age undertow. Ross's jumble of narrow streets zeroes in on the **Market Place**, which is shadowed by the seventeenth-century **Market House**, a sturdy two-storey sandstone structure that sports a medallion bust of a bewigged

Charles II, placed here at the instigation of the pioneering seventeenth-century town planner, John Kyrle.

Veer right at the top of the Market Place, then turn left up Church Street to reach Ross's other noteworthy building, the mostly thirteenth-century **St Mary's Church**, whose sturdy stonework culminates in a slender, tapering spire. In front of the church, at the foot of the graveyard, is a plain but rare **Plague Cross**, commemorating the three hundred or so townsfolk who were buried here by night without coffins during a savage outbreak of the plague in 1637. Inside, the church holds the conspicuous **memorial-tombs** of the Rudhall family, one of which – that of a certain William Rudhall (d.1530) – is a wonderful example of the alabaster sculptures turned out by the specialist masons of Nottingham, whose work was prized right across medieval Europe. Beside the church, to the right of the entrance, **The Prospect** is a neat public garden offering pleasant views out over the river.

Practicalities

There are no trains to Ross, but the **bus station** is handily located on Cantilupe Road, from where it's a couple of minutes' walk west to the Market Place. The **tourist office** is equally convenient, located a few yards west of the Market Place on the corner of High and Edde Cross streets (April–Sept daily 10am–5pm; Oct–March Mon–Sat 10am–4.30pm; ☏01989/562768, ⓦwww.visitherefordshire.co.uk).

Ross is strong on **B&Bs** with one of the best being the ⚘ *Linden House*, in a fetching, three-storey Georgian building opposite St Mary's at 14 Church St (☏01989/565373, ⓦwww.lindenguesthouse.com; ❷). The half-dozen guest rooms here, three of which are en suite, are cosily decorated in pastel shades, plus the breakfasts are delicious – both traditional and vegetarian. A good second choice, just yards from the tourist office at 53 High St, is the *Old Court House* B&B (☏01989/762275, ⓦwww.wyenot.com/oldcthouse01.htm; ❸), which occupies a very old, but sympathetically modernized, stone house with an unusual, warren-like layout.

For **food**, *Nature's Choice*, just north of the Market Place at 17 Broad St, is a pleasant little café selling a tasty range of snacks and light meals. An unusual alternative is the *Gurkha Restaurant*, 1 Brookend St (☏01989/564963; closed Mon), which specializes in Nepalese and Tibetan food with mains from just £6; Brookend is a continuation of Broad Street. Of the **pubs**, the traditional *Man of Ross*, across from the tourist office at the top of Wye Street, wins on atmosphere and serves filling bar food.

The Wye River Valley

Travelling south from Ross along the B4234, it's just five miles to the sullen sandstone mass of **Goodrich Castle** (April–June, Sept & Oct daily 10am–5pm; July & Aug daily 10am–6pm; Nov–March Wed–Sun 10am–4pm; £5.50; EH), which commands wide views over the hills and woods of the **Wye River Valley**. The castle's strategic location guaranteed its importance as a border stronghold from the twelfth century onwards and today the substantial ruins incorporate a Norman keep, a maze of later rooms and passageways and walkable ramparts, complete with murder holes, the slits through which boiling oil or water was poured onto the attackers down below.

The castle stands next to the tiny village of **Goodrich**, from where it's around a mile and half southeast along narrow country lanes to the solitary *Welsh Bicknor Hostel* (☏0845/371 9666, Ⓔwelshbicknor@yha.org.uk; Easter–Oct; dorm beds £12, doubles ❶), in a Victorian rectory in its own grounds above the River Wye.

The hostel has 76 beds in anything from two- to ten-bed rooms, has **camping** facilities and provides evening meals on request. It's a great base (in a no-frills sort of way) for **hikers** with the **Wye Valley Walk** running past the front door.

From Goodrich, it's a couple of miles south along narrow country lanes to a fork in the road – veer right for Symonds Yat East (see below), and keep straight for the wriggly road up to the top of **Symonds Yat Rock**, one of the region's most celebrated viewpoints, rising high above a wooded, hilly loop in the River Wye. Way below is **SYMONDS YAT EAST**, a pretty little hamlet that straggles along the east bank of the river. It's a popular spot and one that offers both canoe rental and regular, forty-minute **river trips** with Kingfisher Cruises (April–Sept; ☎01600/891063, ⊛www.fweb.org.uk/kingfisher). There are also a couple of **places to stay**, including the *Saracens Head Inn* (☎01600/890345, ⊛www .saracensheadinn.co.uk; ❸), where the ten en-suite guest rooms are decorated in pleasant modern style – all wooden floors and pastel-painted walls. There's good **food** here too, both in the restaurant and in the bar, with the menu featuring English and Italian favourites with mains averaging £15.

The road to the village is a dead end, so you have to double back to regain Goodrich (or Symonds Yat Rock), though you can cross the river to **SYMONDS YAT WEST** by means of a hand-pulled rope **ferry** (£1), which leaves from outside the *Saracens Head*. There's a riverside **caravan and camping park** at Symonds Yat West (☎01600/890672, ⊛www.riverwyecamping.com; March–Oct) and another rather more attractive campsite, *Doward Park* (☎01600/890438, ⊛www.doward -park.co.uk), in a wooded location a mile or two to the west.

Hay-on-Wye

Straddling the Anglo–Welsh border about twenty miles west of Hereford, the hilly little town of **HAY-ON-WYE** is known to most people for one thing – **books**. Hay saw its first bookshop open forty years ago and has since become a bibliophile's paradise, with just about every spare inch of the town being given over to the trade, including the old cinema and the ramshackle stone castle. As a consequence, many of Hay's inhabitants are now outsiders, which means that it has little indigenous feel: when the hill farmers come into town on the razzle Hay gets a bit of a (welcome) jolt. In summer, the town plays host to a succession of festivals and fairs, the pick of which is the prestigious **Hay Festival of Literature and the Arts** (box office ☎01497/822629, ⊛www.hayfestival .com), held over ten days at the back end of May, when London's literary world decamps here en masse.

Arrival, information and accommodation
Buses to Hay stop yards from the centre of town on Oxford Road beside the main **car park**. The adjacent **tourist office** (daily: Easter–Sept 10am–1pm & 2–5pm; Oct–Easter 11am–1pm & 2–4pm; ☎01497/820144, ⊛www.hay-on-wye.co.uk) issues free town maps and leaflets outlining what, in general terms at least, each of the town's bookshops stock and their specialisms, if any. The tourist office also sells an exhaustive range of hiking books and maps, and will arrange accommodation.

Accommodation in and around Hay is plentiful, though things get booked up long in advance during the Hay Festival. There are a handful of hotels, but the town's **B&Bs** and **guesthouses** are characteristically a better bet. Of several **campsites**, the pick is *Radnors End* (☎01497/820780), in a pleasant rural setting a fifteen-minute walk from the town centre across the Wye bridge on the Clyro road (the B4351); the site has about twenty pitches and caravans are not allowed.

8

The King of Hay

Richard Booth (b.1938), whose family originates from the Hay area, opened the first of his Hay-on-Wye secondhand bookshops in 1961. Thereafter, and with extraordinary brio, he attracted a bevy of other booksellers to the town, turning it into the greatest market of used books in the world. There are now over thirty such shops in this minuscule town, the largest of which – Booth's own – contains around half a million volumes.

Whereas many of the region's country towns have seen their populations ebb in recent decades, Hay has **boomed** on the strength of its bibliophilic connections. Booth regards this success as a prototype for other endangered communities, placing the emphasis firmly on local initiatives and unusual specialisms. He is unequivocal in his condemnation of government regeneration programmes, which, he asserts, have done little to stem the flow of jobs and people out of the region. This healthy distaste for bureaucracy, coupled with Booth's self-promotional skills and Hay's geographical location slap bang on the Anglo–Welsh border, led him to declare Hay independent of the UK in 1977, with himself, naturally enough, as king. In a flurry of activity, he appointed his own ministers and offered "official" government scrolls, passports and car stickers to bewitched visitors. Although this proclamation of independence carried no official weight, most of the locals rallied behind **King Richard** and were delighted with the publicity – and the visitors. With Hay's success now assured, Booth is no longer so publicity-hungry, but he remains an important and popular local figure, though he failed to get elected when he stood as a candidate for the Wales constituency at the European Parliament election of 2009.

In town

Old Black Lion Lion St ☎01497/820841, ⓦwww.oldblacklion.co.uk. Town-centre pub with ten en-suite guest rooms, including one split-level suite, each of which is decorated in a cheerful, modern style. ❹

Start Bed and Breakfast Hay Bridge ☎01497/821391, ⓦwww.the-start.net. One of the best B&Bs in town, occupying a much modernized old house, near the river just across the Clyro bridge. Has three spick-and-span en-suite guest rooms and everyone raves about the breakfasts. ❸

Woodleigh Cottage Oxford Rd ☎01497/820008, ⓦwww.haycottage.co.uk. This attractive two-bedroom Victorian cottage is neatly decorated in a modern version of period style. Great location, a couple of minutes' walk from the centre, and available as either a B&B or for short-term lets. Minimum two-night stay on the weekend. ❷

Outside town

Llangoed Hall Hotel Llyswen ☎0844/411 9079, ⓦwww.legacy-hotels.co.uk. This deluxe hotel, set in its own Wye Valley grounds eight miles southwest of Hay in Llyswen, has 23 smooth and polished guest rooms decorated in a style suitable for a country mansion that was extensively refashioned in the 1910s. ❼

🏃 **Lower House** Cusop Dingle ☎01497/820773, ⓦwww.lowerhousegardenhay.co.uk. Sympathetically updated, eighteenth-century country home, with beamed ceilings and immaculate gardens, just one mile from the centre of Hay but deep in the country in a forested ravine. Two extremely stylish guest rooms, one with oodles of wood panelling, and a minimum two-night stay for most of the year. Either walk here from Hay on the Offa's Dyke footpath or it's the briefest of drives. ❹

The Town

Hay has an attractive **riverside setting**, amid rolling forested hills, and its narrow, bendy streets, which loop around a steep little mound on top of which squats the castle, are lined with an engaging assortment of old stone houses. But, before you start ambling round the town, visit the tourist office to pick up the free leaflet that gives the lowdown on all of Hay's bookshops together with a street plan.

Across the street from the tourist office, a footpath leads up the slope to the **castle**, a careworn Jacobean mansion built into the walls of an earlier medieval fortress. The castle's western flank holds one of the town's largest bookshops, the

Hay Castle Bookshop (☎01497/820503, ⊛www.richardbooth.demon.co.uk), a rambling dusty affair of creaking shelves crammed with old books and photos. From here, a wooden stairway leads down to Castle Street, where **The Addyman Annexe**, at no. 27 (☎01497/821600, ⊛www.hay-on-wyebooks.com), is strong on art and vintage travel books.

Castle Street slopes down to the oddly shaped main square, **High Town**, and just beyond is Lion Street, where, at no. 44, you'll find **Richard Booth's Bookshop** (☎01497/820322, ⊛www.richardbooth.demon.co.uk), a huge, bookish warehouse of a place offering almost unlimited browsing potential. Just up the street, at 5 Lion St, is one of Hay's most popular specialist bookshops, **Murder & Mayhem** (☎01497/821613, ⊛www.hay-on-wyebooks.com), packed with crime novels of every persuasion, and at the foot is the town's main landmark, the ornate, somewhat Ruritanian, Victorian **clocktower**.

Eating and drinking

The *Three Tuns* (☎01497/821855; closed Mon & Tues), a combined **pub and restaurant** in attractive old premises just along from the clocktower beside the Clyro bridge serves the best food in town, its menu featuring local, seasonal ingredients with the likes of lamb in Guinness and mustard sauce costing £15. One good alternative, located opposite the clocktower on Broad Street, is *The Granary* (☎01497/820790), a rusticated kind of place spread over two floors and serving a wide range of wholefood snacks and soups as well as filling main meals (£8–10); they have a roadside terrace, too, where hikers can kick off their boots and sink a leisurely pint. In the centre also is *Shepherds*, 9 High Town, an old-fashioned **café**

Canoeing and hiking around Hay-on-Wye

Hay-on-Wye's environs are readily and pleasantly explored by **kayak or canoe** along the River Wye. In four to six days, it's possible to paddle your way downriver from Hay to Ross-on-Wye (see p.506), overnighting in tents on isolated stretches of riverbank, or holing up in comfortable B&Bs and pubs along the way. Hay's **Paddles & Pedals**, down by the river on the far side of the Clyro bridge (☎01497/820604, ⊛www.paddlesandpedals.co.uk), is a reputable outfit for **kayak and canoe rental**, full of good ideas and advice. Rental of life jackets and other essential equipment (such as waterproof canisters to carry your gear) is included in the price, which works out at around £40 per canoe for 24 hours, with discounts for longer trips. In addition, Paddles & Pedals will transport their customers to and from the departure and finishing points by minibus; advance reservations are essential.

Hundreds of visitors come to Hay to go **hiking** and the surrounding countryside is latticed with footpaths. One of them is the **Offa's Dyke Path**, a long-distance hiking trail which runs north/south along – or near – the Welsh–English border, from Prestatyn to Chepstow, both of which are in Wales, threading through Hay-on-Wye along the way. Some 180 miles long, the path takes its name from the ditch King Offa of Mercia (broadly central England) had cut along the Anglo–Welsh frontier in the eighth century. Unlike Hadrian's Wall, it was never guarded or patrolled, acting as a boundary marker, not a defensive work. For all that, it was an extraordinary enterprise, though there's precious little to actually see today – the dyke merged with its surroundings centuries ago. The Offa's Dyke Path cuts a varied course, traversing open moorland and agricultural land but also weaving through deep wooded valleys. To the south of Hay it slips through the Black Mountains of Wales, making Hay as good a place as any to sample a section. Hay **tourist office** can supply the prospective hiker with everything from maps to specialist guidebooks; alternatively, consult ⊛www.nationaltrail.co.uk.

with a good line in snacks and mouthwatering, locally made ice cream, or you could sample the well-above-average **bar** food of the *Old Black Lion*, Lion Street, where, for instance, a steak-and-kidney pie will cost you £11.25.

Shropshire

One of England's largest and least populated counties, **Shropshire** stretches from its long and winding border with Wales to the very edge of the urban Black Country. Its most unique attraction is industrial: it was here that the Industrial Revolution made a huge stride forward with the spanning of the River Severn by the very first iron bridge. The assorted industries that subsequently squeezed into the **Ironbridge Gorge** are long gone, but a series of museums celebrate their craftsmanship – from tiles through to iron. The River Severn also flows through the county town of **Shrewsbury**, whose antique centre holds dozens of old half-timbered buildings, though **Ludlow**, further to the south, has the edge when it comes to handsome Tudor and Jacobean architecture. In between the two lie some of the most beautiful parts of Shropshire, namely the twin ridges of **Wenlock Edge** and the **Long Mynd**, both of which are prime hiking areas, readily explored from the attractive little town of **Church Stretton**. Yet, for all its varied attractions, Shropshire remains well off the main tourist routes, its true character best appreciated if you dawdle and doddle rather than simply hop from town to town.

There are fast and frequent **trains** from Birmingham to Telford and Shrewsbury, which is also linked to Church Stretton and Ludlow on the Hereford line. **Bus** services are patchy, but one small step forward has been the creation of the **Shropshire Hills Shuttle bus** service (Ⓦwww.shropshirehillsshuttles.co.uk) aimed at the tourist market and operating from April to September on Saturdays and Sundays only. The shuttle has two routes, the more useful of which noses round the Long Mynd as well as the Stiperstones and drops by Church Stretton; services are hourly and an adult Day Rover ticket, valid on the whole route, costs just £7. Bus timetables are available at most Shropshire tourist offices and on the website.

Ironbridge Gorge

Both geographically and culturally, **Ironbridge Gorge**, the collective title for a cluster of small villages huddled in the Severn Valley to the south of new-town **Telford**, looks to the cities of the West Midlands conurbation rather than to rural Shropshire. Ironbridge Gorge was the crucible of the Industrial Revolution, a process encapsulated by its famous span across the Severn – the world's first **iron bridge**, engineered by **Abraham Darby** and opened on New Year's Day, 1781. Darby was the third innovative industrialist of that name – the first Abraham Darby started iron-smelting here back in 1709 and the second invented the forging process that made it possible to produce massive single beams in iron. Under the guidance of such creative figures as the Darbys and Thomas Telford, the area's factories once churned out engines, rails, wheels and other heavy-duty iron pieces in quantities unmatched anywhere else in the world. Manufacturing has now all but vanished, but the surviving monuments make the gorge the most extensive industrial heritage site in England – and one that has been granted World Heritage Site status by UNESCO.

The Gorge contains several museums and an assortment of other industrial attractions spread along a five-mile stretch of the Severn Valley. A thorough exploration takes a couple of days, but the highlights – the iron bridge itself, the **Museum of Iron** and the **Jackfield Tile Museum** – are easily manageable on a day-trip. Each museum and attraction charges its own admission fee, but if you're intending to visit several, then buy a **Passport Ticket** (£22), which allows access to each of them once in any calendar year. Passport Tickets are available at all the main sights and at the Visitor Information Centre (see below), which also issues local maps and information. **Parking** is free at most of the sights, but not in Ironbridge village itself.

Arrival, getting around and information

Every two hours or so, Monday through Saturday only, **Arriva bus #96** links Shrewsbury bus station with Ironbridge village, at the heart of the gorge; the journey takes half an hour. Once you have reached Ironbridge village, however, there are no connecting buses along the gorge except on weekends from April to October, when the **Gorge Connect bus**, which begins and ends at Telford rail and bus stations, travels along the gorge in both directions, taking in Blists Hill, Coalport, Ironbridge village and Coalbrookdale on the way. Departures are every half-hour (9am–5pm) and single tickets cost 50p, or you can buy a day-ticket for £2.50. Alternatively, **bike rental** is available from the Bicycle Hub (Mon–Fri 10am–5pm, Sat 9am–6pm; ☏01952/883249, ⓦwww.thebicyclehub.co.uk) in the same complex as Jackfield Tile Museum.

The **Ironbridge Visitor Information Centre** (Mon–Fri 9am–5pm, Sat & Sun 10am–5pm; ☏01952/884391, ⓦwww.ironbridge.org.uk) is located in the Museum of the Gorge, approximately 500 yards west of the bridge along the main road.

Accommodation

Most visitors come for the day, but there are several pleasant **B&Bs** in Ironbridge village, which is where you want to be. There's also a **hostel** in Coalport.

Bridge View 10 Tontine Hill, Ironbridge village ☏01952/432541, ⓦwww.ironbridgeview.co.uk. Sympathetically updated eighteenth-century house a stone's throw from the bridge with neat and trim en-suite rooms. ❷

Coalbrookdale Villa 17 Paradise, Coalbrookdale ☏01952/433450, ⓦwww.coalbrookdalevilla.co.uk. This B&B occupies an attractive Victorian ironmaster's house set in its own grounds about half a mile up the hill from Ironbridge village in the tiny hamlet

IRONBRIDGE GORGE

M54 & Telford ▲

Darby Houses ❶
Museum of Iron
Coalbrookdale
COACH ROAD
DALE ROAD
PARADISE
Ⓐ
LINCOLN HILL
CHURCH HILL
BEECH RD
MADELEY RD
Museum of the Gorge ⓘ
Ironbridge village Ⓑ
Ⓒ
Iron Bridge ❷
JACKFIELD BRIDGE
COALFORD
Bedlam Furnace
River Severn
COALPORT RD
Blists Hill
Buildwas & Much Wenlock ◄
N
BALLS LANE
IRONBRIDGE RD
Jackfield Tile Museum
Jackfield
Maws Craft Centre
Tar Tunnel
Coalport
Coalport China Works & Museum Ⓓ

ACCOMMODATION
Bridge View   B
Coalbrookdale Villa A
Coalport YHA D
The Library House C

EATING & DRINKING
Coalbrookdale Inn 1
Restaurant Severn 2

0   500 yds

of Paradise. Sedately decorated, country-house-style, en-suite bedrooms. ❸

Coalport YHA Coalport ☎0845/371 9325, Ⓔironbridge@yha.org.uk. At the east end of the gorge in the former Coalport China factory, this YHA hostel has 80 beds in two- to ten-bed rooms, self-catering facilities, laundry, a shop and a café. Dorm beds £16, doubles ❶

The Library House 11 Severn Bank, Ironbridge village ☎01952/432299, Ⓦwww.libraryhouse.com. Enjoyable B&B, the best in the village, in a charming Georgian villa just yards from the iron bridge. Has three well-appointed double bedrooms decorated in a modern rendition of period style. ❹

Eating and drinking

There is one smashing traditional **pub** in the gorge, the excellent *Coalbrookdale Inn* (☎01952/433953), on the main road across from the Coalbrookdale iron foundry. It offers a selection of real ales plus delicious food, both in the bar and in its restaurant (kitchen closed Sun eve), with mains from about £12. The best **restaurant** hereabouts is *Restaurant Severn*, yards from the bridge at 33 High St (☎01952/432233; closed Mon & Tues). The *Severn*'s menu features local produce – some home-grown – with main courses such as venison in a cognac and cranberry sauce averaging around £16.

Ironbridge village

There must have been an awful lot of nail-biting during the construction of the **iron bridge** over the River Severn in the late 1770s. No one was quite sure how the new material would wear and although the single-span design looked sound, many feared the bridge would simply tumble into the river. To compensate, Abraham Darby used more iron than was strictly necessary, but the end result still manages to appear stunningly graceful, arching between the steep banks with the river far below. The settlement at the north end of the span was promptly renamed **IRONBRIDGE**, and today its brown-brick houses climb prettily up the hill from the bridge. The village is also home to the **Museum of the Gorge** (daily 10am–5pm; £3.60), located in a church-like, neo-Gothic old riverside warehouse about 500 yards west of the bridge along the main road. This provides an introduction to the gorge's industrial history and gives a few environmental pointers too; it's also home to the main visitor centre (see opposite).

Coalbrookdale iron foundry

At the roundabout just to the west of the Museum of the Gorge, turn right for the half-mile trip up to what was once the gorge's big industrial deal, the **Coalbrookdale iron foundry**, which boomed throughout the eighteenth and early nineteenth century, employing up to four thousand men and boys. The foundry has been imaginatively converted into the **Museum of Iron** (daily 10am–5pm; £7.40), with a wide range of displays on iron-making in general and the history of the company in particular. There are superb examples of Victorian and Edwardian ironwork here, including the intricate castings – stags, dogs and even camels – that became the house speciality. Also in the complex, across from the foundry beneath a protective canopy, are the ruins of the **furnace** where Abraham Darby pioneered the use of coke as a smelting fuel in place of charcoal.

From the foundry, it's about a hundred yards up to the two **Darby Houses** (late March to early Nov daily 10am–5pm; £4.60) – Dale House and Rosehill – both attractively restored old ironmasters' homes with Georgian period rooms and a scattering of items that once belonged to the Darby family.

Bedlam Furnace and the Tar Tunnel

Heading east from the iron bridge, it's a third of a mile along the river to the battered brick-and-stone remains of the **Bedlam Furnace** (open access; free), one of the first furnaces to use coke rather than charcoal. It was kept alight round-the-clock and at night its fiery silhouette scared passers-by half to death – hence the name. From here, it's a mile to the turning for Blists Hill (see below) and another 500 yards or so to the **Tar Tunnel** (April–Oct daily 10am–5pm; £2.50), built to transport coal from one part of the gorge to another, but so named after the bitumen that oozes naturally from its walls.

Jackfield

Beside the Tar Tunnel, a **footbridge** spans the Severn to reach **JACKFIELD**, nowadays a sleepy little hamlet whose brown-brick cottages string prettily along the river, but once a sooty, grimy place that hummed to the tune of two large tile factories, Maws and Craven Dunnill. Built in the middle of the nineteenth century to the latest industrial design, the two factories boomed until the 1920s, when they went into decline, but both have survived in good condition. From the footbridge, it's a couple of minutes' walk west to the first of the two, which has been sympathetically converted into the **Maws Craft Centre** (Ⓦ www.mawscraft centre.co.uk), holding over twenty arts, craft and specialist shops, which sell everything from flowers to decorative plasterwork with belly-dancing lessons as a possible add-on. A short walk away, the former Craven Dunnill factory has become the excellent **Jackfield Tile Museum** (daily 10am–5pm; £7.40), whose exhibits begin by providing a potted history of Jackfield and its two factories. Upstairs, beyond a series of period rooms related to the factory, is the superb "Style Gallery", where cabinet after cabinet illustrates the different styles of tile produced here, from Art Deco and Art Nouveau through to Arts and Crafts and the Aesthetic Movement. The museum also offers tile-making workshops and is home to **Fusion**, the collective name for several contemporary arts and crafts workers. Incidentally, tiles are still produced here by Craven Dunnill (Ⓦ www .cravendunnill.co.uk) – there are boxes of new tiles down by reception.

Coalport

Back at the Tar Tunnel, a canal towpath leads east in a couple of minutes to **Coalport China works**, a large brick complex holding the **Coalport China Museum** (daily 10am–5pm; £7.40). The museum kicks off with a couple of rooms crammed full of Coalport wares, the particular highlight being the gaudy and ornate pieces manufactured in the company's Victorian heyday, from around 1820 to 1890 (Coalport moved production to Stoke-on-Trent in 1926). There's also a workshop, where potters demonstrate their skills, and a Social History Gallery, which explores the hard life of the factory's workers, whose health was constantly at risk from the factory's lead-saturated dust. The museum also includes two **bottle-kilns**, those distinctive conical structures that were long the hallmark of the pottery industry. In the base of one is a small display of fine Coalport pieces, while the other explains how the kilns worked – though quite how the firers survived the conditions defies the imagination.

Blists Hill Victorian Town

Doubling back along the river, it's a third of a mile west from Coalport to the clearly signed, mile-long side road that cuts up to the gorge's most popular attraction, the rambling **Blists Hill Victorian Town** (daily 10am–5pm; £14.60). This encloses a substantial number of reconstructed Victorian buildings, most notably a school, a candle-maker's, a doctor's surgery, a gas-lit pub, and wrought-iron works. There's also a string of old shops lining up along **Canal Street**, including a draper's, a photographer's, and, most popular of all, a sweetshop. Jam-packed on most summer days, it's especially popular with school parties, who keep the period-dressed employees very busy.

Much Wenlock

Heading west from Ironbridge village along the northern bank of the River Severn, it's only a couple of miles to the A4169 and three more to **MUCH WENLOCK**, a tiny little town where a medley of Tudor, Jacobean and Georgian buildings dots the High Street – and pulls in the day-trippers by the score. At the foot of the High Street is the **Guildhall**, sitting pretty on sturdy oak columns, but the town's architectural high point is **Wenlock Priory** (March, April, Sept & Oct Wed–Sun 10am–5pm; May–Aug daily 10am–5pm; Nov–Feb Thurs–Sun 10am–4pm; £3.80; EH), a short stroll away to the north. The Saxons built a monastery at Much Wenlock, but today's remains mostly stem from the thirteenth and fourteenth centuries when its successor, a Cluniac monastery founded here in the 1080s, reached the height of its wealth and power. Set amid immaculate gardens and fringed by woodland, the ruins are particularly picturesque, from the peeling stonework of the old priory church's transepts to the shattered bulk of **St Michael's chapel** next to the bare foundations of the church's west door.

It only takes an hour or so to look round the town, but the **tourist office**, on the High Street (Easter–Oct Mon–Sat 10.30am–1pm & 1.30–5pm; ℡01952/727679, Ⓦwww.muchwenlockguide.info), does carry lots of local information, including details of hikes along Wenlock Edge.

Wenlock Edge

Attracting hikers from all over the region, the beautiful and deeply rural **Wenlock Edge** is a limestone escarpment that runs twenty-odd miles southwest from Much Wenlock to the A49. The south side of the escarpment is a gently shelving slope of open farmland, while the thickly wooded north side scarps steeply down to the Shropshire plains. Much of the Edge is owned by the National Trust, which maintains a network of waymarked **trails**, graded by colour according to length and difficulty, that wind through the woodland from a string of car parks along the **B4371**. This minor road hugs the first part of the ridge from Much Wenlock to **Longville-in-the-Dale** before proceeding on to Church Stretton (see p.518). The paths are easy to follow, but it's still a good idea to pick up the appropriate OS map and a copy of the National Trust's very helpful and free *Walks along Wenlock Edge* leaflet. The latter should be available from Much Wenlock tourist office (see above) and *Wilderhope Manor* (see below).

To explore Wenlock Edge, you'll need your own transport. The most obvious base is Ironbridge village, though you might opt instead for one of the YHA's most distinctive **hostels**, *Wilderhope Manor* (Easter to mid-Oct; ℡0845/371 9149, Ⓔwilderhope@yha.org.uk; dorm beds £16, doubles ❶). The hostel, which has recently been upgraded, occupies a remote Elizabethan mansion next to a farm about a mile south of the B4371 – the turning is clearly signed on the edge of Longville-in-the-Dale. Facilities include a self-catering kitchen, a café, a laundry and a cycle store; there are seventy beds in three- to ten-bed rooms.

Shrewsbury

SHREWSBURY, the county town of Shropshire, sits in a tight and narrow loop of the River Severn, a three-hundred-yard spit of land being all that prevents its centre from becoming an island. It would be difficult to design a better defensive site and predictably the Normans built a stone castle here, one which Edward I decided to strengthen and expand in the thirteenth century, though by then the local economy owed as much to the Welsh wool trade as it did to the town's military importance. In Georgian times, Shrewsbury became a fashionable staging post on the busy London–Holyhead route, boasting a lively social season, patronized by the sort of people who could afford to send their offspring to the famous Shrewsbury School. However, those heady days are long gone and nowadays Shrewsbury is an easy-going, middling market town, whose jingle and jangle of narrow lanes, courtyards and alleys fills out the small but hilly loop of land that comprises the town centre. It's the overall feel of the place that is its main appeal rather than any specific sight, though to celebrate the town's associations with **Charles Darwin**, the town is now the possessor of a forty-foot-high sculpture entitled **Quantum Leap**: it cost nigh-on half a million pounds, so most locals are ruing the cost rather than celebrating the artistic vision.

Arrival, information and accommodation

Shrewsbury **train station** stands at the northeast end of the centre and the long-distance **Raven Meadows bus station** is nearby off Smithfield Road. The permanent home of the **tourist office** is right in the centre of town on The Square, but until 2012, when its premises will have been converted into an information centre and museum, it has been moved to Rowley's House, on Barker Street (Mon–Sat 10am–5pm, plus May–Sept Sun 10am–4pm; ☎01743/281200, ⓦwww.visitshrewsbury.com). They operate an **accommodation booking service** and there are several prime places bang in the centre.

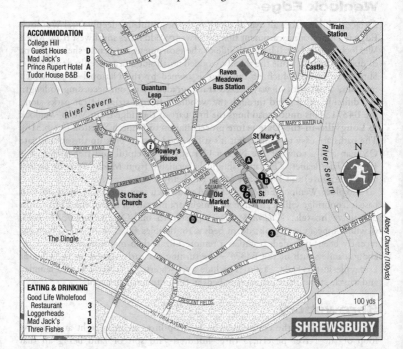

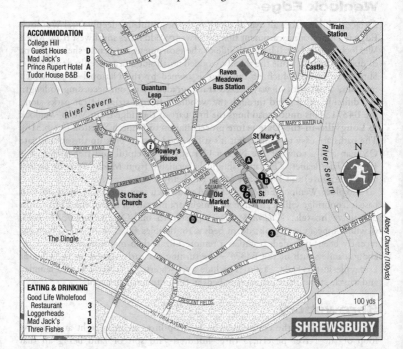**ACCOMMODATION**
College Hill
  Guest House   D
Mad Jack's   B
Prince Rupert Hotel A
Tudor House B&B   C

EATING & DRINKING
Good Life Wholefood
  Restaurant   3
Loggerheads   1
Mad Jack's   B
Three Fishes   2

SHREWSBURY

0   100 yds

Train Station

Castle

River Severn

Quantum Leap

Raven Meadows Bus Station

Rowley's House

St Mary's

St Alkmund's

St Chad's Church

Old Market Hall

The Dingle

WYLE COP

ENGLISH BRIDGE

Abbey Church (100yds)

College Hill Guest House 11 College Hill
ⓣ 01743/365744. Well-maintained seventeenth-
century townhouse with a battery of wooden
beams and a handful of comfortable if slightly
old-fashioned en-suite rooms. No credit cards. ❷

Mad Jack's 15 St Mary's St ⓣ 01743/358870,
ⓦ www.madjacks.uk.com. There are just four
en-suite guest rooms here above the restaurant of
the same name, each decorated in a slick modern
style with shades of brown and cream to the fore.
Smashing central location also. ❸

Prince Rupert Hotel Butcher Row, off Pride Hill
ⓣ 01743/499955, ⓦ www.prince-rupert-hotel.co.uk.

Probably the smartest hotel in Shrewsbury, the
Rupert occupies a cannily converted old building
in the middle of the town centre. There are
seventy bedrooms here and although some are a
tad too fancy for most tastes – ornate bed-head
canopies and so forth – they are undeniably
comfortable. ❸

Tudor House B&B 2 Fish St ⓣ 01743/351735,
ⓦ www.tudorhouseshrewsbury.com. Eminently
cosy B&B with a handful of rooms in an ancient
half-timbered house in the heart of the town. The
rooms are small, but kitted out with care and
considerable attention to detail. ❸

The Town

The logical place to start an exploration of Shrewsbury is the **train station**, built
in a fetching combination of styles, neo-baronial meets country house, in the
1840s. Poking up above the train station are the battered ramparts of the **castle**, a
pale reminder of the mighty medieval fortress that once dominated the town – the
illustrious Thomas Telford turned the castle into the private home of a local
bigwig in the 1780s. **Castle Gates** and its continuation **Castle Street/Pride Hill**
cuts up from the station into the heart of the river loop where the medieval town
took root. Turn left off Castle Street onto St Mary's Street and you soon reach
Shrewsbury's most interesting church, **St Mary's** (Mon–Fri 10am–5pm, Sat
10am–4pm; free), whose architecturally jumbled interior is redeemed by a magnificent east window that rises high above the high altar. Dating from the 1330s and
representing the apogee of the Decorated style, the window's stained glass displays
a superlative **Tree of Jesse**, one of the finest in the country, with Jesse – the
supposed father of David, King of the Israelites – at the bottom with his genealogical tree rising above him, its branches inhabited by Biblical characters.

From St Mary's, it's a couple of minutes' walk to the quiet precincts of
St Alkmund's Church, from where there's a charming view of the fine old
buildings of **Fish Street**, which weaves its way down to the High Street. Turn left
here for Wyle Cop (see below) and right to get to Pride Hill (see above) after
passing The Square, whose narrow confines are inhabited by the **Old Market
Hall**, a heavy-duty stone structure from 1596.

From The Square, High Street snakes down the hill to become **Wyle Cop**, lined
with higgledy-piggledy ancient buildings and leading to the **English Bridge**,
which sweeps across the Severn in grand Georgian style. Beyond the bridge, on
Abbey Foregate, is the stumpy red-stone mass of the **Abbey Church** (Mon–Sat
10.30am–3pm, Sun 11.30am–2.30pm; free), all that remains of the Benedictine
abbey that was a major political and religious force hereabouts until the Dissolution. The church is still in use as a place of worship, hence its good condition, but
the interior is fairly pedestrian, the best feature being the doughty Norman
columns of the nave.

Eating and drinking

The best **café** in town is the *Good Life Wholefood Restaurant* (closed Sun), on
Barracks Passage, just off Wyle Cop; they specialize in salads and vegetarian dishes
with main courses costing around £6. In the evening, head for *Mad Jack's* (see
above), Shrewsbury's best **restaurant**, a smart little place with an outside terrace
serving a wide range of English dishes, from local lamb to mussels, with main
courses averaging £14. Among Shrewsbury's many **pubs**, one of the most distinctive is the *Loggerheads*, an ancient place with several small rooms and great real ales;

it's located near St Alkmund's at 1 Church St. A second good choice is the *Three Fishes*, also in an ancient building, but this time on Fish Street.

Church Stretton and the Long Mynd

Beginning about nine miles south of Shrewsbury, the upland heaths of the **Long Mynd**, some ten miles long and between two and four miles wide, run parallel to and just to the west of the A49. This is prime **walking** territory and the heathlands are latticed with footpaths, the pick of which offer sweeping views over the border to the Black Mountains of Wales. Nestled at the foot of the Mynd beside the A49 is **CHURCH STRETTON**, a tidy little village that makes an ideal base for hiking the area. The village also possesses the dinky parish **church of St Laurence**, parts of which – especially the nave and transepts – are Norman. Look out also for the (badly weathered) fertility symbol over the side door, just to the left of the entrance – it's a genital-splaying **sheela-na-gig**, whose sheer explicitness comes as something of a surprise.

Arrival and information

Church Stretton **train station** is beside the A49 about 600 yards east of the High Street, which is the heart of the village. Most **buses** pull in beside the train station, but some also continue on to the High Street. The **tourist office** is on Church Street immediately to the west of the High Street (April–Sept Mon–Sat 9.30am–5pm; Oct–March Mon–Sat 9.30am–12.30pm & 1.30–5pm; ☎01694/723133, ⓦwww.churchstretton.co.uk). They stock an excellent range of local hiking information and will book accommodation on your behalf.

Accommodation

There are several top-ranking **B&Bs** in and around Church Stretton, the most central of which is the *Victoria House*, 48 High St (☎01694/723823, ⓦwww .bedandbreakfast-shropshire.co.uk; ❷), an extraordinarily cosy little place with six guest rooms above the owners' teashop. The rooms are kitted out in appealing period style with heavy drapes, thick carpets and iron bedsteads; the breakfasts are simply delicious too. Further afield, but equally appealing, is *Jinlye* (☎01694/723243, ⓦwww.jinlye.co.uk; ❸), in an attractively modernized and extended stone cottage on Castle Hill, on the edge of **All Stretton**, one mile or so north of Church Stretton. There are six splendid guest rooms here, each decorated in a homely, vaguely period style.

Hostellers have choices too – *Wilderhope Manor* (see p.515) is only seven miles east of Church Stretton along the B4371, or there's *Bridges Long Mynd* (☎01588/650656, ⓦwww.yha.org.uk; dorm beds £13, doubles ❶), just five miles west of Church Stretton on the edge of tiny **Ratlinghope**. The latter, which occupies a converted village school, has 37 beds in two- to ten-bed rooms, a café, **camping** and a self-catering kitchen, and is a great base for hiking to the Long Mynd or the **Stiperstones**, a remote range of boggy heather dotted with ancient cairns and earthworks.

Eating and drinking

Church Stretton has two smashing **cafés**, the *Victoria House Tea Rooms* (Sat & Sun only), an offshoot of the *Victoria House* B&B (see above), and *Berry's Coffee House*, 17 High St (☎01694/724452), the dinkiest of (licensed) cafés where they serve up delicious salads and light meals during the daytime, diversifying into full dinners on Friday and Saturday nights. The best fully-fledged **restaurant** is *The Studio*, 59 High St (☎01694/722672; Wed–Sat eve only), where the menu is a canny mix of French and English dishes with a two-course set meal costing £25.

Ludlow

LUDLOW, perched on a hill in a loop of the River Teme nearly thirty miles south of Shrewsbury, is one of the most picturesque towns in the West Midlands, if not in England – a gaggle of beautifully preserved black-and-white half-timbered buildings packed around a craggy stone castle, with rural Shropshire forming a drowsy backdrop. These are strong recommendations in themselves, but Ludlow scores even more points by being something of a gastronomic hidey-hole with a clutch of outstanding restaurants and the much-vaunted **Ludlow Food Festival** (Ⓦwww.foodfestival.co.uk), held over three days every September. The other leading event is the **Ludlow Festival** (Ⓣ01584/872150, Ⓦwww .ludlowfestival.co.uk), comprising two weeks of assorted musical and theatrical fun, running from the end of June to early July.

Arrival, information and accommodation

From Ludlow **train station**, it's a fifteen-minute walk southwest to the castle – just follow the signs. Most **buses** stop on Mill Street, just off Castle Square, which is also the site of the **tourist office** (Mon–Sat 10am–5pm, Sun 10.30am–5pm; Oct–March closed Sun; Ⓣ01584/875053, Ⓦwww.ludlow.org.uk). **Accommodation** is plentiful, though rooms still get scarce during the town's two main festivals.

Dinham Hall Hotel Dinham Ⓣ01584/876464, Ⓦwww.dinhamhall.co.uk. Handily located close to the castle, this deluxe hotel occupies a rambling, bow-windowed eighteenth-century stone mansion, which has previously seen service as a boarding house for Ludlow School. It has just thirteen guest rooms, each of which is decorated in an appealing, but never overdone rendition of period style. ❺

Ludlow Bed and Breakfast 35 Lower Broad St Ⓣ01584/876912, Ⓦwww.ludlowbedandbreakfast .blogspot.com. Infinitely cosy B&B in a pair of old terraced cottages that have been carefully knocked into one. Just two doubles, great breakfasts and pick-up from the train station by prior arrangement. In the town centre, a five- to ten-minute walk from the castle. ❷

🏃 **Mr Underhill's** Dinham Weir Ⓣ01584/874431, Ⓦwww.mr-underhills.co .uk. Decorated in fetching shades of brown and cream, the four double rooms and two suites in this immaculate hotel are peaceful and relaxing in equal measure. The hotel occupies a neat and trim mini-complex at the foot of the town centre, beside the River Teme. ❺

The castle

The Saxons were the first to recognize Ludlow's defensive qualities, but it was the Normans who got down to business when Roger Montgomery turned up here with his men in 1085. Over the next few decades, Montgomery's fortifications were elaborated into an immense **castle** (Feb, March, Oct & Nov daily 10am–4pm; April–July & Sept daily 10am–5pm; Aug daily 10am–7pm; Dec & Jan Sat & Sun 10am–4pm; £4.50; Ⓦwww.ludlowcastle.com), seat of the Lord President of the Council of The Marches, as the borders were then known, and strong enough to keep the Welsh at bay. Today, the rambling ruins of the castle are still imposing, incorporating towers and turrets, gatehouses and concentric walls as well as the remains of the 110-foot Norman **keep** and an unusual **Round Chapel** built in 1120. With its spectacular setting high above the river, the castle also makes a fine open-air auditorium during the Ludlow Festival (see above).

The rest of town

The castle entrance abuts **Castle Square**, a rectangular open space that's home to a particularly pleasant open-air **market** on Mondays, Wednesdays, Fridays and Sundays (9am–5pm). The eastern side of the square breaks into several short and narrow lanes, with the one on the left leading through to the gracefully propor-tioned **Church of St Laurence**, whose interior is distinguished by its stained-glass windows. The church also holds an especially fine set of misericords. Carved in oak, they run the gamut from royal emblems and religious scenes to the folkloric and seemingly profane – green men, devils, a fox preaching to geese, a witch, a mermaid, and a woman disappearing into the mouth of hell, bottom first. Back outside the church, it's a few paces to the **Butter Cross**, a Neoclassical extravagance from 1744, and a few more to the **Bull Ring**, home of the **Feathers Hotel**, a fine Jacobean building with the fanciest wooden facade imaginable.

To the south of Castle Square, the gridiron of streets laid out by the Normans has survived intact, though most of the buildings date from the eighteenth century. It's the general appearance that appeals rather than any special sight, but steeply sloping **Broad Street** is particularly attractive, flanked by many of Ludlow's five hundred half-timbered Tudor and red-brick Georgian listed buildings. At the foot of Broad Street is Ludlow's only surviving **medieval gate**, which was turned into a house in the eighteenth century.

Eating and drinking

In recent years, Ludlow and its environs have become something of a gastronomic hot spot with the establishment of a string of much lauded **restaurants**. Predictably enough, none of these prime places comes cheap, but this is a great place to treat yourself, though fortunately there are less wallet-wilting choices too.

DeGreys 5 Broad St. The best tearoom in town, where uniformed staff bustle around a long, narrow and very old beamed room with assorted sandwiches and snacks; the only problem is the prices, which are a little high – the toasties, for one, cost £6.

La Bécasse 17 Corve St ✆01584/872325. This informal, French-influenced, Michelin-starred restaurant has received rave reviews again and again. A two-course *menu du jour* – featuring the likes of mackerel with aubergine purée, artichokes and yoghurt – costs a comparatively reasonable £25. Closed Sun & Mon all day, plus Tues lunch.

Mr Underhill's Dinham Weir ✆01584/874431. Arguably the best

restaurant in town, the menu here is carefully and skilfully crafted with due prominence given to local, seasonal ingredients: English asparagus and garden sorrel risotto soup is a typical starter. Set menus kick off at around £50 and reservations are essential. Closed Mon & Tues.

Olive Branch 2 Old St. Popular, inexpensive café that does a good line in light meals and salads during the daytime. Right in the centre of town, just off the Bull Ring.

Wheatsheaf Inn Lower Broad St. Quaint and friendly little pub a short walk from the main square beside the old town gate. Well-kept ales and filling bar food too.

Birmingham

If anywhere can be described as the first purely industrial conurbation, it has to be **BIRMINGHAM**. Unlike the more specialist industrial towns which grew up across the north and the Midlands, including the **Black Country**, that clutch of towns immediately to the west of Birmingham, "Brum" – and its "Brummies" – turned its hand to every kind of manufacturing, gaining the epithet "the city of 1001 trades". It was here also that the pioneers of the Industrial Revolution – James Watt, Matthew Boulton, Josiah Wedgwood, Joseph Priestley and Erasmus Darwin (grandfather of Charles) – formed the **Lunar Society**, an extraordinary melting-pot of scientific and industrial ideas. They conceived the world's first purpose-built factory, invented gas lighting and pioneered both the distillation of oxygen and the mass production of the steam engine. Thus, a modest Midlands market town mushroomed into the nation's economic dynamo with the population to match: in 1841 there were 180,000 inhabitants; just fifty years later that number had trebled.

Now the second largest city in Britain, with a population of over one million, Birmingham has long outgrown the squalor and misery of its boom years and today its industrial supremacy is recalled – but only recalled – by a crop of **recycled buildings**, from warehouses to an old custard factory, and an extensive network of **canals**. It also boasts a thoroughly multiracial population – this is one of Britain's most cosmopolitan cities. The recent shift to a post-manufacturing economy has been symbolized by an intelligent and far-reaching revamp of the city centre that has included the construction of a glitzy **Convention Centre** and an extravagant revamping of the **Bull Ring**, while the enormous **National Exhibition Centre (NEC)** now inhabits the outskirts near the International Airport. Birmingham has also launched a veritable raft of cultural initiatives, enticing a division of the **Royal Ballet** to take up residence here, and building a fabulous new concert hall for the **City of Birmingham Symphony Orchestra**. Nevertheless, there's no pretending that Birmingham is packed with interesting sights – it isn't – though, along with its first-rate restaurant scene and nightlife, it's well worth at least a couple of days.

Arrival

Birmingham's **International Airport** is eight miles east of the city centre off the A45 and near the M42 (Junction 6); the terminal is beside Birmingham International train station, from where there are regular services into **New Street train station**, right in the heart of the city. New Street station is where all inter-city and the vast majority of local services go, though trains from Stratford-upon-Avon, Warwick, Worcester and Great Malvern usually pull in at either **Snow Hill** or **Moor Street stations**, both about ten minutes' signposted walk from New

---

A weekend in Birmingham

Friday night
Start the weekend in style with a drink in the **Old Joint Stock** followed by a top-notch meal at the **Metro Bar and Grill** before wandering along Broad Street, the centre of Birmingham's hectic nightlife.

Saturday
In the morning, sample the delights of the **Birmingham Museum & Art Gallery**, which possesses the finest collection of Pre-Raphaelite paintings in the world, before heading on to the **Bull Ring** and **The Mailbox** for some retail therapy – from the Rag Market to Selfridges and Jaeger with everything in between. For lunch, head along to the cafés and restaurants of **Brindleyplace** – where *Edmunds* will do very nicely – and then stroll along to Gas Street Basin for a **boat trip** on the city's cobweb of canals. In the evening, enjoy a **balti**, Birmingham's gastronomic speciality, at *Celebrity Balti* and then make your way to the **Factory**, one of the grooviest bars and clubs in town, sited in the old Alfred Bird Custard Factory. The more retiring can opt instead for Birmingham's **Royal Ballet**, a West End production at the Hippodrome, or a film at the oldest cinema around, **The Electric**.

Sunday
Sunday morning is a good time to visit Birmingham's bustling **Chinatown**, down and around Hurst Street, and it's here that you'll also find a street of **Back-to-Back** houses that have been immaculately restored by the National Trust. Finish off with a stroll round one of Birmingham's many **parks** – Edgbaston Park out in the suburbs is one of the prettiest – or, if you're here in summer, you can spend the day being knocked for six at **Edgbaston**, the home of Warwickshire County Cricket Club.

Street to the north and east respectively. National Express **long-distance buses** arrive at the **Digbeth coach station**, from where it's a ten-minute walk northwest to the Bull Ring.

Information and city transport

The city's main **tourist office**, 150 New St, is located beside the Bull Ring at the back of the Rotunda (Mon–Sat 9.30am–5.30pm, Sun 10.30am–4.30pm; ☏0844/888 3883, ⓦwww.visitbirmingham.com). A second, smaller office occupies a **kiosk** in front of New Street station, at the junction of New Street and Corporation Street (Mon–Sat 9am–5pm, Sun 10am–4pm; same number). Both offices issue free town maps and supply public transport timetables. The Rotunda office also sells theatre and concert tickets and operates a free **accommodation booking** service: they are often aware of special deals and discounts, which can slash costs considerably

Birmingham has an excellent public transport system, whose **trains**, **metro** and **buses** delve into almost every urban nook and cranny. Various companies provide these services, but they are all coordinated by **Centro** (☏0121/200 2787, ⓦwww .centro.org.uk).

Accommodation

To see Birmingham at its best, you really need to stay in the centre, preferably in the vicinity of Centenary Square, though **chain hotels** do monopolize the downtown scene. The Rotunda tourist office (see above) operates a free **hotel room booking service**.

Back to Backs Houses 52 Inge St ☏0844/800 2070, ⓦwww.nationaltrustcottages.co.uk. The most distinctive place to stay in town: the National Trust has refurbished a small block of nineteenth-century back-to-back workers' houses conveniently located just to the south of the city centre along Hurst St (see p.528). Part of the complex now holds two small "cottages" – really terraced houses – kitted out in Victorian period style, but with the addition of en-suite and self-catering facilities. Each accommodates two guests and can be rented out for two nights or longer with costs varying with the season: a two-night stay costs £165 in Jan, rising to £246 in July.

Birmingham Central Backpackers 58 Coventry St ☏0121/643 0033, ⓦwww.birminghamcentral backpackers.com. Welcoming hostel with self-catering facilities and a large sociable lounge, a small garden and a café and bar. Acommodation is in dorms, with four to eight bunks per room, both female-only and mixed. A short walk from Digbeth bus station. From £13 per person per night.

Hyatt Regency Birmingham 2 Bridge St ☏0121/643 1234, ⓦwww.birmingham.regency .hyatt.com. The sleek, black skyscraper that towers above Centenary Square is a luxury Hyatt hotel. The central location is hard to beat, the city views from the guest rooms on the upper floors are superlative, and the public area has some pleasant Art Deco touches. Less positively, the rooms are

decorated in uninspiring chain-hotel style and you can't open the windows. Discounts are common-place, but the rack rate is ❺

Malmaison 1 Wharfside St, The Mailbox ☏0121/246 5000, ⓦwww.malmaison -birmingham.com. This impeccably stylish, designer hotel offers first-class accommodation of wit and substance – no wonder it's next door to Harvey Nichols. Every convenience and a central location. ❻

Radisson Blu 12 Holloway Circus ☏0121/654 6000, ⓦwww.birmingham.radissonblu.co.uk. Smart and ultra-polished hotel in a tall and sleek skyrise within a few minutes' walk of the centre. The interior is designed in routine modern-minimalist style, but the green amoeba-like pattern etched onto the acres of glass adds élan, as do the floor-to-ceiling windows of many of the bedrooms. ❺

Staying Cool at Rotunda The Rotunda, New St ☏0121/643 0815, ⓦwww.stayingcool.com. The top three floors of the Rotunda, right at the heart of Birmingham, have been converted into fully furnished, serviced apartments, either small, medium, large or extra large. All are decorated in the full flush of modern style and the ones on the top floor – Floor 20 – come equipped with balconies from which there are panoramic views over the city. The apartments can be rented for one night – no problem. From £109 per night for two people and £149 for four.

▲ Aston, M6 & A38 Lichfield

▲ Museum of the Jewellery Quarter

▲ Moseley, Balsall Heath, M5 & A38

▲ A456 Kidderminster

▼ M5

BIRMINGHAM

ACCOMMODATION

Back to Backs Houses	F
Birmingham Central Backpackers	D
Hyatt Regency Birmingham	B
Malmaison	C
Radisson Blu	E
Staying Cool at Rotunda	A

EATING

Brasserie de Malmaison	C
Celebrity Balti	10
Chez Jules	8
Chung Ying	14
Edmunds	9
Edwardian Tea Room	6
Metro Bar and Grill	5
The Oriental	4
Purnells	13
	3

DRINKING

Actress & Bishop	2
Figure of Eight	11
The Old Fox	16
Old Joint Stock	6
Sunflower Lounge	12
The Wellington	7

LIVE MUSIC & CLUB

Factory Club	15
Gatecrasher	17
The Jam House	1
The Nightingale	19
O2 Academy	18

0   200 yds

N

General Hospital

Police Station

St Chad's Catholic Cathedral

Snow Hill Train Station

Victoria Law Courts

Moor Street Station

Coach Station

Selfridges

St Martin's Church

City Markets

Bull Ring

Rotunda

Electric Cinema

Old Rep Theatre

CHINESE QUARTER

Birmingham Hippodrome

Arcadian Centre

New Street Station

Alexandra Theatre

St Philip's Anglican Cathedral

Waterhall Gallery

Council House

Birmingham Museum & Art Gallery

Town Hall

Paradise Forum

Library

Scotland Street Locks

RBSA

St Paul's

JEWELLERY QUARTER

Hall of Memory

City Library (2013)

Repertory Theatre

International Convention Centre & Symphony Hall

Ikon Gallery

National Sea Life Centre

The Mailbox

Gas St Basin

National Indoor Arena

Crescent Theatre

The City

Many visitors get their first taste of central Birmingham at **New Street Station**, whose unreconstructed ugliness – piles of modern concrete – makes a dispiriting start, though there are plans afoot to give the place a thoroughgoing face-lift. Things soon improve if you cut up east from the station to the newly developed **Bull Ring**, once a 1960s eyesore, but now a gleaming new shopping mall distinguished by the startling design of its leading store, **Selfridges**. Head west along pedestrianized **New Street** from here and it's a brief stroll to the elegantly revamped **Victoria Square**, with its tumbling water fountain, and the adjacent **Chamberlain Square**, where pride of place goes to the **Birmingham Museum and Art Gallery**, the city's finest museum, complete with a stunning collection of Pre-Raphaelite art. Beyond, further west still, is the glossy **International Convention Centre**, from where it's another short hop to the **Gas Street Basin**, the prettiest part of the city's serpentine canal system. Close by is canalside **Brindleyplace**, a smart, brick-and-glass complex sprinkled with slick cafés and bars and holding the enterprising **Ikon Gallery** of contemporary art.

From Brindleyplace, it's a short walk southeast to **The Mailbox**, the immaculately rehabilitated former postal sorting office with yet more chic bars and restaurants, or you can head north along the old towpath of the **Birmingham & Fazeley Canal** as far as Newhall Street. The latter is within easy walking distance of the Georgian delights of **St Philip's Cathedral** and – in the opposite direction – the **Jewellery Quarter**, which holds an excellent museum and scores of jewellery workshops and retail outlets.

Incidentally, one thing that may confuse your ramblings is the name of the **inner ring road**: it's called the Queensway, but individual stretches keep their other names too; for example: Great Charles Street, Queensway.

The Bull Ring and Selfridges

A few steps from New Street Station, Rotunda Square marks the intersection of New and High streets, taking its name from the soaring **Rotunda**, a handsome and distinctive cylindrical tower that is the sole survivor of the notorious **Bull Ring** shopping centre, which fulfilled every miserable cliché of 1960s town planning until its demolition in 2001. The new Bull Ring shopping centre has two strokes of real invention. Firstly, the architects split the Bull Ring shops into two separate sections and in the gap there is now an uninterrupted view of the medieval spire of St Martin's – an obvious contrast between the old and the new perhaps, but still extraordinarily effective. The second coup was the design of **Selfridges'** new store, a billowing organic swell protruding from the Bull Ring's east side, and seen to good advantage from the wide stone stairway that descends from Rotunda Square to St Martin's. Reminiscent of an inside-out octopus, Selfridges shimmers with an architectural chain-mail of thousands of silver discs, altogether a bold and hugely successful attempt to create a popular city landmark.

St Martin's Church and the city markets

Nestling at the foot of the Bull Ring, the newly scrubbed and polished **St Martin's Church** (daily 10am–5pm; free) is a fetching amalgamation of the Gothic and the neo-Gothic, its mighty spire poking high into the sky. The church has had some hard times, bombed by the Luftwaffe and attacked by the Victorians, but the interior, with its capacious three-aisled nave, is saved from mediocrity by a delightful **Burne-Jones stained-glass window**, a richly coloured, finely detailed affair whose panes sport angels, saints, biblical figures and scenes; it's in the south transept.

Across from the church are Birmingham's three main **markets** – two selling fresh produce, one indoor (Mon–Sat 9am–5.30pm), the other outdoor (Tues–Sat

9am–5pm), with the **Rag Market** (Tues, Thurs, Fri & Sat 9am–5pm) in between. There was a time when the Rag Market was crammed with every sort of material you could imagine and then some; its heyday is gone but it still musters up all sorts of knick-knacks, always sold at bargain-basement prices.

New Street, Victoria Square and Chamberlain Square

Stretching west from the Bull Ring, **New Street** is a busy pedestrianized thoroughfare, lined with shops and stores. At its west end, New Street opens out into the handsomely refurbished **Victoria Square**, whose centrepiece is a large and particularly engaging **water fountain** designed by Dhruva Mistry. The fountain's large and distinctive female figure is affectionately known as "the Floozy in the Jacuzzi" by the locals – but there's no such term of endearment for Antony Gormley's rusting *Iron Man* lurking nearby, and leaning at a precarious angle like a Saturday-night drunk. The waterfall outdoes poor old Queen Victoria, whose statue is glum and uninspired, though the thrusting self-confidence of her bourgeoisie is very apparent in the flamboyant **Council House** behind her, all gables and cupolas, columns and towers.

Across the square, and very different, is the **Town Hall** of 1834, whose classical design – by Joseph Hansom, who went on to design Hansom cabs – was based on the Roman temple in Nîmes. The building's simple, flowing lines contrast with much of its surroundings, but it's an appealing structure all the same, erected to house public meetings and musical events in a flush of municipal pride and now, after a recent refit, a performing arts venue.

Victoria Square leads into **Chamberlain Square**, in the middle of which is a dinky neo-Gothic memorial in honour of **Joseph Chamberlain** (1836–1914), who made himself immensely popular hereabouts by taking the city's gas and water supplies into public ownership. His political career ultimately took him from the Birmingham mayor's office to national prominence as leader of the Liberal Unionists and figurehead of the resistance to Irish Home Rule.

The Birmingham Museum and Art Gallery

The **Birmingham Museum and Art Gallery** (**BM&AG**) occupies a rambling, Edwardian building on Chamberlain Square (Mon–Thurs & Sat 10am–5pm, Fri 10.30am–5pm, Sun 12.30–5pm; free; ⓦwww.bmag.org.uk). It possesses a multi-faceted collection divided into several sections, but the bulk is spread over one long floor – Floor 2; this is where you'll find the fine art, which attracts most attention. In 2009, the museum also part-purchased the **Staffordshire Hoard**, the largest collection of Anglo-Saxon gold ever found with over 1500 pieces, mostly related to warfare; at time of writing it's not clear quite where and when the hoard will be displayed, but it's likely that the BM&AG will get a prime spot, so be sure to pick up a plan at reception.

The BM&AG holds a significant sample of **European** paintings and an excellent collection of eighteenth- and nineteenth-century British art, most notably a supreme muster of **Pre-Raphaelite** work, concentrated in Rooms 14 and 17–19. Founded in 1848, the Pre-Raphaelite Brotherhood consisted of seven young artists, of whom Rossetti, Holman Hunt, Millais and Madox Brown are the best known. The name of the group was selected to express their commitment to honest observation, which they thought had been lost with the Renaissance. Two seminal Pre-Raphaelite paintings here are **Dante Gabriel Rossetti**'s stirring *Beata Beatrix* (1870) and **Ford Madox Brown**'s powerful image of emigration, *The Last of England* (1855). The Brotherhood disbanded in the 1850s, but a second wave of artists carried on in its footsteps, most notably **Edward Burne-Jones**, whose *Star of Bethlehem* – in Room 14 – is one of the largest watercolours ever painted; it's a mysterious, almost magical piece with earnest Magi and a film-star-like Virgin Mary.

Sharing Floor 2 is the **Industrial Gallery**, which is set around an expansive atrium whose wrought-iron columns and balconies clamber up towards fancy skylights. The gallery holds a choice selection of ceramics, jewellery and stained glass retrieved from defunct churches the length and breadth of Birmingham. Here also is the *Edwardian Tea Room*, one of the city's more pleasant places for a cuppa (see p.529).

Moving on, Floor 1's cavernous **Gas Hall** is an impressive venue for touring art exhibitions, while the **Waterhall Gallery** (same times), inside the Council House, just across Edmund Street from the main museum building, showcases temporary exhibitions of modern and contemporary art.

Centenary Square

From the north side of Chamberlain Square, walk through the hideously ugly **Paradise Forum** shopping and fast-food complex to get to **Centenary Square**, where there's an unusual World War I war memorial, the **Hall of Memory** (Mon–Sat 10am–4pm; free). Erected in 1923 to commemorate those 13,000 Brummies who had died in World War I, the memorial is an architectural hybrid, a delightful mix of Art Deco and Neoclassical features, whose centrepiece is a domed Remembrance chamber. From the memorial, it's a brief walk west past the construction site where the new city library will eventually appear (in 2013) to the showpiece **International Convention Centre (ICC)** and **Symphony Hall** with the **Birmingham Repertory Theatre** on the right.

Gas Street Basin and The Mailbox

From the ICC, it's a brief stroll along Broad Street to Gas Street, on the left, which leads down to **Gas Street Basin**, the hub of Birmingham's intricate canal system. There are eight canals within the city's boundaries, comprising no less than 32 miles of canal. Canal construction peaked in the late eighteenth century, when almost all heavy goods were transported by water. The railways subsequently made them uneconomic, but the canals struggled on until the 1970s when tourism – and narrowboats – gave them a new lease of life. Much of Birmingham's surviving canal network slices through the city's grimy, industrial bowels, but certain sections have been immaculately restored with Gas Street Basin leading the way. The Basin, which lies at the junction of the Worcester & Birmingham and Birmingham Main Line canals, is edged by a delightful medley of old brick buildings and is almost always crowded by a herd of brightly painted narrowboats. To venture out on the water yourself, walk up the canal to Brindleyplace (see below), where Sherborne Wharf (℡0121/455 6163, ⊛www .sherbornewharf.co.uk) operates a **water bus service** around the central part of the canal system (Easter–Oct daily 10am–5pm; every 30–45min; day-pass £3.50 or 75p per stop); they also do one-hour **canal tours** from beside the ICC (Easter–Oct 4 daily; £6.50).

Follow the towpath along the canal southeast from Gas Street Basin and you soon reach **The Mailbox**, a talented reinvention of Birmingham's old postal sorting office complete with restaurants, hotels, and some of the snazziest shops in the city – including Jaeger and Harvey Nichols.

Brindleyplace and the Ikon Gallery

From the Gas Street Basin, it's a short walk northwest along the canal towpath to the bars, shops and offices of waterside **Brindleyplace**, named after James Brindley, the eighteenth-century engineer responsible for many of Britain's early canals. It's an aesthetically pleasing development where you'll also find the city's much-lauded **Ikon Gallery** (Tues–Sun 11am–6pm; free; Ⓦwww.ikon-gallery .co.uk), housed in a rambling Victorian building and one of the country's most imaginative venues for touring exhibitions of contemporary art.

Along the canal to the National Sea Life Centre and St Paul's

Just beyond Brindleyplace, in front of the huge dome of the National Indoor Arena (NIA), the canal forks: the Birmingham & Fazeley leads northeast (to the right) and the Birmingham Main Line Canal cuts west (to the left), though to complicate matters the latter has a spur loop here, going under Sheepcote Street. Also beside the main canal junction is the shell-like **National Sea Life Centre** (Mon–Fri 10am–4pm, Sat & Sun 10am–5pm; £17.50, children 3 to 14 years £14; Ⓣ0121/643 6777, Ⓦwww.sealifeeurope.com), which can't help but raise a few eyebrows given the city's inland location. Nevertheless, it's an enterprising educational venture, offering Birmingham's landlubbers an opportunity to view and even touch many unusual varieties of fish and sea life – it's so popular with kids that bookings are advised during school holidays.

Beyond the main canal fork, the first part of the **Birmingham & Fazeley Canal** has been attractively restored, its antique brick buildings cleaned of accumulated grime as far as the quaint **Scotland Street Locks**. Further on, the canal cuts past a string of new apartment blocks as well as the (unsigned) flight of steps that leads up to Newhall Street, about half a mile from the main canal junction and just a stone's throw from St Paul's Square, where an attractive ensemble of old houses flank **St Paul's Church**. Dating to the 1770s, the rational symmetries of St Paul's are an excellent illustration of Neoclassical design, though to the people who paid for it (by public subscription), there was much more to the building than aesthetics: gone were the mysteries of the medieval church, replaced by a church of the Enlightenment and one that proved popular with the new industrialists – both Matthew Boulton and James Watt had family pews here, though Watt never actually turned up. Here also, beside the square in Dakota House, on Brook Street, you'll find the **Royal Birmingham Society of Artists** (RBSA; Mon–Fri 10.30am–5.30pm, Sat 10.30am–5pm, Sun 1–5pm; free; Ⓦwww.rbsa.org.uk), which offers an inventive range of fine and applied art exhibitions.

The square is a short haul from St Philip's Cathedral and on the edge of the Jewellery Quarter.

St Philip's Cathedral

One of Birmingham's grandest streets, Colmore Row is framed by a string of fancily carved, High Victorian stone buildings which provide a suitable backdrop for **St Philip's Anglican Cathedral**, a bijou example of English Baroque (Mon–Fri 7.30am–6.30pm, July to early Sept closes 5pm; Sat & Sun 8.30am–5pm; free; Ⓦwww.birminghamcathedral.com). Consecrated in 1715, the church is a handsome affair, its graceful, galleried interior all balance and poise, its harmonies unruffled by the Victorians, who enlarged the original church in the 1880s, when four new stained-glass windows were commissioned from local boy **Edward Burne-Jones**, a leading light of the Pre-Raphaelite movement. The windows are typical of his style – intensely coloured, fastidiously detailed and distinctly sentimental. Three – the *Nativity*, *Crucifixion* and *Ascension* – are at the east end of the church beyond the high altar, the fourth – the *Last Judgement* – is directly opposite.

From the cathedral, it's just a few minutes' walk back to the Rotunda (see p.524).

The Jewellery Quarter

Birmingham's long-established **Jewellery Quarter** (Ⓦwww.the-quarter.com) lies to the northwest of the city centre, beginning just beyond St Paul's Square. Buckle-makers and toy-makers first colonized this area in the 1750s, opening the way for hundreds of silversmiths, jewellers and goldsmiths, and today there are still several hundred jewellery-related companies in the district with most of the **jewellery shops** concentrated along Vittoria Street and its northerly continuation, Vyse Street. The prime attraction hereabouts is the engrossing **Museum of the Jewellery Quarter**, 75–79 Vyse St (Tues–Sat 10.30am–4pm; free), which occupies a former jewellery-maker's that closed down in the early 1980s. What makes it so distinctive is that the owners just shut up shop, leaving everything intact and untouched, down to the dirty teacups. The museum details the rise and fall of the jewellery trade in Birmingham, but it's the old factory that steals the show.

From the museum, it's a couple of minutes' walk back along Vyse Street to the Jewellery Quarter **train station** and **metro stop**, on the Snow Hill line.

The Custard Factory

Below the Bull Ring, **Digbeth** falls away to the southeast. Jammed with traffic and jostled by decrepit industrial buildings, it's hardly enticing, but there are two reasons to venture out here. The first is the coach station on the right; the second – on the left just along and off Gibb Street – is the arts complex that occupies the old **Alfred Bird Custard Factory** (Ⓦwww.custardfactory.co.uk), a handsome, homely affair set around a friendly little courtyard. The **arts complex** offers a fascinating variety of workshops, has gallery space for temporary exhibitions of modern art, and incorporates one of the city's grooviest clubs (see p.530).

Back to Backs

The sheer scale of the industrial boom that gripped nineteenth-century Birmingham is hard to grasp, but the raw statistics speak for themselves: in 1811, there were just 85,000 Brummies, a century later there were literally ten times more. Inevitably, Birmingham's infrastructure could barely cope, particularly in terms of **housing** with the city's newest inhabitants crowded into every conceivable nook and cranny. The concomitant demand for cheap housing spawned the **back-to-back**, quickly erected dwellings that were one room deep and two, sometimes three storeys high, built in groups ("courts") around a courtyard where the communal privies were located. Even by the standards of the time, this was pretty grim stuff and as early as the 1870s Birmingham council banned the construction of any more, though it took several decades to clear those that had already been built. The last Birmingham courts were bulldozed in the 1970s, but one set survived and this, the **Birmingham Back to Backs**, not far from the Bull Ring and on the edge of Chinatown at 55–63 Hurst St, has been restored by the National Trust (Feb–Dec Tues–Sun 10am–5pm; 1hr guided tours on timed ticket; £5.45; bookings on ☎0121/666 7671). The informal guided tour wends its way through four separate homes, each of which represents a different period from the early nineteenth century onwards, with titbits about the families who lived here and lots of period bygones to touch and feel. There is also a room devoted to the history of the back-to-back, and you can even stay here – see p.522 for more.

Eating and drinking

Central Birmingham has a bevy of first-rate **restaurants** with a string of smart, new venues springing up in the slipstream of the burgeoning conference and trade-fair business. Birmingham's gastronomic speciality is the **balti**, a delicious Kashmiri stew cooked and served in a small wok-like dish called a *karahi*, with naan bread instead of cutlery. The original balti houses are concentrated in the gritty suburbs of **Balsall Heath**, **Moseley** and **Sparkhill** to the south of the centre, but nowadays there are now a couple of prime balti houses in the centre too.

City-centre **pubs** vary as much as you'd expect, ranging from slick modern joints catering for a mixed bag of conference delegates and Brummies-out-on-the-ale, to traditional places with hand-pulled real ales and (ersatz) Victorian decor.

Cafés and restaurants

Brasserie de Malmaison 1 Wharfside St, The Mailbox ☏0121/246 5000. Slick and smart brasserie offering a varied menu of both French and English dishes. Prides itself on its use of clearly sourced ingredients. Part of the *Malmaison* hotel (see p.522). Mains £11–18.

Celebrity Balti 44 Broad St ☏0121/643 8969. The days when you had to venture out into the suburbs for a top-ranking balti are over now that this city-centre restaurant is in full swing: the decor may be old-fashioned, but there's little argument about the quality of the food. Baltis cost around £8.

Chez Jules 5a Ethel St, off New St ☏0121/633 4664. Cosy, medium-priced first-floor French restaurant in the city centre, with especially good lunchtime deals. Try the coq au vin; mains average £13 at night, less at lunchtimes. Closed Sun eve.

Chung Ying 16–18 Wrottesley St ☏0121/622 5669. One of the better Cantonese restaurants in the Chinese Quarter, well established – it opened in 1981 – and always busy. Mains £8–12.

Edmunds 6 Central Square, Brindleyplace ☏0121/633 4944. High-style dining in smart contemporary premises with the menu featuring seasonal ingredients – baked turbot with buttered spinach, mussels and Burgundy sauce is typical. A two-course, à la carte meal will set you back £37. Closed Sat lunch & Sun.

Edwardian Tea Room BM&AG, Chamberlain Square. This café-cum-canteen has a great setting in one of the large and fancily decorated halls of the museum's industrial section – hence all the cast-iron columns – but the food is routine.

Metro Bar and Grill 73 Cornwall St ☏0121/200 1911. Slick, very chic Brummie bar/restaurant serving Modern British cuisine with bar plates at just £6. The menu is strong on seasonal, locally sourced ingredients and the long, curved mirror on the back wall adds élan. Mains from £14. Closed Sun.

The Oriental 128 Wharfside St, The Mailbox ☏0121/633 9988. Large and smart restaurant

decorated in a sort of pan-Asian style with a smashing location, down by the canal. The wide-ranging menu features Malay, Thai and Chinese dishes – a place to experiment. Main courses average a very reasonable £10.

Purnells 55 Cornwall St ☏0121/212 9799. Smooth and polished restaurant housed in a Victorian red-brick, though the interior is all soft colours and modern paintings – prestige dining with a three-course à la carte meal costing £45. Brill cooked in coconut milk with Indian red lentils gives the flavour of the menu. Closed Sun, Mon & lunchtime Sat. Reservations essential.

Pubs and bars

Actress & Bishop 35 Ludgate Hill ☏0121/236 7426. Popular bar in a fashionable part of town with a strong line-up of local bands and brews.

Figure of Eight 236 Broad St. Large and popular standard-issue city-centre Wetherspoons pub, but what makes it different is its good-sized beer garden.

The Old Fox 54 Hurst St. Over-modernized but popular pub, with an excellent selection of beers and a boisterous atmosphere. At least the great long windows (of 1891) have survived the updaters.

Old Joint Stock 4 Temple Row West. This delightful pub has the fanciest decor in town – with busts and a balustrade, a balcony and chandeliers, all dating from its days as a bank. Good-quality pub food too.

Sunflower Lounge 76 Smallbrook Queensway. Unusual bar in modern premises on the inner ring road near New Street Station that attracts an indie/student crowd. Covers many bases with quizzes and a big-screen TV plus resident DJs and live gigs. Cool without being pretentious – just as they say on their website.

The Wellington 37 Bennetts Hill. Specialist real-ale pub with a top-notch range of local brews, including those of the much-proclaimed Black Country Brewery, and a central location. Sells ciders too.

Nightlife and entertainment

Nightlife in Birmingham is thriving, and the **club scene** is recognized as one of Britain's best, spanning everything from word-of-mouth underground parties to meat-market mainstream clubs. **Live music** is strong in the city, too, with big-name concerts at several major venues and other, often local bands appearing at some clubs and pubs. Birmingham's showpiece **Symphony Orchestra** and **Royal Ballet** are the spearheads of the city's resurgent **classical scene**.

The social calendar also gets an added fillip from a wide range of upmarket **festivals**, including the **Jazz Festival** (Ⓦwww.birminghamjazzfestival.com) for two weeks in July and the three-day **Artsfest** (Ⓣ0121/464 5678, Ⓦwww.artsfest .org.uk) of film, dance, theatre and music in September.

For current **information** on all events, performances and exhibitions, ask at the tourist office (see p.522) or consult either Ⓦwww.birminghammail.net or Ⓦwww.livebrum.co.uk.

Live music and clubs

Factory Club Custard Factory, Gibb Square, off Digbeth Ⓣ0121/224 7855, Ⓦwww .factoryclub.co.uk. Bar-cum-club in this laid-back, extremely groovy arts complex. Has an eclectic and frequently impeccable music policy, plus juicy live events: one of the best nights out in town.

Gatecrasher 182 Broad St Ⓣ0121/633 1520, Ⓦwww.gatecrasher.com. Birmingham superclub with four levels, six feature areas and nine bars, plus student nights and weekly events. Showcases some real crowd-pleasers like Oakenfold and Faithless.

The Jam House 3 St Paul's Square Ⓣ0121/200 3030, Ⓦwww.thejamhouse.com. Jazz, funk, blues and swing joint pulling in artists from every corner of the globe under the eye of the musical director, Jools Holland. Daily from 6pm.

The Nightingale 18 Kent St Ⓣ0121/622 1718, Ⓦwww.nightingaleclub.co.uk. The king of Brum's gay clubs, but popular with straights too. Five bars, three levels, two discos, a café-bar and even a garden. Just south of the Hippodrome (see below).

O2 Academy 16–18 Horsefair, Bristol St, just south of Holloway Circus Ⓣ0121/622 8250, Ⓦwww .o2academybirmingham.co.uk. State-of-the-art venue with three rooms hosting either gigs or club nights, though the big deal is the top-ranking artists – Ellie Goulding, Paloma Faith, The Courteeners and so forth.

Classical music, theatre, dance and cinema

Birmingham Hippodrome Hurst St Ⓣ0844/338 5000, Ⓦwww.birminghamhippodrome.com.

Lavishly refurbished, the Hippodrome is home to the Birmingham Royal Ballet. Also features touring plays and big pre- and post-West End productions, plus a splendiferous Christmas pantomime.

Birmingham Repertory Theatre Centenary Square, Broad St Ⓣ0121/236 4455, Ⓦwww .birmingham-rep.co.uk. Mixed diet of classics and new work featuring local and experimental writing.

The Crescent Theatre Sheepcote St, Brindley-place Ⓣ0121/643 5858, Ⓦwww.crescent-theatre .co.uk. Adventurous theatre group and venue for visiting companies.

Electric Cinema 47 Station St Ⓣ0121/643 7879, Ⓦwww.theelectric.co.uk. Britain's oldest cinema, housed in a handsome Art Deco building, with an inventive programme of mainstream and art-house films. Sofas and waiter service too.

Old Rep Theatre Station St Ⓣ0121/303 2323, Ⓦwww.oldreptheatre.org.uk. One of Britain's oldest repertory theatres, with regular perform-ances from the imaginative Birmingham Stage Company.

Symphony Hall International Convention Centre, Broad St Ⓣ0121/780 3333, Ⓦwww.thsh.co.uk. Acoustically one of the most advanced concert halls in Europe, home of the acclaimed City of Birmingham Symphony Orchestra (CBSO), as well as a venue for touring music and opera.

Town Hall Broad St Ⓣ0121/780 3333, Ⓦwww .thsh.co.uk. Recently refitted and refurbished, the old Town Hall offers a very varied programme of pop, classical and jazz music through to modern dance and ballet.

Listings

Cricket Warwickshire County Cricket Club play at one of England's most famous grounds, Edgbaston, just to the southwest of the city centre on Edgbaston Rd (Ⓣ0844/635 1902, Ⓦwww .edgbaston.com).

Football Birmingham has three top-flight football teams: Aston Villa, who play at Villa Park, just north of the centre in Aston (Ⓣ0800/612 0970, Ⓦwww .avfc.co.uk); Birmingham City, based at St Andrew's, Small Heath (Ⓣ0844/557 1875,

Ⓦ www.bcfc.com); and West Bromwich Albion, "the
Baggies", who perform at The Hawthorns ground,
northwest of the city in West Bromwich
(☎ 0871/271 9780, Ⓦ www.wba.co.uk).
Internet Free internet access at Birmingham
Central Library, on Chamberlain Square (Mon–Fri

9am–8pm & Sat 9am–5pm; ☎ 0121/303 4511).
Police Steelhouse Lane (☎ 0845/113 5000), near
Snow Hill train station.
Post office 1 Pinfold St, Victoria Square (Mon–Sat
9am–5.30pm).
Taxis Toa Taxis ☎ 0121/427 8888.

Lichfield

Spreading north from the Birmingham conurbation, the miscellaneous landscapes of **Staffordshire** are home to **Alton Towers** (☎ 0871/222 3330, Ⓦ www .altontowers.com; closed mid-Nov to March), the nation's most popular amusement park, with several million visitors annually howling and screaming as they whizz, rattle and plunge around. For quieter mortals, the county has one interesting town, pocket-sized **Lichfield**, about sixteen miles north of Birmingham, which holds a splendid cathedral and was the birthplace of that polymath of all polymaths, **Samuel Johnson**.

Arrival, information and accommodation

Lichfield has **two train stations**: Lichfield City, about five minutes' walk south of the centre, and Lichfield Trent Valley on the eastern fringe of the city, about twenty minutes' walk from the centre. Both have regular services to and from Birmingham New Street. The **bus station** is opposite Lichfield City Station. The **tourist office** shares premises with the Lichfield Garrick Theatre, on Castle Dyke – head south from the Market Square along pedestrianized Baker's Lane and turn right about halfway along (Mon–Sat 9am–5pm; ☎ 01543/412112, Ⓦ www .visitlichfield.com).

Once you've seen the sights, there's no strong reason to hang around, but Lichfield does have a reasonable supply of affordable **B&Bs**. One of the most central is *The Bogey Hole*, an old and well-kept house near the cathedral at 21–23 Dam St (☎ 01543/264303; no credit cards; ❷), with just four guest rooms.

The cathedral

Begun in 1085, but substantially rebuilt on several subsequent occasions, **Lichfield Cathedral** (Mon–Sat 8am–6pm, Sun 8am–5pm; free, but donation requested) is unique in possessing three spires – an appropriate distinction for a bishopric that once extended over virtually all of the Midlands. The church stands on the site of a shrine built for the relics of St Chad, a much-venerated English bishop noted for his humility, who died here in Lichfield in 672.

The cathedral's magnificent **west front** is adorned by over one hundred statues of biblical figures, English kings and the supposed ancestors of Christ, some of them dating back to the thirteenth century, but mostly Victorian replacements of originals destroyed by Cromwell's troops during the Civil War. Inside, the **nave** is supported by two long lines of pointed Gothic arches set beneath an arcaded gallery, which renders the clerestory windows insignificant. The whole effect is rather gloomy, but there's still enough light to admire the soaring **vaulted roof**, which extends without interruption into the choir, looking like the ribcage of a giant beast – a distinctly eerie experience. The **south transept** is earlier than the nave, dating to the 1220s, but the main item of interest here is unreservedly Victorian and imperialist with the railings of **St Michael's Chapel** decorated with replica Zulu shields to celebrate the Staffordshire Regiment's involvement in the

8

THE WEST MIDLANDS AND THE PEAK DISTRICT | Lichfield

Zulu War. Beyond the transepts, most of the choir is resolutely Middle Gothic and on its south side a narrow stone stairway leads up to both a fine **minstrels' gallery** and the **St Chad's Head Chapel**, where the head of the saint was once displayed to cheer up the faithful. Most impressive of all, however, is the **Lady Chapel**, at the far end of the choir, which boasts a set of magnificent sixteenth-century windows, purchased from a Cistercian abbey in Belgium in 1802.

The cathedral's greatest treasure, the **Chad Gospels**, is displayed in the **chapter house**, off the north side of the choir. A rare and exquisite example of Anglo-Saxon artistry dating to the eighth century, this illuminated manuscript contains the complete gospels of Matthew and Mark, and a fragment of the gospel of Luke, written in Latin and with different pages exhibited at different times. The fact that the book ends midway through St Luke means it's almost certainly the first part of a two-volume set – and rare-book specialists have long been on the lookout for the other tome.

The rest of the town

Encircling the cathedral is **The Close**, which, with its good-looking medley of Tudor, Georgian and Victorian buildings, is the prettiest place in town. From the southeast corner of The Close, it's a short walk along **Dam Street** – past the gloomy waters of the Minster Pool – to the **Market Square**, where there's a peculiar little statue of a puck-nosed Boswell and a much better one honouring **Samuel Johnson**, who looks suitably intellectual. The plinth below the statue is carved with three key scenes from Johnson's life. The most revealing shows Johnson making a public penance in Uttoxeter Market Place for the sin – as he saw it – of refusing to work on his father's bookstall fifty years before.

At the back of the Market Place stands St Mary's Church, unremarkable in itself but home to the **Lichfield Heritage Centre** (Mon–Sat 9.30am–4pm, Sun 10am–4pm; £3.50), which tracks the city's history, with an illuminating section on its role in the Civil War. On the outside wall of the church several **plaques** commemorate noteworthy incidents. One of them is a memorial to the unfortunate Edward Wightman, who was burnt at the stake for heresy on this very spot in 1612 – the last Englishman to be so punished for this particular crime. Also on the Market Square is the **Samuel Johnson Birthplace Museum** (daily: April–Sept 10.30am–4.30pm; Oct–March 11am–4.30pm; free). The great man's father – Michael – was a bookseller and this house, a narrow three-storey affair, was both the family home and his place of work. The museum's ground floor still serves as a **bookshop** – with copies of Boswell's biography and many of Johnson's works – while up above, on the first floor, a film provides a well-considered potted introduction to its subject. Thereafter, a series of modest displays explores Johnson's life and times with the top floor holding a small collection of personal memorabilia, including Johnson's favourite armchair, his **chocolate pot** (chocolate was a real delicacy in Georgian times), bib holder, shoe buckles and ivory writing tablets.

Eating, drinking and entertainment

Chapters, next to the cathedral on the south side of The Close, is an old-fashioned **café** with a pleasant atmosphere and inexpensive home-made food. For something more substantial, head for Bird Street, two short blocks southwest of the Market Square, where there is a whole slew of **restaurants**, including *Siam Corner Ma Ma Thai* at no.17 (℡01543/411911; closed Sun & Mon lunch), a smart and modern Thai place serving all the classics; main courses start at about £8. Finally, the **Lichfield Garrick Theatre** (℡01543/412121, ⓦwww.lichfieldgarrick.com), in the centre on Castle Dyke, offers a lively programme of comedy, music, dance and theatre.

Derbyshire and the Peak District

In 1951, the hills and dales of the **Peak District**, at the southern tip of the Pennine range, became Britain's first national park. Wedged between **Derby**, Manchester and Sheffield, it is effectively the backyard for the fifteen million people who live within an hour's drive of its boundaries, though somehow it accommodates the huge influx with minimum fuss and precious little pretension.

Landscapes in the Peak District come in two forms. The brooding high moorland tops of **Dark Peak**, to the east of Manchester, take their name from the underlying gritstone, known as millstone grit for its former use – a function commemorated in the millstones demarcating the park boundary. Windswept, mist-shrouded and inhospitable, the flat tops of these peaks are nevertheless a firm favourite with walkers on the **Pennine Way**, which meanders north from the tiny village of **Edale** to the Scottish border (see box, p.543). Altogether more forgiving, the southern limestone hills of the **White Peak** have been eroded into deep forested dales populated by small stone villages and often threaded by walking trails, some of which follow former rail routes. The limestone is riddled with complex cave systems around **Castleton** and on the periphery of **Buxton**, a charming former spa town lying just outside the park's boundaries and at the end of an industrialized corridor that reaches out from Manchester. Elsewhere, one of the country's most distinctive manorial piles, **Chatsworth House**, stands near **Bakewell**, a town famed locally not just for its cakes but also for its **well dressing**, a possibly pagan ritual of thanksgiving for fresh water that takes place

Samuel Johnson

Eighteenth-century England's most celebrated wit and critic, **Samuel Johnson** was born above his father's bookshop in Lichfield in 1709. From here he went to Pembroke College, Oxford, which he left in 1731 without having completed his degree. Disgruntled with academia, Johnson returned to Staffordshire as a **teacher** and later, after three years in Birmingham, it was here that he opened his own private school. The school was no great success, however, so Johnson abandoned the project and went to London along with his wife and the young **David Garrick**, their star pupil. Journalism and essays were the mainstay of the Johnsons' penurious existence until publisher Robert Dodsley asked Samuel to consider compiling a **Dictionary of the English Language**, a project that nobody had undertaken before, and which was to occupy him for eight years prior to its publication in 1755. Massively learned and full of mordant wit ("lexicographer: a writer of dictionaries; a harmless drudge"), the dictionary is one of Johnson's greatest legacies, although he was financially and emotionally stretched to breaking point by the workload it imposed. The dictionary was widely acclaimed, but, despite his increasing celebrity, **money problems** continued to assail him until the early 1760s when the new king, George III, granted him a bursary of £300 per annum.

In 1763 Johnson met **James Boswell**, a pushy young Scot who clung tenaciously to the cantankerous older man until he learned to like him. Their journey to Scotland resulted in one of the finest travel books ever written, *A Journey to the Western Isles of Scotland* (1775), in which Johnson's fascinated incredulity at the native way of life makes for absorbing reading. Other publications from his final decade included a preface to Shakespeare's plays, a series of political tracts and the magnificent *Lives of the English Poets*. However, the work by which he is now best known is not one that he wrote himself – it's Boswell's *The Life of Samuel Johnson*, commenced on its subject's death in 1784, published in 1791 and still one of the English language's most full-blooded biographies. Johnson was buried in Westminster Abbey.

in about thirty local villages each summer. The well-dressing season starts in May and continues through to mid-September with exact dates and details on ⓦ www.welldressing.com.

There's no obvious **route** around the Peaks, but the one outlined below comes in from the south – from Derby – and then cuts up to Buxton before looping round in a clockwise direction to Castleton, Hathersage, Baslow, Bakewell and points in between. The nearest motorway is the **M1** – come off at either junction 29 or 30 and you're within easy striking distance of workaday **Chesterfield**, whose famous **crooked spire** announces the start of the Peak District in conspicuous style. As for a base, Buxton is your best bet by a (fairly) long chalk, though if you're after hiking and cycling you'll probably prefer one of the area's villages – Edale and Castleton will do very nicely.

Public transport

There are frequent **trains** south from Manchester to end-of-the-line Buxton, and Manchester–Sheffield trains cut through Edale and Hathersage. The main **bus** access is via the Trent Barton bus company's **TransPeak** (ⓦ www.transpeak.co.uk) service from Nottingham to Manchester via Derby, Bakewell and Buxton, which runs every one to two hours daily; the whole journey takes three and a half hours. Otherwise, First (ⓦ www.firstgroup.com) bus #272 runs regularly from Sheffield to Castleton, via Hathersage and Hope, and TM Travel (ⓦ www.tmtravel.co.uk) bus #65 connects Sheffield to Buxton via Eyam. Once you've reached the Peak District, you'll find that **local bus services** are really rather good, though not so much on Sundays and in the depths of winter. Local tourist offices almost always have bus and train timetables, including the encyclopedic *Peak District Bus Timetable*, or go online to ⓦ www.derbysbus.info).

The Peak District has a good network of dedicated **cycle lanes** and trails, sometimes along former railway lines, and the National Park Authority (for contact details, see below) operates three **cycle rental** outlets: at Ashbourne (ⓣ 01335/343156); Derwent, Bamford (ⓣ 01433/651261); and Parsley Hay, Buxton (ⓣ 01298/84493).

Information

The **Peak District National Park Authority** (ⓣ 01629/816200, ⓦ www .peakdistrict.gov.uk) operates four **visitor centres**, including one in Bakewell and another in Castleton, and these supplement a host of town and village tourist offices. A variety of **maps** and **trail guides** is widely available across the Peaks, but for the non-specialist it's hard to beat the **Grate Little Guides**, a series of leaflets which provide hiking suggestions and trail descriptions for a dozen or so localities in a clear and straightforward style. They cost £2.50 each and are on sale at almost every tourist office and information centre, but note that the maps printed on the leaflets are best used in conjunction with an OS map. Finally, there are two other official Peak District **websites**, ⓦ www.visitpeakdistrict.com and www.peak-experience.org.uk.

Accommodation

As you might expect, there's a plethora of **accommodation** in the Peaks, mostly in **B&Bs**, though one of the area's distinctive features is the quality of its **country hotels** – like the ones in Ashford in the Water (see p.549), Baslow (see p.546) and Hassop (see p.548); the greatest concentration of first-rate B&Bs is, however, in Buxton. The Peak District also holds numerous **campsites** and half a dozen or so **YHA hostels** as well as a network of YHA-operated **camping barns**. For further details, consult ⓦ www.yha.org.uk.

Derby

DERBY may be close to the wilds of the Peak District, but it has more in common with its big-city neighbours, Nottingham and Leicester, with whom it shares an industrial tradition, its most famous company being **Rolls-Royce**. For years, Derby city centre was really rather dull, but recent attempts to spruce things up have proved very successful and there's one prime attraction in the centre too, **Derby Museum and Art Gallery**, which holds an outstanding collection of paintings by Joseph Wright. The gallery is located just to the west of the city's spacious, central **Market Place** and to the southwest of the city's most impressive building, the **cathedral**, whose ponderous medieval tower rises high above its modest Victorian surroundings and boasts a wide and particularly graceful Georgian nave. An hour or two will do to see the sights before you hightail it off to the Peak District.

Derby Museum and Art Gallery

Among much else, **Derby Museum and Art Gallery**, in the centre of the city on The Strand (Mon 11am–5pm, Tues–Sat 10am–5pm, Sun 1–4pm; free), exhibits a splendid collection of Derby **porcelain**, several hundred pieces tracking through its different phases and styles from the mid-eighteenth century until today. The museum also has a period room devoted to Charles Edward Stuart – aka **Bonnie Prince Charlie** – who attempted to seize the throne from George II in the Jacobite Rebellion of 1745. Advancing south from Scotland, Charles and his army got as far as Derby, spreading panic in London, but, unable to press their advantage, it was here they turned round for the long and dismal retreat that ended with their defeat at the Battle of Culloden. The museum's star turn, however, is its prime collection of the work of **Joseph Wright** (1734–97), a local artist generally regarded as one of the most talented English painters of his generation. Typical of his style is his portrait of *Sir Richard Arkwright*, looking uncompromising and very porky. More importantly, Wright was one of the few artists of his period to find inspiration in technology and his depictions of the scientific world were hugely influential – as in his *The Alchemist Discovering Phosphorus* and *A Philosopher Lecturing on the Orrery*.

Practicalities

Derby **train station** is a mile to the southeast of the city centre – just follow the signs – but it's a dreary walk, so you're better off taking a taxi. The brand-new **bus station** is more convenient, on Morledge, a couple of minutes' walk southeast of the Market Place, which is where you'll find the **tourist office** (Mon–Sat 9.30am–5pm, Sun 10.30am–2.30pm; ℡01332/255802, ⓦwww.visitderby.co.uk). For light bites and the best **coffee** in town, head for the *Big Blue Coffee Company*, metres from the Derby Museum at 47 Sadler Gate (closed Sun). For something more substantial, make a beeline for the *European Restaurant & Bistro*, above a shop and in an attractive old building just across the street from the cathedral at 22 Irongate (℡01332/368 7320; closed all day Sun & Mon lunch). The menu here is strong on Italian dishes with the likes of *penne con pancetta* costing around £9.

Ashbourne and around

Sitting pretty on the edge of the Peaks twelve miles northwest of Derby, **ASHBOURNE** is an amiable little town, whose stubby, cobbled **Market Place** is flanked by a happy ensemble of old red-brick buildings. Hikers tramp into town from the neighbouring dales to hang around the square's cafés and pubs, and stroll down the hill from the Market Place to take a peek at the suspended wooden beam spanning St John's Street. Once a common feature of English towns, but now a rarity, these **gallows** were not warnings to malcontents, but advertising hoardings.

Walk west along St John's and then Church Street from the gallows and you soon spot the sterling outline of **St Oswald's Church**, an imposing lime- and ironstone structure dating from the thirteenth century. Something of an architectural muddle, the interior of the church is intriguing nonetheless, its columns decorated with all sorts of miniature sculptures and graced by handsome stained-glass windows. In the east aisle of the north transept, the **Cockayne Chapel** is named after the eponymous clan of local landowners who lie buried here. Of the five main table-tombs in and just outside the chapel the earliest dates from 1372, the latest from 1592, and taken together they illustrate changing fashions culminating in the elaborate ruffs and hats that were so very popular with the Elizabethans.

Practicalities

Ashbourne is not on the rail network, but the **bus station** is conveniently located off Dig Street, a couple of minutes' walk from the Market Place, where the **tourist office** (March–Oct daily 10am–5pm; Nov–Feb Mon–Sat 10.30am–4pm; ℡01335/343666, ⓦwww.visitpeakdistrict.com) has reams of hiking maps and guides, including the first-rate *Grate Little Guide to Dovedale* (see p.534). They can also advise on accommodation, though Ashbourne is best regarded as a pit-stop rather than as a base for further wanderings.

Ashbourne boasts a first-rate **delicatessen**, Patrick & Brooksbank, 22 Market Place (closed Sun), which has a superb selection of takeaway food, including local cheeses and hams – perfect for a picnic. The best **café** in town is in Bennetts department store, footsteps from the Market Place at 19 St John St (closed Sun); they do a good line in home-made cakes, scones and sandwiches.

Around Ashbourne: Dovedale

The **River Dove** wriggles its way across the Peak District, cutting a circuitous course from the high hills of Derbyshire to the flatlands southwest of Derby, where it joins the River Trent. The Dove is at its scenic best just four miles north of Ashbourne in the stirring two-mile gorge that comprises **Dovedale** – confusingly, other parts of the river are situated in different dales. To get to Dovedale, head north from Ashbourne along the A515 and then follow the signs to the car park, which is on a narrow country road just beyond the hamlet of Thorpe – and a half-mile or so before you reach minuscule **Ilam**. The **hike** along the gorge is a real pleasure and easy to boot, the only problem being the bogginess of the valley after rain, but be warned that the place heaves with visitors on summer weekends and bank holidays.

Hartington

Best approached from the east, through the boisterous scenery of Hand Dale, **HARTINGTON**, thirteen miles north of Ashbourne via the A515, is one of the prettiest villages in the Peaks, its easy ramble of stone houses zeroing in on a tiny duck pond. The village is also within easy walking distance of the River Dove as well as a sequence of handsome limestone dales – **Biggin Dale** is perhaps the pick. The other excitement is cheese – the village has its own specialist **cheese shop** with a battery of local and international cheeses with chutneys to lighten the gastronomic load.

Buses to Hartington stop a few yards from the duck pond. The village has several **B&Bs**, one of the most attractive of which is the *Parsons House*, in a sympathetically revamped old stone building on Mill Lane (℡01298/84801, ⓦwww.peakdistrictonline.co.uk; ❷). A second good choice is *The Hayloft* (℡01298/84358,

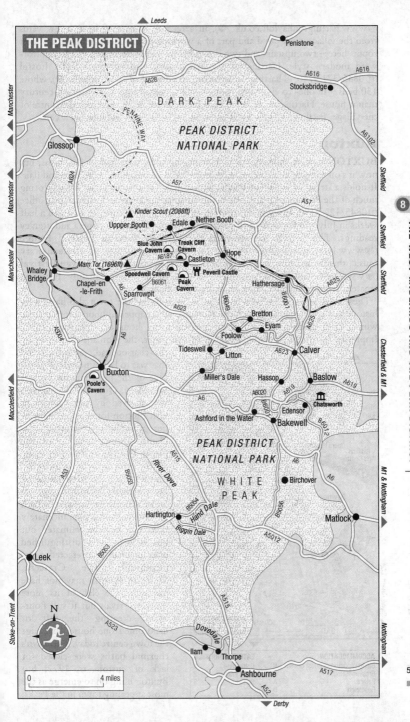

THE PEAK DISTRICT

DARK PEAK

PEAK DISTRICT
NATIONAL PARK

Leeds

Penistone

Stocksbridge

A628

A616

A616

A6102

PENNINE WAY

Glossop

A624

A57

Sheffield

A57

Sheffield

Kinder Scout (2088ft)

Uppper Booth

Edale

Nether Booth

Blue John Cavern

Treak Cliff Cavern

Mam Tor (1696ft)

Castleton

Hope

Whaley Bridge

Speedwell Cavern

Peak Cavern

Peveril Castle

Sheffield

Chapel-en-le-Frith

Sparrowpit

Hathersage

A6187

B6061

A623

B6049

Bretton

Eyam

Foolow

A625

B6001

B625

Tideswell

Litton

A623

Calver

Miller's Dale

Hassop

Baslow

Chesterfield & M1

Buxton

A6

A6020

A619

A619

Poole's Cavern

B600

Edensor

Chatsworth

Ashford in the Water

Bakewell

A6

B6012

A5004

A53

PEAK DISTRICT
NATIONAL PARK

WHITE PEAK

Birchover

A6

M1 & Nottingham

A515

River Dove

B6055

B6054

Hand Dale

Hartington

Biggin Dale

A5012

B6053

Matlock

B6056

Leek

Stoke-on-Trent

Macclesfield

Manchester

Manchester

Manchester

Manchester

A523

N

Dovedale

Ilam

Thorpe

Ashbourne

A515

A517

Nottingham

A52

Derby

0   4 miles

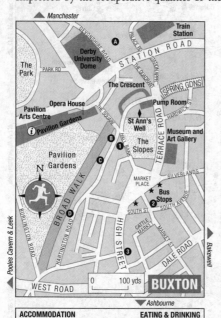

Ⓦ www.hartingtonhayloft.co.uk; ❷), in a recently converted barn, a few yards from the village duck pond and part of a working farm. There are just four guest rooms here – two upstairs and two down below – each decorated in a straightforward modern style. Hartington also has a very well equipped **YHA hostel** (☎ 0845/371 9740, Ⓔ hartington@yha.org.uk; dorm beds £12, doubles ❶), whose 130 beds – in one- to eight-bed rooms – are squeezed into a seventeenth-century manor house, Hartington Hall, on Hall Bank, about 300 yards from the centre of the village. Facilities include a self-catering kitchen, a café and internet access.

Buxton

BUXTON, twelve miles north of Hartington, may have had its doldrums, but now it's on the way up, its centre revamped and reconfigured with care and flair. It holds a string of excellent B&Bs, which makes it a perfect base for exploring much of the Peaks, and it also boasts the outstanding **Buxton Festival** (box office ☎ 0845/127 2190, Ⓦ www.buxtonfestival.co.uk), which runs for two and a half weeks in July and features a full programme of classical music, opera and literary readings. The festival has spawned the first-rate **Buxton Festival Fringe** (Ⓦ www.buxtonfringe.org.uk), also in July, which focuses on contemporary music, theatre and film, but the biggest fiesta is the **Gilbert & Sullivan Festival** (Ⓦ www.gs-festival.co.uk), a three-week affair in August mainly featuring amateur troupes and attracting enthusiastic audiences.

These festivals have added a real zip to Buxton, but the town also has a long history as a **spa**, beginning with the Romans, who happened upon a spring from which 1500 gallons of pure water gushed every hour at a constant 28°C. Impressed by the recuperative qualities of the water, the Romans came here by the chariot-load, setting a trend that was to last hundreds of years. One of the most famous visitors was Mary, Queen of Scots, who was allowed by her captors to visit Buxton for the treatment of her rheumatism; another was Daniel Defoe, who loved the place. The spa's salad days came at the end of the eighteenth century with the **fifth Duke of Devonshire**'s grand design to create a northern answer to Bath or Cheltenham, a plan ultimately thwarted by the climate, but not before some distinguished buildings had been erected, most memorably The Crescent. Victorian Buxton may not have had quite the élan of its more southerly rivals but it still flourished, creating the raft of handsome stone houses that edge the town centre today. The town's **thermal baths** were closed for lack of custom in 1972, but Buxton hung on to emerge as the most appealing town in the Peaks.

ACCOMMODATION		EATING & DRINKING	
Buxton's Victorian Guest House	C	Columbine	1
Grosvenor House	B	Nat's Kitchen	2
Palace	A	Sun Inn	3
Roseleigh	D		

Arrival and information

Hourly trains from Manchester Piccadilly pull into Buxton **train station,** three minutes' walk from the town centre. **Buses,** including the **TransPeak** (see p.534), stop in the Market Place. The permanent home of the **tourist office** is in The Crescent, but during renovation work, which will last till 2012, it has been moved to the Pavilion Gardens, behind the Opera House (daily: April–Oct 9.30am–5pm; Nov–March 10am–4pm; ☎01298/25106, ⍟www.visitbuxton.co.uk). It operates an accommodation booking service and has plentiful information on the town in particular and the Peaks in general.

Accommodation

Buxton town centre is liberally sprinkled with first-rate **B&Bs** and **hotels,** with several of the best located on pedestrianized Broad Walk, where a string of distinguished Edwardian and Victorian stone houses face out onto the Pavilion Gardens. Finding somewhere to stay is rarely a problem, except during the Buxton Festival (see opposite), when advance reservations are well-nigh essential.

Buxton's Victorian Guest House 3a Broad Walk ☎01298/78759, ⍟www.buxtonvictorian.co.uk. Cosy B&B in a grand Victorian house with a handful of well-appointed rooms decorated in a distinctly frilly version of period style from four-posters to Indian-print cushions. Breakfasts feature local produce wherever feasible. ❸

Grosvenor House 1 Broad Walk ☎01298/72439, ⍟www.grosvenorbuxton .co.uk. There are eight en-suite guest rooms – seven doubles and one single – in this friendly B&B in a handsome Victorian townhouse. The rooms are decorated in unfussy period decor – several have lovely quilts – and the pick have gentle views over the gardens. Delicious home-made breakfasts too. ❷

Palace Palace Rd ☎01298/22001, ⍟www .barcelo-hotels.co.uk. Built to impress, the *Palace* was the pride of the Victorian spa, its sweeping stone facade with its pediments, pilasters, balconies and imposing central tower lording it over the town centre from the high ground of Palace Rd. The hotel, which has recently become part of the Barceló chain, is a lot less glamorous today, but there's no gainsaying the grandness of the entrance lobby and the soaring staircase beyond. The bedrooms are very comfortable and although the decor is modern, some have a quirky antique charm, as do the long, echoing corridors. ❹

Roseleigh 19 Broad Walk ☎01298/24904, ⍟www.roseleighhotel.co.uk. This classic, three-storey gritstone Victorian townhouse, overlooking Pavilion Gardens, is an excellent place to stay, its neat and trim public rooms decorated in attractive Victorian style, the en-suite bedrooms beyond similarly well appointed. Family-run and competitively priced. ❸

The Town

The centrepiece of Buxton's hilly, compact centre is **The Crescent**, a broad sweep of Georgian stonework commissioned by the fifth Duke of Devonshire in 1780 and modelled on the Royal Crescent in Bath. It was cleaned and scrubbed a few years ago, but has lain idle ever since, though work will soon start on turning it into a five-star hotel complete with thermal baths. Facing The Crescent, and also currently empty, is the old **Pump Room**, an attractive Victorian building where visitors once sampled the local waters; next to it is a **water fountain**, supplied by St Ann's Well and still used to fill many a local water bottle. For a better view of The Crescent and the town centre, clamber up **The Slopes**, a narrow slice of park that rises behind the Pump Room dotted with decorative urns and a home to a war memorial. From here, it's impossible to miss the enormous **dome** of what was originally the Duke of Devonshire's stables and riding school, erected in 1789. For decades, the building was used as a hospital, but it's now part of Derby University.

Next to The Crescent, the appealing old stone buildings of **The Square** – though square it isn't – nudge up to the grandly refurbished **Buxton Opera House**, an Edwardian extravagance whose twin towers, cherubs and Tiffany glass date from 1903. Stretching back from the Opera House are the **Pavilion Gardens**, a slender string of connected buildings distinguished by their wrought-iron work and culminating in a large and glassy dome, the **Octagon**, which was originally a music hall. The Pavilion Gardens are currently being expanded to include a brand-new concert hall, the **Pavilion Arts Centre**, with a projected completion date of 2011. The adjoining **park**, also known as the Pavilion Gardens and cut across by the River Wye, is particularly pleasant, its immaculate lawns and neat borders graced by a bandstand, ponds, dinky little footbridges and fountains.

The Market Place and the Museum and Art Gallery

From the south end of The Square, the fetching stone terrace that comprises **Hall Bank** scuttles up to the wide and breezy **Market Place**. There's nothing much here to hold the eye, but it's only a few yards back down the hill along Terrace Road to the first-rate **Buxton Museum and Art Gallery** (Tues–Fri 9.30am–5.30pm, Sat 9.30am–5pm, plus Easter–Sept Sun 10.30am–5pm; free). The museum begins well with its ground floor largely devoted to enterprising temporary displays featuring the work of local contemporary artists. There's also a period room dedicated to two Victorian archeologist-cum-geologists – William Boyd Dawkins and Wilfred Jackson – who spent decades exploring and explaining the Peaks. Upstairs, the large and proficient "Wonders of the Peak" display tracks through the history of the region from its geological construction through the Romans and on to the Victorians. The most diverting section here deals with the **petrifactioners**, who turned local semi-precious stones into ornaments and jewellery designed to tickle the fancy of visitors to the town. By the 1840s, Buxton had no less than fourteen petrifactioners' shops, selling every stone trinket imaginable from plates and stone eggs to vases and obelisks. A variety of materials were used, but the two favourites were Blue John fluorspar (also see p.542) and Ashford black marble, actually a dark limestone; the museum displays a superb collection of both.

Poole's Cavern

The Peaks are riddled with cave systems and around half a dozen have become popular tourist attractions. One is **Poole's Cavern** (daily 9.30am–5pm; £8; Ⓦwww.poolescavern.co.uk), whose impressively large chambers are home to a host of orange and blue-grey stalactites and stalagmites. The cavern is located about a mile to the southwest of central Buxton just off Green Lane – take the A53 road towards Macclesfield and Leek and watch for the sign.

Eating and drinking

There are two very good **restaurants** in Buxton beginning with the *Columbine*, a small and intimate place right in the centre at 7 Hall Bank (eve only; closed Sun, plus Tues Nov–March; ℡01298/78752). The menu here is short but imaginative with main courses – such as saddle of monkfish with crab risotto – averaging £14; pre-theatre dinners are available by prior reservation from about 5pm. An excellent second choice is *Nat's Kitchen*, 9 Market St (℡01298/214642; closed Sun eve & Mon), a bright and cheerful little place with an ambitious menu – guinea fowl with vegetable macédoine and foie gras sauce, for example; main courses here cost £11. There's also the *Sun Inn*, a fine old **pub** with antique beamed rooms just south of the Market Place at 33 High St. It offers real ales and first-rate bar food – beef-in-ale pies for instance for just £8.50 – and is also the best place for a pint.

Castleton

The agreeable little village of **CASTLETON**, ten miles northeast of Buxton, lies on the northern edge of the White Peak, its huddle of old stone cottages ringed by hills and set beside a babbling brook. As a starting point for local walks the place is hard to beat, and the hikers resting up in the **Market Place**, just off the main drag behind the church, have the choice of a healthy spread of local accommodation and services. Overseeing the whole caboodle is **Peveril Castle** (April–Oct daily 10am–5pm; Nov–March Mon & Thurs–Sun 10am–4pm; £4.20; EH), from which the village takes its name. William the Conqueror's illegitimate son William Peveril raised the first fortifications here to protect the king's rights to the forest that then covered the district, but most of the remains – principally the ruinous square keep – date to the 1170s. After a stiff climb up to the keep, you can trace much of the surviving curtain wall, which commands great views over the Hope Valley down below.

Arrival and information

The most scenic approach to Castleton is from **Sparrowpit**, about five miles to the west and on the A623, from where the road wiggles through the dramatic **Winnats Pass**, but the principal **bus** service arrives from the east – from Sheffield, Hathersage and Hope (South Yorkshire First bus #272; hourly). There are no **trains** to Castleton – the nearest you'll get is **Hope**, a couple of miles or so to the east along the valley. The **Castleton Visitor Centre** (daily: April–Oct 9.30am–5.30pm; Nov–March 10am–5pm; T01629/816572, W www.visitpeakdistrict .com), a combined museum, community centre and tourist office, stands beside the car park on the west side of the village, just off the main street (also the A6187). They sell **hiking leaflets and maps**, which are invaluable for a string of walking routes that take you up to the swollen hilltops that rise in every direction.

Accommodation

Accommodation in Castleton should be booked in advance at holiday times. Cream of the B&B crop is the *Causeway House*, in an old and well-tended stone cottage just north of the Market Place on Back Street (T01433/623291, W www .causewayhouse.co.uk; ②), which has five guest rooms, three en suite, each tastefully kitted out to make the most of the cottage's original features. A second good choice is *Bargate Cottage*, at the top end of the Market Place (T01433/620201, W www.bargatecottage.co.uk; ②). Also in an old stone cottage, its rooms are rather more traditional and a good bit frillier. Finally, the **YHA hostel** (T0845/371 9628, E castleton@yha.org.uk; dorm beds £14, doubles ①) is housed in Castleton Hall, a capacious if somewhat careworn old stone mansion on the Market Place. The hostel is well equipped with a self-catering kitchen, a café, cycle store and drying room, and its 135 beds are parcelled up into two- to six-bed rooms, many of which are en suite.

Eating and drinking

Castleton's **pubs** are its gastronomic mainstay and there's nowhere better than *The George*, on Castle Street, yards from the Market Place, which offers tasty bar food at affordable prices. The best **tearoom** in town is the *Three Roofs*, beside the main road on the west side of the village, where they have a bash at everything, from big breakfasts to home-made cakes, and they do it very well.

Around Castleton: the caves

The limestone hills pressing in on Castleton are riddled with water-worn **cave systems**, four of which have been developed as tourist attractions. Each can be reached by car or on foot, with Speedwell Cavern accessible via a three-and-a-half-mile circular trail from Castleton that takes two hours. Castleton's tourist office (see above) has the leaflet and sells the maps, though most visitors settle for just one set of caves – either the Peak Cavern or the Treak Cliff Cavern will do very nicely.

The Peak and Speedwell caverns

Peak Cavern is the handiest of the four cave systems (April–Oct daily 10am–5pm; Nov–March Sat & Sun 10am–5pm; £7.75, combined with Speedwell £13; Ⓦwww.peakcavern.co.uk), tucked into a gully at the back of Castleton, its gaping mouth once providing shelter for a rope factory and a small village. Daniel Defoe, visiting in the eighteenth century, noted the cavern's colourful local name, the **Devil's Arse**, a reference to the fiendish fashion in which its interior contours twisted and turned.

Not too far away, 700 yards or so west from the village along the main road, is **Speedwell Cavern** (daily 10am–5pm; £8.25, combined with Peak Cavern £13; Ⓦwww.speedwellcavern.co.uk). At 600 feet below ground, this is the deepest of the cave systems, but the main drama comes with the means of access – down a hundred dripping steps and then by boat through a quarter-mile-long claustrophobic tunnel that was blasted out in search of lead. At the end lies the Bottomless Pit, a pool where 40,000 tonnes of mining rubble were once dumped without raising the water level one iota.

The Treak Cliff and Blue John caverns

The other two caves are the world's only source of the sparkling fluorspar known as **Blue John**. Highly prized for ornaments and jewellery since Georgian times, this semi-precious stone comes in a multitude of hues from blue through deep red to yellow, depending on its hydrocarbon impurities. Before being cut and polished, it is soaked in pine resin, a process originally carried out in France, where the term *bleu et jaune* (after its primary colours) provided its English name. The **Treak Cliff Cavern** (daily 10am–5pm; £7.95; Ⓦwww.bluejohnstone.com), about 800 yards west of Castleton up off a minor road, contains the best examples of the stone *in situ* and a good deal more in the shop. This is also the best cave to visit in its own right, dripping – literally – with ancient stalactites, flowstone and bizarre rock formations, all visible on an entertaining forty-minute walking tour through the main cave system.

Further afield, just two miles or so west of Castleton off the B6061, tours of the **Blue John Cavern** (daily: April–Oct 9.30am–5.30pm; Nov–March 10am–dusk; £8; Ⓦwww.bluejohn-cavern.com) dive deep into the rock, with narrow steps and sloping paths following an ancient watercourse. The tour leads through whirlpool-hollowed chambers to Lord Mulgrave's Dining Room, a cavern where the eponymous lord and owner once put on a banquet for his miners. A goodly sample of Blue John is on sale at the cavern gift shop.

Edale village

There's almost nothing to **EDALE village**, about five miles northwest of Castleton, except for a slender, half-mile trail of stone houses, which march up the main street from the train station with a couple of pubs, an old stone church and a scattering of B&Bs on the way – and it's this somnambulant air that is its immediate appeal. The village is also extremely popular with walkers, who arrive in droves throughout the year to set off on the 268-mile **Pennine Way** (see box opposite) across England's backbone to the Scottish border; the route's starting-point is signposted from outside the *Old Nag's Head* at the head of the village. If that sounds much too daunting, then there are lots of more manageable alternatives, including an excellent **circular walk** (9 miles; 5hr) that takes in the first part of the Pennine Way, leading up onto the bleak, gritstone table-top of **Kinder Scout** (2088ft), below which Edale cowers. This was the site of the famous **Kinder Scout Trespass** of 1932, which began when several hundred ramblers walked onto unused but private land despite the best efforts of the owner's gamekeepers, the owner being the Duke of Devonshire. Afterwards, six of the ramblers were arrested and imprisoned, prompting a huge public outcry and a mass trespass involving no less than ten thousand walkers, a public demonstration that proved to be the turning point in the long fight for public access to open moorland.

Practicalities

Edale village **train station** is on the Sheffield–Manchester line and there is also a Sunday-only **bus** service from Castleton. From Edale train station, it's 400 yards or so up the road to the **Peak District's National Park Moorland Centre** (April–Sept Mon–Fri 9.30am–5pm, Sat & Sun 9.30am–5.30pm; Oct–March Mon–Fri 10am–3.30pm, Sat & Sun 9.30am–4.30pm; ☎01433/670207). The **YHA hostel** (☎0845/371 9514, ✉edale@yha.org.uk; dorm beds £16, doubles ①) is located about two miles east of Edale train station at Rowland Cote, Nether Booth. It's clearly signed from the road into Edale or you can hoof it there across the fields from near the Moorland Centre. The hostel has 157 beds in two- to ten-bed rooms, a good range of facilities from a laundry and a café through to a self-catering kitchen, and also offers an extensive programme of **outdoor activities**, though these need to be booked in advance, as does accommodation. Naturally enough, the hostel is popular with Pennine Way walkers – as is the **campsite** and **camping barn** at *Upper Booth Farm* (☎01433/670250, ⊛www.upperbooth camping.co.uk), west of the village on the way to Kinder Scout. Among several **B&Bs** in the village, the pick is *Stonecroft*, a detached Edwardian house with two pleasantly comfortable guest rooms near the church (☎01433/670262, ⊛www .stonecroftguesthouse.co.uk; ③). The hiker-friendly *Rambler*, yards from the train station at the bottom of the village, serves filling bar **food**.

The Pennine Way

The 268-mile-long **Pennine Way** (⊛www.nationaltrail.co.uk) was the country's first official long-distance footpath, opened in 1965. It stretches north from the boggy plateau of the Peak District's Kinder Scout, through the Yorkshire Dales and Teesdale, crossing Hadrian's Wall and the Northumberland National Park, before entering Scotland to fizzle out at the village of Kirk Yetholm. People had been using a similar route for over thirty years before the official opening, inspired by **Tom Stephenson**, secretary of the Ramblers' Association, who had first identified the need for such a long-distance path in the 1930s. His idea was to stick to the crest of the Pennines where practicable and link up existing tracks, bridleways and footpaths, only descending to the valleys for overnight accommodation and services. The problem was that much of the route lay on private land, so years of negotiation and re-routing were necessary before the Pennine Way could be officially declared open.

Nowadays, the route is one of the most popular walks in the country, whether taken in sections or attempted in one go, which takes two to three weeks, depending on levels of fitness and experience. It's a challenge in the best of weather, since it passes through some of the most remote countryside in England. You must certainly be properly equipped, able to use a map and compass and be prepared to follow local advice about current diversions and re-routing; changes are often made to avoid erosion of the existing trail. The National Trail Guides, *Pennine Way: South* and *Pennine Way: North*, are essential, though some still prefer to stick to Wainwright's *Pennine Way Companion*. Information centres along the route – like the one at Edale village – stock a selection of guides and associated trail leaflets.

Hathersage

Hilly **HATHERSAGE**, six miles east of Castleton, has a hard time persuading people not to shoot straight past on their way to the heart of the Peaks. This little town is, however, worth at least an hour of anyone's time, the prime target being the much-restored **church of St Michael and All Angels**, a good-looking stone structure perched high on the hill on its eastern edge. The views out over the surrounding countryside are delightful and, enclosed within a miniature iron fence in the churchyard, opposite the porch, is the **grave** – or at least what legend asserts to be the grave – of Robin Hood's old sparring partner, **Little John**. In typically English style, Little John wasn't "little" at all and, although no one can be sure if he actually existed, one of the church's Georgian vicars couldn't resist opening up the tomb to check it out. He unearthed the skeleton of a giant of a man, over 7ft tall, quite enough encouragement for the vicar to display a green cap, longbow and arrows in the church, though sadly there is no sign of them today.

In the 1800s, Hathersage became a **needle-making centre** with a string of factories billowing out dust and dirt. The needle grinders were the best paid among the factory workers, but most of them didn't last long – the metallic dust simply killed them off. Those dangerous days are long gone, but the metal-working tradition has been revived by the Sheffield designer **David Mellor**, who has set up his cutlery factory in the distinctive **Round Building**, a gritstone edifice with a sweeping lead roof about half a mile south of town on the B6001. There's a **Design Museum** (Mon–Sat 10am–5pm, Sun 11am–5pm; ⓦwww .davidmellordesign.com) here too as well as a **Country Shop** (same times), which sells the full range of Mellor cutlery, tableware and kitchenware – but you do pay for the quality.

Practicalities

Hathersage is on the Manchester–Sheffield rail line and from the town's **train station** it's about 500 yards north to the scattering of shops, banks and pubs that comprise the centre, strung along the main street, which doubles as the A6187. Among several **buses** to Hathersage, perhaps the most useful is the frequent South Yorkshire First bus #272 linking Sheffield and Castleton, which stops on the main street outside the *George Hotel* (Ⓣ01433/650436, ⓦwww.george-hotel .net; ⑤). This immaculately maintained one-time coaching **inn** remains very much the place to stay with 22 comfortable bedrooms decorated in country-house style. At the other end of the spectrum, Hathersage **YHA hostel** (Ⓣ0845/371 9021, Ⓔhathersage@yha.org.uk; dorm beds £10, doubles ①) occupies a rambling Victorian house on the main road just to the west of the *George*. It has forty beds, in two- to six-bed rooms, and a good range of facilities, including a self-catering kitchen. The *George* also has a first-rate **restaurant** featuring a canny amalgamation of traditional and modern dishes with main courses averaging around £16.

Eyam

Within a year of September 7, 1665, the lonely lead-mining settlement of **EYAM** (pronounced "Eem"), five miles south of Hathersage, had lost almost half of its population of 750 to the bubonic plague, a calamity that earned it the enduring epithet "**The Plague Village**". The first victim was one George Vicars, a journeyman tailor who is said to have released some infected fleas into his lodgings from a package of cloth he had brought here from London. Acutely conscious of the danger to neighbouring villages, **William Mompesson**, the village rector, speedily organized a self-imposed quarantine, arranging for food to be left at places on the parish boundary. Payment was made with coins left in pools of disinfecting vinegar in holes chiselled into the old boundary stones – and these can still be seen at **Mompesson's Well**, half a mile up the hill to the north of the village and accessible by footpath. Mompesson himself survived the plague, though his wife did not – poor reward for a man whose endeavours prevented the plague from spreading across the Peaks.

The village

Long, thin and hilly, Eyam is little more than one main street – Church and then Main Street – which begins at **The Square**, effectively a crossroads overlooked by a few old stone houses. Heading west from The Square along Church Street, it only takes a couple of minutes to get to the **church of St Lawrence** (Easter–Sept Mon–Sat 9am–6pm, Sun 1–5.30pm; Oct–Easter Mon–Sat 9am–4pm, Sun 1–5.30pm; free), of medieval foundation but extensively revamped in the nineteenth century. In the church **graveyard** a few feet from the entrance stands a conspicuous, eighth-century carved Celtic cross and close by is the distinctive table-tomb of Mompesson's wife, whose sterling work nursing sick villagers caused her early death. Rather more cheerful is the grave of one **Harry Bagshawe** (d. 1927), a local cricketer whose tombstone shows a ball breaking his wicket with the umpire's finger raised above, presumably – on this occasion – to heaven. Bagshawe lies buried round the back of the church on the right-hand side

---

Ring a ring o' roses: Eyam and the plague

As the residents of Eyam began to drop like flies from the **plague** in the autumn of 1665, they resorted to **home remedies** and desperate snatches from folkloric memory to stave off the inevitable. There was little understanding in the seventeenth century of why or how the disease spread: Daniel Defoe, in his later journal of London's plague, recorded how the lord mayor ordered the destruction of all the city's pets, believing them to be responsible. Others, thinking it to be a miasma, kept coal braziers alight day and night in the hope that the smoke would push the infection back into the sky from where it was thought to have come. In isolated Eyam, with the plague among them and no way out through the self-imposed cordon, the locals improvised with great invention but little effect. Applications of cold water, herb infusions and draughts of brine or lemon juice were tried; poultices applied; bleeding by leeches was commonplace; and when all else failed, **charms and spells** were wheeled out – the plucked tail of a pigeon laid against the sore supposedly drew out the poison. All, of course, had no effect and the death toll mounted, though occasionally there was coincidental success: one 14-year-old girl mistakenly drank a pitcher of discarded bacon fat, left by her bedside; the fever passed and she recovered.

According to popular myth, the horrors of plague-ridden England may well have been recorded in a children's **nursery rhyme**, whose gruesome verse has been popular ever since:

Ring a ring o' roses
A pocket full of posies
Atishoo, atishoo
We all fall down

The "roses" are the patches which developed on the victim's chest soon after contracting the disease; the "posies" are herbs or flowers, carried as charms; as the fever took hold, sneezing ("atishoo, atishoo") was a common symptom; until, chillingly, at death's door, "we all fall down".

of this part of the graveyard. **Inside** the church, informative panels reveal more of the village's plague history, highlighting a number of associated sites in and around the place.

Immediately to the west of the church stand the so-called **plague cottages**, where plaques explain who died where and when – it was here that Vicars met his maker. Another short hop brings you to **Eyam Hall**, built for a certain Thomas Wright a few years after the plague's visitation, possibly in an attempt to secure his position as the squire of the depleted village. From here, it's a few minutes' walk along Main Street and up Hawkhill Road – follow the signs – to the modest Methodist chapel that now houses the **Eyam Museum** (April–Oct Tues–Sun 10am–4.30pm; £2), which tracks the village's history and has a good section on the bubonic plague – its transmission, symptoms and social aftermath.

Practicalities

Buses to Eyam stop on The Square, and one or two also run along Church/Main Street. The pick of a handful of **B&Bs** is *Crown Cottage*, in a pleasantly maintained old stone building on Main Street (℡01433/630858, ⓌWww.crown-cottage .co.uk; no credit cards; ❷). There are four homely guest rooms here, three doubles and one twin. The most appealing alternative is the well-equipped **YHA hostel** (℡0845/371 9738, ⒺWeyam@yha.org.uk; £18, doubles ❶), which occupies an idiosyncratic Victorian house, whose ersatz medieval towers and turrets overlook Eyam from amid wooded grounds on Hawkhill Road, a stiff, half-mile ramble up from Eyam Museum. The hostel has a café, self-catering facilities, a cycle store and a lounge, and its sixty beds are parcelled up into two- to ten-bed rooms; advance reservations are recommended.

The best **place to eat** is the *Miner's Arms*, in antique premises just off The Square on Water Lane, where they serve filling bar meals as well as very enjoyable traditional British dinners in the restaurant every evening except Sunday.

Baslow

BASLOW, some four miles southeast of Eyam, is an unassuming little village, whose oldest stone cottages string prettily along the River Derwent. The only building of note is **St Anne's Church** whose stone spire pokes up above the Victorian castellations of its nave in between the river and the busy junction of the A623/A619. Baslow may be inconsequential, but it is handy for the nearby Chatsworth estate (see below) and it also possesses one of the Peak's finest **hotels**, *Fischer's Baslow Hall* (℡01246/583259, ⓌWwww.fischers-baslowhall.co.uk; ❻), a mile or so out of the village back towards Eyam along the A623. In its own grounds, the hall is picture-postcard perfect, a handsome Edwardian building made of local stone with matching gables and a dinky canopy over the front door. The interior is suitably lavish and the service attentive, while rooms occupy both the main building and the Garden House annexe next door. The **restaurant** is superb too, and has won several awards for its imaginative cuisine – Modern British at its best – with set meals costing £72. Alternatively, you can pop back into Baslow for a bite at *Charlie's Café & Bistro* (closed Mon), where they serve a tasty range of salads, light meals and afternoon teas in bright, modern surroundings; the café is opposite St Anne's Church.

Chatsworth

One of the finest stately homes in Britain, fantastically popular **Chatsworth House** (mid-March to late Dec daily 11am–5.30pm, last admission 4.30pm; gardens till 6pm, last admission 5pm; house & gardens £11.50, gardens only

Getting to Chatsworth

The best way to get to Chatsworth House is **on foot** along one of the footpaths that network the estate, the obvious departure point being Baslow (see opposite) on the northern edge of the estate. It's easy walking, and The *Grate Little Guide to Chatsworth* (see p.534) describes an especially pleasant four-mile loop that begins and ends in the village, taking in the house on the way. There are also **buses** to Chatsworth House from Sheffield, Baslow and several other Peak District villages with TM Travel (see p.534).

£7.50; ⓦwww.chatsworth.org), just south of Baslow via the A619, was built in the seventeenth century by the first Duke of Devonshire. It has been owned by the family ever since and several of them have done a fair bit of tinkering – the sixth duke, for instance, added the north wing in the 1820s – but the end result is remarkably harmonious. The house is seen to best advantage from the B6012, which meanders across the estate to the west of the house, giving a full view of its vast Palladian frontage, whose clean lines are perfectly balanced by the undulating partly wooded **parkland**, which rolls in from the south and west. The B6012 also gives access to the immaculately maintained estate village of **Edensor**, whose sturdy stone houses are well worth a look in their own right; a signed turning off the same road leads to the house itself.

Many visitors forgo the **house** altogether, concentrating on the gardens instead – an understandable decision given the predictability of the assorted baubles accumulated by the family over the centuries. Nonetheless, among the maze of grandiose rooms and staircases, there are several noteworthy highlights, notably the ornate ceilings of the **State Apartments**, daubed with strikingly energetic cherubs, and, in the State Bedroom, the four-poster bed in which George II breathed his last. And then there are the **paintings**. Among many, Frans Hals, Tintoretto, Veronese and Van Dyck all have a showing and there's even a Rembrandt – *A Portrait of an Old Man* – hanging in the chapel. The sixth duke also added a **Sculpture Gallery** to show all the tackle he had acquired on his travels, mostly large-scale Italian sculptures, but here also is the Chatsworth tazza, probably the largest Blue John vase in the world; for more on this semi-precious stone, see p.542.

Chatsworth's **gardens** are a real treat and owe much to the combined efforts of Capability Brown, who designed them in the 1750s, and Joseph Paxton (designer of London's Crystal Palace), who had a bash seventy years later. Among all sorts of fripperies, there are water fountains, a rock garden, an artificial waterfall, a grotto and a folly as well as a nursery and greenhouses. Afterwards, you can wend your way to the **café** in the handsomely converted former stables.

Bakewell and around

BAKEWELL, flanking the banks of the River Wye four miles southwest of Baslow, is famous for both its puff-pastry **Bakewell Pudding** and its shortcrust Bakewell Tart – the former is the much more distinctive (and less commonplace), being a sweet and slippery, almond-flavoured confection (now with a dab of jam) invented here around 1860 when a cook botched a recipe for strawberry tart. Almost a century before this fortuitous mishap, the Duke of Rutland set out to turn what was then a remote village into a prestigious spa, thereby trumping the work of his rival, the Duke of Devonshire, in Buxton. The frigidity of the water made failure inevitable, leaving only the prettiness of **Bath Gardens** at the heart of the town centre, beside the crossroads Rutland Square, as a reminder of the venture.

Famous pudding and tart apart, Bakewell is an undemanding place today, its main streets too crowded by traffic – and tourists – to be much fun, though it is within easy striking distance of several first-rate attractions, primarily Chatsworth (see p.546). In town, there is some interest in the web of narrow shopping streets around **Water Street**, just off the main drag near Rutland Square, as well as in the nearby **riverside walkway**, but the most agreeable part of Bakewell trails up the hill at the west end of the centre. Here, strolling up North Church Street, with its line of comely stone cottages, you soon reach **All Saints Church**, the result of centuries of architectural fiddling from the Normans onwards, with a rare **Saxon cross**, carved with decorative circles and scrolls, outside in the graveyard.

Practicalities

Buses to Bakewell stop on – or very close to – central Rutland Square; there are no trains. The well-equipped **tourist office** is just a couple of hundred yards from the square, along the main drag – Bridge Street – in the Old Market Hall (daily: April–Oct 9.30am–5.30pm; Nov–Easter 10am–5pm; ℡01629/813227, ⓦwww .visitpeakdistrict.com). There's no overriding reason to overnight in Bakewell, but there is a wide selection of **B&Bs**. One good choice is *Avenue House*, whose three cosily furnished, en-suite rooms occupy a spacious Victorian building just south of the centre on Matlock Street, which doubles as the A6 (℡01629/812467, ⓦwww .bakewell-bed-breakfast.co.uk; ❷).

Bakeries all over town claim to make Bakewell Pudding to the original recipe, but arguably the most authentic are served up at the Old Original Bakewell Pudding Shop, on the main street a few yards from Rutland Square. They sell the pudding in several sizes, from the small and handy to the gargantuan, enough to keep the average family going for a whole day. The best **restaurant** in town is *Piedaniel's*, in a pleasantly renovated old beamed building immediately north of the main drag on Bath Street (℡01629/812687; closed Sun & Mon). The menu here is an inventive mix of English and French cuisines with main courses costing around £15.

Hassop and Ashford in the Water

Hidden away in the heart of the Peaks, about three miles north of Bakewell on the B6001, the tiny hamlet of **HASSOP** has a rugged, solitary feeling. It is also home to one of the region's finest **hotels**, the wonderful 🎋 *Hassop Hall* (℡01629/640488, ⓦwww.hassophall.co.uk; ❸), a handsome stone manor house whose long stone facade ripples with elegant bay windows. The interior has kept faith with the Georgian architecture too – modernization has been kept to a

---

Hiking around Bakewell

Bakewell is a popular starting-point for short hikes out into the easy landscapes that make up the town's surroundings, with one of the most relaxing excursions being a four-mile loop along the banks of the **River Wye** to the south of the centre. Chatsworth (see p.546) is within easy hiking distance too – about seven miles there and back – and so is Ashford in the Water (see opposite), a brief hike away to the northwest along the Wye. Rather more ambitious – and one of the best-known hikes in the national park – is the **Monsal Trail**, which cuts eight miles north and then west through some of Derbyshire's finest limestone dales using part of the old Midland Railway line. The trail begins at Coombs viaduct, one mile southeast of Bakewell, and ends at Blackwell Mill Junction, three miles east of Buxton.

subtle minimum – and the views out over the surrounding parkland are delightful. The hotel **restaurant** (reservations required) is also first class with a two-course set meal costing from around £25.

Minuscule **ASHFORD IN THE WATER**, just over a mile to the west of Bakewell along the River Wye, is one of the prettiest and wealthiest villages in the Peaks, its old stone cottages nuzzling up to a quaint medieval church. It was not always so. Ashford was once a poor lead-mining settlement with sidelines in milling and agriculture, hence the name of the (impossibly picturesque) Sheepwash Bridge. There was, however, a bit of a boom when locals took to polishing the dark limestone found on the edge of the village (and nowhere else), turning it into so-called **Ashford black marble** – much to the delight of Buxton's petrifactioners (see p.540). Today, Ashford possesses an outstanding **hotel**, the plush *Riverside House* (☎01629/814275, ⓦwww.riversidehousehotel .co.uk; ⑨), which occupies a handsome Georgian building by the banks of the Wye. There are a dozen or so extremely well-appointed rooms here, each decorated in a full-blown country-house style, and the hotel takes justifiable pride in both its gardens and its restaurant.

Travel details

For information on all local and national bus services, contact Traveline ☎0871/200 2233, ⓦwww.traveline.org.uk. See p.534 for transport around the Peak District.

Buses

Operated by Trent Barton buses, the **TransPeak bus service** (ⓦwww .transpeak.co.uk) runs from Nottingham to Manchester via Derby, Bakewell and Buxton every one or two hours daily. The whole journey takes 3 hours, 30 minutes.

Birmingham to: Coventry (every 20min; 1hr); Great Malvern (hourly; 2hr 30min); Ludlow (every 2hr; 2hr 10min); Stratford-upon-Avon (hourly; 1hr); Worcester (hourly; 2hr).

Buxton to: Ashbourne (Mon–Sat 6 daily, Sun 1; 40min); Castleton (1 daily; 1hr); Derby (hourly; 2hr).

Derby to: Ashbourne (Mon–Sat 6 daily, Sun 1; 40min); Buxton (hourly; 2hr).

Great Malvern to: Birmingham (hourly; 2hr 30min); Hereford (every 2hr; 2hr); Ledbury (hourly; 30min); Worcester (every 30min; 40min).

Hay-on-Wye to: Hereford (every 2hr; 1hr); Ross-on-Wye (every 2hr; 2hr).

Hereford to: Great Malvern (every 2hr; 2hr); Hay-on-Wye (every 2hr; 1hr); Ledbury (hourly; 30min); Ludlow (every 2hr; 1hr 10min); Ross-on-Wye (hourly; 50min); Worcester (every 1–2hr; 1hr 20min).

Ludlow to: Birmingham (every 2hr; 2hr 10min); Hereford (every 2hr; 1hr 10min); Shrewsbury (hourly; 1hr 30min).

Ross-on-Wye to: Hay-on-Wye (every 2hr; 2hr); Hereford (hourly; 50min); Ledbury (Mon–Sat every 1–2hr, Sun every 2–3hr; 30min).

Shrewsbury to: Ludlow (hourly; 1hr 30min).

Stratford-upon-Avon to: Birmingham (hourly; 1hr); Worcester (hourly; 2hr).

Worcester to: Birmingham (hourly; 2hr); Great Malvern (every 30min; 40min); Hereford (every 1–2hr; 1hr 20min); Stratford-upon-Avon (hourly; 2hr).

Trains

For information on all local and national rail services, contact National Rail Enquiries ☎08457/484950, ⓦwww.nationalrail.co.uk.

Birmingham New Street to: Birmingham International (every 15–30min; 15min); Coventry (3–5 hourly; 25min); Derby (every 30min; 45min); Great Malvern (hourly; 1hr); Hereford (hourly; 1hr 30min); Lichfield City (every 15min; 40min); London (every 30min; 1hr 10min); Shrewsbury (every 30min; 1hr); Telford (Mon–Sat every 30min, Sun hourly; 40min); Worcester (hourly; 40min).

Birmingham Moor Street Station to: Stratford-upon-Avon (hourly; 50min); Warwick (hourly; 30min).

Buxton to: Manchester (hourly; 1hr).

Derby to: Birmingham (every 30min; 45min).

Edale to: Manchester (hourly; 45min).
Great Malvern to: Birmingham (hourly; 1hr); Hereford (hourly; 35min); Ledbury (hourly; 15min); Worcester (every 30min; 15min).
Hathersage to: Manchester (hourly; 1hr).
Hereford to: Birmingham (hourly; 1hr 30min); Great Malvern (hourly; 30min); Ledbury (hourly; 20min); Ludlow (every 30min; 30min); Shrewsbury (hourly; 1hr); Worcester (hourly; 40min).
Hope to: Manchester (hourly; 50min).

Shrewsbury to: Birmingham (every 30min; 1hr); Church Stretton (every 30min; 15min); Hereford (hourly; 1hr); Ludlow (hourly; 30min); Telford (every 30min; 20min).
Stratford-upon-Avon to: Birmingham Moor Street (hourly; 50min); London (every 2hr; 2hr 20min); Warwick (hourly; 15min).
Worcester to: Birmingham (hourly; 40min); Hereford (hourly; 40min).

9

The East Midlands

CHAPTER 9 # Highlights

* **Nottingham Contemporary** Nottingham's brand-new top-ranking art gallery has garnered all sorts of praise for its adventurous shows and exhibitions. **See p.559**

* **Newstead Abbey** One-time home of Lord Byron, this delightful spot has superb period rooms and lovely gardens. **See p.562**

* **Hardwick Hall** A beautifully preserved Elizabethan mansion that was once the home of the formidable Bess of Hardwick. **See p.564**

* **Golden Mile, Leicester** The focus of Leicester's sizeable Asian community is Belgrave Road, where a long strip of authentic restaurants line up for custom. **See p.570**

* **Lincoln Cathedral** One of the finest medieval cathedrals in the land, seen to fine advantage on a rooftop guided tour. **See p.580**

* **Stamford** Lincolnshire's prettiest town, with its cobbled lanes and ancient limestone buildings, well deserves an overnight stay. **See p.589**

▲ Lincoln Cathedral

9

The East Midlands

M any tourists dodge the five counties of the **East Midlands** – Nottinghamshire, Leicestershire, Northamptonshire, Rutland and Lincolnshire – on their way to more obvious destinations, an understandable mistake given that the region is short on star attractions. And indeed it's true that the first three of these counties are pockmarked by industrialization, from the old coalfield of northern Nottinghamshire to the hosiery industry of Leicester, and their county towns – **Nottingham**, **Leicester** and **Northampton** – have also been badly bruised by postwar town planning. Nevertheless, embedded in the modernity is a scattering of fine historical landmarks and even though these are the frills rather than the substance, Nottingham and Leicester certainly have enough character to give them an aesthetic edge. Furthermore, the countryside surrounding these three towns can be delightful, with rolling farmland punctuated by wooded ridges and flowing hills, all sprinkled with prestigious country homes, pretty villages and old market towns. In **Nottinghamshire**, Byron's **Newstead Abbey** is intriguing, though the Elizabethan **Hardwick Hall** (just over the border in Derbyshire but covered in this chapter) is even better, while the eastern reaches of the county hold two appealing market towns – **Southwell** and **Newark**. Heading south, **Leicestershire** offers the fascinating mansion of **Calke Abbey** and lies adjacent to the easy countryside of **Rutland**, the region's smallest county, where you'll find two more pleasant country towns, **Oakham** and **Uppingham**, not to mention the postcard-pretty village of **Lyddington**. Rutland and **Northamptonshire** benefit from the use of limestone as the traditional building material and rural Northamptonshire is studded with handsome stone villages and towns – most notably **Fotheringhay** – as well as a battery of country estates, the best known of which is **Althorp**, the final resting place of Princess Diana.

Lincolnshire is very different in character from the rest of the region, an agricultural backwater that remains surprisingly remote – locals sometimes call it the "forgotten county". This was not always the case: throughout medieval times the county flourished as a centre of the wool trade with Flanders, its merchants and landowners becoming some of the wealthiest in England. Reminders of the high times are legion, beginning with the majestic cathedral that graces **Lincoln**, an old (in part at least) and easy-paced city. Equally enticing is the splendidly intact stone town of **Stamford**, while out in the sticks, Lincolnshire's most distinctive feature is **The Fens**, whose pancake-flat fields, filling out much of the south of the county and extending deep into Cambridgeshire, have been regained from the marshes and the sea. Fenland villages are generally short of charm, but their **parish churches**, whose spires regularly interrupt the wide-skied landscape, are simply stunning, the most impressive of the lot adorning the otherwise humdrum town of **Boston**.

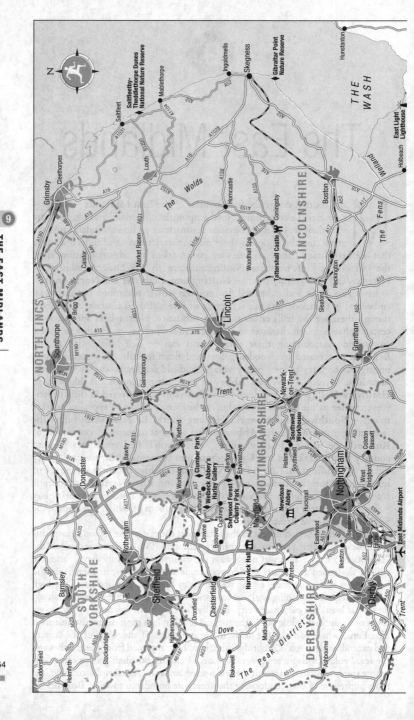

THE EAST MIDLANDS

9

555

In north Lincolnshire, the gentle chalky hills of the **Lincolnshire Wolds** contain the county's most diverse scenery, including woodland clustered round **Woodhall Spa**, and a string of sheltered valleys concentrated in the vicinity of **Louth**, an especially fetching country town. To the east of the Wolds is the **coast**, whose long sandy beach extends, with a few marshy interruptions, from Mablethorpe to **Skegness**, the region's main resort. The coast has long attracted thousands of holiday-makers from the big cities of the East Midlands and Yorkshire, hence its trail of bungalows, campsites and caravan parks – though significant chunks of the seashore are now protected as **nature reserves**.

Nottingham

With a population of around 290,000, **NOTTINGHAM** is one of England's big cities. A longtime manufacturing centre for bikes, cigarettes, pharmaceuticals and lace, it is, however, more famous for Nottingham Forest football team, for the Trent Bridge cricket ground and for its association with **Robin Hood**, the legendary thirteenth-century outlaw. Hood's bitter enemy was, of course, the Sheriff of Nottingham, but unfortunately his home and lair – the city's imposing medieval castle – is long gone, and today Nottingham is at its most diverting in and around its handsome **Market Square**, which is also the centre of a heaving, teeming nightlife each and every weekend.

Some history

Constructed in 1068 by William the Conqueror, Nottingham's **castle** was a military stronghold and royal palace, the equal of the great castles of Windsor and Dover, and every medieval king of England paid regular visits. And it was from the castle that Charles I rode out in 1642 to raise his standard and start the Civil War; not that the locals were overly sympathetic: hardly anyone joined up, even though the king had the ceremony repeated on the next three days.

After the Civil War, the Parliamentarians slighted the castle and, in the 1670s, the ruins were cleared by the Duke of Newcastle to make way for a **palace**, whose continental – and, in English terms, novel – design he chose from a pattern book, probably by Rubens. Beneath the castle lay a market town which, according to Daniel Defoe, was "one of the most beautiful towns in England". In the second half of the eighteenth century, however, the city was transformed by the expansion of the lace and hosiery industries, and within the space of fifty years, Nottingham's population increased from ten thousand to fifty thousand, the resulting slum becoming a hotbed of **radicalism**. In the 1810s, a recession provoked the hard-pressed workers into action. They struck against the employers and, calling themselves **Luddites** after an apprentice-protester by the name of Ned Ludd, raided the factories to smash the knitting machines.

The worst of Nottingham's slums were cleared in the early twentieth century, when the city centre assumed its present structure, with the main commercial area ringed by alternating industrial and residential districts. Thereafter, crass **postwar development** added tower blocks, shopping centres and a ring road, resulting in a disheartening cityscape. The flavour of this postwar industrial city was best described by Arthur Seaton, the factory-worker protagonist of *Saturday Night and Sunday Morning*, the perceptive and forceful novel by Nottingham's own **Alan Sillitoe** (1928–2010): "I'm out for a good time – all the rest is propaganda".

Arrival and information

Nottingham **train station** is on the south side of the city centre, a five- to ten-minute walk from the Market Square – just follow the signs. Most long-distance **buses** arrive at the **Broad Marsh bus station**, down the street from the train station on the way to the centre, but some – including services to north Nottinghamshire – pull in at the **Victoria bus station**, a five-minute walk north of the Market Square.

Nottingham's new(ish) **trams** link the train station with the Market Square, but otherwise are not especially useful for tourists. The city's **tourist office** is on the Market Square, on the ground floor of the Council House, at 1 Smithy Row (Mon–Fri 9am–5.30pm, Sat 9am–5pm, Sun 10am–4pm; ☎0115/915 5330, ⓦwww.visitnottingham.com).

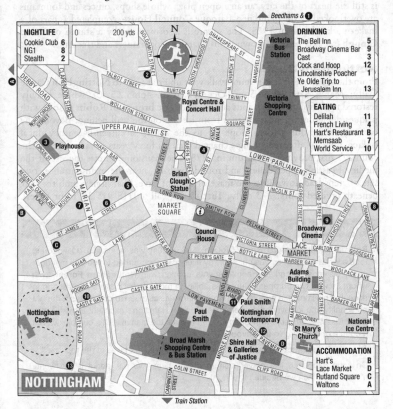

NIGHTLIFE
Cookie Club	6
NG1	8
Stealth	2

DRINKING
The Bell Inn	5
Broadway Cinema Bar	9
Cast	3
Cock and Hoop	12
Lincolnshire Poacher	1
Ye Olde Trip to Jerusalem Inn	13

EATING
Delilah	11
French Living	4
Hart's Restaurant	B
Memsaab	7
World Service	10

ACCOMMODATION
Hart's	B
Lace Market	D
Rutland Square	C
Waltons	A

▲ Beedhams & ❶

NOTTINGHAM

▼ Train Station

Accommodation

Almost all of Nottingham's central **hotels** are chain hotels with the best located being a *Jury's Inn*, in a large tower block near the train station on Station Street. There are two top-quality independent hotels in the centre, but both are a tad pricey.

Hart's Standard Hill, Park Row ℡0115/988 1900, ⓦwww.hartshotel.co.uk. Chic hotel, with comfort and style in equal measure: ultramodern fixtures and fittings, Egyptian cotton bed linen and so forth. It's quite pricey, but the quiet location – near both the castle and the Market Square – is hard to beat. ⑤

Lace Market 29 High Pavement ℡0115/852 3232, ⓦwww.lacemarkethotel.co.uk. In a great location, footsteps from St Mary's Church, this smart hotel has just over forty slick modern rooms decorated in sharp minimalist style – all within a tastefully modernized Georgian house. ⑤

Rutland Square Rutland St, off St James St ℡0115/941 1114, ⓦwww.rutlandsquarehotel .co.uk. Enticing and tastefully furnished modern chain hotel in a good location, just by the castle. Ninety-odd rooms. ❸

Waltons 2 North Rd, The Park ℡0115/947 5215, ⓦwww.waltonshotel.co.uk. Bijou, privately owned hotel (with bar) in a tastefully modernized nineteenth-century lodge on the edge of one of the city's wealthiest neighbourhoods, The Park, which is jam-packed with Victorian mansions. The seventeen plush rooms are mostly in period style. About one mile west of the centre along Derby Rd. ❸

The City

One of the best-looking central squares in England, Nottingham's **Market Square** is still the heart of the city, an airy open plaza whose shops, offices and fountains are overlooked by the grand neo-Baroque **Council House**, completed as part of a make-work scheme in 1928. The square is also overseen by a **statue of Brian Clough** (see box below), shown in his characteristic trainers and tracksuit.

Nottingham Castle

From the square, it's a five-minute walk west up Friar Lane to **Nottingham Castle** (daily: March–Sept 10am–5pm; Oct–Feb 10am–4pm; £5.50), whose heavily restored medieval gateway stands above a folkloric **bronze of Robin Hood**, with plaques depicting legendary scenes from his life on the wall behind. Beyond the gateway, delightful gardens slope up to the squat, seventeenth-century ducal **palace**, which – after remaining a charred shell for forty years – was opened as the country's first provincial museum in 1878. The mansion occupies the site of the medieval castle's upper bailey, and round the back, near the main entrance, two sets of steps lead down into the maze of ancient **caves** that honeycomb the cliff beneath (guided tours: 2–3 daily; 1hr; £2.50; call ℡0115/915 3676 for times).

Brian Clough

Born in Middlesbrough, **Brian Clough** (1935–2004) was a prolific goal-scoring footballer whose career was cut short by injury. He soon turned to football management, his most remarkable achievements coming with **Nottingham Forest**, with whom he won two European Cups. His ability to motivate his players was second to none, but his immense popularity in Nottingham was as much to do with his forthright personality and idiosyncratic utterances. Duncan Hamilton's excellent *Provided You Don't Kiss Me: 20 Years with Brian Clough* reveals the man in all his complexity, but a couple of quotes give the flavour:

"I wouldn't say I was the best manager in the business, but I was in the top one."

On what happened if a player disagreed with him: "We talk about it for twenty minutes and then we decide I was right."

Tours include **Mortimer's Hole**, a three-hundred-foot shaft along which, legend has it, the young Edward III and his chums crept in 1330 to capture the queen mother, Isabella, and her lover, Roger Mortimer. The couple had already polished off Edward III's father, the hapless Edward II, and were intent on usurping the Crown, but the young Edward proved too shrewd for them and Mortimer came to a sticky end.

The interior of the ducal mansion holds the rambling **Castle Museum and Art Gallery**, where a particular highlight is the "Story of Nottingham", a lively and entertaining account of the city's development. Pride of place here goes to a small but exquisite collection of late medieval **alabaster carvings**, an applied art for which Nottingham once had an international reputation. It's worth walking up to the top floor, too, for a turn round the main **picture gallery**, a handsome and spacious room where a curious assortment of mostly English nineteenth-century romantic paintings are displayed. The works are regularly rotated, but look out for the evocative nineteenth-century canvases of Nottingham's own Richard Parkes Bonington, Laslett John Pott's melodramatic *Mary Queen of Scots being led to her Execution*, and the cheerily folksy Nottingham cityscapes of Arthur Spooner. One surprise is a typical industrial scene by Lowry (see p.608), entitled *Industrial Panorama*, another are two meticulously executed canvases by Stanley Spencer.

The Lace Market

The narrow, canyon-like lanes and alleys of the **Lace Market**, beginning a couple of minutes' walk east of the Market Square, are flanked by large and imposing Victorian factories and warehouses. Stoney Street is the Lace Market at its most striking, its star turn being the **Adams Building**, whose handsome stone-and-brick facade combines both neo-Georgian and neo-Renaissance features. Neighbouring Broadway doesn't lag far behind either, with a line of homogeneous red-brick and sandstone-trimmed buildings performing a neat swerve halfway along the street. At the heart of the Lace Market is the **church of St Mary**, a good-looking, mostly fifteenth-century Gothic structure built on top of the hill that was once the Saxon town.

Shire Hall and the Galleries of Justice

St Mary's abuts High Pavement, the administrative centre of Nottingham in Georgian times, and it's here you'll find **Shire Hall**, whose Neoclassical columns, pilasters and dome date from 1770. The facade also bears the marks of a real Georgian cock-up: to the left of the entrance, at street level, the mason carved the word "Goal" onto an arch and then had to have a second bash, turning it into "Gaol"; both versions are clearly visible. The hall now houses the **Galleries of Justice** (daily 10.30am–5pm; £8.75, Mon & Tues £5.75; Ⓦ www.galleriesofjustice.org.uk), whose child-friendly "Crime and Punishment" tour involves lots of role-play. The building is actually much more interesting than the hoopla, incorporating two superbly preserved Victorian courtrooms, an Edwardian police station, some spectacularly unpleasant old cells, a women's prison with bath house and a prisoners' exercise yard.

Nottingham Contemporary and around

Just along the street from the Galleries of Justice is the city's brand-new art gallery, **Nottingham Contemporary** (Tues–Fri 10am–7pm, Sat 10am–6pm, Sun 11am–5pm; free; Ⓦ www.nottinghamcontemporary.org), which – despite the grand assurances of the architects – looks like something assembled from a giant IKEA flat pack. That said, the gallery's temporary exhibitions have proved a real hit with locals, especially the one focusing on David Hockney.

Sausages

For the finest sausages north of the Alps, go to **Beedhams**, an outstanding, family-owned butchers' located about a mile and a half north of the city centre at 556 Mansfield Rd (℡0115/960 5901). There's some great stuff here, everything from boerewors with coriander, paprika and nutmeg, through to the spicy, Hungarian-style "Magyar". Unbeatable.

Near the gallery, on Byard Lane, is the first shop of local lad **Paul Smith**, a major success story of contemporary British fashion, though he also has a much larger, flagship store a hop, skip and jump away at 20 Low Pavement.

Eating

Nottingham boasts at least half a dozen top-quality **restaurants** and, by and large, competition keeps prices down to reasonable levels. All our recommendations are within easy walking distance of the Market Square.

Delilah 15 Middle Pavement. The best deli in town with more cooked meats and cheeses than you can shake a stick at, plus a café-counter for tasty lunches and light meals, though finding a spare seat can be difficult.

French Living 27 King St ℡0115/958 5885. Authentic French cuisine served in an intimate, candle-lit basement. Daytime snacks and baguettes in the ground-floor café too. Evening main courses from £11. Closed Sun & Mon.

Hart's Restaurant Standard Court, Park Row ℡0115/911 0666. One of the city's most acclaimed restaurants, occupying part of the old general hospital and serving an international menu of carefully presented meals. Attractive pastel/modern decor and attentive service; reservations well-nigh essential. Mains from about £17. For something rather less expensive, go next door to the bar of *Hart's* hotel (see p.558), where – among much else – they serve great fish and chips with mushy peas.

Memsaab 12 Maid Marian Way ℡0115/957 0009. One of a new breed of Indian restaurants (to Nottingham at least) – no burgundy wallpaper here, but crisp modern decor and bags of space. The food – canny amalgamations of different Indian cooking styles from different regions – is exquisite. A large and imaginative menu with main courses starting from as little as £10. Evenings only.

World Service Newdigate House, Castle Gate ℡0115/847 5587. Chic restaurant with bags of decorative flair in charming premises up near the castle. A Modern British menu, featuring such delights as pork cutlets with onion marmalade and rack of lamb with butternut squash tarte tatin, is prepared with imagination and close attention to detail. In the evenings, main courses start at around £17, but there are great deals at lunchtimes with two-course set meals costing £13, or £18 for three courses.

Drinking, nightlife and entertainment

Central Nottingham's **pubs** literally heave on the weekend and are not for the faint-hearted – the timid may well see sights they will never forget. For hundreds, the pubs are just the prelude to some serious clubbing and once again no one could call Nottingham's clubs restrained. If you're over thirty (twenty?), you may well prefer the quieter pubs a few minutes' walk out of the centre.

For **live music**, both popular and classical, most big names play at the Royal Centre Concert Hall, on South Sherwood Street (℡0115/989 5555, ⓦwww.royalcentre-nottingham.co.uk). The Broadway, in the Lace Market at 14 Broad St (℡0115/952 6611, ⓦwww.broadway.org.uk), is the best **cinema** in the city, featuring a mixed bag of mainstream and avant-garde films, and there's **theatre** at the Nottingham Playhouse, on Wellington Circus (℡0115/941 9419, ⓦwww.nottinghamplayhouse.co.uk).

Pubs and bars

The Bell Inn 18 Angel Row. Age-old inn, where locals have been tanking up for decades before hitting the brighter lights elsewhere. Lots of wood panelling and tasty guest beers.

Broadway Cinema Bar Broadway Cinema, 14 Broad St. Informal, fashionable (in an arty sort of way) bar serving an eclectic assortment of bottled beers to a cinema-keen clientele. The bar food is, however, very average.

Cast Wellington Circus. The bar of the Nottingham Playhouse is a popular, easy-going spot with courtyard seating on summer nights. Patrons have the advantage of looking at a piece of modern art too – Anish Kapoor's whopping, reflective *Sky Mirror*. There's also an attached deli and (pretty average) restaurant.

Cock and Hoop 25 High Pavement, Lace Market. Smart, small and well-behaved city-centre bar with thick carpets and comfortable chairs. Superior bar food in the main bar at the front and in the cellar-like room at the back. Very different from almost every other pub in the centre. Real ales, too.

Lincolnshire Poacher 161 Mansfield Rd, about half a mile from the Market Square. Very popular and relaxed pub, where most of the customers take their (real) ales fairly seriously. Attracts an older clientele and the decor is pleasantly traditional.

Ye Olde Trip to Jerusalem Inn Below the castle in Brewhouse Yard. Carved into the castle rock, this ancient inn may well have been a meeting point for soldiers gathering for the Third Crusade. Its cave-like bars, with their rough sandstone ceilings, are delightfully secretive and there's a good range of ales too.

Clubs

Cookie Club 22 St James St ⊛ www.cookieclub .co.uk. Central venue casting a wide musical net, from indie/student favourites to Goth and retro.

NG1 76 Lower Parliament St ⊛ www.ng1club .co.uk. Nottingham's leading gay club with four different grooves, three sound systems, two dancefloors and a capacity of 800.

Stealth Masonic Place, Goldsmith St ⊛ www .stealthattack.co.uk. The biggest club in Nottingham – big enough to host live music and a battery of leading DJs.

Around Nottingham: Eastwood

D.H. Lawrence (1885–1930) was born in the coal-mining village of **EASTWOOD**, about eight miles west of Nottingham. The mine closed years ago, and Eastwood is something of a post-industrial eyesore, but Lawrence's childhood home, in the centre of town at 8a Victoria St, off Nottingham Road, has survived: a tiny, red-brick terraced house amid several streets of the same which has been refurbished as the **D.H. Lawrence Birthplace Museum** (Tues–Fri & Sun: April–Oct 10am–5pm; Nov–March 10am–4pm; £2.50). None of the furnishings and fittings are Lawrence originals, which isn't too surprising considering the family moved out when he was two, but it's an appealing evocation of the period interlaced with biographical insights into the author's early life. Afterwards, enthusiasts can follow the two-mile **Blue Line Walk** round those parts of Eastwood with Lawrence associations – his family moved house on several occasions and Lawrence only left Eastwood in 1908. The walk takes an hour or so, and a brochure is available at the museum.

Buses leave Nottingham's Victoria bus station every twenty minutes for the thirty-minute journey to Eastwood.

The rest of Nottinghamshire

Nottingham is flanked to the south by the commuter villages of the Nottingham-shire Wolds and to the north by the gritty towns and villages of what was, until it was decimated by Thatcher and her cronies in the late 1980s, the Nottinghamshire coalfield. Both are unremarkable, but encrusted within the old coalfield are the thin remains of Sherwood Forest, a chunk of which is preserved in the **Sherwood Forest National Nature Reserve**, supposedly where Robin Hood did some canoodling with Maid Marian. The rest of the remaining forest is contained within **the Dukeries**, named after the five dukes who owned most of this area and preserved at least part of the ancient broad-leaved forest. Three of the four remaining estates that comprise the Dukeries – Worksop, Welbeck and Thoresby – are still in private hands, though **Welbeck** has courted the public with the pleasing **Harley Art Gallery**. The fourth estate, **Clumber Park**, is very different, now owned by the National Trust and offering long woodland walks. Also within the confines of the former coalfield are two fascinating country houses, **Newstead Abbey**, one-time home of Byron, and the wonderful Elizabethan extravagance of **Hardwick Hall**.

Without coal, eastern Nottinghamshire escaped the heavy-duty industrialization that fell upon its county neighbours. It remains a largely agricultural area today, its undulating farmland, punctuated by dozens of pint-sized villages, rolling seamlessly over to the River Trent, the boundary with Lincolnshire. By and large, it's prosperous and by no means unpleasant, but for the casual visitor the attractions are distinctly low-key, being essentially confined to a splendid church at **Southwell** and the riverside pleasantries of **Newark**.

Nottingham is the transport hub for the rest of the county with regular **bus** services to all the above with the exception of Hardwick Hall, for which you will need your own transport.

Newstead Abbey

In 1539, **Newstead Abbey**, eight miles north of Nottingham on the A60 (house April–Sept Fri–Mon noon–5pm; grounds daily 9am–6pm or dusk; £8, grounds only £4; ⓦwww.newsteadabbey.org.uk), was granted by Henry VIII to Sir John Byron, who demolished most of the church and converted the monastic buildings into a family home. In 1798, **Lord Byron** inherited the estate, then little more than a ruin. He restored part of the complex during his six-year residence (1808–14), though most of the present structure dates from later renovations, which maintained much of the shape and feel of the medieval original while creating the warren-like mansion that exists today.

Inside, a string of intriguing period rooms begins with the Great Hall, which sets the tone nicely, its high Victorian panelling adorned by oodles of antlers and a solitary suit of armour. Just beyond is Byron's bedroom, one of the few rooms

Top 5: East Midlands country pubs

▶▶ **Martin's Arms** School Lane, Colston Bassett ☏01949/81361. Tastefully renovated pub-cum-restaurant in the tiny hamlet of Colston Bassett, about twelve miles east of Nottingham. The restaurant is a fairly formal affair, decked out in a distinctive Georgian style, while the Victorian-era bar is a lovely spot to grab a pint and settle down to some of the best gastro bar food around. Kitchen closed on Sun eve.

▶▶ **Waggon & Horses** The Turnpike, Halam ☏01636/813109. An award-winning pub and restaurant, and a carbon-neutral one to boot, this friendly, informal place is proud of its pies – try the Robin Hood pie made from local game. Halam is just outside Southwell (see p.565).

▶▶ **The Finches Arms** Hambleton. Traditional country inn close to Rutland Water. See p.574.

▶▶ **The Old White Hart**, Main St, Lyddington. An ancient pub in an ancient village with top-class bar food. See p.575.

▶▶ **The Falcon** Fotheringhay. Rightly celebrated village pub and restaurant in the heart of rural Northamptonshire. See p.579.

to look pretty much like it did when he lived here, and the Library, which holds a small collection of the **poet's possessions**, from letters and an inkstand through to his pistols and boxing gloves. Here also is the flashy black-leather cavalry helmet Byron had made for himself when he set out to liberate the Greeks from their Ottoman overlords – Byron always liked to dress the part, if nothing else. A further room contains a set of satirical, cartoon-like watercolours entitled *The Wonderful History of Lord Byron & his dog* by his friend Elizabeth Pigot, and there's a portrait of the self-same dog, **Boatswain**, further on in the south gallery. The final part of a visit proceeds through the medieval cloisters to which was added a chapel in the full, florid flush of high Victorian design.

At the back of the house is a delightful **walled garden**, on the edge of which is a conspicuous memorial, with an absurdly extravagant inscription, to Boatswain. Beyond lie the main **gardens**, a secretive and subtle combination of lake, Gothic waterfalls, yew tunnels and Japanese-style rockeries, complete with idiosyncratic pagodas.

A fast and frequent Pronto **bus** service (Ⓦwww.prontobus.co.uk) leaves Nottingham's Victoria bus station every twenty minutes or so bound for Mansfield; en route, it stops at the gates of Newstead Abbey, a mile from the house; the journey takes about 25 minutes.

Sherwood Forest National Nature Reserve

Most of **Sherwood Forest**, once a vast royal woodland of oak, birch and bracken covering all of northern Nottinghamshire, was cleared in the eighteenth century and nowadays it's difficult to imagine the protection it provided for generations of outlaws, the most famous of whom was **Robin Hood**. There's no "true story" of Robin's life – the earliest reference to him, in Langland's fourteenth-century *Piers Plowman*, treats him as a fiction – but to the balladeers of fifteenth-century England, who invented most of Hood's folklore, this was hardly the point. For them, Robin was a symbol of yeoman decency, a semi-mythological opponent of corrupt clergymen and evil officers of the law; in the early tales, although Robin shows sympathy for the peasant, he has rather more respect for the decent nobleman, and he's never credited with robbing the rich to give to the poor. This and other parts of the legend, such as Maid Marian and Friar Tuck, were added later.

Robin Hood may lack historical authenticity, but it hasn't discouraged the county council from spending thousands of pounds sustaining the **Major Oak**, the creaky tree where Maid Marian and Robin are supposed to have plighted their troth. The Major Oak is on a pleasant one-mile woodland trail that begins beside the visitor centre at the main entrance to **Sherwood Forest National Nature Reserve** (daily dawn–dusk; free, but weekend & school hols car parking fee £3), which comprises 450 acres of oak and silver birch crisscrossed with footpaths. The visitor centre is half a mile south of the village of Edwinstowe, which is itself about twenty miles north of Nottingham via the A614.

Stagecoach's Sherwood Arrow **bus** #33 (Ⓦwww.stagecoachbus.com) departs for the Sherwood Forest visitor centre from Nottingham's Victoria bus station every two hours.

Clumber Park

Four miles north along the A614 from Ollerton – Edwinstowe's immediate neighbour – is the entrance to **Clumber Park** (daily dawn–dusk; free, but £5.20 entry per vehicle for non-NT members), four thousand acres of park and woodland lying to the south of industrial Worksop. The estate was once the country seat of the dukes of Newcastle, and it was here in the 1770s that they constructed a grand mansion overlooking Clumber Lake. The house was dismantled in 1938, when the duke sold the estate, and today the most interesting survivor of the lakeside buildings – located about two miles west of the A614 – is the Gothic Revival **chapel** (daily: April–Oct 10am–5pm; Nov–March 10am–4pm; free), an imposing edifice with a soaring spire and an intricately carved interior built for the seventh duke in the 1880s. Close by, the old **stable block** now houses a National Trust office, shop and **café** (same hours as chapel), and there's **bike rental** (April–Oct & winter weekends) in an adjacent building. The woods around the lake offer some delightful strolls and bike rides through planted woodland interspersed with the occasional patch of original forest.

Stagecoach's Sherwood Arrow **bus** #33 (ⓦwww.stagecoachbus.com) runs up the west side of Clumber Park en route to Worksop every two hours; ask the driver to stop at Carburton for the 2.5-mile walk to the Clumber Park NT office.

Welbeck Abbey's Harley Art Gallery

Immediately to the west of Clumber Park lies **Welbeck Abbey estate**, which remains firmly in ducal hands. Here, the estate's old gas works, built on the edge of the duke's property in the 1870s, has been imaginatively turned into the **Harley Art Gallery** (daily 10am–5pm; free; ⓦwww.harleygallery.co.uk). The gallery is mainly devoted to temporary exhibitions featuring the work of local living artists, all well presented and intelligently arranged, but there's also a permanent exhibition on the ducal family, variously named Cavendish, Portland and Newcastle. It's a small display – just one room – but includes an appealing assortment of family knick-knacks, from portraits, cameos and rare books through to silverware and paintings. Locally at least, the most famous of the line was the **Fifth Duke of Portland** (1800–1879), known as the "burrowing duke" for the maze of gas-lit tunnels he built underneath his estate. Naturally enough, many thought he was bonkers, but the truth may well be far more complex – an issue explored in Mick Jackson's novel *The Underground Man*, wherein the duke is portrayed as a shy man haunted by his obsessions. Another school of thought puts his burrowing down to the disfiguring effects of a skin disease. The tunnels are not, however, open to the public, which is a real shame. Next to the gallery, a **café** serves reasonably tasty light snacks and there's also a first-rate **farm shop**, which attracts happy eaters from far and wide – the steak pies are especially tasty.

The entrance to the Harley Gallery is on the A60, two miles north of the hamlet of Cuckney, which is itself about five miles from the facilities at Clumber Park. There are no buses to the gallery from Nottingham.

Hardwick Hall

Born the daughter of a minor Derbyshire squire, Elizabeth, Countess of Shrewsbury (1527–1608) – aka **Bess of Hardwick** – became one of the leading figures of Elizabethan England, renowned for her political and business acumen. She also had a penchant for building and her major achievement, **Hardwick Hall** (mid-Feb to Oct Wed–Sun: house 11am–4.30pm; gardens 11am–5pm; house & gardens £9.50, gardens only £5.30; NT), begun when she was 62, has survived in amazingly good condition. The house was the epitome of fashionable taste, a balance of symmetry and ingenious detail in which the rectangular lines of the building are offset by line upon line of windows – there's actually more glass than stone – while up above her giant-sized initials (E.S.) hog every roof line. Inside, the ground floor is relatively routine, but it's here that the Hall's extensive collection of sixteenth- and seventeenth-century needlework is displayed, including several pieces by Mary, Queen of Scots, who was held in custody by the Earl of

Shrewsbury for years. He moaned about the expense incessantly, one of the reasons for the souring of his relationship with Bess, a deterioration that prompted their estrangement.

On the top floor, the **High Great Chamber**, where Bess received her most distinguished guests, boasts an extraordinary plaster frieze, a brightly painted, finely worked affair celebrating the goddess Diana, the virgin huntress – it was, of course, designed to please the Virgin Queen herself. Next door, the **Long Gallery** is simply breathtaking, like an indoor cricket pitch only with exquisite furnishings and fittings from the splendid chimneypieces and tapestries through to a set of portraits, including one each of the queen and Bess. Bess could exercise here while keeping out of the sun – at a time when any hint of a tan was considered decidedly plebeian.

Outside, the **garden** makes for a pleasant wander and, beyond the ha-ha (the animal-excluding low wall and ditch), rare breeds of cattle and sheep graze the surrounding **parkland** (daily 8am–6pm; free). Finally – and rather confusingly – there's **Hardwick Old Hall** (April–Oct Wed–Sun 10am–5pm; £4.50; EH), next to Hardwick Hall. It was Bess's previous home, but is now little more than a broken-down if substantial ruin.

The easiest way to reach Hardwick is along the M1; come off at Junction 29 and follow the signs from the roundabout at the top of the slip road – a three-mile trip.

Southwell

SOUTHWELL, some fourteen miles northeast of Nottingham, is a sedate and well-heeled backwater distinguished by **Southwell Minster** (daily 8am–7pm or dusk, Sun hours depend on services; £5 donation suggested; Ⓦwww.southwell minster.co.uk), whose perky twin towers are visible for miles around, and by the fine Georgian mansions facing it along Church Street. The Normans built the minster at the beginning of the twelfth century and, although some elements were added later, their design predominates, from the imposing west towers through to the dog-tooth decoration and the bull's-eye windows of the clerestory. Inside, the arcaded nave, with its sturdy columns, marches up to the north transept, where there is a remarkably fine alabaster tomb of a long forgotten churchman, one Archbishop Sandys, who died in 1588. The red-flecked alabaster effigy of Sandys is so precise that you can see the furrows on his brow and the crow's feet round his eyes; his children are depicted kneeling below and it's assumed that Sandys was one of the first bishops to marry – and beget – after the break with Rome changed the rules. The nave's Norman stonework ends abruptly at the transepts and beyond lie both the Early English choir and the extraordinary **chapterhouse**. The latter is embellished with naturalistic foliage dating from the late thirteenth century, some of the earliest carving of its type in England. To wet your whistle, the minster's **café** is in the modern annexe just outside the entrance to the church.

About a mile from the minster, out on the road to Newark, stands **Southwell Workhouse** (March–Oct Wed–Sun noon–5pm; £5.80; NT), a substantial three-storey brick building that looks like a prison, but is in fact a rare survivor of the Victorian workhouses that once dotted every corner of the country. They were built as a result of the New Poor Law of 1834, which made a laudable attempt to provide shelter for the destitute. However, the middle classes were concerned that the workers would take advantage of free shelter, so conditions were made hard – as a matter of policy – and the "workhouses" were much feared. Most were knocked down or redeveloped years ago, but the one here at Southwell remained almost untouched, though its bare rooms and barred windows make the whole experience rather depressing.

There are regular NCT (Nottingham City Transport) **buses** to Southwell from Queen Street in central Nottingham. See the box on p.562 for where to **eat** around Southwell

Newark

From Southwell, it's seven miles east to **NEWARK**, an amiable old river port and market town that was once a major staging point on the Great North Road. Fronting the town as you approach from the west are the gaunt riverside ruins of **Newark Castle** (daily dawn–dusk; free), all that's left of the mighty medieval fortress that was pounded to pieces during the Civil War by the Parliamentarians. Opposite, just across the street to the north, is **The Ossington**, a flashy structure whose Tudor appearance is entirely fraudulent – it was built in the 1880s as a temperance hotel by a local bigwig, in an effort to save drinkers from themselves. From here, it's just a couple of minutes' walk east through a network of narrow lanes and alleys to the **Market Place**, an expansive square framed by attractive Georgian and Victorian facades. Just off the square stands the mostly thirteenth-century **church of St Mary Magdalene** (Mon–Sat 8.30am–4.30pm, May–Sept also Sun 2–4.30pm), a handsome if badly weathered structure with a massive spire (236ft) that soars high above the town centre. Inside, look out for the pair of medieval Dance of Death panel paintings, behind the reredos in the choir's Markham Chantry Chapel. One panel has a well-to-do man slipping his hand into his purse, the other shows a carnation-carrying skeleton pointing to the grave – an obvious reminder to the observer of his or her mortality.

Practicalities

Newark has two **train stations**: Newark Castle on the Nottingham–Lincoln line is on the west side of the River Trent, a five-minute walk from the castle, while the larger Newark North Gate Station, on the main London–Edinburgh line, is on Appleton Gate, from where it's a ten-minute walk southwest to the castle. Regular buses from Nottingham pull into the **bus station**, on Lombard Street, from which it's a five-minute walk north along Castlegate to the castle. Newark **tourist office** is in front of the castle on Castlegate (daily 9am–5pm, Oct–March till 4pm; ℡01636/655765).

For **food**, either head for the excellent *Gannets*, 35 Castlegate, a first-rate coffee bar serving delicious daytime snacks and meals, or go to *Café Bleu*, opposite at 14 Castlegate (℡01636/610141), a brilliant French/Modern British restaurant serving top-class meals (main courses average £15) from an inventive menu – try the lasagne of wild mushrooms with squash and truffle dressing or the sea trout and pak choi. It's one of the best restaurants in the county, with an outside terrace and frequent live jazz; the decor – all pastel-painted cheerfulness – is appealing too.

Leicester

At first glance, **LEICESTER**, some 25 miles south of Nottingham, seems a resolutely modern city, but further inspection reveals traces of its medieval and Roman past, situated immediately to the west of the downtown shopping area near the River Soar. The Romans chose this site to keep an eye on the rebellious Corieltauvi tribe, constructing a fortified town beside the Fosse Way (now the A46), the military road running from Lincoln to Cirencester. Later, the **Emperor Hadrian** kitted the place out with huge public buildings, though the Danes, who overran the area in the eighth century, were not overly impressed and didn't even bother to pilfer much of the stone. Later still, the town's medieval castle became the base of the earls of Leicester, the most distinguished of whom was **Simon de Montfort**, who forced Henry III to convene the first English Parliament in 1265.

Since the late seventeenth century, Leicester has been a centre of the **hosiery trade** and it was this industry that attracted hundreds of Asian immigrants to settle here in the 1950s and 1960s. Today, about a third of Leicester's population is Asian and the city elected England's first Asian MP, Keith Vaz, in 1987. The focus of Leicester's **Asian community** is the Belgrave Road and its environs, an area of cramped terrace houses about a mile to the northeast of the city centre. Belgrave celebrates two major Hindu festivals – **Diwali**, the Festival of Light, held in October or November, when six thousand lamps are strung out along Belgrave Road, and **Navrati**, an eight-day celebration in October held in honour of the goddess Ambaji. In addition, the city's sizeable Afro-Caribbean community holds England's second biggest street festival (after the Notting Hill Carnival), the **Leicester Caribbean Carnival** (Ⓦwww.leicestercarnival.com), on the first weekend in August.

Traditionally, Leicester has had a reputation for looking rather glum, but the city centre is very much on the up, especially with the creation of a **Cultural Quarter** equipped with a flashy performance venue, Curve Theatre. Otherwise, pride of municipal place goes to varied collections of the **New Walk Museum and Art Gallery**.

Arrival, information and accommodation

From Leicester **train station**, on London Road, it's a ten-minute walk northwest to the city centre; St Margaret's **bus station** is on the north side of the centre, just off Gravel Street. The centre is signed from both – the large Haymarket shopping centre, between the two, is an easy landmark. The **tourist office** is a short walk to the south of the Haymarket at 7–9 Every St, on Town Hall Square (Mon–Fri 10am–5.30pm, Sat 10am–5pm; Ⓣ0844/888 5181, Ⓦwww.goleicestershire.com).

Leicester has a good crop of business **hotels**, mostly within walking distance of the train station. The tourist office will help fix you up with somewhere to stay, but things rarely get tight except during the Navrati and Diwali festivals.

Belmont De Montfort St Ⓣ0116/254 4773, Ⓦwww.belmonthotel.co.uk. Proficient hotel in a modernized and extended Georgian property about 300 yards south of the train station. Popular with business folk. ❸

Maiyango 13–21 St Nicholas Place Ⓣ0116/251 8898, Ⓦwww.maiyango.com. New kid on the accommodation block, this hotel – the best in town – has fourteen slick modern rooms with wooden floors, plasma TVs, subdued lighting and wide, low-slung beds. Also has a handy location, a brief

walk from the principal sights and Leicester's main shopping centres, the Haymarket and Highcross; has its own first-rate restaurant too (see p.567). ❺–❻

Spindle Lodge 2 West Walk Ⓣ0116/233 8801, Ⓦwww.spindlelodge.com. Well-maintained, family-run hotel in a pleasantly converted, three-storey, ivy-clad Victorian townhouse. The public rooms have period touches and the bedrooms beyond are decorated in plain, unfussy style. On a quiet residential street, a 10min walk south of the train station. ❷

The City

The most conspicuous buildings in Leicester's crowded centre are two large shopping centres, the ultramodern **Highcross** and the clumpy **Haymarket**, but the historic landmark is the Victorian **clocktower** of 1868, standing in front of the Haymarket and marking the spot where seven streets meet. One of the seven is Cheapside, which leads to Leicester's open-air **market** (Mon–Sat), one of the best of its type in the country and the place where the young **Gary Lineker**, now the UK's best-known football pundit, worked on the family stall. Good-hearted Gary remains a popular figure hereabouts and has been made a freeman of the city,

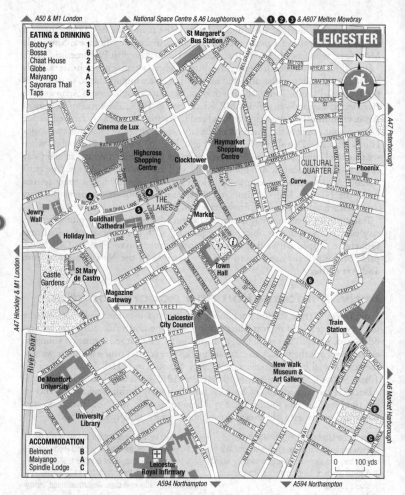

LEICESTER

N

EATING & DRINKING

Bobby's	1
Bossa	6
Chaat House	2
Globe	4
Maiyango	A
Sayonara Thali	3
Taps	5

St Margaret's
Bus Station

Cinema de Lux

Highcross
Shopping
Centre

Clocktower

Haymarket
Shopping
Centre

CULTURAL
QUARTER

Phoenix

Curve

THE
LANES

Market

Jewry
Wall

Guildhall Cathedral

Holiday Inn

St Mary
de Castro

Castle
Gardens

Magazine
Gateway

Town
Hall

Leicester
City Council

Train
Station

De Montfort
University

New Walk
Museum &
Art Gallery

University
Library

ACCOMMODATION

Belmont	B
Maiyango	A
Spindle Lodge	C

Leicester
Royal Infirmary

0   100 yds

9

River Soar

which gives him the right to graze his sheep in front of the town hall. To the east of the clocktower is Leicester's nascent **Cultural Quarter**, whose two main attractions are **Curve Theatre** and the Phoenix cinema (see p.570). There's more to come but this is a good start, no mistake.

The Lanes, the Cathedral and the Guildhall

Another of the seven streets beginning at the clocktower is Silver Street (subsequently Guildhall Lane), which passes through **The Lanes**, where a medley of small, independent shops gives this part of the centre real character. Nearby is **St Martin's Cathedral**, a much modified, eleventh-century structure incorporating two finely carved porches – a stone one at the front and an earlier timber version at the rear. Next door is the **Guildhall** (Feb–Nov Mon–Wed & Sat 11am–4.30pm, Sun 1–4.30pm; free), a half-timbered building that has served, variously, as the town hall, prison and police station. The most interesting part of a visit is the rickety Great Hall, its beams bent with age, but there are a couple of old cells too, plus the town gibbet on which the bodies of the hanged were publicly displayed until the 1840s.

The Jewry Wall and around

From the Guildhall, it's a short walk west to St Nicholas Circle, a large roundabout that is part of the ring road. Beside the roundabout, you'll spot the conspicuous **church of St Nicholas** and beside that, in a little dell, lie the foundations of the Emperor Hadrian's public baths, which culminate in the **Jewry Wall**, a substantial chunk of Roman masonry some 18ft high and 73ft long. The baths were a real irritation to the emperor: the grand scheme was spoilt by the engineers, who miscalculated the line of the aqueduct that was to pipe in the water, and so bathers had to rely on a hand-filled cistern replenished from the river – which wasn't what he had in mind at all.

To St Mary de Castro

From the Jewry Wall, keep on going round St Nicholas Circle – with the *Holiday Inn* on the left – then veer down the first major street on the right and opposite you'll see the entrance to **Castle Gardens**, a narrow strip of a park that runs alongside a canalized portion of the River Soar. The gardens are a pleasant spot, incorporating the overgrown mound where Leicester's Norman castle motte once stood. At the far end, you emerge on The Newarke; turn left and follow the road round, and in a jiffy you'll reach Castle View, a narrow lane spanned by the Turret Gateway, a rare survivor of the city's medieval castle. Just beyond the gateway is **St Mary de Castro** (Easter–Oct Mon–Fri noon–2pm, Sat 2–4pm), a dignified old church with a dainty crocketed spire where Chaucer may well have got married.

Looping round the church you reach the ring road; look right and you can't miss the substantial **Magazine Gateway** (no access), a combined medieval gateway and arsenal that is now ignominiously stranded between the two carriageways.

To the New Walk Museum and Art Gallery

From the Magazine Gateway, it's a short walk east to Town Hall Square, where the grandiloquent **Town Hall** is a real whopper of a building, its red-brick and sandstone-trimmed facade, completed in a sort of chateau style in the 1870s, surmounted by a suitably large clocktower; the square is also the site of the tourist office (see p.567).

From here, it's a brief stroll south to the **New Walk**, a long and pleasant pedestrianized promenade that is home to the city's best museum, the **New Walk Museum and Art Gallery**, 55 New Walk (Mon–Sat 10am–5pm, Sun 11am–5pm; free). The museum covers a lot of ground, from the natural world to geology and beyond, but one highlight is its extensive collection of Ancient Egyptian artefacts, featuring mummies and hieroglyphic tablets brought back to Leicester in the 1880s. The museum also holds an enjoyable collection of paintings and, although these are rotated regularly, you're likely to see works by British artists such as Hogarth, Francis Bacon, Stanley Spencer and Lowry as well as a whole raft of mawkishly romantic Victorian paintings, such as Charles Green's *The Girl I Left Behind Me* (1880). Even better, and this is something of a surprise, there's an outstanding collection of German Expressionist works, mostly sketches, woodcuts and lithographs by the likes of Otto Dix and George Grosz. It's a ten-minute walk from the museum back to the Haymarket.

The National Space Centre

The **National Space Centre**, just off the A6 two miles north of the city centre (term time: Tues–Fri 10am–4pm, Sat & Sun 10am–5pm; school hols: daily

10am–5pm; £13, children (5–16) £11; Ⓦwww.spacecentre.co.uk), is devoted to space, science and astronomy, with a string of themed galleries exploring everything from the planets to orbiting earth. The emphasis is on the interactive, which makes the place very popular with kids. Bus #54 links the train station with Abbey Lane, a five-minute walk from the centre.

Eating, drinking and entertainment

People come from miles around to eat at the **Indian restaurants** along **Belgrave Road**, which begins just beyond the flyover, about a mile to the northeast of the centre. There are top-notch restaurants in the city centre too, and a battery of **bars**, though most of these are chains.

As for the **performing arts**, the leading venue is **Curve Theatre** (Ⓣ0116/242 3560, Ⓦwww.curveonline.co.uk), whose startling glass facade is at the heart of the Cultural Quarter at 60 Rutland St. Curve offers a wide-ranging programme and is just a couple of minutes' walk from the **Phoenix**, an outstanding art-house **cinema**, at 4 Midland St (Ⓣ0116/242 2800, Ⓦwww.phoenix.org.uk). The Phoenix's most distinctive rival is the glittering new **Cinema de Lux**, adjoining the Highcross shopping centre (Ⓣ0871/220 1000, Ⓦwww.cinemadelux.co.uk).

Restaurants, pubs and bars

Bobby's 154 Belgrave Rd Ⓣ0116/266 0106. Run by Gujaratis, this bright, modern restaurant – and takeaway – is strictly vegetarian. A mind-blowing menu covers almost every vegetarian option you can think of, and then some. Mains from as little as £5.

Bossa 110 Granby St. Pocket-sized café-bar with tasty snacks and light meals during the day, Latin/Hispanic beats at night. Popular with the city's gay community.

Chaat House 108 Belgrave Rd Ⓣ0116/266 0513. Opened over thirty years ago, the *Chaat House* is something of a local institution, serving satisfying mounds of vegetarian food to its many customers – the *masala dosas* are wonderful. £20 will cover a meal for two.

Globe 43 Silver St. Traditional pub in an attractive old building at the heart of the city. Smashing range of real ales and filling bar food too.

Maiyango 13–21 St Nicholas Place Ⓣ0116/251 8898. Intimate, chi-chi

lounge-bar and restaurant, beneath the hotel of the same name (see p.567). The restaurant, decorated in rich, warm colours, uses local, seasonal ingredients, put together with style and verve, and the menu is wide-ranging – for example, soy-scented guinea-fowl breast in a sweet-and-sour plum *jus*. First-class service too. Three-course evening menu £28.

Sayonara Thali 49 Belgrave Rd Ⓣ0116/266 5888. Specializes in set *thali* meals, with several different dishes, breads and pickles served together on large steel plates. Full *thalis* from £6.50.

Taps 10 Guildhall Lane Ⓣ0116/253 0904. Inventive bar and restaurant, whose claim to fame is the beer taps at many of the tables – help yourself and pay later (yes, the taps are monitored as they dispense). Excellent range of bottled beers too, plus vaulted cellars that date back yonks, and an above-average menu – chicken breast stuffed with apples and Stilton in a creamy leek sauce, for example, for just £10.25. Closed Sun.

Leicestershire and Rutland

Leicester lies at the heart of the compact county of **Leicestershire**, arguably one of the more anonymous of the English shires, its undulating landscapes comprising an apparently haphazard mix of the industrial and rural. Highlights include the trim charms of tiny **Market Bosworth**, near the site of **Bosworth Field**, where Richard III came an unpleasant cropper to end the Wars of the Roses, and **Ashby-de-la-Zouch**, an amenable little town graced by the substantial remains of its medieval castle. There's also a fine hilltop church at **Breedon-on-the-Hill** as well as **Calke Abbey**, technically over the boundary in Derbyshire and not an abbey at all, but an intriguing country house whose faded charms are witness to the declining fortunes of the landed gentry. To the east of Leicestershire lies England's smallest county, **Rutland**, reinstated in its own right in 1997 following 23 unpopular years of merger with its larger neighbour. Rutland has three places of note: **Oakham**, the county town, and **Uppingham** – both rural centres with some elegant Georgian architecture – and the prettier, much smaller stone hamlet of **Lyddington**.

There are frequent **buses** from Leicester to Market Bosworth, Ashby-de-la-Zouch and Breedon-on-the-Hill, but none to Calke Abbey. There are also **trains** from Leicester to Oakham (and Stamford, see p.589), from where there's a reasonably good bus service on to Uppingham, but nothing much to Lyddington.

Market Bosworth and around

The thatched cottages and Georgian houses of tiny **MARKET BOSWORTH**, some eleven miles west of Leicester, fan out from a dinky **Market Place** that was an important trading centre throughout the Middle Ages. From the sixteenth to the nineteenth century, the dominant family hereabouts was the Dixies, merchant-landlords who mostly ended up buried at the **church of St Peter** (daily 8.30am–dusk; free), a good-looking edifice with a castellated nave and a sturdy square tower, a three-minute walk north of the centre. Heavily revamped by the Victorians, the church's interior is fairly routine, but the chancel does hold the early eighteenth-century **tomb** of John Dixie, one-time rector, who is honoured by a long hagiographic plaque and the effigy of his weeping sister. John apart, the Dixies were not universally admired, however, and the young Samuel Johnson, who taught at the **Dixie Grammar School** – its elongated facade still abuts the Market Place – disliked the founder, Sir Wolstan Dixie, so much that he recalled his time there "with the strongest aversion and even a sense of horror".

There are hourly **buses** from Leicester to Market Bosworth's Market Place. Also on the Market Place is an excellent **hotel**, *Softleys* (☏01455/290464, ⓦwww.softleys.com; ❸), which has three well-appointed bedrooms above an excellent **restaurant** (closed Sun eve & Mon), where the menu is lively and creative – the lamb is especially good; mains average around £16.

The Battle of Bosworth Field

Market Bosworth is best known for the **Battle of Bosworth Field**; the battle was fought on hilly countryside near the village in 1485. This was the last and most decisive battle of the Wars of the Roses, an interminably long-winded and bitterly violent conflict among the nobility for control of the English Crown. The victor was Henry Tudor, subsequently Henry VII, the vanquished Richard III, who famously died on the battlefield. In desperation, Shakespeare's villainous Richard cried out "A horse, a horse, my kingdom for a horse," but in fact the defeated king seems to have been a much more phlegmatic character. Taking a glass of water before the fighting started, he actually said, "I live a king: if I die, I die a king."

The **Bosworth Battlefield Heritage Centre** (daily: April–Oct 10am–5pm; Nov–March 10am–4pm; £6, £1.50 parking), located a couple of miles south of Market Bosworth, features a workmanlike description of the battle and explains its historical context, though the less said about the ersatz medieval village that is beginning to take shape next door the better. The Heritage Centre also has a separate section on recent archeological efforts to find the actual site of the battle: unfortunately, it turns out that the battlefield was a couple of miles further west on what is now private land, which leaves the centre, never mind the adjoining circular two-mile **Battle Trail**, which identifies where tradition had the protagonists meet, somewhat marooned. Nevertheless, the ramble along the trail is pleasant enough and on the way you'll pass **King Richard's Well**, a rough cairn where the king was supposed to have had his final drink.

Ashby-de-la-Zouch and around

ASHBY-DE-LA-ZOUCH, fifteen miles northwest of Leicester, takes its fanciful name from two sources – the town's first Norman overlord was Alain de Parrhoet la Souche, while the rest simply means "place by the ash trees". Nowadays, Ashby is far from rustic, but it's still an amiable little place and its principal attraction, the **castle** (April–June & Sept–Oct Thurs–Mon 10am–5pm; July & Aug daily 10am–5pm; Nov–March Thurs–Mon noon–4pm; £3.90; EH), stands just off the town's main drag, Market Street. Originally a Norman manor house, the stronghold was the work of Edward IV's chancellor, Lord Hastings, who received his licence to crenellate in 1474. Today, the rambling ruins include substantial leftovers from the old fortifications, but the star turn is the hundred-foot-high **Hastings Tower**, a self-contained four-storey stronghold that has survived in reasonably good nick. This tower house represented the latest thinking in castle design: it provided a secure inner fastness for Hastings and his retinue both against any outside enemy and his own mercenaries – who, experience had shown elsewhere, were often a threat to their employer – while also providing much better accommodation than was previously available. Improved living quarters reflecting the power and pride of the nobility were built all over England at this time and this is a rare survivor – witness the large windows on the upper floors, accessible via the tower's well-worn spiral staircase.

There are regular Arriva **buses** (ⓦwww.arrivabus.co.uk) to Ashby's Market Street from Leicester.

Calke Abbey

The eighteenth-century facade of **Calke Abbey**, set deep in the countryside a few miles north of Ashby (house: March–Oct Mon–Wed, Sat & Sun 12.30–5pm; gardens: March–June, Sept & Oct Mon–Wed, Sat & Sun 11am–5pm, July & Aug daily 11am–5pm; park: daily 8am–8.30pm; £8.40 all inclusive, garden only £4.60, park only £1.60; NT), is all self-confidence, its acres of dressed stone and three long lines of windows polished off with an imposing Greek Revival portico. This all cost oodles of money and the Harpurs, and then the Harpur-Crewes, who owned the estate, were doing very well until the finances of the English country estate changed after World War I. Then, at a time when country houses were being demolished by the score, the Harpur-Crewes simply hung on, becoming the epitome of faded gentility and refusing to make all but the smallest of changes to the house – though they did finally plump for electricity in 1962. The last Harpur-Crewe to live here, Charles, died in 1981 and the estate passed in its entirety to the National Trust. Very much to their credit, the Trust decided not to bring in the restorers and have kept the house in its dishevelled state – and this is its real charm.

A visit starts among the old agricultural outbuildings, from where it's a short stroll to the **house**, whose entrance hall adroitly sets the scene, its walls decorated with ancient, moth-eaten stuffed heads from the family's herd of prize cattle. Beyond is the Caricature Room, whose walls are lined with satirical cartoons, some by the leading cartoonists of their day, including Gillray and Cruikshank. Further on, there are more animal heads and glass cabinets of stuffed birds in the capacious Saloon; an intensely cluttered Miss Havisham-like Drawing Room; and a chaotic at-home School Room. After you've finished in the house, you can stroll out into the **gardens**, pop into the Victorian estate **church**, and wander through rolling, wooded **parkland**.

There's no public transport to Calke Abbey, and motorists must follow a long-winded one-way system: from Ashby, take the B587 Melbourne Road and follow the signs – the entrance is at the village of Ticknall to the north of the house; the exit is to the south.

Staunton Harold Church

When you leave Calke Abbey, spare a little time for neighbouring **Staunton Harold Church** (April, May, Sept & Oct Sat & Sun 1–4.30pm; June–Aug Wed–Sun 1–4.30pm; free; NT), though it is a little tricky to find: at the abbey exit, turn right, take the second left into the Staunton Harold estate, and then proceed as far as the garden centre – the church is at the back, behind the Ferrers Arts and Craft Centre. Curiously, Staunton Harold Church is a political rant of a building in which the local lord, the reactionary Robert Shirley, expressed his hatred of Oliver Cromwell. There's no missing Shirley's intentions as he carved them above the church door: "In the year 1653 when all things sacred were throughout the nation either demolished or profaned..." and so he goes on. Whatever the politics, it was certainly an audacious – probably foolhardy – gesture, and sure enough Cromwell had the last laugh when an unrepentant Shirley died in prison three years later. The church itself is a good-looking affair, largely in the Perpendicular style with delightful painted ceilings and wood panelling.

Breedon-on-the-Hill

It's five miles northeast from Ashby to the village of **BREEDON-ON-THE-HILL**, which sits in the shadow of the large, partly quarried hill from which it takes its name. A steep footpath and a winding, half-mile byroad lead up from the village to the summit, from where there are smashing views over the surrounding countryside. Here also is the fascinating **church of St Mary and St Hardulph** (daily 9.30am–4pm, sometimes later in summer; free), which occupies the site of an Iron Age hillfort and an eighth-century Anglo-Saxon monastery. Mostly dating from the thirteenth century, the church is kitted out with Georgian pulpit and pews as well as a large and distinctly rickety box-pew. Much more rare are a number of **Anglo-Saxon carvings**, both individual saints and prophets and wall friezes, where a dense foliage of vines is inhabited by a tangle of animals and humans. The friezes are quite extraordinary, and the fact that the figures look Byzantine rather than Anglo-Saxon has fuelled much academic debate.

Cresswell Coaches (Ⓦwww.cresswellcoaches.com) operate a reasonably frequent **bus** service from Ashby to Breedon village, at the bottom of the hill.

Oakham

Well-heeled **OAKHAM**, 23 miles east of Leicester, is **Rutland**'s county town, its prosperity bolstered by Oakham School, now one of the region's more exclusive private schools, and by its proximity to **Rutland Water**, a large reservoir whose assorted facilities attract cyclists, ramblers, sailors and birdwatchers by the hundred (see box below). Oakham's stone terraces and Georgian villas are too often interrupted to assume much grace, but the town does have its architectural moments, particularly in the L-shaped **Market Place**, where a brace of sturdy awnings shelters the old water pump and town stocks.

A few steps from the north side of the Market Place stands **Oakham Castle** (Tues–Fri 10am–5pm, Sat 10am–4pm; free), a large banqueting hall that was once part of a twelfth-century fortified house. The hall is a good example of Norman domestic architecture and surrounding it are the grassy banks that once served to protect it. Inside, the whitewashed walls are covered with **horseshoes**, the result of an ancient custom by which every lord or lady, king or queen, is obliged to present an ornamental horseshoe when they first set foot in the town.

Oakham School is housed in a series of impressive ironstone buildings that frames the west edge of the Market Place. On the right-hand side of the school, a narrow lane leads to **All Saints' Church**, whose heavy tower and spire rise high above the town. Dating from the thirteenth century, the church is an architectural hybrid, but the airy interior is distinguished by the intense medieval carvings along the columns of the nave and choir, with Christian scenes and symbols set alongside dragons, grotesques, devils and demons.

Practicalities

Oakham **train station** lies on the northwest side of town, a ten-minute walk from the Market Place. **Buses**, including those from Leicester, arrive on John Street, just west of the Market Place. There's nowhere special to stay or even drink in Oakham itself, but the nearby village of **Clipsham**, close to the A1 about six miles to the northeast, has the *Olive Branch* (℡01780/410355, Ⓦwww.theolivebranchpub .com; ❺), a country inn where the food is excellent and there are six deluxe rooms in their adjacent *Beech House*, each decorated to a particular theme – the Berry Room, for example, has splashes of pink and purple and a large and old mahogany bedstead. Also near Oakham, overlooking Rutland Water just a couple of miles to the southeast in tiny **Hambleton**, is one of the region's most opulent hotels, *Hambleton Hall* (℡01572/756991, Ⓦwww.hambletonhall.com; ❽), which occupies an imposing Baronial-Gothic mansion set in its own immaculate grounds. Part of the Relais & Châteaux group, it's seriously expensive; a much more affordable option in Hambleton village is *The Finches Arms* (℡01572/756575, Ⓦwww .finchsarms.co.uk; ❹), whose handful of smart, modern bedrooms have new

---

Outdoors at Rutland Water

Flanked by easy, green hills, the gentle waters of **Rutland Water** (Ⓦwww.rutland water.org.uk) have become a major centre for outdoor pursuits. There's **sailing** at Rutland Sailing Club (Ⓦwww.rutlandsc.co.uk); **cycle hire** from Rutland Water Cycling (via Ⓦwww.rutlandactivities.co.uk); and assorted watersports at Rutland Watersports Centre at Whitwell on the north shore (℡01780/460154, Ⓦwww.anglianwater.co.uk). Rutland Water also attracts a wide range of waterfowl, which prompted the establishment of a **nature reserve** with no fewer than 27 hides and two visitor centres at its west end. The reserve is home to an osprey breeding project, where the first osprey chick to fledge in central England for over a century was hatched in 2001.

wooden floors. It also offers tasty food with the emphasis on local, seasonal ingredients, in both its restaurant and its wood-beamed, stone-flagged bar; mains average around £13.

Uppingham

The narrow main street of **UPPINGHAM**, six miles south of Oakham, has the uniformity of style Oakham lacks, its course flanked by bow-fronted shops and ironstone houses, mostly dating from the eighteenth century. It's the general appearance that pleases, rather than any individual sight, but the town is famous as the home of **Uppingham School**, a bastion of privilege whose imposing, fortress-like building stands on the west side of the High Street. Founded in 1587, the school was distinctly second-rate until the middle of the nineteenth century, when a dynamic headmaster, the Reverend Edward Thring, grabbed enough land to lay out some of the biggest playing fields in England – fitness being, of course, an essential attribute for the rulers of the British Empire.

There's a regular **bus** service (every 2hr; Ⓦ www.rutnet.co.uk) from Oakham to Uppingham; the journey takes forty minutes. Uppingham has one especially good **hotel**, the *Lake Isle*, in a tastefully modernized eighteenth-century townhouse at 16 High Street East (Ⓣ01572/822951, Ⓦ www.lakeislehotel.co.uk; ❸). The rooms here are tastefully decorated in a pleasant rendition of traditional style and the **restaurant** is first-rate too, offering a superb and varied menu from guinea fowl to local venison, with main courses averaging around £15. For a **drink**, head for *The Vaults*, on the minuscule Market Place.

Lyddington

LYDDINGTON, some two miles southeast of Uppingham, is a sleepy little village of honey-coloured cottages straggling along a meandering main street, all backed by plump hills and broadleaf woodland. Early in the twelfth century, the Bishop of Lincoln, whose lands once extended south as far as the Thames, chose this as the site of a small palace – one of thirteen he erected to accommodate himself and his retinue while away on episcopal business. Confiscated during the Reformation, **Lyddington Bede House**, on Church Lane (April–Oct Thurs–Mon 10am–5pm; £3.90; EH), next door to the ironstone bulk of St Andrew's Church, was later converted into almshouses by Lord Burghley and has since been beautifully restored by English Heritage. The highlight is the light and airy Great Chamber, with its exquisitely carved oak cornices, but look out also for the tiny ground-floor rooms, which were occupied by impoverished locals for centuries.

Of the village's pubs, easily the most convivial is *The Old White Hart*, a traditional village **inn** with beamed ceilings on Main Street (Ⓣ01572/821703, Ⓦ www .oldwhitehart.co.uk; ❸). It has ten bright and breezily decorated rooms, two in the inn and eight in the adjoining cottage, and serves delicious food, both in the bar and in the restaurant, where main courses average around £12 (kitchen closed Sun eve in winter).

Northampton

Spreading north from the banks of the River Nene, **NORTHAMPTON** is a workaday modern town whose appearance largely belies its ancient past. Throughout the Middle Ages, this was one of central England's most important centres, a flourishing commercial hub whose now-demolished castle was a popular stopping-off point for travelling royalty. A fire in 1675 burnt most of the medieval city to a cinder, and the Georgian town that grew up in its stead was itself swamped by the Industrial Revolution, when Northampton swarmed with **boot-and shoemakers**. Their products shod almost everyone in the Empire – from Australia to Canada – as well as the British army, though things did go badly awry during the Crimean War. The army ordered two boat-loads of Northampton boots in preparation for the Russian winter, but – for reasons that remain obscure – insisted that all the left boots be shipped in one vessel, the right ones in another. Unfortunately, one of the boats sank en route – and the soldiers were left perplexed by the ways of the army commissariat. Equally perplexed were the Northampton tailors who clothed Errol Flynn, while he was in repertory here in 1933. Always a charmer, Flynn dressed well, but he hightailed it out of town after just a year, leaving a whopping tailors' debt behind him.

The Town

Northampton's compact centre is at its most appealing on and around its main plaza, Market Square, which is where you'll find the town's finest buildings, principally All Saints' Church and the Guildhall, plus an excellent museum holding a fantastic collection of boots and shoes. Half a day is enough for a quick gambol round the sights, but there's no strong reason to stay the night here.

The Market Square

Northampton's expansive **Market Square** has a bustling, self-confident air and is just a few metres from the town's ecclesiastical pride and joy, the **church of All Saints**, whose unusually secular appearance stems from its finely proportioned, pillared portico and towered cupola. A statue of a bewigged Charles II in Roman attire surmounts the portico, a (flattering) thank-you for his donation of a thousand tonnes of timber after the Great Fire of 1675 had incinerated the earlier church. Inside, the handsome interior holds a sweeping timber gallery and a batch of Neoclassical pillars, which lead the eye up to the fancy plasterwork that decorates the ceiling.

Behind the church in St Giles' Square is the **Guildhall**, a flamboyant Victorian edifice constructed in the 1860s to a design by Edward Godwin. Godwin was one of the period's most inventive architects and his Gothic exterior, with its high-pointed windows and dinky turrets and towers, sports kings and queens plus scenes central to the county's history, including the execution of Mary, Queen of Scots, at Fotheringhay (see p.579).

Northampton Museum and Art Gallery

The **Northampton Museum and Art Gallery** (Mon–Sat 10am–5pm, Sun 2–5pm; free), metres from the Guildhall, celebrates the town's industrial heritage with a fabulous collection of **shoes and boots**. Along with silk slippers, clogs and high-heeled nineteenth-century court shoes, there's one of the four boots worn by an elephant during the British Expedition of 1959, which retraced Hannibal's putative route over the Alps into Italy. There's celebrity footwear too, such as the giant DMs Elton John wore in *Tommy*, plus whole cabinets of heavy-duty riding boots, pearl-inlaid raised wooden sandals from Ottoman Turkey, and a couple of cabinets showing just how long high heels have been in fashion. Moving on, the top floor is given over to an excellent display charting the town's history from Roman days to the present, paying particular attention to the significance of the shoe industry, which employed no less than half the town's population in 1920.

Practicalities

From Northampton **train station**, it's a ten-minute walk east to the Market Square. Buses pull into the **bus station** on Greyfriars, behind the Grosvenor shopping centre, immediately to the north of the Market Square. The **tourist office** is located in the former county courthouse, a good-looking seventeenth-century stone building across from All Saints on George Row (Mon–Fri 8.30am–5.30pm; ℡01604/236236, ⓦwww.explorenorthamptonshire.co.uk).

For **accommodation**, the *Best Western Lime Trees Hotel*, 8 Langham Place, Barrack Road (℡01604/632188, ⓦwww.limetreeshotel.co.uk; ➋), has thirty well-equipped modern bedrooms in attractive Georgian premises a little more than half a mile north of the centre on the A508. As for **food**, *The Vineyard*, a pleasantly turned-out little place metres from the Guildhall at 7 Derngate (℡01604/633978; closed Sun), is strong on both seafood and Italian dishes with mains from £10.

The rest of Northamptonshire

Northamptonshire is one of the region's most diverse counties – so diverse in fact that even many Midlanders can't recall what is actually in it and what isn't. Northampton apart, the county possesses three large industrial towns – Wellingborough, Corby and Kettering – but beyond these, amid rolling farmland, lies a battery of stately homes, historic churches and charming villages, the most picturesque of which are built of local limestone. The county's prime tourist attraction is **Althorp**, family home of the Spencers and the burial place of Diana, Princess of Wales. Runners-up include the postcard-pretty hamlet of **Ashby St Ledgers**, one-time haunt of Guy Fawkes and his incendiary cronies, the pretty canal locks of **Stoke Bruerne**, and the delightful hamlet of **Fotheringhay**, where Mary, Queen of Scots, came to an untimely end. The county also has a notable long-distance footpath, the seventy-mile **Nene Way**, which follows the looping course of the river right across the county. Nene Way brochures are available from Northampton tourist office.

Getting to the rural nooks and crannies of Northamptonshire by **public transport** requires some careful planning around patchy bus services.

Althorp

Althorp (July & Aug daily 11am–5pm; £12.50; ℡01604/770107, ⓦwww.althorp.com), the lavish country home and estate of the Spencers, is located about six miles northwest of Northampton off the A428. The Spencers have lived here for centuries, but this was no big deal until one of the tribe, **Diana**, married Prince Charles in 1981. The disintegration of the marriage and Diana's elevation to sainthood is a story known to millions – and most perceptively analysed by Beatrix Campbell in her book, *Diana, Princess of Wales: How Sexual Politics Shook the Monarchy*. The public outpouring of grief following Diana's death in 1997 was quite astounding, and Althorp became the focus of massive media attention as the coffin was brought up the M1 motorway from London to be buried on an island in the grounds of the family estate. Today, visitors troop round the grandiloquent rooms of Althorp house, drop by the **Diana exhibition** in the old stable block, and then take the footpath that leads round a lake in the middle of which is the islet (no access) where Diana is buried.

Ashby St Ledgers

The **Gunpowder Plot** (see box below), which so dismally failed to blow the Houses of Parliament to smithereens in 1605, was hatched in **ASHBY ST LEDGERS**, immediately to the west of the M1 off the A361, about fourteen miles northwest of Northampton. Since those heated conversations, nothing much seems to have happened here, and the village's one and only street, flanked by handsome limestone cottages and a patch of ancient grazing land, still leads to the conspiratorial **manor house** (no access), a beautiful Elizabethan complex set around a wide courtyard. The adjacent **church**, dedicated to St Mary and St Leodegarius (hence Ledger), looks a little stodgy, but its modest fourteenth-century stonework holds some wonderful, if faded, medieval **murals**. The clearest is the large painting in the nave of St Christopher carrying the infant Jesus.

Stoke Bruerne

Heading south out of Northampton on the A508, it's about eight miles to the village of **STOKE BRUERNE**, which sits beside a flight of seven locks on the Grand Union Canal. By water at least, the village is very close to England's longest navigable tunnel, the one-and-three-quarter-miles-long **Blisworth Tunnel**, constructed at the beginning of the nineteenth century. Before the advent of steam tugs in the 1870s, boats were pushed through the tunnel by "legging" – two or more men would push with their legs against the tunnel walls until they emerged to hand over to waiting teams of horses. This exhausting task is fully explained in the village's folksy **museum** (April–Oct daily 10am–5pm; Nov–March Wed–Fri 11am–3pm, Sat & Sun 11am–4pm; £4.75), which is housed in a converted canalside corn mill. The museum delves into two hundred years of canal history with models, exhibits of canal art and spit-and-polish engines.

Over the canal bridge, the *Boat Inn* **pub** (℡01604/862428, ⊛www.boatinn .co.uk) is jam-packed with narrowboat trinkets and serves a good pint and filling bar food. The pub also operates **narrowboat cruises** to the Blisworth Tunnel (Easter–Sept; 30min; £3) as well as longer canal trips; advance booking is advised as sailings do not take place every day.

Guy Fawkes and the Gunpowder Plot

Born in York, **Guy Fawkes** (1570–1606) was a young convert to Catholicism, and his enthusiasm for the old faith induced him to leave Elizabeth I's Protestant England to fight in the Spanish army – against the "heretics" of the Netherlands – in 1593. There he established a reputation as a brave and determined soldier, catching the eye of leading Catholics back home. Cowed by Elizabeth for decades, these same Catholics viewed the queen's death and the accession of **James I** (1603–25) with some optimism, but their hopes were dashed when the new king proved unsympathetic to the Catholic cause. A small group, under the leadership of one **Robert Catesby**, decided that this called for desperate measures and, keen to recruit a military man, one of them popped over to the Netherlands to seek out Fawkes, who signed up and returned to England like a shot. The plan was simple – almost amazingly so: first the conspirators rented a cellar under Parliament and then Fawkes filled it with barrels of gunpowder, enough to blow Parliament sky high. But on November 4, 1605, the eve of the planned attack, the authorities discovered this so-called **Gunpowder Plot** and Fawkes was promptly tortured into giving away the names of his co-conspirators. Fawkes was tried and executed in January 1606, but he is still burnt in effigy all over the country on **Bonfire Night**, November 5.

Fotheringhay

Pocket-sized **FOTHERINGHAY**, by the River Nene about thirty miles to the northeast of Northampton, has long been left to its own devices, but its medieval glory is recalled by the magnificent **church of St Mary and All Saints** (dawn–dusk; free), which rises mirage-like above the green riverine meadows. Begun in 1411 and a hundred and fifty years in the making, the church is a paradigm of the Perpendicular, its exterior sporting wonderful arching buttresses, its nave lit by soaring windows and the whole caboodle topped by a splendid octagonal lantern tower. The interior is a tad bare, but there are two fancily carved medieval pieces to inspect – a painted pulpit and a sturdy stone font. On either side of the altar are the tombs of Elizabeth I's ancestors, the dukes of York, Edward and Richard. Elizabeth found the tombs in disarray in 1573 and promptly had them rebuilt in a smooth white limestone that still looks like new.

Precious little remains of **Fotheringhay Castle** today, but the stronghold witnessed two key events – the birth of Richard III in 1452 and the beheading of **Mary, Queen of Scots**, in 1587. On the orders of Elizabeth I, Mary was executed in the castle's Great Hall with no one to stand in her defence – apart, that is, from her dog, which is said to have rushed from beneath her skirts as her head hit the deck. Thereafter, the castle fell into disrepair and nowadays only a grassy mound and ditch remain to mark its position; it's signposted down a short and narrow lane on the bend of the road as you come into the village from the pretty town of Oundle.

Fotheringhay has an excellent **pub-restaurant**, *The Falcon* (℡01832/226254), which occupies a neat stone building with a modern patio. They offer an imaginative menu here – lamb shank and artichoke for example – with delicious main courses costing around £15.

Lincoln

Reaching high into the sky from the top of a steep hill, the triple towers of **LINCOLN**'s mighty cathedral are visible for miles across the surrounding flatlands. This conspicuous spot was first fortified by the Celts, who called their settlement Lindon, "hillfort by the lake", a reference to the pools formed by the River Witham in the marshy ground below. In 47 AD, the Romans occupied Lindon and built a fortified town, which subsequently became, as Lindum Colonia, one of the four regional capitals of Roman Britain.

Today, only fragments of the Roman city survive, mostly pieces of the third-century town wall, and these are outdone by reminders of Lincoln's medieval heyday, which began during the reign of William the Conqueror with the construction of the **castle** and **cathedral**. Lincoln flourished, first as a Norman power-base and then as a centre of the wool trade with Flanders, until 1369 when the wool market was transferred to neighbouring Boston. It was almost five hundred years before the city revived, the recovery based upon its manufacture of agricultural machinery and drainage equipment for the neighbouring fenlands.

As the nineteenth-century city spread south down the hill and out along the old Roman road – the Fosse Way – so Lincoln became a place of precise class distinctions: the **Uphill** area, spreading north from the cathedral, became synonymous with middle-class respectability, **Downhill** with the proletariat. For the visitor, almost everything of interest is confined to the Uphill part of town and the key sights can be seen in about half a day, though Lincoln does make for a pleasant overnight stop, particularly in December when its open-air **Christmas market** pulls in the punters from far and wide.

Arrival, information and accommodation

Both Lincoln **train station**, on St Mary's Street, and the **bus station**, close by off Melville Street, are located "Downhill" in the city centre. From either, it's a very steep, fifteen-minute walk up to the cathedral, or you can take the **Walk & Ride minibus** (Mon–Sat 10am–5pm, Sun noon–5pm; 3 hourly) from either the train station or the bus stop on Silver Street, just off the High Street. The **tourist office** (Mon–Sat: April–Sept 10.30am–4pm; Oct–March 11am–3pm; ☏01522/545458, ⊕www.visitlincolnshire.com) is at 9 Castle Hill, in between the cathedral and the castle; they have lots of local information and can book accommodation.

Lincoln has a healthy supply of competitively priced **hotels** and **B&Bs**. The best location is Uphill, which is where you'll find all the places detailed below.

Carline Guest House 1–3 Carline Rd ☏01522/530422, ⊕www.carlineguesthouse.co.uk. One of the best B&Bs in the city, *Carline* occupies a neat and trim Edwardian house about 10min walk down from the cathedral – take Drury Lane from in front of the castle and keep going. Breakfasts are very good, and the rooms are large and pleasantly furnished in a traditional style – large headboards and drape curtains. No credit cards. ❷

Hillcrest 15 Lindum Terrace ☏01522/510182, ⊕www.hillcrest-hotel.com. Traditional, very English hotel in a large red-brick house that was originally a Victorian rectory. Sixteen comfortable rooms with all mod cons plus a large, sloping garden. About 10min walk from the cathedral. ❺

St Clements Lodge 21 Langworthgate ☏01522/521532, ⊕www.stclementslodge .co.uk. In an unassuming modern house a short walk from the cathedral, this very friendly B&B has three comfortable, en-suite rooms. Home-made breakfasts too – try the haddock and kippers. ❷

White Hart Bailgate ☏01522/526222, ⊕www.whitehart-lincoln.co.uk. Antique former coaching inn, whose public rooms still have all sorts of hidden nooks and crannies despite a fairly humdrum modern revamp. The bedrooms are in a more traditional style and the pick overlook the cathedral. Great location. ❹, weekends ❺

The cathedral

Not a hill at all, **Castle Hill** is a wide, short and level cobbled street that links Lincoln's castle and cathedral. Its east end is marked by the arches of the medieval **Exchequer Gate**, beyond which soars the glorious west front of **Lincoln Cathedral**, a veritable cliff-face of blind arcading mobbed by decorative carving (July & Aug Mon–Fri 7.15am–8pm, Sat & Sun 7.15am–6pm; Sept–June Mon–Sat 7.15am–6pm, Sun 7.15am–5pm; access restricted during services; £5 including guided tour – see box below; ⊕www.lincolncathedral.com). The west front's apparent homogeneity is, however, deceptive, and further inspection reveals two phases of construction – the small stones and thick mortar of much of the facade belong to the original church, completed in 1092, whereas the longer stones and finer courses date from the early thirteenth century. These were enforced works: in 1185, an earthquake shattered much of the Norman church, which was then rebuilt under the auspices of **Bishop Hugh of Avalon**, the man responsible for most of the present cathedral, with the notable exception of the (largely) fourteenth-century central tower.

The cathedral's cavernous **interior** is a fine example of Early English architecture, with the nave's pillars conforming to the same general design yet differing

The cathedral offers two different **guided tours** daily except Sunday, both free with the price of admission. The first – the **Floor Tour** (2–3 per day) – is a quick gambol round the cathedral's salient features, while the second, the ninety-minute **Roof Tour** (1–2 per day), takes in parts of the church otherwise out of bounds. Both are very popular, so it's a good idea to book in advance on ☏01522/561600.

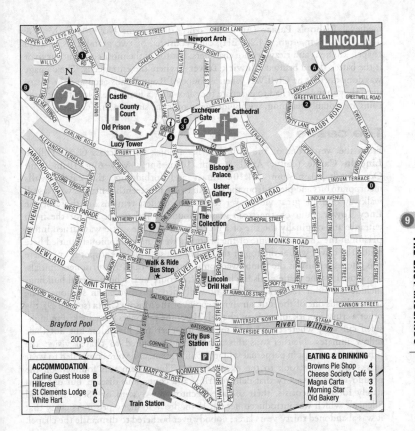

ACCOMMODATION

Carline Guest House	B
Hillcrest	D
St Clements Lodge	A
White Hart	C

EATING & DRINKING

Browns Pie Shop	4
Cheese Society Café	5
Magna Carta	3
Morning Star	2
Old Bakery	1

slightly, their varied columns and bands of dark Purbeck marble contrasting with the oolitic limestone that is the building's main material. Looking back up the nave from beneath the **central tower**, you can also observe a major medieval cock-up: Bishop Hugh's roof is out of alignment with the earlier west front, and the point where they meet has all the wrong angles. It's possible to pick out other irregularities, too – the pillars have bases of different heights, and there are ten windows in the nave's north wall and nine in the south – but these are deliberate features, reflecting a medieval aversion to the vanity of symmetry. Beyond the nave lies **St Hugh's Choir**, whose fourteenth-century misericords carry an eccentric range of carvings, with scenes from the life of Alexander the Great and King Arthur mixed up with biblical characters and folkloric parables. Further on is the open and airy **Angel Choir**, completed in 1280 and famous for the tiny, finely carved Lincoln Imp (see p.582), which embellishes one of its columns. Finally, a corridor off the choir's north aisle leads to the wooden-roofed **cloisters** and the polygonal **chapterhouse**, where Edward I and Edward II convened gatherings that prefigured the creation of the English Parliament.

The Bishop's Palace

Hidden behind a gated wall immediately to the south of the cathedral are the ruins of what would, in its day, have been the city's most impressive building. This, the

581

medieval **Bishop's Palace** (April–Oct daily 10am–5pm; Nov–March Mon & Thurs–Sun 10am–4pm; £4.20; EH), once consisted of two grand halls, a lavish chapel, kitchens and ritzy private chambers, but today the most coherent survivor is the battered and bruised **Alnwick Tower** – where the entrance is. The damage was done during the Civil War when a troupe of Roundheads occupied the palace until they themselves had to evacuate the place after a fierce fire. Nonetheless, the ruins are suitably fetching, with wide views over the surrounding flatlands.

The castle

From the west front of the cathedral, it's a quick stroll across Castle Hill to **Lincoln Castle** (daily: April & Sept 10am–5pm; May–Aug 10am–6pm; Oct–March 10am–4pm; £4.10). Intact and forbidding, the **castle walls** incorporate bits and pieces from the twelfth to the nineteenth centuries with a wall walkway offering great views over town. The earliest remains are those of the **Lucy Tower**, built on the steep grassy mound round to the left of the main entrance and originally the site of a Norman motte. The castle was turned into a **prison** in the 1820s and some of the prisoners were unceremoniously buried here inside the tower wall at the top of the mound – a sad and lonely spot if ever there was one, especially as the tombs were only allowed to carry the prisoners' initials.

Enclosed by the castle walls is a large central courtyard, whose several buildings include the dour red-brick prison, now divided into two main sections. One section holds one of the four surviving copies of the **Magna Carta** (see p.829), the other a truly remarkable **prison chapel**. Here, the prisoners were locked in high-sided cubicles, where they could see the preacher and his pulpit but not their fellow inmates. Neither was this approach just applied to chapel visits: the prisoners were kept in perpetual solitary confinement, and were compelled to wear masks when they took to the exercise yard. This system was founded on the pseudo-scientific theory that defined crime as a contagious disease, but unfortunately for the theorists, their so-called Pentonville System of "Separation and Silence", which was introduced here in 1846, drove so many prisoners crazy that it was abandoned thirty years later; nobody ever bothered to dismantle the chapel.

The rest of the city

The rest of **Uphill Lincoln** is scattered with historic remains, notably several chunks of Roman wall, the most prominent of which is the second-century **Newport Arch** straddling Bailgate and once the main north gate into the city. There's also a bevy of medieval stone houses, most notably on and around the aptly named **Steep Hill** as it cuts down from the cathedral to the city centre.

From Steep Hill, take **Danesgate** and you soon reach the city's prime museum, **The Collection** (daily 10am–4pm; free), which occupies two contrasting buildings – a striking modern structure and a really rather grand 1920s edifice close by. Pride of place in the more modern building is the city's extensive collection of archeological artefacts, from prehistoric times onwards, whereas the older building, aka the **Usher Gallery**, focuses on fine art. The Usher's permanent collection includes some charming paintings of the cathedral and its environs, the best being those by William Logsdail (1859–1944), as well as an eclectic collection of coins, porcelain, watches and clocks. The timepieces were given to the gallery by its benefactor, James Ward Usher, a local jeweller and watchmaker who made a fortune on the back of the **Lincoln Imp**: first, in the 1880s, he devised the legend and then he sold the little trinkets and novelties to match – with such success that the imp became the city's emblem. Usher's tale has a couple of imps hopping around the cathedral, until one of them is turned to stone for trying to talk to the angels carved into the roof of the Angel Choir. His chum made a hasty exit on the back of a witch, but the wind is still supposed to haunt the cathedral awaiting their return.

Eating, drinking and entertainment

Lincoln's **café**, **restaurant and pub** scene is a little patchy, but there's enough to keep you going for a day or so – and all of the best places are within shouting distance of the cathedral. The city's prime arts and entertainment venue is **Lincoln Drill Hall**, Free School Lane (℡01522/873894, ⓦwww.lincolndrill hall.com), which features everything from stand-up and theatre to classical concerts, rock and pop.

Browns Pie Shop 33 Steep Hill ℡01522/527330. Not a pie shop at all, *Browns* is a first-rate restaurant in ancient premises yards from the cathedral. The creative menu puts the emphasis on local ingredients and prices are very reasonable with main courses costing about £11. Save room for the earth-shattering puddings.

Cheese Society Café 1 St Martin's Lane. Bright and breezy little café attached to a superb specialist cheese shop. The café menu does more than cheese too – try the rarebit. Closed Sun.

Magna Carta 1 Exchequergate. A Marston's pub with a good range of real ales, the *Magna Carta*

has traditional decor and a prime location near the cathedral.

Morning Star 11 Greetwellgate. Old-fashioned and friendly locals' pub with a good range of ales. A couple of minutes' walk from the cathedral – if you want something livelier, head for the bars on Bailgate.

Old Bakery 26 Burton Rd ℡01522/576057. Cosy, award-winning restaurant, where the menu is both well considered and inventive – try, for example, the grilled corn polenta and cherry tomatoes with Gorgonzola and green olive purée. Reservations recommended. Mains from £14. Closed Mon.

The Lincolnshire Wolds and the coast

Northeast and east of Lincoln, the **Lincolnshire Wolds** are a narrow band of chalky land whose rolling hills and gentle valleys run southeast from Caistor to just outside Skegness. Here, a string of particularly appealing valleys is concentrated in the vicinity of **Louth**, where conscientious objectors were sent to dig potatoes during World War II and which, with its striking church and old-fashioned centre, is easily the most enticing of the area's towns. A few miles to the south of Louth, the Wolds dip down to both **Woodhall Spa**, a one-time Victorian spa that served as the HQ of the **Dambusters** as they prepared for their celebrated Ruhr raid in 1943, and then the imposing red-brick remains of **Tattershall Castle**. East of the Wolds lies the coast, with its bungalows, campsites and caravans parked behind a sandy beach that extends, with a few marshy interruptions, north from **Skegness**, the main resort, to Mablethorpe and ultimately Cleethorpes. South of Skegness, the **Gibraltar Point Nature Reserve** is a welcome diversion from all the bucket-and-spade/amusement-arcade commercialism.

Louth and around

Henry VIII didn't much care for Lincolnshire, describing it as "one of the most brutal and beestlie counties of the whole realm", his contempt based on the events of 1536, when thousands of northern peasants rebelled against his religious reforms. In Lincolnshire, this insurrection, the **Pilgrimage of Grace**, began in the northeast of the county at **LOUTH**, 25 miles from Lincoln, under the leadership of the local vicar, who was subsequently hanged, drawn and quartered for his pains. There's a commemorative **plaque** in honour of the rebels beside the entrance to the **church of St James** (Easter–Christmas Mon–Sat 10.30am–4pm;

Lincolnshire: transport and information

Getting around Lincolnshire by **public transport** can be tiresome. Lincoln is the hub of the county's limited **rail** network, with regular services to Boston and Skegness via Sleaford. There are also links to Newark, in Nottinghamshire, which is on the main line from London to the northeast, and Stamford in the southwest of the county, which has frequent services to and from Peterborough, Leicester and Oakham. Other than that, you'll be reliant on a patchy network of rural **buses** (℡0845/234 3344, Ⓦwww.lincsinterconnect.com). Services between Lincoln and the county's larger market towns, like Louth and Boston, are pretty good, but you'll struggle to get to the villages without your own transport.

For **information** on all aspects of the county, check the Lincolnshire Tourist Board's helpful website (Ⓦwww.visitlincolnshire.com).

Christmas–Easter Mon, Wed, Fri & Sat 9–11.30am; free), which is the town's one outstanding building, its soaring Perpendicular spire, buttresses, battlements and pinnacles set on a grassy knoll on the west side of the centre. The interior is delightful too, the sweeping symmetries of the nave illuminated by slender windows and capped by a handsome Georgian timber roof decorated with dinky little angels. The roof of the tower vault is, if anything, even finer, its intricate stonework an exercise in geometrical precision.

Next to the church, the well-tended gardens and Georgian houses of **Westgate** make it one of Louth's prettiest streets. Afterwards, it doesn't take long to explore the rest of the town centre, whose cramped lanes and alleys – zeroing in on the **Cornmarket** – are flanked by red-brick buildings mostly dating from the nineteenth century.

Practicalities

Louth **bus station** is on the east side of the centre, a five-minute walk from the Cornmarket at the east end of Queen Street. The **tourist office** is in the Town Hall on Cannon Street, a minute or two north of the Cornmarket (Mon–Fri 9am–5pm, Wed till 4pm, plus Easter to Oct Sat 10am–4pm; ℡01507/609289). They have a list of local B&Bs (❶–❷), but there's nowhere outstanding. For a bite to **eat**, head for the *Cheese Shop*, in the centre at 110 Eastgate, where they serve a good range of sandwiches and baguettes and sell every sort of cheese you can imagine and then some. Neither should you ignore St James's volunteer-run **café** and its home-made cakes – locals set out early to get a slice of the lemon-drizzle. And for a **drink** head to the antique *Wheatsheaf Inn*, yards from St James on Westgate.

Saltfleetby-Theddlethorpe Dunes National Nature Reserve

Heading northeast from Louth, the B1200 cuts across nine miles of farmland on its way to the **coast**. This byroad is built over an old Roman road that was used to transport salt inland from the seashore saltpans, once a lucrative source of income for local traders. At the coast, turn right along the A1031 and, after about half a mile, you reach the (poorly signed) gravel track on the left that leads through to the **Saltfleetby-Theddlethorpe Dunes National Nature Reserve**. Comprising over eight miles of sand dune, salt- and freshwater marsh, the reserve is at its prettiest in midsummer, when the dunes sprout buckthorn bushes and sea heather flowers, forming a carpet of violet spreading down towards the sea. A network of trails navigates the dunes and lagoons, with the latter attracting hundreds of migratory wildfowl in spring and autumn.

From the reserve, it's about thirty miles south along the coastal road to Skegness (see p.586), though you only get the occasional glimpse of the ocean, which is hidden away behind the sea defences.

Woodhall Spa and around

Travelling south from Louth along the A153, it's fourteen miles to Horncastle, which was once famous for its horse fairs, and a further seven miles along the B1191 to **WOODHALL SPA**, an elongated village surrounded by a generous chunk of woodland. Here, the main street – **The Broadway** – is dotted with Victorian/Edwardian houses and shops, reminders of the time when the spring water of this isolated place, rich in iodine and bromine, was a popular tipple, though nowadays the village is kept afloat by its **golf course**, generally reckoned to be one of the best in England.

The Cottage Museum and the Dambusters

The tiny **Cottage Museum** (Easter–Oct Mon–Fri 10am–5pm, Sat & Sun 10.30am–4.30pm; £1.50; Ⓦ www.woodhallspa-museum.co.uk), on Iddesleigh Road off The Broadway, outlines the development of Woodhall Spa and also has a section on the **Dambusters**, who were based at a nearby mansion, **Petwood**, on Stixwould Road, which is now a first-rate hotel (see below). The mansion was built in 1905 for the furniture millionaires, the Maples, then requisitioned by the RAF during World War II, and turned into the Officers' Mess of 617 Squadron, better known as the Dambusters, famous for their bombing raid of May 16, 1943. The raid was planned to deprive German industry of water and electricity by breaching several Ruhrland dams, a mission made possible by Barnes Wallis's famous bouncing bomb. A rusting specimen stands outside the front door of the hotel, which also contains the old **Officers' Bar**, kitted out with memorabilia from bits of aircraft engines to newspaper cuttings.

The Kinema in the Woods

Another unexpected delight is Woodhall Spa's **Kinema in the Woods**, set deep in the forest, yet only five minutes' walk from The Broadway – just follow the signs. Opened in 1922, the Kinema is one of England's few remaining picture houses where the film is projected from behind the screen, and at weekends a 1930s organ rises in front of the screen to play you through the ice-cream break. For details of what's showing, call Ⓣ 01526/352166 or check Ⓦ www.thekinemainthewoods.co.uk.

Practicalities

Most **buses** to Woodhall Spa pull in outside St Hugh's School, from where it's a five-minute walk north to The Broadway. The **tourist office** is inside the Cottage Museum (same times; Ⓣ 01526/353775). The most appealing **hotel** hereabouts is the ⚜ *Petwood* (Ⓣ 01526/352411, Ⓦ www.petwood.co.uk; ❾), set in immaculate gardens, its handsome half-timbered gables sheltering a fine panelled interior and fifty large, well-appointed bedrooms decorated in unfussy, modern style. The all-English breakfasts are excellent and so are the **dinners** – a three-course set menu costing a very reasonable £27 and often featuring local, seasonal ingredients. For lighter wallets, the *Oglee Guest House*, in Edwardian premises off The Broadway at 16 Stanhope Ave (Ⓣ 01526/353512, Ⓦ www.oglee-guesthouse.co.uk; ❷), is a pleasant alternative with three immaculate, en-suite rooms.

Tattershall Castle

From Woodhall Spa, it's about four miles southeast to **Tattershall Castle** (mid-Feb to mid-March & Nov to mid-Dec Sat & Sun 11am–4pm; mid-March to Oct Mon–Wed, Sat & Sun 11am–4pm; £5.30; NT), a massive, moated, red-brick keep that dominates the farmland from beside the main road between Sleaford and Skegness. There's been a castle here since Norman times, but it was Ralph Cromwell, the Lord High Treasurer, who built the present quadrangled tower in the 1440s. A veteran of Agincourt, Cromwell was familiar with contemporary French architecture and it was to France that he looked for his basic design – in England, keeps had been out of fashion since the thirteenth century. Cromwell's quest for style explains Tattershall's contradictions. The castle walls are sixteen feet thick and rise to a height of one hundred feet, but there are no fewer than three ground-floor doorways with low-level windows to match. It's a medieval keep as fashion accessory, a theatricality that continues with the grand chimneypieces inside the castle, though otherwise the interior is almost entirely bare.

The adjacent church of the **Holy Trinity** (April–Sept daily 10am–5pm; free) is a high and mighty fifteenth-century structure, whose soaring nave, with its slender columns and pointed windows, is bright but austere. It now houses a volunteer-run **café**, serving excellent home-made cakes.

Skegness and around

SKEGNESS, some 26 miles east of Tattershall, has been a busy resort ever since the railways reached the Lincolnshire coast in 1875. Its heyday was pre-1960s, before the Brits began to take themselves off to sunnier climes, but it still attracts tens of thousands of city-dwellers who come for the wide, sandy beaches and for a host of attractions ranging from nightclubs to bowling greens. Every inch the traditional English seaside town, Skegness gets the edge over many of its rivals by keeping its beaches sparklingly clean and its parks spick-and-span. Indeed, the resort has a tradition of keeping ahead of its competitors: in 1908 it came up with the ground-breaking "Skegness is So Bracing" slogan beneath a picture of a jolly fisherman, and it was here in 1936 that ex-showman **Billy Butlin** opened his first Butlin's Holiday Camp.

All that said, the seafront, with its rows of souvenir shops and amusement arcades, can be dismal, especially on rainy days, and you may well decide to sidestep the whole affair by heading south three miles along the coast to the **Gibraltar Point National Nature Reserve** (daily dawn–dusk; free; parking from £1). Here, a network of clearly signed footpaths patterns a narrow strip of salt- and freshwater marsh, sand dune and beach that attracts an inordinate number of birds, both resident and migratory. The reserve's smart-looking **visitor centre** has an observation deck equipped with binoculars and a telescope – and their use is free.

Practicalities

Skegness **bus and train stations** are next door to each other about ten minutes' walk from the seashore – cut across the square and go straight up the pedestrianized High Street to the landmark clocktower. The **tourist office** (April–Oct daily 9.30am–5pm; Nov–March Mon–Fri 9.30am–4.30pm; ℡01754/899887, ⓦwww.visitlincolnshire.com) is only yards from the clocktower, on Grand Parade in the Embassy Theatre. Skegness has scores of **hotels**, **B&Bs** and **guest houses**: one of the more appealing is the *Best Western Vine Hotel*, Vine Road (℡01754/610611, ⓦwww.bw-vinehotel.co.uk; ❷), which occupies a rambling old house on a quiet residential street about three-quarters of a mile from the clocktower on the road to Gibraltar Point, though the hotel interior is uninspiringly modern.

The Lincolnshire Fens

The Fens, that great chunk of eastern England extending from Boston in Lincoln-shire right down to Cambridge, encompass some of the most productive farmland in Europe. Give or take the occasional hillock, this pancake-flat, treeless terrain has been painstakingly reclaimed from the marshes and swamps which once drained into **The Wash**, a process that has taken almost two thousand years. In earlier times, outsiders were often amazed by the dreadful conditions hereabouts – as one medieval chroni-cler put it: "There is in the middle part of Britain a hideous fen which [is] oft times clouded with moist and dark vapours having within it divers islands and woods as also crooked and winding rivers." These dire conditions spawned the distinctive culture of the so-called **fen-slodgers**, who embanked small portions of marsh to create pastureland and fields, supplementing their diets by catching fish and fowl and gathering reed and sedge for thatching and fuel. This local economy was threatened by the large-scale land-reclamation schemes of the late fifteenth and sixteenth centuries, and time and again the fenlanders sabotaged progress by breaking down new banks and dams. But the odds were stacked against the saboteurs, and a succes-sion of great landowners eventually drained huge tracts of the fenland – and by the 1790s the fen-slodgers' way of life had all but disappeared.

Nevertheless, the **Lincolnshire Fens** remain a distinctive area, with a scattering of introverted little villages spread across the flatlands within easy striking distance of the A17. Many of these villages are distinguished by their imposing **medieval churches**, whose soaring spires are seen to best advantage in the pale, watery sunlight and wide skies of the fenland evening. The most impressive church of all, however, looms above the largest town hereabouts, the rough-edged old port of **Boston**, which, with a population of around 58,000 is Lincolnshire's second largest settlement.

Boston

As it approaches The Wash, the muddy River Witham weaves its way through **BOSTON**, which is named after St Botolf, the Anglo-Saxon monk-saint who first established a monastery here in 645 AD. In the fourteenth century, Boston expanded to become England's second largest seaport, its flourishing economy dependent on the wool trade with Flanders. Local merchants, revelling in their success, decided to build a church that demonstrated their wealth, the result being the magnificent church of **St Botolph**, whose 272-foot tower still presides over the town and its environs. The church was completed in the early sixteenth century, but by then Boston was in decline as trade drifted west towards the Atlantic and the Witham silted up. The town's fortunes only revived in the late eighteenth century when, after the nearby fens had been drained, it became a minor agricultural centre with a modest port that has, in recent times, been modernized for trade with the EU. A singular mix of fenland town and seaport, Boston is an unusual little place that is at its liveliest on **market days** – Wednesday and Saturday – when you'll hear lots of Polish voices: in recent years, Eastern Europeans have come here in their hundreds to work in food processing and agriculture.

The Market Place and St Botolph's

Mostly flanked by Victorian red-brick buildings, the mazy streets of Boston's cramped and compact centre, on the east side of the River Witham, radiate out from the **Market Place**, a dishevelled square of irregular shape. Just to the west looms the massive bulk of **St Botolph's** (daily 9am–4.30pm; free), whose exterior is embellished by the high-pointed windows and elaborate tracery of the Decorated style. Most of the structure dates from the fourteenth century, but the huge and distinctive tower, whose lack of a spire earned the church the nickname the "Boston Stump", is of later construction. The octagonal lantern is later still, added in the sixteenth century and graced by flying buttresses and pointy pinnacles. Visible from twenty miles away, it once sheltered a beacon that guided travellers in from the fens and the North Sea. A tortuous 365-step spiral **staircase** (Mon–Sat 10am–4pm; £3) leads to a balcony near the top, from where the panoramic views over Boston and the fens amply repay both the price of the ticket and the effort of the climb. Down below, St Botolph's light and airy nave is an exercise in the Perpendicular, all soaring columns and high windows. The sheer purity of design is stunning, its virtuosity heightened by the narrowness of the annexe-like chancel.

St Botolph's most famous vicar was **John Cotton** (1584–1652), who helped stir the Puritan stew during his twenty-year tenure, encouraging a stream of Lincolnshire dissenters to head off to the colonies of New England to found their "New Jerusalem". Cotton emigrated himself in 1633 and soon became the leading light among the **Puritans** of Boston, Massachusetts. The Cotton connection was finally commemorated here in the Stump by the creation of the **Cotton Chapel**, at the west end of the nave, in 1857. The most interesting relic from Cotton's sojourn here is not, however, in the chapel at all, but in the nave in the form of the ornate, wooden pulpit from which he pounded out his three-hour sermons.

The Guildhall

Boston had been alive to religious dissent before John Cotton arrived and, in 1607, two of the **Pilgrim Fathers** were incarcerated here after their failed attempt to escape religious persecution by slipping across to Holland. They were imprisoned for thirty days and, although the location of the prison is much debated, it may have been inside the old **Guildhall** (Wed–Sat 10.30am–3.30pm; £3.35), on South Street, a brief walk south from St Botolph's back through the Market Place. A creaky affair, the Guildhall has a series of modest displays on medieval life in Boston plus the court room and cells where the Pilgrim Fathers may or may not have been tried, sentenced and locked up.

Practicalities

It's ten minutes' walk east from Boston **train station** to the town centre – head straight out of the station along Station Street and keep going until you hit the river and cross the bridge. The **bus station** is also to the west of the river, off West Street, just five minutes' walk away from the Market Place. The **tourist office** (Wed–Sat 10.30am–3.30pm; ☎01205/356656, Ⓦwww.boston.gov.uk) is in the new Haven Gallery, a brief walk south of the Market Place – and a couple of doors down from the Guildhall – at 2 South Square. They have a list of **B&Bs**, but nothing that really catches the eye. Boston is short on good **restaurants** too, the pick of the crop being the chain Italian bistro, *Prezzo*, just north of the Market Place at 20 Wide Bargate (☎01205/356003).

Gedney, Long Sutton and the Peter Scott Walk

Heading south from Boston, it's about six miles to the A17, which runs east across the Lincolnshire Fens bound for King's Lynn (see p.467). En route, it slips past the scattered hamlet of **GEDNEY**, where the massive tower of **St Mary Magdalene** (daily dawn–dusk; free) intercepts the fenland landscape. Seen from a distance, the church seems almost magical, or at least mystical, its imposing lines so much in contrast with its fen-flat surroundings. Close up, the three-aisled nave is simply beautiful, its battery of windows lighting the exquisite Renaissance alabaster effigies of Adlard and Cassandra Welby, who, in death, face each other on the south wall near the chancel.

There's more ecclesiastical excitement just a mile or two to the east in **LONG SUTTON**, a modest farming centre that limps along the road until it reaches its trim Market Place. Here, the **church of St Mary** (daily dawn–dusk; free) has preserved many of its Norman features, with its arcaded tower supporting the oldest lead spire in the country, dating from around 1200. Look out also for the striking stained-glass windows. Long Sutton once lay on the edge of the five-mile-wide mouth of the **River Nene**, where it emptied into The Wash. This was the most treacherous part of the road from Lincoln to Norfolk, and locals had to guide travellers across the mud flats and marshes on horseback, not always without mishap. In 1205, King John was caught by the rising tide, losing his jewels and baggage train in the quicksands somewhere between Long Sutton and Terrington St Clement in Norfolk. In 1831, the River Nene was embanked and then spanned with a wooden bridge at **SUTTON BRIDGE**, a hamlet just two miles east of Long Sutton – and a few miles from King's Lynn (see p.467). The present swing bridge, with its nifty central tower, was completed in 1894.

The muddy, marshy shores of **The Wash** remain wild and desolate. There are several access points, but the best is near Sutton Bridge: cross the bridge over the Nene on the A17 and then turn left along a narrow byroad, which leads north along the river for three miles to **East Light lighthouse** (no public access), where the famous naturalist **Peter Scott** spent much of the 1930s. The picnic spot and car park near the lighthouse mark the start of the ten-mile-long **Peter Scott Walk**, which runs east along the seawall to **Ongar Hill**, where there's a second car park, or you can continue to **West Lynn**, from where a passenger **ferry** (Mon–Sat only; times on ⊕07974/260639) runs over to King's Lynn (see p.467). To do the walk, you'll need proper maps, hiking gear and food and drink.

Stamford

STAMFORD, in the southwest corner of Lincolnshire, is delightful, a handsome little limestone town of yellow-grey seventeenth- and eighteenth-century buildings edging narrow streets which slope up from the River Welland. It was here that the Romans forded this important river, establishing a fortified outpost that the Danes subsequently selected for one of their regional capitals. Later, the town became a centre of the medieval wool and cloth trade, its wealthy merchants funding a series of almshouses known as "**callises**" – after Calais, the English-occupied port through which most of them traded. Stamford was also the home of William Cecil, Elizabeth I's chief minister, who built his splendid mansion, **Burghley House**, close by.

The town survived the collapse of the wool trade, prospering as an inland port after the Welland was made navigable to the sea in 1570, and, in the eighteenth century, as a staging point on the Great North Road from London. More recently, Stamford escaped the three main threats to old English towns – the Industrial Revolution, wartime bombing and postwar development – and was designated the country's first Conservation Area in 1967.

Arrival, information and accommodation

From Stamford **train station**, it's a five- to ten-minute walk north to the town centre, on the other side of the River Welland. The **bus station** is on Sheepmarket in the centre. The **tourist office** is also bang in the centre, in the Stamford Arts

Centre at 27 St Mary's St (Mon–Sat 9.30am–5pm, April–Oct also Sun 10.30am–4pm; ℡01780/755611, Ⓦwww.southwestlincs.com). They have a full list of local accommodation, including a scattering of **B&Bs** (①–③), though most of these are on the edge of town, including the *Elm Guest House*, in a large modern house a ten-minute walk north of the centre on New Cross Road (℡01780/764210, Ⓦwww.elmguesthouse.co.uk; ③). There are four, well-appointed en-suite bedrooms here, each kitted out in a bright and breezy modern style. Stamford also boasts several charming **hotels**, the most celebrated of which is the ⌘ *George Hotel*, 71 High Street St Martin's (℡01780/750750, Ⓦwww.georgehotelofstamford .com; ⑥), an intelligently refurbished coaching inn with flagstone floors and antique furnishings, whose most appealing rooms overlook a cobbled courtyard. Further up the street, the attractive *Garden House Hotel* (℡01780/763359, Ⓦwww .gardenhousehotel.com; ④) also occupies a tastefully modernized, old stone building and has twenty bedrooms decorated in a range of styles.

The Town

Above all, it's the harmony of Stamford's architecture that pleases, rather than any specific sight. There are, nevertheless, a handful of buildings of some special interest among the web of ancient streets and lanes that makes up the town's compact centre.

St Mary's and the Stamford Museum

A convenient place to start an exploration of Stamford is the **church of St Mary** (no regular opening hours), sitting pretty just above the main bridge on St Mary's Street. The church has a splendid spire and a small but airy interior, which incorporates the Corpus Christi chapel, whose intricately embossed, painted and panelled ceiling dates from the 1480s.

Across the street from St Mary's, several lanes thread up to the carefully preserved High Street, from where Ironmonger Street leads north again to the wide and handsome Broad Street, the site of the **Stamford Museum** (Mon–Sat 10am–4pm; free). This holds a series of small displays on the town and its surroundings, plus a thoughtful feature on **Daniel Lambert**, the Leicester fat man who died at Stamford in 1809, aged 39 and weighing 52st 11lb (336kg). Poor old Daniel was regarded as something of a freak and after his death his clothes were displayed in a local inn for visitors to gawp at. One such visitor was the American midget Tom Thumb, otherwise Charles Stratton, who turned up to perform a few party tricks, such as standing in Lambert's waistcoat armhole. Today, a series of panels examine the problems of Daniel's disability – he certainly wasn't fat because he ate too much – alongside his portrait, his top hat and a replica set of his clothes.

Browne's Hospital

Near the museum, also on Broad Street, is **Browne's Hospital** (May–Sept Sat 11am–4pm, Sun 2–4.30pm; £2.50), the most

---

STAMFORD

0   200 yds

N

EATING & DRINKING
George Hotel   B
Hambleton Bakery   1

ACCOMMODATION
Elm Guest House   A
Garden House Hotel   C
George Hotel   B

extensive of the town's almshouses, dating from the late fifteenth century. Not all of the complex is open to the public, though well worth seeing is the first room – the old dormitory – which is capped by a splendid wood-panelled ceiling. The adjacent chapel holds some delightfully folksy misericords and, moving on, the upstairs audit room is illuminated by a handsome set of stained-glass windows. Here also is a small feature on one of the inmates, a certain George Spencer, who lived at Browne's from 1945 until his death in 1963. After his demise, Spencer was found to have stuffed a cake tin with his savings – enough to refurbish a goodly slice of the place.

All Saints
From Browne's, it's a few paces more to Red Lion Square, which is overlooked by the **church of All Saints** (daily dawn–dusk; free). Several centuries in the making, this is a happy amalgamation of Early English and Perpendicular features and one that takes full advantage of its position, perched on a small hillock. Entry is via the south porch, itself an ornate structure with a fine – if badly weathered – crocketed gable, and, although much of the interior is routinely Victorian, the carved capitals are of great delicacy. There's also an engaging folkloric carving of the Last Supper behind the high altar.

Along High Street St Martin's
Down the slope from St Mary's, across the reedy River Welland on **High Street St Martin's**, is the **George Hotel**, a splendid old coaching inn whose Georgian facade supports one end of the gallows that span the street – not a warning to criminals, but a traditional advertising hoarding. Just up the street, the plain and sombre, late fifteenth-century **church of St Martin** (daily 9.30am–4pm; free) shelters the magnificent tombs of the lords Burghley, with a recumbent William Cecil carved beneath twin canopies, holding his rod of office and with a lion at his feet. Just behind, the early eighteenth-century effigies of John Cecil and his wife show the couple as Roman aristocrats, propped up on their elbows, she to gaze at him, John to stare across the nave commandingly.

Burghley House
Burghley House (late March to late Oct daily except Fri 11am–5pm; £11.80, including grounds; ⓦ www.burghley.co.uk), an extravagant Elizabethan mansion standing in parkland landscaped by Capability Brown, is located a mile and a half or so to the southeast of Stamford out along the Barnack Road. Completed in 1587, the house sports a mellow-yellow ragstone exterior, embellished by dainty cupolas, a pyramidal clocktower and skeletal balustrading, all to a plan by **William Cecil**, the long-serving adviser to Elizabeth I. A shrewd and cautious man, Cecil steered his queen through all sorts of difficulties, from the wars against Spain to the execution of Mary, Queen of Scots, vindicating Elizabeth's assessment of his character when she appointed him secretary of state in 1558: "You will not be corrupted with any manner of gifts, and will be faithful to the state."

With the notable exception of the Tudor kitchen, little remains of Burghley's Elizabethan interior. Instead, the house bears the heavy hand of John, fifth Lord Burghley, who toured France and Italy in the late seventeenth century, commissioning furniture, statuary and tapestries, as well as buying up old Florentine and Venetian paintings. To provide a suitable setting for his art, John brought in Antonio Verrio and his assistant Louis Laguerre, who between them covered many of Burghley's walls and ceilings with frolicking gods and goddesses. These gaudy and gargantuan murals are at their most engulfing in the **Heaven Room**, an artfully painted classical temple that adjoins the **Hell Staircase**, where the entrance to the inferno is through the gaping mouth of a cat.

Eating and drinking

For **food**, it has to be the *George Hotel* (see p.590), preferably in the moderately priced and informal *Garden Lounge*, where the emphasis is on British ingredients served in imaginative ways. Main courses here average around £15, less if you eat in the hotel's delightfully antique *York Bar*. For a **sandwich**, the best place in town is the *Hambleton Bakery*, on Ironmonger Street, where the range of freshly baked breads and fillings is outstanding (closed Sun).

Travel details

Buses	Trains
For information on all local and national bus services, contact Traveline ☎0871/200 2233, ⓦwww.traveline.org.uk.	For information on all local and national rail services, contact National Rail Enquiries ☎08457/484950, ⓦwww.nationalrail.co.uk.

Leicester to: Lincoln (1 daily; 1hr 30min); Northampton (5 daily; 1hr); Nottingham (every 30min; 1hr).
Lincoln to: Boston (hourly; 1hr 45min); Gedney (4 daily, with 1 change; 3hr); Leicester (1 daily; 1hr 30min); Long Sutton (4 daily, with 2 changes; 4hr); Louth (every 2hr; 1hr); Nottingham (hourly, with 1 change; 2hr); Skegness (hourly; 1hr 45min); Stamford (1 daily; 1hr 35min); Woodhall Spa (hourly; 50min).
Northampton to: Leicester (5 daily; 1hr); Nottingham (2 daily; 2hr 45min); Oakham (hourly; 2hr 30min with 1 change); Stamford (hourly, with 1 change; 3hr).
Nottingham to: Leicester (every 30min; 1hr); Lincoln (hourly, with 1 change; 2hr); Newark (every 30min; hourly); Northampton (2 daily; 2hr 45min); Oakham (hourly; 1hr 30min); Stamford (hourly, with 1 change; 2hr).
Oakham to: Nottingham (hourly; 1hr 30min); Stamford (every 30min; 20min).
Stamford to: Northampton (hourly, with 1 change; 3hr); Nottingham (hourly, with 1 change; 2hr); Oakham (hourly; 30min).

Leicester to: Birmingham (every 30min; 1hr 15min); Lincoln (hourly; 2hr 20min); London St Pancras (every 30min; 1hr 30min); Nottingham (every 30min; 25min); Oakham (hourly; 30min); Stamford (hourly; 40min).
Lincoln to: Boston (hourly, via Sleaford; 1hr 10min–1hr 40min); Cambridge (hourly, via Peterborough; 2hr 30min–3hr); Leicester (hourly; 2hr 20min); Newark (hourly; 25min); Nottingham (hourly, with 1 change; 2hr); Peterborough (every 2hr; 1hr 30min); Skegness (every 1–2hr, via Sleaford; 2hr).
Northampton to: Birmingham (every 30min; 1hr); London (every 30min; 1hr 15min).
Nottingham to: Birmingham (every 30min; 1hr 20min); Leicester (every 30min; 25min); Lincoln (hourly; 1hr); London St Pancras (hourly; 1hr 40min); Newark (hourly; 40min).
Stamford to: Cambridge (hourly; 1hr); Leicester (hourly; 40min); Oakham (hourly; 15min); Peterborough (hourly; 20min).

The Northwest

CHAPTER 10

Highlights

※ **Chic shopping, Manchester** Enjoy some retail therapy in the city's maze of independent shops. See p.607

※ **Imperial War Museum, Manchester** A startlingly human exploration of the reasons for, and effects of, war. See p.608

※ **City walls, Chester** Survey the handsome old town from the heights of its Roman walls. See p.615

※ **Crosby Beach, Liverpool** Home to Antony Gormley's one hundred eerie, life-size, cast-iron statues, which disappear at high tide. See p.626

※ **Blackpool Pleasure Beach** Scream down the rides at the home of the rollercoaster. See p.630

※ **Lancaster Castle** From dungeons to ornate court rooms, the castle tour is a historical tour-de-force. See p.635

※ **Sunset across Morecambe Bay** Drink in one of the country's finest sunsets at the bar in the Art Deco *Midland Hotel*. See p.637

※ **Sea-kayaking the Calf of Man** Seal colonies, sea birds, and the Isle of Man's stunning rugged coast from a unique perspective. See p.645

▲ *Another Place*, Crosby Beach

The Northwest

A sk most southerners about the **northwest** and their answer will probably involve football, industry and/or the region's loud and unpretentious people. While there is truth in the stereotype, it hides the fact that the region – spearheaded by its two urban powerhouses, Manchester and Liverpool – has become one of the most exciting and cosmopolitan corners of the country. **Manchester**, in particular, surprises many first-time visitors. Where once only a handful of Victorian Gothic buildings lent any grace to the city, Manchester today has been transformed by a rebuilding programme that puts it in the vanguard of modern British urban design. Quite apart from a clutch of top-class attractions the city also boasts a thriving café and club scene, which services its 90,000 or so resident students, and upmarket, fashion-centric shopping. Thirty miles west, **Liverpool** has kept apace of the "northern renaissance" with striking new architecture complementing a revitalized dockside, Georgian terraces, grand civic buildings and museums, and a burgeoning café and restaurant scene.

The southern suburbs of Manchester bump into the steep hills of the Pennine range, but to the southwest the city slides into pastoral **Cheshire**, a county of rolling green countryside, whose dairy farms churn out the crumbly white Cheshire cheese. The county town, **Chester**, with its complete circuit of town walls and partly Tudor centre, is as alluring as any of the country's northern towns, capturing the essence of one of England's wealthiest counties.

The historical county of **Lancashire** reached industrial prominence in the nineteenth century primarily due to the cotton-mill towns around Manchester and the thriving port of Liverpool. Today, neither city is part of the county, and

Regional transport

Manchester's international **airport** picks the city out as a major UK point of arrival, and there are direct train services from the airport to Liverpool, Blackpool, Lancaster, Leeds and York, as well as to Manchester itself. Both Manchester and Liverpool are well served by **trains**, with plentiful connections to the Midlands and London, and up the west coast to Scotland. There's also a frequent rail and **bus** service between both cities, and from each to Chester, allowing an easy loop between Greater Manchester, Merseyside and Cheshire. The major east–west rail lines in the region are the direct routes between Manchester, Leeds and York, and between Blackpool, Bradford, Leeds and York. The Morecambe/Lancaster–Leeds line slips through the Yorkshire Dales (with connections at Skipton for the famous Settle–Carlisle line; see box, p.718); further south, the Manchester–Sheffield line provides a rail approach to the Peak District.

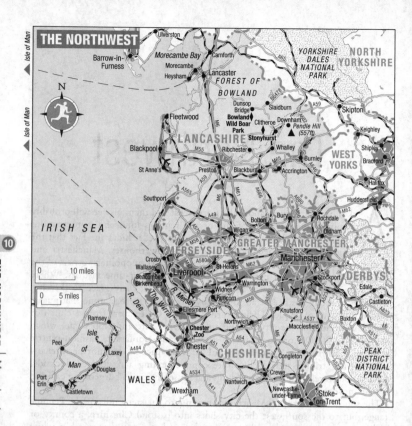

Lancashire's oldest town, and major commercial and administrative centre, is **Preston**, though tourists are perhaps more inclined to linger in the charming towns and villages of the nearby **Ribble Valley**. Along the coast to the west and north of the major cities stretches a line of **resorts** – from Southport to **Morecambe** – which once formed the mainstay of the northern British holiday. Only **Blackpool** is really worth visiting for its own sake, a rip-roaring resort which has stayed at the top of its game by supplying undemanding entertainment with more panache than its neighbours. For anything more culturally invigorating you'll have to continue north to the historically important city of **Lancaster**, with its Tudor castle. Finally, the Crown Dependency of the **Isle of Man**, only 25 miles off the coast, provides a terrain almost as rewarding as that of the Lake District, but without the seasonal overcrowding.

Manchester

MANCHESTER has occupied a place on the global stage for over 150 years, since its days as the world's first industrial city. But today's elegant core of converted warehouses and glass skyscrapers is a far cry from the industrial sprawl George Orwell once described as "the belly and guts of the nation". Its renewed pre-eminence expresses itself in various ways, most swaggeringly in the success of

Manchester United, arguably the most famous football club in the world, and Manchester City, the globe's wealthiest club, but also in a thriving music scene that has given birth to world-beaters as diverse as the Hallé Orchestra and Oasis. Moreover, the city's celebrated concert halls, theatres, clubs and café society feed off the cosmopolitan drive provided by the country's largest student population outside London and a blooming, proud gay community, whose spending power has created a pioneering Gay Village.

Specific attractions may be a little thin on the ground, but the city centre possesses the enjoyable **Manchester Art Gallery** as well as the extensive **Museum of Science and Industry** and the **People's History Museum**, which are both next door to the canal footpaths of the creatively revamped **Castlefield** district. Further out, there's another good art gallery – the **Whitworth** – to the south of the city centre, and to the west, on the **Salford Quays**, are two more prestigious sights, **The Lowry** arts centre and the stirring **Imperial War Museum North**.

Some history

Despite a history stretching back to Roman times, and pockets of surviving medieval and Georgian architecture, Manchester is first and foremost a Victorian manufacturing city with imposing warehouses and towering office buildings. Its rapid growth was equal to any flowering of the Industrial Revolution – from little more than a village in 1750 to the world's major cotton centre in only a hundred years. The spectacular rise of **Cottonopolis**, as it became known, came from the manufacture of vast quantities of competitively priced imitations of expensive Indian calicoes: in 1751 one thousand tonnes of raw cotton was imported into Manchester; this figure had grown to 45,000 by the time of the Battle of Waterloo and no less than a billion tonnes when the industry peaked in 1914. Rapid industrialization brought immense wealth for a few but a life of misery for the majority. The discontent this engendered among the working class came to a head in 1819 when eleven people were killed at **Peterloo**, in what began as a peaceful demonstration against the oppressive Corn Laws, which kept the price of grains at artificially high levels to benefit the aristocracy. Things were even worse when the 23-year-old Friedrich Engels came here in 1842 to work in his father's cotton plant: the grinding **poverty** he recorded in *Condition of the Working Class in England* was a seminal influence on his later collaboration with Karl Marx in the *Communist Manifesto*.

Waterways and railway viaducts formed the matrix into which the city's principal buildings were and still are embedded. In 1772 the Duke of Bridgewater had a canal cut to connect the city to the west Lancashire coal mines, and in 1830 the Manchester–Liverpool railway opened. The **Manchester Ship Canal** was completed in 1894, and played a crucial part in sustaining Manchester's competitiveness. By the late 1950s, however, the docks, mills, warehouses and canals were in dangerous decline. Sporadic efforts were made to pull Manchester out of the economic doldrums in the 1960s and 1970s, but the main engine of change turned out to be the devastating **IRA bomb**, which exploded outside the Arndale shopping centre in June 1996, wiping out a fair slice of the city's commercial infrastructure. Rather than simply patching things up, the city council embarked on an ambitious rebuilding scheme, which also embraced the construction of the facilities needed to host the **Commonwealth Games** in 2002. Rejuvenation projects also took hold of other parts of the city centre, with once-blighted areas now reclaimed for retail and residential use, a process assisted by the burgeoning fashion for loft and apartment city-centre living. Only one blot stains the city's modern reputation: it was in Greater Manchester, Stockport to be precise, that a certain Roy Brooke invented the Sing-along Machine in 1975, later adapted by the Japanese into Karaoke.

Arrival

Manchester Airport (☎0161/489 3000, ⓦwww.manchesterairport.co.uk) is located ten miles south of the city centre. Direct trains depart direct to Manchester's principal station, Manchester Piccadilly (daily 6am–11pm every 10–15min; 11pm–1am & 4–6am every 30min–1hr), some continuing on to the city's Deansgate and Oxford Road train stations. Train tickets from the airport to any of these three city stations cost £3.20 one-way off-peak, £3.80 on weekdays before 9.30am. You can make the same journey by bus (Skyline/Stagecoach bus #43; every 15–30min) and taxi; the latter will cost around £22.

Manchester's three main **train stations** form the points of a triangle that encloses much of the city centre. Most long-distance services pull into **Piccadilly Station**, facing London Road, on the east side of the centre, with some services continuing onto **Oxford Road Station**, just to the south of the centre. Trains from Lancashire and Yorkshire mostly terminate at **Victoria Station** on the north side of the centre. It takes about ten minutes to walk from either Victoria or Oxford Road stations to Albert Square, plumb in the middle of town – on the way you'll pass by several of the city's key attractions; Piccadilly is handier for the city's Northern Quarter, and a twenty-minute hoof from Albert Square. All three stations are connected to other parts of central Manchester via the **Metroshuttle** free bus service; Piccadilly and Victoria are also on the **Metrolink** tram line.

Most long-distance **buses** use **Chorlton Street Coach Station**, about halfway between Piccadilly train station and Albert Square, though some regional buses drop passengers at nearby **Piccadilly Gardens** instead.

Information

The **Manchester Visitor Information Centre** is in the back of the Town Hall, on St Peter's Square (Mon–Sat 10am–5.30pm, Sun 10.30am–4.30pm; ☎0871/222 8223, ⓦwww.visitmanchester.com). They supply a free pocket map of the city centre and a free short-breaks city guide as well as various other useful leaflets and brochures. You can also buy National Express bus tickets, check rail timetables, book guided tours, and reserve accommodation (for more on which, see opposite). They are often knowledgeable about special deals and discounts, too.

To find out **what's on** in the city, check out the *Manchester Evening News* or consult their website, ⓦwww.manchestereveningnews.co.uk.

City transport

About thirty minutes' walk from top to bottom, central Manchester is compact enough to cover on **foot**, though most visitors take to the bus as soon as it starts raining. The **Metroshuttle** free bus service, which runs every five to ten minutes, weaves its way across central Manchester along three routes: Service 1 (Mon–Sat 7am–7pm, Sun 10am–6pm) runs east–west linking Piccadilly Station with Piccadilly Gardens, the Royal Exchange and Deansgate; Service 2 (same times) travels north–south between Victoria and Oxford Road train stations; and Service 3 (Mon–Sat 7am–7pm) links Piccadilly Station with Oxford Street, Peter Street and ultimately Salford Central Station.

There is also the **Metrolink** tram network (every 5–10min Mon–Sat 6am–midnight, Sun 7am–10.30pm; ⓦwww.metrolink.co.uk), which whisks through the city centre bound for the suburbs. There are two routes: one links central Manchester with Bury in the north and Altrincham in the south, the other travels west to Eccles via Salford Quays, the location of the Imperial War Museum North. Metrolink has eight city-centre stops, the most useful of which are at Piccadilly Station, Piccadilly Gardens, St Peter's Square, Market Street and Victoria Station;

Manchester's Blue Badge guides offer a varied, year-round programme of guided walks (2hr; £5), covering everything from **pubs** to Peterloo and Cottonopolis **heritage** tours. Advance bookings are advised in person at the Visitor Centre in Peter's Square (see opposite). There are usually two or three walks a week. If you are keen on the city's "**Madchester**" musical heritage, it's well worth taking the two-hour walking tour run by local musician Craig Gill (May–Sept daily; £5; ℡07958/246917, ℡www .manchestermusictours.com).

note that the Manchester Central convention centre stop is difficult to find – it's among the tangle of elevated rail lines to the rear of the complex. **Tickets** must be purchased from the automatic machines at Metrolink stops before the start of a journey; prices are reasonable.

For information on all Greater Manchester bus and train services, call GMPTE on ℡0871/200 2233, ℡www.gmpte.com.

Accommodation

There is no shortage of budget or more upmarket **hotel chains** in the city – *Jury's Inn*, *Ibis* – making it easy to find a smart, albeit formulaic, en-suite room in central Manchester for around £60–70 at almost any time of the year – except when Manchester United are playing at home, when hotel prices can rocket into the stratosphere. At other times, hotel prices tend to be higher during the week than at the weekend. Manchester is also serviced by some brilliant **youth hostels** occupying prime central locations – but they need to be booked well in advance.

Hotels & B&Bs

Arora 18–24 Princess St ℡0161/236 8999, ℡www.manchester.arorahotels.com. Opposite the city art gallery in a listed building, this four-star has over a hundred neat, modern rooms – five of them themed on part-owner Cliff Richard. Big discounts if booked online. ④–⑤

Castlefield Liverpool Rd ℡0161/832 7073, ℡www.castlefield-hotel.co.uk. Large, modern, red-brick, warehouse-style hotel handily located near the foot of Deansgate in Castlefield, opposite the Museum of Science and Industry and overlooking the canal. Nicely appointed rooms, attached leisure club and pool (free to guests). ④

Didsbury House Didsbury Park, Didsbury Village ℡0161/448 2200, ℡www.didsburyhouse.co.uk. Located about four miles south of the centre in well-heeled Didsbury Village – buses into the centre are fast and frequent – this is a stylish conversion of Victorian premises, with 27 immacu-late/verging-on-minimalist guest rooms, some with dark wooden floors. Great breakfasts. ⑤

Great John Street Great John St ℡0161/831 3211, ℡www.greatjohnst.co.uk. Deluxe hotel in an imaginatively refurbished, old school building not far off Deansgate. Holds thirty individually designed, spacious and comfortable suites, some split-level,

with nifty scholastic names – "Headmaster's Office" and so on. The hotel has a bar-cum-restaurant, equipped with an open fire, wide sofas, and gallery breakfast room up above. Rooftop garden. Substantial discounts are legion, but the rack rate is ⑦.

Luther King House Brighton Grove ℡0161/224 6404, ℡www.lutherkinghouse.co.uk. Set in the peaceful grounds of an academic college three miles south down Oxford Rd, this very reasonable B&B has 45 tidy and homely rooms flanking green quads. Free parking. ②

Midland Peter St ℡0161/236 3333, ℡www .qhotels.co.uk. Once the terminus hotel for Central Station (now the Manchester Central convention centre) this building was the apotheosis of Edwardian style. The public areas today are returned to their former glory, with bedrooms in immaculate chain style. Full raft of leisure facilities, and discounted rates if booked online. ④–⑤

The Palace Oxford Rd ℡0161/288 1111, ℡www .principal-hotels.com. Occupying one of the city's grandest Victorian buildings, *The Palace* is part of a small English chain of luxury hotels. Public rooms have all the stately grandeur you might expect, the foyer coming complete with ersatz Roman pillars and columns. Great location, opposite the Corner-house arts centre. From ④

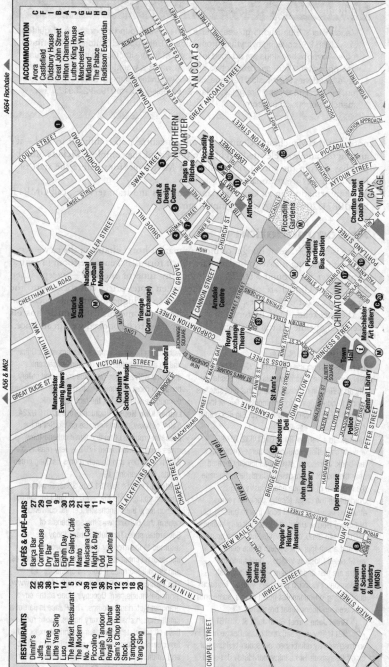

City of Manchester Stadium

ACCOMMODATION
Arora C
Castlefield F
Didsbury House I
Great John Street B
Hilton Chambers A
Luther King House J
Manchester YHA G
Midland E
The Palace H
Radisson Edwardian D

RESTAURANTS
Dimitri's 22
Jaffa 35
Lime Tree 38
Little Yang Sing 17
Luso 5
The Market Restaurant 14
The Modern 1
No. 4 39
Piccolino 16
Punjab Tandoori 41
Royal Suite Darbar 36
Sam's Chop House 37
Stock 12
Tampopo 13
Yang Sing 18
20

CAFÉS & CAFÉ-BARS
Barça Bar 27
Cornerhouse 29
Dry Bar 9
Earth 30
Eighth Day 10
The Gallery Café 33
Manto 21
Musicana Café 41
Night & Day 11
Odd 7
Trof Central 4

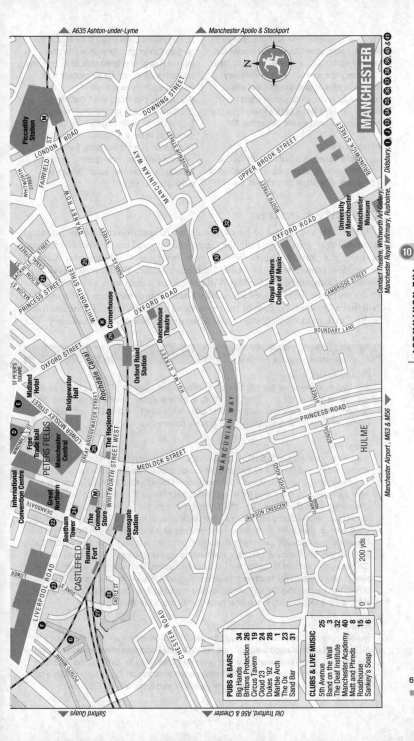

▲ A635 Ashton-under-Lyme   ▲ Manchester Apollo & Stockport

N

Piccadilly Station Ⓜ

DOWNING STREET

LONDON ROAD

FAIRFIELD STREET

WHITWORTH STREET

GRANBY ROW

BROOK STREET

CHARLES STREET

MANCUNIAN WAY

UPPER BROOK STREET

BROSENOR STREET

BOOTH STREET

BRUNSWICK STREET

University of Manchester

Manchester Museum

OXFORD ROAD

CAMBRIDGE STREET

Royal Northern College of Music

BOUNDARY LANE

Cornerhouse Ⓗ

Dancehouse Theatre

Oxford Road Station

HULME STREET

PRINCESS ROAD

BONSALL STREET

HULME

MANCUNIAN WAY

PRINCESS ROAD

MEDLOCK STREET

ROYCE ROAD

JACKSON CRESCENT

CLABURN ROAD

▶ Contact Theatre, Whitworth Art Gallery,
Manchester Royal Infirmary, Rusholme,
▶ Didsbury, ❶, Ⓙ, ㉝ ㉞ ㉟ ㊱ ㊲ ㊳ ㊴ ㊵ & ㊶

Manchester Airport, M63 & M56 ▶

10

THE NORTHWEST

St Peters Square Ⓔ

Midland Hotel

Bridgewater Hall

Rochdale Canal

Oxford Road Station

Free Trade Hall Ⓓ

PETERS FIELDS

WINDMILL STREET

Manchester Central

LOWER MOSLEY STREET

GREAT BRIDGEWATER STREET

The Hacienda

The Hacienda West

WHITWORTH STREET WEST

International Convention Centre

Great Northern

DEANSGATE

CASTLEFIELD

Beetham Tower

Roman Fort

LIVERPOOL ROAD

LOWER

DUKE ST

CASTLE ST

The Comedy Store Ⓜ

Deansgate Station

CHESTER ROAD

POTATO WHARF

Ⓕ   Ⓖ

0   200 yds

PUBS & BARS	
Big Hands	34
Britons Protection	26
Circus Tavern	19
Cloud 23	24
Dukes '92	28
Marble Arch	1
The Ox	23
Sand Bar	31

CLUBS & LIVE MUSIC	
5th Avenue	25
Band on the Wall	3
The Deaf Institute	32
Manchester Academy	40
Matt and Phreds	8
Roadhouse	15
Sankey's Soap	6

▼ Salford Quays   ▼ Old Trafford, A56 & Chester

Radisson Edwardian Peter St ☎0161/835 9929, Ⓦwww.radissonedwardian.com. The Neoclassical facade is all that's left of the Free Trade Hall. Aside from history (see opposite), this five-star luxury hotel has a sleek, modern interior full of natural light, tasteful rooms, all the genteel extras one expects – spa and gym – and the trendy *Opus One* bar looking out under the facade's arches. ❺

Hostels

Hilton Chambers 15 Hilton St ☎0161/236 4414, Ⓦwww.hattersgroup.com/hilton. Part of a small chain operating in the northwest, this recently opened hostel is right in the heart of the Northern Quarter, great for exploring the city's nightlife. A range of different room types, and some cool communal spaces, like their outdoor deck. Dorm beds £19, en-suite doubles ❷

Manchester YHA Potato Wharf, Castlefield ☎0161/839 9960, Ⓔmanchester@yha.org.uk. Excellent hostel overlooking the canal that runs close to the Museum of Science and Industry. There are 35 rooms in total (thirty four-bunk, two five-bunk rooms, and three doubles), all en suite. Facilities include internet access, laundry, self-catering and a café. ❶

The city centre

If Manchester can be said to have a centre, it's **Albert Square** and the buildings surrounding it – the Town Hall, the Central Library and the *Midland Hotel*. South of here, the former Central Station now functions as **Manchester Central** convention centre, with the Hallé Orchestra's home, **Bridgewater Hall**, just opposite. **Chinatown** and the **Gay Village** are just a short walk to the east, while to the northeast the revamped **Piccadilly Gardens** provide access to the so-called **Northern Quarter**, funkiest of the regenerated inner-city areas. To the southwest is the **Castlefield** district, site of the **Museum of Science and Industry**. The

A weekend in Manchester

Friday night

Start your weekend at the city's heights with an early evening Bellini or two at the glamorous **Cloud 23** bar. Then it's off to the **Deansgate Locks** for dancing and comedy or, for the more artistic, a short walk further to the **Cornerhouse** for art-house cinema, and a drink at their equally cultured bar.

Saturday

Get an early tram down to **Salford Quays** for a morning wandering round the Imperial War Museum and The Lowry, before scarves-on time for an afternoon of football – if you can manage to get a ticket – at Manchester United's **Old Trafford**, a short walk from the quays. (A great idea for a match-day eat is to pick up a packed lunch in the city centre from Katsouris Deli, 113 Deansgate – try the gammon and fried onion ciabatta or veggie Zorba sandwich.) Alternatively, for drama of a different kind, head back to the centre for a matinee performance at either the **Royal Exchange** or **Library** theatre (usually beginning at 4pm). From the theatres you're well placed for a pre-dinner stroll around the city's neo-Gothic squares before indulging yourself in **Chinatown** – home of Britain's best Far Eastern cuisine. Refreshed, it's a night on the tiles in the city's funky **Northern Quarter**: begin in the red-brick bars on Thomas Street before heading for an evening of live music at *Matt and Phred's* jazz bar or *Band on the Wall* (which in the later hours turns into a cracking club night).

Sunday

Nurse any aching heads with a veggie breakfast and blueberry-and-banana smoothie at **The Deaf Institute** and then carry on down Oxford Road for a morning stroll through the galleries of the **Whitworth** – which is also an ideal stop for lunch at their majestic café. From here it's a quick bus back to the centre to polish off the afternoon with a bit of **shopping** or a visit to one of the family-friendly museums around Castlefield.

spine of the city, **Deansgate**, begins in Castlefield near the city's most striking new addition, the **Beetham Tower** skyscraper, and runs north to the cathedral, close to which the most dramatic core of urban regeneration in the country is found in the steel-and-glass architecture of **Exchange Square**.

Albert Square and St Peter's Square

Until recently, Manchester's only real claim to architectural merit was its panoply of **neo-Gothic** buildings and monuments, most dating from the second half of the nineteenth century. One of the more fanciful is the shrine-like, canopied **monument** to Prince Albert, Queen Victoria's husband, perched in the middle of the square that bears his name – **Albert Square**. The monument was erected in 1867, six years after Albert's death, supposedly because the prince had always shown an interest in industry. Overlooking the prince is Alfred Waterhouse's magnificent, neo-Gothic **Town Hall** (Mon–Fri 9am–5pm; free), with its mighty clocktower, completed in 1877. The interior is similarly imposing, with echoing stone-vaulted corridors arching above acres of mosaics. Be sure to pop inside the first-floor Great Hall, which boasts stylish iron candelabras, stained-glass windows, a double hammer-beam roof and wall paintings by Ford Madox Brown depicting Manchester's history.

Just to the south of the Town Hall, facing **St Peter's Square**, the circular **Central Library** (Mon–Thurs 10am–8pm, Fri & Sat 9am–5pm) was built in 1934 as the largest municipal library in the world. It's an impressive sight, but Lutyens' mournful **Cenotaph**, in the middle of St Peter's Square, now passes virtually unnoticed.

Footsteps away, over on Peter Street, the grandiose **Midland Hotel** of 1903 is distinguished by its intricate exterior tile-work. The hotel's earlier visitors ventured out for an evening's entertainment to the **Free Trade Hall**, a few yards to the west along Peter Street. Originally built on St Peter's Fields, the site of the "Peterloo Massacre", the hall was the home of the city's Hallé Orchestra for over a century (until the completion of the Bridgewater Hall in 1996). Its Italianate facade survived intense wartime bombing and is now a protected part of the *Radisson Edwardian Hotel*. In 1974 and 1976, the **Lesser Free Trade Hall**, a smaller room upstairs, witnessed performances from the Sex Pistols that electrified Tony Wilson and others, including the Buzzcocks and Joy Division.

Manchester Art Gallery

Presiding over the northeast corner of St Peter's Square on Mosley Street is Charles Barry's porticoed **Manchester Art Gallery** (Tues–Sun 10am–5pm; free; Ⓦwww .manchestergalleries.org), which displays an invigorating collection of eighteenth- and nineteenth-century art on the middle of the gallery's three floors. The paintings are, however, divided by theme rather than by artist, which makes it difficult to appreciate the strength of the collection, especially when it comes to its forte, the Pre-Raphaelite Brotherhood. Pre-Raphaelite highlights include the highly charged eroticism of Rossetti's *Astarte Syrinca* (Gallery 8) and Holman Hunt's *The Light of the World* (Gallery 5), a painting of Jesus standing at the door (of the soul) that was familiar to generations of evangelical Protestants. For families or small children, a fun aside is the interactive gallery on the first floor where you can dress up in imitation of works in the gallery and race model chariots. Worth a look also is the ground floor's Manchester Gallery, which offers a visual history of the city.

South to Bridgewater Hall and Deansgate Locks

South of St Peter's Square, **Lower Mosley Street** runs past **Manchester Central** convention complex, the main part of which occupies what was, until 1969, a train station. Across the street from the complex rises **Bridgewater Hall**, Britain's finest concert hall and home of the world-renowned Hallé Orchestra.

Pressing on, the apartment block at the corner of Lower Mosley Street and Whitworth Street West bears the name of the site's previous occupant, the **Haçienda Club**, the spiritual home of Factory Records, which closed in 1997. In its 1980s heyday, the club showcased live performances by an army of bands, including the likes of the Happy Mondays, Stone Roses, and The Smiths, and pioneered and popularized a new dance craze – "house". Turn right along Whitworth Street West and you'll spot the string of café-bars and restaurants that have been shoehorned along the Rochdale Canal's **Deansgate Locks**, a pattern repeated along and across the street in the old railway arches abutting Deansgate Station. Here also is the base of the 47-storey **Beetham Tower**, home to the city's highest bar (see p.611).

Castlefield

Best approached along Castle Street, just to the west of Deansgate Station, the remarkable tangle of railway viaducts and canals that lie sandwiched between Water Street, Liverpool Road and Deansgate make up the pocket-sized district of **Castlefield**. It was here that the country's first man-made canal, the Bridgewater Canal, brought coal and other raw materials to the city's warehouses throughout the eighteenth century. By the early 1960s, the district was an eyesore, but an influx of money allied to a fair amount of vision cleaned it up, creating Britain's first "urban heritage park" in 1982, now complete with cobbled canalside walks, an outdoor events arena, a youth hostel and attractive café-bars. Curiously enough, Castlefield was also where Manchester started as the **Roman fort** of Mamucium in 79 AD; the Romans abandoned their settlement in around 410 AD and the scant remains – mainly defensive ditches plus a couple of replica walls – are now on display in open ground between the Rochdale Canal and Liverpool Road.

The Museum of Science and Industry (MOSI)

From the remains of the Roman fort, it's a couple of hundred yards north to the extremely popular **Museum of Science and Industry (MOSI)**, whose several different sections spread out along Liverpool Road (daily 10am–5pm; free, but admission charge for special exhibitions; ℡0161/832 2244, ⓦwww.mosi.org.uk). One of the most impressive museums of its type in the country, it mixes technological displays and special blockbuster exhibitions with trenchant analysis of the impact of industrialization. The **Power Hall** trumpets the region's remarkable technological contribution to the Industrial Revolution by means of a hall full of steam engines, some of which are fired up daily. There's more steam just outside the Power Hall in the shape of a working replica of Robert Stephenson's **Planet**, whose original design was based on the *Rocket*, the work of Robert's father George. Built in 1830, the *Planet* reliably attained a scorching 30mph but had no brakes; the museum's version does, and uses them at weekends (noon–4pm), dropping passengers a couple of hundred yards away at the **Station Building**, the world's oldest passenger railway station.

The museum is far more than just a study of industrial technology, with the revamped interactive **Experiment** area a particular delight, in which kids and adults can create giant bubbles, see infinity mirrors, and have a go at surprisingly tricky logic games. The **1830 Warehouse** features a sound-and-light show that delves into the history of the city's warehouses, while the **Air and Space Hall** features vintage planes, cutaway engines and space exploration displays.

Deansgate, John Rylands Library and the People's History Museum

Deansgate cuts through the city centre from the Rochdale Canal to the cathedral. The first major point of interest is the former Great Northern Railway Company's

Goods Warehouse, a great sweep of brickwork dating back to the 1890s that flanks Deansgate between Great Bridgewater and Peter streets. Now incorporated into a modern retail and leisure development called **Great Northern**, the warehouse was originally an integral part of an ambitious trading depot with road and rail links up above and a canal way down below street level.

Continuing north along Deansgate from Peter Street, turn right down either Queen or Brazennose streets for the minute's stroll to tiny, leafy **Lincoln Square**, named after its statue of the American President. The working men of Lancashire were steadfastly against "that foul blot on civilization and Christianity – chattel slavery" and wrote a letter of support to Lincoln, whose moving letter of reply is quoted on the base of the statue.

Across Deansgate, opposite Brazennose Street, is the **John Rylands Library** (Mon & Sun noon–5pm, Tues–Sat 10am–5pm; free, audioguide £2.50), the city's supreme example of Victorian Gothic, though a recent refurbishment has added a modern entrance to the original building. The library takes its name from John Rylands (1801–1888), an extremely wealthy textile merchant, who married the Cuban-born Enriqueta Tennant (1843–1908), when he was 74 and she was 32. After his death, Enriqueta decided to build a library as a memorial to her husband. The library now houses specialist collections of rare books and manuscripts, including a fragment of the Gospel of St John dating back to the second century AD. Close-up public viewings of rare books take place every Thursday at 12.15pm (£2.50; book in advance on ☏0161/306 0555).

Turning down Bridge Street, a few minutes' walk leads you to the **People's History Museum** (daily 10am–5pm; free; ⓦwww.phm.org.uk), on the left just before the River Irwell. The museum is housed in a former pump house and a four-storey ultra-modern extension, the two connected by means of a glass walkway. Unlike MOSI, it explores the social effects of industrialization, tracing the development of workers' political resistance and the freedoms we take for granted today from the Peterloo Massacre of 1819 onwards. As the gallery shows, this moment became the catalyst for agitation that led to the 1832 Reform Act, and subsequent rise of the egalitarian Chartist movement. The later, more interactive galleries focus on the working-class origins of football and pop music, as well as exhibiting one of the finest collections of trade-union banners in the country.

St Ann's Square, the Royal Exchange and Exchange Square

Slender **St Ann's Square** is tucked away off the eastern side of Deansgate, a couple of blocks up from the Rylands Library. Flanking the square's southern side is **St Ann's Church** (daily 9.45am–4.45pm), whose Neoclassical symmetries date from 1709, though the stained-glass windows are firmly Victorian. At the other end of the square is the **Royal Exchange**, which houses the much-lauded **Royal Exchange Theatre**, a space-age theatre-in-the-round pod which sits at the heart of the building's columned hall. When it functioned as the Cotton Exchange, its main trading-floor hall – twice the current size – was the largest room in the world, and employed over seven thousand people. Close of trade at the Royal Exchange was December 31, 1968 – the old trading board still shows the last day's prices for American and Egyptian cotton.

A pedestrian high street – **New Cathedral Street** – runs north from St Ann's Square to **Exchange Square**, the focus of the ambitious city-centre rebuilding programme that followed the IRA bomb of 1996. On the southeast side of the square stands the whopping **Arndale Centre**, modernized and clad in glass, and on the north is the former Corn Exchange, now another converted shopping hub renamed the **Triangle**. Exchange Square may be overloaded with modern shops and stores, but its western corner – straight ahead from New Cathedral Street – abuts two old half-timbered **pubs**, the *Old Wellington Inn* and *Sinclair's Oyster Bar*; both were carefully moved to this new location after the bomb.

Manchester Cathedral to Victoria Station

Manchester Cathedral (Mon–Sat 10am–4.30pm, plus May–Sept Sun 11.30am–4pm; free), standing just beyond Exchange Square from the end of New Cathedral Street, dates back to the fifteenth century, though in truth its Gothic lines have been hacked about too much to have any real architectural coherence. In 1940, a 1000lb bomb all but destroyed the interior, knocking out most of the stained glass, which is why it's so light inside today.

The cathedral's choristers are trained in **Chetham's School of Music** (☏0161/834 7961, ⍵www.chethams.com), on the far side of the cathedral on Long Millgate. This fifteenth-century manor house became a school and a free public library in 1653 and was turned into a music school in 1969. There are free recitals and a calendar of lunchtime concerts during term time and, although there's no public access to most of the complex, you can visit the oak-panelled **Library** (Mon–Fri 9am–12.30pm & 1.30–4.30pm by appointment; free), with its handsome carved eighteenth-century bookcases. Along the side corridor is the main **Reading Room**, where Marx and Engels beavered away on the square table that still stands in the windowed alcove.

Directly opposite Chetham's, the six-storey green building that formerly functioned as Urbis is due to reopen by the end of 2011 as the **National Football Museum** (⍵www.nationalfootballmuseum.com), housing an unparalleled collection of football memorabilia. Behind the museum, down the slope, is **Victoria Station**, the most likeable of the city's several stations with its long, gently curving stone facade. Pop inside for a look at the Art Deco ticket booths and the immaculate tiled map of the Lancashire and Yorkshire Railway network as it was in the 1920s.

Piccadilly Gardens and the Northern Quarter

Just east of the Arndale Centre, about ten minutes' walk from Victoria Station, are **Piccadilly Gardens**, one of Manchester's busiest public spaces. Transformed by Japanese architects during the city's redevelopment, the gardens are an odd mixture – trees, austere-looking statues of Queen Victoria and the Duke of Wellington, a fountain and water jets, and a modern glass-and-stone pavilion – but provide a great space in summer for organized events – it's worth walking through on a weekend to see what's going on. The gardens also provide a major local transport hub and gateway to Oldham Street and the shabby yet fashionable **Northern Quarter**. Traditionally, this is Manchester's garment district and you'll still find shops and wholesalers selling high-street fashions but there are also new design outlets, lots of music stores, and funky bars and cafés.

Chinatown and the Gay Village

From Piccadilly Gardens, it's a short walk to **Chinatown**, whose grid of narrow streets stretch north–south from Charlotte to Princess Street between Portland and Mosley streets, with the inevitable **Dragon Arch**, at the corner of Faulkner and Nicholas streets, providing the focus for the annual Chinese New Year celebrations. Close by, just to the southeast, the side roads off Portland Street lead down to the Rochdale Canal, where Canal Street is the heart of Manchester's thriving **Gay Village**. The pink pound has filled this part of the city with canalside cafés, clubs, bars and businesses. One block west of the Gay Village, at the junction of Oxford Road and Whitworth Street, stands the **Cornerhouse**, the dynamo of the Manchester arts scene (see p.613).

Aside from the high-end boutiques on King Street, and the department-store big boys – Harvey Nichols, Selfridges, House of Fraser – around Market Street and Exchange Square, the city has a plethora of smaller independent stores catering for all tastes. If you're around between mid-November and the week before Christmas, it's well worth making for the city's **German Christmas Market**, which sees Albert Square transformed into a Bavarian picture postcard with hundreds of stalls selling everything from painted wooden toys to iced gingerbread, as well as hot *Glühwein* and *Bratwurst*.

Afflecks 52 Church St. A Manchester institution, where over fifty independent one-room stores spread over four floors mixing everything from Gothic rock outfits to retro cocktail dresses and quirky footwear.

Manchester Craft and Design Centre 17 Oak St. The city's best place to pick up ceramics, fabrics, earthenware, jewellery and decorative art. Closed Sun.

Piccadilly Records 53 Oldham St. The enthusiastic staff, often DJ themselves, are more than willing to help navigate you through the shelves of records to some special gem, whatever your taste.

Rags to Bitches 60 Tib St. This flapper's paradise leads the way as the city's best boutique, selling vintage fashions from the Twenties to the Sixties to stars, and offering courses in dress design and style. Closed Sun.

Oxford Road and points south

Beginning at Whitworth Street, **Oxford Road** cuts a direct route south from the city centre, slicing through a string of impressive Manchester University buildings, one of which houses the **Manchester Museum**, before reaching after about a mile the enjoyable **Whitworth Art Gallery**, situated in the verdant grounds of Whitworth Park.

An endless stream of **buses** runs down Oxford Road from the stops outside the *Palace Hotel*, at the corner of Whitworth Street, putting both the museum and the gallery within easy reach.

The Manchester Museum

From the Whitworth Street/Oxford Road intersection, it's a ten-minute hoof south to the Gothic Revival home of the **Manchester Museum** (Mon & Sun 11am–4pm, Tues–Sat 10am–5pm; free; ⓦ www.museum.manchester.ac.uk), whose diverse collection spreads over five floors. One floor has displays on rocks, minerals and prehistoric life, a second focuses on meteorites and two more concentrate on animal life, the human body and biomedical research. A final floor boasts one of the country's finest collections on **Ancient Egypt** outside of the British Museum.

The Whitworth Art Gallery

Another half-mile away to the south is the university's **Whitworth Art Gallery** (Mon–Sat 10am–5pm, Sun noon–4pm; free; ⓦ www.whitworth.manchester .ac.uk), a large red-brick building at the corner of Oxford and Denmark roads. The gallery is formed of two distinct halves, pre-1880s and modern, with the former collection incorporating a strong assembly of watercolours by Turner, Constable, Cox and Blake as well as Gillray engravings and Hogarth prints. There are also several diverting oddities, most notably Ford Madox Brown's *Execution of Mary Queen of Scots* – his first attempt at a large-scale historical work. The modern collection concentrates on post-1880 British staples, with Moore and Hepworth, Lucien Freud and Francis Bacon, as well as a wonderful set of contributions from lesser-known artists. Given Manchester's cotton connections, it is perhaps not too surprising that the gallery also displays the country's widest range of textiles outside London's Victoria and Albert Museum.

Salford Quays: The Lowry and the Imperial War Museum North

After the Manchester Ship Canal opened in 1894, **Salford docks** played a pivotal role in turning Manchester into one of Britain's busiest seaports. By the 1970s, however, trade had well-nigh collapsed and the docks were forced to close in 1982. Since then, an extraordinarily ambitious redevelopment has transformed **Salford Quays**, as it was rebranded, into a waterfront residential and leisure complex, with gleaming new apartment blocks, shopping mall and arts centre, **The Lowry**, among whose various delights are art galleries that feature the works of the centre's namesake, L.S. Lowry. Also on the quays is the much-praised **Imperial War Museum North**, with its profoundly thoughtful displays on war in general and its effects on the individual in particular.

To get to the quays by public transport, take the **Metrolink** tram (Eccles line) from the city centre to the Harbour City tram stop, from where it is a five-minute walk to both The Lowry and the Imperial War Museum.

The Lowry

Perched on the water's edge, **The Lowry** (Ⓦ www.thelowry.com) is the quays' distinctive shiny steel arts centre, housing one of Manchester's biggest stages, the Lyric. A small part of The Lowry, the **Galleries** (Mon–Fri & Sun 11am–5pm, Sat 10am–5pm; donation), is devoted to displays of fine art. There are some sixteen different exhibitions held here each year, but most of them showcase a selection of the paintings of **Lawrence Stephen Lowry** (1887–1976). Lowry's earlier paintings have a sense of desolation and melancholia in their portrayal of Manchester mill workers, but later he modified his outlook, repeating earlier paintings but changing the greys and sullen browns for lively reds and pinks. Lowry also expanded his repertoire as he grew older, capturing mountain scenes and seascapes and painting full-bodied realistic portraits. A twenty-minute film – *Meet Mr Lowry* – puts further flesh on the artistic bones.

Imperial War Museum North

A footbridge spans the Manchester Ship Canal to link The Lowry with the startling **Imperial War Museum North** (daily: March–Oct 10am–6pm; Nov–Feb 10am–5pm; free; Ⓦ www.north.iwm.org.uk), whose iconic structure, designed by Daniel Libeskind, sees a steel fin striking defiantly upwards into the sky; getting to the top costs 95p. The interior is just as distinct, its angular lines serving as a dramatic backdrop to the displays. Among the hundreds of artefacts displayed in the main hall are six separate exhibition areas – the "Silos" – focusing on everything from women's work in the two world wars to war reporting and the build-up to the Iraq conflict of 2003. It's an ambitious and carefully conceived museum with a mixture of the personal and the general that is nothing less than superb.

The football stadiums

From the War Museum, it's about three quarters of a mile southeast to **Old Trafford**, the self-styled "Theatre of Dreams" and home of **Manchester United** (☎0161/868 8000, Ⓦ www.manutd.com), arguably the most famous football team in the world. The club's following is such that only season-ticket holders can ever attend games, but guided tours of Old Trafford and its **museum** (daily

9.30am–4.30pm; advance booking essential; £12.50) placate out-of-town fans. To get there by public transport, take the Metrolink tram to Old Trafford Station and walk up Warwick Road to Sir Matt Busby Way.

Across the other side of town, United's long-suffering local rivals, **Manchester City** (Ⓦ www.mcfc.co.uk), became the world's richest club in a dramatic twist of fate one evening in 2008, after being bought by the royal family of Abu Dhabi. They play at the **City of Manchester Stadium**, occupying the Commonwealth Games site. It's easier to get tickets for their games.

Eating and drinking

Second only to London in the breadth and scope of its **cafés** and **restaurants**, Manchester has something to suit everyone, from a cheap curry to the most urbane dining. Moreover at both ends of the market your money goes a lot further than it does in London, and smart in Manchester doesn't often mean snobby – the city is much too egalitarian for that. Most city-centre **pubs** dish up something filling at lunchtime, but for a more modish snack or drink, European-style **café-bars** are everywhere.

Restaurants

Manchester's dining scene is expansive and diverse, from slap-up curries to chic restaurants, the latter increasingly featuring high-quality local flavours from around the northwest. If it's a budget lunch or late-night meal you're after, count on **Chinatown**, and there's a gaggle of recommendable restaurants along and off Deansgate. It also pays to visit the suburbs. The **Rusholme** district, a couple of miles south of the centre, is the focus for devotees of the city's South Asian cuisine, a self-named "curry mile" of Indian and Pakistani restaurants that extends along the main drag, Wilmslow Road; it also features some Middle Eastern cafés. From Rusholme it's another couple of miles down Wilmslow Road to **Didsbury**, a leafy, well-heeled suburb, equipped, along with nearby **West Didsbury**, with several excellent Modern British restaurants. Taxis aren't particularly expensive to any of these places, or you can easily take a bus.

City centre

Dimitri's 1 Campfield Arcade, Deansgate Ⓣ 0161/839 3319. Pick and mix from the Greek/Spanish/Italian menu (particularly good for vegetarians), or grab a sandwich, an arcade table and sip a drink – Greek coffee to Lebanese wine. Snacks around £4, tapas £5.

Little Yang Sing 17 George St Ⓣ 0161/228 7722. Celebrated basement restaurant (forerunner to the larger *Yang Sing*) where the emphasis is on down-to-earth Cantonese cooking with lots of choices under £8.

Luso 63 Bridge St Ⓣ 0161/839 5550. Compact restaurant serving a wonderful selection of modern Portuguese, heavy on the pork but also excellent for seafood – try the Gomes de Sá salt cod or the pork and clam cataplana. Portuguese wine specials too. Mains around £15.

The Market Restaurant 104 High St Ⓣ 0161/834 3743. A Northern Quarter institution with a regularly changing menu that puts together contemporary British dishes in adventurous, eclectic fashion, with main courses for around £13–18. Reservations absolutely essential. Closed Mon.

The Modern Cathedral Gardens Ⓣ 0161/685 8282. Above the National Football Museum, this chic and exclusive restaurant has a Taste of Manchester menu and elegantly served British classics like line-caught Shetland cod and bubble-and-squeak cake. From £16 for your main course. A drink in the bar above is essential.

Piccolino 8 Clarence St Ⓣ 0161/835 9860. Just around from the town hall, this is the favoured spot for Manchester's great and good for both lunch and dinner. Proper Italian cuisine, with mains £9–17.

Sam's Chop House Chapel Walks, off Cross St Ⓣ 0161/834 3210. The restaurant attached to this wonderful old-world pub is a real hidden gem. It has a Victorian gas-lit feel, serves a delightful menu of English food, and they know their wine. Mains £14–16.

Stock 4 Norfolk St Ⓣ 0161/839 6644. Superior Italian cooking – the fish is renowned – accompanied by a wine list of serious intent. It's housed in the city's old stock exchange, hence the name. Dress smart. Main courses average £18, less at lunchtimes and from 5 to 7pm. Closed Sun.

Tampopo 16 Albert Square ☎0161/819 1966. Basement noodle bar – Japanese, Thai, Malaysian or Indonesian – with long benches and a fast turnover. Most dishes under £7. One of a small chain.

Yang Sing 34 Princess St ☎0161/236 2200. One of the best Cantonese restaurants in the country, with thoroughly authentic food, from a lunchtime plate of fried noodles to the full works. Stray from the printed menu for the most interesting dishes; ask the friendly staff for advice. Main courses from £11.

Rusholme

Jaffa 185 Wilmslow Rd ☎0161/225 0800. More Lebanese canteen than curry house, this cheap, cheerful place is one of the best spots for meze, lamb kebabs and *shawarma* (no more than £6), and very popular with Asian families.

Punjab Tandoori 177 Wilmslow Rd ☎0161/225 2960. Despite the name, the only distinctively southern Indian – as opposed to Pakistani – restaurant on the strip, *Punjab* is a local favourite without pretensions and has reasonable prices – a full meal should cost no more than £15. Try the special *dosa* starters.

Royal Suite Darbar 65–67 Wilmslow Rd ☎0161/224 4392. Award-winning South Asian food in plain but friendly surroundings. The house speciality is *nihari*, a slow-cooked lamb dish, while other home-style choices appear on Sun; the *karahi gosht* is particularly good. Take your own booze. Main courses from £9.

Didsbury and West Didsbury

Lime Tree 8 Lapwing Lane, West Didsbury ☎0161/445 1217. The finest local food, with a menu that chargrills and oven-roasts as if its life depended on it – the Hardingland suckling pig is a joy. Main courses cost £14 and up in the evening, less at lunchtime. Fashionable, so reservations recommended. Closed lunchtime Mon & Sat.

No. 4 4 Warburton St, Didsbury ☎0161/445 0448. Tucked away off the main road, this cottage-style bolt-hole has two floors of intimate dining. Omelettes and open sandwiches at lunch (around £5) give way to seasonally changing Modern British dinners, with main courses from £12. Closed Sun eve & all day Mon.

Cafés and café-bars

Manchester's recently adopted cosmopolitanism is nowhere more apparent than in its delightful **café-bars**. Many of those in the Gay Village, the Northern Quarter and Castlefield are laid-back, easygoing joints, though evenings always see the atmosphere ratcheted up a notch or two, while among the half-dozen places along Deansgate Locks (Whitworth Street West) the emphasis is more on serious partying. Lots of café-bars have outdoor seating, ideal for an afternoon refresher in the sun. As a general rule, the places listed below are open daily from 11am or noon until around midnight, often later at the weekend or if there's music, but we have also included a couple of daytime-only **cafés**.

Barça Bar Arches 8 & 9, Catalan Square. Love or hate it – and plenty of people do both – this trendy Castlefield café-bar does have a great location, tucked into the old railway arches off Castle St, a stone's throw from the Rochdale Canal. Best on the weekend.

Cornerhouse 70 Oxford St. Slick ground-floor bar and first-floor café-bar in Manchester's premier art-house cinema and arts centre. Tasty, inexpensive snacks and light meals – from around £5 – and a good beer and wine menu.

Dry Bar 28–30 Oldham St. The first of the designer café-bars on the scene, started by Factory Records and the catalyst for much of what has happened since in the Northern Quarter. Still as cool (though not always easy) as they come.

Earth 16–20 Turner St. Never a letdown. Gourmet vegan and organic food and drink – stuffed pancakes, pies, bakes, juices and deli delights – underneath the Manchester Buddhist centre. Daytime only; closed Sun & Mon.

Eighth Day 107–111 Oxford Rd. Manchester's oldest organic-vegetarian café has spanking new premises on its old Oxford Rd site – shop, takeaway and juice bar upstairs, great-value café/restaurant downstairs. Daytime only; closed Sun.

The Gallery Café Whitworth Art Gallery, Oxford Rd. Just inside the elegant entrance, this award-winning café serves a range of locally sourced breakfasts, posh sandwiches and light lunches for no more than £6. Also a fine stop for an afternoon tea and cake after taking in one of the galleries. Daytime only.

Manto 46 Canal St. Probably the most iconic and oldest bar in the Gay Village, constantly reinventing itself since it was established in 1990. Attracts a chic crowd, who lap up the cool sounds and club nights. Inexpensive fusion dishes served daily from noon till 8pm.

Musicana Café 10a Wilmslow Rd. Just on the left as you enter Rusholme, this non-alcoholic bar might feel more at home in Damascus than the northwest. Tables spill out onto the street, where shisha pipes are passed around under the warming glow of outdoor heaters.

Night & Day 26 Oldham St ⓦ www.nightnday.org. Unpretentious café-bar with a late licence and a wide variety of live music most nights from local musicians. Club nights too.

🏃 **Odd** 30–32 Thomas St. Oozes Manchester's cosmopolitan pride in kitsch surroundings. Great food follows the quirky theme – NYPD New York Pastrami Doorstep, for instance. DJ nights most weekends, and a three-page drinks menu.

Trof Central 6–8 Thomas St ⓦ www.trof.co.uk. The epitome of new Manchester: three storeys of cool, relaxed café-bar, populated by trendy young things and ideal for a late breakfast or early afternoon drink. Open-mic nights, poetry readings and DJ sets.

Pubs and bars

Considering the working-class heritage, it's hardly surprising that Manchester has a great selection of classic Victorian **pubs** as well as modern designer joints in imaginatively recycled old buildings. As far as **beer** goes, independent local brewers Hydes, Holts and Robinson's are all favourites.

Big Hands 296 Oxford Rd. In front of the Contact Theatre, this intimate über-cool bar is popular with trendy students, usually post-gig as it has a late licence. Diverse selection of drinks.

🏃 **Britons Protection** 50 Great Bridgewater St. Cosy, old pub with a couple of small rooms and all sorts of Victorian decorative detail – most splendidly the tiles and open fires during the winter months. Also has a backyard beer garden.

Circus Tavern 86 Portland St. Manchester's smallest pub, this Victorian drinking-hole is many people's favourite city-centre pit-stop. You may have to knock on the door to get in; once you do, you're confronted by the landlord in the corridor pulling pints.

Cloud 23 Beetham Tower, 301 Deansgate. Not so much a pub, as Manchester's highest and most popular cocktail bar. Expensive but it's worth paying for the view of the city and Pennines beyond, as well as to stand on the 23rd-floor glass overhang.

Dukes '92 Castle St. Classily revamped former stable-block with art on the walls, terrace seating and a good selection of beers – an ideal spot for a sunny afternoon pint by the picturesque canal lock. Serves great-value food too, including a wide range of pâtés and cheeses.

Marble Arch 73 Rochdale Rd. A little way out of the centre but don't be put off by the surroundings. Beautiful, ornate Victorian tiling and wooden bar, plus its own microbrewery which creates a highly popular ginger beer among the alcoholic brews.

The Ox 71 Liverpool Rd. Pleasant and popular old boozer that dates back to Victorian times – as does some of the tile-work. Good range of cask ales along with well-above-average bar food.

🏃 **Sand Bar** 120–122 Grosvenor St. Between the university and the city centre, this is a brilliant modern take on the traditional pub, where students, lecturers and workers shoot the breeze. Serves a great selection of beers and wines.

Nightlife

Manchester's musical heritage and whopping student population have marked it out as a serious contender to London as the forerunner of Britain's youth culture. **Clubs** often change styles on different nights of the week, and frequently change names; you'll see numerous fly-posters advertising what's on. The city's biggest nocturnal draw, though, is the internationally acclaimed **Warehouse Project** (ⓦ www .thewarehouseproject.com; £20) from October to December, a three-month season of the country's best house acts – 2manydjs, Annie Mac, La Roux – smashing out sessions on Friday and Saturday nights in a warehouse below Piccadilly train station. Tickets are like gold dust, so book well in advance. Of the classic clubs listed below, expect to pay £5–15 cover depending on what's on. Many of the city's hip café-bars also host regular club nights.

Manchester also has an excellent pub and club **live music** scene, with tickets for local bands usually under £5, or more like £10–15 for someone you've heard of.

Mega-star gigs take place at one of the city's major venues, listed below. For the broadest coverage of musical happenings, check out the *Manchester Evening News*.

Smaller live-music and club venues

5th Avenue 121 Princess St ℗0161/236 2754, ⓦ5thavenuemanchester.com. An unashamedly Manc indie club: a fun night of Stone Roses, Oasis and The Smiths, though don't expect much else.

Band on the Wall 25 Swan St ℗0161/834 1786, ⓦwww.bandonthewall.org. Dazzlingly revamped, this legendary Northern Quarter joint remains true to its commitment to "real music": one of the city's best venues to see live bands – from world and folk to jazz and reggae – plus club nights to boot.

The Deaf Institute 135 Grosvenor St ℗0161/276 9350, ⓦwww.thedeafinstitute .co.uk. A mile down Oxford Rd, this bar and music hall sits in a funky bohemian makeover of the elegant Victorian former deaf institute. Music centres around folk, indie and r'n'b, and regularly showcases up-and-coming talent.

Manchester Academy Oxford Rd ℗0161/275 2930, ⓦwww.manchesteracademy.net. Academy 1 is on the university campus, opposite the medical school, Academy 2 & 3 are inside the Students' Union building on Oxford Rd. All three are popular student venues featuring both new and established bands.

Matt and Phreds 64 Tib St ℗0161/831 7002, ⓦwww.mattandphreds.com. The city's finest jazz bar, from jiving dance tunes to gritty New Orleans blues.

Roadhouse 8 Newton St ℗0161/237 9789, ⓦwww.theroadhouselive.co.uk. Regular and varied gigs by local bands plus a succession of club nights.

Sankey's Soap Beehive Mill, Jersey St, Ancoats ℗0161/236 5444, ⓦsankeys.info. Many Mancunians' favourite night out, brought to you by the legendary Tribal Gathering crew, popular for their sleazy house music; other club-night specials too.

Stadium venues

Manchester Apollo Stockport Rd, Ardwick Green ℗0870/991 3913, ⓦwww.manchesterapollo.co .uk. Huge theatre auditorium for all kinds of concerts.

Manchester Central Petersfield ℗0161/834 2700, ⓦwww.manchestercentral.co.uk. Mid-sized city-centre indoor stadium.

Manchester Evening News Arena 21 Hunt's Bank, beside Victoria Station ℗0844/847 8000, ⓦwww.men-arena.com. Indoor stadium seating 20,000 and hosting all the big names.

Arts and culture

Manchester is blessed with the north's most highly prized **orchestra**, the Hallé. Other acclaimed names include the BBC Philharmonic and the Manchester Camerata chamber orchestra (ⓦwww.manchestercamerata.co.uk), which performs at venues across the city. The city's **theatres** also provide for classical tastes as well as exhibiting raw, gritty young talent, while the Cornerhouse is the local "alternative" arts mainstay and the best art-house **cinema** in town.

Concerts and music

Bridgewater Hall Lower Mosley St ℗0161/907 9000, ⓦwww.bridgewater-hall.co.uk. Home of the Hallé and the Manchester Camerata; also sponsors a full programme of chamber, pop, classical and jazz concerts.

Manchester's gay scene

Manchester has one of Britain's most vibrant gay scenes, centred beside the Rochdale Canal between Princess and Chorlton streets, in the so-called **Gay Village**. The café-bars and clubs here are among the city's best. Among gay-specific events, one of the best is **Manchester Pride** (ⓦwww.manchesterpride.com), held every August bank holiday around the city, centred on the village, with a stage that has attracted the likes of Little Boots and Beth Ditto's The Gossip. Other events, including an annual arts festival held every May, are coordinated by **queerupnorth** (℗0161/234 2942, ⓦwww.queerupnorth.com). For further information, try the **Lesbian and Gay Foundation** (daily 6–10pm; ℗0845/330 3030, ⓦwww.lgfoundation.org.uk), which can put you in touch with dozens of other organizations and services.

The Lowry Pier 8, Salford Quays ☎0870/787 5780, ⓦwww.thelowry.com. Full, year-round programme of music events, from opera to country.

Royal Northern College of Music (RNCM) 124 Oxford Rd ☎0161/907 5555, ⓦwww.rncm.ac.uk. Stages top-quality classical and modern-jazz concerts – often at discount rates – including performances by Manchester Camerata.

Opera House Quay St ☎0161/828 1700, ⓦwww.manchesteroperahouse.org.uk. Major venue for touring West End musicals, drama, comedy and concerts.

Theatre, cinema and the arts

Contact Theatre 15 Oxford Rd ☎0161/274 0600, ⓦwww.contact-theatre.org. One of the most outrageous theatre companies in town, housed in provocatively designed premises, and intentionally focusing on young talent. Just west of Oxford Rd, a 5min walk from the Oxford Road/Brunswick Street junction.

Cornerhouse 70 Oxford St ☎0161/200 1500, ⓦwww.cornerhouse.org. Centre for contemporary arts, whose three screens are your best bet for art-house film releases, special screenings and cinema-related talks and events. There are also three floors of changing art exhibitions, recitals, talks, plus bookshop, café and bar.

Dancehouse Theatre 10 Oxford Rd ☎0161/237 9753, ⓦwww.thedancehouse.co.uk. Home of the Northern Ballet School and the eponymous theatre troupe; the best venue in the city for contemporary and classical dance, and they also put on drama and comedy.

Library Theatre Central Library, St Peter's Square ☎0161/236 7110, ⓦwww.librarytheatre.com. Classic drama and new writing in an intimate theatre below the Central Library.

Royal Exchange Theatre St Ann's Square ☎0161/833 9833, ⓦwww.royalexchange.co.uk. The theatre-in-the-round in the Royal Exchange is the most famous stage in the city. There's a Studio Theatre for works by new writers alongside the main stage.

Stand-up comedy

The Comedy Store Arches 3 & 4, Deansgate Locks, Whitworth St West. Bookings on ☎0844/826 0001, ⓦwww.thecomedystore.co.uk. Showcase for the best in nationwide stand-up comedy talent, with gigs most nights. Bar and brasserie too.

Listings

Hospital Manchester Royal Infirmary, Oxford Rd ☎0161/276 1234.
Internet Free at the Central Library, St Peter's Square (Mon–Thurs 9am–8pm, Fri & Sat 9am–5pm).

Police 31 Bootle St ☎0161/872 5050.
Post office 26 Spring Gardens.
Taxis Mantax ☎0161/230 3333; Taxifone ☎0161/232 3333.

Chester and around

In 1779 Boswell wrote to Samuel Johnson: "Chester pleases me more than any town I ever saw" – and although **CHESTER**, forty miles southwest of Manchester, has greatly changed since then, it still has much to recommend it. A glorious two-mile ring of medieval and Roman walls encircles a kernel of Tudor and Victorian buildings, all overhanging eaves, mini-courtyards, and narrow cobbled lanes, which culminate in the unique raised arcades called "**The Rows**". Taken altogether, Chester has enough in the way of sights, restaurants and atmosphere to make it an enjoyable base for a couple of days.

In 79 AD the Romans built Deva Castra here, their largest known fortress in Britain. Later, Ethelfleda, the daughter of King Alfred the Great, extended and refortified the place, only for it to be brutally sacked by William the Conqueror. Trade routes to Ireland made Chester the most prosperous port in the northwest. By the middle of the eighteenth century, however, the silting of the port forced the re-routing of Irish trade through Liverpool and Chester slipped into a genteel decline, which accidentally ensured the survival of many of its old buildings. In Victorian times, the canal and railway networks made the city a regional trading centre of middling importance, a status it retains today.

Arrival and information

Most long-distance and regional **buses** pull in at the stops on Vicar's Lane, a five-minute walk from the city centre. Local buses use the Bus Exchange right in the centre of town. From the **train station**, to the northeast of the centre, it's a ten-minute walk down City Road and Foregate Street to the central Eastgate Clock. A shuttle bus (every 30min: Mon–Sat 8am–6pm; free with rail ticket) links the train station with the Bus Exchange. Drivers should note that city-centre parking is thin on the ground, which makes Chester's **Park and Ride** scheme attractive – just follow the signs on any of the major approach roads.

Chester has two **tourist offices**, one bang in the centre, in the Town Hall on Northgate Street (April–Sept Mon–Sat 9am–5.30pm, Sun 10am–4pm; Oct–March Mon–Fri 10am–4pm, Sat 10am–5pm), a second on Vicar's Lane (same hours plus Oct–March Sun 10am–4pm). They share the same telephone number and website (℗01244/351609, ⓦwww.visitchester.co.uk). At either, you can book accommodation and guided walks (see box above), and pick up a copy of the handy *Chester Visitor Guide*.

Accommodation

Chester is a popular tourist destination and although most of its visitors are day-trippers, enough of them stay overnight to sustain dozens of **B&Bs** and **hotels**. Standards are generally high and the competition keeps prices down to reasonable levels. For most of the year, finding a vacant room presents few problems, but at the height of the summer and on high days and holidays – like Chester Races – advance booking is strongly recommended, whether direct or via the tourist office.

Hotels and B&Bs

The Chester Grosvenor Eastgate St ℗01244/324024, ⓦwww.chestergrosvenor.co.uk. Superbly appointed luxury hotel in an immaculately maintained Victorian building in the centre of town. Extremely comfortable bedrooms and a host of facilities, not least a full-blown spa and an excellent brasserie. Discounts common at the weekend. ❼

Chester Town House B&B 23 King St ℗01244/350021, ⓦwww.chestertownhouse.co.uk. High-standard B&B in a comfortably furnished seventeenth-century townhouse on a cobbled central street off Northgate St. Five en-suite rooms and private parking. ❸

Green Bough 60 Hoole Rd, a mile northeast of the city centre en route to the M53/M56 ℗01244/326241, ⓦwww.greenbough.co.uk. Award-winning, small,

friendly, family-run hotel in a Victorian townhouse. The fifteen rooms each have a distinctive style with thoughtful details. Great breakfasts, a rooftop garden, and a wonderful, though expensive, restaurant. ❻

Grove Villa 18 The Groves ℗01244/341793, ⓦwww.grovevilla.com. Right on the waterfront, this homely Victorian B&B is walking distance from the city walls and stuffed with antiques. There are three cosy, en-suite bedrooms – ask for one overlooking the river. ❷

Hostel

Chester Backpackers 67 Boughton ℗01244/400185, ⓦwww.chesterbackpackers.co.uk. Close to the city walls and 5min walk from the train station in a typically Chester mock-Tudor building. En-suite doubles as well as 18-bed dorms. Dorm beds £17, rooms ❶

The City

Central Chester is a delightful spot readily explored on foot. There are two special highlights, **The Rows**, the picturesque galleries that run above the central shops, and the ancient **city wall**, from the top of which are fetching views of Chester's environs.

The Rows

Intersecting at **The Cross**, where the town crier welcomes visitors to the city (May–Aug Tues–Sat at noon), the four main thoroughfares of central Chester are lined by **The Rows**, galleried shopping arcades that run along the first floor of a wonderful set of half-timbered buildings with another set of shops down below at street level. This engaging tableau is a blend of genuine Tudor houses and Victorian imitations that are hard to separate out. The Rows were first recorded shortly after a fire wrecked Chester in 1278 – it seems likely that the hard bedrock

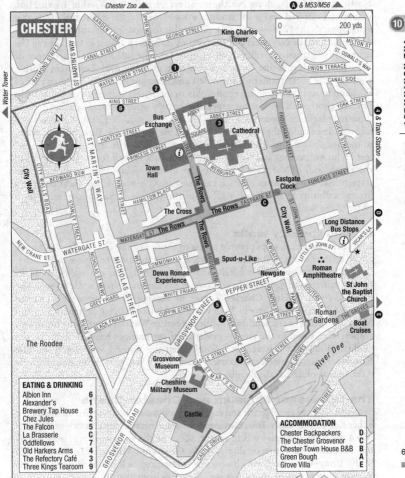

Chester Zoo ▲   **A** & M53/M56 ▲

CHESTER

0   200 yds

King Charles Tower

Bus Exchange

Cathedral

Town Hall

Eastgate Clock

The Cross

The Rows

City Wall

Long Distance Bus Stops

Spud-u-Like

Dewa Roman Experience

Newgate

Roman Amphitheatre

St John the Baptist Church

Roman Gardens

Boat Cruises

The Roodee

Grosvenor Museum

Cheshire Military Museum

Castle

River Dee

EATING & DRINKING

Albion Inn	6
Alexander's	1
Brewery Tap House	8
Chez Jules	2
The Falcon	5
La Brasserie	C
Oddfellows	7
The Refectory Café	4
Three Kings Tearoom	9

ACCOMMODATION

Chester Backpackers	D
The Chester Grosvenor	C
Chester Town House B&B	B
Green Bough	A
Grove Villa	E

that lies underneath the town centre prevented its shopkeepers and merchants from constructing the cellars they required, so they built upwards instead. The finest Tudor buildings are on Watergate Street, though Bridge Street is perhaps the more picturesque and there's a real curiosity here: the *Spud-u-Like* snack bar doesn't look like much from the outside, but wander in, step down into the cellar and you'll spy the substantial remains of a **Roman hypocaust** (under-floor heating system), dating from the first century AD. Opposite *Spud-u-Like*, an alley leads through to the child-friendly **Dewa Roman Experience** (Mon–Sat 9am–5pm, Sun 10am–4pm; £4.95), which attempts to evoke the flavour of Roman Chester with a galley, a reconstruction of a Roman street and some underground remains. Back at The Cross, it's a brief walk along Eastgate Street to one of the old town gates, above which is perched the filigree **Eastgate Clock**, raised in honour of Queen Victoria's Diamond Jubilee.

The Town Hall and the cathedral

North of The Cross, along Northgate Street, rises the neo-Gothic **Town Hall**, whose acres of red and grey sandstone look over to the **cathedral** (Mon–Sat 9am–5pm, Sun 12.30–4pm; £5), a much-modified red-sandstone structure dating back to the Normans and for most of its history a Benedictine abbey. The nave, with its massive medieval pillars, sports on one side a splendid sequence of Victorian Pre-Raphaelite mosaic panels that illustrate Old Testament stories. Close by, the north transept is the oldest and most authentically Norman part of the church, and the adjoining choir holds an intricately carved set of fourteenth-century choir stalls with some especially beastly misericords. Look out for the funerary plaque of Frederick Philips (1720–1785), stuck on a pillar in the south transept. Poor old Philips had been a colonial bigwig in New York, but his loyalty to the British cost him dear during the American War of Independence, when he lost all his possessions and was obliged to hot-foot it back to England. Doors in the north wall of the nave lead into the old abbey buildings, principally the sixteenth-century cloisters, which enclose a small garden whose focal point is a bronze sculpture by Stephen Broadbent of the Woman of Samaria, offering Jesus water at the well.

Around the city walls

East of the cathedral, steps provide access to the top of the **city walls**, a two-mile girdle of medieval and Roman handiwork that is the most complete in Britain – though in places the wall is barely above street level. You can walk past all its towers, turrets and gateways in an hour or so, and most have a tale to tell. The fifteenth-century **King Charles Tower** in the northeast corner is so named because Charles I stood here in 1645 watching his troops being beaten on Rowton Moor, two miles to the southeast, while the earlier **Water Tower** at the northwest corner, once stood in the river – evidence of the changes brought about by the gradual silting of the River Dee. South from the Water Tower you'll see **The Roodee**, England's oldest racecourse. Races are still held here throughout the year – the tourist office has the details.

The Grosvenor Museum and Chester Castle

Scores of sculpted tomb panels and engraved headstones once propped up the wall to either side of the Water Tower, evidence of some nervous repair work undertaken when the Roman Empire was in retreat. Much of this stonework was retrieved by the Victorians and is now on display at the **Grosvenor Museum**, 27 Grosvenor St (daily 10am–4pm; free), which also has interesting background displays on the Roman Empire in general and Roman Chester in particular.

Close by, on Castle Street, the **Cheshire Military Museum** (daily 10am–5pm; £3) inhabits part of the same complex as **Chester Castle** (no public access), built by William the Conqueror, though most of what you see today is resolutely Georgian and used as courts and offices. From the castle, it's an easy five- to ten-minute stroll east to one of the old city gates, **Newgate**, for the Roman Gardens and the Roman amphitheatre.

The Roman Gardens and Roman amphitheatre

Immediately to the east of Newgate, a footpath leads into the **Roman Gardens**, where a miscellany of Roman stonework is on display amid the surrounding greenery. Footsteps away, along Little St John Street, is the shallow, partly excavated bowl that marks the site of the **Roman amphitheatre** (open access), which is estimated to have held seven thousand spectators, making it the largest amphitheatre in Britain. The Roman garrison was 6000 strong in its heyday, and the amphitheatre was used by soldiers of the Twentieth Legion for weapons training as well as entertainment.

St John the Baptist Church and The Groves

A few yards from the amphitheatre, in Grosvenor Park, lurks the **Church of St John the Baptist** (daily 9.30am–5pm; free), which was founded by the Saxon king Ethelred. Rebuilt in its entirety by the Normans and largely untouched thereafter, it's an impressive structure. The east portion of the church was abandoned at the Reformation and left to crumble.

Behind the ruins, steps lead down to **The Groves**, a partly pedestrianized esplanade that stretches out along the muddy River Dee, complete with bandstand, slender iron footbridge of 1923 and ancient willow trees. It's from here that Bithells Boats organize their river cruises (see box, p.614). The Groves leads round to the foot of Lower Bridge Street, from where you can regain the town centre.

Eating and drinking

You can't walk more than a few paces in downtown Chester without coming across somewhere to eat and drink, as often as not housed in a medieval or Tudor building. Standards are very variable, but there is a clutch of first-class **restaurants** and several delightful **pubs**.

Cafés and restaurants

Chez Jules 71 Northgate St ☎01244/400014. There's a classic brasserie menu at this popular spot, housed in an attractive half-timbered black-and-white building. In the evenings, main courses begin at about £10, but they also do a terrific-value, two-course lunch for £7.90. Closed Sun eve.

La Brasserie *Chester Grosvenor* hotel, Eastgate St ☎01244/324024. In the same hotel as *Simon Radley's*, a Michelin-starred gourmet restaurant where the à la carte menu sits at a cool £69, is this much more affordable yet smart brasserie that serves inventive French and fusion cooking. Main courses average £16, and it's also a great place for a coffee and pastry. Daily 7am–10pm.

Oddfellows 20 Lower Bridge St ☎01244/400001. Chic modern brasserie serves a menu of British cuisine, from spiced pumpkin and chestnut risotto, to poached haddock with bubble and squeak. Dinnertime mains for around £18.

The Refectory Café Chester Cathedral, 12 Abbey Square ☎01244/500964. Ideal for afternoon tea and pastry or a simple lunch is the cathedral's medieval dining hall with beautiful stained-glass windows, first used in the early thirteenth century by Benedictine monks. Daytime only; closed Sun.

Three Kings Tearoom 90 Lower Bridge St. Behind the cutest of antique shops, an amenable little tearoom with pleasantly fuddy-duddy decor and tasty food – a filling salad and sandwich combo costs about £4.

Pubs and bars

Albion Inn Corner of Albion and Park sts. An English Victorian terraced pub in the shadow of the city walls reminiscent of the war days: no fruit machines, no children allowed, and Union Jack bunting. Tasty bar food and a great range of ales. **Alexander's** 2 Rufus Court ☎01244/340005, Ⓦwww.alexanderslive.com. Continental-style café-bar with inexpensive tapas – one of the livelier places in town, with live music or comedy most nights.

Brewery Tap House 52–54 Lower Bridge St. Up the cobbled ramp, this converted medieval hall, owned by the royalist Gamul family, serves up a good selection of ales from a local brewery in a tall barn-like room with whitewashed walls.

The Falcon Lower Bridge St. This half-timbered building started out as an aristocrat's townhouse, but now it's a traditional pub with a good range of draught beers.

Old Harkers Arms 1 Russell St, below the City Rd bridge. Canalside gastropub imaginatively sited in a former warehouse about 500 yards northeast of Foregate St. A good selection of real ales and wines, and quality bar food.

Around Chester: Chester Zoo

Chester's most popular attraction is **Chester Zoo** (daily: April–Sept 10am–6pm; Oct–March 10am–4pm; last admission 1hr before closing; £14.95, £11.75 in winter; children aged 3–15 £12.45/£9.95; Ⓦwww.chesterzoo.org), one of the best in Europe. It is also the second largest in Britain (after London's), with over seven thousand animals spread over a hundred landscaped acres. The zoo is well known for its **conservation projects** and has had notable success with its Asiatic lions, jaguars and giant Komodo dragons. Animals are grouped by region in large paddocks viewed from a maze of pathways, from the monorail or from the water bus, with main attractions including the baby animals (elephants, giraffes and orang-utans), the Tropical Realm, Bat Cave and the Chimpanzee Forest with the biggest climbing frame in the country. The zoo entrance is signposted off the A41 just two miles to the north of Chester. To get there by public transport, take bus #1 (Mon–Sat every 20min, Sun hourly) from the Bus Exchange.

Liverpool and around

From the days as empire's second city to urban deprivation in the postwar years, **LIVERPOOL** has always been a city of mixed fortunes. Thanks to the millions invested in regenerating the centre and old docks, the city today is back to strutting its stuff, having claimed the accolade of European Capital of Culture for 2008. Acerbic wit and loyalty to one of the city's two football teams (Liverpool and Everton) are the linchpins of Scouse culture, although Liverpool also makes great play of its musical heritage – reasonable enough from the city that produced The Beatles. It's also the proud owner of a Tate Gallery of its own, a series of innovative museums, and a fascinating social history.

Liverpool gained its charter from King John in 1207, but remained a humble fishing village until the booming slave trade prompted the building of the first dock in 1715. From then until the abolition of slavery in Britain in 1807, Liverpool was the apex of the **slaving triangle**. After the abolition of the trade, the port continued to grow into a seven-mile chain of docks, not only for freight but also to cope with wholesale European **emigration**, which saw nine million people leave for the Americas and Australasia between 1830 and 1930. Immigration from the Caribbean, China and especially Ireland in the wake of the potato famine in the 1840s resulted in one of Britain's earliest multiethnic communities.

The docks had lost their pre-eminence by the middle of the twentieth century and, although the arrival of car manufacturing plants in the 1960s stemmed the decline for a while, during the 1970s and 1980s Liverpool became a byword for

British economic malaise. However, the waterfront area of the city was granted **UNESCO World Heritage** status in 2004, spurring redevelopment and the refurbishment of the city's magnificent municipal and industrial buildings.

Visitors have to plan ahead if they are to get around the sights in two or three days. The **River Mersey** provides one focus, whether crossing on the famous ferry to the **Wirral** peninsula or on a tour of the attractions in **Albert Dock**, such as **Tate Liverpool**. The associated **Beatles** sights can easily occupy another day. If you want a **cathedral**, they've "got one to spare" as the song goes; plus there's a fine showing of British art in the celebrated **Walker Art Gallery**, a multitude of child-friendly exhibits in the **World Museum Liverpool**, and a revitalized arts and nightlife urban quarter centred on **FACT**, Liverpool's showcase for film and the media arts. Not forgetting the stunning, 1000-yard-long Antony Gormley art installation, **Another Place**, at Crosby Beach.

Arrival and information

Mainline trains pull in to **Lime Street Station**, while the suburban **Merseyrail** system (for trains from Chester) calls at four underground stations in the city, including Lime Street, Central (under the main post office on Ranelagh Street) and James Street (for Pier Head and the Albert Dock). National Express **buses** use the station on Norton Street, just northeast of Lime Street, and local buses depart from Queen Square and Liverpool One bus station.

Liverpool John Lennon **airport** (℡0870/129 8484, ⓦwww.liverpoolairport .com) is eight miles southeast of the city centre. From outside the main entrance, the **Airlink #500 bus** (every 30min 6.45am–11.45pm; £2.50) runs into the city centre, stopping at both major bus terminals and at Lime Street; a **taxi** to Lime Street costs around £15. Most **ferries** – from the Isle of Man, Dublin and Belfast – dock at the terminals just north of Pier Head, not far from James Street Merseyrail station, though Norfolkline arrivals are over the water in The Wirral at Twelve Quays, near Woodside ferry terminal (ferry or Merseyrail to Liverpool).

Tourist information – including the free, comprehensive *Liverpool Visitor Guide* – is available from the **central tourist office**, at **08 Place**, 36–38 Whitechapel (Mon–Sat 9am–6/7pm, Sun 11am–4pm; ℡0151/233 2008, accommodation line ℡0844/870 0123; ⓦwww.visitliverpool.com). There are smaller offices in the Anchor Courtyard at the **Albert Dock** (daily 10am–5pm) and at the **airport** (daily 5am–midnight).

City transport and tours

Liverpool city centre is surprisingly compact and easy to handle on foot. Even the walk from the Metropolitan Cathedral through the centre to Albert Dock takes less than half an hour. For an overview take City Sightseeing's open-top **Liverpool Bus Tour** (every 30–90min 10am–4pm; 24hr ticket £8; ⓦwww .city-sightseeing.com). Take a **ferry across the Mersey** (see p.625) at some point if only to be able to say that you've sung *that* song; longer **cruises** (selected days May to mid-Oct; 6hr; £36) run from Woodside along the Manchester Ship Canal to Salford Quays (trip back by bus). The local transport authority is **Merseytravel** (℡0871/200 2233, ⓦwww.merseytravel.gov.uk), which has travel centres at Queen Square and the Liverpool One bus station. A daily off-peak **Saveaway ticket** (£4.50) gives you unlimited travel on buses, trains and ferries, and if you're here for any length of time, consider buying a "Your Ticket for Liverpool" **visitor card** either online or from the Queen Square Travel Centre (£24.99 for one day, £29.99 for three; ℡0870/055 3471, ⓦwww.yourticketforliverpool.com), which gives free and discounted tickets to attractions.

The tourist offices have details of guided **walking tours** of the city (mostly Easter–Sept; from £3), or pick up one of the self-guided trails around sights associated with Liverpool's Jewish or Irish heritage. With children in tow, don't miss a trip on the amphibious **Yellow Duckmarine** (daily 10.30/11am–5.30pm; peak time £11.95, off-peak £9.95; ℡0151/708 7799, ⓦwww.theyellowduck marine.co.uk), which departs from Gower Street, in front of Albert Dock.

Accommodation

It's not difficult to find accommodation in Liverpool, from small-scale apartments to boutique hotels and business-oriented four-stars, particularly around the new Liverpool One complex – though be sure to book in advance if Liverpool FC is playing.

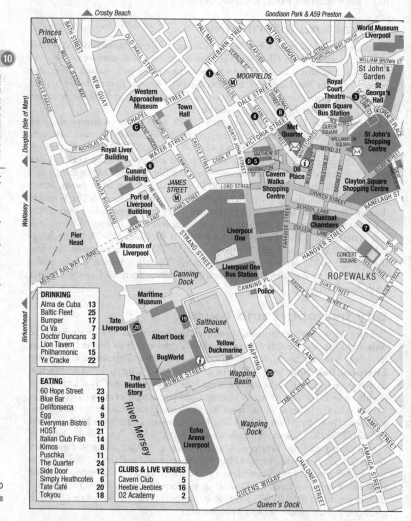

DRINKING

Alma de Cuba	13
Baltic Fleet	25
Bumper	17
Ca Va	7
Doctor Duncans	3
Lion Tavern	1
Philharmonic	15
Ye Cracke	22

EATING

60 Hope Street	23
Blue Bar	19
Delifonseca	4
Egg	9
Everyman Bistro	10
HOST	21
Italian Club Fish	14
Kimos	8
Puschka	11
The Quarter	24
Side Door	12
Simply Heathcotes	6
Tate Café	20
Tokyou	18

CLUBS & LIVE VENUES

Cavern Club	5
Heebie Jeebies	16
O2 Academy	2

Hotels and apartments

Aachen 89–91 Mount Pleasant ☏ 0151/709 3477, Ⓦ www.aachenhotel.co.uk. Recently renovated, this is a solid mid-range choice, with a range of value-for-money rooms (with and without en-suite showers), sizeable breakfasts, and a late bar. ❷

Feathers 113–125 Mount Pleasant ☏ 0151/709 9655, Ⓦ www.feathers.uk.com. A converted, modernized terrace of Georgian houses, with a variety of refurbished rooms. Late bar, 24hr reception, and help-yourself hot-and-cold buffet breakfast included in the price. ❸

Hard Day's Night North John St ☏ 0151/236 1964, Ⓦ www.harddaysnighthotel.com. Large four-star with over 110 guest rooms, close to Mathew St. All rooms are Beatle-themed, though the Lennon and McCartney suites are the tops. Great bar with regular live music. Breakfast not included. ❺, suites ❽

Hope Street 40 Hope St (entrance on Hope Place) ☏ 0151/709 3000, Ⓦ www.hopestreethotel.co.uk. Recently expanded to 89 rooms, this former police station is one of Liverpool's best boutique hotels, with a Scandinavian feel of bare wood, light walls, and open brickwork. Rooms have hardwood

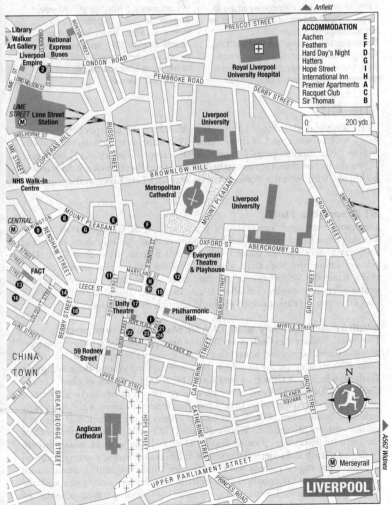

ACCOMMODATION

Aachen	E
Feathers	F
Hard Day's Night	D
Hatters	G
Hope Street	I
International Inn	H
Premier Apartments	A
Racquet Club	C
Sir Thomas	B

▲ Anfield
▲ A562 Widnes
▼ Sefton Park, John Lennon Airport & Speke Hall

LIVERPOOL

floors and luxurious bathrooms. Breakfast not included. **⑤**, suites **⑦**

Premier Apartments 9 Hatton Garden ☎0151/227 9467, ⓦwww.premierapartments .com. Centrally located, spacious one- and two-bedroom apartments, some for families, in a modern glass building. Wi-fi and parking are available. Good deals available online. Two-bedroom apartments from £67 per night.

Racquet Club Hargreaves Building, 5 Chapel St ☎0151/236 6676, ⓦwww.racquetclub .org.uk. A wonderful family-run townhouse boutique hotel, this former gentleman's club has only eight rooms, each mixing good linen and traditional furniture with contemporary art and all mod cons. Breakfast available courtesy of *Ziba*, the hotel's cutting-edge restaurant. **⑤**

Sir Thomas 24 Sir Thomas St ☎0151/236 1366, ⓦwww.sirthomashotel.co.uk. Occupying the old Bank of Liverpool building right in the city centre, this small hotel offers clean, ornate – if a little

cramped – rooms with TV, with breakfast included. Gets a little noisy on weekends, but good discounts. **②–③**

Hostels

Hatters 56–60 Mount Pleasant ☎0151/709 5570, ⓦwww.hattersgroup.com/Liverpool. Though it's housed in the former YMCA building – with an institutional feel and gymnasium-size dining hall – *Hatters* boasts clean rooms, friendly staff and a great location. Standard range of facilities including internet. Dorms £18.50, doubles **①**

International Inn 4 South Hunter St, off Hardman St ☎0151/709 8135, ⓦwww .internationalinn.co.uk. Converted Victorian warehouse in a great location, with modern accommodation for 100 in heated, en-suite rooms sleeping two to ten people. Cool, cosy facilities and internet access in the adjacent café. Dorm beds from £15, twin rooms **①**

The City

The main sights are scattered throughout the centre of Liverpool but you can easily walk between most of them, through cityscapes ranging from restyled city squares to the surviving regal Georgian terraces around Rodney and Hope streets. If you're short on time, the two **cathedrals** and the **Albert Dock** are the standout highlights, with both the **Walker Art Gallery** and **Tate Liverpool** essential for art fans.

St George's Hall

Emerging from Lime Street Station you can't miss **St George's Hall**, one of Britain's finest Greek Revival buildings. Now primarily an exhibition venue, but once Liverpool's premier concert hall and crown court, its vaulted Great Hall features a floor tiled with thirty thousand precious Minton tiles (usually covered over), while the Willis organ is the third largest in Europe. The small heritage centre offers audioguides (Tues–Sun 10am–5pm; free; ☎0151/225 6909), which also show you the darker side of the building, including its prisoner cells.

Walker Art Gallery and World Museum Liverpool

Liverpool's **Walker Art Gallery** on William Brown Street (daily 10am–5pm; free; ⓦwww.thewalker.org.uk) houses one of the country's best provincial art collections. The art is up on the first floor, but don't miss the ground-floor **Sculpture Gallery**, where John Gibson's *Tinted Venus* (1851–56) takes pride of place, nor the **Craft and Design Gallery**, with its displays of glassware, ceramics, fabrics, precious metals and furniture, largely retrieved from the homes of the city's early industrial businessmen. The Walker had its origins in the collection of one such person, eminent Liverpudlian William Roscoe (1753–1831), who acquired much of the early Renaissance art now on display. Liverpool's explosive economic growth in the eighteenth and nineteenth centuries is reflected as British painting begins to occupy centre stage – notably works by George Stubbs, England's greatest animal painter (and native Liverpudlian). The galleries then shift up another gear with the Pre-Raphaelites, John Everett Millais' *Isabella* (1848) leading into a succession of classical pieces by other members of the Brotherhood. Meanwhile, Victorian taste

The Beatles in Liverpool

Mathew Street, ten minutes' walk west of Lime Street Station, is where *The Cavern* used to be – once the womb of Merseybeat, it has become an enclave of Beatles nostalgia, most of it bogus and typified by the **Cavern Walks Shopping Centre**, with a bronze statue of the boys in the atrium. *The Cavern* itself saw 292 Beatles' gigs and was where the band was first spotted by Brian Epstein; the club closed in 1966 and was partly demolished in 1973, though a latter-day successor, the **Cavern Club** at 10 Mathew St, complete with souvenir shop, was rebuilt on half of the original site, using, it's claimed, the original bricks. The **Cavern Pub**, immediately across the way, boasts an exterior "Wall of Fame" highlighting both the names of all the bands who appeared at the club between 1957 and 1973 (etched into bricks) and brass discs commemorating every Liverpool chart-topper since 1952. The soul of Beatlemania is embodied at **The Beatles Shop**, 31 Mathew St (Ⓦ www.thebeatleshop.co.uk), with the "largest range of Beatles gear in the world".

For a personal and social history of the group, it's off to the Albert Dock for **The Beatles Story** in the Britannia Vaults (daily 10am–6pm; £12.50; Ⓦ www.beatlesstory .com), which entertainingly traces The Beatles' rise from the early days at *The Cavern* to their disparate solo careers. Then it's on to the two houses where John Lennon and Paul McCartney grew up, **Mendips** and **20 Forthlin Road** respectively, both now saved by the National Trust. The houses are only accessible on pre-booked tours, which run from both the city centre and Speke Hall (from the city centre: early to mid-March Wed–Sun 10am, 12.30pm & 3pm; mid-March to Oct Wed–Sun 10am & 10.50am; Nov Wed–Fri 3pm; from Speke Hall: mid-March to Oct 2.30pm & 3.20pm; Nov Sat & Sun 3pm; £16.80, NT members £7.90; Ⓣ 0844/800 4791, Ⓦ www.national trust.org.uk/beatles).

Dedicated pilgrims will undoubtedly want to see other famous Beatles' landmarks, like Strawberry Fields (a Salvation Army home) and Penny Lane (an ordinary suburban street). This is best done on an **organized Beatles tour**, and the two best options are listed below. Note that these tours only show you the exteriors of the Lennon and McCartney homes.

Beatles tours

Phil Hughes Ⓣ 0151/228 4565 or 07961/511223, Ⓦ www.tourliverpool.co.uk. Small (8-seater) minibus tours with a guide well versed in The Beatles and Liverpool life. Four-hour tours run daily on demand (£16 per person; private tour £80), with city-centre pick-ups/drop-offs and free refreshments.

Magical Mystery Tour Ⓣ 0151/236 9091, Ⓦ www.cavernclub.org or book at tourist offices. Board a multicoloured Mystery Bus, departing daily throughout the year from The 08 Place and Albert Dock (1hr 45min; £14.95).

---

for melodrama is encapsulated in a work by W.F. Yeames whose English Civil War subject might not be immediately familiar but whose title undoubtedly is – *And when did you last see your father?* (1878). Impressionists and Post-Impressionists, including Degas, Sickert, Cézanne and Monet, pull the collection into more modern times, before the Walker embarks on contemporary British art.

Further along William Brown Street the **World Museum Liverpool** (daily 10am–5pm; free; Ⓦ www.liverpoolmuseums.org.uk/wml) is among the city's favourite family attractions. The dramatic six-storey atrium provides access to an eclectic series of themed exhibits of broad appeal – from natural history to ethnographical collections, insects to antiquities, dinosaurs to space rockets. Standout sections for children include the Bug House, plus the hands-on aquarium and archeology discovery centres. The planetarium and theatre have free daily shows, with times posted at the information desk.

The cathedrals and around

On the hill behind Lime Street, off Mount Pleasant, rises the idiosyncratically shaped Catholic **Metropolitan Cathedral** of Christ the King (daily 8am–6pm; donation requested; Ⓦwww.liverpoolmetrocathedral.org.uk). Built in the wake of the revitalizing Second Vatican Council, it was raised on top of the tentative beginnings of Sir Edwin Lutyens' grandiose project to outdo St Peter's in Rome. World War II brought building work to a halt in 1941, and following subsequent financial constraints the majestic **crypt** (Mon–Sat 10am–3.15pm; £3) was not completed until 1958. The present building, to Sir Frederick Gibberd's spectacular Modernist design, is anchored by sixteen concrete ribs supporting the landmark stained-glass lantern, and was consecrated in 1967.

At the other end of Hope Street, the Anglican **Liverpool Cathedral** (daily 8am–6pm; donation requested; Ⓦwww.liverpoolcathedral.org.uk) looks older but was actually completed eleven years later, in 1978, after 74 years in construction. The last of the great British neo-Gothic structures, Sir Giles Gilbert Scott's masterwork claims a smattering of superlatives: Britain's largest and the world's fifth-largest cathedral, the world's tallest Gothic arches and the highest and heaviest bells. The stark interior is lightened by the beautiful stone tracery in the finely detailed Lady Chapel. On a clear day a trip up the 330-foot **tower** (£5 combined ticket with the Great Space audioguide) is rewarded by views to the Welsh hills.

A couple of minutes' walk from the Anglican cathedral, **59 Rodney Street** (mid-March to Oct Wed–Sun 11am–3.30pm, timed tours only, call Ⓣ0151/709 6261; £6.30; NT) was the home and studio of photographer Edward Chambré Hardman. There's a wide selection of his Liverpool photographs on show.

The city centre

Over the past fifteen years, Liverpool's city centre has witnessed a dramatic transformation. Opened in 2008, **Liverpool One**, enclosed by Strand, Paradise and James streets, forms an impressive multi-layered semi-outdoor complex of shops and café-bars, topped with a tiny park and Ferris wheel. Due east, in the former warehouse and factory district between Bold Street and Duke Street now known as the **RopeWalks**, change has been an evolution, old Victorian brick buildings being renovated into new apartments, urban spaces, and shops. **Concert Square**, just off Bold Street, occupies space once taken up by a factory which was levelled to provide room for warehouse-style bar developments. **FACT** at 88 Wood St (Ⓦwww.fact.co.uk) – Film, Art and Creative Technology – provides a cultural anchor with its galleries for art, video and new-media exhibitions (Tues–Sun 11am–6pm; free), community projects, cinema screens, café and bar.

School Lane, opposite the western end of Wood Street, throws up the beautifully proportioned **Bluecoat Chambers**, originally built in 1717 as an Anglican boarding school for orphans. An integral part of Liverpool's cultural life for years, it has now been enlarged to incorporate artists' studios (Ⓦwww.thebluecoat.org.uk). The associated **Bluecoat Display Centre** (access from College Lane) features contemporary craft in its gallery and shop (Ⓦwww.bluecoatdisplaycentre.com).

On the other side of the city centre towards the Pier Head, the **Western Approaches Museum**, 1 Rumford St, off Chapel Street (Mon–Thurs & Sat 10.30am–4.30pm; £5.50; Ⓦwww.liverpoolwarmuseum.co.uk), reveals an underground labyrinth of rooms, formerly headquarters for the campaign for the Battle of the Atlantic during World War II. The massive Operations Room vividly displays all the technology of a 1940s' nerve centre.

THE NORTHWEST | Liverpool and around

Pier Head, Mersey Ferry and the Three Graces

While the vast quantity of maritime traffic of the eighteenth and nineteenth centuries may have gone, the recently regenerated **Pier Head** landing stage with its modern limestone-clad Ferry Terminal remains the embarkation point for the **Mersey Ferry** (☎0151/330 1444, ⓦwww.merseyferries.co.uk) to Woodside (for Birkenhead) and Seacombe (Wallasey). Straightforward ferry shuttles (£2.40 return) operate during the morning and evening rush hours. At other times the boats run circular fifty-minute "river explorer" **cruises** (hourly: Mon–Fri 10am–3pm, Sat & Sun 10am–6pm; £6.30), which you can combine with a visit to the Spaceport space exploration visitor attraction at Seacombe (see p.626).

The view back across the Mersey to the Liverpool skyline is one of the city's glories. Dominating the waterfront are the so-called **Three Graces** – the Port of Liverpool Building (1907), Cunard Building (1913) and the 322-foot-high **Royal Liver Building** (1910), topped by the "Liver Birds", a couple of cormorants which have become the symbol of the city. Foreshadowing these monuments are the newest additions to the waterfront, the massive Danish-designed cross-shaped **Museum of Liverpool**, due to open in 2011, which will explore the complex history of the city in a global context.

Albert Dock

Albert Dock, five minutes' walk south of Pier Head, was built in 1846 when Liverpool's port was a world leader. It started to decline at the beginning of the twentieth century and last saw service in 1972. A decade later the site was given a complete refit, making it one of Liverpool's most popular stopping points, full of bars, restaurants, museum collections and the high-profile Beatles Story (see box, p.623); there's pay parking – follow the Echo Arena signs – and frequent buses arrive at the Liverpool One bus station from Queen Square.

The **Merseyside Maritime Museum** (daily 10am–5pm; free; ⓦwww .liverpoolmuseums.org.uk/maritime) fills one wing of the Dock; allow at least two hours to peruse the various galleries. The basement houses Seized, an interactive glimpse into smuggling and revenue collection, along with Emigrants to a New World, an illuminating display detailing Liverpool's pivotal role as a springboard for over nine million emigrants. Other galleries tell the story of the three ill-fated liners – the *Titanic*, *Lusitania* and *Empress of Ireland*. On the third floor is the **International Slavery Museum**, which in three parts dissects the trade that brought about the biggest movement of people in history, shipping millions of slaves to sugar plantations in the Americas under the most barbaric conditions. The most impressive section is the Middle Passage Gallery, which tells dehumanizing stories of slavery through an unnerving 360-degree dramatization, with displays of manacles, chains and instruments of torture.

Also on the Dock, **Tate Liverpool** (10am–5.50pm: June–Aug daily; Sept–May Tues–Sun; free, special exhibitions usually £5; ⓦwww.tate.org.uk /liverpool) is the country's national collection of modern art from the north. The main galleries include popular retrospectives of the likes of Mondrian, Dalí, Magritte and Calder, along with an ever-changing display of lesser-known works. There's also a full programme of events, talks and tours – the daily tour at noon is free.

The Dock's newest addition is **BugWorld** (daily 10am–5pm; £10.95, children aged 5–14 £6.25, under-5s free; ⓦwww.bugworldexperience.co.uk), an "Insectorium", which brings you an insect's perspective of the world. It's a fun few hours for families, particularly as the handlers allow you to hold a variety of live bugs.

Speke Hall

Located near Liverpool's airport, six miles southeast of the centre, **Speke Hall** (mid-March to Oct Wed–Sun 11am–5pm, plus Nov to mid-Dec Sat & Sun 1–4.30pm; gardens Tues–Sun 11am–4.30pm; £8.40, gardens only £5; NT) is one of the country's finest examples of Elizabethan timbered architecture. Dating from 1530, the house encloses a beautifully proportioned courtyard overlooked by myriad diamond panes. There are secret priest and spy holes, a wealth of seventeenth-century and Victorian furniture plus ornamental gardens and woodland walks. Any bus to the airport from the city centre runs within half a mile of the entrance.

The Wirral: Spaceport and Port Sunlight

Across the Mersey lies **The Wirral**, the peninsula that sits between Liverpool and Chester, flanked by the Irish Sea and the River Dee. A trip on the Mersey ferry to its Seacombe Terminal at Wallasey brings you to **Spaceport** (Tues–Sun 10.30am–6pm, last entry at 4.30pm; £5, with ferry £9.50; Ⓦwww.spaceport.org.uk), where you can blast off in a space pod to the six interactive galleries of space flight and the universe. Allow two hours, especially if you want to stop for the thirty-minute planetarium show.

Merseyrail trains run under the Mersey and out as far as **Port Sunlight**, a garden village created in 1888 by industrialist William Hesketh Lever for the workers at his soap factory. It's explored at the **Sunlight Vision Museum**, 95 Greendale Rd (daily 10am–5pm; £3.75; Ⓦwww.portsunlightvillage.com), from where a self-guided trail runs through the village, past the houses, church, theatre and gardens.

Crosby Beach

Around seven miles north of the centre is **Crosby Beach**, an innocuous spot until the arrival in 2005 of Antony Gormley's **Another Place** installation: an eerie set of a hundred life-size cast-iron statues looking out to sea, spread along over a thousand yards of beach. Crosby is a twenty-minute train ride from Liverpool Lime Street to Hall Road Station (every 30min; £2.65).

Eating, drinking and nightlife

Top-end **restaurants** sit alongside a fine selection of **cafés** and cheap stops for a bite to eat in Liverpool. Most are in three distinct areas – at Albert Dock, around Hardman and Hope streets, and along Berry and Nelson streets, heart of Liverpool's **Chinatown**. Failing those, take a short taxi ride to **Lark Lane** in Aigburth, close to Sefton Park, where a dozen eating and drinking spots pack into one short street.

Liverpool's **pubs and bars** stay open later than most, with many serving until 1 or 2am. In the RopeWalks area, Fleet, Seel and Wood streets have seen most development, with the action centred on Concert Square. Moving up towards the universities, there's a growing set of bars on Hardman Street and another tranche of places down at Albert Dock.

The city's **clubs** are notable for their lack of pretence, fashion playing second string to dancing and drinking. The evening paper, the *Liverpool Echo* (Ⓦwww .liverpoolecho.co.uk) and the monthly *Liverpool.com* (Ⓦwww.liverpool.com) have events **listings**.

Cafés, bistros and café-bars

Blue Bar Edward Pavilion, Albert Dock ☏0151/702 5830. Brick-vaulted café-bar/lounge with dockside tables and big sofas inside. Attracts the Liverpool soccerati and celebs.

Delifonseca 12 Stanley St ☏0151/255 0808. Upstairs from the deli, this bistro's ever-changing menu offers Italian and British delights, including Welsh black beef salad, or spiced mutton and apricot pie. Mains around £10. Closed Sun.

Egg 16 Newington. Up on the third floor, this plant-strewn bohemian café serves excellent vegan and vegetarian food with good set-meal deals. Also a nice place for a chai tea.

Everyman Bistro 5–9 Hope St. Attracting everyone from students to barristers, this theatre-basement café offers home-made quiche, pies and bakes, pizza and salads at around £10 for two courses. Known for its beers and wines. Bar closes at midnight, or 2am on Fri & Sat. Closed Sun.

Kimos 46 Mount Pleasant. A student fave for mountainous portions of Middle Eastern/Mediterranean-style grills, kebabs, platters, salads and a fine range of breakfasts.

The Quarter 7 Falkner St ☎0151/707 1965. Between the two cathedrals, this wonderful bistro-deli serves pasta, posh pies and gourmet pizza. Alternatively, you can stop by for coffee and excellent pastries outside on the Georgian terrace.

Tate Café Albert Dock. Looking onto the waterfront and serving breakfasts, posh sandwiches and light bites, such as smoked haddock and salmon fishcakes with pea purée.

Tokyou 7 Berry St ☎0871/963 2891. Great-value noodle bar offering a selection of Japanese, Korean and Chinese – a meal all-in shouldn't be more than £10.

Restaurants

60 Hope Street 60 Hope St ☎0151/707 6060. The rising star of the Liverpool gastronomic scene, set in a Georgian terrace, serves British cuisine with creative flourishes – Cumbrian venison with pancetta purée or cod with red-lentil dhal – as well as a vegetarian menu and extensive wine list. Around £20 per main.

HOST 31 Hope St ☎0151/708 5831. Sophisticated Asian fusion cuisine at very reasonable prices. A good stop for hearty, sinus-clearing main dishes, such as sea bass with sweet potato and soybeans, as well as light lunches. Mains usually under £10.

Italian Club Fish 128 Bold St ☎0151/707 2110. Proper Italian seafood place with a menu that adapts to what's fresh – try the *saute di Maurizio*. There are also a few token meat and vegetarian dishes, all around £13. Closed Sun.

Puschka 16 Rodney St ☎0151/708 8698. This small restaurant with chic pink decor serves up a seasonally changing menu of Modern European dishes that continues to excite its high-society

clientele. Mains around £15. Closed Mon, and for lunch Tues–Fri.

Side Door 29a Hope St ☎0151/707 7888. The intimate Georgian townhouse restaurant has settled on a winning combination of Mediterranean food and reasonable prices – with a bargain Saturday lunch deal of £10. Closed Sun.

Simply Heathcotes Beetham Plaza, 25 The Strand ☎0151/236 3536. Many people's favourite Liverpool restaurant: light lunches, grills, Sunday brunch and other delights, all involving Lancashire's best locally sourced ingredients and looking out over the Three Graces. Try the lamb hotpot with red cabbage. Most mains around £18.

Pubs and bars

Alma de Cuba St Peter's Church, Seel St. Far more candles than when it was a church, but the mirrored altar is still the focus of this bar's rich and dark Cuban-themed interior. One of the city's fancier places, so be dressed for it.

Baltic Fleet 33a Wapping. Restored, no-nonsense, quiet pub with age-old shipping connections and an open fire, just south of the Albert Dock. Good food on offer.

Bumper 18 Hardman St. For Liverpool's hip young things, no night is complete without a drink in this cool Americana indie bar. Club nights on weekends. Closed Sun.

Ca Va 4a Wood St. Masses of hip students crowd into this fun-time, dark, loud Mexican bar. Closed Sun.

Doctor Duncans St John's Lane. Local gem with Victorian tiled walls near the station, offering a wide variety of good beer including the local favourite, Caine's.

Lion Tavern 67 Moorfields. Real ale in superbly restored Victorian surroundings, from the tiles to the stained-glass rotunda. Also excellent cheese and pâté lunches (Mon–Fri).

Philharmonic 36 Hope St. Liverpool's finest traditional watering-hole, a former gentleman's club, where the main attractions – beer aside – are the mosaic floors, gilded wrought-iron gates and the marble decor in the toilets.

Ye Cracke 13 Rice St. Crusty backstreet pub off Hope St, much loved by the young Lennon, with a great jukebox and cheap-as-chips food (daytime only).

Clubs and live music

Cavern Club 10 Mathew St ☎0151/236 1965, ⓦwww.cavernclub.org. The self-styled "most famous club in the world" has live bands Wed–Sun.

Heebie Jeebies 80–82 Seel St ☎0151/708 7001. A student favourite with cavernous

Liverpool festivals

Annual **festivals** include ship visits and events at the **Mersey Maritime Festival** (June); the country's largest African arts and music festival, **Africa Oye** (June; Ⓦ www.africaoye.com); the **Summer Pops** (July), when the Royal Philharmonic and top pop names take the stage; the **Liverpool International Street Festival** (July/ Aug), with performances by a host of European theatre, music and dance groups; and **Beatles Week** (last week of Aug) and the **Mathew Street Festival** (Aug bank holiday; Ⓦ www.mathewstreetfestival.co.uk), with half a million visitors dancing to hundreds of local, national and tribute bands.

brick-vaulted ceilings. Puts on a selection of good music sets, mainly indie and soul, and sometimes live bands.

O2 Academy 11–13 Hotham St Ⓣ 0151/707 3200, Ⓦ www.liverpool-academy.co.uk. A good roster of contemporary, indie and rock gigs.

Arts and culture

The Royal Liverpool Philharmonic Orchestra, ranked with Manchester's Hallé as the northwest's best, dominates the city's **classical music** scene. **Theatre** is well entrenched in the city at a variety of venues, while independent **cinema** has found a home at FACT, the city's creative-technology centre.

Echo Arena Liverpool King's Dock Ⓣ 0844/800 0400, Ⓦ www.echoarena.com. Liverpool's space-age dock-front venue hosts large-scale concerts, sports fixtures and conventions.

Everyman Theatre and Playhouse 5–9 Hope St Ⓣ 0151/709 4776, Ⓦ www.everymanplayhouse .com. Showcases many national premieres and has a focus on young talent. Presents everything from Shakespeare to Jarman, plus concerts, exhibitions and dance.

Liverpool Empire Lime St Ⓣ 0870/606 3536, Ⓦ www.liverpool-empire.co.uk. The city's largest theatre, a venue for touring West End shows and large-scale opera and ballet – Welsh National Opera and English National Ballet both perform regularly.

Liverpool Philharmonic Hall Hope St Ⓣ 0151/709 3789, Ⓦ www.liverpoolphil.com.

This beautiful 1930s Art Deco building is the home of the Royal Liverpool Philharmonic Orchestra, and has a lively calendar of classical and popular music. Also shows classic films once a month.

Picturehouse at FACT Wood St Ⓣ 0871/704 2063, Ⓦ www.picturehouses.co.uk. The city's only independent cinema screens, for new films, reruns and festivals.

Royal Court Theatre Roe St Ⓣ 0870/787 1866, Ⓦ www.royalcourtliverpool.co.uk. Theatre and concert hall which sees regular plays, music and comedy acts.

Unity Theatre 1 Hope Place Ⓣ 0151/709 4988, Ⓦ www.unitytheatreliverpool.co.uk. The city's most adventurous range of contemporary works.

Listings

Football Liverpool FC, Anfield Rd (stadium tours every day except match days 10am–3pm; tours Ⓣ 0151/260 6677, tickets Ⓣ 0844/844 0844; Ⓦ www.liverpoolfc.tv). Everton FC, Goodison Rd (Ⓣ 0871/663 1878, Ⓦ www.evertonfc.com).

Hospital Royal Liverpool University Hospital, Prescot St Ⓣ 0151/706 2000; NHS Walk-in Centre, 53 Great Charlotte St Ⓣ 0151/285 3535.

Internet Cafe Latte.net, 4 South Hunter St Ⓣ 0151/708 9610 (Mon–Fri 8am–7pm, Sat & Sun 9am–5.30pm).

Police Canning Place Ⓣ 0151/709 6010.

Post office City-centre office at St John's Shopping Centre.

Taxis Mersey Cabs Ⓣ 0151/298 2222.

Blackpool

With its "Golden Mile" of piers, fortune-tellers, amusement arcades, tram and donkey rides, fish-and-chip shops, candyfloss stalls and fun pubs, **BLACKPOOL** is the archetypal British seaside resort, shamelessly committed to the pursuit of low-brow fun-seeking of the finest kind. From ukulele-strumming George Formby and his "little stick of Blackpool rock" to today's predatory, half-dressed gangs of stag and hen parties, few visitors, then or now, are in any doubt about the point of a holiday here. While the resort-town has seen tourist numbers dwindle in recent years, its seven miles of wide sandy beach, backed by an unbroken chain of hotels and guesthouses, still manages to attract the millions, and it remains one of the country's most popular tourist destinations.

Wealthy visitors were already summer-holidaying in Blackpool by the end of the eighteenth century, but it was the coming of the railway in 1846 that ultimately transformed Blackpool into the world's first seaside resort for working-class folk. From the mid-nineteenth century, whole Lancashire mill towns would descend on the town for the "Wakes Weeks", their annual holiday, spending their hard-saved cash on living the high life for a few days. And Blackpool didn't disappoint: the town wowed crowds with its three piers, Grand Theatre, and, from 1894, its very own seafront "Eiffel Tower", which went up only five years after the Paris original.

Where other British holiday resorts have suffered from the rivalry of cheap foreign packages, Blackpool has endured by shrewdly providing exactly what its visitors want. Underneath the populist veneer there's a sophisticated marketing approach, which balances ever more elaborate attractions with well-grounded traditional entertainment. And when other resorts begin to close up for the winter, Blackpool's main season is just beginning, as over half a million light bulbs are used to create the **Illuminations** which decorate the promenade from the beginning of September to early November.

Arrival and information

Blackpool's main train station is **Blackpool North** (direct trains from Manchester and Preston), with the **bus station** just a few steps away down Talbot Road; alternatively, trains also run hourly from Preston direct to **Blackpool Pleasure Beach** (on the Blackpool South Line). There are **car parks** signposted all over town

BLACKPOOL

ACCOMMODATION		EATING, DRINKING & NIGHTLIFE	
The Big Blue	E	AJ's	3
Four Seasons	D	Blues Brasserie	8
The Imperial	A	Funny Girls	1
Number One	F	Kwizeen	6
Number One South Beach	G	The Lounge	5
Raffles	C	Mitre	4
Ruskin	B	The Syndicate	7
		Yorkshire Fisheries	2

(including on Albert Rd, Talbot Rd, Bank St and Central Drive), and it's best to use them since on-street parking is only short-term. Blackpool's **airport** (Ⓦ www .blackpoolinternational.com) lies two miles south of the centre; there are buses from the bus station or it's a £6 taxi ride.

The **tourist office** is at 1 Clifton St (Mon–Sat 9am–5pm; ℡ 01253/478222, Ⓦ www.visitblackpool.com), on the corner with Corporation Street, and sells **discounted admission tickets** for all major Blackpool attractions (except the Pleasure Beach), as well as Travel Cards (1/3/5/7-day, £6/15.50/21.70/23.80) for use on buses and trams.

Accommodation

Bed-and-breakfast prices are generally low (from £25 per person, even less on a room-only basis or out of season), but rise at weekends and during the Illuminations. In peak season, it's simply a matter of looking for vacancy signs or asking the tourist office for help – anything cheap between North and Central piers is guaranteed to be noisy; for more peace and quiet, look for places along the North Shore, beyond North Pier (the grid west of Warbreck Hill Rd has hundreds of options).

The Big Blue Ocean Boulevard, Blackpool Pleasure Beach ℡ 0845/367 3333, Ⓦ www.bigbluehotel .com. American-resort-style accommodation with spacious family rooms that have separate children's areas, plus boutique-style, dark-wood executive rooms with sofas and fireplaces. Next to the Pleasure Beach (and its train station) and most rooms look onto the rides. ❸

Four Seasons 60 Reads Ave ℡ 01253/752171, Ⓦ www.fourseasons blackpool.co.uk. One of Blackpool's newest and best boutique hotels, a tastefully converted Victorian townhouse with airy rooms and original dark-wood fittings. The four suites are individually furnished, and staff are keen to help – even if that means setting up a Wii in your room. ❺

The Imperial North Promenade ℡ 01253/623971, Ⓦ www.paramount-hotels.co.uk. The politicians' conference favourite, a four-star hotel with sea-facing rooms, pool and gym, the famous oak-panelled *No. 10 Bar* (see box opposite), *Palm Court* restaurant and parking. A short tram ride away from the Tower and the rest of the sights. Special online room-only deals. ❻

Number One 1 St Lukes Rd ℡ 01253/343901, Ⓦ www.numberoneblackpool.com. A lavish boutique experience hosted by the ultra-amiable Mark and Claire. Set in a detached townhouse, the three extravagantly appointed rooms have dark-wood furnishings, crisp Egyptian linen, and large baths facing discreet TVs. ❺

Number One South Beach 4 Harrowside West ℡ 01253/343900, Ⓦ www.numberonesouthbeach .co.uk. *Number One*'s larger sister hotel, just off the seafront, with individually designed rooms that reflect the new Blackpool – bold colours, contemporary style, and low carbon footprint – and a good restaurant attached. ❻

Raffles 73–77 Hornby Rd ℡ 01253/294713, Ⓦ www.raffleshotelblackpool.co.uk. Nice place back from Central Pier and away from the bustle, with well-kept rooms, bar, and traditional tearooms attached. Some parking available. Good winter rates. ❸

Ruskin Albert Rd ℡ 01253/624063, Ⓦ www.ruskin hotel.com. At the prom end of Albert Rd, the *Ruskin* exudes repro-Victorian style and offers smart rooms with decent bathrooms, though it's slightly aged. Bar and brasserie, and parking available. ❸

The Town

With seven miles of sandy beach and accompanying (smartly revamped) promenade, you'll want to jump on and off the electric trams if you plan to get up and down much between the piers. Most of the shops and bars are along the waterfront, though the recently gentrified centre is worth a stroll.

The Pleasure Beach and Sandcastle Waterpark

The major event in town is **Blackpool Pleasure Beach** on the South Promenade (March–Oct daily from 11am though times vary; Ⓦ www.blackpoolpleasurebeach

There's an alternative Blackpool behind the resort's facade – one of history, heritage and even culture. There's evidence of Victorian and Edwardian Blackpool in the **Mitre** pub on West Street, "Blackpool's smallest pub," where for the price of a pint you can examine the collected black-and-white yesteryear photos. Down the prom and up Victoria Street leads directly to the **Winter Gardens** (Coronation St), which opened in 1878. The Gardens house a motley set of cafés, bars and amusements, but don't miss seeing the extraordinary Spanish Hall Suite and the **Opera House** honours board, where you'll find Charlie Chaplin, George Formby and Vera Lynn. The splendid **Grand Theatre** around the corner (Church St) is also worth a look, and has an ornate café and bar of its own.

From in front of the Opera House, follow Abingdon Street to Queen Street and the porticoed Central Library, next to which the **Grundy Art Gallery** (Mon–Sat 10am–5pm; free) might tempt you in to see its Victorian oils and watercolours, contemporary art and special exhibitions. Walking down Queen Street to the promenade you reach **North Pier**, the first pier to be opened (1863) on the Blackpool seafront and now a listed building. At this point, let chance and the trams dictate the tour – Blackpool had the world's first permanent electric street **tramway** (1885). Head northbound and you can get off at the **Imperial Hotel** (North Promenade), whose wood-panelled *No. 10 Bar* is covered with photographs and mementoes of every British prime minister since Lloyd George.

.com), just south of South Pier. Entrance to the amusement park is free, but you'll have to fork out for the superb array of "white knuckle" rides including the "Big One", one of Europe's tallest roller coasters. After these, the wonderful array of antique wooden roller coasters seems like kids' stuff, but each is unique. The original "Big Dipper" was invented at Blackpool in 1923 and still thrills, as does the "Grand National" (1935), whose 3300-foot twin track races you against a parallel car. Recuperate in the park's champagne and oyster bar, which adds a bit of class to the otherwise relentless barrage of fairground noise, shrieking, music and fast food. There are charges for individual rides but best value is to buy an unlimited-ride wristband (£15–28 depending on the season, cheaper if booked online).

After the Pleasure Beach, you might also consider the **Sandcastle Waterpark** (Ⓦ www.sandcastle-waterpark.co.uk), Britain's largest indoor water park, close to the South Pier opposite the Pleasure Beach, which has eighteen waterslides, including one that loops outside the main building.

The seafront and the tower

Pleasure Beach and Sandcastle aside, most of the big-ticket attractions are found near the **Central Pier**, with its 108-foot-high revolving Big Wheel. You'll need a bulging wallet if you plan to do the lot, from the **Sea-Life Centre** (Ⓦ www.sealife.co.uk) to **Louis Tussauds Waxworks** (Ⓦ www.louistussaudswaxworks.co.uk).

Blackpool's elegant cast-iron **piers** strike a more traditional note. They're covered with arcades and amusements, while much of what passes for evening family entertainment – TV comics and variety shows – takes place in the various pier theatres (see above). Between Central and North piers stands the 518-foot **Blackpool Tower** (daily: June–Oct 10am–11pm; Nov–May 10am–6pm; £15.95, £9.95 after 7pm; Ⓦ www.theblackpooltower.co.uk). Paying the hefty entrance fee is the only way to ride up to the top for the stunning view and an unnerving walk on the see-through glass floor. The all-day ticket covers all the other tower attractions, including the gilt Edwardian ballroom, with its Wurlitzer-organ tea dances and big-band evenings, plus aquarium, children's entertainers, cafés, amusements, and a kids' indoor adventure playground. There's also a Moorish-inspired **circus** (2hr shows included in the entry ticket; two daily performances) between the tower's legs. Coming out of the tower, it's worth taking an evening wander down Birley Street to see **Brilliance**, six giant steel arches housing disco lasers and a sound system which, come sundown, make the pedestrianized street feel like a rave club.

Eating

Eating out revolves around the typical British seaside fare of **fish and chips**, available all over town – the best centrally is *Yorkshire Fisheries* at 14–16 Topping St behind the Winter Gardens, where you can sit down or take away. Given the sheer volume of customers, other restaurants don't have to try too hard – you'll have no trouble finding cheap roasts, pizzas, Chinese or Indian food – and though sophistication is harder to come by, there are a few hidden gems. For a quieter night out, head the few miles south to genteel **St Annes** (a taxi's best), where Wood Street has a line of agreeable bars and restaurants.

AJ's 65 Topping St ☎01253/626111. A festival of meat, this unpretentious restaurant is at its best with steaks and grills, though makes some concessions to vegetarians. Non-steak mains around £10.

Blues Brasserie Ocean Boulevard, Blackpool Pleasure Beach ☎0845/367 3333. Looking out onto the roller coasters of the Pleasure Beach, with a good choice of light bites and main meals, as well as a Sunday carvery. Reasonable prices, with mains under a tenner.

Kwizeen 49 King St ☎01253/290045. This friendly, contemporary bistro is the best restaurant in town, with a seasonally changing menu that places a real emphasis on locally sourced produce, from Blackpool tomatoes and Lancashire cheese to Fylde farm ostriches. Mains around £13, though there's a bargain two-course weekday lunch. Closed Sat lunch & Sun, 2 weeks Feb & 1 week Aug.

The Lounge 10a Cedar Square ☎01253/291112. Typical of Blackpool's recent embrace of cosmopolitan café culture, where you can enjoy a posh sandwich and espresso from a moulded plastic chair, looking out over Cedar Square and St John's church. Also serves a selection of light lunches. Closed weekday eve, except Fri.

Drinking, nightlife and entertainment

In all the **pubs and clubs**, young men can expect to have their attire and demeanour given the once-over by the hired hulks at the door, while "girls" and "ladies" can expect free drinks and entry and a lot of largely good-natured amorous jousting. There's a plethora of theme bars and any number of places for karaoke or **dancing** – local opinion favours *The Syndicate*, 120–140 Church St (ⓦwww.thesyndicate.com), the UK's biggest club, which features star DJs throughout the year. *Funny Girls*, a transvestite-run bar at 5 Dickson Rd, off Talbot Road (☎0870/350 2665, ⓦwww.funnygirlsshowbar.co.uk), has nightly shows that attract long (gay and straight) queues. Otherwise, entertainment is based heavily on family shows, musicals, veteran TV comedians, ice shows, tribute bands, crooners and stage spectaculars at a variety of end-of-pier and Pleasure Beach theatres (see p.631), or at historic venues such as the **Grand Theatre** (☎01253/290190, ⓦwww.blackpoolgrand.co.uk) and the **Opera House** (☎0870/380111, ⓦwww.blackpoollive.com), both on Church Street.

Preston and the Ribble Valley

With the siren draws of the Lakes, the Peak District and the Yorkshire Dales so close, the rest of Lancashire often gets bypassed in the rush to the surrounding national parks, and more's the pity. It's true, the old cotton towns of north and east Lancashire might not be first on everyone's must-see list, but **Preston**, 25 miles northwest of Manchester, is one of England's oldest towns, containing a fine museum and some appealing Georgian and Victorian remnants. North of the town is rural Lancashire, at its most bucolic in the ancient villages of the **Ribble Valley** – which inspired such literary giants as Arthur Conan Doyle and J.R.R. Tolkien – and particularly in the **Forest of Bowland**, to which the gateway is the small market town of **Clitheroe**.

Preston

Strategically placed on the banks of the River Ribble, **PRESTON** was already an important market town in Anglo-Saxon times and received its royal charter in 1179. Charles Dickens gathered material here for *Hard Times*, his coruscating attack on the factory system, and some handsome Victorian public buildings survive from the era when it was an industrial boomtown, most notably the majestic Greek Revivalist **Harris Museum and Art Gallery** (Mon–Sat 10am–5pm; free; Ⓦwww.harris museum.org.uk) in the central Market Square. Centred around a three-storey atrium focused on a Foucault's pendulum, the main collections cover fine and decorative art, as well as a renowned collection of photographs that includes many of Roger Fenton's wartime prints of the Crimea. More child-friendly is "The Story of Preston", which presses home the city's role in starting the Industrial Revolution.

On either side of the Harris lies the modern shopping area, converging on Fishergate, the main street through town. Cross Fishergate to explore the handsome Georgian development of **Winckley Square**, once home to the town's richest cotton magnates. Beyond the square, the ground drops away to the River Ribble and **Avenham Park**, one of the country's best examples of a landscaped Victorian park.

The **train station** has regular services to Lancaster, Manchester and Blackpool: a bus connects the train station to the town centre and huge **bus station**; otherwise, follow Fishergate into the centre, a ten-minute walk. The **tourist office** is in the Guild Hall, on Lancaster Road (Mon–Sat 10am–5.30pm; ℡01772/253731, Ⓦwww.visitpreston.com), just round the corner from the Harris Museum. For food, there's Paul Heathcoate's *Olive Press* in Winckley Square.

The Ribble Valley

When the nineteenth-century Lancashire cotton weavers enjoyed a rare break from their industry they took to the bucolic retreats of the **Ribble Valley**, north of Preston, which parades a stream of small market towns and isolated villages set among verdant fields and rolling hills. Much of the northwestern part of the region is occupied by thinly populated grouse moorland known as the **Forest of Bowland**. **Public transport** is limited to the train service from Manchester and Blackburn, or buses from Preston, to the market town of **Clitheroe** on the forest's southern fringes; from here, buses run out to Dunsop Bridge and **Slaidburn** (with connections on to Settle in Yorkshire). Just south, hikers can follow the course of the river from its source to the estuary along the seventy-mile **Ribble Way**, which passes through Clitheroe.

Clitheroe and around

A tidy little market town on the banks of the River Ribble, **CLITHEROE** is best seen from the terrace of its empty **Norman keep** which towers above the Ribble Valley floor. From here, the small centre is laid out before you and you can spend an hour or two sampling its old pubs and browsing around some of Lancashire's best independent food and drink shops; a real delight is the family-owned **D. Byrne and Co. Wine Merchants**, 12 King St, experts on the finer points of the grape since the 1870s. There's been a **market** in town since the thirteenth century, the current affair held off King Street every Tuesday, Thursday and Saturday.

One obvious target hereabouts is **Pendle Hill**, a couple of miles to the east, where the ten **Pendle Witches** allegedly held the diabolic rites that led to their hanging in

1612. The evidence against them came mainly from one small child, but a considerable mythology has grown up around the witches, whose memory is perpetuated by a hilltop gathering each Halloween. The Clitheroe tourist office (℡01200/425566) can provide a self-drive leaflet guiding you around the locality. The best approach is from the charming village of **Downham** on the west of the hill, seemingly untouched by modernity, with its wonderful local pub, the *Assheton Arms*. With a car, you could also run out to the Roman museum at **Ribchester** (southwest) and the ruined Cistercian abbey at **Whalley**, a few miles south of Clitheroe, in which case you could stop for a meal at the 🍴 *Three Fishes* (℡01254/826888), a gastropub focusing on high-quality local produce, in rolling countryside just outside Whalley on the Mitton road.

It was at the ancient spire-donned school of **Stonyhurst**, just three miles southwest of Clitheroe along the road to Hurst Green, that former pupil Arthur Conan Doyle found inspiration for *The Hound of the Baskervilles* and J.R.R. Tolkien wrote part of his *The Lord of the Rings*. The college opens its doors in August to reveal treasures including the desk into which the young Conan Doyle carved his name and a fifteenth-century illuminated manuscript known as the *Book of Hours* (tours: Aug only daily except Fri 1–4.30pm; ℡01254/826345; £6 for school and gardens).

The Forest of Bowland

Heading northwest from Clitheroe on the B6478 brings you to the **Forest of Bowland** (Ⓦwww.forestofbowland.com), designated an Area of Outstanding Natural Beauty, although the name "forest" is used here in its traditional sense of "a royal hunting ground". It's an area of remote fells and farmland and a preserve of rare birds like the hen harrier, ring ouzel and merlin. The website has details of guided walks and events in the area, from dawn-chorus safaris to night-time bat watches. At the duck-riddled riverside hamlet of **Dunsop Bridge**, an old drover's track (now a very minor road) known as the **Trough of Bowland** begins its fifteen-mile slog across the tops to Lancaster, winding through heather- and bracken-clad hills. Those in the know make their way the couple of miles south to the 🍴 *Inn at Whitewell* (℡01200/448222, Ⓦwww.innatwhitewell.com; ❺–❻), which combines cosy, traditionally furnished rooms with fabulous food in both its restaurant (dinner only, reservations essential) and its welcoming bar. Work up an appetite at the **Bowland Wild Boar Park** (daily: March–Oct 10.30am–5pm; Nov–Feb 11am–4pm; £4.50; Ⓦwww.wildboarpark.co.uk), signposted down the Chipping road from Dunsop Bridge, where wild boar roam free in the woodland by the River Hodder.

Northeast of Dunsop Bridge it's a couple of miles to **SLAIDBURN**, where old stone cottages set the tone. The village buildings are largely untouched by modern intrusion – a single family has owned much of the village for 200 years. There's an even older **inn**, the *Hark to Bounty* (℡01200/446246, Ⓦwww.harktobounty.co.uk; ❸), with reasonable rooms and good bar food, as well as a popular **youth hostel** (℡0870/770 6034, Ⓔslaidburn@yha.org.uk; from £16) with beamed ceilings and an open fire.

Lancaster and around

LANCASTER, Lancashire's county town, dates back at least to the Roman occupation, though only scant remains survive from that period. A Saxon church was later built within the ruined Roman walls as the town became a strategic trading centre, and by medieval times a castle had been constructed on the heights above the river. Lancaster became an important port on the slave-trade triangle, and it's the legacy of predominantly Georgian buildings from that time that gives the town its character, particularly in the leafy areas around the castle. It's no surprise that many people choose to spend a night here on the way to the Lakes or Dales to the north. It's also an easy side-trip the few miles west to the resort of **Morecambe** and to neighbouring **Heysham village**, with its ancient churches.

Arrival, information and accommodation

From either the **train station** on Meeting House Lane, or the **bus station** on Cable Street, it's a five-minute walk to the **tourist office** at 29 Castle Hill (Mon–Sat 9.30/10am–4/5pm; ℡01524/32878, ⓦwww.citycoastcountryside.co.uk). Annual **events** include the spectacular Bonfire Night celebrations (Sat nearest Nov 5). For **canal cruises**, including the scheduled waterbus service to Carnforth, contact Lancaster Canal Packet Boats (℡01524/389410, ⓦwww.budgietransport.co.uk).

Accommodation

Royal King's Arms 75 Market St ℡01524/32451, ⓦwww.oxfordhotelsandinns.com. Though slightly faded from glory, the *Royal King's Arms* still provides prettily furnished rooms with smart bathrooms, plus a bar and brasserie. Ask for a castle view. ❹

Shakespeare 96 St Leonard's Gate ℡01524/841041. Hard-working hosts maintain seven cosy en-suite rooms (including two singles)

in this popular townhouse B&B on a central street. Close to several long-stay car parks. No credit cards. ❸

Sun 63 Church St ℡01524/66006, ⓦwww.thesunhotelandbar.co.uk. In a 300-year-old building, the city centre's only four-star hotel has 16 handsome rooms – great value for money and conveniently located, with pay parking nearby. Breakfast and meals available in the bar, one of the best in the city centre. ❸

The City

The site of **Lancaster Castle** (daily: tours every 30min 10.30am–4pm; £5; ⓦwww.lancastercastle.com) has been the city's focal point since Roman times. The Normans built the first castle here in around 1093 in an attempt to protect the region from marauding Scots armies, and it was added to throughout medieval times, becoming a crown court and prison in the thirteenth century, a role it still fulfils today. Currently, about a quarter of the battlemented building can be visited on an entertaining hour-long tour, though court sittings sometimes affect the schedules. The tour begins around the back in the grandiose eighteenth-century Shire Hall, and then moves on to the thirteenth-century Adrian's Tower, with its eight-foot-thick walls encircling a room hung with manacles and leg-irons.

A two-minute walk down the steps between the castle and the neighbouring Priory Church of St Mary brings you to the seventeenth-century **Judges' Lodgings** (Easter–June & Oct Mon–Fri 1–4pm, Sat & Sun noon–4pm; July–Sept Mon–Fri 10am–4pm, Sat & Sun noon–4pm; £3), once used by visiting magistrates. The top floor is given over to a **Museum of Childhood**, with memory-jogging displays of toys and games, and a period (1900) schoolroom.

Down on the banks of the River Lune – which lent Lancaster its name – one of the eighteenth-century quayside warehouses is taken up by part of the **Maritime Museum** (daily 11am/12.30pm–4/5pm; £3). The museum's ample coverage of life on the sea and inland waterways of Lancashire is complemented by the **City Museum** on Market Square back in town (Mon–Sat 10am–5pm; free), which explores the city's history from Neolithic to Georgian times. The grandiose **Town Hall** faces Dalton Square at the top of town, whose **Queen Victoria Memorial** bears a sculpted frieze that's a roll-call of the Victorian great and good – including Lancaster's own Richard Owen, natural scientist and coiner of the word "dinosaur".

For a panorama of the town, Morecambe Bay and the Cumbrian fells, take a bus from the bus station (or a steep 25-minute walk up Moor Lane) to **Williamson**

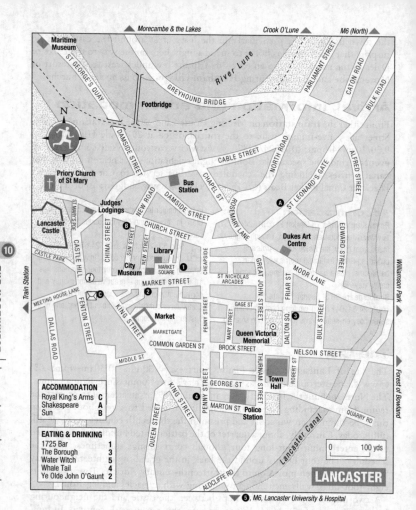

Park (daily 10am–4/5pm; free; ⓦwww.williamsonpark.com), Lancaster's highest point. Funded by local statesman and lino magnate Lord Ashton, the park's centrepiece is the 220-foot-high **Ashton Memorial**, a Baroque folly raised by his son in memory of his second wife.

Eating, drinking and entertainment

The main cultural destination is **The Dukes** on Moor Lane (☎0845/344 0642, ⓦwww.dukes-lancaster.org), the city's principal arts centre, with cinema and theatre; there are also open-air performances in Williamson Park in summer.

Cafés and restaurants

1725 Bar 28 Market St. A tasteful modern conversion joining two of Lancaster's ancient buildings, which serves good-value tapas – meals shouldn't cost more than £15 all in.

The Borough 3 Dalton Square ☎01524/64170. Great for informal dining, this roomy gastropub – in a refurbished 1824 building – has a rigorously sourced local menu, including a fun, two-course "School dinners" list (Mon–Sat till 6.30pm only).

Lancaster promotes itself as a **cycling centre**, and miles of canal towpaths, old railway tracks and riverside paths provide excellent traffic-free routes around the Lune estuary, Lancaster Canal and Ribble Valley. Typical is the easy riverside path to the **Crook O'Lune** beauty spot, where you can reward yourself with a bacon buttie at *Woodies'* famous snack bar. Other good routes are down the **Lune estuary** or along the canal to **Carnforth**, all detailed on a useful free map available at the tourist office or online from Ⓦwww.citycoastcountryside.co.uk.

Otherwise mains, ranging from steak and Thwaites ale pie to "posh" fish and chips cost £12–16. Good choice of beers, with a discount for CAMRA members.
Whale Tail 78a Penny St ⓉⓉ01524/845133. Tucked up a yard on the first floor, this cheery veggie and wholefood café serves good breakfasts, quiche, moussaka, baked potatoes and so on. Garden seating outside on sunny days. Lunch only, closes 5pm.

Pubs

Water Witch Canal towpath. Relaxing canal-side pub named after an old canal packet-boat. A youthful crowd munches burgers, shoots pool and hogs the canal-side tables, but there is an impressive range of real ales and continental lagers.
Ye Olde John O'Gaunt 53 Market St. Terrific city-centre local just up from the Market Square, that's serious about its drinks. Expect a diverse crowd, from old boys to students and aspiring musicians.

Morecambe

MORECAMBE – the seaside town five miles west of Lancaster – rapidly expanded from a small fishing village into a full-blown resort in the nineteenth century with the arrival of the railway. Following a decline of many years, recent times have seen a fair amount of regeneration; the sweep of the bay remains the major attraction, however, with the Lakeland fells visible beyond and the local sunsets a renowned phenomenon. The **Stone Jetty** features bird sculptures, games and motifs – recognizing Morecambe Bay as Britain's most important wintering site for wildfowl and wading birds. A little way along the prom stands the statue of one of Britain's most treasured comedians – Eric Bartholomew, who took the stage name **Eric Morecambe**.

There's a cycle path from Lancaster to Morecambe, while regular buses and trains also make the ten-minute trip. The **tourist office** is just back from the Stone Jetty, in the Old Station Buildings on the Central Promenade (Mon–Sat 9.30am–4/5pm, Sun 10am–4pm; Ⓣ01524/582808, Ⓦwww.citycoastcountryside.co.uk), and can provide information about seasonal **guided walks** taking in the town's Art Deco heritage. The Art Deco *Midland Hotel* (Ⓣ08458/501240, Ⓦwww.elh.co.uk/hotels /midland) has recently reopened for business after a stylish and careful restoration. Rooms are comfortable, extending the modernist theme of the hotel (❻; sea view ❼), but even if you're not staying it's worth popping into the electric-blue bar, and taking a drink onto the terrace to watch the sunset. The **Platform** arts centre (Ⓣ01524/582803, Ⓦwww.lancaster.gov.uk/platformanddome) shares the same building as the tourist office.

Heysham

The main historic interest on the Lancashire side of Morecambe Bay is at **HEYSHAM**, three miles southwest of Morecambe – you can walk here along the promenade from the resort. It's the shoreside **Heysham Village** that's worth seeing, centred on a group of charming seventeenth-century cottages and barns. The proudest relic is the well-preserved Viking hog's-back tombstone in Saxon **St Peter's Church**, set in a romantic churchyard below the headland. Just up the lane, on the headland itself, the even earlier ruins of **St Patrick's Chapel** occupy a superb vantage-point over the bay and to the Lakeland hills beyond. Once you've seen these, all that remains is to step back into a village tearoom for a glass of nettle beer, a local speciality dating from the Victorian era.

The Isle of Man

Almost equidistant between Ireland, England, Wales and Scotland, the **Isle of Man** is one of the most beautiful spots in Britain – a mountainous, cliff-fringed island just thirty-three miles by thirteen, into which are shoehorned wooded glens, sandy beaches and scores of standing stones and Celtic crosses. It takes some effort to reach and the weather is hardly reliable – factors that mean that the Isle of Man has been spared the worst excesses of the British tourist trade. There's peace and quiet in abundance, walks around the unspoilt hundred-mile coastline, rural villages and steam trains, and with an increasing array of outdoor thrills, the Isle makes a great weekend away from it all.

The capital, **Douglas**, is atypical of an island that prides itself on its Celtic and Norse heritage, and it's the vestiges of the distant past – the castles at the former capital **Castletown** and the west-coast port of **Peel** – that make the most obvious destinations. Elsewhere, **Port Erin** has one of the island's best beaches, while to the north **Laxey** is an attractive proposition for its huge waterwheel and the meandering train ride to the barren summit of **Snaefell**, the island's highest peak. From Snaefell's summit you get an idea of the range of the Manx scenery, the finest parts of which are to be found in the seventeen officially designated **National Glens**, most of them linked by the 100-mile **Raad Ny Foillan** (Road of the Gull) coastal footpath, which passes several of the island's numerous hillforts, Viking ship burials and Celtic crosses. The island's wildlife, meanwhile, is best seen on a boat trip to the **Calf of Man**, an islet off the southwest coast with hundreds of breeding birds and seals.

The Isle of Man's main tourist draw, however, is the **TT (Tourist Trophy) motorcycle races** (held in the two weeks around the late-May bank holiday), a frenzy of speed and burning rubber that's shattered the island's peace annually since 1907. Thousands of bikers swamp the place to watch a nonstop parade of maniacs hurtling round the roads on a 37-mile circuit at speeds averaging 126mph. This is only the most famous of a summer-long list of **rallies and races** on the island's roads, and if you want to stay at these times, you must book accommodation well in advance.

Some history

St Patrick is said to have come to the island in the fifth century AD, bringing Christianity, though it was the arrival of the **Vikings**, who established garrisons here in the eleventh century, which changed the face of the Isle of Man. They reigned as **Kings of Mann** – the name derived from that of the island's ancient sea-god, Manannan Mac Lir (Son of the Sea). The Scots wrested power from the Norsemen in 1275, the beginning of an unsuccessful 130-year struggle with the English for control of the island. During the English **Civil War**, James Stanley, seventh Earl of Derby and Lord of Man, raised an army to support Charles II, but in his absence a local militia offered the island to Cromwell. It was a shortlived insurrection: with the restoration of the monarchy, the leaders of the militia were executed and the island returned to Crown control.

The **distinct identity** of the island remained intact, however, and many true Manx inhabitants, who comprise a shade under fifty percent of its 80,000 population, are quick to remind visitors that the Isle of Man is not part of the UK. Indeed, although a Crown dependency, the island has its own government, **Tynwald**, arguably the

Getting there

The **ferries** and the quicker **fastcraft** (Seacats) from England to Douglas are both run by the Isle of Man Steam Packet Company (℡0872/299 2992, Ⓦwww.steam-packet .com), from either Heysham or Liverpool. Heysham (ferry 3hr 30min) has the most frequent service, with two or three sailings a day throughout the year. Liverpool manages one or two fastcraft services a day (2hr 30min), down to one daily at weekends in December. **Fares** start at £18.50 one-way for foot passengers, £206 return for drivers.

Low-budget **flights** are the increasingly popular alternative method to access the island, leaving from numerous British and Irish regional airports, with regular prices starting from £45 one-way. Services are with Aer Arran (Dublin and London; Ⓦwww .aerarann.com); easyJet (Liverpool); Flybe (Birmingham, Bristol, Edinburgh, Glasgow, London Gatwick, Manchester, Liverpool); and Manx2 (Blackpool, Belfast, Leeds Bradford, East Midlands, Newcastle and Gloucester; Ⓦwww.manx2.com).

Getting around

With a car you could see almost everything in a couple of days, but don't miss a trip on one of the two century-old rail services which still provide the best public transport (Ⓦwww.iombusandrail.info) to all the major towns and sights except for Peel. The carriages of the **Steam Railway** (April–Oct regular daily services from Douglas 10.20am–4.20pm; £9.90 return to Port Erin) rock their fifteen-mile course from Douglas to Castletown, Port St Mary and Port Erin at a spirited pace. Resembling a tramway more than a train, the **Manx Electric Railway** (April–Sept daily 9.40am–4.40pm; some later departures in summer; £8.80 return to Ramsey) runs for seventeen miles from Douglas's Derby Castle Station to Ramsey via Laxey. **Buses** are often quicker – routes are given in the text where appropriate. There's also the **Snaefell Mountain Railway** from Laxey to the top of the island's highest mountain, Snaefell (see p.643).

The "**Island Explorer**" ticket gives one (£14), three (£28) or seven (£42) days' unlimited travel on all public transport on the island.

10

THE NORTHWEST | The Isle of Man

world's oldest democratic parliament, which has run continuously since 979 AD. The island has its own sterling currency, its own laws, an independent postal service, and a Gaelic-based language which is taught in schools and seen on dual-language road signs. It's also famous for its four-horned sheep and, of course, its own tailless version of the domestic cat, as well as famously good kippers and queenies (scallops).

Douglas

Dubbed "the Naples of the North" by John Betjeman, **DOUGLAS** has developed since the 1950s heyday of seaside holidaymaking into a major offshore financial centre, but still remains home to the majority of the island's hotels and restaurants. Douglas displays many similarities to Blackpool, just across the water: candy-coloured five-storey terraces back the two-mile-long curve of the promenade and its tram tracks, and the town even makes an attempt to emulate the Illuminations. There's an excellent museum and truly dramatic bay views from the promenade, but you'll need to explore further afield to really see the best of Man.

Arrival, orientation and information

All flights arrive at **Ronaldsway Airport** (℡01624/821600, Ⓦwww.iom-airport .com) at Ballasalla, ten miles south of Douglas, close to Castletown. Buses (every 30min–1hr 6.45am–11.15pm) connect the airport with Douglas as well as Castletown/Port St Mary, while a taxi to Douglas costs around £23. Ferries and Seacats dock by the **Sea Terminal** at the southern end of the Douglas waterfront. Fifty yards beyond the forecourt taxi rank, the Lord Street **bus terminal** is the hub of the island's buses.

North Quay runs three hundred yards west from the bus terminal alongside the fishing port to the Victorian red-brick Douglas Station, the northern terminus of the **Steam Railway** to Port Erin. The waterfront (progressively Loch, Central and Queen's promenades) runs two miles north to Derby Castle Station for the **Electric Railway** to Laxey and Ramsey – take the horse-drawn tram along the promenade or bus #24, #24a, #26 or #26a from North Quay. Bikes can be rented from Eurocycles, 8a Victoria Rd, off Broadway (☎01624/624909; closed Sun).

The **Welcome Centre** in the Sea Terminal building (Mon–Sat 8am–6pm, Sun 10am–2pm; ☎01624/686766 or 662525) has island-wide transport information and sells Island Explorer **travel tickets**. There's a smaller office at the airport, open to meet flight arrivals. The main **websites** for information are Ⓦwww.gov.im and www.visitisleofman.com. The twelve heritage sites and museums are run under the umbrella of Manx National Heritage (Ⓦwww.gov.im/mnh); NT and EH members get in free.

ISLE OF MAN

Accommodation

B&Bs are packed in along Douglas's seafront and up the roads immediately off Harris Promenade, particularly along Broadway, Castle Mona Avenue, Empress Drive and Empire Terrace. Prices start from under £40 for a double and a sea-view room can be had for £50. Note that many places demand a two-night minimum stay in the summer. Given the high numbers doing business here, there is also a set of luxury chains and boutique-style **hotels** in renovated seafront buildings with significantly higher prices.

Admiral House Loch Promenade ☏01624/629551, ⓦwww.admiralhouse.com. Decent mid-range option at the ferry terminal end of the prom, with large rooms; rates rise for a sea view. The town's most expensive restaurant, *Ciapelli's* (closed Sun), is on the ground floor. ❸

Birchfield House York Rd ☏01624/673000, ⓦwww.birchfieldhouse.com. This five-star boutique hotel with only three rooms is the finest Douglas has to offer. Spacious rooms are loaded with antiques and all creature comforts, and it's run by the island's celeb-chef Kevin Woodford, who is keen to make up personalized menus (from £35) and is in permanent residence there. ❻

Dreem Ard Ballanard Rd, 2 miles west of the centre ☏01624/621491. Tranquil, out-of-town B&B with three en-suite rooms, including a family room and large garden suite with its own dressing room and sitting area. No credit cards. ❷

Mereside 1 Empire Terrace, just off the Central Promenade ☏01624/676355, ⓦwww.hqbar.im.

Small, family-owned guesthouse with elegant modern fittings and very well maintained modern rooms. A good bar/restaurant downstairs and breakfast is included. Disabled access. ❸

Sefton Harris Promenade ☏01624/645500, ⓦwww.seftonhotel.co.im. Next to the Gaiety Theatre, this four-star has comfortable rooms offering a sea view or a balcony over the impressive internal water garden. Facilities include pool, gym, internet access, free bikes, bar and restaurant. Book online and you save yourself a tenner. ❺

Welbeck Mona Drive, off Central Promenade ☏01624/675663, ⓦwww.welbeckhotel.com. Mid-sized family-run hotel 100 yards up the hill off the seafront. Accommodation is warmly decorated with modern furniture, and there are six self-catering apartments, and a delightful breakfast-conservatory. ❸, deluxe rooms/apartments ❹

The Town

Douglas's seafront vista has changed little since Victorian times, and is still trodden by heavy-footed carthorses pulling **trams** (May–Sept from 9am; £2 return). On Harris Promenade the opulent **Gaiety Theatre** sports a lush interior that can be seen on ninety-minute-long tours each Saturday at 10.30am (April–Sept only; £6.50). Further up Harris Promenade, approaching Broadway, the spruced-up **Villa Marina** gardens display more Victorian elegance, with their colonnade walk, lawns and bandstand. There's a monthly **farmers' market** here on the first Saturday of the month. Look seaward and you'll see the sandcastle-like **Tower of Refuge** on Conister Rock, built in 1832; for many years it was stocked with fresh water and bread as a safe haven for those thrown overboard.

In the streets nearer the harbour, an attempt has been made to preserve Douglas's "historic quayside". There's not much to it, save a few old pubs, and you might as well head up Victoria Street, past the Manx Legislative Building, to the **Manx Museum**, on the corner of Kingswood Grove and Crellin's Hill (Mon–Sat 10am–5pm; free). The museum makes a good start for anyone wanting to get to grips with Manx culture and heritage, kicking off with the National Art Gallery of Manx painters before revealing Neolithic standing stones, Celtic grave markers and some excellent displays on Viking burials and runic crosses. More recent history is covered with a collection of artefacts made by World War I internees and displays about the TT races, not forgetting the island's natural history and environment.

Out on Douglas Head – the point looming above the southern bay – the town's Victorian **camera obscura** has been restored for visits (Easter week, plus

May–Sept Sat 1–4pm, Sun and bank hols 11am–4pm, weather permitting; £2; ☎01624/686766).

Eating, drinking and entertainment

Douglas has the best choice of **cafés and restaurants** on the island, with plenty of inexpensive places to grab a bite to eat as well as some more sophisticated dining options; note that all the cafés below are open till 5pm and closed on Sunday. Manx-brewed beer is on sale at most **pubs** and brews such as Old Bushy Tail soon revive flagging spirits. The **Villa Marina and Gaiety Theatre** complex (☎01624/694555) is the hub of most entertainment, from orchestral concerts to rock gigs, tea dances to theatrical productions.

Cafés

The Bay Room Manx Museum, Kingswood Grove. Enclosed by the Manx national sculpture collection with wonderful views across the bay, this café serves a selection of soups, sandwiches and pastries.

Greens Douglas Station, North Quay. Plant-filled vegetarian café in the station, serving hot lunches, including a veggie buffet (noon–2.30pm), plus drinks and snacks.

Spill the Beans 1 Market Hill. Douglas's best coffee house, with a choice of brews plus muffins, croissants, cakes and pastries.

Restaurants

Café Tanroagan 9 Ridgeway St ☎07624/472411. The best fish and seafood on the island in a relaxed, contemporary restaurant. Visiting film crews and actors all make a beeline here, for fish straight off the boat. Dinner reservations essential. Mains around £17. Closed Sun.

L'Experience Queen's Promenade ☎01624/623103. Housed in an innocuous whitewashed shack, this long-standing French bistro offers good meat dishes and freshly caught fish (mains average £15). Great lunchtime specials. Closed Sun.

Paparazzi 26 Loch Promenade ☎01624/673222. Large, popular pizzeria-trattoria serving a few more unusual specialities alongside the traditional pizzas, pastas and Italian dishes. Mains around £8.

Pubs and bars

Bar George Hill St. A fashionable haunt housed in a converted Sunday school, opposite St George's church. Closed Sun.

Queen's Hotel Queen's Promenade. The best place for an alfresco drink is this old seafront pub at the top end of the promenade, where the picnic tables look out over the sweeping bay.

Rovers Return 11 Church St. Hidden down a pedestrianized street, this is one of the town's cosiest pubs, with an open fire and good local Manx beer on tap.

Laxey

Hidden in a narrow valley seven miles north of Douglas, the village of **LAXEY** spills down from its train station along a picturesque river to a small harbour and long, pebbly beach, squeezed between two bulky headlands. The Manx Electric Railway from Douglas drops you at the station used by the Snaefell Mountain Railway (see below). Passengers disembark and then head inland and uphill to Laxey's pride, the **"Lady Isabella" Great Laxey Wheel** (April–Oct daily 10am–5pm; £4), which with a diameter of over 72ft is said to be the largest working waterwheel in the world. Otherwise the village is at its best down around the harbour in **Old Laxey**, half a mile below the station, where you can pick up an ice cream from the beachside café and stroll down the shore.

Hourly **buses** #3 and #3A run to Laxey from Douglas. The *Mines Tavern*, by the station, serves **meals** (lunch and dinner), while down at the harbour, **drinking** is done at the *Shore Hotel*, a nice pub by the bridge.

Snaefell, Tholt-y-Will Glen and Sulby Glen

Every thirty minutes, the tramcars of the **Snaefell Mountain Railway** (April–Sept daily 10.15am–3.45pm; £8.40 return) begin their wind from Laxey through increasingly denuded moorland to the island's highest point, the top of **Snaefell** (2036ft) – the Vikings' "Snow Mountain" – from where you can see England, Wales, Scotland and Ireland on a clear day. The four and a half miles of track were built in seven months over the winter of 1895 by two hundred men. Most people are content to take the train back down again, but with a decent map and a clear day, you could walk down, following trails to Laxey (the easiest and most direct route), Sulby Glen or the Peel–Ramsey road.

The road route up, the A18 from Douglas or Ramsey, also makes for a great ride, forming as it does part of the TT course. Where the A18 and A14 (Snaefell–Sulby) meet, just below the summit, there's an isolated railway halt where drivers and hikers can pick up the mountain railway for a truncated ride to the summit and back. Three miles below the summit, down the A14, which sweeps past **Sulby Reservoir**, the road drops into **Tholt-y-Will Glen**, one of the island's more picturesque corners, with its gushing river and walks through the verdant plantations.

The A14 continues north to join the A3 Ramsey road, along a fine route through **Sulby Glen**, with bracken-clad hills flanking the road. At the junction, the *Sulby Glen Hotel* (℡01624/897240, ⓦwww.sulbyglenhotel.net; ➋), an established stop for biking enthusiasts, has Manx beer and food (except Sun and Mon nights).

Maughold, Ramsey and the north

Manx Electric Railway trains stop within a mile and a half of **MAUGHOLD**, seven miles northeast of Laxey, a tiny hamlet just inland from the cliff-side lighthouse at **Maughold Head**. It's an isolated spot which only adds to the attraction of Maughold's parish church, in whose grounds is maintained an outstanding collection of early Christian and Norse **carved crosses** – 44 pieces, dating from the sixth to the thirteenth century. Look inside the church, too, at the old parish cross, fourteenth-century in date and sporting the earliest known picture of the Three Legs of Man apart from that on the twelfth-century Sword of State. Bus #16 comes direct to Maughold from Ramsey (not Sun).

RAMSEY marks the northern terminus of the Electric Railway, 45 minutes beyond Laxey, though it's a dispiriting swatch of build-by-numbers modernity. The only real attraction is **The Grove Museum** (April–Sept daily 10am–5pm; £4), a mile north on the A9. Once the summer home of a Merseyside shipping magnate, it tells the story of three generations of the Gibb family, whose Victorian domestic paraphernalia is all still there. There's a lovely conservatory restaurant too.

You really need a car to see any more of the island beyond Ramsey. Due north at the end of the A16 is the **Point of Ayre** lighthouse, at the northeastern tip of the island, built in 1818. Its hinterland, the Ayres National Nature Reserve, is an important coastal habitat of lichen heath, dune grassland and marsh, where sightings of terns, oystercatchers, cormorants and ringed plovers are common.

St John's, Peel and around

The trans-island A1 (and hourly bus #5 or #6 from Douglas) follows a deep twelve-mile-long furrow between Douglas to Peel. Nine miles along, at the crossroad settlement of **ST JOHN'S**, you reach a small mound topped with a Manx flagpole. This mound marks the original site of **Tynwald**, the ancient Manx government – its name derives from the Norse *Thing Völlr*, meaning "Assembly Field". Nowadays the word refers to the Douglas-based House of Keys and Legislative Council, but acts passed in the capital only become law once they have been proclaimed here on July 5 (ancient Midsummer's Day) in an annual open-air parliament. Until the nineteenth century the local people arrived with their livestock and stayed a week or more to thrash out local issues, play sports, make marriages and hold a fair. Now Tynwald

Day begins with a service in the chapel, followed by a procession to the mound where the offices of state are carried out, after which a fair and concerts begin.

The main settlement on the west coast, **PEEL** immediately captivates, with its sandy beach running the length of its eastern promenade and imposing medieval castle set against the Irish Sea. Its enduring appeal is as one of the most "Manx" of all the island's towns, with an age-old Tuesday **market** in the marketplace above the harbour and a wood-smoke-belching kipper factory along the harbourside. Archeological evidence indicates that **St Patrick's Isle**, which guards the harbour, has had a significant population since Mesolithic times. What probably started out as a flint-working village gained significance with the foundation of a monastery in the seventh or eighth century, parts of which remain inside the ramparts of the red-sandstone **Peel Castle** (April–Oct daily 10am–5pm; £4), the residence of the Kings of Mann until 1220.

It's a fifteen-minute walk from the town around the river harbour and over the bridge to the castle. On the way, you'll have passed the excellent harbourside **House of Manannan heritage centre** (daily 10am–5pm; £6, combined ticket with Peel Castle £8.50), named after the island's ancient sea-god. You should allow at least two hours to get around the museum, which concentrates strongly on participatory exhibits – whether it's examining the contents and occupants of a life-sized Viking ship or walking through a kipper factory. If the seafront cafés and fish-and-chip shops don't appeal, head for the *Creek Inn*, opposite the House of Manannan, or the cheaper *Marine Hotel*.

Out of town, it's a five-mile drive south down the A27 to reach **Dalby**, from where you can take the minor road to **Niarbyl**, a headland framed by clear water and fronted by a flat pebbled beach, above which sits a picture-perfect thatched cottage.

Port Erin, Port St Mary and the Calf of Man

PORT ERIN, at the southwestern tip of the island, 75 minutes' ride from Douglas, unfurls around a wide, fine-sand beach backing a deeply indented bay beneath green hills, which climb northwest to the tower-topped headland of Bradda Head. An arm of holiday apartments stretches out towards the headland, while the far side of town is marked by the breakwater and small harbour. Families relish the beach, nearby coves and time-warped atmosphere, which appears to have altered little in fifty years. For a stretch of the legs, head up the promenade past the golf club to the entrance of **Bradda Glen**, where you can follow the path out along the headland.

The **train station** is on Station Road, a couple of hundred yards above and back from the beach. **Buses** #1 and #2 from Douglas/Castletown, and #8 from Peel/ St John's, stop on Bridson Street, across Station Road. For **accommodation**, the best B&B is *Rowany Cottier* (☎01624/832287; no credit cards; ❸), a detached house overlooking the bay, opposite the entrance to Bradda Glen. Come the evening, your choice is between the bistro at the *Bay Hotel* down by the beach or bar **meals** at the *Falcon's Nest*.

Sea-kayaking around the Isle of Man

The scenery of Man's western coast is some of the most spectacular on the isle, and a great way to explore it is on a **sea-kayaking** trip. **Adventurous Experiences** (☎01624/843034, ⓦ www.adventurousexperiences.com) run trips ranging from an evening paddle (£45) to full-day excursions (£85) and multi-day expeditions involving overnight camping. Particularly recommended are the afternoon trips (£45) covering the sea caves of Bradda Head and around the stunning Calf of Man with its huge seal colonies and multitude of birdlife. All equipment is provided.

Two miles east of Port Erin, the fishing harbour still dominates little **PORT ST MARY**, with its houses strung out in a chain above the busy dockside. The best beach is away to the northeast, reached from the harbour along a well-worked Victorian path that clings to the bay's rocky edge. Regular **steam trains** run to Port Erin or back to Douglas from Port St Mary, with the station a ten-minute walk from the harbour along High Street, Bay View Road and Station Road; hourly **buses** from the harbour serve the same places. Nicest **accommodation** is at ⚘ *Aaron House*, high up on The Promenade (℡01624/835702, ⓦwww.aaron house.co.uk; ❸), a lovingly re-created Victorian experience of brass beds and clawfoot baths, and home-made scones and jam in the parlour. The bay views from the front are superb. **Food** options include *Harbour Lights* restaurant on Queen Street (℡01624/832064; closed Mon–Wed all day & Sun eve) down by the harbour, and *Horizons* on Bay View Road (℡01624/834040; closed Tues & Sun eve), for a more cosmopolitan menu.

From Port St Mary, a minor road runs out along the Meayll peninsula towards **Cregneash**, the oldest village on the island, part of which now forms the **Cregneash Village Folk Museum** (April–Oct daily 10am–5pm; £4), a picturesque cluster of nineteenth-century thatched crofts. This was a real Gaelic-speaking village until well into the twentieth century, but is now peopled with spinners, weavers and smiths in period costumes; you can walk through the seasonal crops and watch horses at work. The local views are stunning – bar, perhaps, the bizarre UFO-looking RAF installation to the southeast – and it's only a short walk south to **The Chasms**, a headland of gaping rock cliffs swarming with gulls and razorbills.

The footpath continues around **Spanish Head**, the island's southern tip, to the turf-roofed **Sound Visitor Centre** (daily 10/11am–4/5pm; free), which also marks the end of the road from Port St Mary. There's an excellent café, with windows looking out across the treacherous waters of The Sound to the Calf of Man beyond.

Calf of Man

It really is worth making the effort to visit the **Calf of Man**, a craggy 600-acre heathland island off the southwest coast that is preserved as a bird sanctuary. Resident wardens monitor the seasonal populations of kittiwakes, puffins, razorbills, shags, guillemots and others, while grey seals can be seen all year round basking on the rocks. Paths run across the island, out to the bird observatory, the lighthouses and various derelict buildings – bring something to eat and drink, and pack warm clothes in case the weather changes.

Charter **boats** to the island operate from Port St Mary, but the most reliable scheduled service (weather permitting) is from the pier at Port Erin (Easter–Sept daily; £13; usually 3 daily starting at 10am; ℡01624/832339); always call in advance as landing numbers are limited.

Castletown and around

From the twelfth century until 1869, **CASTLETOWN** was the island's capital. Its sleepy harbour and low-roofed cottages are dominated by **Castle Rushen** (April–Oct daily 10am–5pm; £5.50), formerly home to the island's legislature and still the site of the investiture of new lieutenant-governors. The rooms – furnished in medieval and seventeenth-century styles – may seem unending, but it's worth pressing on to the rooftop viewpoint to admire the view.

Across the central Market Square and down Castle Street in tiny Parliament Square you'll find the **Old House of Keys**. Built in 1821 this was the site of the Manx parliament, the Keys, until 1874 when it was moved to Douglas. The frock-coated Secretary of the House meets you at the door and shows you into the restored debating chamber, where visitors are included in a highly entertaining participatory session of the House, guided by a hologram Speaker. Visits are conducted on the hour (April–Oct daily 10am–5pm; £4).

The **train station** is five minutes' walk from the centre of Castletown, out along Victoria Road from the harbour; **buses** #8 (from Peel/Port Erin) and #1 (from Douglas) stop in the main square. Best place for **food** is *The Garrison*, across from the hotel at 5 Castle St (℡01624/824885; closes Sun at 5pm), with jolly staff and good seafood tapas. Out of town, at **Santon**, about five miles northeast of Castletown, the *Mount Murray Hotel and Country Club* (℡01624/661111, ⓦwww.mountmurray.com; ⑥) is the highest-rated rural hotel on the island, with its own golf course, pool, health club, bar and restaurant.

Rushen Abbey

The island's most important medieval religious site, **Rushen Abbey** (April–Oct daily 10am–5pm; £4) lies two miles north of Castletown at **Ballasalla** ("place of the willows"). A Cistercian foundation of 1134, it was abandoned by its "White Monks" in the 1540s and in more recent times the site was used as a school. The excavated remains themselves would hold only specialist appeal were it not for the excellent interpretation centre, which explains much about daily life in a Cistercian abbey. Ballasalla is a stop on the Steam Railway, with the abbey a few minutes' walk from the village.

Travel details

Buses

For information on all local and national bus services, contact Traveline ℡0871/200 2233, ⓦwww.traveline.org.uk.

Chester to: Liverpool (every 20min; 1hr 15min); Manchester (3 daily; 1hr 30min).
Lancaster to: Carlisle (4–5 daily; 1hr 20min); Kendal (hourly; 1hr); Manchester (2 daily; 2hr); Windermere (hourly; 1hr 45min).
Liverpool to: Blackpool (1 daily; 1hr 30min); Chester (12 daily; 1hr); Leeds (hourly; 2hr 10min); London (9 daily; 5hr 10min–6hr 40min); Manchester (hourly; 1hr); Preston (2 daily; 1hr).
Manchester to: Birmingham (12 daily; 2hr 40min); Blackpool (3 daily; 1hr 40min); Chester (3 daily; 1hr 15min); Leeds (hourly; 1hr 30min); Liverpool (hourly; 1hr); London (every 1–2hr; 4hr 30min–5hr 20min); Newcastle (6 daily; 5hr); Sheffield (4 daily; 2hr 25min).

Trains

For information on all local and national rail services, contact National Rail Enquiries ℡0845/748 4950, ⓦwww.nationalrail.co.uk.

Blackpool to: Manchester (hourly; 1hr 10min); Preston (hourly; 30min).
Chester to: Liverpool (2 hourly; 45min); London (12 daily; 2hr 45min); Manchester (2 hourly; 1hr–1hr 20min).
Lancaster to: Carlisle (every 30min–1hr; 50min); London (hourly; 2hr 20min); Manchester (hourly; 1hr); Morecambe (every 30min–1hr; 10min); Preston (every 20–30min; 20min).
Liverpool to: Birmingham (hourly; 1hr 40min); Chester (every 30min; 45min); Leeds (hourly; 1hr 40min); London (hourly; 2hr 20min); Manchester (hourly; 50min); Preston (14 daily; 1hr); Sheffield (hourly; 1hr 45min); York (11 daily; 2hr 15min).
Manchester to: Barrow-in-Furness (Mon–Sat 10 daily, Sun 3 daily; 2hr 15min); Birmingham (every 30min; 1hr 30min); Blackpool (hourly; 1hr 20min); Buxton (hourly; 1hr); Carlisle (11 daily; 1hr 50min); Chester (every 30min; 1hr–1hr 20min); Lancaster (14 daily; 1hr); Leeds (hourly; 1hr); Liverpool (every 30min; 50min); London (every 30min; 2hr 15min); Newcastle (hourly; 2hr 40min); Oxenholme (8 daily; 40min–1hr 10min); Penrith (2–6 daily; 1hr 50min); Preston (every 20min; 55min); Sheffield (hourly; 1hr); York (every 30min; 1hr 30min).

Cumbria and the Lakes

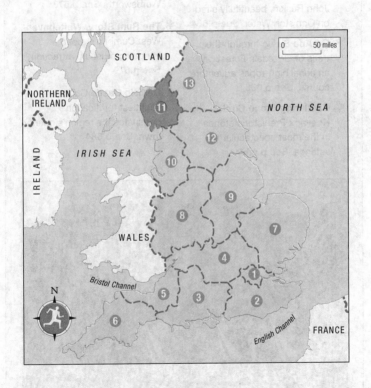

Highlights

✳ **Windermere** Take to the water on England's largest lake. See p.655

✳ **Old Dungeon Ghyll Hotel, Langdale** The hikers' favourite inn – cosy rooms, stone-flagged floors and open fires. See p.660

✳ **Brantwood** The home of John Ruskin, beautifully sited on Coniston Water. See p.664

✳ **Go Ape** Swing through the trees of Grizedale Forest on an aerial high-ropes adventure course. See p.666

✳ **Castlerigg Stone Circle, Keswick** Prehistoric stones in the most spectacular of settings. See p.669

✳ **Honister Pass and Slate Mine** Explore the 300-year-old slate mine and climb the extraordinary Via Ferrata. See p.671

✳ **Wordsworth House, Cockermouth** Step into the eighteenth century at the birthplace of William Wordsworth. See p.673

✳ **The Rum Story, Whitehaven** West Cumbria's most intriguing museum attraction. See p.679

✳ **Carlisle Castle** Cumbria's mightiest fortification dominates the region's county town. See p.684

▲ Sailing on Windermere

Cumbria and the Lakes

T he Lake District is England's most hyped scenic area, and for good reasons. Within an area a mere thirty miles across, sixteen major lakes are squeezed between the steeply pitched faces of the country's highest mountains, an almost alpine landscape that's augmented by waterfalls and picturesque stone-built villages packed into the valleys. Most of what people refer to as the Lake District – or simply the Lakes – lies within the **Lake District National Park**. This, in turn, falls entirely within the northwestern county of **Cumbria**, formed in 1974 from the historic counties of Cumberland and Westmorland, and the northern part of Lancashire. Consequently Cumbria contains more than just its lakes, stretching south and west to the largely unsung **coast**, and north to its historic county town of **Carlisle**. To the east, **Penrith** and the **Eden Valley** separate the Lakes from the near wilderness of the northern Pennines.

Two factors spurred the first waves of **tourism** here: the reappraisal of landscape brought about by such painters as Constable and the writings of **William Wordsworth** and his contemporaries, and the turmoil of the French Revolution, which put paid to the idea of the continental Grand Tour. Indeed, it was Wordsworth who first recognized the special character of the Lakes, writing in his *Guide to the Lakes* (1810) that he desired "a sort of national property, in which every man has a right and interest who has an eye to perceive and a heart to enjoy". His wish finally came to fruition in 1951 when the government designated 880 square miles of the Lake District as England's largest national park.

On any scale, the **National Park** has been wildly successful, attracting millions of visitors every year. This has come at some price, mainly in terms of traffic and environmental pressure, which a forward-thinking integrated transport strategy is attempting to alleviate. There's always been a severe contrast, too, between the touristed villages of the Lakes and the old industrial towns of coastal **West Cumbria**, which have struggled in the past to attract visitors and investment. However, regeneration has been dramatic in recent years, with the reviving fortunes of places like **Whitehaven** giving tourists ever more reason to stray from the Lakes.

The Lake District

Given a week you could easily see most of the famous settlements and lakes – a circuit taking in the towns of Ambleside, Windermere and Bowness, all on **Windermere**, the Wordsworth houses and sites in pretty villages such as **Hawkshead** and **Grasmere**, and the more dramatic northern scenery near **Keswick** and **Ullswater** would give you a fair sample of the whole. But it's away from the crowds that the Lakes really begin to pay dividends, in the dramatic valleys of **Langdale** and **Eskdale**, and the lesser-visited lakes of **Wast Water** and **Buttermere**. Of course, it's only when you start to walk and climb around the Lakes that you can really say you've explored the region. Four peaks top out at over 3000ft – including **Scafell Pike**, the highest in England – but there are hundreds of other mountains, crags and fells to roam.

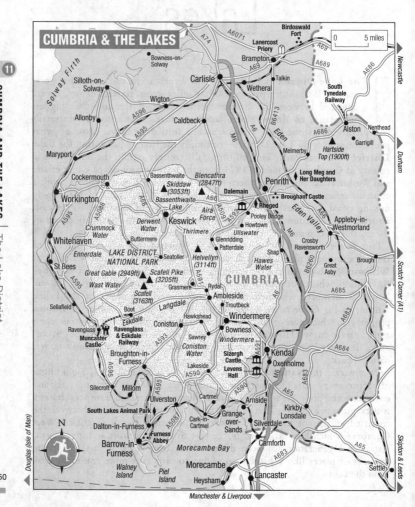

CUMBRIA & THE LAKES

Manchester & Liverpool ▼

National Express **coaches** connect London and Manchester with Windermere, Ambleside, Grasmere and Keswick. **Trains** leave the West Coast main line at **Oxenholme**, north of Lancaster, for the branch-line service to Kendal and Windermere. The only other places directly accessible by train are Penrith and Carlisle, further north on the West Coast line, and the towns along the Cumbrian coast. Of the lakes themselves, Windermere, Coniston Water, Derwent Water and Ullswater have useful **cruise and ferry** services, while the **Cross Lakes Experience** (operates Feb half-term hols, March weekends, then daily Easter–Oct; information from Mountain Goat ⊕015394/45161, or see ⓦwww.lakedistrict.gov.uk) – integrating boats and buses – connects Bowness-on-Windermere with Hawkshead, Hill Top (Beatrix Potter house), Coniston Water and Grizedale Forest.

The one-day Stagecoach **Explorer Ticket** (from £9.75; ⓦwww.stagecoachbus .com/northwest) is valid on the entire local bus network (and available from the driver), and there are also good-value combination bus-and-boat tickets for Windermere, Coniston and Ullswater. Best single deal is the **Lakes Day Ranger** ticket (£18.50; ⓦwww.northernrail.org), which is valid on all Cumbrian Stagecoach buses and regional trains, and includes a free Windermere cruise and other local discounts. The two **main bus services** are the #555 (Kendal–Windermere–Ambleside–Grasmere–Keswick, with connections to Lancaster and Carlisle) and the open-top #599 (Kendal–Windermere–Bowness–Ambleside–Grasmere), but all routes and timetables are available on the Stagecoach website or by contacting **Traveline** (⊕0871/200 2233, ⓦwww.traveline.info).

For more **information** about all aspects of the Lakes, visit ⓦwww.lakedistrict .gov.uk, while the official site of Cumbria Tourism, ⓦwww.golakes.co.uk, has links to all sorts of themed holiday ideas. It's wise to book **accommodation** ahead at any time of year, though local tourist offices pride themselves on always being able to find a bed for anyone arriving without a reservation. For farmhouse accommodation, a Cumbrian speciality, check the websites ⓦwww.farmstayuk.co.uk and ⓦwww.luxuryinafarm.co.uk, while campsites are all covered in depth on the excellent ⓦwww.lakedistrictcamping.co.uk.

Bad weather can move in quickly, even in summer, so always check the **weather forecast** before a hike – many hotels and outdoor shops post a daily forecast – or check on ⊕0844/846 2444 (recorded 24hr line) or ⓦwww.lakedistrict.gov.uk /weatherline.

Kendal and around

The self-billed "Gateway to the Lakes" (though nearly ten miles from Windermere), limestone-grey **KENDAL** offers rewarding rambles along the River Kent and around the "yards" and "ginnels" on both sides of Highgate and Stricklandgate, the main streets. Although the old Market Place long since succumbed to development, traditional stalls still do business outside the Westmorland Shopping Centre every Wednesday and Saturday.

Arrival, information and accommodation

Kendal's **train station** is the first stop on the Windermere branch line, just three minutes from the **Oxenholme** main-line station and a ten-minute walk from the centre. The **bus station** is on Blackhall Road (off Stramongate), while the **tourist office** (Mon–Sat 10am–5pm, Nov–Feb until 4pm; ⊕01539/797516, ⓦwww .kendaltowncouncil.gov.uk) is in the town hall on Highgate.

Standard **B&Bs** are ranged along Milnthorpe Road, a few minutes south of the centre – walk straight down Highgate and Kirkland – but there's also the excellent boutique *Beech House*, 40 Greenside (℡01539/720385, Ⓦwww.beechhouse -kendal.co.uk; ❸, deluxe rooms ❹), which is just a short steep climb up the hill from the town centre. Kendal's biggest **hotel** is the resort-style *Castle Green* (℡01539/734000, Ⓦwww.castlegreen.co.uk; ❺), a mile or so out of the centre, while the smart, bright *Riverside* on Stramongate Bridge (℡01539/734861, Ⓦwww.riversidekendal.co.uk; ❹) was fashioned from one of the former town tanneries. There's also a **youth hostel** at 118 Highgate (℡0845/371 9641, Ⓔkendal@yha.org.uk; dorm beds from £17.95, includes breakfast), attached to the Brewery Arts Centre. Five miles west of town at Crosthwaite, the 🏕 *Punch Bowl Inn* (℡01539/568237, Ⓦwww.the-punchbowl.co.uk; ❽) is a super-stylish operation – the earth-toned rooms have exposed beams and superb bathrooms, while the restaurant serves scrumptious, unpretentious, locally sourced food (pot-roast wood pigeon to local lamb, from around £30).

The Town

The **Kendal Museum**, on Station Road (Thurs–Sat noon–5pm; £2.80; Ⓦwww .kendalmuseum.org.uk), holds the district's natural history and archeological finds, and town history displays. You'll also find the reconstructed office, pen-and-ink drawings and personal effects of **Alfred Wainwright** (1907–91), Kendal's former borough treasurer (and honorary clerk at the museum). Wainwright moved to Kendal in 1941 and, dissatisfied with the accuracy of existing maps, embarked on his series of highly personal walking guides, painstakingly handwritten with delicately drawn maps and views. They have been hugely popular guidebooks ever since, which many treat as gospel in their attempts to "bag" ascents of the 214 fells he recorded. When he died, Wainwright's ashes were scattered on his favourite mountain – Haystacks in Buttermere.

The town's other two museums are at the Georgian **Abbot Hall** (Mon–Sat 10.30am–5pm, Nov–March until 4pm; closed 2 weeks in Dec) by the river near the parish church. The main hall houses the **Art Gallery** (£5.75; Ⓦwww.abbothall.org .uk), which hosts both temporary exhibitions and locally focused collections concentrating in particular on the works of the eighteenth-century "Kendal School" of portrait painters, most famously George Romney. Meanwhile, the former stables contain the **Museum of Lakeland Life and Industry** (£4.75, ticket valid for 1 year; Ⓦwww.lakelandmuseum.org.uk), where reconstructed period house interiors stand alongside trade and craft workshops. There's also a room devoted to the life and work of the children's writer Arthur Ransome, a must for *Swallows and Amazons* fans.

Eating, drinking and entertainment

For inexpensive veggie café **meals** visit *Waterside Wholefood* (closed Sun) on Gulfs Road, by the river at the bottom of Lowther Street. *Déjà-Vu By Day* in Blackhall Yard (closed Sun), opposite the library off Stricklandgate, is a little French-style café with a nice line in baguettes, salads and light lunches, while their dinner-only bistro, *Bistro Déjà-Vu*, 124 Stricklandgate (℡01539/724843; closed Tues),

---

Climb every mountain

Kendal mint cake, a tooth-challenging, energy-giving, solid block of sugar and peppermint oil, was apparently invented by accident in the mid-nineteenth century. The familiar retro-packaged Romney's brand (from Kendal) is on sale throughout the Lakes, and its proudest boast is still that Kendal mint cake was carried to the top of Everest during Hillary's ascent of 1953.

serves three courses for around a tenner (Sun–Thurs all night, Fri & Sat before 7.30pm). Best restaurant in town is generally acknowledged to be the *New Moon*, 129 Highgate (℡01539/729254; closed Sun & Mon), an easy-going contemporary place (lunch £5–7, dinner mains mostly £11–16).

The 🎭 **Brewery Arts Centre**, 122 Highgate (℡01539/725133, ⓦwww .breweryarts.co.uk), is the town's cultural focus. Its *Grain Store Restaurant* and lively *Vats Bar* serve drinks, light lunches, gourmet pizzas and a more elaborate dinner menu (mains £10–15); the centre also has a cinema, theatre, gallery and concert hall. There's live music throughout the year (particularly jazz, world and folk), while the centre also hosts the renowned **Kendal Mountain Festival** in November (ⓦwww.mountainfest.co.uk), Europe's biggest celebration of mountain culture.

Sizergh Castle and Levens Hall

Out of town, bus #555 links Kendal to two stately homes that each make for an enjoyable half-day's visit. Three miles south, **Sizergh Castle** (Easter–Oct Mon–Thurs & Sun noon–5pm; gardens open same days from 11am; £7.15, gardens only £4.50; NT) owes its "castle" epithet to the fourteenth-century peel tower at its core, one of the best examples of the towers built as safe havens during the region's protracted medieval border raids. **Levens Hall** (Easter to mid-Oct Mon–Thurs & Sun noon–5pm; gardens open 10am; £11, gardens only £8; ⓦwww.levenshall.co.uk), two miles south of Sizergh, was refurbished in the classic Elizabethan manner between 1570 and 1640. House stewards are on hand to point out the oddities and curios – for example, the dining room is panelled not with oak but with goat's leather, printed with a deep green floral design. Outside are beautifully trimmed topiary gardens, where yews in the shape of pyramids, peacocks and top hats stand between colourful bedding plants and apple orchards.

Windermere town and around

WINDERMERE town was all but non-existent until 1847 when a railway terminal was built here, making England's longest lake (after which the town is named) an easily accessible resort. All the traffic pours a mile downhill to Windermere's older twin town, Bowness, actually on the lake, but do stay long enough in Windermere to make the twenty-minute stroll up through the woods to **Orrest Head** (784ft), from where there's a 360° panorama sweeping from the Yorkshire fells to Morecambe Bay – the path begins just by the *Windermere Hotel* on the A591, across from Windermere train station.

You should also make time for the **Lake District Visitor Centre at Brockhole** (Easter–Oct daily 10am–5pm; grounds & gardens open all year; free, parking fee charged; ℡015394/46601, ⓦwww.lakedistrict.gov.uk), a lakeshore mansion three miles northwest of Windermere. It's the headquarters of the Lake District National Park and, besides the permanent natural history and geological displays, the centre hosts guided walks, children's trails and activities, special exhibitions and lectures. The landscaped gardens are a real treat and there's also a nice café with an outdoor terrace. Daily **buses** between Windermere and Ambleside run past the visitor centre, or you can get here by Windermere Lake Cruises **launch** from Waterhead, near Ambleside (Easter–Oct; £6.75 return).

Arrival and information

All **buses** stop outside Windermere **train station**, with the **tourist office** (Mon–Sat 9.30am–5pm, Sun 10am–5pm; ℡015394/46499, ⓦwww.lakelandgateway .info) just a hundred yards away at the top of Victoria Street. A one-day **Central Lakes Day Rider** ticket (buy from the driver; from £6.50) gives unlimited travel on any service running between Windermere/Bowness and Grasmere/Coniston, while the **Windermere Bus and Boat Rider** (from £9) combines the open-top #599 bus service with a Windermere lake cruise. For **bike rental**, contact Country Lanes at the train station (☎015394/44544, ⓦwww.countrylaneslake district.co.uk; £20–30 per day), which provides route maps for local rides.

Accommodation, eating and drinking

Good places to look for **B&Bs** are High Street and neighbouring Victoria Street at the top of town near the tourist office, with other concentrations just to the south on College Road, and Oak and Broad streets.

Accommodation

Archway 13 College Rd ☎015394/45613, ⓦwww.the-archway.com. Simply a great B&B, with four trim rooms in a Victorian house known for its breakfasts – try the pancakes, kippers, home-made yoghurt and granola. ❷

Brendan Chase 1–3 College Rd ☎015394/45638, ⓦwww.placetostaywindermere.co.uk. A popular place with backpackers and overseas travellers. Eight comfortable rooms (some en-suite) available – family/group rooms sleep up to five and can bring the price down to around £20 per person. No credit cards. ❷

Coach House Lake Rd ☎015394/44494, ⓦwww .lakedistrictbandb.com. Comfort and contemporary design join hands in this stylish conversion of a Victorian coach house. Five classy rooms feature wrought-iron beds and gleaming bathrooms, and guests can use the local leisure club. ❸

Holbeck Ghyll Holbeck Lane, off A591, 3 miles north ☎015394/32375, ⓦwww.holbeck-ghyll.co .uk. Country-house stalwart offering luxurious rooms either in the main house or the lodge, or suites in the grounds – plus seven acres of gardens and Michelin-starred food. Price – from around £250, lake-view rooms from £310 – includes dinner. ❽

Jerichos at the Waverley College Rd ☎015394/42522, ⓦwww.jerichos.co.uk. Modish but unpretentious restaurant-with-rooms, retaining many original features but adding black leather beds and iPod docks. Downstairs you get seasonally changing menus (mains £16–22), served in a buzzy, stripped-down restaurant (dinner only, not Thurs; reservations advised). ❹

Miller Howe Rayrigg Rd, A592, half-mile west ☎015394/42536, ⓦwww.millerhowe.com. Gorgeous Edwardian house in an elevated position above Windermere, long a byword for lakeland indulgence. The price includes an elegant dinner (otherwise £40 for non-residents), with rates starting at £210 (superior lake-view rooms from £280). Closed 2 weeks in Jan. ❽

Queen's Head A592, Troutbeck, 3 miles north ☎015394/32174, ⓦwww.queensheadhotel.com. Revamped country inn that oozes atmosphere, from the slate floors, oak beams and smoky fires to the carved bar fashioned from a four-poster bed. Dining covers everything from Thai-style mussels to red-onion tarte tatin – most mains cost £11–16. ❺

Windermere YHA High Cross, Bridge Lane, 2 miles north ☎0845/371 9352, ⓔwindermere @yha.org.uk. Built originally as a private mansion, the house has magnificent lake views, while a major refit has smartened up hostel rooms and facilities. The food gets good reviews – you can also buy bottled Cumbrian beers and organic wines. Dorm beds from £13.95.

Cafés and restaurants

First Floor Lakeland Ltd, behind the train station ☎015394/88200. The café inside the home furnishings/design store provides superior snacks, sandwiches and daily specials (£4.50–7.50).

Francine's 27 Main Rd ☎015394/44088. Daytime eats can be anything from a *pain au chocolat* to a big bowl of mussels, while dinner (Wed–Sat only) sees a wide-ranging continental menu, with an emphasis on fish and seafood (most mains £9–14, set menu £17.95). Closed Mon.

Lamplighter Bar *Oakthorpe Hotel*, High St ☎015394/43547. A favoured local spot at night, where bistro meals (gammon, fresh fish, rack of lamb) go for £10–15. Closed Sun lunch & Mon lunch.

Bowness and the lake

BOWNESS-ON-WINDERMERE – to give its full title – is undoubtedly the more attractive of the two Windermere settlements, spilling back from its lakeside piers in a series of terraces lined with guesthouses and hotels. There's been a village here since the fifteenth century and a ferry service across the lake for almost as long – these days, though, you could be forgiven for thinking that Bowness begins and

Windermere cruises

Windermere Lake Cruises (ⓦ www.windermere-lakecruises.co.uk) operate services to Lakeside at the southern tip (£9.45 return) or to Waterhead (for Ambleside) at the northern end (£9.15 return). There's also a direct service from Ambleside to the Lake District Visitor Centre at Brockhole (£6.75 return), and a shuttle service across the lake between Pier 3 at Bowness and Ferry House, Sawrey (£4.50 return). An enjoyable circular **cruise** around Belle Isle and other islands departs several times daily from Bowness (£6.75; 45min), while a 24hr **Freedom-of-the-Lake** ticket costs £16.50. Services on all routes are frequent between Easter and October (every 30min–1hr at peak times), and reduced during the winter – but there are sailings every day except Christmas Day.

ends with **The World of Beatrix Potter** in the Old Laundry on Crag Brow (daily 10am–4.30/5.30pm; £6.75; ⓦ www.hop-skip-jump.com). You either like Beatrix Potter or you don't, but it's safe to say that the elaborate 3D story scenes, Peter Rabbit garden, audiovisual "virtual walks", themed tearoom and gift shop here find more favour with children than the more formal Potter attractions at Hill Top and Hawkshead. The other main sight is the **Windermere Steamboat Museum** (ⓦ www.steamboat.co.uk), a fifteen-minute walk north of the centre on Rayrigg Road. This is currently undergoing a major restoration (though parts may be open during the works – check the website for details), which will not only provide superb new premises for its historic watercraft but also include a marine conservation workshop and lake trips on some of the restored steamboats.

The lake itself – simply **Windermere** (from the Norse, "Vinandr's Lake", and thus never "*Lake* Windermere") – is the heavyweight of Lake District waters, at ten and a half miles long, a mile wide in parts and a shade over two hundred feet deep. Rowing boats are available for rent by the lakeside piers, while Windermere Lake Cruises operates modern cruisers and vintage steamers throughout the year. The traditional **ferry service** is the chain-guided contraption across the water from Ferry Nab on the Bowness side (a ten-minute walk from the cruise piers) to Ferry House, Sawrey (Mon–Sat 7am–10pm, Sun 9am–10pm; departures every 20min; 50p, cars £3.50), providing access to the Beatrix Potter house at Hill Top and to Hawkshead.

Arrival and information

The open-top #599 **bus** from Windermere train station stops at the lakeside piers, also the terminus for the #517 (to Troutbeck and Ullswater). For onward routes to Ambleside and Grasmere you have to return first to Windermere station, though the very useful **Cross Lakes Experience** (Feb half-term hols, March weekends, then daily Easter–Oct) provides a direct connecting boat-and-minibus service from Bowness Pier 3 to Hill Top (£9.20 return), Hawkshead (£10.45), Grizedale (£13.40) and Coniston Water (£18.05). Windermere Canoe & Kayak (ⓣ 015394/44451, ⓦ www.windermerecanoekayak.co.uk), on Ferry Nab Road (on the way to the Sawrey ferry), offers bike and kayak rental (from £20 per day). **Bowness Bay Information Centre** is near the piers on Glebe Road (daily 9.30/10am–4/5.30pm; ⓣ 015394/42895).

Accommodation, eating and drinking

Crag Brow and then Lake Road is the main thoroughfare up from the lake towards Windermere, on and off which you'll find much of the accommodation and services; pedestrianized **Ash Street**, at the foot of Crag Brow, is where to look for restaurants and bars, from fish and chips to tapas.

Accommodation

Angel Inn Helm Rd ☏015394/44080, ⓦwww
.the-angelinn.com. A dozen chic rooms – all
burnished wood and black leather – above a
smooth bar bring a bit of metropolitan style to
Bowness. Posh pub food (mains £10–17) is served
in the bar, restaurant or terraced garden. **⑤**

The Cranleigh Kendal Rd ☏015394/43293,
ⓦwww.thecranleigh.com. Indulge yourself in the
"guesthouse with a difference" – the difference
being the super-stylish rooms and suites (vibrant
fabrics, designer beds, iPod docks and space-
station-like showers). **⑤**, suites **⑥**

Gilpin Lodge Crook Rd, B5284, 2 miles southeast
☏015394/88818, ⓦwww.gilpinlodge.co.uk. A
renowned country-house retreat with fourteen
elegant rooms, and six more contemporary suites
in the grounds with private gardens and hot tubs.
Rates (from £290, suites £440) include dinner in
the Michelin-starred restaurant (otherwise £55,
open to non-guests). **⑧**

Linthwaite House Crook Rd, B5284, 1 mile south
☏015394/88600, ⓦwww.linthwaite.com. Boutique
style grafted onto an ivy-covered country house set
high above Windermere – very comfortable rooms
feature muted fabrics, Shaker-style furniture, king-
sized beds and flat-screen TVs. Rates vary
according to outlook and size (up to £330) and
include dinner. **⑧**

Monties Crag Brow ☏015394/42723,
ⓦwww.montiesbedandbreakfast.com. The
standard rooms here are pretty nice, but three
others have been given an extra-stylish makeover,
with strong colours and decent bathrooms. Prices
include breakfast in the fab *Monties* café
downstairs. **❸**

Number 80 80 Craig Walk ☏015394/43584,
ⓦwww.number80bed.co.uk. Quiet
townhouse offering quirky, stylish B&B in four
rather dramatic earth-toned double rooms. **❸**

Cafés, pubs and restaurants

2 Eggcups 6a Ash St ☏015394/45979. Serves
the best sandwich in Bowness, plus other blackboard specials (£3–7). Daytime only, closed Thurs.

Hole in't Wall Fallbarrow Rd
☏015394/43488. The town's oldest hostelry
is named after the hole the beer used to be passed
through; it's cosy in winter when the fires are lit,
and pleasant in summer when you can sit outside.
The usual bar meals (£9–12) include a daily curry
special.

Jackson's Bistro St Martin's Square
☏015394/46264. The local choice for a family
meal or romantic night out – classic bistro dishes,
including a good-value three-course *table d'hôte*
menu (£14.95) available all night. Dinner only.

Around Bowness

A mile and a half south of Bowness, there's the rare chance to visit a house designed
by one of the major exponents of the Arts and Crafts Movement. Mackay Hugh
Baillie Scott's **Blackwell** (daily 10.30am–5pm, Nov–March until 4pm; closed
2 weeks Jan; £6.30; ⓦwww.blackwell.org.uk) was built in 1900 as a lakeside
holiday home, and Lakeland motifs (particularly trees, flowers, birds and berries) are
visible in virtually every nook and cranny, from the stonework to the stained glass.
You'll also have the chance to see changing exhibitions of Arts and Crafts furniture
and other contemporary pieces, and there's an informative introductory talk
(usually weekdays at 2.30pm), plus tearoom and gardens. You can walk from
Bowness (about 25min), but you'll need to go along a busy road, so take care.

From Bowness piers, boats head to the southern reaches of Windermere at
Lakeside, which is also the terminus of the **Lakeside & Haverthwaite
Railway** (Easter–Oct 6–7 daily; £5.90 return; ☏015395/31594, ⓦwww
.lakesiderailway.co.uk), whose steam-powered engines chuff along four miles
of track through the forests of Backbarrow Gorge. The boat arrivals at Lakeside
connect with train departures throughout the day, and you can buy a joint
boat-and-train ticket at Bowness. Also on the quay at Lakeside is the **Lakes
Aquarium** (daily 9am–5/6pm; £8.95; ⓦwww.lakesaquarium.co.uk), centred
on the fish and animals found along a Lakeland river, including a walk-through
tunnel aquarium containing huge carp and diving ducks. Enthusiastic staff are
on hand to explain what's going on and, again, there's a joint ticket available
with the boat ride from Bowness. Alternatively, contact Country Lanes
(ⓦwww.countrylaneslakedistrict.co.uk) on the quayside, either for full-day

After 30 years located in the old shire-horse stables at Holker Hall, the popular **Lakeland Motor Museum** (daily 10am–5.30pm; Ⓦ www.lakelandmotormuseum .co.uk) has a new purpose-built home at Backbarrow, near Newby Bridge, to show off its 30,000-plus motoring history exhibits. It's a dream for petrol heads and nostalgia buffs alike, while a proposed museum halt on the Lakeside & Haverthwaite Railway should eventually open up the collection to a new generation of visitors.

bike rental (from £20) or a **bike-and-boat** day out (from £17.50) which includes the boat ride from Bowness.

Ambleside

Five miles northwest of Windermere, **AMBLESIDE** is at the heart of the central and southern Lakes region. The thriving centre – more a retail experience than a lakeland town – consists of a cluster of grey-green stone houses either side of the babbling gully of Stock Ghyll, and more outdoor shops, pubs, B&Bs and cafés than you can shake a stick at. Huge car parks soak up the day-trip trade, but actually Ambleside improves with time, boasting some enjoyable local walks and also the best selection of accommodation and restaurants in the area.

For some background on Ambleside's history, stroll a couple of minutes along Rydal Road to the **Armitt Collection** (daily 10am–5pm; £2.50; Ⓦ www.armitt .com), which catalogues the very distinct contribution to Lakeland society made by writers and artists from John Ruskin to Beatrix Potter. The rest of town lies a mile south at **Waterhead**, at the head of the lake, overlooked by grass banks, spreading trees, a couple of little cafés by the pier and the lawns of some imposing hotels.

Arrival and information

Walking up to Ambleside from the ferry piers at Waterhead takes about fifteen minutes, while all **buses** stop on Kelsick Road, opposite the library. The **tourist office** is on Market Cross (daily 9am–5.30pm; Ⓣ 015394/32582, Ⓦ www .lakelandgateway.info). There's **bike rental** (from £20 per day) from Biketreks on Rydal Road (Ⓣ 015394/31245, Ⓦ www.biketreks.net), or Ghyllside Cycles on The Slack (Ⓣ 015394/33592, Ⓦ www.ghyllside.co.uk). Zeffirelli's **cinema** (Ⓦ www .zeffirellis.com) has five screens at three locations in town, while annual festivals include the traditional procession to the church known as the **Rushbearing** (July),

11

Walks from Ambleside

A couple of good walks are accessible straight from the town centre. First, from the footbridge across the river in Rothay Park you can strike up across **Loughrigg Fell** (1099ft). Dropping down to Loughrigg Terrace (2hr), overlooking Grasmere, you then cut south at Rydal on the A591 and follow the minor road back along the River Rothay to Ambleside – a total of 6 miles (4hr).

The walk over **Wansfell to Troutbeck** and back (6 miles; around 4hr) is a little tougher. Stock Ghyll Lane runs up the left bank of the tumbling stream to **Stock Ghyll Force**, one of the more attractive waterfalls in the region. The path then rises steeply to **Wansfell Pike** (1581ft) and down into Troutbeck village, where you can have lunch either at the *Mortal Man* or the nearby *Queen's Head*, both just a short walk from the village centre. The return cuts west onto the flanks of Wansfell and around past the viewpoint at **Jenkin Crag** back to Ambleside.

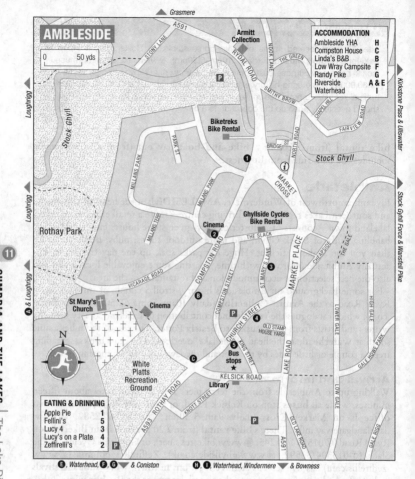

▲ *Grasmere*

AMBLESIDE

0 ——— 50 yds

Armitt Collection

ACCOMMODATION

Ambleside YHA	H
Compston House	C
Linda's B&B	B
Low Wray Campsite	F
Randy Pike	G
Riverside	A & E
Waterhead	I

Kirkstone Pass & Ullswater ▶

Stock Ghyll Force & Wansfell Pike ▶

Loughrigg ◀

Loughrigg ◀

Biketreks Bike Rental

Stock Ghyll

Rothay Park

Ghyllside Cycles Bike Rental

Cinema ②

THE SLACK

③

St Mary's Church

Cinema

Ⓑ

④

White Platts Recreation Ground

Ⓒ

⑤ **Bus stops**

Library

KELSICK ROAD

EATING & DRINKING

Apple Pie	1
Fellini's	5
Lucy 4	3
Lucy's on a Plate	4
Zeffirelli's	2

Ⓔ, *Waterhead,* Ⓕ, Ⓖ ▼ *& Coniston*   Ⓗ, Ⓘ, *Waterhead, Windermere* ▼ *& Bowness*

11

CUMBRIA AND THE LAKES | The Lake District

and the famous annual **Ambleside Sports** gathering (traditional wrestling to fell-running) on the Thursday before the first Monday in August.

Accommodation, eating and drinking

Lake Road, running between Waterhead and Ambleside, is lined with **B&Bs**, with other concentrations on central Church Street and Compston Road. You should usually be able to find something, even in peak season. Both the YHA and Low Wray campsite are hugely popular (reservations advised), while the town is stuffed with cafés, pubs and restaurants for all tastes and budgets.

Accommodation

Ambleside YHA Waterhead, A591, 1 mile south of Ambleside ☎ 0845/371 9620, Ⓔambleside@yha .org.uk. Ambleside's impressive lakeside hostel boasts over 250 beds divided among neatly furnished small dorms and private rooms. Facilities

are first-rate – from private jetty to licensed bar and restaurant. Dorm beds from £15.95, rooms ②
Compston House Compston Rd ☎ 015394/32305, Ⓦwww.compstonhouse.co.uk. There's a breezy New York air in this traditional Lakeland house, with American-style themed rooms and breakfasts

of pancakes and maple syrup. ❸, some rooms and weekends ❹

Linda's B&B Compston Rd ☏ 015394/32999. The cheapest rates in town. The three rooms (a single, double and a twin) all share bathroom facilities, while a room-only stay brings the price down to as little as £15 a night. No credit cards. ❶

Low Wray Campsite Low Wray, off B5286, 3 miles south ☏ 015394/63862, ⓦ www .ntlakescampsites.org.uk. The National Trust site on the western lakeshore is a glam-campers' haven with a choice of wooden camping "pods" (£30–45 per night; contact the campsite), fully furnished tipis (part-week rental from £130, weekends £155; ⓦ www.4windslakelandtipis.co.uk), plus bell-tents and yurts (bell-tents part-week from £235/full week from £355, yurts from £285/385; ⓦ www .long-valley-yurts.co.uk). Bus #505 passes within a mile of the site. Closed Nov–Easter.

Randy Pike B5286 (Hawkshead road), 3 miles south ☏ 015394/36088, ⓦ www.randypike .co.uk. The owners of Grasmere's *Jumble Room* restaurant offer two amazing light-filled B&B suites opening out onto the gardens of what was once a Victorian gentleman's hunting lodge. It's a grown-up, romantic retreat, and you can either stay put or be whizzed down to the *Jumble Room* for dinner. ❻

Riverside Under Loughrigg ☏ 015394/32395, ⓦ www.riverside-at-ambleside.co.uk. Charming guesthouse on a quiet lane, half a mile (10min walk) from town across Rothay Park. Six large, light country-pine-style rooms available, including a river-facing one with four-poster bed. ❹

Waterhead Waterhead ☏ 015394/32566, ⓦ www .elh.co.uk. Lakeshore city chic pretty much sums up this designer townhouse-style hotel opposite the Waterhead piers – there's a champagne menu in each slate-and-marble bathroom, plus garden-bar and positively metropolitan restaurant (mains £12–20). ❼

Cafés, restaurants and bars

Apple Pie Rydal Rd ☏ 015394/33679. The best café and bakery in town, with a secluded patio garden and trademark home-made pies that come savoury or sweet. Dishes £5–6.

Fellinis' Church St ☏ 015394/32487, ⓦ www .fellinisambleside.com. At the gourmet end of veggie dining, but with sensible prices (mains £10.95). Zeffirelli's digital art-house cinema is also on the premises, and a meal-and-movie deal costs £19.95 (see website, reservations essential). Dinner only; restaurant closed Mon in winter.

Lucy's on a Plate Church St ☏ 015394/31191. Really enjoyable bistro offering a daily changing menu with tonnes of choice. By day it's a café, with a Mediterranean-inspired menu (dishes £4–10); dinner (mains £14–19) is "sourced locally, cooked globally", while *Lucy 4* on St Mary's Lane (open daily from 5pm) is their moderately priced tapas-bar offshoot. They also have a nice deli called Lucy's Specialist Grocers on Compston Rd, great for picnic supplies and sandwiches.

Zeffirelli's Compston Rd ☏ 015394/33845. Famous for its wholemeal-based pizzas, but also serving inventive pastas and veggie food (mains £8–10) – there's a sun-trap terrace, cool upstairs jazz bar (with live music a couple of nights a week) and a dinner with cinema-ticket special (£17.95) for screenings at Zeffirelli's cinemas.

Great Langdale

Three miles west of Ambleside along the A593, Skelwith Bridge marks the start of **Great Langdale**, a U-shaped glacial valley overlooked by the prominent rocky summits of the **Langdale Pikes**. It's fantastic hiking country, easily accessible on the #516 Langdale Rambler **bus** from Ambleside, which runs to Elterwater (17min) and on up to the head of the valley at the *Old Dungeon Ghyll Hotel* (30min).

Pretty **ELTERWATER** is centred on a tiny village green overlooked by the excellent *Britannia Inn* (☏ 015394/37210, ⓦ www.britinn.co.uk; ❹, weekends ❺), with comfortable rooms and good food (Cumberland sausage to seared scallops, mains £10–14) served in the bar or dining room – come on a summer's day and the terrace is packed.

A **footpath** from Elterwater runs all the way up the valley; drivers follow the minor B5343 and should make for either of the valley's main car parks. Three miles from Elterwater, at **Stickle Ghyll** car park, Harrison Stickle (2414ft), Pike of Stickle (2326ft) and Pavey Ark (2297ft) form a dramatic backdrop, though many walkers aim no further than **Stickle Tarn**, an hour's climb up from Stickle Ghyll. The other car park, a mile further west up the valley road by the **Old Dungeon**

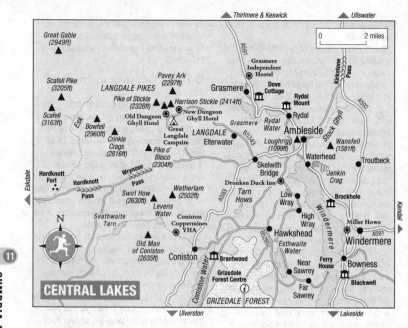

Map labels:

▲ Thirlmere & Keswick   ▲ Ullswater

0   2 miles

Great Gable (2949ft) ▲

Scafell Pike (3205ft) ▲

Pavey Ark (2297ft) ▲

LANGDALE PIKES

Grasmere Independent Hostel

Grasmere   Dove Cottage

Rydal Mount

Pike of Stickle (2326ft) ▲   Harrison Stickle (2414ft) ▲

Scafell (3163ft) ▲

Old Dungeon Ghyll Hotel   New Dungeon Ghyll Hotel

Rydal

Bowfell (2960ft) ▲

Great Langdale Campsite

Grasmere   Rydal Water

Ambleside

Crinkle Crags (2816ft) ▲

LANGDALE   Loughrigg (1099ft)

Wansfell (1581ft) ▲

Elterwater

Esk

Pike o' Blisco (2304ft) ▲

Waterhead

Troutbeck

Hardknott Fort   Hardknott Pass

Wrynose Pass

Skelwith Bridge

Jenkin Crag

Eskdale

Wetherlam (2502ft) ▲

Drunken Duck Inn

Brockhole

Swirl How (2630ft) ▲

Tarn Hows

Low Wray

Levens Water

N   Coniston Coppermines YHA

High Wray

Miller Howe

Seathwaite Tarn

Windermere

A591

Windermere

Old Man of Coniston (2635ft) ▲

Hawkshead

Esthwaite Water

Coniston

Brantwood

Bowness

Near Sawrey

Ferry House

Blackwell

Grizedale Forest Centre ℹ

Coniston Water

Far Sawrey

CENTRAL LAKES

GRIZEDALE FOREST

▼ Ulverston   ▼ Lakeside

Kirkstone Pass   Stock Ghyll   A592   Kendal   B5285

Ghyll Hotel, is the starting-point for a series of more hardcore hikes to resonant Lakeland peaks like Crinkle Crags (2816ft) or Bowfell (2960ft), though **Pike o'Blisco** (2304ft) is the easier prospect – a five-mile, three-hour round-trip from the car park, rewarded by marvellous views.

Best-known accommodation in the valley is the peerless ⚡ *Old Dungeon Ghyll Hotel* (☏015394/37272, ⓦ www.odg.co.uk; ❹), at the end of the B5343, seven miles northwest of Ambleside. It's a traditional, old-school mountain inn, well known to walkers and climbers, with dinner (£25, reservations essential) served in the dining room, though all the action is in the stone-flagged **hikers' bar** (filling meals from £8.50). A short walk away is the National Trust's stupendously sited *Great Langdale* **campsite** (☏015394/63862, ⓦ www.ntlakescampsites.org.uk), with its fancy camping pods (£30–45 per night, contact the campsite) and luxury yurts (part-week from £285/full week £385; ⓦ www.long-valley-yurts.co.uk).

Grasmere and around

Four miles northwest of Ambleside, the village of **GRASMERE** consists of an intimate cluster of grey stone houses on the old packhorse road that runs beside the babbling River Rothay. It's set back from one of the most alluring of the region's small lakes, but it loses some of its charm in summer thanks to the hordes who descend on the trail of the village's most famous former resident, **William Wordsworth** (1770–1850). The poet, his wife Mary, sister Dorothy and other members of his family are buried beneath the yews in **St Oswald's churchyard**, around which the river makes a sinuous curl. At the rear entrance to the church-yard, the schoolhouse where Wordsworth once taught is now Sarah Nelson's Gingerbread Shop. There's little else to the village, save its gift shops, galleries, tearooms and hotels, though the **lake** is just a ten-minute walk away down Redbank Road; tremendous views unfold from **Loughrigg Terrace**, on its southern reaches. The four-mile circuit of Grasmere and adjacent **Rydal Water**

CUMBRIA AND THE LAKES | The Lake District

takes around two hours, though as the route passes Wordsworth houses Rydal Mount and Dove Cottage, it could be turned into an all-day sightseeing venture.

Arrival and information

Grasmere is on the main #555 and #599 **bus** routes, and a **Central Lakes Day Rider ticket** (from £6.50) allows unlimited stops on the return journey between Bowness and Grasmere, allowing you to visit the Wordsworth houses as a day-trip. The big event of the year is **Grasmere Lakeland Sports and Show** (third or fourth Sun in Aug), a great day out showcasing traditional Cumbrian sports and activities.

Accommodation, eating and drinking

Note that as well as the recommended backpackers' hostel, there are two official YHA hostels close to the village (*Butharlyp Howe* and *Thorney How*; see Ⓦwww.yha.org.uk). Various village cafés cater to the daytime crowds; outside the hotels, independent restaurants and bars are thin on the ground but generally of good quality.

Accommodation

Cote How Organic Three miles southeast off A591, Rydal Ⓣ015394/32765, Ⓦwww.cotehow.co.uk. Three B&B rooms retain original fireplaces and antique beds, while in the romantic Rydal Suite you also get a vintage rolltop bath and a skylight for star-gazing. It's a fully certified organic guesthouse, while eco-credentials are unimpeachable (including discounts to anyone who comes by public transport). Tearooms are open weekends and bank holidays. ⑤

Full Circle Yurts Rydal Hall, 2 miles southeast, A591 Ⓣ07975/671928, Ⓦwww.lake-district-yurts.co.uk. Tucked into the lovely grounds of Rydal Hall are four authentic Mongolian yurts, complete with proper beds, rug-strewn floors and wood-burning stoves. From £265 (Mon–Fri or Fri–Mon rental) or £385 (per week), school and bank hols £285/440.

Grasmere Independent Hostel Broadrayne Farm, A591 Ⓣ015394/35055, Ⓦwww.grasmerehostel.co.uk. Just north of the village, past the *Travellers' Rest* pub, this stylish backpackers' is the top budget choice – 24 beds in small, carpeted en-suite rooms, impressive kitchen, laundry facilities and sauna, not to mention gracious hosts. Dorm beds from £19.50.

The Harwood Red Lion Square Ⓣ015394/35248, Ⓦwww.harwoodhotel.co.uk. A boutique "retreat for adults", offering six rustic-chic double rooms with a touch of Swiss-German mountain style. All rooms have a view, a couple also have patios and the duplex suite has a private terrace. ⑤, suite ⑥

How Foot Lodge Town End Ⓣ015394/35366, Ⓦwww.howfoot.co.uk. Spacious Victorian villa, just yards from Dove Cottage, with six charming B&B rooms, one with its own garden-side sun lounge. ③

Lancrigg Vegetarian Country House Easedale Rd Ⓣ015394/35317, Ⓦwww.lancrigg.co.uk.

Relaxed country house, half a mile northwest of the village. A dozen variously sized rooms have been carved from the well-worn interior (one in the former library); a vegetarian four-course dinner is included in the price. ⑥

Moss Grove Organic Corner of College St, opposite the *Wordsworth Hotel* Ⓣ015394/35251, Ⓦwww.mossgrove.com. A Victorian-era hotel redesigned on organic, low-impact lines – rooms have extraordinary handmade beds, wool carpets, duck-down duvets and natural wood blinds. The feel is less hotel and more private house party – you're encouraged to forage in the kitchen for a superior buffet-style breakfast. ⑥

Raise View White Bridge Ⓣ015394/35215, Ⓦwww.raiseviewhouse.co.uk. Lovely fell views from every corner of this superior B&B, plus a warm welcome and seven very comfortable rooms. ④

Rothay Garden Broadgate Ⓣ015394/35334, Ⓦwww.rothaygarden.com. The Lake District's newest four-star hotel is a classy mix of town and country. Urban-style attic "loft suites" have the most cachet, though you can't argue with the bright ground-floor "Grasmere" rooms that open out onto a riverside terrace. Price includes dinner. ⑦, suites ⑧

Cafés, restaurants and pubs

Jumble Room Langdale Rd Ⓣ015394/35188. Funky café-restaurant with an organic touch and a menu that ranges the world – from Thai prawns to local game pie (mains £11–18). Dinner reservations advised. Closed Tues.

Tweedies Langdale Rd Ⓣ015394/35300. Although part of the *Dale Lodge Hotel*, there's more of a country pub feel here than anywhere else in

Grasmere, from the stone-flagged floors to the big beer garden. The locally sourced menu features dishes like slow-cooked pork belly or grilled sea bass (mains £12–20), while Sunday night is usually live music night.

Villa Colombina Town End ☏ 015394/35268. Open during the day for snacks and light meals, followed by an authentic Italian dinner menu (mains £10–17) of pizzas, pastas, steak and chicken. Closed Jan and occasional other days in winter.

Dove Cottage

On Grasmere's southeastern outskirts, just off the A591, stands **Dove Cottage** (daily 9.30am–5.30pm; closed early Jan to early Feb; £7.50; ⓦ www.words worth.org.uk; buses #555 and #599), home to William and Dorothy Wordsworth from 1799 to 1808. Guides bursting with anecdotes lead you around rooms that reflect Wordsworth's guiding principle of "plain living but high thinking" and are little changed now but for the addition of electricity and internal plumbing. Most of the furniture in the cottage belonged to the Wordsworths, while in the upper rooms are various other possessions, including a pair of William's ice skates. The nearby **museum** contains paintings, manuscripts (including that of *Daffodils*) and personal effects once belonging to the Wordsworths, plus mementoes of Robert Southey, Samuel Taylor Coleridge and Thomas De Quincey. Any special **exhibitions** are detailed on the website, while the Wordsworth Trust sponsors readings, family activities and other events throughout the year.

Rydal Mount

Another mile and a half southeast along the A591 from Grasmere, **Rydal Mount** (March–Oct daily 9.30am–5pm; Nov–Feb daily except Tues 10am–4pm, closed 3 weeks in Jan; £6, gardens only £4; ⓦ www.rydalmount.co.uk) was the home of William Wordsworth from 1813 until his death in 1850. The house is now owned by descendants of the poet and you're free to wander around what is essentially still a family home – summer concerts feature poetry readings by Wordsworth family members and there are recent family photos on display alongside more familiar portraits of the poet and his circle. In the drawing room and library is the only known portrait of Dorothy, while for many the highlight is the **garden**, which has been preserved as Wordsworth designed it, complete with terraces where he used to declaim his poetry. Buses #555 and #599 pass the house on the way to Grasmere from Windermere and Ambleside.

Coniston and around

Coniston Water is not one of the most immediately imposing of the lakes, yet it has a quiet beauty that sets it apart from the more popular destinations. The nineteenth-century art critic and social reformer John Ruskin made the lake his home, and his isolated house, **Brantwood**, on the northeastern shore, provides the most obvious target for a day-trip. No one should miss a boat ride on the National Trust's elegant steam yacht, *Gondola*, or on the lake's wooden motor-launches.

Arrival, information and accommodation

Buses – principally the #505 "Coniston Rambler" from Windermere, Ambleside and Hawkshead and the #12 from Ulverston – stop on the main road through Coniston village. A **Ruskin Explorer** ticket (from £14.50, buy on the bus) gets you return travel on the #505 and the Coniston Launch, plus entry to Brantwood. The Cross Lakes Experience minibus service from Bowness runs as far as the *Waterhead Hotel* pier (for Brantwood and lake services), half a mile out of the village. There's a **tourist office** (daily 9.30am–4/5pm; ☎015394/41533, ⓦwww .conistontic.org) in the centre by the main car park, while local accommodation is plentiful – including some excellent nearby country retreats.

Bank Ground Farm Coniston Water, east side ☎015394/41264, ⓦwww.bankground.com. On the lakeshore just north of Brantwood, this beautifully located farmhouse features country-style rooms in the main house, many with sweeping views (room 8 is best), plus self-catering holiday cottages and a farmhouse tearoom. ❸

Beech Tree Guesthouse Yewdale Rd ☎015394/41717. Friendly vegetarian place 150 yards north of the village on the Ambleside road. No credit cards. ❷

Black Bull Inn Coppermines Rd, by the bridge ☎015394/41335. The village's best pub has rooms available in the main building or in the renovated cottages attached. Hearty bar meals feature local lamb, sausage and trout (£9–15), and award-winning beer is brewed on site. ❸, weekends ❹

🚶 **Church House Inn** Torver, 2 miles south ☎015394/41282, ⓦwww.churchhouse inntorver.com. Fine gastropub with five B&B rooms and excellent food served in the snug bar or dining room. Meals are locally sourced and strong on the classics (potted shrimps, local "tattie" hot pot, steak and ale pudding, fish pie). Dishes £12–18. ❸

Coniston Coppermines YHA ☎0845/371 9630, ⓔcoppermines@yha.org.uk. *Holly How* might be the closer hostel to the village, but it's *Copper-mines* that's the hikers' favourite, set dramatically in the mountains a steep mile from the village. It's fairly basic, but meals are available and you can buy local beer or organic wine. Closed Nov–March & some other days in summer season. Dorm beds from £17.95.

Lakeland House Tilberthwaite Ave ☎015394/41303, ⓦwww.lakelandhouse.com. A good, centrally located budget option accus- tomed to walkers and cyclists. Downstairs there's an internet café serving up big breakfasts, burgers, soup and sarnies (£3–7). ❷

🚶 **Yew Tree Farm** A593, 2 miles north ☎015394/41433, ⓦwww.yewtree-farm .com. The classiest farmhouse B&B in the Lakes, with a private outdoor hot tub and three hugely atmospheric rooms with low oak beams. There are walks straight from the gates, and a hikers' and cyclists' tearoom, while fans should note that Yew Tree Farm doubled as Beatrix Potter's house Hill Top in the *Miss Potter* movie starring Renée Zellweger – Potter herself once owned the farm and bought much of the surviving furniture. ❺

Coniston village

The slate-grey village of **CONISTON** hunkers below the craggy bulk of the mountain known as **The Old Man of Coniston** (2628ft), which most fit walkers can climb in under two hours. Having made the climb, and then studied **John Ruskin's grave**, which lies in St Andrew's original churchyard beneath a beautifully worked Celtic cross, you'll have seen all that Coniston has to offer, save for the excellent **Ruskin Museum** on Yewdale Road (Easter to mid-Nov daily 10am–5.30pm; mid-Nov to Easter Wed–Sun 10.30am–3.30pm; £5.25;

ⓦ www.ruskinmuseum.com). This combines local history and geology exhibits with a fascinating look at Ruskin's life and work through his watercolours, manuscripts and personal memorabilia.

Coniston Water

Coniston Water is hidden out of sight, half a mile southeast of the village. Here, the *Bluebird Café* sells ices, snacks and drinks, while at the **Coniston Boating Centre** (☏ 015394/41366) there are rowing boats, sailing dinghies, canoes, electric launches and motorboats. From the pier, the sumptuously upholstered **Steam Yacht Gondola** (Easter–Oct roughly hourly departures 10.30am–4.30pm, weather permitting; £8.50 round trip; ☏ 015394/41288; NT); built in 1859, departs on hour-long circuits of the lake, though you can also stop off at Ruskin's Brantwood. The other lake service is the **Coniston Launch** (Easter–Oct hourly 10.15am–5pm; Nov–Easter up to 5 daily depending on the weather; ☏ 017687/75753, ⓦ www.conistonlaunch.co.uk), which operates wooden solar-powered boats on two routes around the lake, north (£8.90 return) and south (£12.50), both calling at Brantwood. Special **cruises** (Easter–Oct; call for times; £12) concentrate on the various local sites associated with Arthur Ransome's *Swallows and Amazons* and on speed-king Donald Campbell.

Brantwood

Nestling among trees above the eastern shore of Coniston Water, two and a half miles by road from Coniston (off B5285), **Brantwood** (mid-March to mid-Nov daily 11am–5.30pm; mid-Nov to mid-March Wed–Sun 11am–4.30pm; £6.30, gardens only £4.50, combined Coniston Launch ticket available; ⓦ www.brantwood.org.uk) was home to **John Ruskin** from 1872 until his death in 1900.

Ruskin was champion of J.M.W. Turner and the Pre-Raphaelites and foremost Victorian proponent of the supremacy of Gothic architecture. His study – hung with handmade paper to his own design – and dining room boast superlative lake views, bettered only by those from the **Turret Room** where he used to sit in later life in his bathchair. The surviving Turners from Ruskin's own art collection are on show, and other exhibition rooms and galleries display Ruskin-related arts and crafts, while the excellent *Jumping Jenny Tearooms* – named after Ruskin's boat – has an outdoor terrace with lake views. Free guided walks through the **gardens** take place several times a week, while Thursday is "activity day", always a good time to visit.

Hawkshead and around

HAWKSHEAD, midway between Coniston and Ambleside, wears its beauty well, its patchwork of cottages and cobbles backed by woods and fells. Huge car parks at the village edge take the strain, and when the crowds of day-trippers leave, Hawkshead regains its natural tranquillity.

William Wordsworth studied at **Hawkshead Grammar School** (Easter–Oct Mon–Sat 10am–12.30pm & 1.30–5pm, Sun 1–5pm, Oct closes 4pm; £2), located near the main car park, though most visits to Hawkshead focus on the **Beatrix Potter Gallery** on Main Street (Feb half-term to Easter daily except Fri 11am–3.30pm; Easter–Oct daily except Fri 11am–5pm; £4.40; NT), occupying rooms once used by the author's solicitor husband. The gallery contains an annually changing selection of her original sketchbooks, drawings, watercolours and manuscripts, though the less devoted might find displays on her life as a keen naturalist, conservationist and early supporter of the National Trust more diverting – Potter bequeathed her farms and land in the Lake District to the Trust on her death, including the local beauty spot, **Tarn Hows** whose glistening waters are circled by woodland, paths and picnic spots. Tarn Hows is a two-mile walk from Hawkshead (or Coniston) on country lanes and paths, while the seasonal #X31 Tarn Hows Tourer bus (daily Easter–Oct; £3 return) also runs here up to half a dozen times a day from Hawkshead (plus connections from Coniston and Coniston Water). Drivers have to pay to use the National Trust car park.

Arrival, information and accommodation

The main **bus service** to Hawkshead is the #505 Coniston Rambler between Windermere, Ambleside and Coniston, while the seasonal **Cross Lakes Experience** runs from Hawkshead down to the Beatrix Potter house at Hill Top and on to Sawrey for boat connections back to Bowness. The **tourist office** (daily 9am–5pm; T015394/36946, W www.hawksheadtouristinfo.org.uk) is by the main car park. Accommodation within the village is limited, and eating is largely confined to the pubs, though a few delis and cafés also offer daytime meals and snacks.

Ann Tyson's Cottage Wordsworth St T015394/36405, W www.anntysons.co.uk. Some contend that Wordsworth once boarded here – the old cobbled street where the cottage is located has certainly changed little since his era. There are three rooms in the main house, plus a ground-floor single, and one superior room in what was formerly an adjoining chapel. ❷, superior room ❸

Drunken Duck Inn Barngates crossroads, 2 miles north, off B5285 T015394/36347, W www.drunkenduckinn.co.uk. Superb restaurant-with-rooms in a beautifully located 400-year-old inn. The rooms are eminently stylish, and the views

divine, while food shifts from classic sandwiches and bistro meals at lunch to a modish, fab and fresh seasonal dinner menu (mains £14–25). ❺, superior rooms ❻

King's Arms Market Square T015394/36372, W www.kingsarmshawkshead.co.uk. Bags of character in this old inn, with nine rooms retaining their oak beams and idiosyncratic proportions. It's also the best pub in the village, with good-value meals (£9–15) featuring the likes of fell-bred lamb, hot smoked salmon and venison steak. ❹

Yewfield Hawkshead Hill, 2 miles west, off B5285 T015394/36765,

Ⓦwww.yewfield.co.uk. Splendid vegetarian guesthouse set among organic vegetable gardens, orchards and wildflower meadows. The house is a

Victorian Gothic beauty, filled with artefacts and art from the owners' travels. Closed Dec & Jan. ❸, superior rooms ❹

Grizedale Forest

Grizedale Forest extends over the fells separating Coniston Water from Windermere, and the open-air sculptures, children's activities, cycle trails and high-wire adventure course make for a great day out. The best starting point is the **Grizedale Visitor Centre** (daily 10am–4/5pm; free, parking fee charged; ℡01229/860010, Ⓦwww.forestry.gov.uk/grizedaleforestpark), three miles southwest of Hawkshead – the #X30 **Grizedale Wanderer** bus (4 daily Easter–Oct) runs from Hawkshead, and connects with the Cross Lakes Experience service (so you can come direct from Bowness-on-Windermere). There's a good café at the centre, while **Grizedale Mountain Bikes** (daily from 9.30am, last rental at 3pm; ℡01229/860369, Ⓦwww.grizedalemountainbikes.co.uk) rents cycles (from £15 for 4hr, full-day rental from £22) on which to explore the forest's waymarked trails. The **Silurian Way** links most of a remarkable series of ninety-odd stone and wood sculptures that are scattered among the trees, while the challenging 10-mile North Face Trail gets rave reviews from serious mountain-bikers. More adventurous still is the forest high-ropes course known as **Go Ape** (daily Easter–Oct, Nov weekends only, closed Tues in term-time; from £25; advance booking essential, online or by phone ℡0845/643 9215, Ⓦwww.goape.co.uk), which has you frolicking in the tree canopy for a couple of hours – fantastic fun involving zip-wires, Tarzanswings and aerial walkways.

Hill Top

It's two miles from Hawkshead to the hamlet of Near Sawrey, the site of Beatrix Potter's beloved **Hill Top** (Feb half-term to Easter daily except Fri 11am–3.30pm; Easter–Oct daily except Fri 10.30am–4.30pm; £6.50; shop and garden, entry free on Fri when house is closed, and also open Nov & Dec; NT). A Londoner by birth, Potter bought the farmhouse with the proceeds from her first book, *The Tale of Peter Rabbit*, and retained it as her study long after she moved out following her marriage in 1913. Its furnishings and contents have been kept as they were during her occupancy – a condition of Potter's will. Actually, the displays here do little to throw light on Potter's character, but if you love the books then Hill Top and the Sawrey neighbourhood will be familiar as they featured in many scenes. That said, entry is by timed ticket, you'll probably have to wait in line, and sell-outs are possible, especially in school holidays (and you can't book in advance). As there's limited free parking, you're encouraged to use the Cross Lakes Experience bus-and-launch service (from Bowness or Hawkshead). Hill Top's adjacent local pub, the *Tower Bank Arms*, incidentally, is also owned by the National Trust, and is the very model of an English country inn, used by Potter in *The Tale of Jemima Puddle-Duck*.

Keswick and Derwent Water

Standing on the shores of **Derwent Water** at the junction of the main north–south and east–west routes through the Lake District, the small market town of **KESWICK** makes a good base for exploring delightful Borrowdale to the south or the heights of Skiddaw (3053ft) and Blencathra (2847ft), which loom over the town to the north. It's a bustling place with plenty of accommodation, pubs and cafés, while several bus routes get you to the start of even the most challenging local hikes.

Arrival and information

Buses stop in front of Booths supermarket, off Main Street. Disc zones in town allow an hour or two's free parking, but you'll have to use the large signposted car parks if you're staying for the day. The **National Park Information Centre** is in the Moot Hall on Market Square (daily 9.30am–4.30/5.30pm; ☎017687/72645). George Fisher, at 2 Borrowdale Rd (Ⓦwww.georgefisher.co.uk), is one of the most celebrated **outdoors stores** in the Lakes, with a daily weather information service and terrific hiker's café, *Abraham's*. **Guided walks** – from lakeside rambles to mountain climbs – depart from the Moot Hall (Easter–Oct daily 10.15am; £10, longer walks £12); just turn up with a packed lunch. For **bike rental**, there's Keswick Mountain Bikes on Southey Lane (☎017687/75202, Ⓦwww.keswick mountainbikes.co.uk; from £20).

Accommodation

Standard **B&Bs** cluster along Bank and Stanger streets, near the post office, and around Southey, Blencathra and Eskin streets in the grid near the start of the A591 Penrith road. Smarter **guesthouses** line the street known as The Heads, overlooking Hope Park, a couple of minutes south of the centre on the way to the lake.

Café-Bar 26 26 Lake Rd ☎017687/80863, Ⓦwww .cafebar26.co.uk. Four stylish rooms offer a central chintz-free base. Downstairs is a funky café-bar with comfy sofas and good lunches (not Mon). ❸

Castlerigg Hall Rakefoot Lane, off A591, Castlerigg ☎017687/74499, Ⓦwww.castlerigg .co.uk. Not near the lake, but with views to compensate, this award-winning campsite is just over a mile southeast of the centre. Tents and camping pods (standard £34, family pod £39 per night) are kept well away from the caravans and motorhomes, and there's a shop, campers' kitchen and terrace restaurant. Closed Nov–Easter.

Derwentwater YHA Barrow House, Borrowdale, 2 miles south on the B5289 ☎0845/371 9314, Ⓔderwentwater@yha.org.uk. Hostel based in an old mansion with fifteen acres of grounds sloping down to the lake – the Borrowdale bus runs past and the Keswick Launch stops nearby. Dorm beds from £15.95.

Ellergill 22 Stanger St ☎017687/73347, Ⓦwww.ellergill.co.uk. A restored Victorian house with a chic European feel. There are five rooms with leather headboards and chairs, and a splash of deep colour, while magnificent Lakes photography brightens the breakfast room. No credit cards. ❷

Howe Keld 5–7 The Heads ☎017687/72417, Ⓦwww.howekeld.co.uk. The Fishers' boutique guesthouse puts local crafts and materials centre stage, with furniture and floors handcrafted from Lake District trees, plus green-slate bathrooms and Herdwick wool carpets. Breakfast incorporates home-baked organic bread, veggie rissoles and other specialities. ❹

Keswick YHA Station Rd ☎0845/371 9746, Ⓔkeswick@yha.org.uk. Keswick's town YHA, set in a converted woollen mill on the river, has a contemporary look after a major overhaul. The restaurant and bar offer good-value meals. Dorm beds from £17.95 (May–Sept from £21.95), breakfast included.

Powe House Portinscale, 2 miles west, off the A66 ☎017687/73611, Ⓦwww.powehouse.com. For stylish B&B on a budget, you can't beat this detached country house near the head of the lake, where bright, light rooms overlook the gardens. ❸

Ravensworth 29 Station St ☎017687/72476, Ⓦwww.ravensworth-hotel.co.uk. Small town-centre hotel that makes a real effort to please. Lakeland lilies adorn the lounge, while breakfast includes organic tomatoes, locally sourced meats, free-range eggs and the like. ❸

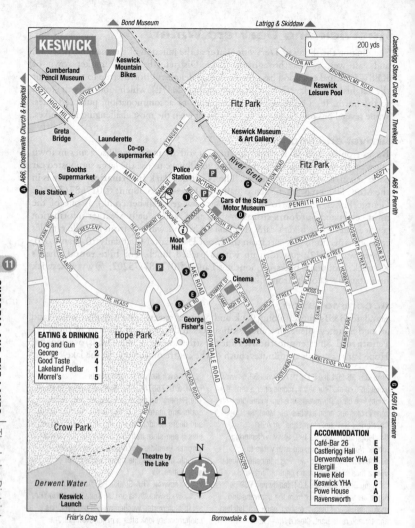

Bond Museum ▲   Latrigg & Skiddaw ▲

KESWICK

0   200 yds

Castlerigg Stone Circle & ▶
Threlkeld ▶

A66 & Penrith ▶

G A591 & Grasmere ▶

Cumberland Pencil Museum
Keswick Mountain Bikes
STATION AVE
BRUNDHOLME ROAD
Keswick Leisure Pool
Fitz Park

SOUTHEY LANE
A5271 HIGH HILL

Greta Bridge
Launderette
Co-op supermarket
STANGER ST.
GRETA SIDE
River Greta
Keswick Museum & Art Gallery
Fitz Park

A66: Crosthwaite Church & Hospital ◀

Booths Supermarket
Bus Station ★
MAIN ST
BANK ST
Police Station
B
OTLEY RD
VICTORIA ST
PACKHORSE CT
P
C

THE CRESCENT
THE HEADLANDS
DERWENT CT
MARKET SQUARE
1
NEW ST
STANDISH ST
STATION ST
Cars of the Stars Motor Museum
D
PENRITH ROAD
A5271

THE HEADS
HEADS ROAD
LAKE RD
Moot Hall
2
BLENCATHRA
GRETA ST
WORDSWORTH STREET
STREET
HELVELLYN STREET
SKIDDAW ST.
ST HERBERT ST.

P
3 **4**
DERWENT ST.
Cinema
SOUTHEY ST.
LEONARD ST.
RATCLIFFE PLACE
ESKIN ST.

E
SEAMS
ST JOHN'S ST.
HIGH ST.
CHURCH STREET
CROSS ST.
ACORN ST.
MANOR PARK

Hope Park
F
5
LAKE ROAD
George Fisher's
St John's
AMBLESIDE ROAD
CASTLEHEAD

EATING & DRINKING
Dog and Gun   3
George   2
Good Taste   4
Lakeland Pedlar   1
Morrel's   5

BORROWDALE ROAD
HEADS ROAD
LAKE ROAD
B5289

P

Crow Park

P
Theatre by the Lake
N

Derwent Water
Keswick Launch

ACCOMMODATION
Café-Bar 26   E
Castlerigg Hall   G
Derwentwater YHA   H
Ellergill   B
Howe Keld   F
Keswick YHA   C
Powe House   A
Ravensworth   D

Friar's Crag ▼   Borrowdale & **H** ▼

11

CUMBRIA AND THE LAKES | The Lake District

The Town

Granted its market charter by Edward I in 1276 – **market day** is Saturday – Keswick was an important wool and leather centre until around 1500, when these trades were supplanted by the discovery of local graphite. Using the Italian idea of putting graphite into wooden holders, Keswick became an important pencil-making town, and remained so until the late eighteenth century, when the French discovered how to make pencil graphite cheaply and broke Keswick's monopoly. The **Cumberland Pencil Museum** at Greta Bridge (daily 9.30am–5pm; £3.25; Ⓦwww.pencilmuseum.co.uk) tells the story entertainingly.

In Fitz Park you'll find the **Keswick Museum and Art Gallery** (Easter–Oct Tues–Sat 10am–4pm; free), a gloriously quirky Victorian collection including (among other things) a set of lion's teeth, ancient dental tools, a 600-year-old mummified cat and the famous "musical stones" which sound in tune when you strike them. Make time, too, for a couple of churches: **St John's**, on St John's Street in the centre, where the novelist Sir Hugh Walpole (of Herries novels fame) is buried; and **Crosthwaite Church**, a fifteen-minute walk northwest of town over Greta Bridge, resting place of the poet Robert Southey.

By way of quite extraordinary contrast, the **Cars of the Stars Motor Museum**, on Standish Street (Easter–Nov daily, weekends only in Dec, plus Feb school hols 10am–5pm; £6; ⓦwww.carsofthestars.com), does no less than its name suggests. The original Batmobile, Emma Peel's Lotus Elan, Mad Max's Ford Falcon, the *Back to the Future* Delorean, Mr Bean's Mini – all of these and more are displayed in glorious incongruity in a restored garage in a Keswick backstreet. Incidentally, the James Bond cars, boats, buggies and props are now all on display in the sister **Bond Museum** (Easter–Oct daily 10am–5pm; £6; ⓦwww.thebondmuseum.com), up behind the Pencil Museum.

Local walks

Latrigg (1203ft), north of town, gets the vote for a quick climb (45min) to a fine viewpoint, while south of town the best half-day walk is to **Walla Crag** (1234ft) and back (5 miles; 4hr), via the wooded peninsula of **Friar's Crag** on Derwent Water. Also, you shouldn't miss Keswick's most mysterious landmark, **Castlerigg Stone Circle**, where 38 hunks of volcanic stone, the largest almost eight feet tall, form a circle a hundred feet in diameter, set against a magnificent mountain backdrop. From the end of Station Road, take the Threlkeld rail-line path (signposted by the *Keswick Country House Hotel*) and follow the signs. The rail path itself continues all the way to **Threlkeld**, three miles from Keswick, providing a delightful riverside walk with the promise of a drink at the end in one of Threlkeld's old pubs.

Derwent Water

The shores of **Derwent Water** lie five minutes' walk south of the centre along Lake Road. It's among the most attractive of the lakes, ringed by crags and studded with islets, and is most easily seen by hopping on the **Keswick Launch** (regular departures Easter–Nov daily, Dec–Easter weekends only; £9 round trip, or cheaper fares per stage, starting at £1.90; ⓦwww.keswick-launch .co.uk). There's also an enjoyable one-hour **evening cruise** (£9) in school summer holidays.

You can hop off the launch at any of the half a dozen piers on Derwent Water for a stroll, but if you've only got time for one hike, make it up **Cat Bells** (take the launch to Hawes End), a superb vantage-point (1481ft) above the lake's western shore – allow two and a half hours for the scramble to the top and a return to the pier along the wooded shore.

Eating, drinking and entertainment

Many of Keswick's **cafés**, **pubs** and **restaurants** cater to a walking crowd, which means large portions and few airs. There's a fair amount of **entertainment** throughout the year, including the jazz festival (ⓦwww.keswickjazzfestival .co.uk) and mountain festival (ⓦwww.keswickmountainfestival.co.uk), both in May, a **beer festival** in June, and the traditional **Keswick Agricultural Show** (August bank holiday; ⓦwww.keswickshow.co.uk). The **Theatre by the Lake** on Lake Road (☎017687/74411, ⓦwww.theatrebythelake.com) hosts drama, concerts and exhibitions, as well as a renowned spring literature festival, Words By The Water (ⓦwww.wayswithwords.co.uk).

Bassenthwaite Lake

Keswick's other lake is **Bassenthwaite**, a couple of miles northwest of town – there are regular buses along its eastern shore, including the #555 and the #73/73A, while the summer-season #74 "Osprey Bus" (all-day ticket £5) runs on a round-Bassenthwaite circuit from Keswick. You'll win any pub quiz if you know that Bassenthwaite is actually the only lake in the Lake District (all the others are known as waters or meres). Families will enjoy both **Mirehouse** stately home (Ⓦwww.mirehouse.com) and **Trotters World of Animals** (Ⓦwww.trottersworld.com), the latter a pioneering wildlife conservation project. There's also the unique attraction of the **Lake District ospreys** (Ⓦwww.ospreywatch.co.uk), which nest and breed each year on the Bassenthwaite shore below Dodd Wood. From a viewing platform at the wood you'll get to see the ospreys fishing and feeding (usually April to late Aug/Sept), or you can get even closer with the nest-cam at nearby **Whinlatter Forest Park**, west of Keswick along the B5292 (the Cockermouth–Buttermere road). This is also a great place for mountain-bikers (rental available), and there's a forest high-ropes Go Ape adventure course here too.

Cafés, restaurants and pubs

🍴 **Dog and Gun** 2 Lake Rd ☏017687/73463. The best pub in town is a real ale, open fire, dog-friendly kind of place, though many come just for the food – the house special is Hungarian goulash with dumplings (£8.50), made every day to a recipe handed down over the years.

George St John's St ☏017687/72076. Keswick's oldest inn has snug bars lined with pictures and curios, and wooden settles in front of the fire. There's a good bistro menu (mains £8–15), available in the restaurant or bar.

Good Taste 19 Lake Rd ☏017687/75973. Delectable deli downstairs, coffee house upstairs, serving classy snacks and meals (£3–7), from home-smoked trout to wild boar burgers. Closed Sun.

🍴 **Lakeland Pedlar** Henderson's Yard, Bell Close, off Main St ☏017687/74492. Keswick's best café serves a tasty range of Mediterranean/Tex-Mex wholefood veggie dishes, like falafel wraps or spicy chilli (£4–8). Daytime only, but also open for dinner (Thurs–Sat until 9pm) in school holidays.

Morrel's 34 Lake Rd ☏017687/72666. At Keswick's top spot, modern styles prevail – from duck on parsnip mash to salmon and *pak choi* salad (mains £11–17, plus Sunday *table d'hôte* menu from £13.95). It's the closest restaurant to the Theatre by the Lake and opens for pre-theatre meals. Dinner only, closed Mon.

Borrowdale

It is difficult to overstate the beauty of **Borrowdale**, with its river flats and yew trees, lying at the head of Derwent Water and overshadowed by Scafell Pike, the highest mountain in England. Public transport access from Keswick is by bus #77A (along the west side of Derwent Water) or #78 Borrowdale Rambler (along the B5289), with a **Borrowdale Day Rider** (from £5.60) giving a day's unlimited travel between Keswick and Seatoller on the #78. Accommodation in the valley also makes a good rustic alternative to staying in Keswick.

A couple of miles south of Keswick, the pier at Ashness Gate provides access to the steep climb to the photogenic **Ashness Bridge**. The minor road ends two miles further south at **Watendlath**, where you'll find an idyllic little tarn and tearooms. Back on the B5289, a signposted path heads to the **Lodore Falls**, a diversion only really worth it after sustained wet weather, while further south is the 1900-tonne **Bowder Stone**, a house-sized lump of rock scaled by way of a wooden ladder and worn to a shine on top by thousands of pairs of feet. Beyond lies the straggling hamlet of **Rosthwaite**, which is a popular base for walkers. Local B&Bs include *Yew Tree Farm* (☏017687/77675, Ⓦwww.borrowdaleherd wick.co.uk; no credit cards; closed Dec & Jan; ❸), favoured on occasion by Prince

Charles on incognito walking trips to the Lakes. There are also comfortable **rooms** at the hiker-friendly *Royal Oak Hotel* (☎017687/77214, ⓦwww.royaloakhotel .co.uk; ❺, includes dinner) though best address is *Hazel Bank* (☎017687/77248, ⓦwww.hazelbankhotel.co.uk; ❻), a country-house hotel set in serene gardens, where a candlelit dinner is included in the price.

Another mile up the valley, eight from Keswick, the bus ends its run at **SEATOLLER**, where *Seatoller House* (☎017687/77218, ⓦwww.seatollerhouse. co.uk; closed Dec–Feb; ❺ with dinner, except Tues) has rooms in an atmospheric seventeenth-century farmhouse. Virtually next door is the welcoming *Yew Tree* café (☎017687/77634; closed Nov to early March), where you can relax in the riverside garden with snacks, soups and cakes.

It's twenty minutes' walk from Seatoller down the minor road to **SEATHWAITE**, where there's a campsite and camping barn at *Seathwaite Farm* (☎017687/77394; bunk beds £6 per person), the hardcore hikers' favourite, last stop before the high fells. For England's highest peak, **Scafell Pike** (3205ft), the approach is through the farmyard and up to **Styhead Tarn** via Stockley Bridge; from the tarn the classic ascent is up the thrilling Corridor Route, then descending via Esk Hause – an arduous eight-mile (6hr) loop walk in all from Seathwaite.

Honister Pass, Slate Mine and Via Ferrata

From Seatoller the B5289 strikes up and over the dramatic **Honister Pass** (bus #77A comes this way). Slate quarrying was well established here by the mid-eighteenth century, and to get an idea of what traditional slate-mining entailed you can don a hard hat and lamp and join one of the hugely entertaining tours of **Honister Slate Mine** (visitor centre daily 9am–5pm; 3 or 4 daily tours, £9.75;

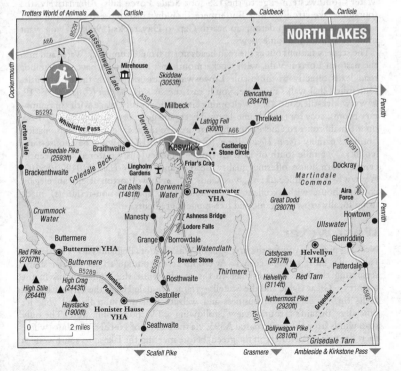

ⓣ017687/77230, ⓦwww.honister-slate-mine.co.uk) – England's last remaining working slate mine – which lead you through narrow tunnels into illuminated, dripping caverns. There's also a nerve-jangling, Alpine-style **Via Ferrata** (£25, all-day pass including mine tour £37; bookings on ⓣ017687/77714 or online) – or "Iron Way" – that guides visitors to the top of Fleetwith Pike (2126ft), above the mines, by means of a fixed cableway and harness. You'll be following the miners' old route up the exposed face of the mountain – and if you opt for the "zip" version of the climb (£35, all-day pass £48) you also get a heart-pounding zip-wire ride across a thousand-foot chasm for good measure.

Buttermere and around

From Honister Pass, the B5289 makes a dramatic descent into the **Buttermere Valley**. The direct bus is the #77 via Whinlatter Pass, while the #77A comes the long way around through Borrowdale, and with a Honister Day Rider ticket (from £6.50) you can use both services all day. At Buttermere village there's a seasonal café, a large car park and two **hotels**, the *Bridge* and the *Fish*, both with bar meals and beer gardens. Best choice on a hot day though is an ice cream from the tearoom at *Syke Farm*, made with milk from their Ayrshire cows. The **youth hostel**, *Buttermere YHA* (ⓣ0845/371 9508, ⓔbuttermere@yha.org.uk; dorm beds from £17.95, includes breakfast), overlooks the lake on the road to Honister Pass, while overlooking nearby Crummock Water, *Wood House* (ⓣ017687/70208, ⓦwww.wdhse.co.uk; no credit cards; closed Nov–March; ④) is an elegant **B&B**, set in woodland and with rowboat rental available.

From the village – set between the two expanses of Buttermere and neighbouring **Crummock Water** – there's an easy two-mile hike out along Crummock Water's southwestern edge to the 125-foot **Scale Force** falls. Alternatively, the four-mile lake stroll circling Buttermere shouldn't take more than a couple of hours; you can always detour up Scarth Gap to **Haystacks** (1900ft) if you want more of a climb and some views.

The scenery flattens out as the road heads north from Crummock Water and into the pastoral **Lorton Vale**, with Cockermouth just a few miles beyond. A minor road leads directly to minuscule **Loweswater**, around which there's a gentle, four-mile (2hr) walk. En route, you'll pass the ⚘ *Kirkstile Inn* (ⓣ01900/85219, ⓦwww.kirkstile.com; ④), a welcoming sixteenth-century place with contemporary rooms, cosy bar (with home-brewed beer) and good food (mains £9–12). Back on the main route to Cockermouth, there are two more excellent accommodation options, namely *New House Farm* (ⓣ07841/159818, ⓦwww.newhouse-farm .co.uk; ⑤), a mile south of **Low Lorton** – a meticulously restored seventeenth-century farmhouse offering quality B&B – and *Winder Hall* (ⓣ01900/85107, ⓦwww.winderhall.co.uk; ⑤, weekends ⑥), in Low Lorton itself, an elegant country house with excellent food (dinner £39, open to non-residents), made using locally grown, organic and free-range ingredients.

Wast Water

Nothing prepares you for the first sight of **Wast Water**, England's deepest lake and Lakeland's most remote corner. Awesome screes plunge to its eastern shore, separating the lake from Eskdale to the south, while the highest peaks in the country – Great Gable and the Scafells – frame Wasdale Head, the tiny settlement at its tip. As every local business and website will undoubtedly tell you, it's officially "Britain's favourite view", following a TV show public vote. The only road winds from the main coastal A595, via the hamlet of **Nether Wasdale** (where there are two small hotels on the green) before meeting the lake at its southwestern

tip at the *Wasdale Hall* **youth hostel** (℡0845/371 9350, ⒺΕ wastwater@yha.org
.uk; from £13.95), a country mansion set in its own lakeside grounds.

The road then hugs the shore of the lake, ending three miles away at **Wasdale
Head**, a Shangri-La-like clearing between the mountain ranges, where there's a
National Trust campsite (open all year; Ⓦwww.ntlakescampsites.org.uk) as well as
the marvellous ⚹ *Wasdale Head Inn* (℡01946/726229, Ⓦwww.wasdale.com; ❾), one
of the most celebrated of all Lakeland hostelries, serving hearty bistro meals in the bar
(£8–11) and a classy four-course dinner (£28) in the oak-panelled dining room.

Eskdale

Best approach to pretty **Eskdale** is from the coast via the Ravenglass & Eskdale
Railway (see p.678), which drops you at Dalegarth Station, right in the heart of
superb walking country around the hamlet of **Boot**. There's a café and bike rental at
the station, while three miles beyond Boot and 800 feet up, the remains of granaries,
bathhouses and the commandant's quarters for **Hardknott Roman Fort** (always
open; free) command a panoramic position. Beyond, over the narrow switchbacks of
Hardknott Pass, the road drops to Cockley Beck, before making the equally
alarming ascent of Wrynose Pass – this is the route back to Langdale and Ambleside.

There are a couple of pubs in Boot, though it's the first-rate ⚹ *Woolpack Inn*
(℡019467/23230, Ⓦwww.woolpack.co.uk; ❸), a mile east of the village on the
Hardknott Pass road, that really stands out – cosy rooms, a beer garden with views,
ale from the pub's own brewery and excellent food (home-smoked trout to
Cumbrian beef fillet; mains £12–18 dinner reservations advised).

Cockermouth

The attractive small town of **COCKERMOUTH** lies midway between the coast
and Keswick. There's a lot to admire about it – impressive Georgian facades, tree-
lined streets and riverside setting – and there's no shortage of local attractions, not
least the logical first stop on the Wordsworth trail. **Wordsworth House** on Main
Street (Easter–Oct Sun–Wed, plus Thurs during local school hols 11am–5pm;
£6.20; Ⓦwww.wordsworthhouse.org.uk) is where William and Dorothy Wordsworth were born and spent their first few years. Rather than a pure period piece it's
presented as a functioning eighteenth-century home – with a costumed cook willing
to share recipes in the kitchen and a clerk completing the ledger with quill and ink.
Afterwards, follow your nose and you're likely to stumble upon **Jennings Brewery**
on Brewery Lane near the river, where the hour-and-a-half-long tour (£6; booking
advisable on ℡0845/129 7190, Ⓦwww.jenningsbrewery.co.uk) culminates in a
real-ale tasting session. It's also always worth checking to see what's on at Castlegate
House (Mon, Fri & Sat 10.30am–5pm; free; Ⓦwww.castlegatehouse.co.uk), a
Georgian mansion and sculpture garden which supports a changing programme of
contemporary art displays, specializing in the work of regional artists.

Practicalities

There's stylish **accommodation** at *Six Castlegate*, 6 Castlegate (℡01900/826786,
Ⓦwww.sixcastlegate.co.uk; ❸), and *Croft House*, 6–8 Challoner St (℡01900/827533,
Ⓦwww.croft-guesthouse.com; closed Feb; ❷), both renovated Georgian houses.
Out of town (two miles southeast), you'll pass a quiet night at the *Old Homestead* at
Byresteads Farm, Hundrith Hill Road, off the B5292 (℡01900/822223, Ⓦwww
.byresteads.co.uk; ❸), a beautifully restored seventeenth-century farmhouse
offering quality B&B.

Merienda **café**, 7a Station St (℡01900/822790; daytime only, though open Fri
night for tapas and music; closed Sun), is the best place for breakfasts, sandwiches

and light meals, or drive out to the *Old Stackyard Tearooms* (℡ 01900/822777), a mile from town, for a family farm, tearoom and walks on the local nature reserve. Vegetarians come from far and wide for the fine-dining experience that is the *Quince and Medlar*, 13 Castlegate (℡ 01900/823579; dinner only, mains £13.95; closed Sun & Mon), while top **pub** is *The Bitter End* on Kirkgate (℡ 01900/828993), housing Cumbria's smallest brewery, and producing ales such as "Cockersnoot" and "Cuddy Lugs". The food is really good here too (mains £9–15), with all the meat sourced from Cumbrian farms.

Ullswater

Ullswater is the second longest lake in the national park (almost eight miles long), with a serpentine shape that's overlooked by soaring fells, none higher than Helvellyn (one of the Lakes' celebrated three-thousand-footers). It's a beautiful spot, with only a couple of small villages to break up the serene views, while some fine walks snake around the water's edge and through the local valleys. There's a year-round steamer cruise service from Glenridding, the chief lakeside settlement, while main public transport is the #108 bus from Penrith, which runs via Pooley Bridge and the celebrated waterfall of Aira Force. An **Ullswater Bus & Boat ticket** (from £13.80) is available for a day's travel between Penrith and Glenridding, using both bus and steamer.

Glenridding

The little village of **GLENRIDDING** features several inexpensive B&Bs, though it's at the *Inn on the Lake* (℡ 017684/82444, ⓦ www.lakedistricthotels.net/innonthelake; ⓞ) that you really begin to appreciate Ullswater's charms. The hotel's 15 acres of gardens stretch down to the water, and there's a lake-view restaurant (*table d'hôte* menu £35) and informal *Ramblers Bar*. The helpful **National Park Information Centre** (daily 9.30am–5.30pm; ℡ 017684/82414) is in the main car park, and there's **camping** and **bunkhouse** accommodation (from £10) half a mile up the valley at *Gillside Caravan & Camping* (℡ 017684/82346, ⓦ www.gillsidecampingandcaravansite.co.uk; no credit cards; closed Nov–Feb). Hikers wanting an early start on Helvellyn stay at *Helvellyn YHA* (℡ 0845/371 9742, ⓔ helvellyn@yha.org.uk; from £11.95; closed Dec), a mile and a half up the valley road from Glenridding.

Around the lake

At **Gowbarrow Park**, three miles north of Glenridding, the hillside still blazes green and gold in spring, as it did when the Wordsworths visited in April 1802; it's thought that Dorothy's recollections of the visit in her diary inspired William to

---

Climbing Helvellyn

The climb to the summit of **Helvellyn** (3114ft) forms part of a day-long circuit from Glenridding. The most frequently chosen approach is via the infamous **Striding Edge**, an undulating rocky ridge offering the most direct access to the summit. The classic return is via the less demanding and less exposed **Swirral Edge**, where a route leads down to **Red Tarn** – the highest Lake District tarn – then follows the beck down to Glenridding past Helvellyn youth hostel; the Swirral Edge route is also the best way *up* Helvellyn if you don't fancy Striding Edge. Either approach makes for around a seven-mile (5–6hr) round walk, though a good alternative descent (total walk 6hr) is to follow the flat ridge south from Helvellyn, past **Nethermost Pike** and **Dollywagon Pike**, after which there's a long scree scramble down to **Grisedale Tarn** and then the gentlest of descents down **Grisedale Valley**.

write his famous *Daffodils* poem. The tearooms (closed Nov–Easter) here mark the start of a brief walk up to **Aira Force** (40min round trip), a seventy-foot fall that's spectacular in spate.

Ullswater Steamers (℡017684/82229, ⓦwww.ullswater-steamers.co.uk) provide a year-round service from Glenridding to Howtown, halfway up the lake's eastern side (40min), and from Howtown to the pretty village of Pooley Bridge, at the northern end of the lake (20min). Any one stage costs £5.60 one-way, £9 return, though there's also a one-day "Freedom of the Lake Pass" (£12.30) as well as a "Walker's Ticket" (£10.70) that lets you travel in three separate stages.

HOWTOWN is tucked into a little clearing at the foot of beautiful Fusedale, where the *Howtown Hotel* has a pocket-sized hikers' bar around the back. A minor road from here hugs the eastern shore of the lake for four miles to **POOLEY BRIDGE**, passing the incomparable *Sharrow Bay* (℡017684/86301, ⓦwww .sharrowbay.com; ❽ with dinner) on the way, one of England's finest country-house hotels – afternoon tea here is a famously lavish affair. Pooley Bridge itself has several local campsites and three pubs, while best place for a lake view without spending a fortune is the *Brackenrigg Inn* (℡017684/86206, ⓦwww.brackenrigginn.co.uk; ❸), a traditional roadside inn at **WATERMILLOCK**, two miles to the west, whose menu emphasizes locally sourced produce, lamb hotpot to lake char (mains £10–18). Three miles north of Pooley Bridge, meanwhile, the *Gate Inn* at **YANWATH** (℡01768/862386; mains from £14) is a highly recommended gastropub, serving inventive dishes like Herdwick lamb in a smoked paprika and garlic marinade.

The Cumbrian coast

South and west of the national park, the Cumbrian coast attracts much less attention than the spectacular scenery inland, but it would be a mistake to write it off. The **Furness peninsulas** area (ⓦwww.lake-district-peninsulas.co.uk) lies only a few miles from Windermere, where varied attractions include the sleepy resort of **Grange-over-Sands**, the monastic priory at **Cartmel** and the pleasant market town of **Ulverston**. Parts of this region share nearby Lancashire's industrial heritage, and in the ship-building port of **Barrow-in-Furness** it's possible to see a slow revival that's only just starting to pay dividends in terms of tourism – though the dramatic ruins of **Furness Abbey** have been attracting visitors for almost two hundred years.

The **Cumbrian coast** itself begins at Silecroft near Millom and stretches for more than sixty miles to the small resort of Silloth, on the shores of the Solway Firth. The estuary village of Ravenglass is the access point for the **Ravenglass & Eskdale Railway**, though if you had to pick just one coastal destination the attractive Georgian port of **Whitehaven** would be the clear winner.

Grange-over-Sands and around

Before the arrival of the railways, the main route to the Lake District was the "road across the sands" from near Lancaster to **GRANGE-OVER-SANDS**. It may look benign, but the sands of Britain's second largest bay are treacherous and many lives have been lost here over the centuries (including, notoriously, a gang of Chinese cockle-pickers caught by the racing tide in 2004). Monks from Cartmel once led intrepid travellers safely across the bay, but from the sixteenth century onwards the route was considered so dangerous that an official guide was appointed by royal command. The tradition continues today and you can sign up for the eight-mile (3hr) cross-bay walk, in the company of the Queen's Guide, Cedric Robinson, at

Grange tourist office (☎015395/34026, ⓦwww.grange-over-sands.com). Walks usually depart every other week between May and September.

Grange itself is a genteel place of floral gardens fronted by a mile-long esplanade, with fine views of the bay. The local train line towards Lancaster offers a pleasant half-day out, running across the rail causeway in five minutes to the pretty bayside settlement of **Arnside**, where a couple of pubs look back at Grange. From the next stop, **Silverdale** (another 5min), you can walk back around the headland to Arnside in around two hours, past isolated stony coves and through the shoreline woods. Or film buffs can stay on one more stop to **Carnforth** (under 20min from Grange; ⓦwww.carnforthstation.co.uk), the station where Celia Johnson and Trevor Howard came over all misty-eyed in the classic David Lean film *Brief Encounter*. The station has been restored in 1940s style, while the refreshment room replicates the tearoom film set.

Cartmel and around

Sheltered several miles inland from Morecambe Bay, **CARTMEL** grew up around its twelfth-century Augustinian priory and is still dominated by the proud Church of St Mary and St Michael, the only substantial remnant to survive the Dissolution. Everything else in the village is modest in scale, centred on the attractive market square, with its Elizabethan cobbles and water pump. On the square, the **Cartmel Village Shop** sells the finest sticky-toffee pudding known to humanity, while the delightful **Cartmel Racecourse** (ⓦwww.cartmel-racecourse.co.uk) is the setting for fashionable race days for the county set each May and August bank holiday weekend.

A couple of miles west of Cartmel, **Holker Hall** (Easter–Oct daily except Sat, house open 11am–4pm, gardens 10.30am–5.30pm; £10, gardens only £6.50; ⓦwww.holker.co.uk) is one of Cumbria's finest stately homes, still in use by the Cavendish family who've owned it since the late seventeenth century. Only the New Wing of the house, rebuilt following a fire in 1871, is open to the public, though it's the impressive 25-acre **gardens** that are the real highlight, featuring sweeping views to the fells and estuary beyond. You don't have to pay the entrance fee in order to visit the excellent Food Hall and *Courtyard Café*, both of which are also open on Saturdays and in winter when Holker Hall is otherwise closed.

Practicalities

Apart from around race days, **accommodation** is easy to find though you will need to book in advance for Cartmel's extraordinary *L'Enclume* on Cavendish Street (☎015395/36362, ⓦwww.lenclume.co.uk; closed first 2 weeks Jan, restaurant closed Mon & Tues lunch; ❺), a highly individual Michelin-starred restaurant-with-rooms with artfully constructed menus at £55, £75 and £95. Chef Simon Rogan also has a casual dining offshoot, *Rogan & Company* on Devonshire Square (☎015395/35917; most dishes £6–15, lunch and dinner), whose bistro menu is beautifully presented and impeccably sourced (the local butcher and milkman get a salute on the blackboard). Meanwhile, there's organic farmhouse B&B at genial *Howbarrow Farm* (☎015395/35746; no credit cards; ❷) a couple of miles west of the village.

Ulverston

The railway line winds westwards to **ULVERSTON**, an attractive place enhanced by its dappled grey limestone cottages and a jumble of cobbled alleys and traditional shops zigzagging off the central **Market Place**. Stalls are still set up here and in the surrounding streets every Thursday and Saturday; on other days (not Wed or Sun), the **market hall** on New Market Street is the centre of commercial life.

Ulverston's most famous son is Stan Laurel (born Arthur Stanley Jefferson), the whimpering, head-scratching half of the comic duo, celebrated in a mind-boggling collection of memorabilia at the **Laurel and Hardy Museum** (daily 10am–4.30pm, closed Jan; £4; Ⓦ www.laurel-and-hardy-museum.co.uk), inside a rear entrance of the Roxy Cinema behind Coronation Hall. It's also worth checking what's on at the **Lanternhouse**, on The Ellers (Ⓦ www.lanternhouse .org), just off the A590 at the bottom of Market Street and across Tank Square (a traffic roundabout). Here, a group of multimedia artists known as Lanternhouse International present imaginative exhibitions, installations and concerts relating to the "participatory arts".

The 70-mile **Cumbria Way** (Ⓦ www.thecumbriaway.info) long-distance footpath from Ulverston to Carlisle starts from The Gill, at the top of Upper Brook Street – a waymarker spire marks the start. There's also a popular annual walking festival held each spring, with ten days of outdoor events, from one-mile strolls to all-day hikes. For a day-walk, pick up the leaflet at the tourist office detailing an 11-mile country-and-coast hike from town.

Practicalities

Ulverston **train station** is a few minutes' walk from the town centre – head down Prince's Street and turn right at the main road for County Square. **Buses** arrive on nearby Victoria Road, while the **tourist office** is in Coronation Hall on County Square (Mon–Sat 10am–4pm; ☏ 01229/587120).

Main choice for Cumbria Way walkers is the *Walker's Hostel* on Oubas Hill (☏ 01229/480511, Ⓦ www.walkershostel.co.uk; £17.50, including breakfast), fifteen minutes' walk from the centre on the A590 near Canal Head, at the foot of the Hoad Monument. Otherwise, let the *Bay Horse Hotel* (☏ 01229/583972, Ⓦ www.thebayhorsehotel.co.uk; ❹, April–Oct ❺), a cosy old inn on the Leven estuary a mile and a half out of town, lull you with gorgeous views and fine Cumbrian cuisine. There's either a monthly changing à la carte menu (mains around £23) or a more bistro-style two/three-course *table d'hôte* (£22/28). At the *Farmers Arms* pub in Market Place, fish is always a good choice (mains £10–15), while *Gillam's*, 64 Market St (daytime only), is an excellent tearoom that's wholly organic, Fair Trade and veggie.

Barrow-in-Furness and around

The gruff, industrial shipbuilding town of **BARROW-IN-FURNESS**, another six miles down the A590 from Ulverston, was once one of England's busiest ports. Despite a significant amount of town-centre regeneration it scarcely figures on anyone's Cumbrian itinerary, though its excellent free **Dock Museum** (Easter–Oct Tues–Fri 10am–5pm, Sat & Sun 11am–5pm; Nov–Easter Wed–Fri 10.30am–4pm, Sat & Sun 11am–4.30pm; Ⓦ www.dockmuseum.org.uk) is definitely worth a visit. Located in the dried-out graving dock where ships were once repaired, the enterprising museum tells the history of Barrow, which is also the history of modern shipbuilding, while popular family events are held here every summer. It's signposted throughout town, and from the train station.

Ruined **Furness Abbey** (April–June & Sept Mon & Thurs–Sun 10am–5pm; July & Aug daily 10am–5pm; Oct–March Sat & Sun 10am–4pm; £3.50; EH) lies a mile and a half out of Barrow on the Ulverston road, hidden in a wooded vale. Founded in 1124, the Cistercian abbey ran sheep farms on the fells, controlled fishing rights, produced grain and leather, smelted iron, dug peat for fuel and manufactured salt and even beer. It became such a prize that the Scots raided it twice, but it survived until April 1536 when Henry VIII chose it to be the first of the large abbeys to be dissolved.

The attacks by the Scots goaded Furness Abbey into protecting itself with Piel Castle on **Piel Island** (ⓌWww.pielisland.co.uk), reached from Roa Island, three miles southeast of Barrow down the A5087 – turn off at Rampside (signposted "Lifeboat station"). From here there's a seasonal weather- and tide-dependent **ferry** across to Piel Island, where the landlord of the island's *Ship Inn* is traditionally known as the King of Piel. The inn is currently under restoration (latest news on the island website), but there's still a bar open for visitors in summer while accommodation is planned for the future.

Whatever you feel about zoos, you're likely to be positively surprised by the **South Lakes Animal Park** (daily 10am–5pm; £11.50, Nov–Feb £8; ⓌWww .wildanimalpark.co.uk), five miles north of Barrow, just outside Dalton-in-Furness. An award-winning conservation zoo, it relies for the most part on ditches and trenches (not cages) to contain its animals and is split into separate habitat areas, ranging from the Australian bush to a tropical rainforest. It's quite something to encounter free-roaming kangaroos in rural Cumbria, while the Sumatran tiger-feeding (encouraging them to climb and jump for their meal) is unique in Europe.

Ravenglass and Muncaster

The single main street of **RAVENGLASS**, twenty miles or so up the coast from Barrow, preserves a row of characterful nineteenth-century cottages facing out across the estuarine mud flats and dunes. Despite appearances, the village dates back to the arrival of the Romans, who established a supply post here in the first century AD for the legions manning Hadrian's Wall. Nothing remains, save the ruins of the "Roman Bath House", 500 yards from the station up a single-track lane.

Cumbrian coastal-line trains stop at Ravenglass, which is also the starting point for the enjoyable **Ravenglass & Eskdale Railway** (March–Oct, at least 6 trains daily; trains also most winter weekends, plus Christmas, New Year and Feb half-term hols; £11.20 return; ☎01229/717171, ⓌWww.ravenglass-railway .co.uk). Opened in 1875 to carry ore from the Eskdale mines to the coastal railway, the 15-inch-gauge track winds seven miles up through the Eskdale Valley to Dalegarth Station near Boot. The full return journey takes an hour and forty minutes, though you can get off and walk from several intermediate stations, while a really good day out is to take your bike up on the train and cycle back from Dalegarth down the traffic-free **Eskdale Trail** (8.5 miles; 2hr) – there's also bike rental available at Dalegarth Station (half-day £8, full day £14) whenever the trains are running.

A mile east of Ravenglass on the A595 spreads the estate of **Muncaster Castle** (Feb half-term hols to first week of Nov; £11, £8.50 without castle entrance; ⓌWww.muncaster.co.uk). Apart from the ghost-ridden rooms of the castle itself (Mon–Fri & Sun noon–4.30pm), there are also seventy acres of well-kept **grounds and gardens**, as well as an **owl centre** (a breeding centre for endangered species) and **meadow vole maze** (each daily 10.30am–6pm or dusk). Here you can learn about the Muncaster voles, follow the hiking trails and see entertaining bird displays (daily 2.30pm) or wild herons feeding (4.30pm, 3.30pm in winter). The castle is closed in winter, though the grounds remain open in November and December for the illuminated Darkest Muncaster experience.

The best local **accommodation** is at 🎐 *The Pennington* (☎01229/717222, ⓌWww.penningtonhotels.com; ❺), a restored seafront hotel in Ravenglass that belongs to the castle; it has an excellent restaurant with a locally sourced menu (mains £9–15) including ingredients from Muncaster's kitchen gardens. There's also B&B at the castle itself (❸) in the converted stable block, while the *Ratty Arms* (☎01229/717676) at Ravenglass mainline train station is the place for a bar meal (£8–10) and pint of real ale.

Sellafield

The main blot on the Cumbrian coast is **Sellafield nuclear reprocessing plant**, midway between Ravenglass and Whitehaven. It's always been controversial, since the site was first developed in the 1950s to produce plutonium for Britain's early nuclear weapons programme. Today, Sellafield contains more than 200 separate nuclear facilities, including redundant defence work (ie, weapons) sites and Calder Hall, the world's first fully commercial nuclear power station (1957–2003). Sellafield was developed quickly at a time when little thought was given to nuclear waste treatment, which has necessitated the current clean-up and decommissioning project at what is, in any view, a dangerous industrial site. Unfortunately, returning Sellafield to a "safe, passive state" will cost billions of pounds and won't be complete until 2150 – none of which will help the government sell its current policy of promoting a new generation of "clean" British nuclear power stations, in an attempt to combat rising greenhouse gas emissions.

St Bees

A nunnery was established in the coastal village of **ST BEES** as early as the seventh century, and was succeeded in the twelfth by St Bees Priory, a structure that still stands today. Long sands lie a few hundred yards west of the village (there's a massive car park, bucket-and-spade shop and café), while the sandstone cliffs of **St Bees Head** to the north are good for windy walks and birdwatching. The headland's lighthouse marks the start of Alfred Wainwright's 190-mile **Coast-to-Coast Walk** to Robin Hood's Bay.

St Bees is on the Cumbrian coast train line and lies just five miles south of Whitehaven, from where there's also a regular bus service. There's good **accommodation** at *Fleatham House*, High House Road (℡01946/822341, ⓦwww.fleathamhouse .com; ❸), a lovely, informal retreat set in its own grounds just five minutes' walk from the station (first left off Main Street).

Whitehaven and the Solway Firth coast

Some fine Georgian houses mark out the centre of **WHITEHAVEN**, one of the few grid-planned towns in England and easily the most interesting destination on Cumbria's west coast. Economic expansion here in the eighteenth century was as much due to the booming slave trade as to the more widely recognized coal traffic, and all the local history is covered in **The Beacon** (Tues–Sun 10am–4.30pm; £5; ⓦwww.thebeacon-whitehaven.co.uk), an entertaining museum on the harbour, with interactive exhibitions on all floors on themes from slaving to smuggling. The **harbour** itself sits at the heart of a renaissance quayside project of promenades, sculptures and heritage trails, while the whole waterfront comes alive during the annual summer festival in June, which usually has a maritime bent. Finally, stroll up Lowther Street to the **Rum Story** (daily 10am–4.30pm; £5.45; ⓦwww.rumstory.co.uk), housed in the eighteenth-century courtyard and warehouses of the Jefferson's rum family. You could easily spend a couple of hours here, learning all about rum, the Navy, temperance and the hideousness of the slaves' Middle Passage, among other matters.

North of Whitehaven, past Workington, it's a fourteen-mile drive – the last part along the **Solway Firth coast** – to Maryport, another eighteenth-century port with a restored harbour and marina, this one featuring the handy rainy-day attraction that is the **Lake District Coast Aquarium** (daily 10am–5pm; £6.95; ⓦwww.lake district-coastaquarium.co.uk). Silloth, another thirteen miles north, is the Solway Firth's nicest small resort with its cobbled streets, seafront promenade, salt marshes and dunes. The **Solway Coast Discovery Centre** (Mon–Thurs 10am–4pm, Fri–Sun

⑪

CUMBRIA AND THE LAKES | The Cumbrian coast

10am–1pm & 2–4pm; £3.50; Ⓦwww.solwaycoastaonb.org.uk) here is another good family-friendly attraction, delving into the history and environment of this area of outstanding natural beauty. You can reach Maryport easily from Whitehaven on the Cumbrian coastal train line; for Silloth, there are daily buses (not Sun) from Maryport.

Practicalities

From the **train station** you can walk around the harbour to The Beacon in less than ten minutes. Buses use a variety of stops around town – Duke Street for St Bees and Ravenglass, Lowther Street for Cockermouth and Carlisle. The **tourist office** is in the Market Hall on Market Place (Mon–Sat 9.30am–4.30pm, plus Sun 11am–3pm in July & Aug; Ⓣ01946/598914, Ⓦwww.rediscoverwhitehaven.com), just back from the harbour. Whitehaven is the start of the 140-mile **C2C cycle route** to Sunderland/Newcastle – a metal cut-out at the harbour marks the spot.

For **accommodation**, pick of the B&Bs is 🌂 *Lowther House*, 13 Inkerman Terrace (Ⓣ01946/63169, Ⓦwww.lowtherhouse-whitehaven.com; ❸), a highly personal, period restoration of an old Whitehaven house with antique French beds and padded window seats. It's a ten-minute walk from the centre (up Lowther St, past the Esso garage) or it's on the way into town from the A595. Two miles north of town, *Moresby Hall* (Ⓣ01946/696317, Ⓦwww.moresbyhall.co.uk; ❺) also provides quality accommodation in an attractive manor house with walled gardens and dinner available (from £25).

Espresso, 22 Market Place (daytime only; Ⓣ01946/591548), Whitehaven's classic old-school espresso bar, is the place for frothy coffees, fry-ups and grills for under a fiver. Otherwise, the town's only real gastro destination is *Zest*, on Low Road (Ⓣ01946/692848; dinner only Wed–Sat; mains £14–17), three-quarters of a mile out of the centre on the B5349 Whitehaven–St Bees road. The sister café-bar, *Zest Harbourside*, on the harbour front, is open daily for superior sarnies, wraps, salads and bistro meals (£6–8).

East Cumbria: Penrith and the Eden Valley

The Lake District might end abruptly with the market town of **Penrith**, ten miles northeast of Ullswater, but Cumbria doesn't. To the east, the **Eden Valley** splits the Pennines from the Lake District fells, and boasts a succession of hardy market towns, prime among which is the former county town of **Appleby-in-Westmorland**. This lies on the magnificent **Settle–Carlisle Railway** (see box, p.718), connecting Cumbria with the Yorkshire Dales. Northeast of Penrith, the A686 leads imperceptibly from Cumbria into Teesdale via a string of offbeat attractions and the high town of **Alston** – a superbly scenic approach to Hexham and Hadrian's Wall.

Penrith and around

The thriving market town of **PENRITH** has more in common with the towns of the North Pennines than the stone villages of south Cumbria, and even the local building materials emphasize the geographic shift. Its deep-red buildings were erected from the same rust-red sandstone used to construct **Penrith Castle** (daily 7.30am–dusk; free) in the fourteenth century, as a bastion against raids from the north; it's now a romantic, crumbling ruin, opposite the train station. The town itself is at its best in the narrow streets, arcades and alleys off **Market Square**, and around **St Andrew's churchyard**, where the so-called "Giant's Grave" is actually a collection of tenth-century Viking crosses and Viking-influenced tombstones.

Potfest (ⓦwww.potfest.co.uk), Europe's biggest ceramics show, takes place in Penrith over two consecutive weekends (late July/early August), with **Potfest in the Park** held in the grounds of Hutton-in-the-Forest country house, followed by the highly unusual **Potfest in the Pens**. This sees potters displaying their creations in the unlikely setting of the cattle-pens at Penrith's cattle market, where the public can talk to the artists and even sign up for free classes.

Three miles southwest lies the country house of **Dalemain** (Feb half-term hols & Easter–Oct Mon–Thurs & Sun 11.15am–4pm, gardens & tearoom same days 10.30am–5pm; Nov to mid-Dec & early Feb–Easter gardens & tearoom only Mon–Thurs & Sun 11.15am–4pm; £9, gardens only £6; ⓦwww.dalemain.com). It started out in the twelfth century as a fortified tower, but has subsequently been added to by successive generations, culminating in the addition of a Georgian facade grafted onto a largely Elizabethan house. Visitors have the run of the public rooms, which the family still uses – hence the photographs and contemporary portraits alongside those of the ancestors – and the servants' corridors and pantries offer a glimpse of life "below stairs".

You also shouldn't miss **Rheged** (daily 10am–5.30pm; free; ⓦwww.rheged .com) at Redhills on the A66, a couple of minutes' drive from the M6 (junction 40); express buses between Penrith and Keswick stop outside. Billed as Europe's largest earth-covered building, it takes its name from the ancient kingdom of Cumbria and features a spectacular atrium-lit underground visitor centre, complete with exhibitions, craft displays, family activities, food hall, restaurant and café. The staple visit, though, is for the big-screen **3D cinema**, showing family-friendly 50-minute movies (£6.50, each extra film £3.50).

Practicalities

Penrith **train station** is five minutes' walk south of Market Square and the main street, Middlegate, while the **bus station** is on Albert Street, behind Middlegate. There are **car parks** signposted around town, though spaces are hard to come by on Tuesdays (market day). The **tourist office** is on Middlegate (Mon–Sat 9.30am–5pm, plus April–Oct Sun 10am–4pm; ☏01768/867466, ⓦwww.visiteden.co.uk).

Portland Place, behind the town hall, has a refined row of **guesthouses**, including the excellent *Brooklands*, 2 Portland Place (☏01768/863395, ⓦwww .brooklandsguesthouse.com; ❸). The traditional choice in town is the *George Hotel*, an old coaching inn by Market Square (☏01768/862696, ⓦwww.lake districthotels.net/georgehotel; ❺). For something more contemporary, drive three miles south down the A6 to Clifton's ⚘ *George and Dragon* (☏01768/865381, ⓦwww.georgeanddragonclifton.co.uk; ❹, superior rooms ❺), a revamped eighteenth-century inn with country-chic guest rooms and an informal bar and restaurant (around £25 for 3 courses), where pretty much everything is sourced from the adjacent Lowther Estate, from organic meat to kitchen-garden veg and herbs. Fifteen miles southeast, *Crake Trees Manor* at Crosby Ravensworth (☏01931/715205, ⓦwww.craketreesmanor.co.uk; closed Jan & Feb; ❹) is a super-stylish barn-conversion B&B in the Eden Valley.

Penrith to Alston

The main routes north from Penrith are the M6 and the rail line to Carlisle, but if you're heading for Hadrian's Wall the highly scenic A686 provides an alternative route into the North Pennines, via Alston.

The prehistoric stone circle known as **Long Meg and Her Daughters** is just outside Little Salkeld, six miles north of Penrith and just over a mile's walk from Langwathby on the Settle–Carlisle Railway. Standing outside a ring of stones nearly 400ft in diameter, Long Meg is the tallest stone at 12ft and has a profile like the face of an austere old lady. Little Salkeld itself is the location of the prettily sited **Little Salkeld Watermill** (daily 10.30am–5pm; closed Jan; free; Ⓦwww.organicmill.co.uk), producer of organic flour – the wholefood veggie tearoom here is worth a stop – while you can also detour into **LANGWATHBY** for the idiosyncratic **Eden Ostrich World** (daily 10.30am–3.30pm, closed Tues in winter; £5.95; Ⓦwww.ostrich-world.com). Chick-hatching season is May to October, though there's always something to do and see.

Back on the A686, it's worth making a point of stopping at **MELMERBY**'s marvellous *Village Bakery* (daily until 5pm; Ⓦwww.village-bakery.com), a pioneer in organic baking, where there's a really good café-restaurant. Having covered an initial stretch of smooth vales and aromatic pine woods, the road then winds steeply up **Hartside Top** (1900ft), which has a welcome café at its summit (closed weekdays Nov–March). Come here on a Sunday and you'll see half of the region's bikers parked up watching the other half zoom by.

Alston

Seven miles below Hartside Top, **ALSTON** commands the head of the South Tyne Valley. It no longer has a market but still has its market cross, beside the cobbled curve of the steep main road. It's a tidily restored town, and the convenient location between Cumbria and the northeast, plus its role as a hiking and biking hub, makes it a popular stopover. Families also come for the narrow-gauge **South Tynedale Railway** (school holidays daily, otherwise weekends and selected days only; £6 return, day-ticket £10; Ⓦwww.strps.org.uk), whose steam engines follow the route of an old coal-carrying branch of the Carlisle–Newcastle line.

There's plenty of local **accommodation** in all price ranges, starting with B&B at *Lowbyer Manor* (Ⓣ01434/381230, Ⓦwww.lowbyer.com; ❸), a Georgian house on the Hexham road, just a hundred yards or so beyond the train station. A town youth hostel caters for Pennine Way walkers, while a couple of miles east on the Nenthead road, the *Lovelady Shield Country House* (Ⓣ01434/381203, Ⓦwww.lovelady.co.uk; ❼ including dinner) is a beautiful Georgian establishment in mature grounds that serves excellent food.

Appleby-in-Westmorland

One-time county town of Westmorland, **APPLEBY-IN-WESTMORLAND** is protected on three sides by a lazy loop in the River Eden. The fourth was defended by the now privately owned **Appleby Castle**, whose Norman keep was restored

Women wanted

Alston hit the headlines in 2005 when a group of local young men – despairing at the paucity of suitable mates – launched the **Alston Moor Regeneration Society** in an attempt to attract women to move to this isolated rural outpost. Their lonely hearts plea struck a chord, as the national press ran with the story and Channel 4 made a documentary on "the town that's looking for love". Gimmick or not, the campaign said something serious about the problems facing many similar towns in the UK, where young locals move away for work – though whether or not Alston really is "the Ibiza of the north" (one of the enticements offered) is for you to decide.

⑪

by Lady Anne Clifford. It's currently closed to the public, but you can pursue the Lady Anne trail at the lovely **almshouses** she founded. These are on Boroughgate, the town's backbone, which runs from High Cross, former site of the cheese market outside the castle, down to Low Cross, previously a butter market but now home of the general Saturday market. **St Lawrence's Church** meanwhile, at Low Cross, holds the tombs of Lady Anne Clifford and her mother.

Practicalities

The **Settle–Carlisle Railway** (Ⓦ www.settle-carlisle.co.uk) is the best way to get to Appleby, although **bus services** from Penrith (#563, every 2–3hr, not Sun) are frequent enough. The **tourist office**, in the Moot Hall on Boroughgate (April–Oct Mon–Sat 9.30am–5pm, Sun 11am–3pm; Nov–March Mon–Thurs 10am–1pm, Fri & Sat 10am–3pm; ☎ 01768/351177, Ⓦ www.applebytown.org .uk), is ten minutes' walk from the station, across the river.

There are a couple of **B&Bs** on Bongate, 500 yards (10min walk) from town, over the river from Low Cross, then south along the Brough road. Also along here you'll find the *Royal Oak* (☎ 01768/351463, Ⓦ www.royaloakappleby.co.uk; ❸), an old inn with some comfortably refurbished rooms, while top hotel in town is the *Tufton Arms* on Market Square (☎ 01768/351593, Ⓦ www.tuftonarmshotel.co.uk; ❹).

Cafés and tearooms in town soak up much of the passing trade, while there's brasserie-style food (mains from £10) at the *Royal Oak*.

Carlisle and around

The county capital of Cumbria and its only city, **CARLISLE** is also the repository of much of the region's history, as it was battled over for more than two thousand years due to its strategic location. The original Celtic settlement was superseded by a Roman town, whose first fort was raised in 72 AD. Carlisle thrived during the construction of Hadrian's Wall and then, long after the Romans had gone, the Saxon settlement was repeatedly fought over. The struggle with the Scots in particular defined the very nature of Carlisle as a border city: William Wallace was repelled in 1297 and Robert the Bruce eighteen years later, but Bonnie Prince Charlie's troops took the city in 1745 after a six-day siege, holding it for six weeks before surrendering to the Duke of Cumberland.

It's not surprising, then, that the city touts itself as "historic Carlisle", and nearby **Talkin Tarn**, the ruins of **Lanercost Priory** and the only surviving bit of Hadrian's Wall in Cumbria, at **Birdoswald Fort**, are all worth a stop. Carlisle is also the terminus of the historic Settle–Carlisle Railway, and Edinburgh is reachable in under two hours.

Arrival and information

From either the **train station** or the **bus station**, it's a five-minute walk to the **tourist office** in the old town hall (Mon–Sat 9.30/10am–4/5.30pm, plus May–Aug Sun 10.30am–4pm; ☎ 01228/625600, Ⓦ www.historic-carlisle.org .uk), where you can find out about **guided tours** highlighting various aspects of the city – medieval and modern Carlisle, say, or a tour of sights associated with Woodrow Wilson, 28th president of the United States, whose mother was born here. Cultural **entertainment** revolves around the concerts, performances, exhibitions and workshops at Tullie House, while the big annual music festival is **Brampton Live** every July (Ⓦ www.bramptonlive.net), a three-day world, folk and roots extravaganza outside the city at Brampton.

Accommodation

Most budget **accommodation** is concentrated in a conservation area in the streets between Victoria Place and Warwick Road. There's also summer-only YHA accommodation in a university hall of residence near the castle.

Acorn Bank Wetheral, 4 miles east of Carlisle, off A69 ℡01228/561434, ⓦwww.acornbank.co.uk. Two lovely rooms available at a country guesthouse in a pretty village. The owners (former restaurateurs) offer dinner on request (£26), as well as cookery demonstrations. No credit cards. ❹

Hallmark Court Square ℡01228/531951, ⓦwww .hallmarkhotels.co.uk. Right outside the train station, the boutique-style *Hallmark* boasts a chic look, sleek rooms with big beds and a contemporary bar and brasserie serving tapas, mussels, pasta and grills (dishes £10–16). ❹

Langleigh House 6 Howard Place ℡01228/530440, ⓦwww.langleighhouse.co.uk.

Nicely presented Victorian townhouse B&B with eight rooms, including a family room that sleeps four. No credit cards. ❸

The Weary Castle Carrock, Brampton, 8 miles east of Carlisle ℡01228/670230, ⓦwww.theweary.com. The inn with the "wow" factor – traditional eighteenth century outside, utterly contemporary (yet unstuffy and informal) inside. Rooms have rich colours and fabrics, and bathrooms with glass basins and inset bath-side TV screens, while a handsome bar-restaurant provides classy dining (bistro meals from £8.50, restaurant mains from £13). ❺

The City

Carlisle's main thoroughfare, **English Street**, is pedestrianized as far as the expansive **Green Market** square, formerly heart of the medieval city, though a huge fire in 1392 destroyed its buildings. The Lanes shopping centre on the east side of the square – its "alleys" lit through a cast-iron-and-glass roof – stands where the medieval city's lanes once ran. Otherwise, the only historic survivors are the **market cross** (1682), the Elizabethan former **town hall** behind it, which now houses the tourist office and, at the southern end of Fisher Street, the timber-framed **Guildhall** (1405).

It's only a few steps along to **Carlisle Cathedral** (Mon–Sat 7.30am–6.15pm, Sun 7.30am–5pm), founded in 1122 but embracing a considerably older heritage. Christianity was established in sixth-century Carlisle by St Kentigern (often known as St Mungo), who became the first bishop and patron saint of Glasgow. Parliamentarian troops during the Civil War caused great destruction, but there's still much to admire in the ornate fifteenth-century choir stalls and the glorious **East Window**, which features some of the finest medieval stained glass in the country. Opposite the main entrance, the reconstructed **Fratry**, or monastic building, houses the *Prior's Kitchen*, a café (9.45am–3.45pm, closed Sun) in what was once the monks' dining hall.

For the lowdown on Carlisle's history, head for the wonderful **Tullie House Museum and Art Gallery** (Mon–Sat 10am–4/5pm, Sun 11am/noon–4/5pm; £5.50; ⓦwww.tulliehouse.co.uk), reached via Castle Street or Abbey Street. This takes a highly imaginative approach to Carlisle's turbulent past, with special emphasis put on life on the edge of the Roman Empire – climbing a reconstruction of part of Hadrian's Wall, you learn about catapults and stone-throwers, while other sections elaborate on domestic life, work and burial practices. There are also changing exhibitions, art shows, and innovative displays devoted to local geology, archeology and architecture, plus a café overlooking the gardens and Monday night art-house movies.

The other historic jewel is **Carlisle Castle** (daily 9.30/10am–4/5pm; £4.50; EH), reached by a public walkway from outside Tullie House. With a thousand years of military occupation of the site, it's loaded with significance – not least as the place where, in 1568, Elizabeth I kept Mary, Queen of Scots, as her "guest".

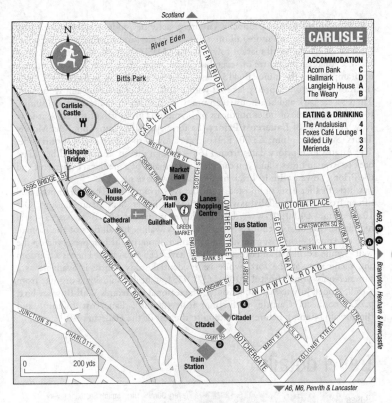

Guided tours (Easter–Oct daily; ask at the entrance) help bring history to life – don't leave without climbing to the battlements for a view of the Carlisle rooftops.

Eating and drinking

The Carlisle restaurant and bar scene has improved immeasurably over the last few years, and there are now plenty of reasonable options, particularly around the Warwick Road/Lowther Street axis.

The Andalusian Warwick Rd ☎01228/810214.
The gorgeous tile-work, carved oak bar, big sofas and fireplaces make for a relaxed meet-and-greet bar, with tapas (£3–7) to share over drinks.
Foxes Café Lounge 18 Abbey St
☎01228/536439. Amiable, idiosyncratic café-bar with an alternative vibe, featuring cakes, bakes and panini for around a fiver, plus film and music nights, exhibitions and events. Daytime only, though also open Fri & Sat nights; closed Sun & Mon.

Gilded Lily 6 Lowther St ☎01228/593600.
Fabulous-looking restaurant and lounge-bar (open until 1am most nights) serving cosmopolitan food at lunch and dinner, noodles to local lamb, burgers to piri-piri prawns (£8–15).
Merienda 12 Treasury Court ☎01228/595259.
Best place for a quality lunch is this superior café-bar with a glass-house extension in a tucked-away alley, where freshly made sandwiches, soups, stews and salads go for around £5–6.

Around Carlisle

Families make a beeline for **Walby Farm Park** (daily 10am–6pm; £5.95; ⓦwww .walbyfarmpark.co.uk), four miles northeast of Carlisle (A689, Brampton road), which combines animal paddocks, childrens' activities, indoor and outdoor play areas, nature trails and more, all on a huge working farm in rolling countryside. Otherwise, it's the small market town of **BRAMPTON** itself, eight miles east of Carlisle, that's at the centre of several other outlying attractions. Two miles south of Brampton, on the minor B6413 (Castle Carrock road), **Talkin Tarn** is the city's traditional bolthole, a pretty lake set within 160 acres of meadow and woodland. There's a car park and boathouse tearoom, with the tarn ringed by an easy (30min) footpath. A couple of miles northeast of Brampton (just north of the A69, at Low Row), the ruins of **Lanercost Priory** (Easter–Sept daily 10am–5pm; Oct Mon & Thurs–Sun 10am–4pm; £3.20; EH) occupy a lovely spot deep in the countryside. The Augustinian priory dates from 1166 – though carved stones found here date back to Roman times – and you can view the remains of a medieval undercroft and the Prior's Tower, with its brick fireplace and ovens *in situ*.

A little further east, signposted from the A69 five miles beyond Brampton and fifteen from Carlisle – **Birdoswald Fort** (daily: Easter–Sept 10am–5.30pm; Oct 10am–4pm; £4.80; ⓦwww.birdoswaldromanfort.org.uk) is the area's real highlight. One of sixteen forts along Hadrian's Wall, it has all tiers of the Roman structure intact – the east gateway, in particular, is one of the best preserved on the wall – while a drill hall and other buildings have been excavated. There's a tearoom and picnic area at the fort, while its residential study centre is available as a summer-only **youth hostel** (ⓣ0845/371 9551, ⓔbirdoswald@yha.org.uk; from £13.95), open July to September only. The seasonal **Hadrian's Wall Bus** (see box, p.772) connects Carlisle with Brampton (20min), Lanercost (30min) and Birdoswald (40min), before continuing to the rest of the Hadrian's Wall sights.

Travel details

Buses

For information on all local and national bus services, contact Traveline ⓣ0871/200 2233, ⓦwww.traveline .info.

Carlisle to: Keswick (3 daily; 1hr 10min); Windermere/Bowness (3 daily; 2hr 20min).

Cross Lakes Experience (Lake District): up to 9 daily services; launch from Bowness connects with minibus from Sawrey to Hill Top (7min) and Hawkshead (15min); connections at Hawkshead for Grizedale Forest (25min). Service daily Easter–Oct.

Kendal to: Ambleside (hourly; 40min); Grasmere (hourly; 1hr); Keswick (hourly; 1hr 30min); Lancaster (hourly; 1hr); Windermere/Bowness (hourly; 30min).

Keswick to: Ambleside (hourly; 45min); Buttermere (2 daily; 30min); Carlisle (3 daily; 1hr 10min); Cockermouth (every 30min–1hr; 30min); Grasmere (hourly; 40min); Honister (Easter–Oct 4 daily; 40min); Kendal (hourly; 1hr 30min); Rosthwaite

(every 30min–1hr; 25min); Seatoller (every 30min–1hr; 30min); Windermere (hourly; 1hr).

Windermere to: Ambleside (hourly; 15min); Bowness (every 20–30min; 15min); Carlisle (3 daily; 2hr 20min); Grasmere (every 20–30min; 30min); Kendal (hourly; 25min); Keswick (hourly; 1hr).

Trains

For information on all local and national rail services, contact National Rail Enquiries ⓣ08457/484950, ⓦwww .rail.co.uk.

Appleby-in-Westmorland to: Carlisle (7 daily; 45min).

Carlisle to: Appleby (7 daily; 45min); Barrow-in-Furness (5 daily; 2hr 20min); Lancaster (every 30min–1hr; 1hr); Newcastle (hourly; 1hr 20min–1hr 40min); Whitehaven (hourly; 1hr 10min).

Windermere to: Kendal (hourly; 15min) and Oxenholme (hourly; 20min) for onward services to Lancaster and Manchester, or Penrith and Carlisle.

12

Yorkshire

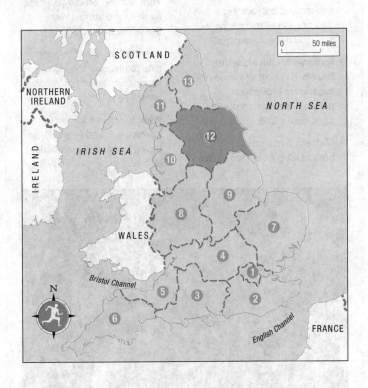

CHAPTER 12

Highlights

* **Winter Garden, Sheffield** Award-winning modern take on a Victorian glasshouse, home to 2000 exotic plants. See p.695

* **Royal Armouries, Leeds** The Tower of London's unique collection, not just the weapons and armour, but jousting, falconry and all manner of swashbuckling. See p.703

* **National Media Museum, Bradford** A host of hands-on experiences for couch potatoes and film fans of all ages. See p.708

* **Malham** Make the breathtaking hike from Malham village to the glorious natural amphitheatre of Malham Cove. See p.717

* **Turkish Baths, Harrogate** The ultimate in personal pampering, among splendid Victorian tilework. See p.730

* **York Minster** Medieval Gothic masterpiece stuffed with treasures. See p.735

* **Jorvik, York** Travel through time to discover the sights, sounds and smells of Viking York. See p.738

* **Whitby** Picturesque port, atmospheric abbey and Bram Stoker's Dracula. Irresistible. See p.761

▲ Winter Garden, Sheffield

Yorkshire

t's easy to be glib about **Yorkshire** – for much of the country, England's largest county is shorthand for "up north" and all its clichéd connotations, from flat caps and factories to tightfisted locals. For their part, many Yorkshire born-and-bred are happy to reinforce the prejudice of southerners, calling it "God's Own County". In its sheer size at least, Yorkshire does have a case for primacy, while its most striking characteristics – from dialect to landscape – derive from a long history of settlement, invention and independence that's still a source of pride today. For every grim suburb and moribund mill there are acres of rolling valley, national park upland and glorious coast, riddled with Viking place-names, medieval abbeys, English Civil War battle sites, and the country homes of nobles and industrialists. As for Yorkshire's other boasts (the beer's better, the air's cleaner, the people are friendlier than "down south" and so on), visitors can make up their own minds.

Yorkshire was once divided into three regions called "**ridings**" (North, East and West), from the Old Norse for "third part", which correspond roughly with the modern divisions of North, East and West Yorkshire, plus South Yorkshire which abuts the Peak District and East Midlands. Differently named administrative authorities confuse the issue further for locals, but for visitors the divisions are a handy guide to the main cities and attractions – South Yorkshire for Sheffield, West Yorkshire for Leeds, Bradford and Haworth, East Yorkshire for Hull, and North Yorkshire for York, moors, dales and coast.

The number-one Yorkshire destination is undoubtedly history-soaked **York**, for centuries England's second city until the Industrial Revolution created new centres of power and influence. York's mixture of medieval, Georgian and Victorian architecture is mirrored in miniature in the prosperous north and east of the county by towns such as **Beverley**, centred on another soaring minster; **Richmond**, banked

Regional transport

Fast **train** services on the East Coast main-line link York to London, Newcastle and Edinburgh. Leeds is also served by regular trains from London, and is at the centre of the integrated Metro bus and train system that covers most of West and South Yorkshire. There are also train services to Scarborough (from York) and Whitby (from Middlesbrough), while the **Settle–Carlisle** line, to the southern and western Yorkshire Dales, can be accessed from Leeds. The **North Country Rover** ticket (any four days in eight; £72) covers unlimited train travel north of Leeds, Bradford and Hull and south of Newcastle and Carlisle. Picturesque private lines with steam trains make good days out, notably the **Keighley & Worth Valley Railway** line to Haworth and the **North Yorkshire Moors Railway** between Pickering and Grosmont.

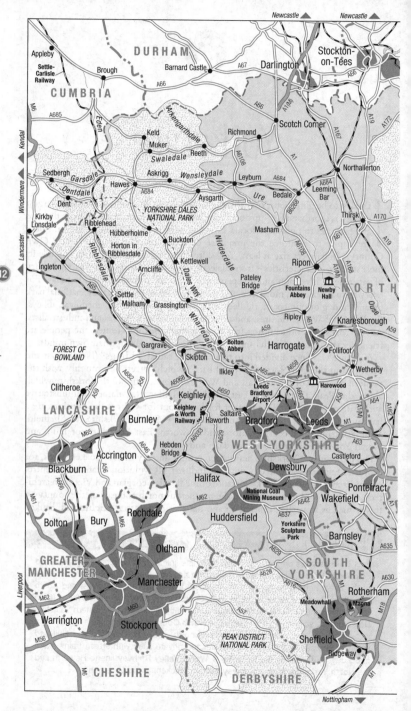

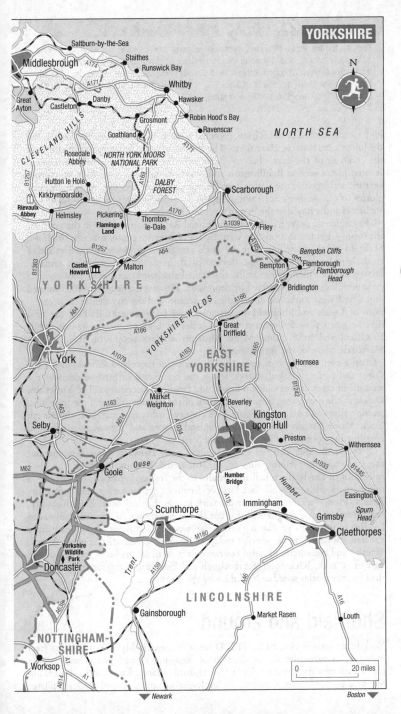

under a crag-bound castle; **Ripon**, gathered around its honey-stoned cathedral; and the historic spa town of **Harrogate**. The Yorkshire coast, too, retains something of the grandeur of the days when its towns were the first to promote themselves as resorts: places such as **Bridlington** and **Scarborough** boomed in the nineteenth century and again in the postwar period, though these days they're living on past glories. It's in smaller resorts with unspoiled historic centres such as **Whitby** and **Robin Hood's Bay** that the best of the coast is to be found today.

The engine of growth during the Industrial Revolution was not in the north of the county, but in the south and west. By the nineteenth century, Leeds, Bradford, Sheffield and their satellites were the world's mightiest producers of textiles and of steel. Ruthless economic logic devastated the area in the twentieth century, leaving only disused textile mills, abandoned steelworks and great soot-covered civic buildings in cities battered by depression. However, a new vigour has infused South and West Yorkshire during the last decade, and the city-centre transformations of **Leeds** and **Sheffield** in particular have been remarkable. Both are now making open play for tourists with a series of high-profile attractions, while **Bradford** and its National Media Museum waylays people on their way to **Haworth**, home of the Brontë sisters.

During even the worst of times, broad swathes of moorland survived above the slum- and factory-choked valleys, and it can come as a surprise to discover the amount of open countryside on Leeds' and Bradford's doorsteps. The **Yorkshire Dales**, to the northwest, form a patchwork of stone-built villages, limestone hills, serene valleys and majestic heights. The county's other national park, the **North York Moors**, is divided into bleak upland moors and a tremendous rugged coastline between Robin Hood's Bay and Staithes.

Of the predictable roster of stately homes **Castle Howard** stands supreme, but there are also imperious relics of the Industrial Revolution, from the civic splendour of Leeds' town hall and arcades to the Italianate pastiche of **Saltaire**, a millworkers' village on the outskirts of Bradford. In an earlier age, before the Reformation, Yorkshire had more monastic houses than any other English county, centres not only of religious retreat but also of a commercial acumen that was to lay the foundations of the region's great woollen industry. Many beautifully situated **monastic ruins** survive today at Fountains, Rievaulx, Bolton Abbey, Whitby and elsewhere, graceful counterpoints to the more solid remains of the **castles** at York, Richmond, Scarborough and Pickering – the foremost of more than twenty castles raised in Yorkshire by the Normans.

Sheffield and around

Yorkshire's second city, **SHEFFIELD** remains inextricably linked with its steel industry, in particular the production of high-quality cutlery. As early as the fourteenth century, the carefully fashioned, hard-wearing knives of hard-working Sheffield enjoyed national repute. Technological advances in steel production later turned the city into one of the country's foremost centres of heavy and specialist engineering. The city suffered heavy bombing in World War II, yet several of its grand civic buildings emerged remarkably unscathed. More damaging though to the city's pre-eminence was the steel industry's subsequent downturn, which by the 1980s had tipped parts of Sheffield into dispiriting decline.

The subsequent economic and cultural revival has been rapid, with the centre in particular – the part, after all, that most tourists see – utterly transformed by flagship architectural projects. As a city-break destination, Sheffield can't fail to surprise, and with the Peak District so close (over a third of the city lies within its boundary), it's easy to escape for the day. A glut of sports facilities backs Sheffield's claim to be considered "National City of Sport". Meanwhile, the city's two universities and large student population lend the alternative shopping, café and nightlife scene a welcome edge.

Steel, of course, still underpins much of what Sheffield is about. The city that gave the world *The Full Monty* – the black comedy about five former steelworkers carving out a new career as a striptease act – also boasts **Meadowhall** shopping centre, located on the site of an old steelworks and billed as one of Europe's biggest malls – it's either Meadowheaven or Meadowhell depending on your point of view. Museum collections tend to specialize in the region's industrial heritage, which is complemented by the startling science-and-adventure exhibits at **Magna** built in a disused steelworks at nearby **Rotherham**.

Arrival and information

Parking is signposted throughout the city from the ring road. Sheffield's **train station** is on the eastern edge of the city centre, by Sheffield Hallam University, with the bus and coach station, known as **Sheffield Interchange**, about two hundred yards to the north – the two are clearly linked, while following Howard Street from the station takes you straight up to the city centre, emerging at Millennium Square. The **tourist office** is just north of here, at 14 Norfolk Row (Mon–Fri 10am–5pm, Sat 10am–4pm; ℡0114/221 1900, ⓦwww.yorkshiresouth.com).

Most local **buses** depart from High Street or Arundel Gate, while the **Supertram** system (ⓦwww.supertram.com) connects the city centre with Meadowhall (northeast), Middlewood (northwest) and Halfway (southeast). For fare and timetable information, visit the **Mini Interchange** travel centre on Arundel Gate, behind the Crucible Theatre (Mon–Fri 7am–6pm, Sat 9am–5pm; ℡01709/515151 or 0114/201 2675, ⓦwww.sypte.co.uk). A Day Tripper (£5.80) gives unlimited travel on buses, trains and trams throughout South Yorkshire.

Accommodation

Sheffield has a fair amount of mid-range central accommodation – even so, the tourist office's room-booking service can come in handy (℡0871/700 0121), especially if you're looking for cheaper **B&Bs** on the outskirts. Self-catering **student rooms** in the Devonshire Quarter (late June to mid-Sept) can be booked through the University of Sheffield (℡0114/289 3500, ⓦwww.victoriahall.com; from £22.50 per night), while a night in the central *Ibis* or *Premier Travel Inn* costs from £50.

Houseboat Hotels Victoria Quays ℡0114/232 6556 or 07974/590264, ⓦwww.houseboathotels.com. Something a little bit different – three moored houseboats, available by the night, very nicely styled, all with en-suite bathrooms and kitchens. Tea and coffee are provided, continental breakfast can be arranged

(£8 extra), parking is included, and there's use of the nearby *Hilton*'s leisure centre. ❷

Leopold 2 Leopold St ℡0114/252 4000, ⓦwww.leopoldhotel.co.uk. Billed as Sheffield's first boutique hotel, the *Leopold* occupies a Grade II-listed building (once a boys' grammar school), the keynote of which is solid luxury allied to quirkiness – many original features have been kept and whimsical touches added. Backs onto tiny but beautifully remodelled Leopold Square, which boasts plenty of places to eat. Limited parking. Breakfast not included. ④

Mercure St Paul's 119 Norfolk St ⓣ 0114/278 2000, ⓦ www.mercure.com. An up-to-the-minute hotel on Millennium Square, with restaurant adjoining the Winter Garden. Bedrooms are minimalist and neutral in tone. Leisure facilities include indoor pool, spa and sauna. ④

Park Inn Blonk St ⓣ 0114/220 4000, ⓦ www.parkinn.co.uk. Breezy, informal business hotel near the river, quays and markets, with a good bar and restaurant. All rooms are stylishly furnished, some with futons – handy for families. Parking. ③

The city centre

New-look Sheffield is at its best around the **Town Hall**, at the junction of Pinstone and Surrey streets. Completed in 1897, it's topped by the figure of Vulcan, the Roman god of fire and metalworking, and the facade sports a fine frieze depicting traditional Sheffield industries. The adjacent **Peace Gardens** feature central water jets that whoosh up intermittently to send children giddy with delight, while rising to the east, a minute's walk away, is the main symbol

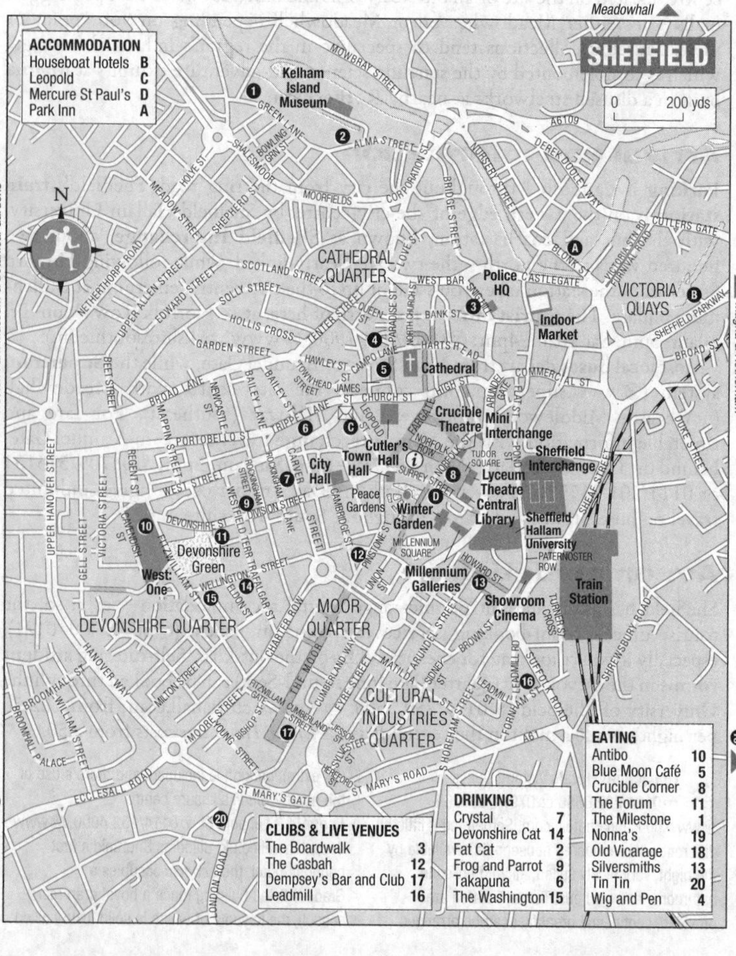

Meadowhall
SHEFFIELD
0 200 yds
ACCOMMODATION
Houseboat Hotels B
Leopold C
Mercure St Paul's D
Park Inn A
N
Kelham Island Museum
MOWBRAY STREET
GREEN LANE
ALMA STREET
A6109
DEREK DOOLEY WAY
NURSERY STREET
CORPORATION ST
BRIDGE STREET
SHALESMOOR
BOWLING GRN ST
MOORFIELDS
HOLLIS CROSS
MEADOW STREET
SHEPHERD ST
NETHERTHORPE ROAD
UPPER ALLEN STREET
EDWARD STREET
SOLLY STREET
SCOTLAND STREET
CATHEDRAL QUARTER
LOVE ST
WEST BAR
Police HQ
CASTLEGATE
SNIG HILL
BLONK ST
CUTLERS GATE
VICTORIA STN RD
FURNIVAL ROAD
VICTORIA QUAYS
SHEFFIELD PARKWAY
BROAD ST
Indoor Market
BANK ST
HARTSHEAD
QUEEN ST
PARADISE ST
NORTH CHURCH ST
TENTER STREET
GARDEN STREET
HAWLEY ST
CAMPO LANE
Cathedral
COMMERCIAL ST
TOWNHEAD STREET
ST JAMES ST
CHURCH ST
HIGH ST
ARUNDEL GATE
FLAT ST
BROAD LANE
NEWCASTLE ST
BAILEY LANE
BAILEY ST
TRIPPET LANE
BEET STREET
MAPPIN STREET
LEOPOLD ST
FARGATE
Crucible Theatre
Mini Interchange
DUKE STREET
PORTOBELLO ST
Cutler's Hall
NORFOLK ROW
TUDOR SQUARE
POND ST
Sheffield Interchange
City Hall
Town Hall
SURREY STREET
NORFOLK ST
Lyceum Theatre
SHEAF STREET
WEST STREET
ROCKINGHAM STREET
ROCKINGHAM LANE
CARVER STREET
Peace Gardens
Winter Garden
Central Library
UPPER HANOVER STREET
REGENT ST
DIVISION STREET
WESTFIELD TERR
CAMBRIDGE ST
PINSTONE ST
Sheffield Hallam University
DEVONSHIRE ST
CAVENDISH ST
VICTORIA STREET
GELL STREET
FITZWILLIAM ST
Devonshire Green
TRAFALGAR STREET
MILLENNIUM SQUARE
PATERNOSTER ROW
Millennium Galleries
HOWARD ST
West One
WELLINGTON ST
ELDON ST
UNION ST
Showroom Cinema
TURNER ST CROSS
Train Station
DEVONSHIRE QUARTER
MOOR QUARTER
CHARTER ROW
ARUNDEL STREET
BROWN ST
SHREWSBURY ROAD
HANOVER WAY
MATILDA ST
SIDNEY ST
LEADMILL RD
SUFFOLK ROAD
BROOMHALL ST
WILLIAM STREET
MILTON STREET
THE MOOR
CUMBERLAND WAY
EYRE STREET
CULTURAL INDUSTRIES QUARTER
LEADMILL ST
FORNHAM ST
BROOMHALL PLACE
MOORE STREET
FITZWILLIAM GATE
CUMBERLAND STREET
JESSOP ST
SHOREHAM STREET
A61
YOUNG STREET
BISHOP ST
SYLVESTER ST
HEREFORD ST
ECCLESALL ROAD
ST MARY'S GATE
ST MARY'S ROAD
LONDON ROAD
Weston Park Museum & Botanical Gardens
Magna & Rotherham
18
19
CLUBS & LIVE VENUES
The Boardwalk 3
The Casbah 12
Dempsey's Bar and Club 17
Leadmill 16
DRINKING
Crystal 7
Devonshire Cat 14
Fat Cat 2
Frog and Parrot 9
Takapuna 6
The Washington 15
EATING
Antibo 10
Blue Moon Café 5
Crucible Corner 8
The Forum 11
The Milestone 1
Nonna's 19
Old Vicarage 18
Silversmiths 13
Tin Tin 20
Wig and Pen 4

of the city regeneration, the stunning **Winter Garden** (daily 8am–6pm, Wed in summer till 9pm; free), an arched steel-and-wood glasshouse almost 200 feet long and over 60 feet high. It's a spectacular public space, filled with plants and shrubs.

Sheffield's **Millennium Galleries** (Mon–Sat 8am–5pm, Sun 11am–5pm, free; visiting exhibitions from 10am, £4; Ⓦ www.museums-sheffield.org.uk) back onto the gardens and contain two permanent displays, both specific to Sheffield and its heritage. In the **Metalworks Gallery** you can discover why the eighteenth-century city's natural endowments (a fast water supply, forests for charcoal and gritstone deposits) ensured the rapid development of the cutlery industry. Not surprisingly, the gallery contains the most extensive collection of Sheffield cutlery in the world, from sixteenth-century knives to designer cleavers. There's also the highly diverting **Ruskin Gallery**, based on the collection founded by John Ruskin in 1875 to improve the working people of Sheffield. A library of classic nineteenth-century texts ("the working man's Bodleian") is complemented by an intriguing selection of watercolours, sketches, minerals, paintings and medieval illuminated manuscripts, and contrasts with Keiko Mukaide's stunning wall-length clouds and water sculpture.

The rest of central Sheffield divides into neat areas, touted rather grandly as "quarters". Southeast of the Winter Garden, clubs and galleries exist alongside arts and media businesses in the **Cultural Industries Quarter**. North of the stations, near the River Don, **Castlegate** has a traditional indoor **market** (closed Sun) while the spruced-up warehouses and cobbled towpaths in the neighbouring canal basin, **Victoria Quays**, house several high-tech businesses, restaurants, hotels and leisure facilities.

Closer to the Town Hall, at the end of Fargate, the city's **Cathedral of St Peter and St Paul** retains elements of its fifteenth-century origins, and is enhanced by its late twentieth-century lantern tower and colourful glass. **Cutler's Hall**, opposite on Church Street, is an imposing reminder of the importance of the cutlery trade – the Company of Cutlers guild was established here as early as 1624 to regulate the affairs of the industry. South of here, down Fargate and across the Peace Gardens, the pedestrianized **Moor Quarter** draws in shoppers, though it's the **Devonshire Quarter**, east of Devonshire Green and centred on Division Street, that is the trendiest shopping area.

Outside the centre

Sheffield's other attractions are all on the outskirts. Fifteen minutes' walk north of the cathedral, the **Kelham Island Museum** on Alma Street (Mon–Thurs 10am–4pm, Sun 11am–4.45pm; £4; Ⓦ www.simt.co.uk) reveals the breadth of the city's industrial output. Many of the old machines are still working, arranged in period workshops where craftspeople demonstrate some of the finer points of cutlery production.

You can then put the city's life and times into perspective a mile or so west at the **Weston Park Museum** (Mon–Sat 10am–5pm, Sun 11am–5pm; free; Ⓦ www .museums-sheffield.org.uk), where the imaginatively themed and family-friendly galleries draw together the city's extensive archeology, natural history, art and social history collections. Catch bus #51 or #52 from High Street and get off at the Children's Hospital/Weston Park stop.

Also on this side of the city are the lovely **Botanical Gardens** (Mon–Fri 8am–dusk, Sat & Sun 10am–dusk, pavilions 11am–3.30/5pm; free; Ⓦ www.sbg.org .uk), where there are nineteen acres of Victorian landscaping, some impressively restored glass pavilions and an early nineteenth-century bear pit. There are two entrances – one on Clarkehouse Road (bus #30 or #40 from High St), the other on Thompson Rd (buses #81 to 86 from High St).

Eating and drinking

Sheffield has plenty of great **café-bars** and **restaurants** in the city centre, while south of the centre London Road is lined with good, authentic East and Southeast Asian restaurants. For the best insight into Sheffield's nightlife, take a night-time walk along **Division Street** and **West Street** where competing theme and retro bars go in and out of fashion. Town and Gown meet at the fancy retail-restaurant-and-leisure development known as West:One (end of Devonshire St, at Fitzwilliam St), while locals and students also frequent the bars and pubs of Ecclesall Road (the so-called "golden mile"), out of the centre to the southwest – best take a taxi.

Cafés and café-bars

Blue Moon Café 2 St James St ☎0114/276 3443. Relax in the skylit dining room, next to the cathedral, and tuck into home-made vegetarian/vegan food, including pies, burritos, a cold-counter selection and organic beers. Shuts at 8pm; closed Sun.

Crucible Corner Tudor Square ☎0114/273 8255. The Crucible Theatre's licensed café/bistro, hived out into a separate building since refurbishment. Sandwiches, salads and bistro classics £5–12. Open till midnight, closed Sun.

The Forum 127–129 Devonshire St ☎0114/272 0569. Long the mainstay of the Devonshire Quarter, *The Forum* has a great menu and laid-back clientele. A sinuous sun-terrace overlooks the green. Till 1am (2am Fri & Sat), with food till 10pm (till 8pm Sat & Sun).

Restaurants

Antibo West:One, Unit 10, Fitzwilliam St ☎0114/272 7222. Classy, contemporary Italian restaurant with on-the-mark pizzas and pastas (around £9) and daily fish specials (£16), swordfish to sea bass.

The Milestone 84 Green Lane ☎0114/272 8327. Close to Kelham Island, in an attractive listed building, the award-winning *Milestone* offers gastropub and fine-dining menus at reasonable prices (pub starters around £5, main courses £10, taster menu £34.95; restaurant £25 for two courses, £30 for three).

Nonna's 535–541 Ecclesall Rd ☎0114/268 6166. Where the Sheffield beautiful hang out, a see-and-be-seen Italian bar and restaurant with a great reputation. Restaurant reservations advised. The deli and ice-cream parlour round the corner in Hickmott Rd (closed Mon & Tues) are worth a visit, too.

Old Vicarage Ridgeway Village, 8km (15min) from the city centre ☎0114/247 5814. The only Michelin-starred restaurant in the region, the *Old Vicarage* does simple set menus (lunch: 2-course £30, 3-course £40; dinner: 4-course £60). Atmosphere, food and wine are all spot on.

Silversmiths 111 Arundel St ☎0114/270 6160. A "kitchen nightmare" turned around in 2008 by Gordon Ramsay, city-centre *Silversmiths* supplies top-notch Yorkshire food from locally sourced ingredients in a 200-year-old ex-silversmith's workshop.

Tin Tin 30–32 London Rd ☎0114/275 8880. Something of an institution in the area, known for quality and value, this London Road Chinese started as a cheap'n'cheerful buffet restaurant, but has gone upmarket.

Wig and Pen Paradise Square ☎0114/276 3988. Just behind the cathedral, a cool and stylish setting for varied and imaginative lunch, tapas, "early bird" (£10 for two courses 6–7.30pm) and dinner menus.

Pubs and bars

Crystal 23–32 Carver St. A former scissors factory provides stunning premises for an airy bar-restaurant-patio, good for food and great for a night out, with a bar until 1.30am.

Devonshire Cat 49 Wellington St, Devonshire Green. Renowned alehouse with a beer menu on every table and good cheap food with drinks matched to every selection.

Fat Cat 23 Alma St. Old-fashioned pub famed for its umpteen real ales and imported bottles, and hearty food. No gaming machines or piped music.

Frog and Parrot 94 Division St. A boisterous pub with big windows onto the Division St scene, lots of beers (including the hellishly strong Roger & Out) and a good jukebox.

Takapuna 52–54 West St. The cool crowd has moved out west to stylish *Takapuna*, for eating, greeting and drinking, with DJs and club nights an added incentive. The bar stays open until 2am.

The Washington 79 Fitzwilliam St. A favoured hangout for musicians, just two minutes across the green from Division St.

Pubs and pints

When you order a pint, you're doing more than having a drink
– you're celebrating English history and heritage from top
to bottom of the glass. Beer has been a staple part of the
local diet for centuries, dating back to times when water was
too dangerous to drink, while in recent years there's been a
renaissance in regional brewing that reflects the wider interest
in locally sourced food and drink. The country has a fantastic
selection of beers these days (the best in the world – no
argument), and there's no excuse not to sample a pint or two
in the nation's one great surviving social institution, the pub.

Behind the beer

Ask simply for a "beer" in an English pub and you'll cause no end of confusion. Although cold, fizzy lager is by far the most popular tipple, England's unique glory is its "**real ale**", a refreshing, non-fizzy, natural-tasting beer brewed with traditional ingredients and served at cellar temperature. The most common ale is known as **bitter**, with a colour ranging from straw-yellow to dark brown, depending on the brew. Other real ales include golden or **pale ales** – summery and light in colour, though often strong – darker and maltier **milds**, **stouts and porters**, and wheat- and fruit-based beers. Whichever you choose, real ale is the stuff that's pumped by hand from a **cask** in the pub's cellar – ignore the chilled and gas-added "smoothflow" beers because if it doesn't say "cask", "cask-conditioned" or "naturally conditioned", it's not the real thing.

A pint of real ale (and the paper) ▲

Beer pumps ▼

Local breweries

While the major international breweries and pub companies are facing the economic squeeze, England's medium-sized and small **microbreweries** are flourishing. Each region has its own independent outfits, brewing beers that are sometimes confined to one particular area or even just one pub. Cumbria alone has over thirty small breweries, with several pioneering one-pub outlets like the *Bitter End* in Cockermouth (Ⓦwww.bitterend.co.uk) or Hesket Newmarket's *Old Crown* (Ⓦwww .theoldcrownpub.co.uk), the latter said to be Britain's first cooperatively owned pub. Elsewhere, many of the big beer names on the bar (like Boddington's of Manchester, or Tetley's from Leeds) started out as local family businesses, though are owned by multinational conglomerates these days. Others with widely available beers (Adnams of Suffolk, Harveys of Sussex, Yorkshire's Black Sheep and Timothy Taylor) are still independently owned and regionally based, though beer aficionados gravitate naturally towards the smaller, more idiosyncratic breweries. The Hook Norton Brewery in Oxfordshire (Ⓦwww.hooknortonbrewery.co.uk) still has a working steam engine used for beer production, while there can't be many more remote ale-making locations than that of the Dent Brewery (Ⓦwww.dentbrewery.co.uk), hidden in a secluded corner of the Yorkshire Dales National Park.

It's all in the name

While the English pub dates back to the wayfarers' hostelries and alehouses of medieval times, it's the nook-and-cranny Tudor taverns and gleaming Victorian gin palaces that fit most people's idea of a classic English pub. What they all have in common is a hanging **pub sign** above the door – vital in the days when most of the English couldn't read, but essentially decorative today. There's a lot of history wrapped up in a simple name, though, as England's oldest inn shows – Nottingham's *Ye Olde Trip to Jerusalem* was an early gathering point for medieval Crusaders. Many pub names have obvious royal connections (*The Crown*, *King's Arms* or *Queen's Head*), while hundreds of others are named after erstwhile local bigwigs – the *Duke of Cambridge*, the *Earl of Gloucester* and so forth. Animals, country pursuits and fox-hunting account for a huge number of rural pub names, while urban tradesmen once clearly spent more time than was strictly wise in assorted *Plumbers'*, *Bricklayers'* and *Carpenters' Arms*. Some names are playful (like the *First In, Last Out*), some archaically patriotic (*John Bull*), and others frankly obscure – make what you like of the *Hit or Miss* pub near Chippenham in Wiltshire or Liverpool's *Ye Cracke*.

▲ Hook Norton Brewery dray and horses

▼ *The Salisbury*, London

▼ Pub sign

Devon cider ▲

Supping a pint of cider at the Great British Beer Festival ▼

Cider, scrumpy and perry

Travel to the West Country, Herefordshire and Worcestershire and the traditional drink is not beer but cider, which is produced from fermented apple juice. As with real ale, the fizzy, sweet keg cider sold in pubs all over England is not the genuine article. It's "real cider" you're looking for, specifically the potent and cloudy beverage known as scrumpy, which is increasingly available in pubs outside its native southwest. Perry (made from pears) is harder to find, though farmers have made it for centuries and most beer festivals carry a range these days.

CAMRA

Based in St Albans, in Hertfordshire, CAMRA, the Campaign for Real Ale, has fought long and hard to protect the traditional beers and ciders of England from extinction. Armed with its annual *Good Beer Guide*, you'll never be stuck anywhere in England for a decent drink.

England's five best beer festivals

▶▶ **Beer on the Wye**, Hereford (July). The best place to try regional ciders and perries, in a lovely riverside setting.

▶▶ **Boot Beer Festival**, Cumbria (June). One isolated Lake District valley, three pubs and over seventy beers.

▶▶ **Cambridge Beer Festival** (May). Beers in the sun (plus a renowned cheese counter) on Jesus Green in the ancient university city.

▶▶ **Great British Beer Festival**, London (August). The Campaign for Real Ale hosts Britain's biggest annual beer fest in the capital.

▶▶ **Kent Beer Festival**, Canterbury (July). Kent's independent breweries offer a rustic "beer on the farm" experience.

Nightlife, music and the arts

Friday's *Sheffield Telegraph* lists the week's performances, events, concerts and films, or there's *Exposed* (Ⓦ www.exposedmagazine.co.uk), a free monthly listings magazine, available from cafés, restaurants, shops and bars across the city.

Clubs and live music

The Boardwalk 39 Snig Hill ☏ 0114/279 9090, Ⓦ www.theboardwalklive.co.uk. Popular venue for indie bands, rock, folk and blues.

The Casbah 1 Wellington St ☏ 0114/275 6077. As in "Rock the…", which tells you what to expect – a stroll down punk/rock memory lane, with current indie and alternative nights as well.

Dempsey's Bar and Club 1 Hereford St ☏ 0114/275 4616, Ⓦ www.dempseys-sheffield .com. The best established gay venue in the city, licensed until the small hours.

Leadmill 6–7 Leadmill Rd ☏ 0114/221 2828, Ⓦ www.leadmill.co.uk. In the Cultural Industries Quarter, this place hosts live bands and DJs most nights of the week.

Arts venues

Crucible, Lyceum & Studio Tudor Square ☏ 0114/249 6000, Ⓦ www.sheffieldtheatres.co.uk. Sheffield's theatres put on a full programme of theatre, dance, comedy and concerts. The Crucible hosts the World Snooker Championships, the annual Music in the Round festival of chamber music (May), and the Sheffield Children's Festival (late June or July).

Sheffield City Hall Barker's Pool ☏ 0114/278 9789, Ⓦ www.sheffieldcityhall.com. Year-round programme of classical music, opera, mainstream concerts, comedy and club nights.

The Showroom 7 Paternoster Row ☏ 0114/275 7727, Ⓦ www.showroom.org.uk. Big independent cinema that also has a relaxed café-restaurant on one side and a great bar on the other.

Listings

Buses Traveline 01709/515151.

Hospital Royal Hallamshire Hospital, Glossop Rd (☏ 0114/271 1900), with NHS Walk-In centre.

Internet At Central Library, Surrey St ☏ 0114/273 4712 (Mon 10am–8pm, Tues & Thurs–Sat 9.30am–5.30pm, Wed 9.30am–8pm).

Police West Bar ☏ 0114/220 2020.

Post office 9 Norfolk Row.

Shopping On the western side of the city, around Devonshire Green and along Ecclesall Rd as far as Hunter's Bar, there are lots of boutiques and specialist shops.

Rotherham: Magna

About six miles northeast of Sheffield, **ROTHERHAM** town centre has been improved over recent years. Locals point to its **churches** as its proudest feature, and certainly the medieval parish church is particularly fine, while in the Chapel of Our Lady on Rotherham Bridge, the town has one of only four surviving examples in England of a medieval bridge chantry. For most visitors, however, these pale in comparison with **Magna** (daily 10am–5pm; closed some Mon Nov–March; Easter–Oct £9.95, Oct–Easter £9; Ⓦ www.visitmagna.co.uk), the UK's first science adventure centre, housed in a former steelworks building on Sheffield Road (A6178) in Templeborough, just off the M1 a mile from the Meadowhall shopping complex. You can get here on bus #69 from either Sheffield or Rotherham interchanges, or it's a fifteen-minute taxi ride from Sheffield.

Entering the bowels of the building confronts you immediately with the half-light, invasive noise and arcane hardware of a massive steelworks. The vast internal space comfortably holds four gadget-packed **pavilions**, themed on the basic elements of earth, air, fire and water. In these you're encouraged to get your hands on interactive exhibits, games and machines – operating a real JCB, filling diggers and barrows, blasting a rock face, firing a water cannon, or investigating a twister. On the hour, everyone decamps to the main hall for the **Big Melt** when the original arc furnace is used in a bone-shaking light-and-sound show that has visitors gripping the railings. The whole experience is an excellent day out – there are free tours of the premises most days, a very large children's play area, plus café and restaurant. Bring warm clothes if you're coming in winter.

Leeds and around

Yorkshire's commercial capital, and one of the fastest-growing cities in the country, **LEEDS** has undergone a radical transformation in recent years. There's still a true northern grit to its character, and in many of its dilapidated suburbs, but the grime has been removed from the impressive Victorian buildings and the city centre now has a chic, urbane feel. Leeds was an early market town, with wool traded here in medieval times by the monks of nearby Kirkstall Abbey. By the eighteenth century, the advent of canals and technical innovations such as the harnessing of steam power turned what had been a cottage industry into a dynamic large-scale economy. Leeds quickly boomed beyond its capacity to support its burgeoning population, and while the textile barons prospered, the city acquired a reputation for grimness that proved hard to shake off. In 1847 Charles Dickens described Leeds as "the beastliest place, one of the noisiest I know".

The renowned **shops, restaurants, bars and clubs** provide one focus of a visit to contemporary Leeds – it's certainly Yorkshire's top destination for a day or two of conspicuous consumption and indulgence. It's also long been the region's **cultural** centre, home to Opera North, the noted West Yorkshire Playhouse and a triennial international piano competition that ranks among the world's top musical events. Museums start with the hugely impressive **Royal Armouries**, which hold the national arms and armour collection, while the **City Art Gallery** has one of the best collections of British twentieth-century art outside London. The city itself deserves the best part of two days, longer if you plan to see any of the outlying attractions, which include the fascinating **Thackray Museum** of medicine, medieval **Kirkstall Abbey** and the art collection and grounds at **Temple Newsam**.

Leeds can also serve as the base for seeing some of West Yorkshire's most notable attractions, the prime example being **Harewood**, one of the country's great Georgian piles, which deserves a day's visit of its own. Two other trips out of the city make equally good excursions, depending on your interests – at the **National Coal Mining Museum** the north's industrial past is brought sharply into focus, while the bucolic **Yorkshire Sculpture Park** presents the country's greatest showing of Henry Moore and Barbara Hepworth.

Arrival, transport and information

Leeds Bradford Airport is eight miles northwest of the city; there's a bus (#757; £2) every thirty minutes to the centre, or a taxi costs £17–20. National and local Metro trains use **Leeds City Station** off City Square, which also houses the **Leeds Visitor Centre** in the Arcade (Mon–Sat 9am–5.30pm, Sun 10am–4pm; ☎0113/242 5242, ⓦwww.visitleeds.co.uk). The **bus station** occupies a site to the east, behind Kirkgate Market, on St Peter's Street. Drivers will eventually be fed onto the City Centre Loop road; there are myriad signposted pay-and-display **car parks**.

The **Metro Travel Centres** at the bus and train stations have up-to-date service details for local transport or call **Metroline** (daily 7am–10pm; ☎0113/245 7676, ⓦwww.wymetro.com). **Passes** are available, and include bus/train DayRovers and a good-value Family DayRover.

Accommodation

There's a good mix of accommodation, including inexpensive **guesthouses** near the university campus and plenty of **hotels**, from budget chain to stylish designer or boutique. Cheaper lodgings lie out to the northwest in the student area of Headingley, though these are a bus or taxi ride away. For short or **weekend breaks** call the tourist office's special booking line (☎0800/808050) – they'll phone around to get you the best deal, and sometimes offer really good discounts. Rooms in self-catering **student apartments** at Clarence Dock (☎0113/343 6100, ⓦwww.meetinleeds.co.uk), near the Royal Armouries, are available every summer holiday (mid-July to early Sept; £24 per night; single occupancy only).

Hotels

42 The Calls 42 The Calls ☎0113/244 0099, ⓦwww.42thecalls.co.uk. Converted riverside grain mill, where rooms come with great beds and sharp bathrooms, though the cheapest rates are for the small "studio" rooms. ⑤

Butlers/Boundary Cardigan Rd, Headingley, 1.5 miles northwest of the centre. Adjacent associated hotels in a leafy suburban street offering good-value accommodation: *Butlers* (☎0113/274 4755, ⓦwww.butlershotel.co.uk) has cosy, smart, traditionally furnished en-suite rooms, while the cheaper lodgings at the *Boundary* (☎0113/275 7700, ⓦwww.boundaryhotel.co.uk) are nicely done with IKEA-style furnishings, though not all en suite. Parking. ①–③

City Inn Granary Wharf ☎0113/241 1000, ⓦcityinn.com/leeds. This impressive addition to Leeds' city-centre hotels has a beautiful setting on Granary Wharf, 5min walk from the train station, luxurious rooms and friendly, committed staff. The ground-floor *City Café* offers a variety of menus, either indoors or on the terrace next to the canal, while the thirteenth-floor *Sky Lounge* has wonderful views (see p.705). Parking under railway arches, or at reduced rate in nearby commercial car park. ⑦

Glengarth 162 Woodsley Rd ☎0113/245 7940, ⓦwww.glengarthhotel.co.uk. The best of the bunch on Woodsley Rd, just behind the university, about a mile from the centre. Rooms are fairly basic, but a bit of care has been taken with the decor, and there's a friendly welcome. Negotiable prices for multi-night stays. Parking. ①

Malmaison 1 Swinegate ☎0113/398 1000, ⓦwww.malmaison.com. Classy restored premises with the signature Malmaison style – plum and aubergine decor, attractive artwork and prints throughout the hotel – plus brasserie and bar. Rooms are uniformly comfortable, with all the services you'd expect. Breakfast not included; weekend deals from £99. ⑥

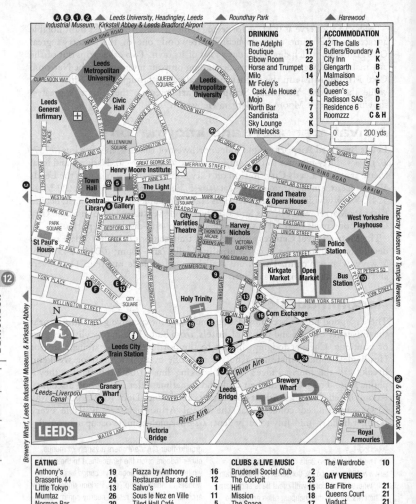

DRINKING

The Adelphi	25
Boutique	17
Elbow Room	22
Horse and Trumpet	8
Milo	14
Mr Foley's	
Cask Ale House	6
Mojo	4
North Bar	7
Sandinista	3
Sky Lounge	K
Whitelocks	9

ACCOMMODATION

42 The Calls	I
Butlers/Boundary	A
City Inn	K
Glengarth	B
Malmaison	J
Quebecs	F
Queen's	G
Radisson SAS	D
Residence 6	E
Roomzzz	C & H

0   200 yds

EATING

Anthony's	19	Piazza by Anthony	16
Brasserie 44	24	Restaurant Bar and Grill	12
Little Tokyo	13	Salvo's	1
Mumtaz	26	Sous le Nez en Ville	11
Norman Bar	20	Tiled Hall Café	5

CLUBS & LIVE MUSIC

Brudenell Social Club	2
The Cockpit	23
Hifi	15
Mission	18
The Space	17

The Wardrobe   10

GAY VENUES

Bar Fibre	21
Queens Court	21
Viaduct	21

Brewery Wharf, Leeds Industrial Museum & Kirkstall Abbey

Thackray Museum & Temple Newsam

& Clarence Dock

Quebecs 9 Quebec St ☎0113/244 8989, ⊛www
.theetoncollection.com. The ultimate city boutique
lodgings, in the former Leeds and County Liberal
Club. The glorious Victorian oak panelling and
stained glass remain, offset by chic rooms with
enormous beds, plumped pillows, and lovely
bathrooms. Breakfast not included; weekend rates
from £95. Very limited parking. ❸

Queen's City Square ☎0845/034 5777,
⊛www.qhotels.co.uk. Refurbished four-star
Art Deco landmark, right in front of the station,
with restaurant and parking. Rates are fairly
flexible – even during the week you can
sometimes get a room from £75 (the code below

is the official rate), while weekend prices include
breakfast. ❹

Radisson SAS No.1 The Light, The Headrow
☎0113/236 6000, ⊛www.radissonblu.co.uk
/hotel-leeds. The Grade II-listed former HQ of the
Leeds Permanent Building Society features snazzy
rooms and suites that reflect high-tech, Art Deco or
modern Italian design. Weekend rates start at £89
room only. ❺

Apartments

Residence 6 3 Infirmary St ☎0113/285 6250,
⊛www.residencesix.com. This award-winning
self-catering apartment hotel is centrally located in

the old post office building, just off City Square. Superb accommodation, with huge high-ceilinged rooms, complimentary wi-fi and games console, state-of-the-art fully equipped kitchen/dining rooms, classy bathroom fittings. Very limited parking – otherwise reduced-rate parking nearby. From £135 per night. **Roomzzz** 12 Swinegate; also at 2 & 361 Burley Rd ☎ 0113/233 0400, ⓦ www.roomzzz.co.uk.

Self-catering one- and two-bedroom apartments in contemporary style, with three locations: Swinegate is the most central, the others are a mile or so west of the train station. All come with great kitchens, memory foam beds, leather sofas, wide-screen TVs and free internet. Good weekend deals. Parking. Burley Rd from £53, Swinegate from £59.

The City

The city's revitalized commercial life is most apparent in the packed pedestrianized streets south of **The Headrow**, where the Victorian and Edwardian buildings glitter with brand names and designer labels, while down along the **Leeds– Liverpool Canal** and **River Aire** a kind of post-industrial chic has infused the converted warehouses and railway arches. Most places – including the Art Gallery, Royal Armouries, markets and shopping arcades – are an easy walk apart, though you'll need transport for the **outlying attractions**.

City Square to The Headrow

Opposite the train station, a prancing statue of Edward, the Black Prince, welcomes you to **City Square**, a smartened-up space that still retains its bronze nymph gas lamps. It's a short walk to the top of East Parade where you can't miss **Leeds Town Hall**, one of the finest expressions of nineteenth-century civic pride in the country and the masterpiece of local architect Cuthbert Broderick. Further up Calverley Street, to the side of the Town Hall and past the Central Library, is **Millennium Square**, handsome enough in its landscaped, contemporary way, but not a patch on nearby **Park Square**. This graceful Georgian ensemble, southwest of the Town Hall, is a peaceful place for a sit-down among the rose bushes, where you can contemplate the flanking bulk of **St Paul's House** (1878), a red-brick, neo-Gothic, former warehouse and cloth-cutting workshop.

East from the Town Hall and you're on **The Headrow**, the city's central spine, with the Art Gallery the major draw.

City Art Gallery and Henry Moore Institute

Leeds' **City Art Gallery** (Mon, Tues, Thurs & Sat 10am–5pm, Wed noon–5pm, Sun 1–5pm; free; ⓦ www.leeds.gov.uk/artgallery) on The Headrow presents changing selections from the permanent collection of nineteenth- and twentieth-century art and sculpture, with an understandable bias towards pieces by Henry Moore and Barbara Hepworth, both former students at the Leeds School of Art; Moore's *Reclining Woman* lounges at the top of the steps outside the gallery. Local painter Atkinson Grimshaw also has a guaranteed showing, along with the founder of the Camden Town Group, Walter Sickert, his younger disciple Spencer Frederick Gore and later artists such as Stanley Spencer and Wyndham Lewis. There's a splendid café in the restored Victorian Tiled Hall (see p.704), and direct access to the **Craft Centre and Design Gallery** below (Tues–Fri 10am–5pm, Sat 10am–4pm; free; ⓦ www.craftcentreleeds.co.uk), where changing displays of contemporary jewellery, ceramics and applied art are on show.

From the City Art Gallery, a slender bridge connects to the adjacent **Henry Moore Institute** (daily 10am–5.30pm, Wed until 9pm; free; ⓦ www.henry -moore.org/hmi), which also has its own entrance on The Headrow. It's devoted to showcasing temporary exhibitions of sculpture from all periods and nationalities,

A weekend in Leeds

Friday night

After a bite to eat – try *Little Tokyo* in Central Road – depending on your taste, see a **play** at the West Yorkshire Playhouse, **opera** or **ballet** at the Grand Theatre and Opera House, or enjoy a few drinks and the **music** at *Boutique* or *The Space* in Hirsts Yard.

Saturday

After breakfast walk along the banks of the River Aire to visit the **Royal Armouries** at Clarence Dock. Pick up a *What's on today* leaflet when you arrive, and decide on an itinerary. Take midday refreshment at the immaculate Clarence Dock *Mumtaz*. In the afternoon make your way along The Headrow from east to west, taking a look at the sculptures exhibited in the **Henry Moore Institute** then visit the **Leeds City Art Gallery**, perhaps buying something nice in the basement Craft Centre and Design Gallery. Take **tea** in the spectacular Victorian Tiled Hall, once the reading room of the library, now the Art Gallery's café and shop. For the evening, take your pick of the city's wonderful pubs, clubs and fine restaurants: the best hunting ground is in the southern part of the city centre, between City Square and the Corn Exchange.

Sunday

Sunday's a good day to sample the city's famous shopping. Make your way down Briggate and pop into the **Victoria Quarter**, where you can pick up top-end designer stuff by Vivienne Westwood, Mulberry, Louis Vuitton et al, and visit iconic Harvey Nichols department store. Then, if it's the first or third Sunday in the month, check out the **farmers' market** in the open area behind Kirkgate Market. There's more delicious food in the stalls that line the brick arches beneath the beautiful elliptical dome in the **Corn Exchange**; once you've worked up an appetite, treat yourself to lunch at **Piazza by Anthony**. In the afternoon, either head a couple of miles northeast to the wonderful **Thackray Museum**, which deals with medical and social advance (a million times more interesting than it sounds), or just a bit further out, work off lunch with a walk in **Roundhay Park**.

and not, as you might imagine, pieces by the masterful Moore himself – for those, best visit the Yorkshire Sculpture Park (see p.707).

Shopping: Briggate, the arcades and markets

Most visitors make a beeline for the brimming, shop-filled arcades on either side of pedestrianized **Briggate**. These nineteenth-century palaces of marble, mahogany, stained glass and mosaics have been magnificently restored and perhaps the most splendid of all is the light-flooded **Victoria Quarter** (ⓦ www.v-q.co.uk) – dubbed the "Knightsbridge of the North" – with Harvey Nichols (107–111 Briggate) as its designer lodestone. Compatriots in style include Gieves & Hawkes (10 Queen Victoria St), Vivienne Westwood (15–17 County Arcade) and Louis Vuitton (98–99 Briggate), while stylish *Anthony's Patisserie* (37 Queen Victoria St) is the favoured place to take the weight off your arms and muse on exactly how much those shoes just cost.

Across Vicar Lane, **Kirkgate Market** (Mon–Sat 9am–5pm; ⓦ www.leeds market.com) is the largest market in the north of England. Housed in a superb Edwardian building, it's a descendant of the medieval woollen markets that were instrumental in making Leeds the early focus of the region's textile industry – if you're after tripe, haberdashery or big knickers, there's no better place. The **open market** behind here (closed Wed & Sun), incidentally, is where Michael Marks set up stall in 1884 with the slogan "Don't ask the price, it's a penny" – an enterprise that blossomed into the present-day retail giant Marks & Spencer. There's also a farmers' market here on the first and third Sunday of the month.

At the bottom of the street, on the corner of Vicar Lane and Duncan Street, the elliptical, domed **Corn Exchange** (W www.cornx.net) was built in 1863, also by Cuthbert Broderick, whose design leaned heavily on his studies of Paris's corn exchange. Following a complete refurbishment, it was reopened in 2008 as a rather posh food emporium, with *Piazza by Anthony* (see p.704) occupying the whole of the open basement floor, and various food shops. Whether a sellout to commercial forces, or a move upmarket in keeping with the city's aspirations, the old place has been buffed up until it shines.

Granary Wharf to the Royal Armouries

The biggest transformation in Leeds has been along both sides of the **Leeds–Liverpool Canal** and **River Aire**, formerly a stagnant relic of industrial decline. At **Granary Wharf**, a couple of minutes' walk from the train station, specialist shops fill the extensive cobbled, vaulted arches (the "Dark Arches"), while every weekend and bank holiday a market with stalls, bands and entertainers spills out onto the canal basin. **Brewery Wharf**, on the south side (or "Left Bank" as Leeds would like it to be known), sports a welter of bars and brasseries, while further east along the river beckons the glass turret and gun-metal grey bulk of the **Royal Armouries** (daily 10am–5pm; free; W www.armouries.org.uk). Purpose-built to house the arms and armour collection from the Tower of London, it's a hugely adventurous museum that requires a leap of faith – discard the notion that all you'll see are casefuls of weapons because you're in for a treat. Themed galleries cover concepts such as "War" and "Hunting", with displays – ranging from gun emplacements to Mughal Indian elephant armour – backed up by intelligent commentary, video exhibits and documentary evidence. Interpretations and demonstrations take place throughout the day, so you might learn smallsword techniques from a Georgian swordsmaster or sixteenth-century javelin skills in the outdoor Tiltyard. It's an easy ten-minute walk along the river to the museum from the centre; there's parking outside.

Outlying attractions

The **Thackray Museum** on Beckett Street (daily 10am–5pm, last admission 3pm; £6.50; W www.thackraymuseum.org), next to St James' Hospital, is sited in a former workhouse a mile east of the city centre; take bus #50 from The Headrow or #42 from Infirmary Street (off City Square). Essentially a medical history museum, it's a hugely entertaining place with displays on subjects as diverse as the history of the hearing aid and the workings of the human intestine. It's gruesome, too, with film of a Victorian limb amputation in a gallery called "Pain, pus and blood". Needless to say, children love it.

For Leeds' industrial past, visit the vast **Leeds Industrial Museum**, two miles west of the centre off Canal Road (Tues–Sat 10am–5pm, Sun 1–5pm; £3.10; W www.leeds.gov.uk/armleymills), which runs between Armley and Kirkstall Road – take bus #5 or #67. There's been a mill on the site since at least the seventeenth century, and the present building was one of the world's largest woollen mills until its closure in 1969.

You should also see the bucolic ruins and cloisters of **Kirkstall Abbey** (dawn to dusk; free; W www.leeds.gov.uk/kirkstallabbey), which was built between 1152 and 1182 by Cistercian monks from Fountains Abbey. The former gatehouse now provides the setting for the family-friendly **Abbey House Museum** (Tues–Fri & Sun 10am–5pm, Sat noon–5pm; £3.60; W www.leeds.gov.uk/abbeyhouse), which takes a look at Victorian Leeds. The abbey lies about three miles northwest of the city centre on Abbey Road; take the first turning right after the abbey, or bus #33, #33A or #670.

Four miles east of the city, the Tudor-Jacobean house of **Temple Newsam** (Tues–Sun: April–Oct 10.30am–5pm; Nov–March 10.30am–4pm; £3.50; Ⓦ www.leeds.gov.uk/templenewsam) shows many of the paintings and much of the decorative art owned by Leeds City Art Gallery. There are over 1500 acres on the estate (park open daily dawn to dusk; free), which also contains Europe's largest **rare-breeds farm** (Tues–Sun: April–Oct 10.30am–5pm; Nov–March 10.30am–4pm; £3.25). There's an hourly Sunday bus service to the house; otherwise, parking costs £4.

Eating, drinking and nightlife

Eating out in Leeds has been transformed in recent years, with many old warehouses and grain mills converted into up-to-the-minute **restaurants and brasseries**. Late-opening central **café-bars** exploit the city's relaxed licensing laws to the full – most are open till midnight during the week, and 1am, 2am or even later at weekends. The best of the city's **pubs** are the ornate Victorian alehouses in which Leeds specializes, and when these close you can move on to one of the city's DJ bars or **clubs**, many of which have a nationwide reputation – not least because Leeds lets you dance until 5 or 6am most weekends. For information about **what's on**, your best bets are the fortnightly listings magazine *The Leeds Guide* (Ⓦ www.leedsguide.co.uk) or the daily *Yorkshire Evening Post*.

Café-bars and restaurants

Anthony's Trevelyan Square, just off Boar Lane ☎ 0113/245 5922. The original award-winning restaurant opened by top local chef Anthony Flinn in 2004. Cool laid-back decor, innovative and imaginative menu, though you do need to know your ceviche from your sous-vide. The emphasis is on fish and poultry, though the meat dishes are excellent as well.

Brasserie 44 44 The Calls ☎ 0113/234 3232. Informal Modern British bar and brasserie, serving everything from pan-fried mackerel to fancied-up duck confit. Most food is locally sourced though not cheap – for example Howden pork fillet (£14.95) and fillet of Yorkshire beef (£22.95). Closed Sun.

Little Tokyo 24 Central Rd ☎ 0113/243 9090. Leeds' favourite Japanese restaurant has an enormous menu – sushi, noodles, curries, grills and salads – with main courses around £7, or bento box set meals from £12.

Mumtaz Clarence Dock ☎ 0113/242 4211. Offshoot of the famous *Mumtaz* restaurant in Bradford – quality Kashmiri food, smart decor and a bustling atmosphere.

Norman Bar 36 Call Lane ☎ 0113/234 3988. A boho-chic interior – cast-iron girders to cuckoo clock – plus juice bar, eclectic food (most dishes £5–10) and varied club nights add up to one of the city's unique spots.

Piazza by Anthony Corn Exchange, Call Lane ☎ 0113/247 0995. Top-quality food and friendly, efficient service in stunningly beautiful surroundings with prices to suit most pockets. Main courses range from £8 to £20. This latest venture of the growing Anthony brand isn't just a restaurant – there's a bakery, patisserie, chocolatier, wine shop, cheese shop and charcuterie as well.

Restaurant Bar and Grill The Old Post Office, 3 City Square ☎ 0113/244 9625. The bank of wine bottles in the huge window draws you into this classy post office makeover. The menu ranges from Old Spot sausages, calves' liver and grills to Italian, Thai and North African dishes, most between £10 and £20.

Salvo's 115 Otley Rd, Headingley ☎ 0113/275 5017. Pizza in Leeds to a local means *Salvo's* – as authentic as they come – though there's a classy menu covering other Italian dishes as well and a choice list of daily specials (pizzas £7.50–10, other mains £15–18.50). It really is worth the trek out from the centre. A daytime café-deli a couple of doors down offers lighter bites.

Sous le Nez en Ville Quebec House, 9 Quebec St ☎ 0113/244 0108. Housed in the splendid red-brick building of the former Liberal Club, this basement wine bar/restaurant is particularly strong on fish – there are always half a dozen starter and main specials (the latter £11–25), plus a wide bistro-style menu. Closed Sun.

Tiled Hall Café City Art Gallery, The Headrow. With granite pillars, tiled walls with relief portraits of Homer, Milton, Burns and others, and a beautifully vaulted mosaic ceiling, you'll not find a more palatial venue for a cup of tea and a bun anywhere in the country.

Bars and pubs

The Adelphi 1–3 Hunslet Rd, just south of the river across the Leeds Bridge. Joshua Tetley's first pub, the splendidly Victorian *Adelphi* is all things to all men (and women), with four contrasting bars, a wide range of draught beers, ciders, wine and food – snacks, pub grub and full meals. There's also a comedy club (Mon) and music (Sat and last Sun of the month), and its wide appeal is reflected in its mixed clientele.

Boutique 11–13 Hirsts Yard, Briggate. Small, perfectly formed venue with outdoor glass-topped tables revealing jelly babies, tennis balls, petals and the like. Expect equally diverse cocktails. Hard to find: the alley is just off Duncan St, between William Hill and 14 Duncan House. Closed Mon & Sun.

Elbow Room 64 Call Lane. Funk and food, and a very cool place to play pool.

Horse and Trumpet 51–53 The Headrow. Across the road from Argos, the *Horse and Trumpet* is a no-nonsense city drinking establishment, divided into small wood-panelled areas and serving unbelievably cheap food (burgers, pies, fish and chips and so on) at from £3–5 all day, every day. No children under 18.

Milo 10–12 Call Lane. Unpretentious, offbeat bar with DJs most evenings, ringing the changes from old soul and reggae to indie and electronica.

Mr Foley's Cask Ale House 159 The Headrow. Super Victorian pub near the Town Hall, with several bars on different levels, draught beers listed on a blackboard with strengths and tasting notes, and international beers. Food at around a fiver.

Mojo 18 Merrion St. A great bar, pure and simple, with classic tunes ("music for the people") and a classy drinks menu to match.

North Bar 24 New Briggate. The city's beer specialist is more new Leeds than old, but the basics are familiar: a massive selection of guest beers (more Belgian than bitter) plus cold meats and cheeses to nibble on.

Sandinista 5/5a Cross Belgrave St ℡0113/305 0372, ⓦwww.sandinistaleeds.co.uk. Award-winning cocktail bar and tapas restaurant. With live music gigs through the week and DJs at the weekend, it's also one of Leeds' foremost late-night venues.

Sky Lounge *City Inn*, Granary Wharf. Situated on the hotel's thirteenth floor, the *Sky Lounge* is often busy, and certainly expensive, but well worth a visit for the wide range of exquisitely prepared cocktails, served with the city's best views available from its wrap-around terrace.

Whitelocks Turk's Head Yard, off Briggate. Leeds' oldest and most atmospheric pub (tucked up an alley) retains its traditional decor and a good choice of beers.

Clubs and live music

Brudenell Social Club 33 Queen's Rd ℡0113/275 2411, ⓦwww.brudenellsocialclub .co.uk. Known for hosting secret gigs for bands like Franz Ferdinand and the Kaiser Chiefs, this former working-men's club champions live music, especially of new bands. Beyond the university, but worth the twenty-minute trip.

The Cockpit Bridgend House, Swinegate ℡0113/244 1573, ⓦwww.thecockpit.co.uk. Live music and club venue, 5min by foot from the train station. It's built into three railway arches, giving the interior its distinctive curved ceilings. Gigs take place most nights of the week, and showcase local and international bands.

Hifi 2 Central Rd ℡0113/242 7353, ⓦwww .thehificlub.co.uk. Small, moodily lit basement club with lots of pine. Live and DJ-led rock, soul, jazz, funk, indie and hip-hop, and a comedy club on Sat nights.

Mission 8 Heaton's Court ℡0870/122 0114, ⓦwww.clubmission.com. Large venue that's recently revamped its bare-brick industrial feel in favour of giving their clientele lasers to reach for. Great range of nights, featuring big-name DJs. Packed to the curved ceilings every weekend.

The Space Hirsts Yard ℡0113/246 1030, ⓦwww .thespaceleeds.com. Literally an underground club, *The Space* is a well-established leader in the Leeds dance music scene. Focuses strongly on house and electro for the discerning listener and serious clubber, shunning the mainstream in favour of darker sounds and richer beats.

The Wardrobe 6 St Peter's Square ℡0113/383 8800, ⓦwww.thewardrobe.co.uk. Stylish restaurant, club, bar and coffee house, with excellent food upstairs and varied jazz/soul/funk on Fri and Sat nights.

Arts, festivals and entertainment

Temple Newsam hosts numerous concerts and events, from plays to rock gigs and opera, while at Kirkstall Abbey every summer there's a **Shakespeare Festival** (ⓦwww.britishshakespeare.com/leeds.html) with open-air productions of the

Leeds' best gay venues are clustered at the lower end of Call Lane.

Bar Fibre 168 Lower Briggate ⓦwww.barfibre.com. Leeds' finest gay bar comes with plenty of attitude plus outside balcony, DJs and dancing most nights.

Queens Court 167 Lower Briggate ⓦwww.queenscourtleeds.com. In the same court-yard as *Bar Fibre* (with which it has wild monthly summer parties), this bar has cool, contemporary design, a basic menu, and an upstairs nightclub (*The Loft*).

Viaduct 11 Briggate ⓦwww.viaductleeds.com. Traditional pub converted into a gay venue with live music.

Bard's works. Roundhay Park is the other large outdoor venue for concerts, while **Millennium Square** hosts gigs, festivals, markets and other events, including the annual Ice Cube, a temporary outdoor ice rink and café (mid-Jan to end Feb). Bramham Park, ten miles east of the city, hosts the annual **Leeds Festival** (ⓦwww.leedsfestival.com) over the August bank holiday weekend with rock/indie music on five stages. The same weekend heralds the **West Indian Carnival** in Chapeltown (ⓦwww.leedscarnival.co.uk), beaten in size only by Notting Hill.

Venues

City Varieties Swan St, Briggate ☎0845/644 1881, ⓦwww.cityvarieties.co.uk. One of the country's last surviving music halls, though these days it hosts more tribute bands, comedians and cabaret – great building and bar though.

Grand Theatre and Opera House 46 New Briggate ☎0844/848 2706, ⓦwww.leeds grandtheatre.com. The regular base of Opera North (ⓦwww.operanorth.co.uk) and Northern Ballet (ⓦwww.northernballettheatre.co.uk) also puts on a full range of theatrical productions.

Hyde Park Picture House Brudenell Rd, Headingley ☎0113/275 2045, ⓦwww.hydeparkpicturehouse .co.uk. The place to come for classic cinema with

independent and art-house shows alongside more mainstream films; bus #28, #96 or #97.

Leeds Town Hall The Headrow ☎0113/247 7989, ⓦwww.leedsconcertseason.com. Supports an annual international concert season of great distinction and is the venue for Leeds' internationally renowned piano competition (ⓦwww.leedspiano.com; next in 2012).

West Yorkshire Playhouse Quarry Hill ☎0113/213 7700, ⓦwww.wyp.org.uk. The city's most innovative theatre has two stages, plus bar, restaurant and café, and hosts a wide range of productions and premieres of local works.

Listings

Airport ☎0871/288 2288, ⓦwww.lbia.co.uk.
Hospital Leeds General Infirmary, Great George St ☎0113/243 2799.
Internet The Internet Café, 64–65 Merrion Indoor Market Centre, off Merrion Way. There's also free access at the Central Library, Calverley St ☎0113/247 8274 (call for hours).

Police Millgarth Police Station, Millgarth St ☎0845/606 0606.
Post office Branches on New York St, opposite Kirkgate market, and on Albion St, junction Merrion St.
Taxis Taxis are available 24hr at the train station, outside the bus station, and on New Briggate.

Out of the city

Give yourself another couple of days in Leeds and you can do justice to the region's major draws, though they're also all easily seen en route to your next destination – **Harewood** lies on the Harrogate road, while the **National Coal Mining Museum** and **Yorkshire Sculpture Park**, both south of Leeds, are easily reached from the M1. Only Harewood can straightforwardly be accessed by public transport from Leeds.

Harewood House

The stately home of **Harewood**, seven miles north of Leeds (early April to Oct daily: state rooms noon–4pm, below stairs – servants' quarters – and gallery 10.30am–4pm, bird garden 10am–5.30pm, grounds 10am–6pm; all attractions July, Aug & bank hol weekends £13, low season £9; below stairs, geopods and grounds only high season £11, low season £7.50; ℡0113/218 1010, ⓦwww .harewood.org), was designed and decorated by one of the greatest architectural teams ever assembled. Conceived in 1759 by York architect John Carr, the building was finished by Robert Adam, the furniture made by Thomas Chippendale and the landscaped gardens laid out by Capability Brown. To cap it all, a sweeping terrace designed by Sir Charles Barry (architect of the Houses of Parliament) overlooks the gardens. It's still the home of the Earl and Countess of Harewood, who let in the great unwashed in return for nothing more than a sizeable chunk of money. To be fair, there's an enormous amount to see and do, with daily tours and talks plus changing exhibitions included in the entrance fee. As well as the grand state and private rooms, the old kitchen and servants' quarters can be viewed, while outside in the magnificent **grounds** are: an adventure playground; the renowned **bird garden**, where four acres of aviaries cage over 150 and you can watch penguins being fed at 2pm; a **Himalayan Garden** (opened in 2009); and three wonderful geodesic domes – the **geopods** – stuffed full of interactive child-friendly science kit and much else. The whole estate has started to go into conservation in a big way, running breeding programmes, monitoring populations on the estate and feeding some endangered species back into their natural habitats.

There are frequent buses to Harewood from Leeds (including the #36, every 20min, 30min on Sun), and if you come by bus or bike you'll get a fifty percent discount on admission (keep your bus ticket). The house is near the junction of the A659 and the A61 Leeds–Harrogate road, and parking is free.

National Coal Mining Museum

While the gentry enjoyed the comforts of life in grand houses like Harewood, generations of Yorkshiremen sweated out a living underground just a few miles distant. Mining is now little more than a memory in most parts of Yorkshire, the industry crushed by government policy in the 1980s, but visitors can get all too vivid an idea of pit life through the ages at the excellent **National Coal Mining Museum** (daily 10am–5pm; free; ⓦwww.ncm.org.uk), about ten miles south of Leeds at Overton, halfway between Wakefield and Huddersfield (on the A642, signposted from the M1). Based in the former Caphouse Colliery, the highlight is an underground tour (90min, warm clothes required; arrive early in school hols; last tour 3.15pm) with a former miner as your guide, though the museum has no shortage of other attractions, from machinery demonstrations to a stableful of retired pit ponies.

Yorkshire Sculpture Park

Another Yorkshire country estate, at West Bretton outside Wakefield, now serves as the **Yorkshire Sculpture Park** (daily: grounds and centre 10am–6pm, restaurant, shop and indoor galleries 10am–5pm; free, but parking £4; ⓦwww.ysp.co.uk), a mile from the M1 (junction 38). Trails and paths run across 500 acres of eighteenth-century parkland, past open-air "gallery spaces" for some of Britain's most famous sculptors. The two big local names represented here are Henry Moore (1898–1986), born in nearby Castleford, and his contemporary Barbara Hepworth (1903–75), from Wakefield, but the works of other artists also rise to the grandeur of the surroundings – in particular the large figurative granite sculptures of Ronald Rae, which adorn the Access Sculpture Trail (possible for wheelchairs/prams). The **visitor** centre near the car park is the place to check on current exhibitions and pick up a park map – the restaurant here has views over Moore's monumental pieces. Exhibitions are held in the Longside Gallery (during exhibitions 11am–4pm; free) – catch the shuttle bus from the YSP car park or it's a two-kilometre walk through the park.

Bradford and around

BRADFORD has always been a working town, booming in tandem with the Industrial Revolution, when it changed from a rural seat of woollen manufacture to a polluted metropolis. In its Victorian heyday it was the world's biggest producer of worsted cloth, its skyline etched black with mill chimneys, and its hills clogged with some of the foulest back-to-back houses of any northern city. Contemporary Bradford is valiantly rinsing away its associations with urban decrepitude, and while it can hardly yet be compared with neighbouring Leeds as a visitor attraction it might ultimately succeed on its own distinct terms. In the meantime, in the **National Media Museum** and nearby **Saltaire**, Bradford has two of West Yorkshire's most compelling attractions. You should also hang around at least long enough to sample one of Bradford's famous **curry houses** – legacy of the city's large population with roots in the Indian subcontinent. Bradford and its textile industry has always been a lure for immigrants: German and Jewish merchants, and Irish workers in the nineteenth century, and significant numbers of men from India, Pakistan and Bangladesh in the 1950s and 1960s. They later sent for their families, making Bradford perhaps the most multicultural centre in the UK outside London.

The City

The focal point of the city is **Centenary Square**, behind which the **City Hall** behind shouts its Victorian credentials, the work of local architects Lockwood and Mawson, who also provided Bradford with **St George's Hall**, a Neoclassical extravaganza on Bridge Street still in use as a concert hall. Edwardian audiences later flocked to the minaret-topped **Alhambra Theatre**, across Princes Way, also splendidly restored.

Just across from here, on the rise, is the **National Media Museum** (Tues–Sun 10am–6pm; free; ☎0870/701 0200, ⓦwww.nationalmediamuseum.org.uk), one of the most visited national museums outside London, which wraps itself around one of Britain's largest cinema screens showing daily **IMAX** and 3D film screenings (£7.75–9). The museum itself is crammed with memorabilia and hardware, including the world's biggest lens, the first example of a moving picture and other superlatives. Exhibitions are devoted to every nuance of film and television, including topics like digital imaging, light and optics, and computer animation, while there are detours into the mechanics of advertising and news-gathering – even a searchable archive of classic British TV. The **Pictureville** cinema at the museum has a year-round repertory programme (films from £4.50), including Bite the Mango, a monthly selection of world cinema, and hosts several major film festivals, notably the Bradford International Film Festival in March.

Back across Centenary Square, a walk past the Venetian-Gothic **Wool Exchange** building on Market Street provides ample evidence of the wealth of nineteenth-century Bradford; it's now almost entirely taken up by a Waterstone's. Over to the east, the tight grid of streets that is **Little Germany** retains an enclave of warehouse and office buildings in which transplanted German and Jewish merchants once plied their wool trade.

For further insights into what once made the city tick, visit the **Bradford Industrial Museum** (Tues–Sat 10am–5pm, Sun noon–5pm; free; Ⓦwww .bradfordmuseums.org/industrialmuseum) in the old Victorian Moorside Mills in Eccleshill, three miles northeast of the centre. The museum documents the city's industrial heritage, alongside working textile machinery, surviving examples of the former workers' cottages, and shire horses hauling a selection of vintage trams and buses. Bus #666 from the Interchange runs to the museum (not Sun).

Practicalities

Trains and buses both arrive at **Bradford Interchange** off Bridge Street, a little to the south of the city-centre grid. There's also a smaller station at **Forster Square**, across the city, for trains to Keighley (for Haworth). The tourist office (Mon 10am–5pm, Tues–Sat 9.30am–5pm; ☎01274/433678, Ⓦwww.visitbradford .com), located in City Hall, is three minutes' signposted walk from the Interchange or five minutes from Forster Square. The major annual event is the **Bradford Mela** (Ⓦwww.bradfordmela.org.uk), a two-day celebration of the arts, culture, food and sports of the Indian subcontinent, held in June or July.

Restaurants

Akbar's 1276–1278 Leeds Rd ☎01274/773311. A buzzing, upmarket balti house (one of a chain of eight) located east of Bradford, on the Leeds Road in Thornbury, a short drive away. Most mains £6–8.

Great Victoria Bridge St ☎01274/728706. If you don't fancy Indian food, try the restaurant at this Victorian station hotel by the architects of the City Hall and St George's Hall. Varied menu, mainly British but with Continental options, served in a spacious, high-ceilinged room. Popular bar.

Kashmir 27 Morley St ☎01274/726513. Two minutes up the road that runs between the

Alhambra and the National Media Museum, this claims to have been Bradford's first curry house. Like many others in town it's unlicensed, though you can take your own booze. Open until 3am. Inexpensive.

Mumtaz 386–400 Great Horton Rd ☎01274/571861. Spacious contemporary restaurant where you buy your dish by weight – 220g or 440g, the larger portion serving two – and the sweet *lassi* is legendary. There's no alcohol allowed, and it's a 20min walk up towards the university, but you won't be disappointed. Open until midnight. Inexpensive.

Saltaire

Three miles out of Bradford towards Keighley, along the A650 to the north, no one should pass up the chance to drop in on **SALTAIRE**, a model industrial village and textile mill built by the industrialist Sir Titus Salt. Trains to Saltaire Station run from Bradford Forster Square, or take bus #623 or #662 from the Interchange, which stops in Saltaire village.

The village (still lived in today) is a perfectly preserved 25-acre realization of one man's vision of an industrial utopia. Saltaire was built between 1851 and 1876, modelled on buildings of the Italian Renaissance, a period evoked because of its perceived similarities with nineteenth-century Britain, insofar as the cultural and social advances of both eras were made possible by the commercial acumen of textile barons. **Salt's Mill**, larger than St Paul's Cathedral in London, was the biggest factory in the world when it opened in 1853, and it remains the fulcrum of the village, the focus of which is the **1853 Gallery** (Mon–Fri 10am–5.30, Sat & Sun 10am–6pm; free; Ⓦwww.saltsmill.org.uk), three floors given over to the world's largest retrospective collection of the works of Bradford-born **David Hockney**. There are art, craft and furniture shops to browse in, plus *Salt's Diner* on the second floor with its Hockney-designed logo, menu and crockery, and the posher *Café Opera* on the third.

Haworth

A quarter of a million visitors swarm annually into the village of **HAWORTH** to tramp the cobbles once trodden by the Brontë sisters. During the summer the steep, cobbled Main Street is lost under huge crowds, herded by multilingual signs around the various stations on the Brontë trail.

Of these, the **Brontë Parsonage Museum**, at the top of the main street (daily April–Sept 10am–5.30pm; Oct–March 11am–5pm; £6.50, Ⓦ www.bronte .info), is the obvious focus, a modest Georgian house bought by Patrick Brontë in 1820 to bring up his family (see box below). The house is furnished as it was in their day, and filled with the sisters' pictures, books, manuscripts and personal treasures. You can see the sofa on which Emily is said to have died in 1848, aged just 28, for example, and the footstool on which she sat outside on fine days writing *Wuthering Heights*.

The **parish church** in front of the parsonage contains the family vault; Charlotte was married here in 1854. At the **Sunday School**, between the parsonage and the church, Charlotte, Anne and even Branwell did weekly teaching stints; Branwell, however, was undoubtedly more at home in the **Black Bull**, a pub within staggering distance of the parsonage near the top of Main Street. He got his opium at the pharmacist's over the road (now a lace shop).

The Brontës at Haworth

The **Brontë family** – the Reverend Brontë, his wife and six children – first settled in Haworth in 1820. Mrs Brontë died within the year and the four oldest girls were sent away to school, but withdrawn after first Maria, then Elizabeth, died after falling ill. The surviving daughters **Charlotte**, **Emily** and **Anne**, and cosseted son **Branwell**, were kept at home, where they amused themselves by making up stories and writing miniature books. As they came of age, the girls took up short-lived jobs as governesses at various local schools; Charlotte and Emily even spent a year in Brussels, learning French. Branwell, meanwhile, was already sowing the dissolute seeds of his disappointing future: having failed, despite a certain talent, to apply himself at the Royal Academy, he got into debt, made himself overly familiar with the beer in the *Black Bull* and began experimenting with drugs.

By 1846, the girls' continued writings had led to the private publication of a series of poems. They used the (male) pseudonyms Currer, Ellis and Acton Bell – corresponding to their own initials – and though few copies of the collection were ever sold, the little volume acted as a catalyst. Keeping the pseudonym, Charlotte wrote a novel the same year, which was rejected by various publishers; but her **Jane Eyre**, submitted in 1847, was an instant success. Emily's **Wuthering Heights** and Anne's **Agnes Grey** received similar acclaim the same year; Anne's second novel, the better-known **Tenant of Wildfell Hall**, was published in 1848. As far as the public was concerned, the brilliant Bell brothers were a publishing sensation.

From there it was all downhill as the family was ravaged by **consumption**. First, Branwell, who had sunk ever deeper into addictive misery and ill health, died in September 1848, followed by Emily in December of that year, and Anne in the following May. Charlotte lived on for another six years, writing two more novels – *Shirley* (1849) and *Villette* (1853) – and becoming something of a literary figure once she had revealed her identity, but she died after nine months of marriage in the early stages of pregnancy. The Reverend Brontë lived on until 1861 – the entire family, except Anne (who is buried in Scarborough), lies in the **Brontë vault** in the village church, next to the house.

The **Keighley & Worth Valley Railway** runs steam trains (Easter week, school hols, July & Aug daily; rest of the year Sat & Sun) along a five-mile stretch of track between Keighley and Oxenhope, stopping at Haworth en route. The restored stations are a delight, with sections of the line etched into the memories of those who recall the film of E. Nesbit's *The Railway Children*, which was shot here in 1970. Valley footpaths run between the stations at Oakworth, Haworth and Oxenhope, allowing you to make a day of your reminiscences. Regular trains from Leeds or Bradford's Forster Square run to Keighley, where you change onto the branch line for the **steam services** (Day Rover ticket £14; ☏01535/645214, recorded information ☏01535/647777, ⓦwww.kwvr.co.uk).

The most popular local walk runs to **Brontë Falls** and **Bridge**, reached via West Lane and a track from the village, and to **Top Withens**, a mile beyond, a ruin fancifully (but erroneously) thought to be the model for Wuthering Heights (allow 3hr for the round trip). The moorland setting, however, beautifully evokes the flavour of the book, and to enjoy it further you could walk on another two and a half miles to **Ponden Hall**, perhaps the Thrushcross Grange of *Wuthering Heights* (this section of path, incidentally, forms part of the Pennine Way).

Practicalities

Haworth is eight miles northwest of Bradford. To get here by bus, take the #662 from Bradford Interchange to Keighley (every 10min), and change there for the #663, #664 or #665 (every 20min), which drop at various points in the streets immediately below the cobbled Main Street. On Sundays, only the #663 and #665 operate (every 30min). However, the nicest way of getting here is on the **Keighley & Worth Valley Railway** (see box above). Steep Main Street and its continuation, **West Lane**, form one long run of gift and teashops, cafés and guesthouses, with the busy Haworth **tourist office** at the top at Main Street (daily: April–Sept 9.30am–5.50pm, Wed from 10am; Oct–March closes 5pm ☏01535/642329, ⓦwww.haworth-village.org.uk).

Accommodation and eating

Aitches 11 West Lane ☏01535/642501, ⓦwww.aitches.co.uk. This stone-built Victorian house offers five stylish rooms with plenty of drapery, and has an attached restaurant that serves meals to residents (set menu £18). ❷

Apothecary 86 Main St ☏01535/643642, ⓦwww.theapothecaryguesthouse.co.uk. Traditional guesthouse opposite the church, whose rear rooms, breakfast room and attached café have splendid moorland views. ❷

Haworth YHA Longlands Hall ☏0870/770 5858, ⓔhaworth@yha.org.uk. The former mansion of a Victorian mill owner, refurbished in 2009, overlooks the village a mile from the centre, off the Keighley road. Bradford buses stop on the main road nearby.

Weekends only Nov to mid-Feb. Dorm beds from £11.95.

Old Registry 2–4 Main St ☏01535/646503, ⓦwww.theoldregistryhaworth.co.uk. Pretty old building at the bottom of Main St, with a four-poster bed in most rooms and tastefully coordinated furnishings throughout. Two-night minimum stay at weekends. ❹

Weaver's 15 West Lane ☏01535/643822, ⓦwww.weaverssmallhotel.co.uk. A renowned restaurant-with-rooms operation housed in a converted row of weavers' cottages. Meals – good modern northern cuisine using local ingredients – are served eve Tues–Sat, plus Wed, Thurs, Fri & Sun lunch. Dinner from around £25 a head, plus drinks. Booking essential. ❹

The Yorkshire Dales

The **Yorkshire Dales** form a varied upland area of limestone hills and pastoral valleys at the heart of the Pennines. Protected as a national park since 1954, there are over twenty main dales covering 680 square miles, crammed with opportunities for outdoor activities, including local hikes and long-distance footpaths, a specially designated cycle way, plus caving, pony-trekking and other more specialist pursuits.

Most approaches are from the industrial towns to the south, via the superbly engineered **Settle–Carlisle Railway**, or along the main A65 road from towns such as **Skipton**, **Settle** and **Ingleton**. This makes southern dales like **Wharfedale** the most visited, while neighbouring **Malhamdale** is also immensely popular, thanks to the fascinating scenery squeezed into its narrow confines around **Malham**, perhaps the single most visited village in the region. **Ribblesdale**, approached from Settle, is more sombre, its villages popular with hikers intent on tackling the Dales' famous **Three Peaks** – the mountains of Pen-y-ghent, Ingleborough and Whernside. To the northwest lies the more remote **Dentdale**, one of the least known but most beautiful of the valleys. Moving north, there are two parallel dales, **Wensleydale** and **Swaledale**, the latter pushing Dentdale as the most rewarding overall target. Both flow east, with Swaledale's lower stretches encompassing **Richmond**, an appealing historic town with a terrific castle. Finally, outside the national park boundary, to the east, is **Nidderdale**, which is relatively seldom visited, even though its beautiful upper reaches stand comparison with its more famous neighbours.

Public transport throughout the Dales is good, with countless special summer weekend and bank holiday services (usually May–Sept, peaking in school holidays) connecting almost everywhere, though bus services are limited in winter. Pick up the free **timetables** (Ⓦwww.dalesbus.org) from the region's tourist offices, or consult Ⓦwww.traveldales.org.uk. Keep your bus ticket and you'll be able to claim discounts at numerous local businesses – look for "Dales Bus Discount" window stickers. Many seasonal weekend bus services also offer **Dales Rover** tickets for unlimited travel, from £7.50 per day – buy on board the bus.

There are useful **National Park Centres** (Ⓦwww.yorkshiredales.org.uk) at Grassington, Aysgarth Falls, Malham, Reeth and Hawes, as well as many **information points** in shops, post offices and cafés. For a different view of the Dales, consult Ⓦwww.outofoblivion.org.uk, which looks in depth at the archeology and history of the national park, and from which you can download walking trails ("podwalks").

The Pennine Way cuts right through the heart of the Dales, and the region is crossed by the Coast-to-Coast Walk, but the principal local route is the **Dales Way** (Ⓦwww.dalesway.org.uk), an 84-mile footpath from Ilkley to Bowness-on-Windermere in the Lake District. Shorter **guided walks** (5–13 miles, every Sun & bank hol Mon, April–Oct) are organized by the National Park Authority and Dalesbus Ramblers (Ⓦwww.dalesbusramblers.org.uk). The Dales also has a network of over five hundred miles of bridleways, byways and other routes for **mountain bikers** to explore (Ⓦwww.mtbthedales.org.uk). The main touring cycle route is the circular 130-mile **Yorkshire Dales Cycle Way** (Ⓦwww.cyclethedales.org.uk), which starts and finishes in Skipton.

Skipton

SKIPTON, southernmost town of the Dales, is best visited on one of its four weekly **market days** (Mon, Wed, Fri & Sat), when the streets and pubs are filled with what seems like half the Dales' population. There's a farmers' market on the

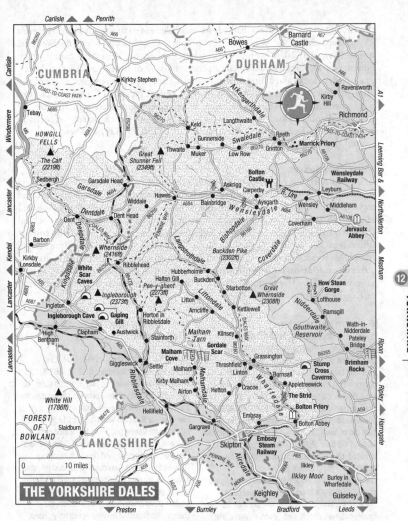

first Sunday of the month, and even a **Mart Theatre** on the outskirts of town (Ⓦwww.themarttheatre.org.uk), the only theatre to operate in a working auction market. Medieval and Christmas markets in December are an enjoyable feature, too.

Sceptone, or "Sheeptown" – the annual Sheep Day (first Sun in July) celebrates its ovine heritage – was a thriving agricultural settlement long before the arrival of the Normans. Their **castle**, at the top of the High Street (March–Sept Mon–Sat 10am–6pm, Sun noon–6pm; Oct–March Mon–Sat 10am–4pm, Sun noon–4pm; £6.20; Ⓦwww.skiptoncastle.co.uk), is among England's best preserved, thanks mainly to the efforts of Lady Anne Clifford, who rebuilt much of her family seat following the pillage of the Civil War. A self-guided tour leads you through the original Norman gateway into the beautiful Conduit Court, where the yew tree was supposedly planted by Lady Anne herself. Further down the High Street, on the first floor of the town hall, don't miss the entertaining **Craven Museum** (April–Sept Mon & Wed–Sat 10am–4pm; Oct–March Mon & Wed–Fri noon–4pm, Sat 10am–4pm; free), whose collection runs the gamut from boneshaker bicycles to policemen's helmets, by way of flints, fossils, snuff boxes, grandfather clocks and a hippopotamus skull. The alleys on the western side of the High Street emerge on to the banks of the **Leeds–Liverpool Canal**, which runs right through the centre of Skipton; a one-hour signposted trail follows the towpath. Pennine Boat Trips at Waterside Court, off Coach Street, offers daily **canal cruises** (Easter–Oct & Dec; £6.50; ☎01756/790829, ⊛www.canaltrips .co.uk) that last around an hour.

Practicalities

The **train** station is on Broughton Road, a ten-minute walk from the centre. The **bus** station is closer in, on Keighley Road, at the bottom of the High Street. Local services run from Skipton to Settle (not Sun) for connections on to Ingleton and Horton, to Malham (not Sun), and to Grassington. The main **car parks** are behind the town hall (off High St) or on Coach Street nearer the canal, while the **tourist office** is at 35 Coach St (April–Oct Mon–Sat 10am–5pm, Sun 11am–3pm; Nov–March Mon–Sat 10am–4pm; ☎01756/792809, ⊛www.skiptononline.co.uk).

    Accommodation is plentiful, with a host of central pubs offering rooms, as well as several B&Bs a few minutes' walk out of the centre, either on Gargrave (west) or Keighley (south) roads.

Accommodation

Chinthurst Otley Rd ☎01756/799264, ⊛www .chinthurst.co.uk. Run by very amenable owners, this elegant detached Victorian house features spacious bathrooms, lovely bed linen and contemporary art on the walls. New conservatory and executive suites recently added. ❸

Craven Heifer Grassington Rd ☎01756/792521, ⊛www.cravenheifer.co.uk. Stone-built Dales inn, a mile out of town (2min drive), with rooms fashioned from an old barn. Buffet continental breakfast included, plus bar, restaurant and parking. No single Sat night bookings. ❷

Woolly Sheep Inn 38 Sheep St, bottom of High St ☎01756/700966, ⊛www.timothytaylor.co.uk. Some of the pine-furnished rooms are a bit tight on space, but have decent beds, good showers, and cafetieres supplied. Downstairs in the public bar

there are Timothy Taylor's beers and meals served daily. Parking. ❸

Restaurants and pubs

Bizzie Lizzies 36 Swadford St ☎01756/701131. The town's award-winning fish-and-chip shop, with the restaurant side of the operation (dining over the canal) open until 9pm every night.

The Narrow Boat 38 Victoria St ☎01756/797922. All you want from a pub – not just varied cask ales and a multitude of Belgian and German beers, but good, inexpensive food (lunch daily, dinner Tues–Sat until 9pm, Sun noon–4pm), and no piped music. It's the recipe for coming for one drink and staying put.

Nosh 1 Devonshire Place ☎01756/700060. Modern bar-brasserie serving moderately priced, fashionable food.

Wharfedale

Wharfedale starts just south and east of Skipton, with **Ilkley** and **Bolton Abbey**, and then continues north in a broad, pastoral sweep scattered with picture-perfect villages. The popular walking centre of **Grassington** is the main village, while upland roads lead from the head of the valley across the watershed into Wensleydale. However, the most attractive itinerary would take you up lonely Littondale to **Arncliffe**, a village almost too good to be true, and then over the tops to either Malham or Ribblesdale. Throughout the year, **buses** run roughly hourly (not Sun in winter) to Grassington from Skipton, and then half a dozen times a day on up the B6160 to Kettlewell, Starbotton and Buckden.

Approaching the Dales from Leeds and the southeast along the A65, it's hard to resist a detour to the small, stone town of Ilkley, once a spa town of some repute though largely known for the brooding moorland above. In the words of a round known to many Yorkshire schoolchildren, windswept **Ilkley Moor** is where "tha's been a-courtin' Mary Jane, on Ilkley Moor baht-'at [without a hat]" – a foolish sartorial omission since, according to the round, you'll catch your death of cold, die, be buried, eaten by worms, which are eaten by ducks, which are eaten by people, until "then we shall all 'ave etten thee".

Bolton Abbey

BOLTON ABBEY, five miles east of Skipton, is the name of a whole village rather than an abbey, a confusion compounded by the fact that the place's main monastic ruin is known as **Bolton Priory** (daily 9am–dusk; free). Turner painted the site, and Ruskin described it as the most beautiful in England, though only the nave, which was incorporated into the village church in 1170, has survived in almost its original state. The priory is the starting point for several popular riverside walks, including a section of the **Dales Way** footpath that follows the river's west bank to take in Bolton Woods and the **Strid** (from "stride"), an extraordinary piece of narrow white water two miles north of the abbey. Beyond the Strid, the path emerges at **Barden Bridge**, four miles from the priory, where the fortified **Barden Tower** shelters a tearoom.

Perhaps the nicest approach to the priory is on the **Embsay & Bolton Abbey Steam Railway** – the Bolton Abbey station is a mile and a half by footpath from the priory ruins. The trains (every 1hr–1hr 30min: summer daily; winter weekends only plus some other days; £8 return; ☎01756/710614, ⓦwww .embsayboltonabbeyrailway.org.uk) start from Embsay, two miles east of Skipton. Alternatively, it costs £6 to park in any of the three estate **car parks**. There's local **information** from the estate office (☎01756/718009, ⓦwww.boltonabbey.com) and an information point at **Cavendish Pavilion**, a mile north of the priory, where there's also a riverside restaurant and café.

At Bolton Abbey the main **hotel** is the sumptuous *Devonshire Arms* (☎01756/710441, ⓦwww.thedevonshirearms.co.uk; ⑨), owned by the Duchess of Devonshire and furnished with antiques from the ancestral pile at Chatsworth; there's a good brasserie and bar open to the public.

Grassington and around

GRASSINGTON, nine miles from Bolton Abbey, has a good Georgian centre, and the surroundings are at their best by the river, where the shallow Linton Falls thunder after rain. The cobbled **Market Square** is home to several inns, a few gift shops and a small local museum. Traditional rural pursuits, as well as music and arts, are celebrated in the annual **Grassington Festival** (ⓦwww.grassington-festival .org.uk), held every June.

The **National Park Centre** is on Hebden Road (April–Oct daily 10am–5pm; Nov–March Fri–Sun 10am–4pm; ☎01756/751690), across from the bus stop; there's a huge pay-and-display **car park** here. Grassington also has the bulk of the dale's **services**, including a bank with ATM.

In summer you should pre-book **accommodation**, and at busy times you may have to look further afield – no hardship since Grassington is surrounded by tiny scenic villages. Tearooms, **cafés and restaurants** abound, but Grassington's best places to eat – a series of country **inns** known for their food – are all slightly out of the centre.

Hotels, inns and B&Bs

Angel Inn/Angel Barn Lodgings Hetton, 4 miles southwest ☎01756/730263, ⓦwww.angelhetton .co.uk. This Dales gastropub par excellence has five immaculate rooms and suites. Over the road in the inn, food is served either in the bar-brasserie (lunch & dinner) or more formal restaurant (Mon–Sat dinner & Sun lunch). ❺

Ashfield House Summers Fold, Grassington ☎01756/752584, ⓦwww.ashfieldhouse.co .uk. Lovely seventeenth-century house, 50yd off the square (behind the *Devonshire Hotel*), boasting immaculate cottage-style decor, comfortable and individual rooms, a walled garden and good breakfasts. Weekend deals. ❸

Devonshire Fell Burnsall, 3 miles southeast ☎01756/729000, ⓦwww.devonshirefell.co.uk. Rooms here have been given the designer treatment – it's a country-house retreat, but definitely not "country" in feel. Views are either of garden and village or fells and river, while a classy bar and bistro complete the experience. Guests can use Bolton Abbey's *Devonshire Arms'* leisure facilities. Weekend two-night minimum. ❺

Grassington Lodge 8 Wood Lane, Grassington ☎01756/752518, ⓦwww.grassingtonlodge.co.uk. A splash of contemporary style – coordinated fabrics, hardwood floors, specially commissioned Dales photography – enhances this comfortable village guesthouse. Many rooms, in the main house and in the new annexe, are spacious, with large beds. Parking available. ❸

Red Lion Burnsall, 3 miles southeast ☎01756/720204, ⓦwww.redlion.co.uk. A real old country inn, with log fires, oak beams, a cosy bar, and river views from its comfortable, traditionally furnished rooms. Inventive meals (in the bar or restaurant) use local ingredients (both expensive; restaurant reservations advised). ❹

Eating and drinking

Fountaine Inn Linton, 1 mile southwest of Grassington ☎01756/752210. The old pub on the green makes a nice target for a walk across the river from Grassington. The food's excellent, with daily specials (local meat, fresh fish and veggie options) that take some beating. Most mains £9–15.

Old Hall Inn Threshfield, 1 mile west of Grassington ☎01756/752441. Stone-flagged inn where you can expect to have to wait for a table before tucking into the likes of salmon, steaks and sausages, all locally sourced. Closed Mon lunch. Similar prices to the *Fountaine Inn.*

Littondale, Kettlewell and upper Wharfedale

Wharfedale's scenery above Grassington grows still more impressive, starting a mile north with ancient Grass Wood, and followed two miles later by glacially carved Kilnsey Crag, popular with climbers. Just beyond, a minor road branches off left into **Littondale**, whose stunning scenery is best appreciated from **Arncliffe**, halfway up the dale, with a nice walkers' pub on the green. The valley-floor footpath from Arncliffe on to **LITTON** (2–3 miles) is a delight, ending at the ancient and unspoilt *Queen's Arms* (☎01756/770208; ❺).

KETTLEWELL is the main centre for the upper dale, with plenty of local B&B accommodation plus a youth hostel in the village centre (☎01756/760232, Ⓔkettlewell@yha.org.uk). The pubs, the *Bluebell* and the *King's Head*, are both cosy. Incidentally, the village was one of the major locations for *Calendar Girls*, the true story of doughty Yorkshire ladies who bared all for a charity calendar.

It's lovely country north of Kettlewell, accessed either via the dale's single lonely road (B6160) or the Dales Way path. There's a good pub at **STARBOTTON**, two miles away, the *Fox & Hounds* (☎01756/760269; closed Mon & first two weeks in Jan), which has ancient flagged floors and a huge fire in winter. Further upstream, the river flows through Langstrothdale to **HUBBERHOLME** and the stone-flagged, whitewashed *George* (☎01756/760223, ⓦwww.thegeorge-inn.co.uk; ❹), the favourite pub of archetypal Yorkshireman J.B. Priestley, who revelled in visiting a hamlet he thought "one of the smallest and pleasantest places in the world". His ashes are buried outside the church of St Michael and All Angels, over the stone bridge from the pub.

Malhamdale

A few miles west of Wharfedale lies **Malhamdale** (ⓦwww.malhamdale.com), with its three outstanding natural features of Malham Cove, Malham Tarn and Gordale Scar. It is classic limestone country, dominated by a mighty escarpment topped by a fractured pavement, and cut through with sheer walls, tumbling waterfalls and dry valleys. All three attractions are within easy hiking distance of **Malham village**, reached by bus from Skipton (Mon–Fri year-round) or on the seasonal **Malham Tarn shuttle** which runs between Settle (Easter–Oct, weekends & bank hols only, several daily departures) and the National Park Centre.

Malham village

MALHAM's couple of hundred inhabitants live in a handful of stone houses on either side of a bubbling river, but the village attracts half a million visitors a year. Provided you're prepared to do some walking you can escape the worst of the crowds, and something of the village's charm can be enjoyed in the evening when most of the trippers have gone. Don't miss the annual agricultural country fair, the **Malham Show** (August bank holiday Saturday).

The car park is by the **National Park Centre**, at the southern edge of the village (April–Oct daily 10am–5pm; Nov–March Sat & Sun 10am–4pm; ⓣ01969/652380). There are several good village **B&Bs**, plus many others dotted up and down dale, while the two **pubs** in Malham also have rooms. The *Buck Inn* has a popular walkers' back-bar, but food is better at the fancier *Lister Arms* over the bridge. As well as the YHA hostel, there are also local campsites and bunkbarns – details from the National Park Centre.

Accommodation

Beck Hall ⓣ01729/830332, ⓦwww.beckhall malham.com. Extended Dales cottage set in streamside gardens, 200yd from the fork in the village centre. A varied mix of en-suite rooms – some with panelling and four-posters, others with stream and field views – plus a cosy lounge and fire, wi-fi access, and all-year daytime café (closed Mon). Parking. ❸

Malham YHA ⓣ0845/371 9529, ⓔmalham@yha .org.uk. Purpose-built hostel that's well known as a walking and cycling centre. Closed Jan. Dorms from £13.95.

Miresfield Farm ⓣ01729/830414, ⓦwww .miresfield-farm.com. The first house in the village, with lovely rural views. Country-pine-style rooms vary in size. There's also a small campsite with toilet and shower. Breakfast available. ❷

Malham Cove, Malham Tarn and Gordale Scar

A mile north of Malham, **Malham Cove** is a white-walled limestone amphitheatre rising three hundred feet above its surroundings. A track leads to the cove, passing some of England's most visible prehistoric field banks. After a breath-sapping haul to the top, the rewards are fine views and the famous limestone pavement, an expanse of clints (slabs) and grykes (clefts) created by water seeping through weaker lines in the limestone rock.

A simple walk (or summer shuttle bus ride) over the moors brings **Malham Tarn** into sight, a lake created by an impervious layer of glacial debris. Its waterfowl are protected by a nature reserve on the west bank, visible from a nature trail which forms part of the Pennine Way. Meanwhile, at **Gordale Scar** (also easily approached direct from Malham village), the cliffs are if anything more spectacular than at Malham Cove, complemented by a deep ravine to the rear caused by the collapse of a cavern roof. A little to the south of the scar, off the road, lies **Janet's Foss**, a peach of a waterfall set amid green-damp rocks and overarching trees. The classic **circuit** takes in cove, tarn and scar in a clockwise walk from Malham (8 miles; 3hr 30min).

The Settle–Carlisle Railway

Often dubbed England's most scenic railway, the **Settle–Carlisle** line is a feat of Victorian engineering that has few equals in Britain. In the six years between 1869 and 1875, when the 72-mile line opened, herculean efforts were made by thousands of navvies to blast a route through the unforgiving Dales mountainsides. Living in squalid shantytowns by the sides of the track, and even in the newly opened railway tunnels themselves, six thousand men built twenty viaducts and bored fourteen tunnels. Construction had a high price – over two hundred workers died, some of disease or in accidents; many now lie buried in the village churches that line the route.

The journey from Settle to Carlisle takes an hour and forty minutes, so it's easy to make a **return trip** (day return £18) along the whole length of the line. If you only have time for a short rail trip, the best section is that between Settle and **Garsdale** (30min). Walkers can access the Dales, Ribble and Pennine ways from the B6255 (Hawes road), just a mile or so east of the line at Ribblehead. There are connections to Settle from Skipton (20min) and Leeds (1hr); full **timetable** details are available from National Rail Enquiries, ☎0845/748 4950, or from the website, ⓦwww.settle-carlisle.co.uk.

Ribblesdale

Ribblesdale, to the west of Malhamdale, is entered from Settle, starting point of the **Settle–Carlisle Railway**, among the most scenic rail routes in the country. The valley's only village of any size is **Horton in Ribblesdale**, a focus not only for the Ribble Way and Pennine Way, but also for those starting the **Three Peaks Walk**, an arduous hike around the Dales' highest peaks.

Settle is the transport junction for Ribblesdale, with daily **trains** heading north through Horton to Carlisle and south to Skipton, Keighley and Leeds. Regular **buses** connect Skipton with Settle, from where there are services three or four times daily (not Sun) north through Stainforth to Horton, and northwest via Clapham to Ingleton in the western Dales.

Settle

Nestled under the wooded knoll of Castleberg, **SETTLE** has a typical seventeenth-century market square, still sporting its split-level arcaded shambles. Other than on Tuesdays, when the market is in full swing, there's not much to see in the few streets behind the square and you might as well make the ten-minute climb up through the woods to the top of Castleberg for views over the town.

The **train station** is less than five signposted minutes' walk from Market Place, down Station Road. The **tourist office** in the town hall, just off Market Place (daily 9.30am–4.30pm; ☎01729/825192), has hiking maps and pamphlets. A seasonal weekend and bank holiday **shuttle bus** (Easter–Oct) runs over the tops to Malham in an hour. As for accommodation, two old inns, the *Royal Oak* on Market Place (☎01729/822561, ⓦwww.royaloaksettle.co.uk; ➋), and the *Golden Lion*, just off Market Place along Duke Street (☎01729/822203, ⓔinfo@goldenlion.yorks .net; ➌), are the most atmospheric **places to stay**. Best of the B&Bs is *Settle Lodge* on Duke Street (☎01729/823258, ⓦwww.settlelodge.co.uk; no credit cards; ➋), a Victorian house with spacious rooms in contemporary style.

Both the inns serve reasonable **food** and decent beer. The *Royal Oak* gets the nod by virtue of its extraordinary carved oak-panelled bar and dining room. During the day, however, it's hard to see anyone resisting the lure of ⚘ *Ye Olde Naked Man Café* on Market Place (☎01729/823230), serving breakfasts, proper coffee and good home-made food; a former undertakers', the café's name refers to the old adage that "You bring now't into t'world and you take now't out".

Horton in Ribblesdale and the Three Peaks

HORTON IN RIBBLESDALE, now a prime walking centre, dates from Norman times – its church, St Oswald's, retains its original proportions in the fine nave – but the village gained a new lease of life in the nineteenth century when the arrival of the Settle–Carlisle Railway allowed it to expand its age-old quarrying operations. Mine workings old and new slightly spoil the west side of the village, but they don't mar the views from the surrounding walking trails.

The village is most convenient for the ascent of sphinx-shaped **Pen-y-ghent** (3–4hr round trip), the most dramatic of the three summits just to the east on the Pennine Way; the other peaks are more easily climbed from Ingleton or Dentdale. The family-owned ⋇ *Pen-y-ghent Café* in the village has filling meals, and is also a networked Tourist Information Centre (summer daily Mon–Fri 9am–5.30pm, Sat 8am–6pm, Sun 8.30–6pm; call ☎01729/860333 for winter hours), headquarters for the famous **Three Peaks Walk** (see box below).

Horton straggles along a mile of the Settle–Ribblehead road (B6479), with the **train station** in the north, and the church in the south. In between are the café, a post office/store and a campsite. The *Crown Hotel* (☎01729/860209, ⒲www .crown-hotel.co.uk; ❸), by the bridge, has plain but cosy **rooms** (some, without attached bath, a bit cheaper) and good bar food. The *Golden Lion* (☎01729/860206, ⒲www.goldenlionhotel.co.uk), at the other end of the road by the church, has both B&B rooms (❷) and bunkhouse beds (from £12; breakfast and packed lunches available).

The western Dales

The **western Dales** run north from **Ingleton**, a village perfectly poised for walks up **Ingleborough** and **Whernside**, and for **Dentdale**, one of the loveliest valleys in the national park. Ingleton has the most accommodation, but **Dent** is by far the best target for a quiet night's retreat, with a cobbled centre barely altered in centuries. **Sedbergh** to the northwest has an interesting arts and crafts centre while just outside the park and county boundary, to the southwest, the pretty market town of **Kirby Lonsdale** features a graceful medieval bridge spanning the River Lune.

Ingleton is linked by **bus** to Kirby Lonsdale, Clapham, Settle (for Skipton) and Horton, while the Settle–Carlisle Railway offers access to scenic upper Dentdale and Garsdale (though it does drop you in the middle of nowhere). Sedbergh is actually easiest to reach from Kendal in the Lake District, and also has the only regular (but fairly limited) bus services to Dent.

Clapham and its caves

CLAPHAM, a seductive little riverside village at the southern foot of Ingleborough, is the starting point for the mile-long (30min) walk to **Ingleborough Cave**

12

YORKSHIRE | The Yorkshire Dales

Extreme peaks

Hiking up any of the Dales' notable Three Peaks – namely Pen-y-ghent (2273ft), Whernside (2416ft) – Yorkshire's highest point – and Ingleborough (2373ft) – would be challenging enough, but a circuit of the lot, the **Three Peaks Walk**, is a staple of the hardcore English walking scene. It's 25 miles and twelve hours of gut-busting effort, though the last Sunday of April sees lunatics *running* the route in the "Three Peaks Race" – what takes normal people the best part of a day to walk takes the winner under three hours – while on the last Sunday in September cyclo-cross enthusiasts take their own crack at the gruelling route, cycling where they can, pushing or carrying their bikes when it gets too steep (⒲www.3peakscyclocross.org.uk).

(mid-Feb to Oct daily 10am–5pm; £6; ⓦwww.ingleboroughcave.co.uk), the Pennines' oldest show cave, discovered in 1837. There's a signposted public footpath to the cave, or the adjacent nature trail (50p) through Clapdale Woods. To make a real walk of it you can continue on the footpath beyond the cave, through the narrow canyon walls of **Trow Gill** and up to the fenced site of **Gaping Gill**, 365ft deep and 450ft long, and the most famous of the Dales' many potholes.

Clapham is equidistant from Settle and Ingleton, just off the A65, around four miles from either; its **train station** (on the Leeds/Skipton–Lancaster line) offers another entry to the Dales, but lies over a mile south of the village. The village has a couple of tearooms and a pub, while a mile or so to the east in **AUSTWICK**, the charms of the *Austwick Traddock* (ⓣ01524/251224, ⓦwww.austwicktraddock.co.uk; ❻, minimum 2-night stay at weekends) are obvious: an elegant Georgian country-house hotel with a cheery demeanour, agreeable rooms with plump beds, and refined food.

Ingleton

The straggling slate-grey village of **INGLETON** sits upon a ridge at the confluence of two streams, the Twiss and the Doe, whose beautifully wooded valleys are easily the area's best features. The four-and-a-half mile **Falls' Walk** (daily 9am–dusk; entrance fee £4.50; ⓦwww.ingletonwaterfallswalk.co.uk) is a lovely circular walk (2hr 30min) taking in both valleys, and providing viewing points over its waterfalls. Serious hikers also tackle both **Ingleborough** and **Whernside** from Ingleton, two of the Three Peaks.

There are a dozen local **B&Bs and guesthouses**, most lying along Main Street. *Riverside Lodge*, 24 Main St (ⓣ01524/241359, ⓦwww.riversideingleton.co.uk; ❷), is the pick of them for its valley-view conservatory, terraced garden and sauna. The centrally located **youth hostel** (ⓣ0845/371 9124, ⓔingleton@yha.org.uk; from £15.95) is an old stone house set in its own gardens, while *Stackstead Farm*, a mile south off the minor road to High Bentham (ⓣ01524/241386, ⓦwww.stackstead farm.co.uk), has a **bunkhouse barn** (from £11, groups only at weekends). The *Inglesport Café* on the first floor of the hiking store on Main Street provides hearty soups and potatoes with everything. In the evening there's *La Tavernetta*, 23 Main St (ⓣ01524/242465; Thurs–Sat only), serving inexpensive Italian meals and pizza.

White Scar Caves

Just a mile and a half out of Ingleton on the Ribblehead/Hawes road (B6255) is the entrance to the **White Scar Caves** (daily 10am–5pm; weekends only Nov–Jan, weather permitting; £7.95; ⓣ01524/241244, ⓦwww.whitescarcave.co.uk), the longest show cave in England. Don't be put off by the steep price – it's worth every penny for the (hourly or so) eighty-minute tour of dank underground chambers, contorted cave formations and glistening stalactites. The cave is lined with steel-grid walkways along which you edge, the thundering of the internal waterfall becoming ever louder the further in you venture. There's a café on site.

Dent

Just over the border in Cumbria, **DENT** is a picture, with its grassy cobbles and huddled stone cottages. In the seventeenth and eighteenth centuries, **Dentdale** (ⓦwww.dentdale.com) supported a flourishing hand-knitting industry, later ruined by mechanization. These days, the hill-farming community supplements its income through tourism and crafts.

Dent's **train station** (on the Settle–Carlisle line) is, oddly, not in Dent at all, but four miles to the east. You can stay at either of the village's two **pubs**, the *Sun Inn* (ⓣ01539/625208; ❶), or the *George & Dragon* (ⓣ01539/625256, ⓦwww.thegeorgeanddragondent.co.uk; ❸), which are virtually next to each other in the centre. The *Sun* is the nicer, welcoming to walkers and with a great traditional feel; that said, the en-suite rooms at the *George & Dragon* have been modernized and are more comfortable. There are a handful of **B&Bs**, most notably *Stone Close Guest House* (℡01539/625231, Ⓔstoneclose@btconnect. com; ❷, en-suite ❸), which has a good tearoom (closed Mon, and Tues in winter). Both the pubs serve bar **meals**. The only other facilities in the village are a post office and small store.

Sedbergh

A few miles northwest of Dent, up on the A684, the small stone-built market town of **SEDBERGH** is tucked under the brooding Howgill Fells. Historically, it's best known for its public school, established in 1525, and its Quaker meeting house of 1675 at nearby Briggflatts, but the **Dales Way** passes through, making it something of a hiking centre, while since 2006 it has been officially recognized as England's "**book town**" (joining Hay-on-Wye on the Anglo–Welsh border and Scotland's Wigtown). Otherwise, call in at **Farfield Mill** (mid-Feb to Dec daily 10.30am–5pm; £3; Ⓦwww.farfieldmill.org), a mile east of town on the Garsdale/ Hawes road (A684 – follow the signs). The former woollen mill is now an enterprising arts and heritage centre – the admission fee allows you to view the historic exhibits, galleries, Victorian weaving looms and artists at work, though there's no charge for the excellent riverside café.

Kirkby Lonsdale

Also in Cumbria, quaint **KIRKBY LONSDALE** sits on a rise above the River Lune. Ten minutes' walk south of town on the A683, the three-arched **Devil's Bridge** once formed the main route into Yorkshire from the Lakes. There's parking by the bridge and a path from here follows the river to the base of a steep flight of steps that re-enters the town behind St Mary's Church.

Kirkby Lonsdale is a handy base for the western Yorkshire Dales, with both Dent (no public transport) and Ingleton only around eight miles away. The **tourist office** is at 24 Main St (℡01524/271437, Ⓦwww.kirkbylonsdale.co.uk), and posts a list of B&Bs in the window when closed, or **stay** at either the *Snooty Fox* on Main Street (℡01524/271308, Ⓔsnootyfoxhotel@talktalk.net; ❷) or the nearby *Sun Hotel*, 6 Market St (℡01524/271965, Ⓦwww.sun-inn.info; ❹), which backs onto the churchyard. Both are also decent places for a drink, and have brasserie-style menus. However, the real gourmet experience is to be found a couple of miles out of town, at lovely *Hipping Hall*, Cowan Bridge (℡01524/271187, Ⓦwww.hippinghall.com; ❻, weekends ❼), with cool and classy rooms and stone and slate bathrooms.

Wensleydale

Best known of the Dales, if only for its cheese, **Wensleydale** (Ⓦwww.wensleydale .org) is also the largest and most serene. It's also familiar to devotees of the **James Herriot** TV series, which was filmed here. Aside from the main town, **Hawes**, there are several well-known waterfalls – notably **Aysgarth Falls** – and, as the dale opens into the Vale of York, historic buildings that range from **castles** at Bolton and Middleham to **abbeys** at Jervaulx and Coverham.

The dale is traversed by the national park's only east–west **main road** (the A684), and linked by high moor roads to virtually all the park's other dales. Year-round **public transport** is provided by post and service buses from Hawes on varied routes via Bainbridge, Askrigg, Aysgarth and Castle Bolton to Leyburn (for Richmond), and the #159 between Masham, Leyburn and Richmond. There are also Sunday and bank holiday services connecting Hawes to Wharfedale (#800).

Hawes

HAWES is Wensleydale's chief town, main hiking centre, and home to its tourism, cheese and rope-making industries. It also claims to be Yorkshire's highest market town, and received its market charter in 1699; the weekly Tuesday market – crammed with farmers and market traders – is still going strong. If you haven't yet bought any **cheese**, the groaning stalls will doubtless persuade you otherwise. The cheese trail invariably leads to the **Wensleydale Creamery** on Gayle Lane (Mon–Sat 10am–5pm, Sun 10am–4.30pm; £2.50; ☎01969/667664, ⓦwww.wensleydale .co.uk), a few hundred yards south of the centre. The Creamery doesn't make cheese every day, so call first to guarantee a viewing. On the Aysgarth side of town, in the former train station and warehouses, the **Dales Countryside Museum** (daily 10am–5pm; £3) embraces lead-mining, farming, peat-cutting, knitting and much else. Alongside it, **Hawes Ropemakers** (Mon–Fri 9am–5.30pm, plus some Sat July–Oct; free) show present-day rope-makers at work.

The **National Park Centre** (daily 10am–5pm; ☎01969/666210) shares the building with the Dales Countryside Museum. **Buses** stop in Market Place (summer-only buses pull up outside the museum), and post buses depart from outside the post office. **Accommodation** is plentiful in local B&Bs, while all the pubs on and around the market square – the *Board*, *Crown*, *Fountain*, *Bull's Head* and *White Hart* – have rooms, too. Traditional **tearooms and cafés** cluster around Market Place – *Beckindales*, by the Ropemakers Museum, has a more contemporary air and an outdoor terrace. **Pub** dining is best at the *Crown* – which has a raised rear garden with valley views; otherwise, you're limited to a couple of hotel dining rooms, an Indian restaurant and a fish-and-chip café.

Accommodation and food

Hawes YHA Lancaster Terrace ☎0870/770 5854, ⓔhawes@yha.org.uk. Modern hostel on the edge of town, at the junction of the main A684 and B6255. Some twin and family rooms available (❶), otherwise dorm beds from £13.95. Closed Nov–Feb.

Herriot's Main St ☎01969/667536, ⓦwww .herriotsinhawes.co.uk. Small B&B, just off Market Place, where a couple of the rooms have fell views. The restaurant here is the best place to eat in town, offering hearty Dales dishes. ❸

The Old Dairy Farm Widdale, 3 miles west of Hawes ☎01969/667070, ⓦwww.olddairyfarm .com. Farmhouse accommodation, but of the luxurious and contemporary kind, with fine dining available (main courses £12.50–16.50). ❺

Rose & Crown Bainbridge, 5 miles east of Hawes ☎01969/650225, ⓦwww.theprideofwensleydale .com. Fifteenth-century coaching inn with restaurant and bar, overlooking an emerald village green. ❷

Askrigg, Aysgarth and Castle Bolton

The mantle of "Herriot country" lies heavy on **ASKRIGG**, six miles east of Hawes, as the TV series *All Creatures Great and Small* was filmed in and around the village. Nip into the *King's Arms* – a cosy old haunt with wood panelling, good beer and bar meals – and you can see stills from the TV series.

The ribbon-village of **AYSGARTH** sucks in Wensleydale's largest number of visitors, courtesy of the **Aysgarth Falls**, half a mile below the village. A marked nature trail runs through the surrounding woodlands and there's a big car park and excellent **National Park Centre** on the north bank (April–Oct daily 10am–5pm; Nov–March Fri–Mon 10am–4pm; ☎01969/662910). The **Upper Falls** and picnic grounds lie just back from here, by the bridge and church; the more spectacular **Middle** and **Lower Falls** are a ten-minute stroll to the east through shaded woodland. The ice cream is good at the park centre **café**; otherwise, the two local **pubs** – the *Palmer Flatts* by the falls turn-off and the *George & Dragon* in the village – both have bar meals and outdoor tables, though the main A684 road does neither of them a favour.

There's a superb **circular walk** northeast from Aysgarth via Bolton Castle (6 miles; 4hr) – or you can simply drive to the castle in about ten minutes. The walk starts at the falls themselves and climbs up through Thoresby, with the foursquare battlements of **Bolton Castle** (March–Nov Tues–Sun 10am–5pm; restricted winter opening, call for details; £6.50; ℡01969/623981, ⓦwww.boltoncastle .co.uk) themselves a magnetic lure from miles away. It's a massive defensive structure in which Mary, Queen of Scots, was imprisoned for six months in 1568. The Great Chamber, a few adjacent rooms and the castle gardens have been restored, and the café (free to enter) is a welcome spot if you've just trudged up from Aysgarth.

Wensley, Leyburn, Middleham and Jervaulx

A few miles east of Aysgarth, Wensleydale broadens into a low-hilled pastoral valley. The church of the **Holy Trinity** at **WENSLEY**, one of the Dales' finest, originates from the thirteenth century but has fabric dating from the following five centuries, the most impressive being an extravagant box pew and a sixteenth-century rood-screen removed from Richmond's Easby Abbey. The market town of **LEYBURN** – a couple of miles east of Wensley and eleven miles southwest of Richmond – occupies almost the last piece of straggling high ground on the valley's north edge, set around three open squares replete with buildings from its eighteenth-century heyday; market day is Friday. Trains run on the scenic **Wensleydale Railway** (℡0845/450 5474, ⓦwww.wensleydalerailway.com; £12.50 day rover) between Leyburn and Leeming Bar, twelve miles to the east (on the A1).

Two miles southeast of Leyburn, the tiny town of **MIDDLEHAM** is approached over an impressive early nineteenth-century castellated bridge. A well-to-do place set around a sloping cobbled square, it's dominated by the imposing ruins of **Middleham Castle** (Easter–Sept daily 10am–6pm; Oct–March Mon–Wed, Sat & Sun 10am–4pm; £4; EH), built by the Normans to guard the route from Skipton to Richmond. Racehorses clip-clopping through the centre are a common sight, with over five hundred trained locally at more than a dozen stables. Several **pubs** vie for custom around the square – the *White Swan*, *Black Swan*, *Richard III* and *Black Bull* all have rooms available; the best food is at the *White Swan*.

Wensleydale all but peters out with the overgrown ruins of **Jervaulx Abbey** (daily dawn–dusk; £2; ⓦwww.jervaulxabbey.com), four miles southeast of Middleham on the A6108 road to Ripon. Founded in 1156, it is the least prepossessing of the great trio of Cistercian abbeys completed by Fountains and Rievaulx, but makes an enjoyable stop for a ramble amid the wildflowers.

Masham

If you're a beer fan, head for **MASHAM** (pronounced Mass'm), home to the **Theakston Brewery** (tours daily on the hour 11am–3pm (July & Aug 11am–4pm; £5.75, reservations advised; ℡01765/680000, ⓦwww.theakstons.co.uk) since 1827, where you can learn the arcane intricacies of the brewer's art and become familiar with the legendary Old Peculier ale. In the early 1990s one of the Theakston family brewing team left to set up the **Black Sheep Brewery**, also based in Masham and offering tours (daily 11am–4pm, but call for availability; £5.95; ℡01765/680100, ⓦwww.blacksheepbrewery.com). Both breweries are just a few minutes' signposted walk out of the centre.

Masham itself is one of the most attractive small towns in Yorkshire, with a huge central marketplace (market days are Wednesday and Saturday), a handsome church and a smattering of local shops and galleries. There's no more agreeable **accommodation** – here, or for many miles around – than ☙ *Swinton Park* (℡01765/680900, ⓦwww.swintonpark.com; ❼), an elegant stately home overlooking the river. There's a fine-dining restaurant, and a cookery school (day

courses available). The *King's Head*, 42 Market Place (℡01765/689295, ⓦwww
.kingsheadmasham.com; ❸, breakfast not included), is the best **place to eat** in
town, more restaurant than pub. There's also a bistro inside the Black Sheep
Brewery (open when the brewery's open and also for dinner most nights). The
local beer's at its best in the *White Bear* (℡01765/689319), the **brewery pub**
attached to Theakston's.

Swaledale

Narrow and steep-sided in its upper reaches, **Swaledale** emerges rocky and rugged
in its central tract before more typically pastoral scenery cuts in at the main village
of Reeth, the dale's best overnight stop. From Richmond, **bus #30** (not Sun) runs
up the valley along the B6270 as far as Keld. It's worth noting the Swaledale
Festival (ⓦwww.swaledale-festival.org.uk) every June, a widespread music and
arts bash at villages up and down the dale.

    Keld, eight miles north of Hawes and at the crossroads of the Pennine Way and
the Coast-to-Coast Path, is no more than a straggle of hardy buildings surrounded
by relics of the lead-mining industry. The Pennine Way shadows the very minor
Stonesdale road for the three or four miles across **Stonesdale Moor** to the *Tan Hill
Inn* (℡01833/628246, ⓦwww.tanhillinn.co.uk; ❹), reputedly the highest pub in
Britain (1732ft above sea level). **Thwaite** is the first hamlet south of Keld, just a
two-mile walk away, while some of the loveliest scenery follows beyond the little
village of **Muker**, a mile or so to the east, where there are a couple of teashops and
a decent pub, the *Farmers Arms*.

    Nine miles or so east, **REETH** is set in a dramatic moorland bowl. It's the dale's
main village and market centre – market day is Friday – and its desirable cottages
are gathered around a triangular green, where you'll find the **National Park
Centre** (April–Oct daily 10am–5pm; Nov–March Sat & Sun 10am–4pm;
℡01748/884059). Reeth has the biggest range of facilities in the dale, including
several B&Bs, a petrol station, two ATMs and a post office, as well as several craft
workshops. The three central **pubs** also have rooms, most notably the *King's Arms*
(℡01748/884259, ⓦwww.thekingsarms.com; ❷; weekend 2-night minimum),
or for superior old-fashioned comforts there's the *Burgoyne Hotel* (℡01748/884292,
ⓦwww.theburgoyne.co.uk; no single Sat night reservations; ❺), lording it over
the top of the green. Reeth Bakery is known for its great chocolate cake; and
there's good food at *Overton House Café* (℡01748/884332; open daytime Wed–Sat,
plus Thurs–Sat dinner), especially for fish.

    East of Reeth lie the romantic ruins of **Marrick Priory** and **Ellerton Priory**,
the latter visible from the B6270. Numerous paths cross the fields on the south
side of the River Swale letting you complete a circular walk from Reeth via
Grinton, whose attractive bridge, church and riverside inn are just a mile away
by road.

Richmond

RICHMOND is the Dales' single most tempting historical town, thanks mainly
to its magnificent castle, whose extensive walls and colossal keep cling to a
precipice above the River Swale. Indeed, the entire town is an absolute gem,
centred on a huge cobbled market square. The town was first dubbed *Riche-Mont*
("noble hill") by the Normans' who first built a castle here in 1071.

Arrival, information and accommodation

Buses stop in the Market Place; there are regular services into Wensleydale and
Swaledale, and to Darlington, ten miles to the northeast, on the main east-coast

train line. There's free two-hour **parking** in Market Place (pick up a disc from local shops), or aim for the pay-and-display Nunn's Close car park on Hurgill Road, off Victoria Road. The **tourist office**, at Friary Gardens, Victoria Road (summer daily 9.30am–5.30pm; winter 9.30am–4.30pm, closed Sun; T01748/828742, Wwww.richmond.org.uk), is helpful in finding accommodation, and also organizes **guided walking tours** around the town in summer (free, donations welcome). The big **events** each year are the Richmond Meet (May), with floats, parades and carnival, the free Richmond Live music festival (August), and September's Walking Festival.

Accommodation

Aislabeck Natural Retreats Hurgill Rd, Aislabeck, 1 mile north of Richmond T0161/242 2970, Wwww.naturalretreats.com. Contemporary wood lodges sleeping up to six, built on sustainable lines and set in a beautifully secluded location. Minimum two-night stay, from £300 (£610 high season).

Frenchgate Guest House 66 Frenchgate T01748/823421, Wwww.66frenchgate.co.uk. The reward for staying in one of the three immaculately presented rooms is breakfast with the best panoramic view in town. ❸

Frenchgate Hotel 59–61 Frenchgate T01748/822087, Wwww.thefrenchgate.co.uk. Georgian townhouse hotel, with eight individually furnished rooms, lots of local artwork and walled gardens. Its food has an excellent reputation. Parking. ❺

Millgate House Millgate T01748/823571, Wwww.millgatehouse.com. Shut the big green door of this Georgian house and enter a world of books, antiques, embroidered sheets, oil paintings in the bathroom, handmade toiletries, scrumptious breakfasts and the finest (and least precious) hosts you could wish for. If this is not enough, there's a haven of a walled garden too. No credit cards. ❺, en-suite ❺

Whashton Springs Near Whashton, 3 miles north, Ravensworth road T01748/822884, Wwww.whashtonsprings.co.uk. This working Dales farm offers a peaceful night in the country in rooms (in the main house or round the courtyard) filled with family furniture. A farmhouse breakfast sets you up for the day, while nearby country pubs are a short drive (or even a walk) away. ❷

The Town

There's no better place to start than **Richmond Castle** (April–Sept daily 10am–6pm; Oct–March Mon & Thurs–Sun 10am–4pm; £4; EH), which retains many original features from its earliest incarnation – the gatehouse, curtain wall and Scolland's Hall, the oldest Norman great hall in the country. There are prodigious views from the keep, which is over a hundred feet high, and from the Great Court, now an open lawn which ends in a sheer fall to the river below. Most of medieval Richmond sprouted around the castle, but much of the town now radiates from the **Market Place**, with the Market Hall alongside; market day is Saturday (farmers' market on the third Saturday of the month). The defunct **Holy Trinity Church** on the square now houses the **Green Howards Museum** (Mon–Sat 10am–4.30pm; £3.50). For local history, visit the charming **Richmondshire Museum** (April–Oct daily 10.30am–4.30pm; £2.50), down Ryder's Wynd, off King Street on the northern side of the square.

In the **Theatre Royal** (1788) the town has a fine piece of Georgian architecture that is one of England's oldest extant theatres. It's open for both **performances** (box office T01748/825252, Wwww.georgiantheatreroyal.co.uk) and **tours** (on the hour: mid-Feb to mid-Dec Mon–Sat 10am–4pm; £3.50), while a museum at the rear gives an insight into eighteenth-century theatrical life.

A signposted walk runs along the north bank of the River Swale out to the beautifully situated church of **St Agatha**, noted for its fine thirteenth-century wall paintings, and the golden stone walls of adjacent **Easby Abbey** (dawn to dusk; free; EH), a mile southeast of the town.

Eating and drinking

By far the best option for eating out is the **restaurant** in the *Frenchgate Hotel* (meals around £34; see p.725), though *A Taste of Thailand* at 15 King St (℡01748/829696) has its strong points, and the *Black Lion* **pub** on Finkle Street is good for daytime food or an evening pint. Alternatively you can drive out into the gentle country to the north where prettily sited pubs like the *Shoulder of Mutton* (℡01748/822772) at **Kirby Hill** (3 miles) or the *Bay Horse Inn* (℡01325/718328) at **Ravensworth** (5 miles) make for a decent night out.

Nidderdale

Nidderdale (ⓦwww.nidderdale.co.uk), the easternmost and probably least known of the Yorkshire Dales, stretches for around twenty miles from the source of the River Nidd on Great Whernside to the village of Ripley in the lower dale, just four miles from Harrogate. The main approach is along the east–west B6265 between Grassington in Wharfedale and Ripon, with the only available route north being along the wild road from Pateley Bridge, the dale's main village, to Masham and, ultimately, Wensleydale.

RIPLEY (bus #36 from Ripon or Harrogate) is an impeccably kept village whose bizarre appearance is due to a whim of Sir William Amcotts Ingilby, who between 1827 and 1854 rebuilt it in the manner of a village he had seen on his travels in Alsace, for no other reason than he liked the style. Summer crowds pile in for the cobbled square, stocks, twee cottages and shops, not to mention the Ingilby house, parkland and **castle** (castle 10am–3pm: Easter–Sept daily; March, Oct & Nov closed Mon, Wed & Fri; Dec–Feb Sat & Sun only; gardens: daily summer 9am–5pm, winter 9am–4.30pm; £8, gardens only £5.50; ⓦwww.ripleycastle.co.uk). The attractive *Boar's Head* (℡01423/771888, ⓦwww.ripleycastle.co.uk/hotel.html; ⑥) has a lovely bar and beer garden, and a high-class restaurant.

The characterful little town of **PATELEY BRIDGE** (bus #24 from Harrogate) serves as the dale's focus, and a base for campers, cavers and visitors of every kind. Make time for the **Panorama Walk** (2 miles; 1hr), signposted from the top of the High Street, and then refuel in one of the tearooms, pubs and restaurants along the High Street. One of the nicest **places to stay** and eat is the *Sportsmans Arms* (℡01423/711306, ⓦwww.sportsmans-arms.co.uk; ④), a couple of miles out off the Nidderdale road at Wath-in-Nidderdale.

Five miles west of the village on the Grassington road lie the **Stump Cross Caverns** (March–Nov daily 10am–6pm; Dec–Feb Sat & Sun 10am–4.45pm; £6; ⓦwww.stumpcrosscaverns.co.uk), one of England's premier show caves, complete with massive stalagmites. About the same distance east of the village, signposted off the B6265, are the extraordinary **Brimham Rocks**, nearly four hundred acres of strangely eroded millstone-grit outcrops scattered over one-thousand-foot-high moors. Views from here are superlative, stretching over the Vale of York, with York Minster visible on clear days.

The Nidderdale scenery is superb north of Pateley Bridge, above the **Gouthwaite Reservoir**. At **RAMSGILL**, at the northern end of the reservoir, the *Yorke Arms* (℡01423/755243, ⓦwww.yorke-arms.co.uk; ⑥) is a renowned restaurant-with-rooms operation. A couple of miles further, seven miles from Pateley Bridge, **How Stean Gorge** (Mon–Fri 10am–5pm, Sat, Sun & school hols 10am–6pm; £5.50; ⓦwww.howstean.co.uk) is an ice-gouged ravine of surging waters and overhanging rocks.

Ripon and around

The attractive market town of **RIPON**, eleven miles north of Harrogate, is centred upon its **cathedral** (daily 8am–6.30pm, depending on services; donation requested; ⊚www.riponcathedral.org.uk), which can trace its ancestry back to its foundation by St Wilfrid in 672; the original crypt is still open to the public. The town's other focus is its **Market Place**, linked by narrow Kirkgate to the cathedral; market day is Thursday, with a farmers' market on the third Sunday of the month. A ninety-foot obelisk built in 1780 dominates the square, topped by a horned weather vane. This is an allusion to the "Blowing of the Wakeman's Horn", a ceremony which may date from 886, when Alfred the Great reputedly granted Ripon a charter and an ox's horn was presented for the setting of the town's watch. The horn is still blown nightly at 9pm at the four corners of the obelisk.

The town makes for an agreeable, relatively traffic-free stroll. Three restored buildings show a different side of the local heritage, under the banner of the Yorkshire Law and Order Museums (all open April–Oct daily: school hols 11am–4pm, other times 1–4pm; combined ticket £7; ⊚www.riponmuseums.co .uk). At the **Prison and Police Museum** on St Marygate behind the cathedral, the cells serve as the backdrop for an informative and engaging exhibition on policing since Anglo-Saxon times, while criminals were tried in the 1830s **Courthouse** on Minster Road. Law-abiding locals often fared little better, with the "undeserving" poor incarcerated in the nearby **Ripon Workhouse** on Allhallowgate.

One of England's most splendid Queen Anne houses, **Newby Hall** (April–Sept Tues–Sun, plus Mon in July & Aug: house noon–4pm, gardens 11am–5pm; £12, gardens only £8.50; ⊚www.newbyhall.com), lies five miles southeast of Ripon near Skelton, south of the B6265. It contains some outstanding decorative plasterwork, lashings of Chippendale furniture and rich eighteenth-century tapestries. The grounds, sculpture park and gardens offer plenty for children, and there's also a tearoom and picnic area.

Practicalities

The **bus station** (#36 from Harrogate, or Leeds) is just off Market Place, while the town's **tourist office** is on Minster Road opposite the cathedral (April–Oct Mon–Sat 10am–5pm, Sun 10am–1pm; Nov–March Thurs & Sat 10am–4pm; ☏01765/604625, ⊚www.visitripon.org). For **B&B**, a longstanding favourite is *Bishopton Grove House*, Bishopton (☏01765/600888, ⊚www.bishoptongrove house.co.uk; no credit cards; ❷), a Georgian house in a peaceful corner of the town. Top honours, though, go to *The Old Deanery* on Minster Road (☏01765/600003, ⊚www.theolddeanery.co.uk; ❺), just across from the cathedral, completely refurbished in contemporary fashion, with excellent rooms and food (reservations advised for dinner; expensive).

Fountains Abbey and Studley Royal

It's tantalizing to imagine how the English landscape might have appeared had Henry VIII not dissolved the monasteries, with all the artistic ruin precipitated by that act. **Fountains Abbey**, four miles southwest of Ripon off the B6265, gives a good idea of what might have been, and is the one Yorkshire monastic ruin you should make a point of seeing. Linked to it are the elegant water gardens of **Studley Royal**, landscaped in the eighteenth century to form a setting for the abbey. The estate is owned by the National Trust, which organizes an ambitious range of activities and events – from opera and firework displays to **free guided tours** (April–Oct daily; ☏01765/608888). Public transport to the abbey is limited, though summer Sunday and bank holiday **bus** services operate from York/Ripon/Grassington (#812); there's also the #139 from Ripon.

The Abbey

Beautifully set in a narrow, wooded valley, **Fountains Abbey** (Feb, March & Oct daily 10am–4pm; April–Sept daily 10am–5pm; Nov–Jan daily except Fri 10am–4pm; £8.50 including Studley Royal and Fountains Hall; ⓦwww .fountainsabbey.org.uk) was founded in 1133 by dissident Benedictine monks and formally adopted by the Cistercian order two years later. Within a hundred years, Fountains had become the wealthiest Cistercian foundation in England and the three main phases of the abbey's development – nave and transepts, the domestic buildings, and the church's east end – all date from this period. After the Dissolution the abbey ultimately became a source of building stone for the nearby Fountains Hall, though further desecration was avoided when in 1768 William Aislabie brought the ruined abbey within the orbit of the Studley Royal Estate.

Most immediately eye-catching is the **abbey church**, in particular the **Chapel of the Nine Altars** at its eastern end, whose delicacy is in marked contrast to the austerity of the rest of the nave. A great sixty-foot-high window rises over the chapel, complemented by a similar window at the nave's western doorway, over 370ft away. Looming over the whole ensemble is the 180ft-high **Perpendicular Tower**, added in the early sixteenth century, perhaps the abbey's greatest period of prosperity. Equally grandiose in scale is the undercroft of the **Lay Brothers' Dormitory** off the cloister, a stunning vaulted space over 300ft long that was used to store the monastery's annual harvest of fleece: some thirteen tonnes of wool was turned over a year, most of it sold to Venetian and Florentine merchants who toured the monasteries.

The size of the lay buildings – including a substantial **Lay Brothers' Infirmary** – gives an idea of the number of lay brothers at the abbey. All are considerably larger than the corresponding monks' buildings, of which the most prepossessing are the **Chapter House** and **Refectory** – notice the huge fireplace of the tiny **Warming Room** alongside the refectory, the only heated space in the entire complex. Outside the abbey perimeter, between the gatehouse and the bridge, are the Abbey Mill and the fine seventeenth-century **Fountains Hall**.

Studley Royal

A bucolic riverside walk (two miles there and back), marked from the visitor centre car park, takes you from Fountains Hall through the abbey to the ponds and ornamental gardens of **Studley Royal** (same times as the abbey; NT), which can also be entered via the village of Studley Roger, where there's a separate car park. This lush medley of lawns, lake, woodland and **Deer Park** (daily dawn–dusk; free) was laid out in 1720. There are some scintillating views of the abbey from the gardens, though it's the cascades and water gardens that command most attention, framed by several aesthetically positioned small temples.

Harrogate

Genteel **HARROGATE** owes its landscaped appearance and early prosperity to the discovery of Tewit Well in 1571. This was the first of over eighty ferrous and sulphurous springs that, by the nineteenth century, were to turn the town into one of the country's leading spas. By the mid-twentieth century, however, spas were passé, and since the early 1970s Harrogate has instead concentrated on hosting conferences, exhibitions and festivals. Monuments to its past splendours still stand dotted around town and Harrogate manages to retain its essential Victorian and Edwardian character. Much of its appeal lies in the splendid parks and gardens – pick up a free "Floral Trail" leaflet from the tourist office – and Harrogate is particularly well known for its **flower shows** (late April and mid-Sept; Ⓦwww .flowershow.org.uk). There's also the three-day **Great Yorkshire Show** (second week in July; Ⓦwww.greatyorkshireshow.com) and various book and antique fairs, music festivals and craft shows.

Arrival, information and accommodation

Bus and **train** stations are conveniently located next to each other on Station Parade, on the eastern edge of the town centre. There's limited-hours **parking** along and around West Park, and there are signposted central car parks on Oxford Street and near the train station. Harrogate's **tourist office** (April–Sept Mon–Sat 9am–5.30pm, Sun 10am–1pm; Oct–March Mon–Sat 9am–5pm; ℡01423/537300, Ⓦwww.enjoyharrogate.com) is in the Royal Baths on Crescent Road.

There are scores of **accommodation** options, though the town fills up quickly during major conferences and festivals. B&Bs line King's Road and Franklin Road, north of the centre, though side streets like Studley Road, off King's Road beyond the conference centre, are quieter.

Acorn Lodge 1 Studley Rd ℡01423/525630, Ⓦwww.acornlodgeharrogate.co.uk. A guesthouse with big hotel ideas (luxury fittings, individual decor, jacuzzi, massage available in room) but B&B tariffs and friendliness. Well placed for town centre (a 5min walk). ❸

Applewood House 55 St George's Rd ℡01423/544549, Ⓦwww.applewoodhouse .co.uk. Imposing Victorian house south of The Stray. Light, airy, spotlessly clean rooms, wonderfully personal service, and impressive rates which include breakfast. An award-winning gem. ❸

Balmoral Hotel Franklin Mount ℡01423/508208, Ⓦwww.balmoralhotel.co.uk. Recently refurbished hotel occupying a rather grand terrace of three Edwardian houses a few minutes' walk from the town centre. Fixtures and fittings are luxurious, rooms spacious and (like black plasma TVs) stylish, modern and individual, and staff pleasant and helpful. ❺

The Bijou 17 Ripon Rd ☎01423/567974, ⓦwww
.thebijou.co.uk. The mellow lounge with a
wood-burning stove sets the tone for this small,
family-run boutique hotel, close to the centre. Good
fresh choices for breakfast. Parking. ❸

The Fountains 27 King's Rd ☎01423/530483,
ⓦwww.thefountainshotel.co.uk. Family-run house
a minute or two from the conference centre.
Rooms have trim little bathrooms, and it's quieter
at the side, where the rooms look over a shady
copse. Parking. ❸

🏃 **Hotel du Vin** Prospect Place
☎01423/856800, ⓦwww.hotelduvin.com.
Beautiful boutique-style rooms overlooking The
Stray (including four stunning "loft suites") featuring
trademark enormous beds and lavish bathrooms.
The handsome bistro is sensibly priced, while public
areas – champagne bar, lounge and snooker room,
courtyard garden – are stylishly turned out.
Breakfast not included; parking available. ❺

🏃 **Rudding Park Hotel** Follifoot, 5km southeast
of Harrogate ☎01423/872100, ⓦwww
.ruddingpark.co.uk. Top-end hotel in a
Grade I-listed building, set in extensive parkland
with its own golf course. Rooms and facilities are
luxurious, the service terrific, and the *Clocktower*
restaurant immaculate (à la carte mains range from
£21–26). Though expensive – it's really a special-
occasion type of place – check the website for
some excellent offers. ❼

The Town

Harrogate's spa heritage begins with the **Royal Baths**, facing Crescent Road, first
opened in 1897 and now restored to their late-Victorian finery. You can experience the beautiful Moorish-style interior during a session at the **Turkish Baths
and Health Spa** (hours vary; call ☎01423/556746; £13–19). The public
entrance is on Parliament Street; allow two hours for the full treatment. Just
along Crescent Road from the Royal Baths stands the **Royal Pump Room**, built
in 1842 over the sulphur well that feeds the baths. From here it's just a hundred
yards to the town's earliest surviving spa building, the old Promenade Room of
1806; it now houses the **Mercer Art Gallery** (Tues–Sat 10am–5pm, Sun 2–5pm;
free), which hosts regularly changing fine-art exhibitions.

Harrogate deserves much credit for the preservation of its green spaces, most
prominent of which is **The Stray**, a jealously guarded green belt that curves
around the south of the town centre. To the southwest (entrance opposite the
Royal Pump Room), the 120-acre **Valley Gardens** are a delight, while many
visitors also make for the botanical gardens at **Harlow Carr** (daily 9.30am–5pm;
£7; ⓦwww.rhs.org.uk), the northern showpiece of the Royal Horticultural
Society. These lie one and a half miles out, on the town's western edge – the nicest
approach is to walk (30min) through the Valley Gardens and pine woods, but bus
#106 (every 20min) will get you there as well. Although laid out with a scientific
purpose – breeding fruit and vegetable stock suited to northern climates – the
gardens are a year-round floral extravaganza, with especially wonderful rose
displays and a notable exhibit of seven historical "Gardens Through Time". The
tea-and-cake specialists *Bettys of Harrogate* provide the meals and drinks at Harlow
Carr's excellent café and teahouse.

Eating and drinking

Most of Harrogate's places to eat and drink are to be found either side of Parliament
Street – to the east in the town centre, to the west in the Montpellier district.
There's a good range of establishments – from tearooms to Thai, fine dining to
seafood, grills to gastropubs.

Bettys 1 Parliament St ☎01423/814070. Very
much a Harrogate institution, established by a
Swiss emigrant in the 1920s. The cakes and tarts
are to die for (takeaway available), but full meals
(mains £10–12) are also served – Alpine macaroni
or *rösti*, say, or changing seasonal specialities.
Closes at 9pm.

Le D2 7 Bower Rd ☎01423/502700. Quality
French food – meat, fish, poultry and vegetarian
– and excellent service in unpretentious

The small town of Knaresborough, four miles east of Harrogate, rises spectacularly above the River Nidd's limestone gorge. It was home to sixteenth-century soothsayer **Mother Shipton** (Ⓦ www.mothershiptonscave.com), who dwelt in a river cave while predicting the defeat of the Armada, the Great Fire of London, world wars, cars, planes and iron ships – only falling short with her claim that "The world to an end will come, in eighteen hundred and eighty one." You can visit the cave today, while close by is the **Petrifying Well**, where dripping, lime-soaked waters coat everyday objects – gloves, hats, coats, toys – in a brownish veneer that sets rock-hard in a few weeks. Regular trains and buses (every 10min) from Harrogate make Knaresborough an easy side trip.

surroundings and at affordable prices (2-course lunch £9.95, dinner £14.95). Closed Sun & Mon.
Old Bell Tavern 6 Royal Parade ℡ 01423/507930. Treat it as a pub – it's the best in town – or come to eat, since there are bar meals and sandwiches served daily and a brasserie upstairs (eve only; closed Sun) dispensing braised lamb shank, steaks, smoked haddock and so on. Mains in both average £8–11.
Orchid 28 Swan Rd ℡ 01423/560425. Wok-wielding chefs conjure up specialities from all corners of Southeast Asia – tempura to Shanghai noodles. There's dim sum at lunch, and sushi and sashimi sets every Tues. Mains average around £16. Closed Sat lunch.

Quantro 3 Royal Parade ℡ 01423/503034. Popular restaurant offering Modern European food and stylish decor, though the layout is a little regimented. Main courses £14–18, and lunchtime/early bird options (2 courses £10.95, 3 courses £13.95).
Rajput 9–11 Cheltenham Parade ℡ 01423/562113. Award-winning and rave-reviewed Indian restaurant serving regional dishes from all over the subcontinent. Moderately priced.
The Tannin Level 5 Raglan St ℡ 01423/560595. Popular town-centre brasserie, smartly under-stated, with a Michelin-trained cook, super locally sourced food and an admirably simple dinner menu – starters and puds all £5, mains all £10, with express menu for lunches and early bird discounts for early evening diners.

York and around

YORK is the north's most compelling city, a place whose history, said George VI, "is the history of England". It stood at the heart of the country's religious and political life for centuries, and until the Industrial Revolution was second only to London in population and importance. These days a more provincial air hangs over the city, except in summer when it draws crowds of tourists. The city's former importance means there are good road and rail connections and plenty of accommodation, and it's also well placed for any number of **day-trips**: the coast is only an hour away by car or train (longer by bus), while Harrogate, Knaresborough, Ripon and Fountains Abbey are all easily accessible. However, if you've only time for one day-trip, it should probably be to **Castle Howard**, the gem among English stately homes.

A brief history of York

The Romans first chose the site of modern-day York for a military camp in 71 AD, and in time this fortress became a city – Eboracum, capital of the empire's northern European territories and the base for Hadrian's northern campaigns. Much fought over after the decline of Rome, the city later became the fulcrum of Christianity in northern England. It was here, on Easter Day in 627, that Bishop Paulinus, on a mission to establish the Roman Church, baptized King Edwin of Northumbria in a small timber chapel. Six years later the church became the first minster and Paulinus the first archbishop of York. In 867 the city fell to the **Danes**, who renamed it **Jorvik**, and later made it the capital of eastern England (Danelaw).

Later Viking raids culminated in the decisive **Battle of Stamford Bridge** (1066), six miles east of the city, where English King Harold defeated Norse King Harald – a pyrrhic victory in the event, for his weakened army was defeated by the Normans just a few days later at the Battle of Hastings.

The **Normans** devastated much of York's hinterland in their infamous "Harrying of the North". Stone walls were thrown up during the thirteenth century, when the city became a favoured Plantagenet retreat and commercial capital, its importance reflected in the new title of Duke of York, bestowed ever since on the monarch's second son. The 48 **York Mystery Plays**, one of only four surviving such cycles, date from this era, created by the powerful guilds that rose with the city's woollen industry.

Although Henry VIII's Dissolution of the Monasteries took its toll on a city crammed with religious houses, York remained strongly wedded to the Catholic cause, and the most famous of the Gunpowder Plot conspirators, **Guy Fawkes**, was born here. The city remained strongly pro-Royalist during the **Civil War**, and Charles I established his court here, inviting a Parliamentarian siege. Royalist troops were routed by Cromwell and Sir Thomas Fairfax at the **Battle of Marston Moor** in 1644, which took place just six miles west of York. It's said that only the fact that Fairfax was a local man saved York from destruction.

In the eighteenth century York emerged as a social centre for the county's landed elite. While the Industrial Revolution largely passed it by, the arrival of the **railways** brought renewed prosperity, thanks to the enterprise of pioneering "Railway King" George Hudson, lord mayor during the 1830s and 1840s. The railway is gradually losing its role as a major employer, as is the declining confectionery industry; incomes are now generated by new service and bioscience industries – not forgetting, of course, the six million annual tourists.

Arrival, information and city transport

Trains arrive at York Station, just outside the city walls, a 750-yard walk from the historic core. National Express **buses** and most other regional bus services drop off and pick up at the train station. Change at Leeds for connections from Leeds/Bradford airport. Frequent **park-and-ride** services operate into the city centre from sites adjacent to the A64, A19, A1079 and A166. Otherwise, drivers should park in one of the **car parks** on the roads shadowing the city walls.

There's a useful **tourist office** at the train station, though the main office is at 1 Museum St, on the corner with Blake Street (Mon–Sat 9am–5/6pm, Sun 10am–4/5pm; ℡01904/550099, ⓦwww.visityork.org). It's well worth investing in a Yorkshire Pass to cover York's attractions (see box, p.692). City **bus** routes are operated by First York (℡01904/883000), but consider renting a **bike** instead, as York is one of the country's most bike-friendly cities – there's a rental outfit listed on p.742.

Tours

York is probably tour capital of Britain, the streets clogged by double-decker buses, guides and carefully shepherded sightseers. Call in the main tourist office to peruse the leaflets. **Bus tours** start at around £10 per person, but much more interesting are the various **guided walks** (around £5.50), most famously the evening ghost walks, but also Viking- and Roman-themed walks (usually in the company of a costumed guide). There's not much to choose between any of these, though one thoroughly recommended option also has the advantage of being **free** – the York Association of Voluntary Guides (℡01904/550098) offers a two-hour guided tour throughout the year (daily at 10.15am), plus additional tours in summer (April,

May & Sept at 2.15pm; June–Aug at 2.15pm & 6.45pm), departing from outside the Art Gallery in Exhibition Square; just turn up. Otherwise, self-guided city walking trails, focusing on Guy Fawkes, the railways and the walls, among others, are available from the tourist office or online at Ⓦ www.visityork.org/explore.

The best river operator is **YorkBoat** (Ⓣ01904/628324, Ⓦ www.yorkboat.co .uk), whose one-hour "cruise on the Ouse" sails daily from King's Staith and Lendal Bridge (Feb–Dec; cruises from £7.50, evening trips £9.50).

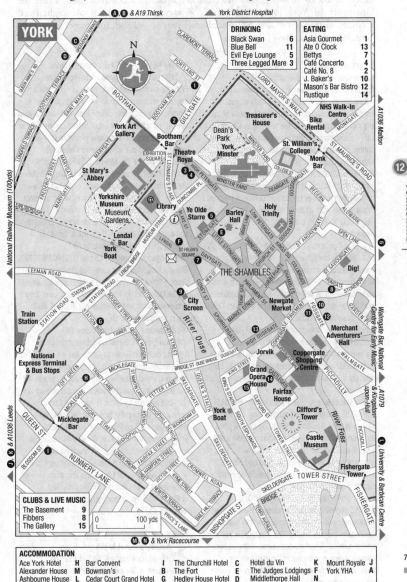

YORK

DRINKING		EATING	
Black Swan	6	Asia Gourmet	1
Blue Bell	11	Ate O Clock	13
Evil Eye Lounge	5	Bettys	7
Three Legged Mare	3	Café Concerto	4
		Café No. 8	2
		J. Baker's	10
		Mason's Bar Bistro	12
		Rustique	14

CLUBS & LIVE MUSIC
The Basement	9
Fibbers	8
The Gallery	15

0 100 yds

12

YORKSHIRE | York and around

ACCOMMODATION

Ace York Hotel	H	Bar Convent	I	The Churchill Hotel	C	Hotel du Vin	K	Mount Royale	J
Alexander House	M	Bowman's	B	The Fort	E	The Judges Lodgings	F	York YHA	A
Ashbourne House	L	Cedar Court Grand Hotel	G	Hedley House Hotel	D	Middlethorpe Hall	N		

Accommodation

Accommodation within the city walls is at a premium, as are prices, but there are some very nice boutique-style **hotels** housed in historic buildings. The main **B&B** concentration is in the side streets off Bootham (immediately west of Exhibition Square, about a 10min walk from the centre). Alternatively, consider the various **budget chains**: *Travelodge*, *Holiday Inn*, *Ramada*, *Novotel* and *Quality Hotel* all have hotels in York. There's good hostel and **backpacker** accommodation, while the University of York (℡01904/432037, ⊛www.york.ac.uk) has overnight B&B accommodation (from £45.50) available all year round and, for longer stays, self-contained flats/houses (July–Sept).

Hotels and B&Bs

Alexander House 94 Bishopthorpe Rd ℡01904/625016, ⊛www.alexanderhouseyork.co.uk. Small, friendly B&B in a lovely Victorian townhouse renovation, a 10min walk south of the city centre. The owners take pride in quality of service, and comfort and cleanliness of accommodation. Plentiful free parking. ❸

Ashbourne House 139 Fulford Rd ℡01904/639912, ⊛www.ashbournehouseyork.co.uk. Hotel-standard facilities, guesthouse prices, halfway between city centre and southern by-pass (it's a 20min walk or 5min bus ride to the city). Deliciously Yorkshire breakfasts. Free off-street parking. ❸

🏃 **Bar Convent** 17 Blossom St ℡01904/643238, ⊛www.bar-convent.org.uk. Grand Georgian building housing a museum and café as well as nine single rooms (£33–37 each), three twins, two double and a family room, self-catering kitchen and guest lounge. Pay-and-display parking over the road. Continental breakfast included. ❸

Bowman's 33 Grosvenor Terrace ℡01904/622204, ⊛www.bowmansguesthouse.co.uk. Six spotlessly clean rooms in a friendly Victorian terrace B&B off Bootham Rd, within easy reach of city centre. Free on-street parking provided. ❸

Cedar Court Grand Hotel Station Rise ℡0845/409 6430, ⊛www.cedarcourtgrand.co.uk. York's new (and only) five-star hotel, a 2min walk from the train station, is housed in what was the 1906 headquarters of the North Eastern Railway. Bags of character, wonderful views of walls and Minster, with uniquely luxurious rooms, fine-dining restaurant and relaxing bar. ❼

The Churchill Hotel 65 Bootham ℡01904/644456, ⊛www.churchillhotel.com. Housed in an early nineteenth-century mansion within walking distance of the city centre, *The Churchill* is historic on the outside, smart contemporary within. Lovely piano bar, and fine-dining restaurant looking out through tall windows onto the front garden. Free parking for guests. ❺

Hedley House Hotel 3 Bootham Terrace ℡01904/637404, ⊛www.hedleyhouse.com. Friendly, comfortable small hotel 10min walk from the train station, known for its breakfasts. Best in summer – there's an outdoor area with sauna/aqua spa on the garden deck – but rooms can be cold in winter, especially in the (separate) annexe. Free car parking on first come, first served basis. ❹

Hotel du Vin 89 The Mount ℡01904/557350, ⊛www.hotelduvin.com. The slick boutique-hotel-and-bistro chain's York address, close to the centre of town. The 44 rooms feature the trademark style, while the courtyard offers alfresco dining. There's also a vast selection of malts for whisky drinkers and a smokers' bothy in the garden. Limited parking £10 per day. Room only ❻

The Judges Lodgings 9 Lendal ℡01904/638733, ⊛www.judgeslodgings.com. Beautifully renovated Grade I-listed building in the centre, which housed Assize Court judges for over 150 years. Luxurious accommodation and attentive but discreet staff. Bar in the basement. ❻

Middlethorpe Hall Bishopsthorpe Rd ℡01904/641241, ⊛www.middlethorpe.com. A grand eighteenth-century mansion a couple of miles south of the city, next to the racecourse. Antiques, wood panelling, superb rooms (some set in a private courtyard), gardens, parkland, pool and spa, and fine dining in the formal *Oak Room* restaurant. Continental breakfast included. ❻

Mount Royale The Mount ℡01904/628856, ⊛www.mountroyale.co.uk. Antique-filled retreat with superb garden suites set around a private garden, together with a heated outdoor pool (open summer only) and hot tub, sauna and steam room. Some less exalted standard rooms are also available. The contemporary restaurant here is well regarded. ❺

Hostels

🏃 **Ace York Hotel** Micklegate House, 88–90 Micklegate ℡01904/627720, ⊛www.acehotelyork.co.uk. Handsome building (the 1752 former home of the High Sheriff of

Yorkshire) for an amiable "boutique hostel" with good facilities – kitchen, laundry, internet, TV and games room, café and cellar bar. High-ceilinged dorms (sleeping 6, 8, 10 and 14) are cheaper for multi-night stays, and there are also twin dorms (with bunks) and double rooms; prices include continental breakfast. Dorms £16, rooms ❸

The Fort Little Stonegate ☎ 01904/620222, ⓦ www.thefortyork.co.uk. Another "boutique hostel" in the city centre, with interesting decor – a log cabin-style room which sleeps 6, plus 4 double/twin bedrooms with different whimsical motifs (futuristic, city walls, underwater, city scenes) – at

a knock-down price (from £20). In the words of the owner, "luxury, funky and easy on the pocket". Dorms £20, rooms ❸

York YHA Water End, Clifton ☎ 0845/371 9051, ⓔ york@yha.org.uk. Large Victorian mansion, 20min walk along Bootham and then a left turn at Clifton Green – or follow the riverside footpath. Beds are mostly in four-bed dorms, though variously priced private rooms are also available (book well in advance). Facilities include a licensed café, internet, large garden, parking and discounts for attractions. Buffet breakfast included. Dorms from £13.95, rooms ❶

The City

Although there are around sixty churches, museums and historic buildings crammed within York's walls, in fact the tally of essential sights is surprisingly limited. Even so, it's hard to get round everything in less than two days, and equally difficult to stick to any rigid itinerary, though see the box on p.736 for some ideas. The **Minster** is the obvious place to start, and you won't want to miss a walk around **the walls**, though after that it very much depends on your interests. The medieval city is at its most evocative around the streets known as **Stonegate** and the **Shambles**, while the earlier Viking city is entertainingly presented at **Jorvik**, perhaps the city's favourite family attraction. Standout historic buildings include the Minster's Treasurer's House, Georgian **Fairfax House**, the **Merchant Adventurers' Hall**, and the stark remnants of York's **castle**. The two major museum collections are the incomparable **Castle Museum** and the **National Railway Museum**, where the appeal goes way beyond railway memorabilia, while the evocative ruins and gardens of St Mary's Abbey house the family-friendly and recently revitalized **Yorkshire Museum**.

York Minster

York Minster (Mon–Sat 9/9.30am–5.30pm, Sun noon–3.45pm, though times vary depending on season and services; Minster, undercroft, treasury and crypt £8, tower an additional £5; ☎ 0844/939 0011, ⓦ www.yorkminster.org), the seat of the Archbishop of York, is Britain's largest Gothic building and home to countless treasures, including an estimated half of all the medieval stained glass in England. In addition to the main body of the church, any tour of the building, which took 250 years to complete, should also include the foundations, crypt, chapterhouse and an ascent of the great central tower.

The first significant foundations were laid around 1080, and it was from the germ of this Norman church that the present structure emerged. The oldest surviving fabric, in the south transept, dates from 1220 during the reign of Archbishop Walter de Grey, who also began work on a new north transept in 1260. A new chapterhouse, in the Decorated style, appeared in 1300, and a new nave in the same style was completed in 1338. The Perpendicular (ie late Gothic) choir was realized in 1450 and the western towers in 1472. In 1480, the thirteenth-century central tower, which had collapsed in 1407, was rebuilt, thereby bringing the Minster to more or less its present state.

Nothing else in the Minster can match the magnificence of the **stained glass** in the nave and transepts. The **West Window** (1338) contains distinctive heart-shaped upper tracery (the "Heart of Yorkshire"), while in the nave's north aisle, the second bay window (1155) contains slivers of the oldest stained glass in the country. Moving down to the crossing, the north transept's **Five Sisters Window** is named after the five fifty-foot lancets, each glazed with thirteenth-century grisaille, a distinctive frosted, silvery-grey glass. Opposite, the south transept contains a sixteenth-century, 17,000-piece **Rose Window**, commemorating the marriage in 1486 of Henry VII and Elizabeth of York, an alliance which marked the end of the Wars of the Roses. The greatest of the church's 128 windows, however, is the majestic **East Window** (1405), at 78ft by 31ft the largest area of medieval stained glass in a single window in the world.

The foundations, or **undercroft**, have been turned into a museum, displaying fragments of the Roman fort which once stood on this site, as well as capitals, sculpture and fabric from the present Minster and its Norman predecessor. Among precious relics in the adjoining **treasury** is the eleventh-century Horn of Ulf, presented to the Minster by a relative of the tide-turning King Canute. There's also access from the undercroft to the **crypt**, which contains sections of the original eleventh-century church, including pillars with fine Romanesque capitals. A small illuminated doorway opens onto the base of a pillar belonging to the guardhouse of the original Roman camp. Access to the undercroft, treasury and crypt is from the south transept, also the entrance to the **central tower** (£5), which you can climb for rooftop views over the city.

Around the Minster

The **Treasurer's House** in Chapter House Street (April–Oct daily except Fri 11am–4.30pm, Nov 11am–3pm; £5.40, cellar £2.40; NT) is a glorious seventeenth-century townhouse restored to reflect four centuries of styles by local industrialist Frank Green, who lived here from 1897 to 1930. His collection adorns the various period rooms, including an authentically kitted-out eighteenth-century kitchen and medieval hall. The cellar tour recounts the tale of the famed ghostly Roman legionaries; there's also a walled garden and nice café.

Just around the corner in College Street stands **St William's College**, an eye-catching half-timbered building erected in 1467 for the Minster's priests. Nearby Goodramgate features even earlier constructions in the form of the houses along **Our Lady's Row**, the oldest in the city (1316). These back onto the quiet churchyard of the delightful **Holy Trinity Church** (Tues–Sun 10am–4pm; free), first built in the twelfth century but much altered since. Look out for the medieval stained glass and Georgian woodwork, notably the jumbled box pews that have subsided with the slabbed floor.

Around the walls

Although much restored, the city's superb **walls** (dawn–dusk; free) date mainly from the fourteenth century, though fragments of Norman work survive, particularly in the gates (known as "bars"), while the northern sections still follow the line of the Roman ramparts. The only break in the walls is along the eastern side, a few hundred yards along from Monk Bar, where the city was first protected by the marshes of the River Foss and later by the deliberately flooded area known as King's Pool.

Monk Bar is as good a point of access as any, tallest of the city's four main gates and host to the small **Richard III Museum** (daily: March–Oct 9am–5pm; Nov–Feb 9.30–4pm; £2.50), where you're invited to decide on the guilt or innocence of England's most maligned king. For just a taste of the walls' best section – with great views of the Minster and acres of idyllic-looking gardens – take the ten-minute stroll west from Monk Bar to Exhibition Square and **Bootham Bar**, the only gate on the site of a Roman gateway and marking the traditional northern entrance to the city. A stroll around the walls' entire two-and-a-half-mile length will also take you past the southwestern **Micklegate Bar**, long considered the most important of the gates since it marked the start of the road to London. The gate was built to a Norman design, reputedly using ancient stone coffins as building stone, and was later used to exhibit the heads of executed criminals and rebels. At the **Micklegate Bar Museum** (daily 10am–3pm; £3; ®www.micklegatebar.com) you can explore the story by way of old lithographs, models, paintings and the odd gruesome skull. Finally, **Walmgate Bar** in the east is the best preserved and the only one with its barbican intact.

Exhibition Square, Art Gallery and Yorkshire Museum

Exhibition Square, outside Bootham Bar, is the site of the **York Art Gallery** (daily 10am–5pm; free; ®www.yorkartgallery.org.uk), housing an extensive collection of early Italian, British and northern European paintings. It's fun to pick out the smattering of York scenes, which include L.S. Lowry's take on Clifford's Tower. Otherwise, the gallery puts on a year-round series of special exhibitions and events, and is noted for its collections of British studio pottery and twentieth-century British painters.

Reopened in 2010 after a major makeover, the **Yorkshire Museum** (daily 10am–5pm; £7; ®www.yorkshiremuseum.org.uk), south of Exhibition Square on Museum Street, has been reorganized into five new galleries – "History of York", a multi-screen audiovisual spectacular; "Extinct", where you can step into a dinosaur footprint or measure yourself against the ten-foot tall Moa bird; "Meet the People of the Empire", in which you can view York's Romans through a virtual doorway, and walk on a real Roman mosaic; "The Power and the Glory", exploring medieval York; and "Enquiry" (in the upstairs gallery), which investigates how archeology and science piece together the past. But a list of contents tells only half the story – it's the exciting visual and hands-on aspects that now make it one of York's main visitor attractions. And if you visit during the summer holidays, take part in all sorts of interactive stuff in the Science and Discovery labs.

Part of the museum basement incorporates the fireplace and chapterhouse of **St Mary's Abbey** (dawn–dusk; free), the ruins of which lie within the attractive museum gardens. Founded around 1080, the abbey later became an important Benedictine foundation – it was from here that disenchanted monks fled to found Fountains Abbey. The fact that the abbey controlled the city's brothels at the time can hardly have helped the Benedictine cause.

Stonegate, the Shambles and around

The two most photographed streets in York lie south of the Minster. **Stonegate** is as ancient as the city itself. Originally the Via Praetoria of Roman York, it's now paved with thick flags of York stone, which were once carried along here to build the Minster, hence the street name. Guy Fawkes' parents lived on Stonegate (there's a plaque opposite Mulberry Hall) and its Tudor buildings retain their considerable charm – **Ye Olde Starre** at no. 40, one of York's original inns, is on every tourist itinerary (you can't miss the sign straddling the street). Look up at the shop under the inn sign for the little red devil – the medieval sign for a printer's premises. Step through an alley known as Coffee Yard (by the *Old Starre*) to find **Barley Hall** (daily 10am–4pm; £4.50; Ⓦ www.barleyhall.org.uk), a fine restoration of a late-medieval townhouse given a hands-on twist – you can learn about fifteenth-century life here by touching the exhibits, playing period games, trying on costumes or attending other special events and festivals.

The Shambles, further to the south, could be taken as the epitome of medieval York. Almost impossibly narrow and lined with perilously leaning timber-framed houses, it was the home of York's butchers (the word "shambles" derives from the Old English for slaughterhouse), and old meat-hooks still adorn the odd house. A little way further south, off Fossgate, the **Merchant Adventurers' Hall** (April–Sept Mon–Thurs 9am–5pm, Fri & Sat 9am–3.30pm, Sun noon–4pm; Oct–March Mon–Sat 9am–3.30pm; £2.50; Ⓦ www.theyorkcompany.co.uk) is one of the finest medieval timber-framed halls in Europe. The beautiful building was raised by the city's most powerful guild: dealers in wool from the Wolds, woollens from the Dales and lead from the Pennines, commodities that were traded for exotica from far and wide.

Jorvik

The city's blockbuster historic exhibit is **Jorvik** (daily 10am–4/5pm; £8.95, joint ticket with Barley Hall, Dig! and Micklegate Bar Museum £13; ☎01904/543402, Ⓦ www.jorvik-viking-centre.co.uk), located by the Coppergate shopping centre; you can avoid queuing by pre-booking your entrance ticket (though a surcharge applies). This multi-million-pound affair propels visitors in "time capsules" on a ride through the tenth-century city of York, presenting not just the sights but the sounds and even the smells of a riverside Viking city. Most of the sites (blacksmiths' to bedrooms) and artefacts (leather shoes to wooden combs) were discovered during the 1976 excavations of Coppergate's real Viking settlement, now largely buried beneath the shopping centre outside. Jorvik shows how the artefacts were used, complete with live-action market and domestic scenes on actual Viking-age streets, with constipated villagers, axe-fighting, and other singular attractions.

Where Jorvik shows what was unearthed at Coppergate, the associated attraction that is **Dig!** (same times; £5.50, pre-booking advised; Ⓦwww.digyork.com) illustrates the science involved. Housed five minutes' walk away in the medieval church of St Saviour, a simulated dig allows you to take part in a range of excavations in the company of archeologists, using authentic tools and methods. Tours (£1) to visit **Dig Hungate** (Ⓦwww.dighungate.com), York's ongoing major archeological site, start from here, though excavations are due to end in 2012.

Fairfax House

Fairfax House on Castlegate (Mon–Thurs & Sat 11am–4.30pm, Sun 1.30–4.30pm; guided tours only on Fri at 11am & 2pm; closed Jan & Feb; £5; Ⓦwww.fairfax house.co.uk) celebrates the wealth of the city's Georgian period. The elegant townhouse, decorated with superb stuccowork, was restored to house the collection of fine arts left by Noel Terry, scion of one of the city's chocolate dynasties. The bulk of the collection consists of eighteenth-century furniture and clocks, though seasonal exhibitions showcase other arts, while every December the popular "Keeping of Christmas" exhibition re-creates a Georgian Christmas in the house.

York Castle and the Castle Museum

Despite the rich architectural heritage elsewhere in the city, there's precious little left of **York Castle**, one of two established by William the Conqueror. Only the perilously leaning **Clifford's Tower** (daily: April–Sept 10am–6pm; Oct 10am–5pm; Nov–March 10am–4pm; £3.50; EH) remains, a stark stone keep built between 1245 and 1262. The old Norman keep was destroyed in 1190 during one of the city's more shameful historical episodes: after an outburst of anti-Semitic rioting, 150 Jews were put inside the tower for their own protection. With no sign of the mob's anger abating, the Jews committed mass suicide by setting the tower on fire.

Immediately east of the tower lies the outstanding **Castle Museum** (daily 9.30am–5pm; £8; Ⓦwww.yorkcastlemuseum.org.uk), a remarkable "collection of bygones" instigated by a Dr Kirk of Pickering, who in the 1920s realized that many of the everyday items used in rural areas were in danger of disappearing, and thus accepted bric-a-brac from his patients in lieu of fees. When the pile of miscellanea grew too large for his own home it was housed in the city's old Debtors' Prison where, incidentally, the infamous highwayman Dick Turpin spent his last night on earth – you can still see his cell. A whole range of early craft, folk and agricultural ephemera is complemented by costumes, toys, machinery, domestic implements and show workshops, plus special exhibitions on subjects as diverse as swimming costumes through the ages and fire engines. Two entire reconstructed Victorian and Edwardian streets are perhaps the highlight, though Kirk's fetishistic collections of truncheons and biscuit moulds are surely unsurpassed. The extensive military displays and Sixties gallery are well worth seeing, as are the rambling dungeons, with stories from prison records projected onto whitewashed walls.

The National Railway Museum

The **National Railway Museum** on Leeman Road (daily 10am–6pm; free; Ⓦwww.nrm.org.uk) is a truly wonderful day out, even if you're not a railway nerd. The heart of the museum lies in the exhibitions of the steam leviathans of the past, and their modern equivalents, in the **Great Hall** (through the tunnel on the right of the museum shop), and the rolling stock and associated exhibits in the **Station Hall** (straight ahead). Look out for the stunningly beautiful *Duchess of Hamilton*, which looks as if it has jumped out of an Art Deco poster; the great turntable; the Japanese

York delights in its independent, stylish and quirky shops – if there's anywhere else in England you can buy a Gothic nesting box and a Ford Capri coal sculpture on the same day, we've yet to find it. For special guidance, the *5 Routes to Shopping Heaven* shopping trail **leaflet** is available from the tourist office.

Otherwise, for **brand and designer names** under one roof start at department stores Browns (Davygate; ⓦwww.brownsyork.co.uk) or Fenwicks (Coppergate Centre), or, a little out of town at Fulford (buses every 10min from the train station), the York Designer Outlet (ⓦwww.yorkdesigneroutlet.com), which houses 120 stores.

The Blue Ballroom (36 Gillygate) stocks **vintage and retro clothing**, and Porta Dextra (1 High Petergate) specializes in innovative contemporary jewellery. **Foodies** can choose their own curry mix from Rafi's Spicebox (17 Goodramgate; ⓦwww .spicebox.co.uk), and bread, Italian-style, from La Via Vecchia (6 Shambles), a shop so good it doesn't even need a sign. Parliament Street, off the Shambles, sees numerous **outdoor markets** throughout the year, including the daily Newgate market, and a farmers' market on the last Friday of the month.

Booklovers will find a wealth of **secondhand/antiquarian bookshops**; favourites include the Barbican Bookshop (24 Fossgate; ⓦwww.barbicanbookshop.co.uk) and the Minster Gate Bookshop (Minster Gates, off High Petergate; ⓦwww.minstergate books.co.uk). The **York National Book Fair** every September (ⓦwww.yorkbookfair .com) is one of the best for antiquarian books in the UK.

bullet train (the only one outside Japan); and assorted royal trains, including Queen Victoria's carriage. If you want to see the *Mallard*, though, you'll have to go to the NRM's other branch, Locomotion, at Shildon in County Durham (see p.780) – it was moved there in 2010. After exploring the Great Hall and Station Hall, don't miss the **Warehouse**, with its huge collection of railway memorabilia, **The Works**, where you can see restoration work in progress, or the **South Yard** with its miniature railway, play and picnic areas. Look out, too, for the talks, activities, demonstrations and events put on each day. There's an excellent shop, a restaurant (in the Station Hall) and a café (in the Great Hall), and you can leave your clutter in one of the lockers in the underpass between them. The museum is ten minutes' walk from the train station, or you can get there on a road train (Easter–Oct every 30min 11.15am–4.15pm) from Duncombe Place, near the Minster.

Eating and drinking

In keeping with much else in the city, many eating and drinking establishments are self-consciously old-fashioned, though there are some real highlights – truly **historic pubs**, the ultimate **teashop** experience that is *Bettys*, and a scattering of well-regarded **restaurants**. Riverside terraces between the Lendal and Ouse bridges have opened up the city for alfresco drinking, and there's a flourishing **café-bar** scene, with some honourable independents alongside the main chains. Every September, the city hosts a huge **food and drink festival** (ⓦwww.yorkfestivaloffoodanddrink.com), with ten days of cookery demonstrations, promotions and events.

Tearooms, cafés, bistros and restaurants

Asia Gourmet 61 Gillygate ☏01904/622728. Small, cheerful restaurant in the city centre with shabby decor but delicious food. Mainly Japanese food (sushi a speciality) though other Asian cuisines available. Sushi £4, main courses average £6.

Ate O Clock 13a High Ousegate ☏01904/644080. Despite the wince-making name, this is an excellent choice for lunch or an evening meal, with good food (Mediterranean with a twist), friendly service and a laid-back atmosphere. Two-course lunch £8.80, dinner mains £13.50–22.

Bettys 6–8 St Helen's Square ☏ 01904/659142. If there are tearooms in heaven they'll be like *Bettys*. Tea, cakes and pastries are the stock-in-trade (pikelets and Yorkshire fat rascals for example), but there are a dozen or so hot dishes, great puddings, and a shop where you can buy fine-grade teas and coffees. Take a look at the wartime flight-crew signatures on the mirror downstairs – they used it as an unofficial mess.

Café Concerto 21 High Petergate. Independent bistro, wallpapered with sheet music, boasting a good reputation and a relaxed atmosphere. Daily until 10pm.

Café No. 8 8 Gillygate ☏ 01904/653074. This wainscotted little bistro, just outside Bootham Bar, has a great summer garden, while the food has progressed since the café's early days to, for example, honey-mustard slow-cooked outdoor-reared pork belly. Evening mains £12–17. Closes at 10pm; closed Sun.

J. Baker's 7 Fossgate ☏ 01904/622688. Innovative food with a sense of humour – "corned beef butty" sounds decidedly plebeian but is actually pretty as a picture – and the Chocolate Room menu offers a fine range of lovely chocolate desserts. If you can't make up your mind, go for the "grazing plate". Reservations essential. Closed Sun & Mon. Expensive.

Mason's Bar Bistro 13 Fossgate ☏ 01904/611919. All-day bar/bistro which offers atmosphere and simple breakfast/lunch/dinner menus. The food is good, with generous portions at medium prices – all burgers are under £10, light bites £4–8 and main courses £8.95–13.95.

Rustique 28 Castlegate ☏ 01904/612744. French-style bistro serving rustic (of course) food in pleasantly risqué surroundings. A la carte and set menus (2 courses £11.95, 3 courses £13.95). Excellent value.

Pubs and bars

Black Swan Peasholme Green. York's oldest (sixteenth-century) pub has some superb stone flagging and wood panelling. The beer's good – you can get the local York Brewery stuff here – and it's also home of the city's folk club (see Ⓦ www .blackswanfolkclub.org.uk for details of gigs).

Blue Bell Fossgate. A tiny, no-frills traditional pub – oak panelling, real ales, no mobile phones, non-tourist clientele.

Evil Eye Lounge 42 Stonegate. Colourful café-bar, where cosmopolitan reigns supreme. Cocktails, beer and music are to the fore, with a backpacker ethos, faintly eastern-mystic decor and ultra-low lighting. Yet the food is really good too – Tibetan dumplings and Japanese chicken vie with traditional Sunday roasts.

Three Legged Mare 15 High Petergate. York Brewery's cosy outlet for its own quality beer and definitely a pub for grown-ups – no jukebox, no video games and no kids. Named after a type of gallows.

Nightlife, culture and entertainment

Cultural entertainment in York is wide and varied. Classical music recitals and concerts are often held in the city's churches and York Minster, while being a university city, York has a fair range of clubs and live music venues; most are within the city centre. For what's on listings see the monthly *What's On York* leaflet or visit the website Ⓦ www.whatsonyork.com; while Ⓦ www.york festivals.com gives the lowdown on the annual festivals and events.

The famous **York Mystery Plays** are traditionally held every four years (next in 2014; Ⓦ www.yorkmysteryplays.co.uk). Major annual events include Jorvik's **Viking Festival** every February and the **Early Music Festival** (Ⓦ www.ncem .co.uk), held in July, perhaps the best of its kind in Britain. There are also noteworthy **Roman** (October) and **Christmas** (December) festivals, with plenty to see and do.

Clubs and live music

The Basement 13–17 Coney St, below City Screen cinema ☏ 01904/612940, Ⓦ www.thebasementyork .co.uk. This intimate venue presents a pleasingly diverse variety of themes, from regular live music to comedy to cabaret and burlesque.

Fibbers Stonebow House, Stonebow ☏ 01904/ 651250, Ⓦ www.fibbers.co.uk. The city's primary music venue which puts on indie, guitar pop, jazz, punk, rock and acoustic gigs. Club nights also feature, with 90s (Fri) and indie/electro (Sat) nights.

The Gallery 12 Clifford St ☏ 01904/647947, Ⓦ www.galleryclub.co.uk/york. York's main nightclub caters to a wide variety of musical tastes, from indie to dance.

Venues

City Screen 13–17 Coney St ☎0871/704 2054, ⓦwww.picturehouses.co.uk. The art-house cinema choice, with three screens, riverside café-bar, and *The Basement* below.

Grand Opera House 4 Cumberland St ☎01904/678700, ⓦwww.grandoperahouseyork .org.uk. Musicals, ballet, pop gigs and family entertainment in all its guises.

The National Centre for Early Music St Margaret's Church, Walmgate ☎01904/658338, ⓦwww.ncem .co.uk. Not just early music, but also contemporary folk, world and jazz.

Theatre Royal St Leonard's Place ☎01904/623568, ⓦwww.yorktheatreroyal.co.uk. Musicals, panto and mainstream theatre.

Listings

Bike rental Bob Trotter, 13–15 Lord Mayor's Walk, at Monkgate ☎01904/622868, ⓦwww.bobtrotter cycles.com. Rates from £15 per day (£13 half-day). Free city cycle maps available.

Bus information East Yorkshire ☎01482/222222 (for Hull, Beverley and Bridlington); Yorkshire Coastliner ☎01653/692556 (for Leeds, Castle Howard, Pickering, Scarborough and Whitby).

Hospital York District Hospital, Wigginton Rd (24hr emergency number ☎01904/631313); bus #2, #5 or #6. NHS Walk-in Centre, 31 Monkgate (daily 7am–10pm).

Internet City Library, off Museum St (Mon–Thurs 9am–8pm, Fri 9am–6pm, Sat 9am–5pm, Sun 11am–4pm, 1st Thurs of the month 1–8pm).

Police Fulford Rd ☎0845/606 0247.

Post office 22 Lendal.

Racing York Racecourse ☎01904/620911, ⓦwww.yorkracecourse.co.uk. One of Britain's finest, York Racecourse has regular meetings during the season (May–Sept), including the John Smith's Cup, the highlight of the annual calendar each July.

Taxis Ranks at Rougier St, Duncombe Place, Exhibition Square, and the train station; or call Station Taxis ☎01904/623332.

Castle Howard

Immersed in the deep countryside of the Howardian Hills, fifteen miles northeast of York off the A64, **Castle Howard** (house March–Oct & late Nov to mid-Dec daily 11am–5pm; gardens open all year 10am–6.30pm, dusk in winter; £12.50, grounds only £8.50; ⓦwww.castlehoward.co.uk) is one of the country's grandest stately homes. It's a pricey visit, but there's no question that it's worth seeing, the grounds especially, and you could easily spend the best part of a day here. The parking, at least, is free, though arriving by public transport is more problematic. The summer Moorsbus (see p.750) comes out here from Helmsley, while some Yorkshire Coastliner buses run from York, Malton or Pickering – it's best to call Traveline (☎0871/200 2233) to check schedules, or consider taking a bus tour from York.

The colossal main house was designed in 1699 by **Sir John Vanbrugh** – odd, since he was best known as a playwright, with no formal architectural training. His only qualification seems to have been membership of the same gentlemen's club as Charles Howard, third Earl of Carlisle, for whom the house was built. Vanbrugh recognized his limitations and called in **Nicholas Hawksmoor** – the pair went on to collaborate on Blenheim Palace. If Hawksmoor's guiding hand can be seen throughout, Vanbrugh's influence is clear in the very theatricality of the building, notably in the palatial **Great Hall**. Other rooms and chambers in endless succession are filled with Dutch porcelain, Roman statuary, furniture by Sheraton and Chippendale, paintings by Gainsborough, Veronese, Rubens and Van Dyck, not to mention trinkety objets d'art, gaudy friezes and monumental pilasters – vulgar in their excess if not provenance.

Vanbrugh also turned his attention to the estate's thousand-acre **grounds**, where he could indulge his playful inclinations – the formal gardens, clipped parkland, towers, obelisks and blunt sandstone follies stretch in all directions, sloping gently to two artificial lakes. The whole is a charming artifice of grand, manicured views – an example of what three centuries, skilled gardeners and pots of money can produce.

Daily outdoor **tours** (call for times; free) concentrate on aspects of the house and garden, and the annual outdoor Proms concert every August is very popular. There are **cafés** in the main house and by the larger lake, though the courtyard café at the main entrance has the nicest food. Facilities round off with a children's playground, nature trails, plant centre, gift shop and even a **camping and caravan** park (ⓣ01653/648316; March–Oct).

Hull, the Humber and the East Yorkshire coast

The character of the historic "**East Riding**" has been shaped by a strong seafaring tradition, boosted by **Hull**'s position on the **Humber** estuary. Beyond Hull, up the East Yorkshire coast, lonely beaches, wild foreshores and forgotten seafront villages draw curious tourists keen to get off the beaten track. The bucket-and-spade resorts of **Bridlington** and **Filey** are the traditional draws, while the cliffs of **Flamborough Head** provide one of the best places in Britain for birdwatching. Inland, historic **Beverley**, with its marvellous minster, is plonked amid the flatlands that stretch northwards from Hull to meet the **Yorkshire Wolds**, a crescent-shaped ridge of hills that falls to the sea at Flamborough. Drivers approaching from Lincolnshire and the south will cross the **Humber Bridge**, an immense single-span suspension bridge opened in 1981; a viewing area allows you to stop and gasp.

Hull

HULL – officially Kingston upon Hull – has a maritime pre-eminence that dates back to 1299, when it was laid out as a seaport by Edward I. It quickly became England's leading harbour, and was still a vital garrison when the gates were closed against Charles I in 1642, the first serious act of rebellion of what was to become the English Civil War. Fishing and seafaring have always been important here, and today's city maintains a firm grip on its heritage while bolstering its attractions for visitors – the dramatic aquarium known as **The Deep**, a superior set of free local **museums** and a revived **Old Town** area – which together provide scope for a good couple of days' worth of sightseeing. Hull's most famous adopted son, the poet and university librarian **Philip Larkin** – the twenty-fifth anniversary of whose death was belatedly commemorated by the opening of a "Larkin Trail" and unveiling of a statue in the Paragon Interchange in 2010 – was being typically curmudgeonly when he wrote, "I wish I could think of just one nice thing to tell you about Hull, oh yes… it's very nice and flat for cycling." This is too harsh – museums aside, he might have mentioned the city's excellent historic pubs, its unique cream telephone boxes, or the various **festivals** that Hull arranges with great flair, notably the colossal Hull Fair (October), the Hull Literature Festival (June) and the Hull Jazz Festival (August).

Arrival, information and accommodation

Hull's **train station** is on the west side of town, on the main drag of Ferensway, with the **bus station** just to the north. Drivers should aim for the **car parks** in the St Stephen's development or Princes Quay shopping centre.

The **tourist office** is on Paragon Street at Queen Victoria Square (Mon–Sat 10am–5pm, Sun 11am–3pm; ⓣ01482/223559, ⓦwww.realyorkshire.co.uk). They coordinate richly anecdotal **guided tours** around the Old Town (April–Oct Mon–Sat at 2pm, Sun 11am; £3) departing from their office, or you can pick up the entertaining *Fish Trail* leaflet, a self-guided trail that kids will love. There's a fair choice of **accommodation** on offer, including several central small hotels and the budget chains *Ibis*, *Campanile* and *Holiday Express*. The tourist office can help – and through them you can get special weekend hotel rates (from around £25 per person per night).

Accommodation

Acorn Guesthouse 719 Beverley Rd ☎01482/853248, ⊛www.acornguesthousehull .co.uk. Big hotel facilities at B&B prices in a suburban semi on the northwest edge of the city, about 4km from the centre. Seven comfortably old-fashioned rooms, with friendly and attentive service, ample parking at the front and a nice garden to the rear. Regular bus service into town. ❷

Earlsmere Hotel 76–78 Sunny Bank, off Spring Bank West ☎01482/341977, ⊛www.earlsmere hotel.co.uk. Old-fashioned guesthouse in a quiet street a mile northwest of the train station. ❶

Kingston Theatre Hotel 1–2 Kingston Square ☎01482/225828, ⊛www.kingstontheatrehotel.com.

Straightforward but good-value hotel rooms on the city's prettiest square, across from Hull New Theatre. It's quiet for the city centre, and for a bit more money you can upgrade to one of the more spacious attached "Victorian Suites". ❷

Little Weghill Farm Preston, about 8km east of The Deep ☎01482/897650, ⊛www.littleweghill farm.co.uk. *Little Weghill Farm* is a beautiful eighteenth-century farmhouse that's kept many original features. Barn conversion rooms are all en suite. Quiet location with many local walks. ❷

Royal Hotel 170 Ferensway ☎01482/325087, ⊛www.hotels-hull.co.uk. Large Victorian hotel near the station that's been fully refurbished, with comfortable rooms, a leisure centre and pool. Room only ❺

The City

The central **Princes Dock** sets the tone for Hull's modern refurbishment, the waters now lined by landscaped brick promenades and café-bars, and overlooked by **Princes Quay**, a multi-tiered, glass-spangled shopping centre, with the marina beyond. To the north, the massive St Stephen's development, housing the new transport interchange and shopping complex, leads off Ferensway.

The Maritime Museum and Trinity Square

The city's maritime legacy is covered in the **Maritime Museum** (Mon–Sat 10am–5pm, Sun 1.30–4.30pm; free), housed in the Neoclassical headquarters of the former Town Docks Offices, on Queen Victoria Square. The main boost to the town's coffers in the eighteenth and nineteenth centuries was whaling, and here you can view a whale skeleton, a blubber pot cauldron, and a fine collection of scrimshaw (items made from whale bones and teeth) alongside model ships, old photographs, and Inuit relics.

Leave Queen Victoria Square by pedestrianized Whitefriargate and, after about 200 yards, turn right down Trinity House Lane for **Holy Trinity** (Tues 11am–3pm, Wed–Fri noon–3pm, Sat 9.30am–noon; free), among the most pleasing parish churches in the country, notable for its early brick transepts and chancel. Trinity Square has long been the place for **markets**: there's the indoor Trinity Market (Mon–Sat 7.30am–5pm) and a farmers' market in the square on the second and fourth Friday of the month. Close by on South Church Side is one of Hull's most revered relics – the **Old Grammar School**, a red-brick edifice built in 1583, which for 120 years doubled as the town's Merchant Adventurers' Hall.

The Old Town

Two blocks east, over towards the River Hull, you reach the **Museums Quarter** (all attractions Mon–Sat 10am–5pm, Sun 1.30–4.30pm; free) and **High Street**, which has been designated an "Old Town" conservation area thanks to its crop of former merchants' houses and narrow cobbled alleys. At its northern end stands **Wilberforce House**, the former home of William Wilberforce, containing some fascinating exhibits on slavery and its abolition, the cause to which he dedicated much of his life. Next door is **Streetlife**, centred on a 1930s street scene of reconstructed shops, railway goods yard, and cycle and motor works. Highlights include a (simulated) ride on a nineteenth-century coach, recorded conversations on a Hull Tram, and the rules of bicycle polo. If this is good, then the adjoining **Hull and East Riding Museum** is even better, full of inventive displays. A life-size mammoth and a walk-through Iron Age village set you up for the showpiece attractions, namely vivid displays of Celtic burials, the unique Bronze Age wooden figures from Roos Carr (complete with appendages the Victorians thought too rude to display) and spectacular Roman mosaics. Dredged from a river, meanwhile, came the Hasholme boat, an oak cargo boat 41 feet long and 2300 years old – now confined within a see-through conservation chamber.

The Deep

Protruding from a promontory overlooking the River Humber looms **The Deep** (daily 10am–6pm, last entry 5pm; £9.50; Ⓦ www.thedeep.co.uk), ten minutes' walk from the Old Town. Its educational displays and videos wrap around an immense thirty-foot-deep, 2.3-million-gallon viewing tank filled with sharks, rays and octopuses. You see into the tank at every level on the ramped walk down – while diverting off to a deep-sea research station or the ice-cold Polar Gallery – and then return by underwater lift. Meanwhile the Twilight Zone extension takes you even further into the ocean's depths – and face-to-face with its deepwater inhabitants.

Eating, drinking and entertainment

Hull has dozens of city-centre **pubs and café-bars**, the best of which are picked out in a *Hull Ale Trail* leaflet available from the tourist office. The upcoming nightlife area is centred on Pearson Park, just north of the centre (take a taxi), where Princes Avenue has a line of popular café-bars and restaurants. Meanwhile, the excellent **Hull Truck Theatre Company** (Ⓣ01482/323638, Ⓦ www.hulltruck.co.uk) on Ferensway is where, among others, many of the plays of award-winning John Godber first see the light of day.

Cafés-bars and restaurants

Cerutti's 10 Nelson St Ⓣ01482/328501. Facing the site of the Victoria Pier, overlooking the river – perfect for a restaurant known for its fish. Mains £14–20, but look out for special 2- and 3-course deals. Closed Sat lunchtime & all day Sun.

Pave Café-Bar 16–20 Princes Ave Ⓣ01482/333181. Nice, laid-back atmosphere with food till 7pm (most main courses well under £10) and lots going on – from live jazz/blues to a Sunday comedy night and readings by the likes of Alexei Sayle, Will Self and Simon Armitage.

Taman Ria Tropicana 45–47 Princes Ave Ⓣ01482/345640. Malay food (*masakan melayu*, or Malayan style) served in contemporary surroundings: go for the "three dishes for £10.50" option if you're not familiar with it. Otherwise mains up to £12.50. Closed Mon.

Wokkas 3 Brook St Ⓣ01482/329626. Unpretentious Chinese restaurant near the train station, known for the promptness and friendliness of its service. Adequate good-value food.

Pubs

George The Land of Green Ginger. Venerable pub found on Hull's most curiously named street – and featuring, if you can find it, England's smallest window.

Minerva Corner of Nelson St and Humber Dock St. Classic marina pub with cosy nooks, outdoor tables and cheap food.

Ye Olde White Harte 25 Silver St. Has a very pleasant courtyard beer garden and a history going back to the seventeenth century – witness the huge fireplaces and the skull behind the bar, found during renovations.

Beverley

BEVERLEY, nine miles north of Hull, ranks as one of northern England's premier towns, with its minster (the superior of many an English cathedral), its tangle of old streets, cobbled lanes and elegant Georgian and Victorian terraces. Over 350 buildings are listed as possessing historical or architectural merit, and though you could see its first-rank offerings in a morning, this is one of a handful of places in this part of the world where you might want to stay.

Arrival, information and accommodation

Beverley's **train station** on Station Square is just a couple of minutes' walk from the minster. The **bus station** is at the junction of Walkergate and Sow Hill Road, with the main street just a minute's walk away. The **tourist office** is at 34 Butcher Row in the main shopping area (Mon–Fri 9.30am–5.30pm, Sat 10am–4.45pm, plus Sun in July & Aug 11am–3pm; ℡01482/391672, ⊛www .realyorkshire.co.uk).

Local **accommodation** includes *Number One*, 1 Woodlands (℡01482/862752, ⊛www.number-one-bedandbreakfast-beverley.co.uk; no credit cards; ❷), a small B&B in a quiet Victorian house two minutes' walk from the market place. The top town-centre hotel is the *Beverley Arms*, North Bar Within (℡01482/869241, ⊛www.brook-hotels.co.uk; ❻), though there are several cheaper options. The **youth hostel** (℡0870/770 5696, ⓔbeverleyfriary@yha.org.uk; from £13.95; closed Nov–March) occupies one of the town's finer buildings, a restored Dominican friary mentioned in the *Canterbury Tales*. It's located in Friar's Lane, off Eastgate, just a hundred yards southeast of the minster.

The Town

Approaches to the town are dominated by the twin towers of **Beverley Minster** (Mon–Sat: March, April, Sept & Oct 9am–5pm, May–Aug 9am–5.30pm, Nov–Feb 9am–4pm; free but donations welcomed; ⊛www.beverleyminster.org), visible for miles around. An early monastery stood on the site but a series of fires, and the collapse of the central tower in 1213, paved the way for two centuries of rebuilding. The result was one of the finest Gothic creations in the country. The **west front**, which crowned the work in 1420, is widely considered without equal, its survival due in large part to architect Nicholas Hawksmoor, who restored much of the church in the eighteenth century. Inside is the fourteenth-century **Percy Tomb** on the north side of the altar, its sumptuously carved canopy one of the masterpieces of medieval European ecclesiastical art, and the **Fridstol**, a Saxon "sanctuary chair", which provided a safe haven for men on the run. Other incidental carving throughout the church is magnificent, particularly the 68 misericords of the oak **choir** (1520–24), one of the largest and most accomplished in England. Much of the decorative work here and elsewhere is on a musical theme. Beverley had a renowned guild of itinerant minstrels, who provided funds in the sixteenth century for the carvings on the transept aisle capitals, where you'll be able to pick out players of lutes, bagpipes, horns and tambourines.

Cobbled Highgate runs from the minster through town, along the pedestrianized shopping streets and past the main Market Square, to Beverley's other great church, **St Mary's** (April–Sept Mon–Fri 9.30am–4.30pm, Sat 10am–4pm, Sun 2–4pm; Oct–March Mon–Fri 9.30am–noon & 1–4pm, Sun outside services only, closed Sat; free; ⊛www.stmarysbeverley.org.uk), which nestles alongside the **North Bar**, sole survivor of the town's five medieval gates. Inside, the chancel's painted panelled ceiling (1445) contains portraits of English kings from Sigebert (623–37) to Henry VI (1421–71), while among the carvings, the favourite novelty is the so-called "Pilgrim's Rabbit", said to have been the inspiration for the White Rabbit in Lewis Carroll's *Alice's Adventures in Wonderland*.

Eating, drinking and entertainment

Cerutti 2, in Station Square (℡01482/866700; closed Sun & Mon), is a sister **brasserie** to the restaurant of the same name in Hull and serves fresh fish; there's also a good deli next door. Otherwise, there's a full complement of tearooms and cafés, or you can eat in the **pubs** – the celebrated *White Horse* (also known as *Nellie's*) on Hengate, near St Mary's, is a thoroughly atmospheric traditional drinking den. The **Beverley Folk Festival** (Ⓦwww.beverleyfestival.com) takes place each June while if you fancy a day at the races, contact **Beverley Racecourse** (℡01482/867488, Ⓦwww.beverley-racecourse.co.uk).

The East Yorkshire coast

The **East Yorkshire coast** curves south in a gentle arc from the mighty cliffs of Flamborough Head to erosion-created Spurn Head. There are few parts of the British coast as dangerous – indeed, the Humber lifeboat station at Spurn Point is the only one in Britain permanently staffed by a professional crew. Between the two points lie tranquil villages, windswept dunes, mudflats, noted bird sanctuaries, and superbly lonely retreats accessible to anyone prepared to cycle or walk.

The two main resorts, **Bridlington** and **Filey** are linked by the regular **train** service between Hull and Scarborough. There's also an hourly bus service between Bridlington, Filey and Scarborough, while the seasonal Sunday **Spurn Ranger** service (Easter–Oct; ℡01482/222222) gives access to the isolated Spurn Head coastline.

Bridlington

Popular **BRIDLINGTON** has maintained its harbour for almost a thousand years, though for much of that time it remained a small-scale place of little consequence. Like many coastal stations, it flourished in Edwardian times as a resort, but has spent recent decades in the same decline as other English bucket-and-spade destinations. Renovations have smartened up the promenade, which looks down upon the town's best asset – its sweeping sandy **beach**. It's an out-and-out family resort, which means plenty of candy-floss, fish and chips, rides, boat trips and amusement arcades.

Bridlington's largely Georgian **Old Town** is a mile inland, and home to the **Bayle Museum** (June–Aug Mon–Fri 10am–4pm; £1), which presents local history in the gateway to a fourteenth-century priory. The Old Town's High Street is a narrow thoroughfare of antique shops and traditional stores – the *Georgian Tea Rooms* at no. 56 has several floors of antiques and a tea garden at the rear.

In late October, the Spa Bridlington on the promenade is home to the renowned **Musicport World Music Festival** (Ⓦwww.musicportfestival.com).

Flamborough Head and Bempton Cliffs

Around fourteen miles of precipitous four-hundred-foot cliffs gird **Flamborough Head**, just to the northeast of Bridlington. The best of the seascapes are visible on the peninsula's north side, accessible by road from Flamborough village. The **lighthouse** (phone in advance for opening hours; £3; ℡01255/245011) just a mile beyond is the latest of a series on this site that date back to the seventeenth century, but which, in earlier times at least, manifestly failed to do their job: between 1770 and 1806, 174 ships went down in the hazardous waters off the headland.

From **Bempton**, two miles north of Bridlington, you can follow the grassy cliff-top path all the way round to Flamborough Head or curtail by cutting up paths to Flamborough village. The *Seabirds*, at the junction of the roads to the two villages, is a nice pub with a good line in fresh-fish bar meals. The RSPB sanctuary at **Bempton Cliffs**, reached along a quiet lane from Bempton, is the best single place to see the area's thousands of cliff-nesting birds. It's also the only mainland gannetry in England and you'll see gannets diving from fifty feet in the air to catch mackerel and herring. Bempton also boasts the second-largest **puffin colony** in the country, with several thousand returning to the cliffs between March and August. Late March and April is the best time to see the puffins, but the **visitor centre** (daily: March–Oct 10am–5pm; Nov–Feb 10am–4pm; parking £3.50; ☎01262/851179, ⓦwww.rspb .org.uk) can advise on other breeds' activities and rent you a pair of binoculars. RSPB puffin and sea-bird **cruises** (mid-May to Sept, times vary, usually on Sat & Sun; £15; ☎01262/850959) are a spectacular way to see the Bempton and Flamborough Head cliffs. They last three to four hours and depart from Bridlington.

Filey

FILEY, half a dozen miles further north up the coast, is at the very edge of the Yorkshire Wolds (and technically in North Yorkshire). It has a good deal more class as a resort than Bridlington, retaining many of its Edwardian features, including some splendid panoramic gardens. It, too, claims miles of wide sandy beach, stretching most of the way south to Flamborough Head and north the mile or so to the jutting rocks of **Filey Brigg**, where a nature trail wends for a couple of miles through the surroundings. **Bus** and **train** stations are just west of the centre on Station Avenue; there's a **car park** behind the bus station. Walk down Station Avenue and Murray Street to **Filey Visitor Centre** on John Street (May–Sept daily 9.30am–5pm; Oct–April Sat & Sun 9.30am–12.30pm & 1–4pm; ☎01723/518003, ⓦwww.discoveryorkshirecoast.com). You'll find a clutch of standard **B&Bs** on Rutland Street, off West Avenue, which runs from the church in the centre of town. A few pricier **hotels** sit among the holiday flats down on the beachfront. *Downcliffe House* (☎01723/513310, ⓦwww.downcliffehouse.com; ❺) is the pick of them, with a sea-view restaurant with outdoor terrace serving a decent menu of fresh fish.

The North York Moors

Virtually the whole of the **North York Moors** (ⓦwww.northyorkmoors.org .uk), from the Hambleton and Cleveland hills in the west to the cliff-edged coastline to the east, is protected as one of the country's finest national parks. The heather-covered, flat-topped hills are cut by deep, steep-sided valleys, and views here stretch for miles, interrupted only by giant cultivated forests, pale shadows of the woodland that covered the region before it was cleared by Neolithic and later peoples. Barrows and ancient forts provide memorials of these early settlers, mingling on the high moorland with the **Roman remains** of Wades Causeway, the battered stone crosses of the first Christian inhabitants and the ruins of great monastic houses such as **Rievaulx Abbey**.

Long-distance footpaths cross the park, notably the **Cleveland Way**, which follows the coast and northern moor, while the steam trains of the **North Yorkshire Moors Railway** run between Pickering and Grosmont and on to Whitby, even more popular since being used as the *Hogwarts Express* in the *Harry Potter* films. At Grosmont you can connect with the regular trains on the **Esk Valley** line, running six miles east to Whitby and the coast and west through more remote country settlements (and ultimately to Middlesbrough).

The main **bus** approaches to the moors are from Scarborough and York to the main towns of **Helmsley** and **Pickering** – pick up the free *Moors Explorer* timetable booklet from tourist offices and park information centres. There are also seasonal

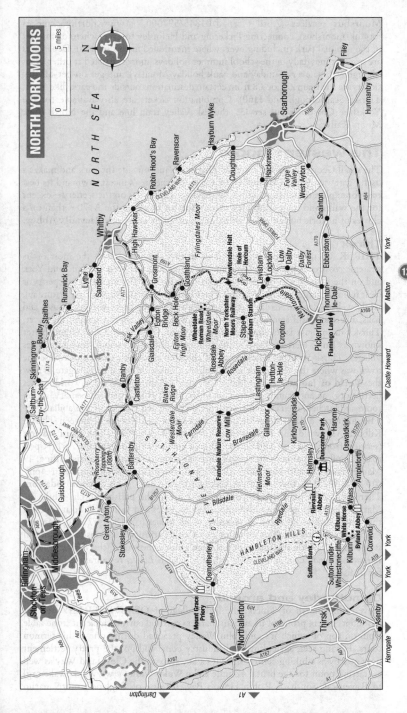

Moorsbus services (April–Oct; ☎01845/597000, ⓦwww.northyorkmoors
.org.uk/moorsbus), connecting Pickering and Helmsley to everywhere of interest
in the national park (including everywhere mentioned in this section). Departures
are several times daily in the school summer holidays, more restricted at other times
(though at least every Sunday and bank holiday Monday), and get-on-get-off day
tickets are a bargain £5, or £8 from certain destinations outside the park (like York,
Thirsk, Scarborough and Hull). Combination tickets are also available for the
Yorkshire Coastliner bus service, the Esk Valley train line and the North York
Moors Railway.

The western moors

The small Georgian market town of **Thirsk** lies just outside the park and makes a
useful gateway, but it's **Helmsley** that is by far the area's nicest town and its best
base for exploration. Most outings are likely to centre less on the scenery – except
for the walks and staggering views from **Sutton Bank** on the A170 – than on a
cluster of historic buildings, of which the most prepossessing is **Rievaulx Abbey**.

Thirsk

THIRSK, 23 miles north of York (and an easy day-trip), made the most of its
strategic crossroads position on the ancient drove road between Scotland and York
and on the historic east–west route from dales to coast. Its medieval prosperity is
clear from the large, cobbled **Market Place** (market days are Monday and Saturday),
while well-to-do citizens later endowed the town with fine Georgian houses and
halls, like those still standing on Kirkgate, which runs off the square. However,
Thirsk's main draw is its attachment to the legacy of local vet Alf Wight, better
known as James Herriot. Despite the confusing claims of various Yorkshire Dales
villages, Thirsk was the "Darrowby" of the Herriot books, not least because the
town was where the vet had his actual surgery. This building, at 23 Kirkgate, is now
the **World of James Herriot** (daily 10/11am–4/5pm; £6; ⓦwww.worldofjames
herriot.org), an entertaining re-creation of the vet's 1940s surgery, dispensary, sitting
room and kitchen, each crammed with period pieces and Herriot memorabilia.

Buses (three a day, Mon–Sat, from York, plus local services between Thirsk,
Kilburn, Coxwold and Helmsley) stop in the Market Place. The **train station**
(services from York and Middlesbrough) is a mile west of town on the A61 (Ripon
road); minibuses connect the station with the town centre. The **tourist office**, 49
Market Place (Easter–Nov daily 10am–5pm; Nov–Easter Mon–Sat 10am–4pm;
☎01845/522755, ⓦwww.visit-thirsk.com), can help with **accommodation**.
There are B&Bs on Kirkgate, on the road up to the parish church, while the
Market Place is ringed by old-fashioned pubs, cafés and tearooms. Four miles to
the south, down the A168 at **Asenby**, *Crab Manor* (☎01845/577286, ⓦwww
.crabandlobster.co.uk; ⑤) is something of a local curiosity – its lavish rooms are all
styled in the fashion of famous hotels from around the world (the *Waldorf Astoria*,
Barbados's *Sandy Lane* and so on) – while its *Crab & Lobster* restaurant is renowned
for its fish.

Osmotherley and around

Eleven miles north of Thirsk, the little village of **OSMOTHERLEY** huddles
around its green, proud of its ancient market cross and curious adjacent stone table
from on top of which it's said John Wesley preached during one of his sermon
tours. Having seen agriculture and industry come and go, the pretty settlement
now gets by as a hiking centre, since it's a key stop on the **Cleveland Way** as well
as starting point for the brutal 42-mile **Lyke Wake Walk** (ⓦwww.lykewake.org)
to Ravenscar, south of Robin Hood's Bay. It's one of England's more macho

long-distance paths, and a highly popular route, so hikers and their back-up teams tend to pack both village youth hostel and campsite year round.

Grouped around Osmotherley's small green are three pubs – the *Three Tuns* (℡01609/883301, Ⓦwww.threetunsrestaurant.co.uk; ❹), the *Queen Catherine Hotel* (℡01609/883209, Ⓦwww.queencatherinehotel.co.uk; ❷) and the *Golden Lion* (℡01609/883526, Ⓦwww.goldenlionosmotherley.co.uk; ❸), all of which offer **food and accommodation** – there's little to choose between them in terms of cost or quality.

Two miles from Osmotherley, the fourteenth-century **Mount Grace Priory** (April–Sept Mon & Thurs–Sun 10am–6pm; Oct–March Thurs–Sun 10am–4pm; £4.50; NT & EH), the most important of England's nine Carthusian ruins, provides a striking contrast to its more grandiose and worldly Cistercian counterparts. The Carthusians took a vow of silence and lived, ate and prayed alone in their two-storey cells, each separated from its neighbour by a privy, small garden and high walls. The foundations of the cells are still clearly visible, together with one that has been reconstructed to suggest its original layout and the monks' way of life. Road access to the priory is straight up the busy A19 from Thirsk, eleven miles to the south; it's reached off a signposted minor road just after the Osmotherley turn-off. Or it's an easy walk from Osmotherley, via Chapel Wood Farm.

Sutton Bank and Kilburn

The main A170 road enters the national park from Thirsk as it climbs five hundred feet in half a mile to **Sutton Bank** (960ft), a phenomenal viewpoint from where the panorama extends across the Vale of York to the Pennines on the far horizon. At the top of the climb stands a huge car park and a North York Moors National Park **Visitor Centre** (Jan to mid-Feb Sat & Sun 11am–4pm; mid-Feb to March, Nov & Dec daily 11am–4pm; April–Oct daily 10am–5pm; ℡01845/597426), full of background on the short waymarked walks and off-road bike rides you can make from here. It has a café, too.

To the south of the A170, the **White Horse Nature Trail** (2–3 miles; 1hr 30min) skirts the crags of Roulston Scar en route to the **Kilburn White Horse**, northern England's only turf-cut figure, 314 feet long and 228 feet high. You could make a real walk of it by dropping a couple of miles down to pretty **KILBURN** village (a minor road also runs from the A170, passing the White Horse car park). The village has been synonymous with woodcarving since the days of "Mouseman" Robert Thompson (1876–1955), whose woodcarvings are marked by his distinctive mouse motif and can be found throughout Yorkshire – in York Minster and Trinity Church, Hull, for instance, and beyond, even in Westminster Abbey. The **Mouseman Visitor Centre** (Easter–Sept daily 10am–5pm; Oct Tues–Sun 10am–5pm; Nov & Dec Wed–Sun 11am–4pm; £4; Ⓦwww.robertthompsons.co.uk) displays examples of Thompson's hand-crafted furniture, and you can recuperate in the village's *Forresters Arms*.

Coxwold and around

Most of the many visitors to the attractive little village of **COXWOLD** come to pay homage to the novelist **Laurence Sterne**, who is buried by the south wall (close to the porch) in the churchyard of **St Michael's**, where he was vicar from 1760 until his death in 1768. The church, with its odd octagonal tower, is worth closer scrutiny – particularly the three-decker pulpit and medieval stained glass – before heading for **Shandy Hall**, 150 yards further up the road beyond the church (May–Sept: house Wed 2–4.30pm, Sun 2.30–4.30pm; gardens daily except Sat 11am–4.30pm; also by appointment; house & gardens £4.50, gardens only £2.50; ℡01347/868465, Ⓦwww.shandean.org). Sterne's home, now a museum crammed with literary memorabilia, it was here that he wrote *A Sentimental Journey through France and Italy* and the wonderfully eccentric *The Life and Opinions of Tristram Shandy, Gentleman*.

Laurence Sterne talked of "A delicious Walk of Romance" from Coxwold to twelfth-century **Byland Abbey** (April–June daily except Tues 11am–6pm; July & Aug daily 11am–6pm; Sept daily except Tues 11am–5pm; £4.20; EH), a mile and a half northeast of the village, a description that captures the appeal of the ruins. The *Abbey Inn*, opposite the priory entrance (☎01347/868204; ❹), has three intimate rooms, and serves coffee and meals (closed Tues), or you can press on the half a mile to **Wass**, where the *Wombwell Arms* is known for its food and beer.

Helmsley

One of the moors' most appealing towns, **HELMSLEY** makes a perfect base for visiting the western moors and Rievaulx Abbey. Local life revolves around a large cobbled market square, dominated by a boastful monument to the second earl of Feversham, whose family was responsible for rebuilding most of the village in the nineteenth century. The old **market cross** now marks the start of the 110-mile Cleveland Way. **Helmsley Castle** (March & Oct daily 10am–5pm; April–Sept daily 10am–6pm; Nov–Feb Mon & Thurs–Sun 10am–4pm; £4.50; EH) is visible from the square, its unique twelfth-century D-shaped keep ringed by massive earthworks. After a three-month siege during the Civil War it was "slighted" by Sir Thomas Fairfax, the Parliamentary commander, and much of its stone was plundered by townspeople for local houses. A visitor centre, exhibition and audioguide fill you in on the full history.

To the southwest of the town, overlooking a wooded meander of the Rye, stands the Fevershams' country seat, **Duncombe Park** (April–Oct Mon–Thurs & Sun: house tours 12.30–3.30pm, garden, parkland & visitor centre 11am–5.30pm; house, gardens & parkland £8.25, gardens £5, parkland £3; ⓦwww .duncombepark.com), built for the Fevershams' ancestor Sir Thomas Duncombe in 1713. The building is by gentleman-architect William Wakefield, though he was probably influenced by Vanbrugh who was working on Castle Howard at about the same time. The grounds are perhaps more appealing than the house, boasting acres of landscaped gardens, including a brace of artfully sited temples.

Practicalities

Buses all stop on or near the Market Place. The useful **tourist office** is at the castle visitor centre (March–Oct daily 10am–5pm; Nov–Feb Fri–Sun 10am–4pm; ☎01439/770173), and has information on both the **Cleveland Way** and the **Ebor Way**, the latter a gentle seventy-mile route to Ilkley that links with the Dales Way.

Market day in Helmsley is Friday, when the town centre is filled with traders. *The Feathers* on the Market Place is the best place for a drink and a **pub** meal, while also on Market Place are two excellent delis, Hunters and Perns, the latter associated with the excellent *Star Inn* at Harome (see opposite). Borogate has several fine little **shops** in ancient houses, including a working smithy and a good secondhand bookshop in the old fire station. At **Helmsley Arts Centre** in the Old Meeting House, off Bridge Street (☎01439/771700, ⓦwww.helmsleyarts.co.uk), there's a full programme of theatre, film, music and other events.

Accommodation and food

Crown Market Place ☎01439/770297, ⓦwww .tchh.co.uk. Of the inns ringing Market Place, this is the best mid-range (two-star) option, a comfortable, old-fashioned (in the best sense), family-run

hotel. The restaurant serves good-value lunches and evening meals. ❸

Feversham Arms 1 High St, behind the church ☎01439/770766, ⓦwww .fevershamarmshotel.com. Combines hip styling

The Cleveland Way

The 110-mile **Cleveland Way**, one of England's premier long-distance national trails, starts at Helmsley in the North York Moors and follows a route that embraces the northern rim of the moors, the Cleveland Hills and the cliff scenery of the North Yorkshire coast. The path hits the sea at Saltburn and then runs south, terminating at Filey, south of Scarborough – though an unofficial "Missing Link" joins Scarborough to Helmsley, through the Tabular Hills, thus completing a circular walk.

Most people complete the Cleveland Way in around nine or ten days, though it's easy to walk short stages instead, particularly on the **coastal section**, where towns, villages and services are closer together. The outstanding high-cliff sections are (from south to north): Hayburn Wyke, near Ravenscar, to Robin Hood's Bay (7 miles); Robin Hood's Bay to Whitby (6 miles); Sandsend to Runswick Bay to Staithes (7 miles); and Staithes to Skinningrove, the section with the highest cliffs (5 miles).

The **Cleveland Way Project** (☎01439/770657) produces a variety of guides, including an annual accommodation guide, which you can download from ⓦwww.nationaltrail.co.uk. *The Cleveland Way* by Ian Sampson (Aurum Press) covers the ground in detail.

with comfort in its spacious rooms and Modern British brasserie. It's favoured by the country-pursuits crowd, but there's also an outdoor pool, gym, tennis court and garden-terrace, a spa and new poolside suites. ❻
Helmsley YHA ☎0845/371 9638, ⓔhelmsley@yha.org.uk. A few hundred yards east of the Market Place – follow Bondgate to Carlton Rd and turn left. Open daily April–Sept. Dorm beds from £13.95.
No. 54 54 Bondgate ☎01439/771533, ⓦwww.no54.co.uk. A delightful cottage-style B&B offering three superior courtyard rooms just 500 yards from

the Market Place. Power showers, fresh flowers, sheltered terrace and garden add up to a relaxing night, and breakfast (free-range eggs, proper bacon, kedgeree) is excellent. Picnics and evening meals also available. ❸
Star Inn Harome, 2 miles south of the A170 ☎01439/770397, ⓦwww.thestaratharome.co.uk. A thatched pub where Michelin-rated food awaits. Should you wish to make a night of it, eight very nice rooms in the adjacent lodge are individually furnished, some with spa baths, a couple with a private garden, and one with its own snooker table. No food Mon lunch. ❻

Rievaulx Abbey and Terrace

From Helmsley you can easily walk across country to **Rievaulx Abbey** (April–Sept daily 10am–6pm; Oct Mon & Thurs–Sun 10am–5pm; Nov–March Thurs–Sun 10am–4pm; £5; EH), once one of England's greatest Cistercian abbeys. The signposted path follows the opening two miles of the Cleveland Way, plus another mile's diversion off the Way, and takes around ninety minutes – a trail leaflet is available from the tourist office in Helmsley.

Founded in 1132, the abbey quickly developed from a series of rough shelters on the wooded banks of the River Rye to become a flourishing community with interests in fishing, mining, agriculture and the woollen industry. At its height, 140 monks and up to 500 lay brothers lived and worked at the abbey, though numbers fell dramatically once the Black Death (1348–49) had done its worst. The end came with the Dissolution, when many of the walls were razed and the roof lead stripped – the beautiful ruins, however, still suggest the abbey's former splendour. A **visitor centre** mounts exhibitions pertaining to the ruins and to monastic life in the valley.

Although it forms some sort of ensemble with the abbey, there's no direct access from the ruins to **Rievaulx Terrace** (late Feb to Oct daily 11am–5pm; £4.75; NT), which is entered from the B1257, a couple of miles northwest of Helmsley.

This half-mile stretch of grass-covered terraces and woodland was laid out as part of Duncombe Park in the 1750s, partly to enhance the views of the abbey. The resulting panorama makes it a great spot for a picnic.

The central moors

The highest and wildest terrain in the North York Moors is in the **central moors**, bounded by Ryedale in the west and by **Rosedale** in the east. Purple swathes of summer heather carpet the tops, where ancient crosses and standing stones provide hints of the moorland's distant past.

Hutton-le-Hole

Lying eight miles northeast of Helmsley, one of Yorkshire's quaintest villages, **HUTTON-LE-HOLE**, has become so great a tourist attraction that you'll have to come off-season to get much pleasure from its stream-crossed, sheep-dotted village green. Apart from the sheer photogenic quality of the place, the big draw is the family-oriented **Ryedale Folk Museum** (daily mid-Jan to early Dec 10am–5.30pm/dusk; £5.50; ⓦwww.ryedalefolkmuseum.co.uk), where local life is explored in a series of reconstructed buildings. Special events and displays throughout the season mean there's always something going on.

The museum also houses a **national park information centre** (same hours as museum; ⓣ01751/417367), while the nearby car park fills quickly in summer as walkers disperse from the village. The information centre has a list of local **B&Bs**, or make for *Burnley House* (ⓣ01751/417548, ⓦwww.burnleyhouse.co.uk; ❸), a hospitable Georgian house on the green with streamside garden. The *Forge Tea Shop* (closed weekdays Nov–Feb) is a renowned stop for tea and cakes, while if you stay the night you'll have plenty of time to become acquainted with the *Crown*, the local **pub**.

Around Hutton-le-Hole

A mile and a half east of Hutton-le-Hole don't miss a look inside the church of **St Mary's** (daily 9am–dusk; free) in the hamlet of **LASTINGHAM**, which preserves its early Norman crypt, one of Yorkshire's great ecclesiastical treasures. Its heavy vaults and carved columns still shelter the head of a ninth-century Anglo-Saxon cross, a Viking "hogsback" tombstone and the original doorposts of the Saxon monastery dating from 654 AD.

A little to the northwest of Hutton-le-Hole the country lanes of **Farndale** are packed in spring as visitors arrive to see the area's wild daffodils, protected by the two-thousand-acre **Farndale Nature Reserve**. The Moorsbus runs a special "Daffodil" service every Sunday in April and over Easter from Hutton-le-Hole. The best area for the flowers is north of **Low Mill**, where roads from Gillamoor and Hutton-le-Hole meet, about four miles north of the latter.

Rosedale Abbey, four miles northeast of Hutton-le-Hole, preserves only a few fragments of the Cistercian priory (1158) that gave it its name, most of them incorporated into **St Lawrence's** parish church. North of Rosedale Abbey is the *Lion Inn* (ⓣ01751/417320, ⓦwww.lionblakey.co.uk; ❸) on **Blakey Ridge**, a couple of miles south of the junction with the Hutton-le-Hole–Castleton road. A truly windswept local (at over 1300ft), the inn has an unbeatable location for an isolated night's stay – though come Sunday lunchtime the car park soon fills up.

Pickering and the eastern moors

The biggest centre for miles around, **Pickering**, self-styled "Gateway to the Moors", is a handy halt if you're touring the villages and dales of the **eastern**

moors. Its undoubted big pull is the **North Yorkshire Moors Railway** (**NYMR**; see box below), which provides a beautiful way of travelling up (and walking from) **Newtondale**, and of connecting with the Esk Valley line in Esk Dale, and with Whitby and the Yorkshire coast.

Pickering

A thriving market town at the junction of the A170 and the transmoor A169 (Whitby road), **PICKERING** is worth an hour or two's stop. Its most attractive feature is its motte-and-bailey **castle** on the hill north of the Market Place (April–June & Sept Thurs–Mon 10am–5pm; July & Aug daily 10am–5pm; £3.70; EH), reputedly used by every English monarch up to 1400 as a base for hunting in nearby Blandsby Park. The other spot worth investigating is the **Beck Isle Museum of Rural Life** on Bridge Street (Feb–Oct daily 10am–5pm; £5; Ⓦwww.beckislemuseum.co.uk), which has reconstructions of a gents' outfitters and a barber's shop, a case full of knickers, and two giant Welsh guardsmen painted by Rex Whistler for a children's party.

Buses stop outside the library and **tourist office** (March–Oct Mon–Sat 9.30am–5pm, Sun 9.30am–4pm; Nov–Feb Mon–Sat 9.30am–4.30pm; Ⓣ01751/473791), opposite the Co-op on The Ropery in the centre of town; the **NYMR train station** is less than five minutes' signposted walk away. The tourist office can help with **B&Bs**, though Whitby, only twenty minutes' drive away on the coast, is the better overnight destination. A couple of the **pubs** also have rooms, top choice being the *White Swan*, on Market Place (Ⓣ01751/472288, Ⓦwww.white-swan .co.uk; Ⓞ), with both contemporary and traditional bedrooms. There are cafés and tearooms throughout town, and a couple of Indian **restaurants**, though it's the *White Swan* that's most serious about its cooking – fine Modern British food at moderate prices. **Market** day in town is Monday, and there's a farmers' market on the first Thursday of the month.

Along the North Yorkshire Moors Railway

The first stop is **LEVISHAM**, perfect for walks to the village a mile and a half to the east, where the *Horseshoe Inn* (Ⓣ01751/460240) is a favourite target, especially for Sunday lunch. A steep winding road continues another mile down across the beck and then up to **LOCKTON**, where there's a youth hostel and a path due north to the **Hole of Horcum**, a bizarre natural hollow gouged by the glacial meltwaters that carved out Newtondale. The paths run back to Levisham Station from here – the entire seven-mile circuit is one of the Moors' best short walks.

The North Yorkshire Moors Railway

The **North Yorkshire Moors Railway** (NYMR; Ⓣ01751/472508, talking timetables Ⓣ01751/473535, Ⓦwww.nymr.co.uk) connects **Pickering** with the Esk Valley (Middlesbrough–Whitby) line at **Grosmont**, eighteen miles to the north. The line was completed by George Stephenson in 1835, just ten years after the opening of the Stockton & Darlington Railway, making it one of the earliest lines in the country. Scheduled **services** operate year-round (limited to weekend and school hols service Nov–Feb), and a **day-return ticket** costs £16. Part of the line's attraction is the **steam trains**, though be warned that diesels are pulled into service when the fire risk in the forests is high. Steam services have also been extended from the end of the NYMR line at Grosmont to the nearby seaside resort of Whitby – departures are usually during school and bank holidays, with a return fare from Pickering of £21.

The second train stop, **Newtondale Halt**, is only a couple of miles southwest of the Hole of Horcum, or you can head off through the extensive woods of **Cropton Forest** to the west on trails marked by the Forestry Commission. At Stape – three miles southwest through the forest – you're just two miles south of the best-preserved stretch of Roman road in Europe, **Wheeldale Roman Road**, a mile of Wade's Causeway that ran from York to bases on the coast: the remains show a twenty-foot-wide stretch of sand and gravel studded by sandstone slabs and edged with kerbs and ditches.

The third NYMR station is at **GOATHLAND**, a highly attractive village set in open moorland beneath the great expanses of Wheeldale and Goathland moors. If it seems oddly familiar – and if it seems unduly crowded – it's because it's widely known as "Aidensfield", the fictional village at the centre of the *Heartbeat* TV series, while the station doubled as "Hogsmeade" in *Harry Potter and the Philosopher's Stone*. Outside summer weekends Goathland can still be a joy to wander, with signposts pointing you to the local sight, the **Mallyan Spout**, a seventy-foot-high waterfall.

A gentle path from Goathland runs the mile through the fields down to **BECK HOLE**, an idyllic hamlet focused on the ✲ *Birch Hall Inn*, one of the finest rural pubs in all England – tiny to the point of claustrophobic, still doubling as a sweet shop and store as it has for a century, and serving great sandwiches. It also serves as a focus for the summer game of quoits, played on the nearby green.

Thornton-le-Dale and Dalby Forest

THORNTON-LE-DALE, two miles east of Pickering, hangs onto its considerable charm despite the main A170 Scarborough road scything through its centre. Most of the houses, pubs and shops are alluring, none more so than the thatched cottage near the parish church, which features in so many ads, magazine covers, chocolate boxes and calendars that it's been described as the most photographed house in Britain.

Minor roads from Thornton-le-Dale and from the A169 (Whitby road) lead into **Dalby Forest**: drivers pay a toll (£7; road closed 9pm–7am) to join the start of a nine-mile forest drive that emerges close to Hackness, just four miles from Scarborough. It's best to make first for the **visitor centre** (daily 10am–5pm; ☏01751/460295, ⓦwww.forestry.gov.uk/dalbyforest) at **Low Dalby**, which has information on the wildlife, picnic spots and the range of marked trails. This is also a great place for mountain biking, and there's high-wire fun and Tarzan swings at the **Go Ape** adventure course (April–Oct daily 9am–5pm, closed Tues in term time; Nov Sat & Sun 9am–12.30/2.30pm; £30; ⓦwww.goape.co.uk), across the road from the visitor centre, where the Moorsbus stops in summer.

The best walks are from a car park about three miles north of Low Dalby at Low Staindale, which include the one-and-a-half mile (1hr) **Bridestones Trail** – to the two great sandstone tors rising out of the heather that have been eroded into unearthly shapes. Similarly named outcrops are found all over the moors, and may be so named because of their connections with ancient fertility rites, or derive from a Norse word meaning "brink", or "boundary" stones.

The Esk Valley

The northernmost reaches of the national park are crossed by the east–west **Esk Valley**, whose pretty river flows into the sea at Whitby. It's a part of the North York Moors overlooked by many visitors – partly because there's not much moorland tramping to be done until you reach the isolated stone village of **DANBY**, one of the finest of all moorland villages. Here, you're within striking distance of some excellent walks, all detailed on trail leaflets available from the **Moors Centre** (mid-Feb to March daily 11am–4pm; April–Oct daily 10am–5pm; Nov–Feb Sat & Sun only

11am–4pm; ☎01439/772737), where there's also a good tearoom. Danby's pub is the *Duke of Wellington*, while the *Stonehouse Bakery & Tea Shop* is great for daytime snacks. A mile out of the village at **AINTHORPE**, the *Fox & Hounds* (☎01287/660218, Ⓦwww.foxandhounds-ainthorpe.com; ❸) looks out over the moors.

You can reach Danby by road (from Whitby via the A169 through Sleights) or by train: the North York Moors Railway connects at Grosmont, where you're on the **Esk Valley line**, which runs between Whitby and Middlesbrough, stopping at **GREAT AYTON**. Here, the North York Moors give way to the **Cleveland Hills**, whose scattered peaks provide the buffer between the rural east of the region and the encroaching industry of Teesside to the west. It is Great Ayton's **Captain Cook** connections, though, that draw most visitors: the town was the boyhood home of England's greatest seaman and explorer, James Cook, between 1736 (when he was 8) and 1745. The young Cook lived at Aireyholme Farm (no public access) on the outskirts of town, though after James left to go to sea his father built a family **cottage** on Bridge Street, which was later dismantled and shipped to Melbourne, Australia, in 1934; its site is marked by an obelisk of Australian granite near Low Green. Other Cook-related sights include **All Saints' Church**, also at Low Green, which the family attended and where Cook's mother Grace is buried; Cook's school on the High Street, now the **Schoolroom Museum** (daily: April–June, Sept & Oct 1–4pm; July & Aug 11am–4pm; £2; Ⓦwww .captaincookschoolroommuseum.co.uk); and a **sculpture** of a youthful Cook – bare-chested and long-locked – on High Green.

A waymarked path runs northeast out of Great Ayton, up to the summit of **Roseberry Topping** (1050ft), the queerly shaped peak visible from all over the locality – beacons were lit on top of here during the threat by the Spanish Armada. It's a stiff climb, followed by a tramp across Easby Moor to the south to the fifty-foot-high **Cook Monument** (1827) for more amazing views, before circling back to Great Ayton.

The North Yorkshire coast

The **North Yorkshire coast** (Ⓦwww.discoveryorkshirecoast.com) is the south-ernmost stretch of a cliff-edged shore that stretches almost unbroken to the Scottish border. **Scarborough** is the biggest town and resort, with a full set of attractions and a terrific beach. Cute **Robin Hood's Bay** is the most popular of the coastal villages, with fishing and smuggling traditions, while bluff **Staithes** – a fishing harbour on the far edge of North Yorkshire – has yet to tip over into full-blown tourist mode. **Whitby**, in between the two, is the best stopover, its fine sands and resort facilities tempered by its abbey ruins, cobbled streets, Georgian buildings and maritime heritage – more than any other local place Whitby celebrates Captain Cook as one of its own. **Walkers** should note that two of the best parts of the **Cleveland Way** depart from Whitby: southeast to Robin Hood's Bay (six miles) and northwest to Staithes (eleven miles), both along thrilling high-cliff sections.

Scarborough

The oldest resort in the country, **SCARBOROUGH** first attracted visitors to its newly discovered mineral springs in the early seventeenth century. By the 1730s, the more enterprising spa-goers were also venturing onto the sweeping local sands and dipping themselves in the bracing North Sea, popularizing the racy pastime of sea-bathing. Still fashionable in Victorian times – when it was "the Queen of the Watering Places" – Scarborough saw its biggest transformation after World War II, when it (and many other resorts) became a holiday haven for workers from the industrial heartlands. In the 1950s, three million visitors a year thronged the beaches, rode on the donkeys and paddled in the rock pools. All the traditional ingredients of a beach resort are still here in force, from superb clean sands and kitsch amusement arcades to the more refined pleasures of its tight-knit old town streets and a genteel round of parks and gardens.

Arrival, information and accommodation

The **train station** is at the top of town facing Westborough; **buses** pull up outside or in the surrounding streets, though the National Express services (direct from London) stop in the car park behind the station. Scarborough's **tourist offices** are located inside the Brunswick Shopping Centre on Westborough (Mon–Sat 9am–5.30pm, April–Oct also Sun 10.30am–4pm; ☎01723/383637) and by the harbour on Sandside (April–Sept daily 9.30am–9pm; Oct–Feb Sat & Sun only 9.30am–5pm). To reach the harbour and castle, walk straight down Westborough, Newborough and Eastborough, through the main shopping streets. Open-top **seafront buses** (Easter–Sept daily from 9.30am, March weekends only; £1.60), meanwhile, run from North Bay to the Spa Complex in South Bay.

Scarborough is crammed with inexpensive **hotels and guesthouses**. Happy hunting grounds include North Bay's Queen's Parade, where most of the guesthouses have sweeping bay views and parking, and Blenheim Terrace, which is closer to the castle. The cheapest places in town are those without the sea views – try along central Aberdeen Walk (off Westborough), or on North Marine Road and Trafalgar Square, behind Queen's Parade. Above South Bay, hotels tend to be pricier, though there's a clutch of B&Bs along and around West Street. If you're stuck, call the tourist office.

Crown Spa Esplanade ☎01723/357400, ⓦwww .crownspahotel.com. In a Regency terrace built in 1847 above South Bay, the *Crown* makes the most of its period features, views and genteel feel. There's a gym, pool and brasserie. ⓺

Helaina 14 Blenheim Terrace ☎01723/375191, ⓦwww.hotelhelaina.co.uk. Victorian terraced house on North Bay; bedrooms are on the small side, but beautifully furnished in contemporary style. Great sea views, and ample breakfasts. Parking. ⓶

Interludes 32 Princess St ☎01723/360513, ⓦwww.interludeshotel.co.uk. Quiet Georgian townhouse in the old-town streets behind the harbour. Bay views from the upper floors, and theatre memorabilia, antiques, fresh flowers and traditional English decor throughout; call for details of Stephen Joseph Theatre breaks. It's a gay-friendly place, though all (except children) are welcome. ⓶

Riviera St Nicholas Cliff ☎01723/372277, ⓦwww.riviera-scarborough.co.uk. Restored Georgian townhouse opposite the *Grand* with bay views and refurbished rooms featuring crisp white bedding and colourful cushions. ⓶

Scarborough YHA Burniston Rd, Scalby Mills, 2 miles north of town ☎0845/371 9657, ⓔscarborough@yha.org.uk. Occupies a converted watermill, off the A165, a 10min walk from the sea; the Cleveland Way passes close by. Closed Nov–Easter. Dorm beds from £11.95.

Windmill Mill St, off Victoria Rd ☎01723/372735, ⓦwww.windmill-hotel.co.uk. Eighteenth-century windmill incongruously sited in the town centre, with country-style rooms (upper-floor ones with veranda) ranged around a cobbled courtyard; you take breakfast inside the mill dining-room amid the owner's amazing toy collection. Parking. ⓷

The Town

There's no better place to get an overview of the town than from the walls of **Scarborough Castle** (April–Sept daily 10am–6pm; Oct–March Mon & Thurs–Sun 10am–4pm; £4.50; EH), mounted on a headland between two golden-sanded bays. Bronze and Iron Age relics have been found on the wooded castle crag, together with fragments of a fourth-century Roman signalling station, Saxon and Norman chapels and a Viking camp, reputedly built by one Scardi (or "harelip"), from which the town's name derives. As you leave the castle, drop into the **church of St Mary** (1180), immediately below on Castle Road, whose graveyard contains the tomb of Anne Brontë, buried here in 1849.

The town's **museums** (all Tues–Sun 10am–5pm; ⓦ www.scarboroughmuseums trust.co.uk) – the Art Gallery (£2), Rotunda Museum (£4.50) and Scarborough Collections (£3) – are worth seeing, especially the **Rotunda**. Constructed to the plans of William Smith, the founder of English geology, it's a fascinating building in its own right and has recently been updated to include in its venerable shell very modern displays on geology and local history. The Dinosaur Coast Gallery is particularly child-friendly. All three museums have lots of activities during the summer – check the website.

Otherwise, the chief cultural distraction is the unexpected concentration of Pre-Raphaelite art in the **church of St-Martin-on-the-Hill** (1863) on Albion Road. The Victorian-Gothic pile has a roof by William Morris, a triptych by Burne-Jones, a pulpit with four printed panels by Rossetti, stained glass by Morris, Burne-Jones and Ford Madox Brown, and an east wall whose tracery provides the frames for angels by Morris and *The Adoration of the Magi* by Burne-Jones.

The bays

The miniature North Bay Railway (daily Easter–Sept) runs up to the **Sea Life Centre and Marine Sanctuary** at Scalby Mills (daily 10am–6pm; £11.60), distinguished by its white pyramids, but the most enjoyable **amusements and rides** are the old-fashioned ones on the harbour, where creaky dodgems, helter-skelter and shooting galleries compete for custom. From the harbourside in summer you'll be able to take one of the short **cruises and speedboat trips** out into the bay. For unique entertainment, head for **Peasholm Park**, where naval warfare, in the shape of miniature man-powered naval vessels, battle it out on the lake (Mon, Thurs & Sat in July and Aug; full details from the tourist office).

The **South Bay** is more refined, backed by the pleasant Valley Gardens and the Italianate meanderings of the South Cliff Gardens, and topped by an esplanade from which a **hydraulic lift** (April–Sept daily 10am–5pm; 70p) chugs down to the beach. Here, Scarborough's Regency and Victorian glories are still in evidence, most impressively of all in the six million bricks and fifty-two chimneys of the **Grand Hotel**, built in 1867. Views from its (neglected) terrace are superb.

Eating, drinking and entertainment

Cafés, fish-and-chip shops and **tearooms** are great in number and variable in quality and popularity. There's a more discerning selection when it comes to **restaurants**, not least because the town has a fair-sized Italian population – including the descendants of several POWs who settled in Scarborough after the war. Virtually every street has a **pub** – two of the best are the *Golden Ball*, 31 Sandside (ⓣ01723/353899), down by the harbour, and the *Scalby Mills*, Scalby Mills Road (ⓣ01723/500449), just beyond the Sea Life Centre.

Whatever the posters and advertising suggest, the cultural heart of Scarborough is neither the Spa Complex nor the Futurist Theatre, with their end-of-pier summer shows, but the renowned **Stephen Joseph Theatre** on Westborough (ⓣ01723/370541, ⓦ www.sjt.uk.com). Housed in a former Art Deco cinema, the theatre premieres every new work of local playwright **Alan Ayckbourn** and promotes strong seasons of theatre and film; there's also a good café/restaurant and the bar is open daily except Sunday.

Cafés and restaurants

Café Fish 19 York Place, at the intersection with Somerset Terrace ☎01723/500301. For a more sophisticated way with fish than most Scarborough restaurants. Gets busy at weekends. Mains from £15; dinner only.

Café Italia 36 St Nicholas Cliff. Utterly charming, microscopic Italian coffee bar next to the *Grand*, where good coffee, focaccia slices and ice cream keep a battery of regulars happy. Shuts at 4pm; closed Sun.

Gianni's 13 Victoria Rd ☎01723/507388. The most immediately welcoming of the town's Italian restaurants, where the good-natured staff bustle up and down stairs, delivering quality pizzas, pastas (£8–10) and quaffable wine by the carafe. Dinner only.

Golden Grid 4 Sandside. The harbourside's choicest fish-and-chip establishment, "catering for the promenader since 1883". Offers grilled fish (£9–11), crab and lobster, a *fruits-de-mer* platter and a wine list alongside the standard crispy-battered fry-up.

Lanterna 33 Queen St ☎01723/363616. Long-established, special-night-out destination, featuring traditional, seasonal Italian cooking in quiet, formal surroundings. Mains from £12.50; dinner only; closed Sun.

Robin Hood's Bay and around

Although known as Robbyn Huddes Bay as early as Tudor times, there's nothing except half-remembered myth to link **ROBIN HOOD'S BAY** with Sherwood's legendary bowman – locals anyway prefer the old name, Bay Town or simply Bay. The best-known and most heavily visited spot on the coast, the village fully lives up to its reputation, with narrow streets and pink-tiled cottages toppling down the cliff-edge site, evoking the romance of a time when this was both a hard-bitten fishing community and a nest of smugglers. So packed together are the houses, legend has it, that contraband could be passed up the hill from cottage to cottage without the pursuing king's men being any the wiser.

From the upper village, lined with Victorian villas, now mostly B&Bs, it's a very steep walk down the hill to the harbour. The **Old Coastguard Station** (March to late July & early Sept to Oct daily 10am–5pm; late July to early Sept Tues–Sun 10am–5pm; Nov–March Sat & Sun 10am–4pm; free; ☎01947/885900; NT) has been turned into a visitor centre with displays relating to the area's geology and sealife. When the tide is out, the massive rock beds below are exposed, split by a geological fault line and studded with fossil remains. There's an easy circular walk (2.5 miles) to **Boggle Hole** and its youth hostel (see below), a mile south, returning inland via the path along the old Scarborough–Whitby railway line.

Practicalities

Drivers will have to leave their cars in one of two **car parks** in the upper part of the village, which is also where the buses stop. Whitby has the nearest train station and tourist office.

Many people see the village as a day-trip from Whitby: you can check on Bay accommodation in the tourist office there, or simply stroll the streets of the old part of the village to see if any of the small cottage **B&Bs** has vacancies. Boggle Hole's **youth hostel** is one of Yorkshire's most popular, a former mill located in a wooded ravine about a mile south of Robin Hood's Bay at Mill Beck (☎0845/371 9504, ❸bogglehole@yha.org.uk; from £13.95). A torch is essential after dark, and you can't access the hostel along the beach once the tide is up.

You'll probably end up **eating** in one of the pubs in the lower village – try the *Bay Hotel*, right on the harbour (☎01947/880278), which is the traditional start or end of the Coast-to-Coast Walk. Alternatively, the *Swell Café* in the Old Chapel, Chapel Street (☎01947/880180), serves a good range of daytime dishes and has great coastal views from its terrace tables; you can catch family cinema shows in summer here too. The eighteenth-century *Dolphin* in King Street is the oldest in the village, and has folk nights every Friday.

A couple of miles northwest of Robin Hood's Bay at **HAWKSER**, on the A171, Trailways (℡01947/820207, Ⓦwww.trailways.info) is a **bike-rental** outfit based in the old Hawsker train station, perfectly placed for day-trips in either direction along the disused railway line. They'll deliver or pick up from local addresses (including *Boggle Hole* youth hostel); there's also a refreshments kiosk at the station, and a small campsite and bunkhouse (call for details).

Whitby

If there's one essential stop on the North Yorkshire coast it's **WHITBY**, whose historical associations, atmospheric ruins, fishing harbour and intrinsic charm make it many people's favourite northern resort. The seventh-century cliff-top abbey here made Whitby one of the key foundations and centres of learning of the early Christian period. Below, for a thousand years the local herring boats landed their catch on the banks of the River Esk, until the great whaling boom of the eighteenth century transformed the fortunes of the town. Melville's *Moby Dick* makes much of Whitby whalers such as William Scoresby, while James Cook took his first seafaring steps from the town in 1746, on his way to becoming a national hero. All four of Captain Cook's ships of discovery – the *Endeavour*, *Resolution*, *Adventure* and *Discovery* – were built in Whitby.

Divided by the Esk and joined by a swing bridge, Whitby divides into the cobbled **old town** to the east, and the newer (mostly eighteenth- and nineteenth-century) **West Cliff** to the west, which is home to the quayside, most of the hotels and shops, and the few arcades, amusements and souvenir stalls that have been allowed to proliferate. Virtually everything you want to see is in or above the old town on the east side, principally the **abbey ruins** and the **Captain Cook Memorial Museum**.

Arrival, information and accommodation

The **train station** is a couple of hundred yards south of the bridge. Special school- and bank-holiday steam train services also stop here, departing from the NYMR station at Grosmont. The bus station is adjacent and there's a **Travel Centre** (Mon–Fri 8.30am–4pm; ℡01947/602146) in the train station for all local transport enquiries. Whitby's **tourist office** (daily: May & June 9.30am–5pm; July & Aug 9.30am–7pm; Sept–April 10am–4.30pm; ℡01723/383637, Ⓦwww.discovery orkshirecoast.com) is on the corner of Langborne Road and New Quay Road.

The main **B&B** concentration is on West Cliff, in the streets stretching back from the elegant Royal Crescent. Across the river in the old town, several pubs have rooms, as does the *Moon and Sixpence* (see p.765), while if you're prepared to travel a couple of miles out of Whitby you can find some pleasant inns and hotels in relaxed country surroundings. *The Old Boatman's Shelter Apartments* (℡01947/811089, Ⓦwww.oldboatmansshelter.co.uk) are superior **holiday apartments** right by the waterside, available nightly at £75, or £550 per week.

Hotels, B&Bs and guesthouses

Dunsley Hall Dunsley ℡01947/893437, Ⓦwww.dunsleyhall.com. This stately oak-panelled pile (the choice of visiting celebs) has fine gardens, pool, sauna and leisure club, and a very cosy bar. It's a couple of miles inland (west) of town. ❻

Estbek House Sandsend ℡01947/893424, Ⓦwww.estbekhouse.co.uk. Georgian house overlooking the stream at Sandsend, 2 miles from

Whitby and just yards from the beach. There are four pretty double/twin rooms, while the relaxed restaurant (expensive; reservations recommended) is well known for its meals of fresh fish and seafood. ❺

La Rosa Hotel 5 East Terrace ℡01947/606981, Ⓦwww.larosa.co.uk. Eccentric B&B with eight rooms done out in extravagantly individual style – think French naughty nineties courtesy of eBay and car boot sales. A breakfast picnic delivered in a basket to your door. Great fun and terrific views. ❸

Number Five 5 Havelock Place ☏ 01947/606361. Amiable West Cliff B&B that provides a good breakfast (veggie options available). There are five doubles and three singles, with small but smart shower rooms. No credit cards. ❷

Shepherd's Purse 95 Church St ☏ 01947/820228, ⓔ shepherdspursewhitby@googlemail.com. Popular wholefood store combined with clothes and gift shop. Its best rooms (with brass bedsteads and pine furniture) are set around a galleried courtyard; the two pricier doubles on the upper level are nicest, and one has its own balcony. ❷

White Horse & Griffin 87 Church St ☏ 01947/604857, ⓦ www.whitehorseandgriffin .co.uk. A welcoming eighteenth-century coaching inn with stylishly decorated en-suite rooms (some have antique panelling, others a rooftop view), open fires and a good bistro restaurant serving local fish, meat and game. They also have self-catering cottages in the old town. ❷

White Linen 24 Bagdale ☏ 01947/603635, ⓦ www.whitelinenguesthouse.co.uk. Superior B&B in a restored Georgian house – nine individually styled rooms with contemporary colours and furnishings and good shower rooms. Garden at the front, courtyard out back. ❸

Hostels

Harbour Grange Spital Bridge, Church St ☏ 01947/600817, ⓦ www.whitbybackpackers .co.uk. Backpackers' hostel right on the river (eastern side) with 24 beds in five small dorms (£17, plus £1 for bedding if required). Self-catering kitchen and lounge; curfew at 11.30pm.

Whitby YHA Abbey House, East Cliff ☏ 0845/371 9049, ⓔ whitby@yha.org.uk. Fairly recently opened flagship hostel, located in a Grade I-listed building right next to the Abbey Visitor Centre. Stunning views, Victorian conservatory, tearoom and restaurant, and every facility. Rates include breakfast and entry to the abbey. Dorm beds from £19.95, though more expensive in summer, twin rooms ❷

The old town

Cobbled **Church Street** is the old town's main thoroughfare, barely changed since the eighteenth century, though now lined with tearooms and gift shops. Parallel Sandgate has more of the same, the two streets meeting at the small marketplace where souvenirs and trinkets are sold; there's a farmers' market here every Thursday.

Whitby, understandably, likes to make a fuss of Captain Cook who served an apprenticeship here from 1746 to 1749 under John Walker, a Quaker ship-owner. The **Captain Cook Memorial Museum** (last two weeks Feb Sat & Sun 11am–3pm; March daily 11am–3pm; April–Oct daily 9.45am–5pm; £4.50; ⓦ www.cook museumwhitby.co.uk), housed in Walker's house in Grape Lane, contains memorabilia including ships' models, letters, and paintings by artists seconded to Cook's voyages. The 18-year-old Cook assisted on the coal runs between Newcastle and London, learning his seafaring skills in flat-bottomed craft called "cats". Designed for inshore and river work their specifications were to prove perfect for Cook's later surveys of the South Sea Islands and the Australian coast. When he wasn't at sea, Cook, together with the other apprentices, slept in Walker's attic.

At the north end of Church Street, you climb the famous **199 steps** – now paved, but originally a wide wooden staircase built for pallbearers carrying coffins to the church of St Mary. The views over the harbour and town are magnificent, while a search will reveal the grave of William Scoresby Sr, master whaler and inventor of the crow's nest.

The bizarre parish **church of St Mary** at the top of the steps is an architectural amalgam dating back to 1110, boasting a Norman chancel arch, a profusion of eighteenth-century panelling, box pews unequalled in England and a triple-decker pulpit – note the built-in ear trumpets, added for the benefit of a nineteenth-century rector's deaf wife.

Whitby Abbey

The cliff-top ruins of **Whitby Abbey** (April–Sept daily 10am–6pm; Oct–March Mon & Thurs–Sun 10am–4pm; £5.50; EH), beyond St Mary's, are some of the most evocative in England, the nave, soaring north transept and lancets of the east

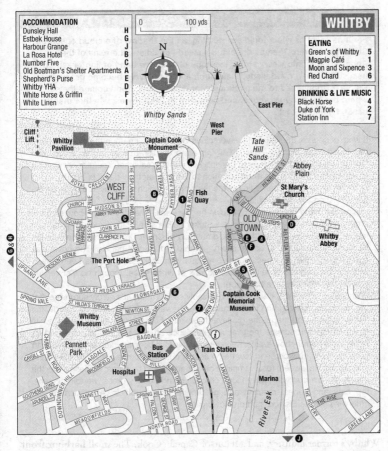

The map shows:

ACCOMMODATION

Dunsley Hall	H
Estbek House	G
Harbour Grange	J
La Rosa Hotel	B
Number Five	C
Old Boatman's Shelter Apartments	A
Shepherd's Purse	E
Whitby YHA	D
White Horse & Griffin	F
White Linen	I

WHITBY

0 — 100 yds

N

EATING

Green's of Whitby	5
Magpie Café	1
Moon and Sixpence	3
Red Chard	6

DRINKING & LIVE MUSIC

Black Horse	4
Duke of York	2
Station Inn	7

Whitby Sands · West Pier · East Pier · Cliff Lift · Whitby Pavilion · Captain Cook Monument · Tate Hill Sands · Abbey Plain · St Mary's Church · ROYAL CRESCENT · THE ESPLANADE · EAST TERRACE · KHYBER PASS · PIER ROAD · Fish Quay · HENRIETTA ST · TATE HILL · WEST CLIFF · CHURCH SQUARE · HUDSON ST · ABBEY TERRACE · HAVELOCK PL · WELLINGTON TERRACE · JOHN ST · CLARENCE PL · CLIFF STREET · ST ANNE'S STAITH · 199 STEPS · CHURCH LA. · OLD TOWN · SANDGATE · GROPE LANE · Whitby Abbey · LE FLEDA TERRACE · CRESCENT AVENUE · ABINGDON TERRACE · SKINNER STREET · SILVER ST · The Port Hole · UPGANG LANE · BACK ST HILDAS TERRACE · FLOWERGATE · BRIDGE ST · NEW QUAY RD · Captain Cook Memorial Museum · SPRING VALE · ST. HILDA'S TERRACE · NEWTON ST · BRUNSWICK ST · BAXTERGATE · WALKER STREET · BAGDALE · Whitby Museum · Pannett Park · CHUBB HILL ROAD · CAYGILL HILL ROAD · Bus Station · Train Station · WINDSOR TERRACE · Marina · SPRING HILL · Hospital · SOUTHEND GDNS · DOWNDINNER HILL · ARUNDEL PL · PANNETT WAY · BROOMFIELD · SPRING HILL TERRACE · ALBION PL · MEADOWFIELDS · TALBOT ST · GEORGE ST · GRAY ST · NORTH ROAD · LANGBOURNE ROAD · River Esk · THE ROPERY · THE RISE · GREEN LANE · WEST CLIFF · **YORKSHIRE** | The North Yorkshire coast · 12

end giving a hint of the building's former delicacy and splendour. Its monastery was founded in 657, and by 664 had become important enough to host the **Synod of Whitby**, an event of seminal importance in the development of English Christianity. It settled once and for all the question of determining the date of Easter, and adopted the rites and authority of the Roman rather than the Celtic Church. The original abbey was destroyed by the Danes in 867 and refounded by the Benedictines in 1078, though most of the present ruins date from between 1220 and 1539. You'll discover all this and more in the **visitor centre** (hours as above), housed in the shell of the adjacent mansion, built after the Dissolution using material from the plundered abbey. Ongoing archeological work on the headland has yielded finds dating back to Anglo-Saxon times, while audiovisual displays concentrate both on life at the medieval abbey and at the house, whose seventeenth-century geometric "hard" garden has been restored.

West Cliff

Whitby developed as a holiday resort in the nineteenth century following the arrival of the railway. Wide streets, elegant crescents, boarding houses and hotels were laid on the heights of **West Cliff**, topped by a whalebone arch, commemorating

Bram Stoker and Dracula

For a moment or two I could see nothing, as the shadow of a cloud obscured
St Mary's Church. Then as the cloud passed I could see the ruins of the
Abbey coming into view; and as the edge of a narrow band of light as sharp
as a sword-cut moved along, the church and churchyard became gradually
visible... [It] seemed to me as though something dark stood behind the seat
where the white figure shone, and bent over it. What it was, whether man or
beast, I could not tell.

Dracula, Bram Stoker

It was, of course, the figure of the voracious Count, feasting upon the blood of Lucy.
Her friend Mina Murray – despite "flying along the fish-market to the bridge" and
"toiling" up the endless steps to the abbey – failed to save her. The story of *Dracula*
is well known, but it's this exact attention to the geographical detail of Whitby – little
changed since Bram Stoker first wrote the words – which has proved a huge attraction to visitors on the Dracula trail.

Using first-hand observation of a town he knew well – he stayed at a house on the
West Cliff, now marked by a plaque – Stoker built a story that mixed real locations,
legend, myth and historical fact: the grounding of Count Dracula's ship on Tate Hill
Sands was based on an actual event reported in the local papers. The novel was
published in 1897 and became synonymous with Stoker's name; it's been filmed,
with varying degrees of faithfulness, dozens of times since, though no film version
has yet used Whitby as a backdrop.

With many of the early chapters recognizably set in Whitby, it's hardly surprising that
the town has cashed in on its **Dracula Trail**. The various sites – Tate Hill Sands, the
abbey, church and steps, the graveyard, Stoker's house – can all be visited, while
down on the harbourside the Dracula Experience attempts to pull in punters to its
rather lame horror-show antics. Keen interest has also been sparked among the **Goth**
fraternity, who now come to town en masse a couple of times a year (in late spring
and around Halloween) for a vampire's ball, concerts and readings; at these times the
streets are overrun with pasty-faced characters in Regency dress, wedding gowns,
top hats and capes, meeting and greeting at their unofficial headquarters, the
otherwise sedate *Elsinore* pub on Flowergate.

Whitby's former industry, and a statue of Captain Cook. The small **harbour front**
below, along Pier Road, sports an active fish market and a run of arcades and chip
shops, leading to the twin, pincered piers and lighthouses. Various short boat trips
and cruises depart from Pier Road throughout the day. When the tide's out, the
broad, clean sands to the west stretch for three miles to **Sandsend** (where the beer
garden of the *Hart Inn* makes a tempting target).

Final port of call should be the gloriously eclectic **Whitby Museum** in Pannett
Park (Tues–Sun 9.30am–4.30pm, plus bank hols; £3; Ⓦwww.whitbymuseum
.org.uk), up the hill from the train station. There's more Cook memorabilia,
including various objects and stuffed animals brought back as souvenirs by his
crew, as well as exhibits devoted to Whitby's seafaring tradition, its whaling
industry in particular. Some of the best and largest fossils of Jurassic-period
reptiles unearthed on the east coast are also preserved here.

Eating, drinking and entertainment

Unsurprisingly, Whitby is well known for its freshly caught fish. A multitude of
cafés around town – especially along Pier Road and Bridge Street – serve fish and
chips, bread and tea for around £5; the same thing in most of the **restaurants** costs
a few pounds more.

Whitby has a strong local **music scene**, with especially good folk nights in some of its pubs – English folk's first family, the Waterson/Carthys, are from nearby Robin Hood's Bay. First fest of the year is the **Moor and Coast** (Ⓦwww.moorandcoast .co.uk), a weekend over the May bank holiday, though this is eclipsed by the annual **Whitby Folk Week** (Ⓦwww.whitbyfolk.co.uk) in August (the week immediately preceding the bank holiday). Best place to find out more is at The Port Hole, 16 Skinner St (Ⓣ01947/603475), a fair-trade craft shop that's also the HQ of local collective **Musicport** (Ⓦwww.musicportfestival.com) who put on weekly gigs from big names in the world/folk scene, as well as the Musicport Festival in Bridlington.

Finally, the **Regatta** every August (moveable dates) is a noisy weekend of fairground rides, spectacular harbourside fireworks and boat races.

Restaurants

Green's of Whitby 13 Bridge St Ⓣ01947/600284. Great food in friendly unpretentious surroundings, a few yards from the swing bridge. Thought by many to be the best restaurant in Whitby, *Green's* has a lively bistro downstairs (mains around £20) and a fine-dining restaurant (two courses £35.95) on the first floor offering dinner. Food is locally sourced, with lots of fish and meat.

Magpie Café 14 Pier Rd Ⓣ01947/602058. The traditional fish-and-chip choice in town (£10–15, depending on size) for over forty years, and with a wide-ranging menu in case you don't want something battered and fried. In summer you'll have to queue to eat in or even for the takeaways. Closes 9pm.

Moon and Sixpence 5 Marine Parade Ⓣ01947/604416, Ⓦwww.moon-and-sixpence .co.uk. Fish is outstanding here, but this contemporary spot on the quayside dishes up lots more besides, such as local game; champagne cocktails

are on offer too. Main courses around £15. There are also luxury rooms above the restaurant, with jacuzzi and double shower (with TV) from ❸.

Red Chard 22 Flowergate Ⓣ01947/606660. Relaxed place for coffee or a glass of wine, or dig into dishes ranging from prawn cocktail and bubble-and-squeak to saffron pappardelle. Mains £11–19. Closed Mon, plus Sat lunch.

Pubs and live music

Black Horse 91 Church St. Lovely old pub (parts date from the seventeenth century) in the heart of the old town, with real ale, Yorkshire cheeses, seafood and snuff.

Duke of York Church St. Classic Whitby pub, at the bottom of the 199 steps, with harbour views and a mixed clientele of tourists and locals who come for the good-value food and occasional music.

Station Inn New Quay Rd. A real-ale haunt, with a changing selection of guest beers and live music on Fri.

Staithes

Beyond the beach at Sandsend, a fine coastal walk through pretty Runswick Bay leads in around four hours to the picturesque fishing village of **STAITHES**. James Cook first worked here in a draper's shop before moving to Whitby and he's remembered in the **Captain Cook and Staithes Heritage Centre**, on the High Street (daily 10am–5pm, weekends only Jan to Feb half-term; £2.75), which re-creates an eighteenth-century street among other interesting exhibits. Other than this, you'll have to content yourself with pottering about the rocks near the harbour – there's no beach to speak of – or clambering the nearby cliffs for spectacular views; at **Boulby**, a mile-and-a-half's trudge up the coastal path (45min), you're walking on the highest cliff (670ft) on England's east coast.

Practicalities

The road into Staithes, off the A174, puts drivers into a **car park** at the top of the hill leading down into the old village; don't ignore the signs and drive down, since there's nowhere to park and it's hard work turning round again.

The best **accommodation** is at *Endeavour House* (Ⓣ01947/841735, Ⓦwww .endeavour-restaurant.co.uk; ❸), in the old village, which four rooms, each with self-catering facilities. Alternatively, drive the three miles south (back towards Whitby) to

Runswick Bay, a tiny little one-pub-village-and-beach, where the *Cliffemount Hotel* (℡01947/840103, ⓦwww.cliffemounthotel.co.uk; ④) glories in its elevated position. It has a good sea-facing restaurant too.

Travel details

Buses

Details of minor and seasonal local bus services are frequently given in the text. It's essential to pick up either the *Dales Explorer* or *Moors Explorer* timetable booklets from a local tourist office if visiting those parts of the county. For details of the Moorsbus in the North York Moors National Park, see p.750. For information on all other local and national bus services, contact Traveline ℡0871/200 2233, ⓦwww.yorkshiretravel.net.

Harrogate to: Knaresborough (every 10min; 15–25min); Leeds (every 20min–1hr; 40min); Pateley Bridge (hourly; 50min); Ripon (every 20min; 30min).

Helmsley to: Pickering (hourly; 40min); Scarborough (hourly; 1hr 30min); York (Mon–Sat 3 daily; 1hr 30min).

Pickering to: Helmsley (hourly; 40min); Scarborough (hourly; 1hr); Whitby (4 daily; 55min); York (hourly; 1hr 15min).

Richmond to: Masham (Mon–Sat 2 hourly; 55min); Ripon (Mon–Sat 2 hourly; 1hr 15min).

Scarborough to: Bridlington (every 30min; 1hr 15min); Filey (every 30min; 30min); Helmsley (hourly; 1hr 30min); Hull (hourly; 2hr 50min); Leeds (hourly; 2hr 40min); Pickering (hourly; 1hr); Robin Hood's Bay (every 30min; 45min); Whitby (every 30min; 1hr); York (hourly; 1hr 35min).

Skipton to: Grassington (Mon–Sat hourly; 30min); Malham (Mon, Wed & Fri 4 daily, otherwise 2 daily; 40min); Settle (Mon–Sat hourly; 40min).

Whitby to: Robin Hood's Bay (every 30min; 25min); Staithes (hourly; 30min); York (4 daily; 2hr).

York to: Beverley (Mon–Sat hourly, Sun 7 daily; 30min); Hull (Mon–Sat hourly; Sun 7 daily; 1hr 45min); Leeds (every 30min; 55min); Pickering (hourly; 1hr 15min); Scarborough (hourly; 1hr 35min); Whitby (4 daily; 2hr).

Trains

Main routes and services are given below, and check timetables on ⓦwww.nationalrail.co.uk. For more detailed information about specific lines, see the boxes on the Settle–Carlisle Railway (box, p.718), North Yorkshire Moors Railway (box, p.755) and Keighley & Worth Valley Railway (box, p.711).

Harrogate to: Knaresborough (every 30min; 10min); Leeds (every 30min; 35min); York (hourly; 40min).

Hull to: Beverley (Mon–Sat every 30min, Sun 6 daily; 13min); Leeds (hourly; 1hr); London (6 daily; 2hr 45min); Scarborough (every 2hr; 1hr 30min); York (9 daily; 1hr).

Knaresborough to: Harrogate (every 30min; 10min); Leeds (every 30min; 45min); York (hourly; 30min).

Leeds to: Bradford (every 15min; 20min); Carlisle (3–7 daily; 2hr 40min); Harrogate (every 30min; 35min); Hull (hourly; 1hr); Knaresborough (every 30min; 45min); Lancaster (4 daily; 2hr); Liverpool (hourly; 1hr 50min); London (every 30min; 2hr 20min); Manchester (every 15min; 1hr); Scarborough (every 30min–1hr; 1hr 20min); Settle (3–8 daily; 1hr); Sheffield (every 30min; 40min–1hr); Skipton (hourly; 45min); York (every 10–15min; 25min).

Pickering to: Grosmont (April–Oct 5–8 daily, plus limited winter service; 1hr 10min).

Scarborough to: Bridlington (5–9 daily; 30min); Filey (5–9 daily; 15min); Hull (every 2hr; 1hr 30min); Leeds (hourly; 1hr 20min); York (hourly; 50min).

Sheffield to: Leeds (every 30min; 40min–1hr); London (hourly; 2hr 20min); York (every 30min–1hr; 1hr).

Whitby to: Danby (4–5 daily; 40min); Great Ayton (4–5 daily; 1hr 5min); Grosmont (4–5 daily; 15min); Middlesbrough (4–5 daily; 1hr 30min).

York to: Bradford (hourly; 1hr); Durham (every 30min; 50min); Harrogate (hourly; 40min); Hull (9 daily; 1hr); Leeds (every 5–15min; 25min); London (every 30min; 2hr); Manchester (every 30min; 1hr 30min); Newcastle (every 10min; 1hr); Scarborough (hourly; 50min); Sheffield (every 30min–1hr; 1hr).

13

The Northeast

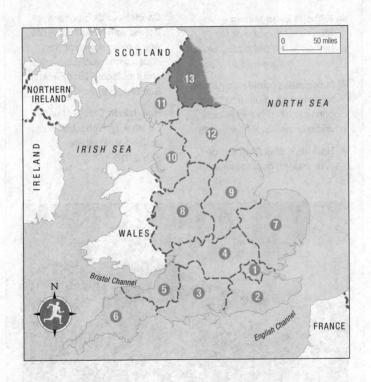

❉ **Durham Cathedral**
Awe-inspiring Romanesque
church towering above the
River Wear. See p.775

❉ **Beamish Museum** The
northeast's industrial past
poignantly re-created.
See p.779

❉ **Killhope Lead Mining
Museum** An excellent family
day out – put the kids to work
down t'pit. See p.783

❉ **Newcastle nightlife** Something
for everybody, from traditional
pubs to chilled-out indie bars
and raucous clubs. See p.795

❉ **Hadrian's Wall Path** Put on
your walking boots to make

the most of this extraordinary
monument. See p.802

❉ **Northumberland National
Park** A huge windswept
swathe of land, home to
beautiful river valleys and the
mighty Kielder Water reservoir.
See p.807

❉ **Castles** Northumberland is
littered with beautiful castles,
which tell of a violent past,
ridden with ferocious battles
and embittered family feuds.
See box, p.812

❉ **Holy Island** Cradle of early
Christianity, with a brooding,
isolated atmosphere.
See p.818

▲ Dunstanburgh Castle

13

The Northeast

ngland's **northeast** (principally the counties of Durham and Northumberland) contains some of the country's most important historic and natural attractions. In many ways a land apart from the rest of England – more remote, less affluent, its accents often impenetrable to outsiders – it also has the very stuff of English history etched across its landscapes. Romans, Vikings and Normans all left dramatic evidence of their colonization, while the Industrial Revolution exploited to the limit the northeast's natural resources and its people. Consequently, heritage centres, wildlife tours, national park hikes, stately homes and gardens all vie with the standard "castles and coast" itinerary that most tourists follow.

The essential sights start with one of England's most evocative ruins – the World Heritage site of **Hadrian's Wall**, built by the **Romans** between the North Sea and the west coast to monitor their population and trade. When the Romans departed, the northeast was divided into unstable Saxon principalities until order was restored by the kings of Northumbria, who dominated the region from 600 until the 870s. It was they who nourished the region's early Christian tradition, which achieved its finest flowering with the creation of the **Lindisfarne Gospels** on what is now known as Holy Island. The monks abandoned their island at the end of the ninth century, in advance of the Vikings' destruction of the Northumbrian kingdom, and only after the Norman Conquest did the northeast again become part of a greater England. The **Norman** kings and their successors repeatedly attempted to subdue Scotland, passing effective regional control to powerful local lords, whose authority is recalled by a sequence of formidable fortresses dotted along the coast.

Long after the northeast had ceased to be a critical military zone, its character and appearance were transformed by the **Industrial Revolution**. Towards the end of the eighteenth century two main coalfields were established – one dominating County Durham from the Pennines to the sea, the other stretching north along the Northumberland coast from the Tyne. The world's first railway, the Stockton & Darlington Railway, was opened in 1825 to move coal to the nearest port for export, while local coal and ore also fuelled the foundries that supplied the shipbuilding and heavy-engineering companies of Tyneside.

Most tourists dodge the industrial areas, bypassing the towns along the **Tees Valley** – Darlington, Stockton, Middlesbrough and Hartlepool – on the way to **Durham**, a handsome university city dominated by its magnificent twelfth-century cathedral. From Durham it's a short hop to **Newcastle upon Tyne**, distinguished by some fine Victorian buildings, the revitalized Quayside, and a burgeoning cultural scene and nightlife. North, past the old colliery villages, the **Northumberland coast** boasts some superb castles – most impressively at

THE NORTHEAST

0 _____ 10 miles

N

NORTH SEA

Edinburgh

Berwick-upon-Tweed

Holy Island

Scremerston

Waren Mill

Bamburgh

Seahouses

Beadnell

Newton-by-the-Sea

Embleton

Dunstanburgh Castle

Craster

Farne Islands

Bead

Belford

B6525

B6354

B6354

Etal

Ford

Crookham

Etal Castle

Heatherslaw Light Railway

Norham Castle

Coldstream

Cornhill-on-Tweed

Branxton

Kirk Yetholm

SCOTLAND

Tweed

A697

A698

A68

Chillingham Castle

Wooler

Eglingham

Alnwick

A1

B1340

Newton-on-the-Moor

Cragside

Rothbury

A697

Warkworth

Amble

Woodhorn

Ashington

Bedlington

Blyth

A1

Morpeth

A697

Cambo

Wallington

NORTHUMBERLAND

The Cheviot (2674ft)

NORTHUMBERLAND NATIONAL PARK

THE CHEVIOT HILLS

Byrness

Redesdale

Otterburn

Greenhaugh

Tarset

Bellingham

N. Tyne

A68

KIELDER FOREST PARK

Kielder

Kielder Water

Belvedere

Falstone

Leaplish

Tower Knowe

Stannersburn

Edinburgh

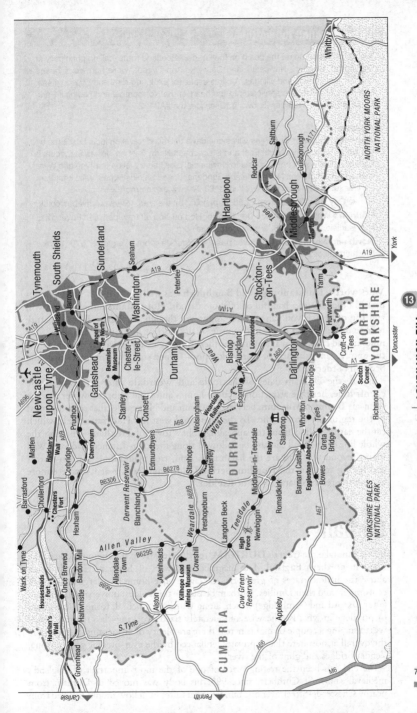

NORTH
YORKSHIRE

► York

► Doncaster

DURHAM

CUMBRIA

YORKSHIRE DALES
NATIONAL PARK

NORTH YORK MOORS
NATIONAL PARK

Whitby

Saltburn

Guisborough

Redcar

Middlesbrough

Marton

Hartlepool

Stockton-
on-Tees

Yarm

Hurworth

Croft-on-
-Tees

Scotch
Corner

Richmond

Darlington

Piercebridge

Gretna
Bridge

Bowes

Whorlton

Barnard Castle

Egglestone Abbey

Staindrop

Raby Castle

Middleton-in-Teesdale

Romaldkirk

Newbiggin

Langdon Beck

High
Force

Cow Green
Reservoir

Appleby

Bishop
Auckland

Locomotion

Escomb

Weardale
Railway

Wolsingham

Wear

Frosterley

Stanhope

Wear

Consett

Edmundbyers

Ireshopeburn

Cowshill

Killhope Lead
Mining Museum

Allenheads

Alston

S. Tyne

Allendale
Town

Allen Valley

Weardale

Teesdale

A689

A67

A66

A66

A68

A68

A69

A696

A19

A19

A19

A171

A1(M)

A1

M6

A66

Durham

Chester-
le-Street

Beamish Museum

Angel of
the North

Washington

Peterlee

Seaham

Sunderland

South Shields

Tynemouth

Jarrow

Wallsend

Newcastle
upon Tyne

Gateshead

Stanley

Prudhoe

Matfen

Barrasford

Corbridge

Cherryburn

Hexham

Chollerford

Chesters
Fort

Bardon Mill

Haltwhistle

Once Brewed

Housesteads
Fort

Greenhead

Wark on Tyne

Hadrian's Wall

Hadrian's
Wall

Blanchland

Derwent Reservoir

Blanchland

B6306

B6278

B6295

A696

► Carlisle

► Penrith

Tees

Tees

Wear

Tees

Warkworth, **Dunstanburgh** and **Bamburgh** – as well as a string of superb dune-backed beaches and a handful of offshore islands. **Holy Island** is the best known, and the only one you can stay the night on, though the **Farne Islands** nature reserve makes a great day-trip from the small resort of Seahouses. **Alnwick**, four miles inland from the sea, features another stunning castle and a fine garden, while the extravagant ramparts of **Berwick-upon-Tweed** signal the imminence of the Scottish border.

Inland, the Durham dales of **Teesdale** and **Weardale** offer a mix of scenic countryside, heritage attractions, stately homes and rural pubs. However, it's the open-air **Beamish Museum**, between Durham and Newcastle, that soaks up most of the regional visitor traffic. To the north and west lies **Hadrian's Wall**, which can be easily visited from the appealing abbey town of **Hexham** – though the whole line of the Wall can also be followed along the long-distance Hadrian's Wall Path. Beyond the Wall are the harsh moorland, tree plantations, country towns and hiking trails of the **Northumberland National Park** – at its most remote around the reservoir and forest of **Kielder**.

Durham

If you can, take the train to **DURHAM**, for the view from the station is one of the finest in northern England. The magnificent towers of Durham Cathedral soar above the little terraces of grey-brick cottages, once home to a large number of coal-miners and their families. Durham boasts the third oldest university in England (after Oxford and Cambridge) which, along with the cathedral, forms a little island of privilege in what is otherwise a moderately sized, working-class town. It's well worth staying a couple of nights here – there are plenty of attractions, but it's more the overall atmosphere that captivates, enhanced by the ever-present golden stone, slender bridges and glint of the river.

The city has been the resting place of one of the most important of England's medieval saints, St Cuthbert, since 995; his body was moved to Durham from nearby Chester-le-Street over one hundred years after his fellow monks had fled from

Lindisfarne in fear of the Vikings, carrying his coffin with them. Cuthbert's hallowed remains made Durham a place of pilgrimage for both the Saxons and the Normans, who began work on the present cathedral at the end of the eleventh century. Subsequently, the bishops of Durham were granted extensive powers to control the troublesome northern marches of the kingdom, ruling as semi-independent Prince Bishops. They reached the peak of their power in the fourteenth century, but there-after the office went into decline, especially in the wake of the Reformation, yet they clung to the vestiges of their authority until 1836, when they ceded them to the Crown. They abandoned Durham Castle for their palace in Bishop Auckland and transferred their old home to the fledgling university.

Arrival and information

From either Durham **train station**, or the **bus station** on North Road, it's a ten-minute walk to the city centre, across the River Wear. The "Cathedral" **bus** (every 20min; 50p for all-day ticket) links train and bus stations with the Market Place (for the tourist office) and the cathedral. Drivers should note that the peninsula road (to the castle and cathedral) is a toll road during the daytime (Mon–Sat 10am–4pm; £2).

The **tourist office** (Mon–Sat 9.30am–5.30pm, Sun 11am–4pm; ☎0191/384 3720, ⓦwww.thisisdurham.com) is located at **Millennium Place**, off Claypath, in the Walkergate development, which also incorporates a theatre, cinema, public library, bar and café. To get out onto the river, either rent a **rowing boat** (£4 per person plus refundable £10 deposit; 1hr) from Brown's Boathouse, Elvet Bridge, or take a **cruise** aboard the *Prince Bishop* (☎0191/386 9525; £5; 1hr), which has regular summer departures, again from Elvet Bridge. Free **internet** access is available at the Clayport Library, opposite the tourist office on Millennium Place.

You can **rent bicycles** at Freeman's Quay Leisure Centre (☎0191/301 8306) in the Walkergate complex. Rental is free, though you need to give 24 hours advance notice.

Trails and tracks

Pennine Way The main long-distance footpath, which cuts up from the Yorkshire Dales, runs parallel to Hadrian's Wall from Greenhead to Housesteads, and then climaxes in a climb through the Northumberland National Park.

Hadrian's Wall Path An 84-mile waymarked trail following the line of the Wall (see box, p.802).

St Cuthbert's Way 63-mile pilgrim's route, which links Melrose, where St Cuthbert started his ministry just across the border in Scotland, with Holy Island.

Teesdale Way Waymarked route running 92 miles from Appleby-in-Westmorland in Cumbria to Teesmouth (just beyond Middlesbrough).

Weardale Way Trail covering 78 miles, from Cowshill at the head of the valley to the coast at Sunderland.

Cycle routes

Sea to Sea (C2C) 140-mile trail from Whitehaven/Workington to Sunderland/ Newcastle that drops into the northeast just beyond Alston and links Allenheads, Stanhope and Consett with either town. ⓦwww.c2c-guide.co.uk.

Walney to Wear (W2W) Cross-country route from Cumbria that diverges at Barnard Castle northwards to Durham city and Sunderland (150 miles) or eastwards through Darlington to Whitby (170 miles). ⓦwww.cyclingw2w.info.

Hadrian's Cycleway Runs the length of Hadrian's Wall.

Something for the kids

Beamish Children will love exploring the reconstructed cottages, farm and trams – County Durham just as it was during the eighteenth and nineteenth centuries. See p.779.

Locomotion Marvellous railway museum with interactive children's exhibits, summer steam rides, rallies and shows. See p.780.

Hartlepool Maritime Experience Educational and entertaining, this is a brilliantly re-created eighteenth-century quayside with period shops, costumed guides and nautical games, plus a tour of HMS *Trincomalee*, a navy training ship built in 1817 (daily 10am–5pm; £7.75, children £4.75; ⓦwww.hartlepoolsmaritimeexperience.com).

Seven Stories Colourful, inventive museum focusing on children's literature. See p.793.

Kielder Water Plenty of watersports, from kayaking and swimming to waterskiing. See p.808.

Heatherslaw Light Railway Jump aboard the toy railway that runs from Heatherslaw Mill to Etal village, around ten miles south of Berwick-upon-Tweed (mid-March to Oct daily 11am–3pm, hourly service; £6 return, children £4; ⓣ01890/820244, ⓦwww .ford-and-etal.co.uk).

Accommodation

Durham's **accommodation** includes a budget *Premier Travel Inn* in the Walkergate development, and a *Radisson SAS* on the opposite side of the River Wear. There are private rooms at the colleges of **Durham University** (Jan, Easter & July–Sept; from £28.50 per person, or £39.50 in en-suite rooms, breakfast included), all within walking distance of the centre; contact the Conference and Tourism Office (ⓣ0800/289970, ⓦwww.dur.ac.uk/conference_tourism). University College has rooms inside the castle – two of which are available all through the year (from £50) – while St Chad's, next to the cathedral, accepts **YHA bookings** in the same periods (ⓣ0191/334 3358, ⓔchads@durham.ac.uk; from £22.50).

Castle View Guest House 4 Crossgate ⓣ0191/386 8852, ⓦwww.castle-view.co.uk. Mint-green and white townhouse on a cobbled terrace next to St Margaret's Church, with pretty rooms and a quiet courtyard garden. Plus, of course, great castle views. ❸

🏃 **Fallen Angel** 34 Old Elvet ⓣ0191/384 1037, ⓦwww.fallenangelhotel.com. Boutique hotel with ten exquisite rooms following different themes, from the gothic Cruella room, which drips with faux-diamonds and is plastered with black wallpaper, to the sumptuous Russian Bride suite with its beautiful carved bed, lace curtains and private sauna. There's also a huge, New York-themed penthouse that can sleep four and a lively café/restaurant. ❺

Marriott Hotel Royal County Old Elvet ⓣ0191/386 6821, ⓦwww.marriotthotels.com.

Luxury hotel with its own riverside leisure centre and pool, and large, comfortable rooms. Also restaurant, brasserie, bar and parking. Breakfast not included except with special/weekend rate. Parking. ❹

🏃 **Seaham Hall** Lord Byron's Walk, Seaham, 10 miles northeast of Durham ⓣ0191/516 1400, ⓦwww.seaham-hall.com. Hip, holistic spa hotel that makes a great coastal base for city sightseeing – Durham is only a 20min drive away. There's a well-regarded restaurant, and beaches and coastal walks nearby. ❾

Victoria Inn 86 Hallgarth St ⓣ0191/386 5269, ⓦwww.victoriainn-durhamcity.co.uk. Six charming rooms with iron bedsteads and floral quilts above a family-run pub (see p.778) just a few minutes from the centre. Parking available. ❷

The City

Surrounded on three sides by the River Wear, Durham's compact centre is approached by two road bridges that lead from the western, modern part of town across the river to the spur containing castle and cathedral. The commercial heart of this "old town" area is the triangular **Market Place**, flanked by the Guildhall and St Nicholas' Church.

Durham Cathedral

From Market Place, it's a five-minute walk up cobbled Saddler Street to **Durham Cathedral** (Mon–Sat 9.30am–6pm, Sun 12.30–5.30pm; mid-July to Aug Mon–Sat 9.30am–8pm, Sun 12.30–8pm; guided tours 3 daily Easter week & mid-July to mid-Sept; access sometimes restricted, call ℡0191/386 4266 to check; £4 suggested donation, tours £4; ⓦwww.durhamcathedral.co.uk), facing the castle across the manicured Palace Green. Standing on the site of an early wooden Saxon cathedral, built to house the remains of St Cuthbert, the present cathedral – a supreme example of the Norman-Romanesque style – was completed in 1133, and has survived the centuries pretty much intact. The awe-inspiring **nave**, completed

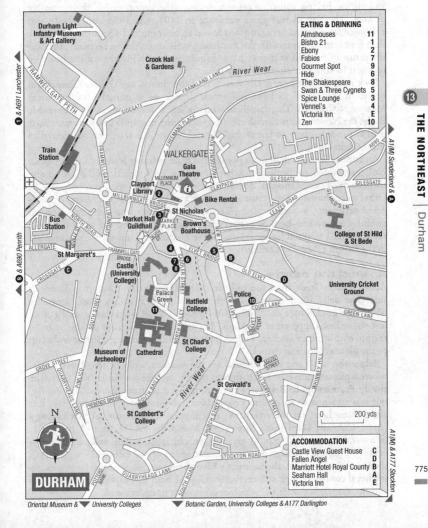

EATING & DRINKING

Almshouses	11
Bistro 21	1
Ebony	2
Fabios	7
Gourmet Spot	9
Hide	6
The Shakespeare	8
Swan & Three Cygnets	5
Spice Lounge	3
Vennel's	4
Victoria Inn	E
Zen	10

ACCOMMODATION

Castle View Guest House	C
Fallen Angel	D
Marriott Hotel Royal County	B
Seaham Hall	A
Victoria Inn	E

0   200 yds

DURHAM

N

Oriental Museum & ▼ University Colleges   ▼ Botanic Garden, University Colleges & A177 Darlington

in 1128, used pointed arches for the first time in England, raising the vaulted ceiling to new and dizzying heights. The weight of the stone is borne by massive pillars, their heaviness relieved by striking Moorish-influenced geometric patterns. A door gives access to the **tower** (April–Sept Mon–Sat 10am–4pm; Oct–March Mon–Sat 10am–3pm; £4), from where there are fine views of the city.

Separated from the nave by a Victorian marble screen is the **choir**, where the dark-stained Restoration stalls are overshadowed by the vainglorious **bishop's throne**, reputedly the highest in medieval Christendom, built on the orders of the fourteenth-century Bishop Hatfield, whose militaristic alabaster tombstone lies just below. Beyond, the **Chapel of the Nine Altars** dates from the thirteenth century, its Early English stonework distinguished by its delicacy of detail. Here, and around the adjoining **Shrine of St Cuthbert**, much of the stonework is of local Weardale marble, each dark shaft bearing its own fancy pattern of fossils. Cuthbert himself lies beneath a plain marble slab, his presence and shrine having gained a reputation over the centuries for their curative powers. The legend was given credence in 1104, when the saint's body was exhumed for reburial here, and was found to be completely uncorrupted, more than four hundred years after his death on Lindisfarne. Almost certainly, this was the result of his fellow monks having (unintentionally) preserved the body by laying it in sand containing salt crystals.

Back near the entrance, at the west end of the church, the **Galilee Chapel** was begun in the 1170s, its light and exotic decoration in imitation of the Great Mosque of Córdoba. The chapel contains the simple tombstone of the **Venerable Bede**, the Northumbrian monk credited with being England's first historian. Bede died at the monastery of Jarrow in 735, and his remains were first transferred to the cathedral in 1020.

An ancient wooden doorway opposite the main entrance leads into the spacious **cloisters**, which are flanked by what remains of the monastic buildings, among them an oak-beamed **monks' dormitory** (Mon–Sat 10am–4pm, Sun 1–4pm; £1). Other riches housed in the cathedral include a collection of St Cuthbert's embroidered vestments, as well as altar plates and manuscripts, the cathedral's original twelfth-century lion-head **Sanctuary Knocker** (the one on the main door is a replica), and a splendid facsimile copy of the Lindisfarne Gospels (the originals are in the British Library in London).

Around the centre

Across Palace Green from the cathedral, **Durham Castle** (Christmas, Easter & July–Sept daily 10am–noon & 2–5pm; rest of the year daily 2–4pm; access by 45-minute guided tour only; £5; ℡0191/334 3800, Ⓦwww.durhamcastle.com) lost its medieval appearance long ago. The highlights of the tour include visits to the fifteenth-century kitchen, a climb up the enormous hanging staircase and a trip to the gloomy Norman chapel.

Below the castle and the cathedral are the wooded banks of the **River Wear**, where a pleasant one-mile footpath runs right round the peninsula. You'll pass the sturdy **Framwellgate Bridge**, which originally dates from the twelfth century, but was widened to its present proportions in the mid-nineteenth century. Just along from here, on the riverbank, the university's **Museum of Archeology** (April–Oct daily 11am–4pm; Nov–March Mon & Fri–Sun 11.30am–3.30pm; £1; Ⓦwww.dur.ac.uk/fulling.mill) occupies an old stone fulling mill. Eighteenth-century **Prebends Bridge** boasts celebrated views of the cathedral, and the path then continues round to the handsome **Elvet Bridge**, again widened far beyond its medieval course, though still retaining traces of both its erstwhile bridge-houses and the chapel, St Andrew's, which once stood at its eastern end.

Walk through town to the Victorian **Market Hall** (closed Sun), buried in the vaults of the buildings that line the west side of the Market Place. There's an outdoor market here every Saturday, as well as farmers' markets on the third Thursday of the month (10am–4pm). The hall also provides access to **Fowlers Yard**, an interesting collection of creative workshops housed in quaint, flower-decorated warehouses; you're welcome to watch the artists and craftspeople at work here, which includes a goldsmith's, traditional embroiderers and even a microbrewery.

Crook Hall and the Durham Light Infantry Museum

It's worth making time for a visit to the idyllic **Crook Hall** (Easter weekend & May–Sept Wed–Sun 11am–5pm; £5.50; ⓦ www.crookhallgardens.co.uk), situated on Frankland Lane, Sidegate, north of the centre a couple of minutes' walk along the river from the *Radisson* hotel. The thirteenth-century hall is made up of a tangle of atmospheric rooms, including the haunted Jacobean Room. Surrounding the house is a series of rambling enclosed **gardens** (times as above) with their own personality and name; wander from the shimmering Silver and White garden, into the Orchard and Secret Walled gardens, and tackle the circular maze in the wild meadow.

From Crook Hall it's a ten-minute walk to the **Durham Light Infantry Museum and Art Gallery** (April–Oct daily 10am–5pm; Nov–March daily 10am–4pm; £3.25; ⓦ www.durham.gov.uk/dli), at Aykley Heads, whose temporary art exhibitions are bolstered by fascinating galleries telling the story of the DLI regiment, from World War I (when it lost 12,000) to its last parade in 1968.

The Oriental Museum and Botanic Garden

The university's **Oriental Museum** (Mon–Fri 10am–5pm, Sat & Sun noon–5pm; £1.50; ⓦ www.dur.ac.uk/oriental.museum) is set among college buildings a couple of miles south of the city centre on Elvet Hill Road (take bus #5 or #6 to South Road). Highlights of its wide-ranging collection include outstanding displays of Chinese jade and ceramics, Arabic calligraphy, a magnificent Chinese bed and Japanese wood-block prints. After the museum, continue to the nearby **Botanic Garden** (daily 10am–4pm, March–Oct open until 5pm; £4), whose glasshouses, café and visitor centre are set in eighteen acres of woodland, grassland and gardens near Collingwood College; buses run back to the centre from either Elvet Hill Road or South Road.

Eating, drinking and entertainment

As a student and tourist haven, Durham has plenty of inexpensive pizza and pasta places, but there are a few more upmarket **restaurants** dotted around, too. The usual chain bars and restaurants vie for attention in the modern Walkergate complex. Regular **classical concerts** are held at venues around the city, including the cathedral, while the Gala Theatre on Millennium Place (☏ 0191/332 4041, ⓦ www.galadurham.co.uk) hosts music of all kinds, plus theatre, cinema, dance and comedy. The **Miner's Gala** takes place on the second Saturday in July, celebrating the international labour movement with an energetic street parade of traditional lodge banners.

Cafés and restaurants

Almshouses Palace Green. Simple quiches, sandwiches, pasta dishes and the like for around £5–6, served in a historic building in the shadow of the cathedral. Sept–June 9am–5pm, July & Aug 9am–8pm.

Bistro 21 Aykley Heads ☏ 0191/384 4354. Excellent bistro cooking in a converted farmhouse north of the centre, a ten-minute walk from the DLI Museum and Art Gallery; courtyard seating in summer and good-value set menus at lunchtime. Mains are pricey at around £18. Closed Sun.

Gourmet Spot The Avenue, 15min walk from the Market Place ☎0191/384 6655. Durham's boldest and most extravagant restaurant. Dishes could include pan-roast scallops with a beetroot mousse, and goats' cheese and truffle *millefeuille* with wild sorrel, along with some sensational puddings like mango cheesecake with ginger crumble and cracked black pepper ice cream. The two-course menu costs £27, while those with an appetite can opt for seven courses (£50). Open Tues–Sun eve only.

Hide 39 Saddler St ☎0191/384 1999. The best of the café-bars with foodie pretensions, *Hide* serves a pizza, salad or brunch-style menu during the day, with prices rising to around £10 for a main course – sirloin steak, home-made beef burger and the like – at night.

Spice Lounge St Nicholas Cottage, Market Place ☎0191/383 0927. The most popular Indian restaurant in Durham, with an extensive menu that includes all the standards, from chicken tikka and lamb *rogan josh* to tandoori king prawn. Service is very friendly. Booking recommended. Mains around £7.95. Look for the little sandwich board in the Market Place that points down a narrow passageway. Daily 6pm–midnight.

Vennel's Saddler's Yard, 71 Saddler St. Named after the skinny alley or "vennel" where it stands – near the junction with Elvet Bridge – this rambling two-storey café dispenses appetizing sandwiches, quiche, pastas and cakes in its sixteenth-century courtyard. Daily 9.30am–5pm.

Zen Court Lane ☎0191/384 9588. Tucked away just off New Elvet, this cool Thai restaurant is ensconced in a cloud of delicious-smelling incense and decked out with myriad Buddha statues and red lamps. Serves coffee, light meals, dinner (mains around £15) and cocktails.

Bar and pubs

Ebony 8 Walkergate. Chic little bar in the middle of Walkergate, with a good drinks menu including champagne, wines, beers and cocktails, as well as bar snacks.

Fabios 66 Saddler St. Hidden above the student-filled Italian restaurant, *La Spaghettata*, this lively, down-to-earth bar has three quirky rooms with wooden floorboards, walls covered in zebra skins and battered sofas. There are weekly jazz sessions, often played out on the resident piano. Food is served in the "middle room", but best to come here for the cocktails (£3.80) and perhaps an impromptu dance on the bar.

The Shakespeare 63 Saddler St. One of the oldest and most traditional pubs in Durham, *The Shakespeare* serves real ales to a local crowd.

Swan & Three Cygnets Elvet Bridge. Town and gown converge in this popular riverside pub with a full-to-the-brim outdoor terrace.

Victoria Inn 86 Hallgarth St. With its etched-glass windows, William Morris wallpaper, cosy coal fire and narrow wooden tables, this pub emanates Victoriana. Half a dozen well-kept ales are on offer.

The rest of County Durham

In the 1910s, **County Durham** produced 41 million tonnes of coal each year, raised from three hundred pits by 170,000 miners. This was the heyday of an industry that since the 1830s had transformed the county's landscape, spawning scores of pit villages that matted the rolling hills from the Pennines to the North Sea. The miners, waging a long struggle against serf-like pay and conditions, achieved a gradual improvement of their lot, but could not prevent the slow decline of the Durham coalfield from the 1920s: just 127 mines were left when the industry was nationalized in 1947, only 34 in 1969, and today not a single pit remains. As a consequence, the old colliery villages have lost their sense of purpose and structure, some becoming godforsaken terraces in the middle of nowhere, others being swallowed up by neighbouring towns. For a taste of the old days, most people visit the reconstructed colliery village at the open-air **Beamish Museum**, north of Durham, while for the region's considerable railway heritage you shouldn't miss **Locomotion**, south of Durham, near Bishop Auckland – a fascinating outpost of York's National Railway Museum.

Away from the old coalfields and railway works the rest of County Durham's attractions form a neat triangle. The two main towns are the ecclesiastical residence of **Bishop Auckland** and the well-to-do market town of **Barnard**

Castle, beyond which – to the west – lie the isolated Pennine valleys of **Teesdale** and **Weardale**. It's easy to construct a circuit by car to see both, calling in at the valleys' small heritage centres, Methodist chapels and natural highlights; onward routes are then west via nearby Alston into Cumbria or north across the moors on minor roads from Weardale – the latter direction dropping into Northumberland, either through the bucolic **Allen Valley** or via the delightful stone village of **Blanchland**, tucked away in the Derwent River valley.

Beamish Museum

The open-air **Beamish Museum** (April–Oct daily 10am–5pm; Nov–April Tues–Thurs, Sat & Sun 10am–4pm; admission £16, £7.50 in winter; ℗0191/370 4000, ⓦwww.beamish.org.uk) spreads out over three hundred acres beside the A693, about ten miles north of Durham. Buildings from all over the region have been painstakingly reassembled in six main sections, linked by restored trams and buses. Shopkeepers, workers and householders in period dress can answer your questions – many of the costumed guides are recruited for their real-life experience – and you can walk through many of the buildings and workshops to find out about daily life a century or two ago. Four of the sections show life in 1913: a pint-sized **colliery village**, complete with drift mine (regular tours throughout the day), cottages, Methodist chapel and school; a **farm** inhabited by breeds of livestock that were popular in the period; a **train station** and goods shed; and a large-scale re-creation of a market **town**, its High Street lined by shops, offices, garage, stables, sweet factory and Masonic Hall. The other two areas date to 1825, at the beginning of the northeast's industrial development: a **manor house**, with horse yard, formal gardens, vegetable plots and orchards; and the **Pockerley Waggonway**, where you can ride behind a replica of George Stephenson's *Locomotion*, the first passenger-carrying steam train in the world. There's a great deal to see, and what with the summertime Victorian funfair, the *Sun Inn* pub and tearooms, and **special events** (from ploughing matches to leek shows), most people make a day of it – reckon on at least four hours to get round the lot in summer, two in winter when usually only the town and train station are open.

To **get there**, drivers should follow signs to the museum off the A1(M) Chester-le-Street exit, then follow the signs along the A693 to Stanley. Half-hourly direct **bus** services – appropriately named "The Waggonway" – from Newcastle drop you close to the main entrance, though from Durham you'll need to change at Chester-le-Street.

Bishop Auckland and around

Eleven miles southwest of Durham city, **BISHOP AUCKLAND** has been the country home of the bishops of Durham since the twelfth century and their official residence for more than a hundred years. Their palace, the gracious **Auckland Castle** (Easter–June & Sept Sun & Mon 2–5pm; July & Aug Mon & Wed 11–5pm, Sun 2–5pm; £4; ⓦwww.auckland-castle.co.uk), standing in eight-hundred-acre grounds, is approached through an imposing gatehouse just off the town's large Market Place. Most rooms are rather sparsely furnished, save the splendid seventeenth-century marble-and-limestone chapel and the long dining room, with its thirteen paintings of Jacob and his sons by Francisco de Zurbarán, commissioned in the 1640s for a monastery in South America. After you've seen the castle stroll into the adjacent **Bishop's Deer Park** (daily dawn–dusk; free), where an eighteenth-century deer house survives.

The town itself plays second fiddle to the castle, though don't leave until you've followed the mile-long lane from behind the town hall (signposted by the *Sportsman*

Inn) to the remains of **Binchester Roman Fort** (daily: April–June 11am–5pm; July & Aug 10am–5pm; £2.25). Only a small portion of Roman Vinovia (the fort's Roman name) has been excavated (with most of the finds displayed in the Bowes Museum at Barnard Castle), but a stretch of cobbled Dere Street has been uncovered (a fortified supply route stretching from York to Corbridge on Hadrian's Wall) and so has the country's best example of a **hypocaust**, built to warm the private bath suite of the garrison's commanding officer. The fort was abandoned in the fifth century and many of its stones found their way to the hamlet of **ESCOMB**, two miles west of Bishop Auckland (bus #86 and #87 from town), where they were used to build a seventh-century **Saxon church** (daily: May–Sept 9am–8pm; Oct–April 9am–4pm; free; ⓦ www.escombsaxonchurch.com).

Locomotion

The first passenger train (as opposed to freight) in the world left from the station at Shildon in 1825 – making the small County Durham town, around five miles southeast of Bishop Auckland, the world's oldest railway town. It's a heritage explored in the magnificently realized **Locomotion**, otherwise known as the **National Railway Museum at Shildon** (April–Oct daily 10am–5pm; Nov–March Wed–Sun 10am–4pm; free; ⓣ 01388/777999, ⓦ www.nrm.org.uk/locomotion); follow the signs off the B6282 (from Bishop Auckland) or the A6072 (from the A68/A1(M)). Bus #1 runs half-hourly from Darlington town centre (Sun hourly).

This regional outpost of York's National Railway Museum traces two hundred years of railway history and is spread out around a kilometre-long site, with the attractions linked by free bus from the reception building (where there's parking). You can visit the house of the first railway works' manager – Timothy Hackworth – with its reconstructed rooms decked out in original 1830s garb, as well as amusing interactive displays that tell the story of the railway's development. Dotted about the site are depots, sidings, junctions and coal drops, that all lead you to the **Collection** – a gargantuan steel hangar containing an extraordinary and vast array of locomotives, dating from the very earliest days of steam; shining star is the *Mallard*, recently moved here from York Railway Museum, which made history in the 1930s by reaching speeds in excess of 120mph. Accompanied by an intoxicating aroma of oil and grease, you're free to explore Britain's rail heritage up close. There's usually something interactive going on most days, often geared towards kids – talks, guided tours, model railway demonstrations, steam-engine rallies and the like.

Barnard Castle and around

Fifteen miles southwest of Bishop Auckland, the attractive market town of **BARNARD CASTLE** is overlooked by the skeletal remains of its **castle** (April–Oct daily 10am–6pm; Nov–March Sat & Sun 10am–4pm; £4; EH), poking out from a cliff high above the River Tees. First fortified in the eleventh century, the castle was long a stronghold of the Balliols, a Norman family interminably embroiled in the struggle for the Scottish Crown. However, by the seventeenth century it had outlived its usefulness and the Vanes of nearby Raby Castle (see opposite) were quarrying its stone to repair their premises.

Castle aside, the prime attraction is the grand French-style chateau that constitutes the **Bowes Museum** (daily 10am–5pm; £8; ⓦ www.bowesmuseum.org.uk), half a mile east of the centre, signposted along Newgate. Begun in 1869, the chateau was commissioned by John and Josephine Bowes, a local businessman and MP and his French actress wife, who spent much of their time in Paris collecting ostentatious treasures and antiques. They shipped the whole lot back to County Durham and turned the house into a museum for the enlightenment of the Teesdale public (though neither lived to see its formal opening in 1892). It's a hugely rewarding collection, showcasing French decorative and religious art, as well as one of the most important Spanish collections in the UK, including El Greco's *The Tears of St Peter*. There are also tapestries, lace, ceramics, costumes and dresses dating from the eighteenth century and incidental curiosities, notably a late eighteenth-century mechanical silver swan, which sits upstairs on the first floor and still performs his daily preen in a brief forty-second melodic burst at 2pm.

Practicalities

Buses stop on either side of central Galgate – once the road out to the town gallows, hence the name. Market day is Wednesday. The **tourist office** (April–Oct Mon–Sat 9.30am–5pm, Sun 10am–4pm; Nov–March Mon–Sat 10am–3pm; ℡01833/696356, Ⓦwww.exploreteesdale.co.uk) is on Flatts Road, at the end of Galgate by the castle. **B&Bs** include the welcoming *Homelands*, 85 Galgate (℡01833/638757, Ⓦwww.homelandsguesthouse.co.uk; ❷), and ⚲ *34 The Bank* (℡01833/631304, Ⓦwww.number34.com; ❷; no credit cards), housed in a beautiful old building replete with creaky floorboards, pretty quilts and exposed wooden beams. Cafés and tearooms line Barney's pleasant streets, while the top **restaurant** is *Blagraves House*, 30–32 The Bank (℡01833/637668; closed Sun & Mon; main meals around £15). Three miles away, in the little village of Whorlton, is *Bridge End Inn* (℡01833/627341), a handsome pub serving high-quality, no-nonsense dishes such as roast rump of lamb with hot potato cake (£15).

Around Barnard Castle

It's a fine mile-and-a-half walk from the castle, southeast (downriver) through the fields above the banks of the Tees, to the glorious shattered ruins of **Egglestone Abbey** (dawn–dusk; free; EH), a minor foundation dating from 1195. Turner painted here on one of his three visits to Teesdale, and also at nearby **Rokeby Park** (bank hols & June–Aug Mon & Tues 2–5pm; £6.50), a Palladian country house where Walter Scott wrote his ballad *Rokeby*. You can get to the hall directly on bus #79 from Barnard Castle, which also runs to Abbey Bridge End, for Egglestone Abbey.

Around seven miles northeast of town, up the A688, the splendid, sprawling battlements of **Raby Castle** (castle 1–5pm: May, June & Sept Sun–Wed; July & Aug daily except Sat; bank hol weekends also Sat; gardens same days 11am–5.30pm; £9.50, park & gardens only £5; Ⓦwww.rabycastle.com) mostly date from the fourteenth century, reflecting the power of the Neville family, who ruled the local roost until 1569. It was then that Charles Neville helped plan the "Rising of the North", the abortive attempt to replace Elizabeth I with Mary, Queen of Scots. The revolt was a dismal failure, and Neville's estates were confiscated, with Raby subsequently passing to the Vane family in 1626. On the first floor, the spectacular octagonal drawing room reflects the elaborate taste of the 1840s. Outside are the walled gardens, where peaches, apricots and pineapples once flourished under the careful gaze of forty gardeners.

Teesdale

Extending twenty-odd miles northwest from Barnard Castle, **Teesdale** begins calmly enough, though the pastoral landscapes of its lower reaches are soon replaced by wilder Pennine scenery. There's a regular bus service as far as Middleton-in-Teesdale, the valley's main settlement, with infrequent services (Mon–Sat) on to the spectacular High Force waterfall (see box, p.782) and Langdon Beck.

It's a 3.5-mile hike from Bowlees Visitor Centre to **High Force waterfall**. Cross over the B6277 from the centre and follow the path over the river at Wynch suspension bridge. Bear right and follow the riverside path upstream, passing through a gate, for approximately 1.5 miles. You'll then see High Force, a seventy-foot cascade that rumbles over an outcrop of Whin Sill ridge. The waterfall is on private Raby land, and visitors must pay £1.50 to view the falls. If you don't want to walk, there's a car park nearby (£2), by the B6277.

MIDDLETON-IN-TEESDALE was once the archetypal "company town", owned lock, stock and barrel by the Quaker-run London Lead Company, which began mining here in 1753. The firm built stone cottages for its workforce, who in return were obliged to send their children to Sunday school and keep off the booze. Not that the Quakers were over-mindful of working conditions: lead miners suffered bronchial complaints brought on by the contaminated air in the mines, illnesses compounded by long hours and an early start – "washerboys", who sorted the lead ore from the rock for ten hours a day and more, began at eight years old. For local information, call in at the **tourist office** (daily 10am–1pm; ☏01833/641001) in the central Market Place. Otherwise, head three miles back down the road towards Barnard Castle, to the charming village of **ROMALD-KIRK**, where the ivy-clad ⚘ *Rose & Crown* (☏01833/650213, ⓦwww.rose -and-crown.co.uk; ❺) has beautiful rooms with exposed wooden beams and antique furniture, and serves fantastic food: you can eat in the cheaper brasserie (mains from £10) or the candle-lit restaurant (four-course dinner £32.50).

Past Middleton, the countryside becomes harsher and the Tees more vigorous as the B6277 travels the three miles on to **Bowlees Visitor Centre** (April–Sept daily 11.30am–4pm; ☏01833/622292), from where there are various walks, including one to the enchanting **Gibson's Caves**, 200 yards from the visitor centre, and another to **High Force waterfall** (see box above). Six miles upstream from Bowlees is the **Cauldron Snout waterfall**, where the river rolls 200ft down a rock stairway as it leaves **Cow Green Reservoir**. To reach the reservoir by car, turn off the main road at **Langdon Beck** and follow the three-mile-long lane to the car park – the Snout is a mile's walk away.

Weardale

Weardale is an easy day out in a car from Durham, though seeing the dramatic high dale scenery by public transport can be a frustrating business. Bus #101 runs roughly hourly between Bishop Auckland and **Stanhope**, the main village. Buses to **Killhope**, where there's a fascinating lead-mining museum, are run by Weardale Travel ☏01388/528235, ⓦweardale-travel.co.uk); in the summer they run direct to the museum (by request), but in the winter you'll be dropped off 2.5 miles east at Cowshill, unless you arrange an alternative route with them. There's B&B accommodation in Stanhope and elsewhere in the dale, but the better overnight stop is actually Alston (see p.682), just over the border in Cumbria, seven miles from Killhope. The delightful **Weardale steam railway** runs from Stanhope to Bishop Auckland via Frosterley (3 daily; £8).

Stanhope and around

Weardale's main settlement, **STANHOPE**, lies about halfway up the valley. It's an elongated village that makes a useful halt for hikes on the local moors, including the enjoyable five-mile circuit from the town centre, up through the woods of **Stanhope Dene**, after which in summer you can cool off with a splash in the open-air heated swimming pool (£2.90). The village has a castle (closed to the public), built for a local MP in 1798, whose walled gardens now house the **Durham Dales Centre** – on the main road through Stanhope – in which you'll find the **tourist office** (daily: April–Oct 10am–5pm; Nov–March 10am–4pm; T01388/527650, Wwww.durhamdalescentre.co.uk) and a tearoom. Take a quick look at the 250-million-year-old **fossilized tree trunk** in the grounds of St Thomas's Church, on the main road near the Dales Centre. The best **food** hereabouts is served at the ★ *Black Bull* (May–Oct Wed–Sun; Nov–April Thurs–Sun; T01388/527784; booking essential) in the traditional, fawn-coloured village of **Frosterley**, three miles southeast of Stanhope. The menu is small and thoughtfully selected – the owners always source the ingredients from local suppliers first – while the beers are all from nearby breweries. Mains start from £10, and puddings are around £6 – their honey, whisky and Drambuie crème brûlée is especially tempting.

Nine miles upstream from Stanhope, at Ireshopeburn, the **Weardale Museum** (Easter, May–Oct Wed–Sun 2–5pm; Aug daily 2–5pm; £2) tells the story of the dale, in particular its lead mining and Methodism (the faith of most of County Durham's lead-miners). **High House Chapel**, built in 1760, next to the museum (entry included), claims to be the world's oldest Methodist chapel in continuous weekly use.

Killhope Lead Mining Museum

Lead and iron-ore mining flourished in and around Weardale from the 1840s to the 1880s, leaving today's landscape scarred with old workings. One of the bigger mines, situated about five miles west of Ireshopeburn is now the **Killhope Lead Mining Museum** (April–Oct daily 10.30am–5pm; £4.50, £6.50 including mine visit; Wwww.killhope.org.uk), a terrific attraction that presents the nineteenth-century buildings and machinery in a way that really brings home the hardships of a mining life – investigating the cramped "mineshop", where the workers lived away from their families all week, visiting the huge clanking waterwheel, or trying your hand as a washerboy on the old washing floor. The highlight is descending **Park Level Mine** (1hr tour; T01388/537505 call for times) with wellies, hard-hat and lamp in the company of a guide who expounds entertainingly about the realities of life underground, notably the perils of the "Black Spit", a lung disease which killed many men by their mid-forties. Expect to spend at least a couple of hours at the museum; there's a café on site.

The Allen Valley

The B6295 climbs north out of Weardale into Northumberland, soon dropping into the **Allen Valley**, where heather-covered moorland shelters small settlements that once made their living from lead mining. The dramatic surroundings are still easily viewed today from a series of river walks accessible from either of the main settlements.

At **ALLENHEADS**, at the top of the valley, twelve miles from Stanhope, handsome stone buildings stand close to the river. A heritage centre details the village's erstwhile industry, while a short nature trail guides you through the woodland around the East Allen River. The *Allenheads Inn* (T01434/685200, Wwww.allenheadsinn.co.uk; ❶), a popular stop for cyclists on the C2C route, provides beer and inexpensive bar meals, and has seven rooms which get booked up quickly in summer.

ALLENDALE TOWN, another four miles north, also goes about its quiet, rural way – New Year's Eve excepted, when the villagers celebrate pagan-style by throwing barrels of burning tar onto a huge, spluttering bonfire. This is a good place to base yourself for the local walking, with a small supermarket and several friendly pubs and small hotels, all centred on the market square. A very good path connects Allenheads to Allendale (around nine miles one way), leaving or crossing the river on occasion, though connoisseurs rate higher the northern section, from Allendale to the River Tyne (eight miles one way), which is at its most dramatic when passing through the beautiful, tree-clad **Allen Gorge**, watched over by Staward Peel, a medieval fortified tower-house; there's road access at **Plankey Mill**, around which the river becomes full of splashing families on summer weekends.

Blanchland and around

The other trans-moorland route into Northumberland is the B6278 which cuts north from Weardale at Stanhope for ten wild miles to **BLANCHLAND**, a handful of lichen-stained stone cottages huddled round an L-shaped square that was once the outer court of a twelfth-century abbey. The village has been preserved since 1721, when Lord Crewe bequeathed his estate to trustees on condition that they restored the old buildings, as Blanchland had slowly fallen into disrepair after the abbey's dissolution. Nothing but the faintest whiff of subsequent centuries has been allowed to intrude, the last concession being the construction of a pint-sized shelter in celebration of Queen Victoria's Diamond Jubilee. It's the ⚔ *Lord Crewe Arms Hotel* (☎01434/675251, Ⓦwww.lordcrewe hotel.com; ❸) that now steals the show. Once the abbot's lodge, the hotel's nooks and crannies are an enticing mixture of medieval and eighteenth-century Gothic, including the dark vaulted basements, two big fireplaces left over from the canons' kitchen and a priest's hideaway stuck inside the chimney. You can eat in the restaurant (mains £14–20), or more cheaply in the fine public bar in the undercroft.

The Tees Valley

That the **River Tees** is so far off the contemporary tourist map as to be invisible is hardly the fault of towns whose livelihood largely disappeared once iron- and steel-making and shipbuilding became things of the past in England. But this area was one of the great engines of British economic power in the late nineteenth century. It was from **Darlington**, twenty miles south of Durham city, that George Stephenson's *Locomotion* made its inaugural run and where it is now on permanent display. The railway line ran first to Stockton-on-Tees and was then extended to ports at **Middlesbrough** and Hartlepool, to enable ever-increasing amounts of Durham coal to be unloaded and exported. Iron from the local Cleveland Hills supported a shipbuilding industry, which in Hartlepool at least had been flourishing since the eighteenth century.

In truth, few tourists stop at any of these towns. But, for those that do, Darlington is the most surprisingly attractive, and you'd have to be hard-hearted not to derive some pleasure from Middlesbrough's fine new art gallery or Hartlepool's historic quay (see box, p.774). Once out on the coast at the Victorian resort of **Saltburn**, or inland beyond Guisborough, you're very quickly in the heart of the North York Moors. In particular, note the Esk Valley train line from Middlesbrough to Whitby, which runs via Grosmont, northern terminal point of the North Yorkshire Moors Railway (see p.755).

Darlington

DARLINGTON hit the big time in 1825, when George Stephenson's "Number 1 Engine", later called *Locomotion*, hurtled from here to nearby Stockton-on-Tees at the terrifying speed of fifteen miles per hour, with the inventor at the controls and flag-carrying horsemen riding ahead to warn of the onrushing train. This novel form of transport soon proved popular with passengers, an unlooked-for bonus for Edward Pease, the line's instigator: he had simply wanted a fast and economical way to transport coal from the Durham pits to the docks at Stockton. Subsequently, Darlington grew into a rail engineering centre, and didn't look back till the closure of the works in 1966.

Top attraction here is, unsurprisingly, the **Head of Steam** museum (April–Sept Tues–Sun 10am–4pm; Oct–March Fri–Sun 11am–3.30pm; Ⓦwww.darlington .gov.uk/culture/headofsteam; £4.85), housed in Darlington's North Road Station, which was completed in 1842; it's a twenty-minute walk up Northgate from the central Market Place. The museum is packed with lively interactive and audio exhibits, while its absolute pride and joy is the original *Locomotion*, actually built in Newcastle, which continued in service until 1841.

The origins of the rest of Darlington lie deep in Saxon times. The monks carrying St Cuthbert's body from Ripon to Durham stopped here, the saint lending his name to the graceful riverside church of **St Cuthbert**. One of England's largest market squares spreads beyond the church up to the restored Victorian covered **market** (Mon–Sat 8am–5pm, with a large outdoor market Mon & Sat), next to the clocktower, both designed by Alfred Waterhouse, the architect responsible for Manchester's town hall and London's Natural History Museum. The pedestrianized **Market Place** has been given back to the people and while it may not be Rome, you can sip a cappuccino at one of several cafés and pubs that spill tables outside at the first hint of sunshine.

Practicalities

Darlington's **train station** is on the main line from London to Scotland (via Durham and Newcastle). From the station, walk up Victoria Road to the round-about and turn right down Feethams for the central Market Place. **Buses** stop opposite the town hall on Feethams. The **tourist office** (Mon–Fri 9am–5pm, Sat 9am–3pm; ℡01325/388666, Ⓦwww.visitdarlington.com) is housed in the Dolphin Leisure Centre on Horsemarket.

You're best off **staying** out of town in the attractive surrounding countryside. Two miles south in Croft-on-Tees, the welcoming *Clow Beck House* (℡01325/721075, Ⓦwww.clowbeckhouse.co.uk; ❺) has six individually decorated rooms and serves delicious breakfasts and evening meals (mains from £15), while if you're after a swanky place to rest your head, *Rockliffe Hall* (℡01325/729999, Ⓦwww.rockliffe hall.com; ❺), between the villages of Croft-on-Tees and Hurworth, has cool and luxurious rooms, a spa, and no fewer than three restaurants. It also lays claim to having the UK's longest golf course.

Good **eating** options in town include *Oven* (℡01325/466668; mains around £15; closed Mon), at 30 Duke St, which serves finely executed fish and meat dishes with a French twist, and *Ochis* (℡01325/282675; mains from £5.50), 30 Bondgate, a quirky, good-value Caribbean restaurant. Outside of Darlington, head for the handsome ⚡*Bay Horse*, just south of town in Hurworth village. Proud owner of a Michelin star, this exquisite pub has a roaring fire, exposed wooden beams, comfy bar stools and chalked-up menus. Tuck into delicious meals such as posh crayfish cocktail (£5.95), beef and suet pudding with pancetta and creamed mashed potato (£11.95) and make sure you leave room for their delectable puddings; the sticky toffee pudding with banana ice cream (£5.50) is particularly good.

Middlesbrough

MIDDLESBROUGH, Teesside's largest town, fifteen miles east of Darlington, is entirely a product of the early industrial age, with nineteenth-century iron and steel barons throwing up factories and housing almost as fast as they could ship their products out of the docks. What was a hamlet at the turn of the nineteenth century was a thriving industrial town of 100,000 people by the turn of the twentieth. When iron and steel declined in importance and the local shipbuilding industry collapsed (the last shipyard closed in 1986), Middlesbrough took to light engineering and the chemical industry, the belching plants of which still surround the outskirts. For visitors, none of this is as easily celebrated as the "heritage industry" of the coalfields further west, though in the stunning **Middlesbrough Institute of Modern Art** (Tues–Sat & bank hols 10am–5pm, Sun noon–4pm; free; ⓦwww.visitmima.com), in Centre Square, the town finally has a major tourist draw. The museum has brought together its municipal art collections for the first time, while changing exhibitions concentrate on fine arts and crafts (ceramics and jewellery in particular) from the early twentieth century to the present day. Coming here is also a good excuse to ride on Middlesbrough's famous **Transporter Bridge** (60p per pedestrian; £1.20 per car), built in 1911 and the sole working example left in the country. The **Newport Bridge** (1934), the first vertical lift bridge built in England, also recalls past feats of engineering.

Saltburn

South of the Tees estuary along the coast, it's not a difficult decision to bypass the kiss-me-quick tackiness of Redcar in favour of **SALTBURN**, twelve miles east of Middlesbrough, a graceful Victorian resort in a dramatic setting overlooking extensive sands and mottled red sea-cliffs. Soon after the railway arrived in 1861 to ferry Teessiders out to the seaside on high days and holidays, Saltburn became a rather fashionable spa town boasting a hydraulic **inclined tramway**, which still connects upper town to pier and promenade, and ornate **Italian Gardens** that are laid out beneath the eastern side of town. The **Smugglers Heritage Centre** (April–Sept Wed–Sun 10am–6pm; £2), set in fishermen's cottages to the east of the pier, is a vivid re-creation of Saltburn's darker past.

There are regular **train** services from Newcastle and Durham via Darlington and Middlesbrough, while frequent **buses** from Middlesbrough stop outside the train station. The **tourist office** (Tues–Sat 9am–5pm, closes lunch hour; Oct–May closed Sun & Mon; ⓣ01287/622422, ⓦwww.redcar-cleveland.gov.uk) is in the railway station buildings and has a list of **accommodation** vacancies. *Vista Mar* (ⓣ01287/623771) **restaurant** on Saltburn Bank serves good fish dishes (around £10) day and night, and has lovely seaside views.

Newcastle upon Tyne

De facto capital of the northeast, **NEWCASTLE UPON TYNE** has steadily emerged from its years of grimy, industry-focused existence to become a vibrant and stylish metropolis, packed with a huge variety of cultural attractions that warrant at least a couple of days' attention.

The Romans were the first to bridge the river here, and the "new castle" appeared as long ago as 1080. In the seventeenth century a regional monopoly on coal export brought wealth and power to Newcastle and engendered its other great industry, shipbuilding. At one time, 25 percent of the world's shipping was built here, and the first steam train and steam turbine also emerged from local factories. In its nineteenth-century heyday, Newcastle's engineers and builders gave the city an elegance that has survived today in the impressive buildings of Grainger Town – indeed, only London and Bath have more listed classical buildings.

Newcastle's revival after a tough post-industrial decline is most prominently exemplified in the enormous **Angel of the North**, Antony Gormley's magnificent steel sculpture that welcomes anyone approaching from the south by rail or road. These days visitors are encouraged to think of the city not as Newcastle upon Tyne but as "NewcastleGateshead" – the two sides part of some of the same entity straddling the Tyne. On **Gateshead Quays** are the BALTIC contemporary arts centre and Norman Foster's Sage music centre, while Newcastle's **Quayside** is scene of much of the city's contemporary nightlife. Add to these some impressive **museums and galleries** – including the unique Centre for Life, the Laing Art Gallery and Seven Stories, the Centre for Children's Books – and it seems Newcastle has firmly stamped its authority on the cultural map.

Arrival

Central Station, on Neville Street, is a five-minute walk from the city centre or Quayside and has a useful Metro station. National Express services arrive at the **coach station** on St James's Boulevard, not far from Central Station, while most regional bus services use the **Haymarket bus station** (Haymarket Metro). Many other city and local bus services arrive at and depart from the bus station in **Eldon Square Shopping Centre**. There are **car parks** signposted all over the city (including on the Quayside, under the High Level and Swing bridges); street parking is usually free between 6.30pm and 8am.

Newcastle's **airport**, six miles north of the city, is linked by Metro to Central Station (5.50am–11.10pm, every 7–15min; 23min; £2.90) and beyond. Alternatively, take a taxi into the centre (around £16). **Ferry arrivals** from Scandinavia and Holland dock at Royal Quays, North Shields, seven miles east of the city – there are connecting bus services or a taxi to the city costs around £16.

Information, city transport and tours

The two main **tourist offices** (ⓦwww.visitnewcastlegateshead.com) are at **Central Arcade**, Market Street (Mon–Fri 9–5pm, Sat 9am–4pm; ☎0191/277 8000), and in **The Sage** (daily 10am–5pm; ☎0191/478 4222).

Bright yellow **Quaylink** buses link Newcastle and Gateshead centres (daily 7am–midnight; 80p). The region also has an efficient commuter rail system, the **Metro** (daily 5.15am–11.30pm, services every 3–15min), with the landmark Grey's Monument marking the city centre and the site of **Monument**, the main interchange for the Metro's two lines: the green line for South Shields, Jarrow, Gateshead, Jesmond and the airport; and the yellow line for Wallsend, Tynemouth and Whitley Bay, plus a southern branch to Gateshead and Sunderland. The most useful discount pass is the **Metro Day Saver** for unlimited rides (£3.50 after 9am Mon, Tues, Thurs & Fri, plus all day Sat & Sun; £2.50 after 9am Wed; or £2 after 6pm any day), available from ticket machines at every station. For all public transport enquiries, contact **Nexus Traveline** (T 0191/203 3333, W www.nexus .org.uk) or visit the Nexus Travelshops at the Central Station, Haymarket, Monument or Gateshead Metro stations.

River Escapes Cruises' one-, two- and three-hour **sightseeing cruises** (£6/10/12; T 0167/078 5666, W www.riverescapes.co.uk) depart most weekends throughout the year from Newcastle's Quayside. Finally, a hop-on, hop-off, open-top **sightseeing bus** departs from Central Station (Easter–Nov daily 10am–3.30pm; Dec Sat & Sun 10am–3pm; departures every 30min–1hr; £8; T 0191/228 8900, W www.city-sightseeing.com).

Accommodation

Hotel chains, among them *Premier Travel Inn*, *Jury's*, *Quality*, *Travelodge*, *Holiday Inn* and a stupendously sited *Hilton* that overlooks the Tyne, are scattered about the city centre and on the Quayside. The biggest concentration of small hotels and **guesthouses** is a mile north of the centre in Jesmond, along and off Osborne Road: take bus #30B, #31B or #80 from Central Station or Haymarket. There's a free **room-booking service** available at the tourist offices to personal callers. In addition, both the University of Newcastle (T 0191/222 6318) and University of Northumbria (T 0191/227 4499) have hundreds of **student rooms** available at various locations from June to September, from around £28 per person.

Hotels and guesthouses

Adelphi 63 Fern Ave, off Osborne Rd, Jesmond T 0191/281 3109, W www.adelphihotelnewcastle .co.uk. Cheery and neat family-run B&B, in a quiet residential street. Five of the seven rooms are ensuite, and there are a couple of family rooms. ❷

Copthorne The Close, Quayside T 0191/222 0333, W www.millenniumhotels.com. This four-star hotel has Tyne views from most of its well-appointed rooms. Breakfast not included except for weekend packages; discounts via online booking. ❺

Grey Street 2 Grey St T 0191/230 6777, W www .greystreethotel.com. This hotel, housed in a former bank, couldn't be more central (triple-glazed windows bar the traffic noise). The slick, minimalist rooms can be on the small size – upgrade to a suite to get more space. Pay parking nearby. ❹

Hotel du Vin City Rd, Ouseburn Valley T 0191/229 2200, W www.hotelduvin.com. Housed in a beautifully converted former shipping warehouse and overlooking the river, the *Hotel du Vin* has spectacular rooms with all mod-cons, including iPod docks and flat-screen TVs. There's a smart bistro, complete with dinky wine-tasting room. Parking. Good deals at the weekends – check the website. ❻

Jesmond Dene House Jesmond Dene Rd, Jesmond T 0191/212 3000, W www .jesmonddenehouse.co.uk. An imposing Arts and Crafts house in a wooded valley with big beds, big bathrooms and bold decoration. Bedrooms all have digital radios, flat-screen TVs and wi-fi, and service is impeccable. There's fine dining in the garden-room restaurant. Parking. ❼

Malmaison Quayside T 0191/245 5000, W www .malmaison.com. Chic lodgings in the former Co-op building, right on the Quayside. Jazzy sounds, crushed-velvet sofas, brasserie, bar, spa and gym provide the signature backdrop. Breakfast not included. ❻

New Northumbria 61–69 Osborne Rd, Jesmond T 0191/281 4961, W www.newnorthumbria.com. Contemporary boutique-style lodgings offering spacious rooms, big beds, warm decor and lovely panelled bathrooms with power showers. Café-bar and Italian restaurant attached. ❹

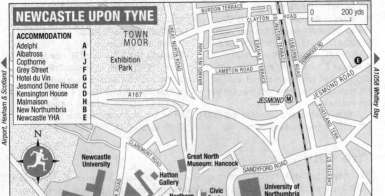

NEWCASTLE UPON TYNE

ACCOMMODATION

Adelphi	A
Albatross	I
Copthorne	J
Grey Street	F
Hotel du Vin	G
Jesmond Dene House	C
Kensington House	D
Malmaison	H
New Northumbria	B
Newcastle YHA	E

0   200 yds

TOWN MOOR

Exhibition Park

BURDON TERRACE
CLAYTON ROAD
BRANDLING PARK
LAMBTON ROAD
ESKDALE TERRACE
OSBORNE ROAD
ISLINGTON TERRACE
FERNWOOD RD

GREAT NORTH ROAD
A167

JESMOND Ⓜ
JESMOND ROAD
PORTLAND TERR
A1058 Whitley Bay

Ⓔ

13

THE NORTHEAST

Newcastle University
Hatton Gallery
Great North Museum: Hancock
SANDYFORD ROAD
Civic Centre
Northern Stage
University of Northumbria

CLAREMONT ROAD
KING'S WALK
QUEEN VICTORIA ROAD
RICHARDSON ROAD
ST THOMAS STREET
BARRAS BRIDGE

Royal Victoria Infirmary
HAYMARKET Ⓜ
ST MARY'S PLACE
City Hall
Bus Station
NORTHUMBERLAND ROAD

Leazes Park

Newcastle Utd F.C.

LEAZES PARK ROAD
PERCY STREET
STRAWBERRY PLACE
ST JAMES' BOULEVARD

NORTHUMBERLAND STREET
COLLEGE STREET
PERCY STREET

Eldon Square Shopping Centre & Bus Station
Grey's Monument
Laing Art Gallery
❷

NEW BRIDGE STREET

The Hyena
ST JAMES' Ⓜ
GALLOWGATE
BLACKETT STREET

MONUMENT Ⓜ
NELSON ST.
Grainger Market
Theatre Royal
Police Station
❺
MARKET ST
CARLIOL ST
MANORS Ⓜ
STEPNEY LANE

Morden Tower
The Gate
Blackfriars
⑩
Tyneside Cinema
❹
GRAINGER STREET
CLAYTON STREET
LOW FRIAR ST
NEWGATE STREET
BIGG MKT
ⓘ
❼
SHAKESPEARE STREET
WORSWICK ST
Globe Gallery
CITY ROAD
CITY ROAD

❽
MARKET ST
PILGRIM STREET
MOSLEY ST.
HIGH BRIDGE
GREY STREET
CLOTH MKT
⑬
PANDON

Journal Tyne Theatre
WESTGATE ROAD
Newcastle Arts Centre
⑭ Ⓘ
⑲
FRIARS ST
STOWELL STREET
⑰
⑱
PINK LANE
NEVILLE ST.
Cathedral
WESTGATE RD
COLLINGWOOD ST
ST NICHOLAS ST
⑮
THE SIDE
Live Theatre
❷⓿
DEAN ST
BROAD CHARE
⑯
Ⓗ
Ⓖ, ⑪, ⑫

Discovery Museum
⑳❶
BLANDFORD SQUARE
WATERLOO ST
❷❹
CLAYTON ST
ORCHARD ST
⑫
Castle
❷❸
Side Gallery
Millennium Bridge
BALTIC
ⓘ
The Sage Gateshead

WESTMORLAND ROAD
Coach Station
Centre for Life
❷❺
CENTRAL STATION Ⓜ
Central Station
Hanover Gardens
Guildhall
SANDHILL
TYNE BRIDGE
QUAYSIDE
SOUTH SHORE

Metro Radio Arena
ST JAMES' BOULEVARD
SCOTSWOOD ROAD
FORTH STREET
FORTH BANKS
HANOVER ST
THE CLOSE
High Level Bridge
Swing Bridge
A187 Tynemouth

Ⓙ
Metro Bridge
GATESHEAD Ⓜ
GATESHEAD
A1(M), Durham & Bus Station

A69 Hexham

Airport, Hexham & Scotland

Ouseburn Valley & Ferry Terminal (7 miles)

EATING & DRINKING						**CLUBS & LIVE MUSIC VENUES**	
As You Like It	1	El Coto	3	Popolo	8	Black Swan	17
Baby Lynch	15	Forth Hotel	18	Starters & Puds	6	The Cluny	12
Barn Asia	21	Free Trade	11	Tokyo	22	Digital	25
Blackfriars	10	Head of Steam	19	Vineyard	13	O2 Academy	14
Café 21	16	Kaffeccinos	9	Vujon	20	Powerhouse	24
Café Royal	4	Pani Café	7			Trillians Rock Bar	2
Crown Posada	23	Paradiso	8			World Headquarters	5

Hostels and apartments

Albatross 51 Grainger St ☏ 0191/233 1330, ⓦ www.albatrossnewcastle.co.uk. This award-winning 177-bed backpackers' hostel has a great central location and is immaculate throughout. It's a very welcoming place, with 24/7 reception, parking and internet, and free tea, toast and coffee. Dorm beds from £16.50; two-bed dorm ❶

 Kensington House 5 Osborne Rd ☏ 0191/281 8175, ⓦ www.kensingtonaparthotel.com.

An elegant townhouse at the bottom of Osborne Road, moments from Jesmond Metro, with 23 sophisticated apartments that can accommodate up to four people. £208.

Newcastle YHA 107 Jesmond Rd, near Jesmond Metro ☏ 0870/770 5972, ⓔ newcastle@yha.org .uk. The traditional hostel choice in the city, the *YHA* has fifty beds available in a converted townhouse. Breakfast and cheap evening meals served, though no laundry facilities. Closed Christmas to mid-Jan. Dorm beds from £17.95.

The City

The city splits into several distinct areas, though it's only a matter of minutes to walk between them. **Castle** and **cathedral** occupy the heights immediately above the River Tyne, whose Newcastle and Gateshead **quaysides** form the biggest single attraction in the city. North of the cathedral lies **Grainger Town**, the city-centre district of listed Victorian buildings that is at its most dramatic along Grey Street. West of the centre is Chinatown and the two big draws of the Discovery Museum and the Centre for Life; east is the renowned Laing Gallery; and north the university and open parkland known as Town Moor. Further east along the

A weekend in Newcastle

Friday night

There's no point in wasting time: put on your glad rags and head into town for a raucous night out, Geordie-style. Warm up with a glass of wine at the cosy **Vineyard** bar or a pint at the **Crown Posada**, and then move on to one of the **Mr Lynch** bars – try *Florita's* or *Baby Lynch* – for a cocktail or three and some dancing. Hardcore party people can finish up their night in one of the busy **nightclubs** – *World Headquarters* and *Digital* are the pick of the bunch.

Saturday

Blow the cobwebs away with a breezy walk along the **Quayside**, admiring the melee of beautifully constructed bridges and striking modern buildings that fringe the riverbank. Spend an hour or two in the contemporary art museum, **The BALTIC**, and then pop back over the river to the old town, stopping off at the diminutive **Side Gallery**. After all that art, it's time for lunch at lively Sardinian café, *Pani*. In the afternoon, indulge your inner child at the colourful **Seven Stories** literature museum in the Ouseburn Valley. While you're in the area, don't miss a visit to the **Biscuit Factory**, if only for a cup of coffee and a cake in their cute café. The best place to spend Saturday night is at the artsy **Cluny** bar, particularly if there's live music or a theatre recital going on.

Sunday

Explore Newcastle's architectural heritage – take a trip up to the gloomy **castle** and the adjacent **cathedral**, and then follow the ruins of the old city wall and medieval towers along **Stowell Street**. For lunch you could choose one of the many **Chinese restaurants** near the wall, or tuck into a large Sunday roast at the snug and tradi-tional *Blackfriars*. Walk off your meal and expand your scientific knowledge at the **Centre of Life** museum, and the nearby **Discovery Museum**. If you're all partied and museumed out, put your feet up and munch on popcorn at Newcastle's art-house cinema, **The Tyneside**.

river, the old industrial **Ouseburn Valley** district has emerged as a cultural quarter, focusing on the Seven Stories children's books centre.

Castle and cathedral

Anyone arriving by train from the north will get a sneak preview of the **castle** (Mon–Sat 10am–5pm, Sun noon–5pm; £4), as the rail line splits the keep from its gatehouse, the Black Gate, on St Nicholas Street. A wooden fort was built here over an Anglo-Saxon cemetery by Robert Curthose, illegitimate eldest son of William the Conqueror, but the present keep dates from the twelfth century. Down in the garrison room, prisoners were incarcerated during the sixteenth to eighteenth centuries, while locals rushed to its deep shelter in World War II to sit out German bombing. There's a great view from the rooftop over the river and city.

Further along St Nicholas Street stands the **cathedral** (free), dating mainly from the fourteenth and fifteenth centuries and remarkable chiefly for its tower – erected in 1470, it is topped with a crown-like structure of turrets and arches supporting a lantern. Inside, behind the high altar, is one of the largest funerary brasses in England; it was commissioned by Roger Thornton, the Dick Whittington of Newcastle, who arrived in the city penniless and died its richest merchant in 1430.

Along the River Tyne

From between the castle and the cathedral a road known simply as The Side – formerly the main road out of the city – descends to Newcastle's **Quayside**. There have been fixed river crossings over the River Tyne since Roman times and today it's spanned by seven bridges in close proximity, the most prominent being the looming **Tyne Bridge** of 1928, which bears a striking resemblance to the roughly contemporaneous Sydney Harbour Bridge – not surprising really, as both were built by Dorman Long of Middlesbrough. Immediately west is the hydraulic **Swing Bridge**, erected in 1876 by Lord Armstrong so that larger vessels could reach his shipyards upriver, while modern road and rail lines cross the river on the adjacent **High Level Bridge**, built by Robert Stephenson in 1849 – Queen Victoria was one of the first passengers to cross, promoting the railway revolution.

Beyond the Tyne Bridge, riverside apartments, a landscaped promenade, public sculpture and pedestrianized squares have paved the way for a series of fashionable bars and restaurants, centred on the graceful **Gateshead Millennium Bridge**, the world's first tilting span, designed to pivot to allow ships to pass. For tilting times see the information boards at either side of the bridge or visit Ⓦ www.gateshead .gov.uk/bridge.

You can cross the bridge over to the **Gateshead Quays**, and **BALTIC**, the dramatic Centre for Contemporary Art (Mon & Wed–Sun 10am–6pm, Tues 10.30am–6pm; free; Ⓦ www.balticmill.com), fashioned from a brick flour-mill built in the 1940s. This has been converted into a huge visual "art factory", second only in scale to London's Tate Modern. There's no permanent collection here, though the galleries display a robust series of specially commissioned or invited art exhibitions, local community projects and other displays. Alongside the galleries, the BALTIC accommodates artists' studios, education workshops, an art performance space and cinema, plus a restaurant on the roof with uninterrupted views of the Newcastle skyline.

The BALTIC is complemented on the Gateshead side by **The Sage Gateshead** (Ⓦ www.thesagegateshead.org), an extraordinary billowing steel, aluminium and glass concert hall complex, best seen at night when it glows with many colours. It's home to the Northern Sinfonia orchestra and Folkworks, an organization promoting British and international traditional music.

Grainger Town and the city centre

By the mid-nineteenth century, Newcastle's centre of balance had shifted away from the river, uphill to the rapidly expanding Victorian town. In a few short years, businessmen-builders and architects such as Richard Grainger, Thomas Oliver and John Dobson fashioned the best-designed Victorian town in England, with classical facades of stone lining splendid new streets, most notably **Grey Street** – "that descending, subtle curve", as John Betjeman described it. The street takes its name from the Northumberland dynasty of political heavyweights whose most illustrious member was the second Earl Grey (he of the tea), prime minister from 1830 to 1834. In the middle of his term in office he carried the Reform Bill through parliament, an act commemorated by **Grey's Monument** at the top of the street.

Grey Street today still shows off much of its Victorian elegance, best exemplified by the **Theatre Royal**, halfway down. Other streets fell to the municipal butchers in the 1960s and 1970s – Eldon Square, once a model of Victorian balance, now a shopping centre, is a case in point – though not all was lost. The restored **Grainger Market** (Mon & Wed 9am–5pm, Tues–Sat 9am–5.30pm), near Grey's Monument, was Europe's largest undercover market when built in the 1830s, while John Dobson's nearby **Central Station**, facing Neville Street, trumpets the confidence of the railway age with its soaring interior spaces and curved ironwork.

West of here, behind Gallowgate, is the most complete stretch of the old **city walls**, leading down to Westgate Road. These once encircled the whole of medieval Newcastle, but were plundered for building stone after the sixteenth century. However, several towers remain, including the **Morden Tower** (once the haunt of Beat poets) alongside Stowell Street, where the outer defensive ditch has been restored. Stowell Street is Newcastle's **Chinatown**, lined with restaurants and supermarkets. Across Stowell Street from the tower, at Friar's Green, is the tranquil courtyard of **Blackfriars**, a thirteenth-century stone monastery with ruined cloistered grounds, now lovingly restored to house a crafts centre and restaurant (see p.795).

Discovery Museum

On the south side of Westgate Road, the **Discovery Museum** in Blandford Square (Mon–Sat 10am–5pm, Sun 2–5pm; free; Ⓦ www.twmuseums.org.uk) puts into context the city's history in a series of impressive interactive displays. You are confronted on arrival by the 35m-long *Turbinia*, the world's first steam-turbine-powered ship, built by a brilliant local engineer, Charles Parsons. Galleries on three floors surround the *Turbinia*, with standout attractions including the "Newcastle Story", a walk through the city's past with tales from animated characters along the way, and the "Science Maze" which focuses on Newcastle's pioneering inventors (including one Joseph Swan who, according to locals at least, beat Edison to the invention of the light bulb). Elsewhere in the museum, there are walk-through fashion galleries, displaying some of the eight thousand costume items in the collection, and old favourites like the talking regimental horse and barking drill-sergeant in "The Soldier's Life" exhibition.

Centre for Life

Heading back towards the Central Station along Westmorland Road, you can't miss the **Centre for Life** (Mon–Sat 10am–6pm, Sun 11am–6pm, last admission 4pm; £7.65; Ⓦ www.life.org.uk), whose sleek buildings reach around the sweeping expanse of Times Square. This ambitious "science village" project combines bioscience and genetics research centres with a science visitor centre which aims to convey the secrets of life using the latest entertainment technology. Highlights include 3D motion-simulator rides and a blockbuster exhibit on the history of human life. The centre is always adding new attractions and in winter an open-air **ice rink** is unveiled (mid-Nov to mid-Feb; £7.50). Children find the whole thing enormously rewarding – expect to spend a good three hours here, if not more.

Laing Art Gallery

The northeast's premier art collection is the **Laing Art Gallery** on New Bridge Street (Mon–Sat 10am–5pm, Sun 2–5pm; free; ⓦ www.twmuseums.org.uk), off John Dobson Street, behind the library. Local pottery, glassware, costume and sculpture all play their part, while on permanent display is a sweep through British art from Reynolds to John Hoyland, with a smattering of Pre-Raphaelites, so admired by English industrial barons.

The real treat here is the work of **John Martin** (1789–1854), a self-taught Northumberland painter with a penchant for massive biblical and mythical scenes. He came from a rather dysfunctional family – his elder brother wore a tortoiseshell hat, another brother set fire to York Minster – and with the benefit of twenty-first-century psychological hindsight, it's easy to imagine what demons drove him in his work. Outside the Laing's front door is the somewhat faded **Blue Carpet** – a public art installation whose tiles fold back on themselves to form unusual benches.

The Great North: Hancock Museum and Town Moor

The **Great North: Hancock Museum** (ⓦ www.twmuseums.org.uk) is a rather clunkily named amalgamation of four museums, the most worthwhile of which are the Great North Museum, housed in the Hancock building, and the nearby Hatton Gallery. In the Hancock building (Mon–Sat 10am–5pm, Sun 2–5pm; free) you can wander round engaging collections focusing on the natural world and archeology, including a bony-looking T-Rex, a replica of Hadrian's Wall and a planetarium (from £2.50). A two-minute walk away, on the university campus, is the small **Hatton Gallery** (Mon–Fri 10am–5.30pm, Sat 10am–5pm; free), famous for housing the only surviving example of German Dadaist Kurt Schwitters' *Merzbau* (a sort of architectural collage); it also hosts a wide variety of temporary exhibitions.

Beyond the University of Newcastle, through the landscaped **Exhibition Park**, you reach the **Town Moor**, 1200 acres of common land where freemen of the city, including Jimmy Carter, Nelson Mandela and Bob Geldof, are entitled to graze their cattle. It's the site of the annual "Hoppings" in the last week of June: a huge week-long fair of rides, stalls and other attractions which keeps the cows awake until well after dark.

Ouseburn Valley

Ten minutes' walk up the River Tyne from Millennium Bridge, or a less attractive route via busy New Bridge Street, the old Victorian mills and warehouses of the **Ouseburn Valley** that were once the epicentre of Newcastle's industry are gradually being given a new lease of life. Check out The Biscuit Factory (Britain's largest commercial art gallery; see p.796), 36 Lime Street (artist's studio group); enjoyable music bar, *The Cluny* (see p.796), and the imaginative **Seven Stories**, 30 Lime St (Mon–Sat 10am–5pm, Sun 10am–4pm; £6; ☏ 0845/271 0777, ⓦ www.sevenstories.org.uk). This national centre for children's literature spreads across seven floors of a converted riverside mill, showcasing a unique collection of original manuscripts, documents and artwork – including Phillip Pullman's early books, material from Nina Bawden, the drawings from Noel Streatfeild's *Ballet Shoes*, and illustrations from *Charlie and the Chocolate Factory*, among much else. Changing exhibitions explore every facet of children's literature, with plenty of interactive engagement and events thrown in. There's also a café and an excellent children's bookshop.

Angel of the North

For over a decade Antony Gormley's **Angel of the North** has stood sentinel over the A1 at Gateshead. Situated on what used to be a colliery's pithead baths, it has become the symbol of Tyneside and the country's most viewed sculpture. Gormley himself wanted to remind people that miners worked underground here for two centuries, and to him the angel symbolizes an embracing celebration of industry. It's the sheer scale of its 175-foot wingspan, which inclines slightly forward, that makes the most impact, and it's even more imposing close up, when the ribbed structure of the body and rough, rusty texture gradually become apparent. The Angel is accessible by car from the A167 (signed Gateshead South; there's a parking lay-by), and by frequent buses (#21 or #21A) that run from Pilgrim Street in Newcastle and from the Gateshead Interchange bus station in the centre of Gateshead (Gateshead Metro; green or yellow lines).

Eating

At the budget end of the market Italian, Indian and Chinese food dominate the scene, while at the top end of the scale the city has attracted some inventive chefs. The very cheapest places are found around **Bigg Market**, while in Stowell Street in **Chinatown** there are plenty of all-you-can-eat buffets as well as more refined Cantonese restaurants. Many city-centre restaurants offer **early bird/happy hour** deals before 7pm.

Cafés and café-bars

Café Royal 8 Nelson St. Bright and buzzy café with great smoothies, coffees and delectable home-made breads and cakes – try the gooey Baileys brownies (£2.50). Closed Sun.
Kaffeccinos 54 Grainger St. Everything at this relaxed café – from the good-value toasties (£3.95) to the tasty milkshakes (£2.50) – uses Fairtrade and organic ingredients.

Pani Café 61–65 High Bridge, off Grey St ☎0191/232 4366. Up a side-street below the Theatre Royal, this buzzy Sardinian café has a loyal clientele, who come day and night (it's open until 10pm) for authentic, good-value stuffed sandwiches, antipasti, pasta and salads. Closed Sun.
Paradiso 1 Market Lane ☎0191/221 1240. Unpretentious café-bar hidden down an alley off Pilgrim St – snacky food during the day, more

---

Traditional Northeastern grub

Stottie cakes Gargantuan bread rolls, made with a heavy dough, today often found drizzled with olive oil and stuffed with Parma ham and chargrilled veg.

Newcastle Brown Ale Also known as "Dog", this caramel-coloured brew with a slighty nutty, malty taste hails from the Toon.

Craster kippers You can buy traditionally smoked kippers at Robson's factory in this tiny village. See p.815.

Alnwick stew Once a lunchtime staple, this hearty concoction is made with potatoes, bacon or gammon, and veg. You might find it on menus in traditional restaurants and pubs.

Lindisfarne Mead Brewed only on Holy Island, and supped by the original Holy Island monks, this is a sweet, fortified wine made with honey and herbs. See p.818.

substantial meals at night (like home-made fish cakes or Moroccan tagine). Alfresco dining when the weather's good up on the sun deck. Closed Sun.

Restaurants

Barn Asia Waterloo Square ☎0191/221 1000. Inventive pan-Asian food, such as Chiang Rai curry with snow peas and sticky rice (£11), served in a lively, foliage-filled restaurant. Closed Sun & Mon.

Blackfriars Friars St ☎0191/261 5945. Housed in a beautiful stone building dating back to 1239, *Blackfriars* offers superb traditional British dishes using locally produced ingredients, such as pan-fried County Durham pork chop, sausage and haricot bean stew (£9), and for pudding an irresistible Friars dark chocolate cake with Lindisfarne Mead marmalade ice cream (£5).

Café 21 Trinity Gardens, 1 Broad Chare ☎0191/222 0755. Stylish Parisian-influenced bistro with crisp white tablecloths, leather banquettes, a classic French menu, and slick service. Expect dishes like roasted scallops with cauliflower purée (£22.50) and sautéed Northumbrian venison with winter fruits (£19.80).

El Coto 21 Leazes Park Rd ☎0191/261 0555. Cute and cosy, the city's best tapas place has an extensive and good-value menu – dishes cost around £4, though paella goes for £10 per person.

Starters & Puds 2–9 Shakespeare St ☎0191/233 2515. It's all in the name – this warm and inviting restaurant only offers mini, tapas-style starters (£4–9) and tempting puddings (£4.70) – these, thankfully, of normal size. You could eat your starters, pop to the theatre and come back for pud.

Vujon 29 Queen St ☎0191/221 0601. The city's classiest Indian restaurant with dishes a cut above the ordinary, from lamb *rezala* with green peppers, ground almonds and tomatoes (£10.90) to pheasant *tarkhari* (£14.90).

Drinking, nightlife and music

Newcastle's boisterous pubs, bars and clubs are concentrated in several distinct areas: between Grainger Street and the cathedral in the area called the **Bigg Market**; around the **Quayside** and in the developing **Ouseburn Valley** area, where the bars tend to be quirkier and more sophisticated; and in the mainstream leisure-and-cinema complex known as **The Gate** (Newgate Street). It's difficult to escape the weekend mayhem, though the bars around **Central Station** and nearby **Pink Lane** at least start off the evening with more civilized intent, while in **Jesmond**, there's a thriving strip of student-filled café-bars along Osborne Road. The **"Gay Quarter"** centres on the Centre for Life, spreading out to Waterloo Street and Westmorland and Scotswood roads.

There's something going on most nights in the city, with gigs, club nights and the gay scene reviewed exhaustively in *The Crack* (free; ⓦwww.thecrackmagazine .com), a monthly **listings magazine** available in shops, pubs and bars.

Pubs and bars

As You Like It Archbold Terrace ☎0191/281 2277. Incongruously sitting beneath an ugly tower block, this funky bar-restaurant has a relaxed vibe, exposed brick walls and mishmash furniture. The best bar in the Jesmond area, and part of the *Mr Lynch* chain (see below), which is actually opposite *AYLI*.

Baby Lynch 26 Collingwood St. Part of a Newcastle-based chain (includes *As You Like It, Nancy Bordellos, Floritas, Madame Koo* and *Mr Lynch*), but still cool for it, *Baby Lynch* oozes seventies chic with its retro wooden floorboards, cosy booths and bamboo loungers. The cocktails are good but pricey (around £9). Usually busy later on, with the overspill from next-door *Floritas*.

Crown Posada 31 The Side. A proper old man's pub: local beers and guest ales in a small wood-and-glass-panelled Victorian boozer. You might fancy the dark, malty Hadrian's Gladiator or opt for the golden, hoppy Tyneside Blonde.

Forth Hotel Pink Lane. Honest city-centre pub with a fine jukebox, varied crowd, good lunchtime food and a decent range of wines by the glass.

Free Trade St Lawrence Rd. Walk along the Newcastle Quayside past the Millennium Bridge and look for the shabby pub on the hill, where you are invited to "drink beer, smoke tabs" with the city's pub cognoscenti. Cask beer from local microbreweries, a great jukebox and superb river views from the beer garden.

Head of Steam 2 Neville St. In an unpromising modern building (but a whole lot better-looking inside), this relaxed drinking den has good sounds and big sofas. Usually live gigs in the basement from 8pm.

Popolo 82–84 Pilgrim St. This casual American-style bar is a firm city favourite, and is known for its large variety of tasty mojitos, which go for £3.95 on Wed (from £5 otherwise).

Tokyo 17 Westgate Rd. The dark main bar's handsome enough, but follow the tea-lights up the stairs to the outdoor "garden" bar. A pre-club favourite for Shindig (see *Digital*, below).

Vineyard 1 Grey St. Small bar with charming, eclectic decor – think painted tiles, barrels, giant flowers and rickety stools – and a decent wine list.

Clubs

Digital Centre for Life, Times Square ⓦwww .yourfutureisdigital.com. The city's top club with an amazing sound system pumping out a variety of tunes, from house and retro to cheesy classics. The big draw is Saturday's house music-fest Shindig (ⓦwww.shindiguk.com).

Powerhouse 7–19 Westmorland Rd ⓦwww .clubph.co.uk. Spread over four floors, this is Newcastle's biggest and most popular gay club. Closed Tues & Wed.

World Headquarters Carliol Square ☎0191/281 3445, ⓦwww.welovewhq.com.

Mellow two-storey bar and club playing funk, soul and hip-hop every Friday and Saturday, plus regular DJ slots, indie to electro.

Live music venues

Black Swan Newcastle Arts Centre, 69 Westgate Rd ☎0191/261 5618. Cellar bar with live music up to five nights a week – rock, folk, world and jazz – and a rollicking Friday-night salsa session. Late bar until 2am.

The Cluny 36 Lime St, Ouseburn Valley ☎0191/230 4474, ⓦwww.theheadofsteam .co.uk. The best small venue in the city is out in the eastern sticks (20min walk from Quayside or take the Q2 yellow bus), with gigs almost every night from 8pm, real ales and a great bar courtesy of the *Head of Steam*. At the time of writing, the *Cluny 2*, right next door to *The Cluny*, was being prepped as a theatre, live music and comedy venue (check the *Head of Steam* website for details).

O2 Academy Westgate Rd ☎0191/260 2020, ⓦwww.o2academynewcastle.co.uk. Hosts big-name bands, plus wannabes.

Trillians Rock Bar Princess Square ☎0191/232 1619, ⓦwww.myspace.com/trillians. Headbangers of the world unite – local and national rock acts play this pub venue, which also hosts rock DJ nights (Fri & Sat).

Arts and culture

Theatrical and cultural life in the city varies from the offerings at the splendid Victorian Theatre Royal to those of smaller contemporary theatre companies and local, independent **cinemas**. The Sage and City Hall are the main **classical music** concert venues, but you'll also find performances throughout the year at Newcastle University's King's Hall and in churches around town. Contemporary **art** is a growing scene in Newcastle, with new galleries and workshops popping up all the time, particularly in the Ouseburn Valley area.

Galleries

The Biscuit Factory 16 Stoddart St, Ouseburn Valley ☎0191/261 1103, ⓦwww.thebiscuitfactory .com. Britain's biggest commercial centre for art. There's also a little café serving tasty coffees and cakes on the top floor. Free entry.

Globe Gallery Curtis Mayfield House, Carliol Square ☎0191/222 1666, ⓦwww.globegallery.org. Fashionable warehouse gallery, with regular exhibitions and one-off events.

Mushroom Works St Lawrence Rd, Ouseburn Valley ☎0191/224 4011, ⓦwww.mushroomworks .com. Interesting artist-led gallery and studio space – open Wed–Sat noon–5pm for a stroll around and a chat with the artists. Free entry.

Northern Print Stepney Bank, Ouseburn Valley ☎0191/261 7000, ⓦwww.northernprint.org.uk.

Little gallery that sells affordable prints by local artists. You can also learn how to make prints at the studio's workshop. Open Wed–Sat noon–4pm. Free entry.

Side Gallery 5–9 Side ☎0191/232 2208, ⓦwww .amber-online.com. Small, independent gallery displaying high-quality changing photographic exhibitions, which explore hard-hitting social themes such as women's incarceration. The gallery is also home to an independent cinema, which usually shows films linked to the current exhibition. Free entry. Tues–Sat 11am–5pm.

Cinemas

Star and Shadow Cinema Stepney Bank, Ouseburn Valley ☎0191/261 0066, ⓦwww.starandshadow .org.uk. Independent programme of art, classic and

Shop till you drop

The celebrated **MetroCentre** at Gateshead (ⓦwww.metrocentre-gateshead.co.uk) is Europe's largest shopping and leisure venue, with over 300 shops, a huge number of restaurants and cafés, multi-screen cinema and indoor theme park. Should you balk at that, there are plenty of shopping choices in the city centre:

Art Biscuit Factory (see opposite); Art Works Galleries (Stepney Bank); Waygood Art Boutique (31–39 High Bridge); Opus Gallery (Church Hall, West Ave); Northern Print (see opposite).

Department stores Fenwick's (Northumberland St); John Lewis (Eldon Square).

Designer labels Vivienne Westwood (1 Hood St); Cruise stores (Princess Square); Jules B (50–54 Acorn Rd).

Markets Quayside market (under Tyne bridge; Sun am); Grainger Market (daily except Sun; plus arts and crafts market 2nd Sat of month); Armstrong Bridge arts and crafts market (Jesmond; Sun from 10am); farmers' market (Grey's Monument; 1st Fri of each month); Tynemouth antiques market (Tynemouth Metro; every weekend, plus farmers' market on 3rd Sat of month).

Vintage Attica (20 Old George Yard, off High Bridge); Period Clothing Warehouse (29 High Bridge).

political films as well as exhibitions, bands and live art. Films every Thurs & Sun at 7.30pm.

Tyneside Cinema 10 Pilgrim St ⓣ0191/232 8289, ⓦwww.tynesidecinema.co.uk. Central art-house cinema, with a wide-ranging international programme. There's coffee, light meals and movie talk in the Art Deco cinema café (closes 9pm).

Concert venues

City Hall Northumberland Rd ⓣ0191/261 2606, ⓦwww.newcastlecityhall.org. Orchestras from around the world, as well as mainstream rock, pop and comedy acts.

Journal Tyne Theatre 111 Westgate Rd ⓣ0870/145 1200, ⓦwww.tynetheatre.co.uk. Beautifully restored Victorian theatre with a wide range of shows (including children's performances and pantomime), comedy and gigs.

Metro Radio Arena Arena Way, 10min walk from Central Station ⓣ0844/493 4567, ⓦwww.metro radioarena.co.uk. Big names and big shows – ice shows, basketball matches and blockbuster musicals – take the stage at the largest venue in the northeast.

The Sage Gateshead South Shore Rd, Gateshead Quays ⓣ0191/443 4661, ⓦwww.thesagegates head.org. Stunning international music centre, home of the Northern Sinfonia and Folkworks, hosting a full programme of classical, folk, world and jazz music. Tickets from £9.

Theatre, dance and comedy

The Hyena 17 Leazes Park Rd ⓣ0191/232 6030, ⓦwww.thehyena.com. Stand-up comedy with visiting national and international acts every Fri and Sat night from 6.30pm.

Live Theatre Broad Chare ⓣ0191/232 1232, ⓦwww.live.org.uk. Enterprising theatre company promoting local actors and writers (Lee Hall gave his boy-ballet movie, *Billy Elliot*, its first reading here). The attached *Caffè Vivo* is good for coffee by day and pre-theatre meal deals by night.

Northern Stage Barras Bridge, Haymarket ⓣ0191/230 5151, ⓦwww.northernstage.co.uk. The company stages its own "visually driven" productions here as well as co-producing innovative work from Europe and beyond.

Theatre Royal 100 Grey St ⓣ0191/244 2500, ⓦwww.theatreroyal.co.uk. Drama, opera, dance, musicals and comedy; also hosts the annual RSC season in Nov.

Listings

Bike hire Grange Rd, Newburn ⓣ0191/264 0014. Mon–Fri 9am–10pm, Sat & Sun 9am–5pm. £16/day.

Football Newcastle United play at St James' Park (ticket office ⓣ0844/372 1892, ⓦwww.nufc .co.uk) in front of the country's most long-suffering supporters. You're unlikely to get a ticket for the big matches against major rivals, but seats do go on general sale for some games. Don't, under any circumstances, wear anything red (the colour of hated local rivals Sunderland).

Hospital Newcastle General Hospital, Westgate Rd
℡0191/233 6161.
Police Corner of Market and Pilgrim sts
℡0191/214 6555.

Taxis Ranks at Haymarket, Bigg Market, and
outside Central Station. Call Noda Taxis
(℡0191/222 1888) at Central Station for advance
bookings.

Around Newcastle

The Metro runs east along both banks of the **River Tyne**, connecting Newcastle with several historic attractions, and with the sandy beaches at Tynemouth and Whitley Bay. To make a round trip of it, you can cross the river between North Shields and South Shields on the **Shields Ferry** (every 30min: Mon–Sat 7am–10.50pm, Sun 10.30am–6pm; 7min; £1 one-way); there are Metro stations on either side, a short walk from the ferry terminals. A **Metro Day Saver ticket** is valid for most buses in the county of Tyne and Wear and for the Shields ferry.

Wallsend and Segedunum

As the name tells you, **WALLSEND**, four miles east of Newcastle, was the last outpost of Hadrian's great border defence. **Segedunum**, the "strong fort" a couple of minutes' signposted walk from the Metro station (daily: April–Oct 10am–5pm; Nov–March 10am–3pm; £4.35; Ⓦwww.twmuseums.org.uk/segedunum), has been admirably developed as one of the prime attractions along the Wall. A range of activities takes place year-round, including summer re-enactments of Roman drill and equipment, and the grounds contain a fully reconstructed bathhouse, complete with heated pools and colourful frescoes. The museum combines excavated finds with interactive computer displays to give a strong flavour of life at the fort, as well as bringing the history of the site up to the present day with displays on coal mining and shipbuilding. To complete the picture, climb the 110-foot tower for a spectacular overview of the remains and the adjacent ship repair yards. The "wall's end" itself is visible at the edge of the site, close to the river and Swan Hunter shipyard, and it's from here that the **Hadrian's Wall Path** (see p.802) runs for 84 miles to Bowness-on-Solway in Cumbria; you can get your walk "passport" stamped inside the museum.

Bede's World

JARROW, five miles east of Newcastle, and south of the Tyne, has been ingrained on the national consciousness since the celebrated 1936 **Jarrow Crusade**, which saw two hundred men march the 290 miles to London to present a petition to Parliament in the wake of the devastation wrought on the shipbuilding industry during the Depression. It is also well-known for being the site of **Bede's World** (Mon–Sat 10am–5pm, Sun noon–5pm; £5.50; Ⓦwww.bedesworld.co.uk), which encompasses a fascinating museum, a reconstructed Anglo-Saxon farm with an assortment of rare-breeds farm animals, a typical medieval herb garden and some monastic ruins. All this endeavours to explore the life and times of the **Venerable Bede** (673–735 AD), who lived here as a boy, growing to become one of Europe's greatest scholars. Bede is also regarded as England's first historian – his *History of the English Church and People*, describing the struggles of the island's early Christians, was completed at Jarrow in 731. His other writings were many and varied – poetry, scientific works on chronology and the calendar, lives of St Cuthbert, historical and geographical treatises – and his influence was immense, prompting a European-wide revival in monastic learning. The complex also incorporates **St Paul's** (Mon–Sat 10am–4pm, Sun

⑬

THE NORTHEAST | Around Newcastle

2.30–4pm) with its original seventh-century dedication stone (dated 23 April,
685 AD, the earliest in England) inside, set in the arch above the chancel. Access
to the church and monastery ruins is free – you have to pay to get into the
museum and farm.

St Paul's and Bede's World are a signposted fifteen-minute walk through an
industrial estate from **Bede Metro station**. Alternatively, buses #526 or #527 run
roughly every thirty minutes from Neville Street (Central Station) in Newcastle or
Jarrow Metro station, and stop in front of the church. The site is a little way off
the A185, at the south end of the Tyne tunnel; follow the signs at the A185/A19
roundabout junction.

Wearside

There is an intense rivalry between Newcastle and **Sunderland**, twelve miles to
the southeast: both cities outraged about being lumped together in the municipal
appellation Tyne *and* Wear; both Geordies (from Newcastle) and Mackems (from
Sunderland) indignant at being taken for the other by know-nothing southerners; supporters of both local football teams jubilant at the old enemy's
misfortunes. To an outsider it can seem at times a bewildering argument over
nothing at all, but whisper in Wearside at your peril the obviously superior
charms of Newcastle as a city. Yet Sunderland and the River Wear do have their
attractions, and in the adjacent new town of **Washington** one of the more
intriguing historic sites of the northeast.

Sunderland

SUNDERLAND shares Newcastle's long history, river setting and industrial
heritage but cannot match its architectural splendour. Formed from three medieval
villages flanking the Wear, it was one of the wealthiest towns in England by 1500
and later supported the Parliamentary cause in the Civil War. The twentieth
century made and broke the town: from being the largest shipbuilding centre in
the world, Sunderland slumped after ferocious bombing during World War II.
Depression and recession did the rest.

However, it's worth a trip to visit the **Sunderland Museum** (Mon–Sat
10am–5pm, Sun 2–5pm; free; ⓦ www.twmuseums.org.uk/sunderland), easily
accessible by Metro from Newcastle. It does a very good job of telling the city's
history, while its **Winter Gardens**, housed in a steel-and-glass hothouse, invite a
treetop walk to view the impressive polished-steel column of a water sculpture.
The museum relates how Sunderland ships were once sent around the world – a

trade, incidentally, which gave the city inhabitants their "Mackem" nickname, derived from a stage in the shipbuilding process. The museum also has much to say about the city's other major trades, notably its production of lustreware (shown in the excellent Pottery Gallery) and particularly its glass industry, which dates back to the seventh century when workshops turned out stained glass for the north's monastic houses.

Across the River Wear, the landscaped **Riverside** is actually the oldest settled part of the city: walk up Fawcett Street and then Bridge Street from the centre and cross Wearmouth Bridge (around 20min). Along the north bank of the river, in front of the university buildings, the early Christian church of **St Peter** (674 AD) is the elder sibling of St Paul's Church at Jarrow and displays fragments of the oldest stained glass in the country.

The main stop for Metros from Newcastle (30–35min) is in the central train station opposite The Bridges shopping centre. The tourist office (Mon–Sat 9am–5pm, bank hols 10am–4pm; ☎0191/553 2000, ⓌWwww.visitsunderland.com) is behind the central station on the main shopping drag at 50 Fawcett St.

Washington

Five miles west of Sunderland, the River Wear keeps to the south of the new town of **WASHINGTON**, focus of much of the area's contemporary investment and manufacture. Split into planned, numbered districts and organized on American lines, it's not an obvious stop, although the original **old village** has been zealously preserved as a conservation area.

Just off the village green stands the ancestral home of the family that spawned the first US president. The "de Wessyngtons" – later the Washingtons – originally came over with William the Conqueror and by 1183 were based at the **Old Hall** (mid-March to Oct Mon–Wed & Sun 11am–5pm; £4.60; NT), where they lived until 1613. Carefully preserved as a Jacobean showpiece, the stone-flagged house has a fine kitchen, Great Hall and garden, and some exemplary wood panelling, and although none of the furniture is original to the Washington family, it is contemporaneous. Washington himself probably knew little of his family's northeast English origins – the Old Hall had passed into other hands well before the future president's great-grandfather emigrated to Virginia in 1656, an exile after the English Civil War.

The other main attraction in the area is the **Washington Wildfowl and Wetlands Centre** (April–Oct daily 9.30am–5.30pm; Nov–March 9.30am–4.30pm; £7.95; ⓌWwww.wwt.org.uk), east of town and north of the River Wear in District 15, its hundred acres designed by Sir Peter Scott and acting as a winter habitat for migratory birds, including geese, ducks, herons and flamingos. It's signposted off most local roads, four miles from the A1(M), one mile from the A19.

Hadrian's Wall

In 55 and 54 BC, Julius Caesar successfully launched two swift invasions of southeast England from his base in Gaul. The full-scale assault began under Claudius in 43 AD and, within forty years, Roman troops had reached the Firth of Tay in modern Scotland. In 83 AD, the Roman governor Agricola ventured farther north, but Rome subsequently transferred part of its army to the Danube, and the remaining legions withdrew to the frontier that was marked by the **Stanegate**, a military roadway linking Carlisle and Corbridge.

Emperor Hadrian, who toured Roman Britain in 122 AD, found this informal arrangement unsatisfactory. He wanted the empire to live at peace within stable frontiers, most of which were defined by geographical features. In northern Britain, however, there was no natural barrier and so Hadrian decided to create his own by constructing a **wall** from the Tyne to the Solway Firth. It was not intended to be an impenetrable fortification, but rather a base for patrols that could push out into hostile territory and a barrier to inhibit movement. Built up to a height of fifteen feet in places, it was punctuated by **milecastles**, which served as gates, depots and mini-barracks, and by observation **turrets**, two of which stood between each pair of milecastles. Before the Wall was even completed, major modifications were made: the bulk of the garrison were moved from Stanegate up to the Wall, occupying a chain of new **forts**, which straddled it at six- to nine-mile intervals. Simultaneously, a military zone was defined by the digging of a broad ditch, or **vallum**, on the south side of the Wall, crossed by causeways to each of the forts, turning them into the main points of access and rendering the milecastles, in this respect, largely redundant. The revised structure remained in operation until the late fourth century AD, though centralized Roman rule in Britain had broken down by then.

Most of Hadrian's Wall disappeared centuries ago, yet walking or cycling its length remains a popular pastime, following the waymarked Hadrian's Wall Path that partly shares its route with Hadrian's Cycleway. Approached from Newcastle along the valley of the Tyne, via the Roman museum and site at **Corbridge**, the cobbled market town of **Hexham** makes a good base. Most visitors stick to the best-preserved portions of the Wall, which are concentrated between **Chesters Roman Fort**, four miles north of Hexham, and **Haltwhistle**, sixteen miles to the west. Scattered along this section are a variety of key archeological sites and museums, notably the remains of **Housesteads Fort** and **Vindolanda**, the milecastle remains at **Cawfields** and, further west, the **Roman Army Museum** near Greenhead.

Information and transport

You can pick up a comprehensive Hadrian's Wall **public transport timetable** from Newcastle, Hexham, Carlisle and Haltwhistle tourist offices and the very informative **Once Brewed National Park Visitor Centre** (March–Sept daily 9.30am–5.30pm; Nov–Feb Sat & Sun 10am–3pm; ℡01434/344396), which also has exhibitions on both the Wall and the national park, or contact the **Hadrian's Wall information line** (℡01434/609700, Ⓦwww.hadrians-wall.org).

Drivers use the A69 (Hexham to Carlisle) to flit between major towns, though it's the narrower B6318 (known as the **Military Road**) that actually follows the line of the Wall from Chollerford to Greenhead. A special **Hadrian's Wall bus**, the #AD122, runs from Newcastle to Corbridge, Hexham and all the Wall sites and villages, and then on to Carlisle and Bowness-on-Solway (the end of the

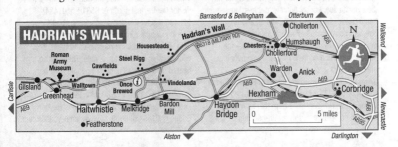

The 84-mile **Hadrian's Wall Path** (ⓦwww.nationaltrail.co.uk/hadrianswall) runs from Wallsend in the east to Bowness-on-Solway in the west, shadowing the line of the Wall, with over forty other linear or circular walks accessible en route. You could walk the main route in four days, but that's allowing little or no time to explore the archeological sites, towns and villages on the way, so a week is a more realistic timescale. To prove you made it, a "path passport" is available, which you get stamped at seven locations along the way. Contact the Hadrian's Wall information line (see p.801) for an official free **walking and accommodation guide**; there's also the *Hadrian's Wall Path: National Trail Guide* (Aurum Press), which details the route in exhaustive detail. It's essential to book accommodation ahead (see below) and be prepared to spend some nights a few miles from the end of your day's walk, though the Hadrian's Wall bus service is a boon in this respect. The walk is best tackled between May and October, as the wet winter months are not only heavier going but also contribute to erosion and archeological damage. For the same reason, keep off the Wall itself at all times.

Hadrian's Wall Path). This operates between Easter and October, up to five times a day in each direction; a typical one-way ticket, from Hexham to Vindolanda, costs £2.90, though **Day Rover** tickets (1/3/7 days £8/16/32) are better value. There's also a year-round hourly service on the #685 bus between Newcastle and Carlisle, and other local services from Carlisle and Hexham, which provide access to various points on the Wall. The nearest **train** stations are on the Newcastle–Carlisle line at Corbridge, Hexham, Bardon Mill and Haltwhistle – a combination Rail Rover ticket with the Hadrian's Wall bus allows travel between Newcastle and Carlisle. The best place to **park and ride** is at Once Brewed visitor centre, where there's all-day parking and a bus stop for the Hadrian's Wall bus. The side road beyond the centre continues for half a mile down to Vindolanda and then runs on to the A69, where you turn left for Haydon Bridge and Hexham or right for Haltwhistle.

Accommodation, eating and drinking

In addition to the B&Bs and pubs in the countryside around the Wall, Corbridge (see p.806), Hexham (see p.805) and Haltwhistle (see p.804) have a good selection of accommodation and places to eat and drink.

Carraw B&B Military Rd, Humshaugh ☏01434/689857, ⓦwww.carraw.co.uk. It's not often you can say "I've slept on Hadrian's Wall", but here you can – this beautiful B&B, run by a friendly couple, is built slap bang on Hadrian's masterpiece and boasts stunning views as far as the eye can see. Lovely homely touches, like home-made shortbread and cake on arrival, hot-water bottles and luxurious toiletries make this place really special. Delicious breakfasts – the nutty granola is a winner. Three-course evening meals £25. ❸

Grindon Cartshed 4 miles north of Haydon Bridge ☏01434/684273, ⓦwww.grindon-cartshed.co.uk. There are wonderful views from this cosy B&B, which is complemented by a self-catering farmhouse barn next door. Evening meals (£19) are available on request. Suitable for wheelchair users – ask for details. Self-catering Oct–March (1 week £330–370). ❶

Hadrian's Wall Camping and Caravan Site 1 mile southwest of Once Brewed National Park Visitor Centre, just south of B6318 ☏01434/320495, ⓦwww.romanwallcamping.co.uk. Friendly, family-run site half a mile from the Wall, with showers, washing machine and dryer, and bike storage; breakfast available. There's also a heated bunk barn sleeping 10 people (£15 per person). Open all year. £10 per tent, plus £2 per person; campervan £12.50, plus £2 per person. **Langley Castle** A686, 2 miles south of Haydon Bridge ☏01434/688888, ⓦwww.langleycastle.com.

Appropriately regal rooms – four-poster beds, sumptuous furnishings and beautiful bathrooms with saunas and spa baths – in this turreted medieval castle. The cheaper rooms are in the grounds, looking onto the castle. There's also an atmospheric restaurant, cocktail bar, lounge and gardens. ❸, castle rooms ❺

Once Brewed YHA Military Rd, Once Brewed ☎0845/3719753, ✉oncebrewed@yha.org.uk. Next to the visitor centre, providing walking leaflets, packed lunches, three-course dinners, kitchen and lounge. Dorms (from £11.95) are small (mostly four-bed), with modern facilities. Closed Dec & Jan.

Twice Brewed Inn Military Rd ☎01434/344534. Friendly community pub, 50 yards up from Once Brewed visitor centre and hostel, with simple rooms, food served all day, beer garden, local beers on tap and perhaps the northeast's largest selection of rums (there's a choice of 54). En suites are slightly pricier. ❷

Willowford Farm 2.5 miles west of Greenhead ☎016977/47962, ⓦwww .willowford.co.uk. Just over the Northumbrian border in Cumbria, this farmhouse B&B makes a lovely, tranquil base to explore the Wall. Rooms are in converted farm buildings and decked out with pretty wooden beams and large beds. Closed Nov–March. No credit or debit cards. ❸

Eating and drinking

Barrasford Arms Barrasford, 9 miles north of Hexham ☎01434/681237. Endearingly ramshackle, welcoming and homely, this pub serves great traditional British food with a French twist; dishes could include mixed-game pie with juniper and orange and a suet pastry crust (£13.50), and apple and local hedgerow fruit crumble with Calvados ice cream (£5). Booking advisable. Closed Mon lunch.

Battlesteads Country Inn and Restaurant Wark on Tyne, 12 miles north of Hexham ☎01434/230209. In a charming little village by a trickling stream, this locally renowned restaurant with a lovely beer garden uses fresh produce sourced from within a 30-mile radius. Make sure you leave room for their famed whisky-and-marmalade bread-and-butter pudding (£5.75). Best to book.

General Havelock Inn Haydon Bridge ☎01434/684376. Eighteenth-century country inn that specializes in tasty food, from mushroom tagliatelle and fish pie to summer pudding and ice cream sundaes. Main meals average around £17.

Milecastle Inn Military Rd, 2 miles south of Haltwhistle ☎01434/321372. Just off the Wall, this place is known for its great home-cooked pies – the game one is popular, but there's also fish and wild boar.

Housesteads to Cawfields

Overlooking the bleak Northumbrian moors from the top of the Whin Sill, **Housesteads Roman Fort** (daily: April–Sept 10am–6pm; Oct–March 10am–4pm; £4.80; EH & NT), has long been the most popular site on the Wall. It's an unorthodox building for its time, as forts were usually constructed to straddle the line of the Wall, encroaching purposefully onto barbarian territory. Housesteads is instead built on a slope; its foundations follow the edge of the cliff, and use the Wall as its northern defensive wall. Access is via the tiny **museum**, from where you stroll across to the south gate, beside which lie the remains of the civilian settlement that was dependent on the one thousand infantrymen stationed within. The fort is also home to some of the best-preserved Roman latrines in Britain.

You don't need to pay for entrance to Housesteads if you simply intend to walk west along the Wall from here. The three-mile hike past the lovely wooded **Crag Lough** to **Steel Rigg** (car park) offers the most fantastic views, especially when you spy the course of the Wall as it threads over the crags ahead. Leaving the Wall at Steel Rigg, it's roughly half a mile south to the main road (B6318) and the visitor centre at **Once Brewed** (see p.801). Otherwise, Wall-walkers can continue another three miles west from Steel Rigg to **Cawfields** (free access), where the remains of another milecastle are perched on one of the most rugged crags on this section. There's a car park and picnic site at Cawfields, while if you make your way the mile or so south to the main B6318 you can recuperate at the *Milecastle Inn* (see above).

Vindolanda

The excavated garrison fort of **Vindolanda** actually predates the Wall itself, though most of what you see today dates from the second to third century AD, when the fort was a thriving metropolis of five hundred soldiers with its own civilian settlement attached. The site (daily: mid-Feb to March & Oct 10am–5pm; April–Sept 10am–6pm; £5.90, joint admission with Roman Army Museum £9; Ⓦwww.vindolanda.com) is operated by the private Vindolanda Trust, which has done an excellent job of imaginatively presenting its finds.

The ongoing **excavations** at Vindolanda are spread over a wide area, with civilian houses, inn, guest quarters, administrative building, commander's house and main gates all clearly visible. The path through the excavations descends to what's termed the **open-air museum**, where you can walk into reconstructions of a shrine to the water nymphs, a shop and a house, all with lively sound commentaries. Beyond lies the café, shop and **museum**, the latter housing the largest collection of Roman leather items ever discovered on a single site – dozens of shoes, belts, even a pair of baby boots – which were preserved in the black silt of waterlogged ditches. The most intriguing sections cover the excavated hoard of **writing tablets**, which will be returning home to Vindolanda from the British Museum in 2011. Between 1973 and 1992, two hundred significant texts were discovered on the site, dealing with subjects as diverse as clerical filing systems and children's schoolwork. Then, in 1993, final excavations from a bonfire site revealed more tablets, apparently discarded when the garrison received orders in 103–104 AD to move to the Danube to participate in Emperor Trajan's Second Dacian War. The writings depict graphically the realities of military life in Northumberland: soldiers' requests for more beer, birthday party invitations, court reports, even letters from home containing gifts of underwear for freezing frontline troops.

Roman Army Museum

Trekking four miles further west from Cawfields takes you past the remains of Great Chesters Fort before reaching a spectacular section of the Wall, known as the **Walltown Crags**. The views from here are marvellous and there's a handy nearby car park, picnic site and simple tea-and-ice-cream café. Very near the crags, at Carvoran, you can call into the Vindolanda Trust's **Roman Army Museum** (same hours as Vindolanda; £4.50, joint ticket with Vindolanda £9; Ⓦwww .vindolanda.com), which tells you everything there is to know about life in the Roman army by way of exhibits, dioramas, reconstructions and games. There's also a virtual-reality aerial "flight" along the Wall.

Haltwhistle

A couple of miles off the Wall, **HALTWHISTLE** is home to the only full set of amenities (ATMs, supermarket, shops and cafés) near the Wall west of Hexham and also has a lively **market** each Thursday. It also claims to be the very centre of Britain, something you could debate with the **tourist office** (hours subject to change but most likely Easter–Oct Mon–Sat 9.30am–12.30pm & 1–5pm, Sun 11am–3pm; Nov–Easter daily 9.30am–noon & 1–4.30pm; ℡01434/322002), which at the time of writing was in the old train station on the western edge of town, close to the A69, though it is likely to move to the library on Westgate.

Accommodation is dotted about the town and includes: the *Centre of Britain* hotel (℡01434/322422, Ⓦwww.centre-of-britain.org.uk; ❶) on Main Street, which has tasteful rooms and a popular restaurant; and *Ashcroft B&B* (℡01434/320213, Ⓦwww.ashcroftguesthouse.co.uk; ❸), housed in an elegant former vicarage on Lantys Lonnen – a turn off Main Street, by the Working Men's

Club. A mile and a half to the west of town is *Wyndon Farm* (℡ 01434/321702, Ⓦ www.wydon-haltwhistle.co.uk; ❷), a working farm with three spacious and attractive rooms. For good **food** in a pretty setting, try *The Wallace Arms*, at Rowfoot, near Featherstone, a couple of miles south of Haltwhistle.

Hexham and around

In 671, on a bluff above the Tyne, sixteen miles east of Haltwhistle and four miles west of Corbridge, St Wilfrid founded a Benedictine monastery whose church was, according to contemporary accounts, the finest to be seen north of the Alps. Unfortunately, its gold and silver proved irresistible to the Vikings, who savaged the place in 876, but the church was rebuilt in the eleventh century as part of an Augustinian priory and the town of **HEXHAM** grew up in its shadow. It's a handsome market town – the only significant stop between Newcastle and Carlisle – and however focused you are on seeing the Wall, you'd do well to give Hexham a night or even make it your base.

Arrival, information and accommodation

The **bus station** is off Priestpopple, a few minutes' stroll east of the abbey, while the **train station** sits on the northeastern edge of the town centre, a ten-minute walk from the abbey; the **tourist office** (mid-May to Oct Mon–Sat 9am–6pm, Sun 10am–5pm; Oct to mid-May Mon–Sat 9am–5pm; ℡ 01434/652220) is halfway between the two, in the pay-and-display **car park** at Waitrose. Central **accommodation** includes the *Beaufort Hotel* (℡ 01434/602331, Ⓦ www .bestwestern.co.uk; ❷), on Beaumont Street, where the rooms are functional but clean and comfortable, and *Hallbank* (℡ 01434/605567, Ⓦ www.hallbankguest house.com; ❹), tucked away behind the Old Gaol, a pretty guesthouse that serves evening meals – book in advance.

The Town

The stately exterior of **Hexham Abbey** (daily 9.30am–5pm; free), properly the Priory Church of St Andrew, still dominates the west side of the Market Place. Entry is through the south transept, where there's a bruised but impressive first-century tombstone honouring Flavinus, a standard-bearer in the Roman cavalry. The memorial lies at the foot of the broad, well-worn steps of the canons' **night stair**, one of the few such staircases – providing access from the monastery to the church – to have survived the Dissolution. Beyond, most of the high-arched nave dates from an Edwardian restoration and it's here that you gain access to the **crypt**, a Saxon structure made out of old Roman stones, where pilgrims once viewed the abbey's reliquaries. At the end of the nave is the splendid sixteenth-century rood-screen, whose complex tracery envelops the portraits of local bishops. Behind the screen, the chancel displays the inconsequential-looking **frith-stool**, an eighth-century stone chair that was once believed to have been used by St Wilfrid, rendering it holy enough to serve as the medieval sanctuary stool.

The rest of Hexham's large and irregularly shaped **Market Place** (main market day is Tuesday, farmers' market second and fourth Sunday of the month) is peppered with remains of its medieval past. The massive walls of the fourteenth-century **Moot Hall** were built to serve as the gatehouse to "The Hall", a well-protected enclosure that was garrisoned against the Scots. The archbishops also built their own prison nearby, a formidable fortified tower dating from 1330 and constructed using stones plundered from the Roman ruins at Corbridge. Known as the **Old Gaol**, this accommodates Hexham's local history museum (April–June daily 10am–4.30pm; July–Sept Tues–Sat 11am–4.30pm; Oct, Nov, Feb & March Tues & Sat 11am–4.30pm; Ⓦ www.tynedaleheritage.org; £3.95).

Eating and drinking

Hexham has plenty of **cafés**, delis and a few Indian **restaurants**, but if you don't mind heading out of town, there are a couple of great **pubs** nearby.

Boatside Inn Warden, 3 miles northwest of Hexham ☎01434/602233. Pretty countryside pub with hearty meals and real ales on tap.

Bouchon Bistrot 4 Gilesgate ☎01434/609943. Stylish restaurant that serves sophisticated French dishes, such as duck confit with *lyonnaise* potatoes (£14.50) and *griottines clafoutis* with pistachio ice cream (£5.50). Closed Sun & Mon.

Danielle's Bistro 12 Eastgate ☎01434/601122.

Simple, good-value French–Italian food; three courses go for £16. Closed Sun.

Dipton Mill Inn Dipton Mill Rd, 2 miles south of Hexham ☎01434/606577. A lovely, traditional country pub that serves wholesome bar meals and its own-brewed beer.

Rat Inn Anick, 2 miles northeast of Hexham ☎01434/602814. In a glorious hillside location, this quaint pub has a roaring fire in winter, pretty summer garden and fine food (mains from £10).

Chesters Roman Fort

Four miles north of Hexham – and half a mile west of present-day Chollerford – **Chesters Roman Fort** (April–Sept daily 10am–6pm; Oct–March 10am–4pm; £4.80; EH), otherwise known as Cilurnum, was built to guard the Roman bridge over the river. Enough remains of the original structure to pick out the design of the fort, and each section has been clearly labelled, but the highlight is down by the river where the vestibule, changing room and steam range of the garrison's **bathhouse** are still visible, along with the furnace and the latrines. The **museum** at the entrance has an excellent collection of Roman stonework – in particular, look out for Juno (now headless) in a delicately pleated dress standing on a cow, one of the finest pieces of statuary found along the Wall.

Corbridge and around

CORBRIDGE is a quiet and well-heeled commuter town overlooking the River Tyne from the top of a steep ridge. This spur of land was first settled by the Saxons, and their handiwork survives in parts of the **church of St Andrew**, on the central Market Place, but it's the adjacent **Vicar's Pele** that catches the eye, an unusually well-preserved late-medieval fortified tower-house in which the priest could hole up in times of strife.

There's plenty of **accommodation** in and around town but the shining light is the *Angel Inn* on Main Street (☎01434/632119, ⓦwww.theangelofcorbridge.com; ❹), which has classy rooms above a very popular restaurant (mains £10–15). They also have an annexe – the *Angel Radcliffe* (same contact details; ❹) – across the road. A couple of miles north of town, signposted from Matften village, is *Matfen Hall* ☎01661/886500, ⓦwww.primahotels.co.uk/matfen; ❻), an elegant pile with a 27-hole golf course, spa and swimming pool. The *Valley Restaurant* (☎01434/633434; closed Sun), in the creeper-covered station house, right on the railway line, serves delicious Indian **meals**, while *Brocksbushes* farm shop and tearooms, on the A69 a mile or two outside of town, is a great place to pick up picnic food, organic fruit and veg or even pick your own strawberries and raspberries in the summer.

Corbridge Roman Site

One mile west of the Market Place, accessible either by road or along the riverside footpath, lies **Corbridge Roman Site** (April–Sept daily 10am–6pm; Oct daily 10am–4pm; Nov–March Sat & Sun 10am–4pm; £4.80; EH), which was first established as a supply base for the Roman advance into Scotland in 80 AD and thus predates the Wall itself. It remained in regular military use until the end of the second century, after which a town quickly developed around it – most of the visible archeological remains date from this period, when "Corstopitum" served as the nerve centre of Hadrian's Wall, guarding the bridge at the intersection of Stanegate and Dere Street. The extensive remains provide an insight into the layout of the civilian town, showing the foundations of temples, public baths, garrison headquarters, workshops and houses as well as the best-preserved **Roman granaries** in Britain. In the site **museum** the celebrated Lion and Stag fountain-head – the so-called "Corbridge Lion" – gets pride of place; to the Romans, the lion and its prey symbolized the triumph of life over death.

Cherryburn, Prudhoe and Wylam

The local Roman remains are the big draw, but it's also an easy drive from Corbridge to three small-scale attractions along the eastern Tyne valley road (A695), which can make a good half-day's outing by car.

Around six miles east of Corbridge, close to the south bank of the Tyne and signposted off the A695 at Mickley Square, **Cherryburn** (mid-March to Oct daily except Wed 11am–5pm; £4; NT) was the birthplace of Thomas Bewick, England's greatest engraver (1753–1828). Still offering beautiful views of the rolling landscape that inspired Bewick, the simple cottage sits below a farmhouse gallery, which contains displays that tell the story of his far-reaching legacy. Sunday is the big day here, with afternoon demonstrations of printing and woodblock engraving, and traditional Northumbrian music in the garden.

Back on the A695 through Prudhoe, moated **Prudhoe Castle** (April–Sept Mon & Thurs–Sun 10am–5pm; £4.20; EH) is worth a quick stop. Occupied continuously since the twelfth century – and the only castle in Northumberland never to have been taken by the Scots – its handsome grounds make an ideal place for a picnic. Finally, a couple of miles beyond Prudhoe at **WYLAM**, a whitewashed miner's cottage near the old Wylam Colliery is preserved as the **Birthplace of George Stephenson** (April–Oct Thurs–Sun noon–5pm; £2; NT), the celebrated railway engineer. He was born here in 1781 and furnishings inside reflect the period – the whole family living in one room.

Northumberland National Park

Northwest Northumberland, the great triangular chunk of land between Hadrian's Wall and the coastal plain, is dominated by the wide-skied landscapes of **Northumberland National Park** (Ⓦ www.northumberland-national-park.org.uk), whose four hundred windswept square miles rise to the Cheviot Hills on the Scottish border. These uplands are interrupted by great slabs of forest, mostly the conifer plantations of the Forestry Commission, and a string of river valleys, of which Coquetdale, Tynedale and Redesdale are the longest. Remote from lowland law and order, these dales were once the homelands of the **Border Reivers**, turbulent clans who ruled the local roost from the thirteenth to the sixteenth century. The Reivers took advantage of the struggles between England and Scotland to engage in endless cross-border rustling and general brigandage, activities recalled by the ruined bastles (fortified farmhouses) and peels (defensive tower-houses) that lie dotted across the landscape.

The most popular hiking trail is the **Pennine Way**, which, entering the national park at Hadrian's Wall, cuts up through **Bellingham**, a pleasant town on the banks of the North Tyne, on its way to **The Cheviot**, the park's highest peak at 2674ft, and finishes at Kirk Yetholm, over the border in Scotland; as an introduction it's hard to beat the lovely moorland scenery of the fifteen-mile stretch between Housesteads and Bellingham. Bellingham is also the gateway to **Kielder Water**, a massive pine-surrounded reservoir, nature reserve and watersports centre. Further north, Victorian **Rothbury**, in Coquetdale, is convenient for walks in the Simonside Hills and for visits to the country estates of **Cragside** and **Wallington**, while footpaths lead into the Cheviot Hills from the hiking centre of **Wooler**. Idiosyncratically restored **Chillingham**, with its gruesome torture chambers and rooms stuffed with antiques, offers a different view of a stately home; the estate also accommodates an equally unusual herd of wild cattle.

Bellingham

The stone terraces of **BELLINGHAM** (pronounced Bellinjum) slope up from the banks of the Tyne on the eastern edge of the Northumberland National Park. There's nothing outstanding about the place, but it is a restful spot set in rural surroundings, and it does contain the medieval **church of St Cuthbert**, which has an unusual stone-vaulted roof – designed (successfully) to prevent raiding Border Reivers from burning the church to the ground.

Buses from Hexham stop on Market Place, a few hundred yards down from the helpful **tourist office** on Main Street (April–Oct Mon–Sat 9.30am–1pm & 2–5.30pm, Sun 1–5pm; Nov–March Mon–Fri 1–4pm; ☎01434/220616), housed in Bellingham's former Poor House building. **Accommodation** in the area includes the *Riverdale Hall Hotel* (☎01434/220254, ⓦwww.riverdalehallhotel.co.uk; ❷), a country house on the village's western edge, with an indoor swimming pool and extensive grounds, and *Bridgeford Farm* (☎01434/220940, ⓦwww.bridgefordfarm bandb.co.uk; ❷), two miles south of the village, a working farm with three en-suite rooms. Bellingham has a bank with an ATM, small supermarket and a couple of **cafés**, though otherwise you're dependent on the bar meals served at the pubs.

Kielder Water and Forest

The road from Bellingham follows the North Tyne River west and skirts the forested edge of **Kielder Water** (ⓦwww.kielder.org), passing the assorted visitor centres, waterside parks, picnic areas and anchorages that fringe its southern shore. The reservoir – built originally to service the needs of a now largely defunct steel industry – and the surrounding forest make a good day out: there's great cycling and hiking, along with plenty of watersports such as yachting, windsurfing and waterskiing.

Tower Knowe visitor centre (daily: April–June & Sept 10am–5pm; July & Aug 10am–6pm; Oct 10am–4pm; ☎0845/155 0236), eight miles from Bellingham, has a café and an exhibition on the history of the valley and reservoir. Another four miles west, the **Leaplish** waterside park, bar and restaurant (opening hours vary; ☎01434/251000) is the focus of most of Kielder's outdoor activities and accommodation (see box opposite). There's also a heated indoor pool and sauna, and the **Bird of Prey Centre** (☎01434/250400) lays on entertaining flying demonstrations (daily 10.30am–4.30pm; demonstrations May–Sept 1.30pm & 3pm, Oct–April 2pm; £6).

Five miles from Leaplish at the top of the reservoir and just three miles from the Scottish border, the forestry settlement of KIELDER VILLAGE is dominated by Kielder Castle, built in 1775 as the hunting lodge of the Duke of Northumberland and now the **Kielder Castle Visitor Centre** (April–Oct daily 10am–5pm; Nov Sat & Sun 11am–4pm; Dec daily 11am–4pm; ☎01434/250209), where free exhibitions appraise the work of the Forestry Commission. There's also a café and a full programme of events and activities.

The castle is at the heart of **Kielder Forest Park**, Britain's largest forest, comprising several million spruce trees, crisscrossed by trails and home to red squirrels, deer, otters and countless birds, including goshawks, merlins and ospreys. Several clearly marked footpaths and bike trails lead from the castle into the forest, or you can explore some of the contemporary sculptures that Kielder is increasingly known for – like the **Minotaur Maze**, near the castle, or the **Skyspace** (1.5 miles from the castle), a light-and-space chamber – visit at dusk or dawn.

Practicalities

You really need your **own transport** to see much of Kielder, especially on a short visit. Otherwise, you're dependent on the local bus from Bellingham, which calls at Tower Knowe, Leaplish and Kielder, and less regularly at Stannersburn and Falstone. Kielder village has a general store, garage, post office, tearoom and pub (Oct–April closed Mon).

As well as the **accommodation** options listed below, there are several other B&Bs in Kielder village and the surrounding area – the visitor centres can assist. The forest also has a number of basic **campsites** (℡01434/220242; no facilities; no vehicle access) – bring plenty of midge repellent.

Accommodation and eating

Falstone Barns Falstone, 3 miles east of Kielder Water ℡01434/240251, @www.falstonebarns .com. Set in a large, private and tranquil estate, these four glamorous holiday apartments have been beautifully converted from barn buildings – you could stay in the fresh and airy French Bourgeois apartment or go for the cosy Romantic Medieval suite. ❹

Hollybush Inn Greenhaugh, 12 miles east of Kielder Water ℡01434/240391, @www .thehollybushinn.net. Rustic old B&B in a remote location, with four attractive rooms and good, hearty breakfasts. ❸

Kielder Lodges Leaplish Waterside Park ℡01434/251000, @www.nwl.co.uk/kielder. Luxurious Scandinavian-style self-catering lodges for £290–1095 per week depending on size and season (cheaper 3-night stays available all year) – all have lovely views over the lake and forest, and facilities onsite include pool, sauna and mini-golf.

Kielder YHA Kielder village ℡0845/371 9126, @kielder@yha.org.uk. Well-equipped activity-based hostel, with some two- and three-bed rooms plus small dorms. Ring ahead in winter to check that it's open. Dorm beds from £15.95. ❶

Pheasant Inn Stannersburn, 2 miles east of Kielder Water ℡01434/240382, @www .thepheasantinn.com. The food and the relaxed ambience are the main draws at this lovely seventeenth-century inn – specialities include locally sourced fish dishes (around £12) and home-made game pie (£11.95). They also have eight very comfortable bedrooms. ❸

Snabdough Farm Tarset, 5 miles west of Bellingham ℡01434/240239, @snabdoughfishinginfo.com. Lovely stone farmhouse B&B with three bedrooms and excellent salmon fishing in the river nearby. Residents can rent fishing rods for £40 (non-residents £50). Call for directions. Closed Nov–Easter. No credit cards. ❶

Rothbury and around

ROTHBURY, straddling the River Coquet thirty miles northeast of Hexham, prospered as a late Victorian resort because it gave ready access to the forests, burns and ridges of the **Simonside Hills**. In the centre, where the High Street widens to form a broad triangle, there are hints of past pretensions in the assertive facades overlooking the Rothbury Cross, erected in 1902. It's a popular spot for walkers, with several of the best local trails beginning from the Simonside Hills car park, a couple of miles southwest of Rothbury. The town is also a handy base for visiting two of the northeast's most interesting landed estates, while each July a renowned **traditional music festival** (ⓦwww.rothbury-traditional-music.co.uk) brings folk into town from all over the region for Northumbrian pipe music, dancing and story-telling.

The **Tourist Information and National Park Visitor Centre** (April–Oct daily 10am–5pm; Nov–March Sat & Sun 10am–3pm; ⓣ01669/620887, ⓦwww .visit-rothbury.co.uk) is near the cross on Church Street. With Alnwick (twelve miles) and the coast so close, there's no particular need to **stay**, although a good choice is *The Queen's Head* (ⓣ01669/620470, ⓦwww.queensheadrothbury .com; ❷, including breakfast), a traditional pub with seven surprisingly modern, boutique-style rooms. There are a few places to **eat and drink** – two or three cafés, delis and a couple of pubs – dotted along the High Street.

Cragside

Victorian Rothbury was dominated by Sir William, later the first **Lord Armstrong**, the immensely wealthy nineteenth-century arms manufacturer, shipbuilder and engineer who built his country home at **Cragside** (mid-March to Oct Tues–Sun & bank hols 1–5pm; opens 11am during school hols; £12.60, gardens only £9; NT), a mile to the east of the village. He hired Richard Norman Shaw, one of the period's top architects, who produced a grandiose Tudor-style mansion that is entirely out of place in the Northumbrian countryside. The interior is stuffed with Armstrong's dark furnishings and fittings, enlivened by the William Morris stained glass in the library and the dining-room inglenook. Later extensions catered for Armstrong's numerous hobbies and diversions – his natural history and shell collection was placed in the gallery, a billiard room was added, while the marble-decked drawing room was completed in time for the visit of the Prince and Princess of Wales in 1884. Doubtless, they were too well brought up to comment on Shaw's "masterpiece", the spectacularly hideous Renaissance-style marble chimneypiece, which uses ten tonnes of the stuff to overly sentimental effect. Armstrong was also an avid innovator, and in 1880 he managed to make Cragside the first house in the world to be lit by hydro-electric power. The remains of the original pumping system are still visible in the **grounds**, which, together with the splendid formal gardens, have longer opening hours (mid-March to Oct Tues–Sun 10.30am–5pm; Nov to mid-Dec Wed–Sun 11am–4pm). Over at the visitor centre there's a café/restaurant.

Wallington

Around thirteen miles south of Rothbury, down the B6342 and a mile out of Cambo, stands **Wallington** (March–Oct Mon & Wed–Fri 1–5pm, Sat & Sun 11am–5pm; £9.20, gardens only £7.10; NT), an ostentatious mansion rebuilt in the 1740s by Sir Walter Blackett, the coal- and lead-mine owner. The house is known for its Rococo plasterwork and William Bell Scott's Pre-Raphaelite murals of scenes from Northumbrian history. Children will love the collection of dolls' houses, one of which has 36 rooms and was originally fitted with running water and a working lift. However, it's the magnificent **gardens and grounds** (daily dawn–dusk) that are the real delight, with lawns, woods and lakes that are traced by easy-to-follow footpaths. A leisurely circuit of the estate might take you a couple of hours, depending on how long you spend in the magical **walled garden** (daily 10am–7pm), exploring its terracing, conservatories, arbours and water features. There are events, concerts and activities throughout the year, as well as a café and farm shop on site.

Wooler

Stone-terraced **WOOLER**, a grey one-street market town twenty miles north of Rothbury, may have been wholly rebuilt after a calamitous fire in the 1860s, but its hillside setting high above Harthope Burn and its proximity to the Cheviot Hills do much to lift the spirits. For the most extensive views you'll have to tackle the trek to **The Cheviot** (2674ft) itself, seven miles to the southwest, which is the highest point in the Cheviot Hills. Starting out from *Wooler Youth Hostel* at 30 Cheviot St, count on four hours up, a little less back – from Hawsen Burn, the nearest navigable point, it's still two hours walking there and back. Wooler is also a staging-post on **St Cuthbert's Way**, the trans-Cheviot route, which runs west from the town to Kirk Yetholm and beyond or northeast to Holy Island.

Frequent buses link Wooler with Berwick-upon-Tweed and Alnwick, the two nearest towns, and the **bus station** is set back off the High Street. At the other end of the High Street, off Burnhouse Road (by the free car park), you'll find the **tourist office** (Easter–Oct Mon–Sat 10am–1.30pm & 2–4.30pm, Sun 10am–1.30pm & 2–6pm; Oct–Easter Sat & Sun 10am–2pm; ℡01668/282123), which has a list of the surrounding **B&Bs**. One of the best is the snug *Tilldale House* (℡01668/281450, Ⓦwww.tilldalehouse.co.uk; ❷) in the middle of the High Street, while there's also the *Tankerville Arms* (℡01668/281581, Ⓦwww.tankervillehotel.co.uk; ❷), just off the A697 below town, a welcoming seventeenth-century coaching inn. The top **restaurant** in town is *Milan* (℡01668/283692; booking essential), which serves excellent-value French and Italian food, including pizza and pasta for around £10. The restaurant at the *Tankerville Arms* is a good alternative.

Chillingham

Six miles southeast of Wooler, **Chillingham Castle** (Easter–Oct daily except Sat noon–5pm, gardens and tearooms from noon; £7; Ⓦwww.chillingham-castle .com) provides a refreshing counterpoint to the high-minded tidiness of most stately homes. Starting life as an eleventh-century tower, the castle was augmented at regular intervals until the nineteenth century, but then from 1933 was largely left to the elements for fifty years, until the present owner set about restoring it in his own eccentric way: bedrooms, living rooms and even a grisly torture chamber (designed to "cause maximum shock") are decorated with all manner of historical paraphernalia to give an idea of how the place would have looked through the ages. Several self-catering **apartments** within the castle are available, either by the night (℡01668/215359; ❺) or by the week.

In 1220, the adjoining 365 acres of parkland were enclosed to protect the local wild cattle for hunting and food. And so the **Chillingham Wild Cattle** (visits Easter–Oct daily except Sat 10am–noon & 2–4pm; £5; ℡01668/215250, Ⓦwww .chillinghamwildcattle.com) – a fierce, primeval herd with white coats, black muzzles and black tips to their horns – have remained to this day, cut off from mixing with domesticated breeds. You can visit these unique relics, who number about seventy, but only in the company of a warden, as the animals are potentially dangerous and need to be protected from outside infection. The visit takes two hours and involves a short country walk before viewing the cattle at a safe distance, as the warden expands upon their history, heritage and even their DNA. The site is signposted from the A1 and A697; bring strong shoes or walking boots if it's wet.

The Northumberland coast

The low-lying **Northumberland coast** stretches 64 miles north from Newcastle to the Scottish border. In its heyday at the beginning of the twentieth century this area employed a quarter of Britain's colliers, but the mines closed years ago and entire local communities were devastated – you can revisit those days at **Woodhorn**, where the colliery has now been reborn as an evocative museum complex.

Beyond Amble and its marina, you emerge into the best part of the coast, a pastoral, gently wooded landscape that spreads over the thirty-odd miles to Berwick-upon-Tweed. On the way there's a succession of mighty fortresses, beginning with **Warkworth** and **Alnwick castles**, former and present strongholds of the Percys, the county's biggest landowners. Further along, there's the formidable fastness of **Bamburgh** and then, last of all, the magnificent Elizabethan ramparts surrounding **Berwick-upon-Tweed**. In between you'll find splendid sandy beaches – notably at Warkworth, Bamburgh and the tiny seaside resort of **Alnmouth** – as well as the site of the Lindisfarne monastery on **Holy Island** and the sea-bird and nature reserve of the **Farne Islands**, reached by boat from Seahouses.

Public transport connections are good – only Holy Island is tricky to reach, an infrequent bus from Berwick-upon-Tweed being the sole connection. **By car**, the A1 from Alnwick (and, before that, from Newcastle) provides the fastest route to Berwick, though it runs inland, away from the coast. The B1340 from Alnwick and its offshoots – signposted "Coastal Route" – are the prettier ones to follow.

Woodhorn

Although mining in Woodhorn stopped in 1981, you can still visit the old colliery buildings as part of the fantastic **Woodhorn Northumberland Museum** (Wed–Sun: April–Oct 10am–5pm; Nov–March 10am–4pm; free, £2.50 parking; ⓦwww.experiencewoodhorn.com). You can trace the lot of a miner, down the pit or in his pigeon loft, while a display in the East Gallery shows intimate and touching paintings of daily life by the **Ashington Art Group** – miners who learned to paint at night school in the 1930s. The museum is fifteen miles north of Newcastle, signposted off the A189.

Warkworth

WARKWORTH, a coastal hamlet set in a loop of the River Coquet a couple of miles from Amble, is best seen from the north, from where the grey stone terraces of the long main street slope up towards the commanding remains of **Warkworth Castle** (April–Sept daily 10am–5pm; Oct daily 10am–4pm; Nov–March Mon, Sat & Sun

Top 5 Northumbrian castles

▶▶ **Chillingham** Grand old medieval castle, home to some wonderful cattle and, so they say, a fleet of ghosts and ghoulies. See p.811.

▶▶ **Warkworth** The keep here is made up of a maze of marvellously echoey rooms, twisting staircases and dark niches, perfect for a game of hide and seek. See p.812.

▶▶ **Alnwick** Scene of many a *Harry Potter* escapade, this imposing castle is crammed with suitably luxurious rooms, and complete with stunning grounds. See p.813.

▶▶ **Dunstanburgh** This enormous crumbling pile crouches on a spectacular headland overlooking the golden Embleton sands. See p.815.

▶▶ **Bamburgh** Sits regally on a rocky plateau and is home to an impressive armoury, dungeon and the colossal King's Hall with an exquisite teak ceiling. See p.817.

10am–4pm; £4.50; EH), which has a remarkably well-preserved keep. Mostly built in the fourteenth century, it's a fine example of the designs developed by the castle-builders of Plantagenet England. It was here that most of the Percy family, earls of Northumberland, chose to live throughout the fourteenth and fifteenth centuries.

The main street sweeps down into the attractive village, flattening out at Dial Place and the Church of St Lawrence before curving right to cross the River Coquet. Just over the bridge, a signposted quarter-mile lane leads to the **beach**, which stretches for five miles from Amble to Alnmouth.

Accommodation in the village includes the very comfortable B&B, *Roxbro House* (T01665/711416, Wwww.roxbrohouse.co.uk; ❸), at 5 Castle Terrace, just a stone's throw from the castle.

Alnmouth

It's just three miles north from Warkworth to the seaside resort of **ALNMOUTH**, with its charming, narrow centre backing onto a beautiful, sandy beach and rolling dunes. Alnmouth was a prosperous port up until 1806, when the sea, driven by a freakish gale, broke through to the river and changed its course, moving the estuary from the south to the north side of Church Hill and rendering the original harbour useless. Alnmouth never really recovered, though it has been a low-key holiday spot since Victorian times, as attested by the elegant seaside villas at the south end of town. Many come for the golf: the village's splendid nine-hole course, right on the coast, was built in 1869, and dune-strollers really do have to heed the "Danger – Flying Golf Balls" signs that adorn Marine Road.

There are local **bus services** from Alnwick and Warkworth, while the regular Newcastle–Alnwick bus also passes through Alnmouth and calls at its **train station** at Hipsburn, a mile and a half west of the centre. Most of the **accommodation** lies along or just off the main Northumberland Street. At no. 56, the friendly *Beaches* (T01665/830006, Wwww.beachesbyo.co.uk; no credit cards; ❷) has a variety of en-suite rooms and a good **restaurant** (dinner only), where mains such as local smoked haddock, home-made steak pie and the like go for around £15 a head; you can take your own wine. Alternatively, there's the *Red Lion* (T01665/830584, Wwww.redlionalnmouth.com; ❸) at no. 22, which has six fresh and spacious rooms above a snug, traditional pub that serves decent meals from £9.

Alnwick

ALNWICK (pronounced "Annick"), thirty miles north of Newcastle and four miles inland from Alnmouth, is renowned for its castle and gardens – seat of the dukes of Northumberland – which overlook the River Aln. You'll need a full day to do these justice, and as the biggest town between Hadrian's Wall and the Scottish border Alnwick itself warrants an overnight stop in any case. It's an appealing market town of cobbled streets and Georgian houses, centred on the old cross in Market Place, site of weekly markets (Thursdays and Saturdays) since the thirteenth century, and a farmers' market on the last Friday of the month.

Arrival, information and accommodation

Drivers should park in the **car park** around the back of the castle and gardens on Greenwell Road, a right turn just before the Bondgate arch as you come in from the A1. There are regular bus services to and from Alnmouth, Warkworth and Newcastle, as well as inland to Wooler and up the coast to Bamburgh. Alnwick **bus station** is on Clayport Street, a couple of minutes' walk west of the Market Place, where you'll find the **tourist office** (April–June, Sept & Oct Mon–Sat 9am–5pm, Sun 10am–4pm; July & Aug Mon–Sat 9am–6pm, Sun 10am–4pm; Nov–March Mon–Fri 9.30am–4.30pm, Sat 10am–4pm; ☎01665/510665, ⓦwww.visitalnwick .org.uk), in the arcaded Shambles.

Blackmore's Bondgate Without ☎01665/ 602395, ⓦwww.blackmoresofalnwick.com. Decked out in leather and dark wood, this place is contemporary and youthful – but has a slightly corporate feel. The restaurant and bar are very popular in the evening. ❹

The Old School Newton-on-the-Moor, 6 miles south of Alnwick ☎01665/575767, ⓦwww.northumberlandbedandbreakfast.co.uk. In a quaint little village just outside Alnwick is this superb B&B, housed in a venerable eighteenth-century building surrounded by tranquil gardens. The rooms – an attractive blend of country and modern decor – come complete with indecently fluffy dressing gowns, delicious-smelling toiletries, flat-screen TVs and wi-fi. In the morning wake up to a fantastic cooked breakfast. ❹

Tankerville Arms Eglingham, 8 miles northwest of Alnwick ☎01665/578444, ⓦwww.tankerville arms.com. Three delightful bedrooms in this traditional country inn, with enormous beds and

en-suite bathrooms. There's also a restaurant (see opposite). ❸

Tower Restaurant & Accommodation 10 Bondgate Within ☎01665/603888, ⓦwww .tower-alnwick.co.uk. Just inside the gate, this place has bright, tasteful rooms; the pine-furnished restaurant below serves licensed evening meals. Parking around the back. ❶

West Acre House On the outskirts of Alnwick, off the Alnmouth Rd ☎01665/510374, ⓦwww .westacrehouse.co.uk. A luxurious Edwardian mansion with four large rooms and all the trimmings – big beds, flat-screen TVs and DVD players. Usually minimum 2-night stay. ❶

White Swan Bondgate Within ☎01665/602109, ⓦwww.classiclodges.co.uk. Alnwick's main hotel, where you might want to pop in at least for coffee or a meal – there's a comfortable lounge, while the hotel's fine oak-panelled dining room was swiped from an old ocean liner, the *Olympic*, the twin of the *Titanic*. Parking. ❸

Alnwick Castle and Garden

The Percys – who were raised to the dukedom of Northumberland in 1750 – have owned **Alnwick Castle** (April–Oct daily 10am–6pm, last admission 4.15pm; £12.50; ⓦwww.alnwickcastle.com) since 1309. In the eighteenth century, the castle was badly in need of a refit, so the first duke had the interior refurbished by Robert Adam in an extravagant Gothic style – which in turn was supplanted by the gaudy Italianate decoration preferred by the fourth duke in the 1850s. As you enter, look up to the sturdy battlements, which sport a number of stone soldiers – a piece of eighteenth-century flummery replacing the figurines of medieval times – set up there to ward off the evil eye.

There's plenty to see inside, though the **interior** is not to everyone's taste and it can be crowded at times. The most lavish decoration is in the red drawing room, where the rich polygonal panels of the ceiling bear down on damask-covered walls and some magnificent ebony cabinets rescued from Versailles during the French Revolution. Three of the perimeter towers contain **museum** collections – the Regimental Museum of the Royal Northumberland Fusiliers in the Abbot's Tower; early British and Roman finds in the Postern Tower; and an exhibition dedicated to the Percy Tenantry Volunteers, a private force raised by the second duke during the Napoleonic Wars, in the Constable's Tower – but the bucolic garden walks and Capability Brown-designed **grounds** are a more profitable use of time once you've seen the main rooms.

Signs lead you out of the grounds for the short walk to the **Alnwick Garden** (April–Sept 10am–6pm; Oct–March 10am–4pm; £9.50; Ⓦ www.alnwickgarden .com), which draws crowds to marvel at its sheer scale and invention. At its heart is the computerized Grand Cascade, which shoots water jets in a regular synchronized display, while special features include a bamboo labyrinth maze and the popular Poison Garden – filled with the world's deadliest plants. Superior ices, teas and snacks are available from the *Garden Café*, while Europe's biggest **treehouse** also houses a café and restaurant.

The rest of town

Other than castle and gardens, the main sight in Alnwick is the small-scale **Bailiff-gate Museum**, 14 Bailiffgate (Easter–Oct daily 10am–5pm; Nov–Easter Tues–Sun 10am–4pm; £2.50; Ⓦ www.bailiffgatemuseum.co.uk), housed in the former church of St Mary, just around the corner from the castle's main entrance, which tells the history of the town and its trades. The principal remains of the medieval town walls are on view at the **gatehouses** on Pottergate and Bondgate, while you can't miss the grandiose **Percy Tenantry Column** just to the southeast of the centre along Bondgate Without. A little further on, housed in the Victorian train station, **Barter Books** (Ⓦ www.barterbooks.co.uk), one of the largest secondhand bookshops in England, is definitely worth a call – not just books, but sofas, murals, open fire, coffee and biscuits, and a model railway that runs on top of the stacks.

Eating, drinking and entertainment

Alnwick has plenty of bakeries, tearooms and **restaurants**, but the standout is the chic little *Louis' Steakhouse* (Ⓣ 01665/606947) in the Market Place – they do a great line in steaks (from around £13) in their upstairs steakhouse (eve only; closed Sun), as well as a good breakfast menu, paninis, omelettes and salads (all around £5) downstairs in the bistro (daytime only; closed Sun). Alternatively you could head out of town to the village of Eglingham, where the ivy-clad *Tankerville Arms* (see opposite) serves big meals such as bangers and mash and "Tanky's burger" with cheese (both around £10).

Alnwick Playhouse, just through the arch on Bondgate Without (Ⓣ 01665/ 510785, Ⓦ www.alnwickplayhouse.co.uk), is a venue for theatre, music and film throughout the year. It's also host to concerts during the town's annual **International Music Festival** every August and the **Alnwick Northumbrian Gathering** of traditional music in November.

Craster, Dunstanburgh, Newton and Beadnell

Heading northeast out of Alnwick along the B1340, it's a six-mile hop to the tiny fishing village of **CRASTER**. Half a dozen buses a day run here from Alnwick; the service continues to Seahouses and Bamburgh. The *Jolly Fisherman*, the **pub** above the harbour, features sea views from its back window and garden and serves famously good crab sandwiches. **Kippers** are the thing to sample here, though see box, p.794.

Most spectacularly, however, Craster provides access to **Dunstanburgh Castle** (April–Sept daily 10am–5pm; Oct daily 10am–4pm; Nov–March Mon & Thurs–Sun 10am–4pm; £2.90; NT & EH), whose shattered medieval ruins occupy a magnificent promontory about thirty minutes' windy walk up the coast – there's a car park in Craster. Originally built in the fourteenth century, parts of the surrounding walls survive – offering heart-stopping views down to the crashing sea below – though the dominant feature is the massive keep-gatehouse, which stands out from miles around on the bare coastal spur.

Many think that the coastline beyond Dunstanburgh is as good as Northumberland gets. Long sandy beaches backing Embleton and Beadnell bays are windswept and deserted in winter, busier in summer though rarely overly so. A minor road cuts down to the beachside hamlet of **NEWTON-BY-THE-SEA**, where the rustic *Ship Inn* (℡01665/576262; dinner reservations advised), on a square of old cottages, just yards from the beach, serves terrific fresh fish meals.

A couple of miles north around the next bay, **BEADNELL** also has a pub and fine beaches, which offer the finest windsurfing on the northeast coast. The best place to stay is at the welcoming *Beach Court* (℡01665/720225, ⓦwww.beachcourt.com; ❷), right next to the harbour, with glorious bay views, an oak-panelled drawing room and three lovely rooms with big bathrooms – the most expensive of which is a "turret" suite with a crow's-nest observatory. You can walk from the front door along the beach to the *Ship* at Newton (two miles) or even on to Dunstanburgh (seven miles).

Seahouses and the Farne Islands

From Beadnell, it's three miles north to the fishing port of **SEAHOUSES**, the only place on the local coast that could remotely be described as a resort. Arrive in poor weather, with the rain lashing against the windows of the fish-and-chip shops, and you might wonder why you had bothered. But clear skies above the dunes to the north – Bamburgh Castle a distant viewpoint – changes perspectives, as does the exciting possibility of a boat trip out to the windswept **Farne Islands**, a rocky archipelago lying a few miles offshore. Owned by the National Trust and maintained as a nature reserve, the Farnes are the summer refuge of hundreds of thousands of migrating sea birds, notably puffins, guillemots, terns, eider ducks and kittiwakes, and home to a grey seal colony.

Weather permitting, several operators run **boat trips** (April–Oct; around 2–4hr; from £10) from Seahouses quayside usually starting at around 10am. It's best to book in advance – contact either the **National Trust Shop**, 16 Main St (℡01665/721099), by the Seahouses traffic roundabout, or the **tourist office** (April–Oct daily 10am–5pm; ℡01665/720884, ⓦwww.seahouses.org), in the nearby main car park – but you can just wander down to the quayside and pick a departure. There are frequent landings on the islands in April, and from August to October, but during the bird breeding season (May–July) landings are restricted to morning trips to **Staple Island** and afternoons to **Inner Farne**. All landings incur a separate National Trust fee: during the breeding season it is £6; otherwise it's £5. On Inner Farne, you can visit a restored fourteenth-century chapel built in honour of St Cuthbert, who spent much of his life and died here. Most operators also offer "sail around" cruises, which get close to the birds and seals without landing, or you can take a trip to **Longstone Island** (not a bird sanctuary, so no landing fee), whose single attraction is the lighthouse from where Grace Darling (see box opposite) launched her daring rescue.

There are regular buses to both Alnwick and Berwick-upon-Tweed, so it's unlikely you'd **stay** for the night. If you do, however, the top choice is ⚜ *St Cuthbert's House* (℡01665/720456, ⓦwww.stcuthbertshouse.com; ❹), at 192 Main St, a warm and welcoming B&B housed in a beautifully converted church. For **food** in Seahouses, your choice will be limited to an unhealthy quantity of fish and chips, although *The Olde Ship* pub down by the harbour and the neighbouring *Bamburgh Castle Hotel* do offer some respite. For the local catch, the *Fisherman's Kitchen*, 2 South St, sells smoked kippers, shellfish and salmon from its traditional smokehouse.

Bamburgh

Flanking a triangular green in the lee of its castle, the tiny village of **BAMBURGH**, three miles north of Seahouses, is only a five-minute walk from two splendid sandy beaches, backed by rolling, tufted dunes. From the sands – in fact from everywhere – **Bamburgh Castle** (March–Oct daily 10am–5pm; Nov–Feb Sat & Sun 11am–4.30pm; £8, parking £1; ⓦ www.bamburghcastle.com) is a spectacular sight, its elongated battlements crowning a formidable basalt crag high above the beach. As an early Anglo-Saxon stronghold, it was one-time capital of Northumbria and the protector of the preserved head and hand of St Oswald, the seventh-century king who invited St Aidan over from Iona to convert his subjects. To the Normans, however, Bamburgh was just one of many border fortresses administered by second-rank vassals. In centuries-long decline – rotted by sea spray and buffeted by winter storms – the castle struggled on until 1894, when it was bought by Lord Armstrong (of Rothbury's Cragside; see p.810), who demolished most of the structure to replace it with a hybrid castle-mansion. In the ground floor of the keep, the stone-vaulted ceiling maintains its Norman appearance; here the huge chains which once pulled wrecked ships ashore make the most impact.

Inside the castle there's plenty to explore, including the sturdy keep that houses an unnerving armoury packed with vicious-looking pikes, halberds, helmets and muskets; the King's Hall, with its beautiful teak ceiling that was imported from Siam (Thailand) and carved in Victorian times; and a medieval kitchen complete with jugs, pots and pans.

Practicalities

A regular **bus** service links Alnwick and Berwick-upon-Tweed with Bamburgh, stopping on Front Street by the green. There's a public **car park** on the road below the castle and another at the castle itself for visitors. Book **accommodation** in advance, particularly in the summer. Options include the smart *Victoria Hotel* (ⓣ 01668/214431, ⓦ www.victoriahotel.net; ●), at the top of the village green, which has a couple of relaxing bars and a more expensive brasserie (dinner & Sun lunch only; three courses £25). Further down Front Street is the traditional *Lord Crewe Hotel* (ⓣ 01668/214243, ⓦ www.lordcrewe.co.uk; ●; closed Dec to mid-Feb), a comfortable old inn with oak beams, open fires, public bar and restaurant. The large country pile, *Waren House Hotel* (ⓣ 01668/214581, ⓦ www.warenhousehotel .co.uk; ●), two miles northwest of Bamburgh in the hamlet of Waren Mill, has large rooms with four-poster beds, chintzy decor and an excellent restaurant.

Darling of the seas

Bamburgh is the burial place of the widely celebrated English heroine **Grace Darling**, who rests beneath a Gothic Revival memorial in the churchyard of thirteenth-century St Aidan's. In September 1838, a gale dashed the steamship *Forfarshire* against the rocks of the Farne Islands. Nine passengers struggled onto a reef, where they were subsequently saved by Grace and her lighthouseman father, William, who left the safety of the Longstone lighthouse to row out to them. *The Times* trumpeted Grace's bravery, offers of marriage and requests for locks of her hair streamed into the Darlings' lighthouse home, and for the rest of her brief life Grace was plagued by unwanted visitors – she died of tuberculosis aged 26 in 1842. The story is told on any Farne Islands boat trip from Seahouses (see opposite), while the enlightening **RNLI Grace Darling Museum** opposite the church in Bamburgh (Easter–Oct daily 10am–5pm; Oct–Easter Tues–Sun 10am–4pm; £2.75; ⓣ 01668/214910) goes into more detail.

Food-wise, there are a couple of tearooms – specializing in fresh, warm crab sandwiches – a small deli, and a butcher's selling home-made pies, while for something a bit more substantial, alongside the *Victoria* there's little *Blackett's* at 1 Lucker St (℡01668/214714; closed Sun eve; reservations advised), which serves anything from a delicious plate of Northumbrian cheeses (£6.50) to roast beef and Yorkshire pudding (£9.95).

Holy Island

It's a dramatic approach to **Holy Island**, past the barnacle-encrusted marker poles that line the causeway and on towards the brooding lump of a castle that rears up from its flat surroundings. Small (just one and a half miles by one), sandy and bare, in the winter Holy Island can be a bleak spot, but come summer, day-trippers clog the car parks as soon as the causeway is open. Even then, though, the island has a distinctive and isolated atmosphere. Give the place time and, if you can, stay overnight, when you'll be able to see the historic remains without hundreds of others cluttering the views.

It was on Lindisfarne (as the island was once known) that St Aidan of Iona founded a monastery at the invitation of King Oswald of Northumbria in 634. The monks quickly established a reputation for scholarship and artistry, the latter exemplified by the **Lindisfarne Gospels**, the apotheosis of Celtic religious art, now kept in the British Library. The monastery had sixteen bishops in all, the most celebrated being the reluctant **St Cuthbert**, who never settled here – within two years, he was back in his hermit's cell on the Farne Islands (see p.816), where he died in 687. His colleagues rowed the body back to Lindisfarne, which became a place of pilgrimage until 875, when the monks abandoned the island in fear of marauding Vikings, taking Cuthbert's remains with them. In 1082 Lindisfarne was colonized by Benedictines from Durham, but the monastery was a shadow of its former self, a minor religious house with only a handful of attendant monks, the last of whom was evicted at the Dissolution.

Arrival, information and accommodation

The island is cut off for about five hours every day, so consult the **tide timetables** at one of the region's tourist offices, in the local newspapers or online at Ⓦwww.lindisfarne.org.uk. The #477 **bus** from Berwick-upon-Tweed to Holy Island is something of a law unto itself given the interfering tides, but basically service is daily in August and twice weekly the rest of the year, and the journey takes thirty minutes.

It's imperative to book **accommodation** in advance. Straightforward B&B is on offer at *Bamburgh View* (℡01289/389212, Ⓔbamburghview@btinternet.com; ❸), Fenkle Street, or there are a couple of traditional hotels, the *Lindisfarne* (℡01289/389273; ❸) and the *Manor House* (℡01289/389207, Ⓦwww.manorhouse lindisfarne.com; ❹; closed Jan), the latter overlooking the priory.

The island

There's not much to the **village**, just a couple of streets radiating out from a small green and church cross, everything within a five-minute walk of everything else. Park in one of the large signposted car parks – the castle shuttle-bus runs every twenty minutes from the main car park.

Just off the green, the pinkish sandstone ruins of **Lindisfarne Priory** (Feb & March daily 10am–4pm; April–Sept daily 9.30am–5pm; Oct daily 9.30am–4pm; Nov–Jan Sat–Mon 10am–2pm; £4.50; EH) are from the Benedictine foundation. Behind lie the scant remains of the monastic buildings while adjacent is the mostly thirteenth-century **Church of St Mary the Virgin**, whose delightful churchyard overlooks the ruins. The **museum** (same times as priory; entrance included in priory fee) features an interesting collection of incised stones that constitute all that remains of the first monastery.

Stuck on a small pyramid of rock half a mile away from the village, past the dock and along the seashore, **Lindisfarne Castle** (April–Oct Tues–Sun, hours vary according to tide but always include noon–3pm; £6; NT; ☏01289/389244) was built in the middle of the sixteenth century to protect the island's harbour from the Scots. It was, however, merely a decaying shell when Edward Hudson, the founder of *Country Life* magazine, stumbled across it in 1901. Hudson bought the castle and turned it into a holiday home to designs by Edwin Lutyens, who used the irregular levels of the building to create the L-shaped living quarters that survive today. Lutyens kept the austere spirit of the castle alive in the great fireplaces, stone walls, columns and rounded arches that dominate the main rooms. He regularly collaborated with the garden designer Gertrude Jekyll, whose charming walled **garden** (£1 suggested donation) makes a pleasant place for contemplation.

A **walk** around the island's perimeter is a fine way to spend a couple of hours. Most of its northwestern portion is maintained as a **nature reserve**: from a bird hide you can spot terns, fulmars and plovers and then plod through the dunes and grasses to your heart's content. The island even supports a seal colony, though sightings by visitors are rare.

Eating and drinking

The top place to **eat** on the island is at the diminutive and homely *Café Beangoose* (☏012893/89083; May–Oct only), on the green. Meals are substantial – Northumberland beef and ale stew, local sea trout and the like for around £11 – and locally sourced. The best pub on the island is *The Ship* on Marygate, which serves basic pub meals (around £10). If you're keen to sample some of the world-famous **Lindisfarne mead** (see box, p.794), head to St Aidan's Winery, in the modern building behind the green. They also sell home-made chutneys, biscuits and jams.

Berwick-upon-Tweed and around

Before the union of the English and Scottish crowns in 1603, **BERWICK-UPON-TWEED**, twelve miles north of Holy Island, was the quintessential frontier town, changing hands no fewer than fourteen times between 1174 and 1482, when the Scots finally ceded the stronghold to the English. Interminable cross-border warfare ruined Berwick's economy, turning the prosperous Scottish port of the thirteenth century into an impoverished English garrison town. By the late sixteenth century, Berwick's fortifications were in a dreadful state of repair and Elizabeth I, apprehensive of the resurgent alliance between France and Scotland, had the place rebuilt in line with the latest principles of military architecture. Berwick's ramparts – one and a quarter miles long and still in pristine condition – are no more than twenty feet high but incredibly thick: a facing of ashlared stone protects ten to twelve feet of rubble, which, in turn, backs up against a vast quantity of earth.

The town is a useful staging-post between England and Scotland, and it's worth spending the night. It's not a large place but there's a fair choice of accommodation and services, and its quality-of-life charms have been recognized with its **"Cittaslow"** designation, a movement that has strong links with the Slow Food network.

Arrival, information and tours

From Berwick **train station** it's ten minutes' walk down Castlegate and Marygate to the town centre. Most regional **buses** stop closer in on Golden Square (where Castlegate meets Marygate), on the approach to the Royal Tweed Bridge, though some may also stop in front of the station. The main **car parks** are just outside the walls off Castlegate and down below the quay walls at the bottom of Sandgate.

The **tourist office** (Mon–Sat: April–June, Sept & Oct 10am–5pm; July & Aug 10am–6pm; Nov–March 10am–noon & 1–4pm; ☎01289/330733) at 106 Marygate can book you onto one-hour **walking tours** of town (Easter–Oct Mon–Fri 3 daily; £4). For **bike rental**, contact Tweed Cycles, 17a Bridge St (☎01289/331476) – you can get details of a scenic route to Holy Island (24 miles return) either here or from the tourist office.

Accommodation

Apart from our choices below, you'll find others ranged along Church Street and Ravensdowne (off Woolmarket, the continuation of Marygate); or head north up Castlegate, past the station, to North Road. Other concentrations are found in **Tweedmouth**, just on the other side of the bridge (10min walk), or near the beach at **Spittal** (bus from Golden Square).

Berwick Backpackers 56–58 Bridge St ☎01289/331481, ⊛www.berwickbackpackers .co.uk. This rambling place (once part of a shoe factory) has simple but smartly decorated en-suite rooms (available as single, double, triple or family), one with a gallery, another with a private kitchen, all tastefully done. There's a fully equipped kitchen/ lounge, plus wi-fi; prices include continental breakfast. ❷

Clovelly House 58 West St ☎01289/302337, ⊛www.clovelly53.freeserve.co.uk. Centrally located B&B on a steep cobbled street by the arts centre (free parking provided nearby). Rooms are very smart, and equipped with little luxuries like chocolate biscuits, fluffy dressing gowns and slippers, while breakfast is superb. No credit cards. ❷

Coach House Crookham, 10 miles southwest of Berwick ☎01890/820293, ⊛www.coachhouse crookham.com. Eleven beautiful rooms with exposed beams, king-sized beds and sparkling bathrooms in a beautifully converted coach house. Guests are pampered with afternoon tea on arrival, and there are generous three-course dinners (£21.95; summer only). ❸

No.1 Sallyport Bridge St ☎01289/308827, ⊛www.sallyport.co.uk. Berwick's most luxurious B&B, with two spacious rooms and four

lavish suites – including the romantic Mulberry Suite and the airy Manhattan Loft – in a seventeenth-century house; all are elegantly and individually furnished. They also have a little café stuffed with delicious goodies, and serve simple dinners in the evenings. Reservations essential. Rooms ❹, suites ❺

Old Vicarage Guest House 24 Church Rd, Tweedmouth ☎01289/306909, ⊛www .oldvicarageberwick.co.uk. The finest choice in Tweedmouth, a delightful Victorian villa with spacious rooms. ❷

Pot-a-Doodle-Do Wigwam Village Borewell, Scremerston, 3 miles south of Berwick ☎01289/307107, ⊛www.northumbrianwigwams .com. These quirky wooden wigwams sleep up to five people, and have a fridge, heating and light. From July to Sept, yurts are available for three-night stays too. Good facilities and activities on hand, plus a Finnish barbecue hut with reindeer skins. Closed Jan to mid-Feb. ❶

Queen's Head 6 Sandgate ☎01289/307852, ⊛www.queensheadberwick.co.uk. The best pub in town has six good rooms, including a family room. Downstairs is a welcoming restaurant that serves well-executed dishes such as wild sea trout with pak choi (£15.95) and banana crème brûlée (£4.95). ❸

The Town

Berwick's **walls** – protected by ditches on three sides and the Tweed on the fourth – are strengthened by immense bastions. Begun in 1558, the defences were completed after eleven years at a cost of £128,000, more than Elizabeth I paid for all her other fortifications put together. And, as it turned out, it was all a waste of time and money: the French didn't attack and, once England and Scotland were united, Berwick was stuck with a white elephant. Today, the easy circuit along the top of the walls and ramparts (allow an hour) offers a succession of fine views out to sea, across the Tweed and over the orange-tiled rooftops of a town that's distinguished by its elegant **Georgian mansions**. These, dating from Berwick's resurgence as a seaport between 1750 and 1820, are the town's most attractive feature, with the tapering Lions' House on Windmill Hill and the daintily decorated facades of Quay Walls, beside the river, of particular note. The three **bridges** spanning the Tweed are worth a look, too – the huge arches of the Royal Border Railway Bridge, built in the manner of a Roman aqueduct by Robert Stephenson in the 1840s, contrasting with the desultory concrete of the Royal Tweed, completed in 1928, and the modest seventeenth-century Berwick Bridge.

Within the ramparts, the Berwick skyline is punctured by the stumpy spire of the eighteenth-century **town hall** (April–Sept Mon–Fri tours at 10.30am & 2pm; £2) at the bottom of Marygate, right at the heart of the compact centre. This retains its original jailhouse on the upper floor, now housing the **Cell Block Museum**, entertaining tours of which dwell on tales of crime and punishment in Berwick. Unruly visitors can spend a reflective minute or two locked in the condemned cell. From here, it's a couple of minutes' walk along Church Street to **Holy Trinity Church**, one of the few churches built during the Commonwealth, the absence of a tower supposedly reflecting the wishes of Cromwell, who found them irreligious.

Opposite the church, the finely proportioned **Barracks** (April–Sept Wed–Sun 10am–5pm; £3.70; EH), designed by Nicholas Hawksmoor (1717), were in use until 1964, when the King's Own Scottish Borderers regiment decamped. Inside, there's a regimental museum, as well as the "By Beat of Drum" exhibition, which in a series of picture boards and dioramas traces the life of the British infantryman from the sixteenth to the nineteenth century. These are of rather specialist interest, though most will warm to the temporary exhibitions of contemporary art in the **Gymnasium Gallery** and the borough museum and art gallery, sited in the **Clock Block**. Geared up for school parties, the museum features imaginative displays of local traditional life.

Eating, drinking and entertainment

Berwick has plenty of **cafés and tearooms**, while the **dining** scene is on the up, spearheaded by distinctive *Café Curios*. The town's **arts centre**, The Maltings, Eastern Lane (℡01289/330999, ⓦwww.maltingsberwick.co.uk), has a year-round programme of music, theatre, comedy, film and dance, as well as river views from its licensed café.

Amaryllis 7 West St ℡01289/331711. Contemporary, spacious brasserie serving sandwiches and salads as well as bigger meals and great puddings – not least the key lime pie (£4.50). Dinner reservations advised.

Café Curios 52 Bridge St ℡01289/302666. With its daily changing menu that ensures top quality and fresh ingredients, this little restaurant is run by a committed husband-and-wife team, who are fans of the Slow Food movement. As well as à la carte, they serve a four-course "surprise menu" (£25 per head) and wine comes by recommendation only (there's no list). Expect delights such as lamb with chickpeas and cinnamon, and porcini mushroom risotto with fennel. The restaurant itself is absolutely beautiful, packed with twinkling candles, antique china (that's all for sale – watch out for the Wedgwood) and has a warm, comfortable atmosphere. Cash or cheque only.

Foxton's 26 Hide Hill ℡01289/303939. This pleasant brasserie has a lengthy wine list and opens early in the mornings for coffees and light snacks. Cuisine is predominantly Mediterranean.

Villa Spice 34 Ravensdowne ℡01289/306836. Superior Indian restaurant run by a passionate chef. Try the king prawn *bhaji* (£5.95) or their special lamb *bhuna gost* (£7.95).

Around Berwick-upon-Tweed

The village of **ETAL**, ten miles southwest of Berwick on the B6354, is home to the tranquil **Etal Castle** (April–Sept daily 11am–4.30pm; £3.70; EH), built in 1340 on the banks of the quiet River Till. Here you'll also find the *Black Bull*, the only thatched pub in Northumberland. Bearing further west, just beyond Crookham, a minor road leads a mile to the hamlet of **BRANXTON**, above which is the site of the English victory at the **Battle of Flodden** (1513). It was one of the most decisive of sixteenth-century conflicts: up to ten thousand Scots died in battle, including James IV and most of the contemporary Scottish nobility. The bodies were dumped in pits in Branxton churchyard, their passing now remembered by a simple granite memorial on the hill inscribed "To the brave of both nations".

The A697 runs four miles west of Branxton to reach the **border** where the ruins of **Norham Castle** (mid-March to Sept Sat, Sun & bank hols only 10am–5pm; free; EH) overlook the tumbling Tweed (signposted off the A698), its pink sandstone walls and foursquare keep celebrated in paint by J.M.W. Turner and in verse in Sir Walter Scott's *Marmion*.

Travel details

Buses

For more information on all local and national bus services, contact Traveline ℡0871/200 2233, Ⓦwww.traveline.org.uk.

Alnwick to: Bamburgh (Mon–Fri 8 daily, Sat 9, Sun 2; 1hr); Berwick-upon-Tweed (Mon–Sat 5 daily; 1hr).

Bamburgh to: Alnwick (Mon–Fri 8 daily, Sat 10, Sun 3; 1hr); Craster (Mon–Sat 8 daily, Sun 3; 30–40min); Seahouses (Mon–Sat hourly; 10–20min).

Barnard Castle to: Bishop Auckland (Mon–Sat am hourly, pm 1 every 2hr; 1hr); Darlington (frequent; 40min); Middleton-in-Teesdale (Mon–Sat hourly, Sun 4 daily; 35–45min); Raby Castle (9 daily; 30min).

Berwick-upon-Tweed to: Holy Island (Aug 2 daily, rest of the year 2 weekly; 35min); Newcastle (Mon–Sat 9 daily, Sun 4; 2hr 25min); Wooler (Mon–Sat hourly; 50min).

Darlington to: Barnard Castle (every 20min; 45min); Bishop Auckland (every 30min; 50min); Durham (every 30min; 1hr 15min).

Durham to: Bishop Auckland (every 30min; 35min); Darlington (frequent; 1hr 15min); Newcastle (frequent; 1hr); Sunderland (frequent; 1hr 10min); Washington (every 30min; 45min).

Haltwhistle to: Alston (Mon–Sat 4 daily; 40min); Hexham (hourly; 35min).

Hexham to: Allendale (Mon–Sat 9 daily; 25min); Allenheads (Mon–Sat 5 daily; 45min); Bellingham (Mon–Sat 9 daily; 45min); Haltwhistle (hourly; 35min).

Middlesbrough to: Newcastle (Mon–Sat frequent, Sun hourly; 1hr); Saltburn (frequent; 40min).

Newcastle to: Alnmouth (hourly; 1hr 40min); Alnwick (frequent; 1hr 20min–1hr 50min); Bamburgh (3 daily; 2hr 30min); Beamish (daily every 30min; 1hr); Berwick-upon-Tweed (Mon–Sat 7 daily, Sun 5; 2hr 30min); Carlisle (Mon–Sat hourly;

2hr 10min); Durham (frequent; 1hr); Hexham (hourly; 50min); Middlesbrough (Mon–Sat frequent, Sun hourly; 1hr); Seahouses (4 daily; 2hr 30min); Sunderland (frequent; 1hr 20min); Warkworth (hourly; 1hr 30min); Washington (half-hourly; 45min).

Sunderland to: Durham (frequent; 1hr 10min); Newcastle (frequent; 1hr 20min); Washington (frequent; 45min).

Washington to: Durham (every 30min; 45min); Newcastle (every 30min; 45min); Sunderland (frequent; 45min).

Wooler to: Alnwick (Mon–Sat hourly; 45min); Berwick-upon-Tweed (Mon–Sat hourly; 50min).

Trains

For information on all local and national rail services, check Ⓦwww.transportdirect.info.

Darlington to: Bishop Auckland (10 daily; 25min); Durham (frequent; 20min); Newcastle (frequent; 30min).

Durham to: Darlington (frequent; 20min); London (hourly; 3hr); Newcastle (frequent; 15min); York (frequent; 50min).

Hexham to: Carlisle (hourly; 50min); Haltwhistle (hourly; 20min); Newcastle (every 20min; 40min).

Middlesbrough to: Durham (often involves change at Darlington; every 30min; 50min); Grosmont, for North York Moors Railway (see p.755; 4 daily; 1hr 5min); Newcastle (hourly; 1hr 20min); Saltburn (every 40min; 25min).

Newcastle to: Alnmouth (hourly; 30min); Berwick-upon-Tweed (hourly; 45min); Carlisle (hourly; 1hr 30min); Corbridge (hourly; 35min); Darlington (frequent; 30min); Durham (frequent; 15min); Haltwhistle (hourly; 1hr); Hexham (every 20min; 40min); London (hourly; 2hr 45min–3hr 30min); York (frequent; 1hr).

Contexts

Contexts

History

England's history is long and densely woven, and events within this small nation have had an influence far outweighing the country's modest size. From obscure beginnings, England came to play a leading role in European affairs and more latterly, with the expansion of the British Empire, the whole globe. What follows is therefore a necessarily brief introduction to a complex subject: for some recommendations for more detailed accounts, see our "Books and literature" section on p.855.

Stone Age and Bronze Age England

England has been inhabited for the best part of half a million years, though the earliest archeological evidence dates from around **250,000 BC**, comprising the meagre remains, found near Tilbury just outside London, of one of the migrant communities whose comings and goings were dictated by the fluctuations of the several Ice Ages. The next traces – mainly roughly worked flint implements – were left much later, around **40,000 BC**, by cave-dwellers at Creswell Crags in Derbyshire, Kent's Cavern near Torquay and Cheddar Cave in Somerset. The last spell of intense cold began about 17,000 years ago, and it was the final thawing of this **last Ice Age** around 5000 BC that caused the British Isles to separate from the European mainland.

The sea barrier did nothing to stop further migrations of nomadic hunters, drawn by the rich forests that covered ancient Britain. In about 3500 BC a new wave of colonists arrived from the Continent, probably via Ireland, bringing with them a **Neolithic culture** based on farming and the rearing of livestock. These tribes were the first to make some impact on the environment, clearing forests, enclosing fields, constructing defensive ditches around their villages and digging mines to obtain flint used for tools and weapons. Fragments of Neolithic pottery have been found near Peterborough and in Wiltshire, but the most profuse relics of this culture are their graves, usually stone-chambered, turf-covered mounds (called **long barrows**). These are scattered throughout the country, but the most impressive are at Belas Knap in Gloucestershire and at Wayland's Smithy in Berkshire.

The transition from the Neolithic to the **Bronze Age** began around 2000 BC with the importation from northern Europe of artefacts attributed to the **Beaker Culture** – named from the distinctive cups found at many burial sites. In Britain as elsewhere, the spread of the Beaker Culture along European trade routes helped stimulate the development of a comparatively well-organized social structure with an established aristocracy. Many of Britain's stone circles were completed at this time, including **Avebury** and **Stonehenge** in Wiltshire, while many others belong entirely to the Bronze Age – for example, the Hurlers and the Nine Maidens on Cornwall's Bodmin Moor. Large numbers of earthwork forts were also built in this period, suggesting endemic tribal warfare, a situation further complicated by the appearance of bands of **Celts**, who arrived in numbers from central Europe in around 600 BC, though some historians have disputed the whole notion of a Celtic migration, preferring instead the notion of cultural diffusion along well-established trade routes.

The Iron Age and the Romans

By 500 BC, the **Britons** – whether with or without a significant Celtic infusion – had established a sophisticated farming economy and a social hierarchy that was dominated by a druidic priesthood. Familiar with Mediterranean artefacts through their far-flung trade routes, they gradually developed better methods of metal-working, ones that favoured **iron** rather than bronze, from which they forged not just weapons but also coins and ornamental works, thus creating the first recognizable English art. Their principal contribution to the landscape was a network of hill forts and other defensive works stretching over the entire country, the greatest of them at **Maiden Castle** in Dorset, a site first fortified during the Neolithic period.

Maiden Castle was also one of the first British fortifications to fall to the **Roman** legions in 43 AD. Coming at the end of a long period of commercial probing, the Roman invasion had begun hesitantly, with small cross-Channel incursions led by **Julius Caesar** in 55 and 54 BC. Britain's rumoured mineral wealth was a primary motive, but the immediate spur to the eventual conquest that came nearly a century later was anti-Roman collaboration between the British Celts and their cousins in France. The subtext was that the **Emperor Claudius**, who led the invasion, owed his power to the army and needed a military triumph. The death of the king of southeast England, Cunobelin – Shakespeare's Cymbeline – presented Claudius with a golden opportunity and in August 43 AD a substantial Roman force landed in Kent, from where it fanned out, soon establishing a base along the estuary of the Thames. Joined by a menagerie of elephants and camels for the major battle of the campaign, the Romans soon reached **Camulodunum** (Colchester) – the region's most important city – and within four years were dug in on the frontier of south Wales.

Some determined resistance did occur, notably from the Catuvellauni chief, **Caractacus**, who conducted a guerrilla campaign from Wales until he was captured in about 50 AD, but this was nothing when compared with the revolt of the East Anglian Iceni, under their queen **Boudica** (or Boadicea) in 60 AD. The Iceni sacked Camulodunum and Verulamium (St Albans), and even reached the undefended new port of Londinium (London), but the Romans rallied and exacted a terrible revenge. The rebellion turned out to be an isolated act of resistance, and it would seem that most of the southern tribes acquiesced to their absorption into the empire. In the next decades, the Romans extended their control, subduing Wales and the north of England by 80 AD. They did not, however, manage to conquer Scotland and eventually gave up – as signified by the construction of **Hadrian's Wall** in 130 AD. Running from the Tyne to the Solway, the wall marked the northern limit of the Roman Empire, and stands today as England's most impressive remnant of the Roman occupation.

The written history of England begins with the Romans, whose rule lasted nearly four centuries. For the first time, the country began to emerge as a clearly identifiable entity with a defined political structure. Peace also brought prosperity. Commerce flourished and cities prospered, including the most northerly Roman town of Eboracum (York) and **Londinium**, which soon assumed a pivotal role in the commercial and administrative life of the colony. Although Latin became the language of the Romano-British ruling elite, local traditions were allowed to coexist alongside imported customs, so that Celtic gods were often worshipped at the same time as Roman ones, and sometimes merged with them. Perhaps the most important legacy of the Roman occupation, however, was the introduction of **Christianity** from the third century on, becoming firmly entrenched after its official recognition by the Emperor Constantine in 313.

Anglo-Saxon England and the Danes

From the early fourth century, Roman England was subject to **raids** by Germanic Saxons, and by the middle of the fourth century – with the Romans on the run –

Picts from Scotland and Scots from northern Ireland were harrying inland areas in the north and west. As economic life declined and rural areas became depopulated, individual military leaders began to usurp local authority. Indeed, by the start of the fifth century England had become irrevocably detached from what remained of the Roman Empire and within fifty years the **Saxons** had begun settling England themselves. This marked the start of a gradual conquest that culminated in the defeat of the native Britons in 577 at the Battle of Dyrham (near Bath) and, despite the despairing efforts of such semi-mythical figures as King Arthur, the last independent Britons were driven deep into Cumbria, Wales and the southwest. The Saxons all but eliminated Romano-British culture and by the end of the sixth century the rest of England was divided into the **Anglo-Saxon kingdoms** of Northumbria, Mercia, East Anglia, Kent and Wessex. So complete was the Anglo-Saxon domination of England, through conquest and intermarriage, that some ninety percent of English place names today have an Anglo-Saxon derivation.

Only in the westerly extremities of the country did the ancient Romano-British traditions survive and was Christian worship kept alive, though the countrywide revival of Christianity was driven mainly by **St Augustine**, who was despatched by Pope Gregory I and landed on the Kent coast in 597, accompanied by forty monks. **Ethelbert**, the overlord of all the English south of the River Humber, received the missionaries and gave Augustine permission to found a monastery at **Canterbury** (on the site of the present cathedral), where the king himself was then baptized, followed by ten thousand of his subjects at a grand Christmas ceremony. Despite some short-term reversals thereafter, the Christianization of England proceeded quickly, so that by the middle of the seventh century all of the Anglo-Saxon kings had at least nominally adopted the faith. Tensions and clashes between the Augustinian missionaries and the Romano-British (Celtic) monks inevitably arose, but were resolved by the **Synod of Whitby** in 663, when it was agreed that the English Church should follow the rule of Rome, thereby ensuring a realignment with the European cultural mainstream.

The central English region of **Mercia** became the dominant Anglo-Saxon kingdom in the eighth century under **King Offa**, who was responsible for the greatest public work of the Anglo-Saxon period, **Offa's Dyke**, an earthwork marking the border with Wales from the River Dee to the River Severn. Yet, after Offa's death, **Wessex** gained the upper hand, and by 825 the Wessex kings had conquered or taken allegiance from all the other English kingdoms. The triumph of Wessex was, however, short-lived. Carried here by their remarkable longboats, the **Vikings** – at this time mostly **Danes** – had started to raid the east coast towards the end of the eighth century. Emboldened by their success, these raids grew in size and then turned into a migration. In 865, a substantial Danish army landed in East Anglia, and within six years they had conquered Northumbria, Mercia and East Anglia. The Danes then set their sights on Wessex, whose new king was the formidable and exceptionally talented **Alfred the Great**. Despite the odds, Alfred successfully resisted the Danes and eventually the two warring parties signed a truce, which fixed an uneasy border between Wessex and Danish territory – the **Danelaw** – to the north. Ensconced in northern England and what is today the East Midlands, the Danes soon succumbed to Christianity and internal warfare, while Alfred modernized his kingdom and strengthened its defences.

Alfred died in 899, but his successor, **Edward the Elder**, capitalized on his efforts, establishing Saxon supremacy over the Danelaw to become the de facto overlord of all England. The relative calm continued under Edward's son, **Athelstan** and his son, **Edgar**, who became the first ruler to be crowned **king of England** in 973. However, this was but a lull in the Viking storm. Returning in force, the Vikings milked Edgar's son **Ethelred the Unready** ("lacking counsel") for all the money they could, but the ransom (the Danegeld) paid brought only temporary relief and in 1016 Ethelred hot-footed it to Normandy, leaving the Danes in command.

The first Danish king of England was **Canute**, a shrewd and gifted ruler, but his two disreputable sons quickly dismantled his carefully constructed Anglo-Scandinavian empire. Thereafter, the Saxons regained the initiative, installing Ethelred's son, **Edward the Confessor**, on the throne in 1042. It was a poor choice. Edward was more suited to be a priest than a king and he allowed power to drift into the hands of his most powerful subject, Godwin, Earl of Wessex, and his son Harold. On Edward's death, the Witan – a sort of council of elders – confirmed **Harold** as king, ignoring several rival claims including that of William, Duke of Normandy. William's claim was a curious affair, but he always insisted – however improbable it may seem – that the childless Edward the Confessor had promised him his crown. Unluckily for Harold, his two main rivals struck at the same time. First up was his alienated brother **Tostig** along with his ally King Harald of Norway, a giant of a man reliably reckoned to be seven feet tall. They landed with a Viking army in Yorkshire and Harold hurriedly marched north to meet them. Harold won a crushing victory at the battle of Stamford Bridge, but then he heard that **William of Normandy** had invaded the south. Rashly, Harold did not pause to muster more men, but dashed south, where William famously routed the Saxons – and killed Harold – at the **Battle of Hastings** in 1066. On Christmas Day, William the Conqueror was installed as king in Westminster Abbey.

The Normans and the early Plantagenets

William I imposed a Norman aristocracy on his new subjects, reinforcing his rule with a series of strongholds, the grandest of which was the **Tower of London**. Initially, there was some resistance, but William crushed these sporadic rebellions with great brutality – Yorkshire and the north were ravished and the fenland resistance of Hereward the Wake was brought to a savage end. Perhaps the single most effective controlling measure was the compilation of the **Domesday Book** in 1085 and 1086. Recording land ownership, type of cultivation, the number of inhabitants and their social status, it afforded William an unprecedented body of information about his subjects, providing a framework for the administration of taxation, the judicial structure and ultimately feudal obligations.

William died in 1087, and was succeeded by his son **William Rufus**, an ineffectual ruler but a notable benefactor of religious foundations. Rufus died in mysterious circumstances – killed by an unknown assailant's arrow while hunting in the New Forest – and the throne passed to **Henry I**, William I's youngest son. Henry spent much of his time struggling with his unruly barons, but at least he proved to be more conciliatory in his dealings with the Saxons, even marrying into one of their leading families. On his death in 1135, the accession was contested, initiating a long-winded civil war that was only ended when **Henry II**, the first of the **Plantagenets**, secured the throne. Energetic and far-sighted, Henry kept his barons firmly in check and instigated profound administrative reforms, most notably the introduction of trial by jury. Nor was England Henry's only concern, his inheritance bequeathing him great chunks of France. This territorial entanglement was to create all sorts of problems for his successors, but Henry himself was brought low by his attempt to subordinate Church to Crown. This went terribly awry in 1170, when he sanctioned the murder in Canterbury Cathedral of his erstwhile drinking companion **Thomas à Becket**, whose canonization just three years later created an enduring Europe-wide cult.

The last years of Henry's reign were riven by quarrels with his sons, the eldest of whom, **Richard I** (or Lionheart), spent most of his ten-year reign crusading in the Holy Land. Neglected, England fell prey to the scheming of Richard's brother

John, the villain of the Robin Hood tales, who became king in his own right after Richard died of a battle wound in France in 1199. Yet John's inability to hold on to his French possessions and his rumbling dispute with the Vatican over control of the English Church alienated the English barons, who eventually forced him to consent to a charter guaranteeing their rights and privileges, the **Magna Carta**, which was signed in 1215 at Runnymede, on the Thames.

The later Plantagenets

The power struggle with the barons continued into the reign of **Henry III**, but Henry's successor, **Edward I**, who inherited the throne in 1272, was much more in control of his kingdom than his predecessor. Edward was a great law-maker, but he also became obsessed by military matters, spending years subduing Wales and imposing English jurisdiction over Scotland. Fortunately for the Scots – it was too late for Wales – the next king of England, **Edward II**, proved to be completely hopeless and in 1314 Robert the Bruce inflicted a huge defeat on his guileless army at the battle of **Bannockburn**. This reverse spelt the beginning of the end for Edward, who was ultimately murdered by his wife Isabella and her lover Roger Mortimer in 1327.

Edward III began by sorting out the Scottish imbroglio before getting stuck into his main preoccupation – his (essentially specious) claim to the throne of France. Starting in 1337, the resultant **Hundred Years War** kicked off with several famous English victories, principally Crécy in 1346 and Poitiers in 1356, but was interrupted by the outbreak of the **Black Death** in 1349. The plague claimed about one and a half million English souls – some one third of the population – and the scarcity of labour that followed gave the peasantry more economic clout than they had ever had before. Predictably, the landowners attempted to restrict the concomitant rise in wages, thereby provoking the widespread rioting that culminated in the **Peasants' Revolt** of 1381. The rebels marched on London under the delusion that they could appeal to the king – now **Richard II** – for fair treatment, but they soon learnt otherwise. The king did indeed meet a rebel deputation in person, but his aristocratic bodyguards took the opportunity to kill the peasants' leader, **Wat Tyler**, the prelude to the enforced dispersal of the crowds and mass slaughter.

Running parallel with this social unrest were the clerical reforms demanded by the scholar **John Wycliffe** (1320–1384), whose acolytes made the first translation of the Bible into English in 1380. Another sign of the elevation of the common language was the success enjoyed by **Geoffrey Chaucer** (c.1343–1400), a wine merchant's son, whose *Canterbury Tales* was the first major work written in the vernacular and one of the first English books to be printed.

The houses of Lancaster and York

In 1399, **Henry IV**, the first of the **Lancastrian** kings, supplanted the weak and indecisive Richard II. Henry died in 1413 to be succeeded by his son, the bellicose **Henry V**, who promptly renewed the Hundred Years War with vigour. Henry famously defeated the French at the battle of **Agincourt**, a comprehensive victory that forced the French king to acknowledge Henry as his heir in the Treaty of Troyes of 1420. However, Henry died just two years later and his son, **Henry VI** – or rather his regents – all too easily succumbed to a French counter-attack inspired by **Joan of Arc** (1412–1431); by 1454, only Calais was left in English hands.

It was soon obvious that **Henry VI** was mentally unstable, and consequently, as the new king drifted in and out of insanity, two aristocratic factions attempted to squeeze control: the Yorkists, whose emblem was the white rose, and the Lancastrians, represented by the red rose – hence the protracted **Wars of the Roses**. The

Yorkist **Edward IV** seized the crown in 1471 and held on to it until his death in 1483, when he was succeeded by his 12-year-old son **Edward V**, whose reign was cut short after only two months: he and his younger brother were murdered in the Tower of London, probably at the behest of their uncle, the Duke of Gloucester, who was crowned **Richard III**. In 1485, Richard was famously toppled at Bosworth Field by Henry Tudor, Earl of Richmond, who took the throne as Henry VII.

The Tudors

The opening of the **Tudor** period brought radical transformations. A Lancastrian through his mother's line, **Henry VII** promptly reconciled the Yorkists by marrying Edward IV's daughter Elizabeth, thereby ending the Wars of the Roses at a stroke. It was a shrewd gambit and others followed. Henry married his daughter off to James IV of Scotland and his son to Catherine, the daughter of Ferdinand and Isabella of Spain – and by these means England began to assume the status of a major European power. There were economic stirrings too, with the burgeoning wool and cloth trades spawning an increasingly prosperous merchant class.

Henry's son, **Henry VIII** is best remembered for his multiple marriages – and all the rumpuses that went along with them – but much more significant was his separation of the English Church from Rome and his establishment of an independent Protestant Church – the **Church of England**. This is not without its ironies. Henry was not a Protestant himself and such was his early orthodoxy that the pope even gave him the title "Defender of the Faith" for a pamphlet he wrote attacking Luther's treatises. In fact, the schism between Henry and the pope was triggered not by doctrinal issues but by the failure of his wife **Catherine of Aragon** – widow of his elder brother – to provide Henry with male offspring. Failing to obtain a decree of nullity from Pope Clement VII, he dismissed his long-time chancellor Thomas Wolsey and turned instead to **Thomas Cromwell**, who helped make the English Church recognize Henry as its head. One of the consequences was the **Dissolution of the Monasteries**, which conveniently gave both king and nobles the chance to get their hands on valuable monastic property in the late 1530s.

In his later years Henry became a corpulent, syphilitic wreck, six times married but at last furnished with an heir, **Edward VI**, who was only nine years old when he ascended the throne in 1547. His short reign saw Protestantism established on a firm footing, with churches stripped of their images and Catholic services banned, yet on Edward's death most of the country readily accepted his half-sister **Mary**, daughter of Catherine of Aragon and a fervent Catholic, as queen. She returned England to the papacy and married the future Philip II of Spain, forging an alliance whose immediate consequence was war with France. The marriage was deeply unpopular and so was Mary's foolish decision to begin persecuting Protestants, executing the leading lights of the English Reformation – Hugh Latimer, Nicholas Ridley and **Thomas Cranmer**, the archbishop of Canterbury who was largely responsible for the first English prayer book, published in 1549.

When she came to the throne in 1558 on the death of her half-sister, **Elizabeth I** looked very vulnerable. The country was divided by religion – Catholic against Protestant – and threatened from abroad by Philip II of Spain, the most powerful ruler in Europe. Famously, Elizabeth eschewed marriage and, although a Protestant herself, steered a delicate course between the two religious groupings. Her prudence rested well with the English merchant class, who were becoming the greatest power in the land, its members mostly opposed to foreign military entanglements. An exception was, however, made for the piratical activities of the great English seafarers of the day, sea captains like Walter Raleigh, Martin Frobisher, John Hawkins and Francis Drake, who made a fortune raiding Spain's American colonies. Inevitably,

Philip II's irritation took a warlike turn, but the **Spanish Armada** he sent in 1588 was defeated, thereby establishing England as a major European sea power. Elizabeth's reign also saw the efflorescence of a specifically English Renaissance – **William Shakespeare** (1564–1616) is the obvious name – the only major blip being the queen's reluctant execution of her cousin and rival **Mary, Queen of Scots,** in 1587.

The early Stuarts and the Commonwealth

The son of Mary, Queen of Scots, James VI of Scotland, succeeded Elizabeth as **James I** of England in 1603, thereby uniting the English and Scottish crowns.

Kings and queens

House of Wessex
Egbert 802–39
Ethelwulf 839–55
Ethelbald 855–60
Ethelbert 860–66
Ethelred I 866–71
Alfred the Great 871–99
Edward the Elder 899–924
Athelstan 924–39
Edmund I 939–46
Eadred 946–55
Eadwig 955–59
Edgar 959–75
Edward the Martyr 975–78
Ethelred II (Ethelred the Unready) 978–1016
Edmund II (Edmund Ironside) 1016

House of Skjoldung
Canute 1016–35
Harold I 1035–40
Harthacanute 1040–42

House of Wessex
Edward the Confessor 1042–66
Harold II 1066

House of Normandy
William I (William the Conqueror) 1066–87
William II (William Rufus) 1087–1100
Henry I 1100–35
Stephen 1135–54

House of Plantagenet
Henry II 1154–89
Richard I (Richard the Lionheart) 1189–99
John 1199–1216
Henry III 1216–72
Edward I 1272–1307
Edward II 1307–27
Edward III 1327–77
Richard II 1377–99

House of Lancaster
Henry IV 1399–1413
Henry V 1413–22
Henry VI 1422–61 & 1470

House of York
Edward IV 1461–70 &1471–83
Edward V 1483
Richard III 1483–85

House of Tudor
Henry VII 1485–1509
Henry VIII 1509–47
Edward VI 1547–53
Mary I 1553–58
Elizabeth I 1558–1603

House of Stuart
James I 1603–25
Charles I 1625–49
Commonwealth and Protectorate 1649–60
Charles II 1660–85
James II 1685–88
William III and Mary II 1688–94
William III 1694–1702
Anne 1702–14

House of Hanover
George I 1714–27
George II 1727–60
George III 1760–1820
George IV 1820–30
William IV 1830–37
Victoria 1837–1901

House of Saxe-Coburg
Edward VII 1901–10

House of Windsor
George V 1910–36
Edward VIII 1936
George VI 1936–52
Elizabeth II 1952–

James quickly moved to end hostilities with Spain and adopted a policy of toleration towards the country's Catholics. Inevitably, both initiatives offended many Protestants, whose worst fears were confirmed in 1605 when **Guy Fawkes** and a group of Catholic conspirators were discovered preparing to blow up king and Parliament in the so-called **Gunpowder Plot**. During the ensuing hue and cry, many Catholics met an untimely end and Fawkes himself was hanged, drawn and quartered. At the same time, many Protestants felt the English state was irredeemably corrupt and some of the more dedicated **Puritans** fixed their eyes on establishing a "New Jerusalem" in North America following the foundation of the first permanent **colony** in Virginia in 1608. Twelve years later, the **Pilgrim Fathers** landed in New England, establishing a colony that would absorb about a hundred thousand Puritan immigrants by the middle of the century.

Meanwhile, James was busy alienating his landed gentry. He clung to an absolutist vision of the monarchy – the divine right of kings – that was totally out of step with the Protestant leanings of the majority of his subjects and he also relied heavily on court favourites. It was a recipe for disaster, but it was to be his successor, **Charles I**, who reaped the whirlwind. Charles inherited James's dislike of the Protestants and liking for absolutism, ruling without Parliament from 1629 to 1640. But he overstepped himself when he tried to impose a new Anglican prayer book on the Scots, who rose in revolt, forcing Charles to recall Parliament to raise the money for an army. This was Parliament's chance and they were not going to let it slip. The **Long Parliament**, as it became known, impeached several of Charles's allies – most notably Archbishop Laud, who was hung out to dry by the king and ultimately executed – and compiled its grievances in the Grand Remonstrance of 1641.

Facing the concerted hostility of Parliament, the king withdrew to Nottingham where he raised his standard, the opening act of the **Civil War**. The Royalist forces ("Cavaliers") were initially successful, leading to the complete overhaul of key regiments of the Parliamentary army ("Roundheads") by **Oliver Cromwell** and his officer allies. The **New Model Army** Cromwell created was something quite unique: singing psalms as they went into battle and urged on by preachers and "agitators", this was an army of believers whose ideological commitment to the parliamentary cause made it truly formidable. Cromwell's revamped army cut its teeth at the battle of Naseby and thereafter simply brushed the Royalists aside. Attempting to muddy the political waters, Charles surrendered himself to the Scots, but they finally handed him over to the English Parliament, by whom – after prolonged negotiations, endless royal shenanigans and more fighting – he was ultimately executed in January 1649.

For the next eleven years England was a **Commonwealth** – at first a true republic, then, after 1653, a **Protectorate** with Cromwell as the Lord Protector and commander in chief. Cromwell reformed the government, secured advantageous commercial treaties with foreign nations and used his New Model Army to put the fear of God into his various enemies. The turmoil of the Civil War and the pre-eminence of the army unleashed a furious legal, theological and political debate in every corner of the country. This milieu spawned a host of leftist sects, the most notable of whom were the **Levellers**, who demanded wholesale constitutional reform, and the more radical **Diggers**, who proposed common ownership of all land. Nonconformist religious groups also flourished, prominent among them the pacifist **Quakers**, led by the much persecuted George Fox (1624–91), and the **Dissenters**, to whom the most famous writers of the day, John Milton (1608–74) and John Bunyan (1628–88), both belonged.

Cromwell died in 1658 to be succeeded by his son **Richard**, who ruled briefly and ineffectually, leaving the army unpaid while one of its more ambitious commanders, General Monk, conspired to restore the monarchy. Charles II, the exiled son of the previous king, entered London in triumph in May 1660.

The Restoration and the later Stuarts

A Stuart was back on the English throne, but **Charles II** had few absolutist illusions – the terms of the **Restoration** were closely negotiated and included a general amnesty for all those who had fought against the Stuarts, with the exception of the regicides: those who had signed Charles I's death warrant. Nonetheless, there was a sea-change in public life with the re-establishment of a royal court and the foundation of the **Royal Society**, whose scientific endeavours were furthered by Isaac Newton (1642–1727). The low points of Charles's reign were the **Great Plague** of 1665 and the 1666 **Great Fire of London**, though the London that rose from the ashes was an architectural showcase for Christopher Wren (1632–1723) and his fellow classicists. Politically, there were still underlying tensions between the monarchy and Parliament, but the latter was more concerned with the struggle between the **Whigs** and **Tories**, political factions representing, respectively, the low-church gentry and the high-church aristocracy. There was a degree of religious toleration too, but its brittleness was all too apparent in the anti-Catholic riots of 1678.

James II, the brother of Charles II, came to the throne in 1685. He was a Catholic, which made the bulk of his subjects uneasy, but there was still an indifferent response when the Protestant **Duke of Monmouth**, the favourite among Charles II's illegitimate sons, raised a rebellion in the West Country. Monmouth was defeated at Sedgemoor, in Somerset, in 1685, but if James felt secure he was mistaken. A foolish man, James showed all the traditional weaknesses of his family, from his enthusiasm for the divine right of kings to an over-reliance on sycophantic favourites. Even worse, as far as the Protestants were concerned, he built up a massive standing army, officered it with Roman Catholics and proposed a **Declaration of Indulgence**, removing anti-Catholic restrictions. When James's queen gave him a son, securing a Catholic succession, the most powerful Protestants in the land begged **William of Orange**, the Dutch husband of Mary, the Protestant daughter of James II, to save them from Catholic tyranny – and that was precisely what he did. William landed in Devon in 1688 and, as James's forces simply melted away, he speedily took control of London in the **Glorious Revolution**. This was the final postscript to the Civil War – although it was a couple of years before James and his Jacobite army were finally defeated in Ireland at the **Battle of the Boyne**.

William and Mary were made joint sovereigns after they agreed a **Bill of Rights** defining the limitations of the monarchy's power and the rights of its subjects. This, together with the **Act of Settlement of 1701** made Britain a **constitutional monarchy**, in which the roles of legislature and executive were separate and interdependent. The model was broadly consistent with that outlined by the philosopher and political thinker John Locke (1632–1704), whose essentially Whig doctrines of toleration and social contract were gradually embraced as the new orthodoxy. Ruling alone after Mary's death in 1694, William regarded England as a prop in his defence of Holland against France, a stance that defined England's political alignment in Europe for the next sixty years. In the reign of **Anne**, second daughter of James II, English armies won a string of remarkable victories on the Continent, beginning with the Duke of Marlborough's triumph at Blenheim in 1704, followed the next year by the capture of Gibraltar, establishing a British presence in the Mediterranean once and for all. These military escapades were part of the Europe-wide **War of the Spanish Succession**, which rumbled on until the Treaty of Utrecht in 1713 – a treaty which all but settled the European balance of power for the rest of the eighteenth century. Otherwise Anne's reign was distinguished mainly for the 1707 **Act of Union**, uniting the English and Scottish parliaments.

With none of her children surviving into adulthood, Anne was the last of the Stuarts and, when she died in 1714, the succession passed – in accordance with the terms of the Act of Settlement – to the Duke of Hanover, a non-English-speaking, Protestant German who became **George I** of England.

The Hanoverians

As power leaked away from the monarchy into the hands of the Whig oligarchy, the king ceased to attend Cabinet meetings, his place being taken by his chief minister. Most prominent of these ministers was **Robert Walpole** (1676–1745), regarded as England's **first prime minister**. To all intents and purposes, Walpole governed from 1721 to 1742, a tranquil period politically, with the country standing aloof from foreign affrays. Peace ended in the reign of **George II**, when England declared war on Spain in 1739 at the start of yet another dynastic squabble, the eight-year War of the Austrian Succession. Then, in 1745, the Young Pretender, Charles Stuart, invaded England and Scotland in the second and most dangerous of the Jacobite rebellions (the first had failed dismally in 1715). So-called **Bonnie Prince Charlie** and his Highland army managed to reach Derby, just 120 miles from London, creating pandemonium in the capital, but their lines of supply were over-extended and they were obliged to retreat north. It all ended in Jacobite tears, when a Hanoverian army under the brutal Duke of Cumberland caught up with them and hacked them to pieces at Culloden, in Scotland. Otherwise, the **Seven Years War** harvested England further overseas territory in India and Canada at the expense of France and, in 1768, **Captain James Cook** sailed to New Zealand and Australia, thereby netting another chunk of the globe.

In 1760, **George III** succeeded his father. The early years of his sixty-year reign saw a revived struggle between king and Parliament, enlivened by the intervention of John Wilkes, first of a long and increasingly vociferous line of parliamentary radicals. The contest was exacerbated by the deteriorating relationship with the thirteen colonies of North America, a situation brought to a head by the **American Declaration of Independence** and Britain's subsequent defeat in the Revolutionary War. Chastened by this disaster, Britain chose not to interfere in the momentous events taking place across the Channel, where France, long its most consistent foe, was convulsed by revolution. Out of the turmoil emerged the most daunting of enemies, **Napoleon** (1769–1821), whose stunning military progress was interrupted by Nelson at **Trafalgar** in 1805 and finally stopped ten years later by the Duke of Wellington at **Waterloo**.

The Industrial Revolution

England's triumph over Napoleon was underpinned by its financial strength, which was itself born of the **Industrial Revolution**, the switch from an agricultural to a manufacturing economy that completely changed the face of the country in the space of a hundred years. The earliest mechanized production was in the Lancashire **cotton mills**, where cotton-spinning was transformed from a cottage industry into a highly productive factory-based system. Initially, river water powered the mills, but the technology changed after James Watt patented his **steam engine** in 1781. Watt's engines needed **coal**, which made it convenient to locate mills and factories near coal mines, a tendency that was accelerated as **ironworks** took up coal as a smelting fuel, vastly increasing the output from their furnaces. Accordingly, there was a shift of population towards the Midlands and north of England, where the great coal reserves were located, and as the industrial economy boomed and diversified, so these regions' towns mushroomed at an extraordinary rate. There were steel towns like **Sheffield**, huge cotton warehouses in **Manchester**, pottery in **Stoke-on-Trent** and vast dock facilities in **Liverpool**, where raw materials from India and the Americas came in and manufactured goods went out. Commerce and industry were also served by improving transport facilities, such as the building of a network of **canals**, but the great leap forward came with the arrival of the **railway**, heralded by the Stockton–Darlington line in 1825 and followed five years later by the Liverpool–Manchester railway, as travelled by George Stephenson's *Rocket*.

Boosted by a vast influx of immigrant workers, the country's population rose from about seven and a half million at the beginning of George III's reign to more than fourteen million by its end. As the factories and their attendant towns expanded, so the rural settlements of England declined, inspiring the elegiac pastoral yearnings of Samuel Taylor Coleridge and William Wordsworth, the first great names of the **Romantic movement**. Later Romantic poets such as Percy Bysshe Shelley and Lord Byron took a more socially engaged position, but much more dangerous to the ruling class were the nation's factory workers, who grew restless when mechanization put thousands of them out of work. The discontent coalesced in the **Chartists**, a broad-based popular movement that demanded parliamentary reform – the most important of the industrial boom towns were still unrepresented in Parliament – and the repeal of the hated **Corn Laws**, which kept the price of bread artificially high to the advantage of the large landowners.

The following year, a weak, blind and insane George III finally died to be succeeded, in fairly rapid succession, by two of his sons, **George IV** and then **William IV**. Tensions continued to run high throughout the 1820s, and in retrospect it seems that the country may have been saved from a French-style revolution by a series of judicious parliamentary acts: the **Reform Act** of 1832 established the principle (if not actually the practice) of popular representation; the **Poor Law** of 1834 did something to alleviate the condition of the most destitute; and the repeal of the Corn Laws in 1846 cut the cost of bread. Furthermore, there was such a furore after five Dorset labourers – the **Tolpuddle Martyrs** – were transported to Australia in 1834 for joining an agricultural trade union, that the judiciary decided it was prudent to overturn the judgement six years later. Significant sections of the middle classes were just as eager to see progressive reform as the working classes, as evidenced by the immense popularity of **Charles Dickens** (1812–70), whose novels railed against poverty and injustice. Dickens' social concerns had been anticipated in the previous century by John Wesley (1703–91) and his **Methodists**, who – along with other Nonconformist Christians – led the anti-slavery campaign. As a result of their efforts, **slavery** was banned throughout the British Empire in 1833 – long after the seaports of Bristol and Liverpool had grown rich on the backs of the trade.

Victorian England

In 1837, William IV was succeeded by his niece, **Victoria**, whose long reign witnessed the zenith of British power. For much of the period, the economy boomed – typically the nation's cloth manufacturers boasted that they supplied the domestic market before breakfast, the rest of the world thereafter. The British trading fleet was easily the mightiest in the world and it underpinned an empire upon which, in that famous phrase of the time, "the sun never set". There were extraordinary intellectual achievements too – as typified by the publication of Charles Darwin's *On the Origin of Species* in 1859 – and the country came to see itself as both a civilizing agent and, on occasion, the hand of (a very Protestant) God on earth. Britain's industrial and commercial prowess was best embodied by the great engineering feats of **Isambard Kingdom Brunel** (1806–1859) and by the **Great Exhibition** of 1851, a display of manufacturing achievements without compare.

With trade at the forefront of the agenda, much of the political debate crystallized into a conflict between the Free Traders – led by the Whigs, who formed the **Liberal Party** – and the Protectionists under Bentinck and **Disraeli**, guiding light of the **Conservatives**, descended from the Tories. Parliament itself was long dominated by the duel between Disraeli and the Liberal leader **Gladstone**, the pre-eminent statesmen of the day. It was Disraeli who eventually passed the Second Reform Bill in 1867, further extending the electoral franchise, but it was Gladstone's first ministry of 1868–74 that ratified some of the century's most far-reaching legislation, including compulsory education, the full legalization of trade unions and an Irish Land Act.

There were foreign entanglements, too. In 1854 troops were sent to protect the Ottoman empire against the Russians in the **Crimea**, an inglorious debacle whose horrors were relayed to the public by the first-ever press coverage of a military campaign and by the revelations of Florence Nightingale, who was appalled by the lack of medical care for wounded and sick soldiers. The **Indian Mutiny** of 1857 was a further shock to the imperial system, exposing the fragility of Britain's hold over the Indian subcontinent, though the status quo was eventually restored. Thereafter, the British army was flattered by a series of minor wars against poorly armed Asian and African opponents, but promptly came unstuck when it faced the Dutch settlers of South Africa in the **Boer War** (1899–1902). The British ultimately fought their way to a sort of victory, but the discreditable conduct of the war prompted a military shake-up at home that was to be of significance in the coming European war.

From World War I to World War II

Victoria died in 1901, to be succeeded by her son, **Edward VII**, whose leisurely lifestyle has sometimes been seen as the epitome of the complacent era to which he gave his name. This complacency came to an abrupt end on August 4, 1914, when the Liberal government, honouring the Entente Cordiale signed with France in 1904, declared war on Germany. Hundreds of thousands volunteered for the British army, but their enthusiastic nationalism was not enough to ensure a quick victory and **World War I** dragged on for four miserable years, its key engagements fought in the trenches that zigzagged across northern France and west Belgium. Britain and her allies eventually prevailed, but the number of dead beggared belief, undermining the authority of the British ruling class, whose generals had shown a particularly lethal combination of incompetence and indifference to the plight of their men. Many looked admiringly at the Soviet Union, where the workers had rid themselves of the Tsar and seized control in 1917 under the leadership of Lenin and his Bolsheviks.

At the war's end in 1918 the political fabric of England was changed dramatically when the sheer weight of public opinion pushed Parliament into extending the **vote** to all men over 21 and to women over 30. This tardy liberalization of women's rights owed much to the efforts of the radical **Suffragettes**, led by Emmeline Pankhurst and her daughters Sylvia and Christabel, but the process was only completed in 1929 when women were at last granted the vote at 21, on equal terms with men.

During this period, the **Labour Party** supplanted the Liberals as the second largest party, its strength built on an alliance between the working-class trade unions and middle-class radicals. Labour formed its first government in 1923 under Ramsay MacDonald (1866–1937), but the publication of the **Zinoviev**

Letter, a forged document that purported to be a letter from the Soviets urging British leftists to promote revolution, undermined MacDonald's position and the Conservatives were returned with a large parliamentary majority in 1924. Two years later, in a time of acute economic difficulty, a bitter dispute between the nation's pit men and the owners of the coal mines spread to the railways, the newspapers and the iron and steel industries, escalating into a **General Strike**. The strike lasted nine days and involved half a million workers, provoking the government into draconian action – the army was called in, and the strike was broken. The economic situation deteriorated even further after the crash of the New York Stock Exchange in 1929, which precipitated a worldwide depression. Unemployment reached over 2.8 million in 1931, generating a series of mass demonstrations, which peaked with the **Jarrow March** from the northeast to London in 1936.

Abroad, the structure of the **British Empire** had undergone profound changes since World War I. The status of **Ireland** had been partly resolved following the electoral gains of the nationalist Sinn Féin in 1918. Their success led to the establishment of the Irish Free State in 1922, though (and this was to cause endless problems thereafter) the six counties of the mainly Protestant North (Ulster) chose to "contract out" and stay part of the United Kingdom. Four years later, the **Imperial Conference** recognized the autonomy of the British dominions, comprising all the major countries that had previously been part of the Empire. This agreement was formalized in the 1931 Statute of Westminster, whereby each dominion was given an equal footing in a Commonwealth of Nations, each still recognized the British monarch. The royal family itself was shaken in 1936 by the **abdication of Edward VIII**, following his decision to marry a twice-divorced American, Wallis Simpson. In the event, the succession passed smoothly to his brother **George VI**, but the royals had to play catch-up to regain their popularity among the population as a whole.

Non-intervention in both the Spanish Civil War and the Sino–Japanese War was paralleled by a policy of appeasement towards **Adolf Hitler**, who began to rearm Germany in earnest in the mid-1930s. This policy was epitomized by the antics of Prime Minister Neville Chamberlain, who returned from meeting Hitler at Munich in 1938 with an assurance of good intentions that he took at face value. Consequently, when **World War II** broke out in September 1939, Britain was seriously unprepared. In May 1940 the discredited Chamberlain stepped down in favour of a national coalition government headed by the charismatic **Winston Churchill** (1874–1965), whose bulldog steadfastness and heroic speeches provided the inspiration needed in the backs-against-the-wall mood of the time. Partly through Churchill's manoeuvrings, the United States became a supplier of foodstuffs and munitions to Britain and this, combined with the US's breaking off of trade links with Japan in June (in protest at their attacks on China), may have helped precipitate the Japanese bombing of Pearl Harbor on December 7, 1941. Once attacked, the US immediately joined the war, declaring against both Japan and Germany, and its intervention, combined with the heroic efforts of the Soviet Red Army, swung the military balance. In terms of the number of casualties, World War II was not as calamitous as World War I, but its impact upon the civilian population of Britain was much greater. In its first wave of **bombing** of the UK, the Luftwaffe caused massive damage to industrial centres such as London, Coventry, Manchester, Liverpool, Southampton and Plymouth. In later raids, intended to shatter morale rather than factories and docks, the cathedral cities of Canterbury, Exeter, Bath, Norwich and York all took a battering too. At the end of the fighting, nearly one in three of all the houses in the nation had been destroyed or damaged, nearly a quarter of a million members of the British armed forces and over 58,000 civilians had lost their lives.

Postwar England

The end of the war in 1945 was quickly followed by a general election. Hungry for change (and demobilization), the electorate replaced Churchill with a Labour government under **Clement Attlee** (1883–1967), who, with a large parliamentary majority, set about a radical programme to **nationalize** the coal, gas, electricity, iron and steel industries. Building on the plans for a social security system presented in Sir William Beveridge's report of 1943, the National Insurance Act and the National Health Service Act were both passed early in the Labour administration, giving birth to what became known as the **welfare state**. But despite substantial American aid, the huge problems of rebuilding the economy made **austerity** the keynote, with the rationing of food and fuel remaining in force long after 1945. This cost the Labour Party dear in the general election of 1951, which returned the Conservatives to power with a modest majority under the leadership of an ageing Churchill. The following year, King George VI died and was succeeded by one of his daughters, who, as **Queen Elizabeth II**, remains on the throne today.

Meanwhile, in April 1949, Britain, the United States, Canada, France and the Benelux countries signed the **North Atlantic Treaty** as a counterbalance to Soviet power in Eastern Europe, thereby defining the country's postwar international commitments. Yet confusion regarding Britain's post-imperial role was shown up by the **Suez Crisis** of 1956, when Anglo-French and Israeli forces invaded Egypt to secure control of the Suez Canal, only to be hastily recalled following international (American) condemnation. The Suez incident revealed severe limitations on the country's capacity for independent action, and resulted in the resignation of Churchill's successor as Conservative prime minister, Anthony Eden. Nonetheless, his successor, the more pragmatic **Harold Macmillan** (1894–1986), maintained a nuclear policy that suggested a continued desire for an international role, and nuclear testing went on against a background of widespread marches under the auspices of the Campaign for Nuclear Disarmament (CND).

The 1960s were dominated by the Labour premiership of **Harold Wilson** (1916–1995), and saw a boom in consumer spending, some pioneering social legislation (primarily on the legalization of homosexuality and abortion), and a cultural upswing, with London becoming the hippest city on the planet. The good times lasted barely a decade. Though Tory prime minister Edward Heath led Britain into the brave new world of the **European Economic Community** (**EEC**), the 1970s were a decade of recession and industrial strife. A succession of public-sector strikes and mistimed decisions by James Callaghan's Labour government handed the 1979 general election to the Conservatives under **Margaret Thatcher** (b.1925), who four years earlier had ousted Heath to become the first woman to lead a major political party in Britain.

1979 to 1997: Thatcher and Major

Thatcher went on to win three general elections, but pushed the UK into a period of sharp social polarization. While taxation policies and easy credit fuelled a consumer boom for the professional classes, the erosion of manufacturing industry and the weakening of the welfare state impoverished a great swathe of the population. Thatcher won an increased majority in the 1983 election, largely thanks to the successful recapture of the **Falkland Islands**, a remote British dependency in the south Atlantic, retrieved from the occupying Argentine army in 1982. Her electoral domination was also assisted by the fragmentation of the Labour opposition, particularly following the establishment of the short-lived

Social Democratic Party, which had split in panic at what it perceived as the radicalization of the Labour Party, but ended up amalgamating with what remained of the Liberal Party to form the **Liberal Democrats** in 1988.

Social and political tensions surfaced in sporadic urban rioting and the year-long **miners' strike** (1984–85) against colliery closures, a bitter industrial dispute in which the police were given unprecedented powers to restrict the movement of citizens. The violence in Northern Ireland also intensified, and in 1984 the bombing campaign of the **IRA** came close to killing the entire Cabinet when they blew up the Brighton hotel where the Conservatives were staying during their annual conference. The divisive politics of Thatcherism reached their apogee with the introduction of the **Poll Tax**, a desperately unpopular tax scheme that led ultimately to Thatcher's overthrow by Conservative colleagues who feared annihilation should she lead them into another general election. The beneficiary was **John Major** (b.1943), a notably uninspiring figure who nonetheless managed to win the Conservatives a fourth term of office in 1992, albeit with a much reduced Parliamentary majority. While his government presided over a steady growth in economic performance, they gained little credit amid allegations of mismanagement, incompetence and feckless leadership, all overlaid by endless tales of Tory "sleaze", with revelations of extramarital affairs and financial crookery gleefully blazed by the British press. There was also the small matter of ties with Europe: a good chunk of the Conservative Party wanted a European free-trade zone, but nothing more, whereas the **Maastricht Treaty** of 1992, which the UK government signed, had the spank of political/federal union with the EEC rebranded as the **European Union (EU)**; right-wing Tories were apoplectic and their frequent and very public demonstrations of disloyalty further hobbled the Major government.

Also in trouble by the mid-1990s was the **Royal Family**, whose credibility fissured with the break-up of the marriage of Prince Charles and Diana. Revelations about the cruel treatment of Diana by both the prince and his family badly damaged the royals' reputation and suddenly the institution itself seemed an anachronism, its members stiff, old-fashioned and dim-witted. By contrast, **Diana**, who was formally divorced from Charles in 1994, appeared warm-hearted and glamorous, so much so that her death in a car accident in Paris in 1997 may actually have saved the Royal Family as an institution. In the short term, Diana's death had a profound impact on the British, who joined in a media-orchestrated exercise in public grieving unprecedented in modern times.

1997 to 2007: The Blair years

Wracked by factionalism in the 1980s, the **Labour Party** regrouped under Neil Kinnock and then John Smith, though neither of them reaped the political rewards. These dropped into the lap of a new and dynamic young leader, **Tony Blair** (b.1953), who soon began to push the party further and further away from traditional left-wing socialism. Blair's mantle of idealistic, media-friendly populism worked to devastating effect, sweeping the Labour Party to power in the **general election of May 1997** on a wave of genuine popular optimism. There were immediate rewards in enhanced relations with the EU and progress in the Irish peace talks, and Blair's electoral touch was soon repeated in Labour-sponsored **devolution referenda**, whose results semi-detached Scotland and Wales from their larger neighbour in the form of a Scottish Parliament and Welsh Assembly.

Labour won the **general election of June 2001** with another parliamentary landslide. This second victory was, however, accompanied by little of the optimism of before. Few voters fully trusted Blair and his administration had by then established an unenviable reputation for the laundering of events to present the government in the best possible light. Nonetheless, the ailing Conservative Party failed to capitalize on these failings, leaving Blair streets ahead of his political rivals in the opinion polls when the hijacked planes hit New York's World Trade Center on **September 11, 2001**. Blair rushed to support President Bush, joining in the attack on Afghanistan and then, to the horror of millions of Brits, sending British forces into **Iraq** alongside the Americans in 2003. Saddam Hussein was deposed with relative ease, but neither Bush nor Blair had a coherent exit strategy, and back home Blair was widely seen as having spun Britain into the war by exaggerating the danger Saddam presented with his supposed – indeed nonexistent – **WMDs** (Weapons of Mass Destruction).

On the domestic front Blair proceeded with a massive and much-needed investment in **public services** during his second term, with education and health being the prime beneficiaries, and a concerted attempt to lift (many of) the country's poorer citizens out of poverty, though against a background of unpopularity these achievements did not secure the recognition they deserved. This was partly a consequence of the method: though committed to public service investment, Labour failed to trust its employees. The result was a top-down, command-and-control system in which central government imposed all sorts of targets – performance indicators and the like – in a welter of initiatives and regulation that confused almost everyone.

However, with the Conservatives still at reactionary sixes and sevens, Blair managed to win a **third general election in May 2005**, though not before he had promised to step down before the next general election thereafter – by any standard, a rather odd way to secure victory. After the election, Blair teased and tormented his many political enemies with promises of his imminent departure, but finally, in June 2007, he did indeed move on, and was succeeded uncontested by his arch-rival, the Chancellor of the Exchequer, **Gordon Brown** (b.1951).

2007 to the present

A deeply obsessive man, Brown proved to be an extraordinarily clumsy Prime Minister with a tin ear for the public mood. Blundering around, he failed to create a coherent narrative for either himself or his government, even managing to secure little credit for his one major achievement, the staving off of a banking collapse during the worldwide **financial crisis** that hit the UK hard in the autumn of 2007–08. Brown's bold decision to keep public investment high by borrowing vast sums of money almost certainly prevented a comprehensive economic collapse in 2008 and 2009, though equally his failure to properly regulate the banks beforehand helped create the crisis in the first place.

In the build-up to the **general election of 2010**, both main political parties – Conservative and Labour – as well as the Liberal Democrats, spoke of the need to cut public spending more or less drastically, manoeuvring the electorate away from blaming the bankers, if not indeed capitalism per se. In the event, none of the three was able to secure a Parliamentary majority in the election, but an impasse was avoided when the Liberal Democrats swapped principles for power to join a **Conservative–Liberal Democrat coalition**, which took office in May 2010 with the Conservative **David Cameron** (b.1966) as Prime Minister. Cameron has made a confident and sure-footed start. He is a very personable man with considerable charm and a leader who keeps his ideology (if indeed he has one) well hidden, but in the background his henchmen – and a woman or two – are, at time of writing, limbering up for a savage attack on the public sector under the cover of a need to reduce the national debt. How much of this the Liberal Democrats will stomach is hard to say, but at the moment they seem resolute allies.

Architecture

f England sometimes seems like a historic theme park, jam-packed with **monuments** and **buildings** recalling a fascinating past, then it's because physical evidence of its long history is so ubiquitous. Despite the best efforts of Victorian modernizers, the Luftwaffe and twentieth-century town planners, every corner of the country has some landmark worthy of attention, whether it be a Neolithic burial site or a postmodern addition to a world-famous gallery.

Pre-1066 origins

The oldest traces of building in England date from the **fourth millennium BC**, in the form of habitations – consisting of concentric rings of ditches and banks – and **long barrows** (burial sites) left by **Neolithic** peoples. The most famous of all English prehistoric monuments, the stone circle of **Stonehenge** on Salisbury Plain, was initiated in around 3000 BC and extensively modified over the next thousand years. This, and nearby **Avebury** probably had an astronomical and sacred significance. Less grandiose **stone circles and rows** survive from the Lake District to Bodmin Moor, while **hut circles** on the moors of the West Country are associated with the Bronze Age – **Grimspound**, on Dartmoor, is one of the best examples, dating from about 1200 BC. The **Celtic** invaders who arrived from around 700 BC left behind a series of hill-top defensive works, ranging from simple circular earthworks to the vast complex of **Maiden Castle** in Dorset. The best preserved Iron Age village of this period is **Chysauster**, Cornwall, consisting of stone houses arranged in pairs. The **Romans** brought order, peace and a slew of **public buildings**, including the surviving amphitheatre in **Chester** and baths in **Bath**. Two of Roman Britain's principal towns, **Colchester** and **St Albans**, retain impressive remains, while the palace at **Fishbourne** in West Sussex, built around 75 AD, is a prime example of a wealthy provincial villa. The most enduring relics of **Anglo-Saxon** construction were **stone-built churches**, though those that survived were subject to constant modifications, as was the case with two of the earliest English churches, both in **Canterbury** – St Peter and St Paul, and the town's first cathedral, both dating from around 600. The most impressive of all Saxon churches, however, lies in the Midlands, at **Brixworth** in Northamptonshire, erected around 670, and distinguished by the systematic use of arches. The later Anglo-Saxon era was characterized by Viking incursions and general disorder, though an emergent native style can be discerned in the churches and monasteries erected in the tenth century, many of which show a penchant for quirky decoration, as in the spiral columns in the crypt at St Wystan's Church in Repton, Derbyshire.

Norman architecture

The early eleventh century marks the turning point when England's architectural insularity faded away as Continental influences wafted across the Channel. When Edward the Confessor rebuilt **Westminster Abbey** (1050–65), he followed the Norman – or Romanesque – style, while French architectural styles became the dominant influence in both castles and churches following the Norman conquest of 1066. The earliest Norman castles followed a "motte and bailey" design, consisting of a central tower (or keep) placed on a mound (the motte) encircled by one or more courts (the baileys). Most such castles were built of wood until the time of the Plantagenet Henry II, though some were stone-constructed from the beginning, including those at **Rochester** and **Colchester** and the **White Tower** at the **Tower of London**, the most formidable of all the Norman strongholds.

Once the country had been secured, the Normans set about transforming the English Church. Many – for example at **Canterbury**, **York**, **St Albans**, **Winchester**, **Worcester** and **Ely** – were rebuilt along Romanesque lines, with cruciform ground plans and massive cylindrical columns topped by semicircular arches. The finest Norman church was **Durham Cathedral**, begun in 1093 and boasting Europe's first example of large-scale ribbed vaulting. An increasing love of decoration was evident in the spectacular zigzag and diamond patterns on its colossal piers, in the elaborately carved capitals and blind arcading in Canterbury Cathedral, and in the beakhead moulding in Lincoln Cathedral.

The Transitional and Early English styles

The twelfth century brought a dramatic increase in the wealth and power of England's **monastic houses**. The **Cistercians** were responsible for some of the most splendid foundations, establishing an especially grand group of self-sufficient monasteries in Yorkshire – **Fountains**, **Rievaulx** and **Jervaulx** – which all featured examples of the pointed arch, an idea imported from northern France. The reforming Cistercians favoured a plain style, but the native penchant for decoration gradually infiltrated their buildings, as at **Kirkstall Abbey** (c.1152), near Leeds. Other orders, such as the **Cluniacs**, showed a preference for greater elaboration from much earlier, as in the extravagantly ornate west front of Norfolk's **Castle Acre** priory (1140–50).

Profuse carved decoration and pointed arches were distinctive elements in the evolution of a **Transitional style**, which, from the middle of the twelfth century, represented a shift away from purely Romanesque forms. The use of the pointed arch, alongside improvements in masonry techniques and the introduction of new systems of buttressing and vaulting, meant taller buildings, proportionally larger windows and more slender piers.

Gothic architecture began in earnest in the last quarter of the twelfth century, when Gothic motifs were used at **Roche Abbey** and **Byland**, both in Yorkshire, but it was the French-designed **choir** at **Canterbury Cathedral** (1175–84) that really established the new style. This first phase of English Gothic, lasting through most of the thirteenth century, is known as **Early English** (or Pointed or Lancet), and was given its full expression in what is regarded as the first truly Gothic cathedral in England, **Wells**, largely completed by 1190.

Begun shortly afterwards, **Lincoln Cathedral** takes the process of vertical emphasis further, with wall-shafts soaring all the way to the ceiling, while adding an even greater profusion of decoration. The strong influence of Lincoln, however, was resisted by the builders of **Salisbury Cathedral** (1220–65), one of the most homogeneous of the Early English churches.

A transitional phase in the evolution of Gothic architecture is represented by the **rebuilding of Westminster Abbey** in 1220. This became the most French of English churches, as shown in the flying buttresses added to support its greater height and in the lavish use of **window tracery**, created by subdividing each window with moulded ribs (or mullions).

The Decorated and Perpendicular styles

The development of complicated **tracery** is one of the chief characteristics of the **Decorated** style, which reached its apotheosis around the end of the thirteenth century and the beginning of the fourteenth, when the cathedral at **Exeter** was almost completely rebuilt with a dense exuberance of rib vaulting and multiple moulding on the arches and piers. **York Minster**, rebuilt from 1225 and the largest of all English Gothic churches, introduced **lierne vaulting**, whereby a subsidiary, mainly ornamental, rib is added to the roof complex. Intricately carved roof bosses and capitals are other common features of Decorated Gothic, as is the use of the **ogee curve** – a curve with a double bend in it.

The prevalent style in the second half of the fourteenth century, the **Perpendicular**, was the first post-Conquest architecture unique to England, emphasizing a more rectilinear and less flamboyant design. In **Gloucester Cathedral** (rebuilt 1337–57), for example, this can be seen in the massive east window, in which the maximization of light is paramount and the tracery organized in vertical compartments, while the cloister features the first fully developed **fan vault**.

The Wars of the Roses meant that few new "prestige" buildings were commissioned in the second half of the fifteenth century, though parish churches eagerly embraced the new Perpendicular style. Tudor rule saw a resurgence of royal patronage and the construction of three splendid chapels during the reign of Henry VII – **St George's Chapel**, Windsor; **King's College Chapel**, Cambridge; and **Henry VII's Chapel** in Westminster Abbey. At King's College, the fan vaulting extended over the whole nave and harmonized with the windows and wall panelling, but it was the densely sculptured Chapel of Henry VII that took such vaulting to the limit, with the lavish use of decorative pendants – a rare element in English design.

The Renaissance

The impact of **Renaissance** architecture during the Tudor era was largely confined to small decorative features, such as the Italianate embellishments at **Hampton Court Palace**. The dissemination of the latest ideas in design and decoration came about chiefly through individual commissions from courtiers and statesmen in such mansions as **Burghley House**, Lincolnshire (1552–87), **Longleat**, Wiltshire (1568–80), and **Hardwick Hall** in Derbyshire (1591–96) – celebrated in local rhyme as "Hardwick Hall, more glass than wall".

The full spirit of the Renaissance did not find full expression in England until **Inigo Jones** (1573–1652) began to apply the lessons learned from his visits to Italy, and in particular from his familiarity with Palladio's rules of proportion and symmetry. Appointed Royal Surveyor in 1615, Jones changed the direction of English architecture, with prominent London works including the **Banqueting House**, Whitehall (1619–22); the **Queen's House** at Greenwich (1617–35); and **St Paul's Church**, Covent Garden (1630s), the focal point of the first planned city square in England.

Wren and the Baroque

The artistic heir of Inigo Jones, **Christopher Wren** (1632–1723) had already established himself as a mathematician and astronomer before turning to architecture shortly after the Restoration of 1660. Wren's work was never so wholeheartedly Italianate as that of Jones, and his first building, Oxford's **Sheldonian Theatre**, demonstrated an eclectic style that combined orthodox classicism with **Baroque** inventiveness and French and Dutch elements.

The bulk of Wren's achievement is to be seen in London, where the **Great Fire of 1666** led to a commission for the building of no less than 53 churches. The most striking of these buildings display a remarkable elegance and harmony, notably **St Bride** in Fleet Street, **St Mary-le-Bow** in Cheapside, **St Stephen Walbrook** alongside Mansion House and, most monumental of all, **St Paul's Cathedral** (1675–1710), with its massive central dome.

Glossary of architectural terms

Aisle Clear space parallel to the nave, usually with lower ceiling than the nave.

Altar Table at which the Eucharist is celebrated, at the east end of the church.

Ambulatory Covered passage around the outer edge of the choir of a church.

Apse The curved or polygonal east end of a church.

Arcade Row of arches on top of columns or piers, supporting a wall.

Art Deco Geometrical style of art and architecture popular in the 1930s.

Art Nouveau Style of art, architecture and design based on highly stylized vegetal forms. Especially popular in the early part of the twentieth century.

Ashlar Dressed building-stone worked to a smooth finish.

Bailey Area enclosed by castle walls.

Balustrade An ornamental rail, running, almost invariably, along the top of a building.

Barbican Defensive structure built in front of a main gate.

Barrel vault Continuous rounded vault, like a semi-cylinder.

Boss A decorative carving at the meeting point of the lines of a vault.

Box pew Form of church seating in which each row is enclosed by high, thin wooden panels.

Buttress Stone support for a wall; some buttresses are wholly attached to the wall, others take the form of an outer support with a connecting half-arch, known as a "flying buttress".

Capital Upper section of a column, usually carved.

Chancel The eastern part of a church, often separated from the nave by a screen (see "Rood-screen"). Contains the choir and ambulatory.

Chantry Small chapel in which masses were said for the soul of the person who financed its construction; none built after the Reformation as Protestants rejected the doctrine of prayers for the dead.

Choir Area in which the church service is conducted; next to or the same as the chancel.

Classical Architectural style incorporating Greek and Roman elements – pillars, domes, colonnades etc – at its height in the seventeenth century and revived, as Neoclassical (see opposite), in the nineteenth.

Clerestory Upper story of a church, with windows.

Crenellations Battlements with square indentations.

Crossing (church) The intersection of the nave, choir and transepts.

Decorated Middle Gothic style; about 1280–1380.

Dormer Window raised out of the main roof.

Early English First phase of Gothic architecture in England; about 1150–1280.

Fan vaulting Late Gothic form of vaulting, in which the area between the walls and ceiling is covered with stone ribs in the shape of an open fan.

Finial Any decorated tip of an architectural feature.

Fresco Wall painting – durable through application to wet plaster.

Gargoyle Grotesque exterior carving, usually a decorative form of water spout.

Gothic Architectural style of the thirteenth to sixteenth centuries, characterized by pointed arches, rib vaulting, flying buttresses and a general emphasis on verticality. See also "Decorated", "Early English" and "Perpendicular".

Wren also rebuilt, extended or altered several royal palaces, including the south and east wings of **Hampton Court** (1689–1700). Other secular works include **Trinity College Library**, Cambridge (1676–84), the **Tom Tower of Christ**

Hammerbeam Type of ceiling in which horizontal brackets support vertical struts that connect to the roof timbers.

Jesse Tree Christian legend asserts that Jesse, the father of King David, was the ancestor of Jesus, and Jesse windows trace the genealogical tree by means of their stained-glass pictures.

Keep Main structure of a castle.

Lady Chapel Chapel dedicated to the Virgin, often found at the east end of major churches.

Lancet Tall, narrow and plain window.

Lantern Upper part of a dome or tower, often glazed.

Misericord Ledge on choir stall on which the occupant can be supported while standing; often carved with secular subjects.

Motte Mound on which a castle keep stands.

Mullion Vertical post between the panes of a window.

Nave Main body of a church.

Neoclassical A style of classical architecture (see opposite) revived in the nineteenth century.

Neo-Gothic Revived Gothic style of architecture popular in the late eighteenth and nineteenth centuries.

Ogee Double curve; distinctive feature of Decorated style.

Oriel Projecting window.

Palladian Seventeenth- and eighteenth-century classical style adhering to the principles of Andrea Palladio.

Pediment Triangular space above a window or doorway.

Perpendicular Late Gothic style; about 1380–1550.

Pier A massive column, often consisting of several fused smaller columns.

Renaissance The period of European history, begun in Italy, marking the end of the medieval period and the rise of the modern world. Defined, among many criteria, by an increase in classical scholarship, geographical discovery, the rise of secular values and the growth of individualism.

Reredos Painted or carved panel behind an altar.

Retable Altarpiece.

Romanesque Early medieval architecture distinguished by squat, heavy forms, rounded arches and naive sculpture.

Rood-screen Decorative screen separating the nave from the chancel.

Rose window Large circular window, divided into vaguely petal-shaped sections.

Stalls Seating for clergy in the choir area of a church.

Tracery Pattern formed by narrow bands of stone in a window or on a wall surface.

Transept Arms of a cross-shaped church, placed at ninety degrees to nave and chancel.

Triptych Carved or painted work on three panels. Often used as an altarpiece.

Tympanum Sculpted, usually recessed, panel above a door.

Vault An arched ceiling or roof.

Church, Oxford (1681–82) – a rare work in the Gothic mode – and, grandest of all, **Greenwich Hospital** (1694–98), a magnificent foil to the Queen's House built by Inigo Jones, and to Wren's own Royal Observatory (1675).

Work at Greenwich Hospital was continued by Wren's pupil, **Nicholas Hawksmoor** (1661–1736), whose distinctively muscular form of the Baroque is seen to best effect in his London churches, such as **St George-in-the-East** (1715–23) and **Christ Church**, Spitalfields (1723–29). His exercises in Gothic pastiche include the western towers of **Westminster Abbey** (1734) and **All Souls College**, Oxford (1716–35), while the mausoleum at Castle Howard in Yorkshire (1729) shows close affinities with the Roman Baroque.

The third great English architect of the Baroque era was **John Vanbrugh** (1664–1726), primarily known as a dramatist and lacking any architectural training when he was commissioned to design a new country seat at **Castle Howard** (1699–1726). More flamboyant than either Hawksmoor or Wren, Vanbrugh went on to design numerous other grandiose houses, of which the outstanding example is the gargantuan **Blenheim Palace** (1705–20), the culminating point of English Baroque.

Gibbs and Palladianism

The period of peace that followed the Treaty of Utrecht (1713) allowed English aristocrats and artisans to travel on the Continent and absorb European influences. The most obvious effect was the rebirth in England of the **Palladian** architecture introduced by Inigo Jones a century before – a style that was to dominate the secular architecture of the eighteenth century. The Palladian movement was championed by a Whig elite led by **Lord Burlington** (1694–1753), whose own masterpiece was **Chiswick House** in London (1725), a domed villa closely modelled on Palladio's Villa Rotonda. Burlington collaborated with the decorator, garden designer and architect **William Kent** (1685–1748) on such stately piles as **Holkham Hall** in Norfolk (1734), whose imposing portico and ordered composition typify the break with Baroque dramatics.

In the field of church architecture, the most influential architect of the time was **James Gibbs** (1682–1754), whose masterpiece, **St Martin-in-the-Fields** in London (1722–26), with its steeple sprouting above a pedimented portico, was widely imitated as a model of how to combine the Classical with the Gothic. Elsewhere, Gibbs designed **Senate House** (1722–30) and the **Fellows' Building** at King's College (1723–49), both in Cambridge, and Oxford's **Radcliffe Camera** (1737–49), which drew heavily on his knowledge of Roman styles.

The Palladian idiom was further disseminated by such men as **John Wood** (1704–54), designer of **Liverpool Town Hall** (1749–54) but better known for the work he did in **Bath**, helping to transform the city into a paragon of town planning. His showpieces there are **Queen Square** (1729–36) and the **Circus** (1754), the latter completed by his son, **John Wood the Younger** (1728–81), who went on to design Bath's **Royal Crescent** (1767–74). Georgian Bath was further developed by **Robert Adam** (1728–92), the most versatile and refined architect of his day, who designed the city's **Pulteney Bridge** (1769–74). Adam's forte, however, was in designing elaborate decorative interiors, best displayed in **Syon House** (1762–69) and **Osterley Park** (1761–80), both on the western outskirts of London, and **Kenwood** (1767–79) on the edge of Hampstead Heath. Adam's chief rival was the more fastidious **William Chambers** (1723–96), whose masterpiece, **Somerset House** on London's Strand (1776–98), is an academic counterpoint to Adam's dashing originality.

One area in which English designers excelled in the eighteenth century was **landscape gardening**, whose greatest exponent was **Capability Brown** (1716–83). All over England, Brown and his acolytes modified the estates of the landed gentry into idealized "Picturesque" landscapes, often enhancing the view with a romantic "ruin" or some exotic structure such as a Chinese pagoda or Indian temple. One of Brown's earliest and most spectacular designs was at **Stowe** in Buckinghamshire, while **Chatsworth** in the Peak District combined his vision with the talents of **Joseph Paxton**, who contributed to the estate in the following century.

The nineteenth century

The greatest architect of the late eighteenth and early nineteenth centuries was **John Nash** (1752–1835), whose Picturesque country houses were built in collaboration with the landscapist **Humphrey Repton** (1752–1818). Nash is associated above all with the style favoured during the **Regency** of his friend and patron the Prince of Wales (afterwards George IV), a decorous style that made plentiful use of stucco. A prolific worker, Nash was responsible for much of the present-day appearance of such **resorts** as Weymouth, Cheltenham, Clifton (in Bristol), Tunbridge Wells and Brighton, site of his orientalized Gothic palace, the **Brighton Pavilion**. In central **London**, his constructions include the **Haymarket Theatre** (1820), the church of **All Souls**, Langham Place (1822–25), and **Clarence House** (1825), not to mention the layout of **Regent's Park** and **Regent Street** (from 1811), and the remodelling of **Buckingham Palace** (1826–30). The pared-down Classical experiments of Nash's contemporary, **Sir John Soane** (1753–1837), presented a serious-minded contrast to Nash's extrovert creations. Little remains of his greatest masterpiece, the **Bank of England** (1788–1833), but his idiosyncratic style is well illustrated by two other buildings in London – his own home, **Sir John Soane's Museum** on Lincoln's Inn Fields (1812–13) and **Dulwich Art Gallery** (1811–14).

Nash and other exponents of the Picturesque also dabbled in a version of the Gothic style, and when Parliament voted a million pounds for the construction of new Anglican churches in 1818, two-thirds of these were built in a Gothic or near-Gothic style, inaugurating the so-called **Gothic Revival**. The pre-eminence of neo-Gothic was confirmed when the **Houses of Parliament** were rebuilt in that style after the fire of 1834. The contract was given to Charles Barry (1795–1860), the designer of the classical Reform Club, but his collaborator, **Augustus Welby Pugin** (1812–52), was to become the unswerving apostle of the neo-Gothic. Another eminent architect, **George Gilbert Scott** (1811–78) vented his neo-Gothic predilections in the extravaganzas of **St Pancras Station** (1868–74) and the **Albert Memorial** (1863–72), both based on Flemish and north Italian Gothic models, while **Truro Cathedral** (1880–1910) was a scholarly exercise in French-influenced Gothic.

Nonetheless, the Victorian age was nothing if not eclectic: many public buildings continued to draw on Renaissance and Classical influences – notably the town halls of Birmingham and Leeds (1832–50 & 1853–58) – and the Catholic **Westminster Cathedral** (1895–1903) was a neo-Byzantine design. The architectural stew was further enriched by a string of engineer-architects, who employed cast iron and other industrial materials in such works as Joseph Paxton's glass-and-iron **Crystal Palace** (1851, burned down in 1936). The potential of iron and glass was similarly exploited in **Newcastle Central Station** (1846–55), the first of a generation of monumental railway stations incorporating classical motifs and rib-vaulted iron roofs.

John Ruskin (1819–1900) and his disciple **William Morris** (1834–96), leader of the Arts and Crafts Movement, rejected these industrial technologies in favour of traditional materials – such as brick, stone and timber – worked in traditional ways. Morris was not an architect himself, but he did plan the interior of his own home, the Red House in Bexley, Kent (1854), from designs by Philip Webb (1831–1915). The Arts and Crafts Movement also influenced **Charles Voysey** (1851–1941), whose clean-cut cottages and houses eschewed all ostentation, depending instead on the meticulous and subtle use of local materials for their effect. The originality of

Voysey's work and that of his contemporaries M.H. Baillie Scott (1865–1945) and Ernest Newton (1856–1922) was later debased by scores of speculative suburban builders, though not before their refreshingly simple style had found recognition first in Germany and then across the rest of Europe.

The twentieth century

Revivalist tendencies prevailed in England throughout the early decades of the twentieth century, typified by **Edwin Lutyens** (1869–1944), whose work moved from the Arts and Crafts style through to classicized structures, neo-Georgianism and the one-off faux-medieval **Castle Drogo** on Dartmoor (1910–30). An awareness of more radical trends surfaced in isolated projects in the 1930s, for example **Senate House** in London's Bloomsbury (1932), designed by **Charles Holden** (1875–1960), who was also responsible for some of London's Underground stations, notably **Arnos Grove** (1932). The **Tecton group**, led by the Russian immigrant Lubetkin, also created several successful examples of the austere International Modern style, most notably London Zoo's **Penguin Pool** (1934). The UK's first public building built in the modernist style was the sleek, streamlined **De La Warr Pavilion** in Bexhill-on-Sea, Sussex, designed by Erich Mendelsohn and Serge Chermayeff in 1935, and described by Mendelsohn as a "horizontal skyscraper".

Nonetheless, there was no general acceptance of architectural modernism in England before the 1951 **Festival of Britain** on London's South Bank, which showcased the latest technological marvels. Many of the festival pavilions were designed by **Basil Spence** (1907–76), whose best-known work was the replacement of the bombed **Coventry Cathedral** (1951–59), incorporating defiantly modernist detail into a neo-Gothic structure. The only architectural survivor of the Festival of Britain is the **Royal Festival Hall** (1949–51), a triumphant modernist departure from the traditional model for classical music venues. The site was later augmented by the addition of the far less attractive **National Theatre** (1967–77) by the Tecton architect **Denys Lasdun** (1914–2001). Prestige projects apart, the bombs of World War II had helped create a national **housing crisis** of immense proportions. The problem was that speed of reconstruction – rather than quality – was too often the key criterion and the consequent use of **prefabricated units** produced generally dire results. **Tower blocks** sprouted up by the score, creating the desolate urban wastelands that are a characteristic feature of English cities today, while the wholesale restructuring of scores of city centres led to roads being ploughed through willy-nilly, to service yet more concrete office blocks and shopping centres. The general situation might have been desperate, but some interesting 1960s architecture was created at the new "red-brick" universities, notable examples being Spence's **Sussex University** at Brighton (1961) and Lasdun's **University of East Anglia** at Norwich (1963).

The universities were also where a new generation of architects cut their teeth, most notably **James Stirling** (1926–92), **Norman Foster** (b.1935) and **Richard Rogers** (b.1933), who reacted against the general urban desolation with such buildings as Rogers' bold, high-tech **Lloyd's Building** (1978–86), Stirling's postmodern extension for the **Tate Gallery** (1989) – both in London – and Foster's glass-tent terminal at **Stansted Airport** (1991). During this period, the architectural scene was stranded between a popular dislike for the modern and a general reluctance among architects to return to the architectural past. **Prince Charles** also entered the debate: his notorious comment on plans for the new Sainsbury Wing at London's National Gallery ("a monstrous carbuncle on the face of a much-loved and elegant friend") resulted in a replacement of the original design with a much safer Neoclassical pastiche, and a general backtracking on architectural modernism. The general public, however, generally responded enthusiastically to new buildings exhibiting wit and/or sinuosity, such as **Michael Hopkins'** eye-catching Mound Stand for Lord's Cricket Ground (1985–87) and his wood-panelled auditorium at the **Glyndebourne Opera House** (1994).

The 2000s and beyond

In London, the turn of the century saw Rogers' **Millennium Dome** (1999, now the O2 arena) erected in Greenwich; the spectacular transformation of Giles Gilbert Scott's South Bank power station into **Tate Modern** (2000) by Herzog & de Meuron; and, by the Norman Foster group, the **Great Court** (2000) at the British Museum, the **Greater London Assembly** (2002) and **The Gherkin** (officially 30 St Mary Axe; 2004) in the City. Exciting and fresh work can appear in the unlikeliest of places, as within the hallowed Victorian frontage of **St Pancras Station**, overhauled and reopened to grand acclaim in 2007, at Richard Rogers' controversial but ultimately triumphant **Terminal 5** at Heathrow Airport (2008), and – on a smaller scale – in the thrilling transformation of **Whitechapel Gallery** (Robbrecht en Daem, 2009). Outside the capital, a number of formerly industrial cities have similarly rebranded themselves by means of such eye-catching developments as Gateshead's **BALTIC** arts centre (Ellis Williams Architects, 2002) and **Sage Gateshead** (Foster and Partners, 2004); Manchester's striking **Imperial War Museum North** (Libeskind, 2002); Birmingham's **Selfridges** department store (Future Systems, 2003); **Nottingham Contemporary** art gallery (Caruso St John, 2009); and the redevelopment of Liverpool's Paradise Street as **Liverpool One**, opened in 2008–09.

Meanwhile back in London, skyscrapers came back into vogue in the late 2000s, with an array of new constructions set to transform the city's skyline, such as Kohn Pederson Fox's **Heron Tower** and **Pinnacle** and Renzo Piano's **Shard**, which will be the country's tallest building when complete in 2012. Sustainability is the buzzword of most new projects these days, from museums and galleries to schools and libraries, often incorporating the ideas of "organic architecture" – harmonizing individual and local needs and using environmentally friendly materials – though how many new public schemes survive the recession remains to be seen. Certain to be completed, however, are the new venues currently under construction for the 2012 Olympic Games in London. And while some have questioned the supposedly sustainable credentials of the **Olympic Stadium** or Zaha Hadid's **Aquatic Centre**, many of the less flamboyant buildings planned for the Games will highlight their eco-worthiness while showcasing cutting-edge designs.

Books and literature

A tour of literary England could take many lifetimes. Many of the world's most famous writers were born, lived and died here, leaving footprints that reach into every corner of the country. Writers' birthplaces, houses, libraries and graves are a staple of local tourist industries, while in places like Stratford-upon-Avon or Grasmere literature and tourism have formed an unbreakable symbiosis. England even has one quintessential bookish destination, Hay-on-Wye, the town on the Anglo–Welsh border that is entirely devoted to the buying, selling and enjoyment of books – its annual literary festival (every May) is the nation's biggest book-related jamboree.

Literary England

For readers and book-lovers of all ages, there's something deeply satisfying about immersing yourself in English literature's natural fabric, whether it's tramping the Yorkshire moors with the Brontë sisters or exploring the streets of Dickens' Rochester. And for every over-trumpeted sight in "Shakespeare Country" or "Beatrix Potter's Lakeland" there are dozens of other locales that contemporary English writer have made unquestionably their own, from Martin Amis's London to P.D. James's East Anglia. Here's our pick of the best places to follow in the footsteps of your favourite author.

Shakespeare Country

Warwickshire in the West Midlands is – as the road signs attest – "Shakespeare Country", though to all intents and purposes it's a county with just one destination – **Stratford-upon-Avon**, birthplace in 1564 of England's greatest writer. So few facts about Shakespeare's life are known that Stratford can be a disappointment for the serious literary pilgrim, its buildings and sights hedged with "reputedlys" and "maybes" – after 500 years, still the only incontrovertible evidence is that he was born in Stratford, and lived, married, had children and died there. Real Shakespeare country could just as easily be London, where his plays were written and performed (there was no theatre in Stratford in Shakespeare's day). But, from the house where he was born (probably) to the church in which he's buried (definitely), Stratford at least provides a coherent centre for England's Shakespeare industry – and it's certainly the most atmospheric place to see a production by the Royal Shakespeare Company.

Wordsworth's Lake District

William Wordsworth and the **Lake District** are inextricably linked, and in the streets of Cockermouth (where he was born), Hawkshead (where he went to school) and Grasmere (where he lived most of his life), you're never very far from a sight associated with the poet and his circle. Wordsworth's views on nature and the natural world stood at the very heart of all his poetry, and it's still a jolt to encounter the very views that inspired him – from his carefully tended garden at Rydal Mount to the famous daffodils of Gowbarrow Park. It wasn't just Wordsworth either. The "Lake Poets" of popular description – Wordsworth, Samuel Taylor Coleridge and Robert Southey – formed a clique of fluctuating friendships with a shared passion for the Lakes at its core.

Poetic England

From the *Canterbury Tales* onwards, English poets have taken inspiration from the country's people and landscape. Traditionally, much was made of England's rural lives and trades, by poets as diverse as Northamptonshire "peasant poet" John Clare and A.E. Housman, whose nostalgic *A Shropshire Lad* is one of English poetry's most favoured works. For poets like Cumbria's Norman Nicholson it was working people, their dialect and industry that inspired, while in Yorkshire-born (and later Devon resident) Ted Hughes, savage English nature found a unique voice. Perhaps there's something about the north in particular that engages and enrages poets: Philip Larkin, famously, spent the last thirty years of his life in Hull; the self-proclaimed "bard of Salford", John Cooper Clarke, skewered Manchester in his early machine-gun-style punk poems; and Huddersfield-born Simon Armitage continues to report "from the long, lifeless mud of the River Colne". Meanwhile, dub poet Linton Kwesi Johnson uses Jamaican patois in devastating commentaries on the English social condition ("Inglan is a bitch").

Haworth and the Brontës

Quite why the sheltered life of the Brontë sisters, Charlotte, Emily and Anne, should exert such a powerful fascination is a puzzle, though the contrast of their pinched provincial existence in the Yorkshire village of **Haworth** with the brooding moors and tumultuous passions of their novels may well form part of the answer. Their old home in the village parsonage and the family vault in the parish church only tell half the story. As Charlotte later recalled, "resident in a remote district... we were wholly dependent on ourselves and each other, on books and study, for the enjoyments and occupations of life". Charlotte's *Jane Eyre*, the harrowing story of a much-put-upon governess, sprang from this domestic isolation, yet it was out on the bleak moors above Haworth that inspiration often struck, and where works like Emily's *Wuthering Heights* and Anne's *The Tenant of Wildfell Hall* progressed from mere parlour entertainments to melodramatic studies of emotion and obsession.

Dickensian England

Charles Dickens' name has passed into the language as shorthand for a city's filthy stew of streets and gallery of grotesques. But although any dark alley or old curiosity shop in London might still be considered "Dickensian", it's a different matter trying to trace the author through his works. He was born in **Portsmouth**, though spent his younger years in **Chatham** and **Rochester**, in Kent (and set most of his last book, *The Mystery of Edwin Drood*, in the latter). Is this Dickensian England? Perhaps, though many of the most famous books – including *Oliver Twist*, *David Copperfield*, *Bleak House* and *Little Dorrit* – are set or partly set in a **London** that Dickens unquestionably made his own. His unhappy early experiences of the city – the boot-blacking factory at the age of twelve, his father's spell in a debtors' prison, working as a law clerk – form the basis of many of Dickens' most trenchant pieces of social analysis. Yet only one of his London houses survives (now the Charles Dickens Museum in Bloomsbury), and he only lived in that for two years. To the north then, finally, for Dickensian England, to the fictional "Coketown" of *Hard Times*. Dickens went to Preston and other **Lancashire** mill towns to gather material for his "state-of-the-nation" satire about the social and economic conditions of factory workers, while in **Barnard Castle** (County Durham) he found a heartbreaking neglect of schoolchildren that underpinned the magnificent *Nicholas Nickleby*.

Criminal England

Contemporary crime writers have moved well beyond the enclosed country-house mysteries of Agatha Christie. Colin Dexter's morose Inspector Morse flits between Town and Gown in university **Oxford** in a cerebral series of whodunnits, while in the elegantly crafted novels of P.D. James it's the remote coast and isolated villages of **East Anglia** that often provide the backdrop. The other English "Queen of Crime", Ruth Rendell, sets her long-running Inspector Wexford series in "Kingsmarkham" – inspired by Midhurst in **West Sussex**, surely the most crime-ridden town in the country after over twenty Wexford novels. **London**, of course, preoccupies many writers, from Derek Raymond or Jake Arnott re-creating Sixties villainy to Rendell again, writing as Barbara Vine, at home with the capital's suburban misfits, drop-outs and damaged. Val McDermid, and her sassy private eye, Kate Brannigan, nail contemporary **Manchester**, and the seedier side of the city also gets a good kicking in the noir novels of Nicholas Blincoe. **Yorkshire** of the 1970s and 1980s is dissected in David Peace's majestic Red Riding quartet about corrupt police; Reginald Hill's popular Dalziel and Pascoe series portrays a more traditional pair of Yorkshire detectives, but in his Joe Sixsmith private-eye novels it's a re-imagined **Luton** that forms the backdrop. Graham Greene gave us seedy **Brighton** first; Peter James' policeman, Roy Grace, digs further into its underbelly, while in **Portsmouth** it's Graham Hurley's Joe Faraday charged with keeping the peace. Britain's rural areas don't escape the escalating body count either. Peter Robinson's Inspector Banks series is set in the **Yorkshire Dales**, and for Stephen Booth and his Derbyshire detective Ben Cooper it's the wilds of the **Peak District**.

Recommended books

Whether you're looking for light holiday reading, historical background, classic literature or an insight into what it is to be English, you should find something appealing in the list of books reviewed below. It's necessarily selective, and entirely subjective – feel free to disagree. Most of the books reviewed are currently in print, though if local bookshops can't help then the online bookseller Amazon almost certainly can (⊛www.amazon.co.uk, ⊛www.amazon.com).

Travels and places

Peter Ackroyd *London: The Biography*; *Albion*. The capital is integral to many of Ackroyd's works, novels to biographies, and in *London* the great city itself is presented as a living organism, with themed chapters covering its fables, follies and foibles. Meanwhile, in the massively erudite *Albion*, Ackroyd traces the very origins of English culture and imagination.

Bill Bryson *Notes From A Small Island*. After twenty years living and working in England, Bryson set off on one last tour of Britain before returning to the States – his snort-with-laughter observations set the tone for his future

travel, popular science and language best-sellers.

Paul Kingsnorth *Real England*. Kingsnorth's personal journey through his own "private England" is partly a lament for what's being lost – village greens, apple varieties, independent shops, waterways, post offices – and partly a heartfelt howl against globalization.

Stuart Maconie *Pies and Prejudice*; *Adventures on the High Teas*. A Lancastrian exile explores the north of England in *Pies*, in which you can find out where the north starts (Crewe

Windows onto England's past

In his celebrated diary, **Samuel Pepys** recorded an eyewitness account of daily life in London from 1660 until 1669, covering momentous events like the Great Plague and the Great Fire. The plague of 1665 also takes centre stage in *Journal of a Plague Year* by **Daniel Defoe** (author of *Robinson Crusoe*), a fictional "observation" of London's trials actually written sixty years later, while the same author's *Tour Through the Whole Island of Great Britain* (1724) was an early sort of economic guide to the country in the years immediately before the Industrial Revolution. Later, the changing seasons in a Hampshire village were recorded by **Gilbert White**, whose *Natural History of Selborne* (1788) is still seen as a masterpiece of nature writing. By 1830, **William Cobbett** was bemoaning the death of rural England and its customs in *Rural Rides*, while decrying both the growth of cities and the iniquities suffered by the exploited urban poor. These last were given magnificent expression in *The Condition of the Working Class in England*, an unforgettable portrait of life in England's hellish industrial towns, published in 1844 as **Friedrich Engels** worked in his father's Manchester cotton mills. Journalist **Henry Mayhew** would later do something similar for the Victorian capital's downtrodden in his mighty *London Labour and the London Poor* (1851). **George Orwell** was therefore following in a well-worn path when he published his dissections of 1920s' and 1930s' working-class and under-class life, *Down and Out in Paris and London* (1933) and *The Road to Wigan Pier* (1937), giving respectively a tramp's-eye view of the world and the brutal effects of the Great Depression on the industrial communities of Lancashire and Yorkshire. A later period of English transformation was recorded in *Akenfield* (1969), the surprising best-seller by **Ronald Blythe** that presented life in a rural Suffolk village on the cusp of change. Craig Taylor's update, *Return to Akenfield* (2006), and **Richard Askwith**'s *The Lost Village* (2008) show that interest in ordinary English rural life endures today, while in *The Plot* (2009), **Madeleine Bunting** presents an innovative through-the-ages biography of a secluded acre of land owned by her father that gets to the very heart of the English spirit.

station, apparently) and unravel the arcane mysteries of northern dialect, dress and delicacies. *Adventures* continues his engaging investigation of the country, this time of the mythical "Middle England" so beloved of social commentators.

Ian Marchant *The Longest Crawl*. The pub – so central to English life and landscape – is dissected in this highly entertaining account of a month-long crawl across the country, involving pork scratchings, funny beer names and lots of falling over.

Harry Pearson *Racing Pigs and Giant Marrows*; *The Far Corner*. The subtitles tell you all you need to know about content – "Travels Around North Country Fairs" and "A Mazy Dribble Through North-East Football" respectively – though they don't tell you that you'll laugh until you're sick.

J.B. Priestley *English Journey*. The Bradford-born playwright and

author's record of his travels around England in the 1930s say nothing about contemporary England, but in many ways its quirkiness and eye for English eccentricity formed the blueprint for the later Brysons and Therouxs.

W.G. Sebald *Rings of Saturn*. Intriguing, ruminative book that is a heady mix of novel, travel and memoir, focusing ostensibly on the author's walking tour of Suffolk.

Iain Sinclair *London Orbital*. After spending a couple of years walking around the "concrete necklace" of the M25, the erudite Sinclair delves into the dark and mysterious heart of suburban London.

Paul Theroux *The Kingdom by the Sea*. Travelling around the British coast in its entirety in 1982 to find out what the British are really like leaves Theroux thoroughly bad tempered. No change there then.

Guidebooks

Simon Jenkins *England's Thousand Best Churches*; *England's Thousand Best Houses*. A lucid, witty pick of England's churches and houses, divided by county and with a star rating – for the houses book Jenkins includes all sorts of curiosities, from caves in Nottingham to prefabs in Buckinghamshire.

Sam Jordison and Dan Kieran *The Idler Book of Crap Towns*; *Crap Towns II*. The books that made local councils all over England as mad as hell – utterly prejudiced but hilarious accounts of the worst places to live in the country. We daren't even repeat the names of the "winners", we'll only get letters of complaint.

Iain Pattinson *Lyttleton's Britain*. Great British jazz man and bandleader Humphrey Lyttleton presented the roving radio comedy panel game *I'm Sorry I Haven't A Clue* for 40 years until

his death in 2008. His barbed town introductions ("...from the Malvern Hills... it is possible to catch a sight of Birmingham, despite the many, clearly posted warning signs") form a laugh-out-loud gazetteer to many of England's historic towns and cities.

Nikolaus Pevsner *The Buildings of England*. If you want to know who built what, when, why and how, look no further than this popular architectural series, in 46 county-by-county volumes. The magisterial project was initially a one-man show, but after Pevsner died in 1983 later authors revised his text, inserting newer buildings but generally respecting the founder's personal tone.

A. Wainwright *A Pictorial Guide to the Lakeland Fells* (7 vols). More than mere guidebooks could ever be, the beautifully produced small-format volumes of handwritten notes and sketches (produced between 1952 and 1966) have led generations up the Lake District's mountains. The originals have now been revised to take account of changing routes and landscapes.

History, society, people and politics

Andy Beckett *When the Lights Went Out*. Enough time has elapsed to make 1970s Britain seem like a different world (the title is reference to the power cuts during the industrial unrest of 1974), but Beckett's lively history brings the period to life.

John Campbell *Margaret Thatcher*. Campbell has been mining the Thatcher seam for several years now and this abridged paperback version hits many political nails right on the head. By the same author, and equally engaging, is *Aneurin Bevan and the Mirage of British Socialism*.

Antonia Fraser *The Weaker Vessel*; *The Six Wives of Henry VIII*; *Warrior Queens*. The women of England tend to get short shrift in mainstream history books, but not so with Fraser – *The Weaker Vessel* is a tour de force exploring the lives of women in seventeenth-century England; *The Six Wives* shifts the emphasis firmly away from the corpulent Henry; while *Warrior Queens* celebrates Boudica and Elizabeth I among others.

Lynsey Hanley *Estates*. The story of social housing (the council "estates" of the title) hardly sounds like a winning topic, but Hanley's "intimate history" brilliantly reveals how class structure is built into the very English landscape (albeit a land that tourists rarely see).

David Horspool *Why Alfred Burned the Cakes*. Little is known of the life of Alfred the Great, king of Wessex, and arguably the first king of what would become "England", but Horspool adds a welcome new dimension to the myths and legends. And in case you were wondering about the cakes, Alfred probably didn't.

Roy Jenkins *Churchill: A Biography*. Churchill biographies abound (and the man himself, of course, wrote up his own life), but politician and statesman Jenkins adds an extra level of understanding. Jenkins specialized in political biogs of men of power, so you can also read his take on Gladstone, Asquith, various Chancellors of the Exchequer and others.

David Kynaston *Austerity Britain, 1945–51*. Comprehensive vox pop that gives the real flavour of postwar England. Everything is here, from the skill of a Dennis Compton cricket innings through to the difficulties and dangers of hewing coal down the pit, all in a land where there were "no supermarkets, no teabags, no Formica, no trainers ... and just four Indian restaurants". Also recommended is Kynaston's follow-up volume *Family Britain, 1951–1957*.

Andrew Morton *Diana: Her True Story*. The biography of the "People's Princess" that started all the hullabaloo – and now they won't let it lie. Morton's is still the one they all aspire to join in mega-sales nirvana, but if he won't do, there are always books by the butler (Paul Burrell), the bodyguard (Trevor Rees-Jones), the feminist (Beatrix Campbell), the magazine editor (Tina Brown), Uncle Tom Cobbley and all.

Katie Price *Being Jordan*. If you don't know who Katie Price/Jordan is, you're not English, don't watch reality television or never read the tabloids, simple as that. Even more points are deducted if you're not interested in books by or about Peter, Alex, Cheryl or whoever else is currently dancing around the slimy pole of C-list celebrity.

Francis Pryor *Britain BC; Britain AD; Britain in the Middle Ages*. The sometimes arcane field discoveries of working archeologists are given fascinating new exposure in Pryor's lively archeological histories of Britain. Everything from before the Romans to the sixteenth century is examined through the archeologist's eye, unearthing a more sophisticated native culture than was formerly thought along the way.

Diane Purkiss *The English Civil War: A People's History*. The English story of revolution, given a human face – the clue is in the subtitle, as Purkiss gets away from battles and armies, focusing instead on the men who fought and the women who had to feed and tend them.

Andrew Rawnsley *The End of the Party*. Arguably Britain's most acute political journalist, Rawnsley cross-examines and dissects New Labour under Blair and Brown to withering effect.

Simon Schama *A History of Britain* (3 vols). British history, from 3000 BC to 2001, delivered by the country's major TV historical popularizer (the books followed the series). Schama's the best at this kind of stuff, though plenty of others have weighed in recently with similar TV-and-book history tie-ins, most notably Andrew Marr (*A History of Modern Britain*).

W.C. Sellar and R.J. Yeatman *1066 And All That*. The classic alternative history of England was first published in 1930, and subsequent generations have rejoiced in its parodic litany of "Good Things" and "Bad Kings".

Zeitgeist novels

Which English novels since the war best capture the spirit of the age in which they were written? Here's our choice.

1984, George Orwell (1949). When the clocks strike thirteen in the first sentence, you know something's wrong with wartime England.

Lucky Jim, Kingsley Amis (1954). "Angry Young Man" writes funniest book of the century.

Saturday Night and Sunday Morning, Alan Sillitoe (1958). Factory life and sexual shenanigans in working-class Nottingham.

Billy Liar, Keith Waterhouse (1959). Cloying Yorkshire provincialism meets laugh-out-loud fantasy on the eve of the Swinging Sixties.

A Clockwork Orange, Anthony Burgess (1962). Droogs, crime and violence in a dystopian England.

The History Man, Malcolm Bradbury (1975). The "campus novel" par excellence.

London Fields, Martin Amis (1989). Literary London's favourite bad boy writes ferociously witty, baleful satire or pretentious drivel – you decide.

The Buddha of Suburbia, Hanif Kureishi (1990). Youth culture, identity and the immigrant experience.

Fever Pitch, Nick Hornby (1992). The modern masculine obsession with football started here.

Bridget Jones's Diary, Helen Fielding (1996). Thirtysomething female neurosis, rehashed from an original newspaper column (and then again in film).

White Teeth, Zadie Smith (2000). Mixed families, mixed races, mixed religions, mixed England.

Saturday, Ian McEwan (2005). England's finest contemporary writer addresses the state of the nation and upper-middle-class angst.

South of the River, Blake Morrison (2007). The first heavyweight literary despatch from the decade of Blair and New Labour.

James Sharpe *Remember Remember the Fifth of November; Dick Turpin*. A crisp retelling of the Gunpowder Plot of 1605 also helps put the English phenomenon that is Bonfire Night into context – and explains why Guy Fawkes (not even the leader of this "failed act of terrorism") is the plotter remembered still each year. In *Dick Turpin*, subtitled "The myth of the English highwayman", Sharpe stands and delivers a broadside to the commonly accepted notion of Turpin and his ilk – not romantic robbers but brutal villains after all.

Lytton Strachey *Queen Victoria*. Strachey is often credited with establishing a warmer, wittier, more all-encompassing form of biography, with his *Queen Victoria* (1921) following on from the ground-breaking *Eminent Victorians*. Many others have followed in trying to understand Britain's longest reigning monarch – Christopher Hibbert and Elizabeth Longford being two of the most recent and respected – but few match Strachey's economy and wit.

E.P. Thompson *The Making of the English Working Class*. A seminal text – essential reading for anyone who wants to understand the fabric of English society – tracing the birth of England's working-class society between 1780 and 1832.

Michael Wood *In Search of England: Journeys into the English Past*. Historian Wood was also an early TV historical popularizer and consequently his books are highly readable. *In Search of England* delves into the myths and historical record behind the notion of England and Englishness, while other "In search of…" titles shed new light on the Dark Ages and the Domesday Book.

Being English

Julian Baggini *Welcome to Everytown: A Journey into the English Mind*. Baggini's "Everytown" is Rotherham, South Yorkshire, supposedly containing the most typical mix of household types in the country. As a philosopher, his six-month stay there wasn't in search of the English character, but rather their "folk philosophy" (ie, what they think). The result? A surprising, illuminating view of mainstream English life.

Michael Collins *The Likes of Us*. Baggini's main finding – "England's culture remains predominantly working class" – is underpinned by this celebration of the white working class, as Collins weaves family history into the story of England's urban development.

A.A. Gill *The Angry Island*. Gill's self-confessed "collection of prejudice" seeks to explain what England and the English like. Not everyone will like his conclusions ("They have a unique national habit of bringing out the worst in each other"), but you'll certainly keep reading.

Sarah Lyall *A Field Guide to the English*. The *New York Times* reporter and long-time London resident concentrates on English institutions, attitudes and eccentricities – House of Lords, the NHS, cricket, being posh, alcohol abuse – in an anecdote-filled examination of the national character.

Sarfraz Manzoor *Greetings From Bury Park*. You have to know your Springsteen to appreciate fully the title, though journalist Manzoor's memoir of "race, religion and rock and roll" in Bury Park, Luton, is a terrific introduction to the second-generation immigrant experience.

Jeremy Paxman *The English: A Portrait of a People*. The acerbic journalist and newsman presents the character of the English as he sees it – from attitudes to sex and sport to the emotionalism of Princess Diana's funeral.

Fifty years of English pop

England's fifty-year-plus heritage as a source of inspirational rock'n'roll is indisputable: the country's historic role as the hub of the British Empire, absorbing immigrants from around the world, and its openness to US culture have allowed it to assimilate diverse styles and rhythms – jazz, blues, ska, soul and reggae – and bred a distinctive domestic brand of popular music. Local acts soaked up the delicious musical juices seeping out of the shebeens, developing, for example, a taste for ska matched only in Kingston, Jamaica, and a white audience for US black music that Tamla Motown would envy.

England's best music has come from its cities, nourished by fashions from the urban stews and flavoured from the cultural melting pot. Here is a brief survey of some of its major cities, region by region, and the musical legacies they have created.

London

Inevitably, **London** has the bulk of the history and is home to the widest range of international influences. Traditionally, artists on the way up had to make the trek to the capital to perform, to record and to sign a contract. Management and publishing companies lurked on the cheaper outskirts of the West End theatre and entertainment district, and there was a domestic "Tin Pan Alley", centred on **Denmark Street** in London's West End. In the 1950s, entrepreneurs such as Larry Parnes created menacing-sounding stage personae (**Tommy Steele**, **Marty Wilde** and **Billy Fury** for example) and stalked the cappuccino bars of Soho to find compliant star material they could reshape as the ideal "all-round entertainer". The whole sordid scene was spoofed in the 1959 film, *Espresso Bongo*, starring **Cliff Richard**.

As the industry blossomed in the early 1960s, the demonic, London-based **Rolling Stones** provided contrast and foil to The Beatles' thumbs-up attitude, bringing shade and cool to the otherwise permanent sunshine of pop music. Acts such as **The Who** and **The Small Faces** were among the most successful of the "**beat groups**" who terrified the locals before heading to the US, following in the wake of the Fab Four, in a "British Invasion". The archetypal Sixties' London band, **The Kinks**, recorded some of the most thoughtful, poignant and enduring pop charmers of the era, in between bouts of breaking equipment and scrapping onstage.

Swinging London was still the place to be when a wave of hippy lifestyles and free love washed over England from sunny California, while the now-demolished UFO on Tottenham Court Road kick-started British psychedelia, booking **Pink Floyd** – originally a blues outfit from Cambridge – and **Soft Machine** in as house bands, hosting the first "light show" and promoting the **14 Hour Technicolor Dream** at Alexandra Palace in 1967 – London's most notorious gig of the decade.

When the beautiful dreams wore off, English pop returned to primitive stomping with **glam rock** and **glitter**. For a while, East-End-boy-turned-bopping-elf **Marc Bolan** and his band T. Rex ruled the roost, but **David Bowie** proved more enduring. The latter's theatrical flirtations with gayness/bisexuality and Weimar Republic decadence mutated almost beyond recognition in the mid- to late Seventies into **punk rock**, a movement whose roots lay both in US garage bands and early 1960s British pop. Typically those swastika-toting, bondage-clad rockers had no interest in politics at all, however, and would just as happily have worn a hammer and sickle if the Cold War enemy had been as potent a tool for baiting the bourgeoisie. The iconoclastic **Sex Pistols** were joined by such bands as **The Clash**, **The Damned**, **The Jam** and **Siouxsie & The Banshees**, and for a few ecstatic months, punk ruled. The flame burned out quickly, however, and was followed by a confusing mix of **post-punk** scenes pulling in different directions, from rockabilly to a skinhead revival with a taste for high-speed **ska**.

Those left unmoved by the lack of glamour or style shown by most of these new movements turned by default back to the superficial fashion wars of nightclubs, and a squadron of **New Romantics** headed by such London-formed acts such as **Duran Duran**, **Spandau Ballet**, **Culture Club** and **Adam & The Ants**. Chart success led to world-cracking tours, with George Michael even taking **Wham!** from London to Beijing in 1985, becoming the first western pop act to gig in Red China.

In the late 1980s, the rise of ecstasy and the affection for the **house** and **techno** scenes of Chicago and Detroit laid the roots for the UK's enduring dance music culture, which for many began at Danny Rampling's euphoric *Shoom* night in Southwark. And in the mainstream, the frills and ruffles of the decade eventually gave way to a search for "roots" and a "back to basics" movement in which the substance of lyrics and melody were considered more important than looks. As the Eighties' "me generation" attitude faded, the quest for authenticity in music in the Nineties threw up big names, including **Blur**, **Suede** and **Elastica** in London, and saw Camden reinvented as the capital of "**Britpop**".

The Camden school endures in reduced form to the present day, recent graduates including **The Libertines** (and their offshoots **Dirty Pretty Things** and **Babyshambles**), but arguably, the most vital of today's music centres on the harsh,

England's pop shrines

Alley of love, Brighton Hometown of some of England's finest pop stars, Brighton was also the location of the main beachfront action in the movie of The Who's mod opera, *Quadrophenia*.

Glastonbury Home to the country's biggest and oldest festival (which actually takes place on a farm some miles away), Glasto is one of the few places where you can still see people busking on the sackbut for spare change.

Town & Country Club, Leeds The city's best-loved major venue for the final years of the last millennium (now corporatized as the O2 Academy).

Eric's, Liverpool Crucible of the alternative and underground scene from the Seventies onward; on the same street as *The Cavern*.

Abbey Road Studios, London The Beatles' permanent recording HQ in the capital, and birthplace to countless classic recordings from Pink Floyd to Radiohead.

Soho, London Stand in the centre of Soho Square, throw a brick in any direction and you'll hit a revered institution, recording company office, musicians' unlicensed club or aspiring superstar. Seek out 23 Heddon St for that essential Ziggy Stardust tribute pic.

Isle of Wight Following the notorious 1970 festival, the largest human gathering of its time, it was 32 years before the island dared to host another such event. Somewhat better organized, the Isle of Wight Festival's modern-day successor, and more alternative and diverse Bestival, are key stops on the festival trail.

Salford Lads' Club, Manchester Featured on the cover of The Smiths' album *The Queen Is Dead*, the club once boasted Allan Clarke of The Hollies among its members.

Twisted Wheel Club, Manchester Northern Soul venue par excellence, the *Twisted Wheel* played it fast, loud, heavy and all night long. The list of visiting bands reads like a Motown/Stax greatest-hits set.

Leadmill Club, Sheffield Boasting more than 25 years as the city's top venue, the *Leadmill* has been an A-listed must-play gig for acts as diverse as Cabaret Voltaire, Killing Joke and The Fall in the Eighties to today's sleek young turns such as The Long Blondes and Reverend & The Makers.

hectic East London **grime** sound and South London's more minimal **dubstep**, both bastardized fusions of hip-hop, R&B and the weirder end of the dance spectrum. The London scene is broad enough, though, to take in a gamut of other musical styles currently making waves, from folk-influenced acts such as **Mumford and Sons**, **Laura Marling** and **Noah and the Whale**, to the smart, provocative pop of **Florence and the Machine** and **Lily Allen**, and the acoustic rap of **Plan B**.

The northwest

As one of England's major port cities, postwar **Liverpool** was home to substantial immigrant populations – of Chinese, Irish and West Indians in particular – with strong commercial links to the New York pop scene owing to the maritime traffic between the two cities. When they hit big in 1963, **The Beatles** brought moptops, R&B and genuine passion to a pop scene stuffed with insipid novelty tunes and crooning balladry. From *Please Please Me* to *Hey Jude*, their music furnished a constant reassuring backing track to the rest of the decade. Their success put the whole Merseyside music scene into the glare of a short-lived countrywide spotlight of interest, from **Cilla Black** to **Billy J. Kramer & The Dakotas**, but when The Beatles made the long drive down to London, the media attention moved away. Britain's most influential and long-serving DJ **John Peel** flew the flag for Liverpool in the 1970s, but Liverpudlian pop had to wait until the next decade for its resurgence, in the form of **The Teardrop Explodes** and **Echo And The Bunnymen**. Throughout the Eighties and Nineties, kids would hook up at Probe Records before moving on for a night raving at local superclub, *Cream*. Meanwhile, Beatle-influenced melodic pop echoed back to the singalong romanticism much enjoyed in the Irish side of the community with the love songs to heroin of **The La's** and robust beauties of **The Boo Radleys**, living on in the 2000s in such flavours as **The Zutons** and **The Coral**, and more recently bands such as **The Wombats**.

Manchester's contribution to English pop music is even more impressive than Liverpool's. The city boasts Morrissey's beloved Salford Lads' Club, Factory Records, Granada TV and the BBC's main northern studios, while *Wigan Casino* – home of Northern Soul – is not far away, though it's the hedonistic nights at *The Haçienda* that excite the most wistful smiles. Furthermore, the list of Manchester bands is endless, from Sixties pop success stories such as **Herman's Hermits** to more recent chart-toppers such as **The Ting Tings**, the city's role as musical capital of the north continues unchallenged. Manchester and its environs was the second city of English punk, and it nurtured a more sardonic, thoughtful crop of post-punk acts, including **Buzzcocks**, **The Fall** and Macclesfield's **Joy Division** (who morphed into New Order on the death of singer Ian Curtis), that showed more genuine artistry and greater resilience than the perhaps more fashion-led London bands. From the Eighties, two bands, **The Smiths** and **New Order**, despite coming from opposite ends of the pop spectrum, stand out in particular. While Morrissey's ruminations on confused sexuality, shyness and solitude gave a voice to a generation left cold by the mainstream pop world of the mid-80s, it was New Order that had the more far-reaching effect. Having embraced the new hedonism of synth-powered dance music, their music inspired an ecstasy-driven dance-all-night lifestyle that ultimately created local superclub The Haçienda. From this developed the "**Madchester**" scene that threw up **The Happy Mondays**, **The Stone Roses**, **The Charlatans** and **James**. After "Madchester", the Manchester scene lost some of its energy – the early Nineties' most successful Mancunian act was manufactured boy band, **Take That**. But the city retained its swagger in the soap-opera squabbles of **Oasis**'s Gallagher brothers, and its taste for downbeat realism with bands such as **The Verve**, and more recently, **Doves**, **Elbow** and Wigan's **Starsailor**.

The Midlands and the West Country

While **Brumbeat** donated its fair share of acts to the early to mid-Sixties scenes – with **Spencer Davis Group** and **Traffic** deserving special attention for pushing basic beat music forward to the edge of psychedelia – it was not till the era of **Black Sabbath** and **Led Zeppelin**, at the end of the decade, that Brummie pop came alive. Then as chart pop grew to thrive on hairstyles, glitter and dinosaur stomp, local boy **Roy Wood** escaped The Move and Electric Light Orchestra to emerge as front man to **Wizzard**, while **Slade**'s Noddy Holder sported trousers even more raucous than his gravelly voice. At the tail-end of the Seventies, **The Beat** and Coventry's **The Specials** were at the forefront of a ska revival, and a decade later, all the best "Grebo" (a term coined by **Pop Will Eat Itself**'s Clint Mansell, for a brand of pop aimed at wannabe motorcycle outlaws) bands talked like they had day jobs as Brummie diesel mechanics.

England's southwest has always had a reputation for left-field mavericks, from Dorset's **PJ Harvey** to Cornwall's dance iconoclast **Aphex Twin**. The region's biggest city, and one of England's great ports, **Bristol** has been associated since the 1990s with trip-hop, a catch-all term encompassing artists as diverse as **Portishead**, **Tricky** and **Massive Attack**, who rejected the guitar-led Britpop scene in favour of a darker, spacier and more down-tempo sound.

The northeast and Yorkshire

Newcastle's pop pedigree ranges from **The Animals** in the 1960s through to folk/rock band **Lindisfarne**, punk heroes **Penetration** and Police front man **Sting** in the late Seventies, **Dubstar** in the Nineties and **Maximo Park** in the 2000s. **Durham** sent us the mixed charm and cynicism of **Prefab Sprout** in the Eighties, while down the coast in **Hull**, local boys Mick Ronson and Mick Woodmansey were the linchpins of Bowie's **Spiders From Mars** in the early Seventies, and silken balladry reached new heights in the artistry of **Scritti Politti** and **Everything But The Girl** in the Eighties. In contrast, pop punks and local darlings **The Housemartins** delighted in articulating the depressing realities normally scorned by chart acts.

Leeds responded with such politicized bands as **The Mekons**, **Gang of Four** and **Chumbawamba**, while **Soft Cell** and **Sisters of Mercy** provided a counterpart to the pop cheeriness of the post-punk era, paving the way for **The Wedding Present**'s guitar onslaught. More recently, the **Kaiser Chiefs** and the **Pigeon Detectives** have spearheaded a new wave of Leeds-based indie rockers.

Dave Berry and **Joe Cocker** led **Sheffield**'s Steel City invasion in the Sixties, with the punishing stylings of **Def Leppard**, **Cabaret Voltaire** and others maintaining the city's metal-bashing traditions long after the cutlery factories had closed down. The city has also given us a more stylish brand of pop than other regional conurbations in the form of the glossy magazine tunes of **The Human League** and elegant sophistication of **ABC**. **Pulp**'s domination of the thinking-teen's playlist kept the city in the limelight in the 1990s, while **Warp Records** championed an eclectic selection of techno, ambient and rock music. By the late 2000s, though, the baton of elegant sneering, backed up by solid musicianship, had been passed to **Arctic Monkeys**, and frontman Alex Turner's side band, **The Last Shadow Puppets**.

Al Spicer

Film

E

ngland has produced some of the world's greatest films, and most famous actors and directors, but for all that try getting critics to agree what constitutes an English film (or indeed, where English film stops and British film starts). Take sci-fi-horror classic *Alien* – a 20th Century Fox movie that launched the career of Sigourney Weaver, but was filmed at London's Shepperton Studios, directed by Tyne and Wear-born Ridley Scott and starred English RADA-trained classical actor John Hurt. Or the multi-garlanded *Slumdog Millionaire*, set in Mumbai with an Indian cast but adapted for the screen and directed by Englishmen Simon Beaufoy and Danny Boyle and entirely financed in the UK. While you might not know instinctively where to place these films, others are easier – if it's scripted or directed by Richard Curtis, sports Kenneth Branagh on a Shakespearian battlefield or plonks Emma Thompson and Hugh Grant in a country house, it's a safe bet you're in England (or England, Europe, as Hollywood might have it). We've sidestepped the issue in many ways, and have concentrated on covering films that are at least set in England (with one or two rare exceptions). Most also depict a particular aspect of English life, whether reflecting the immigrant experience, exploring the country's history or examining the national sense of humour. Fetch the popcorn, dim the lights, switch off your mobile and enjoy.

Real England

There's a familiar face to England on film that follows a mainstream line from stiff-upper-lip classics like *Brief Encounter* (David Lean, 1945) to the rom-com machinations of *Love Actually* (Richard Curtis, 2003). But you won't find out much about real English life from these movies, and you need to turn elsewhere for a view that's more kitchen sink than cream tea and village green.

Saturday Night and Sunday Morning (Karel Reisz, 1960) ushered in the "new wave", capturing the grit and dead-end grind of Albert Finney's work in a Nottingham factory. This kind of social realism underpinned much of the best in British film in the 1960s and made stars out of actors like Finney, Richard Harris, Tom Courtenay and Alan Bates. It's a style best exemplified by the work of director Ken Loach, who has documented the country's working- and under-class since his film debut **Poor Cow** (1967) and the unforgettable **Kes** (1970), the story of a Yorkshire schoolboy who finds liberation in the training of a kestrel. Recognizably real people continue to inhabit Loach's universe, from embattled railway workers in **The Navigators** (2001) to the Manchester postman in thrall to footballer-philosopher Eric Cantona in **Looking For Eric** (2009).

Elsewhere, the 1980s' Britain of Mrs Thatcher was incisively dissected in **Made in Britain** (Alan Clarke, 1982), a downbeat odyssey of job centres, drugs and racism, and the decade was revisited in similar fashion in **This is England** (Shane Meadows, 2007). Meadows is at home in the Midlands, where many of his films are set. Other directors to mine regional roots to add gritty realism to their work include Andrea Arnold, whose **Fish Tank** (2009) details troubled relationships on an Essex council estate. Meanwhile, in director Mike Leigh, England has a true virtuoso of slice-of-life ensemble drama, from his much-admired **Secrets and Lies** (1996), charting a dysfunctional family's hidden secrets, to lighter but still socially grounded films like **Happy-Go-Lucky** (2008), which celebrates the relentless cheeriness of a likeable primary-school teacher.

Made in Yorkshire

England's biggest county is also big in film. It's a favoured shoot location for domestic, Hollywood and Bollywood productions, while **Bradford** – home of the National Media Museum – was declared the world's first UNESCO City of Film in 2009. This probably didn't cause too many sleepless nights in LA or Cannes, but the West Yorkshire city got the vote on the back of a proud film heritage, starting with **Room at the Top** (Jack Clayton, 1959) and **Billy Liar** (John Schlesinger, 1963). It's also been the backdrop to films as diverse as immigrant culture-clash comedy-drama **My Son the Fanatic** (Udayan Prasad, 1997) and classic family weepie **The Railway Children** (Lionel Jeffries, 1970), filmed at the nearby Keighley & Worth Valley Railway. Another famous Yorkshire heritage railway, the North York Moors Railway, got a huge boost from its appearance in the first Harry Potter film, **Harry Potter and the Philosopher's Stone** (Chris Columbus, 2001). Rolling Yorkshire countryside gets an outing in both coming-of-age tale **My Summer of Love** (Pawel Pawlikowski, 2004) and in the middle-aged women kit-off hit **Calendar Girls** (Nigel Cole, 2003), while it's back to the unsung towns of Barnsley, Doncaster and Halifax for **Brassed Off** (Mark Herman, 1996), the crossover comedy about the tribulations of a colliery brass band. At the seaside, Scarborough is the backdrop to the

Big-screen kings and queens

Catch up on your English history, from bruising battles to comic capers, in this rundown of ten movie monarchs.

Arthur The "Once and Future King", as portrayed by Richard Harris in *Camelot* (Joshua Logan, 1967) and Nigel Terry in the far grittier *Excalibur* (John Boorman, 1981) – while Graham Chapman is far sillier in *Monty Python and the Holy Grail* (Terry Gilliam and Terry Jones, 1975).

Henry II Want a Henry II? Call for Peter O'Toole, who does the definitive job in *Becket* (Peter Glenville, 1964) and *The Lion in Winter* (Anthony Harvey, 1968).

Richard I The most ubiquitous film king turns up in every Robin Hood romp, and Patrick Stewart in particular has a ball in Mel Brooks' genre-skewering *Robin Hood: Men in Tights* (1993).

Henry V The young Kenneth Branagh's bravura *Henry V* (he also directed, 1989) is a worthy successor to Laurence Olivier's rousing wartime interpretation (1944).

Richard III With the action transposed to a 1930s' Fascist England, Ian McKellen is a snarling *Richard III* (Richard Loncraine, 1995) in this renowned stage-to-screen production.

Henry VIII *A Man for All Seasons* (Fred Zinneman, 1966) pits Robert Shaw's Henry against Paul Scofield's Sir Thomas More in one of English history's great moral confrontations.

Elizabeth I They've all played Good Queen Bess, from Bette Davis to Dame Judi Dench, but in Shekhar Kapur's visually stunning *Elizabeth* (1998) and *Elizabeth: The Golden Age* (2007) Cate Blanchett adds a darker tone.

George III Nigel Hawthorne's endearing turn as the loopy king lights up *The Madness of King George* (Nicholas Hytner, 1994).

Victoria In *Mrs Brown* (John Madden, 1997), Dame Judi Dench's Queen-in-mourning finds solace in the friendship of her faithful Scottish servant John Brown.

Elizabeth II Diana's dead, the monarchy's wobbling and Tony Blair is at the gates – a majestic Helen Mirren attempts to reconcile public and private anguish in *The Queen* (Stephen Frears, 2006).

virtuoso performance by Jane Horrocks in **Little Voice** (Mark Herman, 1998), while atmospheric Whitby – an original location in the Bram Stoker novel *Dracula* – appeared on film as early as 1931 with Bela Lugosi in the title role.

Don't Look Now

From bucket-of-blood Gothic Hammer horrors to souped-up twenty-first-century zombies, there's always been something unpleasant lurking in the darkest corners of English film. Production company Hammer hit its stride as the "House of Horror" in the late 1950s, pairing scare-meister stalwarts Peter Cushing and Christopher Lee in **The Curse of Frankenstein** (Terence Fisher, 1957) and **Dracula** (Terence Fisher, 1958), and continued to shock with assorted devils, monsters, mummies and zombies until well into the 1970s. Most of these films of the period revisited classic Hollywood themes and characters but in the creepy slasher-movie forerunner **Peeping Tom** (Michael Powell, 1960) English film had a genuine horror pioneer. Werewolves got a domestic rebranding in **An American Werewolf in London** (John Landis, 1981) – in which tourists learned never to drink in any pub called *The Slaughtered Lamb* – while **The Company of Wolves** (Neil Jordan, 1984) was a classy interpretation of fantasy writer Angela Carter's stories of loss of innocence. English horror writer Clive Barker turned director with his feature debut, the very nasty **Hellraiser** (1987) – filmed in England, conceived in Hell – while Newcastle's Neil Marshall burst onto the scene with cult werewolf horror **Dog Soldiers** (2002), followed later by his post-apocalypse virus-chiller **Doomsday** (2008). Most of Marshall's films are, admittedly, largely set in Scotland, but Mancunian Danny Boyle went for iconic English settings in London and the Lake District in his landmark zombie reinvention **28 Days Later** (2002), featuring virus-infected crazies who can run, very, very fast. The zombies were rather more typically shuffling and shambolic in cult horror-romp **Shaun of the Dead** (Edgar Wright, 2004), the zom-com that proved that there are loud laughs in the living dead.

Colliding cultures

As film-makers started to explore multicultural England, unfamiliar lives and experiences began to be portrayed on screen. In **Babylon** (Franco Rosso, 1980), the experiences of London's disaffected black youth took centre-stage, while films by pioneering film-maker Horace Ové addressed head-on the black–white culture clash – with wry humour in the case of **Playing Away** (1987), a comedy of manners pitching inner city against English village in a charity cricket match. Breakthrough film featuring the Asian immigrant experience, **My Beautiful Laundrette** (Stephen Frears, 1985) – based on the novel by Hanif Kureishi – explored racial, sexual and class dynamics in an unforgiving London, though later popular successes mined the rich comic seam inherent in contrasting cultures, like the delightful **Bhaji on the Beach** (Gurinder Chadha, 1993), in which a group of Asian women head off on a day-trip to Blackpool. The lively comedy **East is East** (Damien O'Donnell, 1999) sets a 1970s' Salford Pakistani chip-shop owner against his more independent, British-born children, and there's more comedy and Asian–English cultural conflict in **Anita and Me** (Metin Hüseyin, 2002). Meanwhile in **Bend It Like Beckham** (2002), Gurinder Chadha scored a huge coming-of-age hit about a football-loving Punjabi girl (and launched Keira Knightley as a megastar to boot).

It's a funny old England

You have to laugh, but English film comedies have pretty much come full circle – in the 1930s and 1940s they were built around the well-honed characters of

Atonement (Joe Wright, 2007). Too soon to call Ian McEwan's 2001 novel a classic? Possibly, but not so the critically acclaimed film evoking 1930s' and 1940s' England.

Brighton Rock (John Boulting, 1947). Film noir menace – and a genuinely scary Richard Attenborough – in Graham Greene's adaptation of his own novel.

Far From the Madding Crowd (John Schlesinger, 1967). Julie Christie shines in the Dorset-filmed version of Thomas Hardy's doom-laden tale.

Great Expectations (David Lean, 1946). One of England's finest directors with a haunting, definitive rendition of Dickens' greatest novel.

Howards End (James Ivory, 1992). A theatrical period piece carved from E.M. Forster's meditation on social class.

Jane Eyre (Robert Stevenson, 1944). Joan Fontaine and Orson Welles in "A Love Story Every Woman Would Die A Thousand Deaths to Live!"

Rebecca (Alfred Hitchcock, 1940). Hitch does du Maurier – his first Hollywood picture, perfectly paced and beautifully shot.

Sense and Sensibility (Ang Lee, 1995). Jane Austen's sprightly story of love, money and behaviour given wings by a classy English cast.

Wuthering Heights (Peter Kosminsky, 1992). Atmospheric Yorkshire scenery and brooding Ralph Fiennes as Heathcliff in Emily Brontë's passionate tale.

1984 (Michael Radford, 1984). A heavyweight Brit cast (Richard Burton, John Hurt) rewrites history in Orwell's peculiarly English totalitarian future.

established music-hall stars like George Formby, Arthur Askey and Will Hay, while in *The Invention of Lying* (2009) and *Cemetery Junction* (2010) we encounter today's equivalent of the megastar music-hall act in the TV-age genius of prickly comic, writer and director Ricky Gervais. If there was a Golden Age of comedy, many would point to the films of **Ealing Studios** between 1948 and 1955, which poked a satirical finger at English society in classics like *Kind Hearts and Coronets* (Robert Hamer, 1949), *The Man in the White Suit* (Alexander Mackendrick, 1951) and *The Ladykillers* (Alexander Mackendrick, 1955). The **Boulting bothers**, John and Roy, picked up where Ealing left off, directing a series of sharp comedies addressing English class, society and institutions, starting with *Private's Progress* (1956) – the sequel, *I'm All Right Jack* (1959) was an early hit for Peter Sellers. The lethal boarding-school girls of **St Trinian's** and gaffe-prone medics of the **Doctor** series were both first seen on screen in 1954, and each ran to half a dozen sequels, while the equally loved-and-mocked **Carry On** series launched in 1958 with National Service farce *Carry On Sergeant*; Gerald Thomas directed thirty Carry Ons in all, employing a regular crew of English comedy actors (Kenneth Williams, Sid James, Charles Hawtrey, Joan Sims, Hattie Jacques et al) in saucy japes, spoofs and single entendres.

What links all these films, good, bad or indifferent, is their very sense of national character, place and humour – a trait that resurfaces in every classic English comedy since. Consider the verbal duelling between Julie Walters and Michael Caine in **Educating Rita** (Lewis Gilbert, 1983); the gloriously seedy excesses of **Withnail and I** (Bruce Robinson, 1986); the John Cleese crime caper **A Fish Called Wanda** (Charles Crichton, 1988); the tale of unemployed Sheffield steel workers turned male strippers, **The Full Monty** (Peter Cattaneo, 1997); the feel-good boy-ballet comedy-drama **Billy Elliot** (Stephen Daldry, 2000); or Alan Bennett's wit-laden adaptation of his northern grammar-school play **The History Boys** (Nicholas Hytner, 2006) – all very funny, all undeniably English.

Gangsters, villains and bad guys

Hollywood bad guys nearly always have an English accent – think Alan Rickman, hamming it up as the Sheriff of Nottingham in *Robin Hood: Prince of Thieves*, Peter Cushing in command of the Death Star in the original *Star Wars*, or Sir Ian McKellen as Magneto in the *X-Men* franchise. For real villainy in a real English film, though, Ben Kingsley is the usual choice of current critics for his role as one of the hardest, meanest criminals ever in **Sexy Beast** (Jonathan Glazer, 2000). Film-goers of a certain age stand instead by a monumentally savage Michael Caine in the seminal British mobster movie **Get Carter** (Mike Hodges, 1971). In between, there's been Bob Hoskins doing his turn as a maniacal East End gang boss in **The Long Good Friday** (John Mackenzie, 1980), and Sting, Sean Bean and Tommy Lee Jones covering Newcastle in blood in **Stormy Monday** (Mike Figgis, 1988), while gangland heavies got a "geezer" reboot in the since much-copied heist movie **Lock, Stock and Two Smoking Barrels** (Guy Ritchie, 1998). Malcolm McDowell's sociopathic Alex dominated the adaptation of Anthony Burgess's **A Clockwork Orange** (Stanley Kubrick, 1971) – a film considered so disturbingly violent it was withdrawn from circulation in the UK for over 25 years. Finally, there's "Master of Suspense" Alfred Hitchcock, who made what's usually considered to be Britain's first "talkie" in 1929, the thriller *Blackmail*; his penultimate film, and the last shot in England, **Frenzy** (1972), proved a hit return to his psycho-thriller heyday, with Barry Foster committing London's grisly "neck-tie" murders.

Small print and
Index

A Rough Guide to Rough Guides

Published in 1982, the first Rough Guide – to Greece – was a student scheme that became a publishing phenomenon. Mark Ellingham, a recent graduate in English from Bristol University, had been travelling in Greece the previous summer and couldn't find the right guidebook. With a small group of friends he wrote his own guide, combining a highly contemporary, journalistic style with a thoroughly practical approach to travellers' needs.

The immediate success of the book spawned a series that rapidly covered dozens of destinations. And, in addition to impecunious backpackers, Rough Guides soon acquired a much broader and older readership that relished the guides' wit and inquisitiveness as much as their enthusiastic, critical approach and value-for-money ethos.

These days, Rough Guides include recommendations from shoestring to luxury and cover more than 200 destinations around the globe, including almost every country in the Americas and Europe, more than half of Africa and most of Asia and Australasia. Our ever-growing team of authors and photographers is spread all over the world, particularly in Europe, the US and Australia.

In the early 1990s, Rough Guides branched out of travel, with the publication of Rough Guides to World Music, Classical Music and the Internet. All three have become benchmark titles in their fields, spearheading the publication of a wide range of books under the Rough Guide name.

Including the travel series, Rough Guides now number more than 350 titles, covering: phrasebooks, waterproof maps, music guides from Opera to Heavy Metal, reference works as diverse as Conspiracy Theories and Shakespeare, and popular culture books from iPods to Poker. Rough Guides also produce a series of more than 120 World Music CDs in partnership with World Music Network.

Visit www.roughguides.com to see our latest publications.

SMALL PRINT

Rough Guide credits

Text editors: Edward Aves, Lara Kavanagh
Layout: Umesh Aggarwal, Jessica Subramanian
Cartography: Swati Handoo, Lokamata Sahu
Picture editor: Harriet Mills
Production: Rebecca Short
Proofreader: Diane Margolis
Cover design: Nicole Newman, Dan May
Photographers: Tim Draper, Diana Jarvis,
Suzanne Porter, Helena Smith, Natascha Sturny,
Mark Thomas
Editorial: London Andy Turner, Keith Drew,
Alice Park, Lucy White, Jo Kirby, James Smart,
Natasha Foges, Róisín Cameron, James Rice,
Emma Beatson, Emma Gibbs, Kathryn Lane,
Monica Woods, Mani Ramaswamy, Harry Wilson,
Lucy Cowie, Alison Roberts, Eleanor Aldridge,
Ian Blenkinsop, Joe Staines, Matthew Milton,
Tracy Hopkins; **Delhi** Madhavi Singh,
Jalpreen Kaur Chhatwal
Design & Pictures: London Scott Stickland, Dan
May, Diana Jarvis, Mark Thomas, Nicole Newman,
Sarah Cummins, Emily Taylor; **Delhi** Ajay Verma,
Ankur Guha, Pradeep Thapliyal, Sachin Tanwar,
Anita Singh, Nikhil Agarwal, Sachin Gupta

Production: Liz Cherry, Louise Daly, Erika Pepe
Cartography: London Ed Wright, Katie Lloyd-
Jones; **Delhi** Rajesh Chhibber, Ashutosh Bharti,
Rajesh Mishra, Animesh Pathak, Jasbir Sandhu,
Deshpal Dabas
Online: London Faye Hellon, Jeanette Angell,
Fergus Day, Justine Bright, Clare Bryson,
Aine Fearon, Adrian Low, Ezgi Celebi;
Delhi Amit Verma, Rahul Kumar, Narender Kumar,
Ravi Yadav, Debojit Borah, Rakesh Kumar,
Ganesh Sharma, Shisir Basumatari
Marketing & Publicity: London Liz Statham,
Jess Carter, Vivienne Watton, Anna Paynton,
Rachel Sprackett, Laura Vipond; **New York** Katy
Ball; **Delhi** Aman Arora
Digital Travel Publisher: Peter Buckley
Reference Director: Andrew Lockett
Operations Assistant: Becky Doyle
Operations Manager: Helen Atkinson
Publishing Director (Travel): Clare Currie
Commercial Manager: Gino Magnotta
Managing Director: John Duhigg

Publishing information

This ninth edition published January 2011 by
Rough Guides Ltd,
80 Strand, London WC2R 0RL
11, Community Centre, Panchsheel Park,
New Delhi 110017, India
Distributed by the Penguin Group

Penguin Books Ltd,
80 Strand, London WC2R 0RL

Penguin Group (USA)
375 Hudson Street, New York 10014, USA

Penguin Group (Australia)
250 Camberwell Road, Camberwell,
Victoria 3124, Australia

Penguin Group (NZ)
67 Apollo Drive, Mairangi Bay, Auckland 1310,
New Zealand

Rough Guides is represented in Canada by
Tourmaline Editions Inc. 662 King Street West,
Suite 304, Toronto, Ontario M5V 1M7

Cover concept by Peter Dyer.

Typeset in Bembo and Helvetica to an original
design by Henry Iles.

Printed in Italy by L.E.G.O. S.p.A, Lavis (TN)
© Robert Andrews, Jules Brown, Rob Humphreys
and Phil Lee 2011
Maps © Rough Guides
No part of this book may be reproduced in any
form without permission from the publisher except
for the quotation of brief passages in reviews.
888pp includes index
A catalogue record for this book is available from
the British Library
ISBN: 978-1-84836-601-5

Help us update

We've gone to a lot of effort to ensure that the
ninth edition of **The Rough Guide to England**
is accurate and up-to-date. However, things
change – places get "discovered", opening hours
are notoriously fickle, restaurants and rooms raise
prices or lower standards. If you feel we've got it
wrong or left something out, we'd like to know,
and if you can remember the address, the price,
the hours, the phone number, so much the better.

Please send your comments with the subject
line "Rough Guide England Update" to ©mail
@uk.roughguides.com. We'll credit all
contributions and send a copy of the next edition
(or any other Rough Guide if you prefer) for the
very best emails.

Find more travel information, connect with
fellow travellers and book your trip at ®www
.roughguides.com

Acknowledgements

Matthew Hancock and Amanda Tomlin would like to thank Verity Chamley at *Hotel du Vin*.

Phil Lee would like to thank his editor, Ed Aves, for his thorough and very diligent attention to detail during the preparation of this new edition of the *Rough Guide to England*. Special thanks also to Kate Eccles at Marketing Birmingham; Ellen at the *Adelphi Guest House*; Michelle Marriott-Lodge at the *Castle Hotel*; Pat and Joan Chapman at *Grosvenor House*; Regis Crepy at the *Great House*, Lavenham; and Emma Rees for the chance to eat a squirrel.

Claire Saunders Thanks to Ian, Tom and Mia for putting up with my continual disappearances, and to Tara, who saved me from setting foot in a nightclub for the first time in twenty years.

Jos Simon would like to thank Andrew Denton at Welcome to Yorkshire for lots of practical support,

Catherine and Matt for help with research, and Ed Aves for highly diplomatic editing.

Matthew Teller would like to thank Chris Dee of Cotswolds Tourism, Hayley Beer at Oxfordshire Cotswolds, Heather Armitage and colleagues at Visit Oxford, Phil Lee and, in particular, Kedi Simpson for such brilliant help and support.

Lucy White would like to thank all those who helped with the creation of her chapter, including Flan, Poddy and Anna Hartley for their excellent Newcastle suggestions; Scott Cooper for everything Durham-related; Kevin and Leah Vigahs for a great stay in their beautiful B&B on the Wall; and not forgetting Mum, Dad and Inca for countless lovely trips to the Northumberland coast. Moral support as usual from Chris. Thanks also to Ed for being a lovely editor (hope I've inspired you to visit the chilly north one day).

Readers' letters

Thanks to all the readers who took the trouble to write and email in with their comments and suggestions. In the particular, our thanks to:

Tom Allen; Derek Bigland; Robin Boothroyd; Stewart Bristow; Merlyn Chesterman; Ron Clarke; Beth Clinton; Sue & David Collingwood; Laura Currie; Patrick De Backer; James Derounian; Emma Drury; Luke Dunstan; Waltraud Englefield; Rolf Fruin; Natasha Galilee; Marcus Gomm; Ben Goodhall; Sigrid Grawert; Nicola Greaves; Fay Gregory; David Hattersley; Ellen Harvey; Lian Hazewinkel; Steve Hudson; Arnelle Kendall; Harmony Kirtley; Alex Lambley; Abbie Lawson;

Steve Locke; Jonas Ludvigsson; Charlie Mason-Pearson; Ted & Tilly Maxwell; Gary Newborough; Alison O'Malley; Ian Parri; Fiona Pouchard; Ruth Pragnell; Jim Vander Putten; Jennifer Randall; Jim Rayner; Mandy Revel; Katherine Rich; Susannah Rose; Susana Rowles; Gill & Alec Saville; Hermann Schoenecker; Judy Smith; Tyson Smith; Sian Thomas; Paul Wales; Chris Watkins; Helen Welsh; Janice Wilkinson; Amy Williams; Jonathan Worrell; A Wyle; Simon Zeal.

Photo credits

All photos © Rough Guides except the following:

Title page
Newcastle waterfront © Guy Edwardes/Getty

Full page
Palace Pier, Brighton © Craig Roberts/Britain on View/Photolibrary

Introduction
Mugs of tea © Image Source/Corbis
Christ Church Gate, Canterbury © Chris Parker/Axiom Photo
Naunton, Gloucestershire © White/Photodisc/Photolibrary
Ice skating at Somerset House, London © Mark Thomas/Axiom Photo

Things not to miss
01 Wast Water, Lake District © George Kavanagh/Stone
02 Sharpitor, Dartmoor © Peter Chadwick/Alamy
04 Broadway, Worcestershire © Paul Quayle/Axiom Photo
05 Alnwick Castle © Joe Cornish/DK Images
06 Radcliffe Camera, Oxford © Imagestate/Tips Images
07 Hay-on-Wye literary festival © Andrew Fox/Alamy
08 Avebury stone circle © Imagestate/Tips Images
09 Hadrian's Wall, Northumberland © Peter Adams/Corbis
10 Glastonbury Festival 2010 © Tabatha Fireman/Redferns/Getty
11 Surfers at Fistral Beach, Newquay © Alan Copson/JAI/Corbis
12 Royal Circus, Bath © Image Source/Getty
15 Lizard Point, Cornwall © Ben Pipe/The Travel Library/Photolibrary
17 Ponies in the New Forest © Adam Burton/Robert Harding/Getty
18 Borough Market © Road Trippin'/Alamy
19 Durham Cathedral and Castle © Horst Puschmann/istockphoto.com
20 Jousting, Royal Armouries, Leeds © 2010 Board of Trustees of the Royal Armouries
21 Tate St Ives and Porthmeor Beach © Peter Barritt/Alamy
22 Punting on the River Cam, Cambridge © Peter Adams/Corbis
23 Climbers at Stanage Edge, Peak District © Paul Harris/JAI/Corbis
24 York Minster © Nigel Kirby/Loop Images/Photolibrary
26 Blenheim Palace © Michael Freeman/Getty
27 Canterbury Cathedral © Imagestate/Tips Images
28 Southwold beach huts © Gideon Mendel/Corbis

29 Clubbing in Biggs Market, Newcastle © Mike Goldwater/Alamy
30 Brighton Pavillion © Rob Reichenfeld/DK Images
31 Tate Modern Turbine Hall, London © Mike Kemp/In Pictures/Corbis
32 The Seven Sisters © John Harper/Terra/Corbis

Coastal England colour section
The Needles, Isle of Wight © Britain on View/Photolibrary
Bamburgh beach and castle, Northumberland © Alan Copson/JAI/Corbis
Par Beach, St Martins, Isles of Scilly © Way Out West Photography/Alamy
Minnack Theatre, Porthcurno © courtesy www.minack.com
South West Coast Path near Durdle Door, Dorset © Terry Yarrow Photography/Flickr /Getty
Southwold beach huts © Diana Jarvis
Thrift flowers, Calf of Man, Isle of Man © Oxford Scientific/Photolibrary

Pints and Pubs colour section
Interior of the *Falkland Arms*, Great Tew, Oxfordshire © Andy Williams/Britain on View/Photolibrary
Pint in a pub garden © Peter Denton/Getty
Hook Norton Brewery dray and horses © David McGill/Alamy
The Queens Head pub sign © Dallas and John Heaton/Photolibrary
Heron Valley cider, Devon © Mark Bolton/Corbis
CAMRA campaign at The Great British Beer Festival © Cate Gillon/Getty

Black and whites
p.62 Great Court, British Museum © Michael Betts/Getty
p.152 Mermaid Street, Rye © Rob Reichenfeld/DK Images
p.208 Corfe Castle, Dorset © Gavin Hellier/Robert Harding World Imagery/Corbis
p.262 Riding through Chipping Camden © Richard Klune/Corbis
p.312 Hot-air balloons over Clifton Suspension Bridge, Bristol © Julian Finney/Getty
p.486 RSC performance of *Julius Caesar*, Stratford-upon-Avon © Robbie Jack/Corbis
p.552 West front of Lincoln Cathedral © Florian Monheim/Arcaid/Corbis
p.594 Antony Gormley's *Another Place*, Crosby Beach © Alan Copson/JAI/Corbis
p.648 Yacht-racing on Lake Windermere © Anthony West/Corbis
p.688 Winter Garden, Sheffield © N&J Clark/Robert Harding World Imagery/Corbis
p.768 Dunstanburgh Castle © Tim Hurst/Getty

Index

Map entries are in colour.

INDEX

Z

INDEX

Map symbols

maps are listed in the full index using coloured text

▬▬	Motorway	◆	Point of interest
▥▥▥	Toll motorway	✞	Public gardens
═══	Major road	♜	Castle
═══	Minor road	⊙	Memorial/statue
▬▬	Pedestrianized street	⌂	Abbey
-----	Path	✝	Church (regional maps)
▥▥▥	Steps	▥	Mosque
▬▬	Wall	✡	Synagogue
▬▪▬	Railway	⊠—⊠	Gate
▥▥▥	Private railway	▣	Parking
— —	Ferry route	⊖	London Underground station
▬▬	River	✈	Airport
▬▬▬	National boundary	★	Bus stop
▬▬▪	County boundary	@	Internet access
▬▬▬	Chapter boundary	ⓘ	Tourist information
▲	Mountain peak	⊠	Post office
⋏⋏	Mountain range	⊞	Hospital
⌇	Rocks	⊛	Swimming pool
)(	Bridge	◉	Accommodation (regional maps)
⌇	Gorge	▬▬	Building
⌇	Waterfall	⊞	Church/cathedral
⌇	Lighthouse	▭	Market
⌒	Caves	◯	Stadium
∴	Ruin	▧	Park/national park
⚔	Battlefield	⊹	Cemetery
♦	Museum	▱	Marshland
⏚	Stately home/historic house	▧	Beach

Contains Ordnance Survey data © Crown copyright and database rights 2011

Over 100 award-winning camp sites for you to enjoy

The
Camping and
Caravanning
Club
The Friendly Club

Slapton Sands Club Site

If you love camping as much as we do, you'll love staying on one of The Camping and Caravanning Club's 110 UK Club Sites. Each of our sites are in great locations and are an ideal base for exploring the UK.

There's just one thing: once you've discovered the friendly welcome, the excellent facilities and clean, safe surroundings, you'll probably want to join anyway!

- More choice of highly maintained, regularly inspected sites
- Friendly sites that are clean and safe, so great for families
- Preferential rates – recoup your membership fee in just 6 nights' stay
- Reduced site fees for 55's and over and special deals for families
- Exclusive Member Services including specialist insurance and advice.

To book your adventure or to join The Club
call **0845 130 7633**
quoting code **3036** or visit
www.thefriendlyclub.co.uk